COLLEGE MATHEMATICS

FOR MANAGEMENT, LIFE, AND SOCIAL SCIENCES   FOURTH EDITION

COLLEGE MATHEMATICS

FOR MANAGEMENT, LIFE, AND SOCIAL SCIENCES   FOURTH EDITION

RAYMOND A. BARNETT
Merritt College

MICHAEL R. ZIEGLER
Marquette University

DELLEN PUBLISHING COMPANY
San Francisco, California

COLLIER MACMILLAN PUBLISHERS
London

Divisions of Macmillan, Inc.

Permissions: Dellen Publishing Company
               400 Pacific Avenue
               San Francisco, California 94133

Orders: Dellen Publishing Company
               c/o Macmillan Publishing Company
               Front and Brown Streets
               Riverside, New Jersey 08075

Collier Macmillan Canada, Inc.

Library of Congress Cataloging-in-Publication Data

Barnett, Raymond A.
   College mathematics for management, life, and social sciences.

   Includes indexes.
   1. Mathematics — 1961–   . 2. Social sciences —
Mathematics. 3. Biomathematics. I. Ziegler, Michael R.
II. Title.
QA37.2.B376 1987   510   86–24209
ISBN 0–02–306251–7

Printing: 1 2 3 4 5 6 7 8   Year: 6 7 8 9 0

ISBN 0-02-306251-7

Contents

CHAPTER 3   Mathematics of Finance   279

CHAPTER 4   Probability   321

CHAPTER 5   Additional Topics in Probability   389

CHAPTER 10   Integration   731

CHAPTER 11   Additional Integration Topics   791

CHAPTER 12   Multivariable Calculus   841

APPENDIX A   Special Topics   913

APPENDIX B	Tables	961

Chapter Dependencies

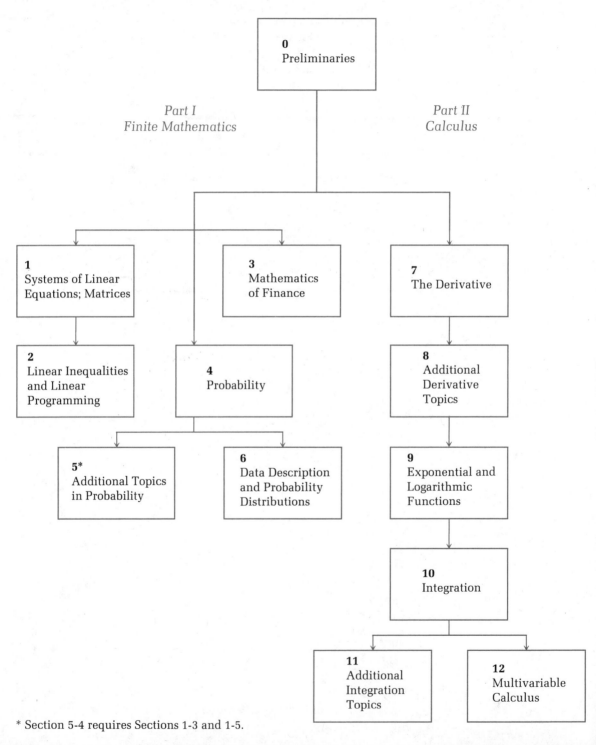

0 Preliminaries

Part I
Finite Mathematics

Part II
Calculus

1 Systems of Linear Equations; Matrices

3 Mathematics of Finance

7 The Derivative

2 Linear Inequalities and Linear Programming

4 Probability

8 Additional Derivative Topics

5* Additional Topics in Probability

6 Data Description and Probability Distributions

9 Exponential and Logarithmic Functions

10 Integration

11 Additional Integration Topics

12 Multivariable Calculus

* Section 5-4 requires Sections 1-3 and 1-5.

Preface

Many colleges and universities now offer mathematics courses that emphasize topics that are most useful to students in business and economics, life sciences, and social sciences. Because of this trend, the authors have surveyed instructors, course outlines, and college catalogs from a large number of colleges and universities, and on the basis of these surveys, selected the topics, applications, and emphasis found in this text.

The material in this book is suitable for a 1 year mathematics course beyond intermediate algebra that includes topics from finite mathematics and calculus. The first part of the book (Chapters 1–6) contains ample material for a one-semester finite mathematics course covering the topics that have become standard in this area: mathematics of finance, linear systems, matrices, linear programming, and probability. The second part (Chapters 7–12) contains material for a one-semester course on the calculus for functions of one variable, including the exponential and logarithmic functions, followed by an introduction to multivariable calculus. The choice and organization of topics in both parts make the book readily adaptable to a variety of courses. (See the diagram on page x for chapter dependencies.)

The book is designed for students who have had $1\frac{1}{2}$–2 years of high school algebra or the equivalent. However, because much of this material is forgotten due to lack of use, Chapter 0 contains a review of the basic topics in intermediate algebra that are most pertinent to the course, and portions of Appendix A review some more fundamental concepts. Any of this material can be studied systematically at the beginning of either part of the book, or referred to as needed. In addition, certain key topics are reviewed immediately before their use (see Section 1-1 or Section 9-3), while others are discussed in Appendix A.

■ Major Changes from the Third Edition

The fourth edition of *College Mathematics for Management, Life, and Social Sciences* reflects the experiences and recommendations of a large number of the users of the first three editions. Much of the material has been reorganized to provide a more efficient presentation of the topics. In addition, certain topics of marginal importance have been deleted. The result is a shorter book that permits a broader coverage of the topics most relevant to its intended audience. Many examples and exercises have been changed to provide clear illustrations of mathematical concepts without undue algebraic complexity. Special attention has been paid to increasing the quantity and quality of applications throughout the book. It is impossible to use actual real-world models in many applied problems, but it is possible to provide simplified versions of such models that reflect the important features of the application and involve mathematical operations appropriate for the level of this book. Such simplified, yet realistic, applications have been included in every chapter of the book.

The intermediate algebra material has been reorganized. Chapter 0 now contains the most frequently used algebra topics, including quadratic equations and logarithmic and exponential functions, and accurately reflects the level of algebraic ability necessary for the material in the remainder of the book. Portions of Appendix A review more fundamental algebra concepts for students whose algebraic skills have become rusty due to lack of use.

In Chapter 1, the section on Leontieff input–output analysis has been rewritten and the exercise set greatly expanded.

In Chapter 2, the geometric approach to linear programming has been modified to eliminate dependence on the use of level lines in the solution process. In the simplex method, the discussion of the pivot operation has been expanded and the terminology has been simplified.

In Chapter 3, simple discounts have been eliminated and many new and up-to-date applications have been added.

The probability material in Chapters 4–6 has been reorganized to provide more efficient coverage. The material on counting techniques has been simplified, a discussion of odds has been added, and the treatment of independent events and tree diagrams has been rewritten to provide sharper focus.

The material on differentiation (Chapters 7–9) has been reorganized, the treatment of limits and asymptotes has been simplified, the chain rule has been moved to the chapter on exponential and logarithmic functions (Chapter 9), and the sections on implicit differentiation, related rates, higher-order derivatives, and elasticity of demand have been eliminated.

In Chapters 10 and 11, integration by substitution is now covered earlier (Section 10-2) and in a more fundamental manner, the section on integral tables has been deleted, and the Riemann sum approach to integration has been moved to Chapter 11. The discussion of consumers' and producers' surplus has been expanded and placed in a new section (Section 11-2), along with a discussion of continuous income streams.

A section on the method of least squares has been added to the chapter on multivariable calculus (Chapter 12).

■ General Comments

The first part of the book (Chapters 1–6) deals with three areas that are independent of each other (see the diagram on page x). Chapters 1 and 2 cover topics from linear algebra and linear programming. Elementary row operations are used for solving systems of equations, inverting matrices, and solving linear programming problems. The material on linear programming is organized so as to provide the instructor with maximum flexibility. Those who want a good intuitive introduction to the subject can cover only the material up to the dual method. On the other hand, those who wish to emphasize the development of computational skills can also cover the dual method or the big M method (or both). Finally, those who wish to concentrate on problem solving (setting up problems) and applications can cover the applications in Section 2-5 or Section 2-6 (or both) and omit the computational methods entirely. In order to facilitate these approaches, the answer section contains an appropriate model for each applied problem, as well as the numerical solution. Section 2-6 also contains optional applications which lead to linear programming problems that are too complex to solve by hand. These applications provide a natural place to introduce the use of a computer program to solve linear programming problems. Such a program is available to institutions adopting this book at no charge from the publisher.

The mathematics of finance is presented in Chapter 3. Simple discounts have been eliminated, and new, up-to-date applications have been added. Most of the exercises can be solved using either the tables in the back of the book or a hand calculator.

Chapters 4–6 consist of topics from probability and statistics. Chapter 4 covers counting techniques and the basic concepts of probability. The interplay between empirical and theoretical probability is carefully explained. Chapter 5 then takes up some more advanced probability topics, while Chapter 6 deals with methods of describing data and the use of probability distributions. Either Chapter 5 or Chapter 6 can follow Chapter 4. (See the diagram on page x.)

In the second part of the book, Chapters 7–9 present the differential calculus for functions of one variable, including the exponential and logarithmic functions. (Trigonometric functions are not discussed in this book.) Limits and continuity are presented in an intuitive fashion, utilizing numerical approximations and graphical concepts. The basic rules of differentiation for algebraic functions are covered in Chapter 7. The relationship between derivatives and graphs is discussed in Sections 8-1 and 8-2, and then applied to optimization problems in Section 8-3 and to curve sketching in Section 8-4. A short section on differentials is included to facilitate the use of differentials in integration by substitution (Chapter 10) and integration by parts (Chapter 11). The chain rule is covered in the chapter on exponential and logarithmic functions (Chapter 9), the first place where its use is really required.

Chapters 10 and 11 deal with integral calculus. Differential equations and exponential growth and decay are included as an application of antidifferentiation. In Chapter 10, the definite integral is intuitively introduced in terms of an area function and then, in Chapter 11, it is formally defined as the limit of a Riemann sum. Integration by parts, some additional applications of integration, and improper integrals are also covered in Chapter 11.

Chapter 12 introduces multivariable calculus, including partial derivatives, optimization, Lagrange multipliers, least squares, and double integrals. If desired, this chapter can be covered immediately after Chapter 10. (See the diagram on page x.)

■ Important Features

Emphasis

Emphasis is on computational skills, ideas, and problem solving rather than mathematical theory. Most derivations and proofs are omitted except where their inclusion adds significant insight into a particular concept. General concepts and results are usually presented only after particular cases have been discussed.

Examples and Matched Problems

Over 350 completely worked examples are included. Each example is followed by a similar problem for the student to work while reading the material. This actively involves the student in the learning process. The answers to these matched problems are included at the end of each section for easy reference.

Exercise Sets

This book contains over 3,700 exercises. Each exercise set is designed so that an average or below-average student will experience success and a very capable student will be challenged. Exercise sets are mostly divided into A (routine, easy mechanics), B (more difficult mechanics), and C (difficult mechanics and some theory) levels.

Applications

Enough applications are included to convince even the most skeptical student that mathematics is really useful. The majority of the applications are included at the end of exercise sets and are generally divided into business and economics, life science, and social science groupings. An instructor with students from all three disciplines can let them choose applications from their own field of interest; if most students are from one of the three areas, then special emphasis can be placed there. Most of the applications are simplified versions of actual real-world problems taken from professional journals and professional books. No specialized experience is required to solve any of the applications in this book.

■ Student and Instructor Aids

Student Aids

Dashed **"think boxes"** are used to enclose steps that are usually performed mentally (see Section 0-2).

Examples and developments are often **annotated** to help students through critical stages (see Section 0-2).

A **second color** is used to indicate key steps (see Section 0-2).

Boldface type is used to introduce new terms and highlight important comments.

Answers to odd-numbered problems are included in the back of the book.

Chapter review sections include a review of all important terms and symbols and a comprehensive review exercise. Answers to all review exercises are included in the back of the book.

A **student's solutions manual** is available at a nominal cost through a book store. The manual includes detailed solutions to all odd-numbered problems and all review exercises.

A **computer applications supplement** is available at a nominal cost through a book store. The supplement contains examples, computer program listings, and exercises that demonstrate the use of a computer to solve a variety of problems in finite mathematics and calculus. No previous computing experience is necessary to use this supplement.

Instructor Aids

A unique **computer-generated random test system** is available to instructors without cost. The system, utilizing an IBM PC computer and a number of commonly used dot matrix printers, will generate an almost unlimited number of chapter tests and final examinations, each different from the other, quickly and easily. At the same time, the system produces an answer key and a student worksheet with an answer column that exactly matches the answer column on the answer key. Graphing grids are included on the answer key and on the student worksheet for problems requiring graphs.

A **printed and bound test battery** is also available to instructors without cost. The battery contains several chapter tests for each chapter, answer keys, and student worksheets with answer columns that exactly match the answer columns on the answer keys. Graphing grids are included on the answer key and on the student worksheet for problems requiring graphs.

An **instructor's answer manual** containing answers to the even-numbered problems not included in the text is available to instructors without charge.

A **solutions manual** (see Student Aids) is available to instructors without charge from the publisher

A **computer applications supplement** (see Student Aids) is available to instructors without charge from the publisher. The programs in this supplement are also available on diskettes for APPLE II and IBM PC computers. The publisher will supply one of these diskettes without charge to institutions using this book.

■ Related Books in the Series

This book is one of three books in a series by the same authors. All of the material in *College Mathematics* is also available in two separate volumes:

Finite Mathematics for Management, Life, and Social Sciences, Fourth Edition: A text designed for a one-quarter or one-semester course in finite mathematics. Contents consist of Chapters 0–6 of *College Mathematics* plus a chapter on games and decision theory.

Calculus for Management, Life, and Social Sciences, Fourth Edition: A text designed for a one-quarter or one-semester course in calculus. Contents consist of Chapter 0 and Chapters 7–12 of *College Mathematics* plus a chapter on trigonometric functions.

■ Acknowledgments

In addition to the authors, many others are involved in the successful publication of a book. We wish to thank personally: Ronald Barnes, University of Houston–Downtown; Carl Bedell, Philadelphia College of Textiles and Science; Paul Boonstra, Calvin College; Miriam Connellan, Marquette University; Edward Connors, University of Massachusetts at Amherst; William Conway, University of Arizona; John Daly, Saint Louis University; Ryness Doherty, Metropolitan State College; Garry Etgen, University of Houston; Jeremiah Farrell, Butler University; James Flynn, Cleveland State University; Gerald Goff, Oklahoma State University; Paul Lawrisuk, Moraine Valley Community College; Roy Luke, Pierce College; Carolyn Meitler, Marquette University; Donald Minassian, Butler University; Robert Moreland, Texas Tech University; Frank Shirley, University of Texas; Martha Sklar, Los Angeles City College; Louis Talman, Metropolitan State College; Vance Underhill, East Texas State University; Wiley Williams, University of Louisville; T. D. Worosz, Metropolitan State College; and Robert Zahn, San Jose State University.
We also wish to thank:

John Williams for a strong and effective cover design.

John Drooyan for the many sensitive and beautiful photographs seen throughout the book.

Phillip Bender and Stephen Merrill for carefully checking all examples and problems (a tedious but extremely important job).

Phyllis Niklas and Janet Bollow for another outstanding book design and for guiding the book smoothly through all production details.

Don Dellen, the publisher, who continues to provide all the support services and encouragement an author could hope for.

Producing this new edition with the help of all these extremely competent people has been a most satisfying experience.

R. A. Barnett
M. R. Ziegler

Preliminaries

CHAPTER 0   Contents

This chapter and Appendix A are provided for those of you whose prerequisite skills are a little rusty. Depending on the degree of your rust, you can either refer to selected sections briefly as needed, you can review certain sections in depth at the start of the course, or you can study them in depth at appropriate points of the course.

0-1   Sets

- Set Properties and Set Notation
- Set Operations
- Application

In this section we will review a few key ideas from set theory. Set concepts and notation not only help us talk about certain mathematical ideas with greater clarity and precision, but are indispensable to a clear understanding of probability.

■ Set Properties and Set Notation

We can think of a **set** as any collection of objects specified in such a way that we can tell whether any given object is or is not in the collection. Capital letters, such as A, B, and C, are often used to designate particular sets. Each object in a set is called a **member** or **element** of the set. Symbolically,

$a \in A$	means	"a is an element of set A"
$a \notin A$	means	"a is not an element of set A"

A set without any elements is called the **empty** or **null set.** For example, the set of all people over 10 feet tall is an empty set. Symbolically,

$\varnothing$ represents   "the empty or null set"

A set is usually described either by listing all its elements between braces { } or by enclosing a rule within braces that determines the elements of the set. Thus, if $P(x)$ is a statement about x, then

$S = \{x|P(x)\}$ means   "S is the set of all x such that $P(x)$ is true"

Recall that the vertical bar in the symbolic form is read "such that." The following example illustrates the rule and listing methods of representing sets.

Example 1   *Rule*   *Listing*

$\{x|x \text{ is a weekend day}\} = \{\text{Saturday, Sunday}\}$

$\{x|x^2 = 4\} = \{-2, 2\}$

$\{x|x \text{ is an odd positive counting number}\} = \{1, 3, 5, \ldots\}$

The three dots . . . in the last set in Example 1 indicate that the pattern established by the first three entries continues indefinitely. The first two sets in Example 1 are **finite sets** (we intuitively know that the elements can be counted); the last set is an **infinite set** (we intuitively know that there is no end in counting the elements). When listing the elements in a set, we do not list an element more than once.

Problem 1   Let G be the set of all numbers such that $x^2 = 9$.*

(A)   Denote G by the rule method.
(B)   Denote G by the listing method.
(C)   Indicate whether the following are true or false: $3 \in G$, $9 \notin G$.

If each element of a set A is also an element of set B, we say that A is a **subset** of B. For example, the set of all women students in a class is a subset of the whole class. Note that the definition allows a set to be a subset of itself. If set A and set B have exactly the same elements, then the two sets are said to be **equal.** Symbolically,

* Answers to matched problems are found near the end of each section just before the exercise set.

$A \subset B$	means	"A is a subset of B"
$A = B$	means	"A and B have exactly the same elements"
$A \not\subset B$	means	"A is not a subset of B"
$A \neq B$	means	"A and B do not have exactly the same elements"

It can be proved that $\varnothing$ **is a subset of every set.**

Example 2   If $A = \{-3, -1, 1, 3\}$, $B = \{3, -3, 1, -1\}$, and $C = \{-3, -2, -1, 0, 1, 2, 3\}$, then each of the following statements is true:

$A = B$	$A \subset C$	$A \subset B$
$C \neq A$	$C \not\subset A$	$B \subset A$
$\varnothing \subset A$	$\varnothing \subset C$	$\varnothing \not\subset A$

Problem 2   Given $A = \{0, 2, 4, 6\}$, $B = \{0, 1, 2, 3, 4, 5, 6\}$, and $C = \{2, 6, 0, 4\}$, indicate whether the following relationships are true (T) or false (F):

(A) $A \subset B$ (B) $A \subset C$ (C) $A = C$
(D) $C \subset B$ (E) $B \not\subset A$ (F) $\varnothing \subset B$

Example 3   List all the subsets of the set $\{a, b, c\}$.

Solution $\{a, b, c\}, \{a, b\}, \{a, c\}, \{b, c\}, \{a\}, \{b\}, \{c\}, \varnothing$

Problem 3   List all the subsets of the set $\{1, 2\}$.

■ Set Operations

The **union** of sets A and B, denoted by $A \cup B$, is the set of all elements formed by combining all the elements of A and all the elements of B into one set. Symbolically,

Union

$$A \cup B = \{x | x \in A \quad \text{or} \quad x \in B\}$$

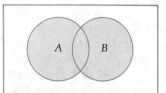

Figure 1 $A \cup B$ is the shaded region.

Here we use the word *or* in the way it is always used in mathematics; that is, x may be an element of set A or set B or both.

Venn diagrams are useful in visualizing set relationships. The union of two sets can be illustrated as shown in Figure 1. Note that

$$A \subset A \cup B \quad \text{and} \quad B \subset A \cup B$$

The **intersection** of sets A and B, denoted by $A \cap B$, is the set of elements in set A that are also in set B. Symbolically,

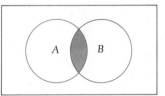

Figure 2 $A \cap B$ is the shaded region.

Intersection

$$A \cap B = \{x \mid x \in A \quad \textbf{and} \quad x \in B\}$$

This relationship is easily visualized in the Venn diagram shown in Figure 2. Note that

$$A \cap B \subset A \quad \text{and} \quad A \cap B \subset B$$

If $A \cap B = \varnothing$, then the sets A and B are said to be **disjoint;** this is illustrated in Figure 3.

The set of all elements under consideration is called the **universal set** U. Once the universal set is determined for a particular discussion, all other sets in that discussion must be subsets of U.

We now define one more operation on sets, called the *complement*. The **complement** of A (relative to U), denoted by A', is the set of elements in U that are not in A (see Fig. 4). Symbolically,

---

Complement

$$A' = \{x \in U \mid x \notin A\}$$

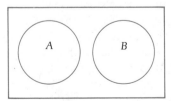

Figure 3 $A \cap B = \varnothing$

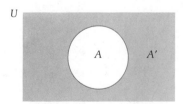

Figure 4 The complement of A is A'.

Example 4 If $A = \{3, 6, 9\}$, $B = \{3, 4, 5, 6, 7\}$, $C = \{4, 5, 7\}$, and $U = \{1, 2, 3, 4, 5, 6, 7, 8, 9\}$, then

$$A \cup B = \{3, 4, 5, 6, 7, 9\}$$
$$A \cap B = \{3, 6\}$$
$$A \cap C = \varnothing \quad \text{A and C are disjoint}$$
$$B' = \{1, 2, 8, 9\}$$

Problem 4 If $R = \{1, 2, 3, 4\}$, $S = \{1, 3, 5, 7\}$, $T = \{2, 4\}$, and $U = \{1, 2, 3, 4, 5, 6, 7, 8, 9\}$, find:

(A) $R \cup S$ (B) $R \cap S$ (C) $S \cap T$ (D) S'

■ Application

Example 5 From a survey of 100 college students, a marketing research company found that 75 students owned stereos, 45 owned cars, and 35 owned cars and stereos.

(A) How many students owned either a car or a stereo?
(B) How many students did not own either a car or a stereo?

Solutions Venn diagrams are very useful for this type of problem. If we let

$U = $ Set of students in sample (100)
$S = $ Set of students who own stereos (75)
$C = $ Set of students who own cars (45)
$S \cap C = $ Set of students who own cars and stereos (35)

then

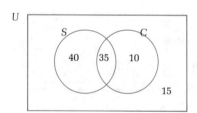

Place the number in the intersection first, then work outward:

$$40 = 75 - 35$$
$$10 = 45 - 35$$
$$15 = 100 - (40 + 35 + 10)$$

(A) The number of students who own either a car or a stereo is the number of students in the set $S \cup C$. You might be tempted to say that this is just the number of students in S plus the number of students in C, $75 + 45 = 120$, but this sum is larger than the sample we started with! What is wrong? We have actually counted the number in the intersection (35) twice. The correct answer, as seen in the Venn diagram, is

$$40 + 35 + 10 = 85$$

(B) The number of students who do not own either a car or a stereo is the number of students in the set $(S \cup C)'$; that is, 15.

Problem 5 Referring to Example 5:

(A) How many students owned a car but not a stereo?

(B) How many students did not own both a car and a stereo?

Note in Example 5 and Problem 5 that the word *and* is associated with intersection and the word *or* is associated with union.

Answers to Matched Problems

1. (A) $\{x|x^2 = 9\}$ (B) $\{-3, 3\}$ (C) True, True

2. All are true

3. $\{1, 2\}, \{1\}, \{2\}, \varnothing$

4. (A) $\{1, 2, 3, 4, 5, 7\}$ (B) $\{1, 3\}$ (C) $\varnothing$ (D) $\{2, 4, 6, 8, 9\}$

5. (A) 10 [the number in $S' \cap C$]   (B) 65 [the number in $(S \cap C)'$]

Exercise 0-1

A *Indicate true (T) or false (F).*

1. $4 \in \{2, 3, 4\}$
2. $6 \notin \{2, 3, 4\}$
3. $\{2, 3\} \subset \{2, 3, 4\}$
4. $\{3, 2, 4\} = \{2, 3, 4\}$
5. $\{3, 2, 4\} \subset \{2, 3, 4\}$
6. $\{3, 2, 4\} \in \{2, 3, 4\}$
7. $\varnothing \subset \{2, 3, 4\}$
8. $\varnothing = \{0\}$

In Problems 9–14 write the resulting set using the listing method.

9. $\{1, 3, 5\} \cup \{2, 3, 4\}$
10. $\{3, 4, 6, 7\} \cup \{3, 4, 5\}$
11. $\{1, 3, 4\} \cap \{2, 3, 4\}$
12. $\{3, 4, 6, 7\} \cap \{3, 4, 5\}$
13. $\{1, 5, 9\} \cap \{3, 4, 6, 8\}$
14. $\{6, 8, 9, 11\} \cap \{3, 4, 5, 7\}$

B *In Problems 15–20 write the resulting set using the listing method.*

15. $\{x|x - 2 = 0\}$
16. $\{x|x + 7 = 0\}$
17. $\{x|x^2 = 49\}$
18. $\{x|x^2 = 100\}$
19. $\{x|x$ is an odd number between 1 and 9, inclusive$\}$
20. $\{x|x$ is a month starting with $M\}$
21. For $U = \{1, 2, 3, 4, 5\}$ and $A = \{2, 3, 4\}$, find A'.
22. For $U = \{7, 8, 9, 10, 11\}$ and $A = \{7, 11\}$, find A'.

U

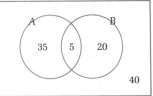

35 5 20

40

Problems 23–34 refer to the Venn diagram in the margin. How many elements are in each of the indicated sets?

23. A	**24.** U	**25.** A'	**26.** B'
27. $A \cup B$	**28.** $A \cap B$	**29.** $A' \cap B$	**30.** $A \cap B'$
31. $(A \cap B)'$	**32.** $(A \cup B)'$	**33.** $A' \cap B'$	**34.** U'

35. If $R = \{1, 2, 3, 4\}$ and $T = \{2, 4, 6\}$, find:

(A) $\{x | x \in R \text{ or } x \in T\}$ (B) $R \cup T$

36. If $R = \{1, 3, 4\}$ and $T = \{2, 4, 6\}$, find:

(A) $\{x | x \in R \text{ and } x \in T\}$ (B) $R \cap T$

37. For $P = \{1, 2, 3, 4\}$, $Q = \{2, 4, 6\}$, and $R = \{3, 4, 5, 6\}$, find $P \cup (Q \cap R)$.

38. For P, Q, and R in Problem 37, find $P \cap (Q \cup R)$.

C Venn diagrams may be of help in Problems 39–44.

39. If $A \cup B = B$, can we always conclude that $A \subset B$?
40. If $A \cap B = B$, can we always conclude that $B \subset A$?
41. If A and B are arbitrary sets, can we always conclude that $A \cap B \subset B$?
42. If $A \cap B = \varnothing$, can we always conclude that $B = \varnothing$?
43. If $A \subset B$ and $x \in A$, can we always conclude that $x \in B$?
44. If $A \subset B$ and $x \in B$, can we always conclude that $x \in A$?
45. How many subsets does each of the following sets have? Also, try to discover a formula in terms of n for a set with n elements.

(A) $\{a\}$ (B) $\{a, b\}$ (C) $\{a, b, c\}$

46. How do the sets $\varnothing$, $\{\varnothing\}$, and $\{0\}$ differ from each other?

Applications

Business & Economics

Problems 47–58 refer to the following survey: A marketing survey of 1,000 car commuters found that 600 listen to the news, 500 listen to music, and 300 listen to both. Let

$N =$ Set of commuters in the sample who listen to news

$M =$ Set of commuters in the sample who listen to music

Following the procedures in Example 5, find the number of commuters in each set described below.

47. $N \cup M$	**48.** $N \cap M$	**49.** $(N \cup M)'$
50. $(N \cap M)'$	**51.** $N' \cap M$	**52.** $N \cap M'$

53. Set of commuters who listen to either news or music
54. Set of commuters who listen to both news and music
55. Set of commuters who do not listen to either news or music

56. Set of commuters who do not listen to both news and music
57. Set of commuters who listen to music but not news
58. Set of commuters who listen to news but not music
59. The management of a company, a president and three vice-presidents, denoted by the set $\{P, V_1, V_2, V_3\}$, wish to select a committee of two people from among themselves. How many ways can this committee be formed; that is, how many two-person subsets can be formed from a set of four people?
60. The management of the company in Problem 59 decides for or against certain measures as follows: The president has two votes and each vice-president has one vote. Three favorable votes are needed to pass a measure. List all minimal winning coalitions; that is, list all subsets of $\{P, V_1, V_2, V_3\}$ that represent exactly three votes.

Life Sciences *Blood types.* When receiving a blood transfusion, a recipient must have all the antigens of the donor. A person may have one or more of the three antigens A, B, and Rh, or none at all. Eight blood types are possible, as indicated in the following Venn diagram, where U is the set of all people under consideration:

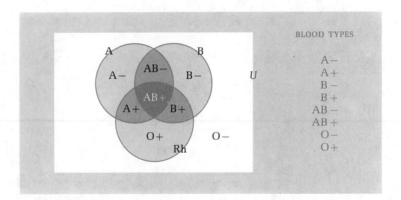

An A— person has A antigens but no B or Rh; an O+ person has Rh but neither A nor B; an AB— person has A and B antigens but no Rh; and so on.

Using the Venn diagram, indicate which of the eight blood types are included in each set.

61. $A \cap Rh$
62. $A \cap B$
63. $A \cup Rh$
64. $A \cup B$
65. $(A \cup B)'$
66. $(A \cup B \cup Rh)'$
67. $A' \cap B$
68. $Rh' \cap A$

Social Sciences *Group structures.* R. D. Luce and A. D. Perry, in a study on group structure (*Psychometrika*, 1949, 14: 95–116), used the idea of sets to formally define the notion of a clique within a group. Let G be the set of all persons in the group and let $C \subset G$. Then C is a clique provided that:

1. C contains at least three elements.
2. For every $a, b \in C$, $a \, \mathsf{R} \, b$ and $b \, \mathsf{R} \, a$.
3. For every $a \notin C$, there is at least one $b \in C$ such that $a \, \bcancel{\mathsf{R}} \, b$ or $b \, \bcancel{\mathsf{R}} \, a$ or both.

[*Note:* Interpret "$a \, \mathsf{R} \, b$" to mean "a relates to b," "a likes b" "a is as wealthy as b," and so on. Of course, "$a \, \bcancel{\mathsf{R}} \, b$" means "$a$ does not relate to b," and so on.]

69. Translate statement 2 into ordinary English.
70. Translate statement 3 into ordinary English.

0-2 Linear Equations and Inequalities in One Variable

- Linear Equations
- The Real Number Line
- Linear Inequalities
- Applications

The equation

$$3 - 2(x + 3) = \frac{x}{3} - 5$$

and the inequality

$$\frac{x}{2} + 2(3x - 1) \geqslant 5$$

are both first degree (linear) in one variable.* A **solution** of an equation (or inequality) involving a single variable is a number that when substituted for the variable makes the equation (or inequality) true. The set of all solutions is called the **solution set.** When we say that we **solve an equation** (or inequality), we mean that we find its solution set.

Knowing what is meant by the solution set is one thing; finding it is another. We start by recalling the idea of equivalent equations and equivalent inequalities. If we perform an operation on an equation (or inequality) that produces another equation (or inequality) with the same solution set, then the two equations (or inequalities) are said to be **equivalent.** The basic idea in solving equations and inequalities is to perform operations on these

---

* An equation (or inequality) is **first degree (linear)** in one variable if it can be transformed into an equation (or inequality) where the left side is of the form $ax + b$, $a \neq 0$, and the right side is zero.

forms that produce simpler equivalent forms, and to continue the process until we obtain an equation or inequality with an obvious solution.

■ Linear Equations

The following properties of equality produce equivalent equations when applied:

Equality Properties

For a, b, and c real numbers:

1. If $a = b$, then $a + c = b + c$.   Addition property
2. If $a = b$, then $a - c = b - c$.   Subtraction property
3. If $a = b$, then $ca = cb$, $c \neq 0$.   Multiplication property
4. If $a = b$, then $\dfrac{a}{c} = \dfrac{b}{c}$, $c \neq 0$.   Division property

---

Several examples should remind you of the process of solving.

Example 6   Solve $8x - 3(x - 4) = 3(x - 4) + 6$.

Solution
$$8x - 3(x - 4) = 3(x - 4) + 6$$
$$8x - 3x + 12 = 3x - 12 + 6$$
$$5x + 12 = 3x - 6$$
$$2x = -18$$
$$x = -9$$

Problem 6   Solve $3x - 2(2x - 5) = 2(x + 3) - 8$.

Example 7   What operations can we perform on

$$\frac{x + 2}{2} - \frac{x}{3} = 5$$

to eliminate the denominators? If we can find a number that is exactly divisible by each denominator, then we can use the multiplication property of equality to clear the denominators. The LCD (least common denominator)* of the fractions, 6, is exactly what we are looking for! Actually, any common denominator will do, but the LCD results in a simpler equivalent equation. Thus, we multiply both sides of the equation by 6:

---

* Recall that the **least common denominator** (LCD) of two or more natural number denominators is the smallest natural number exactly divisible by each denominator.

$$6\left(\frac{x+2}{2} - \frac{x}{3}\right) = 6 \cdot 5$$

$$\overset{3}{\cancel{6}} \cdot \frac{(x+2)}{\cancel{2}} - \overset{2}{\cancel{6}} \cdot \frac{x}{\cancel{3}} = 30$$

$$3(x+2) - 2x = 30$$

$$3x + 6 - 2x = 30$$

$$x = 24$$

Problem 7   Solve $\dfrac{x+1}{3} - \dfrac{x}{4} = \dfrac{1}{2}$.

In many applications of algebra, formulas or equations must be changed to alternate equivalent forms. The following examples are typical.

Example 8   Solve the amount formula for simple interest, $A = P + Prt$ (which will be discussed in Chapter 3), for:

(A) r in terms of the other variables
(B) P in terms of the other variables

Solutions   (A) $A = P + Prt$

$\qquad\qquad P + Prt = A$ Reverse equation

$\qquad\qquad\quad Prt = A - P$ Now isolate r on the left side

$\qquad\qquad\qquad r = \dfrac{A - P}{Pt}$ Divide both members by Pt

(B) $A = P + Prt$

$\qquad\qquad P + Prt = A$ Reverse equation

$\qquad\qquad P(1 + rt) = A$ Factor out P (note the use of the distributive property)

$\qquad\qquad\qquad P = \dfrac{A}{1 + rt}$ Divide by $(1 + rt)$

Problem 8   Solve $M = Nt + Nr$ for: (A) t (B) N

■ The Real Number Line

Figure 5 breaks down the **set of real numbers** into its important subsets

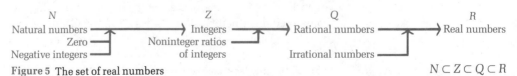

Figure 5 The set of real numbers $N \subset Z \subset Q \subset R$

* The dashed boxes indicate steps that are usually done mentally.

A one-to-one correspondence exists between the set of real numbers and the set of points on a line; that is, each real number corresponds to exactly one point, and each point to exactly one real number. A line with a real number associated with each point, and vice versa, as in Figure 6, is called a **real number line,** or simply a **real line.** Each number associated with a point is called the **coordinate** of that point. The point with coordinate zero is called the **origin.** The arrow indicates a positive direction; the coordinates of all points to the right of the origin are called **positive real numbers,** and those to the left of the origin are called **negative real numbers.**

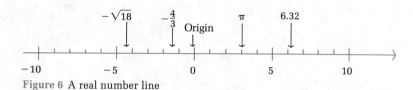

Figure 6 A real number line

■ Linear Inequalities

Before we start solving linear inequalities, let us recall what we mean by $<$ (less than) and $>$ (greater than). If a and b are real numbers, then we write

$a < b$

if there exists a positive number p such that $a + p = b$. Certainly, we would expect that if a positive number was added to any real number, the sum would be larger than the original. That is essentially what the definition states. We write

$b > a$

if $a < b$.

Example 9   (A) $3 < 5$ Since $3 + 2 = 5$
(B) $-6 < -2$ Since $-6 + 4 = -2$
(C) $0 > -10$ Since $-10 < 0$

Problem 9   Replace each question mark with either $<$ or $>$.

(A) $2 ? 8$ (B) $-20 ? 0$ (C) $-3 ? -30$

The inequality symbols have a very clear geometric interpretation on the real number line. If $a < b$, then a is to the left of b on the number line; if $c > d$, then c is to the right of d (Fig. 7).

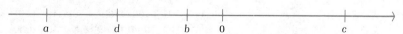

Figure 7 $a < b, c > d$

Now let us turn to the problem of solving linear inequalities in one variable. Recall that a solution of an inequality involving one variable is a number that, when substituted for the variable, makes the inequality true. The set of all solutions is called the solution set. When we say that we solve an inequality, we mean that we find its solution set. The procedures used to solve linear inequalities in one variable are almost the same as those used to solve linear equations in one variable but with two important exceptions (as will be noted below). The following properties of inequalities produce equivalent inequalities when applied:

Inequality Properties

For a, b, and c real numbers:

1. If $a > b$, then $a + c > b + c$.
2. If $a > b$, then $a - c > b - c$.
3. If $a > b$ and c is positive,   then $ca > cb$. ⎫
4. If $a > b$ and c is negative,   then $ca < cb$. ⎭   Note difference

5. If $a > b$ and c is positive,   then $\dfrac{a}{c} > \dfrac{b}{c}$. ⎫

6. If $a > b$ and c is negative,   then $\dfrac{a}{c} < \dfrac{b}{c}$. ⎭   Note difference

---

Similar properties hold if each inequality sign is reversed or if $>$ is replaced with $\geq$ (greater than or equal to) and $<$ is replaced with $\leq$ (less than or equal to). Thus, we can perform essentially the same operations on inequalities that we perform on equations with the exception that *the sense of the inequality reverses if we multiply or divide both sides by a negative number.* Otherwise, the sense of the inequality does not change. For example, if we start with the true statement

$$-3 > -7$$

and multiply both sides by 2, we obtain

$$-6 > -14$$

and the sense of the inequality stays the same. But if we multiply both sides of $-3 > -7$ by -2, then the left side becomes 6 and the right side becomes 14, so we must write

$$6 < 14$$

to have a true statement. Thus, the sense of the inequality reverses.

Recall that the double inequality $a \leq x \leq b$ means that $a \leq x$ **and** $x \leq b$.

Other variations, as well as a useful interval notation, are indicated in Table 1. Note that an end point on a line graph has a square bracket through it if it is included in the inequality and a parenthesis through it if it is not.

Table 1

Interval Notation	Inequality Notation	Line Graph
$[a, b]$	$a \leq x \leq b$	$\overset{\longleftarrow\;\;[\underline{\qquad\qquad}]\;\;\longrightarrow}{\,a\qquad\;\;b}\;x$
$[a, b)$	$a \leq x < b$	$\overset{\longleftarrow\;\;[\underline{\qquad\qquad})\;\;\longrightarrow}{\,a\qquad\;\;b}\;x$
$(a, b]$	$a < x \leq b$	$\overset{\longleftarrow\;\;(\underline{\qquad\qquad}]\;\;\longrightarrow}{\,a\qquad\;\;b}\;x$
(a, b)	$a < x < b$	$\overset{\longleftarrow\;\;(\underline{\qquad\qquad})\;\;\longrightarrow}{\,a\qquad\;\;b}\;x$
$(-\infty, a]$	$x \leq a$	$\overset{\longleftarrow\underline{\qquad\qquad}]\;\;\longrightarrow}{\qquad\qquad\;a}\;x$
$(-\infty, a)$	$x < a$	$\overset{\longleftarrow\underline{\qquad\qquad})\;\;\longrightarrow}{\qquad\qquad\;a}\;x$
$[b, \infty)$*	$x \geq b$	$\overset{\longleftarrow\;\;[\underline{\qquad\qquad}\longrightarrow}{\qquad\;\,b}\;x$
(b, ∞)	$x > b$	$\overset{\longleftarrow\;\;(\underline{\qquad\qquad}\longrightarrow}{\qquad\;\,b}\;x$

* The symbol ∞ (read "infinity") is not a number. When we write $[b, \infty)$, we are simply referring to the interval starting at b and continuing indefinitely to the right. We would never write $[b, \infty]$.

Example 10 Solve and graph $2(2x + 3) < 6(x - 2) + 10$.

Solution
$$2(2x + 3) < 6(x - 2) + 10$$
$$4x + 6 < 6x - 12 + 10$$
$$4x + 6 < 6x - 2$$
$$-2x + 6 < -2$$
$$-2x < -8$$
$$x > 4 \quad \text{or} \quad (4, \infty)$$

Notice that the sense of the inequality reverses when we divide both sides by -2

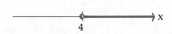

Notice that in the graph of $x > 4$, we use a parenthesis through 4, since the point 4 is not included in the graph.

Problem 10   Solve and graph $3(x - 1) \leqslant 5(x + 2) - 5$.

Example 11   Solve and graph $-3 < 2x + 3 \leqslant 9$.

Solution   We are looking for all numbers x such that $2x + 3$ is between -3 and 9, including 9 but not -3. We proceed as above except that we try to isolate x in the middle:

$$-3 < 2x + 3 \leqslant 9$$
$$-3 - 3 < 2x + 3 - 3 \leqslant 9 - 3$$
$$-6 < 2x \leqslant 6$$
$$\frac{-6}{2} < \frac{2x}{2} \leqslant \frac{6}{2}$$
$$-3 < x \leqslant 3 \quad \text{or} \quad (-3, 3]$$

Problem 11   Solve and graph $-8 \leqslant 3x - 5 < 7$.

Note that a linear equation usually has exactly one solution, while a linear inequality usually has infinitely many solutions.

■ Applications

To realize the full potential of algebra, we must be able to translate real-world problems into mathematical forms. In short, we must be able to do *word problems*.

Example 12

Break-even Analysis   It costs a record company $9,000 to prepare a record album — recording costs, album design costs, etc. These costs represent a one-time **fixed cost.** Manufacturing, marketing, and royalty costs (all **variable costs**) are $3.50 per album. If the album is sold to record shops for $5 each, how many must be sold for the company to **break even?**

Solution   Let $x =$ Number of records sold

$C =$ Cost for producing x records

$R =$ Revenue (return) on sales of x records

The company breaks even if $R = C$, with

$C =$ Fixed costs $+$ Variable costs

$= \$9,000 + \$3.50x$

$R = \$5x$

Find x such that $R = C$; that is, such that

$$5x = 9,000 + 3.5x$$
$$1.5x = 9,000$$
$$x = 6,000$$

Check   For x = 6,000,

$$C = 9,000 + 3.5x \qquad \text{and} \qquad R = 5x$$
$$= 9,000 + 3.5(6,000) \qquad\qquad = 5(6,000)$$
$$= \$30,000 \qquad\qquad\qquad = \$30,000$$

Thus, the company must sell 6,000 records to break even; any sales over 6,000 will produce a profit; any sales under 6,000 will result in a loss.

Problem 12   What is the break-even point in Example 12 if fixed costs are \$9,900, variable costs are \$3.70 per record, and the records are sold for \$5.50 each?

Algebra has many different types of applications—so many, in fact, that no single approach applies to all. However, the following suggestions may help you get started:

Suggestions for Solving Word Problems

1. Read the problem very carefully.
2. Write down important facts and relationships.
3. Identify unknown quantities in terms of a single letter, if possible.
4. Write an equation or inequality relating the unknown quantities and the facts in the problem.
5. Solve the equation (or inequality).
6. Write all solutions asked for in the original problem.
7. Check the solution(s) in the original problem.

Example 13   The consumer price index for several years is given in Table 2.

Consumer Price
Index (CPI)

Table 2 CPI (1967 = 100)

Year	Index
1950	72
1955	80
1960	89
1965	95
1970	116
1975	161
1980	247

What net monthly salary in 1980 would have the same purchasing power as a net monthly salary of \$900 in 1950? Compute the answer to the nearest dollar.

Solution To have the same purchasing power, the ratio of a salary in 1980 to a salary in 1950 would have to be the same as the ratio of the CPI in 1980 to the CPI in 1950. Thus, if x is the net monthly salary in 1980, we solve the equation.

$$\frac{x}{900} = \frac{247}{72}$$

$$x = 900 \cdot \frac{247}{72}$$

$$= \$3{,}088 \text{ per month}$$

Problem 13 What net monthly salary in 1960 would have the same purchasing power as a net monthly salary of \$2,000 in 1975? Compute the answer to the nearest dollar.

Answers to
Matched Problems

6. $x = 4$ 7. $x = 2$

8. (A) $t = \dfrac{M - Nr}{N}$ (B) $N = \dfrac{M}{t + r}$

9. (A) $<$ (B) $<$ (C) $>$

10. $x \geqslant -4$ or $[-4, \infty)$

11. $-1 \leqslant x < 4$ or $[-1, 4)$

12. 5,500 13. \$1,106

Exercise 0-2

A *Solve.*

1. $2m + 9 = 5m - 6$ 2. $3y - 4 = 6y - 19$
3. $x + 5 < -4$ 4. $x - 3 > -2$
5. $-3x \geqslant -12$ 6. $-4x \leqslant 8$

Solve and graph.

7. $-4x - 7 > 5$ 8. $-2x + 8 < 4$
9. $2 \leqslant x + 3 \leqslant 5$ 10. $-3 < y - 5 < 8$

Solve.

11. $\dfrac{y}{7} - 1 = \dfrac{1}{7}$ 12. $\dfrac{m}{5} - 2 = \dfrac{3}{5}$

13. $\dfrac{x}{3} > -2$ 14. $\dfrac{y}{-2} \leqslant -1$

15. $\dfrac{y}{3} = 4 - \dfrac{y}{6}$ 16. $\dfrac{x}{4} = 9 - \dfrac{x}{2}$

B 17. $10x + 25(x - 3) = 275$ 18. $-3(4 - x) = 5 - (x + 1)$
   19. $3 - y \leqslant 4(y - 3)$ 20. $x - 2 \geqslant 2(x - 5)$

   21. $\dfrac{x}{5} - \dfrac{x}{6} = \dfrac{6}{5}$ 22. $\dfrac{y}{4} - \dfrac{y}{3} = \dfrac{1}{2}$

   23. $\dfrac{m}{5} - 3 < \dfrac{3}{5} - m$ 24. $u - \dfrac{2}{3} > \dfrac{u}{3} + 2$

   25. $0.1(x - 7) + 0.05x = 0.8$ 26. $0.4(u + 5) - 0.3u = 17$

   Solve and graph.

   27. $2 \leqslant 3x - 7 < 14$ 28. $-4 \leqslant 5x + 6 < 21$
   29. $-4 \leqslant \frac{9}{5}C + 32 \leqslant 68$ 30. $-1 \leqslant \frac{2}{3}t + 5 \leqslant 11$

C *Solve for the indicated variable.*

   31. $3x - 4y = 12$, for y 32. $y = -\frac{2}{3}x + 8$, for x
   33. $Ax + By = C$, for y $(B \neq 0)$ 34. $y = mx + b$, for m
   35. $F = \frac{9}{5}C + 32$, for C 36. $C = \frac{5}{9}(F - 32)$, for F
   37. $A = Bm - Bn$, for B 38. $U = 3C - 2CD$, for C

   Solve and graph.

   39. $-3 \leqslant 4 - 7x < 18$ 40. $-1 < 9 - 2u \leqslant 5$

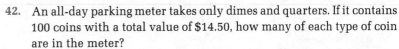

Applications

Business & Economics

41. A jazz concert brought in $60,000 on the sale of 8,000 tickets. If the tickets sold for $6 and $10 each, how many of each type of ticket were sold?

42. An all-day parking meter takes only dimes and quarters. If it contains 100 coins with a total value of $14.50, how many of each type of coin are in the meter?

43. You have $12,000 to invest. If part is invested at 10% and the rest at 15%, how much should be invested at each rate to yield 12% on the total amount?

44. An investor has $20,000 to invest. If part is invested at 8% and the rest at 12%, how much should be invested at each rate to yield 11% on the total amount?

45. *Inflation.* If the price change of cars parallels the change in the CPI (see Table 2 in Example 13), what would a car sell for in 1980 if a comparable model sold for $3,000 in 1965?

46. *Break-even analysis.* For a business to realize a profit, it is clear that revenue R must be greater than costs C; that is, a profit will result only if $R > C$ (the company breaks even when $R = C$). A record manufacturer has a weekly cost equation $C = 300 + 1.5x$ and a revenue equation $R = 2x$, where x is the number of records produced and sold in a week. How many records must be sold for the company to make a profit?

Life Sciences

47. *Wildlife management.* A naturalist for a fish and game department estimated the total number of rainbow trout in a certain lake using the popular capture–mark–recapture technique. He netted, marked, and released 200 rainbow trout. A week later, allowing for thorough mixing, he again netted 200 trout and found 8 marked ones among them. Assuming that the proportion of marked fish in the second sample was the same as the proportion of all marked fish in the total population, estimate the number of rainbow trout in the lake.

48. *Ecology.* If the temperature for a 24 hour period at an Antarctic station ranged between $-49°F$ and $14°F$ (that is, $-49 \leq F \leq 14$), what was the range in degrees Celsius? [*Note:* $F = \frac{9}{5}C + 32$.]

Social Sciences

49. *Psychology.* The IQ (intelligence quotient) is found by dividing the mental age (MA), as indicated on standard tests, by the chronological age (CA) and multiplying by 100. For example, if a child has a mental age of 12 and a chronological age of 8, the calculated IQ is 150. If a 9-year-old girl has an IQ of 140, compute her mental age.

50. *Anthropology.* In their study of genetic groupings, anthropologists use a ratio called the *cephalic index*. This is the ratio of the breadth of the head to its length (looking down from above) expressed as a percentage. Symbolically,

$$C = \frac{100B}{L}$$

where C is the cephalic index, B is the breadth, and L is the length. If an Indian tribe in Baja California (Mexico) had an average cephalic index of 66 and the average breadth of their heads was 6.6 inches, what was the average length of their heads?

0-3 Quadratic Equations

- Solution by Square Root
- Solution by Factoring
- Quadratic Formula

A **quadratic equation** in one variable is any equation that can be written in the form

$$ax^2 + bx + c = 0 \qquad a \neq 0$$

where x is a variable and a, b, and c are constants. We will refer to this form as the **standard form.** The equations

$$5x^2 - 3x + 7 = 0 \qquad \text{and} \qquad 18 = 32t^2 - 12t$$

are both quadratic equations since they are either in the standard form or can be transformed into this form.

We will restrict our review to finding real solutions to quadratic equations. Square root radicals are reviewed in Appendix A.

■ Solution by Square Root

The easiest type of quadratic equation to solve is the special form where the first-degree term is missing:

$$ax^2 + c = 0 \qquad a \neq 0$$

The method makes use of the definition of square root given in Appendix A.

Example 14 Solve by the square root method.

(A) $x^2 - 7 = 0$ (B) $2x^2 - 10 = 0$ (C) $3x^2 + 27 = 0$

Solutions (A) $x^2 - 7 = 0$

$x^2 = 7$ What real number squared is 7?

$x = \pm\sqrt{7}$ Short for $\sqrt{7}$ and $-\sqrt{7}$

(B) $2x^2 - 10 = 0$

$2x^2 = 10$

$x^2 = 5$ What real number squared is 5?

$x = \pm\sqrt{5}$

(C) $3x^2 + 27 = 0$

$3x^2 = -27$

$x^2 = -9$ What real number squared is -9?

No real solution. (Why?)

Problem 14 Solve by the square root method.

(A) $x^2 - 6 = 0$ (B) $3x^2 - 12 = 0$ (C) $x^2 + 4 = 0$

■ Solution by Factoring

If the left side of a quadratic equation when written in standard form can be factored, then the equation can be solved very quickly. The method of solution by factoring rests on the following important property of real numbers: *If a and b are real numbers, then ab = 0 if and only if a = 0 or b = 0 (or both).*

Example 15 Solve by factoring, if possible.

(A) $3x^2 - 6x - 24 = 0$ (B) $3y^2 = 2y$ (C) $x^2 - 2x - 1 = 0$

Solutions   (A) $3x^2 - 6x - 24 = 0$ Divide both sides by 3, since 3 is a
                                               factor of each coefficient

$$x^2 - 2x - 8 = 0$$ Factor the left side, if possible

$$(x - 4)(x + 2) = 0$$

$$x - 4 = 0 \quad \text{or} \quad x + 2 = 0$$

$$x = 4 \quad \text{or} \qquad x = -2$$

(B) $3y^2 = 2y$ We lose the solution $y = 0$ if both
                                sides are divided by y ($3y^2 = 2y$ and
$$3y^2 - 2y = 0$$ $3y = 2$ are not equivalent)

$$y(3y - 2) = 0$$

$$y = 0 \quad \text{or} \quad 3y - 2 = 0$$

$$3y = 2$$

$$y = \tfrac{2}{3}$$

(C) $x^2 - 2x - 1 = 0$

This equation cannot be factored using integer coefficients. We will
solve this type of equation by another method, considered below.

Problem 15   Solve by factoring, if possible.

(A) $2x^2 + 4x - 30 = 0$ (B) $2x^2 = 3x$ (C) $2x^2 - 8x + 3 = 0$

The factoring and square root methods are fast and easy to use when they
apply. However, there are quadratic equations that look simple but cannot
be solved by either method. For example, as was noted in Example 15C, the
polynomial in

$$x^2 - 2x - 1 = 0$$

cannot be factored using integer coefficients. This brings us to the well-
known and widely used quadratic formula.

■ Quadratic Formula

There is a method called *completing the square* that will work for all
quadratic equations. After briefly reviewing this method, we will then use
it to develop the famous quadratic formula—a formula that will enable us
to solve any quadratic equation quite mechanically.

The method of **completing the square** is based on the process of transforming a quadratic equation in standard form,

$$ax^2 + bx + c = 0$$

into the form

$$(x + A)^2 = B$$

where A and B are constants. Then, this last equation can easily be solved (if it has a real solution) by the square root method discussed above.

Consider the equation

$$x^2 - 2x - 1 = 0 \tag{1}$$

Since the left side does not factor using integer coefficients, we add 1 to each side to remove the constant term from the left side:

$$x^2 - 2x = 1 \tag{2}$$

Now we try to find a number that we can add to each side to make the left side a square of a first-degree polynomial. Note the following two squares:

$$(x + m)^2 = x^2 + 2mx + m^2 \qquad (x - m)^2 = x^2 - 2mx + m^2$$

We see that the third term on the right is the square of one-half the coefficient of x in the second term on the right. To complete the square in equation (2), we add the square of one-half the coefficient of x, $(-\frac{2}{2})^2 = 1$, to each side. (This rule works only when the coefficient of x^2 is 1, that is, $a = 1$.) Thus,

$$x^2 - 2x + 1 = 1 + 1$$

The left side is the square of $x - 1$, and we write

$$(x - 1)^2 = 2$$

What number squared is 2?

$$x - 1 = \pm\sqrt{2}$$
$$x = 1 \pm \sqrt{2}$$

And equation (1) is solved!

Let us try the method on the general quadratic equation

$$ax^2 + bx + c = 0 \qquad a \neq 0 \tag{3}$$

and solve it once and for all for x in terms of the coefficients a, b, and c. We start by multiplying both sides of (3) by $1/a$ to obtain

$$x^2 + \frac{b}{a}x + \frac{c}{a} = 0$$

Add $-c/a$ to both members:

$$x^2 + \frac{b}{a}x = -\frac{c}{a}$$

Now we complete the square on the left side by adding the square of one-half the coefficient of x, that is, $(b/2a)^2 = b^2/4a^2$, to each side:

$$x^2 + \frac{b}{a}x + \frac{b^2}{4a^2} = \frac{b^2}{4a^2} - \frac{c}{a}$$

Writing the left member as a square and combining the right side into a single fraction, we obtain

$$\left(x + \frac{b}{2a}\right)^2 = \frac{b^2 - 4ac}{4a^2}$$

Now we solve by the square root method:

$$x + \frac{b}{2a} = \pm\sqrt{\frac{b^2 - 4ac}{4a^2}}$$

$$x = -\frac{b}{2a} \pm \frac{\sqrt{b^2 - 4ac}}{2a}$$

When this is written as a single fraction, it becomes the quadratic formula:

Quadratic Formula

If $ax^2 + bx + c = 0$, $a \neq 0$, then

$$x = \frac{-b \pm \sqrt{b^2 - 4ac}}{2a}$$

This formula is generally used to solve quadratic equations when the square root or factoring methods do not work. The quantity $b^2 - 4ac$ under the radical is called the **discriminant,** and it gives us the useful information about solutions listed in Table 3.

Table 3

$b^2 - 4ac$	$ax^2 + bx + c = 0$
Positive	Two real solutions
Zero	One real solution
Negative	No real solutions

Example 16 Solve $x^2 - 2x - 1 = 0$ using the quadratic formula.

Solution $x^2 - 2x - 1 = 0$

$$x = \frac{-b \pm \sqrt{b^2 - 4ac}}{2a} \qquad \begin{aligned} a &= 1 \\ b &= -2 \\ c &= -1 \end{aligned}$$

$$= \frac{-(-2) \pm \sqrt{(-2)^2 - 4(1)(-1)}}{2(1)}$$

$$= \frac{2 \pm \sqrt{8}}{2} = \frac{2 \pm 2\sqrt{2}}{2} = 1 \pm \sqrt{2}$$

Check $x^2 - 2x - 1 = 0$
When $x = 1 + \sqrt{2}$,

$$(1 + \sqrt{2})^2 - 2(1 + \sqrt{2}) - 1 = 1 + 2\sqrt{2} + 2 - 2 - 2\sqrt{2} - 1 = 0$$

When $x = 1 - \sqrt{2}$,

$$(1 - \sqrt{2})^2 - 2(1 - \sqrt{2}) - 1 = 1 - 2\sqrt{2} + 2 - 2 + 2\sqrt{2} - 1 = 0$$

Problem 16   Solve $2x^2 - 4x - 3 = 0$ using the quadratic formula.

If we try to solve $x^2 - 6x + 11 = 0$ using the quadratic formula, we obtain

$$x = \frac{6 \pm \sqrt{-8}}{2}$$

which is not a real number. (Why?)

Answers to   14.   (A) $\pm\sqrt{6}$ (B) ± 2 (C)   No real solution
Matched Problems   15.   (A) $-5, 3$ (B) $0, \frac{3}{2}$
      (C)   Cannot be factored using integer coefficients
16. $(2 \pm \sqrt{10})/2$

Exercise 0-3

Find only real solutions in the problems below. If there are no real solutions, say so.

A   Solve by the square root method.

1. $x^2 - 4 = 0$ 2. $x^2 - 9 = 0$
3. $2x^2 - 22 = 0$ 4. $3m^2 - 21 = 0$

Solve by factoring.

5. $2u^2 - 8u - 24 = 0$ 6. $3x^2 - 18x + 15 = 0$
7. $x^2 = 2x$ 8. $n^2 = 3n$

Solve by using the quadratic formula.

9. $x^2 - 6x - 3 = 0$ 10. $m^2 + 8m + 3 = 0$
11. $3u^2 + 12u + 6 = 0$ 12. $2x^2 - 20x - 6 = 0$

B   Solve, using any method.

13. $2x^2 = 4x$ 14. $2x^2 = -3x$
15. $4u^2 - 9 = 0$ 16. $9y^2 - 25 = 0$
17. $8x^2 + 20x = 12$ 18. $9x^2 - 6 = 15x$
19. $x^2 = 1 - x$ 20. $m^2 = 1 - 3m$
21. $2x^2 = 6x - 3$ 22. $2x^2 = 4x - 1$
23. $y^2 - 4y = -8$ 24. $x^2 - 2x = -3$
25. $(x + 4)^2 = 11$ 26. $(y - 5)^2 = 7$

C   27.   · Solve $A = P(1 + r)^2$ for r in terms of A and P; that is, isolate r on the left side of the equation (with coefficient 1) and end up with an algebraic expression on the right side involving A and P but not r. Write the answer using positive square roots only.
28.   Solve $x^2 + mx + n = 0$ for x in terms of m and n.

Applications

Business & Economics

29. *Supply and demand.* The demand equation for a certain brand of popular records is $d = 3{,}000/p$. Notice that as the price (p) goes up, the number of records people are willing to buy (d) goes down, and vice versa. The supply equation is given by $s = 1{,}000p - 500$. Notice again, as the price (p) goes up, the number of records a supplier is willing to sell (s) goes up. At what price will supply equal demand; that is, at what price will $d = s$? In economic theory the price at which supply equals demand is called the **equilibrium point**—the point where the price ceases to change.

30. If P dollars is invested at $100r$ percent compounded annually, at the end of 2 years it will grow to $A = P(1 + r)^2$. At what interest rate will $100 grow to $144 in 2 years? [*Note:* If $A = 144$ and $P = 100$, find r.]

Life Sciences

31. *Ecology.* An important element in the erosive force of moving water is its velocity. To measure the velocity v (in feet per second) of a stream we have only to find a hollow L-shaped tube, place one end under the water pointing upstream and the other end pointing straight up a couple of feet out of the water. The water will then be pushed up the tube a certain distance h (in feet) above the surface of the stream. Physicists have shown that $v^2 = 64h$. Approximately how fast is a stream flowing if $h = 1$ foot? If $h = 0.5$ foot?

Social Sciences

32. *Safety research.* It is of considerable importance to know the least number of feet d in which a car can be stopped, including reaction time of the driver, at various speeds v (in miles/hour). Safety research has produced the formula $d = 0.044v^2 + 1.1v$. If it took a car 550 feet to stop, estimate the car's speed at the moment the stopping process was started. You might find a hand calculator of help in this problem.

0-4   Cartesian Coordinate System and Straight Lines

- Cartesian Coordinate System
- Graphing Linear Equations in Two Variables
- Slope
- Equations of Lines—Special Forms
- Application

■ Cartesian Coordinate System

Recall that a **Cartesian (rectangular) coordinate system** in a plane is formed by taking two mutually perpendicular real number lines intersecting at their origins **(coordinate axes)**, one horizontal and one vertical, and then assigning unique **ordered pairs** of numbers **(coordinates)** to each point P in the plane (Fig. 8). The first coordinate **(abscissa)** is the distance of P from the vertical axis, and the second coordinate **(ordinate)** is the distance of P from the horizontal axis. In Figure 8, the coordinates of point P are (a, b). By reversing the process, each ordered pair of real numbers can be associated with a unique point in the plane. The coordinate axes divide the plane into four parts **(quadrants)**, numbered I to IV in a counterclockwise direction.

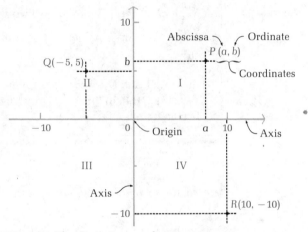

Figure 8 The Cartesian coordinate system

■ Graphing Linear Equations in Two Variables

A linear equation in two variables is an equation that can be written in the form

$$Ax + By = C \qquad \text{Standard form}$$

with A and B not both zero. For example,

$$2x - 3y = 5 \qquad x = 7 \qquad y = \tfrac{1}{2}x - 3 \qquad y = -3$$

can all be considered linear equations in two variables. The first is in standard form, while the other three can be written in standard form as follows:

Standard form

$x = 7$	$x + 0y = 7$
$y = \tfrac{1}{2}x - 3$	$-\tfrac{1}{2}x + y = -3 \quad \text{or} \quad x - 2y = 6$
$y = -3$	$0x + y = -3$

A **solution** of an equation in two variables is an ordered pair of real numbers that satisfy the equation. For example, $(0, -3)$ is a solution of $3x - 4y = 12$. The **solution set** of an equation in two variables is the set of all solutions of the equation. When we say that we **graph an equation** in two variables, we mean that we graph its solution set on a rectangular coordinate system.

We state the following important theorem without proof:

Theorem 1

Graph of a Linear Equation in Two Variables

The graph of any equation of the form

$$Ax + By = C \qquad \text{Standard form} \tag{1}$$

where A, B, and C are constants (A and B not both zero), is a straight line. Every straight line in a Cartesian coordinate system is the graph of an equation of this type.

Also, the graph of any equation of the form

$$y = mx + b \tag{2}$$

where m and b are constants, is a straight line. Form (2) is simply a special case of (1) for $B \neq 0$. To graph either (1) or (2), we plot any two points of their solution set and use a straightedge to draw the line through these two points. The points where the line crosses the axes—called the **intercepts** —are often the easiest to find when dealing with form (1). To find the **y intercept,** we let $x = 0$ and solve for y; to find the **x intercept,** we let $y = 0$ and solve for x. It is sometimes wise to find a third point as a check.

Example 17 (A) The graph of $3x - 4y = 12$ is

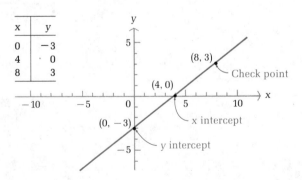

x	y
0	-3
4	0
8	3

(B)   The graph of $y = 2x - 1$ is

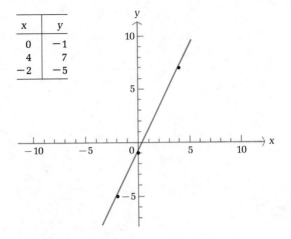

x	y
0	−1
4	7
−2	−5

Problem 17   Graph: (A) $4x - 3y = 12$ (B) $y = \dfrac{x}{2} + 2$

■ Slope

It is very useful to have a numerical measure of the "steepness" of a line. The concept of slope is widely used for this purpose. The **slope** of a line through the two points (x_1, y_1) and (x_2, y_2) is given by the following formula:

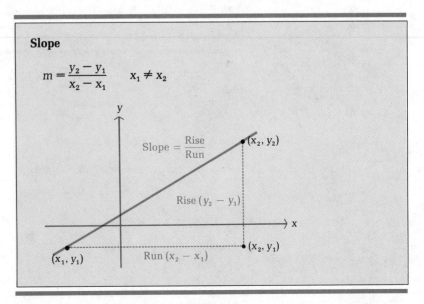

Slope

$$m = \frac{y_2 - y_1}{x_2 - x_1} \qquad x_1 \neq x_2$$

Slope $= \dfrac{\text{Rise}}{\text{Run}}$

(x_2, y_2)

Rise $(y_2 - y_1)$

(x_1, y_1) (x_2, y_1)

Run $(x_2 - x_1)$

The slope of a vertical line is not defined. (Why? See Example 18B.)

Example 18 Find the slope of the line through each pair of points:

(A) $(-2, 5), (4, -7)$ (B) $(-3, -1), (-3, 5)$

Solutions   (A) Let $(x_1, y_1) = (-2, 5)$ and $(x_2, y_2) = (4, -7)$. Then

$$m = \frac{y_2 - y_1}{x_2 - x_1} = \frac{-7 - 5}{4 - (-2)} = \frac{-12}{6} = -2$$

Note that we also could have let $(x_1, y_1) = (4, -7)$ and $(x_2, y_2) = (-2, 5)$, since this simply reverses the sign in both the numerator and the denominator and the slope does not change:

$$m = \frac{5 - (-7)}{-2 - 4} = \frac{12}{-6} = -2$$

(B) Let $(x_1, y_1) = (-3, -1)$ and $(x_2, y_2) = (-3, 5)$. Then

$$m = \frac{y_2 - y_1}{x_2 - x_1} = \frac{5 - (-1)}{-3 - (-3)} = \frac{6}{0} \qquad \text{Not defined!}$$

Notice that $x_1 = x_2$. This is always true for a vertical line, since the abscissa (first coordinate) of every point on a vertical line is the same. Thus, the slope of a vertical line is not defined (that is, the slope does not exist).

Problem 18 Find the slope of the line through each pair of points:

(A) $(3, -6), (-2, 4)$ (B) $(-7, 5), (3, 5)$

In general, the slope of a line may be positive, negative, zero, or not defined. Each of these cases is interpreted geometrically in Table 4.

Table 4 Going from Left to Right

Line	Slope	Example
Rising	Positive	
Falling	Negative	
Horizontal	Zero	
Vertical	Not defined	

■ Equations of Lines — Special Forms

The constants m and b in the equation

$$y = mx + b \tag{3}$$

have special geometric significance.

If we let $x = 0$, then $y = b$, and we observe that the graph of (3) crosses the y axis at $(0, b)$. The constant b is the y *intercept*. For example, the y intercept of the graph of $y = -4x - 1$ is -1.

To determine the geometric significance of m, we proceed as follows: If $y = mx + b$, then by setting $x = 0$ and $x = 1$, we conclude that $(0, b)$ and $(1, m + b)$ lie on its graph (a line). Hence, the slope of this graph (line) is given by:

$$\text{Slope} = \frac{y_2 - y_1}{x_2 - x_1} = \frac{(m + b) - b}{1 - 0} = m$$

Thus, m is the slope of the line given by $y = mx + b$.

Slope – Intercept Form

The equation

$$y = mx + b \qquad \begin{array}{l} m = \text{Slope} \\ b = y \text{ intercept} \end{array} \tag{4}$$

is called the **slope – intercept form** of an equation of a line.

Example 19   (A) Find the slope and y intercept, and graph $y = -\tfrac{2}{3}x - 3$.

(B) Write the equation of the line with slope $\tfrac{2}{3}$ and y intercept -2.

Solutions   (A) $\text{Slope} = m = -\tfrac{2}{3}$ (B) $m = \tfrac{2}{3}$ and $b = -2$;
$y \text{ intercept} = b = -3$ thus, $y = \tfrac{2}{3}x - 2$

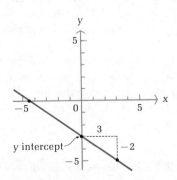

Problem 19 Write the equation of the line with slope $\frac{1}{2}$ and y intercept -1. Graph.

Suppose a line has slope m and passes through a fixed point (x_1, y_1). If the point (x, y) is any other point on the line (Fig. 9), then

$$\frac{y - y_1}{x - x_1} = m$$

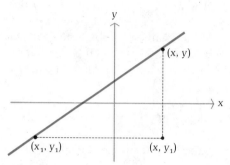

Figure 9

that is,

$$y - y_1 = m(x - x_1)$$

We now observe that (x_1, y_1) also satisfies this equation and conclude that this is an equation of a line with slope m that passes through (x_1, y_1).

Point–Slope Form

An equation of a line with slope m that passes through (x_1, y_1) is

$$y - y_1 = m(x - x_1) \qquad\qquad (5)$$

which is called the **point–slope form** of an equation of a line.

The point–slope form is extremely useful, since it enables us to find an equation for a line if we know its slope and the coordinates of a point on the line or if we know the coordinates of two points on the line.

Example 20 · (A) Find an equation for the line that has slope $\frac{1}{2}$ and passes through $(-4, 3)$. Write the final answer in the form $Ax + By = C$.

(B) Find an equation for the line that passes through the two points $(-3, 2)$ and $(-4, 5)$. Write the resulting equation in the form $y = mx + b$.

Solutions (A) $y - y_1 = m(x - x_1)$

Let $m = \frac{1}{2}$ and $(x_1, y_1) = (-4, 3)$. Then

$$y - 3 = \tfrac{1}{2}[x - (-4)]$$

$$y - 3 = \tfrac{1}{2}(x + 4) \qquad \text{Multiply by 2}$$

$$2y - 6 = x + 4$$

$$-x + 2y = 10 \quad \text{or} \quad x - 2y = -10$$

(B) First, find the slope of the line by using the slope formula:

$$m = \frac{y_2 - y_1}{x_2 - x_1} = \frac{5 - 2}{-4 - (-3)} = \frac{3}{-1} = -3$$

Now use

$$y - y_1 = m(x - x_1)$$

with $m = -3$ and $(x_1, y_1) = (-3, 2)$:

$$y - 2 = -3[x - (-3)]$$

$$y - 2 = -3(x + 3)$$

$$y - 2 = -3x - 9$$

$$y = -3x - 7$$

Problem 20 (A) Find an equation for the line that has slope $\tfrac{2}{3}$ and passes through $(6, -2)$. Write the resulting equation in the form $Ax + By = C$, $A > 0$.

(B) Find an equation for the line that passes through $(2, -3)$ and $(4, 3)$. Write the resulting equation in the form $y = mx + b$.

The simplest equations of a line are those for horizontal and vertical lines. A **horizontal line** has slope 0; thus its equation is of the form

$$y = 0x + c \qquad \text{Slope} = 0, \quad y \text{ intercept } c$$

or simply

$$y = c$$

Figure 10 illustrates the graph of $y = 3$ and $y = -2$.

If a line is vertical, then its slope is not defined. All x values (abscissas) of points on a vertical line are equal, while y can take on any value (Fig. 11).

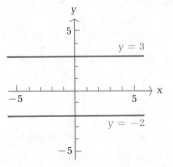

Figure 10

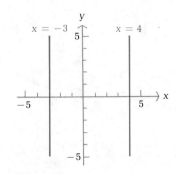

Figure 11

Thus, a **vertical line** has an equation of the form

$x + 0y = c$ x intercept c

or simply

$x = c$

Figure 11 illustrates the graph of $x = -3$ and $x = 4$.

Equations of Horizontal and Vertical Lines

Horizontal line with y intercept c: $y = c$

Vertical line with x intercept c: $x = c$

Example 21   The equation of a horizontal line through $(-2, 3)$ is $y = 3$, and the equation of a vertical line through the same point is $x = -2$.

Problem 21   Find the equations of the horizontal and vertical lines through $(4, -5)$.

It can be shown that if two nonvertical lines are parallel, then they have the same slope. And if two lines have the same slope, they are parallel. It can also be shown that if two nonvertical lines are perpendicular, then their slopes are the negative reciprocals of each other (that is, $m_2 = -1/m_1$, or, equivalently, $m_1 m_2 = -1$). And if the slopes of two lines are the negative reciprocals of each other, the lines are perpendicular. Symbolically:

Parallel and Perpendicular Lines

Given nonvertical lines L_1 and L_2 with slopes m_1 and m_2, respectively, then

$L_1 \| L_2$ if and only if $m_1 = m_2$

$L_1 \perp L_2$ if and only if $m_1 m_2 = -1$ or $m_2 = -\dfrac{1}{m_1}$

[Note: $\|$ means "is parallel to" and $\perp$ means "is perpendicular to."]

Example 22   Given the line $x - 2y = 4$, find the equation of a line that passes through $(2, -3)$ and is:

(A)   Parallel to the given line   (B)   Perpendicular to the given line

Write final equations in the form $y = mx + b$.

Solution First find the slope of the given line by writing $x - 2y = 4$ in the form $y = mx + b$:

$$x - 2y = 4$$
$$y = \tfrac{1}{2}x - 2$$

The slope of the given line is $\tfrac{1}{2}$.

(A) The slope of a line parallel to the given line is also $\tfrac{1}{2}$. We have only to find the equation of a line through $(2, -3)$ with slope $\tfrac{1}{2}$ to solve part A:

$$y - y_1 = m(x - x_1) \qquad m = \tfrac{1}{2} \text{ and } (x_1, y_1) = (2, -3)$$
$$y - (-3) = \tfrac{1}{2}(x - 2)$$
$$y + 3 = \tfrac{1}{2}x - 1$$
$$y = \tfrac{1}{2}x - 4$$

(B) The slope of the line perpendicular to the given line is the negative reciprocal of $\tfrac{1}{2}$; that is, -2. We have only to find the equation of a line through $(2, -3)$ with slope -2 to solve part B:

$$y - y_1 = m(x - x_1) \qquad m = -2 \text{ and } (x_1, y_1) = (2, -3)$$
$$y - (-3) = -2(x - 2)$$
$$y + 3 = -2x + 4$$
$$y = -2x + 1$$

Problem 22 Given the line $2x = 6 - 3y$, find the equation of a line that passes through $(-3, 9)$ and is:

(A) Parallel to the given line   (B) Perpendicular to the given line

Write final equations in the form $y = mx + b$.

■ Application

We will now see how equations of lines occur in certain applications.

Example 23 The management of a company that manufactures roller skates has fixed costs (costs at zero output) of $300 per day and total costs of $4,300 per day at an output of 100 pairs of skates per day. Assume that cost C is linearly related to output x.

(A) Find the slope of the line joining the points associated with outputs of 0 and 100; that is, the line passing through $(0, 300)$ and $(100, 4,300)$.

(B) Find an equation of the line relating output to cost. Write the final answer in the form $C = mx + b$.

(C) Graph the cost equation from part B for $0 \leqslant x \leqslant 200$.

Solutions   (A) $m = \dfrac{y_2 - y_1}{x_2 - x_1} = \dfrac{4{,}300 - 300}{100 - 0} = \dfrac{4{,}000}{100} = 40$

(B) We must find an equation of the line that passes through (0, 300) with slope 40. We use the slope–intercept form:

$$C = mx + b$$
$$C = 40x + 300$$

(C)

x	C
0	300
100	4,300
200	8,300

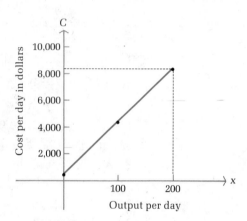

Output per day

Problem 23   Answer parts A and B in Example 23 for fixed costs of $250 per day and total costs of $3,450 per day at an output of 80 pairs of skates per day.

Answers to
Matched Problems

17. (A)   (B)

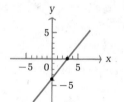   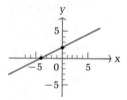

18. (A) -2 (B) 0 (Zero is a number—it exists! It is the slope of a horizontal line.)

19. $y = \frac{1}{2}x - 1$ 20. (A) $2x - 3y = 18$
                                                                    (B) $y = 3x - 9$

21. $y = -5$, $x = 4$ 22. (A) $y = -\frac{2}{3}x + 7$
                                                                    (B) $y = \frac{3}{2}x + \frac{27}{2}$

23. (A) $m = 40$ (B) $C = 40x + 250$

Exercise 0-4

A   *Graph in a rectangular coordinate system.*

1. $y = 2x - 3$
2. $y = \dfrac{x}{2} + 1$
3. $2x + 3y = 12$
4. $8x - 3y = 24$

Find the slope and y intercept of the graph of each equation.

5. $y = 2x - 3$
6. $y = \dfrac{x}{2} + 1$
7. $y = -\tfrac{2}{3}x + 2$
8. $y = \tfrac{3}{4}x - 2$

Write an equation of the line with the indicated slope and y intercept.

9.   Slope $= -2$
y intercept $= 4$
10.   Slope $= -\tfrac{2}{3}$
y intercept $= -2$
11.   Slope $= -\tfrac{3}{5}$
y intercept $= 3$
12.   Slope $= 1$
y intercept $= -2$

B   *Graph in a rectangular coordinate system.*

13. $y = -\tfrac{2}{3}x - 2$
14. $y = -\tfrac{3}{2}x + 1$
15. $3x - 2y = 10$
16. $5x - 6y = 15$
17. $x = 3$ and $y = -2$
18. $x = -3$ and $y = 2$

Find the slope of the graph of each equation. (First write the equation in the form y = mx + b.)

19. $3x + y = 5$
20. $2x - y = -3$
21. $2x + 3y = 12$
22. $3x - 2y = 10$

Write an equation of the line through each indicated point with the indicated slope. Transform the equation into the form y = mx + b.

23. $m = -3$, $(4, -1)$
24. $m = -2$, $(-3, 2)$
25. $m = \tfrac{2}{3}$, $(-6, -5)$
26. $m = \tfrac{1}{2}$, $(-4, 3)$

Find the slope of the line that passes through the given points.

27. $(1, 3)$ and $(7, 5)$
28. $(2, 1)$ and $(10, 5)$
29. $(-5, -2)$ and $(5, -4)$
30. $(3, 7)$ and $(-6, 4)$

Write an equation of the line through each indicated pair of points. Write the final answer in the form Ax + By = C, A > 0.

31. $(1, 3)$ and $(7, 5)$
32. $(2, 1)$ and $(10, 5)$
33. $(-5, -2)$ and $(5, -4)$
34. $(3, 7)$ and $(-6, 4)$

Write equations of the vertical and horizontal lines through each point.

35. $(3, -5)$ **36.** $(-2, 7)$ **37.** $(-1, -3)$ **38.** $(6, -4)$

Find an equation of the line, given the information in each problem. Write the final answer in the form $y = mx + b$.

39. Line passes through $(-2, 5)$ with slope $-\frac{1}{2}$.
40. Line passes through $(3, -1)$ with slope $-\frac{2}{3}$.
41. Line passes through $(-2, 2)$ and is
   (A) Parallel   (B) Perpendicular to $y = -\frac{1}{2}x + 5$.
42. Line passes through $(-4, -3)$ and is
   (A) Parallel   (B) Perpendicular to $y = 2x - 3$.
43. Line passes through $(-2, -1)$ and is
   (A) Parallel   (B) Perpendicular to $x - 2y = 4$.
44. Line passes through $(-3, 2)$ and is
   (A) Parallel   (B) Perpendicular to $2x + 3y = -6$.

C   **45.** Graph $y = mx - 2$ for $m = 2$, $m = \frac{1}{2}$, $m = 0$, $m = -\frac{1}{2}$, and $m = -2$, all on the same coordinate system.
46. Graph $y = -\frac{1}{2}x + b$ for $b = -4$, $b = 0$, and $b = 4$, all on the same coordinate system.

Write an equation of the line through the indicated points. Be careful!

47. $(2, 7)$ and $(2, -3)$ **48.** $(-2, 3)$ and $(-2, -1)$
49. $(2, 3)$ and $(-5, 3)$ **50.** $(-3, -3)$ and $(0, -3)$

Applications

Business & Economics

51. *Simple interest.* If $\$P$ (the principal) is invested at an interest rate of r, then the amount A that is due after t years is given by

$$A = Prt + P$$

If $\$100$ is invested at 6% ($r = 0.06$), then $A = 6t + 100$, $t \geq 0$.

(A) What will $\$100$ amount to after 5 years? After 20 years?
(B) Graph the equation for $0 \leq t \leq 20$.
(C) What is the slope of the graph? (The slope indicates the increase in the amount A for each additional year of investment.)

52. *Cost equation.* The management of a company manufacturing surfboards has fixed costs (zero output) of $\$200$ per day and total costs of $\$1,400$ per day at a daily output of twenty boards.

(A) Assuming the total cost per day (C) is linearly related to the total output per day (x), write an equation relating these two quantities. [*Hint:* Find an equation of the line that passes through (0, 200) and (20, 1,400).]

(B) What are the total costs for an output of twelve boards per day?

(C) Graph the equation for $0 \leq x \leq 20$.

[*Note:* The slope of the line found in part A is the increase in total cost for each additional unit produced and is called the *marginal cost*. More will be said about the concept of marginal cost later.]

53. *Demand equation.* A manufacturing company is interested in introducing a new power mower. Its market research department gave the management the demand-price forecast listed in the table.

Price	Estimated Demand
$ 70	7,800
$120	4,800
$160	2,400
$200	0

(A) Plot these points, letting d represent the number of mowers people are willing to buy (demand) at a price of $p each.

(B) Note that the points in part A lie along a straight line. Find an equation of that line.

[*Note:* The slope of the line found in part B indicates the decrease in demand for each $1 increase in price.]

54. *Depreciation.* Office equipment was purchased for $20,000 and is assumed to have a scrap value of $2,000 after 10 years. If its value is depreciated linearly (for tax purposes) from $20,000 to $2,000:

(A) Find the linear equation that relates value (V) in dollars to time (t) in years.

(B) What would be the value of the equipment after 6 years?

(C) Graph the equation for $0 \leq t \leq 10$.

[*Note:* The slope found in part A indicates the decrease in value per year.]

Life Sciences

55. *Nutrition.* In a nutrition experiment, a biologist wants to prepare a special diet for the experimental animals. Two food mixes, A and B, are available. If mix A contains 20% protein and mix B contains 10% protein, what combination of each mix will provide exactly 20 grams of protein? Let x be the amount of A used and let y be the amount of B used. Then write a linear equation relating x, y, and 20. Graph this equation for $x \geq 0$ and $y \geq 0$.

56. *Ecology.* As one descends into the ocean, pressure increases linearly. The pressure is 15 pounds per square inch on the surface and 30 pounds per square inch 33 feet below the surface.

(A) If p is the pressure in pounds and d is the depth below the surface in feet, write an equation that expresses p in terms of d. [*Hint:* Find an equation of the line that passes through (0, 15) and (33, 30).]

(B) What is the pressure at 12,540 feet (the average depth of the ocean)?

(C) Graph the equation for $0 \leqslant d \leqslant 12{,}540$.

[*Note:* The slope found in part A indicates the change in pressure for each additional foot of depth.]

Social Sciences

57. *Psychology.* In an experiment on motivation, J. S. Brown trained a group of rats to run down a narrow passage in a cage to obtain food in a goal box. Using a harness, he then connected the rats to an overhead wire that was attached to a spring scale. A rat was placed at different distances d (in centimeters) from the goal box, and the pull p (in grams) of the rat toward the food was measured. Brown found that the relationship between these two variables was very close to being linear and could be approximated by the equation

$$p = -\tfrac{1}{5}d + 70 \qquad 30 \leqslant d \leqslant 175$$

(See J. S. Brown, *Journal of Comparative and Physiological Psychology,* 1948, 41:450–465.)

(A) What was the pull when $d = 30$? When $d = 175$?

(B) Graph the equation.

(C) What is the slope of the line?

0-5 Functions and Graphs

- Definition of a Function
- Functions Specified by Equations
- Function Notation
- Linear Functions and Their Graphs
- Quadratic Functions and Their Graphs
- Application: Market Research

The function concept is one of the most important concepts in mathematics. The idea of correspondence plays a central role in its formulation. You have already had experiences with correspondences in everyday life. For example:

To each person there corresponds an annual income.

To each item in a supermarket there corresponds a price.

To each day there corresponds a maximum temperature.

For the manufacture of x items there corresponds a cost.

For the sale of x items there corresponds a revenue.

To each square there corresponds an area.

To each number there corresponds its cube.

One of the most important aspects of any science (managerial, life, social, physical, etc.) is the establishment of correspondences among various types of phenomena. Once a correspondence is known, predictions can be made. A cost analyst would like to predict costs for various levels of output in a manufacturing process; a medical researcher would like to know the correspondence between heart disease and obesity; a psychologist would like to predict the level of performance after a subject has repeated a task a given number of times; and so on.

■ Definition of a Function

What do all of the preceding examples have in common? Each deals with the matching of elements from one set with the elements in a second set. Consider the following three tables of the cube, square, and square root.

Table 5		Table 6		Table 7	
Domain (Number)	**Range (Cube)**	**Domain (Number)**	**Range (Square)**	**Domain (Number)**	**Range (Square Root)**
0 ⟶ 0		−2 ⟶ 4		0 ⟶ 0	
1 ⟶ 1		−1 ⟶ 1		1 ⟶ 1, −1	
2 ⟶ 8		0 ⟶ 0		4 ⟶ 2, −2	
		1		9 ⟶ 3, −3	
		2			

Tables 5 and 6 specify functions, but Table 7 does not. The very important term *function* is now defined.

> **Definition of a Function**
>
> A **function** is a rule (process or method) that produces a correspondence between one set of elements, called the **domain,** and a second set of elements, called the **range,** such that to each element in the domain there corresponds *one and only one* element in the range.

Tables 5 and 6 are functions, since to each domain value there corresponds exactly one range value (for example, the square of -2 is 4 and no other number). On the other hand, Table 7 is not a function, since to at least one domain value there corresponds more than one range value (for example, to the domain value 9 there corresponds -3 and 3, both square roots of 9).

Since in a function elements in the range are paired with elements in the domain by some rule or process, this correspondence (pairing) can be illustrated by using ordered pairs of elements where the first component represents a domain element and the second component a corresponding range element. Thus, we can write functions 1 and 2 (Tables 5 and 6) as follows:

Function 1 $= \{(0, 0), (1, 1), (2, 8)\}$

Function 2 $= \{(-2, 4), (-1, 1), (0, 0), (1, 1), (2, 4)\}$

As a consequence of these definitions, we find that a function can be specified in many different ways: by an equation, by a table, by a set of ordered pairs of elements, and by a graph, to name a few of the more common ways (see Table 8). All that matters is that we are given a set of elements called the domain and a rule (method or process) of obtaining unique corresponding range values for each domain value. (Incidentally, the **graph of a function** specified by an equation in two variables is the graph of the set of all ordered pairs of real numbers that satisfies the equation.)

Table 8 Common Ways of Specifying Functions

Method	Illustration	Example
Equation	$y = x^2 + x \qquad x \in R^*$	If $x = 2$, then $y = 6$.
Table		If $p = 4$, then $C = 18$.

p	C
2	14
4	18
6	22

Method	Illustration	Example
Set of ordered pairs of elements	$\{(2, 14), (4, 18), (6, 22)\}$	6 corresponds to 22.
Graph		If $x = 4$, $y = 2$.

* Recall that R is the set of real numbers.

■ Functions Specified by Equations

Frequently, domains and ranges of functions are sets of numbers, and the rules associating range values with domain values are equations in two variables. Consider the equation

$$y = x^2 - x \qquad x \in R$$

For each **input** x we obtain one **output** y. For example,

If $x = 3$,   then $y = 3^2 - 3 = 6$.

If $x = -\frac{1}{2}$, then $y = (-\frac{1}{2})^2 - (-\frac{1}{2}) = \frac{1}{4} + \frac{1}{2} = \frac{3}{4}$.

The input values are domain values and the output values are range values. The equation (a rule) assigns each domain value x a range value y. The variable x is called an *independent variable* (since values are "independently" assigned to x from the domain), and y is called a *dependent variable* (since the value of y "depends" on the value assigned to x). In general, any variable used as a placeholder for domain values is called an **independent variable;** any variable that is used as a placeholder for range values is called a **dependent variable.**

When does an equation specify a function?

Equations and Functions

In an equation in two variables, if there corresponds exactly one value of the dependent variable (output) to each value of the independent variable (input), then the equation specifies a function. If there is more than one output for at least one input, then the equation does not specify a function.

Unless stated to the contrary, we shall adhere to the following convention regarding domains and ranges for functions specified by equations.

Agreement on Domains and Ranges

If a function is specified by an equation and the domain is not indicated, then we shall assume that the domain is the set of all real number replacements of the independent variable (inputs) that produce real values for the dependent variable (outputs). The range is the set of all outputs corresponding to input values.

■ Function Notation

We have just seen that a function involves two sets of elements, a domain and a range, and a rule of correspondence that enables one to assign to each element in the domain exactly one element in the range. We use different letters to denote names for numbers; in essentially the same way, we will now use different letters to denote names for functions. For example, f and g may be used to name the two functions

$$f: \quad y = 2x + 1$$
$$g: \quad y = x^2 + 2x - 3$$

If x represents an element in the domain of a function f, then we will often use the symbol

$$f(x)$$

in place of y to designate the number in the range of the function f to which x is paired (Fig. 12).

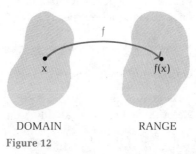

DOMAIN   RANGE

Figure 12

It is important not to think of $f(x)$ as the product of f and x. The symbol $f(x)$ is read "f of x" or "the value of f at x." The variable x is an independent variable; both y and $f(x)$ are dependent variables.

This function notation is extremely important, and its use should be mastered as quickly as possible. For example, in place of the more formal representation of the functions f and g above, we can now write

$$f(x) = 2x + 1 \quad \text{and} \quad g(x) = x^2 + 2x - 3$$

The function symbols $f(x)$ and $g(x)$ have certain advantages over the variable y in certain situations. For example, if we write $f(3)$ and $g(5)$, then each symbol indicates in a concise way that these are range values of particular functions associated with particular domain values. Let us find $f(3)$ and $g(5)$.

To find $f(3)$, we replace x by 3 wherever x occurs in

$$f(x) = 2x + 1$$

and evaluate the right side:

$$f(3) = 2 \cdot 3 + 1$$
$$= 6 + 1$$
$$= 7$$

Thus,

$f(3) = 7$ The function f assigns the range value 7 to the domain value 3; the ordered pair (3, 7) belongs to f

To find g(5), we replace x by 5 whenever x occurs in

$$g(x) = x^2 + 2x - 3$$

and evaluate the right side:

$$g(5) = 5^2 + 2 \cdot 5 - 3$$
$$= 25 + 10 - 3$$
$$= 32$$

Thus,

$g(5) = 32$ The function g assigns the range value 32 to the domain value 5; the ordered pair (5, 32) belongs to g

It is very important to understand and remember the definition of $f(x)$:

The $f(x)$ Symbol

For any element x in the domain of the function f, the symbol $f(x)$ represents the element in the range of f corresponding to x in the domain of f. If x is an input value, then $f(x)$ is the corresponding output value; or, symbolically, $f: x \longrightarrow f(x)$. The ordered pair $(x, f(x))$ belongs to the function f.

Figure 13 on the next page, which illustrates a "function machine," may give you additional insight into the nature of functions and the symbol $f(x)$. We can think of a function machine as a device that produces exactly one output (range) value for each input (domain) value on the basis of a set of instructions such as those found in an equation, graph, or table. (If more than one output value was produced for an input value, then the machine would not be a function machine.)

For the function $f(x) = 2x + 1$, the machine takes each domain value (input), multiplies it by 2, then adds 1 to the result to produce the range

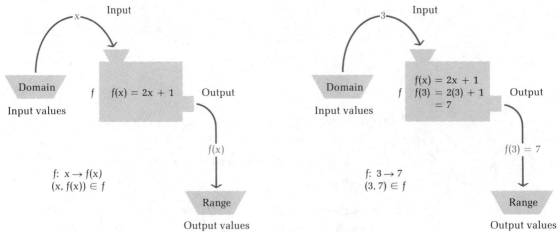

Figure 13 Function machine—exactly one output for each input

value (output). Different rules inside the machine result in different functions.

Example 24   If

$$f(x) = \frac{12}{x-2} \qquad g(x) = 1 - x^2 \qquad h(x) = \sqrt{x-1}$$

then:

(A) $f(6) = \dfrac{12}{6-2} = \dfrac{12}{4} = 3$

(B) $g(-2) = 1 - (-2)^2 = 1 - 4 = -3$

(C) $f(0) + g(1) - h(10) = \dfrac{12}{0-2} + (1 - 1^2) - \sqrt{10-1}$

$$= \frac{12}{-2} + 0 - \sqrt{9}$$

$$= -6 - 3 = -9$$

Problem 24   Use the functions f, g, and h in Example 24 to find:

(A) $f(-2)$ (B) $g(-1)$ (C) $f(3)/h(5)$

Example 25   Find the domains of f, g, and h in Example 24.

Domain f $12/(x - 2)$ represents a real number for all replacements of x by real numbers except for $x = 2$ (division by 0 is not defined). Thus, the domain of f is the set of all real numbers except 2. We would often indicate this by writing

$$f(x) = \frac{12}{x - 2} \qquad x \neq 2$$

Domain g   The domain is all real numbers R, since $1 - x^2$ represents a real number for all replacements of x by real numbers.

Domain h   The domain is $[1, \infty)$, since $\sqrt{x - 1}$ represents a real number for all real x such that $x - 1$ is not negative; that is, such that

$$x - 1 \geq 0$$
$$x \geq 1$$

Problem 25   Find the domains of F, G, and H defined by

$$F(x) = x^2 - 3x + 1 \qquad G(x) = \frac{5}{x + 3} \qquad H(x) = \sqrt{2 - x}$$

Example 26   For $f(x) = 2x - 3$, find:

(A) $f(a)$ (B) $f(a + h)$ (C) $\dfrac{f(a + h) - f(a)}{h}$

Solutions   (A) $f(a) = 2a - 3$
(B) $f(a + h) = 2(a + h) - 3 = 2a + 2h - 3$

(C) $\dfrac{f(a + h) - f(a)}{h} = \dfrac{[2(a + h) - 3] - (2a - 3)}{h}$

$$= \frac{2a + 2h - 3 - 2a + 3}{h} = \frac{2h}{h} = 2$$

Problem 26   Repeat Example 26 for $f(x) = 3x - 2$.

■ Linear Functions and Their Graphs

We aleady know how to graph **linear functions** — that is, functions specified by equations of the form

$$f(x) = mx + b$$

This is equivalent to graphing the equation

$$y = mx + b \qquad \text{Slope} = m, \quad y \text{ intercept} = b$$

which we studied in detail in Section 0-4.

Graph of $f(x) = mx + b$

The graph of a linear function f is a nonvertical straight line with slope m and y intercept b.

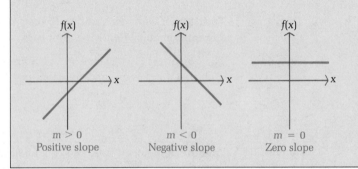

$m > 0$	$m < 0$	$m = 0$
Positive slope	Negative slope	Zero slope

Example 27   Graph the linear function defined by

$$f(x) = -\frac{x}{2} + 3$$

and indicate its slope and y intercept.

Solution

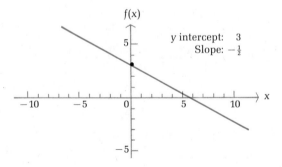

y intercept: 3
Slope: $-\frac{1}{2}$

Problem 27   Graph the linear function defined by

$$f(x) = \frac{x}{3} + 1$$

and indicate its slope and y intercept.

■ Quadratic Functions and Their Graphs

Any function defined by an equation of the form

$$f(x) = ax^2 + bx + c \qquad a \neq 0$$

where a, b, and c are constants and x is a variable, is called a **quadratic function.**

Let us start by graphing the simple quadratic function:

$$f(x) = x^2$$

We evaluate this function for integer values from its domain, find corresponding range values, then plot the resulting ordered pairs and join these points with a smooth curve. The first two steps are usually done mentally or on scratch paper.

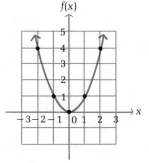

Figure 14

Graphing $f(x) = x^2$

Domain Values	Range Values	Elements of f
x	$y = f(x)$	$(x, f(x))$
-2	$y = f(-2) = (-2)^2 = 4$	$(-2, 4)$
-1	$y = f(-1) = (-1)^2 = 1$	$(-1, 1)$
0	$y = f(0) = 0^2 = 0$	$(0, 0)$
1	$y = f(1) = 1^2 = 1$	$(1, 1)$
2	$y = f(2) = 2^2 = 4$	$(2, 4)$

The curve shown in Figure 14 is called a **parabola.** It is shown in a course in analytic geometry that the graph of any quadratic function is also a parabola. In general:

Graph of $f(x) = ax^2 + bx + c$, $a \neq 0$

The graph of a quadratic function f is a parabola that has its **axis** (line of symmetry) parallel to the vertical axis. It opens upward if $a > 0$ and downward if $a < 0$. The intersection point of the axis and parabola is called the **vertex.**

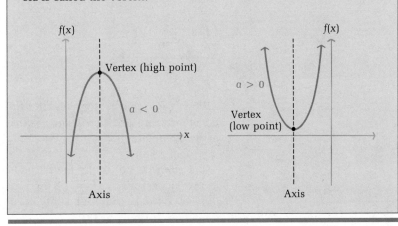

In addition to the point-by-point method of graphing quadratic functions described above, let us consider another approach that will give us added insight into these functions. (A brief review of completing the square, which is discussed in Section 0-3, may prove useful first.) We illustrate the method through an example, and then generalize the results.

Consider the quadratic function given by

$$f(x) = 2x^2 - 8x + 5$$

If we can find the vertex of the graph, then the rest of the graph can be sketched with relatively few points. In addition, we will then have found the maximum or minimum value of the function. We start by transforming the equation into the form

$$f(x) = a(x - h)^2 + k \qquad a, h, k \text{ constants}$$

by completing the square:

$f(x) = 2x^2 - 8x + 5$ Factor the coefficient of x^2 out of the first two terms

$f(x) = 2(x^2 - 4x) + 5$

$ = 2(x^2 - 4x + ?) + 5$ Complete the square within parentheses

$ = 2(x^2 - 4x + 4) + 5 - 8$ We added 4 to complete the square inside the parentheses; but because of the 2 on the outside we have actually added 8, so we must subtract 8

$ = 2(x - 2)^2 - 3$ The transformation is complete

Thus,

$$f(x) = \underbrace{2(x - 2)^2}_{\substack{\text{Never negative} \\ \text{(Why?)}}} - 3$$

When $x = 2$, the first term on the right vanishes, and we add 0 to -3. For *any* other value of x we will add a positive number to -3, thus making $f(x)$ larger. Therefore, $f(2) = -3$ is the minimum value of $f(x)$ for *all* x. A very important result!

The point $(2, -3)$ is the lowest point on the parabola and is also the vertex. The vertical line $x = 2$ is the axis of the parabola. We plot the vertex and the axis and a couple of points on either side of the axis to complete the graph (Fig. 15).

x	f(x)
2	−3
1	−1
3	−1
0	5
4	5

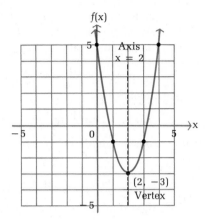

Figure 15

Note the important results we have obtained with this approach. We have found:

1. Axis of the parabola
2. Vertex of the parabola
3. Minimum value of $f(x)$
4. Graph of $y = f(x)$

By proceeding in essentially the same way with the general quadratic function given by

$$f(x) = ax^2 + bx + c \qquad a \neq 0$$

we can obtain the following general results:

Quadratic Function $f(x) = ax^2 + bx + c, \quad a \neq 0$

1. Axis (of symmetry) of the parabola:

$$x = -\frac{b}{2a}$$

2. Maximum or minimum value of $f(x)$:

$$f\left(-\frac{b}{2a}\right) \qquad \begin{array}{l}\text{Minimum if } a > 0 \\ \text{Maximum if } a < 0\end{array}$$

3. Vertex of the parabola:

$$\left(-\frac{b}{2a}, f\left(-\frac{b}{2a}\right)\right)$$

To graph a quadratic function using the method of completing the square, we can either actually complete the square as in the earlier example or use the properties listed in the box—some people can more readily remember a formula, others a process. We will use the boxed properties in the next example.

Example 28 Graph by finding axis of symmetry, maximum or minimum of $f(x)$, and vertex:

$$f(x) = 12x - 2x^2 \qquad 0 \leqslant x \leqslant 6$$

Solution Axis of symmetry:

$$x = -\frac{b}{2a} = -\frac{12}{2(-2)} = 3$$

Maximum value of $f(x)$ (since $a = -2 < 0$):

$$f(3) = 12(3) - 2(3)^2 = 18$$

Vertex: (3, 18)

x	$f(x)$
3	18
2	16
4	16
1	10
5	10
0	0
6	0

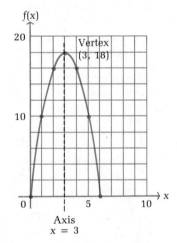

Axis
$x = 3$

Problem 28 Graph as in Example 28.

$$f(x) = x^2 - 2x - 3 \qquad -1 \leqslant x \leqslant 4$$

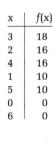

■ Application: Market Research

The market research department of a company recommended to management that the company manufacture and market a promising new product. After extensive surveys, the research department backed up the recommendation with the **demand equation**

$$x = f(p) = 6,000 - 30p \tag{1}$$

where x is the number of units that retailers are likely to buy per month at

$p per unit. Notice that as the price goes up, the number of units goes down. From the financial department, the following **cost equation** was obtained:

$$C = g(x) = 72,000 + 60x \tag{2}$$

where $72,000 is the fixed cost (tooling and overhead) and $60 is the variable cost per unit (materials, labor, marketing, transportation, storage, etc.). The **revenue equation** (the amount of money, R, received by the company for selling x units at $p per unit) is

$$R = xp \tag{3}$$

And, finally, the **profit equation** is

$$P = R - C \tag{4}$$

where P is profit, R is revenue, and C is cost.

We notice that the cost equation (2) expresses C as a function of x and the demand equation (1) expresses x as a function of p. Substituting (1) into (2), we obtain cost C as a linear function of price p:

$$\begin{aligned} C &= 72,000 + 60(6,000 - 3p) \qquad \text{Linear function} \\ &= 432,000 - 1,800p \end{aligned} \tag{5}$$

Similarly, substituting (1) into (3), we obtain revenue R as a quadratic function of price p:

$$\begin{aligned} R &= (6,000 - 30p)p \qquad \text{Quadratic function} \\ &= 6,000p - 30p^2 \end{aligned} \tag{6}$$

Now let us graph equations (5) and (6) in the same coordinate system. We obtain Figure 16 on the next page. Notice how much information is contained in this graph. Let us compute the **break-even points;** that is, the prices at which cost equals revenue (the points of intersection of the two graphs in Figure 16). Find p so that

$$C = R$$
$$432,000 - 1,800p = 6,000p - 30p^2$$
$$30p^2 - 7,800p + 432,000 = 0$$
$$p^2 - 260p + 14,400 = 0 \qquad \text{Solve using the}$$
$$p = \frac{260 \pm \sqrt{260^2 - 4(14,400)}}{2} \qquad \begin{array}{l}\text{quadratic} \\ \text{formula} \\ \text{(Section 0-3)}\end{array}$$
$$= \frac{260 \pm 100}{2}$$
$$= \$80, \quad \$180$$

Thus, at a price of $80 or $180 per unit the company will break even. Between these two prices it is predicted that the company will make a profit.

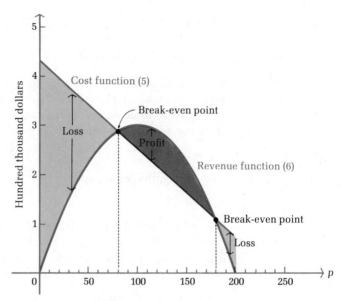

Figure 16

At what price will a **maximum profit** occur? To find out, we write

$$P = R - C$$
$$= (6{,}000p - 30p^2) - (432{,}000 - 1{,}800p)$$
$$= -30p^2 + 7{,}800p - 432{,}000$$

Since this is a quadratic function, the maximum profit occurs at

$$p = -\frac{b}{2a} = -\frac{7{,}800}{2(-30)} = \$130$$

Note that this is not the price at which the maximum revenue occurs. The latter occurs at $p = \$100$, as shown in Figure 16.

Answers to Matched Problems

24. (A) -3 (B) 0   (C) 6
25. Domain of F: $\mathbb{R}$
     Domain of G: All $\mathbb{R}$ except -3
     Domain of H: $x \leqslant 2$ Inequality notation
                    $(-\infty, 2]$ Interval notation
26. (A) $3a - 2$ (B) $3a + 3h - 2$ (C) 3
27.

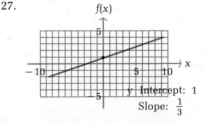

y Intercept: 1
Slope: $\frac{1}{3}$

28. Minimum: $f(1) = -4$

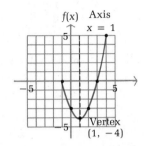

Exercise 0-5

A *Indicate whether each table specifies a function.*

1. | Domain | Range |
    |--------|-------|
    | 3 ⟶ 0 | |
    | 5 ⟶ 1 | |
    | 7 ⟶ 2 | |

2. | Domain | Range |
    |--------|-------|
    | −1 ⟶ 5 | |
    | −2 ⟶ 7 | |
    | −3 ⟶ 9 | |

3. | Domain | Range |
    |--------|-------|
    | 3 ⟶ 5 | |
    | ⟶ 6 | |
    | 4 ⟶ 7 | |
    | 5 ⟶ 8 | |

4. | Domain | Range |
    |--------|-------|
    | 8 ⟶ 0 | |
    | 9 ⟶ 1 | |
    | ⟶ 2 | |
    | 10 ⟶ 3 | |

5. | Domain | Range |
    |--------|-------|
    | 3 | |
    | 6 ⟶ 5 | |
    | 9 | |
    | 12 ⟶ 6 | |

6. | Domain | Range |
    |--------|-------|
    | −2 | |
    | −1 ⟶ 6 | |
    | 0 | |
    | 1 | |

Indicate whether each graph specifies a function.

7.
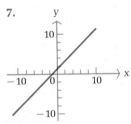

8.
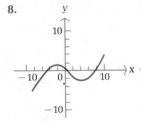

9.
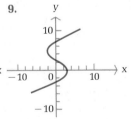

10.
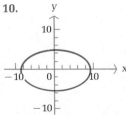

11.
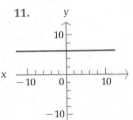

12.
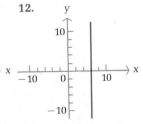

If $f(x) = 3x - 2$ and $g(x) = x - x^2$, find each of the following:

13. $f(2)$ 14. $f(1)$ 15. $f(-1)$

16. $f(-2)$ 17. $g(3)$ 18. $g(1)$

19. $f(0)$ 20. $f(\frac{1}{3})$ 21. $g(-3)$

22. $g(-2)$ 23. $f(1) + g(2)$ 24. $g(1) + f(2)$

25. $g(2) - f(2)$ 26. $f(3) - g(3)$ 27. $g(3) \cdot f(0)$

28. $g(0) \cdot f(-2)$ 29. $g(-2)/f(-2)$ 30. $g(-3)/f(2)$

Graph each linear function, and indicate its slope and y intercept.

31. $f(x) = 2x - 4$ 32. $g(x) = \dfrac{x}{2}$

33. $h(x) = 4 - 2x$ 34. $f(x) = -\dfrac{x}{2} + 3$

35. $g(x) = -\frac{2}{3}x + 4$ 36. $f(x) = 3$

B *If $f(x) = 2x + 1$, $g(x) = x^2 - x$, and $k(x) = \sqrt{x}$, find each of the following:*

37. $f(3) + g(-2)$ 38. $g(-1) - f(1)$ 39. $k(9) - g(-2)$

40. $g(-2) - k(4)$ 41. $f[k(4)]$ 42. $k[f(4)]$

43. $k[g(2)]$ 44. $g[k(9)]$ 45. $g(e)$

46. $f(a)$ 47. $k(u)$ 48. $g(t)$

49. $g(2 + h)$ 50. $f(2 + h)$ 51. $f(a + h)$

52. $g(a + h)$ 53. $\dfrac{f(2 + h) - f(2)}{h}$ 54. $\dfrac{f(a + h) - f(a)}{h}$

55. $\dfrac{g(2 + h) - g(2)}{h}$ 56. $\dfrac{g(a + h) - g(a)}{h}$

Find the domain of each function in Problems 57–62.

57. $f(x) = \sqrt{x}$ 58. $f(x) = 1/\sqrt{x}$

59. $f(x) = \dfrac{x - 3}{(x - 5)(x + 3)}$ 60. $f(x) = \dfrac{x + 1}{x - 2}$

61. $f(x) = \sqrt{x + 5}$ 62. $f(x) = \sqrt{7 - x}$

Graph each quadratic function, and include the axis of symmetry, vertex, and maximum or minimum value.

63. $f(x) = x^2 + 8x + 16$ 64. $h(x) = x^2 - 2x - 3$

65. $f(u) = u^2 - 2u + 4$ 66. $f(x) = x^2 - 10x + 25$

67. $h(x) = 2 + 4x - x^2$ 68. $g(x) = -x^2 - 6x - 4$

69. $f(x) = 6x - x^2$ 70. $G(x) = 16x - 2x^2$

71. $F(s) = s^2 - 4$ 72. $g(t) = t^2 + 4$

73. $F(x) = 4 - x^2$ 74. $G(x) = 9 - x^2$

C   **75.** If
$$f(x) = \begin{cases} x^2 & \text{when} \quad x < 1 \\ 2x & \text{when} \quad x \geq 1 \end{cases}$$
find: (A) $f(-1)$ (B) $f(0)$ (C) $f(1)$ (D) $f(3)$

76. If
$$f(x) = \begin{cases} -x & \text{when} \quad x \leq 0 \\ x & \text{when} \quad x > 0 \end{cases}$$
find: (A) $f(-3)$ (B) $f(-1)$ (C) $f(0)$ (D) $f(5)$

Graph each quadratic function, and include the axis of symmetry, vertex, and maximum or minimum value.

77. $f(x) = x^2 - 7x + 10$ **78.** $g(t) = t^2 - 5t + 2$
79. $g(t) = 4 + 3t - t^2$ **80.** $h(x) = 2 - 5x - x^2$

Applications

Business & Economics

81. *Cost equation.* The cost equation (in dollars) for a particular company that produces stereos is found to be

$$C = g(n) = 96{,}000 + 80n$$

where $96,000 represents fixed costs (tooling and overhead) and $80 is the variable cost per unit (material, labor, etc.). Graph this function for $0 \leq n \leq 1{,}000$.

82. *Demand equation.* After extensive surveys, the research department of a stereo manufacturing company produced the demand equation

$$n = f(p) = 8{,}000 - 40p \qquad 100 \leq p \leq 200$$

where n is the number of units that retailers are likely to purchase per week at a price of $p per unit. Graph the function for the indicated domain.

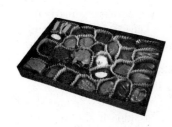

83. *Packaging.* A candy box is to be made out of a piece of cardboard that measures 8 by 12 inches. Equal-sized squares x inches on a side will be cut out of each corner, and then the ends and sides will be folded up to form a rectangular box.

(A) Express the volume of the box $V(x)$ in terms of x.
(B) What is the domain of the function V (determined by the physical restrictions)?
(C) Complete the table:

x	V(x)
1	
2	
3	

Notice how the volume changes with different choices of x

84. *Packaging.* A parcel delivery service will only deliver packages with length plus girth (distance around) not exceeding 108 inches. A rectangular shipping box with square ends, x inches on a side, is to be used.

   (A) If the full 108 inches is to be used, express the volume of the box $V(x)$ in terms of x.

   (B) What is the domain of the function V (determined by the physical restrictions)?

   (C) Complete the table:

x	$V(x)$
5	
10	
15	
20	
25	

    Notice how the volume changes with different choices of x

85. Suppose that in the market research example in this section the demand equation (1) is changed to $x = 9,000 - 30p$ and the cost equation (2) is changed to $C = 90,000 + 30x$.

   (A) Express cost C as a linear function of price p.

   (B) Express revenue R as a quadratic function of price p.

   (C) Graph the cost and revenue functions found in parts A and B in the same coordinate system, and identify the regions of profit and loss on your graph.

   (D) Find the break-even points; that is, find the prices to the nearest dollar at which $R = C$. (A hand calculator might prove useful here.)

   (E) Find the price that produces the maximum revenue.

Life Sciences

86. *Air pollution.* On an average summer day in a large city, the pollution index at 8:00 AM is 20 parts per million and it increases linearly by 15 parts per million each hour until 3:00 PM. Let $P(x)$ be the amount of pollutants in the air x hours after 8:00 AM.

   (A) Express $P(x)$ as a linear function of x.

   (B) What is the air pollution index at 1:00 PM?

   (C) Graph the function P for $0 \leq x \leq 7$.

   (D) What is the slope of the graph? (The slope is the amount of increase in pollution for each additional hour of time.)

Social Sciences

87. *Psychology—sensory perception.* One of the oldest studies in psychology concerns the following question: Given a certain level of stimulation (light, sound, weight lifting, electric shock, and so on), how much should the stimulation be increased for a person to notice

the difference? In the middle of the nineteenth century, E.H. Weber (a German physiologist) formulated a law that still carries his name: If Δs is the change in stimulus that will just be noticeable at a stimulus level s, then the ratio of Δs to s is a constant:

$$\frac{\Delta s}{s} = k$$

Hence, the amount of change that will be noticed is a linear function of the stimulus level, and we note that the greater the stimulus, the more it takes to notice a difference. In an experiment on weight lifting, the constant k for a given individual was found to be $\frac{1}{30}$.

(A) Find Δs (the difference that is just noticeable) at the 30-pound level; at the 90-pound level.

(B) Graph $\Delta s = s/30$ for $0 \leqslant s \leqslant 120$.

(C) What is the slope of the graph?

0-6 Exponential Functions

- Exponential Functions and Their Graphs
- Base e
- Basic Exponential Properties

Exponential Functions and Their Graphs

Many students, if asked to graph equations such as $y = 2^x$ or $y = 2^{-x}$, would not hesitate at all. [Note: $2^{-x} = 1/2^x = (\frac{1}{2})^x$.] They would likely make up tables by assigning integers to x, plot the resulting points, and then join these points with a smooth curve as in Figure 17. The only catch is that 2^x

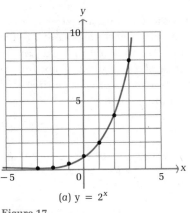

(a) $y = 2^x$

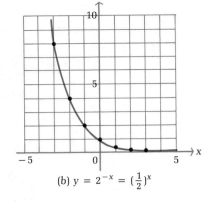

(b) $y = 2^{-x} = (\frac{1}{2})^x$

Figure 17

has not been defined at this point for all real numbers. From Appendix A we know what 2^5, 2^{-3}, $2^{2/3}$, $2^{-3/5}$, $2^{1.4}$, and $2^{-3.15}$ all mean (that is, 2^p, where p is a rational number), but what does

$$2^{\sqrt{2}}$$

mean? The question is not easy to answer at this time. In fact, a precise definition of $2^{\sqrt{2}}$ must wait for more advanced courses, where we can show that

$$2^x$$

names a real number for x any real number, and that the graph of $y = 2^x$ is as indicated in Figure 17A. We can also show that for x irrational, 2^x can be approximated as closely as we like by using rational number approximations for x. Since $\sqrt{2} = 1.414213 \ldots$, for example, the sequence

$$2^{1.4}, \ 2^{1.41}, \ 2^{1.414}, \ \ldots$$

approximates $2^{\sqrt{2}}$, and as we move to the right the approximation improves.

Both $y = 2^x$ and $y = 2^{-x}$ are examples of *exponential functions*. (Do not confuse $y = 2^x$ with $y = x^2$; the latter is a quadratic function.) In general, an **exponential function** is a function defined by an equation of the form:

Exponential Function

$$f(x) = b^x \qquad b > 0, \quad b \neq 1$$

---

where b is a constant, called the base, and the exponent x is a variable. The replacement set for the exponent, the **domain of f,** is the set of real numbers R (with the assumption that we "know" what b^x means for x irrational). The **range of f** is the set of positive real numbers. We require b to be positive to avoid nonreal quantities such as $(-2)^{1/2}$ and 0^0. It is useful to note that the graph of

$$f(x) = b^x \qquad b > 1$$

will look very much like Figure 17A, and the graph of

$$f(x) = b^x \qquad 0 < b < 1$$

will look very much like Figure 17B. [*Note:* In both cases, the graphs approach, but never touch, the horizontal axis.]

Example 29 Graph $y = \left(\dfrac{1}{2}\right) 4^x$ for $-3 \leqslant x \leqslant 3$.

Solution

x	y
-3	0.01
-2	0.03
-1	0.13
0	0.50
1	2.00
2	8.00
3	32.00

Problem 29 Graph $y = \left(\dfrac{1}{2}\right) 4^{-x}$ for $-3 \leqslant x \leqslant 3$.

A great variety of growth phenomena can be described by exponential functions, which is the reason such functions are often referred to as **growth functions.** They are used to describe the growth of money at compound interest; population growth of people, animals, and bacteria; radioactive decay (negative growth); and the growth of learning a skill such as typing or swimming relative to practice.

■ Base e

For introductory purposes, the bases 2 and $\frac{1}{2}$ were convenient choices; however, a certain irrational number, denoted by e, is by far the most frequently used exponential base for both theoretical and practical purposes. In fact,

$$f(x) = e^x$$

is often referred to as *the* exponential function because of its widespread use. The reasons for the preference for e as a base is made clear in the study of calculus. And at that time, it is shown that e is approximated by $(1 + 1/n)^n$ to any decimal accuracy desired by making n (an integer) sufficiently large. The irrational number e to eight decimal places is

$$e \approx 2.718\ 281\ 83$$

Since, for large n,

$$\left(1 + \frac{1}{n}\right)^n \approx e$$

we can raise each side to the xth power to obtain

$$\left(1 + \frac{1}{n}\right)^{nx} \approx e^x$$

Thus, for any x, e^x can be approximated as close as we like by making n (an integer) sufficiently large in

$$\left(1 + \frac{1}{n}\right)^{nx}$$

Because of the importance of e^x and e^{-x}, tables for their evaluation are readily available. In fact, all scientific and financial calculators can evaluate these functions directly.* A short table for evaluating e^x and e^{-x} is provided in Table I of Appendix B. The important constant e, along with two other important constants — $\sqrt{2}$ and π — are shown on the number line in Figure 18A. The graph of $y = e^x$ is shown in Figure 18B.

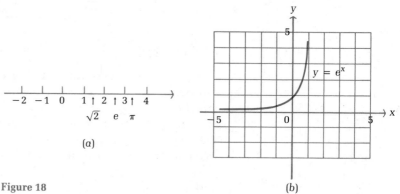

(a)

Figure 18   (b)

Example 30   If $P is invested at 100r% compounded continuously, then the amount A in the account at the end of t years is given by (from the mathematics of finance and calculus):

$$A = Pe^{rt}$$

If $100 is invested at 12% compounded continuously, graph the amount in the account relative to time for a period of 10 years. [*Note:*   Many financial institutions use continuous compounding; look at rates in any financial publication to find some examples.]

Solution   We wish to graph

$$A = 100e^{0.12t} \qquad 0 \le t \le 10$$

We make up a table of values using a calculator, graph the points from the table, and then join the points with a smooth curve.

---

* Consult the manual for your calculator to determine the procedure for evaluating e^x. Some calculators do not have a key labeled e^x. Instead they use a combination of two keys, such as INV and ln x, to evaluate e^x.

t	A
0	100
1	113
2	127
3	143
4	162
5	182
6	205
7	232
8	261
9	294
10	332

Problem 30   Repeat Example 30 with \$5,000 invested at 20% compounded continuously.

■ Basic Exponential Properties

In Appendix A we discussed five laws for integer and rational exponents. It can be shown that these laws also hold for irrational exponents. Thus, we now assume that all five laws of exponents hold for *any* real exponents as long as the involved bases are positive. In addition,

$$b^m = b^n \quad \text{if and only if} \quad m = n, \quad b > 0, \quad b \neq 1$$

Thus, if $2^{15} = 2^{3x}$, then $3x = 15$ and $x = 5$.

**Answers to
Matched Problems**

29. $y = \left(\dfrac{1}{2}\right) 4^{-x}$

x	y
−3	32.00
−2	8.00
−1	2.00
0	0.50
1	0.13
2	0.03
3	0.01

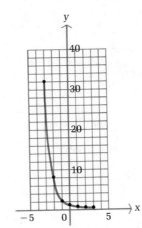

30. $A = 5{,}000e^{0.2t}$

t	A
0	5,000
1	6,107
2	7,459
3	9,111
4	11,128
5	13,591
6	16,601
7	20,276
8	24,765
9	30,248
10	36,945

Exercise 0-6

A   *Graph each equation for* $-3 \leqslant x \leqslant 3$. *Plot points using integers for x, and then join the points with a smooth curve.*

1. $y = 3^x$

2. $y = 10 \cdot 2^x$
   [Note: $10 \cdot 2^x \neq 20^x$]

3. $y = \left(\dfrac{1}{3}\right)^x = 3^{-x}$

4. $y = 10 \cdot \left(\dfrac{1}{2}\right)^x = 10 \cdot 2^{-x}$

5. $y = 10 \cdot 3^x$

6. $y = 10 \cdot \left(\dfrac{1}{3}\right)^x = 10 \cdot 3^{-x}$

B   *Graph each equation for* $-3 \leqslant x \leqslant 3$. *Use Table I of Appendix B or a calculator if the base is e. Plot points using integers for x, and then join the points with a smooth curve.*

7. $y = 10 \cdot 2^{2x}$

8. $y = 10 \cdot 2^{-3x}$

9. $y = e^x$

10. $y = e^{-x}$

11. $y = 10e^{0.2x}$

12. $y = 100e^{0.1x}$

13. $y = 100e^{-0.1x}$

14. $y = 10e^{-0.2x}$

C   15.   Graph $y = e^{-x^2}$ for $x = -1.5, -1.0, -0.5, 0, 0.5, 1.0, 1.5$, and then join these points with a smooth curve. Use Table I of Appendix B or a calculator. (This is a very important curve in probability and statistics.)

16. Graph $y = y_0 2^x$, where y_0 is the value of y when $x = 0$. (Express the vertical scale in terms of y_0.)

17. Graph $y = 2^x$ and $x = 2^y$ on the same coordinate system.

18. Graph $y = 10^x$ and $x = 10^y$ on the same coordinate system.

Applications

Business & Economics

19. *Exponential growth.* If we start with 2¢ and double the amount each day, we would have 2^n¢ after n days. Graph $f(n) = 2^n$ for $1 \leqslant n \leqslant 10$. (Label the vertical scale so that the graph will not go off the paper.)

20. *Compound interest.* If a certain amount of money P (the principal) is invested at $100r\%$ interest compounded annually, the amount of money (A) after t years is given by

$$A = P(1 + r)^t$$

Graph this equation for $P = \$100$, $r = 0.10$, and $0 \leqslant t \leqslant 6$. How much money would a person have after 10 years if no interest were withdrawn? (Technically t should be restricted to nonnegative integers. However, as a visual aid in observing compound growth, join the points with a smooth curve.)

Life Sciences

21. *Bacteria growth.* A single cholera bacterium divides every $\frac{1}{2}$ hour to produce two complete cholera bacteria. If we start with 100 bacteria, in t hours (assuming adequate food supply) we will have

$$A = 100 \cdot 2^{2t}$$

bacteria. Graph this equation for $0 \leqslant t \leqslant 5$.

22. *Ecology.* The atmospheric pressure (P, in pounds per square inch) may be calculated approximately from the formula

$$P = 14.7e^{-0.21h}$$

where h is the altitude above sea level in miles. Graph this equation for $0 \leqslant h \leqslant 12$.

Social Sciences

23. *Learning curves.* The performance record of a particular person learning to type is given approximately by

$$N = 100(1 - e^{-0.1t})$$

where N is the number of words typed per minute and t is the number of weeks of instruction. Graph this equation for $0 \leqslant t \leqslant 40$. What does N approach as t approaches ∞?

24. *Small group analysis.* After a lengthy investigation, sociologists Stephan and Mischler found that if the members of a discussion group of ten were ranked according to the number of times each participated,

then the number of times, $N(k)$, the kth-ranked person participated was given approximately by

$$N(k) = N_1 e^{-0.11(k-1)} \qquad 1 \leqslant k \leqslant 10$$

where N_1 was the number of times the top-ranked person participated in the discussion. Graph the equation assuming $N_1 = 100$. [For a general discussion of this phenomenon, see J. S. Coleman, *Introduction to Mathematical Sociology* (London: The Free Press of Glencoe, 1964), pp. 28–31.]

0-7 Logarithmic Functions

- Definition of Logarithmic Functions
- From Logarithmic to Exponential Form and Vice Versa
- Properties of Logarithmic Functions
- Calculator Evaluation of Common and Natural Logarithms
- Application

Now we are ready to consider logarithmic functions, which are closely related to exponential functions.

■ Definition of Logarithmic Functions

If we start with an exponential function f defined by

$$y = 2^x \tag{1}$$

and interchange the variables, we obtain an equation that defines a new relation g defined by

$$x = 2^y \tag{2}$$

Any ordered pair of numbers that belongs to f will belong to g if we interchange the order of the components. For example, (3, 8) satisfies equation (1) and (8, 3) satisfies equation (2). Thus, the domain of f becomes the range of g and the range of f becomes the domain of g. Graphing f and g on the same coordinate system (Figure 19), we see that g is also a function. We call this new function the **logarithmic function with base 2,** and write

$$y = \log_2 x \qquad \text{if and only if} \qquad x = 2^y$$

Note that if we fold the paper along the dashed line $y = x$ in Figure 19, the two graphs match exactly.

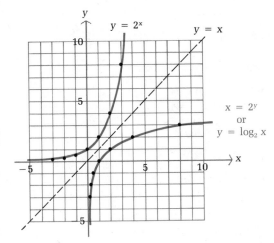

Exponential Function		Logarithmic Function	
x	$y = 2^x$	$x = 2^y$	y
-3	$1/8$	$1/8$	-3
-2	$1/4$	$1/4$	-2
-1	$1/2$	$1/2$	-1
0	1	1	0
1	2	2	1
2	4	4	2
3	8	8	3

Ordered pairs reversed

Figure 19

In general, we define the logarithmic functions with base b as follows:

Logarithmic Function

$y = \log_b x$ if and only if $x = b^y$ $b > 0$, $b \neq 1$

In words, **the logarithm of a number x to a base b ($b > 0$, $b \neq 1$) is the exponent to which b must be raised to equal x.** It is important to remember that $y = \log_b x$ and $x = b^y$ describe the same function, while $y = b^x$ is the related exponential function. Look at Figure 19 again.

Since the domain of an exponential function includes all real numbers and its range is the set of positive real numbers, the **domain** of a logarithmic function is the set of all positive real numbers and its **range** is the set of all real numbers. Remember that **the logarithm of 0 or a negative number is not defined.**

■ From Logarithmic to Exponential Form and Vice Versa

We now consider the matter of converting logarithmic forms to equivalent exponential forms and vice versa.

Example 31   Change from logarithmic form to exponential form.

(A) $\log_5 25 = 2$ is equivalent to $25 = 5^2$
(B) $\log_9 3 = 1/2$ is equivalent to $3 = 9^{1/2}$
(C) $\log_2 (1/4) = -2$ is equivalent to $1/4 = 2^{-2}$

Problem 31   Change to an equivalent exponential form.

(A) $\log_3 9 = 2$ (B) $\log_4 2 = 1/2$ (C) $\log_3 (1/9) = -2$

Example 32   Change from exponential form to logarithmic form.

(A) $64 = 4^3$ is equivalent to $\log_4 64 = 3$
(B) $6 = \sqrt{36}$ is equivalent to $\log_{36} 6 = 1/2$
(C) $1/8 = 2^{-3}$ is equivalent to $\log_2 (1/8) = -3$

Problem 32   Change to an equivalent logarithmic form.

(A) $49 = 7^2$ (B) $3 = \sqrt{9}$ (C) $1/3 = 3^{-1}$

Example 33   Find y, b, or x.

(A) $y = \log_4 16$ (B) $\log_2 x = -3$
(C) $y = \log_8 4$ (D) $\log_b 100 = 2$

Solutions   (A) $y = \log_4 16$ is equivalent to $16 = 4^y$. Thus,

$$y = 2$$

(B) $\log_2 x = -3$ is equivalent to $x = 2^{-3}$. Thus,

$$x = \frac{1}{2^3} = \frac{1}{8}$$

(C) $y = \log_8 4$ is equivalent to

$$4 = 8^y \quad \text{or} \quad 2^2 = 2^{3y}$$

Thus,

$$3y = 2$$

$$y = \frac{2}{3}$$

(D) $\log_b 100 = 2$ is equivalent to $100 = b^2$. Thus,

$$b = 10 \quad \text{Recall that } b \text{ cannot be negative.}$$

Problem 33   Find y, b, or x.

(A) $y = \log_9 27$ (B) $\log_3 x = -1$ (C) $\log_b 1,000 = 3$

Example 34   Graph $y = \log_2(x + 1)$ by converting to an equivalent exponential form first.

Solution   Changing $y = \log_2(x + 1)$ to an equivalent exponential form, we have

$$x + 1 = 2^y \quad \text{or} \quad x = 2^y - 1$$

Even though x is the independent variable and y is the dependent variable, it is easier to assign y values and solve for x.

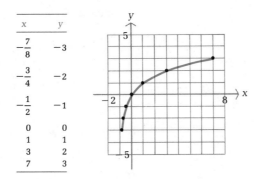

x	y
$-\dfrac{7}{8}$	-3
$-\dfrac{3}{4}$	-2
$-\dfrac{1}{2}$	-1
0	0
1	1
3	2
7	3

Problem 34   Graph $y = \log_3 (x - 1)$ by converting to an equivalent exponential form first.

■ Properties of Logarithmic Functions

Logarithmic functions have several very useful properties that follow directly from their definitions. These properties will enable us to convert multiplication problems into addition problems, division problems into subtraction problems, and power and root problems into multiplication problems. We will also be able to solve exponential equations such as $2 = 1.06^n$.

Logarithmic Properties

$(b > 0, \quad b \neq 1, \quad M > 0, \quad N > 0)$

1. $\log_b b^x = x$
2. $\log_b MN = \log_b M + \log_b N$
3. $\log_b \dfrac{M}{N} = \log_b M - \log_b N$
4. $\log_b M^p = p \log_b M$
5. $\log_b M = \log_b N$ if and only if $M = N$
6. $\log_b 1 = 0$

The first property follows directly from the definition of a logarithmic function. Here, we will sketch a proof for property 2. The other properties are established in a similar way. Let

$$u = \log_b M \quad \text{and} \quad v = \log_b N$$

Or, in equivalent exponential form,

$$M = b^u \quad \text{and} \quad N = b^v$$

Now, see if you can provide reasons for each of the following steps:

$$\log_b MN = \log_b b^u b^v = \log_b b^{u+v} = u + v = \log_b M + \log_b N$$

Example 35   (A) $\log_b \dfrac{wx}{yz} = \log_b wx - \log_b yz$

$$= \log_b w + \log_b x - (\log_b y + \log_b z)$$

$$= \log_b w + \log_b x - \log_b y - \log_b z$$

(B) $\log_b(wx)^{3/5} = \dfrac{3}{5} \log_b wx$

$$= \dfrac{3}{5}(\log_b w + \log_b x)$$

Problem 35   Write in simpler logarithmic forms, as in Example 35.

(A) $\log_b \dfrac{R}{ST}$ (B) $\log_b \left(\dfrac{R}{S}\right)^{2/3}$

The following examples and problems, though somewhat artificial, will give you additional practice in using basic logarithmic properties.

Example 36   Find x so that

$$\dfrac{3}{2} \log_b 4 - \dfrac{2}{3} \log_b 8 + \log_b 2 = \log_b x$$

Solution

$$\dfrac{3}{2} \log_b 4 - \dfrac{2}{3} \log_b 8 + \log_b 2 = \log_b x$$

$$\log_b 4^{3/2} - \log_b 8^{2/3} + \log_b 2 = \log_b x \qquad \text{Property 4}$$

$$\log_b 8 - \log_b 4 + \log_b 2 = \log_b x$$

$$\log_b \dfrac{8 \cdot 2}{4} = \log_b x \qquad \text{Properties 2 and 3}$$

$$\log_b 4 = \log_b x$$

$$x = 4 \qquad \text{Property 5}$$

Problem 36   Find x so that

$$3 \log_b 2 + \dfrac{1}{2} \log_b 25 - \log_b 20 = \log_b x$$

Example 37   Solve $\log_{10} x + \log_{10}(x + 1) = \log_{10} 6$.

Solution $\log_{10} x + \log_{10}(x + 1) = \log_{10} 6$

$\log_{10} x(x + 1) = \log_{10} 6$ Property 2

$x(x + 1) = 6$ Property 5

$x^2 + x - 6 = 0$ Solve by factoring.

$(x + 3)(x - 2) = 0$

$x = -3, 2$

We must exclude $x = -3$, since negative numbers are not in the domains of logarithmic functions; hence,

$x = 2$

is the only solution.

Problem 37   Solve $\log_3 x + \log_3(x - 3) = \log_3 10$.

■ Calculator Evaluation of Common and Natural Logarithms

Of all possible logarithmic bases, the base e and the base 10 are used almost exclusively. Before we can use logarithms in certain practical problems, we need to be able to approximate the logarithm of any number either to base 10 or to base e. And conversely, if we are given the logarithm of a number to base 10 or base e, we need to be able to approximate the number. Historically, tables such as Tables II and III of Appendix B were used for this purpose, but now with inexpensive scientific hand calculators readily available, most people will use a calculator, since it is faster and far more accurate.

Common logarithms (also called **Briggsian logarithms**) are logarithms with base 10. **Natural logarithms** (also called **Napierian logarithms**) are logarithms with base e. Most scientific calculators have a button labeled "log"·(or "LOG") and a button labeled "ln" (or "LN"). The former represents a common (base 10) logarithm and the latter a natural (base e) logarithm. In fact, "log" and "ln" are both used extensively in mathematical literature, and whenever you see either used in this book without a base indicated they will be interpreted as follows:

Logarithmic Notation

$\log x = \log_{10} x$

$\ln x = \log_e x$

Finding the common or natural logarithm using a scientific calculator is very easy: you simply enter a number from the domain of the function and push the log or ln button.

Example 38   Use a scientific calculator to find each to six decimal places:

(A)   log 3,184   (B)   ln 0.000 349   (C)   log(−3.24)

Solutions	*Enter*	*Press*	*Display*
(A)	3184	log	3.502973
(B)	0.000 349	ln	−7.960439
(C)	−3.24	log	Error

An error is indicated in part C because −3.24 is not in the domain of the log function.

Problem 38   Use a scientific calculator to find each to six decimal places:

(A)   log 0.013 529   (B)   ln 28.693 28   (C)   ln(−0.438)

We now turn to the second problem to be discussed in this section: Given the logarithm of a number, find the number. We make direct use of the logarithmic–exponential relationships, which follow directly from the definition of logarithmic functions at the beginning of this section.

Logarithmic–Exponential Relationships

$\log x = y$ is equivalent to $x = 10^y$

$\ln x = y$ is equivalent to $x = e^y$

Example 39   Find x to three significant digits, given the indicated logarithms:

(A) $\log x = -9.315$ (B) $\ln x = 2.386$

Solutions   (A) $\log x = -9.315$ Change to equivalent exponential form.

$x = 10^{-9.315}$

$x = 4.84 \times 10^{-10}$ The answer is displayed in scientific notation in the calculator.

(B) $\ln x = 2.386$ Change to equivalent exponential form.

$x = e^{2.386}$

$x = 10.9$

Problem 39 Find x to four significant digits, given the indicated logarithms.

(A) $\ln x = -5.062$ (B) $\log x = 12.082\ 1$

■ Application

If P dollars are invested at $100i\%$ interest per period for n periods, and interest is paid to the account at the end of each period, then the amount of money in the account at the end of period n is given by

$$A = P(1 + i)^n \qquad \text{Compound interest formula}$$

The fact that interest paid to the account at the end of each period earns interest during the following periods is the reason this is called a **compound interest** formula.

Example 40
Doubling Time

How long (to the next whole year) will it take money to double if it is invested at 20% interest compounded annually?

Solution   Find n for $A = 2P$ and $i = 0.2$.

$$A = P(1 + i)^n$$
$$2P = P(1 + 0.2)^n$$
$$1.2^n = 2 \qquad \text{Solve for } n \text{ by taking the natural or common log of both sides.}$$
$$\ln 1.2^n = \ln 2$$
$$n \ln 1.2 = \ln 2 \qquad \text{Property 4}$$
$$n = \frac{\ln 2}{\ln 1.2} \qquad \text{Use a calculator or a table.}$$
$$= 3.8 \text{ years} \qquad \left[\text{Note: } \frac{\ln 2}{\ln 1.2} \neq \ln 2 - \ln 1.2 \right]$$
$$\approx 4 \text{ years} \qquad \text{To the next whole year}$$

When interest is paid at the end of 3 years, the money will not be doubled; when paid at the end of 4 years, the money will be slightly more than doubled.

Problem 40 How long (to the next whole year) will it take money to double if it is invested at 13% interest compounded annually?

It is interesting and instructive to graph the doubling times for various rates compounded annually. We proceed as follows:

$$A = P(1 + i)^n$$
$$2P = P(1 + i)^n$$
$$2 = (1 + i)^n$$

$$(1 + i)^n = 2$$
$$\ln(1 + i)^n = \ln 2$$
$$n \ln(1 + i) = \ln 2$$
$$n = \frac{\ln 2}{\ln(1 + i)}$$

Figure 20 shows the graph of this equation (doubling times in years) for interest rates compounded annually from 1% to 70%. Note the dramatic changes in doubling times from 1% to 20%.

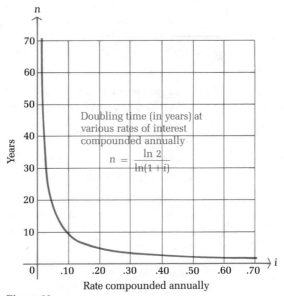

Figure 20

31. (A) $9 = 3^2$ (B) $2 = 4^{1/2}$ (C) $1/9 = 3^{-2}$
32. (A) $\log_7 49 = 2$ (B) $\log_9 3 = 1/2$ (C) $\log_3 (1/3) = -1$
33. (A) $y = 3/2$ (B) $x = 1/3$ (C) $b = 10$
34. $y = \log_3(x - 1)$ is equivalent to $x = 3^y + 1$

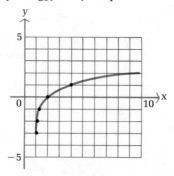

35. (A) $\log_b R - \log_b S - \log_b T$ (B) $(2/3)(\log_b R - \log_b S)$
36. $x = 2$
37. $x = 5$
38. (A) $-1.868\ 734$ (B) $3.356\ 663$ (C) Not defined
39. (A) 6.333×10^{-3} (B) 1.208×10^{12}
40. 6 years

Exercise 0-7

A *Rewrite in exponential form.*

1. $\log_3 27 = 3$
2. $\log_2 32 = 5$
3. $\log_{10} 1 = 0$
4. $\log_e 1 = 0$
5. $\log_4 8 = \dfrac{3}{2}$
6. $\log_9 27 = \dfrac{3}{2}$

Rewrite in logarithmic form.

7. $49 = 7^2$
8. $36 = 6^2$
9. $8 = 4^{3/2}$
10. $9 = 27^{2/3}$
11. $A = b^u$
12. $M = b^x$

Find each of the following:

13. $\log_{10} 10^3$
14. $\log_{10} 10^{-5}$
15. $\log_2 2^{-3}$
16. $\log_3 3^5$
17. $\log_{10} 1,000$
18. $\log_6 36$

Write in terms of simpler logarithmic forms as in Example 35.

19. $\log_b \dfrac{P}{Q}$
20. $\log_b FG$
21. $\log_b L^5$
22. $\log_b w^{15}$
23. $\log_b \dfrac{p}{qrs}$
24. $\log_b PQR$

B *Find x, y, or b.*

25. $\log_3 x = 2$
26. $\log_2 x = 2$
27. $\log_7 49 = y$
28. $\log_3 27 = y$
29. $\log_b 10^{-4} = -4$
30. $\log_b e^{-2} = -2$
31. $\log_4 x = \dfrac{1}{2}$
32. $\log_{25} x = \dfrac{1}{2}$
33. $\log_{1/3} 9 = y$
34. $\log_{49} \dfrac{1}{7} = y$
35. $\log_b 1,000 = \dfrac{3}{2}$
36. $\log_b 4 = \dfrac{2}{3}$

Write in terms of simpler logarithmic forms going as far as you can with logarithmic properties (see Example 35).

37. $\log_b \dfrac{x^5}{y^3}$

38. $\log_b x^2 y^3$

39. $\log_b \sqrt[3]{N}$

40. $\log_b \sqrt[5]{Q}$

41. $\log_b x^2 \sqrt[3]{y}$

42. $\log_b \sqrt[3]{\dfrac{x^2}{y}}$

43. $\log_b (50 \cdot 2^{-0.2t})$

44. $\log_b (100 \cdot 1.06^t)$

45. $\log_b P(1+r)^t$

46. $\log_e Ae^{-0.3t}$

47. $\log_e 100 e^{-0.01t}$

48. $\log_{10} (67 \cdot 10^{-0.12x})$

Find x.

49. $\log_b x = \dfrac{2}{3} \log_b 8 + \dfrac{1}{2} \log_b 9 - \log_b 6$

50. $\log_b x = \dfrac{2}{3} \log_b 27 + 2 \log_b 2 - \log_b 3$

51. $\log_b x = \dfrac{3}{2} \log_b 4 - \dfrac{2}{3} \log_b 8 + 2 \log_b 2$

52. $\log_b x = 3 \log_b 2 + \dfrac{1}{2} \log_b 25 - \log_b 20$

53. $\log_b x + \log_b (x-4) = \log_b 21$
54. $\log_b (x+2) + \log_b x = \log_b 24$
55. $\log_{10}(x-1) - \log_{10}(x+1) = 1$
56. $\log_{10}(x+6) - \log_{10}(x-3) = 1$

Graph by converting to exponential form first.

57. $y = \log_2 (x-2)$

58. $y = \log_3 (x+2)$

In Problems 59 and 60, evaluate to five decimal places using a scientific calculator.

59. (A) $\log 3{,}527.2$ (B) $\log 0.006\ 913\ 2$
    (C) $\ln 277.63$ (D) $\ln 0.040\ 883$

60. (A) $\log 72.604$ (B) $\log 0.033\ 041$
    (C) $\ln 40{,}257$ (D) $\ln 0.005\ 926\ 3$

In Problems 61 and 62, find x to four significant digits.

61. (A) $\log x = 3.128\ 5$ (B) $\log x = -2.049\ 7$
    (C) $\ln x = 8.776\ 3$ (D) $\ln x = -5.887\ 9$

62. (A) $\log x = 5.083\ 2$ (B) $\log x = -3.157\ 7$
    (C) $\ln x = 10.133\ 6$ (D) $\ln x = -4.328\ 1$

C   63. Find the logarithm of 1 for any permissible base.

64. Why is 1 not a suitable logarithmic base? [*Hint:*   Try to find $\log_1 8$.]

65. Write $\log_{10} y - \log_{10} c = 0.8x$ in an exponential form that is free of logarithms.

66. Write $\log_e x - \log_e 25 = 0.2t$ in an exponential form that is free of logarithms.

■

Applications

Business & Economics

67. *Doubling time.* How long (to the next whole year) will it take money to double if it is invested at 6% interest compounded annually?

68. *Doubling time.* How long (to the next whole year) will it take money to double if it is invested at 3% interest compounded annually?

69. *Tripling time.* Write a formula similar to the doubling time formula in Figure 20 for the tripling time of money invested at $100i\%$ interest compounded annually.

70. *Tripling time.* How long (to the next whole year) will it take money to triple if invested at 15% interest compounded annually?

Life Sciences

71. *Sound intensity—decibels.* Because of the extraordinary range of sensitivity of the human ear (a range of over 1,000 million millions to 1), it is helpful to use a logarithmic scale, rather than an absolute scale, to measure sound intensity over this range. The unit of measure is called the *decibel,* after the inventor of the telephone, Alexander Graham Bell. If we let N be the number of decibels, I the power of the sound in question (in watts per square centimeter), and I_0 the power of sound just below the threshold of hearing (approximately 10^{-16} watt per square centimeter), then

$$I = I_0 10^{N/10}$$

Show that this formula can be written in the form

$$N = 10 \log \frac{I}{I_0}$$

72. *Sound intensity—decibels.* Use the formula in Problem 71 (with $I_0 = 10^{-16}$ watt/cm^2) to find the decibel ratings of the following sounds:

(A)   Whisper: 10^{-13} watt/cm^2

(B)   Normal conversation: 3.16×10^{-10} watt/cm^2

(C)   Heavy traffic: 10^{-8} watt/cm^2

(D)   Jet plane with afterburner: 10^{-1} watt/cm^2

Social Sciences

73. *World population.* If the world population is now 4 billion (4×10^9) people and if it continues to grow at 2% per year compounded an-

nually, how long will it be before there is only 1 square yard of land per person? (The earth contains approximately 1.68×10^{14} square yards of land.)

74. *Archaeology—carbon-14 dating.* Cosmic-ray bombardment of the atmosphere produces neutrons, which in turn react with nitrogen to produce radioactive carbon-14. Radioactive carbon-14 enters all living tissues through carbon dioxide which is first absorbed by plants. As long as a plant or animal is alive, carbon-14 is maintained at a constant level in its tissues. Once dead, however, it ceases taking in carbon and the carbon-14 diminishes by radioactive decay according to the equation

$$A = A_0 e^{-0.000124t}$$

where t is time in years. Estimate the age of a skull uncovered in an archaeological site if 10% of the original amount of carbon-14 is still present. [*Hint:* Find t such that $A = 0.1A_0$.]

0-8 Chapter Review

function, quadratic function, parabola, axis of a parabola, vertex of a parabola, maximum, minimum, demand equation, cost equation, revenue equation, profit equation, break-even point, $f(x)$, $f(x) = ax + b$, $f(x) = ax^2 + bx + c$, $a \neq 0$

0-6 *Exponential functions.* Exponential function, graphs of exponential functions, base e, exponential properties, b^x, e^x

0-7 *Logarithmic functions.* Logarithmic function, logarithmic properties, common logarithms, natural logarithms, calculator evaluation, $\log_b x$, $\log x$, $\ln x$

Exercise 0-8 Chapter Review

Work through all the problems in this chapter review and check your answers in the back of the book. (Answers to all review problems are there.) Where weaknesses show up, review appropriate sections in the text.

A

1. True (T) or false (F)?

   (A) $7 \notin \{4, 6, 8\}$ (B) $\{8\} \subset \{4, 6, 8\}$
   (C) $\varnothing \in \{4, 6, 8\}$ (D) $\varnothing \subset \{4, 6, 8\}$

2. Solve $\dfrac{u}{5} = \dfrac{u}{6} + \dfrac{6}{5}$.

3. Solve and graph on a real number line: $2(x + 4) > 5x - 4$

4. Solve $x^2 = 5x$.

5. Graph the equation below in a rectangular coordinate system. Indicate the slope and the y intercept.

   $$y = \frac{x}{2} - 2$$

6. Write the equation of a line that passes through $(4, 3)$ with slope $\frac{1}{2}$. Write the final answer in the form $y = mx + b$.

7. Graph $x - y = 2$ in a rectangular coordinate system. Indicate the slope.

8. For $f(x) = 2x - 1$ and $g(x) = x^2 - 2x$, find $f(-2) + g(-1)$.

9. Graph the linear function f given by the equation

   $$f(x) = \tfrac{2}{3}x - 1$$

   Indicate the slope of the graph.

10. Write $\log_{10} y = x$ in exponential form.

11. Write $\log_b \dfrac{wx}{y}$ in terms of simpler logarithms.

B   12. If $A = \{1, 2, 3\}$ and $B = \{2, 3, 4\}$, find

  (A) $A \cup B$ (B) $\{x | x \in A \quad \text{and} \quad x \in B\}$

13. If $U = \{2, 4, 5, 6, 8\}$, $M = \{2, 4, 5\}$, and $N = \{5, 6\}$, find

  (A) $M \cup N$ (B) $M \cap N$ (C) $(M \cup N)'$ (D) $M \cap N'$

14. Indicate true (T) or false (F) for U, M, and N in Problem 13.

  (A) $N \subset M$ (B) $\varnothing \subset U$ (C) $6 \notin M$ (D) $5 \in N$

15. Given the Venn diagram shown with the number of elements indicated in each part, determine how many elements are in each of the following sets:

  (A) $M \cup N$ (B) $M \cap N$ (C) $(M \cup N)'$ (D) $M \cap N'$

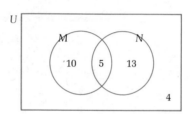

16. In a freshman class of 100 students, 70 are taking English, 45 are taking math, and 25 are taking English and math.

  (A) How many students are taking either English or math?
  (B) How many students are taking English and not math?

17. Solve $\dfrac{x}{12} - \dfrac{x-3}{3} = \dfrac{1}{2}$.

Solve and graph on a real number line.

18. $1 - \dfrac{x-3}{3} \leqslant \dfrac{1}{2}$

19. $-2 \leqslant \dfrac{x}{2} - 3 < 3$

Solve for y in terms of x.

20. $2x - 3y = 6$

21. $xy - y = 3$

Solve problems 22–24.

22. $3x^2 - 21 = 0$ 23. $x^2 - x - 20 = 0$ 24. $2x^2 = 3x + 1$

25. Graph $3x + 6y = 18$ in a rectangular coordinate system. Indicate the slope, x intercept, and y intercept.

26. Find an equation of the line that passes through $(-2, 3)$ and $(6, -1)$. Write the answer in the form $Ax + By = C, A > 0$. What is the slope of the line?

27. Write the equations of the vertical line and the horizontal line that pass through $(-5, 2)$. Graph both equations on the same coordinate system.

28. Find an equation of the line that passes through $(-2, 5)$ and $(2, -1)$. Write the answer in the form $y = mx + b$.

29. For $f(x) = 10x - 7$, $g(t) = 6 - 2t$, $F(u) = 3u^2$, and $G(v) = v - v^2$, find

   (A) $2g(-1) - 3G(-1)$ (B) $4G(-2) - g(-3)$

   (C) $\dfrac{f(2) \cdot g(-4)}{G(-1)}$ (D) $\dfrac{F(-1) \cdot G(2)}{g(-1)}$

30. For $f(x) = \sqrt{x}$ and $g(x) = x^2 + 2x$, find

   (A) $f[g(2)]$ (B) $g[f(a)]$

31. Find the domains of the functions f and g if

$$f(x) = 2x - x^2 \qquad g(x) = \frac{1}{x - 2}$$

32. Graph $g(x) = 8x - 2x^2$, $x \geqslant 0$, in a rectangular coordinate system. Write the coordinates of the vertex and the equation of the axis. What is the maximum or minimum value of $g(x)$?

33. Graph $y = 10 \cdot 2^{3x}$ and $y = 10 \cdot 2^{-3x}$, $-2 \leqslant x \leqslant 2$, on the same coordinate system.

34. Graph $y = 100e^{-0.1x}$, $0 \leqslant x \leqslant 10$, using a calculator or a table.

35. (A) Find b: $\log_b 9 = 2$ (B) Find x: $\log_4 x = -3$

36. Write in terms of simpler logarithmic forms:

   $\log_b(100 \cdot 1.06^t)$

37. Find x: $\log_b x = 3 \log_b 2 - \frac{3}{2} \log_b 4 - \frac{1}{2} \log_b 36$.

38. Evaluate to five decimal places using a scientific calculator.

   (A) $\log 0.009\,108\,5$ (B) $\ln 9{,}843.3$

39. Find x to four significant digits.

   (A) $\log x = -3.805\,5$ (B) $\ln x = 12.814\,3$

40. Solve for x: $\ln x + \ln(x - 3) = \ln 28$.

C 41. If $A \cap B = A$, then is it always true that $A \subset B$?

42. Solve $x^2 + jx + k = 0$ for x in terms of j and k.

43. Write an equation of the line that passes through the points $(4, -3)$ and $(4, 5)$.

44. Write an equation of the line that passes through $(2, -3)$ and is (A) parallel (B) perpendicular to $2x - 4y = 5$. Write the final answers in the form $Ax + By = C$, $A > 0$.

45. Find the domain of the function f specified by each equation.

   (A) $f(x) = \dfrac{5}{x - 3}$ (B) $f(x) = \sqrt{x - 1}$

46.   For $f(x) = 2x - 1$, find $\dfrac{f(3 + h) - f(3)}{h}$.

47.   Find t: $240 = 80e^{0.12t}$.

48.   Write $\ln y - \ln c = -0.2x$ in an exponential form free of logarithms.

◼ Applications

Business & Economics

49.   *Marketing survey.* A survey company sampled 1,000 students at a university. Out of the sample, 550 students smoked cigarettes, 820 drank alcoholic beverages, and 470 did both.

(A)   How many smoked or drank?

(B)   How many drank but did not smoke?

50.   *Investment.* An investor has $60,000 to invest. If part is invested at 8% and the rest at 14%, how much should be invested at each rate to yield 12% on the total amount?

51.   *Inflation.* If the CPI was 89 in 1960 and 247 in 1980, how much would a net salary of $800 in 1960 have to be in 1980 in order to keep up with inflation? Set up an equation and solve.

52.   *Finance.* If P dollars is invested at $100r\%$ compounded annually, at the end of 2 years it will grow to $A = P(1 + r)^2$. At what interest rate will $1,000 grow to $1,210 in 2 years?

53.   *Linear depreciation.* A word-processing system was purchased by a company for $12,000 and is assumed to have a salvage value of $2,000 after 8 years (for tax purposes). If its value is depreciated linearly from $12,000 to $2,000:

(A)   Find the linear equation that relates value V in dollars to time t in years.

(B)   What would be the value of the system after 5 years?

54.   *Pricing.* A sporting goods store sells a tennis racket that cost $30 for $48 and a pair of jogging shoes that cost $20 for $32.

(A)   If the markup policy of the store for items that cost over $10 is assumed to be linear and is reflected in the pricing of these two items, write an equation that relates retail price R to cost C.

(B)   What should be the retail price of a pair of skis that cost $105?

55.   *Construction.* A Wyoming rancher has 20 miles of fencing to enclose a rectangular piece of grazing land along a river.

(A)   If no fence is required along the river and x is the width of the rectangle (at right angles to the river), express the area $A(x)$ of the rectangle in terms of x.

(B)   What is the domain of the function A (due to physical restrictions)?

(C)   Complete the table:

x	A(x)
2	
4	
5	
6	
8	

56.   *Finance.* Find the tripling time (to the next higher year if not exact) for money invested at 15% compounded annually $[A = P(1 + r)^t]$.

57.   *Finance.* Find the doubling time (to two decimal places) for money invested at 10% compounded continuously $[A = Pe^{rt}]$.

Systems of Linear Equations; Matrices

CHAPTER 1	Contents

In this chapter we will first review how systems of equations are solved by using techniques learned in elementary algebra. These techniques are suitable for systems involving two or three variables, but they are not suitable for systems involving larger numbers of variables. After this review, we will introduce techniques that are more suitable for solving systems with larger numbers of variables. These new techniques form the basis for computer solutions of large-scale systems.

1-1 Review: Systems of Linear Equations

- Systems in Two Variables
- Applications
- Systems in Three Variables
- Applications

■ Systems in Two Variables

To establish basic concepts, consider the following simple example: If two adult tickets and one child ticket cost $8, and if one adult ticket and three child tickets cost $9, what is the price of each?

Let x = Price of adult ticket

  y = Price of child ticket

Then $2x + y = 8$

  $x + 3y = 9$

We now have a system of two linear equations and two unknowns. To solve this system, we find all ordered pairs of real numbers that satisfy both equations at the same time. In general, we are interested in solving linear systems of the type

$$ax + by = h$$
$$cx + dy = k$$

where a, b, c, d, h, and k are real constants. A pair of numbers $x = x_0$ and $y = y_0$ [also written as an ordered pair (x_0, y_0)] is a **solution** of this system if each equation is satisfied by the pair. The set of all such ordered pairs of numbers is called the **solution set** for the system. To **solve** a system is to find its solution set. We will consider three methods of solving such systems, each having certain advantages in certain situations.

Solution by Graphing   To solve the ticket problem above by graphing, we graph both equations in the same coordinate system. The coordinates of any points that the graphs have in common must be solutions to the system, since they must satisfy both equations.

Example 1   Solve the ticket problem by graphing:

$$2x + y = 8$$
$$x + 3y = 9$$

Solution

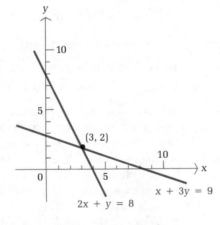

$x = \$3$ Adult ticket

$y = \$2$ Child ticket

Check

$2x + y = 8$	$x + 3y = 9$
$2(3) + 2 \overset{?}{=} 8$	$3 + 3(2) \overset{?}{=} 9$
$8 \overset{\checkmark}{=} 8$	$9 \overset{\checkmark}{=} 9$

Problem 1   Solve by graphing and check:

$$2x - y = -3$$
$$x + 2y = -4$$

It is clear that the above example (and problem) has exactly one solution, since the lines have exactly one point of intersection. In general, lines in a rectangular coordinate system are related to each other in one of the three ways illustrated in the next example.

Example 2   Solve each of the following systems by graphing:

(A) $x - 2y = 2$ (B) $x + 2y = -4$ (C) $2x + 4y = 8$
       $x + y = 5$ $2x + 4y = 8$ $x + 2y = 4$

Solutions

(A)

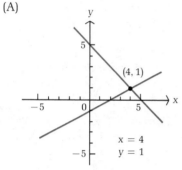

Intersection at one point
only — exactly one solution

(B)

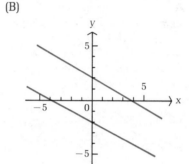

Lines are parallel (each
has slope $-\frac{1}{2}$) — no solutions

(C)

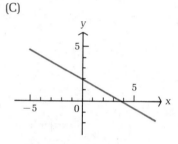

Lines coincide — infinite
number of solutions

Problem 2   Solve each of the following systems by graphing:

(A) $x + y = 4$ (B) $6x - 3y = 9$ (C) $2x - y = 4$
        $2x - y = 2$ $2x - y = 3$ $6x - 3y = -18$

By geometrically interpreting a system of two linear equations in two unknowns, we gain useful information about solutions to the system. Since two lines in a coordinate system must intersect at exactly one point, be parallel, or coincide, we conclude that the system has (A) exactly one solution, (B) no solution, or (C) infinitely many solutions. In addition, graphs of problems frequently reveal relationships that might otherwise be hidden. Generally, however, graphic methods only give us rough approximations of solutions. The methods of substitution and elimination by addition yield results to any decimal accuracy desired — assuming that solutions exist.

Solution by Substitution   Choose one of two equations in a system and solve for one variable in terms of the other. (Make a choice that avoids fractions, if possible.) Then substitute the result into the other equation and solve the resulting linear equation in one variable. Now substitute this result back into either of the original equations to find the second variable. An example should make the process clear.

Example 3   Solve by substitution:

$$5x + y = 4$$
$$2x - 3y = 5$$

Solution   Solve either equation for one variable in terms of the other; then substitute into the remaining equation. In this problem we can avoid fractions by choosing the first equation and solving for y in terms of x.

$$5x + y = 4 \qquad \text{Solve first equation for } y \text{ in terms of } x$$
$$y = \underline{4 - 5x} \qquad \text{Substitute into second equation}$$

$$2x - 3y = 5 \qquad \text{Second equation}$$
$$2x - 3(4 - 5x) = 5 \qquad \text{Solve for } x$$
$$2x - 12 + 15x = 5$$
$$17x = 17$$
$$x = 1$$

Now, replace x with 1 in $y = 4 - 5x$ to find y:

$$y = 4 - 5x$$
$$y = 4 - 5(1)$$
$$y = -1$$

Check

$$5x + y = 4 \qquad\qquad 2x - 3y = 5$$
$$5(1) + (-1) \stackrel{?}{=} 4 \qquad\qquad 2(1) - 3(-1) \stackrel{?}{=} 5$$
$$4 \stackrel{\checkmark}{=} 4 \qquad\qquad\qquad 5 \stackrel{\checkmark}{=} 5$$

Problem 3   Solve by substitution:

$$3x + 2y = -2$$
$$2x - y = -6$$

Solution by Elimination by Addition   Now we turn to **elimination by addition.** This is probably the most important method of solution, since it is readily generalized to higher-order systems. The method involves replacing systems of equations with simpler *equivalent systems* (by performing appropriate operations) until we obtain a system with an obvious solution. **Equivalent systems** of equations are, as you would expect, systems that have exactly the same solution set. Theorem 1 lists the operations that produce equivalent systems.

Theorem 1

> A system of linear equations is transformed into an equivalent system if:
>
> (A) Two equations are interchanged.
> (B) An equation is multiplied by a nonzero constant.
> (C) A constant multiple of another equation is added to a given equation.

Parts B and C of Theorem 1 will be of most use to us now; part A becomes useful when we generalize the theorem for larger systems. The use of the theorem is best illustrated by examples.

Example 4   Solve the following system using elimination by addition:

$$3x - 2y = 8$$
$$2x + 5y = -1$$

Solution   We use the theorem to eliminate one of the variables, thus obtaining a system with an obvious solution:

$$3x - 2y = 8$$
$$2x + 5y = -1$$
$$15x - 10y = 40$$
$$\underline{4x + 10y = -2}$$
$$19x \qquad = 38$$
$$x = 2$$

If we multiply the top equation by 5 and the bottom by 2 and then add, we can eliminate y

Now substitute $x = 2$ back into either of the original equations, say the second equation, and solve for y ($x = 2$ paired with either of the two original equations produces an equivalent system):

$$2(2) + 5y = -1$$
$$5y = -5$$
$$y = -1$$

Check

$$3x - 2y = 8 \qquad\qquad 2x + 5y = -1$$
$$3(2) - 2(-1) \overset{?}{=} 8 \qquad\qquad 2(2) + 5(-1) \overset{?}{=} -1$$
$$8 \overset{\checkmark}{=} 8 \qquad\qquad\qquad -1 \overset{\checkmark}{=} -1$$

Problem 4   Solve the system:

$$5x - 2y = 12$$
$$2x + 3y = 1$$

Let us see what happens in the elimination process when a system has either no solution or infinitely many solutions. Consider the following system:

$$2x + 6y = -3$$
$$x + 3y = 2$$

Multiplying the second equation by -2 and adding, we obtain

$$2x + 6y = -3$$
$$\underline{-2x - 6y = -4}$$
$$0 = -7$$

We have obtained a contradiction. The assumption that the original system has solutions must be false (otherwise we have proved that $0 = -7$). Thus, the system has no solutions. The graphs of the equations are parallel. Systems with no solutions are said to be **inconsistent.**

Now consider the system

$$x - \tfrac{1}{2}y = 4$$
$$-2x + y = -8$$

If we multiply the top equation by 2 and add the result to the bottom equation, we obtain

$$2x - y = 8$$
$$\underline{-2x + y = -8}$$
$$0 = 0$$

Obtaining $0 = 0$ by addition implies that the equations are equivalent; that is, their graphs coincide. Hence, the two equations have the same solution set, and the system has infinitely many solutions. If $x = k$, then using either equation, we obtain $y = 2k - 8$; that is, $(k, 2k - 8)$ is a solution for any real number k. Such a system is said to be **dependent.** The variable k is called a **parameter;** replacing it with any real number produces a particular solution to the system.

▪ Applications

Many real-world problems are readily solved by applying two-equation–two-unknown methods. We shall discuss two applications in detail.

Example 5

Diet

A dietitian in a hospital is to arrange a special diet comprised of two foods, M and N. Each ounce of food M contains 8 units of calcium and 2 units of iron. Each ounce of food N contains 5 units of calcium and 4 units of iron. How many ounces of foods M and N should be used to obtain a food mix that contains 74 units of calcium and 35 units of iron?

Solution   It is convenient to first summarize the quantities involved in a table:

	Food *M*	Food *N*	Total Needed
Calcium	8	5	74
Iron	2	4	35

Let $x =$ Number of ounces of food *M*

   $y =$ Number of ounces of food *N*

$$\begin{pmatrix} \text{Calcium in} \\ x \text{ oz of food } M \end{pmatrix} + \begin{pmatrix} \text{Calcium in} \\ y \text{ oz of food } N \end{pmatrix} = \begin{pmatrix} \text{Total calcium} \\ \text{needed} \end{pmatrix}$$

$$\begin{pmatrix} \text{Iron in } x \text{ oz} \\ \text{of food } M \end{pmatrix} + \begin{pmatrix} \text{Iron in } y \text{ oz} \\ \text{of food } N \end{pmatrix} = \begin{pmatrix} \text{Total iron} \\ \text{needed} \end{pmatrix}$$

$$8x + 5y = 74$$
$$2x + 4y = 35$$

Solve by elimination by addition:

$$\begin{aligned} 8x + 5y &= 74 \\ -8x - 16y &= -140 \\ \hline -11y &= -66 \end{aligned}$$

$$y = 6 \text{ oz of food } N$$

$$2x + 4(6) = 35$$
$$2x = 11$$
$$x = 5.5 \text{ oz of food } M$$

Check

$$8x + 5y = 74 \qquad\qquad 2x + 4y = 35$$
$$8(5.5) + 5(6) \stackrel{?}{=} 74 \qquad 2(5.5) + 4(6) \stackrel{?}{=} 35$$
$$74 \stackrel{\checkmark}{=} 74 \qquad\qquad 35 \stackrel{\checkmark}{=} 35$$

Problem 5   Repeat Example 5 given that each ounce of food *M* contains 10 units of calcium and 4 units of iron, each ounce of food *N* contains 6 units of calcium and 4 units of iron, and the mix of *M* and *N* must contain 92 units of calcium and 44 units of iron.

Example 6

Supply and Demand

The quantity of a product that people are willing to buy during some period of time depends on its price. Generally, the higher the price, the less the demand; the lower the price, the greater the demand. Similarly, the quantity of a product that a supplier is willing to sell during some period of time also depends on the price. Generally, a supplier will be willing to supply more of a product at higher prices and less of a product at lower prices. The simplest supply and demand model is a linear model where the graphs of a demand equation and a supply equation are straight lines.

Suppose in a given city on a given day supply and demand equations for cherries are given by

$$p = -0.2q + 4 \qquad \text{Demand equation (consumer)}$$

$$p = 0.07q + 0.76 \qquad \text{Supply equation (supplier)}$$

where q represents the quantity in thousands of pounds and p represents the price in dollars. For example, we see that consumers will purchase 10 thousand pounds $(q = 10)$ when the price is $p = -0.2(10) + 4 = \$2$ per pound. On the other hand, suppliers will be willing to supply 17.714 thousand pounds of cherries at \$2 per pound (solve $2 = 0.07q + 0.76$). Thus, at \$2 per pound the suppliers are willing to supply more cherries than consumers are willing to purchase. The supply exceeds the demand at that price and the price will come down. At what price will cherries stabilize for the day? That is, at what price will supply equal demand? This price, if it exists, is called the **equilibrium price,** and the quantity sold at that price is called the **equilibrium quantity.** How do we find these quantities? We solve the linear system

$$p = -0.2q + 4 \qquad \text{Demand equation}$$

$$p = 0.07q + 0.76 \qquad \text{Supply equation}$$

We solve this system using substitution (substituting $p = -0.2q + 4$ into the second equation).

$$-0.2q + 4 = 0.07q + 0.76$$

$$-0.27q = -3.24$$

$$q = 12 \text{ thousand pounds (equilibrium quantity)}$$

Now substitute $q = 12$ back into either of the original equations in the system and solve for p (we choose the first equation):

$$p = -0.2(12) + 4$$

$$p = \$1.60 \text{ per pound (equilibrium price)}$$

These results are interpreted geometrically in the figure.

Equilibrium quantity = 12 thousand pounds

Equilibrium price = \$1.60 per pound

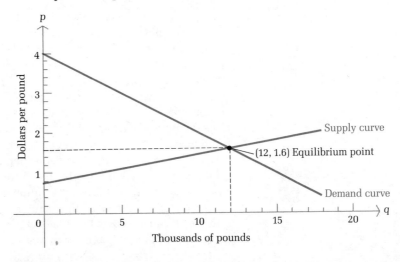

If the price was above the equilibrium price of $1.60 per pound, the supply would exceed the demand and the price would come down. If the price was below the equilibrium price of $1.60 per pound, the demand would exceed the supply and the price would rise. Thus, the price would reach equilibrium at $1.60. At this price, suppliers would supply 12 thousand pounds of cherries and consumers would purchase 12 thousand pounds.

Problem 6   Repeat Example 6 (including drawing the graph) given:

$$p = -0.1q + 3 \qquad \text{Demand equation}$$
$$p = 0.08q + 0.66 \qquad \text{Supply equation}$$

■ Systems in Three Variables

Any equation that can be written in the form

$$ax + by = c$$

where a, b, and c are constants (not both a and b zero) is called a **linear equation in two variables.** Similarly, any equation that can be written in the form

$$ax + by + cz = k$$

where a, b, c, and k are constants (not all a, b, and c zero) is called a **linear equation in three variables.** (A similar definition holds for a linear equation in four or more variables.)

Now that we know how to solve systems of linear equations in two variables, there is no reason to stop there. Systems of the form

$$a_1x + b_1y + c_1z = k_1$$
$$a_2x + b_2y + c_2z = k_2 \qquad\qquad (1)$$
$$a_3x + b_3y + c_3z = k_3$$

as well as higher-order systems are encountered frequently. In fact, systems of equations are so important in solving real-world problems that whole courses are devoted to this one topic. A triplet of numbers $x = x_0$, $y = y_0$, and $z = z_0$ [also written as an ordered triplet (x_0, y_0, z_0)] is a **solution** of system (1) if each equation is satisfied by this triplet. The set of all such ordered triplets of numbers is called the **solution set** of the system. If operations are performed on a system and the new system has the same solution set as the original, then both systems are said to be **equivalent.**

Linear equations in three variables represent planes in a three-dimensional space. Trying to visualize how three planes can intersect will give you insight as to what kind of solution sets are possible for system (1). Figure 1 shows several of the many ways in which three planes can intersect. It can be shown that system (1) will have exactly one solution, no solutions, or infinitely many solutions.

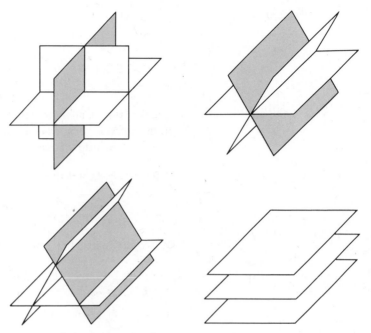

Figure 1 Three intersecting planes

In this section we will use an extension of the method of elimination discussed above to solve systems in the form of (1). In the next section we will consider techniques for solving linear systems that are more compatible with solving such systems with computers. In practice, most linear systems involving more than three variables are solved with the aid of a computer.

Steps in Solving Systems of Form (1)

1.   Choose two equations from the system and eliminate one of the three variables using elimination by addition. The result is generally one equation in two unknowns.
2.   Now eliminate the same variable from the unused equation and one of those used in step 1. We (generally) obtain another equation in two variables.
3.   The two equations from steps 1 and 2 form a system of two equations and two unknowns. Solve as described in the earlier part of this section.
4.   Substitute the solution from step 3 into any of the three original equations and solve for the third variable to complete the solution of the original system.

Example 7 Solve:

$$3x - 2y + 4z = 6 \tag{2}$$
$$2x + 3y - 5z = -8 \tag{3}$$
$$5x - 4y + 3z = 7 \tag{4}$$

Solution Step 1. We look at the coefficients of the variables and choose to eliminate y from equations (2) and (4) because of the convenient coefficients -2 and -4. Multiply equation (2) by -2 and add to equation (4):

$$
\begin{array}{ll}
-6x + 4y - 8z = -12 & -2[\text{equation (2)}] \\
\underline{5x - 4y + 3z = 7} & \text{Equation (4)} \\
-x - 5z = -5 & \tag{5}
\end{array}
$$

Step 2. Now we eliminate y (the same variable) from equations (2) and (3):

$$
\begin{array}{ll}
9x - 6y + 12z = 18 & 3[\text{equation (2)}] \\
\underline{4x + 6y - 10z = -16} & 2[\text{equation (3)}] \\
13x + 2z = 2 & \tag{6}
\end{array}
$$

Step 3. From steps 1 and 2 we obtain the system

$$-x - 5z = -5 \tag{5}$$
$$13x + 2z = 2 \tag{6}$$

[It has been shown that equations (5) and (6) along with (2), (3), or (4) form a system equivalent to the original system.] We solve system (5) and (6) as in the earlier part of this section:

$$
\begin{array}{ll}
-13x - 65z = -65 & 13[\text{equation (5)}] \\
\underline{13x + 2z = 2} & \text{Equation (6)} \\
 - 63z = -63 & \\
 z = 1 &
\end{array}
$$

Substitute $z = 1$ back into either equation (5) or (6) [we choose equation (5)] to find x:

$$
\begin{array}{ll}
-x - 5z = -5 & \tag{5} \\
-x - 5(1) = -5 & \\
-x = 0 & \\
x = 0 &
\end{array}
$$

Step 4. Substitute $x = 0$ and $z = 1$ back into any of the three original equations [we choose equation (2)] to find y:

$$3x - 2y + 4z = 6 \qquad\qquad (2)$$
$$3(0) - 2y + 4(1) = 6$$
$$-2y + 4 = 6$$
$$-2y = 2$$
$$y = -1$$

Thus, the solution to the original system is $(0, -1, 1)$ or $x = 0, y = -1, z = 1$.

Check To check the solution, we must check *each* equation in the original system:

$$3x - 2y + 4z = 6 \qquad\qquad 2x + 3y - 5z = -8$$
$$3(0) - 2(-1) + 4(1) \overset{?}{=} 6 \qquad\qquad 2(0) + 3(-1) - 5(1) \overset{?}{=} -8$$
$$6 \overset{\checkmark}{=} 6 \qquad\qquad\qquad -8 \overset{\checkmark}{=} -8$$

$$5x - 4y + 3z = 7$$
$$5(0) - 4(-1) + 3(1) \overset{?}{=} 7$$
$$7 \overset{\checkmark}{=} 7$$

Problem 7 Solve:

$$2x + 3y - 5z = -12$$
$$3x - 2y + 2z = 1$$
$$4x - 5y - 4z = -12$$

In the process described above, if we encounter an equation that states a contradiction, such as $0 = -2$, then we must conclude that the system has no solution (that is, the system is inconsistent). On the other hand, if one of the equations turns out to be $0 = 0$, the system has either infinitely many solutions or none. We must proceed further to determine which. Notice how this last result differs from the two-equation–two-unknown case. There, when we obtained $0 = 0$, we *knew* that there were infinitely many solutions. We shall have more to say about this in Section 1-3.

■ Applications

Now let us consider a real-world problem that leads to a system of three equations and three unknowns.

Example 8
Production Scheduling

A garment industry manufactures three shirt styles. Each style shirt requires the services of three departments as listed in the table on the next page. The cutting, sewing, and packaging departments have available a maximum of 1,160, 1,560, and 480 labor-hours per week, respectively. How many of each style shirt must be produced each week for the plant to operate at full capacity?

	Style *A*	Style *B*	Style *C*	Time Available
Cutting department	0.2 hr	0.4 hr	0.3 hr	1,160 hr
Sewing department	0.3 hr	0.5 hr	0.4 hr	1,560 hr
Packaging department	0.1 hr	0.2 hr	0.1 hr	480 hr

Solution   Let x = Number of style *A* produced per week

y = Number of style *B* produced per week

z = Number of style *C* produced per week

Then $0.2x + 0.4y + 0.3z = 1{,}160$ Cutting department

$0.3x + 0.5y + 0.4z = 1{,}560$ Sewing department

$0.1x + 0.2y + 0.1z = \phantom{1{,}}480$ Packaging department

We clear the system of decimals by multiplying each side of each equation by 10. Thus,

$$2x + 4y + 3z = 11{,}600 \tag{7}$$

$$3x + 5y + 4z = 15{,}600 \tag{8}$$

$$x + 2y + z = 4{,}800 \tag{9}$$

Let us start by eliminating z from equations (7) and (9):

$$
\begin{array}{ll}
2x + 4y + 3z = 11{,}600 & \text{Equation (7)} \\
\underline{-3x - 6y - 3z = -14{,}400} & -3[\text{equation (9)}] \\
{-x} - 2y = {-2{,}800} & \tag{10}
\end{array}
$$

We now eliminate z from equations (8) and (9):

$$
\begin{array}{ll}
3x + 5y + 4z = 15{,}600 & \text{Equation (8)} \\
\underline{-4x - 8y - 4z = -19{,}200} & -4[\text{equation (9)}] \\
{-x} - 3y = {-3{,}600} & \tag{11}
\end{array}
$$

Equations (10) and (11) form a system of two equations and two unknowns:

$$-x - 2y = -2{,}800 \tag{10}$$

$$-x - 3y = -3{,}600 \tag{11}$$

We solve as in the earlier part of this section:

$$
\begin{array}{ll}
-x - 2y = -2{,}800 & \text{Equation (10)} \\
\underline{x + 3y = 3{,}600} & (-1)[\text{equation (11)}] \\
y = 800 &
\end{array}
$$

Substitute $y = 800$ into either (10) or (11) to find x:

$$-x - \quad 2y = -2,800 \tag{10}$$
$$-x - 2(800) = -2,800$$
$$-x - \quad 1,600 = -2,800$$
$$-x = -1,200$$
$$x = \quad 1,200$$

Now use either (7), (8), or (9) to find z:

$$2x + \quad 4y + 3z = 11,600 \tag{7}$$
$$2(1,200) + 4(800) + 3z = 11,600$$
$$2,400 + \quad 3,200 + 3z = 11,600$$
$$3z = \quad 6,000$$
$$z = \quad 2,000$$

Thus, each week, the company should produce 1,200 style *A* shirts, 800 style *B* shirts, and 2,000 style *C* shirts to operate at full capacity. The check of the solution is left to the reader.

Problem 8 Repeat Example 8 with the cutting, sewing, and packaging departments having available a maximum of 1,180, 1,560, and 510 labor-hours per week, respectively.

Answers to Matched Problems

1.

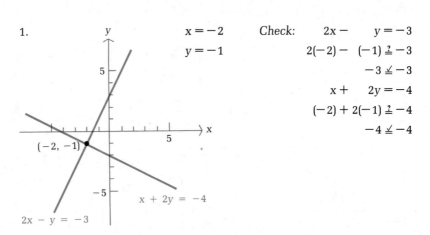

$x = -2$
$y = -1$

Check: $2x - \quad y = -3$
$$2(-2) - (-1) \overset{?}{=} -3$$
$$-3 \overset{\checkmark}{=} -3$$
$$x + \quad 2y = -4$$
$$(-2) + 2(-1) \overset{?}{=} -4$$
$$-4 \overset{\checkmark}{=} -4$$

2. (A) $x = 2, y = 2$ (B) Infinitely many solutions
   (C) No solution
3. $x = -2, y = 2$ 4. $x = 2, y = -1$
5. 6.5 oz of food *M*, 4.5 oz of food *N*

6. Equilibrium quantity = 13 thousand pounds
   Equilibrium price = $1.70 per pound

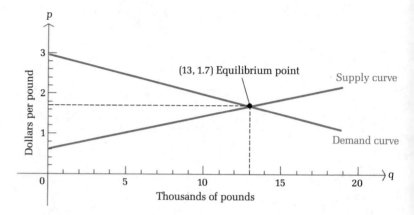

7. $x = -1, y = 0, z = 2$ 8. 900 style *A*; 1,300 style *B*; 1,600 style *C*

Exercise 1-1

A   *Solve by graphing.*

1. $x + y = 5$
   $x - y = 1$

2. $x - y = 2$
   $x + y = 6$

3. $3x - y = 2$
   $x + 2y = 10$

4. $3x - 2y = 12$
   $7x + 2y = 8$

5. $m + 2n = 4$
   $2m + 4n = -8$

6. $3u + 5v = 15$
   $6u + 10v = -30$

Solve using substitution.

7. $y = 2x - 3$
   $x + 2y = 14$

8. $y = x - 4$
   $x + 3y = 12$

9. $2x + y = 6$
   $x - y = -3$

10. $3x - y = 7$
    $2x + 3y = 1$

Solve using elimination by addition.

11. $3u - 2v = 12$
    $7u + 2v = 8$

12. $2x - 3y = -8$
    $5x + 3y = 1$

13. $2m - n = 10$
     $m - 2n = -4$

14. $2x + 3y = 1$
     $3x - y = 7$

Solve using substitution or elimination by addition.

15. $9x - 3y = 24$
     $11x + 2y = 1$

16. $4x + 3y = 26$
     $3x - 11y = -7$

17. $2x - 3y = -2$
     $-4x + 6y = 7$

18. $3x - 6y = -9$
     $-2x + 4y = 12$

19. $3x + 8y = 4$
     $15x + 10y = -10$

20. $7m + 12n = -1$
     $5m - 3n = 7$

21. $-6x + 10y = -30$
     $3x - 5y = 15$

22. $2x + 4y = -8$
     $x + 2y = 4$

23. $y = 0.07x$
     $y = 80 + 0.05x$

24. $y = 0.08x$
     $y = 100 + 0.04x$

B   *Solve using substitution or elimination by addition.*

25. $0.2x - 0.5y = 0.07$
     $0.8x - 0.3y = 0.79$

26. $0.3u - 0.6v = 0.18$
     $0.5u + 0.2v = 0.54$

27. $4y - z = -13$
     $3y + 2z = 4$
     $6x - 5y - 2z = 0$

28. $2x + z = -5$
     $x - 3z = -6$
     $4x + 2y - z = -9$

29. $2x + y - z = 5$
     $x - 2y - 2z = 4$
     $3x + 4y + 3z = 3$

30. $x - 3y + z = 4$
     $-x + 4y - 4z = 1$
     $2x - y + 5z = -3$

31. $2a + 4b + 3c = 6$
     $a - 3b + 2c = -7$
     $-a + 2b - c = 5$

32. $3u - 2v + 3w = 11$
     $2u + 3v - 2w = -5$
     $u + 4v - w = -5$

C   *Solve using substitution or elimination by addition.*

33. $2x - 3y + 3z = -15$
     $3x + 2y - 5z = 19$
     $5x - 4y - 2z = -2$

34. $3x - 2y - 4z = -8$
     $4x + 3y - 5z = -5$
     $6x - 5y + 2z = -17$

35. $x - 8y + 2z = -1$
     $x - 3y + z = 1$
     $2x - 11y + 3z = 2$

36. $-x + 2y - z = -4$
     $4x + y - 2z = 1$
     $x + y - z = -4$

Applications

Business & Economics

37. *Supply and demand.* Suppose the supply and demand equations for printed T-shirts in a resort town for a particular week are

$$p = 0.7q + 3 \qquad \text{Supply equation}$$
$$p = -1.7q + 15 \qquad \text{Demand equation}$$

where p is the price in dollars and q is the quantity in hundreds.

(A) Find the equilibrium price and quantity.

(B) Graph the two equations in the same coordinate system and identify the equilibrium point, supply curve, and demand curve.

38. *Supply and demand.* Repeat Problem 37 with the following supply and demand equations:

$$p = 0.4q + 3.2 \qquad \text{Supply equation}$$
$$p = -1.9q + 17 \qquad \text{Demand equation}$$

39. *Break-even analysis.* A small company manufactures portable home computers. The plant has fixed costs (leases, insurance, and so on) of $48,000 per month and variable costs (labor, materials, and so on) of $1,400 per unit produced. The computers are sold for $1,800 each. Thus, the cost and revenue equations are

$$C = 48{,}000 + 1{,}400x$$
$$R = 1{,}800x$$

where x is the total number of computers produced and sold each month, and C and R are, respectively, monthly costs and revenue in dollars.

(A) How many units must be manufactured and sold each month for the company to break even? (This is actually a three-equation–three-unknown problem with the third equation $R = C$. It can be solved by using the substitution method.)

(B) Graph both equations in the same coordinate system and show the break-even point. Interpret the regions between the lines to the left and to the right of the break-even point.

40. *Break-even analysis.* Repeat Problem 39 with the cost and revenue equations

$$C = 65{,}000 + 1{,}100x$$
$$R = 1{,}600x$$

41. *Production scheduling.* A small manufacturing plant makes three types of inflatable boats: one-person, two-person, and four-person models. Each boat requires the services of three departments as listed in the table. The cutting, assembly, and packaging departments have available a maximum of 380, 330, and 120 labor-hours per week, respectively. How many boats of each type must be produced each week for the plant to operate at full capacity?

	One-Person Boat	Two-Person Boat	Four-Person Boat
Cutting department	0.6 hr	1.0 hr	1.5 hr
Assembly department	0.6 hr	0.9 hr	1.2 hr
Packaging department	0.2 hr	0.3 hr	0.5 hr

42. *Production scheduling.* Repeat Problem 41 assuming the cutting, assembly, and packaging departments have available a maximum of 260, 234, and 82 labor-hours per week, respectively.

Life Sciences **43.** *Nutrition.* Animals in an experiment are to be kept under a strict diet. Each animal is to receive, among other things, 20 grams of protein and 6 grams of fat. The laboratory technician is able to purchase two food mixes of the following compositions: Mix A has 10% protein and 6% fat; mix B has 20% protein and 2% fat. How many grams of each mix should be used to obtain the right diet for a single animal?

44. *Diet.* In an experiment involving mice, a zoologist needs a food mix that contains, among other things, 23 grams of protein, 6.2 grams of fat, and 16 grams of moisture. She has on hand mixes of the following compositions: Mix A contains 20% protein, 2% fat, and 15% moisture; mix B contains 10% protein, 6% fat, and 10% moisture; and mix C contains 15% protein, 5% fat, and 5% moisture. How many grams of each mix should be used to get the desired diet mix?

Social Sciences **45.** *Psychology — approach and avoidance.* People often approach certain situations with "mixed emotions." For example, public speaking often brings forth the positive response of recognition and the negative response of failure. Which dominates? J. S. Brown, in an experiment on approach and avoidance, trained rats by feeding them from a goal box. Then the rats received mild electric shocks from the same goal box. This established an approach–avoidance conflict relative to the goal box. Using appropriate apparatus, Brown arrived at the following relationships:

$$p = -\tfrac{1}{5}d + 70$$
$$a = -\tfrac{4}{3}d + 230 \qquad 30 \leqslant d \leqslant 175$$

Here p is the pull in grams toward the food goal box when the rat is placed d centimeters from it. The quantity a is the pull in grams away (avoidance) from the shock goal box when the rat is placed d centimeters from it.

(A)   Graph the two equations above in the same coordinate system.

(B)   Find d when $p = a$. (This is actually a three-equation—three-unknown problem with the third equation $p = a$. It can be solved by using the substitution method.)

(C)   What do you think the rat would do when placed the distance d from the box found in part B?

(For additional discussion of this phenomenon, see J. S. Brown, "Gradients of Approach and Avoidance Responses and Their Relation to Motivation," *Journal of Comparative and Physiological Psychology*, 1948, 41:450–465.)

1-2   Systems of Linear Equations and Augmented Matrices — Introduction

- Introduction
- Augmented Matrices
- Solving Linear Systems

■ Introduction

Most linear systems of any consequence involve large numbers of equations and unknowns. These systems are solved with computers, since hand methods would be impractical (try solving even a five-equation–five-unknown problem and you will understand why). However, even if you have a computer facility to help solve a problem, it is still important for you to know how to formulate the problem so that it can be solved by a computer. In addition, it is helpful to have at least a general idea of how computers solve these problems. Finally, it is important for you to know how to interpret the results.

Even though the procedures and notation introduced in this and the next section are more involved than those used in the preceding section, it is important to keep in mind that our objective is not to find an efficient hand method for solving large-scale systems (there are none), but rather to find a process that generalizes readily for computer use. It turns out that you will receive an added bonus for your efforts, since several of the processes developed in this and the next section will be of considerable value in Sections 1-6, 1-7, 2-4, 2-5, and 2-6.

■ Augmented Matrices

In solving systems of equations by elimination, the coefficients of the variables and the constant terms played a central role. The process can be made more efficient for generalization and computer work by the introduction of a mathematical form called a *matrix*. A **matrix** is a rectangular array of numbers written within brackets. Some examples are

$$\begin{bmatrix} 3 & 5 \\ 0 & -2 \end{bmatrix} \qquad \begin{bmatrix} 2 \\ -3 \\ 0 \end{bmatrix} \qquad [1 \quad -1 \quad 0 \quad 5]$$

$$\begin{bmatrix} -1 & 2 & -5 & 0 \\ 0 & 3 & 2 & 1 \end{bmatrix} \qquad \begin{bmatrix} 1 & 0 & 0 \\ 0 & 1 & 0 \\ 0 & 0 & 1 \end{bmatrix}$$

Each number in a matrix is called an **element** of the matrix.
   Associated with the system

$$2x - 3y = 5$$
$$x + 2y = -3$$

(1)

is the *augmented matrix*

$$\begin{bmatrix} 2 & -3 & \bigm| & 5 \\ 1 & 2 & \bigm| & -3 \end{bmatrix}$$

which contains the essential parts of the system—namely, the coefficients
of the variables and the constant terms. (The vertical bar is included only to
separate the coefficients of the variables from the constant terms.)
   For ease of generalization to the larger systems in the following sections,
we are now going to change the notation for the variables in (1) to a
subscript form (we could soon run out of letters, but we could not run out of
subscripts). That is, in place of x and y, we will use x_1 and x_2 and (1) will be
written as

$$2x_1 - 3x_2 = 5$$
$$x_1 + 2x_2 = -3$$

In general, associated with each linear system of the form

$$a_1x_1 + b_1x_2 = k_1$$
$$a_2x_1 + b_2x_2 = k_2$$

(2)

where x_1 and x_2 are variables, is the **augmented matrix** of the system:

$$
\begin{array}{l}
\text{Column 1 } (C_1) \\
\quad \text{Column 2 } (C_2) \\
\qquad \text{Column 3 } (C_3)
\end{array}
$$

$$\begin{bmatrix} a_1 & b_1 & \bigm| & k_1 \\ a_2 & b_2 & \bigm| & k_2 \end{bmatrix} \begin{array}{l} \leftarrow \text{Row 1 } (R_1) \\ \leftarrow \text{Row 2 } (R_2) \end{array}$$

This matrix contains the essential parts of system (2). Our objective is to
learn how to manipulate augmented matrices in order to solve system (2), if

a solution exists. The manipulative process is a direct outgrowth of the elimination process discussed in Section 1-1.

Recall that two linear systems are said to be **equivalent** if they have exactly the same solution set. How did we transform linear systems into equivalent linear systems? We used Theorem 1, which we restate here.

Theorem 1

A system of linear equations is transformed into an equivalent system if:

(A)   Two equations are interchanged.
(B)   An equation is multiplied by a nonzero constant.
(C)   A constant multiple of another equation is added to a given equation.

Paralleling the discussion above, we say that two augmented matrices are **row-equivalent,** denoted by the symbol ~ placed between the two matrices, if they are augmented matrices of equivalent systems of equations. (Think about this.) How do we transform augmented matrices into row-equivalent matrices? We use Theorem 2, which is a direct consequence of Theorem 1:

Theorem 2

An augmented matrix is transformed into a row-equivalent matrix if:

(A)   Two rows are interchanged ($R_i \leftrightarrow R_j$).
(B)   A row is multiplied by a nonzero constant ($kR_i \rightarrow R_i$).
(C)   A constant multiple of another row is added to a given row

$(R_i + kR_j \rightarrow R_i)$.

[*Note:*   The arrow $\rightarrow$ means "replaces."]

■ Solving Linear Systems

The use of Theorem 2 in solving systems in the form of (2) is best illustrated by examples.

Example 9   Solve using augmented matrix methods:

$$3x_1 + 4x_2 = 1$$
$$x_1 - 2x_2 = 7$$

(3)

Solution   We start by writing the augmented matrix corresponding to (3)

$$\begin{bmatrix} 3 & 4 & | & 1 \\ 1 & -2 & | & 7 \end{bmatrix} \tag{4}$$

Our objective is to use row operations from Theorem 2 to try to transform (4) into the form

$$\begin{bmatrix} 1 & 0 & | & m \\ 0 & 1 & | & n \end{bmatrix} \tag{5}$$

where m and n are real numbers. The solution to system (3) will then be obvious, since matrix (5) will be the augmented matrix of the following system:

$$x_1 \quad = m$$
$$x_2 = n$$

We now proceed to use row operations to transform (4) into form (5).

Step 1.   To get a 1 in the upper left corner, we interchange Rows 1 and 2 (Theorem 2A):

$$\begin{bmatrix} 3 & 4 & | & 1 \\ 1 & -2 & | & 7 \end{bmatrix} \quad \begin{array}{c} R_1 \leftrightarrow R_2 \\ \sim \end{array} \quad \begin{bmatrix} 1 & -2 & | & 7 \\ 3 & 4 & | & 1 \end{bmatrix}$$

Now you see why we wanted Theorem 1A!

Step 2.   To get a 0 in the lower left corner, we multiply R_1 by (-3) and add to R_2 (Theorem 2C) — this changes R_2 but not R_1. Some people find it useful to write $(-3)R_1$ outside the matrix to help reduce errors in arithmetic, as shown: ·

$$\begin{array}{ccc} -3 & 6 & -21 \longleftarrow \end{array}$$
$$\begin{bmatrix} 1 & -2 & | & 7 \\ 3 & 4 & | & 1 \end{bmatrix} \begin{array}{c} R_2 + (-3)R_1 \rightarrow R_2 \\ \sim \end{array} \begin{bmatrix} 1 & -2 & | & 7 \\ 0 & 10 & | & -20 \end{bmatrix}$$

Step 3.   To get a 1 in the second row, second column, we multiply R_2 by $\frac{1}{10}$ (Theorem 2B):

$$\begin{bmatrix} 1 & -2 & | & 7 \\ 0 & 10 & | & -20 \end{bmatrix} \begin{array}{c} \frac{1}{10}R_2 \rightarrow R_2 \\ \sim \end{array} \begin{bmatrix} 1 & -2 & | & 7 \\ 0 & 1 & | & -2 \end{bmatrix}$$

Step 4.   To get a 0 in the first row, second column, we multiply R_2 by 2 and add the result to R_1 (Theorem 2C) — this changes R_1 but not R_2:

$$\begin{array}{ccc} 0 & 2 & -4 \longleftarrow \end{array}$$
$$\begin{bmatrix} 1 & -2 & | & 7 \\ 0 & 1 & | & -2 \end{bmatrix} \begin{array}{c} R_1 + 2R_2 \rightarrow R_1 \\ \sim \end{array} \begin{bmatrix} 1 & 0 & | & 3 \\ 0 & 1 & | & -2 \end{bmatrix}$$

We have accomplished our objective! The last matrix is the augmented matrix for the system

$$
\begin{aligned}
x_1 &= 3 \\
x_2 &= -2
\end{aligned}
\tag{6}
$$

Since system (6) is equivalent to system (3), our starting system, we have solved (3); that is, $x_1 = 3$ and $x_2 = -2$.

Check

$$
\begin{array}{ll}
3x_1 + 4x_2 = 1 & x_1 - 2x_2 = 7 \\
3(3) + 4(-2) \overset{?}{=} 1 & 3 - 2(-2) \overset{?}{=} 7 \\
\quad\quad 9 - 8 \overset{\checkmark}{=} 1 & \quad\quad 3 + 4 \overset{\checkmark}{=} 7
\end{array}
$$

The above process is written more compactly as follows:

Step 1:
Need a 1 here
$$
\begin{bmatrix} 3 & 4 & | & 1 \\ 1 & -2 & | & 7 \end{bmatrix} \quad R_1 \leftrightarrow R_2
$$

Step 2:
Need a 0 here
$$
\sim \begin{bmatrix} 1 & -2 & | & 7 \\ 3 & 4 & | & 1 \\ -3 & 6 & & -21 \end{bmatrix} \quad R_2 + (-3)R_1 \to R_2
$$

Step 3:
Need a 1 here
$$
\sim \begin{bmatrix} 1 & -2 & | & 7 \\ 0 & 10 & | & -20 \end{bmatrix} \quad \tfrac{1}{10}R_2 \to R_2
$$

Step 4:
Need a 0 here
$$
\sim \begin{bmatrix} 1 & -2 & | & 7 \\ 0 & 1 & | & -2 \\ 0 & 2 & & -4 \end{bmatrix} \quad R_1 + 2R_2 \to R_1
$$

$$
\sim \begin{bmatrix} 1 & 0 & | & 3 \\ 0 & 1 & | & -2 \end{bmatrix}
$$

Therefore, $x_1 = 3$ and $x_2 = -2$.

Problem 9   Solve using augmented matrix methods:

$$
\begin{aligned}
2x_1 - x_2 &= -7 \\
x_1 + 2x_2 &= 4
\end{aligned}
$$

Example 10   Solve using augmented matrix methods:

$$
\begin{aligned}
2x_1 - 3x_2 &= 6 \\
3x_1 + 4x_2 &= \tfrac{1}{2}
\end{aligned}
$$

Solution

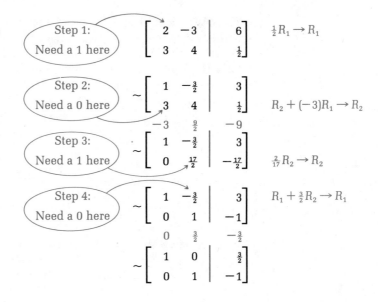

Step 1:
Need a 1 here

$$\begin{bmatrix} 2 & -3 & | & 6 \\ 3 & 4 & | & \frac{1}{2} \end{bmatrix}$$ $\frac{1}{2}R_1 \to R_1$

Step 2:
Need a 0 here

$$\sim \begin{bmatrix} 1 & -\frac{3}{2} & | & 3 \\ 3 & 4 & | & \frac{1}{2} \end{bmatrix}$$ $R_2 + (-3)R_1 \to R_2$

$$\begin{array}{ccc} -3 & \frac{9}{2} & -9 \end{array}$$

Step 3:
Need a 1 here

$$\sim \begin{bmatrix} 1 & -\frac{3}{2} & | & 3 \\ 0 & \frac{17}{2} & | & -\frac{17}{2} \end{bmatrix}$$ $\frac{2}{17}R_2 \to R_2$

Step 4:
Need a 0 here

$$\sim \begin{bmatrix} 1 & -\frac{3}{2} & | & 3 \\ 0 & 1 & | & -1 \end{bmatrix}$$ $R_1 + \frac{3}{2}R_2 \to R_1$

$$\begin{array}{ccc} 0 & \frac{3}{2} & -\frac{3}{2} \end{array}$$

$$\sim \begin{bmatrix} 1 & 0 & | & \frac{3}{2} \\ 0 & 1 & | & -1 \end{bmatrix}$$

Thus, $x_1 = \frac{3}{2}$ and $x_2 = -1$.

Problem 10   Solve using augmented matrix methods:

$$5x_1 - 2x_2 = 11$$
$$2x_1 + 3x_2 = \tfrac{5}{2}$$

Example 11   Solve using augmented matrix methods:

$$2x_1 - x_2 = 4 \tag{7}$$
$$-6x_1 + 3x_2 = -12$$

Solution

$$\begin{bmatrix} 2 & -1 & | & 4 \\ -6 & 3 & | & -12 \end{bmatrix}$$

$\frac{1}{2}R_1 \to R_1$ (this produces a 1 in the upper left corner)

$\frac{1}{3}R_2 \to R_2$ (this simplifies R_2)

$$\sim \begin{bmatrix} 1 & -\frac{1}{2} & | & 2 \\ -2 & 1 & | & -4 \end{bmatrix}$$

$R_2 + 2R_1 \to R_2$ (this produces a 0 in the lower left corner)

$$\begin{array}{ccc} 2 & -1 & 4 \end{array}$$

$$\sim \begin{bmatrix} 1 & -\frac{1}{2} & | & 2 \\ 0 & 0 & | & 0 \end{bmatrix}$$

The last matrix corresponds to the system

$$x_1 - \tfrac{1}{2}x_2 = 2 \tag{8}$$
$$0x_1 + 0x_2 = 0$$

This system is equivalent to the original system. Geometrically, the graphs of the two original equations coincide and there are infinitely many solutions. In general, if we end up with a row of zeros in an augmented matrix for a two-equation–two-unknown system, the system is dependent and there are infinitely many solutions.

There are several ways of representing the infinitely many solutions to system (7). For example, solving the first equation in (8) for either variable in terms of the other (we solve for x_1 in terms of x_2), we obtain

$$x_1 = \tfrac{1}{2}x_2 + 2 \tag{9}$$

Thus, for any real number x_2,

$$(\tfrac{1}{2}x_2 + 2, \, x_2)$$

is a solution. Another way to represent the infinitely many solutions—a way that is convenient for the larger-scale systems we will be solving later in this chapter—is as follows: We choose another variable called a **parameter,** say t, and set the variable on the right of equation (9), x_2, equal to it. Then for t any real number,

$$\begin{aligned} x_1 &= \tfrac{1}{2}t + 2 \\ x_2 &= t \end{aligned} \tag{10}$$

represents a solution. For example, if $t = 8$, then

$$\begin{aligned} x_1 &= \tfrac{1}{2}(8) + 2 = 6 \\ x_2 &= 8 \end{aligned}$$

That is, $(6, 8)$ is a solution of (7). If $t = -3$, then

$$\begin{aligned} x_1 &= \tfrac{1}{2}(-3) + 2 = \tfrac{1}{2} \\ x_2 &= -3 \end{aligned}$$

That is, $(\tfrac{1}{2}, -3)$ is a solution of (7). Other solutions can be obtained in a similar manner. The following is a check that (10) provides a solution for (7) for any real number t:

Check
$$\begin{array}{ll} 2x_1 - x_2 = 4 & -6x_1 + 3x_2 = -12 \\ 2(\tfrac{1}{2}t + 2) - t \overset{?}{=} 4 & -6(\tfrac{1}{2}t + 2) + 3t \overset{?}{=} -12 \\ t + 4 - t \overset{?}{=} 4 & -3t - 12 + 3t \overset{?}{=} -12 \\ 4 \overset{\checkmark}{=} 4 & -12 \overset{\checkmark}{=} -12 \end{array}$$

Problem 11   Solve using augmented matrix methods:

$$\begin{aligned} -2x_1 + 6x_2 &= 6 \\ 3x_1 - 9x_2 &= -9 \end{aligned}$$

Example 12   Solve using augmented matrix methods:

$$2x_1 + 6x_2 = -3$$
$$x_1 + 3x_2 = 2$$

Solution
$$\begin{bmatrix} 2 & 6 & \bigm| & -3 \\ 1 & 3 & \bigm| & 2 \end{bmatrix} \quad R_1 \leftrightarrow R_2$$

$$\sim \begin{bmatrix} 1 & 3 & \bigm| & 2 \\ 2 & 6 & \bigm| & -3 \end{bmatrix} \quad R_2 + (-2)R_1 \rightarrow R_2$$

$$ \quad -2 \quad -6 \quad\quad -4$$

$$\sim \begin{bmatrix} 1 & 3 & \bigm| & 2 \\ 0 & 0 & \bigm| & -7 \end{bmatrix} \quad R_2 \text{ implies the contradiction } 0 = -7$$

This is the augmented matrix of the system

$$x_1 + 3x_2 = 2$$
$$0x_1 + 0x_2 = -7$$

The second equation is not satisfied by any ordered pair of real numbers. Hence, the original system is inconsistent and has no solution — otherwise we have proved that $0 = -7$! Thus, if in a row of an augmented matrix we obtain all zeros to the left of the vertical bar and a nonzero number to the right, then the system is inconsistent and there are no solutions.

Problem 12   Solve using augmented matrix methods:

$$2x_1 - x_2 = 3$$
$$4x_1 - 2x_2 = -1$$

Summary

Form 1 A Unique Solution	Form 2 Infinitely Many Solutions (Dependent)	Form 3 No Solution (Inconsistent)
$\begin{bmatrix} 1 & 0 & \bigm| & m \\ 0 & 1 & \bigm| & n \end{bmatrix}$	$\begin{bmatrix} 1 & m & \bigm| & n \\ 0 & 0 & \bigm| & 0 \end{bmatrix}$	$\begin{bmatrix} 1 & m & \bigm| & n \\ 0 & 0 & \bigm| & p \end{bmatrix}$

m, n, p. real numbers; $p \neq 0$

The process of solving systems of equations described in this section is referred to as **Gauss–Jordan elimination.** We will use this method to solve larger-scale systems in the next section, including systems where the number of equations and the number of variables are not the same.

9. $x_1 = -2$, $x_2 = 3$

10. $x_1 = 2$, $x_2 = -\frac{1}{2}$

11. The system is dependent. For t any real number,
$$x_1 = 3t - 3$$
$$x_2 = t$$
is a solution.

12. Inconsistent—no solution

Exercise 1-2

A *Perform each of the indicated row operations on the following matrix:*

$$\begin{bmatrix} 1 & -3 & \bigm| & 2 \\ 4 & -6 & \bigm| & -8 \end{bmatrix}$$

1. $R_1 \leftrightarrow R_2$
2. $\frac{1}{2}R_2 \rightarrow R_2$
3. $-4R_1 \rightarrow R_1$
4. $-2R_1 \rightarrow R_1$
5. $2R_2 \rightarrow R_2$
6. $-1R_2 \rightarrow R_2$
7. $R_2 + (-4)R_1 \rightarrow R_2$
8. $R_1 + (-\frac{1}{2})R_2 \rightarrow R_1$
9. $R_2 + (-2)R_1 \rightarrow R_2$
10. $R_2 + (-3)R_1 \rightarrow R_2$
11. $R_2 + (-1)R_1 \rightarrow R_2$
12. $R_2 + (1)R_1 \rightarrow R_2$

Solve using augmented matrix methods.

13. $x_1 + x_2 = 5$
    $x_1 - x_2 = 1$

14. $x_1 - x_2 = 2$
    $x_1 + x_2 = 6$

B *Solve using augmented matrix methods.*

15. $x_1 - 2x_2 = 1$
    $2x_1 - x_2 = 5$

16. $x_1 + 3x_2 = 1$
    $3x_1 - 2x_2 = 14$

17. $x_1 - 4x_2 = -2$
    $-2x_1 + x_2 = -3$

18. $x_1 - 3x_2 = -5$
    $-3x_1 - x_2 = 5$

19. $3x_1 - x_2 = 2$
    $x_1 + 2x_2 = 10$

20. $2x_1 + x_2 = 0$
    $x_1 - 2x_2 = -5$

21. $x_1 + 2x_2 = 4$
    $2x_1 + 4x_2 = -8$

22. $2x_1 - 3x_2 = -2$
    $-4x_1 + 6x_2 = 7$

23. $2x_1 + x_2 = 6$
    $x_1 - x_2 = -3$

24. $3x_1 - x_2 = -5$
    $x_1 + 3x_2 = 5$

25. $3x_1 - 6x_2 = -9$
    $-2x_1 + 4x_2 = 6$

26. $2x_1 - 4x_2 = -2$
    $-3x_1 + 6x_2 = 3$

27. $4x_1 - 2x_2 = 2$
    $-6x_1 + 3x_2 = -3$

28. $-6x_1 + 2x_2 = 4$
    $3x_1 - x_2 = -2$

C *Solve using augmented matrix methods.*

29. $3x_1 - x_2 = 7$
$2x_1 + 3x_2 = 1$

30. $2x_1 - 3x_2 = -8$
$5x_1 + 3x_2 = 1$

31. $3x_1 + 2x_2 = 4$
$2x_1 - x_2 = 5$

32. $4x_1 + 3x_2 = 26$
$3x_1 - 11x_2 = -7$

33. $0.2x_1 - 0.5x_2 = 0.07$
$0.8x_1 - 0.3x_2 = 0.79$

34. $0.3x_1 - 0.6x_2 = 0.18$
$0.5x_1 - 0.2x_2 = 0.54$

1-3 Gauss–Jordan Elimination

- Reduced Matrices
- Solving Systems by Gauss–Jordan Elimination
- Application

Now that you have had some experience with row operations on simple augmented matrices, we will consider systems involving more than two variables. In addition, we will not require that a system have the same number of equations as variables.

■ Reduced Matrices

Our objective is to start with the augmented matrix of a linear system and transform it by using row operations from Theorem 2 in the preceding section into a simple form where the solution can be read by inspection. The simple form so obtained is called the *reduced form,* and we define it as follows:

Reduced Matrix

A matrix is in **reduced form** if:

1. Each row consisting entirely of zeros is below any row having at least one nonzero element.
2. The leftmost nonzero element in each row is 1.
3. The column containing the leftmost 1 of a given row has zeros above and below the 1.
4. The leftmost 1 in any row is to the right of the leftmost 1 in the row above.

Example 13   The following matrices are in reduced form. Check each one carefully to convince yourself that the conditions in the definition are met.

$$\left[\begin{array}{cc|c} 1 & 0 & 2 \\ 0 & 1 & -3 \end{array}\right] \qquad \left[\begin{array}{ccc|c} 1 & 0 & 0 & 2 \\ 0 & 1 & 0 & -1 \\ 0 & 0 & 1 & 3 \end{array}\right]$$

$$\left[\begin{array}{cc|c} 1 & 0 & 3 \\ 0 & 1 & -1 \\ 0 & 0 & 0 \end{array}\right] \qquad \left[\begin{array}{cccc|c} 1 & 4 & 0 & 0 & -3 \\ 0 & 0 & 1 & 0 & 2 \\ 0 & 0 & 0 & 1 & 6 \end{array}\right]$$

$$\left[\begin{array}{ccc|c} 1 & 0 & 4 & 0 \\ 0 & 1 & 3 & 0 \\ 0 & 0 & 0 & 1 \end{array}\right]$$

Problem 13   The matrices below are not in reduced form. Indicate which condition in the definition is violated for each matrix.

(A) $\left[\begin{array}{cc|c} 1 & 0 & 2 \\ 0 & 3 & -6 \end{array}\right]$ (B) $\left[\begin{array}{ccc|c} 1 & 5 & 4 & 3 \\ 0 & 1 & 2 & -1 \\ 0 & 0 & 0 & 0 \end{array}\right]$

(C) $\left[\begin{array}{ccc|c} 0 & 1 & 2 & -3 \\ 1 & -2 & 3 & 0 \\ 0 & 0 & 1 & 2 \end{array}\right]$ (D) $\left[\begin{array}{ccc|c} 1 & 2 & 0 & 3 \\ 0 & 0 & 0 & 0 \\ 0 & 0 & 1 & 4 \end{array}\right]$

Example 14   Write the linear system corresponding to each reduced augmented matrix and solve.

(A) $\left[\begin{array}{ccc|c} 1 & 0 & 0 & 2 \\ 0 & 1 & 0 & -1 \\ 0 & 0 & 1 & 3 \end{array}\right]$ (B) $\left[\begin{array}{ccc|c} 1 & 0 & 4 & 0 \\ 0 & 1 & 3 & 0 \\ 0 & 0 & 0 & 1 \end{array}\right]$

(C) $\left[\begin{array}{ccc|c} 1 & 0 & 2 & -3 \\ 0 & 1 & -1 & 8 \\ 0 & 0 & 0 & 0 \end{array}\right]$ (D) $\left[\begin{array}{ccccc|c} 1 & 4 & 0 & 0 & 3 & -2 \\ 0 & 0 & 1 & 0 & -2 & 0 \\ 0 & 0 & 0 & 1 & 2 & 4 \end{array}\right]$

Solutions   (A) $x_1 \qquad = 2$
$\qquad\qquad x_2 \quad = -1$
$\qquad\qquad\qquad x_3 = 3$

The solution is obvious: $x_1 = 2$, $x_2 = -1$, $x_3 = 3$.

(B) $x_1 \quad\quad + 4x_3 = 0$

$\quad\quad\quad x_2 + 3x_3 = 0$

$0x_1 + 0x_2 + 0x_3 = 1$

The last equation implies $0 = 1$, which is a contradiction. Hence, the system is inconsistent and has no solution.

(C) $x_1 \quad + 2x_3 = -3$ We disregard the equation corresponding to the

$\quad\quad x_2 - \ x_3 = \ \ 8$ third row in the matrix, since it is satisfied by

all values of x_1, x_2, and x_3

When a reduced system (a system corresponding to a reduced augmented matrix) has more variables than equations and contains no contradictions, the system is dependent and has infinitely many solutions. To represent these solutions, we note that the first variable in each equation appears in only one equation in the reduced system. Since these variables correspond to leftmost 1's in the reduced augmented matrix, we call the first variable in each equation of a reduced system a **leftmost variable.** The definition of reduced form insures that each leftmost variable will appear in exactly one equation of the reduced system and that no two leftmost variables will appear in the same equation. Thus, it is always easy to solve for each leftmost variable in terms of the remaining variables. Returning to our original system, we solve for the leftmost variables x_1 and x_2 in terms of the remaining variable x_3:

$x_1 = -2x_3 - 3$

$x_2 = x_3 + 8$

If we let $x_3 = t$, then for any real number t,

$x_1 = -2t - 3$

$x_2 = t + 8$

$x_3 = t$

is a solution. For example,

If $t = 0$, then   If $t = -2$, then

$\quad x_1 = -2(0) - 3 = -3$ $\quad x_1 = -2(-2) - 3 = 1$

$\quad x_2 = 0 + 8 = 8$ $\quad x_2 = -2 + 8 = 6$

$\quad x_3 = 0$ $\quad x_3 = -2$

is a solution.   is a solution.

(D) $x_1 + 4x_2 \quad\quad + 3x_5 = -2$

$\quad\quad\quad x_3 \ - 2x_5 = \ \ 0$

$\quad\quad\quad\quad x_4 + 2x_5 = \ \ 4$

Solve for x_1, x_3, and x_4 (leftmost variables) in terms of x_2 and x_5 (remaining variables):

$$x_1 = -4x_2 - 3x_5 - 2$$
$$x_3 = 2x_5$$
$$x_4 = -2x_5 + 4$$

If we let $x_2 = s$ and $x_5 = t$, then for any real numbers s and t,

$$x_1 = -4s - 3t - 2$$
$$x_2 = s$$
$$x_3 = 2t$$
$$x_4 = -2t + 4$$
$$x_5 = t$$

is a solution. The system is dependent and has infinitely many solutions. Can you find two?

Problem 14   Write the linear system corresponding to each reduced augmented matrix and solve.

(A) $\begin{bmatrix} 1 & 0 & 0 & | & -5 \\ 0 & 1 & 0 & | & 3 \\ 0 & 0 & 1 & | & 6 \end{bmatrix}$ (B) $\begin{bmatrix} 1 & 2 & -3 & | & 0 \\ 0 & 0 & 0 & | & 1 \\ 0 & 0 & 0 & | & 0 \end{bmatrix}$

(C) $\begin{bmatrix} 1 & 0 & -2 & | & 4 \\ 0 & 1 & 3 & | & -2 \\ 0 & 0 & 0 & | & 0 \end{bmatrix}$ (D) $\begin{bmatrix} 1 & 0 & 3 & 2 & | & 5 \\ 0 & 1 & -2 & -1 & | & 3 \\ 0 & 0 & 0 & 0 & | & 0 \end{bmatrix}$

■ Solving Systems by Gauss–Jordan Elimination

We are now ready to outline the Gauss–Jordan elimination method for solving systems of linear equations. The method systematically transforms an augmented matrix into a reduced form from which we can write the solution to the original system by inspection, if a solution exists. The method will also reveal when a solution fails to exist (see Example 14B).

Example 15   Solve by Gauss–Jordan elimination:

$$2x_1 - 2x_2 + x_3 = 3$$
$$3x_1 + x_2 - x_3 = 7$$
$$x_1 - 3x_2 + 2x_3 = 0$$

Solution   Write the augmented matrix and follow the steps indicated at the right.

Need a 1 here

$$\begin{bmatrix} 2 & -2 & 1 & | & 3 \\ 3 & 1 & -1 & | & 7 \\ 1 & -3 & 2 & | & 0 \end{bmatrix} \begin{matrix} R_1 \leftrightarrow R_3 \end{matrix}$$

Step 1. Choose leftmost nonzero column and get a 1 at the top.

Need 0's here

$$\sim \begin{bmatrix} 1 & -3 & 2 & | & 0 \\ 3 & 1 & -1 & | & 7 \\ 2 & -2 & 1 & | & 3 \end{bmatrix} \begin{matrix} \\ R_2 + (-3)R_1 \rightarrow R_2 \\ R_3 + (-2)R_1 \rightarrow R_3 \end{matrix}$$

Step 2. Use multiples of the first row to get zeros below the 1 obtained in step 1.

Need a 1 here

$$\sim \begin{bmatrix} 1 & -3 & 2 & | & 0 \\ 0 & 10 & -7 & | & 7 \\ 0 & 4 & -3 & | & 3 \end{bmatrix} \begin{matrix} \\ \frac{1}{10}R_2 \rightarrow R_2 \end{matrix}$$

Step 3. Mentally delete R_1 and C_1, then repeat steps 1 and 2 with the **submatrix** (the matrix that remains after deleting the top row and first column). Continue the above process (steps 1–3) until it is not possible to go further; then proceed with step 4.

Need a 0 here

$$\sim \begin{bmatrix} 1 & -3 & 2 & | & 0 \\ 0 & 1 & -\frac{7}{10} & | & \frac{7}{10} \\ 0 & 4 & -3 & | & 3 \end{bmatrix} \begin{matrix} \\ \\ R_3 + (-4)R_2 \rightarrow R_3 \end{matrix}$$

Need a 1 here

$$\sim \begin{bmatrix} 1 & -3 & 2 & | & 0 \\ 0 & 1 & -\frac{7}{10} & | & \frac{7}{10} \\ 0 & 0 & -\frac{1}{5} & | & \frac{1}{5} \end{bmatrix} \begin{matrix} \\ \\ (-5)R_2 \rightarrow R_2 \end{matrix}$$

Mentally delete R_1, R_2, C_1, and C_2.

Need 0's here

$$\sim \begin{bmatrix} 1 & -3 & 2 & | & 0 \\ 0 & 1 & -\frac{7}{10} & | & \frac{7}{10} \\ 0 & 0 & 1 & | & -1 \end{bmatrix} \begin{matrix} R_1 + (-2)R_3 \rightarrow R_1 \\ R_2 + \frac{7}{10}R_3 \rightarrow R_2 \\ \\ \end{matrix}$$

Since steps 1–3 cannot be carried further, proceed to step 4.

Step 4. Return deleted rows and columns. Begin with the bottom nonzero row and use appropriate multiples of it to get zeros above the leftmost 1. Continue the process, moving up row by row, until the matrix is in reduced form.

Need a 0 here

$$\sim \begin{bmatrix} 1 & -3 & 0 & | & 2 \\ 0 & 1 & 0 & | & 0 \\ 0 & 0 & 1 & | & -1 \end{bmatrix} \begin{matrix} R_1 + 3R_2 \rightarrow R_1 \\ \\ \end{matrix}$$

$$\sim \begin{bmatrix} 1 & 0 & 0 & | & 2 \\ 0 & 1 & 0 & | & 0 \\ 0 & 0 & 1 & | & -1 \end{bmatrix}$$

The matrix is in reduced form, and we can write the solution to the original system by inspection.

Solution: $x_1 = 2$, $x_2 = 0$, $x_3 = -1$. It is left to the reader to check this solution.

Steps 1–4 outlined in the solution of Example 15 are referred to as *Gauss–Jordan elimination*. The steps are summarized in the box below for easy reference:

Gauss–Jordan Elimination

1. Choose the leftmost nonzero column and use appropriate row operations to get a 1 at the top.

2. Use multiples of the first row to get zeros in all places below the 1 obtained in step 1.

3. Delete (mentally) the top row and first column of the matrix. Repeat steps 1 and 2 with the **submatrix** (the matrix that remains after deleting the top row and first column). Continue this process (steps 1–3) until it is not possible to go further.

4. Consider the whole matrix obtained after mentally returning all the rows and columns to the matrix. Begin with the bottom nonzero row and use appropriate multiples of it to get zeros above the leftmost 1. Continue this process, moving up row by row, until the matrix is finally in reduced form.

[*Note:* If at any point in the above process we obtain a row with all zeros to the left of the vertical line and a nonzero number to the right, we can stop, since we will have a contradiction ($0 = n$, $n \neq 0$). We can then conclude that the system has no solution.]

Problem 15   Solve by Gauss–Jordan elimination:

$$3x_1 + x_2 - 2x_3 = 2$$
$$x_1 - 2x_2 + x_3 = 3$$
$$2x_1 - x_2 - 3x_3 = 3$$

Example 16   Solve by Gauss–Jordan elimination:

$$2x_1 - x_2 + 4x_3 = -2$$
$$3x_1 + 2x_2 - x_3 = 1$$

Solution

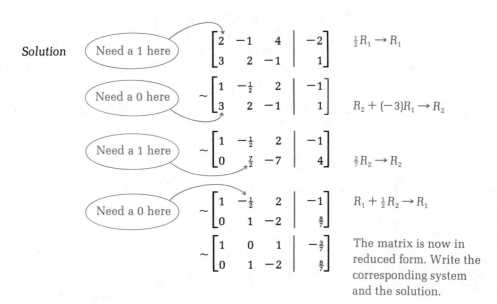

$$x_1 \quad + \quad x_3 = -\tfrac{3}{7}$$
$$x_2 - 2x_3 = \quad \tfrac{8}{7}$$

Solve for the leftmost variables x_1 and x_2 in terms of the remaining variable x_3:

$$x_1 = -x_3 - \tfrac{3}{7}$$
$$x_2 = 2x_3 + \tfrac{8}{7}$$

If $x_3 = t$, then for t any real number,

$$x_1 = -t - \tfrac{3}{7}$$
$$x_2 = 2t + \tfrac{8}{7}$$
$$x_3 = t$$

is a solution.

Remark: In general, it can be proved that a system with more variables than equations cannot have a unique solution.

Problem 16 Solve by Gauss–Jordan elimination:

$$3x_1 + 6x_2 - 3x_3 = \quad 2$$
$$2x_1 - \quad x_2 + 2x_3 = -1$$

Example 17 Solve by Gauss-Jordan elimination:

$$2x_1 - \quad x_2 = -4$$
$$2x_1 + 4x_2 = \quad 6$$
$$3x_1 - \quad x_2 = -1$$

Solution

$$\begin{bmatrix} 2 & -1 & | & -4 \\ 2 & 4 & | & 6 \\ 3 & -1 & | & -1 \end{bmatrix} \quad R_1 \leftrightarrow R_2$$

Interchanging R_1 and R_2 and then multiplying by $\frac{1}{2}$ will avoid fractions and simplify calculations.

$$\sim \begin{bmatrix} 2 & 4 & | & 6 \\ 2 & -1 & | & -4 \\ 3 & -1 & | & -1 \end{bmatrix} \quad \tfrac{1}{2}R_1 \rightarrow R_1$$

$$\sim \begin{bmatrix} 1 & 2 & | & 3 \\ 2 & -1 & | & -4 \\ 3 & -1 & | & -1 \end{bmatrix} \quad \begin{array}{l} R_2 + (-2)R_1 \rightarrow R_2 \\ R_3 + (-3)R_1 \rightarrow R_3 \end{array}$$

$$\sim \begin{bmatrix} 1 & 2 & | & 3 \\ 0 & -5 & | & -10 \\ 0 & -7 & | & -10 \end{bmatrix} \quad -\tfrac{1}{5}R_2 \rightarrow R_2$$

$$\sim \begin{bmatrix} 1 & 2 & | & 3 \\ 0 & 1 & | & 2 \\ 0 & -7 & | & -10 \end{bmatrix} \quad R_3 + 7R_2 \rightarrow R_3$$

$$\sim \begin{bmatrix} 1 & 2 & | & 3 \\ 0 & 1 & | & 2 \\ 0 & 0 & | & 4 \end{bmatrix}$$

We stop the Gauss–Jordan elimination, even though the matrix is not in a reduced form, since the last row produces a contradiction.

The last row implies $0 = 4$, which is a contradiction; therefore, the system has no solution.

Problem 17   Solve by Gauss–Jordan elimination:

$$3x_1 + x_2 = 5$$
$$2x_1 + 3x_2 = 1$$
$$2x_1 - 2x_2 = 6$$

■ Application

Example 18   A casting company produces three different bronze sculptures. The casting department has available a maximum of 350 labor-hours per week, and the finishing department has a maximum of 150 labor-hours available per week. Sculpture A requires 30 hours for casting and 10 hours for finishing; sculpture B requires 10 hours for casting and 10 hours for finishing; and sculpture C requires 10 hours for casting and 30 hours for finishing. If the plant is to operate at maximum capacity, how many of each sculpture should be produced each week?

Solution   First, we summarize the relevant manufacturing data in a table:

	Labor-Hours per Sculpture			Maximum Labor-Hours Available per Week
	A	B	C	
Casting department	30	10	10	350
Finishing department	10	10	30	150

Let x_1 = Number of sculpture *A* produced per week

x_2 = Number of sculpture *B* produced per week

x_3 = Number of sculpture *C* produced per week

Then $30x_1 + 10x_2 + 10x_3 = 350$ Casting department

$10x_1 + 10x_2 + 30x_3 = 150$ Finishing department

Now we can form the augmented matrix of the system and solve by using Gauss–Jordan elimination:

$$\begin{bmatrix} 30 & 10 & 10 & | & 350 \\ 10 & 10 & 30 & | & 150 \end{bmatrix} \quad \begin{matrix} \tfrac{1}{10}R_1 \to R_1 \\ \tfrac{1}{10}R_2 \to R_2 \end{matrix} \qquad \text{Simplify each row}$$

$$\sim \begin{bmatrix} 3 & 1 & 1 & | & 35 \\ 1 & 1 & 3 & | & 15 \end{bmatrix} \quad R_1 \leftrightarrow R_2$$

$$\sim \begin{bmatrix} 1 & 1 & 3 & | & 15 \\ 3 & 1 & 1 & | & 35 \end{bmatrix} \quad R_2 + (-3)R_1 \to R_2$$

$$\sim \begin{bmatrix} 1 & 1 & 3 & | & 15 \\ 0 & -2 & -8 & | & -10 \end{bmatrix} \quad -\tfrac{1}{2}R_2 \to R_2$$

$$\sim \begin{bmatrix} 1 & 1 & 3 & | & 15 \\ 0 & 1 & 4 & | & 5 \end{bmatrix} \quad R_1 + (-1)R_2 \to R_1$$

$$\sim \begin{bmatrix} 1 & 0 & -1 & | & 10 \\ 0 & 1 & 4 & | & 5 \end{bmatrix} \quad \begin{matrix}\text{Matrix is in reduced} \\ \text{form}\end{matrix}$$

$$\begin{matrix} x_1 & - & x_3 = 10 \\ & x_2 + 4x_3 = 5 \end{matrix} \quad \text{or} \quad \begin{matrix} x_1 = x_3 + 10 \\ x_2 = -4x_3 + 5 \end{matrix}$$

Let $x_3 = t$. Then for *t* any real number,

$x_1 = t + 10$

$x_2 = -4t + 5$

$x_3 = t$

is a solution — or is it? We cannot produce a negative number of sculptures. If we also assume that we cannot produce a fractional number of sculptures, then *t* must be a nonnegative whole number. And because of the middle equation ($x_2 = -4t + 5$), t can only assume the values 0 and 1. Thus, for $t = 0$, we have $x_1 = 10$, $x_2 = 5$, $x_3 = 0$; and for $t = 1$, we have $x_1 = 11$, $x_2 = 1$, $x_3 = 1$. These are the only possible production schedules that utilize the full capacity of the plant.

Problem 18   Repeat Example 18 given a casting capacity of 400 labor-hours per week and a finishing capacity of 200 labor-hours per week.

Answers to   13. (A) Condition 2 is violated: The 3 in the second row should be a 1.
Matched Problems   (B) Condition 3 is violated: In the second column, the 5 should be a 0.
        (C) Condition 4 is violated: The leftmost 1 in the second row is not to the right of the leftmost 1 in the first row.
        (D) Condition 1 is violated: The all-zero second row should be at the bottom.

14. (A) $x_1 \qquad\quad = -5$ (B) $x_1 + 2x_2 - 3x_3 = 0$

$\qquad\qquad x_2 \quad = \quad 3$ $0x_1 + 0x_2 + 0x_3 = 1$

$\qquad\qquad\qquad x_3 = \quad 6$ $0x_1 + 0x_2 + 0x_3 = 0$

Solution: Inconsistent; no solution.

$x_1 = -5$, $x_2 = 3$, $x_3 = 6$

(C) $x_1 \quad - 2x_3 = \quad 4$ (D) $x_1 \quad + 3x_3 + 2x_4 = 5$

$\qquad\quad x_2 + 3x_3 = -2$ $x_2 - 2x_3 - \quad x_4 = 3$

Dependent: let $x_3 = t$.   Dependent: let $x_3 = s$ and $x_4 = t$.

Then for any real t,   Then for any real s and t,

$x_1 = 2t + 4$ $x_1 = -3s - 2t + 5$

$x_2 = -3t - 2$ $x_2 = 2s + t + 3$

$x_3 = t$ $x_3 = s$

is a solution. $x_4 = t$

                        is a solution.

15. $x_1 = 1$, $x_2 = -1$, $x_3 = 0$

16. $x_1 = -\frac{3}{5}t - \frac{4}{15}$, $x_2 = \frac{4}{5}t + \frac{7}{15}$, $x_3 = t$, t any real number

17. $x_1 = 2$, $x_2 = -1$

18. $x_1 = t + 10$, $x_2 = -4t + 10$, $x_3 = t$, where $t = 0, 1, 2$; that is, $(x_1, x_2, x_3) = (10, 10, 0)$, $(11, 6, 1)$, or $(12, 2, 2)$

Exercise 1-3

A   *Indicate whether each matrix is in reduced form.*

1. $\begin{bmatrix} 1 & 0 & | & 2 \\ 0 & 1 & | & -1 \end{bmatrix}$ 2. $\begin{bmatrix} 0 & 1 & | & 2 \\ 1 & 0 & | & -1 \end{bmatrix}$

3. $\begin{bmatrix} 1 & 0 & 2 & 3 \\ 0 & 0 & 0 & 0 \\ 0 & 1 & -1 & 4 \end{bmatrix}$

4. $\begin{bmatrix} 1 & 0 & 0 & -2 \\ 0 & 1 & 0 & 0 \\ 0 & 0 & 1 & 1 \end{bmatrix}$

5. $\begin{bmatrix} 0 & 1 & 0 & 2 \\ 0 & 0 & 3 & -1 \\ 0 & 0 & 0 & 0 \end{bmatrix}$

6. $\begin{bmatrix} 1 & 3 & 0 & 0 \\ 0 & 0 & 1 & 0 \\ 0 & 0 & 0 & 1 \end{bmatrix}$

7. $\begin{bmatrix} 1 & 2 & 0 & 3 & 2 \\ 0 & 0 & 1 & -1 & 0 \end{bmatrix}$

8. $\begin{bmatrix} 0 & 1 & 2 & 1 \\ 1 & 0 & -3 & 2 \end{bmatrix}$

Write the linear system corresponding to each reduced augmented matrix and solve.

9. $\begin{bmatrix} 1 & 0 & 0 & -2 \\ 0 & 1 & 0 & 3 \\ 0 & 0 & 1 & 0 \end{bmatrix}$

10. $\begin{bmatrix} 1 & 0 & 0 & 0 & -2 \\ 0 & 1 & 0 & 0 & 0 \\ 0 & 0 & 1 & 0 & 1 \\ 0 & 0 & 0 & 1 & 3 \end{bmatrix}$

11. $\begin{bmatrix} 1 & 0 & -2 & 3 \\ 0 & 1 & 1 & -5 \\ 0 & 0 & 0 & 0 \end{bmatrix}$

12. $\begin{bmatrix} 1 & -2 & 0 & -3 \\ 0 & 0 & 1 & 5 \\ 0 & 0 & 0 & 0 \end{bmatrix}$

13. $\begin{bmatrix} 1 & 0 & 0 \\ 0 & 1 & 0 \\ 0 & 0 & 1 \end{bmatrix}$

14. $\begin{bmatrix} 1 & 0 & 5 \\ 0 & 1 & -3 \\ 0 & 0 & 0 \end{bmatrix}$

15. $\begin{bmatrix} 1 & -2 & 0 & -3 & -5 \\ 0 & 0 & 1 & 3 & 2 \end{bmatrix}$

16. $\begin{bmatrix} 1 & 0 & -2 & 3 & 4 \\ 0 & 1 & -1 & 2 & -1 \end{bmatrix}$

B *Use row operations to change each matrix to reduced form.*

17. $\begin{bmatrix} 1 & 2 & -1 \\ 0 & 1 & 3 \end{bmatrix}$

18. $\begin{bmatrix} 1 & 3 & 1 \\ 0 & 2 & -4 \end{bmatrix}$

19. $\begin{bmatrix} 1 & 0 & -3 & 1 \\ 0 & 1 & 2 & 0 \\ 0 & 0 & 3 & -6 \end{bmatrix}$

20. $\begin{bmatrix} 1 & 0 & 4 & 0 \\ 0 & 1 & -3 & -1 \\ 0 & 0 & -2 & 2 \end{bmatrix}$

21. $\begin{bmatrix} 1 & 2 & -2 & -1 \\ 0 & 3 & -6 & 1 \\ 0 & -1 & 2 & -\frac{1}{3} \end{bmatrix}$

22. $\begin{bmatrix} 0 & -2 & 8 & 1 \\ 2 & -2 & 6 & -4 \\ 0 & -1 & 4 & \frac{1}{2} \end{bmatrix}$

Solve using Gauss–Jordan elimination.

23. $\begin{aligned} 2x_1 + 4x_2 - 10x_3 &= -2 \\ 3x_1 + 9x_2 - 21x_3 &= 0 \\ x_1 + 5x_2 - 12x_3 &= 1 \end{aligned}$

24. $\begin{aligned} 3x_1 + 5x_2 - x_3 &= -7 \\ x_1 + x_2 + x_3 &= -1 \\ 2x_1 + 11x_3 &= 7 \end{aligned}$

25. $3x_1 + 8x_2 - x_3 = -18$
$2x_1 + x_2 + 5x_3 = 8$
$2x_1 + 4x_2 + 2x_3 = -4$

26. $2x_1 + 7x_2 + 15x_3 = -12$
$4x_1 + 7x_2 + 13x_3 = -10$
$3x_1 + 6x_2 + 12x_3 = -9$

27. $2x_1 - x_2 - 3x_3 = 8$
$x_1 - 2x_2 = 7$

28. $2x_1 + 4x_2 - 6x_3 = 10$
$3x_1 + 3x_2 - 3x_3 = 6$

29. $2x_1 + 3x_2 - x_3 = 1$
$x_1 - 2x_2 + 2x_3 = -2$

30. $x_1 - 3x_2 + 2x_3 = -1$
$3x_1 + 2x_2 - x_3 = 2$

31. $2x_1 + 2x_2 = 2$
$x_1 + 2x_2 = 3$
$-3x_2 = -6$

32. $2x_1 - x_2 = 0$
$3x_1 + 2x_2 = 7$
$x_1 - x_2 = -1$

33. $2x_1 - x_2 = 0$
$3x_1 + 2x_2 = 7$
$x_1 - x_2 = -2$

34. $x_1 - 3x_2 = 5$
$2x_1 + x_2 = 3$
$x_1 - 2x_2 = 5$

35. $3x_1 - 4x_2 - x_3 = 1$
$2x_1 - 3x_2 + x_3 = 1$
$x_1 - 2x_2 + 3x_3 = 2$

36. $3x_1 + 7x_2 - x_3 = 11$
$x_1 + 2x_2 - x_3 = 3$
$2x_1 + 4x_2 - 2x_3 = 10$

37. $3x_1 - 2x_2 + x_3 = -7$
$2x_1 + x_2 - 4x_3 = 0$
$x_1 + x_2 - 3x_3 = 1$

38. $2x_1 + 3x_2 + 5x_3 = 21$
$x_1 - x_2 - 5x_3 = -2$
$2x_1 + x_2 - x_3 = 11$

39. $2x_1 + 4x_2 - 2x_3 = 2$
$-3x_1 - 6x_2 + 3x_3 = -3$

40. $3x_1 - 9x_2 + 12x_3 = 6$
$-2x_1 + 6x_2 - 8x_3 = -4$

C   *Solve using Gauss–Jordan elimination*

41. $2x_1 - 3x_2 + 3x_3 = -15$
$3x_1 + 2x_2 - 5x_3 = 19$
$5x_1 - 4x_2 - 2x_3 = -2$

42. $3x_1 - 2x_2 - 4x_3 = -8$
$4x_1 + 3x_2 - 5x_3 = -5$
$6x_1 - 5x_2 + 2x_3 = -17$

43. $5x_1 - 3x_2 + 2x_3 = 13$
$2x_1 + 4x_2 - 3x_3 = -9$
$4x_1 - 2x_2 + 5x_3 = 13$

44. $4x_1 - 2x_2 + 3x_3 = 0$
$3x_1 - 5x_2 - 2x_3 = -12$
$2x_1 + 4x_2 - 3x_3 = -4$

45. $x_1 + 2x_2 - 4x_3 - x_4 = 7$
$2x_1 + 5x_2 - 9x_3 - 4x_4 = 16$
$x_1 + 5x_2 - 7x_3 - 7x_4 = 13$

46. $2x_1 + 4x_2 + 5x_3 + 4x_4 = 8$
$x_1 + 2x_2 + 2x_3 + x_4 = 3$

Applications

Solve all of the following problems using Gauss–Jordan elimination.

Business & Economics   47. *Production scheduling.* A small manufacturing plant makes three types of inflatable boats: one-person, two-person, and four-person models. Each boat requires the services of three departments, as listed in the table. The cutting, assembly, and packaging departments have available a maximum of 380, 330, and 120 labor-hours per week, respectively. How many boats of each type must be produced each week for the plant to operate at full capacity?

	One-Person Boat	Two-Person Boat	Four-Person Boat
Cutting department	0.5 hr	1.0 hr	1.5 hr
Assembly department	0.6 hr	0.9 hr	1.2 hr
Packaging department	0.2 hr	0.3 hr	0.5 hr

48. *Production scheduling.* Repeat Problem 47 assuming the cutting, assembly, and packaging departments have available a maximum of 350, 330, and 115 labor-hours per week, respectively.

49. *Production scheduling.* Work Problem 47 assuming the packaging department is no longer used.

50. *Production scheduling.* Work Problem 48 assuming the packaging department is no longer used.

51. *Production scheduling.* Work Problem 47 assuming the four-person boat is no longer produced.

52. *Production scheduling.* Work Problem 48 assuming the four-person boat is no longer produced.

53. *Income tax.* A company has a taxable income of $1,664,000. The federal income tax is 25% of the portion of the income that remains after the state and local taxes have been deducted. The state income tax is 10% of the portion of the income that remains after the federal and local taxes have been deducted, and the local tax is 5% of the portion of the income that remains after the federal and state taxes have been deducted. Find the company's federal, state, and local income taxes.

54. *Income tax.* Repeat Problem 53 if local taxes are not deducted before computing the federal and state taxes.

Life Sciences   **55.** *Nutrition.* A dietitian in a hospital is to arrange a special diet composed of three basic foods. The diet is to include exactly 340 units of calcium, 180 units of iron, and 220 units of vitamin A. The number of units per ounce of each special ingredient for each of the foods is indicated in the table. How many ounces of each food must be used to meet the diet requirements?

	Units per Ounce		
	Food A	Food B	Food C
Calcium	30	10	20
Iron	10	10	20
Vitamin A	10	30	20

56. *Nutrition.* Repeat Problem 55 if the diet is to include exactly 400 units of calcium, 160 units of iron, and 240 units of vitamin A.

57. *Nutrition.* Solve Problem 55 with the assumption that food C is no longer available.

58. *Nutrition.* Solve Problem 56 with the assumption that food C is no longer available.

59. *Nutrition.* Solve Problem 55 with the assumption that the vitamin A requirement is deleted.

60. *Nutrition.* Solve Problem 56 with the assumption that the vitamin A requirement is deleted.

61. *Nutrition–plants.* A farmer can buy four types of plant food. Each barrel of mix A contains 30 pounds of phosphoric acid, 50 pounds of nitrogen, and 30 pounds of potash; each barrel of mix B contains 30 pounds of phosphoric acid, 75 pounds of nitrogen, and 20 pounds of potash; each barrel of mix C contains 30 pounds of phosphoric acid, 25 pounds of nitrogen, and 20 pounds of potash; and each barrel of mix D contains 60 pounds of phosphoric acid, 25 pounds of nitrogen, and 50 pounds of potash. Soil tests indicate that a particular field needs 900 pounds of phosphoric acid, 750 pounds of nitrogen, and 700 pounds of potash. How many barrels of each type of food should the farmer mix together to supply the necessary nutrients for the field?

62. *Nutrition–animals.* In a laboratory experiment, rats are to be fed 5 packets of food containing a total of 80 units of vitamin E. There are four different brands of food packets that can be used. A packet of brand A contains 5 units of vitamin E, a packet of brand B contains 10 units of vitamin E, a packet of brand C contains 15 units of vitamin E, and a packet of brand D contains 20 units of vitamin E. How many packets of each brand should be mixed and fed to the rats?

Social Sciences

63. *Sociology.* Two sociologists have grant money to study school busing in a particular city. They wish to conduct an opinion survey using 600 telephone contacts and 400 house contacts. Survey company A has personnel to do 30 telephone and 10 house contacts per hour; survey company B can handle 20 telephone and 20 house contacts per hour. How many hours should be scheduled for each firm to produce exactly the number of contacts needed?

64. *Sociology.* Repeat Problem 63 if 650 telephone contacts and 350 house contacts are needed.

1-4   Matrices—Addition and Multiplication by a Number

- Basic Definitions
- Sum and Difference
- Product of a Number k and a Matrix M
- Application

In the last two sections we introduced the important new idea of matrices. In this and the following sections, we shall develop this concept further.

■ Basic Definitions

Recall that we defined a **matrix** as any rectangular array of numbers enclosed within brackets. The **size** or **dimension of a matrix** is important to operations on matrices. We define an $m \times n$ **matrix** (read "m by n matrix") to be one with m rows and n columns. It is important to note that the number of rows is always given first. If a matrix has the same number of rows and columns, it is called a **square matrix.** A matrix with only one column is called a **column matrix,** and one with only one row is called a **row matrix.** These definitions are illustrated by the following:

$$
\begin{array}{cccc}
3 \times 2 & 3 \times 3 & 4 \times 1 & 1 \times 4 \\
\begin{bmatrix} -2 & 5 \\ 0 & -2 \\ 3 & 6 \end{bmatrix} &
\begin{bmatrix} 0.5 & 0.2 & 1.0 \\ 0.0 & 0.3 & 0.5 \\ 0.7 & 0.0 & 0.2 \end{bmatrix} &
\begin{bmatrix} 3 \\ -2 \\ 1 \\ 0 \end{bmatrix} &
\begin{bmatrix} 2 & \frac{1}{2} & 0 & -\frac{2}{3} \end{bmatrix}
\end{array}
$$

Square matrix (under 3×3); Row matrix (under 1×4); Column matrix (under 4×1)

Two matrices are **equal** if they have the same dimension and their corresponding elements are equal. For example,

$$
\begin{array}{cc}
2 \times 3 & 2 \times 3 \\
\begin{bmatrix} a & b & c \\ d & e & f \end{bmatrix} = \begin{bmatrix} u & v & w \\ x & y & z \end{bmatrix}
\end{array}
\quad \text{if and only if} \quad
\begin{array}{ccc}
a = u & b = v & c = w \\
d = x & e = y & f = z
\end{array}
$$

■ Sum and Difference

The **sum of two matrices of the same dimension** is a matrix with elements that are the sum of the corresponding elements of the two given matrices. **Addition is not defined for matrices with different dimensions.**

Example 19   (A) $\begin{bmatrix} a & b \\ c & d \end{bmatrix} + \begin{bmatrix} w & x \\ y & z \end{bmatrix} = \begin{bmatrix} (a+w) & (b+x) \\ (c+y) & (d+z) \end{bmatrix}$

(B) $\begin{bmatrix} 2 & -3 & 0 \\ 1 & 2 & -5 \end{bmatrix} + \begin{bmatrix} 3 & 1 & 2 \\ -3 & 2 & 5 \end{bmatrix} = \begin{bmatrix} 5 & -2 & 2 \\ -2 & 4 & 0 \end{bmatrix}$

Problem 19   Add:

$$\begin{bmatrix} 3 & 2 \\ -1 & -1 \\ 0 & 3 \end{bmatrix} + \begin{bmatrix} -2 & 3 \\ 1 & -1 \\ 2 & -2 \end{bmatrix}$$

Because we add two matrices by adding their corresponding elements, it follows from the properties of real numbers that matrices of the same dimension are commutative and associative relative to addition. That is, if A, B, and C are matrices of the same dimension, then

$$A + B = B + A \qquad \text{Commutative}$$
$$(A + B) + C = A + (B + C) \qquad \text{Associative}$$

A matrix with elements that are all zeros is called a **zero matrix.** For example,

$$[0 \quad 0 \quad 0] \qquad \begin{bmatrix} 0 & 0 \\ 0 & 0 \end{bmatrix} \qquad \begin{bmatrix} 0 \\ 0 \\ 0 \\ 0 \end{bmatrix} \qquad \begin{bmatrix} 0 & 0 & 0 & 0 \\ 0 & 0 & 0 & 0 \\ 0 & 0 & 0 & 0 \end{bmatrix}$$

are zero matrices of different dimensions. [*Note:* "0" is often used to denote the zero matrix of an arbitrary dimension.] The **negative of a matrix M,** denoted by $-M$, is a matrix with elements that are the negatives of the elements in M. Thus, if

$$M = \begin{bmatrix} a & b \\ c & d \end{bmatrix} \qquad \text{then} \qquad -M = \begin{bmatrix} -a & -b \\ -c & -d \end{bmatrix}$$

Note that $M + (-M) = 0$ (a zero matrix).

If A and B are matrices of the same dimension, then we define **subtraction** as follows:

$$A - B = A + (-B)$$

Thus, to subtract matrix B from matrix A, we simply subtract corresponding elements.

Example 20

$$\begin{bmatrix} 3 & -2 \\ 5 & 0 \end{bmatrix} - \begin{bmatrix} -2 & 2 \\ 3 & 4 \end{bmatrix} = \begin{bmatrix} 3 & -2 \\ 5 & 0 \end{bmatrix} + \begin{bmatrix} 2 & -2 \\ -3 & -4 \end{bmatrix} = \begin{bmatrix} 5 & -4 \\ 2 & -4 \end{bmatrix}$$

Problem 20

Subtract: $\begin{bmatrix} 2 & -3 & 5 \end{bmatrix} - \begin{bmatrix} 3 & -2 & 1 \end{bmatrix}$

▪ Product of a Number k and a Matrix M

Finally, the **product of a number k and a matrix M,** denoted by kM, is a matrix formed by multiplying each element of M by k. This definition is partly motivated by the fact that if M is a matrix, then we would like $M + M$ to equal $2M$.

Example 21

$$-2 \begin{bmatrix} 3 & -1 & 0 \\ -2 & 1 & 3 \\ 0 & -1 & -2 \end{bmatrix} = \begin{bmatrix} -6 & 2 & 0 \\ 4 & -2 & -6 \\ 0 & 2 & 4 \end{bmatrix}$$

Problem 21

Find: $10 \begin{bmatrix} 1.3 \\ 0.2 \\ 3.5 \end{bmatrix}$

▪ Application

Example 22

Ms. Smith and Mr. Jones are salespeople in a new-car agency that sells only two models. August was the last month for this year's models, and next year's models were introduced in September. Gross dollar sales for each month are given in the following matrices:

	August sales	
	Compact	Luxury
Ms. Smith	$18,000	$36,000
Mr. Jones	$36,000	0

$= A$

	September sales	
	Compact	Luxury
	$72,000	$144,000
	$90,000	$108,000

$= B$

(For example, Ms. Smith had $18,000 in compact sales in August, and Mr. Jones had $108,000 in luxury car sales in September.)

(A) What was the combined dollar sales in August and September for each person and each model?
(B) What was the increase in dollar sales from August to September?
(C) If both salespeople receive 5% commissions on gross dollar sales, compute the commission for each person for each model sold in September.

Solutions   (A) $A + B =$
$$\begin{bmatrix} \$90{,}000 & \$180{,}000 \\ \$126{,}000 & \$108{,}000 \end{bmatrix} \begin{matrix} \text{Ms. Smith} \\ \text{Mr. Jones} \end{matrix}$$
(Compact Luxury)

(B) $B - A =$
$$\begin{bmatrix} \$54{,}000 & \$108{,}000 \\ \$54{,}000 & \$108{,}000 \end{bmatrix} \begin{matrix} \text{Ms. Smith} \\ \text{Mr. Jones} \end{matrix}$$
(Compact Luxury)

(C) $0.05B =$
$$\begin{bmatrix} (0.05)(\$72{,}000) & (0.05)(\$144{,}000) \\ (0.05)(\$90{,}000) & (0.05)(\$108{,}000) \end{bmatrix}$$
$$= \begin{bmatrix} \$3{,}600 & \$7{,}200 \\ \$4{,}500 & \$5{,}400 \end{bmatrix} \begin{matrix} \text{Ms. Smith} \\ \text{Mr. Jones} \end{matrix}$$

In Example 22 we chose a relatively simple example involving an agency with only two salespeople and two models. Consider the more realistic problem of an agency with nine models and perhaps seven salespeople— then you can begin to see the value of matrix methods.

Problem 22   Repeat Example 22 with
$$A = \begin{bmatrix} \$36{,}000 & \$36{,}000 \\ \$18{,}000 & \$36{,}000 \end{bmatrix} \quad \text{and} \quad B = \begin{bmatrix} \$90{,}000 & \$108{,}000 \\ \$72{,}000 & \$108{,}000 \end{bmatrix}$$

Answers to Matched Problems
19. $\begin{bmatrix} 1 & 5 \\ 0 & -2 \\ 2 & 1 \end{bmatrix}$ 20. $\begin{bmatrix} -1 & -1 & 4 \end{bmatrix}$ 21. $\begin{bmatrix} 13 \\ 2 \\ 35 \end{bmatrix}$

22. (A) $\begin{bmatrix} \$126{,}000 & \$144{,}000 \\ \$90{,}000 & \$144{,}000 \end{bmatrix}$ (B) $\begin{bmatrix} \$54{,}000 & \$72{,}000 \\ \$54{,}000 & \$72{,}000 \end{bmatrix}$

(C) $\begin{bmatrix} \$4{,}500 & \$5{,}400 \\ \$3{,}600 & \$5{,}400 \end{bmatrix}$

Exercise 1-4

A   *Problems 1–18 refer to the following matrices:*

$$A = \begin{bmatrix} 2 & -1 \\ 3 & 0 \end{bmatrix} \qquad B = \begin{bmatrix} -3 & 1 \\ 2 & -3 \end{bmatrix} \qquad C = \begin{bmatrix} 2 \\ -3 \\ 0 \end{bmatrix}$$

$$D = \begin{bmatrix} 1 \\ 3 \\ 5 \end{bmatrix} \qquad E = \begin{bmatrix} -4 & 1 & 0 & -2 \end{bmatrix} \qquad F = \begin{bmatrix} 2 & -3 \\ -2 & 0 \\ 1 & 2 \\ 3 & 5 \end{bmatrix}$$

1. What are the dimensions of B? Of E?
2. What are the dimensions of F? Of D?
3. What element is in the third row and second column of matrix F?
4. What element is in the second row and first column of matrix F?
5. Write a zero matrix of the same dimension as B.
6. Write a zero matrix of the same dimension as E.
7. Identify all column matrices.
8. Identify all row matrices.
9. Identify all square matrices.
10. How many additional columns would F have to have to be a square matrix?
11. Find $A + B$.
12. Find $C + D$.
13. Write the negative of matrix C.
14. Write the negative of matrix B.
15. Find $D - C$.
16. Find $A - A$.
17. Find $5B$.
18. Find $-2E$.

B   *In Problems 19–26 perform the indicated operations.*

19.
$$\begin{bmatrix} 3 & -2 & 0 & 1 \\ 2 & -3 & -1 & 4 \\ 0 & 2 & -1 & 6 \end{bmatrix} + \begin{bmatrix} -2 & 5 & -1 & 0 \\ -3 & -2 & 8 & -2 \\ 4 & 6 & 1 & -8 \end{bmatrix}$$

20.
$$\begin{bmatrix} 4 & -2 & 8 \\ 0 & -1 & -4 \\ -6 & 5 & 2 \\ 1 & 3 & -6 \end{bmatrix} + \begin{bmatrix} -6 & -2 & -3 \\ 5 & 2 & 4 \\ 8 & 3 & -4 \\ 1 & -5 & 0 \end{bmatrix}$$

21. $\begin{bmatrix} 1.3 & 2.5 & -6.1 \\ 8.3 & -1.4 & 6.7 \end{bmatrix} - \begin{bmatrix} -4.1 & 1.8 & -4.3 \\ 0.7 & 2.6 & -1.2 \end{bmatrix}$

22. $\begin{bmatrix} 2.6 & 3.8 \\ -1.9 & 7.3 \\ 5.6 & -0.4 \end{bmatrix} - \begin{bmatrix} 4.8 & -2.1 \\ 3.2 & 5.9 \\ -1.5 & 2.2 \end{bmatrix}$ 23. $1,000\begin{bmatrix} 0.25 & 0.36 \\ 0.04 & 0.35 \end{bmatrix}$

24. $100\begin{bmatrix} 0.32 & 0.05 & 0.17 \\ 0.22 & 0.03 & 0.21 \end{bmatrix}$

25. $0.08\begin{bmatrix} 24,000 & 35,000 \\ 12,000 & 24,000 \end{bmatrix} + 0.03\begin{bmatrix} 12,000 & 22,000 \\ 14,000 & 13,000 \end{bmatrix}$

26. $0.05\begin{bmatrix} 430 & 212 \\ 210 & 165 \\ 435 & 315 \end{bmatrix} + 0.07\begin{bmatrix} 234 & 436 \\ 160 & 212 \\ 410 & 136 \end{bmatrix}$

C   27. Find a, b, c, and d so that

$$\begin{bmatrix} a & b \\ c & d \end{bmatrix} + \begin{bmatrix} 2 & -3 \\ 0 & 1 \end{bmatrix} = \begin{bmatrix} 1 & -2 \\ 3 & -4 \end{bmatrix}$$

28. Find w, x, y, and z so that

$$\begin{bmatrix} 4 & -2 \\ -3 & 0 \end{bmatrix} + \begin{bmatrix} w & x \\ y & z \end{bmatrix} = \begin{bmatrix} 2 & -3 \\ 0 & 5 \end{bmatrix}$$

29. Find x and y so that

$$\begin{bmatrix} 2x & 4 \\ -3 & 5x \end{bmatrix} + \begin{bmatrix} 3y & -2 \\ -2 & -y \end{bmatrix} = \begin{bmatrix} -5 & 2 \\ -5 & 13 \end{bmatrix}$$

30. Find x and y so that

$$\begin{bmatrix} 5 & 3x \\ 2x & -4 \end{bmatrix} + \begin{bmatrix} 1 & -4y \\ 7y & 4 \end{bmatrix} = \begin{bmatrix} 6 & -7 \\ 5 & 0 \end{bmatrix}$$

Applications

Business & Economics   31. *Cost analysis.* A company with two different plants manufactures guitars and banjos. Its production costs for each instrument are given in the following matrices:

	Plant X			Plant Y	
	Guitar	Banjo		Guitar	Banjo
Materials	$30	$25 $= A$		$36	$27 $= B$
Labor	$60	$80		$54	$74

Find $\frac{1}{2}(A + B)$, the average cost of production for the two plants.

Life Sciences

32. *Heredity.* Gregor Mendel (1822–1884), an Austrian monk and botanist, made discoveries that revolutionized the science of genetics. In one experiment, he crossed dihybrid yellow round peas (yellow and round are dominant characteristics; the peas also contained genes for the recessive characteristics green and wrinkled) and obtained 560 peas of the types indicated in the matrix:

$$
\begin{array}{c} \\ \text{Yellow} \\ \text{Green} \end{array}
\begin{array}{cc} \text{Round} & \text{Wrinkled} \end{array}
\begin{bmatrix} 319 & 101 \\ 108 & 32 \end{bmatrix} = M
$$

Suppose he carried out a second experiment of the same type and obtained 640 peas of the types indicated in this matrix:

$$
\begin{array}{c} \\ \text{Yellow} \\ \text{Green} \end{array}
\begin{array}{cc} \text{Round} & \text{Wrinkled} \end{array}
\begin{bmatrix} 370 & 124 \\ 110 & 36 \end{bmatrix} = N
$$

If the results of the two experiments are combined, write the resulting matrix $M + N$. Compute the percentage of the total number of peas (1,200) in each category of the combined results. [*Hints:* Compute $(1/1{,}200)(M + N)$.]

Social Sciences

33. *Psychology.* Two psychologists independently carried out studies on the relationship between height and aggressive behavior in women over 18 years of age. The results of the studies are summarized in the following matrices:

Professor Aldquist

$$
\begin{array}{c} \\ \text{Passive} \\ \text{Aggressive} \end{array}
\begin{array}{ccc} \text{Under 5 ft} & 5-5\frac{1}{2}\text{ ft} & \text{Over } 5\frac{1}{2}\text{ ft} \end{array}
\begin{bmatrix} 70 & 122 & 20 \\ 30 & 118 & 80 \end{bmatrix} = A
$$

Professor Kelley

$$
\begin{array}{c} \\ \text{Passive} \\ \text{Aggressive} \end{array}
\begin{array}{ccc} \text{Under 5 ft} & 5-5\frac{1}{2}\text{ ft} & \text{Over } 5\frac{1}{2}\text{ ft} \end{array}
\begin{bmatrix} 65 & 160 & 30 \\ 25 & 140 & 75 \end{bmatrix} = B
$$

The two psychologists decided to combine their results and publish a joint paper. Write the matrix $A + B$ illustrating their combined results. Compute the percentage of the total sample in each category of the combined study. [*Hint:* Compute $(\frac{1}{935})(A + B)$.]

1-5 Matrix Multiplication

- Dot Product
- Application
- Matrix Product
- Arithmetic of Matrix Products
- Application

In this section, we are going to introduce two types of matrix multiplication that will seem rather strange at first. In spite of this apparent strangeness, these operations are well founded in the general theory of matrices and, as we will see, are extremely useful in many practical problems.

Historically, matrix multiplication was introduced by the English mathematician Arthur Cayley (1821–1895) in his studies of systems of linear equations and linear transformations. In the next section you will see how matrix multiplication is central to the process of expressing systems of linear equations as matrix equations and to the process of solving matrix equations. Matrix equations and their solutions provide us with a very powerful method of solving linear systems.

■ Dot Product

We start by defining the **dot product** of two special matrices, a $1 \times n$ row matrix and an $n \times 1$ column matrix:

$$
\underset{1 \times n}{[a_1 \quad a_2 \cdots a_n]} \cdot \underset{n \times 1}{\begin{bmatrix} b_1 \\ b_2 \\ \cdot \\ \cdot \\ \cdot \\ b_n \end{bmatrix}} = a_1b_1 + a_2b_2 + \cdots + a_nb_n \qquad \text{A real number}
$$

The dot product is a real number, not a matrix. The dot between the two matrices is important. If the dot is omitted, the multiplication is of another type, which we will consider below.

Example 23
$$
[2 \quad -3 \quad 0] \cdot \begin{bmatrix} -5 \\ 2 \\ -2 \end{bmatrix} = (2)(-5) + (-3)(2) + (0)(-2)
$$
$$
= -10 - 6 + 0 = -16
$$

Problem 23

$$[-1 \quad 0 \quad 3 \quad 2] \cdot \begin{bmatrix} 2 \\ 3 \\ 4 \\ -1 \end{bmatrix} = ?$$

- Application

Example 24

A factory produces a slalom water ski that requires 4 labor-hours in the fabricating department and 1 labor-hour in the finishing department. Fabricating personnel receive $8 per hour and finishing personnel receive $6 per hour. Total labor cost per ski is given by the dot product:

$$[4 \quad 1] \cdot \begin{bmatrix} 8 \\ 6 \end{bmatrix} = (4)(8) + (1)(6) = 32 + 6 = \$38 \text{ per ski}$$

Problem 24

If the factory in Example 24 also produces a trick water ski that requires 6 labor-hours in the fabricating department and 1.5 labor-hours in the finishing department, write a dot product between appropriate row and column matrices that will give the total labor cost for this ski. Compute the cost.

- Matrix Product

It is important to remember that the dot product of a row matrix and a column matrix is a real number and not a matrix. We now define a matrix product for certain matrices. First, the product of two matrices A and B is defined only if the number of columns of A is equal to the number of rows of B. If A is an $m \times p$ matrix and B is a $p \times n$ matrix, then the **matrix product** of A and B, denoted by AB (not BA), is an $m \times n$ matrix whose element in the ith row and jth column is the dot product of the ith row matrix of A and the jth column matrix of B.

It is important to check dimensions before starting the multiplication process. If matrix A has dimension $a \times b$ and matrix B has dimension $c \times d$, then if $b = c$, the product AB will exist and have dimension $a \times d$. This is shown schematically in Figure 2. The definition is not as complicated as it might seem at first. An example should help to clarify the process. For

Must be the same
$(b = c)$

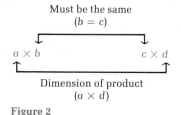

$a \times b$ $\qquad c \times d$

Dimension of product
$(a \times d)$

Figure 2

$$A = \begin{bmatrix} 2 & 3 & -1 \\ -2 & 1 & 2 \end{bmatrix} \quad \text{and} \quad B = \begin{bmatrix} 1 & 3 \\ 2 & 0 \\ -1 & 2 \end{bmatrix}$$

A is 2×3, B is 3×2, and AB will be 2×2. The four dot products used to produce the four elements in AB (usually calculated mentally or with the aid of a hand calculator) are shown in the dashed box at the top of the next page. The shaded portions highlight the steps involved in computing the element in the first row and second column of the product matrix.

$$\underset{2\times 3}{\begin{bmatrix} 2 & 3 & -1 \\ -2 & 1 & 2 \end{bmatrix}} \underset{3\times 2}{\begin{bmatrix} 1 & 3 \\ 2 & 0 \\ -1 & 2 \end{bmatrix}} = \begin{bmatrix} [2\ \ 3\ \ -1]\cdot\begin{bmatrix} 1 \\ 2 \\ -1 \end{bmatrix} & [2\ \ 3\ \ -1]\cdot\begin{bmatrix} 3 \\ 0 \\ 2 \end{bmatrix} \\ [-2\ \ 1\ \ 2]\cdot\begin{bmatrix} 1 \\ 2 \\ -1 \end{bmatrix} & [-2\ \ 1\ \ 2]\cdot\begin{bmatrix} 3 \\ 0 \\ 2 \end{bmatrix} \end{bmatrix} = \underset{2\times 2}{\begin{bmatrix} 9 & 4 \\ -2 & -2 \end{bmatrix}}$$

Example 25 Find the product AB, given

$$A = \begin{bmatrix} 2 & 1 \\ 1 & 0 \\ -1 & 2 \end{bmatrix} \quad \text{and} \quad B = \begin{bmatrix} 1 & -1 & 0 & 1 \\ 2 & 1 & 2 & 0 \end{bmatrix}$$

Solution A convenient way to carry out the multiplication is to arrange the matrices as shown below. The rows and columns in the product matrix will then be determined automatically.

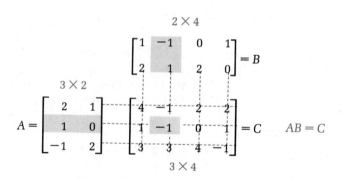

Problem 25 Find the product AB, given

(A) $A = \begin{bmatrix} 1 & -1 & 0 \\ 2 & 1 & 2 \end{bmatrix} \quad \text{and} \quad B = \begin{bmatrix} 2 & -1 \\ 1 & 0 \\ -1 & 2 \end{bmatrix}$

(B) $A = [3 \quad 2 \quad -1] \quad \text{and} \quad B = \begin{bmatrix} -2 \\ 0 \\ 3 \end{bmatrix}$

[*Note:* This is a matrix product, not a dot product. The result is a matrix, not a real number.]

▪ Arithmetic of Matrix Products

Relative to addition, in the last section we noted that

$$A + B = B + A \qquad \text{Commutative}$$

$$A + (B + C) = (A + B) + C \qquad \text{Associative}$$

where A, B, and C are matrices of the same dimension. Do similar properties hold for multiplication? What about the commutative property? Let us compute AB and BA for

$$A = \begin{bmatrix} -3 & 5 \\ 2 & 0 \end{bmatrix} \quad \text{and} \quad B = \begin{bmatrix} 2 & -1 \\ 4 & 3 \end{bmatrix}$$

$$2 \times 2 \qquad\qquad\qquad 2 \times 2$$

$$\begin{bmatrix} 2 & -1 \\ 4 & 3 \end{bmatrix} = B \qquad\qquad \begin{bmatrix} -3 & 5 \\ 2 & 0 \end{bmatrix} = A$$

$$2 \times 2 \qquad\qquad\qquad 2 \times 2$$

$$A = \begin{bmatrix} -3 & 5 \\ 2 & 0 \end{bmatrix} \begin{bmatrix} 14 & 18 \\ 4 & -2 \end{bmatrix} = C \qquad B = \begin{bmatrix} 2 & -1 \\ 4 & 3 \end{bmatrix} \begin{bmatrix} -8 & 10 \\ -6 & 20 \end{bmatrix} = D$$

$$2 \times 2 \qquad\qquad\qquad 2 \times 2$$

$$AB = C \qquad\qquad\qquad BA = D$$

Thus, $AB \neq BA$. Only in some very special cases will matrix products commute; therefore, we must always be careful about the order in which matrix multiplication is performed — we cannot indiscriminately reverse order as in the arithmetic of real numbers. In fact, BA is often not even defined, even though AB is. Thus, $AB \neq BA$ in general.

Another important difference between matrix products and real number products is found in the zero property for real numbers:

For all real numbers a and b,
   $ab = 0$ **if and only if** $a = 0$ **or** $b = 0$ **(or both)**

For A and B matrices it is possible for $AB = 0$ and neither A nor B be 0. For example,

$$\begin{bmatrix} 2 & -6 \\ -3 & 9 \end{bmatrix} = B$$

$$A = \begin{bmatrix} 3 & 2 \\ 6 & 4 \end{bmatrix} \begin{bmatrix} 0 & 0 \\ 0 & 0 \end{bmatrix} = 0 \qquad \text{Zero matrix}$$

Here we see that $AB = 0$ and $A \neq 0$ and $B \neq 0$.

Matrix products do have some of the same types of properties as real number products. We state four important properties without proof. If all products and sums are defined for the indicated matrices A, B, and C, then for k a real number:

1. $(AB)C = A(BC)$ Associative property
2. $A(B + C) = AB + AC$ Left-hand distributive property
3. $(B + C)A = BA + CA$ Right-hand distributive property
4. $k(AB) = (kA)B = A(kB)$

Since matrix multiplication is not commutative, properties 2 and 3 must be listed as distinct properties.

■ Application

Example 26

Let us combine the time requirements for slalom and trick water skis discussed in Example 24 and Problem 24 into one matrix:

$$
\begin{array}{c}
\\
\text{Trick ski} \\
\text{Slalom ski}
\end{array}
\begin{array}{cc}
\text{Fabricating} & \text{Finishing} \\
\text{department} & \text{department} \\
\left[\begin{array}{cc}
6\text{ hr} & 1.5\text{ hr} \\
4\text{ hr} & 1\text{ hr}
\end{array}\right] = A
\end{array}
$$

Now suppose the company has two manufacturing plants X and Y in different parts of the country and that their hourly rates for each department are given in the following matrix:

$$
\begin{array}{c}
\\
\text{Fabricating department} \\
\text{Finishing department}
\end{array}
\begin{array}{cc}
\text{Plant X} & \text{Plant Y} \\
\left[\begin{array}{cc}
\$8 & \$7 \\
\$6 & \$4
\end{array}\right] = B
\end{array}
$$

To find the total labor costs for each ski at each factory, we multiply A and B:

$$
AB = \overset{2 \times 2}{\begin{bmatrix} 6 & 1.5 \\ 4 & 1 \end{bmatrix}} \overset{2 \times 2}{\begin{bmatrix} 8 & 7 \\ 6 & 4 \end{bmatrix}} = \overset{\text{X} \qquad \text{Y}}{\begin{bmatrix} \$57 & \$48 \\ \$38 & \$32 \end{bmatrix}} \begin{array}{l} \text{Trick ski} \\ \text{Slalom ski} \end{array}
$$

Notice that the dot product of the first row matrix of A and the first column matrix of B gives us the labor costs, $57, for a trick ski manufactured at plant X; the dot product of the second row matrix of A and the second column matrix of B gives us the labor costs, $32, for manufacturing a slalom ski at plant Y; and so on.

Example 26 is, of course, overly simplified. Companies manufacturing many different items in many different plants deal with matrices that have very large numbers of rows and columns.

Problem 26   Repeat Example 26 with

$$A = \begin{bmatrix} 7 \text{ hr} & 2 \text{ hr} \\ 5 \text{ hr} & 1.5 \text{ hr} \end{bmatrix} \quad \text{and} \quad B = \begin{bmatrix} \$10 & \$8 \\ \$6 & \$4 \end{bmatrix}$$

Answers to   23. 8   24. $\begin{bmatrix} 6 & 1.5 \end{bmatrix} \cdot \begin{bmatrix} 8 \\ 6 \end{bmatrix} = \$57$
Matched Problems

25. (A) $\begin{bmatrix} 1 & -1 \\ 3 & 2 \end{bmatrix}$ (B) $\begin{bmatrix} -9 \end{bmatrix}$ 26. $\begin{matrix} X & Y \\ \begin{bmatrix} \$82 & \$64 \\ \$59 & \$46 \end{bmatrix} & \begin{matrix} \text{Trick} \\ \text{Slalom} \end{matrix} \end{matrix}$

Exercise 1-5

A   *Find the dot products.*

1. $\begin{bmatrix} 2 & 4 \end{bmatrix} \cdot \begin{bmatrix} 3 \\ 1 \end{bmatrix}$ 2. $\begin{bmatrix} 3 & 1 \end{bmatrix} \cdot \begin{bmatrix} 2 \\ 4 \end{bmatrix}$

3. $\begin{bmatrix} -3 & 2 \end{bmatrix} \cdot \begin{bmatrix} -1 \\ -2 \end{bmatrix}$ 4. $\begin{bmatrix} 3 & -2 \end{bmatrix} \cdot \begin{bmatrix} -4 \\ -1 \end{bmatrix}$

Find the matrix products.

5. $\begin{bmatrix} 2 & 5 \end{bmatrix} \begin{bmatrix} 1 & -1 \\ 2 & 3 \end{bmatrix}$ 6. $\begin{bmatrix} 1 & 3 \end{bmatrix} \begin{bmatrix} 2 & 3 \\ 1 & -4 \end{bmatrix}$

7. $\begin{bmatrix} 3 & 4 \\ -1 & -2 \end{bmatrix} \begin{bmatrix} -1 \\ 2 \end{bmatrix}$ 8. $\begin{bmatrix} -1 & 1 \\ 2 & -3 \end{bmatrix} \begin{bmatrix} 4 \\ -2 \end{bmatrix}$

9. $\begin{bmatrix} 2 & -3 \\ 1 & 2 \end{bmatrix} \begin{bmatrix} 1 & -1 \\ 0 & -2 \end{bmatrix}$ 10. $\begin{bmatrix} -3 & 2 \\ 4 & -1 \end{bmatrix} \begin{bmatrix} -2 & 5 \\ -1 & 3 \end{bmatrix}$

11. $\begin{bmatrix} 1 & -1 \\ 0 & -2 \end{bmatrix} \begin{bmatrix} 2 & -3 \\ 1 & 2 \end{bmatrix}$ 12. $\begin{bmatrix} -2 & 5 \\ -1 & 3 \end{bmatrix} \begin{bmatrix} -3 & 2 \\ 4 & -1 \end{bmatrix}$
(Compare with Problem 9.)   (Compare with Problem 10.)

13. $\begin{bmatrix} 5 & -2 \end{bmatrix} \begin{bmatrix} -3 \\ -4 \end{bmatrix}$ 14. $\begin{bmatrix} -4 & 3 \end{bmatrix} \begin{bmatrix} -2 \\ 1 \end{bmatrix}$

15. $\begin{bmatrix} -3 \\ -4 \end{bmatrix} \begin{bmatrix} 5 & -2 \end{bmatrix}$ 16. $\begin{bmatrix} -2 \\ 1 \end{bmatrix} \begin{bmatrix} -4 & 3 \end{bmatrix}$

B   *Find the dot products.*

17. $[-1 \quad -2 \quad 2] \cdot \begin{bmatrix} 2 \\ -1 \\ 3 \end{bmatrix}$

18. $[-2 \quad 4 \quad 0] \cdot \begin{bmatrix} -1 \\ -3 \\ 2 \end{bmatrix}$

19. $[-1 \quad -3 \quad 0 \quad 5] \cdot \begin{bmatrix} 4 \\ -3 \\ -1 \\ 2 \end{bmatrix}$

20. $[-1 \quad 2 \quad 3 \quad -2] \cdot \begin{bmatrix} 3 \\ -2 \\ 0 \\ 4 \end{bmatrix}$

Find the matrix products.

21. $\begin{bmatrix} 2 & -1 & 1 \\ 1 & 3 & -2 \end{bmatrix} \begin{bmatrix} 1 & 3 \\ 0 & -1 \\ -2 & 2 \end{bmatrix}$

22. $\begin{bmatrix} -1 & -4 & 3 \\ 2 & 0 & 1 \end{bmatrix} \begin{bmatrix} 2 & -3 \\ 1 & 2 \\ 0 & -1 \end{bmatrix}$

23. $\begin{bmatrix} 1 & 3 \\ 0 & -1 \\ -2 & 2 \end{bmatrix} \begin{bmatrix} 2 & -1 & 1 \\ 1 & 3 & -2 \end{bmatrix}$

24. $\begin{bmatrix} 2 & -3 \\ 1 & 2 \\ 0 & -1 \end{bmatrix} \begin{bmatrix} -1 & -4 & 3 \\ 2 & 0 & 1 \end{bmatrix}$

25. $[3 \quad -2 \quad -4] \begin{bmatrix} 1 \\ 2 \\ -3 \end{bmatrix}$

26. $[1 \quad -2 \quad 2] \begin{bmatrix} 2 \\ -1 \\ 1 \end{bmatrix}$

27. $\begin{bmatrix} 1 \\ 2 \\ -3 \end{bmatrix} [3 \quad -2 \quad -4]$

28. $\begin{bmatrix} 2 \\ -1 \\ 1 \end{bmatrix} [1 \quad -2 \quad 2]$

29. $\begin{bmatrix} 2 & -1 & 3 & 0 \\ -3 & 4 & 2 & -1 \\ 0 & -2 & 1 & 4 \end{bmatrix} \begin{bmatrix} 2 & -3 & -2 \\ 1 & 0 & 1 \\ -1 & 2 & 0 \\ 2 & -2 & -3 \end{bmatrix}$

(Compare with Problem 30.)

30. $\begin{bmatrix} 2 & -3 & -2 \\ 1 & 0 & 1 \\ -1 & 2 & 0 \\ 2 & -2 & -3 \end{bmatrix} \begin{bmatrix} 2 & -1 & 3 & 0 \\ -3 & 4 & 2 & -1 \\ 0 & -2 & 1 & 4 \end{bmatrix}$

(Compare with Problem 29.)

C **31.** $\begin{bmatrix} 2.1 & 3.2 & -1.1 \\ -0.8 & 5.7 & -4.3 \end{bmatrix} \begin{bmatrix} -4.5 & 3.7 \\ 1.1 & -2.6 \\ -2.0 & 4.3 \end{bmatrix}$

32. $\begin{bmatrix} 6.4 & 2.0 \\ -2.8 & 3.9 \\ -1.5 & -2.4 \end{bmatrix} \begin{bmatrix} -6.3 & 3.6 \\ -2.7 & 2.2 \end{bmatrix}.$

In Problems 33–36 verify each statement by using the following matrices:

$$A = \begin{bmatrix} 1 & 2 \\ 0 & 1 \end{bmatrix} \qquad B = \begin{bmatrix} 1 & 1 \\ 2 & 3 \end{bmatrix} \qquad C = \begin{bmatrix} -3 & 1 \\ -1 & 2 \end{bmatrix}$$

33. $AB \neq BA$ **34.** $(AB)C = A(BC)$

35. $A(B + C) = AB + AC$ **36.** $(B + C)A = BA + CA$

Applications

Business & Economics

37. *Labor costs.* A company with manufacturing plants located in different parts of the country has labor-hour and wage requirements for the manufacturing of three types of inflatable boats as given in the following two matrices:

Labor-hours per boat

	Cutting department	Assembly department	Packaging department	
$M =$	0.6 hr	0.6 hr	0.2 hr	One-person boat
	1.0 hr	0.9 hr	0.3 hr	Two-person boat
	1.5 hr	1.2 hr.	0.4 hr	Four-person boat

Hourly wages

	Plant I	Plant II	
$N =$	\$6	\$7	Cutting department
	\$8	\$10	Assembly department
	\$3	\$4	Packaging department

(A) Find the labor costs for a one-person boat manufactured at plant I. That is, find the dot product

$$[0.6 \quad 0.6 \quad 0.2] \cdot \begin{bmatrix} 6 \\ 8 \\ 3 \end{bmatrix}$$

(B) Find the labor costs for a four-person boat manufactured at plant II. Set up a dot product as in part A and multiply.

(C) What is the dimension of MN?

(D) Find MN and interpret.

38. *Inventory value.* A personal computer retail company sells five differ-ent computer models through three stores located in a large metropol-itan area. The inventory of each model on hand in each store is summarized in matrix M. Wholesale (W) and retail (R) values of each model computer are summarized in matrix N.

Model

$$
M = \begin{bmatrix} A & B & C & D & E \\ 4 & 2 & 3 & 7 & 1 \\ 2 & 3 & 5 & 0 & 6 \\ 10 & 4 & 3 & 4 & 3 \end{bmatrix} \begin{matrix} \text{Store 1} \\ \text{Store 2} \\ \text{Store 3} \end{matrix}
$$

$$
N = \begin{bmatrix} W & R \\ \$700 & \$840 \\ \$1,400 & \$1,800 \\ \$1,800 & \$2,400 \\ \$2,700 & \$3,300 \\ \$3,500 & \$4,900 \end{bmatrix} \begin{matrix} A \\ B \\ C \\ D \\ E \end{matrix}
$$

(A) What is the retail value of the inventory at store 2?

(B) What is the wholesale value of the inventory at store 3?

(C) Compute MN and interpret.

39. (A) Multiply M in Problem 38 by [1   1   1] and interpret. (The multiplication only makes sense in one direction.)

(B) Multiply MN in Problem 38 by [1   1   1] and interpret. (The multiplication only makes sense in one direction.)

Life Sciences

40. *Nutrition.* A nutritionist for a cereal company blends two cereals in different mixes. The amounts of protein, carbohydrate, and fat (in grams per ounce) in each cereal are given by matrix M. The amounts of each cereal used in the three mixes are given by matrix N.

$$
M = \begin{bmatrix} \text{Cereal } A & \text{Cereal } B \\ 4 \text{ g} & 2 \text{ g} \\ 20 \text{ g} & 16 \text{ g} \\ 3 \text{ g} & 1 \text{ g} \end{bmatrix} \begin{matrix} \text{Protein} \\ \text{Carbohydrate} \\ \text{Fat} \end{matrix}
$$

$$
N = \begin{bmatrix} \text{Mix } X & \text{Mix } Y & \text{Mix } Z \\ 15 \text{ oz} & 10 \text{ oz} & 5 \text{ oz} \\ 5 \text{ oz} & 10 \text{ oz} & 15 \text{ oz} \end{bmatrix} \begin{matrix} \text{Cereal } A \\ \text{Cereal } B \end{matrix}
$$

(A) Find the amount of protein in mix X by computing the dot product

$$[4 \quad 2] \cdot \begin{bmatrix} 15 \\ 5 \end{bmatrix}$$

(B) Find the amount of fat in mix Z. Set up a dot product as in part A and multiply.

(C) What is the dimension of MN?

(D) Find MN and interpret.

(E) Find $\frac{1}{20} MN$ and interpret.

Social Sciences

41. *Politics.* In a local California election, a group hired a public relations firm to promote its candidate in three ways: telephone calls, house calls, and letters. The cost per contact is given in matrix M:

Cost per
contact

$$M = \begin{bmatrix} \$0.40 \\ \$0.75 \\ \$0.25 \end{bmatrix} \begin{matrix} \text{Telephone call} \\ \text{House call} \\ \text{Letter} \end{matrix}$$

The number of contacts of each type made in two adjacent cities is given in matrix N:

	Telephone call	House call	Letter	
$N =$	1,000	500	5,000	Berkeley
	2,000	800	8,000	Oakland

(A) Find the total amount spent in Berkeley by computing the dot product

$$[1{,}000 \quad 500 \quad 5{,}000] \cdot \begin{bmatrix} \$0.40 \\ \$0.75 \\ \$0.25 \end{bmatrix}$$

(B) Find the total amount spent in Oakland by computing the dot product of appropriate matrices.

(C) Compute NM and interpret.

(D) Multiply N by the matrix $[1 \quad 1]$ and interpret.

1-6   Inverse of a Square Matrix; Matrix Equations

- Identity Matrix for Multiplication
- Inverse of a Square Matrix
- Matrix Equations
- Application

▪ Identity Matrix for Multiplication

We know that

$$1a = a1 = a$$

for all real numbers a. The number 1 is called the **identity** for real number multiplication. Does the set of all matrices of a given dimension have an identity element for multiplication? The answer, in general, is no. However, the set of all **square matrices of order n** (dimension $n \times n$) does have an identity, and it is given as follows: The **identity element for multiplication** for the set of all square matrices of order n is the square matrix of order n, denoted by I, with 1's along the **main diagonal** (from the upper left corner to the lower right) and 0's elsewhere. For example,

$$\begin{bmatrix} 1 & 0 \\ 0 & 1 \end{bmatrix} \quad \text{and} \quad \begin{bmatrix} 1 & 0 & 0 \\ 0 & 1 & 0 \\ 0 & 0 & 1 \end{bmatrix}$$

are the identity matrices for all square matrices of order 2 and 3, respectively.

Example 27

(A) $\begin{bmatrix} 1 & 0 & 0 \\ 0 & 1 & 0 \\ 0 & 0 & 1 \end{bmatrix} \begin{bmatrix} a & b & c \\ d & e & f \\ g & h & i \end{bmatrix} = \begin{bmatrix} a & b & c \\ d & e & f \\ g & h & i \end{bmatrix}$

(B) $\begin{bmatrix} a & b & c \\ d & e & f \\ g & h & i \end{bmatrix} \begin{bmatrix} 1 & 0 & 0 \\ 0 & 1 & 0 \\ 0 & 0 & 1 \end{bmatrix} = \begin{bmatrix} a & b & c \\ d & e & f \\ g & h & i \end{bmatrix}$

(C) $\begin{bmatrix} 1 & 0 \\ 0 & 1 \end{bmatrix} \begin{bmatrix} a & b & c \\ d & e & f \end{bmatrix} = \begin{bmatrix} a & b & c \\ d & e & f \end{bmatrix}$

(D) $\begin{bmatrix} a & b & c \\ d & e & f \end{bmatrix} \begin{bmatrix} 1 & 0 & 0 \\ 0 & 1 & 0 \\ 0 & 0 & 1 \end{bmatrix} = \begin{bmatrix} a & b & c \\ d & e & f \end{bmatrix}$

Problem 27   Multiply:

(A) $\begin{bmatrix} 1 & 0 \\ 0 & 1 \end{bmatrix}\begin{bmatrix} 2 & -3 \\ 5 & 7 \end{bmatrix}$ and $\begin{bmatrix} 2 & -3 \\ 5 & 7 \end{bmatrix}\begin{bmatrix} 1 & 0 \\ 0 & 1 \end{bmatrix}$

(B) $\begin{bmatrix} 1 & 0 & 0 \\ 0 & 1 & 0 \\ 0 & 0 & 1 \end{bmatrix}\begin{bmatrix} 4 & 2 \\ 3 & -5 \\ 6 & 8 \end{bmatrix}$ and $\begin{bmatrix} 4 & 2 \\ 3 & -5 \\ 6 & 8 \end{bmatrix}\begin{bmatrix} 1 & 0 \\ 0 & 1 \end{bmatrix}$

In general, we can show that if M is a square matrix of order n and I is the identity matrix of order n, then

$$IM = MI = M$$

If M is an $n \times m$ matrix that is not square ($n \neq m$), it is still true that

$$IM = M \quad \text{and} \quad MI = M$$

However, the identity matrices in these two equations cannot have the same order. (Why?)

■ Inverse of a Square Matrix

In the set of real numbers, we know that for each real number a (except zero) there exists a real number a^{-1} such that

$$a^{-1}a = 1$$

The number a^{-1} is called the **inverse** of the number a relative to multiplication, or the **multiplicative inverse** of a. For example, 2^{-1} is the multiplicative inverse of 2, since $2^{-1} \cdot 2 = 1$. For each square matrix M, does there exist matrix M^{-1} (read "M inverse") such that the following relation is true?

$$M^{-1}M = MM^{-1} = I$$

If M^{-1} exists for a given matrix M, then M^{-1} is called the **inverse of M relative to multiplication.*** Let us use this definition to find M^{-1} for

$$M = \begin{bmatrix} 2 & 3 \\ 1 & 2 \end{bmatrix}$$

---

* If a is a nonzero real number, then, because of the laws of exponents for real numbers, $a^{-1} = 1/a$, and both a^{-1} and $1/a$ represent the multiplicative inverse of $a [a^{-1} \cdot a = a^0 = 1$ and $(1/a)(a) = a/a = 1]$. Matrices do not have the same exponent laws as real numbers. For example, $M^{-1} \neq 1/M$ for M a matrix ($1/M$ is meaningless, since we have not defined matrix division). For a given matrix M, the matrix symbol "M^{-1}" simply represents a matrix with the property $M^{-1}M = MM^{-1} = I$. If M^{-1} exists, then it is called the (multiplicative) inverse of M, or M inverse.

We are looking for

$$M^{-1} = \begin{bmatrix} a & c \\ b & d \end{bmatrix}$$

such that

$$MM^{-1} = M^{-1}M = I$$

Thus, we write

$$\overset{M}{\begin{bmatrix} 2 & 3 \\ 1 & 2 \end{bmatrix}} \overset{M^{-1}}{\begin{bmatrix} a & c \\ b & d \end{bmatrix}} = \overset{I}{\begin{bmatrix} 1 & 0 \\ 0 & 1 \end{bmatrix}}$$

and try to find a, b, c, and d so that the product of M and M^{-1} is the identity matrix I. Multiplying M and M^{-1} on the left side, we obtain

$$\begin{bmatrix} (2a + 3b) & (2c + 3d) \\ (a + 2b) & (c + 2d) \end{bmatrix} = \begin{bmatrix} 1 & 0 \\ 0 & 1 \end{bmatrix}$$

which is true only if

$$\begin{matrix} 2a + 3b = 1 & \qquad 2c + 3d = 0 \\ a + 2b = 0 & \qquad c + 2d = 1 \end{matrix}$$

Solving these two systems, we find that $a = 2$, $b = -1$, $c = -3$, and $d = 2$. Thus,

$$M^{-1} = \begin{bmatrix} 2 & -3 \\ -1 & 2 \end{bmatrix}$$

as is easily checked:

$$\overset{M}{\begin{bmatrix} 2 & 3 \\ 1 & 2 \end{bmatrix}} \overset{M^{-1}}{\begin{bmatrix} 2 & -3 \\ -1 & 2 \end{bmatrix}} = \overset{I}{\begin{bmatrix} 1 & 0 \\ 0 & 1 \end{bmatrix}} = \overset{M^{-1}}{\begin{bmatrix} 2 & -3 \\ -1 & 2 \end{bmatrix}} \overset{M}{\begin{bmatrix} 2 & 3 \\ 1 & 2 \end{bmatrix}}$$

Inverses do not always exist for square matrices. For example, if

$$M = \begin{bmatrix} 2 & 1 \\ 4 & 2 \end{bmatrix}$$

then, proceeding as above, we are led to the systems

$$\begin{matrix} 2a + b = 1 & \qquad 2c + d = 0 \\ 4a + 2b = 0 & \qquad 4c + 2d = 1 \end{matrix}$$

These are both inconsistent and have no solution. Hence, M^{-1} does not exist.

Finding inverses (when they exist) leads to direct and simple solutions to many practical problems. At the end of this section, we shall show how inverses can be used to solve systems of linear equations.

The method outlined above for finding M^{-1}, if it exists, gets very involved for matrices of order larger than 2. Now that we know what we are looking for, we can introduce the idea of the augmented matrix (considered in Section 1-2) to make the process more efficient. For example, to find the inverse (if it exists) of

$$M = \begin{bmatrix} 1 & -1 & 1 \\ 0 & 2 & -1 \\ 2 & 3 & 0 \end{bmatrix}$$

we start as before and write

$$\overset{M}{\begin{bmatrix} 1 & -1 & 1 \\ 0 & 2 & -1 \\ 2 & 3 & 0 \end{bmatrix}} \overset{M^{-1}}{\begin{bmatrix} a & d & g \\ b & e & h \\ c & f & i \end{bmatrix}} = \overset{I}{\begin{bmatrix} 1 & 0 & 0 \\ 0 & 1 & 0 \\ 0 & 0 & 1 \end{bmatrix}}$$

which is true only if

$$\begin{array}{lll} a - b + c = 1 & d - e + f = 0 & g - h + i = 0 \\ 2b - c = 0 & 2e - f = 1 & 2h - i = 0 \\ 2a + 3b = 0 & 2d + 3e = 0 & 2g + 3h = 1 \end{array}$$

Now we write augmented matrices for each of the three systems:

$$\overset{First}{\left[\begin{array}{ccc|c} 1 & -1 & 1 & 1 \\ 0 & 2 & -1 & 0 \\ 2 & 3 & 0 & 0 \end{array}\right]} \quad \overset{Second}{\left[\begin{array}{ccc|c} 1 & -1 & 1 & 0 \\ 0 & 2 & -1 & 1 \\ 2 & 3 & 0 & 0 \end{array}\right]} \quad \overset{Third}{\left[\begin{array}{ccc|c} 1 & -1 & 1 & 0 \\ 0 & 2 & -1 & 0 \\ 2 & 3 & 0 & 1 \end{array}\right]}$$

Since each matrix to the left of the vertical bar is the same, exactly the same row operations can be used on each total matrix to transform it into a reduced form. We can speed up the process substantially by combining all three augmented matrices into the single augmented matrix form

$$\left[\begin{array}{ccc|ccc} 1 & -1 & 1 & 1 & 0 & 0 \\ 0 & 2 & -1 & 0 & 1 & 0 \\ 2 & 3 & 0 & 0 & 0 & 1 \end{array}\right] = [M|I] \tag{1}$$

We now try to perform row operations on matrix (1) until we obtain a row-equivalent matrix that looks like matrix (2):

$$\left[\begin{array}{ccc|ccc} 1 & 0 & 0 & a & d & g \\ 0 & 1 & 0 & b & e & h \\ 0 & 0 & 1 & c & f & i \end{array}\right] \tag{2}$$

with headers I over the left block and B over the right block.

If this can be done, then the new matrix to the right of the vertical bar will be M^{-1}! Now let us try to transform (1) into a form like (2).

$$
\begin{array}{cc}
M & I \\
\left[\begin{array}{ccc|ccc}
1 & -1 & 1 & 1 & 0 & 0 \\
0 & 2 & -1 & 0 & 1 & 0 \\
2 & 3 & 0 & 0 & 0 & 1
\end{array}\right] & R_3 + (-2)R_1 \rightarrow R_3
\end{array}
$$

$$
\sim
\begin{array}{cc}
\left[\begin{array}{ccc|ccc}
1 & -1 & 1 & 1 & 0 & 0 \\
0 & 2 & -1 & 0 & 1 & 0 \\
0 & 5 & -2 & -2 & 0 & 1
\end{array}\right] & \tfrac{1}{2}R_2 \rightarrow R_2
\end{array}
$$

$$
\sim
\begin{array}{cc}
\left[\begin{array}{ccc|ccc}
1 & -1 & 1 & 1 & 0 & 0 \\
0 & 1 & -\tfrac{1}{2} & 0 & \tfrac{1}{2} & 0 \\
0 & 5 & -2 & -2 & 0 & 1
\end{array}\right] & R_3 + (-5)R_2 \rightarrow R_3
\end{array}
$$

$$
\sim
\begin{array}{cc}
\left[\begin{array}{ccc|ccc}
1 & -1 & 1 & 1 & 0 & 0 \\
0 & 1 & -\tfrac{1}{2} & 0 & \tfrac{1}{2} & 0 \\
0 & 0 & \tfrac{1}{2} & -2 & -\tfrac{5}{2} & 1
\end{array}\right] & 2R_3 \rightarrow R_3
\end{array}
$$

$$
\sim
\begin{array}{cc}
\left[\begin{array}{ccc|ccc}
1 & -1 & 1 & 1 & 0 & 0 \\
0 & 1 & -\tfrac{1}{2} & 0 & \tfrac{1}{2} & 0 \\
0 & 0 & 1 & -4 & -5 & 2
\end{array}\right] &
\begin{array}{l}
R_1 + (-1)R_3 \rightarrow R_1 \\
R_2 + \tfrac{1}{2}R_3 \rightarrow R_2
\end{array}
\end{array}
$$

$$
\sim
\begin{array}{cc}
\left[\begin{array}{ccc|ccc}
1 & -1 & 0 & 5 & 5 & -2 \\
0 & 1 & 0 & -2 & -2 & 1 \\
0 & 0 & 1 & -4 & -5 & 2
\end{array}\right] & R_1 + R_2 \rightarrow R_1
\end{array}
$$

$$
\begin{array}{cc}
I & B \\
\sim
\left[\begin{array}{ccc|ccc}
1 & 0 & 0 & 3 & 3 & -1 \\
0 & 1 & 0 & -2 & -2 & 1 \\
0 & 0 & 1 & -4 & -5 & 2
\end{array}\right] &
\end{array}
$$

Converting back to systems of equations equivalent to our three original systems (we don't have to do this step in practice), we have

$$
\begin{array}{ccc}
a = 3 & d = 3 & g = -1 \\
b = -2 & e = -2 & h = 1 \\
c = -4 & f = -5 & i = 2
\end{array}
$$

And these are just the elements of M^{-1} that we are looking for! Hence,

$$
M^{-1} =
\begin{bmatrix}
3 & 3 & -1 \\
-2 & -2 & 1 \\
-4 & -5 & 2
\end{bmatrix}
$$

Note that this is the matrix to the right of the vertical line in the last augmented matrix above. (You should check that $MM^{-1} = I$.)

Inverse of a Square Matrix M

If $[M|I]$ is transformed by row operations into $[I|B]$, then the resulting matrix B is M^{-1}. However, if we obtain all zeros in one or more rows to the left of the vertical line, then M^{-1} does not exist.

Example 28 Find M^{-1}, given: $M = \begin{bmatrix} 3 & -1 \\ -4 & 2 \end{bmatrix}$

Solution $\begin{bmatrix} 3 & -1 & | & 1 & 0 \\ -4 & 2 & | & 0 & 1 \end{bmatrix}$ $\frac{1}{3} R_1 \rightarrow R_1$

$\sim \begin{bmatrix} 1 & -\frac{1}{3} & | & \frac{1}{3} & 0 \\ -4 & 2 & | & 0 & 1 \end{bmatrix}$ $R_2 + 4 R_1 \rightarrow R_2$

$\sim \begin{bmatrix} 1 & -\frac{1}{3} & | & \frac{1}{3} & 0 \\ 0 & \frac{2}{3} & | & \frac{4}{3} & 1 \end{bmatrix}$ $\frac{3}{2} R_2 \rightarrow R_2$

$\sim \begin{bmatrix} 1 & -\frac{1}{3} & | & \frac{1}{3} & 0 \\ 0 & 1 & | & 2 & \frac{3}{2} \end{bmatrix}$ $R_1 + \frac{1}{3} R_2 \rightarrow R_1$

$\sim \begin{bmatrix} 1 & 0 & | & 1 & \frac{1}{2} \\ 0 & 1 & | & 2 & \frac{3}{2} \end{bmatrix}$

Thus,

$$M^{-1} = \begin{bmatrix} 1 & \frac{1}{2} \\ 2 & \frac{3}{2} \end{bmatrix} = \frac{1}{2} \begin{bmatrix} 2 & 1 \\ 4 & 3 \end{bmatrix}$$

Check by showing that $M^{-1}M = I^*$

$$\frac{1}{2} \begin{bmatrix} 2 & 1 \\ 4 & 3 \end{bmatrix} \begin{bmatrix} 3 & -1 \\ -4 & 2 \end{bmatrix} = \frac{1}{2} \begin{bmatrix} 2 & 0 \\ 0 & 2 \end{bmatrix} = \begin{bmatrix} 1 & 0 \\ 0 & 1 \end{bmatrix} = I$$

Problem 28 Find M^{-1}, given: $M = \begin{bmatrix} 2 & -6 \\ 1 & -2 \end{bmatrix}$

---

* Technically, we should check if $M^{-1}M = I$ and if $MM^{-1} = I$. However, it can be shown that if one of these equations is valid, then the other is also valid. Thus, for checking purposes, it is sufficient to compute $M^{-1}M$ or MM^{-1} — you need not do both.

Example 29 Find M^{-1}, given: $M = \begin{bmatrix} 2 & -4 \\ -3 & 6 \end{bmatrix}$

Solution $\begin{bmatrix} 2 & -4 & | & 1 & 0 \\ -3 & 6 & | & 0 & 1 \end{bmatrix} \sim \begin{bmatrix} 1 & -2 & | & \frac{1}{2} & 0 \\ -3 & 6 & | & 0 & 1 \end{bmatrix}$

$\sim \begin{bmatrix} 1 & -2 & | & \frac{1}{2} & 0 \\ 0 & 0 & | & \frac{3}{2} & 1 \end{bmatrix}$

We have all zeros in the second row to the left of the vertical bar; therefore, the inverse does not exist.

Problem 29 Find M^{-1}, given: $M = \begin{bmatrix} -6 & 3 \\ -4 & 2 \end{bmatrix}$

Example 30 Find M^{-1}, given: $M = \begin{bmatrix} -1 & 2 & 0 \\ 3 & 2 & -1 \\ 4 & 0 & 3 \end{bmatrix}$

Solution $\begin{bmatrix} -1 & 2 & 0 & | & 1 & 0 & 0 \\ 3 & 2 & -1 & | & 0 & 1 & 0 \\ 4 & 0 & 3 & | & 0 & 0 & 1 \end{bmatrix}$

$\sim \begin{bmatrix} 1 & -2 & 0 & | & -1 & 0 & 0 \\ 3 & 2 & -1 & | & 0 & 1 & 0 \\ 4 & 0 & 3 & | & 0 & 0 & 1 \end{bmatrix}$

$\sim \begin{bmatrix} 1 & -2 & 0 & | & -1 & 0 & 0 \\ 0 & 8 & -1 & | & 3 & 1 & 0 \\ 0 & 8 & 3 & | & 4 & 0 & 1 \end{bmatrix}$

$\sim \begin{bmatrix} 1 & -2 & 0 & | & -1 & 0 & 0 \\ 0 & 1 & -\frac{1}{8} & | & \frac{3}{8} & \frac{1}{8} & 0 \\ 0 & 8 & 3 & | & 4 & 0 & 1 \end{bmatrix}$

$\sim \begin{bmatrix} 1 & -2 & 0 & | & -1 & 0 & 0 \\ 0 & 1 & -\frac{1}{8} & | & \frac{3}{8} & \frac{1}{8} & 0 \\ 0 & 0 & 4 & | & 1 & -1 & 1 \end{bmatrix}$

$$\sim \begin{bmatrix} 1 & -2 & 0 & \bigm| & -1 & 0 & 0 \\ 0 & 1 & -\frac{1}{8} & \bigm| & \frac{3}{8} & \frac{1}{8} & 0 \\ 0 & 0 & 1 & \bigm| & \frac{1}{4} & -\frac{1}{4} & \frac{1}{4} \end{bmatrix}$$

$$\sim \begin{bmatrix} 1 & -2 & 0 & \bigm| & -1 & 0 & 0 \\ 0 & 1 & 0 & \bigm| & \frac{13}{32} & \frac{3}{32} & \frac{1}{32} \\ 0 & 0 & 1 & \bigm| & \frac{1}{4} & -\frac{1}{4} & \frac{1}{4} \end{bmatrix}$$

$$\sim \begin{bmatrix} 1 & 0 & 0 & \bigm| & -\frac{3}{16} & \frac{3}{16} & \frac{1}{16} \\ 0 & 1 & 0 & \bigm| & \frac{13}{32} & \frac{3}{32} & \frac{1}{32} \\ 0 & 0 & 1 & \bigm| & \frac{1}{4} & -\frac{1}{4} & \frac{1}{4} \end{bmatrix}$$

Thus,

$$M^{-1} = \begin{bmatrix} -\frac{3}{16} & \frac{3}{16} & \frac{1}{16} \\ \frac{13}{32} & \frac{3}{32} & \frac{1}{32} \\ \frac{1}{4} & -\frac{1}{4} & \frac{1}{4} \end{bmatrix} = \frac{1}{32}\begin{bmatrix} -6 & 6 & 2 \\ 13 & 3 & 1 \\ 8 & -8 & 8 \end{bmatrix}$$

Check $$\frac{1}{32}\begin{bmatrix} -6 & 6 & 2 \\ 13 & 3 & 1 \\ 8 & -8 & 8 \end{bmatrix}\begin{bmatrix} -1 & 2 & 0 \\ 3 & 2 & -1 \\ 4 & 0 & 3 \end{bmatrix} = \frac{1}{32}\begin{bmatrix} 32 & 0 & 0 \\ 0 & 32 & 0 \\ 0 & 0 & 32 \end{bmatrix}$$

$$= \begin{bmatrix} 1 & 0 & 0 \\ 0 & 1 & 0 \\ 0 & 0 & 1 \end{bmatrix}$$

Problem 30   Find M^{-1}, given: $M = \begin{bmatrix} 2 & -1 & 3 \\ 1 & 0 & 2 \\ 3 & 2 & 1 \end{bmatrix}$

■ Matrix Equations

We will now show how certain systems of equations can be solved by using inverses of square matrices.

Example 31   Solve the system

$$-x_1 + 2x_2 \qquad = k_1$$
$$3x_1 + 2x_2 - \ x_3 = k_2 \qquad\qquad (3)$$
$$4x_1 \qquad + 3x_3 = k_3$$

for:

(A) $k_1 = 2$, $k_2 = -1$, $k_3 = 3$ (B) $k_1 = -1$, $k_2 = 3$, $k_3 = -2$
(C) $k_1 = 0$, $k_2 = 2$, $k_3 = 6$

Solutions   Once we obtain the inverse of the coefficient matrix

$$A = \begin{bmatrix} -1 & 2 & 0 \\ 3 & 2 & -1 \\ 4 & 0 & 3 \end{bmatrix}$$

we will be able to solve parts A, B, and C very easily. To see why, we convert system (3) into the following equivalent **matrix equation:**

$$\overset{A}{\begin{bmatrix} -1 & 2 & 0 \\ 3 & 2 & -1 \\ 4 & 0 & 3 \end{bmatrix}} \overset{X}{\begin{bmatrix} x_1 \\ x_2 \\ x_3 \end{bmatrix}} = \overset{B}{\begin{bmatrix} k_1 \\ k_2 \\ k_3 \end{bmatrix}} \qquad\qquad (4)$$

Now we see another important reason for defining matrix multiplication as it was defined. You should check that matrix equation (4) is equivalent to system (3) by multiplying the left side and then equating corresponding elements on the left with those on the right.

We are now interested in finding a column matrix X that will satisfy the matrix equation

$$AX = B$$

To solve this equation, we multiply both sides by A^{-1} (if it exists) to isolate X on the left side:

$$
\begin{array}{ll}
AX = B & \text{Multiply both sides by } A^{-1} \\
A^{-1}(AX) = A^{-1}B & \text{Use the associative property} \\
(A^{-1}A)X = A^{-1}B & A^{-1}A = I \\
IX = A^{-1}B & IX = X \\
X = A^{-1}B &
\end{array}
$$

The inverse of A was found in Example 30 to be

$$A^{-1} = \frac{1}{32}\begin{bmatrix} -6 & 6 & 2 \\ 13 & 3 & 1 \\ 8 & -8 & 8 \end{bmatrix}$$

Thus,

$$
\begin{matrix} X \\[2pt] \begin{bmatrix} x_1 \\ x_2 \\ x_3 \end{bmatrix} \end{matrix}
=
\frac{1}{32}
\begin{matrix} A^{-1} \\[2pt] \begin{bmatrix} -6 & 6 & 2 \\ 13 & 3 & 1 \\ 8 & -8 & 8 \end{bmatrix} \end{matrix}
\begin{matrix} B \\[2pt] \begin{bmatrix} k_1 \\ k_2 \\ k_3 \end{bmatrix} \end{matrix}
$$

To solve parts A, B, and C, we simply replace k_1, k_2, and k_3 with the given values and multiply.

(A) $\begin{bmatrix} x_1 \\ x_2 \\ x_3 \end{bmatrix} = \frac{1}{32} \begin{bmatrix} -6 & 6 & 2 \\ 13 & 3 & 1 \\ 8 & -8 & 8 \end{bmatrix} \begin{bmatrix} 2 \\ -1 \\ 3 \end{bmatrix} = \begin{bmatrix} -\frac{12}{32} \\ \frac{26}{32} \\ \frac{48}{32} \end{bmatrix}$

Thus, $x_1 = -\frac{3}{8}$, $x_2 = \frac{13}{16}$, and $x_3 = \frac{3}{2}$.

(B) $\begin{bmatrix} x_1 \\ x_2 \\ x_3 \end{bmatrix} = \frac{1}{32} \begin{bmatrix} -6 & 6 & 2 \\ 13 & 3 & 1 \\ 8 & -8 & 8 \end{bmatrix} \begin{bmatrix} -1 \\ 3 \\ 2 \end{bmatrix} = \begin{bmatrix} \frac{28}{32} \\ -\frac{2}{32} \\ -\frac{16}{32} \end{bmatrix}$

Thus, $x_1 = \frac{7}{8}$, $x_2 = -\frac{1}{16}$, and $x_3 = -\frac{1}{2}$.

(C) $\begin{bmatrix} x_1 \\ x_2 \\ x_3 \end{bmatrix} = \frac{1}{32} \begin{bmatrix} -6 & 6 & 2 \\ 13 & 3 & 1 \\ 8 & -8 & 8 \end{bmatrix} \begin{bmatrix} 0 \\ -2 \\ 6 \end{bmatrix} = \begin{bmatrix} 0 \\ 0 \\ \frac{64}{32} \end{bmatrix}$

Thus, $x_1 = 0$, $x_2 = 0$, and $x_3 = 2$.

Problem 31 Solve the system

$$
\begin{aligned}
2x_1 - \;\; x_2 + 3x_3 &= k_1 \\
x_1 \qquad\quad + 2x_3 &= k_2 \\
3x_1 + 2x_2 + \;\; x_3 &= k_3
\end{aligned}
$$

by using the inverse of the coefficient matrix (found in Problem 30 above). Find the particular solutions of the system for:

(A) $k_1 = 2$, $k_2 = 0$, $k_3 = -3$ (B) $k_1 = -1$, $k_2 = 1$, $k_3 = 2$
(C) $k_1 = 3$, $k_2 = -3$, $k_3 = 0$

Computer programs are readily available for finding the inverse of square matrices. A great advantage of using an inverse to solve a system of linear equations is that once the inverse is found, it can be used to solve any new system formed by changing the constant terms. However, this method is not suited for cases where the number of equations and the number of unknowns are not the same. (Why?)

■ Application

The following application will illustrate the usefulness of the inverse method for solving systems of equations.

Example 32

An investment advisor currently has two types of investments available for clients; a conservative investment A that pays 10% per year and an investment B of higher risk that pays 20% per year. Clients may divide their investments between the two to achieve any total return desired between 10% and 20%. However, the higher the desired return, the higher the risk. How should each client listed in the table invest to achieve the indicated return?

	Client			
	1	2	3	k
Total investment	$20,000	$50,000	$10,000	k_1
Annual return desired	$ 2,400	$ 7,500	$ 1,300	k_2
	(12%)	(15%)	(13%)	

Solution

We will solve the problem for an arbitrary client k by using inverses. Then we will apply the result to the three specific clients.

Let $x_1 = $ Amount invested in A

   $x_2 = $ Amount invested in B

Then $x_1 + \quad x_2 = k_1$ Total invested

   $0.1x_1 + 0.2x_2 = k_2$ Total annual return desired

Write as a matrix equation:

$$\overset{A}{\begin{bmatrix} 1 & 1 \\ 0.1 & 0.2 \end{bmatrix}} \overset{X}{\begin{bmatrix} x_1 \\ x_2 \end{bmatrix}} = \overset{B}{\begin{bmatrix} k_1 \\ k_2 \end{bmatrix}}$$

If A^{-1} exists, then

$X = A^{-1}B$

We now find A^{-1} by starting with $[A|I]$ and proceeding as discussed earlier in this section:

$$\begin{bmatrix} 1 & 1 & | & 1 & 0 \\ 0.1 & 0.2 & | & 0 & 1 \end{bmatrix} \quad 10R_2 \to R_2$$

$$\sim \begin{bmatrix} 1 & 1 & | & 1 & 0 \\ 1 & 2 & | & 0 & 10 \end{bmatrix} \quad R_2 + (-1)R_1 \to R_2$$

$$\sim \begin{bmatrix} 1 & 1 & | & 1 & 0 \\ 0 & 1 & | & -1 & 10 \end{bmatrix} \quad R_1 + (-1)R_2 \rightarrow R_1$$

$$\sim \begin{bmatrix} 1 & 0 & | & 2 & -10 \\ 0 & 1 & | & -1 & 10 \end{bmatrix}$$

Thus,

$$A^{-1} = \begin{bmatrix} 2 & -10 \\ -1 & 10 \end{bmatrix} \quad Check: \quad \overset{A^{-1}}{\begin{bmatrix} 2 & -10 \\ -1 & 10 \end{bmatrix}} \overset{A}{\begin{bmatrix} 1 & 1 \\ 0.1 & 0.2 \end{bmatrix}} = \overset{I}{\begin{bmatrix} 1 & 0 \\ 0 & 1 \end{bmatrix}}$$

and

$$\overset{X}{\begin{bmatrix} x_1 \\ x_2 \end{bmatrix}} = \overset{A^{-1}}{\begin{bmatrix} 2 & -10 \\ -1 & 10 \end{bmatrix}} \overset{B}{\begin{bmatrix} k_1 \\ k_2 \end{bmatrix}}$$

To solve each client's investment problem, we replace k_1 and k_2 with appropriate values from the table and multiply by A^{-1}:

Client 1

$$\begin{bmatrix} x_1 \\ x_2 \end{bmatrix} = \begin{bmatrix} 2 & -10 \\ -1 & 10 \end{bmatrix} \begin{bmatrix} 20,000 \\ 2,400 \end{bmatrix} = \begin{bmatrix} 16,000 \\ 4,000 \end{bmatrix}$$

Solution: $x_1 = \$16,000$ in A, $x_2 = \$4,000$ in B

Client 2

$$\begin{bmatrix} x_1 \\ x_2 \end{bmatrix} = \begin{bmatrix} 2 & -10 \\ -1 & 10 \end{bmatrix} \begin{bmatrix} 50,000 \\ 7,500 \end{bmatrix} = \begin{bmatrix} 25,000 \\ 25,000 \end{bmatrix}$$

Solution: $x_1 = \$25,000$ in A, $x_2 = \$25,000$ in B

Client 3

$$\begin{bmatrix} x_1 \\ x_2 \end{bmatrix} = \begin{bmatrix} 2 & -10 \\ -1 & 10 \end{bmatrix} \begin{bmatrix} 10,000 \\ 1,300 \end{bmatrix} = \begin{bmatrix} 7,000 \\ 3,000 \end{bmatrix}$$

Solution: $x_1 = \$7,000$ in A, $x_2 = \$3,000$ in B

Problem 32 Repeat Example 32 with investment A paying 8% and investment B paying 24%.

Answers to Matched Problems

27. (A) $\begin{bmatrix} 2 & -3 \\ 5 & 7 \end{bmatrix}$ (B) $\begin{bmatrix} 4 & 2 \\ 3 & -5 \\ 6 & 8 \end{bmatrix}$

28. $\begin{bmatrix} -1 & 3 \\ -\frac{1}{2} & 1 \end{bmatrix} = \frac{1}{2} \begin{bmatrix} -2 & 6 \\ -1 & 2 \end{bmatrix}$

29. Does not exist

30. $M^{-1} = \frac{1}{7} \begin{bmatrix} 4 & -7 & 2 \\ -5 & 7 & 1 \\ -2 & 7 & -1 \end{bmatrix}$

31. (A) $x_1 = \frac{2}{7}, x_2 = -\frac{13}{7}, x_3 = -\frac{1}{7}$ (B) $x_1 = -1, x_2 = 2, x_3 = 1$
    (C) $x_1 = \frac{33}{7}, x_2 = -\frac{36}{7}, x_3 = -\frac{27}{7}$

32. $A^{-1} = \begin{bmatrix} 1.5 & -6.25 \\ -0.5 & 6.25 \end{bmatrix}$ Client 1: $15,000 in A and $5,000 in B
    Client 2: $28,125 in A and $21,875 in B
    Client 3: $6,875 in A and $3,125 in B

Exercise 1-6

A   In Problems 1–4, find IM and MI, given M as indicated.

1. $\begin{bmatrix} 2 & -3 \\ 4 & 5 \end{bmatrix}$

2. $\begin{bmatrix} 6 & -8 & 4 \\ 9 & 2 & 0 \end{bmatrix}$

3. $\begin{bmatrix} -2 & 1 & 3 \\ 2 & 4 & -2 \\ 5 & 1 & 0 \end{bmatrix}$

4. $\begin{bmatrix} 7 & 2 \\ 1 & -3 \\ 6 & -9 \end{bmatrix}$

For each problem, show that the two matrices are inverses of each other by showing that their product is the identity matrix I.

5. $\begin{bmatrix} 3 & -4 \\ -2 & 3 \end{bmatrix} \begin{bmatrix} 3 & 4 \\ 2 & 3 \end{bmatrix}$

6. $\begin{bmatrix} 5 & -7 \\ -2 & 3 \end{bmatrix} \begin{bmatrix} 3 & 7 \\ 2 & 5 \end{bmatrix}$

7. $\begin{bmatrix} 1 & -1 & 1 \\ 0 & 2 & -1 \\ 2 & 3 & 0 \end{bmatrix}, \begin{bmatrix} 3 & 3 & -1 \\ -2 & -2 & 1 \\ -4 & -5 & 2 \end{bmatrix}$

8. $\begin{bmatrix} 3 & 3 & -1 \\ -2 & -2 & 1 \\ -4 & -5 & 2 \end{bmatrix} \begin{bmatrix} 1 & -1 & 1 \\ 0 & 2 & -1 \\ 2 & 3 & 0 \end{bmatrix}$

Find x_1 and x_2.

9. $\begin{bmatrix} x_1 \\ x_2 \end{bmatrix} = \begin{bmatrix} 3 & -2 \\ 1 & 4 \end{bmatrix} \begin{bmatrix} -2 \\ 1 \end{bmatrix}$

10. $\begin{bmatrix} x_1 \\ x_2 \end{bmatrix} = \begin{bmatrix} -2 & 1 \\ -1 & 2 \end{bmatrix} \begin{bmatrix} 3 \\ -2 \end{bmatrix}$

11. $\begin{bmatrix} x_1 \\ x_2 \end{bmatrix} = \begin{bmatrix} -2 & 3 \\ 2 & -1 \end{bmatrix} \begin{bmatrix} 3 \\ 2 \end{bmatrix}$

12. $\begin{bmatrix} x_1 \\ x_2 \end{bmatrix} = \begin{bmatrix} 3 & -1 \\ 0 & 2 \end{bmatrix} \begin{bmatrix} -2 \\ 1 \end{bmatrix}$

B Given M as indicated, find M^{-1} and show that $M^{-1}M = I$.

13. $\begin{bmatrix} 1 & 2 \\ 1 & 3 \end{bmatrix}$

14. $\begin{bmatrix} 2 & 1 \\ 5 & 3 \end{bmatrix}$

15. $\begin{bmatrix} 1 & 3 \\ 2 & 7 \end{bmatrix}$

16. $\begin{bmatrix} 2 & 1 \\ 1 & 1 \end{bmatrix}$

17. $\begin{bmatrix} 1 & -3 & 0 \\ 0 & 3 & 1 \\ 2 & -1 & 2 \end{bmatrix}$

18. $\begin{bmatrix} 2 & 9 & 0 \\ 1 & 2 & 3 \\ 0 & -1 & 1 \end{bmatrix}$

19. $\begin{bmatrix} 1 & 1 & 0 \\ 0 & 3 & -1 \\ 1 & 0 & 1 \end{bmatrix}$

20. $\begin{bmatrix} 1 & 0 & -1 \\ 2 & -1 & 0 \\ 1 & 1 & 1 \end{bmatrix}$

Write each system as a matrix equation and solve by using inverses.
[Note: The inverses were found in Problems 13–20.]

21. $x_1 + 2x_2 = k_1$
    $x_1 + 3x_2 = k_2$

   (A) $k_1 = 1, \quad k_2 = 3$
   (B) $k_1 = 3, \quad k_2 = 5$
   (C) $k_1 = -2, \quad k_2 = 1$

22. $2x_1 + x_2 = k_1$
    $5x_1 + 3x_2 = k_2$

   (A) $k_1 = 2, \quad k_2 = 13$
   (B) $k_1 = 2, \quad k_2 = 4$
   (C) $k_1 = 1, \quad k_2 = -3$

23. $x_1 + 3x_2 = k_1$
    $2x_1 + 7x_2 = k_2$

   (A) $k_1 = 2, \quad k_2 = -1$
   (B) $k_1 = 1, \quad k_2 = 0$
   (C) $k_1 = 3, \quad k_2 = -1$

24. $2x_1 + x_2 = k_1$
    $x_1 + x_2 = k_2$

   (A) $k_1 = -1, \quad k_2 = -2$,
   (B) $k_1 = 2, \quad k_2 = 3$
   (C) $k_1 = 2, \quad k_2 = 0$

25. $x_1 - 3x_2 \qquad = k_1$
    $3x_2 + x_3 = k_2$
    $2x_1 - x_2 + 2x_3 = k_3$

   (A) $k_1 = 1, \quad k_2 = 0, \quad k_3 = 2$
   (B) $k_1 = -1, \quad k_2 = 1, \quad k_3 = 0$
   (C) $k_1 = 2, \quad k_2 = -2, \quad k_3 = 1$

26. $2x_1 + 9x_2 \qquad = k_1$
    $x_1 + 2x_2 + 3x_3 = k_2$
    $- x_2 + x_3 = k_3$

   (A) $k_1 = 0, \quad k_2 = 2, \quad k_3 = 1$
   (B) $k_1 = -2, \quad k_2 = 0, \quad k_3 = 1$
   (C) $k_1 = 3, \quad k_2 = 1, \quad k_3 = 0$

27. $\begin{aligned} x_1 + x_2 \quad\;\; &= k_1 \\ 3x_2 - x_3 &= k_2 \\ x_1 \quad\;\; + x_3 &= k_3 \end{aligned}$

  (A) $k_1 = 2, \quad k_2 = 0, \quad k_3 = 4$
  (B) $k_1 = 0, \quad k_2 = 4, \quad k_3 = -2$
  (C) $k_1 = 4, \quad k_2 = 2, \quad k_3 = 0$

28. $\begin{aligned} x_1 \qquad - x_3 &= k_1 \\ 2x_1 - x_2 \quad\;\; &= k_2 \\ x_1 + x_2 + x_3 &= k_3 \end{aligned}$

  (A) $k_1 = 4, \quad k_2 = 8, \quad k_3 = 0$
  (B) $k_1 = 4, \quad k_2 = 0, \quad k_3 = -4$
  (C) $k_1 = 0, \quad k_2 = 8, \quad k_3 = -8$

C   *Find the inverse of each matrix, if it exists.*

29. $\begin{bmatrix} 3 & 9 \\ 2 & 6 \end{bmatrix}$

30. $\begin{bmatrix} 2 & -4 \\ -3 & 6 \end{bmatrix}$

31. $\begin{bmatrix} 3 & 1 \\ 4 & 2 \end{bmatrix}$

32. $\begin{bmatrix} -5 & 3 \\ 2 & -2 \end{bmatrix}$

33. $\begin{bmatrix} -5 & -2 & -2 \\ 2 & 1 & 0 \\ 1 & 0 & 1 \end{bmatrix}$

34. $\begin{bmatrix} 2 & 0 & 1 \\ 1 & 1 & 0 \\ 1 & 0 & 1 \end{bmatrix}$

35. $\begin{bmatrix} 2 & 1 & 1 \\ 1 & 1 & 0 \\ -1 & -1 & 0 \end{bmatrix}$

36. $\begin{bmatrix} 1 & -1 & 0 \\ 2 & -1 & 1 \\ 0 & 1 & 1 \end{bmatrix}$

37. $\begin{bmatrix} -1 & -2 & 2 \\ 4 & 2 & 0 \\ 4 & 0 & 4 \end{bmatrix}$

38. $\begin{bmatrix} 3 & 0 & 2 \\ 4 & 2 & 0 \\ 5 & 0 & 5 \end{bmatrix}$

39. Show that $(A^{-1})^{-1} = A$ for

$$A = \begin{bmatrix} 3 & 4 \\ 2 & 3 \end{bmatrix}.$$

40. Show that $(AB)^{-1} = B^{-1}A^{-1}$ for

$$A = \begin{bmatrix} 3 & 4 \\ 2 & 3 \end{bmatrix} \quad \text{and} \quad B = \begin{bmatrix} 3 & 7 \\ 2 & 5 \end{bmatrix}$$

Applications

Solve using systems of equations and inverses.

Business & Economics   41. *Resource allocation.* A concert hall has 10,000 seats. If tickets are $4 and $8, how many of each type of ticket should be sold (assuming all seats can be sold) to bring in each of the returns indicated in the table? Use decimals in computing the inverse.

	Concert		
	1	2	3
Tickets sold	10,000	10,000	10,000
Return required	$56,000	$60,000	$68,000

42. *Production scheduling.* Labor and material costs for manufacturing two guitar models are given in the table below:

Guitar Model	Labor Cost	Material Cost
A	$30	$20
B	$40	$30

If a total of $3,000 a week is allowed for labor and material, how many of each model should be produced each week to use exactly each of the allocations of the $3,000 indicated in the following table? Use decimals in computing the inverse.

	Weekly Allocation		
	1	2	3
Labor	$1,800	$1,750	$1,720
Material	$1,200	$1,250	$1,280

Life Sciences **43.** *Diets.* A biologist has available two commercial food mixes containing the following percentages of protein and fat:

Mix	Protein (%)	Fat (%)
A	20	2
B	10	6

How many ounces of each mix should be used to prepare each of the diets listed in the following table?

	Diet		
	1	2	3
Protein	20 oz	10 oz	10 oz
Fat	6 oz	4 oz	6 oz

1-7   Leontief Input–Output Analysis (Optional)

- Introduction
- Two-Industry Model

■ Introduction

A very important application of matrices and their inverses is found in the relatively recently developed branch of applied mathematics called **input —output analysis.** Wassily Leontief, the primary force behind these new developments, was awarded the Nobel Prize in economics in 1973 because of the significant impact his work had on economic planning for industrialized countries. Among other things, he conducted a comprehensive study of how 500 sectors of the American economy interacted with each other. Of course, large-scale computers played an important role in this analysis.

Our investigation will be more modest. In fact, we will start with an economy comprised of only two industries. From these humble beginnings, ideas and definitions will evolve that can be readily generalized for more realistic economies. Input–output analysis attempts to establish equilibrium conditions under which industries in an economy have just enough output to satisfy each other's demands in addition to final (outside) demands. Given the internal demands within the industries for each other's output, the problem is to determine output levels that will meet various levels of final (outside) demands.

■ Two-Industry Model

To make the problem concrete, let us start with a hypothetical economy with only two industries—electric company E and water company W. Output for both companies is measured in dollars. The electric company uses both electricity and water (input) in the production of electricity (output) and the water company uses both electricity and water (input) in the production of water (output). Suppose that the production of each dollar's worth of electricity requires $0.10 worth of electricity and $0.30 worth of water, and the production of each dollar's worth of water requires $0.40 worth of electricity and $0.20 worth of water. If the final demand from the outside sector of the economy (the demand from all other users of electricity and water) is

$d_1 = \$12$ million for electricity

$d_2 = \$6$ million for water

how much electricity and water should be produced to meet this final demand? To begin, suppose the electricity company produces $12 million worth of electricity and the water company produces $6 million worth of water (the final demand). Then the production processes of the companies would require

Electricity required to produce electricity | Electricity required to produce water

$$0.1(12) \quad + \quad 0.4(6) \quad = \$3.6 \text{ million of electricity}$$

and

Water required to produce electricity | Water required to produce water

$$0.3(12) \quad + \quad 0.2(6) \quad = \$4.8 \text{ million of water}$$

leaving only $8.4 million of electricity and $1.2 million of water left to satisfy the final demand of the outside sector. Thus, in order to meet the internal demands of both companies and to end up with enough electricity for the final outside demand, both companies must produce more than just the amount demanded by the outside sector. In fact, they must produce exactly enough to meet their own internal demands plus that demanded by the outside sector.

We now state the main problem of input–output analysis.

Basic Input–Output Problem

Given the internal demands for each industry's output, determine output levels for the various industries that will meet a given final (outside) level of demand as well as the internal demand.

If

$x_1 =$ Total output from electric company

and

$x_2 =$ Total output from water company

then reasoning as above, the internal demands are

$0.1x_1 + 0.4x_2$ Internal demand for electricity
$0.3x_1 + 0.2x_2$ Internal demand for water

Combining the internal demand with the final demand produces the following system of equations

Total output | Internal demand | Final demand

$$x_1 = 0.1x_1 + 0.4x_2 + d_1$$
$$x_2 = 0.3x_1 + 0.2x_2 + d_2$$

(1)

or, in matrix form

$$\begin{bmatrix} x_1 \\ x_2 \end{bmatrix} = \begin{bmatrix} 0.1 & 0.4 \\ 0.3 & 0.2 \end{bmatrix} \begin{bmatrix} x_1 \\ x_2 \end{bmatrix} + \begin{bmatrix} d_1 \\ d_2 \end{bmatrix}$$

or

$$X = MX + D$$

(2)

where

$$D = \begin{bmatrix} d_1 \\ d_2 \end{bmatrix} \qquad \text{Final demand matrix}$$

$$X = \begin{bmatrix} x_1 \\ x_2 \end{bmatrix} \qquad \text{Output matrix}$$

$$M = \begin{array}{c} \\ E \\ W \end{array} \begin{array}{c} E \qquad W \\ \begin{bmatrix} 0.1 & 0.4 \\ 0.3 & 0.2 \end{bmatrix} \end{array} \qquad \text{Technology matrix}$$

The **technology matrix** is the heart of input–output analysis. The elements in the technology matrix are determined as follows:

Row E, Column E—Electricity input required to produce \$1 of electricity
Row W, Column E—Water input required to produce \$1 of electricity
Row E, Column W—Electricity input required to produce \$1 of water
Row W, Column W—Water input required to produce \$1 of water

Now our problem is to solve equation (2) for X. We proceed as in the preceding section:

$$X = MX + D$$
$$X - MX = D$$
$$IX - MX = D$$
$$(I - M)X = D \qquad\qquad I = \begin{bmatrix} 1 & 0 \\ 0 & 1 \end{bmatrix}$$
$$X = (I - M)^{-1}D$$

(3)

assuming $I - M$ has an inverse. Since

$$I - M = \begin{bmatrix} 0.9 & -0.4 \\ -0.3 & 0.8 \end{bmatrix}$$

and

$$(I - M)^{-1} = \begin{bmatrix} \frac{4}{3} & \frac{2}{3} \\ \frac{1}{2} & \frac{3}{2} \end{bmatrix}$$

We convert decimals to fractions in this example to work with exact forms

we have

$$\begin{bmatrix} x_1 \\ x_2 \end{bmatrix} = \begin{bmatrix} \frac{4}{3} & \frac{2}{3} \\ \frac{1}{2} & \frac{3}{2} \end{bmatrix} \begin{bmatrix} d_1 \\ d_2 \end{bmatrix} \tag{4}$$

$$= \begin{bmatrix} \frac{4}{3} & \frac{2}{3} \\ \frac{1}{2} & \frac{3}{2} \end{bmatrix} \begin{bmatrix} 12 \\ 6 \end{bmatrix}$$

$$= \begin{bmatrix} 20 \\ 15 \end{bmatrix}$$

Therefore, the electric company must have an output of $20 million and the water company an output of $15 million so that each company can meet both internal and final demands.

Check   We use equation (2) to check our work.

$$X = MX + D$$

$$\begin{bmatrix} 20 \\ 15 \end{bmatrix} \stackrel{?}{=} \begin{bmatrix} 0.1 & 0.4 \\ 0.3 & 0.2 \end{bmatrix} \begin{bmatrix} 20 \\ 15 \end{bmatrix} + \begin{bmatrix} 12 \\ 6 \end{bmatrix}$$

$$\begin{bmatrix} 20 \\ 15 \end{bmatrix} \stackrel{?}{=} \begin{bmatrix} 8 \\ 9 \end{bmatrix} + \begin{bmatrix} 12 \\ 6 \end{bmatrix}$$

$$\begin{bmatrix} 20 \\ 15 \end{bmatrix} \stackrel{\checkmark}{=} \begin{bmatrix} 20 \\ 15 \end{bmatrix}$$

Actually, (4) solves the original problem for arbitrary final demands d_1 and d_2. This is very useful, since (4) gives a quick solution not only for the final demands stated but also to the original problem for various other projected final demands. If we had solved (1) by elimination, then we would have to start over for each new set of final demands.

Suppose in the original problem that the projected final demands 5 years from now were $d_1 = 18$ and $d_2 = 12$. Determine each company's output for this projection. We simply substitute these values into (4) and multiply:

$$\begin{bmatrix} x_1 \\ x_2 \end{bmatrix} = \begin{bmatrix} \frac{4}{3} & \frac{2}{3} \\ \frac{1}{2} & \frac{3}{2} \end{bmatrix} \begin{bmatrix} 18 \\ 12 \end{bmatrix}$$

$$= \begin{bmatrix} 32 \\ 27 \end{bmatrix}$$

We summarize these results for convenient reference.

Solution to a Two-Company Input–Output Problem

Given two companies C_1 and C_2 with

Technology matrix	Output matrix	Final demand matrix

$$M = \begin{array}{c} \\ C_1 \\ C_2 \end{array} \begin{array}{cc} C_1 & C_2 \\ \left[\begin{array}{cc} a_{11} & a_{12} \\ a_{21} & a_{22} \end{array} \right] \end{array} \qquad X = \left[\begin{array}{c} x_1 \\ x_2 \end{array} \right] \qquad D = \left[\begin{array}{c} d_1 \\ d_2 \end{array} \right]$$

where a_{ij} is the input required from C_i to produce a dollar's worth of output for C_j. The solution to the input–output matrix equation

Total output	Internal demand	Final demand

$$X \quad = \quad MX \quad + \quad D \tag{2}$$

is

$$X = (I - M)^{-1}D \tag{3}$$

assuming $I - M$ has an inverse.

Another consequence of expressing the input–output problem in matrix form (2) is that matrix equation (2) and its solution (3) are the same for a three-industry economy, a four-industry economy, or an economy with n industries (where n is any natural number), since the steps we took going from (2) to (3) hold for arbitrary matrices as long as they are dimensionally correct and $(I - M)^{-1}$ exists.

Exercise 1-7

A *Problems 1–6 pertain to the following input–output model: Assume an economy is based on two industrial sectors–agriculture (A) and energy (E). The technology matrix M and final demand matrices are (in billions of dollars)*

$$\begin{array}{c} \\ A \\ E \end{array} \begin{array}{cc} A & E \\ \left[\begin{array}{cc} 0.4 & 0.2 \\ 0.2 & 0.1 \end{array} \right] = M \end{array} \qquad D_1 = \left[\begin{array}{c} 6 \\ 4 \end{array} \right] \qquad D_2 = \left[\begin{array}{c} 8 \\ 5 \end{array} \right] \qquad D_3 = \left[\begin{array}{c} 12 \\ 9 \end{array} \right]$$

1. How much input from A and E are required to produce a dollar's worth of output for A?

2. How much input from A and E are required to produce a dollar's worth of output for E?
3. Find $I - M$ and $(I - M)^{-1}$.
4. Find the output for each sector that is needed to satisfy the final demand D_1.
5. Repeat Problem 4 for D_2.
6. Repeat Problem 4 for D_3.

B Problems 7–12 pertain to the following input–output model: Assume an economy is based on three industrial sectors — agriculture (A), building (B), and energy (E). The technology matrix M and final demand matrices (in billions of dollars) are

$$
\begin{array}{c} \\ A \\ B \\ E \end{array}
\begin{array}{ccc} A & B & E \\ \left[\begin{array}{ccc} 0.3 & 0.2 & 0.2 \\ 0.1 & 0.1 & 0.1 \\ 0.2 & 0.1 & 0.1 \end{array}\right] = M \end{array}
$$

$$
D_1 = \begin{bmatrix} 5 \\ 10 \\ 15 \end{bmatrix} \qquad D_2 = \begin{bmatrix} 20 \\ 15 \\ 10 \end{bmatrix}
$$

7. How much input from A, B, and E is required to produce a dollar's worth of output for B?
8. How much of each of B's output dollars is required as input for each of the three sectors?
9. Show that

$$
I - M = \begin{bmatrix} 0.7 & -0.2 & -0.2 \\ -0.1 & 0.9 & -0.1 \\ -0.2 & -0.1 & 0.9 \end{bmatrix}.
$$

10. Given

$$
(I - M)^{-1} = \begin{bmatrix} 1.6 & 0.4 & 0.4 \\ 0.22 & 1.18 & 0.18 \\ 0.38 & 0.22 & 1.22 \end{bmatrix}
$$

show that

$$
(I - M)^{-1}(I - M) = I.
$$

11. Use $(I - M)^{-1}$ in Problem 10 to find the output for each sector that is needed to satisfy the final demand D_1.
12. Repeat Problem 11 for D_2.

In Problems 13–16, find $(I - M)^{-1}$ and X.

13. $M = \begin{bmatrix} 0.2 & 0.2 \\ 0.3 & 0.3 \end{bmatrix}$ $D = \begin{bmatrix} 10 \\ 25 \end{bmatrix}$

14. $M = \begin{bmatrix} 0.4 & 0.1 \\ 0.2 & 0.3 \end{bmatrix}$ $D = \begin{bmatrix} 15 \\ 20 \end{bmatrix}$

C   15. $M = \begin{bmatrix} 0.3 & 0.1 & 0.3 \\ 0.2 & 0.1 & 0.2 \\ 0.1 & 0.1 & 0.1 \end{bmatrix}$ $D = \begin{bmatrix} 20 \\ 5 \\ 10 \end{bmatrix}$

16. $M = \begin{bmatrix} 0.3 & 0.2 & 0.3 \\ 0.1 & 0.1 & 0.1 \\ 0.1 & 0.2 & 0.1 \end{bmatrix}$ $D = \begin{bmatrix} 10 \\ 25 \\ 15 \end{bmatrix}$

Applications

17.   An economy is based on two industrial sectors, coal and steel. Production of a dollar's worth of coal requires an input of $0.10 from the coal sector and $0.20 from the steel sector. Production of a dollar's worth of steel requires an input of $0.20 from the coal sector and $0.40 from the steel sector. Find the output for each sector that is needed to satisfy a final demand of $20 billion for coal and $10 billion for steel.

18.   An economy is based on two sectors, transportation and manufacturing. Production of a dollar's worth of transportation requires $0.10 of input from each sector and production of a dollar's worth of manufacturing requires an input of $0.40 from each sector. Find the output for each sector that is needed to satisfy a final demand of $5 billion for transportation and $20 billion for manufacturing.

19.   An economy is based on three sectors, agriculture, manufacturing, and energy. Production of a dollar's worth of agriculture requires inputs of $0.20 from agriculture, $0.20 from manufacturing, and $0.20 from energy. Production of a dollar's worth of manufacturing requires inputs of $0.40 from agriculture, $0.10 from manufacturing, and $0.10 from energy. Production of a dollar's worth of energy requires inputs of $0.30 from agriculture, $0.10 from manufacturing, and $0.10 from energy. Find the output for each sector that is needed to satisfy a final demand of $10 billion for agriculture, $15 billion for manufacturing, and $20 billion for energy.

20.   A large energy company produces electricity, natural gas, and oil. The production of a dollar's worth of electricity requires inputs of $0.30 from electricity, $0.10 from natural gas, and $0.20 from oil. Production of a dollar's worth of natural gas requires inputs of $0.30 from electricity, $0.10 from natural gas, and $0.20 from oil. Production of a

dollar's worth of oil requires inputs of $0.10 from each sector. Find the output for each sector that is needed to satisfy a final demand of $25 billion for electricity, $15 billion for natural gas, and $20 billion for oil.

1-8 Chapter Review

Important Terms and Symbols

1-1 *Review: systems of linear equations.* Graphing method, substitution method, elimination by addition, equivalent systems, inconsistent systems, dependent systems, parameter, equilibrium price, equilibrium quantity, linear equation in two variables, linear equation in three variables, solution of a system, solution set

1-2 *Systems of linear equations and augmented matrices — introduction.* Matrix, element, augmented matrix, column, row, equivalent systems, row-equivalent matrices, row operations, $R_i \leftrightarrow R_j$, $kR_i \rightarrow R_i$, $R_i + kR_j \rightarrow R_i$

1-3 *Gauss–Jordan elimination.* Reduced matrix, leftmost variables, submatrix, Gauss–Jordan elimination

1-4 *Matrices — addition and multiplication by a number.* Size or dimension of a matrix, $m \times n$ matrix, square matrix, column matrix, row matrix, equal matrices, sum of two matrices, zero matrix, negative of a matrix M, subtraction of matrices, product of a number k and a matrix M

1-5 *Matrix multiplication.* Dot product, matrix product, associative property, distributive properties

1-6 *Inverse of a square matrix; matrix equations.* Inverse of a number, multiplicative inverse of a number, identity matrix, multiplicative inverse of a matrix, matrix equation, M^{-1}

1-7 *Leontief input–output analysis (optional).* Input–output analysis, technology matrix, final demand matrix, output matrix

Exercise 1-8 Chapter Review

Work through all the problems in this chapter review and check your answers in the back of the book. (Answers to all review problems are there.) Where weaknesses show up, review appropriate sections in the text.

A

1. Solve the following system by graphing:

$$2x - y = 4$$
$$x - 2y = -4$$

2. Solve the system in Problem 1 by substitution.

In Problems 3–11 perform the operations that are defined, given the following matrices:

$$A = \begin{bmatrix} 1 & 2 \\ 3 & 1 \end{bmatrix} \qquad B = \begin{bmatrix} 2 & 1 \\ 1 & 1 \end{bmatrix} \qquad C = \begin{bmatrix} 2 & 3 \end{bmatrix} \qquad D = \begin{bmatrix} 1 \\ 2 \end{bmatrix}$$

3. $A + B$
4. $B + D$
5. $A - 2B$
6. AB
7. AC
8. AD
9. DC
10. $C \cdot D$
11. $C + D$

12. Find the inverse of the matrix A given below by appropriate row operations on $[A \mid I]$. Show that $A^{-1}A = I$.

$$A = \begin{bmatrix} 3 & 2 \\ 4 & 3 \end{bmatrix}$$

13. Solve the following system by elimination by addition:

$$3x_1 + 2x_2 = 3$$
$$4x_1 + 3x_2 = 5$$

14. Solve the system in Problem 13 by performing appropriate row operations on the augmented matrix of the system.

15. Solve the system in Problem 13 by writing the system as a matrix equation and using the inverse of the coefficient matrix (see Problem 12). Also, solve the system if the constants 3 and 5 are replaced by 7 and 10, respectively. By 4 and 2, respectively.

B In Problems 16–21 perform the specified operations given the following matrices:

$$A = \begin{bmatrix} 2 & -2 \\ 1 & 0 \\ 3 & 2 \end{bmatrix} \qquad B = \begin{bmatrix} -1 \\ 2 \\ 3 \end{bmatrix} \qquad C = \begin{bmatrix} 2 & 1 & 3 \end{bmatrix}$$

$$D = \begin{bmatrix} 3 & -2 & 1 \\ -1 & 1 & 2 \end{bmatrix} \qquad E = \begin{bmatrix} 3 & -4 \\ -1 & 0 \end{bmatrix}$$

16. $A + D$
17. $E + DA$
18. $DA - 3E$
19. $C \cdot B$
20. CB
21. $AD - BC$

22. Find the inverse of the matrix A given below by appropriate row operations on $[A \mid I]$. Show that $A^{-1}A = I$.

$$A = \begin{bmatrix} 1 & 2 & 3 \\ 2 & 3 & 4 \\ 1 & 2 & 1 \end{bmatrix}$$

23. Solve by Gauss–Jordan elimination:

(A) $\quad x_1 + 2x_2 + 3x_3 = 1$ (B) $\quad x_1 + 2x_2 - x_3 = \quad 2$

$\qquad 2x_1 + 3x_2 + 4x_3 = 3$ $2x_1 + 3x_2 + x_3 = -3$

$\qquad \; x_1 + 2x_2 + \; x_3 = 3$ $3x_1 + 5x_2 \qquad = -1$

24. Solve the system in Problem 23A by writing the system as a matrix equation and using the inverse of the coefficient matrix (see Problem 22). Also, solve the system if the constants 1, 3, and 3 are replaced by 0, 0, and −2, respectively. By −3, −4, and 1, respectively.

C   25. Find the inverse of the matrix A given below. Show that $A^{-1}A = I$.

$$A = \begin{bmatrix} 4 & 5 & 6 \\ 4 & 5 & -6 \\ 1 & 1 & 1 \end{bmatrix}$$

26. Solve the system

$$0.04x_1 + 0.05x_2 + 0.06x_3 = \quad 360$$
$$0.04x_1 + 0.05x_2 - 0.06x_3 = \quad 120$$
$$x_1 + \quad x_2 + \quad x_3 = 7{,}000$$

by writing as a matrix equation and using the inverse of the coefficient matrix. (Before starting, multiply the first two equations by 100 to eliminate decimals. Also, see Problem 25.)

27. Solve Problem 26 by Gauss–Jordan elimination.

Applications

Business & Economics   28. *Resource allocation.* A mining company has two mines with ore compositions as given in the table. How many tons of each ore should be used to obtain 4.5 tons of nickel and 10 tons of copper? Set up a system of equations and solve using Gauss–Jordan elimination.

Ore	Nickel (%)	Copper (%)
A	1	2
B	2	5

29. (A) Set up Problem 28 as a matrix equation and solve using the inverse of the coefficient matrix.

(B) Solve Problem 28 (as in part A) if 2.3 tons of nickel and 5 tons of copper are needed.

30. *Material costs.* A metal foundry wishes to make two different bronze alloys. The quantities of copper, tin, and zinc needed are indicated in matrix M. The costs for these materials in dollars per pound from two suppliers is summarized in matrix N. The company must choose one supplier or the other.

$$M = \begin{bmatrix} \overset{\text{Copper}}{4,800 \text{ lb}} & \overset{\text{Tin}}{600 \text{ lb}} & \overset{\text{Zinc}}{300 \text{ lb}} \\ 6,000 \text{ lb} & 1,400 \text{ lb} & 700 \text{ lb} \end{bmatrix} \begin{matrix} \text{Alloy 1} \\ \text{Alloy 2} \end{matrix}$$

$$N = \begin{bmatrix} \overset{\text{Supplier } A}{\$0.75} & \overset{\text{Supplier } B}{\$0.70} \\ \$6.50 & \$6.70 \\ \$0.40 & \$0.50 \end{bmatrix} \begin{matrix} \text{Copper} \\ \text{Tin} \\ \text{Zinc} \end{matrix}$$

(A)   Find MN and interpret.   (B)   Find $[1 \quad 1]MN$ and interpret.

31. *Labor costs.* A company with manufacturing plants in California and Texas has labor-hour and wage requirements for the manufacturing of two inexpensive hand calculators as given in matrices M and N below:

Labor-Hours per Calculator

$$M = \begin{bmatrix} \overset{\underset{\text{department}}{\text{Fabricating}}}{0.15 \text{ hr}} & \overset{\underset{\text{department}}{\text{Assembly}}}{0.10 \text{ hr}} & \overset{\underset{\text{department}}{\text{Packaging}}}{0.05 \text{ hr}} \\ 0.25 \text{ hr} & 0.20 \text{ hr} & 0.05 \text{ hr} \end{bmatrix} \begin{matrix} \text{Model } A \\ \text{Model } B \end{matrix}$$

Hourly Wages

$$N = \begin{bmatrix} \overset{\underset{\text{plant}}{\text{California}}}{\$15} & \overset{\underset{\text{plant}}{\text{Texas}}}{\$12} \\ \$12 & \$10 \\ \$ 4 & \$ 4 \end{bmatrix} \begin{matrix} \text{Fabricating department} \\ \text{Assembly department} \\ \text{Packaging department} \end{matrix}$$

(A)   What is the labor cost for producing one model *B* calculator in California? Set up a dot product and multiply.

(B)   Find MN and interpret.

32. *Investment analysis.* A person has $5,000 to invest, part at 5% and the rest at 10%. How much should be invested at each rate to yield $400 per year? Set up a system of equations and solve using augmented matrix methods.

33. *Investment analysis.* Solve Problem 32 by using a matrix equation and the inverse of the coefficient matrix.

Linear Inequalities and Linear Programming

CHAPTER 2   Contents

In this chapter we will discuss linear inequalities in two and more variables; in addition, we will introduce a relatively new and powerful mathematical tool called *linear programming* that will be used to solve a variety of interesting practical problems. The row operations on matrices introduced in Chapter 1 will be particularly useful in Sections 2-4, 2-5, and 2-6.

2-1   Systems of Linear Inequalities in Two Variables

- Graphing Linear Inequalities in Two Variables
- Solving Systems of Linear Inequalities Graphically
- Special Definitions Pertaining to Solution Regions
- Application

- ### Graphing Linear Inequalities in Two Variables

Having graphed linear equations such as

$$y = -2x + 3 \quad \text{and} \quad 2x - 3y = 12$$

we now turn to **graphing linear inequalities in two variables** such as

$$y \leq -2x + 3 \quad \text{and} \quad 2x - 3y > 12$$

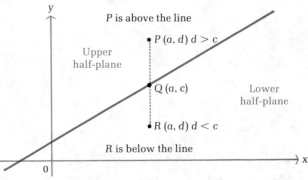

Figure 1

172

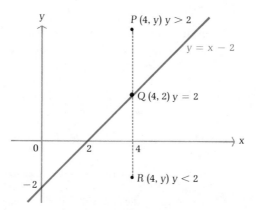

Figure 2

Graphing inequalities of this type is almost as easy as graphing equations. The following discussion leads to a simple solution of the problem.

A vertical line divides a plane into left and right *half-planes*; a nonvertical line divides a plane into **upper** and **lower half-planes** (Fig. 1).

Let us compare the graphs of

$$y < x - 2 \qquad y = x - 2 \qquad y > x - 2$$

We start by graphing $y = x - 2$ (Fig. 2). It is clear from Figure 2 that for $x = 4$, any point P above Q will satisfy $y > 2$, and any point R below Q will

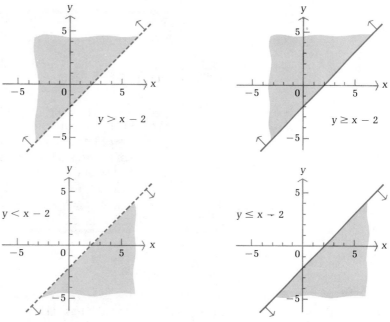

Figure 3

satisfy $y < 2$. Since the same result holds for each x, we conclude that the graph of $y > x - 2$ is the upper half-plane determined by the graph of $y = x - 2$, and $y < x - 2$ is the lower half-plane.

To graph $y > x - 2$, we show the line $y = x - 2$ as a broken line (Fig. 3), indicating that the line is not part of the graph. In graphing $y \geq x - 2$, we show the line $y = x - 2$ as a solid line, indicating that it is part of the graph. Four typical cases are illustrated in Figure 3 (on the preceding page).

The above discussion suggests the following theorem, which is stated without proof:

Theorem 1

The graph of the linear inequality

$$Ax + By < C \quad \text{or} \quad Ax + By > C$$

with $B \neq 0$ is either the upper half-plane or the lower half-plane (but not both) determined by the line $Ax + By = C$. If $B = 0$, the graph of

$$Ax < C \quad \text{or} \quad Ax > C$$

is either the left or right half-plane (but not both) as determined by the line $Ax = C$.

As a consequence of this theorem, we state a simple and fast mechanical procedure for graphing linear inequalities.

Procedure for Graphing Linear Inequalities

1. First graph $Ax + By = C$ as a broken line if equality is not included in the original statement or as a solid line if equality is included.
2. Choose a test point anywhere in the plane not on the line [the origin $(0, 0)$ often requires the least computation] and substitute the coordinates into the inequality.
3. The graph of the original inequality includes the half-plane containing the test point if the inequality is satisfied by that point or the half-plane not containing the test point if the inequality is not satisfied by that point.

Example 1   Graph $2x - 3y \leq 6$.

Solution   First graph the line $2x - 3y = 6$ as a solid line. Choose a convenient test point above or below the line. The origin $(0, 0)$ requires the least computation. So, substituting (0, 0) into the inequality, we see that $2(0) - 3(0) \leq 6$ is true. Hence, the graph of the inequality is the upper half-plane.

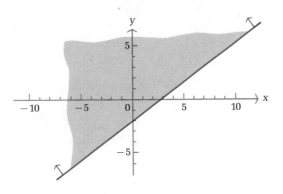

Problem 1 Graph $6x - 3y > 18$.

If you were asked to graph an inequality such as $y \leq 5$, the first question you would need to ask is "Is the graph to be done in a one- or two-dimensional coordinate system?" We have already graphed linear inequalities of this type in a one-dimensional coordinate system (see Section 0-2); now we turn to their graphs in a two-dimensional coordinate system.

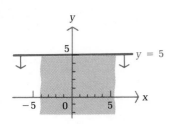

In graphing $y \leq 5$ in an xy-coordinate system, we are actually asking for the graph of all ordered pairs of real numbers (x, y) such that $0x + y \leq 5$. Since x has a zero coefficient, it can be any real number in the ordered pair (x, y) as long as y is less than or equal to 5. Conclusion? The graph is the lower half-plane determined by the line $y = 5$.

Example 2 Graph: (A) $x > -3$ (B) $-2 \leq y < 3$

Solutions   (A) $x = -3$

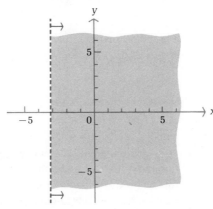

(B)   Graphing $-2 \leqslant y < 3$ in an xy-coordinate system is the same as graphing $-2 \leqslant 0x + y < 3$. Thus, x in (x, y) can be any real number as long as y is between -2 and 3, including -2 but not 3.

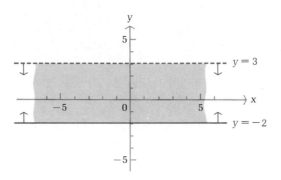

Problem 2   Graph: (A) $y < 4$ (B) $-3 < x \leqslant 3$

■ Solving Systems of Linear Inequalities Graphically

We will now consider systems of linear inequalities such as

$$x \geqslant 0 \quad \text{and} \quad 6x + 2y \leqslant 36$$
$$y \geqslant 0 \qquad\qquad 2x + 4y \leqslant 32$$
$$x \leqslant 8 \qquad\qquad\quad x \geqslant 0$$
$$y \leqslant 4 \qquad\qquad\quad y \geqslant 0$$

We wish to **solve** such systems **graphically,** that is, to find the graph of all ordered pairs of real numbers (x, y) that simultaneously satisfy all inequalities in the system. The graph is called the **solution region** for the system. To find the solution region, we graph each inequality in the system and then take the intersection of all of the graphs.

Example 3   Solve the following linear system graphically:

$$x \geqslant 0$$
$$y \geqslant 0$$
$$x \leqslant 8$$
$$y \leqslant 4$$

Solution   Graph all the inequalities in the same coordinate system and shade in the region that satisfies all four inequalities—that is, the intersection of all four graphs. The coordinates of any point in the shaded region will simultaneously satisfy all the original inequalities.

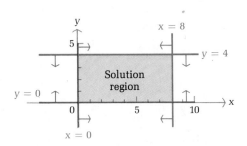

Problem 3 Solve the following linear system graphically:

$x \geqslant 2$

$x \leqslant 6$

$y \leqslant 5$

$y \geqslant 2$

Example 4 Solve the following linear system graphically:

$6x + 2y \leqslant 36$

$2x + 4y \leqslant 32$

$x \geqslant 0$

$y \geqslant 0$

Solution Graph all the inequalities in the same coordinate system and shade in the intersection of all four graphs. The coordinates of any point in the shaded region of the accompanying figure specify a solution to the system. For example, (0, 0), (3, 4), and (2.35, 3.87) are three of infinitely many solutions, as can easily be checked.

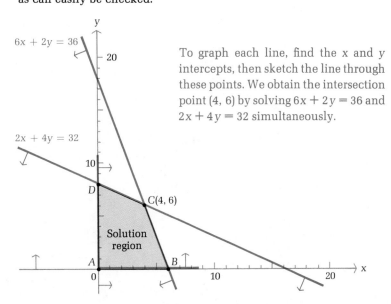

To graph each line, find the x and y intercepts, then sketch the line through these points. We obtain the intersection point (4, 6) by solving $6x + 2y = 36$ and $2x + 4y = 32$ simultaneously.

Problem 4 Solve by graphing:

$$3x + 2y \geqslant 24$$
$$x + 2y \geqslant 12$$
$$x \geqslant 0$$
$$y \geqslant 0$$

Example 5 Solve the system

$$2x + y \leqslant 20$$
$$10x + y \geqslant 36$$
$$2x + 5y \geqslant 36$$

graphically and find the coordinates of the intersection points of the boundary of the solution region.

Solution The solution region is the intersection of the graphs of the three inequalities, as shown in the figure below.

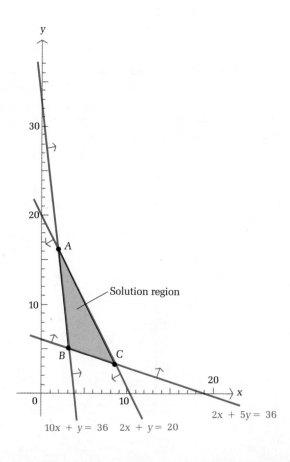

Coordinates of A   Solve the system

$$10x + y = 36$$
$$2x + y = 20$$

to obtain (2, 16).

Coordinates of B   Solve the system

$$10x +\ \ y = 36$$
$$2x + 5y = 36$$

to obtain (3, 6).

Coordinates of C   Solve the system

$$2x +\ \ y = 20$$
$$2x + 5y = 36$$

to obtain (8, 4).

Problem 5   Solve the system

$$3x + 4y \leqslant 48$$
$$x -\ \ y \leqslant 2$$
$$x \geqslant 4$$

graphically and find the coordinates of the intersection points of the boundary of the solution region.

▪ Special Definitions Pertaining to Solution Regions

The following definitions pertain to the solution regions of systems of linear inequalities such as those found in the above examples and matched problems.

1. A solution region of a system of linear inequalities in two variables is **bounded** if it can be enclosed within a circle; if it cannot be enclosed within a circle, then it is **unbounded.** (The solution regions for Examples 4 and 5 are bounded; the solution region for Problem 4 is unbounded.)
2. A **corner point** of a solution region is a point in the solution region that is the intersection of two boundary lines. [The corner points of the solution region in Example 5 are (2, 16), (3, 6), and (8, 4).]

That is enough new terminology for the moment. These definitions will be important to us in the next section. For now, let us introduce two applications that will be developed more fully as we proceed through this chapter.

■ Application

Example 6   A patient in a hospital is required to have at least 84 units of drug A and 120 units of drug B each day (assume that an overdosage of either drug is harmless). Each gram of substance M contains 10 units of drug A and 8 units of drug B, and each gram of substance N contains 2 units of drug A and 4 units of drug B. How many grams of substances M and N can be mixed to meet the minimum daily requirements?

Solution   To clarify relationships, we summarize the information in the following table:

	Amount of Drug per Gram		**Minimum Daily Requirement**
	Substance M	Substance N	
Drug A	10 units	2 units	84 units
Drug B	8 units	4 units	120 units

Let x = Number of grams of substance M used

y = Number of grams of substance N used

Then $10x$ = Number of units of drug A in x grams of substance M

$2y$ = Number of units of drug A in y grams of substance N

$8x$ = Number of units of drug B in x grams of substance M

$4y$ = Number of units of drug B in y grams of substance N

The following conditions must be satisfied to meet daily requirements:

$$\begin{pmatrix} \text{Number of units of} \\ \text{drug } A \\ \text{in } x \text{ grams of substance } M \end{pmatrix} + \begin{pmatrix} \text{Number of units of} \\ \text{drug } A \\ \text{in } y \text{ grams of substance } N \end{pmatrix} \geq 84$$

$$\begin{pmatrix} \text{Number of units of} \\ \text{drug } B \\ \text{in } x \text{ grams of substance } M \end{pmatrix} + \begin{pmatrix} \text{Number of units of} \\ \text{drug } B \\ \text{in } y \text{ grams of substance } N \end{pmatrix} \geq 120$$

$$\begin{pmatrix} \text{Number of grams of} \\ \text{substance } M \text{ used} \end{pmatrix} \geq 0$$

$$\begin{pmatrix} \text{Number of grams of} \\ \text{substance } N \text{ used} \end{pmatrix} \geq 0$$

Converting these verbal statements into symbolic statements by using the variables x and y introduced above, we obtain the system of linear inequalities

$$10x + 2y \geqslant 84 \qquad \text{Drug } A \text{ restriction}$$
$$8x + 4y \geqslant 120 \qquad \text{Drug } B \text{ restriction}$$
$$x \geqslant 0 \qquad \text{Cannot use a negative amount of } M$$
$$y \geqslant 0 \qquad \text{Cannot use a negative amount of } N$$

Graphing this system of linear inequalities, we obtain the set of **feasible solutions,** or the **feasible region,** as shown in the following figure.* Thus, any point in the shaded area (including the straight line boundaries) will meet the daily requirements; any point outside the shaded area will not. (Note that the feasible region is unbounded.)

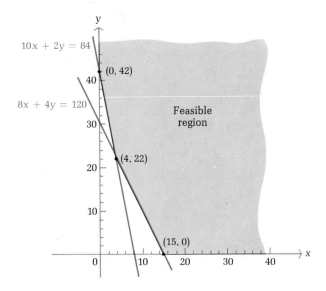

Problem 6 A manufacturing plant makes two types of inflatable boats, a two-person boat and a four-person boat. Each two-person boat requires 0.9 labor-hour in the cutting department and 0.8 labor-hour in the assembly department. Each four-person boat requires 1.8 labor-hours in the cutting department and 1.2 labor-hours in the assembly department. The maximum labor-hours available each month in the cutting and assembly departments are 864 and 672, respectively.

(A) Summarize this information in a table.

(B) If x two-person boats and y four-person boats are manufactured each month, write a system of linear inequalities that reflect the conditions indicated. Find the set of feasible solutions graphically.

* For problems of this type and for linear programming problems in general (Sections 2-2 through 2-6), solution regions are often referred to as feasible regions.

**Answers to
Matched Problems**

1. Graph $6x - 3y = 18$ as a broken line (since equality is not included). Choosing the origin $(0, 0)$ as a test point, we see that $6(0) - 3(0) > 18$ is a false statement; thus, the lower half-plane (determined by $6x - 3y = 18$) is the graph of $6x - 3y > 18$.

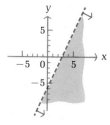

2. (A)

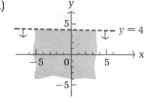

(B)

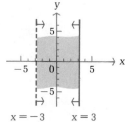

3.

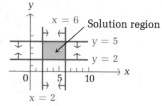

4.

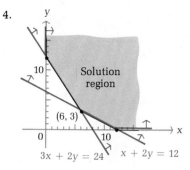

5.

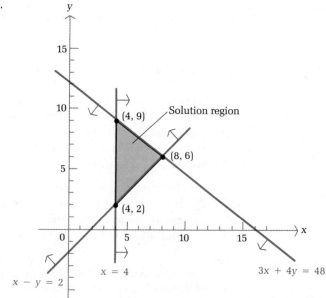

6. (A)

	Labor-Hours Required		Maximum Labor-Hours Available per Month
	Two-Person Boat	Four-Person Boat	
Cutting department	0.9	1.8	864
Assembly department	0.8	1.2	672

(B)
$$0.9x + 1.8y \leqslant 864$$
$$0.8x + 1.2y \leqslant 672$$
$$x \geqslant 0$$
$$y \geqslant 0$$

Exercise 2-1

Graph each inequality.

A
1. $y \leqslant x - 1$
2. $y > x + 1$
3. $3x - 2y > 6$
4. $2x - 5y \leqslant 10$
5. $x \geqslant -4$
6. $y < 5$
7. $-4 \leqslant y < 4$
8. $0 \leqslant x < 6$
9. $10x + 2y \geqslant 84$
10. $8x + 4y \geqslant 120$
11. $0.9x + 1.8y \leqslant 864$
12. $0.8x + 1.2y \leqslant 672$

Solve the following linear systems graphically:

13. $x \geqslant 3$
 $x \leqslant 7$
 $y \geqslant 0$
 $y \leqslant 4$

14. $x \geqslant 0$
 $x \leqslant 4$
 $y \geqslant 3$
 $y \leqslant 7$

15. $2x + 3y \leqslant 12$
 $x \geqslant 0$
 $y \geqslant 0$

16. $3x + 4y \leqslant 24$
 $x \geqslant 0$
 $y \geqslant 0$

17. $2x + y \leqslant 10$
   $x + 2y \leqslant 8$
   $x \geqslant 0$
   $y \geqslant 0$

18. $6x + 3y \leqslant 24$
   $3x + 6y \leqslant 30$
   $x \geqslant 0$
   $y \geqslant 0$

19. $2x + y \geqslant 10$
   $x + 2y \geqslant 8$
   $x \geqslant 0$
   $y \geqslant 0$

20. $4x + 3y \geqslant 24$
   $3x + 4y \geqslant 8$
   $x \geqslant 0$
   $y \geqslant 0$

B   Solve the following systems graphically and indicate whether each solution set is bounded or unbounded. Find the coordinates of each corner point.

21. $2x + y \leqslant 10$
   $x + y \leqslant 7$
   $x + 2y \leqslant 12$
   $x \geqslant 0$
   $y \geqslant 0$

22. $3x + y \leqslant 21$
   $x + y \leqslant 9$
   $x + 3y \leqslant 21$
   $x \geqslant 0$
   $y \geqslant 0$

23. $2x + y \geqslant 16$
   $x + y \geqslant 12$
   $x + 2y \geqslant 14$
   $x \geqslant 0$
   $y \geqslant 0$

24. $3x + y \geqslant 24$
   $x + y \geqslant 16$
   $x + 3y \geqslant 30$
   $x \geqslant 0$
   $y \geqslant 0$

25. $x + 4y \leqslant 32$
   $3x + y \leqslant 30$
   $4x + 5y > 51$

26. $x + y < 11$
   $x + 5y \geqslant 15$
   $2x + y \geqslant 12$

27. $4x + 3y < 48$
   $2x + y \geqslant 24$
   $x < 9$

28. $2x + 3y > 24$
   $x + 3y < 15$
   $y > 4$

29. $x - y \leqslant 0$
   $2x - y \leqslant 4$
   $0 \leqslant x \leqslant 8$

30. $2x + 3y \geqslant 12$
   $-x + 3y \leqslant 3$
   $0 \leqslant y \leqslant 5$

C   Solve the following systems graphically and indicate whether each solution set is bounded or unbounded. Find the coordinates of each corner point.

31. $-x + 3y \geqslant 1$
   $5x - y \geqslant 9$
   $x + y \leqslant 9$
   $x \leqslant 5$

32. $x + y \leqslant 10$
   $5x + 3y \geqslant 15$
   $-2x + 3y \leqslant 15$
   $2x - 5y \leqslant 6$

33. $0.6x + 1.2y \leq 960$
$0.03x + 0.04y \leq 36$
$0.3x + 0.2y \leq 270$
$x \geq 0$
$y \geq 0$

34. $1.8x + 0.9y \geq 270$
$0.3x + 0.2y \geq 54$
$0.01x + 0.03y \geq 3.9$
$x \geq 0$
$y \geq 0$

Applications

Business & Economics

35. *Manufacturing—resource allocation.* A manufacturing company makes two types of water skis, a trick ski and a slalom ski. The trick ski requires 6 labor-hours for fabricating and 1 labor-hour for finishing. The slalom ski requires 4 labor-hours for fabricating and 1 labor-hour for finishing. The maximum labor-hours available per day for fabricating and finishing are 108 and 24, respectively. If x is the number of trick skis and y is the number of slalom skis produced per day, write a system of inequalities that indicates appropriate restraints on x and y. Find the set of feasible solutions graphically for the number of each type of ski that can be produced.

Life Sciences

36. *Nutrition.* A dietitian in a hospital is to arrange a special diet using two foods. Each ounce of food M contains 30 units of calcium, 10 units of iron, and 10 units of vitamin A. Each ounce of food N contains 10 units of calcium, 10 units of iron, and 30 units of vitamin A. The minimum requirements in the diet are 360 units of calcium, 160 units of iron, and 240 units of vitamin A. If x is the number of ounces of food M used and y is the number of ounces of food N used, write a system of linear inequalities that reflects the conditions indicated above. Find the set of feasible solutions graphically for the amount of each kind of food that can be used.

Social Sciences

37. *Psychology.* In an experiment on conditioning, a psychologist uses two types of Skinner (conditioning) boxes with mice and rats. Each mouse spends 10 minutes per day in box A and 20 minutes per day in box B. Each rat spends 20 minutes per day in box A and 10 minutes per day in box B. The total maximum time available per day is 800 minutes for box A and 640 minutes for box B. We are interested in the various numbers of mice and rats that can be used in the experiment under the conditions stated. If we let x be the number of mice used and y the number of rats used, write a system of inequalities that indicates appropriate restrictions on x and y. Find the set of feasible solutions graphically.

2-2   Linear Programming in Two Dimensions—A Geometric Approach

- A Linear Programming Problem
- Linear Programming—A General Description
- Geometric Solution of Linear Programming Problems
- Application

Several problems in the last section are related to a more general type of problem—a *linear programming problem*. Linear programming is a mathematical process that has been developed to help management in decision-making, and it has become one of the most widely used and best-known tools of management science. We will introduce this topic by considering an example in detail, using an intuitive geometric approach. Insight gained from this approach will prove invaluable when we later consider an algebraic approach that is less intuitive but necessary in solving most real-world problems.

Notation Change

For efficiency of generalization in later sections, we will now change variable notation from letters such as x and y to subscript forms such as x_1 and x_2.

A Linear Programming Problem

Example 7   A manufacturer of lightweight mountain tents makes a standard model and an expedition model. Each standard tent requires 1 labor-hour from the cutting department and 3 labor-hours from the assembly department. Each expedition tent requires 2 labor-hours from the cutting department and 4 labor-hours from the assembly department. The maximum labor-hours available per week in the cutting department and the assembly department are 32 and 84, respectively. In addition, the distributor, because of demand, will not take more than 12 expedition tents per week. If the company makes a profit of $50 on each standard tent and $80 on each expedition tent, how many tents of each type should be manufactured each week to maximize the total weekly profit?

Solution   This is an example of a *linear programming problem*. To see relationships more clearly, let us summarize the manufacturing requirements, objectives, and restrictions in table form (see Table 1 on the next page).

In addition, as stated above, the weekly production of expedition tents cannot exceed 12.

Table 1

	Labor-Hours per Tent		Maximum Labor-Hours Available per Week
	Standard Model	Expedition Model	
Cutting department	1	2	32
Assembly department	3	4	84
Profit per tent	$50	$80	

We now proceed to formulate a mathematical model for the problem and then to solve it by using geometric methods.

Objective Function

The *objective* of management is to *decide* how many of each tent model should be produced each week so as to maximize profit. Let

x_1 = Number of standard tents produced per week

x_2 = Number of expedition tents produced per week

} Decision variables

The following equation gives the total profit for x_1 standard tents and x_2 expedition tents manufactured each week, assuming all tents manufactured are sold:

$$P = 50x_1 + 80x_2 \quad \text{Objective function}$$

Mathematically, the management needs to decide on values for the **decision variables** (x_1, x_2) that achieve its objective, that is, maximizing the **objective function** (profit) $P = 50x_1 + 80x_2$. It appears that the profit can be made as large as we like by manufacturing more and more tents—or can it?

Constraints

Any manufacturing company, no matter how large or small, has manufacturing limits imposed by available resources, plant capacity, demand, and so forth. These limits are referred to as **problem constraints.**

Cutting department constraint:

$$\begin{pmatrix} \text{Weekly cutting} \\ \text{time for } x_1 \\ \text{standard tents} \end{pmatrix} + \begin{pmatrix} \text{Weekly cutting} \\ \text{time for } x_2 \\ \text{expedition tents} \end{pmatrix} \leq \begin{pmatrix} \text{Maximum labor-} \\ \text{hours available} \\ \text{per week} \end{pmatrix}$$

$$1x_1 \quad + \quad 2x_2 \quad \leq \quad 32$$

Assembly department constraint:

$$\begin{pmatrix} \text{Weekly assembly} \\ \text{time for } x_1 \\ \text{standard tents} \end{pmatrix} + \begin{pmatrix} \text{Weekly assembly} \\ \text{time for } x_2 \\ \text{expedition tents} \end{pmatrix} \leq \begin{pmatrix} \text{Maximum labor-} \\ \text{hours available} \\ \text{per week} \end{pmatrix}$$

$$3x_1 \quad + \quad 4x_2 \quad \leq \quad 84$$

Demand constraints. The distributor will not take more than 12 expedition tents per week; thus,

$$x_2 \leqslant 12$$

Nonnegative constraints. It is not possible to manufacture a negative number of tents; thus, we have the **nonnegative constraints**

$$x_1 \geqslant 0$$
$$x_2 \geqslant 0$$

which we usually write in the form

$$x_1, x_2 \geqslant 0$$

Mathematical Model   We now have a **mathematical model** for the problem under consideration:

Maximize	$P = 50x_1 + 80x_2$	Objective function
Subject to	$x_1 + 2x_2 \leqslant 32$	
	$3x_1 + 4x_2 \leqslant 84$	Problem constraints
	$x_2 \leqslant 12$	
	$x_1, x_2 \geqslant 0$	Nonnegative constraints

Graphical Solution   **Solving** the set of linear inequality constraints **graphically** (see the last section), we obtain the feasible region for production schedules (Fig. 4).

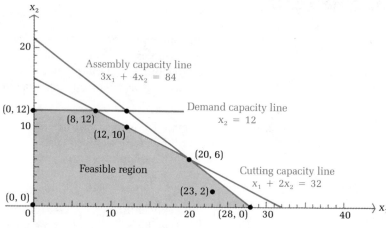

Figure 4

By choosing a production schedule (x_1, x_2) from the feasible region, a profit can be determined using the objective function

$$P = 50x_1 + 80x_2$$

For example, if $x_1 = 12$ and $x_2 = 10$, then the profit for the week would be

$$P = 50(12) + 80(10)$$
$$= \$1,400$$

Or if $x_1 = 23$ and $x_2 = 2$, then the profit for the week would be

$$P = 50(23) + 80(2)$$
$$= \$1{,}310$$

The question is, out of all possible production schedules (x_1, x_2) from the feasible region, which schedule(s) produces the maximum profit? Thus, we have a **maximization problem.** Since point-by-point checking is impossible (there are infinitely many points to check), we must find another way.

By assigning P in

$$P = 50x_1 + 80x_2$$

a particular value and plotting the resulting equation in Figure 4, we obtain a **constant-profit line (isoprofit line).** Every point in the feasible region on this line represents a production schedule that will produce the same profit. By doing this for a number of values for P, we obtain a family of constant-profit lines (Fig. 5) that are parallel to each other, since they all have the same slope. To see that they all have the same slope, we write $P = 50x_1 + 80x_2$ in the slope–intercept form

$$x_2 = -\frac{5}{8} x_1 + \frac{P}{80}$$

and note that for any profit P, the constant-profit line has slope $-\frac{5}{8}$. We also observe that as the profit P increases, the x_2 intercept $(P/80)$ increases, and the line moves away from the origin.

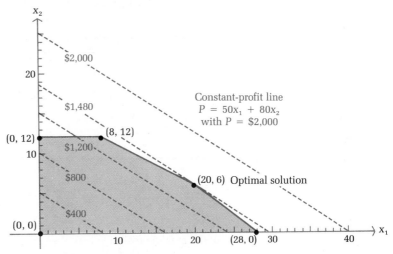

Figure 5 Constant-profit lines

Thus, the maximum profit occurs at a point where a constant-profit line is the farthest from the origin but still in contact with the feasible region. In this example, this occurs at (20, 6), as is seen in Figure 5. Thus, if the manufacturer makes 20 standard tents and 6 expedition tents per week, the profit will be maximized at

$$P = 50(20) + 80(6)$$
$$= \$1{,}480$$

The point (20, 6) is called an **optimal solution** to the problem, because it maximizes the objective (profit) function and is in the feasible region. In general, it appears that a maximum profit occurs at one of the corner points. We also note that the minimum profit ($P = 0$) occurs at the corner point (0, 0).

Problem 7   We now convert the boat problem in the preceding section (Problem 6) into a linear programming problem. A manufacturing plant makes two types of inflatable boats, a two-person boat and a four-person boat. Each boat requires the services of two departments as listed in the table. In addition, the distributor will not take more that 750 two-person boats each month. Management wants to determine a production schedule that will maximize the monthly profit.

(A)   Identify the decision variables.
(B)   Write the objective function P.
(C)   Write the problem constraints and the nonnegative constraints.
(D)   Graph the feasible region. Include graphs of the objective function for $P = 5{,}000$, $P = 10{,}000$, $P = 15{,}000$, and $P = 21{,}600$.
(E)   How many boats of each type should be manufactured each month to maximize the profit? What is the maximum profit?

	Labor-Hours Required		Maximum Labor-Hours Available per Month
	Two-Person Boat	Four-Person Boat	
Cutting department	0.9	1.8	864
Assembly department	0.8	1.2	672
Profit per boat	$25	$40	

▪ Linear Programming—A General Description

In Example 7 and Problem 7, the optimal solution occurs at a corner point of the feasible region. Is this always the case? The answer is a qualified yes, as will be seen in the important theorem stated below. First, we state a few general definitions.

A **linear programming problem** is one that is concerned with finding the maximum or minimum value of a linear **objective function** of the form

$$z = c_1 x_1 + c_2 x_2 + \cdots + c_n x_n$$

where the **decision variables** $x_1, x_2, \ldots, x_n$ are subject to **problem constraints** in the form of linear inequalities and equations. In addition, the decision variables must satisfy the **nonnegative constraints** $x_i \geqslant 0$, $i = 1, 2, \ldots, n$. The set of points satisfying both the problem constraints and the nonnegative constraints is called the **feasible region** for the problem.

Theorem 2

> **Fundamental Theorem of Linear Programming**
>
> If a linear programming problem has an optimal solution, then this solution must occur at one (or more) of the corner points of the feasible region.

Theorem 2 provides a simple procedure for solving a linear programming problem, *provided the problem has a solution—but not all do*. In order to use Theorem 2, we must know that the problem under consideration has a solution. Theorem 3 provides some conditions that will insure that a linear programming has a solution.

Theorem 3

> **Existence of Solutions**
>
> Given a linear programming problem with feasible region S and objective function $z = ax_1 + bx_2$:
>
> (A) If S is bounded, then z has both a maximum and a minimum value on S. That is, both
>
> > maximize z over S
>
> and
>
> > minimize z over S
>
> have solutions.
>
> (B) If S is unbounded and $a > 0$ and $b > 0$, then z has a minimum value over S, but no maximum value over S. That is,
>
> > minimize z over S
>
> has a solution, but
>
> > maximize z over S
>
> has no solution.
>
> (C) If S is the empty set (that is, there are no points that satisfy all the constraints), then z has neither a maximum value nor a minimum value over S.

Theorem 3 does not cover all possibilities. For example, what happens if S is unbounded and one (or both) of the coefficients of the objective function are negative? Problems of this type require special techniques which we will not discuss. Since virtually all applied problems satisfy one of the conditions listed in Theorem 3, we will only consider problems of this type.

■ Geometric Solution of Linear Programming Problems

The discussion above leads to the following procedure for solving linear programming problems geometrically.

Geometrical Solution of a Linear Programming Problem

1. Form a mathematical model for the problem:
    (A) Introduce decision variables and write a linear objective function.
    (B) Write problem constraints using linear inequalities and/or equations.
    (C) Write nonnegative constraints.
2. Graph the feasible region and find the corner points.
3. Use Theorem 3 to determine if an optimal solution exists.
4. If an optimal solution exists, evaluate the objective function at each corner point to determine the optimal solution.

Before we consider additional applications, let us use this procedure to solve some linear programming problems where the model has already been determined.

Example 8

(A) Minimize and maximize

$$z = 3x_1 + x_2$$

Subject to

$$2x_1 + x_2 \leq 20$$
$$10x_1 + x_2 \geq 36$$
$$2x_1 + 5x_2 \geq 36$$
$$x_1, x_2 \geq 0$$

(B) Minimize and maximize

$$z = 10x_1 + 20x_2$$

Subject to

$$6x_1 + 2x_2 \geq 36$$
$$2x_1 + 4x_2 \geq 32$$
$$x_2 \leq 20$$
$$x_1, x_2 \geq 0$$

Solution

(A) Graph the feasible region S.

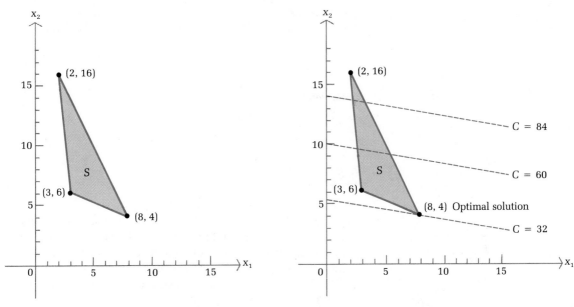

Since S is bounded, z will have both a maximum and a minimum on S [Theorem 3(A)] and these will both occur at corner points (Theorem 2).

Corner Point

(x_1, x_2)	$P = 3x_1 + x_2$	
(3, 6)	15	Minimum value of z
(2, 16)	22	
(8, 4)	28	Maximum value of z

Examining the values in the table, we see that the minimum value of z is 15 at (3, 6) and the maximum value of z is 28 at (8, 4).

(B) Graph the feasible set S.

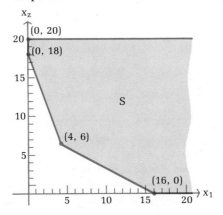

Since S is unbounded and the coefficients of the objective function are positive, z has a minimum value on S but no maximum value [Theorem 3(B)].

Corner Point	
(x_1, x_2)	$z = 10x_1 + 20x_2$
(0,20)	400
(0,18)	360
(4, 6)	160
(16, 0)	160

$\begin{cases} \text{Multiple optimal} \\ \text{solution} \end{cases}$

Thus, the minimum value of z is 160 at (4, 6) and at (16, 0). This is a **multiple optimal solution.** In general, *if two corner points are both optimal solutions to a linear programming problem, then any point on the line segment joining them is also an optimal solution.* This is the only time that optimal solutions also occur at noncorner points.

Problem 8 (A) Maximize and minimize $z = 4x_1 + 2x_2$ subject to the constraints in Example 8(A).

(B) Maximize and minimize $z = 20x_1 + 5x_2$ subject to the constraints in Example 8(B).

For an illustration of Theorem 3(C), consider the following:

Maximize $P = 2x_1 + 3x_2$

Subject to $x_1 + x_2 \geqslant 8$
$x_1 + 2x_2 \leqslant 8$
$2x_1 + x_2 \leqslant 10$
$x_1, x_2 \geqslant 0$

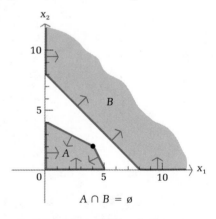

$A \cap B = \emptyset$

The intersection of the graphs of the constraint inequalities is the empty set; hence, the feasible region is empty. If this happens, then the problem should be reexamined to see if it has been formulated properly. If it has, then the management may have to reconsider items such as labor-hours, overtime, budget, and supplies allocated to the project in order to obtain a nonempty feasible region and a solution to the original problem.

■ Application

Example 9

We now convert the drug example in the preceding section (Example 6) into a linear programming problem. A patient in a hospital is required to have at least 84 units of drug D_1 and 120 units of drug D_2 each day. Two substances M and N contain each of these drugs; however, in addition, suppose both M and N contain an undesirable drug D_3. The relevant information is contained in the table. How many grams each of substances M and N should be mixed to meet the minimum daily requirement and at the same time minimize the intake of drug D_3? How many units of the undesirable drug D_3 will be in this mixture?

	Amount of Drug per Gram		Minimum Daily Requirement
	Substance M	Substance N	
Drug D_1	10 units	2 units	84 units
Drug D_2	8 units	4 units	120 units
Drug D_3	3 units	1 unit	

Solution

Let $x_1 =$ Number of grams of substance M used

$x_2 =$ Number of grams of substance N used

⎫ Decision variables ⎬ ⎭

We form the linear objective function

$$C = 3x_1 + x_2$$

which gives the amount of the undesirable drug D_3 in x_1 grams of M and x_2 grams of N. Proceeding as in Example 7, we formulate the following mathematical model for the problem:

Minimize	$C = 3x_1 + x_2$	Objective function
Subject to	$10x_1 + 2x_2 \geq 84$	Drug D_1 constraint
	$8x_1 + 4x_2 \geq 120$	Drug D_2 constraint
	$x_1, x_2 \geq 0$	Nonnegative constraints

Solving the system of constraint inequalities graphically, we obtain the feasible region shown in Figure 6 on the next page. Since the feasible region is unbounded and the coefficients of the objective function are positive, this minimization problem has a solution.

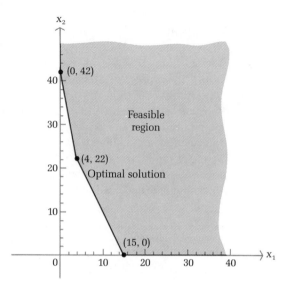

Figure 6

Corner Point

(x_1, x_2)	$C = 3x_1 + x_2$
(0, 42)	42
(4, 22)	34
(15, 0)	45

The optimal solution is $C = 34$ at the corner point (4, 22). Thus, if we use 4 grams of substance M and 22 grams of substance N, we shall supply the minimum daily requirements for drugs D_1 and D_2 and minimize the intake of undesirable drug D_3 at 34 units. Any other combination of M and N from the feasible region will result in a larger amount of the undesirable drug D_3.

Problem 9   A chicken farmer can buy a special food mix A at 20¢ per pound and a special food mix B at 40¢ per pound. Each pound of mix A contains 3,000 units of nutrient N_1 and 1,000 units of nutrient N_2; each pound of mix B contains 4,000 units of nutrient N_1 and 4,000 units of nutrient N_2. If the minimum daily requirements for the chickens collectively are 36,000 units of nutrient N_1 and 20,000 units of nutrient N_2, how many pounds of each food mix should be used each day to minimize daily food costs while meeting (or exceeding) the minimum daily nutrient requirements? What is the minimum daily cost?

Answers to Matched Problems

7. (A) x_1 = Number of two-person boats produced each month
        x_2 = Number of four-person boats produced each month
   (B) $P = 25x_1 + 40x_2$

(C) $0.9x_1 + 1.8x_2 \leqslant 864$
$0.8x_1 + 1.2x_2 \leqslant 672$
$x_1 \qquad\qquad \leqslant 750$
$x_1, x_2 \geqslant 0$

(D)

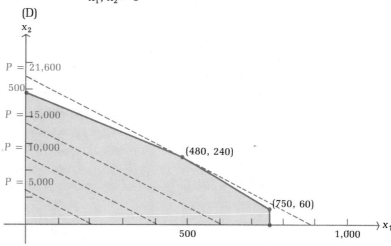

(E) 480 two-person boats, 240 four-person boats; Max $P = \$21,600$ per month

8. (A) Min $z = 24$ at $(3, 6)$; Max $z = 40$ at $(2, 16)$ and $(8, 4)$ (multiple optimal solution)

(B) Min $z = 90$ at $(0, 18)$; no maximum value

9. 8 pounds of mix A, 3 pounds of mix B; Min $C = \$2.80$ per day

Exercise 2-2

A *Solve the following linear programming problems:*

1. Maximize $P = 5x_1 + 5x_2$
Subject to $2x_1 + x_2 \leqslant 10$
$x_1 + 2x_2 \leqslant 8$
$x_1, x_2 \geqslant 0$

2. Maximize $P = 3x_1 + 2x_2$
Subject to $6x_1 + 3x_2 \leqslant 24$
$3x_1 + 6x_2 \leqslant 30$
$x_1, x_2 \geqslant 0$

3. Minimize and maximize
$z = 2x_1 + 3x_2$
Subject to $2x_1 + x_2 \geqslant 10$
$x_1 + 2x_2 \geqslant 8$
$x_1, x_2 \geqslant 0$

4. Minimize and maximize
$z = 8x_1 + 7x_2$
Subject to $4x_1 + 3x_2 \geqslant 24$
$3x_1 + 4x_2 \geqslant 8$
$x_1, x_2 \geqslant 0$

B

5. Maximize $P = 30x_1 + 40x_2$
    Subject to
    $$2x_1 + x_2 \leq 10$$
    $$x_1 + x_2 \leq 7$$
    $$x_1 + 2x_2 \leq 12$$
    $$x_1, x_2 \geq 0$$

6. Maximize $P = 20x_1 + 10x_2$
    Subject to
    $$3x_1 + x_2 \leq 21$$
    $$x_1 + x_2 \leq 9$$
    $$x_1 + 3x_2 \leq 21$$
    $$x_1, x_2 \geq 0$$

7. Minimize and maximize
    $$z = 10x_1 + 30x_2$$
    Subject to
    $$2x_1 + x_2 \geq 16$$
    $$x_1 + x_2 \geq 12$$
    $$x_1 + 2x_2 \geq 14$$
    $$x_1, x_2 \geq 0$$

8. Minimize and maximize
    $$z = 400x_1 + 100x_2$$
    Subject to
    $$3x_1 + x_2 \geq 24$$
    $$x_1 + x_2 \geq 16$$
    $$x_1 + 3x_2 \geq 30$$
    $$x_1, x_2 \geq 0$$

9. Minimize and maximize
    $$P = 30x_1 + 10x_2$$
    Subject to
    $$2x_1 + 2x_2 \geq 4$$
    $$6x_1 + 4x_2 \leq 36$$
    $$2x_1 + x_2 \leq 10$$
    $$x_1, x_2 \geq 0$$

10. Minimize and maximize
    $$P = 2x_1 + x_2$$
    Subject to
    $$x_1 + x_2 \geq 2$$
    $$6x_1 + 4x_2 \leq 36$$
    $$4x_1 + 2x_2 \leq 20$$
    $$x_1, x_2 \geq 0$$

11. Minimize and maximize
    $$P = 3x_1 + 5x_2$$
    Subject to
    $$x_1 + 2x_2 \leq 6$$
    $$x_1 + x_2 \leq 4$$
    $$2x_1 + 3x_2 \geq 12$$
    $$x_1, x_2 \geq 0$$

12. Minimize and maximize
    $$P = -x_1 + 3x_2$$
    Subject to
    $$2x_1 - x_2 \geq 4$$
    $$-x_1 + 2x_2 \leq 4$$
    $$x_2 \leq 6$$
    $$x_1, x_2 \geq 0$$

13. Minimize and maximize
    $$P = 20x_1 + 10x_2$$
    Subject to
    $$2x_1 + 3x_2 \geq 30$$
    $$2x_1 + x_2 \leq 26$$
    $$-2x_1 + 5x_2 \leq 34$$
    $$x_1, x_2 \geq 0$$

14. Minimize and maximize
    $$P = 12x_1 + 14x_2$$
    Subject to
    $$-2x_1 + x_2 \geq 6$$
    $$x_1 + x_2 \leq 15$$
    $$3x_1 - x_2 \geq 0$$
    $$x_1, x_2 \geq 0$$

15. Maximize $P = 20x_1 + 30x_2$
Subject to $0.6x_1 + 1.2x_2 \leqslant 960$
$0.03x_1 + 0.04x_2 \leqslant 36$
$0.3x_1 + 0.2x_2 \leqslant 270$
$x_1, x_2 \geqslant 0$

16. Minimize $C = 30x_1 + 10x_2$
Subject to $1.8x_1 + 0.9x_2 \geqslant 270$
$0.3x_1 + 0.2x_2 \geqslant 54$
$0.01x_1 + 0.03x_2 \geqslant 3.9$
$x_1, x_2 \geqslant 0$

C **17.** The corner points for the bounded feasible region determined by the system of inequalities

$$x_1 + 2x_2 \leqslant 10$$
$$3x_1 + x_2 \leqslant 15$$
$$x_1, x_2 \geqslant 0$$

are $O = (0, 0)$, $A = (0, 5)$, $B = (4, 3)$, and $C = (5, 0)$. If $P = ax_1 + bx_2$ and $a, b > 0$, determine conditions on a and b which will ensure that the maximum value of P occurs:

(A) Only at A (B) Only at B (C) Only at C
(D) At both A and B (E) At both B and C

18. The corner points for the feasible region determined by the system of inequalities

$$x_1 + 4x_2 \geqslant 30$$
$$3x_1 + x_2 \geqslant 24$$
$$x_1, x_2 \geqslant 0$$

are $A = (0, 24)$, $B = (6, 6)$, and $D = (30, 0)$. If $C = ax_1 + bx_2$ and $a, b > 0$, determine conditions on a and b which will ensure that the minimum value of C occurs:

(A) Only at A (B) Only at B (C) Only at D
(D) At both A and B (E) At both B and D

Applications

Business & Economics

19. *Manufacturing — resource allocation.* A manufacturing company makes two types of water skis, a trick ski and a slalom ski. The relevant manufacturing data are given in the table on the next page. How many of each type of ski should be manufactured each day to realize a maximum profit? What is the maximum profit?

	Labor-Hours per Ski		Maximum Labor-Hours Available per Day
	Trick Ski	Slalom Ski	
Fabricating department	6	4	108
Finishing department	1	1	24
Profit per ski	$40	$30	

20. *Manufacturing — resource allocation.* A furniture manufacturing company manufactures dining room tables and chairs. The relevant manufacturing data are given in the accompanying table.

(A) How many tables and chairs should be manufactured each day to realize a maximum profit? What is the maximum profit?

(B) Repeat part A if the marketing department of the company has decided that the number of chairs produced should be at least four times the number of tables produced.

	Labor-Hours per Unit		Maximum Labor-Hours Available per Day
	Table	Chair	
Assembly department	8	2	400
Finishing department	2	1	120
Profit per unit	$90	$25	

21. *Manufacturing — production scheduling.* A furniture company has two plants that produce the lumber used in manufacturing tables and chairs. In one day of operation, Plant A can produce the lumber required to manufacture 20 tables and 60 chairs and Plant B can produce the lumber required to manufacture 25 tables and 50 chairs. The company needs enough lumber to manufacture at least 200 tables and 500 chairs.

(A) If it costs $1,000 to operate Plant A for one day and $900 to operate Plant B for one day, how many days should each plant be operated in order to produce a sufficient amount of lumber at a minimum cost? What is the minimum cost?

(B) Repeat part A if the daily cost of operating Plant A is reduced to $600.

(C) Repeat part A if the daily cost of operating Plant B is reduced to $800.

22. *Manufacturing — resource allocation.* An electronics firm manufactures two types of personal computers, a standard model and a porta-

ble model. The production of a standard computer requires a capital expenditure of $400 and 40 hours of labor. The production of a portable computer requires a capital expenditure of $250 and 30 hours of labor. The firm has $20,000 capital and 2,160 labor-hours available for production of standard and portable computers.

(A) What is maximum number of computers the company is capable of producing?

(B) If each standard computer contributes a profit of $320 and each portable computer contributes a profit of $220, how many of each type of computer should the firm produce in order to maximize profit? What is the maximum profit?

23. *Transportation.* The officers of a high school senior class are planning to rent buses and vans for a class trip. Each bus can transport 40 students, requires 3 chaperones, and costs $1,200 to rent. Each van can transport 8 students, requires 1 chaperone, and costs $100 to rent. Since there are 400 students in the senior class that may be eligible to go on the trip, the officers must plan to accommodate at least 400 students. Since only 36 parents have volunteered to serve as chaperones, the officers must plan to use at most 36 chaperones. How many vehicles of each type should the officers rent in order to minimize the transportation costs? What are the minimal transportation costs?

24. *Investment.* An investor has $24,000 to invest in bonds of AAA and B qualities. The AAA bonds yield on the average 6% and the B bonds yield 10%. The investor's policy requires that she invest at least three times as much money in AAA bonds as in B bonds. How much should she invest in each type of bond to maximize her return? What is the maximum return?

25. *Pollution control.* Because of new federal regulations on pollution, a chemical plant introduced a new, more expensive process to supplement or replace an older process used in the production of a particular chemical. The older process emitted 15 grams of sulfur dioxide and 40 grams of particulate matter into the atmosphere for each gallon of chemical produced. The new process emits 5 grams of sulfur dioxide and 20 grams of particulate matter for each gallon produced. The company makes a profit of 30¢ per gallon and 20¢ per gallon on the old and new processes, respectively. If the government allows the plant to emit no more than 10,500 grams of sulfur dioxide and no more than 30,000 grams of particulate matter daily, how many gallons of the chemical should be produced by each process to maximize daily profit? What is the maximum profit?

26. *Capital expansion.* A fast food chain plans to expand by opening several new restaurants. The chain operates two types of restaurants, drive-through and full-service. A drive-through restaurant costs $100,000 to construct, requires 5 employees, and has an expected

annual revenue of $200,000. A full-service restaurant costs $150,000 to construct, requires 15 employees, and has an expected annual revenue of $500,000. The chain has $2,400,000 in capital available for expansion. Labor contracts require that they hire no more than 210 employees and licensing restrictions require that they open no more than 20 new restaurants. How many restaurants of each type should the chain open in order to maximize the expected revenue? What is the maximum expected revenue? How much of their capital will they use and how many employees will they hire?

Life Sciences

27. *Nutrition — plants.* A fruit grower can use two types of fertilizer in his orange grove, Brand *A* and Brand *B*. The amounts (in pounds) of nitrogen, phosphoric acid, and chlorine in a bag of each brand are given in the accompanying table. Tests indicate that the grove needs at least 1,000 pounds of phosphoric acid and at most 400 pounds of chlorine.

(A) If the grower wants to maximize the amount of nitrogen added to the grove, how many bags of each mix should be used? How much nitrogen will be added?

(B) If the grower wants to minimize the amount of nitrogen added to the grove, how many bags of each mix should be used? How much nitrogen will be added?

| | **Pounds per Bag** | |
	Brand *A*	Brand *B*
Nitrogen	8	3
Phosphoric acid	4	4
Chlorine	2	1

28. *Nutrition — people.* A dietitian in a hospital is to arrange a special diet composed of two foods, *M* and *N*. Each ounce of food *M* contains 30 units of calcium, 10 units of iron, 10 units of vitamin A, and 8 units of cholesterol. Each ounce of food *N* contains 10 units of calcium, 10 units of iron, 30 units of vitamin A, and 4 units of cholesterol. If the minimum daily requirements are 360 units of calcium, 160 units of iron, and 240 units of vitamin A, how many ounces of each food should be used to meet the minimum requirements and at the same time minimize the cholesterol intake? What is the minimum cholesterol intake?

29. *Nutrition — plants.* A farmer can buy two types of plant food, mix *A* and mix *B*. Each cubic yard of mix *A* contains 20 pounds of phosphoric acid, 30 pounds of nitrogen, and 5 pounds of potash. Each cubic yard of mix *B* contains 10 pounds of phosphoric acid, 30 pounds of nitrogen, and 10 pounds of potash. The minimum monthly requirements are 460 pounds of phosphoric acid, 960 pounds of nitrogen, and 220 pounds of potash. If mix *A* costs $30 per cubic yard and mix *B* costs $35

per cubic yard, how many cubic yards of each mix should the farmer blend to meet the minimum monthly requirements at a minimal cost? What is this cost?

30. *Nutrition—animals.* A laboratory technician in a medical research center is asked to formulate a diet from two commercially packaged foods, food A and food B, for a group of animals. Each ounce of food A contains 8 units of fat, 16 units of carbohydrate, and 2 units of protein. Each ounce of food B contains 4 units of fat, 32 units of carbohydrate, and 8 units of protein. The minimum daily requirements are 176 units of fat, 1,024 units of carbohydrate, and 384 units of protein. If food A costs 5¢ per ounce and food B costs 5¢ per ounce, how many ounces of each food should be used to meet the minimum daily requirements at the least cost? What is the cost for this amount of food?

Social Sciences

31. *Psychology.* In an experiment on conditioning, a psychologist uses two types of Skinner boxes with mice and rats. The amount of time in minutes each mouse and each rat spends in each box per day is given in the table. What is the maximum number of mice and rats that can be used in this experiment? How many mice and how many rats produce this maximum?

	Time		Maximum Time Available per Day
	Mice	Rats	
Skinner box A	10 min	20 min	800 min
Skinner box B	20 min	10 min	640 min

32. *Sociology.* A city council voted to conduct a study on inner-city community problems. A nearby university was contacted to provide sociologists and research assistants. Allocation of time and costs per week are given in the accompanying table. How many sociologists and how many research assistants should be hired to minimize the cost and meet the weekly labor-hour requirements? What is the minimum weekly cost?

	Labor-Hours		Minimum Labor-Hours Needed per Week
	Sociologist	Research Assistant	
Fieldwork	10	30	180
Research center	30	10	140
Costs per week	$500	$300	

2-3 A Geometric Introduction to the Simplex Method

- Slack Variables
- Basic Feasible Solutions
- Basic Feasible Solutions and the Simplex Method

The geometric method of solving linear programming problems provided us with an overview of the subject and some useful terminology. But, practically speaking, the method is only useful for problems involving two decision variables and relatively few problem constraints. What happens when we need more decision variables or have many problem constraints? We use an algebraic approach called the *simplex method*. Using matrix methods and row operations, the simplex method is readily adapted to computer computation, and the method is commonly used to solve problems with hundreds and even thousands of variables.

The algebraic procedures utilized in the simplex method require the problem constraints to be written as equations rather than inequalities. This new form of the problem also prompts the use of some new terminology. We introduce this new form of a linear program and associated terminology through a simple example and an appropriate geometric interpretation. From this example we can illustrate what the simplex method does geometrically before we immerse ourselves in the algebraic details of the process.

■ Slack Variables

Let us return to the tent production problem in Example 7 from the last section. Recall the mathematical model for the problem:

$$
\begin{array}{lll}
\text{Maximize} & P = 50x_1 + 80x_2 & \text{Objective function} \\
\text{Subject to} & x_1 + 2x_2 \leq 32 & \text{Cutting department constraint} \\
& 3x_1 + 4x_2 \leq 84 & \text{Assembly department constraint} \\
& x_2 \leq 12 & \text{Demand constraint} \\
& x_1, x_2 \geq 0 & \text{Nonnegative constraints}
\end{array} \qquad (1)
$$

where x_1 and x_2 are the number of standard and expedition tents, respectively, produced each week.

To take advantage of matrix methods in solving systems of equations (which is part of the algebraic process we will discuss in the next section), we convert the problem constraint inequalities in a linear program into a system of linear equations by using a simple device called a *slack variable*. In particular, to convert the system of problem constraint inequalities from (1)

$$x_1 + 2x_2 \leqslant 32$$
$$3x_1 + 4x_2 \leqslant 84 \tag{2}$$
$$x_2 \leqslant 12$$

into a system of equations, we add nonnegative quantities s_1, s_2, and s_3 to the left members of (2) to obtain

$$x_1 + 2x_2 + s_1 \qquad = 32$$
$$3x_1 + 4x_2 \qquad + s_2 \qquad = 84 \tag{3}$$
$$x_2 \qquad + s_3 = 12$$

The variables s_1, s_2, and s_3 are called **slack variables** because each makes up the difference (takes up the slack) between the left and right sides of the inequalities in (2). It is important to remember that **slack variables are nonnegative.**

Notice that system (3) has infinitely many solutions—just solve for s_1, s_2, and s_3 in terms of x_1 and x_2 and then assign x_1 and x_2 arbitrary values. Certain solutions to system (3) have an interesting relationship to the feasible region (see Fig. 4, page 188) for the original linear program (1).

In system (3), set any two variables equal to zero and solve, if possible, for the remaining three. The results of carrying out this project systematically are summarized in Table 2 on the next page. Carefully compare the results in Table 2 with Figure 7.

■ Basic Feasible Solutions

Table 2 contains interesting and useful information, and in conjunction with Figure 7, it leads to several important definitions.

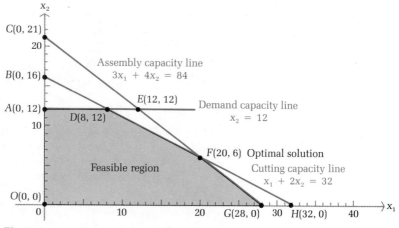

Figure 7

Table 2

x_1	x_2	s_1	s_2	s_3	Intersection Point	Feasible?
0	0	32	84	12	O	Yes
0	16	0	20	−4	B	No
0	21	−10	0	−9	C	No
0	12	8	36	0	A	Yes
32	0	0	−12	12	H	No
28	0	4	0	12	G	Yes
	0*			0*		No
20	6	0	0	6	F	Yes
8	12	0	12	0	D	Yes
12	12	−4	0	0	E	No

* Leads to an inconsistent system.

The solutions in Table 2, obtained by setting two variables equal to zero and solving for the other three, are referred to as *basic solutions* of system (3). Each basic solution corresponds to an intersection point of two of the original constraint equations (including the nonnegativity constraints).

For example, the basic solution $x_1 = 0$, $x_2 = 21$, $s_1 = -10$, $s_2 = 0$, $s_3 = -9$ corresponds to the point $C(0, 21)$, the intersection of the assembly capacity line and the x_2 axis. Even though there is a technical distinction between a point in the plane (like C) and the corresponding basic solution to system (3), we will use the two concepts interchangeably to simplify our discussion. With this understanding, we can say that the basic solutions *are* the intersection points of the constraint equations taken two at a time.

Now note that the set of corner points (including the optimal solution) corresponds to a subset of the set of basic solutions. We refer to the basic solutions (O, A, D, F, and G) in Table 2, which correspond to corner points of the feasible region, as *basic feasible solutions* of system (3). In general,

Basic and Basic Feasible Solutions

Given a system of m linear equations with n variables, $n > m$, and assuming the system has infinitely many solutions, then the solution (if it exists) obtained by setting $n - m$ variables equal to zero and solving for the remaining m variables is called a **basic solution.** When a linear system is associated with a linear programming problem and a basic solution of the system has no negative values (that is, corresponds to a corner point of the feasible region), we refer to that solution as a **basic feasible solution.** The $n - m$ variables set equal to zero in obtaining a basic solution are called **nonbasic variables;** the m remaining variables are called **basic variables.**

Thus, in Table 2 when we set x_1 and x_2 equal to zero, then x_1 and x_2 become nonbasic variables and s_1, s_2, and s_3 become basic variables; if we set x_1 and s_1 equal to zero, then x_1 and s_1 become nonbasic variables and x_2, s_2, and s_3 become basic variables; and so on.

Looking again at Table 2, we notice some negative entries for some variables. **Any basic solution with a negative value for one or more variables is infeasible** (recall that all decision variables and slack variables must be nonnegative). These infeasible basic solutions correspond to points B, C, E, and H in Figure 7, which are outside of the feasible region. Thus, we see that we may subdivide basic solutions into two mutually exclusive sets: *basic feasible solutions* and *basic infeasible solutions*. The following important theorem [which is equivalent to the fundamental theorem (Theorem 2) in the preceding section] is stated without proof:

Theorem 4

> If a linear program has an optimal solution, then it must be one (or more) of the basic feasible solutions.

Thus, to solve a linear programming problem (if a solution exists), we need only concern ourselves with basic feasible solutions (that is, corner points of the feasible region).

Let us carefully compare a couple of the basic feasible solutions in Table 2. If we choose the origin as a basic feasible solution, then we will not produce any tents, and the values of the slack variables represent 32 unused labor-hours in the cutting department, 84 unused labor-hours in the assembly department, and 12 units of unused demand for expedition tents. If we choose the basic feasible solution $D(8, 12)$, then we will produce 8 standard tents and 12 expedition tents. However, there will still be slack in the assembly department; that is, there will be 12 unused labor-hours in that department. There is no cutting department slack nor demand slack. Interpret the value of each slack variable at the optimal solution $F(20, 6)$.

The values of slack variables at optimal solutions provide management with useful information regarding resource utilization. For example, it would be useful to know after deciding on an optimal production schedule if there were any unused (slack) labor-hours in the cutting or assembly departments that could be utilized for other purposes.

■ Basic Feasible Solutions and the Simplex Method

What does all of the above discussion have to do with the simplex method? The **simplex method** is an iterative (repetitive) algebraic procedure that moves automatically from one basic feasible solution to another, improving the situation each time until an optimal solution is reached (if it exists). Geometrically, the simplex method moves from one corner point of the feasible region (see Fig. 7) to another corner point, improving the situation each time until an optimal solution is reached (if it exists). With this background, we are now ready to discuss the details of the simplex method.

Exercise 2-3

A   1. Listed in the table below are all the basic solutions for the system

$$2x_1 + 3x_2 + s_1 \qquad = 24$$
$$4x_1 + 3x_2 \qquad + s_2 = 36$$

For each basic solution, identify the nonbasic variables and the basic variables, then classify each basic solution as feasible or not feasible.

	x_1	x_2	s_1	s_2
(A)	0	0	24	36
(B)	0	8	0	12
(C)	0	12	-12	0
(D)	12	0	0	-12
(E)	9	0	6	0
(F)	6	4	0	0

2. Repeat Problem 1 for the system

$$2x_1 + \ x_2 + s_1 \qquad = 30$$
$$x_1 + 5x_2 \qquad + s_2 = 60$$

whose basic solutions are given in the following table:

	x_1	x_2	s_1	s_2
(A)	0	0	30	60
(B)	0	30	0	-90
(C)	0	12	18	0
(D)	15	0	0	45
(E)	60	0	-90	0
(F)	10	10	0	0

3. Listed in the table below are all the possible choices of nonbasic variables for the system

$$2x_1 + \ x_2 + s_1 \qquad = 50$$
$$x_1 + 2x_2 \qquad + s_2 = 40$$

In each case, find the value of the basic variables and determine if the basic solution is feasible.

	x_1	x_2	s_1	s_2
(A)	0	0	?	?
(B)	0	?	0	?
(C)	0	?	?	0
(D)	?	0	0	?
(E)	?	0	?	0
(F)	?	?	0	0

4. Repeat Problem 3 for the system

$$x_1 + 2x_2 + s_1 \qquad = 12$$
$$3x_1 + 2x_2 \qquad + s_2 = 24$$

B *Graph the following systems of inequalities. Introduce slack variables to convert each system of inequalities to a system of equations and find all the basic solutions of the system. Construct a table (like Table 2) listing each basic solution, the corresponding point on the graph, and whether the basic solution is feasible.*

5. $x_1 + x_2 \le 16$
   $2x_1 + x_2 \le 20$
   $x_1, x_2 \ge 0$

6. $5x_1 + x_2 \le 35$
   $4x_1 + x_2 \le 32$
   $x_1, x_2 \ge 0$

7. $2x_1 + x_2 \le 22$
   $x_1 + x_2 \le 12$
   $x_1 + 2x_2 \le 20$
   $x_1, x_2 \ge 0$

8. $4x_1 + x_2 \le 28$
   $2x_1 + x_2 \le 16$
   $x_1 + x_2 \le 13$
   $x_1, x_2 \ge 0$

2-4 The Simplex Method: Maximization with ≤ Problem Constraints

- Standard Maximization Problems
- An Algebraic Introduction to the Simplex Method
- The Simplex Tableau and Method
- Application

■ Standard Maximization Problems

We start our discussion with the tent problem considered in the last two sections (Example 7). Recall the mathematical model for the problem:

$$\text{Maximize} \quad P = 50x_1 + 80x_2 \qquad \text{Objective function}$$

$$\text{Subject to} \quad \left.\begin{array}{r} x_1 + 2x_2 \leq 32 \\ 3x_1 + 4x_2 \leq 84 \\ x_2 \leq 12 \end{array}\right\} \quad \text{Problem constraints} \qquad (1)$$

$$x_1, x_2 \geq 0 \qquad \text{Nonnegative constraints}$$

Notice that all the problem constraints involve $\leq$ inequalities with positive constants to the right of the inequality. Maximization problems that satisfy this condition are called *standard maximization problems*.

Standard Maximization Problems

A linear programming problem is said to be a **standard maximization problem** if it is a maximization problem and each problem constraint can be written in the form:

$$a_1x_1 + a_2x_2 + \cdots + a_nx_n \leq b, \qquad b \geq 0$$

In this section we will restrict our attention to standard maximization problems.

Using (nonnegative) slack variables s_1, s_2, and s_3, we convert the problem constraint inequalities in (1) into equations:

$$\begin{array}{rcl} x_1 + 2x_2 + s_1 & & = 32 \\ 3x_1 + 4x_2 & + s_2 & = 84 \\ x_2 & + s_3 & = 12 \end{array} \qquad (2)$$

From our discussion in the last section, we know that out of the infinitely many solutions to the system of problem constraint equations (2), an optimal solution will be among the basic feasible solutions, which are the corner points of the feasible region. In that discussion, we found basic solutions by setting any two variables equal to zero and solving for the other three. If all the values in a basic solution are nonnegative, then the basic solution is also feasible.

■ An Algebraic Introduction to the Simplex Method

We will now discuss an algebraic method of moving from one basic feasible solution to another until the optimal solution is found. We will then streamline this process by introducing and using matrix methods. An important feature of this method is that it will not require us to find all the basic solutions of (2) or even all the basic feasible solutions. Instead we will only have to find a subset of the basic feasible solutions. To start, we write (1) in the following **initial form:**

$$
\begin{aligned}
x_1 + 2x_2 + s_1 \qquad\qquad\quad &= 32 \\
3x_1 + 4x_2 \qquad + s_2 \qquad\quad &= 84 \\
x_2 \qquad + s_3 \quad &= 12 \\
-50x_1 - 80x_2 \qquad\qquad + P &= 0
\end{aligned}
\tag{3}
$$

The fourth equation is simply the objective function $P = 50x_1 + 80x_2$ written with all variables on the left.

Adding the objective function equation to the system of problem constraints requires a slight modification of the definitions of basic and basic feasible solutions. Specifically, **a basic solution of (3) must have P as one of the basic variables.** If we then delete the P part of this solution, the remaining variables will form a basic solution of (2). If a basic solution of (2) [formed by deleting P from a basic solution of (3)] is feasible, we say that the corresponding solution of (3) is also feasible, regardless of the sign of P. Thus, **a basic feasible solution of (3) can contain a negative number, but only if it is the value of P,** the objective function variable.

Our objective is to find a solution of (3) that maximizes P. We will not attempt to list all the basic solutions to (3), as we did for (2) in the preceding section. Instead, we begin by finding just one solution, called the *obvious basic solution.*

Obvious Basic Feasible Solution

When a linear program is written in initial form [as in (3)] with m equations and n variables, then choose m variables such that each occurs in one and only one equation and no two occur in the same equation. These m variables are the basic variables. (The objective function variable P will always be chosen as a basic variable.) The remaining $n - m$ variables (each usually occurring in more than one equation) are then nonbasic variables. The solution obtained by setting these $n - m$ nonbasic variables equal to zero and solving (by inspection) for the m basic variables will be referred to as an **obvious basic solution.** If no number in the solution is negative except possibly P, then the solution is an **obvious basic feasible solution.**

Notice that an obvious basic solution is just a basic solution where the basic variables are selected so that each one occurs in only one equation and no two occur in the same equation. A system such as (3) will have many basic solutions, but usually has only one obvious basic solution.

To obtain an obvious basic solution to (3), we choose s_1, s_2, s_3, and P as basic variables (since each occurs in exactly one equation and no two appear in the same equation). This leaves x_1 and x_2 (each occurring in more than one equation) as nonbasic variables. Setting the nonbasic variables equal to zero, a basic feasible solution to (3) can be obtained by inspection (thus the name "obvious basic feasible solution"):

$$
\begin{array}{ccccccccc}
& \overset{0}{} & & \overset{0}{} & & & & & \\
x_1 & + & 2\,x_2 & + s_1 & & & & = 32 \\
3\,x_1 & + & 4\,x_2 & & + s_2 & & & = 84 \\
& & x_2 & & & + s_3 & & = 12 \\
-50\,x_1 & - & 80\,x_2 & & & & + P & = 0
\end{array}
$$

$$x_1 = 0, \quad x_2 = 0, \quad s_1 = 32, \quad s_2 = 84, \quad s_3 = 12, \quad P = 0$$

We would certainly expect a profit of zero if we do not produce any tents! We can improve the situation by increasing either x_1 or x_2 or both. Let us start by increasing the decision variable that contributes most to the profit for each unit increase in the variable. Referring to the objective function $P = 50x_1 + 80x_2$, we see that each unit increase in x_2 increases the profit by \$80, while each unit increase in x_1 increases the profit by only \$50, so we increase x_2 first. How much can we increase x_2 in (3), holding $x_1 = 0$, without causing s_1, s_2, or s_3 to become negative? (Remember that if any of the variables except P become negative, we no longer have a feasible solution.) To see how much x_2 can be increased, rewrite the first three equations in (3), with $x_1 = 0$, as follows:

$$s_1 = 32 - 2x_2$$
$$s_2 = 84 - 4x_2$$
$$s_3 = 12 - x_2$$

We can increase x_2 in the first equation to 16 without causing s_1 to become negative, to 21 in the second equation without causing s_2 to become negative, and to 12 in the third equation without causing s_3 to become negative. Thus, we can increase x_2 to 12 (the minimum of 16, 32, and 12) without causing *any* of the variables s_1, s_2, or s_3 to become negative.

So that $x_2 = 12$ can be read directly (by inspection) as part of an obvious basic feasible solution, we eliminate x_2 from all equations in (3) but the third (then x_2 will change from a nonbasic variable to a basic variable). To do this, we multiply the third equation by -2 and add it to the first equation; then we multiply the third equation by -4 and add it to the second equation; finally, we multiply the third equation by 80 and add it to the fourth equation. (The third equation is not changed in this process.) Completing these operations on (3), we obtain the following equivalent system:

$$
\begin{aligned}
x_1 + s_1 \quad\;\; - 2s_3 &= 8 \\
3x_1 \quad\;\; + s_2 - 4s_3 &= 36 \\
+ x_2 \quad\;\; + \;\; s_3 &= 12 \\
-50x_1 \quad\;\; + 80s_3 + P &= 960
\end{aligned}
\tag{4}
$$

To obtain an obvious basic solution to (4), which variables should be basic and which nonbasic? Since each variable x_2, s_1, s_2, and P occurs in exactly one equation and no two appear in the same equation, they will be chosen as basic. Thus, x_1 and s_3 will be nonbasic. Assigning x_1 and s_3 zero values and solving (by inspection) for x_2, s_1, s_2, and P, we obtain the obvious basic feasible solution

$$
\begin{aligned}
x_1 + s_1 \quad\;\; - 2\,s_3 &= 8 \\
3\,x_1 \quad\;\; + s_2 - 4\,s_3 &= 36 \\
+ x_2 \quad\;\; + \;\; s_3 &= 12 \\
-50\,x_1 \quad\;\; + 80\,s_3 + P &= 960
\end{aligned}
$$

$$x_1 = 0, \quad x_2 = 12, \quad s_1 = 8, \quad s_2 = 36, \quad s_3 = 0, \quad P = \$960$$

Increasing x_2 to 12 has increased the profit to \$960, a marked improvement! But is this the best we can do? Rewriting the objective function (fourth equation) in (4) in the form

$$P = 50x_1 - 80s_3 + 960$$

we see that P can be increased still further if we can increase x_1, holding $s_3 = 0$, without making x_2, s_1, and s_2 negative. To see how far we can increase x_1 under these conditions, rewrite the first three equations in (4), with $s_3 = 0$, in the form

$$
\begin{aligned}
s_1 &= 8 - x_1 \\
s_2 &= 36 - 3x_1 \\
x_2 &= 12
\end{aligned}
$$

We can increase x_1 in the first equation to 8, in the second equation to 12, and in the third equation indefinitely without causing s_1, s_2, or s_3, respectively, to become negative. Thus, we can increase x_1 to 8 (the minimum of 8 and 12) without causing any of the variables s_1, s_2, or x_2 to become negative.

So that $x_1 = 8$ can be read by inspection as part of an obvious basic feasible solution, we eliminate x_1 from all equations in (4) but the first (then x_1 will change from a nonbasic variable to a basic variable). Notice that x_2 does not lose its status as a basic variable in the process. (Why?) Proceeding as above, we eliminate x_1 from all equations in (4) except the first to obtain the equivalent system:

$$
\begin{aligned}
x_1 \;+\; s_1 \;-\; 2s_3 &= 8 \\
-\,3s_1 + s_2 + 2s_3 &= 12 \\
+\,x_2 \qquad\quad +\; s_3 &= 12 \\
+\,50s_1 \qquad -\,20s_3 + P &= 1{,}360
\end{aligned}
\tag{5}
$$

which has the obvious basic feasible solution (s_1 and s_3 are nonbasic variables set equal to zero):

$$
x_1 = 8, \quad x_2 = 12, \quad s_1 = 0, \quad s_2 = 12, \quad s_3 = 0, \quad P = \$1{,}360
$$

Increasing x_1 to 8 has increased the profit to $\$1{,}360$, another marked improvement. Can we do any better? Rewriting the objective function in (5) in the form

$$
P = -50s_1 + 20s_3 + 1{,}360
$$

we see that P can be increased still further if we increase s_3, holding $s_1 = 0$, without making x_1, x_2, or s_2 negative. To see how far we can increase s_3 under these conditions, rewrite the first three equations in (5), with $s_1 = 0$, in the form

$$
\begin{aligned}
x_1 &= 8 + 2s_3 \\
s_2 &= 12 - 2s_3 \\
x_2 &= 12 - s_3
\end{aligned}
$$

We can increase s_3 in the first equation indefinitely, to 6 in the second equation, and to 12 in the third equation without causing x_1, s_2, or x_2, respectively, to become negative. Thus, we can increase s_3 to 6 (the minimum of 6 and 12) without causing any of the variables x_1, s_2, or x_2 to become negative.

So that $s_3 = 6$ can be read by inspection as part of an obvious basic feasible solution, we multiply the second equation in (5) by $\frac{1}{2}$ (so that the coefficient of s_3 is 1), then use the second equation to eliminate s_3 from the first, third, and fourth equations. In the process, s_3 will change from a nonbasic variable to a basic variable, while x_1 and x_2 do not lose their status as basic variables. (Why?) Carrying out the elimination, we obtain the equivalent system:

$$
\begin{aligned}
x_1 \;-\; 2s_1 + \; s_2 &= 20 \\
-\,1.5s_1 + 0.5s_2 + s_3 &= 6 \\
+\,x_2 + 1.5s_1 - 0.5s_2 &= 6 \\
20s_1 + 10\,s_2 \qquad + P &= \$1{,}480
\end{aligned}
\tag{6}
$$

which has the obvious basic feasible solution

$$x_1 = 20, \quad x_2 = 6, \quad s_1 = 0, \quad s_2 = 0, \quad s_3 = 6, \quad P = \$1,480$$

And P has been improved even further. Have we found the production schedule that maximizes P? To find out, we write the objective function in (6) in the form

$$P = -20s_1 - 10s_2 + \$1,480$$

and note that any increase in s_1 or s_2 will reduce P.

It can be shown that when this situation occurs, we have found the optimal solution. Hence, P is a maximum when 20 standard tents and 6 expedition tents are produced (as we found geometrically in Section 2-2). Since s_1 and s_2 are both zero, there are no labor-hours (slack) left in the cutting or assembly departments. However, there is a slack in demand, since $s_3 = 6$. That is, a weekly demand of 6 expedition tents is left unfilled.

Listing the obvious basic feasible solution we considered at each stage above in table form (Table 3) and comparing the results with the corners of the feasible region discussed in the last section (Fig. 8), we see that the algebraic process moved from one corner point of the feasible region to another, improving P each time until the optimal solution $F(20, 6)$ was reached.

Table 3 Obvious Basic Feasible Solutions

x_1	x_2	s_1	s_2	s_3	P	Corner Point
0	0	32	84	12	$ 0	O
0	12	8	36	0	960	A
8	12	0	12	0	1,360	D
20	6	0	0	6	1,480	F

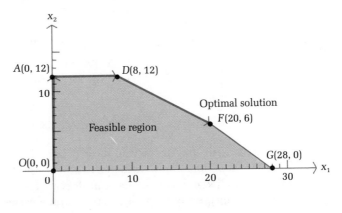

Figure 8

Notice that we did not have to find all the basic feasible solutions and we did not have to find any of the basic infeasible solutions. This very important property of the algebraic process permits generalization to larger systems where it is not practical to find all the basic solutions.

■ The Simplex Tableau and Method

The above process can be made substantially more efficient by using the matrix methods discussed in the last chapter. We start with the original linear program:

$$\begin{aligned} \text{Maximize} \quad & P = 50x_1 + 80x_2 && \text{Objective function} \\ \text{Subject to} \quad & \left. \begin{array}{l} x_1 + 2x_2 \leqslant 32 \\ 3x_1 + 4x_2 \leqslant 84 \\ x_2 \leqslant 12 \end{array} \right\} && \text{Problem constraints} \\ & x_1, x_2 \geqslant 0 && \text{Nonnegative constraints} \end{aligned} \qquad (7)$$

Now we introduce slack variables $s_1 \geqslant 0$, $s_2 \geqslant 0$, and $s_3 \geqslant 0$ and convert (7) into the initial form:

$$\begin{aligned} x_1 + \ 2x_2 + s_1 \qquad\qquad\qquad &= 32 \\ 3x_1 + \ 4x_2 \qquad + s_2 \qquad\qquad &= 84 \\ x_2 \qquad\quad + s_3 \qquad &= 12 \\ -50x_1 - 80x_2 \qquad\qquad\qquad + P &= 0 \\ x_1, x_2, s_1, s_2, s_3 \ &\geqslant 0 \end{aligned} \qquad (8)$$

Let us again state our objective: Out of the infinitely many solutions to system (8), we are interested in finding a solution that maximizes the profit P by using matrix methods.

Our first step is to write the augmented matrix, called the **simplex tableau,** for system (8):

$$\begin{array}{cccccc} x_1 & x_2 & s_1 & s_2 & s_3 & P \\ \left[\begin{array}{cccccc|c} 1 & 2 & 1 & 0 & 0 & 0 & 32 \\ 3 & 4 & 0 & 1 & 0 & 0 & 84 \\ 0 & 1 & 0 & 0 & 1 & 0 & 12 \\ \hline -50 & -80 & 0 & 0 & 0 & 1 & 0 \end{array}\right] \end{array} \qquad (9)$$

Indicators are shown in color

The row below the dashed line always corresponds to the objective function. The values in this row to the left of the solid vertical line are called **indicators.** The indicators are the coefficients of the variables in the objective function equation in (8) and we will see that these values indicate the variable that produces the largest increase in the value of the objective function.

The basic variables for the system of equations corresponding to a simplex tableau are easy to determine by examining the columns in the tableau.

Basic Variables and the Simplex Tableau

Given a simplex tableau for a linear programming problem, the basic variables correspond to the columns in the simplex tableau that have one nonzero element (usually a 1). Furthermore, no two columns corresponding to basic variables can have their nonzero elements in the same row.

Examining (9), we see that s_1, s_2, s_3, and P are the basic variables, x_1 and x_2 are the nonbasic variables, and the obvious basic feasible solution is:

$$
\begin{array}{c}
\quad\ 0 \qquad\quad 0 \\
\begin{array}{c|cccccc|c}
 & x_1 & x_2 & s_1 & s_2 & s_3 & P & \\
\hline
 & 1 & 2 & 1 & 0 & 0 & 0 & 32 \\
 & 3 & 4 & 0 & 1 & 0 & 0 & 84 \\
 & 0 & 1 & 0 & 0 & 1 & 0 & 12 \\
\hline
 & -50 & -80 & 0 & 0 & 0 & 1 & 0
\end{array}
\end{array}
$$

$$x_1 = 0, \quad x_2 = 0, \quad s_1 = 32, \quad s_2 = 84, \quad s_3 = 12, \quad P = 0$$

We would like to transform (9) into a row-equivalent matrix that has an obvious basic feasible solution with a larger value for P. Looking at the objective function $P = 50x_1 + 80x_2$, we observed that the change in P per unit increase in x_2 is greater than the change in P per unit increase in x_1. We can see this in (9) by looking for the most negative indicator in the fourth row, the objective function row. The column with the most negative indicator is called the **pivot column.** Now, how much can x_2 be increased when $x_1 = 0$ without causing s_1, s_2, or s_3 to become negative? We found this value by a process that is equivalent to dividing each *positive* element in the pivot column above the dashed line into the corresponding element in the last column and choosing the minimum value. Carrying out the calculations

$$\tfrac{32}{2} = 16 \qquad \tfrac{84}{4} = 21 \qquad \tfrac{12}{1} = 12$$

we see that the minimum quotient is 12, which is associated with the third row. This row is called the **pivot row.** The element in the pivot column (Column 2) and in the pivot row (Row 3) is called the **pivot element,** and we circle it:

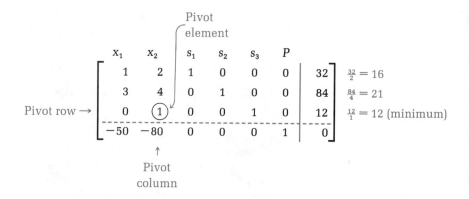

We will use row operations to transform the nonbasic variable associated with the pivot column into a basic variable. This procedure, called a *pivot operation*, is summarized in the box.

Performing a Pivot Operation

A **pivot operation** or **pivoting** consists of performing row operations as follows:

1. Multiply the pivot row by the reciprocal of the pivot element to transform the pivot element into a 1. (If the pivot element is already a 1, omit this step.)
2. Add multiples of the pivot row to other rows in the tableau to transform all other nonzero elements in the pivot column into 0's.

[*Note:* We cannot interchange rows while performing a pivot operation.]

Performing a pivot operation has the following effects:

1. The variable associated with the pivot column is changed from a nonbasic variable to a basic variable.
2. One of the basic variables is changed to a nonbasic variable.
3. The value of the objective function is increased (or, in some cases, remains the same).

We now carry out the pivot operation. Since the pivot element is already a 1, step 1 is omitted.

$$
\begin{array}{cccccc|c}
x_1 & x_2 & s_1 & s_2 & s_3 & P & \\
1 & 2 & 1 & 0 & 0 & 0 & 32 \\
3 & 4 & 0 & 1 & 0 & 0 & 84 \\
0 & ① & 0 & 0 & 1 & 0 & 12 \\
\hline
-50 & -80 & 0 & 0 & 0 & 1 & 0
\end{array}
$$

Step 2.
$R_1 + (-2)R_3 \rightarrow R_1$
$R_2 + (-4)R_3 \rightarrow R_2$

$R_4 + 80R_3 \rightarrow R_4$

$$
\sim
\begin{array}{cccccc|c}
1 & 0 & 1 & 0 & -2 & 0 & 8 \\
3 & 0 & 0 & 1 & -4 & 0 & 36 \\
0 & 1 & 0 & 0 & 1 & 0 & 12 \\
\hline
-50 & 0 & 0 & 0 & 80 & 1 & 960
\end{array}
$$

After completing the pivot operation, we write the obvious basic feasible solution for the resulting tableau (x_1 and s_3 are now nonbasic variables assigned zero values):

$$x_1 = 0 \quad x_2 = 12, \quad s_1 = 8, \quad s_2 = 36, \quad s_3 = 0, \quad P = \$960$$

This is an improvement over our earlier solution, but we can improve P still further since a negative indicator remains in the fourth row. (Write out the fourth row using variables to see why the negative indicator indicates that P can still be increased.)

We repeat the above sequence of steps using another pivot element. To locate the pivot element, we see that the pivot column is the first column in the matrix (since it contains the most negative indicator in the fourth row). To find the pivot row, divide each *positive* element in the pivot column above the dashed line into the corresponding element in the last column and choose the minimum value. The row corresponding to this value is the pivot row.

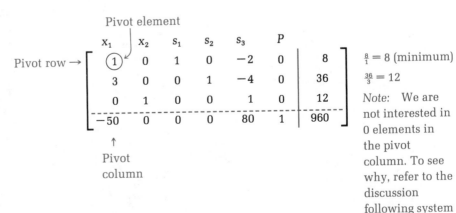

Pivot element

Pivot row →

$$
\begin{array}{cccccc|c}
x_1 & x_2 & s_1 & s_2 & s_3 & P & \\
① & 0 & 1 & 0 & -2 & 0 & 8 \\
3 & 0 & 0 & 1 & -4 & 0 & 36 \\
0 & 1 & 0 & 0 & 1 & 0 & 12 \\
\hline
-50 & 0 & 0 & 0 & 80 & 1 & 960
\end{array}
$$

$\frac{8}{1} = 8$ (minimum)
$\frac{36}{3} = 12$
Note: We are not interested in 0 elements in the pivot column. To see why, refer to the discussion following system (4) earlier in this section.

↑
Pivot column

We now perform another pivot operation. Once again, step 1 is omitted, since the pivot element is already a 1. (The nonbasic variable x_1 will then be transformed into a basic variable.)

$$
\begin{bmatrix}
x_1 & x_2 & s_1 & s_2 & s_3 & P & \\
\fbox{1} & 0 & 1 & 0 & -2 & 0 & 8 \\
3 & 0 & 0 & 1 & -4 & 0 & 36 \\
0 & 1 & 0 & 0 & 1 & 0 & 12 \\
\hdashline
-50 & 0 & 0 & 0 & 80 & 1 & 960
\end{bmatrix}
\begin{matrix}
\text{Step 2} \\[1.5em]
\\
R_2 + (-3)R_1 \rightarrow R_2 \\[1em]
\\
R_4 + 50R_1 \rightarrow R_4
\end{matrix}
$$

$$
\sim
\begin{bmatrix}
1 & 0 & 1 & 0 & -2 & 0 & 8 \\
0 & 0 & -3 & 1 & 2 & 0 & 12 \\
0 & 1 & 0 & 0 & 1 & 0 & 12 \\
\hdashline
0 & 0 & 50 & 0 & -20 & 1 & 1{,}360
\end{bmatrix}
$$

The obvious basic feasible solution is (choosing s_1 and s_3 as nonbasic variables set equal to zero):

$$x_1 = 8, \quad x_2 = 12, \quad s_1 = 0, \quad s_2 = 12, \quad s_3 = 0, \quad P = \$1{,}360$$

Since the fourth row in the matrix (the objective function row) still has a negative indicator, P can be improved still further. We find the pivot element as before and complete the pivot operation:

$$
\begin{array}{c}
\hspace{7em} \text{Pivot element} \\
\begin{array}{cccccc}
x_1 & x_2 & s_1 & s_2 & s_3 & P
\end{array}
\end{array}
$$

$$
\text{Pivot row} \rightarrow
\begin{bmatrix}
1 & 0 & 1 & 0 & -2 & 0 & 8 \\
0 & 0 & -3 & 1 & \fbox{2} & 0 & 12 \\
0 & 1 & 0 & 0 & 1 & 0 & 12 \\
\hdashline
0 & 0 & 50 & 0 & -20 & 1 & 1{,}360
\end{bmatrix}
\begin{matrix}
\\
\frac{12}{2} = 6 \text{ (minimum)} \\[0.5em]
\frac{12}{1} = 12
\end{matrix}
$$

$$
\begin{array}{c}
\uparrow \\
\text{Pivot} \\
\text{column}
\end{array}
$$

Note: The minimum positive quotient is our only interest. To see why $8/(-2) = -4$ does not enter in, see the last part of the algebraic solution to this problem earlier in this section.

We now perform the pivot operation:

$$
\begin{bmatrix}
x_1 & x_2 & s_1 & s_2 & s_3 & P & \\
1 & 0 & 1 & 0 & -2 & 0 & 8 \\
0 & 0 & -3 & 1 & \fbox{2} & 0 & 12 \\
0 & 1 & 0 & 0 & 1 & 0 & 12 \\
\hdashline
0 & 0 & 50 & 0 & -20 & 1 & 1{,}360
\end{bmatrix}
\begin{matrix}
\text{Step 1} \\[1.5em]
\\
0.5R_2 \rightarrow R_2
\end{matrix}
$$

$$
\begin{array}{cccccc}
x_1 & x_2 & s_1 & s_2 & s_3 & P \\
\end{array}
$$

$$
\sim \left[\begin{array}{cccccc|c}
1 & 0 & 1 & 0 & -2 & 0 & 8 \\
0 & 0 & -1.5 & 0.5 & 1 & 0 & 6 \\
0 & 1 & 0 & 0 & 1 & 0 & 12 \\
\hdashline
0 & 0 & 50 & 0 & -20 & 1 & 1{,}360
\end{array}\right]
\qquad
\begin{array}{l}
\text{Step 2} \\
R_1 + 2R_2 \to R_1 \\[4pt]
R_3 + (-1)R_2 \to R_3 \\
R_4 + 20R_2 \to R_4
\end{array}
$$

$$
\sim \left[\begin{array}{cccccc|c}
1 & 0 & -2 & 1 & 0 & 0 & 20 \\
0 & 0 & -1.5 & 0.5 & 1 & 0 & 6 \\
0 & 1 & 1.5 & -0.5 & 0 & 0 & 6 \\
\hdashline
0 & 0 & 20 & 10 & 0 & 1 & 1{,}480
\end{array}\right]
$$

The obvious basic feasible solution is

$$
x_1 = 20, \quad x_2 = 6, \quad s_1 = 0, \quad s_2 = 0, \quad s_3 = 6, \quad P = \$1{,}480
$$

Since the fourth row (the objective function row) has no more negative indicators, P cannot be made larger by increasing any of the variables. This is seen more clearly by converting the fourth row back into the equation form

$$
P = -20s_1 - 10s_2 + 1{,}480
$$

So we are through, because any increase in s_1 or s_2 will reduce P.

Let us review the critical steps in the simplex method so that the process can be mechanized. The key idea in the matrix transformation centers on the selection of the pivot element, which we summarize here:

Selecting the Pivot Element

1. Locate the most negative indicator in the bottom row of the tableau (the negative number to the left of the vertical line with the largest absolute value). The column containing this element is the *pivot column*. If there is a tie for most negative, choose either.

2. Divide each <u>positive</u> element in the pivot column above the dashed line into the corresponding element in the last column. The *pivot row* is the row corresponding to the smallest quotient. If there is a tie for the smallest quotient, choose either. If the pivot column above the dashed line has no positive elements, then there is no solution and we stop.

3. The *pivot* (or *pivot element*) is the element in the pivot column and in the pivot row. [*Note:* The pivot element is always positive and is never in the bottom row.]

We now summarize the important parts of the simplex method.

Simplex Method

Key Steps for Standard Maximization Problems

(Problem constraints are of the $\leq$ form with nonnegative constants on the right.)

1. Introduce slack variables and write the initial form.
2. Write the simplex tableau associated with the initial form.
3. Determine the pivot element (if it exists).
4. Perform the pivot operation.
5. Repeat steps 3 and 4 until all indicators in the bottom row are nonnegative. When this occurs, we stop the process and read the optimal solution.

Remark   Note that there are two different reasons for stopping the simplex method:

1. If we cannot select a new pivot column, we stop because the optimal solution has been found (see step 5 in the key steps for the simplex method).
2. If we select a new pivot column and then are unable to select a new pivot row, we stop because the problem has no solution (see step 2 in selecting the pivot element).

Example 10   Solve the following linear programming using the simplex method:

$$\text{Maximize} \quad P = 10x_1 + 5x_2$$
$$\text{Subject to} \quad 6x_1 + 2x_2 \leq 36$$
$$2x_1 + 4x_2 \leq 32$$
$$x_1, x_2 \geq 0$$

Solution   Introduce slack variables s_1 and s_2 and write the initial form:

$$6x_1 + 2x_2 + s_1 \qquad\qquad = 36$$
$$2x_1 + 4x_2 \qquad + s_2 \qquad = 32$$
$$-10x_1 - 5x_2 \qquad\qquad + P = 0$$
$$x_1, x_2, s_1, s_2 \geq 0$$

Write the simplex tableau and identify the first pivot element:

$$
\begin{array}{ccccc|c}
x_1 & x_2 & s_1 & s_2 & P & \\
\hline
⑥ & 2 & 1 & 0 & 0 & 36 \\
2 & 4 & 0 & 1 & 0 & 32 \\
\hline
-10 & -5 & 0 & 0 & 1 & 0
\end{array}
\qquad
\begin{array}{l}
\frac{36}{6} = 6 \\[4pt]
\frac{32}{2} = 16
\end{array}
$$

Perform the pivot operation:

$$
\begin{array}{ccccc}
x_1 & x_2 & s_1 & s_2 & P
\end{array}
$$

$$
\left[
\begin{array}{ccccc|c}
⑥ & 2 & 1 & 0 & 0 & 36 \\
2 & 4 & 0 & 1 & 0 & 32 \\
\hline
-10 & -5 & 0 & 0 & 1 & 0
\end{array}
\right]
\qquad \tfrac{1}{6}R_1 \to R_1
$$

$$
\sim
\left[
\begin{array}{ccccc|c}
1 & \frac{1}{3} & \frac{1}{6} & 0 & 0 & 6 \\
2 & 4 & 0 & 1 & 0 & 32 \\
\hline
-10 & -5 & 0 & 0 & 1 & 0
\end{array}
\right]
\qquad
\begin{array}{l}
R_2 + (-2)R_1 \to R_2 \\
R_3 + 10R_1 \to R_3
\end{array}
$$

$$
\sim
\left[
\begin{array}{ccccc|c}
1 & \frac{1}{3} & \frac{1}{6} & 0 & 0 & 6 \\
0 & \frac{10}{3} & -\frac{1}{3} & 1 & 0 & 20 \\
\hline
0 & -\frac{5}{3} & \frac{5}{3} & 0 & 1 & 60
\end{array}
\right]
$$

Since there still is a negative indicator in the last row, we repeat the process by finding a new pivot element:

$$
\begin{array}{ccccc}
x_1 & x_2 & s_1 & s_2 & P
\end{array}
$$

$$
\left[
\begin{array}{ccccc|c}
1 & \frac{1}{3} & \frac{1}{6} & 0 & 0 & 6 \\
0 & \left(\frac{10}{3}\right) & -\frac{1}{3} & 1 & 0 & 20 \\
\hline
0 & -\frac{5}{3} & \frac{5}{3} & 0 & 1 & 60
\end{array}
\right]
\qquad
\begin{array}{l}
6 \div \frac{1}{3} = 18 \\[4pt]
20 \div \frac{10}{3} = 6
\end{array}
$$

Performing the pivot operation, we obtain

$$
\begin{array}{ccccc}
x_1 & x_2 & s_1 & s_2 & P
\end{array}
$$

$$
\left[
\begin{array}{ccccc|c}
1 & \frac{1}{3} & \frac{1}{6} & 0 & 0 & 6 \\
0 & \left(\frac{10}{3}\right) & -\frac{1}{3} & 1 & 0 & 20 \\
\hline
0 & -\frac{5}{3} & \frac{5}{3} & 0 & 1 & 60
\end{array}
\right]
\qquad \tfrac{3}{10}R_2 \to R_2
$$

$$
\sim
\left[
\begin{array}{ccccc|c}
1 & \frac{1}{3} & \frac{1}{6} & 0 & 0 & 6 \\
0 & 1 & -\frac{1}{10} & \frac{3}{10} & 0 & 6 \\
\hline
0 & -\frac{5}{3} & \frac{5}{3} & 0 & 1 & 60
\end{array}
\right]
\qquad
\begin{array}{l}
R_1 + (-\frac{1}{3})R_2 \to R_1 \\[6pt]
R_3 + \frac{5}{3}R_2 \to R_3
\end{array}
$$

$$
\sim
\left[
\begin{array}{ccccc|c}
1 & 0 & \frac{1}{5} & -\frac{1}{10} & 0 & 4 \\
0 & 1 & -\frac{1}{10} & \frac{3}{10} & 0 & 6 \\
\hline
0 & 0 & \frac{3}{2} & \frac{1}{2} & 1 & 70
\end{array}
\right]
$$

Since all the indicators in the last row are nonnegative, we stop and read the solution:

$$
\text{Max } P = 70 \quad \text{at} \quad x_1 = 4, \quad x_2 = 6, \quad s_1 = 0, \quad s_2 = 0
$$

(If this still is not clear, write the system of equations corresponding to the last matrix and see what happens to P when you try to increase s_1 or s_2.)

Problem 10   Solve the following linear programming problem using the simplex method:

$$\text{Maximize}\quad P = 2x_1 + x_2$$
$$\text{Subject to}\quad 4x_1 + x_2 \leqslant 8$$
$$2x_1 + 2x_2 \leqslant 10$$
$$x_1, x_2 \geqslant 0$$

Example 11   Solve using the simplex method:

$$\text{Maximize}\quad P = 6x_1 + 3x_2$$
$$\text{Subject to}\quad -2x_1 + 3x_2 \leqslant 9$$
$$-x_1 + 3x_2 \leqslant 12$$
$$x_1, x_2 \geqslant 0$$

Solution   Write the initial form using the slack variables s_1 and s_2:

$$-2x_1 + 3x_2 + s_1 \qquad\qquad = 9$$
$$-x_1 + 3x_2 \qquad + s_2 \qquad = 12$$
$$-6x_1 - 3x_2 \qquad\qquad + P = 0$$

Write the simplex tableau and identify the first pivot element:

$$
\begin{array}{ccccc}
x_1 & x_2 & s_1 & s_2 & P \\
\end{array}
$$
$$
\left[
\begin{array}{ccccc|c}
-2 & 3 & 1 & 0 & 0 & 9 \\
-1 & 3 & 0 & 1 & 0 & 12 \\
\hline
-6 & -3 & 0 & 0 & 1 & 0 \\
\end{array}
\right]
$$

↑
Pivot column

Since both elements in the pivot column above the dashed line are negative, we are unable to select a pivot row. We stop and conclude that there is no solution. Notice that we do not try to continue with the simplex method by using a different column for the pivot column. The pivot column must correspond to the most negative indicator in the bottom row. Once the pivot column has been selected, either there is a pivot row and the simplex method can be continued, or there is no pivot row and the simplex method stops.

Problem 11   Solve using the simplex method:

$$\text{Maximize}\quad P = 2x_1 + 3x_2$$
$$\text{Subject to}\quad -3x_1 + 4x_2 \leqslant 12$$
$$x_2 \leqslant 9$$
$$x_1, x_2 \geqslant 0$$

▪ Application

Example 12

A farmer owns a 100 acre farm and plans to plant at most three crops. The seed for crops A, B, and C costs $40, $20, and $30 per acre, respectively. A maximum of $3,200 can be spent on seed. Crops A, B, and C require 1, 2, and 1 workdays per acre, respectively, and there are a maximum of 160 workdays available. If the farmer can make a profit of $100 per acre on crop A, $300 per acre on crop B, and $200 per acre on crop C, how many acres of each crop should be planted to maximize profit?

Solution

Let

$x_1 = $ Number of acres of crop A

$x_2 = $ Number of acres of crop B

$x_3 = $ Number of acres of crop C

$P = $ Total profit

Then we have the following linear programming problem:

Maximize $P = 100x_1 + 300x_2 + 200x_3$

Subject to $\left.\begin{array}{l} x_1 + x_2 + x_3 \leq 100 \\ 40x_1 + 20x_2 + 30x_3 \leq 3,200 \\ x_1 + 2x_2 + x_3 \leq 160 \end{array}\right\}$ Problem constraints

$x_1, x_2, x_3 \geq 0 \}$ Nonnegative constraints

Next, we introduce slack variables:

$$x_1 + x_2 + x_3 + s_1 \qquad\qquad = 100$$
$$40x_1 + 20x_2 + 30x_3 \qquad + s_2 \qquad = 3,200$$
$$x_1 + 2x_2 + x_3 \qquad\qquad + s_3 \qquad = 160$$
$$-100x_1 - 300x_2 - 200x_3 \qquad\qquad\qquad + P = 0$$

$$x_1, x_2, x_3, s_1, s_2, s_3 \geq 0$$

Now we form the simplex tableau and solve by the simplex method:

x_1	x_2	x_3	s_1	s_2	s_3	P		
1	1	1	1	0	0	0	100	
40	20	30	0	1	0	0	3,200	
1	②	1	0	0	1	0	160	$0.5R_3 \to R_3$
−100	−300	−200	0	0	0	1	0	

x_1	x_2	x_3	s_1	s_2	s_3	P		
1	1	1	1	0	0	0	100	$R_1 + (-1)R_3 \to R_1$
40	20	30	0	1	0	0	3,200	$R_2 + (-20)R_3 \to R_2$
0.5	1	0.5	0	0	0.5	0	80	
−100	−300	−200	0	0	0	1	0	$R_4 + 300R_3 \to R_4$

$$\sim \begin{bmatrix} x_1 & x_2 & x_3 & s_1 & s_2 & s_3 & P \\ 0.5 & 0 & \boxed{0.5} & 1 & 0 & -0.5 & 0 & 20 \\ 30 & 0 & 20 & 0 & 1 & -10 & 0 & 1{,}600 \\ 0.5 & 1 & 0.5 & 0 & 0 & 0.5 & 0 & 80 \\ \hdashline 50 & 0 & -50 & 0 & 0 & 150 & 1 & 24{,}000 \end{bmatrix}$$

$2R_1 \to R_1$

$$\sim \begin{bmatrix} 1 & 0 & 1 & 2 & 0 & -1 & 0 & 40 \\ 30 & 0 & 20 & 0 & 1 & -10 & 0 & 1{,}600 \\ 0.5 & 1 & 0.5 & 0 & 0 & 0.5 & 0 & 80 \\ \hdashline 50 & 0 & -50 & 0 & 0 & 150 & 1 & 24{,}000 \end{bmatrix}$$

$R_2 + (-20)R_1 \to R_2$
$R_3 + (-0.5)R_1 \to R_3$
$R_4 + 50R_1 \to R_4$

$$\sim \begin{bmatrix} 1 & 0 & 1 & 2 & 0 & -1 & 0 & 40 \\ 10 & 0 & 0 & -40 & 1 & 10 & 0 & 800 \\ 0 & 1 & 0 & -1 & 0 & 1 & 0 & 60 \\ \hdashline 100 & 0 & 0 & 100 & 0 & 100 & 1 & 26{,}000 \end{bmatrix}$$

All indicators in the bottom row are nonnegative, and we can now read the optimal solution:

$$x_1 = 0, \quad x_2 = 60, \quad x_3 = 40, \quad s_1 = 0, \quad s_2 = 800, \quad s_3 = 0, \quad P = \$26{,}000$$

Thus, if the farmer plants 60 acres in crop B, 40 acres in crop C, and no crop A, the maximum profit of \$26,000 will be realized. The fact that $s_2 = 800$ tells us (look at the second row in the equations at the start) that this maximum profit is reached by using only \$2,400 of the \$3,200 available for seed; that is, we have a slack of \$800 that can be used for some other purpose.

Problem 12 Repeat Example 12 modified as follows:

	Investment per Acre			Maximum Available
	Crop A	Crop B	Crop C	
Seed cost	\$24	\$40	\$30	\$3,600
Workdays	1	2	2	160 workdays
Profit	\$140	\$200	\$160	

Remarks 1. Refer to the second problem constraint in the model for Example 12:

$$40x_1 + 20x_2 + 30x_3 \leqslant 3{,}200$$

Multiplying both sides of this inequality by $\frac{1}{10}$ before introducing a slack variable simplifies subsequent calculations. However, performing this operation has a side effect — it changes the units of the slack variable from dollars to tens of dollars. Compare the equations

$$40x_1 + 20x_2 + 30x_3 + s_2 = 3{,}200 \qquad s_2 \text{ represents dollars}$$

and

$$4x_1 + 2x_2 + 3x_3 + s_2' = 320 \qquad s_2' \text{ represents tens of dollars}$$

to see why this happens. In general, if you multiply a problem constraint by a number, remember to take this into account when you interpret the value of the slack variable for that constraint.

2. It is important to realize that in order to keep this introduction as simple as possible, we have purposely avoided certain degenerate cases that lead to difficulties. Discussion and resolution of these problems is left to a more advanced treatment of the subject.

Answers to Matched Problems

10. Max $P = 6$ when $x_1 = 1$ and $x_2 = 4$
11. No solution
12. 40 acres of crop A, 60 acres of crop B, no crop C; Max $P = \$17{,}600$ (since $s = 240$, \$240 out of the \$3,600 will not be spent)

Exercise 2-4

A   For the simplex tableaus in Problems 1–4,

(A) Identify the basic and nonbasic variables.
(B) Find the obvious basic solution.
(C) Determine whether the optimal solution has been found, an additional pivot is required, or the problem has no solution.

1.

x_1	x_2	s_1	s_2	P	
2	1	0	3	0	12
3	0	1	−2	0	15
−4	0	0	4	1	20

2.

x_1	x_2	s_1	s_2	P	
1	4	−2	0	0	10
0	2	3	1	0	25
0	5	6	0	1	35

3.

x_1	x_2	x_3	s_1	s_2	s_3	P	
−2	0	1	3	1	0	0	5
0	1	0	−2	0	0	0	15
−1	0	0	4	1	1	0	12
−4	0	0	2	4	0	1	45

4.

$$
\begin{array}{ccccccc}
x_1 & x_2 & x_3 & s_1 & s_2 & s_3 & P \\
\end{array}
$$

$$
\left[\begin{array}{ccccccc|c}
0 & 2 & -1 & 1 & 4 & 0 & 0 & 5 \\
0 & 1 & 2 & 0 & -2 & 1 & 0 & 2 \\
1 & 3 & 0 & 0 & 5 & 0 & 0 & 11 \\
\hline
0 & -5 & 4 & 0 & -3 & 0 & 1 & 27
\end{array}\right]
$$

In Problems 5–8, find the pivot element and perform one pivot operation.

5.

$$
\begin{array}{ccccc}
x_1 & x_2 & s_1 & s_2 & P \\
\end{array}
$$

$$
\left[\begin{array}{ccccc|c}
1 & 4 & 1 & 0 & 0 & 4 \\
3 & 5 & 0 & 1 & 0 & 24 \\
\hline
-8 & -5 & 0 & 0 & 1 & 0
\end{array}\right]
$$

6.

$$
\begin{array}{ccccc}
x_1 & x_2 & s_1 & s_2 & P \\
\end{array}
$$

$$
\left[\begin{array}{ccccc|c}
1 & 6 & 1 & 0 & 0 & 36 \\
3 & 1 & 0 & 1 & 0 & 5 \\
\hline
-1 & -2 & 0 & 0 & 1 & 0
\end{array}\right]
$$

7.

$$
\begin{array}{cccccc}
x_1 & x_2 & s_1 & s_2 & s_3 & P \\
\end{array}
$$

$$
\left[\begin{array}{cccccc|c}
2 & 1 & 1 & 0 & 0 & 0 & 4 \\
3 & 0 & 1 & 1 & 0 & 0 & 8 \\
0 & 0 & 2 & 0 & 1 & 0 & 2 \\
\hline
-4 & 0 & -3 & 0 & 0 & 1 & 5
\end{array}\right]
$$

8.

$$
\begin{array}{ccccccc}
x_1 & x_2 & x_3 & s_1 & s_2 & P \\
\end{array}
$$

$$
\left[\begin{array}{cccccc|c}
0 & 0 & 2 & 1 & 1 & 0 & 2 \\
1 & 0 & -4 & 0 & 1 & 0 & 3 \\
0 & 1 & 5 & 0 & 2 & 0 & 11 \\
\hline
0 & 0 & -6 & 0 & -5 & 1 & 18
\end{array}\right]
$$

In Problems 9–12:

(A) Write the linear programming problem in initial form using slack variables.

(B) Write the simplex tableau and circle the first pivot.

(C) Use the simplex method to solve the problem.

9. Maximize $P = 15x_1 + 10x_2$

Subject to $2x_1 + x_2 \leqslant 10$

$x_1 + 2x_2 \leqslant 8$

$x_1, x_2 \geqslant 0$

10. Maximize $P = 3x_1 + 2x_2$

Subject to $6x_1 + 3x_2 \leqslant 24$

$3x_1 + 6x_2 \leqslant 30$

$x_1, x_2 \geqslant 0$

11. Repeat Problem 9 with the objective function changed to
$P = 30x_1 + x_2$.

12. Repeat Problem 10 with the objective function changed to
$P = x_1 + 3x_2$.

B *Solve the following linear programming problems using the simplex method:*

13. Maximize $P = 30x_1 + 40x_2$
Subject to $2x_1 + x_2 \leqslant 10$
$x_1 + x_2 \leqslant 7$
$x_1 + 2x_2 \leqslant 12$
$x_1, x_2 \geqslant 0$

14. Maximize $P = 20x_1 + 10x_2$
Subject to $3x_1 + x_2 \leqslant 21$
$x_1 + x_2 \leqslant 9$
$x_1 + 3x_2 \leqslant 21$
$x_1, x_2 \geqslant 0$

15. Maximize $P = 2x_1 + 3x_2$
Subject to $-2x_1 + x_2 \leqslant 2$
$-x_1 + x_2 \leqslant 5$
$x_2 \leqslant 6$
$x_1, x_2 \geqslant 0$

16. Repeat Problem 15 with
$P = -x_1 + 3x_2$.

17. Maximize $P = -x_1 + 2x_2$
Subject to $-x_1 + x_2 \leqslant 2$
$-x_1 + 3x_2 \leqslant 12$
$x_1 - 4x_2 \leqslant 4$
$x_1, x_2 \geqslant 0$

18. Repeat Problem 17 with
$P = x_1 + 2x_2$.

19. Maximize
$P = 5x_1 + 2x_2 - x_3$
Subject to
$x_1 + x_2 - x_3 \leqslant 10$
$2x_1 + 4x_2 + x_3 \leqslant 30$
$x_1, x_2, x_3 \geqslant 0$

20. Maximize
$P = 4x_1 - 3x_2 + 2x_3$
Subject to
$x_1 + 2x_2 - x_3 \leqslant 5$
$3x_1 + 2x_2 + 2x_3 \leqslant 22$
$x_1, x_2, x_3 \geqslant 0$

21. Maximize
$P = 2x_1 + 3x_2 + 4x_3$
Subject to
$x_1 + x_3 \leqslant 4$
$x_2 + x_3 \leqslant 3$
$x_1, x_2, x_3 \geqslant 0$

22. Maximize
$P = x_1 + x_2 + 2x_3$
Subject to
$x_1 - 2x_2 + x_3 \leqslant 9$
$2x_1 + x_2 + 2x_3 \leqslant 28$
$x_1, x_2, x_3 \geqslant 0$

23. Maximize
$$P = 4x_1 + 3x_2 + 2x_3$$
Subject to
$$3x_1 + 2x_2 + 5x_3 \leqslant 23$$
$$2x_1 + x_2 + x_3 \leqslant 8$$
$$x_1 + x_2 + 2x_3 \leqslant 7$$
$$x_1, x_2, x_3 \geqslant 0$$

24. Maximize
$$P = 4x_1 + 2x_2 + 3x_3$$
Subject to
$$x_1 + x_2 + x_3 \leqslant 11$$
$$2x_1 + 3x_2 + x_3 \leqslant 20$$
$$x_1 + 3x_2 + 2x_3 \leqslant 20$$
$$x_1, x_2, x_3 \geqslant 0$$

C **25.** Maximize
$$P = 20x_1 + 30x_2$$
Subject to
$$0.6x_1 + 1.2x_2 \leqslant 960$$
$$0.03x_1 + 0.04x_2 \leqslant 36$$
$$0.3x_1 + 0.2x_2 \leqslant 270$$
$$x_1, x_2 \geqslant 0$$

26. Repeat Problem 25 with
$$P = 20x_1 + 20x_2.$$

27. Maximize
$$P = x_1 + 2x_2 + 3x_3$$
Subject to
$$2x_1 + 2x_2 + 8x_3 \leqslant 600$$
$$x_1 + 3x_2 + 2x_3 \leqslant 600$$
$$3x_1 + 2x_2 + x_3 \leqslant 400$$
$$x_1, x_2, x_3 \geqslant 0$$

28. Maximize
$$P = 10x_1 + 50x_2 + 10x_3$$
Subject to
$$3x_1 + 3x_2 + 3x_3 \leqslant 66$$
$$6x_1 - 2x_2 + 4x_3 \leqslant 48$$
$$3x_1 + 6x_2 + 9x_3 \leqslant 108$$
$$x_1, x_2, x_3 \geqslant 0$$

In Problems 29 and 30, first solve the linear programming problem by the simplex method, keeping track of the obvious basic solution at each step. Then graph the feasible region and illustrate the path to the optimal solution determined by the simplex method.

29. Maximize $P = 2x_1 + 5x_2$
Subject to $x_1 + 2x_2 \leqslant 40$
$$x_1 + 3x_2 \leqslant 48$$
$$x_1 + 4x_2 \leqslant 60$$
$$x_2 \leqslant 14$$
$$x_1, x_2 \geqslant 0$$

30. Maximize $P = 5x_1 + 3x_2$
Subject to $5x_1 + 4x_2 \leqslant 100$
$$2x_1 + x_2 \leqslant 28$$
$$4x_1 + x_2 \leqslant 42$$
$$x_1 \leqslant 10$$
$$x_1, x_2 \geqslant 0$$

Applications

Formulate each of the following as a linear programming problem. Then solve the problem using the simplex method.

Business & Economics

31. *Manufacturing—resource allocation.* A small company manufactures three different electronic components for computers. Compo-

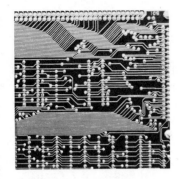

nent A requires 2 hours of fabrication and 1 hour of assembly; component B requires 1 hour of fabrication and 2 hours of assembly; and component C requires 2 hours of fabrication and 2 hours of assembly. The company has up to 1,000 labor-hours of fabrication time and 800 labor-hours of assembly time available per week. The profit on each component, A, B, and C, is $7, $9, and $10, respectively. How many components of each type should the company manufacture each week in order to maximize its profit (assuming all components that it manufactures can be sold)? What is the maximum profit?

32. *Manufacturing—resource allocation.* Repeat Problem 31 under the additional assumption that the combined total number of components produced by the company cannot exceed 550.

33. *Investment.* An investor has at most $100,000 to invest in government bonds, mutual funds, and money market funds. The average yields for government bonds, mutual funds, and money market funds are 8%, 13%, and 15%, respectively. The investor's policy requires that the total amount invested in mutual and money market funds not exceed the amount invested in government bonds. How much should be invested in each type of investment in order to maximize the return? What is the maximum return?

34. *Investment.* Repeat Problem 33 under the additional assumption that no more than $30,000 can be invested in money market funds.

35. *Advertising.* A department store chain has up to $20,000 to spend on television advertising for a sale. All ads will be placed with one television station where a thirty-second ad costs $1,000 on daytime TV and is viewed by 14,000 potential customers, $2,000 on prime-time TV and is viewed by 24,000 potential customers, and $1,500 on late-night TV and is viewed by 18,000 potential customers. The television station will not accept a total of more than 15 ads in all three time periods. How many ads should be placed in each time period in order to maximize the number of potential customers who will see the ads? How many potential customers will see the ads? (Ignore repeated viewings of the ad by the same potential customer.)

36. *Advertising.* Repeat Problem 35 if the department store increases its budget to $24,000 and requires that at least half of the ads be placed in prime-time shows.

37. *Construction—resource allocation.* A contractor is planning to build a new housing development consisting of colonial, split-level, and ranch style houses. A colonial house requires one-half acre of land, $60,000 capital, and 4,000 labor-hours to construct, and returns a profit of $20,000. A split-level house requires one-half acre of land, $60,000 capital, and 3,000 labor-hours to construct, and returns a profit of $18,000. A ranch house requires one acre of land, $80,000 capital, and 4,000 labor-hours to construct, and returns a profit of $24,000. The contractor has available 30 acres of land, $3,200,000 capital, and 180,000 labor-hours. How many houses of each type

should be constructed to maximize the contractor's profit? What is the maximum profit?

38. *Manufacturing—resource allocation.* A company manufactures three-speed, five-speed, and ten-speed bicycles. Each bicycle passes through three departments, fabrication, painting & plating, and final assembly. The revelant manufacturing data is given in the table. How many bicycles of each type should the company manufacture per day in order to maximize its profit? What is the maximum profit?

	Labor-Hours per Bicycle			Maximum Labor-Hours Available per Day
	Three-Speed	Five-Speed	Ten-Speed	
Fabrication	3	4	5	120
Painting & plating	5	3	5	130
Final assembly	4	3	5	120
Profit per bicycle	80	70	100	

39. *Packaging—product mix.* A candy company makes three types of candy, solid center, fruit-filled, and cream-filled, and packages these candies in three different assortments. A box of Assortment I contains 4 solid center, 4 fruit-filled, and 12 cream-filled candies and sells for $9.40. A box of Assortment II contains 12 solid center, 4 fruit-filled, and 4 cream-filled candies and sells for $7.60. A box of Assortment III contains 8 solid center, 8 fruit-filled, and 8 cream-filled candies and sells for $11.00. The manufacturing costs per piece of candy are $0.20 for solid center, $0.25 for fruit-filled, and $0.30 for cream-filled. The company can manufacture 4,800 solid center, 4,000 fruit-filled, and 5,600 cream-filled candies weekly. How many boxes of each type should they produce each week in order to maximize their profit? What is the maximum profit?

40. *Scheduling—resource allocation.* A small accounting firm prepares tax returns for three types of customers: individual, commercial, and industrial. The tax preparation process begins with a one-hour interview with the customer. The data collected during this interview are entered into a time-sharing computer system, which produces the customer's tax return. It takes one hour to enter the data for an individual customer, two hours for a commercial customer, and an hour and a half for an industrial customer. It takes 10 minutes of computer time to process an individual return, 25 minutes to process a commercial return, and 20 minutes to process an industrial return. The firm has one employee who conducts the initial interview and two who enter the data into the computer. The interviewer can work a maximum of 50 hours a week and each of the data-entry employees can work a maximum of 40 hours a week. The computer is available for a maximum of 1,025 minutes a week. The firm makes a profit of $50 on each individual customer, $65 on each commercial customer, and $60 on each industrial customer. How many customers of each type should the firm schedule each week in order to maximize its profit? What is the maximum profit?

Life Sciences   **41.** *Nutrition—animals.* The natural diet of a certain animal consists of three foods, A, B, and C. The number of units of calcium, iron, and protein in 1 gram of each food and the average daily intake are given in the table. A scientist wants to investigate the effect of increasing the protein in the animal's diet while not allowing the units of calcium and iron to exceed their average daily intakes. How many grams of each food should be used to maximize the amount of protein in the diet? What is the maximum amount of protein?

| | Units per Gram | | | Average Daily Intake |
	Food A	Food B	Food C	
Calcium	1	3	2	30
Iron	2	1	1	24
Protein	3	3	5	60

42. *Nutrition—animals.* Repeat Problem 41 if the scientist wants to maximize the daily calcium intake while not allowing the intake of iron or protein to exceed the average daily intake.

Social Sciences   **43.** *Opinion survey.* A political scientist has received a grant to fund a research project involving voting trends. The budget of the grant includes $1,620 for conducting door-to-door interviews the day before an election. Undergraduate students, graduate students, and faculty members will be hired to conduct the interviews. Each undergraduate student will conduct 18 interviews and be paid $60. Each graduate student will conduct 25 interviews and be paid $90. Each faculty member will conduct 30 interviews and be paid $120. Due to limited transportation facilities, no more than 20 interviewers can be hired. How many undergraduate students, graduate students, and faculty members should be hired in order to maximize the number of interviews that will be conducted? What is the maximum number of interviews?

44. *Opinion survey.* Repeat Problem 43 if one of the requirements of the grant is that at least 50% of the interviewers be undergraduate students.

2-5 The Dual; Minimization with $\geq$ Problem Constraints

- Formation of the Dual Problem
- Solution of Minimization Problems
- Application: A Transportation Problem

In the last section we restricted ourselves to maximization problems with $\leq$ problem constraints. Now we will consider minimization problems with $\geq$ problem constraints. These two types of problems turn out to be very closely related.

■ Formation of the Dual Problem

Associated with each minimization problem is a maximization problem called the **dual problem.** To illustrate the procedure for finding the dual problem, we will use Example 9 from Section 2-2. There we solved the following linear programming problem geometrically. Now we will form its dual, and later we will solve the problem using the dual and the simplex method.

$$
\begin{array}{ll}
\text{Minimize} & C = 3x_1 + x_2 \\
\text{Subject to} & 10x_1 + 2x_2 \geq 84 \\
& 8x_1 + 4x_2 \geq 120 \\
& x_1, x_2 \geq 0
\end{array}
\tag{1}
$$

The first step in forming the dual problem is to construct a matrix by using the problem constraints and the objective function written in the following form:

$$
\begin{array}{c}
10x_1 + 2x_2 \geq 84 \\
8x_1 + 4x_2 \geq 120 \\
3x_1 + x_2 = C
\end{array}
\qquad
A = \left[\begin{array}{cc|c}
10 & 2 & 84 \\
8 & 4 & 120 \\
\hline
3 & 1 & 1
\end{array}\right]
$$

Be careful not to confuse this matrix with the simplex tableau. We use a solid horizontal line in the matrix to help distinguish the dual matrix from the simplex tableau. No slack variables are involved in matrix A, and the coefficient of C is in the same column as the constants from the problem constraints.

Now we will form a second matrix B by using the rows of A as the columns of B. [Technically, B is called the *transpose of* A. In general, the **transpose** of a given matrix is formed by interchanging its rows and corresponding columns (first row with first column, second row with second column, and so on.)]

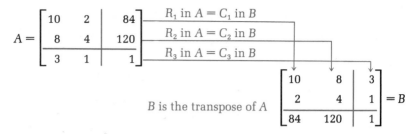

$$A = \begin{bmatrix} 10 & 2 & \bigm| & 84 \\ 8 & 4 & \bigm| & 120 \\ 3 & 1 & \bigm| & 1 \end{bmatrix}$$

R_1 in $A = C_1$ in B

R_2 in $A = C_2$ in B

R_3 in $A = C_3$ in B

B is the transpose of A

$$\begin{bmatrix} 10 & 8 & \bigm| & 3 \\ 2 & 4 & \bigm| & 1 \\ 84 & 120 & \bigm| & 1 \end{bmatrix} = B$$

Finally, we use the rows of B to define a new linear programming problem. This new problem will always be a maximization problem with $\leqslant$ problem constraints. To avoid confusion, we shall use different variables in this new problem:

$$\begin{array}{ll} 10y_1 + 8y_2 \leqslant 3 \\ 2y_1 + 4y_2 \leqslant 1 \\ 84y_1 + 120y_2 = P \end{array} \qquad B = \begin{array}{c} \ y_1 y_2 \\ \begin{bmatrix} 10 & 8 & \bigm| & 3 \\ 2 & 4 & \bigm| & 1 \\ 84 & 120 & \bigm| & 1 \end{bmatrix} \end{array}$$

The dual of the minimization problem (1) is:

Maximize $\quad P = 84y_1 + 120y_2$

Subject to $\quad 10y_1 + 8y_2 \leqslant 3$

$$2y_1 + 4y_2 \leqslant 1$$

$$y_1, y_2 \geqslant 0$$

This procedure is summarized in the box below:

Formation of the Dual Problem

Given a minimization problem with $\geqslant$ problem constraints:

1. Use the coefficients of the problem constraints and the objective function to form a matrix A with the coefficients of the objective function in the last row.
2. Use the *rows* of the matrix A as the *columns* of a second matrix B (matrix B is the transpose of A).
3. Use the *rows* of B to form a maximization problem with $\leqslant$ problem constraints.

Example 13   Form the dual problem:

Minimize $\quad C = 40x_1 + 12x_2 + 40x_3$

Subject to $\quad 2x_1 + x_2 + 5x_3 \geqslant 20$

$$4x_1 + x_2 + x_3 \geqslant 30$$

$$x_1, x_2, x_3 \geqslant 0$$

Solution   Step 1.   Form the matrix A:

$$A = \begin{bmatrix} 2 & 1 & 5 & 20 \\ 4 & 1 & 1 & 30 \\ 40 & 12 & 40 & 1 \end{bmatrix}$$

Step 2.   Form the matrix B (the transpose of A):

$$B = \begin{bmatrix} 2 & 4 & 40 \\ 1 & 1 & 12 \\ 5 & 1 & 40 \\ 20 & 30 & 1 \end{bmatrix}$$

Step 3.   State the dual problem:

$$\text{Maximize} \quad P = 20y_1 + 30y_2$$
$$\text{Subject to} \quad 2y_1 + 4y_2 \leq 40$$
$$y_1 + y_2 \leq 12$$
$$5y_1 + y_2 \leq 40$$
$$y_1, y_2 \geq 0$$

Problem 13   Find the dual problem:

$$\text{Minimize} \quad C = 16x_1 + 9x_2 + 21x_3$$
$$\text{Subject to} \quad x_1 + x_2 + 3x_3 \geq 16$$
$$2x_1 + x_2 + x_3 \geq 12$$
$$x_1, x_2, x_3 \geq 0$$

■ Solution of Minimization Problems

The following theorem establishes the relationship between the solution of a minimization problem and the solution of its dual:

Theorem 5

A minimization problem has a solution if and only if its dual problem has a solution. If a solution exists, then the optimal value of the minimization problem is the same as the optimal value of the dual problem.

In Section 2-4 we saw that the simplex method can be used to solve standard maximization problems (problem constraints of the $\leq$ form with nonnegative constants on the right). When the dual of a minimization problem is formed, the coefficients of the objective function in the minimization problem (the last row in A) become the constants in the problem constraints in the dual problem (the last column in B). **Thus, a minimization problem with $\geqslant$ problem constraints whose objective function has nonnegative coefficients can be solved by applying the simplex method to the dual.** To illustrate this, let's return to Example 9 in Section 2-2, whose dual was found earlier in this section.

Original Problem	*Dual Problem*

Minimize $C = 3x_1 + x_2$	Maximize $P = 84y_1 + 120y_2$
Subject to $10x_1 + 2x_2 \geqslant 84$	Subject to $10y_1 + 8y_2 \leqslant 3$
$8x_1 + 4x_2 \geqslant 120$	$2y_1 + 4y_2 \leqslant 1$
$x_1, x_2 \geqslant 0$	$y_1, y_2 \geqslant 0$

Now we will use the simplex method to solve the dual problem. For reasons that will become clear later, we will use the variables x_1 and x_2 from the original problem as the slack variables in the dual:

$$10y_1 + 8y_2 + x_1 \qquad\qquad = 3$$
$$2y_1 + 4y_2 \qquad + x_2 \qquad = 1$$
$$-84y_1 - 120y_2 \qquad\qquad + P = 0$$

$$
\begin{array}{ccccc}
y_1 & y_2 & x_1 & x_2 & P
\end{array}
$$

$$
\left[\begin{array}{ccccc|c}
10 & 8 & 1 & 0 & 0 & 3 \\
2 & \textcircled{4} & 0 & 1 & 0 & 1 \\
\hline
-84 & -120 & 0 & 0 & 1 & 0
\end{array}\right] \quad \tfrac{1}{4}R_2 \to R_2
$$

$$
\sim\left[\begin{array}{ccccc|c}
10 & 8 & 1 & 0 & 0 & 3 \\
\tfrac{1}{2} & 1 & 0 & \tfrac{1}{4} & 0 & \tfrac{1}{4} \\
\hline
-84 & -120 & 0 & 0 & 1 & 0
\end{array}\right] \quad \begin{array}{l} R_1 + (-8)R_2 \to R_1 \\[6pt] R_3 + 120R_2 \to R_3 \end{array}
$$

$$
\sim\left[\begin{array}{ccccc|c}
\textcircled{6} & 0 & 1 & -2 & 0 & 1 \\
\tfrac{1}{2} & 1 & 0 & \tfrac{1}{4} & 0 & \tfrac{1}{4} \\
\hline
-24 & 0 & 0 & 30 & 1 & 30
\end{array}\right] \quad \tfrac{1}{6}R_1 \to R_1
$$

$$
\sim\left[\begin{array}{ccccc|c}
1 & 0 & \tfrac{1}{6} & -\tfrac{1}{3} & 0 & \tfrac{1}{6} \\
\tfrac{1}{2} & 1 & 0 & \tfrac{1}{4} & 0 & \tfrac{1}{4} \\
\hline
-24 & 0 & 0 & 30 & 1 & 30
\end{array}\right] \quad \begin{array}{l} R_2 + (-\tfrac{1}{2})R_1 \to R_2 \\[6pt] R_3 + 24R_1 \to R_3 \end{array}
$$

$$
\sim\left[\begin{array}{ccccc|c}
1 & 0 & \tfrac{1}{6} & -\tfrac{1}{3} & 0 & \tfrac{1}{6} \\
0 & 1 & -\tfrac{1}{12} & \tfrac{5}{12} & 0 & \tfrac{1}{6} \\
\hline
0 & 0 & 4 & 22 & 1 & 34
\end{array}\right]
$$

Since all indicators in the bottom row are nonnegative, the solution to the dual problem is

$$y_1 = \tfrac{1}{6}, \quad y_2 = \tfrac{1}{6}, \quad x_1 = 0, \quad x_2 = 0, \quad P = 34$$

and the maximum value of P is 34. According to Theorem 5, the minimum value of C must also be 34. This agrees with the solution we found in Section 2-2, where we used a geometric approach.

If we examine the geometric solution, we see that the minimum value of C occurred at $x_1 = 4$ and $x_2 = 22$, which are the numbers in the bottom row of the final simplex tableau. This is no accident. **The entire solution to the minimization problem can always be obtained from the bottom row of the final simplex tableau for the dual problem.** Thus, from the row

$$\begin{matrix} & & & x_1 & x_2 & & \\ [0 & 0 & 4 & 22 & 1 & | & 34] \end{matrix}$$

we can conclude that the solution to the minimization problem is

$$\text{Min } C = 34 \quad \text{at} \quad x_1 = 4, \quad x_2 = 22$$

Now we can see that using x_1 and x_2 as slack variables in the dual problem makes it easy to identify the solution of the original problem.

Solution of a Minimization Problem

Given a minimization problem with nonnegative coefficients in the objective function:

1. Write all problem constraints as $\geq$ inequalities. (This may introduce negative numbers on the right side of some problem constraints.)
2. Form the dual problem.
3. Write the initial form of the dual problem, using the variables from the minimization problem as slack variables.
4. Use the simplex method to solve the dual method.
5. Read the solution of the minimization problem from the bottom row of the final simplex tableau in step 4. [*Note:* If the dual problem has no solution, then the minimization problem has no solution.]

Example 14   Solve the following minimization problem by maximizing the dual (see Example 13).

$$\begin{aligned} \text{Minimize} \quad & C = 40x_1 + 12x_2 + 40x_3 \\ \text{Subject to} \quad & 2x_1 + x_2 + 5x_3 \geq 20 \\ & 4x_1 + x_2 + x_3 \geq 30 \\ & x_1, x_2, x_3 \geq 0 \end{aligned}$$

Solution   From Example 13, the dual is

Maximize $\quad P = 20y_1 + 30y_2$

Subject to $\quad 2y_1 + 4y_2 \leqslant 40$

$\qquad\qquad y_1 + \ y_2 \leqslant 12$

$\qquad\qquad 5y_1 + \ y_2 \leqslant 40$

$\qquad\qquad\quad y_1, y_2 \geqslant 0$

Using x_1, x_2, and x_3 for slack variables, we obtain

$$2y_1 + \ 4y_2 + x_1 \qquad\qquad\qquad = 40$$

$$y_1 + \ \ y_2 \qquad + x_2 \qquad\qquad = 12$$

$$5y_1 + \ \ y_2 \qquad\qquad + x_3 \qquad = 40$$

$$-20y_1 - 30y_2 \qquad\qquad\qquad + P = 0$$

Now we form the simplex tableau and solve the dual problem.

y_1	y_2	x_1	x_2	x_3	P		
2	④	1	0	0	0	40	$\frac{1}{4}R_1 \to R_1$
1	1	0	1	0	0	12	
5	1	0	0	1	0	40	
-20	-30	0	0	0	1	0	

$\sim$

$\frac{1}{2}$	1	$\frac{1}{4}$	0	0	0	10	
1	1	0	1	0	0	12	$R_2 + (-1)R_1 \to R_2$
5	1	0	0	1	0	40	$R_3 + (-1)R_1 \to R_3$
-20	-30	0	0	0	1	0	$R_4 + 30R_1 \to R_3$

$\sim$

$\frac{1}{2}$	1	$\frac{1}{4}$	0	0	0	10	
①/②	0	$-\frac{1}{4}$	1	0	0	2	$2R_2 \to R_2$
$\frac{9}{2}$	0	$-\frac{1}{4}$	0	1	0	30	
-5	0	$\frac{15}{2}$	0	0	1	300	

$\sim$

$\frac{1}{2}$	1	$\frac{1}{4}$	0	0	0	10	$R_1 + (-\frac{1}{2})R_2 \to R_1$
1	0	$-\frac{1}{2}$	2	0	0	4	
$\frac{9}{2}$	0	$-\frac{1}{4}$	0	1	0	30	$R_3 + (-\frac{9}{2})R_2 \to R_3$
-5	0	$\frac{15}{2}$	0	0	1	300	$R_4 + 5R_2 \to R_4$

$\sim$

0	1	$\frac{1}{2}$	-1	0	0	8	
1	0	$-\frac{1}{2}$	2	0	0	4	
0	0	2	-9	1	0	12	
0	0	5	10	0	1	320	

From the bottom row of this tableau, we see that

$$\text{Min } C = 320 \quad \text{at} \quad x_1 = 5, \quad x_2 = 10, \quad \text{and} \quad x_3 = 0$$

Problem 14   Solve the following minimization problem by maximizing the dual (see Problem 13):

$$\text{Minimize} \quad C = 16x_1 + 9x_2 + 21x_3$$
$$\text{Subject to} \quad x_1 + x_2 + 3x_3 \geqslant 16$$
$$2x_1 + x_2 + x_3 \geqslant 12$$
$$x_1, x_2, x_3 \geqslant 0$$

In Section 2-4, we noted that multiplying a problem constraint by a number (usually in order to simplify calculations) changes the units of the slack variable. This requires some special interpretation of the value of the slack variable in the optimal solution, but causes no serious problems. However, when using the dual method, multiplying a problem constraint in the dual problem by a number can have some very serious consequences—the bottom row of the final simplex tableau may no longer give the correct solution to the minimization problem. To see this, refer to the first problem constraint of the dual problem in Example 14:

$$2y_1 + 4y_2 \leqslant 40$$

If we multiply this constraint by $\frac{1}{2}$ and then solve, the final tableau is (verify this):

$$\begin{bmatrix}
y_1 & y_2 & x_1 & x_2 & x_3 & P & \\
0 & 1 & 1 & -1 & 0 & 0 & 8 \\
1 & 0 & -1 & 2 & 0 & 0 & 4 \\
0 & 0 & 4 & -9 & 1 & 0 & 12 \\
\hdashline
0 & 0 & 10 & 10 & 0 & 1 & 320
\end{bmatrix}$$

The bottom row of this tableau indicates that the optimal solution to the minimization problem is $C = 320$ at $x_1 = 10$ and $x_2 = 10$. This is not the correct answer ($x_1 = 5$ in the correct answer). Thus, **you should never multiply a problem constraint in a maximization problem by a number if that maximization problem is being used to solve a minimization problem.** You may still simplify problem constraints in a minimization problem before forming the dual problem.

Example 15   Solve the following minimization problem by maximizing the dual:

$$\text{Minimize} \quad C = 5x_1 + 10x_2$$
$$\text{Subject to} \quad x_1 - x_2 \geqslant 1$$
$$-x_1 + x_2 \geqslant 2$$
$$x_1, x_2 \geqslant 0$$

Solution
$$A = \begin{bmatrix} 1 & -1 & 1 \\ -1 & 1 & 2 \\ \hline 5 & 10 & 1 \end{bmatrix} \qquad B = \begin{bmatrix} 1 & -1 & 5 \\ -1 & 1 & 10 \\ \hline 1 & 2 & 1 \end{bmatrix}$$

The dual problem is

Maximize $P = y_1 + 2y_2$

Subject to $\quad y_1 - y_2 \leq 5$

$\qquad\qquad -y_1 + y_2 \leq 10$

$\qquad\qquad y_1, y_2 \geq 0$

Introduce slack variables x_1 and x_2:

$$y_1 - \ y_2 + x_1 \qquad\qquad = 5$$
$$-y_1 + \ y_2 \qquad + x_2 \qquad = 10$$
$$-y_1 - 2y_2 \qquad\qquad + P = 0$$

Form the simplex tableau and solve:

$$\begin{array}{ccccc} y_1 & y_2 & x_1 & x_2 & P \end{array}$$

$$\begin{bmatrix} 1 & -1 & 1 & 0 & 0 & 5 \\ -1 & \boxed{1} & 0 & 1 & 0 & 10 \\ \hline -1 & -2 & 0 & 0 & 1 & 0 \end{bmatrix} \qquad R_1 + R_2 \to R_1$$

$$R_3 + 2R_2 \to R_3$$

$$\sim \begin{bmatrix} 0 & 0 & 1 & 1 & 0 & 15 \\ -1 & 1 & 0 & 1 & 0 & 10 \\ \hline -3 & 0 & 0 & 2 & 1 & 20 \end{bmatrix}$$

$\uparrow$

Pivot
column

No positive elements
above dashed line in
pivot column

The -3 in the bottom row indicates that Column 1 is the pivot column. Since no positive elements are in the pivot column above the dashed line, we are unable to select a pivot row. We stop the pivot operation and conclude that this maximization problem has no solution (see Section 2-4, page 221). Theorem 5 now implies that the original minimization problem has no solution. The graph of the inequalities in the minimization problem (see Fig. 9 on the next page) shows that the feasible region is empty; thus, it is not surprising that an optimal solution does not exist.

Problem 15   Solve the following minimization problem by maximizing the dual:

Minimize $\quad C = 2x_1 + 3x_2$

Subject to $\qquad x_1 - 2x_2 \geq 2$

$\qquad\qquad -x_1 + \ x_2 \geq 1$

$\qquad\qquad x_1, x_2 \geq 0$

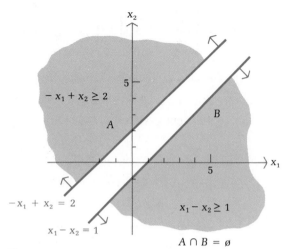

Figure 9

■ Application: A Transportation Problem

One of the first applications of linear programming was to the problem of minimizing the cost of transporting materials. Problems of this type are referred to as **transportation problems.**

Example 16

A computer manufacturing company has two assembly plants, plant A and plant B, and two distribution outlets, outlet I and outlet II. Plant A can assemble at most 700 computers a month, and plant B can assemble at most 900 computers a month. Outlet I must have at least 500 computers a month and outlet II must have at least 1,000 computers a month. Transportation costs for shipping one computer from each plant to each outlet are as follows: $6 from plant A to outlet I; $5 from plant A to outlet II; $4 from plant B to outlet I; $8 from plant B to outlet II. Find a shipping schedule that will minimize the total cost of shipping the computers from the assembly plants to the distribution outlets. What is this minimum cost?

Solution

First we summarize the relevant data in a table:

Assembly Plant	Distribution Outlet		Assembly Capacity
	I	II	
A	$6	$5	700
B	$4	$8	900
Minimum required	500	1,000	

In order to find a shipping schedule, we must determine the number of computers that should be shipped from each plant to each outlet. This will require the use of four decision variables:

x_1 = Number of computers shipped from plant A to outlet I

x_2 = Number of computers shipped from plant A to outlet II

x_3 = Number of computers shipped from plant B to outlet I

x_4 = Number of computers shipped from plant B to outlet II

The total number of computers shipped from plant A is $x_1 + x_2$. Since this cannot exceed the assembly capacity at A, we have

$x_1 + x_2 \leqslant 700$ Number shipped from plant A

Similarly, the total number shipped from plant B must satisfy

$x_3 + x_4 \leqslant 900$ Number shipped from plant B

The total number shipped to each outlet must satisfy

$x_1 + x_3 \geqslant 500$ Number shipped to outlet I

and

$x_2 + x_4 \geqslant 1,000$ Number shipped to outlet II

Using the shipping charges in the table, the total shipping charges are

$C = 6x_1 + 5x_2 + 4x_3 + 8x_4$

Thus, we must solve the following linear programming problem:

Minimize $C = 6x_1 + 5x_2 + 4x_3 + 8x_4$

Subject to $x_1 + x_2 \qquad\qquad \leqslant 700$ Available from A

$\qquad\qquad\quad x_3 + x_4 \leqslant 900$ Available from B

$\qquad x_1 \quad + x_3 \qquad \geqslant 500$ Required at I

$\qquad\quad x_2 \quad + x_4 \geqslant 1,000$ Required at II

$\qquad x_1, x_2, x_3, x_4 \geqslant 0$

Before we can solve this problem, we must multiply the first two constraints by -1 so that all the problem constraints are of the $\geqslant$ type. This will introduce negative constants into the minimization problem but not into the dual. Since the coefficients of C are nonnegative, the constants in the dual problem will be nonnegative and the dual will be a standard maximization problem. The problem can now be stated as

$$\text{Minimize} \quad C = 6x_1 + 5x_2 + 4x_3 + 8x_4$$

$$
\begin{aligned}
\text{Subject to} \quad -x_1 - x_2 \qquad\qquad &\geqslant -700 \\
-x_3 - x_4 &\geqslant -900 \\
x_1 \qquad + x_3 \qquad &\geqslant 500 \\
x_2 \qquad + x_4 &\geqslant 1{,}000 \\
x_1, x_2, x_3, x_4 &\geqslant 0
\end{aligned}
$$

$$
A = \left[\begin{array}{cccc|c}
-1 & -1 & 0 & 0 & -700 \\
0 & 0 & -1 & -1 & -900 \\
1 & 0 & 1 & 0 & 500 \\
0 & 1 & 0 & 1 & 1{,}000 \\
\hline
6 & 5 & 4 & 8 & 1
\end{array}\right]
$$

$$
B = \left[\begin{array}{cccc|c}
-1 & 0 & 1 & 0 & 6 \\
-1 & 0 & 0 & 1 & 5 \\
0 & -1 & 1 & 0 & 4 \\
0 & -1 & 0 & 1 & 8 \\
\hline
-700 & -900 & 500 & 1{,}000 & 1
\end{array}\right]
\qquad B \text{ is the transpose of } A
$$

The dual problem is

$$\text{Maximize} \quad P = -700y_1 - 900y_2 + 500y_3 + 1{,}000y_4$$

$$
\begin{aligned}
\text{Subject to} \quad -y_1 \qquad + y_3 \qquad &\leqslant 6 \\
-y_1 \qquad\qquad + y_4 &\leqslant 5 \\
-y_2 + y_3 \qquad &\leqslant 4 \\
-y_2 \qquad + y_4 &\leqslant 8 \\
y_1, y_2, y_3, y_4 &\geqslant 0
\end{aligned}
$$

Introduce slack variables x_1, x_2, x_3, and x_4:

$$
\begin{aligned}
-y_1 \qquad + \quad y_3 \qquad\qquad + x_1 \qquad\qquad\qquad\quad &= 6 \\
-y_1 \qquad\qquad + \quad y_4 \quad + x_2 \qquad\qquad\quad &= 5 \\
-y_2 + \quad y_3 \qquad\qquad\qquad + x_3 \qquad &= 4 \\
-y_2 \qquad + \quad y_4 \qquad\qquad + x_4 &= 8 \\
700y_1 + 900y_2 - 500y_3 - 1{,}000y_4 \qquad\qquad\qquad + P &= 0
\end{aligned}
$$

Form the simplex tableau and solve:

$$
\begin{bmatrix}
\begin{array}{ccccccccc|c}
y_1 & y_2 & y_3 & y_4 & x_1 & x_2 & x_3 & x_4 & P & \\
-1 & 0 & 1 & 0 & 1 & 0 & 0 & 0 & 0 & 6 \\
-1 & 0 & 0 & \boxed{1} & 0 & 1 & 0 & 0 & 0 & 5 \\
0 & -1 & 1 & 0 & 0 & 0 & 1 & 0 & 0 & 4 \\
0 & -1 & 0 & 1 & 0 & 0 & 0 & 1 & 0 & 8 \\
\hline
700 & 900 & -500 & -1{,}000 & 0 & 0 & 0 & 0 & 1 & 0
\end{array}
\end{bmatrix}
\begin{array}{l}
\\ \\ \\ \\
R_4 + (-1)R_2 \rightarrow R_4 \\
R_5 + 1{,}000R_2 \rightarrow R_5
\end{array}
$$

$$
\sim
\begin{bmatrix}
\begin{array}{ccccccccc|c}
-1 & 0 & 1 & 0 & 1 & 0 & 0 & 0 & 0 & 6 \\
-1 & 0 & 0 & 1 & 0 & 1 & 0 & 0 & 0 & 5 \\
0 & -1 & \boxed{1} & 0 & 0 & 0 & 1 & 0 & 0 & 4 \\
1 & -1 & 0 & 0 & 0 & -1 & 0 & 1 & 0 & 3 \\
\hline
-300 & 900 & -500 & 0 & 0 & 1{,}000 & 0 & 0 & 1 & 5{,}000
\end{array}
\end{bmatrix}
\begin{array}{l}
R_1 + (-1)R_3 \rightarrow R_1 \\
\\ \\ \\
R_5 + 500R_3 \rightarrow R_5
\end{array}
$$

$$
\sim
\begin{bmatrix}
\begin{array}{ccccccccc|c}
-1 & 1 & 0 & 0 & 1 & 0 & -1 & 0 & 0 & 2 \\
-1 & 0 & 0 & 1 & 0 & 1 & 0 & 0 & 0 & 5 \\
0 & -1 & 1 & 0 & 0 & 0 & 1 & 0 & 0 & 4 \\
\boxed{1} & -1 & 0 & 0 & 0 & -1 & 0 & 1 & 0 & 3 \\
\hline
-300 & 400 & 0 & 0 & 0 & 1{,}000 & 500 & 0 & 1 & 7{,}000
\end{array}
\end{bmatrix}
\begin{array}{l}
R_1 + R_4 \rightarrow R_1 \\
R_2 + R_4 \rightarrow R_2 \\
\\ \\
R_5 + 300R_4 \rightarrow R_5
\end{array}
$$

$$
\sim
\begin{bmatrix}
\begin{array}{ccccccccc|c}
0 & 0 & 0 & 0 & 1 & -1 & -1 & 1 & 0 & 5 \\
0 & -1 & 0 & 1 & 0 & 0 & 0 & 1 & 0 & 8 \\
0 & -1 & 1 & 0 & 0 & 0 & 1 & 0 & 0 & 4 \\
1 & -1 & 0 & 0 & 0 & -1 & 0 & 1 & 0 & 3 \\
\hline
0 & 100 & 0 & 0 & 0 & 700 & 500 & 300 & 1 & 7{,}900
\end{array}
\end{bmatrix}
$$

From the bottom row of this tableau, we have

$$\text{Min } C = 7{,}900 \quad \text{at} \quad x_1 = 0, \quad x_2 = 700, \quad x_3 = 500, \quad x_4 = 300$$

The shipping schedule that minimizes the shipping charges is

700 from plant A to outlet II
500 from plant B to outlet I
300 from plant B to outlet II

The total shipping cost is $7,900.

Problem 16 Repeat Example 16 if the shipping charge from plant A to outlet I is increased to $7 and the shipping charge from plant B to outlet II is decreased to $3.

Answers to Matched Problems

13. Maximize $P = 16y_1 + 12y_2$

    Subject to $y_1 + 2y_2 \leqslant 16$

    $y_1 + y_2 \leqslant 9$

    $3y_1 + y_2 \leqslant 21$

    $y_1, y_2 \geqslant 0$

14. Min $C = 132$ at $x_1 = 0$, $x_2 = 10$, $x_3 = 2$

15. Dual problem:

    Maximize $P = 2y_1 + y_2$

    Subject to $y_1 - y_2 \leqslant 2$

    $-2y_1 + y_2 \leqslant 3$

    $y_1, y_2 \geqslant 0$

    No solution

16. 600 from plant A to outlet II, 500 from plant B to outlet I, 400 from plant B to outlet II; total shipping cost $6,200

Exercise 2-5

A   In Problems 1–2:

(A) Form the dual problem.
(B) Write the initial form for the dual problem.
(C) Write the first simplex tableau for the dual problem and label the columns of the tableau.

1. Minimize $C = 8x_1 + 9x_2$

   Subject to $x_1 + 3x_2 \geqslant 4$

   $2x_1 + x_2 \geqslant 5$

   $x_1, x_2 \geqslant 0$

2. Minimize $C = 12x_1 + 5x_2$

   Subject to $2x_1 + x_2 \geqslant 7$

   $3x_1 + x_2 \geqslant 9$

   $x_1, x_2 \geqslant 0$

In Problems 3–4, a minimization problem, the corresponding dual problem, and the final simplex tableau in the solution of the dual problem are given.

(A) Find the optimal solution of the dual problem.
(B) Find the optimal solution of the minimization problem.

3. Minimize $C = 21x_1 + 50x_2$

   Subject to $2x_1 + 5x_2 \geqslant 12$

   $3x_1 + 7x_2 \geqslant 17$

   $x_1, x_2 \geqslant 0$

   Maximize $P = 12y_1 + 17y_2$

   Subject to $2y_1 + 3y_2 \leqslant 21$

   $5y_1 + 7y_2 \leqslant 50$

   $y_1, y_2 \geqslant 0$

y_1	y_2	x_1	x_2	P	
0	1	5	-2	0	5
1	0	-7	3	0	3
0	0	1	2	1	121

4. Minimize $C = 16x_1 + 25x_2$

   Subject to $3x_1 + 5x_2 \geqslant 30$

   $\qquad\qquad 2x_1 + 3x_2 \geqslant 19$

   $\qquad\qquad x_1, x_2 \geqslant 0$

   Maximize $P = 30y_1 + 19y_2$

   Subject to $3y_1 + 2y_2 \leqslant 16$

   $\qquad\qquad 5y_1 + 3y_2 \leqslant 25$

   $\qquad\qquad y_1, y_2 \geqslant 0$

y_1	y_2	x_1	x_2	P	
0	1	5	-3	0	5
1	0	-3	2	0	2
0	0	5	3	1	155

In Problems 5–12:

(A) Form the dual problem.

(B) Find the solution to the original problem by applying the simplex method to the dual problem.

5. Minimize $C = 9x_1 + 2x_2$

    Subject to $4x_1 + x_2 \geqslant 13$

    $\qquad\qquad 3x_1 + x_2 \geqslant 12$

    $\qquad\qquad x_1, x_2 \geqslant 0$

6. Minimize $C = x_1 + 4x_2$

    Subject to $x_1 + 2x_2 \geqslant 5$

    $\qquad\qquad x_1 + 3x_2 \geqslant 6$

    $\qquad\qquad x_1, x_2 \geqslant 0$

7. Minimize $C = 7x_1 + 12x_2$

    Subject to $2x_1 + 3x_2 \geqslant 15$

    $\qquad\qquad x_1 + 2x_2 \geqslant 8$

    $\qquad\qquad x_1, x_2 \geqslant 0$

8. Minimize $C = 3x_1 + 5x_2$

    Subject to $2x_1 + 3x_2 \geqslant 7$

    $\qquad\qquad x_1 + 2x_2 \geqslant 4$

    $\qquad\qquad x_1, x_2 \geqslant 0$

9. Minimize $C = 11x_1 + 4x_2$

    Subject to $2x_1 + x_2 \geqslant 8$

    $\qquad\qquad -2x_1 + 3x_2 \geqslant 4$

    $\qquad\qquad x_1, x_2 \geqslant 0$

10. Minimize $C = 40x_1 + 10x_2$

    Subject to $2x_1 + x_2 \geqslant 12$

    $\qquad\qquad 3x_1 - x_2 \geqslant 3$

    $\qquad\qquad x_1, x_2 \geqslant 0$

11. Minimize $C = 7x_1 + 9x_2$

    Subject to $-3x_1 + x_2 \geqslant 6$

    $\qquad\qquad x_1 - 2x_2 \geqslant 4$

    $\qquad\qquad x_1, x_2 \geqslant 0$

12. Minimize $C = 10x_1 + 15x_2$

    Subject to $-4x_1 + x_2 \geqslant 12$

    $\qquad\qquad 12x_1 - 3x_2 \geqslant 10$

    $\qquad\qquad x_1, x_2 \geqslant 0$

B   Solve the following linear programming problems by applying the simplex method to the dual problem.

13. Minimize $C = 3x_1 + 9x_2$

    Subject to $2x_1 + x_2 \geqslant 8$

    $\qquad\qquad x_1 + 2x_2 \geqslant 8$

    $\qquad\qquad x_1, x_2 \geqslant 0$

14. Minimize $C = 2x_1 + x_2$

    Subject to $x_1 + x_2 \geqslant 8$

    $\qquad\qquad x_1 + 2x_2 \geqslant 4$

    $\qquad\qquad x_1, x_2 \geqslant 0$

15. Minimize $C = 7x_1 + 5x_2$
    Subject to $x_1 + x_2 \geqslant 4$
    $x_1 - 2x_2 \geqslant -8$
    $-2x_1 + x_2 \geqslant -8$
    $x_1, x_2 \geqslant 0$

16. Minimize $C = 10x_1 + 4x_2$
    Subject to $2x_1 + x_2 \geqslant 6$
    $x_1 - 4x_2 \geqslant -24$
    $-8x_1 + 5x_2 \geqslant -24$
    $x_1, x_2 \geqslant 0$

17. Minimize $C = 10x_1 + 30x_2$
    Subject to $2x_1 + x_2 \geqslant 16$
    $x_1 + x_2 \geqslant 12$
    $x_1 + 2x_2 \geqslant 14$
    $x_1, x_2 \geqslant 0$

18. Minimize $C = 40x_1 + 10x_2$
    Subject to $3x_1 + x_2 \geqslant 24$
    $x_1 + x_2 \geqslant 16$
    $x_1 + 3x_2 \geqslant 30$
    $x_1, x_2 \geqslant 0$

19. Minimize $C = 5x_1 + 7x_2$
    Subject to $x_1 \geqslant 4$
    $x_1 + x_2 \geqslant 8$
    $x_1 + 2x_2 \geqslant 10$
    $x_1, x_2 \geqslant 0$

20. Minimize $C = 4x_1 + 5x_2$
    Subject to $2x_1 + x_2 \geqslant 12$
    $x_1 + 2x_2 \geqslant 18$
    $x_2 \geqslant 6$
    $x_1, x_2 \geqslant 0$

21. Minimize
    $C = 10x_1 + 7x_2 + 12x_3$
    Subject to
    $x_1 + x_2 + 2x_3 \geqslant 7$
    $2x_1 + x_2 + x_3 \geqslant 4$
    $x_1, x_2, x_3 \geqslant 0$

22. Minimize
    $C = 18x_1 + 8x_2 + 20x_3$
    Subject to
    $x_1 + x_2 + 3x_3 \geqslant 6$
    $3x_1 + x_2 + x_3 \geqslant 9$
    $x_1, x_2, x_3 \geqslant 0$

23. Minimize
    $C = 5x_1 + 2x_2 + 2x_3$
    Subject to
    $x_1 - 4x_2 + x_3 \geqslant 6$
    $-x_1 + x_2 - 2x_3 \geqslant 4$
    $x_1, x_2, x_3 \geqslant 0$

24. Minimize
    $C = 6x_1 + 8x_2 + 3x_3$
    Subject to
    $-3x_1 - 2x_2 + x_3 \geqslant 4$
    $x_1 + x_2 - x_3 \geqslant 2$
    $x_1, x_2, x_3 \geqslant 0$

C   25. Minimize
    $C = 16x_1 + 8x_2 + 4x_3$
    Subject to
    $3x_1 + 2x_2 + 2x_3 \geqslant 16$
    $4x_1 + 3x_2 + x_3 \geqslant 14$
    $5x_1 + 3x_2 + x_3 \geqslant 12$
    $x_1, x_2, x_3 \geqslant 0$

26. Minimize
    $C = 6x_1 + 8x_2 + 12x_3$
    Subject to
    $x_1 + 3x_2 + 3x_3 \geqslant 6$
    $x_1 + 5x_2 + 5x_3 \geqslant 4$
    $2x_1 + 2x_2 + 3x_3 \geqslant 8$
    $x_1, x_2, x_3 \geqslant 0$

27. Minimize

$$C = 5x_1 + 4x_2 + 5x_3 + 6x_4$$

Subject to

$$x_1 + x_2 \leqslant 12$$
$$x_3 + x_4 \leqslant 25$$
$$x_1 + x_3 \geqslant 20$$
$$x_2 + x_4 \geqslant 15$$
$$x_1, x_2, x_3, x_4 \geqslant 0$$

28. Repeat Problem 27 with

$$C = 4x_1 + 7x_2 + 5x_3 + 6x_4.$$

Applications

Formulate each of the following as a linear programming problem. Then solve the problem by applying the simplex method to the dual problem.

Business & Economics

29. *Manufacturing—production scheduling.* A food processing company produces regular and deluxe ice cream at three plants. Per hour of operation, the plant in Cedarburg produces 20 gallons of regular ice cream and 10 gallons of deluxe ice cream, the Grafton plant 10 gallons of regular and 20 gallons of deluxe, and the West Bend plant 20 gallons of regular and 20 gallons of deluxe. It costs $70 per hour to operate the Cedarburg plant, $75 per hour to operate the Grafton plant, and $90 per hour to operate the West Bend plant. The company needs at least 300 gallons of regular ice cream and at least 200 gallons of deluxe ice cream each day. How many hours per day should each plant operate in order to produce the required amounts of ice cream and minimize the cost of production? What is the minimum production cost?

30. *Mining—production scheduling.* A mining company operates two mines, which produce three grades of ore. The West Summit mine can produce 4 tons of low-grade ore, 3 tons of medium-grade ore, and 2 tons of high-grade ore per hour of operation. The North Ridge mine can produce 1 ton of low-grade ore, 1 ton of medium-grade ore, and 2 tons of high-grade ore per hour of operation. It costs $1,000 per hour to operate the mine at West Summit and $300 per hour to operate the North Ridge mine. To satisfy existing orders, the company needs at least 48 tons of low-grade ore, 45 tons of medium-grade ore, and 31 tons of high-grade ore. How many hours should each mine be operated to supply the required amounts of ore and minimize the cost of production? What is the minimum production cost?

31. *Purchasing.* Acme Micros markets computers with single-sided and double-sided disk drives. The disk drives are supplied by two other companies, Associated Electronics and Digital Drives. Associated Electronics charges $250 for a single-sided disk drive and $350 for a double-sided disk drive. Digital Drives charges $290 for a single-sided disk drive and $320 for a double-sided disk drive. Each month Associated Electronics can supply at most 1,000 disk drives in any combination of single-sided and double-sided drives. The combined monthly total supplied by Digital Drives cannot exceed 2,000 disk drives. Acme Micros needs at least 1,200 single-sided drives and at least 1,600 double-sided drives each month. How many disk drives of each type should Acme Micros order from each supplier in order to meet its monthly demand and minimize the purchase cost? What is the minimum purchase cost?

32. *Transportation.* A feed company stores grain in elevators located in Ames, Iowa, and Bedford, Indiana. Each month the grain is shipped to processing plants in Columbia, Missouri, and Danville, Illinois. The monthly supply (in tons) of grain at each elevator, the monthly demand (in tons) at each processing plant, and the cost per ton for transporting the grain are given in the table. Determine a shipping schedule that will minimize the cost of transporting the grain. What is the minimum cost?

Originating Elevators	Shipping Cost per Ton		Supply in Tons
	Columbia	Danville	
Ames	$22	$38	700
Bedford	$46	$24	500
Demand in tons	400	600	

Life Sciences

33. *Nutrition — people.* A dietitian in a hospital is to arrange a special diet using three foods, L, M, and N. Each ounce of food L contains 20 units of calcium, 10 units of iron, 10 units of vitamin A, and 20 units of cholesterol. Each ounce of food M contains 10 units of calcium, 10 units of iron, 20 units of vitamin A, and 24 units of cholesterol. Each ounce of food N contains 10 units of calcium, 10 units of iron, 10 units of vitamin A, and 18 units of cholesterol. If the minimum daily requirements are 300 units of calcium, 200 units of iron, and 240 units of vitamin A, how many ounces of each food should be used to meet the minimum requirements and at the same time minimize the cholesterol intake? What is the minimum cholesterol intake?

34. *Nutrition — plants.* A farmer can buy three types of plant food, mix A, mix B, and mix C. Each cubic yard of mix A contains 20 pounds of phosphoric acid, 10 pounds of nitrogen, and 5 pounds of potash. Each cubic yard of mix B contains 10 pounds of phosphoric acid, 10 pounds of nitrogen, and 10 pounds of potash. Each cubic yard of mix C contains 20 pounds of phosphoric acid, 20 pounds of nitrogen, and 5 pounds of potash. The minimum monthly requirements are 480 pounds of phosphoric acid, 320 pounds of nitrogen, and 225 pounds of potash. If mix A costs $30 per cubic yard, mix B $36 per cubic yard,

and mix *C* $39 per cubic yard, how many cubic yards of each mix should the farmer blend to meet the minimum monthly requirements at a minimal cost? What is the minimum cost?

Social Sciences

35. *Education — resource allocation.* A metropolitan school district has two high schools that are overcrowded and two that are under-enrolled. In order to balance the enrollment, the school board has decided to bus students from the overcrowded schools to the under-enrolled schools. North Division High School has 300 more students than it should have, and South Division High School has 500 more students than it should have. Central High School can accommodate 400 additional students and Washington High School can accommodate 500 additional students. The weekly cost of busing a student from North Division to Central is $5, from North Division to Washington is $2, from South Division to Central is $3, and from South Division to Washington is $4. Determine the number of students that should be bused from each of the overcrowded schools to each of the under-enrolled schools in order to balance the enrollment and minimize the cost of busing the students. What is the minimum cost?

36. *Education — resource allocation.* Repeat Problem 35 if the weekly cost of busing a student from North Division to Washington is $7 and all the other information remains the same.

2-6 Maximization and Minimization with Mixed Problem Constraints (Optional)

- An Introduction to the Big M Method
- The Big M Method
- Minimization by the Big M Method
- Summary of Methods of Solution
- Larger Problems — A Refinery Application

An Introduction to the Big M Method

In the preceding two sections, we have seen how to solve two types of linear programming problems: maximization problems with ⩽ problem constraints and nonnegative constants on the right side of each problem constraint, and minimization problems with ⩾ problem constraints and nonnegative coefficients in the objective function. In this section we will present a generalized version of the simplex method that will solve both maximization and minimization problems with any combination of ⩽, ⩾, and = problem constraints. The only requirement is that each problem constraint have a nonnegative constant on the right side.

To illustrate this new method, we will consider the following problem, which has one $\leq$ problem constraint and one $\geq$ problem constraint:

Maximize $P = 2x_1 + x_2$

Subject to $x_1 + x_2 \leq 10$

$-x_1 + x_2 \geq 2$ (1)

$x_1, x_2 \geq 0$

To form an equation out of the first inequality, we introduce a nonnegative slack variable s_1, as before, and write:

$x_1 + x_2 + s_1 = 10$

How can we form an equation out of the second inequality? We introduce a second nonnegative variable s_2 and subtract it from the left side so that we can write

$-x_1 + x_2 - s_2 = 2$

The variable s_2 is called a **surplus variable** because it is the amount (surplus) by which the left side of the inequality exceeds the right side. **Surplus variables are always nonnegative quantities.**

We now express the linear programming problem (1) as a system of equations.

$$\begin{aligned}
x_1 + x_2 + s_1 &= 10 \\
-x_1 + x_2 \quad - s_2 &= 2 \\
-2x_1 - x_2 \quad\quad\quad + P &= 0 \\
x_1, x_2, s_1, s_2 &\geq 0
\end{aligned} \qquad (2)$$

The obvious basic solution (found by setting the nonbasic variables x_1 and x_2 equal to zero) is:

$x_1 = 0, \quad x_2 = 0, \quad s_1 = 10, \quad s_2 = -2, \quad P = 0$

This basic solution is infeasible. The surplus variable s_2 is negative, a violation of the nonnegative requirement for all variables except P. The simplex method works only when the obvious basic solution for each tableau is feasible, so we cannot solve this problem by writing the tableau for (2) and starting pivot operations.

In order to use the simplex method on a problem with mixed constraints, we must modify the problem. First, we introduce a second nonnegative variable a_1 in the equation involving the surplus variable s_2:

$-x_1 + x_2 - s_2 + a_1 = 2$

The variable a_1 is called an **artificial variable,** since it has no actual relationship to any of the variables in the original problem. **Artificial**

variables are always nonnegative quantities. Next we add the term $-Ma_1$ to the objective function:

$$P = 2x_1 + x_2 - Ma_1$$

The number M is a very large positive constant whose value can be made as large as we wish. We now have a new problem, which we shall call the **modified problem:**

Maximize $P = 2x_1 + x_2 - Ma_1$

Subject to
$$
\begin{aligned}
x_1 + x_2 + s_1 \quad\quad\quad &= 10 \\
-x_1 + x_2 \quad\quad -s_2 + a_1 &= 2 \\
x_1, x_2, s_1, s_2, a_1 &\geqslant 0
\end{aligned}
$$
(3)

The initial form for the modified problem (3) is

$$
\begin{aligned}
x_1 + x_2 + s_1 \quad\quad\quad\quad &= 10 \\
-x_1 + x_2 \quad -s_2 + \quad a_1 \quad\quad &= 2 \\
-2x_1 - x_2 \quad\quad\quad + Ma_1 + P &= 0
\end{aligned}
$$
(4)

Again we see that the obvious basic solution is not feasible. (Setting the nonbasic variables x_1, x_2, and a_1 equal to zero, we see that s_2 is still negative.) We must find a system equivalent to (4) whose obvious basic solution is feasible. It is easier to work with the augmented coefficient matrix for (4), which we call the **preliminary simplex tableau for the modified problem.**

$$
\begin{array}{cccccc c}
x_1 & x_2 & s_1 & s_2 & a_1 & P & \\
\left[\begin{array}{cccccc|c}
1 & 1 & 1 & 0 & 0 & 0 & 10 \\
-1 & 1 & 0 & -1 & 1 & 0 & 2 \\
\hline
-2 & -1 & 0 & 0 & M & 1 & 0
\end{array}\right]
\end{array}
$$

Let us eliminate M from the a_1 column so that a_1 will become a basic variable in an obvious basic solution. If the resulting obvious basic solution is also feasible, we can start pivot operations.

$$
\begin{array}{cccccc c}
x_1 & x_2 & s_1 & s_2 & a_1 & P & \\
\left[\begin{array}{cccccc|c}
1 & 1 & 1 & 0 & 0 & 0 & 10 \\
-1 & 1 & 0 & -1 & 1 & 0 & 2 \\
\hline
-2 & -1 & 0 & 0 & M & 1 & 0
\end{array}\right]
\end{array}
\quad R_3 + (-M)R_2 \rightarrow R_3
$$

$$
\sim
\left[\begin{array}{cccccc|c}
1 & 1 & 1 & 0 & 0 & 0 & 10 \\
-1 & 1 & 0 & -1 & 1 & 0 & 2 \\
\hline
M-2 & -M-1 & 0 & M & 0 & 1 & -2M
\end{array}\right]
$$

The obvious basic solution (setting the nonbasic variables x_1, x_2, and s_2 equal to zero) is

$$x_1 = 0, \quad x_2 = 0, \quad s_1 = 10, \quad s_2 = 0, \quad a_1 = 2, \quad P = -2M$$

Since this solution is feasible, we have found an initial simplex tableau and can commence with pivot operations.

The pivot column is determined by the most negative indicator in the bottom row of the tableau. Since M is a positive number, $-M - 1$ is certainly a negative indicator. What about the indicator $M - 2$? Remember that M is a very large positive number. We will assume that M is so large that any expression of the form $M - k$ is positive. Thus, the only negative indicator in the bottom row is $-M - 1$.

	x_1	x_2	s_1	s_2	a_1	P		
	1	1	1	0	0	0	10	$R_1 + (-1)R_2 \to R_1$
Pivot row →	-1	①	0	-1	1	0	2	
	$M - 2$	$-M - 1$	0	M	0	1	$-2M$	$R_3 + (M + 1)R_2 \to R_3$

Pivot column ↑

	x_1	x_2	s_1	s_2	a_1	P		
~	②	0	1	1	-1	0	8	$\frac{1}{2}R_1 \to R_1$
	-1	1	0	-1	1	0	2	
	-3	0	0	-1	$M + 1$	1	2	

	x_1	x_2	s_1	s_2	a_1	P		
~	1	0	$\frac{1}{2}$	$\frac{1}{2}$	$-\frac{1}{2}$	0	4	
	-1	1	0	-1	1	0	2	$R_2 + R_1 \to R_2$
	-3	0	0	-1	$M + 1$	1	2	$R_3 + 3R_1 \to R_3$

	x_1	x_2	s_1	s_2	a_1	P		
~	1	0	$\frac{1}{2}$	$\frac{1}{2}$	$-\frac{1}{2}$	0	4	
	0	1	$\frac{1}{2}$	$-\frac{1}{2}$	$\frac{1}{2}$	0	6	
	0	0	$\frac{3}{2}$	$\frac{1}{2}$	$M - \frac{1}{2}$	1	14	

Since all the indicators in the last row are nonnegative ($M - \frac{1}{2}$ is nonnegative because M is a very large positive number), we can stop and write the optimal solution:

$$\text{Max } P = 14 \quad \text{at} \quad x_1 = 4, \quad x_2 = 6, \quad s_1 = 0, \quad s_2 = 0, \quad a_1 = 0$$

This is an optimal solution to the modified problem (3). How is it related to the original problem (2)? Since $a_1 = 0$ in this solution,

$$x_1 = 4, \quad x_2 = 6, \quad s_1 = 0, \quad s_2 = 0, \quad P = 14 \tag{5}$$

is certainly a feasible solution for (2). [You can verify this by direct substitution into (2).] Surprisingly, it turns out that (5) is an optimal solution to the original problem. To see that this is true, suppose that we were able to find feasible values of x_1, x_2, s_1, and s_2 that satisfy the original system (2) and produce a value of $P > 14$. Then by using these same values in (3) along with $a_1 = 0$, we have found a feasible solution of (3) with $P > 14$. This contradicts the fact that $P = 14$ is the maximum value of P for the modified problem. Thus (5) is an optimal solution for the original problem.

As this example illustrates, if $a_1 = 0$ in an optimal solution for the modified problem, then deleting a_1 produces an optimal solution for the original problem. What happens if $a_1 \neq 0$ in the optimal solution for the modified problem? In this case, it can be shown that the original problem has no solution because its feasible set is empty.

In larger problems, each $\geq$ problem constraint will require the introduction of a surplus variable and an artificial variable. If one of the problem constraints is an equation rather than an inequality, there is no need to introduce a slack or surplus variable. However, each $=$ problem constraint will require the introduction of another artificial variable. Finally, each artificial variable must also be included in the objective function for the modified problem. The same constant M can be used for each artificial variable. Because of the role that the constant M plays in this approach, this method is often called the **big M method.**

■ The Big M Method

We now summarize the key steps used in the big M method and use them to solve several problems.

The Big M Method—Introducing Slack, Surplus, and Artificial Variables to Form the Modified Problem

1. If any problem constraints have negative constants on the right side, multiply both sides by -1 to obtain a constraint with a nonnegative constant. (If the constraint is an inequality, this will reverse the direction of the inequality.)
2. Introduce a slack variable in each $\leq$ constraint.
3. Introduce a surplus variable and an artificial variable in each $\geq$ constraint.
4. Introduce an artificial variable in each $=$ constraint.
5. For each artificial variable a_i, add $-Ma_i$ to the objective function. Use the same constant M for all artificial variables.

Example 17   Find the modified problem for the following linear programming problem. Do not attempt to solve the problem.

$$\text{Maximize} \quad P = 2x_1 + 5x_2 + 3x_3$$
$$\text{Subject to} \quad x_1 + 2x_2 - x_3 \leqslant 7$$
$$-x_1 + x_2 - 2x_3 \leqslant -5$$
$$x_1 + 4x_2 + 3x_3 \geqslant 1$$
$$2x_1 - x_2 + 4x_3 = 6$$
$$x_1, x_2, x_3 \geqslant 0$$

Solution   First, we multiply the second constraint by -1 to change -5 to 5:

$$(-1)(-x_2 + x_2 - 2x_3) \geqslant (-1)(-5)$$
$$x_1 - x_2 + 2x_3 \geqslant 5$$

Next, we introduce the slack, surplus, and artificial variables according to the rules stated in the box:

$$x_1 + 2x_2 - x_3 + s_1 \qquad = 7$$
$$x_1 - x_2 + 2x_3 \qquad - s_2 + a_1 \qquad = 5$$
$$x_1 + 4x_2 + 3x_3 \qquad - s_3 + a_2 \quad = 1$$
$$2x_1 - x_2 + 4x_3 \qquad + a_3 = 6$$

Finally, we add $-Ma_1$, $-Ma_2$, and $-Ma_3$ to the objective function:

$$P = 2x_1 + 5x_2 + 3x_3 - Ma_1 - Ma_2 - Ma_3$$

The modified problem is

$$\text{Maximize} \quad P = 2x_1 + 5x_2 + 3x_3 - Ma_1 - Ma_2 - Ma_3$$
$$\text{Subject to} \quad x_1 + 2x_2 - x_3 + s_1 \qquad = 7$$
$$x_1 - x_2 + 2x_3 \qquad - s_2 + a_1 \qquad = 5$$
$$x_1 + 4x_2 + 3x_3 \qquad - s_3 + a_2 \quad = 1$$
$$2x_1 - x_2 + 4x_3 \qquad + a_3 = 6$$
$$x_1, x_2, x_3, s_1, s_2, s_3, a_1, a_2, a_3 \geqslant 0$$

Problem 17   Repeat Example 17 for:

$$\text{Maximize} \quad P = 3x_1 - 2x_2 + x_3$$
$$\text{Subject to} \quad x_1 - 2x_2 + x_3 \geqslant 5$$
$$-x_1 - 3x_2 + 4x_3 \leqslant -10$$
$$2x_1 + 4x_2 + 5x_3 \leqslant 20$$
$$3x_1 - x_2 - x_3 = -15$$
$$x_1, x_2, x_3 \geqslant 0$$

The Big M Method—Solving the Problem

1. Form the preliminary simplex tableau for the modified problem.
2. Use row operations to eliminate the M's in the bottom row of the preliminary simplex tableau in the columns corresponding to the artificial variables. The resulting tableau is the initial simplex tableau.
3. Solve the modified problem by applying the simplex method to the initial simplex tableau found in step 2.
4. Relate the solution of the modified problem to the original problem.
   a. If the modified problem has no solution, then the original problem has no solution.
   b. If all artificial variables are zero in the solution to the modified problem, then delete the artificial variables to find a solution to the original problem.
   c. If any artificial variables are nonzero in the solution to the modified problem, then the original problem has no solution.

Example 18   Solve the following linear programming problem using the big M method:

$$\text{Maximize}\quad P = x_1 - x_2 + 3x_3$$
$$\text{Subject to}\quad x_1 + x_2 \quad\ \leqslant 20$$
$$x_1 \qquad\ + x_3 = 5$$
$$x_2 + x_3 \geqslant 10$$
$$x_1, x_2, x_3 \geqslant 0$$

Solution   State the modified problem:

$$\text{Maximize}\quad P = x_1 - x_2 + 3x_3 - Ma_1 - Ma_2$$
$$\text{Subject to}\quad x_1 + x_2 \qquad + s_1 \qquad\qquad\qquad = 20$$
$$x_1 \qquad + x_3 \qquad\quad + a_1 \qquad\qquad = 5$$
$$x_2 + x_3 \qquad\qquad - s_2 + a_2 = 10$$
$$x_1, x_2, x_3, s_1, s_2, a_1, a_2 \geqslant 0$$

Write the preliminary simplex tableau for the modified problem and find the initial simplex tableau.

$$
\begin{array}{ccccccccc}
x_1 & x_2 & x_3 & s_1 & a_1 & s_2 & a_2 & P & \\
\left[\begin{array}{ccccccccc|c}
1 & 1 & 0 & 1 & 0 & 0 & 0 & 0 & 20 \\
1 & 0 & 1 & 0 & 1 & 0 & 0 & 0 & 5 \\
0 & 1 & 1 & 0 & 0 & -1 & 1 & 0 & 10 \\
\hline
-1 & 1 & -3 & 0 & M & 0 & M & 1 & 0
\end{array}\right]
\end{array}
$$

Eliminate M from the a_1 column

$R_4 + (-M)R_2 \rightarrow R_4$

$$
\begin{array}{cccccccc}
x_1 & x_2 & x_3 & s_1 & a_1 & s_2 & a_2 & P \\
\end{array}
$$

$$
\sim
\left[
\begin{array}{cccccccc|c}
1 & 1 & 0 & 1 & 0 & 0 & 0 & 0 & 20 \\
1 & 0 & 1 & 0 & 1 & 0 & 0 & 0 & 5 \\
0 & 1 & 1 & 0 & 0 & -1 & 1 & 0 & 10 \\
\hline
-M-1 & 1 & -M-3 & 0 & 0 & 0 & M & 1 & -5M
\end{array}
\right]
$$

Eliminate M from the a_2 column

$R_4 + (-M)R_3 \to R_4$

$$
\sim
\left[
\begin{array}{cccccccc|c}
1 & 1 & 0 & 1 & 0 & 0 & 0 & 0 & 20 \\
1 & 0 & 1 & 0 & 1 & 0 & 0 & 0 & 5 \\
0 & 1 & 1 & 0 & 0 & -1 & 1 & 0 & 10 \\
\hline
-M-1 & -M+1 & -2M-3 & 0 & 0 & M & 0 & 1 & -15M
\end{array}
\right]
$$

The obvious basic solution (setting the nonbasic variables x_1, x_2, x_3, and s_2 equal to zero) is

$$x_1 = 0, \quad x_2 = 0, \quad x_3 = 0, \quad s_1 = 20,$$
$$a_1 = 5, \quad s_2 = 0, \quad a_2 = 10, \quad P = -15M$$

Since this basic solution is feasible, we have found the initial simplex tableau and can commence with pivot operations to find the optimal solution. (It can be shown that except for some degenerate cases which we will not consider here, if the modified linear programming problem has a solution, then the obvious basic solution resulting after M has been eliminated from the artificial variable columns will be feasible. We can then perform pivot operations to find the optimal solution if it exists.)

$$
\begin{array}{cccccccc}
x_1 & x_2 & x_3 & s_1 & a_1 & s_2 & a_2 & P \\
\end{array}
$$

$$
\left[
\begin{array}{cccccccc|c}
1 & 1 & 0 & 1 & 0 & 0 & 0 & 0 & 20 \\
1 & 0 & 1 & 0 & 1 & 0 & 0 & 0 & 5 \\
0 & 1 & 1 & 0 & 0 & -1 & 1 & 0 & 10 \\
\hline
-M-1 & -M+1 & -2M-3 & 0 & 0 & M & 0 & 1 & -15M
\end{array}
\right]
$$

$R_3 + (-1)R_2 \to R_3$

$R_4 + (2M+3)R_2 \to R_4$

$$
\sim
\left[
\begin{array}{cccccccc|c}
1 & 1 & 0 & 1 & 0 & 0 & 0 & 0 & 20 \\
1 & 0 & 1 & 0 & 1 & 0 & 0 & 0 & 5 \\
-1 & 1 & 0 & 0 & -1 & -1 & 1 & 0 & 5 \\
\hline
M+2 & -M+1 & 0 & 0 & 2M+3 & M & 0 & 1 & -5M+15
\end{array}
\right]
$$

$R_1 + (-1)R_3 \to R_1$

$R_4 + (M-1)R_3 \to R_4$

$$
\sim
\left[
\begin{array}{cccccccc|c}
2 & 0 & 0 & 1 & 1 & 1 & -1 & 0 & 15 \\
1 & 0 & 1 & 0 & 1 & 0 & 0 & 0 & 5 \\
-1 & 1 & 0 & 0 & -1 & -1 & 1 & 0 & 5 \\
\hline
3 & 0 & 0 & 0 & M+4 & 1 & M-1 & 1 & 10
\end{array}
\right]
$$

Since the bottom row has no negative indicators, we can stop and write the optimal solution to the modified problem:

$$x_1 = 0, \quad x_2 = 5, \quad x_3 = 5, \quad s_1 = 15, \quad a_1 = 0, \quad s_2 = 0, \quad a_2 = 0, \quad P = 10$$

Since $a_1 = 0$ and $a_2 = 0$, the solution to the original problem is

$$\text{Max } P = 10 \quad \text{at} \quad x_1 = 0, \quad x_2 = 5, \quad x_3 = 5$$

Problem 18 Solve the following linear programming problem using the big M method:

$$\text{Maximize} \quad P = x_1 + 4x_2 + 2x_3$$
$$\text{Subject to} \qquad x_2 + x_3 \leqslant 4$$
$$x_1 \qquad\quad - x_3 = 6$$
$$x_1 - x_2 - x_3 \geqslant 1$$
$$x_1, x_2, x_3 \geqslant 0$$

Example 19 Solve the following linear programming problem using the big M method:

$$\text{Maximize} \quad P = 3x_1 + 5x_2$$
$$\text{Subject to} \quad 2x_1 + x_2 \leqslant 4$$
$$x_1 + 2x_2 \geqslant 10$$
$$x_1, x_2 \geqslant 0$$

Solution Introducing slack, surplus, and artificial variables, we obtain the modified problem:

$$2x_1 + x_2 + s_1 \qquad\qquad\qquad = 4$$
$$x_1 + 2x_2 \qquad - s_2 + a_1 \qquad = 10 \qquad \text{Modified problem}$$
$$-3x_1 - 5x_2 \qquad\qquad + Ma_1 + P = 0$$

$$\begin{array}{cccccc|c}
x_1 & x_2 & s_1 & s_2 & a_1 & P & \\
2 & 1 & 1 & 0 & 0 & 0 & 4 \\
1 & 2 & 0 & -1 & 1 & 0 & 10 \\
\hline
-3 & -5 & 0 & 0 & M & 1 & 0
\end{array}$$

Preliminary simplex tableau:
Eliminate M in the a_1 column

$$R_3 + (-M)R_2 \rightarrow R_3$$

$$\sim \begin{array}{cccccc|c}
2 & \boxed{1} & 1 & 0 & 0 & 0 & 4 \\
1 & 2 & 0 & -1 & 1 & 0 & 10 \\
\hline
-M-3 & -2M-5 & 0 & M & 0 & 1 & -10M
\end{array}$$

Initial simplex tableau.
Begin pivot operations:

$$R_2 + (-2)R_1 \rightarrow R_2$$
$$R_3 + (2M+5)R_1 \rightarrow R_3$$

$$\sim \begin{array}{cccccc|c}
2 & 1 & 1 & 0 & 0 & 0 & 4 \\
-3 & 0 & -2 & -1 & 1 & 0 & 2 \\
\hline
3M+7 & 0 & 2M+5 & M & 0 & 1 & -2M+20
\end{array}$$

The optimal solution of the modified problem is

$$x_1 = 0, \quad x_2 = 4, \quad s_1 = 0, \quad s_2 = 0, \quad a_1 = 2, \quad P = -2M + 20$$

Since a_1 is not zero, the original problem has no solution. Figure 10 on the next page shows that the feasible region for the original problem is empty.

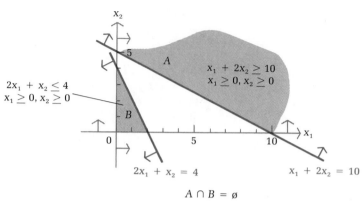

Figure 10

Problem 19 Solve the following linear programming problem using the big M method:

Maximize $P = 3x_1 + 2x_2$

Subject to $x_1 + 5x_2 \leqslant 5$

$2x_1 + x_2 \geqslant 12$

$x_1, x_2 \geqslant 0$

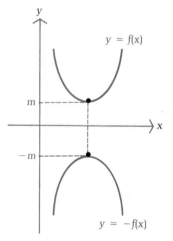

Figure 11

■ Minimization by the Big M Method

In addition to solving any maximization problem, the big M method can also be used to solve minimization problems. To minimize an objective function, we have only to maximize its negative. Figure 11 illustrates the fact that the minimum value of a function f occurs at the same point as the maximum value of the function $-f$. Furthermore, if m is the minimum value of f, then $-m$ is the maximum value of $-f$, and conversely. Thus, we can find the minimum value of a function f by finding the maximum value of $-f$ and then changing the sign of the maximum value.

Example 20 A small jewelry manufacturing company employs a person who is a highly skilled gem cutter, and it wishes to use this person at least 6 hours per day for this purpose. On the other hand, the polishing facilities can be used in any amounts up to 8 hours per day. The company specializes in three kinds of semiprecious gemstones, P, Q, and R. Relevant cutting, polishing, and cost requirements are listed in the table. How many gemstones of each type

should be processed each day to minimize the cost of the finished stones? What is the minimum cost?

	P	Q	R
Cutting	2 hr	1 hr	1 hr
Polishing	1 hr	1 hr	2 hr
Cost per stone	$30	$30	$10

Solution   If we let x_1, x_2, and x_3 represent the number of type P, Q, and R stones finished per day, respectively, then we have the following linear programming problem to solve, where C is the cost of the stones:

Minimize $C = 30x_1 + 30x_2 + 10x_3$ Objective function

Subject to $2x_1 + x_2 + x_3 \geqslant 6$

$\left. \right\}$ Problem constraints

$x_1 + x_2 + 2x_3 \leqslant 8$

$x_1, x_2, x_3 \geqslant 0$ Nonnegative constraints

We convert this to a maximization problem by letting

$$P = -C = -30x_1 - 30x_2 - 10x_3$$

Thus, we get:

Maximize $P = -30x_1 - 30x_2 - 10x_3$

Subject to $2x_1 + x_2 + x_3 \geqslant 6$

$x_1 + x_2 + 2x_3 \leqslant 8$

$x_1, x_2, x_3 \geqslant 0$

and Min $C = -$Max P. To solve, we first state the modified problem:

$$2x_1 + x_2 + x_3 - s_1 + a_1 = 6$$
$$x_1 + x_2 + 2x_3 + s_2 = 8$$
$$30x_1 + 30x_2 + 10x_3 + Ma_1 + P = 0$$
$$x_1, x_2, x_3, s_1, s_2, a_1 \geqslant 0$$

$$\begin{array}{ccccccc}
x_1 & x_2 & x_3 & s_1 & a_1 & s_2 & P \\
\end{array}$$

$$\left[\begin{array}{ccccccc|c}
2 & 1 & 1 & -1 & 1 & 0 & 0 & 6 \\
1 & 1 & 2 & 0 & 0 & 1 & 0 & 8 \\
\hline
30 & 30 & 10 & 0 & M & 0 & 1 & 0 \\
\end{array}\right]$$

Eliminate M in the a_1 column

$R_3 + (-M)R_1 \rightarrow R_3$

Begin pivot operations. Assume M is so large that $-2M + 30$, $-M + 30$, and $-M + 10$ are all negative.

$$\sim \left[\begin{array}{ccccccc|c}
② & 1 & 1 & -1 & 1 & 0 & 0 & 6 \\
1 & 1 & 2 & 0 & 0 & 1 & 0 & 8 \\
\hline
-2M+30 & -M+30 & -M+10 & M & 0 & 0 & 1 & -6M \\
\end{array}\right]$$

$\frac{1}{2}R_1 \rightarrow R_1$

$$\sim \begin{bmatrix}
x_1 & x_2 & x_3 & s_1 & a_1 & s_2 & P & \\
1 & \frac{1}{2} & \frac{1}{2} & -\frac{1}{2} & \frac{1}{2} & 0 & 0 & 3 \\
1 & 1 & 2 & 0 & 0 & 1 & 0 & 8 \\
-2M+30 & -M+30 & -M+10 & M & 0 & 0 & 1 & -6M
\end{bmatrix} \quad \begin{array}{l} R_2 + (-1)R_1 \to R_2 \\ R_3 + (2M-30)R_1 \to R_3 \end{array}$$

$$\sim \begin{bmatrix}
1 & \frac{1}{2} & \frac{1}{2} & -\frac{1}{2} & \frac{1}{2} & 0 & 0 & 3 \\
0 & \frac{1}{2} & \boxed{\frac{3}{2}} & \frac{1}{2} & -\frac{1}{2} & 1 & 0 & 5 \\
0 & 15 & -5 & 15 & M-15 & 0 & 1 & -90
\end{bmatrix} \quad \frac{2}{3}R_2 \to R_2$$

$$\sim \begin{bmatrix}
1 & \frac{1}{2} & \frac{1}{2} & -\frac{1}{2} & \frac{1}{2} & 0 & 0 & 3 \\
0 & \frac{1}{3} & 1 & \frac{1}{3} & -\frac{1}{3} & \frac{2}{3} & 0 & \frac{10}{3} \\
0 & 15 & -5 & 15 & M-15 & 0 & 1 & -90
\end{bmatrix} \quad \begin{array}{l} R_1 + (-\frac{1}{2})R_2 \to R_1 \\ R_3 + 5R_2 \to R_3 \end{array}$$

$$\sim \begin{bmatrix}
1 & \frac{1}{3} & 0 & -\frac{2}{3} & \frac{2}{3} & -\frac{1}{3} & 0 & \frac{4}{3} \\
0 & \frac{1}{3} & 1 & \frac{1}{3} & -\frac{1}{3} & \frac{2}{3} & 0 & \frac{10}{3} \\
0 & \frac{50}{3} & 0 & \frac{50}{3} & M-\frac{50}{3} & \frac{10}{3} & 1 & -\frac{220}{3}
\end{bmatrix}$$

Since the bottom row has no negative indicators, the optimal solution for the modified problem is

$$x_1 = \tfrac{4}{3}, \quad x_2 = 0, \quad x_3 = \tfrac{10}{3}, \quad s_1 = 0, \quad a_1 = 0, \quad s_2 = 0, \quad P = -\tfrac{220}{3}$$

Since $a_1 = 0$, deleting a_1 produces the solution to the original maximization problem and also to the minimization problem. Thus

$$\text{Min } C = -\text{Max } P = -(-\tfrac{220}{3}) = 73\tfrac{1}{3} \quad \text{at} \quad x_1 = \tfrac{4}{3}, \quad x_2 = 0, \quad x_3 = \tfrac{10}{3}$$

That is, a minimum cost of $73\frac{1}{3}$ for gemstones will be realized if $1\frac{1}{3}$ type A, no type B, and $3\frac{1}{3}$ type C stones are processed each day. The fractional values for production make sense if we think of them as average daily production figures.

Problem 20 Repeat Example 20 with $C = 40x_1 + 40x_2 + 10x_3$.

■ Summary of Methods of Solution

The big M method can be used to solve any minimization problem, including those that can be solved by the dual method. (Note that Example 20 could have been solved by the dual method.) Both methods of solving minimization problems are important. You will be instructed to solve most minimization problems in Exercise 2-6 by the big M method in order to gain more experience with that method. If the method of solution is not specified, then the dual method is usually easier.

The following summary should help you select the proper method of solution for any linear programming problem.

Summary of Methods

Type of Problem	*Method of Solution*
1. Standard maximization problem: maximization, ⩽ problem constraints, nonnegative constants on right side of problem constraints	Simplex method with slack variables
2. Minimization, ⩾ problem constraints, nonnegative coefficients in objective function.	Form dual and solve by method 1
3. Maximization, mixed constraints, nonnegative constants on right side of problem constraints	Form modified problem with slack, surplus, and artificial variables and solve by the big M method
4. Minimization, mixed constraints, nonnegative constants on right side of problem constraints	Maximize negative of objective function by method 3

■ Larger Problems — A Refinery Application

Up to this point, all of the problems could be solved by hand. The simplex method will solve problems with a large number of variables and constraints; however, a computer is generally used to perform the actual pivot operations. As a final application, we will consider a problem that would require the use of a computer to complete the solution.

Example 21 A refinery produces two grades of gasoline, regular and premium, by blending together two components, A and B. Component A has an octane rating of 90 and costs $28 a barrel. Component B has an octane rating of 110 and costs $32 a barrel. The octane rating for regular gasoline must be at least 95, and the octane rating for premium must be at least 105. Regular gasoline sells for $34 a barrel and premium sells for $40 a barrel. Currently, the company has 30,000 barrels of component A and 20,000 barrels of component B. It also has orders for 20,000 barrels of regular and 10,000 barrels of premium that it must fill. Assuming that all the gasoline produced can be sold, determine the maximum possible profit.

Solution   First we will organize the information given in the problem in tabular form (Table 4).

Table 4

Component	Octane Rating	Cost	Available Supply
A	90	$28	30,000 barrels
B	110	$32	20,000 barrels

Grade	Minimum Octane Rating	Selling Price	Existing Orders
Regular	95	$34	20,000 barrels
Premium	105	$40	10,000 barrels

Let

x_1 = Number of barrels of component A used in regular gasoline

x_2 = Number of barrels of component A used in premium gasoline

x_3 = Number of barrels of component B used in regular gasoline

x_4 = Number of barrels of component B used in premium gasoline

The total amount of component A used is $x_1 + x_2$. This cannot exceed the available supply. Thus, one constraint is

$$x_1 + x_2 \leq 30,000$$

The corresponding inequality for component B is

$$x_3 + x_4 \leq 20,000$$

The amounts of regular and premium gasoline produced must be sufficient to meet the existing orders:

$$x_1 + x_3 \geq 20,000 \quad \text{Regular}$$
$$x_2 + x_4 \geq 10,000 \quad \text{Premium}$$

Now let's consider the octane ratings. The octane rating of a blend is simply the proportional average of the octane ratings of the components. Thus, the octane rating for regular gasoline is

$$90 \frac{x_1}{x_1 + x_3} + 110 \frac{x_3}{x_1 + x_3}$$

where $x_1/(x_1 + x_3)$ is the percentage of component A used in regular gasoline and $x_3/(x_1 + x_3)$ is the percentage of component B. The final octane rating of regular gasoline must be at least 95; thus,

$$90\,\frac{x_1}{x_1+x_3}+110\,\frac{x_3}{x_1+x_3}\geqslant 95 \qquad \text{Multiply by } x_1+x_3$$

$$90x_1+110x_3\geqslant 95(x_1+x_3) \qquad \text{Collect like terms on the left side}$$

$$-5x_1+\ 15x_3\geqslant 0$$

The corresponding inequality for premium gasoline is

$$90\,\frac{x_2}{x_2+x_4}+110\,\frac{x_4}{x_2+x_4}\geqslant 105$$

$$90x_2+110x_4\geqslant 105(x_2+x_4)$$

$$-15x_2+\ 5x_4\geqslant 0$$

The cost of the components used is

$$C=28(x_1+x_2)+32(x_3+x_4)$$

The revenue from selling all the gasoline is

$$R=34(x_1+x_3)+40(x_2+x_4)$$

and the profit is

$$P=R-C$$
$$=34(x_1+x_3)+40(x_2+x_4)-28(x_1+x_2)-32(x_3+x_4)$$
$$=(34-28)x_1+(40-28)x_2+(34-32)x_3+(40-32)x_4$$
$$=6x_1+12x_2+2x_3+8x_4$$

To find the maximum profit, we must solve the following linear programming problem:

Maximize
$$P=6x_1+12x_2+2x_3+8x_4 \qquad \text{Profit}$$

Subject to

x_1+	x_2		$\leqslant 30{,}000$	Available A
		$x_3+\ x_4$	$\leqslant 20{,}000$	Available B
x_1		$+\ x_3$	$\geqslant 20{,}000$	Required regular
	x_2	$+\ x_4$	$\geqslant 10{,}000$	Required premium
$-5x_1$		$+15x_3$	$\geqslant 0$	Octane for regular
	$-15x_2$	$+5x_4$	$\geqslant 0$	Octane for premium

$$x_1,x_2,x_3,x_4\geqslant 0$$

The tableau for this problem would have seven rows and sixteen columns. Solving this problem by hand is possible but would require considerable effort. Instead, we used a computer program to solve this problem. [The computer program can be found in the computer supplement for this text (see Preface).] The output from this program is displayed in Table 5 on the next page.

Table 5

Input to Program	Output from Program
NUMBER OF VARIABLES = 4	DECISION VARIABLES
NUMBER OF CONSTRAINTS = 6	X1 = 26250
2 OF THE FORM <=	X2 = 3750
4 OF THE FORM >=	X3 = 8750
0 OF THE FORM =	X4 = 11250
CONSTRAINTS	SLACK VARIABLES
1 1 0 0 30000	S1 = 0
	S2 = 0
0 0 1 1 20000	
	SURPLUS VARIABLES
1 0 1 0 20000	S3 = 15000
	S4 = 5000
0 1 0 1 10000	S5 = 0
	S6 = 0
-5 0 1 5 0 0	
	MAXIMUM VALUE OF OBJECTIVE FUNCTION
0 -15 0 5 0	310000
OBJECTIVE FUNCTION	
6 12 2 8	

According to the output in Table 5, the refinery should blend 26,250 barrels of component A and 8,750 barrels of component B to produce 35,000 barrels of regular. They should blend 3,750 barrels of component A and 11,250 barrels of component B to produce 15,000 barrels of premium. This will result in a maximum profit of $310,000.

Problem 21 Suppose the refinery in Example 21 has 35,000 barrels of component A, which costs $25 a barrel, and 15,000 barrels of component B, which costs $35 a barrel. If all the other information is unchanged, formulate a linear programming problem whose solution is the maximum profit. Do not attempt to solve the problem (unless you have access to a computer and a program that solves linear programming problems).

Answers to Matched Problems

17. Maximize $P = 3x_1 - 2x_2 + x_3 - Ma_1 - Ma_2 - Ma_3$

Subject to
$$x_1 - 2x_2 + x_3 - s_1 + a_1 = 5$$
$$x_1 + 3x_2 - 4x_3 - s_2 + a_2 = 10$$
$$2x_1 + 4x_2 + 5x_3 + s_3 = 20$$
$$-3x_1 + x_2 + x_3 + a_3 = 15$$
$$x_1, x_2, x_3, s_1, a_1, s_2, a_2, s_3, a_3 \geq 0$$

18. Max $P = 22$ at $x_1 = 6$, $x_2 = 4$, $x_3 = 0$
19. No solution
20. Min $C = \$86\frac{2}{3}$ at $x_1 = \frac{4}{3}$, $x_2 = 0$, $x_3 = \frac{10}{3}$
21. Maximize $P = 9x_1 + 15x_2 - x_3 + 5x_4$

$$
\begin{array}{rrrrr}
\text{Subject to} & x_1 + & x_2 & & \leqslant 35{,}000 \\
& & & x_3 + & x_4 \leqslant 15{,}000 \\
& x_1 & + & x_3 & \geqslant 20{,}000 \\
& & x_2 & + & x_4 \geqslant 10{,}000 \\
& -5x_1 & + 15x_3 & & \geqslant 0 \\
& & -15x_2 & + 5x_4 & \geqslant 0 \\
& & x_1,\, x_2,\, x_3,\, x_4 & \geqslant 0
\end{array}
$$

Exercise 2-6

A   In Problems 1–8:

(A) Introduce slack, surplus, and artificial variables and form the modified problem.
(B) Write the preliminary simplex tableau for the modified problem and find the initial simplex tableau.
(C) Find the optimal solution of the modified problem by applying the simplex method to the initial simplex tableau.
(D) Find the optimal solution of the original problem, if it exists.

1. Maximize $P = 5x_1 + 2x_2$
   Subject to $x_1 + 2x_2 \leqslant 12$
   $x_1 + x_2 \geqslant 4$
   $x_1, x_2 \geqslant 0$

2. Maximize $P = 3x_1 + 7x_2$
   Subject to $2x_1 + x_2 \leqslant 16$
   $x_1 + x_2 \geqslant 6$
   $x_1, x_2 \geqslant 0$

3. Maximize $P = 3x_1 + 5x_2$
   Subject to $2x_1 + x_2 \leqslant 8$
   $x_1 + x_2 = 6$
   $x_1, x_2 \geqslant 0$

4. Maximize $P = 4x_1 + 3x_2$
   Subject to $x_1 + 3x_2 \leqslant 24$
   $x_1 + x_2 = 12$
   $x_1, x_2 \geqslant 0$

5. Maximize $P = 4x_1 + 3x_2$
   Subject to $-x_1 + 2x_2 \leqslant 2$
   $x_1 + x_2 \geqslant 4$
   $x_1, x_2 \geqslant 0$

6. Maximize $P = 3x_1 + 4x_2$
   Subject to $x_1 - 2x_2 \leqslant 2$
   $x_1 + x_2 \geqslant 5$
   $x_1, x_2 \geqslant 0$

7. Maximize $P = 5x_1 + 10x_2$
   Subject to $x_1 + x_2 \leqslant 3$
   $2x_1 + 3x_2 \geqslant 12$
   $x_1, x_2 \geqslant 0$

8. Maximize $P = 4x_1 + 6x_2$
   Subject to $x_1 + x_2 \leqslant 2$
   $3x_1 + 5x_2 \geqslant 15$
   $x_1, x_2 \geqslant 0$

B   *Use the big M method to solve the following problems:*

9. Minimize and maximize

$$P = 6x_1 - 2x_2$$

Subject to $x_1 + x_2 \leqslant 10$

$3x_1 + 2x_2 \geqslant 24$

$x_1 \; x_2 \geqslant 0$

10. Minimize and maximize

$$P = -4x_1 + 16x_2$$

Subject to $3x_1 + x_2 \leqslant 28$

$x_1 + 2x_2 \geqslant 16$

$x_1, x_2 \geqslant 0$

11. Maximize $P = 2x_1 + 5x_2$

Subject to $x_1 + 2x_2 \leqslant 18$

$2x_1 + x_2 \leqslant 21$

$x_1 + x_2 \geqslant 10$

$x_1, x_2 \geqslant 0$

12. Maximize $P = 6x_1 + 2x_2$

Subject to $x_1 + 2x_2 \leqslant 20$

$2x_1 + x_2 \leqslant 16$

$x_1 + x_2 \geqslant 9$

$x_1, x_2 \geqslant 0$

13. Maximize

$$P = 10x_1 + 12x_2 + 20x_3$$

Subject to

$3x_1 + x_2 + 2x_3 \geqslant 12$

$x_1 - x_2 + 2x_3 = 6$

$x_1, x_2, x_3 \geqslant 0$

14. Maximize

$$P = 5x_1 + 7x_2 + 9x_3$$

Subject to

$x_1 - x_2 + x_3 \geqslant 20$

$2x_1 + x_2 + 3x_3 = 36$

$x_1, x_2, x_3 \geqslant 0$

15. Minimize

$$C = -5x_1 - 12x_2 + 16x_3$$

Subject to

$x_1 + 2x_2 + x_3 \leqslant 10$

$2x_1 + 3x_2 + x_3 \geqslant 6$

$2x_1 + x_2 - x_3 = 1$

$x_1, x_2, x_3 \geqslant 0$

16. Minimize

$$C = -3x_1 + 15x_2 - 4x_3$$

Subject to

$2x_1 + x_2 + 3x_3 \leqslant 24$

$x_1 + 2x_2 + x_3 \geqslant 6$

$x_1 - 3x_2 + x_3 = 2$

$x_1, x_2, x_3 \geqslant 0$

17. Maximize

$$P = 3x_1 + 5x_2 + 6x_3$$

Subject to

$2x_1 + x_2 + 2x_3 \leqslant 8$

$2x_1 + x_2 - 2x_3 = 0$

$x_1, x_2, x_3 \geqslant 0$

18. Maximize

$$P = 3x_1 + 6x_2 + 2x_3$$

Subject to

$2x_1 + x_2 + 3x_3 \leqslant 12$

$2x_1 - 2x_2 + x_3 = 0$

$x_1, x_2, x_3 \geqslant 0$

19. Maximize

$$P = 2x_1 + 3x_2 + 4x_3$$

Subject to

$x_1 + 2x_2 + x_3 \leqslant 25$

$2x_1 + x_2 + 2x_3 \leqslant 60$

$x_1 + 2x_2 - x_3 \geqslant 10$

$x_1, x_2, x_3 \geqslant 0$

20. Maximize

$$P = 5x_1 + 2x_2 + 9x_3$$

Subject to

$2x_1 + 4x_2 + x_3 \leqslant 150$

$3x_1 + 2x_2 + x_3 \leqslant 90$

$-x_1 + 5x_2 + x_3 \geqslant 120$

$x_1, x_2, x_3 \geqslant 0$

21. Maximize
$$P = x_1 + 2x_2 + 5x_3$$
Subject to
$$x_1 + 3x_2 + 2x_3 \leqslant 60$$
$$2x_1 + 5x_2 + 2x_3 \geqslant 50$$
$$x_1 - 2x_2 + x_3 \geqslant 40$$
$$x_1, x_2, x_3 \geqslant 0$$

22. Maximize
$$P = 2x_1 + 4x_2 + x_3$$
Subject to
$$2x_1 + 3x_2 + 5x_3 \leqslant 280$$
$$2x_1 + 2x_2 + x_3 \geqslant 140$$
$$2x_1 + x_2 \geqslant 150$$
$$x_1, x_2, x_3 \geqslant 0$$

C   *Problems 23 – 30 are mixed. Some can be solved by the methods presented in Sections 2-4 and 2-5, while others must be solved by the big M method.*

23. Minimize
$$C = 10x_1 - 40x_2 - 5x_3$$
Subject to
$$x_1 + 3x_2 \leqslant 6$$
$$4x_2 + x_3 \leqslant 3$$
$$x_1, x_2, x_3 \geqslant 0$$

24. Maximize
$$P = 7x_1 - 5x_2 + 2x_3$$
Subject to
$$x_1 - 2x_2 + x_3 \geqslant -8$$
$$x_1 - x_2 + x_3 \leqslant 10$$
$$x_1, x_2, x_3 \geqslant 0$$

25. Maximize
$$P = -5x_1 + 10x_2 + 15x_3$$
Subject to
$$2x_1 + 3x_2 + x_3 \leqslant 24$$
$$x_1 - 2x_2 - 2x_3 \geqslant 1$$
$$x_1, x_2, x_3 \geqslant 0$$

26. Minimize
$$C = -5x_1 + 10x_2 + 15x_3$$
Subject to
$$2x_1 + 3x_2 + x_3 \leqslant 24$$
$$x_1 - 2x_2 - 2x_3 \geqslant 1$$
$$x_1, x_2, x_3 \geqslant 0$$

27. Minimize
$$C = 10x_1 + 40x_2 + 5x_3$$
Subject to
$$x_1 + 3x_2 \geqslant 6$$
$$4x_2 + x_3 \geqslant 3$$
$$x_1, x_2, x_3 \geqslant 0$$

28. Maximize
$$P = 8x_1 + 2x_2 - 10x_3$$
Subject to
$$x_1 + x_2 - 3x_3 \leqslant 6$$
$$4x_1 - x_2 + 2x_3 \leqslant -7$$
$$x_1, x_2, x_3 \geqslant 0$$

29. Maximize
$$P = 12x_1 + 9x_2 + 5x_3$$
Subject to
$$x_1 + 2x_2 + x_3 \leqslant 40$$
$$2x_1 + x_2 + 3x_3 \leqslant 60$$
$$x_1, x_2, x_3 \geqslant 0$$

30. Minimize
$$C = 10x_1 + 12x_2 + 28x_3$$
Subject to
$$4x_1 + 2x_2 + 3x_3 \geqslant 20$$
$$5x_1 - x_2 - 4x_3 \leqslant 10$$
$$x_1, x_2, x_3 \geqslant 0$$

Applications

In Problems 31–38, formulate each problem as a linear programming problem and solve by using the big M method.

Business & Economics

31. *Manufacturing — resource allocation.* An electronics company manufactures two types of add-on memory modules for microcomputers, a 16K module and a 64K module. Each 16K module requires 10 minutes for assembly and 2 minutes for testing. Each 64K module requires 15 minutes for assembly and 4 minutes for testing. The company makes a profit of $18 on each 16K module and $30 on each 64K module. The assembly department can work a maximum of 1,500 minutes per day, and the testing department can work a maximum of 500 minutes a day. In order to satisfy current orders, the company must produce at least 50 16K modules per day. How many units of each module should the company manufacture each day in order to maximize the daily profit? What is the maximum profit?

32. *Manufacturing — resource allocation.* Repeat Problem 31 if the assembly department can work a maximum of 2,100 minutes daily.

33. *Advertising.* A company planning an advertising campaign to attract new customers wants to place a total of at most ten ads in three newspapers. Each ad in the *Sentinel* costs $200 and will be read by 2,000 people. Each ad in the *Journal* costs $200 and will be read by 500 people. Each ad in the *Tribune* costs $100 and will be read by 1,500 people. The company wants at least 16,000 people to read its ads. How many ads should it place in each paper in order to minimize the advertising costs? What is the minimum cost?

34. *Advertising.* Repeat Problem 33 if the *Tribune* is unable to accept more than 4 ads from the company.

Life Sciences

35. *Nutrition — people.* An individual on a high-protein, low-carbohydrate diet requires at least 100 units of protein and at most 24 units of carbohydrates daily. The diet will consist entirely of three special liquid diet foods, *A*, *B*, and *C*. The contents and cost of the diet foods are given in the table. How many bottles of each brand of diet food should be consumed daily in order to meet the protein and carbohydrate requirements at minimal cost? What is the minimum cost?

	Units per Bottle		
	A	*B*	*C*
Protein	10	10	20
Carbohydrates	2	3	4
Cost per bottle	$0.60	$0.40	$0.90

36. *Nutrition — people.* Repeat Problem 35 if brand *C* liquid diet food costs $1.50 a bottle.

37. *Nutrition — plants.* A farmer can use three types of plant food, mix *A*, mix *B*, and mix *C*. The amounts (in pounds) of nitrogen, phosphoric acid, and potash in a cubic yard of each mix are given in the table. Tests performed on the soil in a large field indicate that the field needs at least 800 pounds of potash. The tests also indicate that no more than 700 pounds of phosphoric acid should be added to the field. The farmer plans to plant a crop that requires a great deal of nitrogen. How many cubic yards of each mix should he add to the field in order to satisfy the potash and phosphoric acid requirements and maximize the amount of nitrogen added? What is the maximum amount of nitrogen?

	Pounds per Cubic Yard		
	A	*B*	*C*
Nitrogen	12	16	8
Phosphoric acid	12	8	16
Potash	16	8	16

38. *Nutrition — plants.* Repeat Problem 37 if the field should have no more than 1,000 pounds of phosphoric acid.

In Problems 39–45, formulate each problem as a linear programming problem. Do not solve the linear programming problem.

Business & Economics

39. *Manufacturing — production scheduling.* A company manufactures car and truck frames at plants in Milwaukee and Racine. The Milwaukee plant has a daily operating budget of $50,000 and can produce at most 300 frames daily in any combination. It costs $150 to manufacture a car frame and $200 to manufacture a truck frame at the Milwaukee plant. The Racine plant has a daily operating budget of $35,000, can produce a maximum combined total of 200 frames daily, and produces a car frame at a cost of $135 and a truck frame at a cost of $180. Based on past demand, the company wants to limit production to a maximum of 250 car frames and 350 truck frames per day. If the company realizes a profit of $50 on each car frame and $70 on each truck frame, how many frames of each type should be produced at each plant to maximize the daily profit?

40. *Finances — loan distributions.* A savings and loan company has $3 million to lend. The types of loans and annual returns offered by the company are given in the table. State laws require that at least 50% of the money loaned for mortgages must be for first mortgages and that at least 30% of the total amount loaned must be for either first or second mortgages. Company policy requires that the amount of signature and automobile loans cannot exceed 25% of the total amount loaned and that signature loans cannot exceed 15% of the total amount loaned. How much money should be allocated to each type of loan in order to maximize the company's return?

Type of Loan	Annual Return
Signature	18%
First mortgage	12%
Second mortgage	14%
Automobile	16%

41. *Blending — petroleum.* A refinery produces two grades of gasoline, regular and premium, by blending together three components, A, B, and C. Component A has an octane rating of 90 and costs $28 a barrel, component B has an octane rating of 100 and costs $30 a barrel, and component C has an octane rating of 110 and costs $34 a barrel. The octane rating for regular must be at least 95 and the octane rating for premium must be at least 105. Regular gasoline sells for $38 a barrel and premium sells for $46 a barrel. The company has 40,000 barrels of component A, 25,000 barrels of component B, and 15,000 barrels of component C and must produce at least 30,000 barrels of regular and 25,000 barrels of premium. How should they blend the components in order to maximize their profit?

42. *Blending — food processing.* A company produces two brands of trail mix, regular and deluxe, by mixing dried fruits, nuts, and cereal. The recipes for the mixes are given in the table. The company has 1,200 pounds of dried fruits, 750 pounds of nuts, and 1,500 pounds of cereal to be used in producing the mixes. The company makes a profit of $0.40 on each pound of regular mix and $0.60 on each pound of deluxe mix. How many pounds of each ingredient should be used in each mix in order to maximize the company's profit?

Type of Mix	Ingredients
Regular	At least 20% nuts
	At most 40% cereal
Deluxe	At least 30% nuts
	At most 25% cereal

Life Sciences   43. *Nutrition — people.* A dietitian in a hospital is to arrange a special diet using the foods L, M, and N. The table below gives the nutritional contents and the cost of one ounce of each food. The daily requirements for the diet are at least 400 units of calcium, at least 200 units of iron, at least 300 units of vitamin A, at most 150 units of cholesterol, and at most 900 calories. How many ounces of each food should be used in order to meet the requirements of the diet at minimal cost?

	Units per Ounce		
	L	M	N
Calcium	30	10	30
Iron	10	10	10
Vitamin A	10	30	20
Cholesterol	8	4	6
Calories	60	40	50
Cost per ounce	$0.40	$0.60	$0.80

44. *Nutrition — feed mixtures.* A farmer grows three crops, corn, oats, and soybeans, which he mixes together to feed his cows and pigs. At least 40% of the feed mix for the cows must be corn. The feed mix for the pigs must contain at least twice as much soybeans as corn. He has harvested 1,000 bushels of corn, 500 bushels of oats, and 1,000 bushels of soybeans. He needs 1,000 bushels of each feed mix for his livestock. The unused corn, oats, and soybeans can be sold for $4, $3.50, and $3.25 a bushel, respectively (thus, these amounts also represent the cost of the crops used to feed the livestock). How many bushels of each crop should be used in each feed mix in order to produce sufficient food for the livestock at minimal cost?

Social Sciences 45. *Education — resource allocation.* Three towns are forming a consolidated school district with two high schools. Each high school has a maximum capacity of 2,000 students. Town A has 500 high school students, town B has 1,200, and town C has 1,800. The weekly costs of transporting a student from each town to each school are given in the table. In order to keep the enrollment balanced, the school board has decided that each high school must enroll at least 40% of the total student population. Furthermore, no more than 60% of the students in any town should be sent to the same high school. How many students from each town should be enrolled in each school in order to meet these requirements and minimize the cost of transporting the students?

	Weekly Transportation Cost per Student	
	School I	School II
Town A	$4	$8
Town B	6	4
Town C	3	9

2-7 Chapter Review

<table>
<tr>
<td>Important Terms
and Symbols</td>
<td>2-1</td>
<td>*Systems of linear inequalities in two variables.* Graph of a linear inequality in two variables, upper half-plane, lower half-plane, graphical solution, solution region, bounded regions, unbounded regions, corner point, feasible solution, feasible region</td>
</tr>
<tr>
<td></td>
<td>2-2</td>
<td>*Linear programming in two dimensions—a geometric approach.* Linear programming problem, decision variables, objective function, problem constraints, nonnegative constraints, mathematical model, graphical solution, maximization problem, constant-profit line, isoprofit line, optimal solution, minimization problem, linear function, multiple optimal solutions, empty feasible region, unbounded objective function</td>
</tr>
<tr>
<td></td>
<td>2-3</td>
<td>*A geometric introduction to the simplex method.* Slack variables, basic solution, basic feasible solution, nonbasic variables, basic variables, simplex method</td>
</tr>
<tr>
<td></td>
<td>2-4</td>
<td>*The simplex method: maximization with ≤ problem constraints.* Standard maximization problem, initial form, obvious basic solution, obvious basic feasible solution, simplex tableau, indicators, pivot column, pivot row, pivot element, pivot operation</td>
</tr>
<tr>
<td></td>
<td>2-5</td>
<td>*The dual; minimization with ≥ problem constraints.* Dual problem, transpose, solution of minimization problems, transportation problem</td>
</tr>
<tr>
<td></td>
<td>2-6</td>
<td>*Maximization and minimization with mixed problem constraints.* Surplus variable, artificial variable, modified problem, preliminary simplex tableau, initial simplex tableau, big M method</td>
</tr>
</table>

Exercise 2-7   Chapter Review

Work through all the problems in this chapter review and check your answers in the back of the book. (Answers to all review problems are there.) Where weaknesses show up, review appropriate sections in the text.

A   1.   Solve the system of linear inequalities graphically:

$$3x_1 + x_2 \leq 9$$
$$2x_1 + 6x_2 \leq 18$$
$$x_1, x_2 \geq 0$$

2. Solve the linear programming problem geometrically:

   Maximize $P = 6x_1 + 2x_2$

   Subject to $2x_1 + x_2 \leqslant 8$

   $$x_1 + 2x_2 \leqslant 10$$

   $$x_1, x_2 \geqslant 0$$

3. Convert the problem constraints in Problem 2 into a system of equations using slack variables.

4. Find all basic solutions for the system in Problem 3 and determine which basic solutions are feasible.

5. Write the simplex tableau for Problem 2 and circle the pivot element.

6. Solve Problem 2 using the simplex method.

7. Identify the basic and nonbasic variables. Find the pivot element and perform one pivot operation.

$$
\begin{bmatrix}
x_1 & x_2 & x_3 & s_1 & s_2 & s_3 & P & \\
2 & 1 & 3 & -1 & 0 & 0 & 0 & 20 \\
3 & 0 & 4 & 1 & 1 & 0 & 0 & 30 \\
2 & 0 & 5 & 2 & 0 & 1 & 0 & 10 \\
\hline
-8 & 0 & -5 & 3 & 0 & 0 & 1 & 50
\end{bmatrix}
$$

8. Find the obvious basic solution for each tableau. Determine whether the optimal solution has been reached, additional pivoting is required, or the problem has no solution.

   (A)
$$
\begin{bmatrix}
x_1 & x_2 & s_1 & s_2 & P & \\
4 & 1 & 0 & 0 & 0 & 2 \\
2 & 0 & 1 & 1 & 0 & 5 \\
\hline
-2 & 0 & 3 & 0 & 1 & 12
\end{bmatrix}
$$

   (B)
$$
\begin{bmatrix}
-1 & 3 & 0 & 1 & 0 & 7 \\
0 & 2 & 1 & 0 & 0 & 0 \\
\hline
-2 & 1 & 0 & 0 & 1 & 22
\end{bmatrix}
$$

   (C)
$$
\begin{bmatrix}
1 & -2 & 0 & 4 & 0 & 6 \\
0 & 2 & 1 & 6 & 0 & 15 \\
\hline
0 & 3 & 0 & 2 & 1 & 10
\end{bmatrix}
$$

9. Solve the linear programming problem geometrically:

   Minimize $C = 5x_1 + 2x_2$

   Subject to $x_1 + 3x_2 \geqslant 15$

   $$2x_1 + x_2 \geqslant 20$$

   $$x_1, x_2 \geqslant 0$$

10. Form the dual of Problem 9.

11. Write the initial form for the dual in Problem 10.

12. Write the first simplex tableau for the dual in Problem 10 and label the columns.

13. Use the simplex method to find the optimal solution of the dual in Problem 10.

14. Use the final simplex tableau in Problem 13 to find the optimal solution of Problem 9.

B 15. Solve the linear programming problem geometrically:

$$\text{Maximize} \quad P = 3x_1 + 4x_2$$
$$\text{Subject to} \quad 2x_1 + 4x_2 \leq 24$$
$$3x_1 + 3x_2 \leq 21$$
$$4x_1 + 2x_2 \leq 20$$
$$x_1, x_2 \geq 0$$

16. Solve Problem 15 using the simplex method.

17. Solve the linear programming problem geometrically:

$$\text{Minimize} \quad C = 3x_1 + 8x_2$$
$$\text{Subject to} \quad x_1 + x_2 \geq 10$$
$$x_1 + 2x_2 \geq 15$$
$$x_2 \geq 3$$
$$x_1, x_2 \geq 0$$

18. Form the dual of Problem 17.

19. Solve Problem 18 by applying the simplex method.

Solve the following linear programming problems:

20. $\text{Maximize} \quad P = 5x_1 + 3x_2 - 3x_3$

$$\text{Subject to} \quad x_1 - x_2 - 2x_3 \leq 3$$
$$2x_1 + 2x_2 - 5x_3 \leq 10$$
$$x_1, x_2, x_3 \geq 0$$

21. $\text{Maximize} \quad P = 5x_1 + 3x_2 - 3x_3$

$$\text{Subject to} \quad x_1 - x_2 - 2x_3 \leq 3$$
$$x_1 + x_2 \leq 5$$
$$x_1, x_2, x_3 \geq 0$$

C *Solve the following minimization problems by the dual method.*

22. Minimize $C = 2x_1 + 3x_2$

Subject to $2x_1 + x_2 \leq 20$

$2x_1 + x_2 \geq 10$

$x_1 + 2x_2 \geq 8$

$x_1, x_2 \geq 0$

23. Minimize $C = 15x_1 + 12x_2 + 15x_3 + 18x_4$

Subject to $x_1 + x_2 \qquad\qquad \leq 240$

$x_3 + x_4 \leq 500$

$x_1 \qquad + x_3 \qquad \geq 400$

$x_2 \qquad + x_4 \geq 300$

$x_1, x_2, x_3, x_4 \geq 0$

Applications

Business & Economics

Formulate the following as linear programming problems but do not solve:

24. *Manufacturing — resource allocation.* South Shore Sail Loft manufactures regular and competition sails. Each regular sail takes 2 hours to cut and 4 hours to sew. Each competition sail takes 3 hours to cut and 9 hours to sew. The Loft makes a profit of $100 on each regular sail and $200 on each competition sail. If there are 150 hours available in the cutting department and 360 hours available in the sewing department, how many sails of each type should the company manufacture in order to maximize their profit?

25. *Transportation — shipping schedule.* A company produces motors for washing machines at factory *A* and factory *B*. Factory *A* can produce 1,500 motors a month and factory *B* can produce 1,000 motors a month. The motors are then shipped to one of three plants, where the washing machines are assembled. In order to meet anticipated demand, plant *X* must assemble 500 washing machines a month, plant *Y* must assemble 700 washing machines a month, and plant *Z* must assemble 800 washing machines a month. The shipping charges for one motor are given in the table. Determine a shipping schedule that will minimize the cost of transporting the motors from the factories to the assembly plants.

| | **Shipping Charges** | | |
	Plant *X*	Plant *Y*	Plant *Z*
Factory *A*	$5	$8	$12
Factory *B*	$9	$7	$ 6

Life Sciences

26. *Nutrition — animals.* A special diet for laboratory animals is to contain at least 300 units of vitamins, 200 units of minerals, and 900 calories. There are two feed mixes available, mix A and mix B. A gram of mix A contains 3 units of vitamins, 2 units of minerals, and 6 calories. A gram of mix B contains 4 units of vitamins, 5 units of minerals, and 10 calories. Mix A costs $0.02 per gram and mix B costs $0.04 per gram. How many grams of each mix should be used to satisfy the requirements of the diet at minimal cost?

Mathematics of Finance

3

CHAPTER 3 — Contents

This chapter is independent of the others; you can study it at any time. Table V in Appendix B can be used to solve most of the problems on compound interest, annuities, amortization, and so on. However, if you have a financial or scientific calculator (both types are now available for under $20) you will be able to work all the problems without tables. Even if you use tables, an inexpensive hand calculator that has at least $+, -, \times, \div$, and y^x keys will take most of the drudgery out of the calculations. This chapter includes a number of problems that do require the use of a financial or scientific calculator; these are clearly marked, and may be omitted without loss of continuity.

If time permits, you may wish to cover arithmetic and geometric progressions, discussed in Appendix A, before beginning this chapter. Though not necessary, these topics will provide additional insight into some of the topics covered.

To avoid repeating the statement many times, we now point out:

Throughout the chapter, interest rates are to be converted to decimal form before they are used in a formula.

3-1 Simple Interest

Simple interest is generally used only on short-term notes—often of duration less than one year. The concept of simple interest, however, forms the basis of much of the rest of the material developed in this chapter, for which time periods may be much longer than a year.

If you deposit a sum of money P in a savings account or if you borrow a sum of money P from a lending agent, then P is referred to as the **principal.** When money is borrowed—whether it is a savings institution borrowing from you when you deposit money in your account or you borrowing from a lending agent—a fee is charged for the money borrowed. This fee is rent paid for the use of another's money, just as rent is paid for the use of another's house. The fee is called **interest.** It is usually computed as a percentage (called the **interest rate**)* of the principal over a given period of time. The interest rate, unless otherwise stated, is an annual rate. Simple interest is given by the following formula:

Simple Interest

$$I = Prt \qquad (1)$$

where

$P = $ Principal

$r = $ Annual simple interest rate (written as a decimal)

$t = $ Time in years

For example, the interest on a loan of $100 at 12% for 9 months would be

$I = Prt$

$= (100)(0.12)(0.75)$ Convert 12% to a decimal (0.12)

$= \$9$ and 9 months to years ($\frac{9}{12} = 0.75$)

At the end of 9 months, the borrower would repay the principal ($100) plus the interest ($9), or a total of $109.

In general, if a principal P is borrowed at a rate 100r%, then after t years the borrower will owe the lender an amount A that will include the principal P (the **face value** of the note) plus the interest I (the rent paid for the use of the money). Since P is the amount that is borrowed now and A is the amount that must be paid back in the future, P is often referred to as the **present value** and A as the **future value**. The formula relating A and P is as follows:

Amount—Simple Interest

$$A = P + Prt$$
$$= P(1 + rt) \qquad (2)$$

where

$P = $ Principal, or present value

$r = $ Annual simple interest rate (written as a decimal)

$t = $ Time in years

$A = $ Amount, or future value

---

* If r is the interest rate written as a decimal, then 100r% would be the rate using %. For example, if r = 0.12, then using the percent symbol, %, we would have 100r% = 100(0.12)% = 12%. The expressions 0.12 and 12% are equivalent.

Given any three of the four variables A, P, r, and t in (2), we should be able to solve for the fourth. The following examples illustrate several types of common problems that can be solved by using formula (2).

Example 1   Find the total amount due on a loan of $800 at 18% simple interest at the end of 4 months.

Solution   To find the amount A (future value) due in 4 months, we use formula (2) with $P = 800$, $r = 0.18$, and $t = \frac{4}{12} = \frac{1}{3}$ year. Thus,

$$A = P(1 + rt)$$
$$= 800[1 + 0.18(\tfrac{1}{3})]$$
$$= 800(1.06)$$
$$= \$848$$

Problem 1   Find the total amount due on a loan of $500 at 12% simple interest at the end of 30 months.

Example 2   If you want to earn an annual rate of 10% on your investments, how much (to the nearest cent) should you pay for a note that will be worth $5,000 in 9 months?

Solution   We again use formula (2), but now we are interested in finding the principal P (present value), given $A = \$5,000$, $r = 0.1$, and $t = \frac{9}{12} = 0.75$ year. Thus,

$$A = P(1 + rt)$$
$$5{,}000 = P[1 + 0.1(0.75)] \qquad \text{Replace } A, r, \text{ and } t \text{ with the}$$
$$5{,}000 = (1.075)P \qquad\qquad\; \text{given values and solve for } P.$$
$$P = \$4{,}651.16$$

Problem 2   Repeat Example 2 with a time period of 6 months.

Example 3   If you must pay $960 for a note that will be worth $1,000 in 6 months, what annual simple interest rate will you earn? (Compute the answer to two decimal places.)

Solution   Again we use formula (2), but this time we are interested in finding r, given $P = \$960$, $A = \$1,000$, and $t = \frac{6}{12} = 0.5$ year. Thus,

$$A = P(1 + rt)$$
$$1{,}000 = 960[1 + r(0.5)]$$
$$1{,}000 = 960 + 960r(0.5)$$
$$40 = 480r$$
$$r = \frac{40}{480} \approx 0.0833 \quad \text{or} \quad 8.33\%$$

Problem 3   Repeat Example 3 assuming you have paid $952 for the note.

Example 4 Suppose after buying a new car you decide to sell your old car to a friend. You accept a 270-day note for $3,500 at 10% simple interest as payment. (Both principal and interest will be paid at the end of 270 days.) Sixty days later you find that you need the money and sell the note to a third party for $3,550. What annual interest rate will the third party receive for the investment? (Compute 100r% to three decimal places.)

Solution Step 1. Find the amount that will be paid at the end of 270 days to whomever has the note. (Some financial institutions use a 365-day year and others a 360-day year. In all of the problems in this section involving days, we assume a 360-day year. In other sections we will use a 365-day year. The choice will always be clearly stated.)

$$A = P(1 + rt)$$

$$= \$3,500 \left[1 + (0.1) \left(\frac{270}{360} \right) \right]$$

$$= \$3,762.50$$

Step 2. For the third party we are to find the annual rate of interest r required to make $3,550 grow to $3,762.50 in 210 days $(270 - 60)$; that is, we are to find r (which is to be converted to 100r%), given $A = \$3,762.50$, $P = \$3,550$, and $t = (210/360)$.

$$A = P + Prt \qquad \text{Solve for } r.$$

$$r = \frac{A - P}{Pt}$$

$$r = \frac{3,762.50 - 3,550}{(3,550) \left(\dfrac{210}{360} \right)} = 0.102\ 62 \text{ or } 10.262\%$$

Problem 4 Repeat Example 4 assuming that the note was sold to the third party for $3,500, ninety days after it was initially signed.

Answers to 1. $650   2. $4,761.90   3. 10.08%
Matched Problems 4. 15.0%

Exercise 3-1

A *Using formula (1) for simple interest, find each of the indicated quantities.*

1. $P = \$500$, $r = 8\%$, $t = 6$ months, $I = ?$
2. $P = \$900$, $r = 10\%$, $t = 9$ months, $I = ?$
3. $I = \$80$, $P = \$500$, $t = 2$ years, $r = ?$
4. $I = \$40$, $P = \$400$, $t = 4$ years, $r = ?$

B   Use formula (2) in an appropriate form to find the indicated quantities.

5. $P = \$100$, $r = 8\%$, $t = 18$ months, $A = ?$
6. $P = \$6,000$, $r = 6\%$, $t = 8$ months, $A = ?$
7. $A = \$1,000$, $r = 10\%$, $t = 15$ months, $P = ?$
8. $A = \$8,000$, $r = 12\%$, $t = 7$ months, $P = ?$

C   Solve each formula for the indicated variable.

9. $I = Prt$,   for r 10. $I = Prt$,   for P
11. $A = P + Prt$,   for P 12. $A = P + Prt$,   for r

■

Applications*

Business & Economics

In all problems involving days, a 360-day year is assumed. When annual rates are requested as an answer, compute 100r% to three decimal places.

13. If \$3,000 is loaned for 4 months at a 14% annual rate, how much interest is earned?
14. If \$5,000 is loaned for 10 months at a 10% annual rate, how much interest is earned?
15. How much interest will you have to pay for a one-month overdue credit card balance of \$554, if a 20% annual rate is charged?
16. A department store charges an 18% annual rate for overdue accounts. How much interest will be owed on an \$835 account 2 months overdue?
17. A loan of \$7,250 was repaid at the end of 8 months. What size repayment check (principal and interest) was written, if a 9% annual rate of interest was charged?
18. A loan of \$10,000 was repaid at the end of 14 months. What amount (principal and interest) was repaid if a 12% annual rate of interest was charged?
19. A loan of \$4,000 was repaid at the end of 8 months with a check for \$4,270. What annual rate of interest was charged?
20. A check for \$3,262.50 was used to retire a \$3,000 15-month loan. What annual rate of interest was charged?
21. If you paid \$30 to a loan company for the use of \$1,000 for 60 days, what annual rate of interest did they charge?
22. If you paid \$120 to a loan company for the use of \$2,000 for 90 days, what annual rate of interest did they charge?
23. A radio commercial for a loan company states: "You only pay 50 cents a day for each \$500 borrowed." If you borrow \$1,500 for 120 days, what annual interest rate is the company actually charging?

---

* The authors wish to thank Professor Roy Luke of Pierce College for his many useful suggestions of applications in this chapter.

24. George finds a company that charges $.70 per day for each $1,000 borrowed. If he borrows $3,000 for 60 days, what annual interest rate will he be paying the company?

25. You are interested in buying a 13-week T-bill (treasury bill) from the United States Treasury Department. If you buy a bill with a maturity value of $10,000 for $9,776.94, what annual interest rate will you earn?

26. If you buy a 26-week T-bill with a maturity value of $10,000 for $9,562.56 from the Treasury Department, what annual interest rate will you earn?

27. If an investor wants to earn an annual interest rate of 12.63% on a 13-week T-bill with a maturity value of $10,000, how much should the investor pay for the bill?

28. If an investor wants to earn an annual interest rate of 10.58% on a 26-week T-bill with a maturity value of $10,000, how much should the investor pay for the bill?

29. An attorney accepts a 90-day note for $5,500 at 12% simple interest from a client for services rendered. (Both interest and principal will be repaid at the end of 90 days.) Wishing to have use of her money sooner, the attorney sells the note to a third party for $5,500 after 30 days. What annual interest rate will the third party receive for the investment?

30. To complete the sale of a house, the seller accepts a 180-day note for $10,000 at 10% simple interest. (Both interest and principal will be repaid at the end of 180 days.) Wishing to have use of the money sooner for the purchase of another house, the seller sells the note to a third party for $10,100 after 60 days. What annual interest rate will the third party receive for the investment?

In Problems 31 and 32, use the following buying and selling commission schedule from a well-known discount brokerage house. Example: The commission on 500 shares at $15 per share is $84.50.

Dollar Range per Transaction	Commission	
$0–2,500	$19 + 1.6%	of principal amount
$2,501–6,000	$44 + 0.6%	of principal amount
$6,001–22,000	$62 + 0.3%	of principal amount
$22,001–50,000	$84 + 0.2%	of principal amount
$50,001–500,000	$134 + 0.1%	of principal amount
$500,001+	$234 + 0.08%	of principal amount

31. An investor purchased 500 shares of a stock at $14.20 a share. After holding the stock for 39 weeks, it was sold for $16.84 a share. Taking in to consideration the buying and selling commissions charged by the

discount brokerage house (see table on the preceding page), what annual rate of interest was earned by the investor?

32. An investor purchased 450 shares of a stock at $64.84 a share. After holding the stock for 26 weeks, it was sold for $72.08 a share. Taking in to consideration the buying and selling commissions charged by the discount brokerage house (see table above), what annual rate of interest was earned by the investor?

3-2 Compound Interest

- Compound Interest
- Effective Rate
- Growth and Time

■ Compound Interest

If at the end of a payment period the interest due is reinvested at the same rate, then the interest as well as the original principal will earn interest during the next payment period. Interest paid on interest reinvested is called **compound interest.**

For example, suppose you deposit $1,000 in a bank that pays 8% compounded quarterly. How much will the bank owe you at the end of a year? *Compounding quarterly* means that earned interest is paid to your account at the end of each 3 month period and that interest as well as the principal earns interest for the next quarter. Using the simple interest formula (2) from the previous section, we compute the amount in the account at the end of the first quarter after interest has been paid:

$A = P(1 + rt)$

$\quad = 1,000[1 + 0.8(\tfrac{1}{4})]$

$\quad = 1,000(1.02) = \$1,020$

Now, $1,020 is your new principal for the second quarter. At the end of the second quarter, after interest is paid, the account will have

$A = \$1,020[1 + 0.08(\tfrac{1}{4})]$

$\quad = \$1,020(1.02) = \$1,040.40$

Similarly, at the end of the third quarter, you will have

$A = \$1,040.40[1 + 0.8(\tfrac{1}{4})]$

$\quad = \$1,040.40(1.02) = \$1,061.21$

Finally, at the end of the fourth quarter, the account will have

$$A = \$1,061.21[1 + 0.08(\tfrac{1}{4})]$$
$$= \$1,061.21(1.02) = \$1,082.43$$

How does this compound amount compare with simple interest? The amount with simple interest would be

$$A = P(1 + rt)$$
$$= \$1,000[1 + 0.08(1)]$$
$$= \$1,000(1.08) = \$1,080$$

We see that compounding quarterly yields $2.43 more than simple interest would provide.

Let us look over the above calculations for compound interest to see if we can uncover a pattern that might lead to a general formula for computing compound interest for arbitrary cases.

$A = 1,000(1.02)$	End of first quarter
$A = [1,000(1.02)](1.02) = 1,000(1.02)^2$	End of second quarter
$A = [1,000(1.02)^2](1.02) = 1,000(1.02)^3$	End of third quarter
$A = [1,000(1.02)^3](1.02) = 1,000(1.02)^4$	End of fourth quarter

It appears that at the end of n quarters, we would have

$A = 1,000(1.02)^n$	End of nth quarter

or

$$A = 1,000[1 + 0.08(\tfrac{1}{4})]^n$$
$$= 1,000\left[1 + \frac{0.08}{4}\right]^n$$

where $0.08/4 = 0.02$ is the interest rate per quarter. Since interest rates are generally quoted as annual nominal rates, the **rate per compound period** is found by dividing the annual nominal rate by the number of compounding periods per year.

In general, if P is the principal earning interest compounded m times a year at an annual rate of r, then (by repeated use of the simple interest formula, using $i = m/r$, the rate per period) the amount A at the end of each period is

$A = P(1 + i)$	End of first period
$A = [P(1 + i)](1 + i) = P(1 + i)^2$	End of second period
$A = [P(1 + i)^2](1 + i) = P(1 + i)^3$	End of third period
$\cdot$	
$\cdot$	
$\cdot$	
$A = [P(1 + i)^{n-1}](1 + i) = P(1 + i)^n$	End of nth period

We summarize this important result in the following box:

Amount—Compound Interest

$$A = P(1 + i)^n \tag{1}$$

where

$$i = \frac{r}{m}$$

and

$r = $ Annual nominal rate*
$m = $ Number of compounding periods per year
$n = $ Total number of compounding periods
$i = $ Rate per compounding period
$P = $ Principal (present value)
$A = $ Amount (future value) at end of n periods

* This is often shortened to "annual rate" or just "rate."

Several examples will illustrate different uses of formula (1). If any three of the four variables in (1) are given, we can solve for the fourth. The power form $(1 + i)^n$ in formula (1) can be evaluated for various values of i and n by using any calculator with a y^x key or Table V in Appendix B.

Example 5   If $1,000 is invested at 8% compounded

(A) annually   (B) semiannually   (C) quarterly

what is the amount after 5 years? Write answers to the nearest cent.

Solutions   (A) Compounding annually means that there is one interest payment period per year. Thus, $n = 5$ and $i = r = 0.08$.

$$A = P(1 + i)^n$$
$$= 1,000(1 + 0.08)^5 \qquad \text{Use a calculator (or Table V)}$$
$$= 1,000(1.469\ 328)$$
$$= \$1,469.33 \qquad\qquad \text{Interest earned} = A - P = \$469.33$$

(B) Compounding semiannually means that there are two interest payment periods per year. Thus, the number of payment periods in 5 years is $n = 2(5) = 10$ and the interest rate per period is

$$i = \frac{r}{m} = \frac{0.08}{2} = 0.04$$

So,

$$A = P(1 + i)^n$$
$$= 1{,}000(1 + 0.04)^{10} \qquad \text{Use a calculator (or Table V)}$$
$$= 1{,}000(1.480\ 244)$$
$$= \$1{,}480.24 \qquad \text{Interest earned} = A - P = \$480.24$$

(C) Compounding quarterly means that there are four interest payments per year. Thus, $n = 4(5) = 20$ and $i = 0.08/4 = 0.02$. So,

$$A = P(1 + i)^n$$
$$= 1{,}000(1 + 0.02)^{20} \qquad \text{Use a calculator (or Table V)}$$
$$= 1{,}000(1.485\ 947)$$
$$= \$1{,}485.95 \qquad \text{Interest earned} = A - P = \$485.95$$

Problem 5   Repeat Example 5 with an annual interest rate of 6% over an 8 year period.

Notice the rather significant increase in interest earned in going from annual compounding to quarterly compounding. One might wonder what happens if we compound daily, or every minute, or every second, and so on. Figure 1 shows the relative effect of increasing the number of compounding periods in a year. A limit is reached at compounding *continuously*, which is not a great deal larger than that obtained through monthly compounding. Continuous compounding is discussed in the study of calculus. Compare the results in Figure 1 with simple interest earned over the same time period:

$$I = Prt = 1{,}000(0.08)5 = \$400$$

Figure 1 Rent on $1,000 for 5 years at 8% compounded at different periods

Another use of the compound interest formula is in determining how much you should invest now to have a given amount at a future date.

Example 6 How much should you invest now at 10% compounded quarterly to have $8,000 to buy a car in 5 years?

Solution We are given a future value $A = \$8,000$ for a compound interest investment, and we need to find the present value (principal P) given $i = 0.10/4 = 0.025$ and $n = 4(5) = 20$.

$$A = P(1 + i)^n$$

$$8{,}000 = P(1 + 0.025)^{20}$$

$$P = \frac{8{,}000}{(1 + 0.025)^{20}} \qquad \text{Use a calculator (or Table V)}$$

$$= \frac{8{,}000}{1.638\ 616} = \$4{,}882.17$$

Problem 6 How much should new parents invest now at 8% compounded semiannually to have $16,000 toward their child's college education in 17 years?

■ **Effective Rate**

Suppose you read in the newspaper that one investment pays 15% compounded monthly and another pays 15.2% compounded semiannually. Which has the better return? An effective way to compare investments is to determine their **effective rates,** the simple interest rates that would produce the same returns in one year had the same principal been invested at simple interest without compounding. (Effective rates are also called **annual yields** or **true interest rates**).

If principal P is invested at an annual (nominal rate) r, compounded m times a year, then in one year

$$A = P(1 + r/m)^m$$

What simple interest rate will produce the same amount A in one year? We call this simple interest rate the effective rate, and denote it by r_e. To find r_e we proceed as follows:

$$\begin{pmatrix} \text{Amount at} \\ \text{simple interest} \\ \text{after 1 year} \end{pmatrix} = \begin{pmatrix} \text{Amount at} \\ \text{compound interest} \\ \text{after 1 year} \end{pmatrix}$$

$$P(1 + r_e) = P\left(1 + \frac{r}{m}\right)^m \qquad \text{Divide both sides by } P$$

$$1 + r_e = \left(1 + \frac{r}{m}\right)^m \qquad \text{Isolate } r_e \text{ on the left side}$$

$$r_e = \left(1 + \frac{r}{m}\right)^m - 1$$

> **Effective Rate**
>
> If principal P is invested at the (annual nominal) rate r, compounded m times a year, then the effective rate, r_e, is given by
>
> $$r_e = \left(1 + \frac{r}{m}\right)^m - 1$$

Example 7 A savings and loan pays 8% compounded quarterly. What is the effective rate? (Compute $100r_e\%$ to three decimal places.)

Solution
$$r_e = \left(1 + \frac{r}{m}\right)^m - 1$$
$$= \left(1 + \frac{0.08}{4}\right)^4 - 1$$
$$= (1.02)^4 - 1 \qquad\qquad \text{Use a calculator (or Table V)}$$
$$= 1.082\ 432 - 1$$
$$= 0.082\ 432 \qquad \text{or} \qquad 8.243\%$$

This shows that money invested at 8.243% simple interest earns the same amount of interest in one year as money invested at 8% compounded quarterly. Thus, the effective rate of 8% compounded quarterly is 8.243%.

Problem 7 What is the effective rate of money invested at 6% compounded quarterly?

Example 8 An investor has an opportunity to purchase two different notes: Note A pays 15% compounded monthly, and note B pays 15.2% compounded semiannually. Which is the better investment, assuming all else is equal?

Solution Nominal rates with different compounding periods cannot be compared directly. We must first find the effective rate of each nominal rate and then compare the effective rates to determine which investment will yield the larger return.

Effective Rate for Note A:
$$r_e = \left(1 + \frac{r}{m}\right)^m - 1$$
$$= \left(1 + \frac{0.15}{12}\right)^{12} - 1$$
$$= (1.0125)^{12} - 1 \qquad\qquad \text{Use a calculator (or Table V)}$$
$$= 1.160\ 755 - 1$$
$$= 0.160\ 755 \qquad \text{or} \qquad 16.076\%$$

Effective Rate for Note B:

$$r_e = \left(1 + \frac{r}{m}\right)^m - 1$$

$$= \left(1 + \frac{0.152}{2}\right)^2 - 1$$

$$= (1.076)^2 - 1$$

$$= 1.157\ 776 - 1$$

$$0.157\ 776 \qquad \text{or} \qquad 15.778\%$$

Since the effective rate for Note A is greater than the effective rate for Note B, Note A is the preferred investment.

Problem 8   Repeat Example 8 if Note A pays 9% compounded monthly and Note B pays 9.2% compounded semiannually.

■ Growth and Time

Investments are also compared by computing their **growth time** — the time it takes a given principal to grow to a particular value (the shorter the time, the greater the return on the investment). Example 9 illustrates two methods for making this calculation.

Example 9   How long will it take $10,000 to grow to $12,000 if it is invested at 9% compounded monthly?

Solution
$$A = P(1 + i)^n$$
$$12{,}000 = 10{,}000\left(1 + \frac{0.09}{12}\right)^n$$
$$1.2 = (1.0075)^n$$

Now solve for n:

Method 1.   Use Table V in Appendix B. Look down the $(1 + i)^n$ column on the page that has $i = 0.0075$ ($\frac{3}{4}$%). Find the value in this column that is closest to and greater than 1.2 and take the n value that corresponds to it. In this case, $n = 25$ months, or 2 years and 1 month.

Method 2.   Use logarithms and a calculator.

$$1.2 = 1.0075^n$$

$\ln 1.2 = \ln 1.0075^n$ Log to any base can be used; here we

$\ln 1.2 = n \ln 1.0075$ choose the natural logarithm (base e)

$$n = \frac{\ln 1.2}{\ln 1.0075}$$ Use a calculator

$$= \frac{0.1823}{0.0075} = 24.31 \approx 25 \text{ months or 1 year and 1 month}$$

[*Note:* 24.31 is rounded up to 25 to guarantee reaching $12,000, since interest is paid at the end of each month.]

Problem 9 How long will it take $10,000 to grow to $25,000 if it is invested at 18% compounded quarterly?

Answers to 5. (A) $1,593.85 (B) $1,604.71 (C) $1,610.32
Matched Problems 6. $4,216.83 7. 6.136%
8. Note B (effective rate of Note A is 9.38% and of Note B is 9.412%)
9. 20.78 ≈ 21 quarters or 5 years and 3 months

Exercise 3-2

Use the compound interest formula (1) and a calculator or Table V (or both) to find each of the indicated values (to two decimal places where applicable). (A small discrepancy between calculator produced answers and table produced answers may result because of roundoff errors.)

A
1. $P = \$100$, $i = 0.01$, $n = 12$, $A = ?$
2. $P = \$1,000$, $i = 0.015$, $n = 20$, $A = ?$
3. $P = \$800$, $i = 0.06$, $n = 25$, $A = ?$
4. $P = \$10,000$, $i = 0.08$, $n = 30$, $A = ?$
5. $A = \$10,000$, $i = 0.03$, $n = 48$, $P = ?$
6. $A = \$1,000$, $i = 0.015$, $n = 60$, $P = ?$
7. $A = \$18,000$, $i = 0.01$, $n = 90$, $P = ?$
8. $A = \$50,000$, $i = 0.005$, $n = 70$, $P = ?$

B
9. If $100 is invested at 6% compounded

   (A) annually (B) quarterly (C) monthly

   what is the amount after 4 years? How much interest is earned?
10. If $2,000 is invested at 7% compounded

    (A) annually (B) quarterly (C) monthly

    what is the amount after 5 years? How much interest is earned?
11. If $5,000 is invested at 18% compounded monthly, what is the amount after

    (A) 2 years? (B) 4 years?
12. If $20,000 is invested at 6% compounded monthly, what is the amount after

    (A) 5 years? (B) 8 years?
13. If an investment company pays 8% compounded semiannually, how much should you deposit now to have $10,000

    (A) 5 years from now? (B) 10 years from now?

14. If an investment company pays 10% compounded quarterly, how much should you deposit now to have $6,000

   (A) 3 years from now?   (B) 6 years from now?

15. What is the effective rate of interest for money invested at

   (A) 10% compounded quarterly?
   (B) 12% compounded monthly?

16. What is the effective rate of interest for money invested at

   (A) 6% compounded monthly?
   (B) 14% compounded semiannually?

17. How long will it take $4,000 to grow to $9,000 if it is invested at 15% compounded monthly?

18. How long will it take $5,000 to grow to $7,000 if it is invested at 8% compounded quarterly?

C
19. $A = 2P$, $i = 0.06$, $n = ?$
20. $A = 2P$, $i = 0.05$, $n = ?$
21. How long will it take money to double if it is invested at

   (A) 10% compounded quarterly?
   (B) 12% compounded quarterly?

22. How long will it take money to double if it is invested at

   (A) 14% compounded semiannually?
   (B) 10% compounded semiannually?

Applications

Business & Economics

Solve Problems 23–34 using a calculator or Table V (or both). Find values to two decimal places, unless directed otherwise. (A small discrepancy between calculator produced answers and table produced answers may result because of roundoff errors.)

23. A newborn child receives a $5,000 gift towards a college education from her grandparents. How much will the $5,000 be worth in 17 years if it is invested at 9% compounded quarterly?

24. A person with $8,000 is trying to decide whether to purchase a car now or to invest the money at 12% compounded semiannually, and then buy a more expensive car. How much will be available for the purchase of a car at the end of 3 years?

25. What will a $110,000 house cost 10 years from now if the inflation rate over that period averages 6% compounded annually?

26. If the inflation rate averages 8% per year compounded annually for

the next 5 years, what will a car costing $10,000 now cost 5 years from now?

27. Rental costs for office space has been going up at 7% per year compounded annually for the past 5 years. If office space rent is now $20 per square foot per month, what were the rental rates 5 years ago?

28. In a suburb of a city, housing costs have been increasing at 8% per year compounded annually for the past 8 years. A house with a $160,000 value now would have had what value 8 years ago?

29. If the population in a particular third world country is growing at 4% compounded annually, how long will it take the population to double? (Round up to the next higher year if not exact.)

30. If the world population is now about 5 billion people and is growing at 2% compounded annually, how long will it take the population to grow to 8 billion people? (Round up to the next higher year if not exact.)

31. Which is the better investment and why: 9% compounded monthly or 9.3% compounded annually?

32. Which is the better investment and why: 8% compounded quarterly or 8.3% compounded annually?

33. You have saved $7,000 towards the purchase of a car costing $9,000. How long will the $7,000 have to be invested at 9% compounded monthly to grow to $9,000? (Round up to the next higher month if not exact.)

34. A newly married couple has $15,000 towards the purchase of a house. For the type of house they are interested in buying, they estimate that a $20,000 down payment will be necessary. How long will the money have to be invested at 10% compounded quarterly to grow to $20,000? (Round up to the next higher quarter if not exact.)

The following problems require the use of a calculator with a y^x button. (Use a 365-day year and compute answers to two decimal places, unless directed otherwise.)

35. An Individual Retirement Account (IRA) has $20,000 in it and the owner decides not to add any more money to the account other than interest earned at 8% compounded daily. How much will be in the account 35 years from now when the owner reaches retirement age?

36. If one dollar had been placed in a bank account at the birth of Christ and forgotten until now, how much would be in the account at the end of 1990 if money earned 2% interest compounded annually? 2% simple interest? (Now you can see the power of compounding and see why inactive accounts are closed after a relatively short period of time.)

37. How long will it take money to double if it is invested at 14% compounded daily? 15% compounded annually? (Compute answers in years to three decimal places.)

38. How long will it take money to triple if it is invested at 10% compounded daily? 11% compounded annually? (Compute answers in years to three decimal places.)

*Problems 39–42 refer to zero coupon bonds. (A **zero coupon bond** is a bond that is sold now at a discount and will pay its face value at some time in the future when it matures—no interest payments are made.)*

39. Parents wishing to have enough money for their child's college education 17 years from now decide to buy a $30,000 face value zero coupon bond. If money is worth 10% compounded annually, what should they pay for the bond?

40. How much should a $20,000 face value zero coupon bond, maturing in 10 years, be sold for now if its rate of return is to be 8% compounded annually?

41. If the parents in Problem 39 pay $6,844.79 for the $30,000 face value zero coupon bond, what annual compound rate of return will they be receiving?

42. If you pay $5,893.24 for a $12,000 face value zero coupon bond that matures in 7 years, what is your annual compound rate of return?

43. *Barron's* (a national business and financial weekly) published the following "Top Savings Deposit Yields" for money market deposit accounts:

    (A) Virginia Beach Fed S&L   8.28% compounded monthly
    (B) Franklin Svgs   8.25% compounded daily
    (C) Guaranty Fed Svgs   8.25% compounded monthly

    What is the effective yield for each?

44. *Barron's* also published the following "Top Savings Deposit Yields" for one-year CD accounts:

    (A) Spindletop Savings   9.00% compounded daily
    (B) Alamo Svgs of Texas   9.10% compounded quarterly
    (C) Unity S&L   9.00% compounded quarterly

    What is the effective yield for each?

45. If you just sold a stock for $32,456.32 (net) that cost you $24,766.81 (net) 2 years ago, what annual compound rate of return did you make on your investment?

46. If you just sold a stock for $27,339.79 (net) that cost you $14,664.76 (net) 4 years ago, what annual compound rate of return did you make on your investment?

- Future Value of an Annuity
- Sinking Funds

■ Future Value of an Annuity

An **annuity** is any sequence of equal periodic payments. If payments are made at the end of each time interval, then the annuity is called an **ordinary annuity.** We will only consider ordinary annuities in this book. The amount, or **future value,** of an annuity is the sum of all payments plus all interest earned.

Suppose you decide to deposit $100 every 6 months into an account that pays 6% compounded semiannually. If you make six deposits, one at the end of each interest payment period, over 3 years, how much money will be in the account after the last deposit is made? To solve this problem, let us look at it in terms of a time line. Using the compound amount formula $A = P(1 + i)^n$, we can find the value of each deposit after it has earned compound interest up through the sixth deposit, as shown in Figure 2.

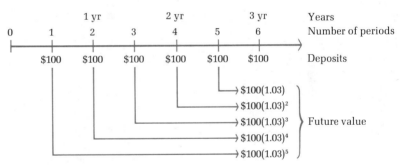

Figure 2

We could, of course, evaluate each of the future values in Figure 2 using Table V or a calculator and then add the results to find the amount in the account at the time of the sixth deposit—a tedious project at best. Instead, we take another approach that leads directly to a formula that will produce the same result in a few steps (even when the number of deposits is very large). We start by writing the total amount in the account after the sixth deposit in the form

$$S = 100 + 100(1.03) + 100(1.03)^2 + 100(1.03)^3 + 100(1.03)^4$$
$$+ 100(1.03)^5 \tag{1}$$

We would like a simple way to sum these terms. Let us multiply each side of (1) by 1.03 to obtain

$$1.03S = 100(1.03) + 100(1.03)^2 + 100(1.03)^3 + 100(1.03)^4$$
$$+ 100(1.03)^5 + 100(1.03)^6 \tag{2}$$

Subtracting (1) from (2), left side from left side and right side from right side, we obtain

$$1.03S - S = 100(1.03)^6 - 100 \qquad \text{Notice how many terms drop out}$$

$$0.03S = 100[(1.03)^6 - 1]$$

$$S = 100\frac{(1 + 0.03)^6 - 1}{0.03} \qquad \begin{array}{l}\text{We write } S \text{ in this form to observe} \\ \text{a general pattern}\end{array} \tag{3}$$

In general, if R is the periodic deposit, i the rate per period, and n the number of periods, then the future value is given by

$$S = R + R(1 + i) + R(1 + i)^2 + \cdots + R(1 + i)^{n-1} \qquad \begin{array}{l}\text{Note how this} \\ \text{compares to (1)}\end{array}$$

and proceeding as in the above example, we obtain the general formula for the future value of an ordinary annuity:*

$$S = R\frac{(1 + i)^n - 1}{i} \qquad \text{Note how this compares to (3)} \tag{4}$$

It is common practice to use the symbol

$$s_{\overline{n}|i} = \frac{(1 + i)^n - 1}{i}$$

for the fractional part of (4). The symbol $s_{\overline{n}|i}$, read "s angle n at i," is evaluated in Table V for various values of n and i. A financial or scientific calculator can also be used to calculate S. The advantage of a calculator, of course, is that it can handle many more situations than any table, no matter how large the table.

Returning to the example above, we now use Table V to complete the problem:

$$S = 100\frac{(1.03)^6 - 1}{0.03}$$

$$= 100s_{\overline{6}|0.03} \qquad \text{Use Table V with } i = 0.03 \text{ and } n = 6$$

$$= 100(6.468\ 410)$$

$$= \$646.84$$

[Note: Using a calculator with a y^x key, we would evaluate $(1.03)^6$ first and then complete the problem using the arithmetic operations indicated. A financial calculator is even more convenient (see the instruction manual for your particular financial calculator if you have one).]

---

* This formula can also be obtained by using the formula in Appendix A for the sum of the first n terms in a geometric progression.

It is common to use *FV* (future value) for *S* and *PMT* (payment) for *R* in formula (4). Making these changes, we have

Future Value of an Ordinary Annuity

$$FV = PMT\,\frac{(1 + i)^n - 1}{i} = PMTs_{\overline{n}|i}$$ (5)

where

PMT = Periodic payment

i = Rate per period

n = Number of payments (periods)

FV = Future value (amount)

(Payments are made at the end of each period.)

Example 10   What is the value of an annuity at the end of 5 years if $100 per month is deposited into an account earning 9% compounded monthly? How much of this value is interest?

Solution   To find the value of the annuity, use formula (5) with $PMT = \$100$, $i = 0.09/12 = 0.0075$, and $n = 12(5) = 60$.

$$FV = PMT\,\frac{(1 + i)^n - 1}{i} \quad \text{or} \quad PMTs_{\overline{n}|i}$$

$$= 100\frac{(1.0075)^{60} - 1}{0.0075} \quad \text{or} \quad 100s_{\overline{60}|0.0075} \qquad \text{Use a calculator (or Table V)}$$

$$= 100(75.424\ 137)$$

$$= \$7,542.41$$

To find the interest, subtract the total amount deposited in the annuity from the value of the annuity:

Deposits $= 60(100)$

$\qquad = \$6,000$

Interest $=$ Value $-$ Deposits

$\qquad = 7,542.41 - 6,000$

$\qquad = \$1,542.41$

Problem 10   What is the value of an annuity at the end of 10 years if $1,000 is deposited every 6 months into an account earning 8% compounded semiannually? How much of this value is interest?

■ Sinking Funds

The formula for the future value of an ordinary annuity has another important application. Suppose the parents of a newborn child decide that on each of the child's birthdays up to the seventeenth year, they will deposit $PMT in an account that pays 6% compounded annually. The money is to be used for college expenses. What should the annual deposit PMT be in order for the amount in the account to be $16,000 after the seventeenth deposit?

We are given FV, i, and n in formula (5), and our problem is to find PMT. Thus,

$$FV = PMT\,\frac{(1+i)^n - 1}{i} \quad \text{or} \quad PMTs_{\overline{n}|i}$$

$$16{,}000 = PMT\,\frac{(1.06)^{17} - 1}{0.06} \quad \text{or} \quad PMTs_{\overline{17}|0.06} \qquad \text{Solve for } PMT$$

$$PMT = 16{,}000\,\frac{0.06}{(1.06)^{17} - 1} \quad \text{or} \quad 16{,}000\,\frac{1}{s_{\overline{17}|0.06}} \qquad \begin{array}{l}\text{Use a calculator or}\\ \text{Table V}\end{array}$$

$$= 16{,}000(0.035\ 445)$$

$$= \$567.12 \text{ per year}$$

An annuity of seventeen $567.12 annual deposits at 6% compounded annually will amount to approximately $16,000 in 17 years.

This is one of many examples of a similar type that are referred to as *sinking fund problems*. In general, any account that is established for accumulating funds to meet future obligations or debts is called a **sinking fund**. If the payments are to be made in the form of an ordinary annuity, then we have only to solve for PMT in formula (5) to find the periodic payment into the fund. Doing this, we obtain the general formula:

Sinking Fund Payment

$$PMT = FV\,\frac{i}{(1+i)^n - 1} = \frac{FV}{s_{\overline{n}|i}} \tag{6}$$

where

PMT = Sinking fund payment

FV = Value of annuity after n payments (future value)

n = Number of payments (periods)

i = Rate per period

[Note: Payments are made at the end of each period.]

Example 11   A company estimates that it will have to replace a piece of equipment at a cost of $10,000 in 5 years. To have this money available in 5 years, a sinking fund is established by making fixed monthly payments into an account paying 6% compounded monthly. How much should each payment be?

Solution   We use formula (6) with $FV = \$10,000$, $i = 0.06/12 = 0.005$, and $n = 5(12) = 60$:

$$PMT = FV \frac{i}{(1 + i)^n - 1} \quad \text{or} \quad \frac{FV}{s_{\overline{n}|i}}$$

$$PMT = (10,000) \frac{0.005}{(1.005)^{60} - 1} \quad \text{or} \quad 10,000 \frac{1}{s_{\overline{60}|0.005}} \quad \text{Use a calculator or Table V}$$

$$PMT = 10,000(0.014\ 333)$$
$$= \$143.33 \text{ per month}$$

Problem 11   A bond issue is approved for building a marina in a city. The city is required to make regular payments every 6 months into a sinking fund paying 6% compounded semiannually. At the end of 10 years, the bond obligation will be retired at a cost of $5,000,000. What should each payment be?

Answers to   10.   Value: $29,778.08; interest: $9,778.08
Matched Problems   11. $186,078.54 every 6 months for 10 years

---

Exercise 3-3

In Problems 1–20 use formula (5) or (6) and a calculator or Table V (or both) to solve each problem. (Answers may vary slightly depending on whether you use a calculator or Table V.)

A   1. $FV = ?$, $n = 20$, $i = 0.03$, $PMT = \$500$
2. $FV = ?$, $n = 25$, $i = 0.04$, $PMT = \$100$
3. $FV = ?$, $n = 40$, $i = 0.02$, $PMT = \$1,000$
4. $FV = ?$, $n = 30$, $i = 0.01$, $PMT = \$50$

B   5. $FV = \$3,000$, $n = 20$, $i = 0.02$, $PMT = ?$
6. $FV = \$8,000$, $n = 30$, $i = 0.03$, $PMT = ?$
7. $FV = \$5,000$, $n = 15$, $i = 0.01$, $PMT = ?$
8. $FV = \$2,500$, $n = 10$, $i = 0.08$, $PMT = ?$

C   9. $FV = \$4,000$, $i = 0.02$, $PMT = 200$, $n = ?$
10. $FV = \$8,000$, $i = 0.04$, $PMT = 500$, $n = ?$

Applications

Business & Economics

11. What is the value of an ordinary annuity at the end of 10 years if $500 per quarter is deposited into an account earning 8% compounded quarterly? How much of this value is interest?

12. What is the value of an ordinary annuity at the end of 20 years if $1,000 per year is deposited into an account earning 7% compounded annually? How much of this value is interest?

13. In order to accumulate enough money for a down payment on a house, a couple deposits $300 per month into an account paying 6% compounded monthly. If payments are made at the end of each period, how much money will be in the account in 5 years?

14. A self-employed person has a Keogh retirement plan. (This type of plan is free of taxes until money is withdrawn.) If deposits of $7,500 are made each year into an account paying 8% compounded annually, how much will be in the account after 20 years?

15. In 5 years a couple would like to have $25,000 for a down payment on a house. What fixed amount should be deposited each month into an account paying 9% compounded monthly?

16. A person wishes to have $200,000 in an account for retirement 15 years from now. How much should be deposited quarterly in an account paying 8% compounded quarterly?

17. A company estimates it will need $100,000 in 8 years to replace a computer. If it establishes a sinking fund by making fixed monthly payments into an account paying 12% compounded monthly, how much should each payment be?

18. Parents have set up a sinking fund in order to have $30,000 in 15 years for their children's college education. How much should be paid semiannually into an account paying 10% compounded semiannually?

19. Beginning in January, a person plans to deposit $100 at the end of each month into an account earning 9% compounded monthly. Each year taxes must be paid on the interest earned during that year. Find the interest earned during each year for the first three years.

20. If $500 is deposited each quarter into an account paying 12% compounded quarterly for 3 years, find the interest earned during each of the 3 years.

Use a calculator with a y^x button (or a financial calculator) to solve Problems 21–26.

21. Why does it make sense to open an Individual Retirement Account (IRA) early in one's life? (Money deposited into an IRA and earnings

from an IRA are tax deferred until withdrawal.) Compare the following:

(A)   Jane deposits $2,000 a year into an IRA account earning 9% compounded annually. She makes her first deposit on her 24th birthday and her last deposit on her 31st birthday (8 deposits in all). Making no additional deposits, she leaves the accumulated amount from the 8 deposits in the account, earning interest at 9% compounded annually, until her 65th birthday. How much (to the nearest dollar) will be in her account on her 65th birthday?

(B)   John, procrastinating, doesn't make his first $2,000 deposit into an IRA account until he is 32, but then he continues to deposit $2,000 on every birthday until he is 65 (34 deposits in all). If his account also earns 9% compounded annually, how much (to the nearest dollar) will he have in his account when he makes his last deposit on his 65th birthday?

(Surprise — Jane will have more money than John!)

22.   Starting on his 24th birthday, and continuing on every birthday up to and including his 65th, a person deposits $2,000 a year into an IRA. How much (to the nearest dollar) will be in the account on the 65th birthday, if the account earns:

(A)   6% compounded annually?
(B)   8% compounded annually?
(C)   10% compounded annually?
(D)   12% compounded annually?

23.   You wish to have $10,000 in 4 years to buy a car. How much should you deposit each month into an account paying 8% compounded monthly? How much interest will the account earn in the 4 years?

24.   A company establishes a sinking fund to upgrade a plant in 5 years at an estimated cost of $1,500,000. How much should be invested each quarter into an account paying 9.15% compounded quarterly? How much interest will the account earn in the 5 years?

25.   You can afford monthly deposits of only $150 into an account that pays 8.5% compounded monthly. How long will it be until you have $7,000 to buy a boat? (Round to the next higher month if not exact.)

26.   A company establishes a sinking fund for upgrading office equipment with monthly payments of $1,000 into an account paying 10% compounded monthly. How long will it be before the account has $100,000? (Round up to the next higher month if not exact.)

3-4 Present Value of an Annuity; Amortization

- Present Value of an Annuity
- Amortization
- Amortization Schedules

■ Present Value of an Annuity

How much should you deposit in an account paying 6% compounded semiannually in order to be able to withdraw $1,000 every 6 months for the next 3 years? (After the last payment is made, no money is to be left in the account.)

Actually, we are interested in finding the **present value** of each $1,000 that is paid out during the 3 years. We can do this by solving for P in the compound interest formula

$$A = P(1 + i)^n$$

$$P = \frac{A}{(1 + i)^n} = A(1 + i)^{-n}$$

The rate per period is $i = 0.06/2 = 0.03$. The present value P of the first payment is $1,000(1.03)^{-1}$, the second payment is $1,000(1.03)^{-2}$, and so on. Figure 3 shows this in terms of a time line.

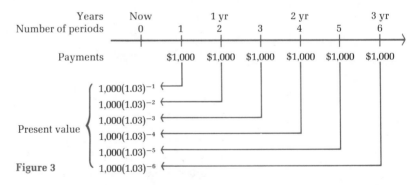

Figure 3

We could evaluate each of the present values in Figure 3 using a calculator or Table V and add the results to find the total present values of all the payments (which will be the amount that is needed now to buy the annuity). Since this is generally a tedious process, particularly when the number of payments is large, we will use the same device we used in the last section to produce a formula that will accomplish the same result in a couple of steps. We start by writing the sum of the present values in the form

$$P = 1,000(1.03)^{-1} + 1,000(1.03)^{-2} + \cdots + 1,000(1.03)^{-6} \tag{1}$$

Multiplying both sides of (1) by (1.03), we obtain

$$1.03P = 1{,}000 + 1{,}000(1.03)^{-1} + \cdots + 1{,}000(1.03)^{-5} \qquad (2)$$

Now subtract (1) from (2):

$1.03P - P = 1{,}000 - 1{,}000(1.03)^{-6}$ Notice how many terms drop out

$$0.03P = 1{,}000[1 - (1 + 0.03)^{-6}]$$

$P = 1{,}000\dfrac{1 - (1 + 0.03)^{-6}}{0.03}$ We write P in this form   (3)
to observe a general pattern

In general, if R is the periodic payment, i the rate per period, and n the number of periods, then the present value of all payments is given by

$P = R(1 + i)^{-1} + R(1 + i)^{-2} + \cdots + R(1 + i)^{-n}$ Note how this
compares to (1)

Proceeding as in the above example, we obtain the general formula for the present value of an ordinary annuity:*

$P = R\dfrac{1 - (1 + i)^{-n}}{i}$ Note how this compares to (3)   (4)

It is common practice to use the symbol

$$a_{\overline{n}|i} = \dfrac{1 - (1 + i)^{-n}}{i}$$

for the fractional part of (4). The symbol $a_{\overline{n}|i}$, read "a angle n at i," is evaluated for various values of n and i in Table V. The present value P can also be evaluated using a financial or scientific calculator. As we said before, a calculator can handle far more situations than any table, no matter how large the table.

Returning to the example above, we now use Table V to complete the problem:

$P = 1{,}000\dfrac{1 - (1.03)^{-6}}{0.03}$

$= 1{,}000a_{\overline{6}|0.03}$ Use Table V with $i = 0.03$ and $n = 6$

$= 1{,}000(5.417\ 191)$

$= \$5{,}417.19$

[*Note:* Using a scientific calculator, we would evaluate $(1.03)^{-6}$ first and then complete the calculation using the arithmetic operations indicated. A financial calculator performs the task with even fewer steps (read the instruction manual for your particular calculator if you have one). For improved accuracy, keep all values in the calculator until the end, then round to the required number of decimal places.]

---

* This formula can also be obtained by using the formula in Appendix A for the sum of the first n terms in a geometric progression.

It is common to use PV (present value) for P and PMT (payment) for R in formula (4). Making these changes, we have:

Present Value of an Ordinary Annuity

$$PV = PMT \frac{1 - (1 + i)^{-n}}{i} = PMTa_{\overline{n}|i} \qquad (5)$$

where

PMT = Periodic payment

i = Rate per period

n = Number of periods

PV = Present value of all payments

[*Note:* Payments are made at the end of each period.]

Example 12 What is the present value of an annuity that pays $200 per month for 5 years if money is worth 6% compounded monthly?

Solution To solve this problem, use formula (5) with $PMT = \$200$, $i = 0.06/12 = 0.005$, and $n = 12(5) = 60$:

$$PV = PMT \frac{1 - (1 + i)^{-n}}{i} \quad \text{or} \quad PMTa_{\overline{n}|i}$$

$$= 200 \frac{1 - (1.005)^{-60}}{0.005} \quad \text{or} \quad 200a_{\overline{60}|0.005} \qquad \text{Use a calculator (or Table V)}$$

$$= 200(51.725\ 561)$$

$$= \$10,345.11$$

Problem 12 How much should you deposit in an account paying 8% compounded quarterly in order to receive quarterly payments of $1,000 for the next 4 years?

■ Amortization

The present value formula for an ordinary annuity (5) has another important use. Suppose you borrow $5,000 from a bank to buy a car and agree to repay the loan in 36 equal monthly payments, including all interest due. If the bank charges 1% per month on the unpaid balance (12% per year compounded monthly), how much should each payment be to retire the total debt including interest in 36 months?

Actually, the bank has bought an annuity from you. The question is, If the bank pays you $5,000 (present value) for an annuity paying them $PMT per month for 36 months at 12% interest compounded monthly, what are the monthly payments PMT? (Note that the value of the annuity at the end of 36 months is zero.) To find PMT, we have only to use formula (5) with $PV = \$5,000$, $i = 0.01$, and $n = 36$:

$$PV = PMT\,\frac{1 - (1 + i)^{-n}}{i} \quad \text{or} \quad PMTa_{\overline{n}|i}$$

$$5{,}000 = PMT\,\frac{1 - (1.01)^{-36}}{0.01} \quad \text{or} \quad PMTa_{\overline{36}|0.01} \qquad \text{Use Table V or a cal-}$$
$$\text{culator; then solve for } PMT$$

$$PMT = 5{,}000(0.033\ 214)$$
$$= \$166.07 \text{ per month}$$

At $166.07 per month, the car will be yours after 36 months. That is, you have *amortized* the debt in 36 equal monthly payments. (*Mort* means "death"; you have "killed" the loan in 36 months.) In general, **amortizing a debt** means that the debt is retired in a given length of time by equal periodic payments that include compound interest. We are usually interested in computing the equal periodic payment. Solving the present value formula (5) for PMT in terms of the other variables, we obtain the following amortization formula:

Amortization Formula

$$PMT = PV\,\frac{i}{1 - (1 + i)^{-n}} = PV\,\frac{1}{a_{\overline{n}|i}} \qquad (6)$$

where

$$PV = \text{Amount of loan (present value)}$$
$$i = \text{Rate per period}$$
$$n = \text{Number of payments (periods)}$$
$$PMT = \text{Periodic payment}$$

[*Note:* Payments are made at the end of each period.]

Example 13   Assume that you buy a television set for $800 and agree to pay for it in 18 equal monthly payments at $1\frac{1}{2}\%$ interest per month on the unpaid balance.

(A) How much are your payments?

(B) How much interest will you pay?

Solutions

(A) Use formula (6) with $PMT = \$800$, $i = 0.015$, and $n = 18$:

$$PMT = PV \frac{i}{1 - (1 + i)^{-n}} \quad \text{or} \quad PV \frac{1}{a_{\overline{n}|i}}$$

$$= 800 \frac{0.015}{1 - (1.015)^{-18}} \quad \text{or} \quad 800 \frac{1}{a_{\overline{18}|0.015}} \qquad \begin{matrix}\text{Use a calculator} \\ \text{or Table V}\end{matrix}$$

$$= 800(0.063\ 806)$$

$$= \$51.04 \text{ per month}$$

(B) Total interest paid = Amount of all payments − Initial loan

$$= 18(\$51.04) - \$800$$

$$= \$118.72$$

Problem 13   If you sell your car to someone for $2,400 and agree to finance it at 1% per month on the unpaid balance, how much should you receive each month to amortize the loan in 24 months? How much interest will you receive?

■ Amortization Schedules

What happens if you are amortizing a debt with equal periodic payments and at some point decide to pay off the remainder of the debt in one lump sum payment? This occurs each time a home with an outstanding mortgage is sold. In order to understand what happens in this situation, we must take a closer look at the amortization process. We begin with an example that is simple enough to allow us to examine the effect each payment has on the debt.

Example 14   If you borrow $500 that you agree to repay in 6 equal monthly payments at 1% interest per month on the unpaid balance, how much of each monthly payment is used for interest and how much is used to reduce the unpaid balance?

Solution   First, we compute the required monthly payment using formula (6) with $PV = \$500$, $i = 0.01$, and $n = 6$:

$$PMT = PV \frac{i}{1 - (1 + i)^{-n}} \quad \text{or} \quad PV \frac{1}{a_{\overline{n}|i}}$$

$$= 500 \frac{0.01}{1 - (1.01)^{-6}} \quad \text{or} \quad 500 \frac{1}{a_{\overline{6}|0.01}} \qquad \text{Use a calculator or Table V}$$

$$= 500(0.172\ 548)$$

$$= \$86.27 \text{ per month}$$

At the end of the first month, the interest due is

$$\$500(0.01) = \$5.00$$

The amortization payment is divided into two parts, payment of the interest due and reduction of the unpaid balance (repayment of principal):

Monthly payment		Interest due		Unpaid balance reduction
$86.27	=	$5.00	+	$81.27

The unpaid balance for the next month is

Previous unpaid balance		Unpaid balance reduction		New unpaid balance
$500.00	−	$81.27	=	$418.73

At the end of the second month, the interest due on the unpaid balance of $418.73 is

$$\$418.73(0.01) = \$4.19$$

The monthly payment is divided into

$$\$86.27 = \$4.19 + \$82.08$$

and the unpaid balance for the next month is

$$\$418.73 - \$82.08 = \$366.65$$

This process continues until all payments have been made and the unpaid balance is reduced to zero. The calculations for each month are listed in Table 1, which is referred to as an **amortization schedule**.

Table 1 Amortization Schedule

Payment Number	Payment	Interest	Unpaid Balance Reduction	Unpaid Balance
0				$500.00
1	$ 86.27	$ 5.00	$ 81.27	418.73
2	86.27	4.19	82.08	336.65
3	86.27	3.37	82.90	253.75
4	86.27	2.54	83.73	170.02
5	86.27	1.70	84.57	85.45
6	86.30	0.85	85.45	0.00
Total	$517.65	$17.65	$500.00	

Notice that the last payment had to be increased by $0.03 in order to reduce the unpaid balance to zero. This small discrepancy is due to round-off errors that occur in the computations. In almost all cases, the last payment must be adjusted slightly in order to obtain a final unpaid balance of exactly zero.

Problem 14   Construct the amortization schedule for a $1,000 debt that is to be amortized in 6 equal monthly payments at 1.25% interest per month on the unpaid balance.

Example 15   A family purchased a home 10 years ago for $80,000. The home was financed by paying 20% down and signing a 9% 30 year mortgage on the unpaid balance. The market value of the house is now $120,000 and the family wishes to sell the house. How much equity (to the nearest dollar) does the family have in the house now after making 120 monthly payments? [*Note:* **Equity** = (current market value) − (unpaid loan balance).]

Solution   How can we find the unpaid loan balance after 10 years or 120 monthly payments? One way to proceed would be to construct an amortization schedule, but this would require a table with 120 lines. Fortunately, there is an easier way. The unpaid balance after 120 payments is the amount of the loan that can be paid off with the remaining 240 monthly payments (20 remaining years on the loan). Since the lending institution views a loan as an annuity that they bought from the family, **the unpaid balance of a loan with n remaining payments is the present value of that annuity and can be computed by using formula (5).** Since formula (5) requires knowledge of the monthly payment, we compute that first using formula (6).

Step 1:   Find the monthly payment.

$$PMT = PV \frac{i}{1 - (1 + i)^{-n}}$$

$PV = (0.80)(\$80,000)$
$\quad = \$64,000$
$i = 0.09/12 = 0.0075$
$n = 12(30) = 360$

$$= 64,000 \frac{0.0075}{1 - (1.0075)^{-360}}$$ Use a calculator

$$= \$514.96 \text{ per month}$$

Step 2:   Find the present value of a $514.96 per month 20 year annuity.

$$PV = PMT \frac{1 - (1 + i)^{-n}}{i}$$

$PMT = \$514.96$
$n = 12(20) = 240$
$i = 0.09/12 = 0.0075$

$$= 514.96 \frac{1 - (1.0075)^{-240}}{0.0075}$$ Use a calculator.

$$= \$57,235 \text{ Unpaid loan balance}$$

Step 3.   Find the equity.

$$\text{Equity} = (\text{Current market value}) - (\text{Unpaid loan balance})$$
$$= \$120,000 - \$57,235$$
$$= \$62,765$$

Thus, if the family sells the house for $120,000, they will have $62,765 after paying off the unpaid loan balance of $57,235.

Problem 15 A couple purchased a home 20 years ago for $65,000. The home was financed by paying 20% down and signing an 8% 30 year mortgage on the unpaid balance. The market value of the house is now $130,000 and the couple wishes to sell the house. How much equity (to the nearest dollar) does the couple have in the house now after making 240 monthly payments?

The answer to Example 15 may seem a surprisingly large amount to owe after having made payments for 10 years, but long-term amortizations start out with very small reductions in the unpaid balance. For example, the interest due at the end of the very first period of the loan in Example 15 was

$64,000(0.0075) = 480.00$

The first monthly payment was divided into

| Monthly payment | Interest due | Unpaid balance reduction |

$514.96 - $480.00 = 34.96

Thus, only $34.96 was applied to the unpaid balance.

Answers to Matched Problems

12. $13,577.71

13. $PMT = 112.98 per month; total interest = $311.52

14.

Payment Number	Payment	Interest	Unpaid Balance Reduction	Unpaid Balance
0				$1,000.00
1	$ 174.03	$12.50	$ 161.53	838.47
2	174.03	10.48	163.55	674.92
3	174.03	8.44	165.59	509.33
4	174.03	6.37	167.66	341.67
5	174.03	4.27	169.76	171.91
6	174.06	2.15	171.91	0.00
Total	$1,044.21	$44.21	$1,000.00	

15. $98,551

Exercise 3-4

Use formula (5) or (6) and a calculator or Table V (or both) to solve each problem. (Answers may vary slightly depending on whether you use a calculator or Table V.)

A 1. $PV = ?$, $n = 30$, $i = 0.04$, $PMT = 200
2. $PV = ?$, $n = 40$, $i = 0.01$, $PMT = 400

3. $PV = ?$, $n = 25$, $i = 0.025$, $PMT = \$250$
4. $PV = ?$, $n = 60$, $i = 0.0075$, $PMT = \$500$

B   5. $PV = \$6,000$, $n = 36$, $i = 0.01$, $PMT = ?$
6. $PV = \$1,200$, $n = 40$, $i = 0.025$, $PMT = ?$
7. $PV = \$40,000$, $n = 96$, $i = 0.0075$, $PMT = ?$
8. $PV = \$14,000$, $n = 72$, $i = 0.005$, $PMT = ?$
9. $PV = \$5,000$, $i = 0.01$, $PMT = \$200$, $n = ?$
10. $PV = \$20,000$, $i = 0.0175$, $PMT = \$500$, $n = ?$

Applications

Business & Economics

11. A relative wills you an annuity paying $4,000 per quarter for the next 10 years. If money is worth 8% compounded quarterly, what is the present value of this annuity?

12. How much should you deposit in an account paying 12% compounded monthly in order to receive $1,000 per month for the next 2 years?

13. Parents of a college student wish to set up an annuity that will pay $350 per month to the student for 4 years. How much should they deposit now at 9% interest compounded monthly to establish this annuity? How much will the student receive in the 4 years?

14. A person pays $120 per month for 48 months for a car, making no down payment. If the loan costs 1.5% interest per month on the unpaid balance, what was the original cost of the car? How much total interest will be paid?

15. (A) If you buy a stereo set for $600 and agree to pay for it in 18 equal installments at 1% interest per month on the unpaid balance, how much are your monthly payments? How much interest will you pay?
    (B) Repeat part A for 1.5% interest per month on the unpaid balance.

16. (A) A company buys a large copy machine for $12,000 and finances it at 12% interest compounded monthly. If the loan is to be amortized in 6 years in equal monthly payments, how much is each payment? How much interest will be paid?
    (B) Repeat part A with 18% interest compounded monthly.

17. A sailboat costs $16,000. You pay 25% down and amortize the rest with equal monthly payments over a 6 year period. If you must pay 1.5% interest per month on the unpaid balance (18% compounded monthly), what is your monthly payment? How much interest will you pay over the 6 years?

18. A law firm buys a computerized word-processing system costing

$10,000. If it pays 20% down and amortizes the rest with equal monthly payments over 5 years at 9% compounded monthly, what will be the monthly payment? How much interest will the firm pay?

19. Construct the amortization schedule for a $5,000 debt that is to be amortized in 8 equal quarterly payments at 4.5% interest per quarter on the unpaid balance.

20. Construct the amortization schedule for a $10,000 debt that is to be amortized in 6 equal quarterly payments at 3.5% interest per quarter on the unpaid balance.

21. A person borrows $6,000 at 12% compounded monthly, which is to be amortized over 3 years in equal monthly payments. For tax purposes, he needs to know the amount of interest paid during each year of the loan. Find the interest paid during the first year, the second year, and the third year of the loan. [*Hint:* Find the unpaid balance after 12 payments and after 24 payments.]

22. A person establishes an annuity for retirement by depositing $50,000 into an account that pays 9% compounded monthly. Equal monthly withdrawals will be made each month for 5 years, at which time the account will have a zero balance. Each year taxes must be paid on the interest earned by the account during that year. How much interest was earned during the first year? [*Hint:* The amount in the account at the end of the first year is the present value of a 4 year annuity.]

Use a financial or scientific calculator to solve each of the following problems.

23. Some friends tell you that they paid $25,000 down on a new house and are to pay $525 per month for 30 years. If interest is 9.8% compounded monthly, what was the selling price of the house? How much interest will they pay in 30 years?

24. A family is thinking about buying a new house costing $120,000. They must pay 20% down, and the rest is to be amortized over 30 years in equal monthly payments. If money costs 9.6% compounded monthly, what will their monthly payment be? How much total interest will be paid over the 30 years?

25. A student receives a federally backed student loan of $6,000 at 3.5% interest compounded monthly. After finishing college in 2 years, the student must amortize the loan in the next 4 years by making equal monthly payments. What will the payments be and what total interest will the student pay? [*Hint:* This is a two-part problem. First find the amount of the debt at the end of the first 2 years; then amortize this amount over the next 4 years.]

26. A person establishes a sinking fund for retirement by contributing $7,500 per year at the end of each year for 20 years. For the next 20 years, equal yearly payments are withdrawn, at the end of which time the account will have a zero balance. If money is worth 9% com-

pounded annually, what yearly payments will the person receive for the last 20 years?

27. A family has a $75,000, 30 year mortgage at 13.2% compounded monthly. Find the monthly payment. Also find the unpaid balance after

    (A) 10 years   (B) 20 years   (C) 25 years

28. A family has a $50,000, 20 year mortgage of 10.8% compounded monthly. Find the monthly payment. Also find the unpaid balance after

    (A) 5 years   (B) 10 years   (C) 15 years

29. A family has a $30,000, 20 year mortgage at 15% compounded monthly.

    (A) Find the monthly payment and the total interest paid.
    (B) Suppose the family decides to add an extra $100 to its mortgage payment each month starting with the very first payment. How long will it take the family to pay off the mortgage? How much interest will the family save?

30. At the time they retire, a couple has $200,000 in an account that pays 8.4% compounded monthly.

    (A) If they decide to withdraw equal monthly payments for 10 years, at the end of which time the account will have a zero balance, how much should they withdraw each month?
    (B) If they decide to withdraw $3,000 a month until the balance in the account is zero, how many withdrawals can they make?

31. A couple wish to borrow money using the equity in their home for collateral. A loan company will loan them up to 70% of their equity. They purchased their home 12 years ago for $79,000. The home was financed by paying 20% down and signing a 12% 30 year mortgage on the unpaid balance. Equal monthly payments are made to amortize the loan over the 30 year period. The market value of the house is now $100,000. After making their 144th payment, they applied to the loan company for the maximum loan. How much (to the nearest dollar) will they receive?

3-5   Chapter Review

Important Terms and Symbols

3-1   *Simple interest.* Principal, interest, interest rate, simple interest, face value, present value, future value, simple interest note, $I = Prt$, $A = P(1 + rt)$

3-2 *Compound interest.* Compound interest, rate per compound period, principal (present value), amount (future value), nominal rate, effective rate (or annual yield), $A = P(1 + i)^n$, $i = r/m$, $P = A(1 + i)^{-n}$

3-3 *Future value of an annuity; sinking funds.* Annuity, ordinary annuity, future value, sinking fund,

$$FV = PMT\frac{(1 + i)^n - 1}{i} = PMTs_{\overline{n}|i} \qquad \text{(future value)}$$

$$PMT = FV\frac{i}{(1 + i)^n - 1} = \frac{FV}{s_{\overline{n}|i}} \qquad \text{(sinking fund)}$$

3-4 *Present value of an annuity; amortization.* Present value, amortizing a debt, amortization schedule, equity

$$PV = PMT\frac{1 - (1 + i)^{-n}}{i} = PMTa_{\overline{n}|i} \qquad \text{(present value)}$$

$$PMT = PV\frac{i}{1 - (1 + i)^{-n}} = \frac{PV}{a_{\overline{n}|i}} \qquad \text{(amortization)}$$

Exercise 3-5 Chapter Review

Work through all the problems in this chapter review and check your answers in the back of the book. (Answers to all review problems are there.) Where weaknesses show up, review appropriate sections in the text.

Solve each problem using a calculator or Table V (or both).

A *Find the indicated quantity, given $A = P(1 + rt)$.*

1. $A = ?$, $P = \$100$, $r = 9\%$, $t = 6$ months
2. $A = \$808$, $P = ?$, $r = 12\%$, $t = 1$ month
3. $A = \$212$, $P = \$200$, $r = 8\%$, $t = ?$
4. $A = \$4,120$, $P = \$4,000$, $r = ?$, $t = 6$ months

B *Find the indicated quantity, given $A = P(1 + i)^n$ and $P = A/(1 + i)^n$.*

5. $A = ?$, $P = \$1,200$, $i = 0.005$, $n = 30$
6. $A = \$5,000$, $P = ?$, $i = 0.0075$, $n = 60$

Find the indicated quantity, given

$$FV = PMT\frac{(1 + i)^n - 1}{i} = PMTs_{\overline{n}|i} \qquad \text{and} \qquad PMT = FV\frac{i}{(1 + i)^n - 1} = \frac{FV}{s_{\overline{n}|i}}$$

7. $FV = ?$, $PMT = \$1,000$, $i = 0.005$, $n = 60$
8. $FV = \$8,000$, $PMT = ?$, $i = 0.015$, $n = 48$

Find the indicated quantity, given

$$PV = PMT\frac{1 - (1 + i)^{-n}}{i} = PMTa_{\overline{n}|i} \quad \text{and} \quad PMT = PV\frac{i}{1 - (1 + i)^{-n}} = \frac{PV}{a_{\overline{n}|i}}$$

9. $PV = ?$, $PMT = \$2,500$, $i = 0.02$, $n = 16$
10. $PV = \$8,000$, $PMT = ?$, $i = 0.0075$, $n = 60$

C   *Use a calculator or Table V (or both) to solve for n to the nearest integer.*

11. $2,500 = 1,000(1.06)^n$ 12. $5,000 = 100\dfrac{(1.01)^n - 1}{0.01} = 100s_{\overline{n}|0.01}$

Applications

Business & Economics   *Solve Problems 13–36 using a calculator or Table V.*

13. If you borrow \$3,000 at 14% simple interest for 10 months, how much will you owe in 10 months? How much interest will you pay?
14. A credit card company charges a 22% annual rate for overdue accounts. How much interest will be owed on a \$635 account 1 month overdue?
15. A loan of \$2,500 was repaid at the end of 10 months with a check for \$2,812.50. What annual rate of interest was charged?
16. If you paid \$100 to a loan company for the use of \$1,500 for 120 days, what annual rate of interest did they charge? (Use a 360-day year.)
17. A loan company advertises in the paper that you will pay only 8 cents a day for each \$100 borrowed. What annual rate of interest are they charging? (Use a 360-day year.)
18. If you buy a 13-week T-bill with a maturity value of \$5,000 for \$4,899.08 from the Treasury Department, what annual interest rate will you earn?
19. If an investor wants to earn an annual interest rate of 10.76% on a 26-week T-bill with a maturity value of \$5,000, how much should the investor pay for the bill?
20. Grandparents deposited \$6,000 into a grandchild's account towards her college education. How much money (to the nearest dollar) will be in the account 17 years from now if the account earns 9% compounded monthly?
21. How much should you deposit initially in an account paying 10% compounded semiannually in order to have \$25,000 in 10 years?
22. What will an \$8,000 car cost (to the nearest dollar) 5 years from now if the inflation rate over that period averages 5% compounded annually?

23. What would the $8,000 car in Problem 22 have cost (to the nearest dollar) 5 years ago if the inflation rate over that period had averaged 5% compounded annually?

24. You have $2,500 towards the purchase of a boat that will cost $3,000. How long will it take the $2,500 to grow to $3,000 if it is invested at 9% compounded quarterly? (Round up to the next higher quarter if not exact.)

25. How long will it take money to double if it is invested at 12% compounded monthly? 18% compounded monthly? (Round up to the next higher month if not exact.)

26. A savings and loan company pays 9% compounded monthly. What is the effective rate?

27. Which is the better investment and why: 9% compounded quarterly or 9.25% compounded annually?

28. What is the value of an ordinary annuity at the end of 8 years if $200 per month is deposited into an account earning 9% compounded monthly? How much of this value is interest?

29. A company decides to establish a sinking fund to replace a piece of equipment in 6 years at an estimated cost of $50,000. To accomplish this, they decide to make fixed monthly payments into an account that pays 9% compounded monthly. How much should each payment be?

30. In order to save enough money for the down payment on a condominium, a young couple deposits $200 each month into an account that pays 9% interest compounded monthly. If they need $10,000 for a down payment, how many deposits will they have to make?

31. A scholarship committee wishes to establish a scholarship that will pay $1,500 per quarter to a student for 2 years. How much should they deposit now at 8% compounded quarterly to establish this scholarship? How much will the student receive in the 2 years?

32. A state-of-the-art compact disk stereo system costs $3,000. You pay one-third down and amortize the rest with equal monthly payments over a 2-year period. If you are charged 1.5% interest per month on the unpaid balance, what is your monthly payment? How much interest will you pay over the 2 years?

33. Construct the amortization schedule for a $1,000 debt that is to be amortized in 4 equal quarterly payments at 2.5% interest per quarter on the unpaid balance.

34. Two years ago you borrowed $10,000 at 12% interest compounded monthly, which was to be amortized over 5 years. Now you have acquired some additional funds and decide that you want to pay off this loan. What is the unpaid balance after making payments for 2 years?

35. A business borrows $80,000 at 15% interest compounded monthly for 8 years.

(A) What is the monthly payment?
(B) What is the unpaid balance at the end of the first year?
(C) How much interest was paid during the first year?

36. An individual wants to establish an annuity for retirement purposes. He wants to make quarterly deposits for 20 years so that he can then make quarterly withdrawals of $5,000 for 10 years. The annuity earns 12% interest compounded quarterly.

(A) How much will have to be in the account at the time he retires?
(B) How much should be deposited each quarter for 20 years in order to accumulate the required amount?
(C) What is the total amount of interest earned during the 30-year period?

Problems 37–50 require the use of a scientific or financial calculator.

37. A $10,000 retirement account is left to earn interest at 7% compounded daily. How much money will be in the account 40 years from now when the owner reaches 65? (Use a 365-day year and round answer to the nearest dollar.)

38. How long will it take money to double if it is invested at 10% compounded daily? 10% compounded annually? (Express answer in years to two decimal places and assume a 365-day year.)

39. Security S & L pays 9.38% compounded monthly and West Lake S & L pays 9.35% compounded daily. Which is the better investment? Compute the effective yield for each using a 365-day year.

40. How much should a $5,000 face value zero coupon bond, maturing in 5 years, be sold for now, if its rate of return is to be 9.5% compounded annually?

41. If you pay $4,476.20 for a $10,000 face value zero coupon bond that matures in 10 years, what is your annual compound rate of return?

42. If you just sold a stock for $17,388.17 (net) that cost you $12,903.28 (net) 3 years ago, what annual compound rate of return did you make on your investment?

43. Starting on his 21st birthday, and continuing on every birthday up to and including his 65th, John deposits $2,000 a year into an IRA. How much (to the nearest dollar) will be in the account on the 65th birthday, if the account earns:

(A) 7% compounded annually?
(B) 11% compounded annually?

44. A company establishes a sinking fund for plant retooling in 6 years at an estimated cost of $850,000. How much should be invested semiannually into an account paying 8.76% compounded semiannually? How much interest will the account earn in the 6 years?

45. You can afford monthly deposits of only $200 into an account that pays 7.98% compounded monthly. How long will it be until you will have $2,500 to purchase a used car? (Round to the next higher month if not exact.)

46. A car salesperson tells you that you can buy the car you are looking at for $3,000 down and $200 a month for 48 months. If interest is 14% compounded monthly, what is the selling price of the car and how much interest will you pay during the 48 months?

47. A student receives a student loan for $8,000 at 5.5% interest compounded monthly to help her finish the last 1.5 years of college. One year after finishing college, the student must amortize the loan in the next 5 years by making equal monthly payments. What will the payments be and what total interest will the student pay?

48. (A) A person deposits $2,000 in an IRA on his 21st birthday and on each subsequent birthday up to and including his 29th (9 deposits in all). The account earns 8% compounded annually. If he then leaves the money in the account without making any more deposits, how much will he have on his 65th birthday, assuming the account continues to earn the same rate of interest?

    (B) How much would be in the account (to the nearest dollar) on his 65th birthday had he started the deposits on his 30th birthday and continued making deposits on each birthday until (and including) his 65th birthday?

49. In a new housing development, the houses are selling for $100,000 and require a 20% down payment. The buyer is given a choice of 30-year or 15-year financing, both at 10.75% compounded monthly.

    (A) What is the monthly payment for the 30-year choice? For the 15-year choice?

    (B) What is the unpaid balance after 10 years for the 30-year choice? For the 15-year choice?

50. A loan company will loan up to 60% of the equity in a home. A family purchased their home 8 years ago for $83,000. The home was financed by paying 20% down and signing an 11.25% 30 year mortgage for the balance. Equal monthly payments are made to amortize the loan over the 30 year period. The market value of the house is now $95,000. After making their 96th payment, the family applied to the loan company for the maximum loan. How much (to the nearest dollar) will they receive?

Probability

CHAPTER 4　　　Contents

Probability, like many branches of mathematics, evolved out of practical considerations. Girolamo Cardano (1501–1576), a gambler and physician, produced some of the best mathematics of his time, including a systematic analysis of gambling problems. In 1654 another gambler, the Chevalier de Méré, plagued with bad luck, approached the well-known French philosopher and mathematician Blaise Pascal (1623–1662) regarding certain dice problems. Pascal became interested in these problems, studied them, and discussed them with Pierre de Fermat (1601–1665), another French mathematician. Thus, out of the gaming rooms of western Europe probability was born.

In spite of this lowly birth, probability has matured into a highly respected and immensely useful branch of mathematics. It is used in practically every field. Probability can be thought of as the science of uncertainty. If, for example, a card is drawn from a deck of 52 cards, it is uncertain which card will be drawn. But suppose a card is drawn and replaced in the deck and a card is again drawn and replaced, and this action is repeated a large number of times. A particular card, say the ace of spades, will be drawn over the long run with a relative frequency that is approximately predictable. Probability theory is concerned with determining the long-run frequency of the occurrence of a given event.

How do we assign probabilities to events? There are two basic approaches to this problem, one theoretical and the other empirical. An example will illustrate the difference between the two approaches.

Suppose you were asked, "What is the probability of obtaining a 2 on a single throw of a die?" Using a *theoretical approach,* we would reason as follows: Since there are six *equally likely* ways the die can turn up (assuming the die is fair) and there is only one way a 2 can turn up, then the probability of obtaining a 2 is $\frac{1}{6}$. Here we have arrived at a probability assignment without even rolling a die once; we have used certain assumptions and a reasoning process.

What does the result have to do with reality? We would expect that in the long run (after rolling a die many times) the 2 would appear approximately $\frac{1}{6}$ of the time. With the *empirical approach,* we make no assumption about the equally likely ways in which the die can turn up. We simply set up an experiment and roll the die a large number of times. Then we compute the percentage of times the 2 appears and use this number as an estimate of the probability of obtaining a 2 on a single roll of the die. Each approach has advantages and drawbacks; these will be discussed in the following sections.

We will first consider the theoretical approach and develop procedures that will lead to the solution of a large variety of interesting problems. These procedures require counting the number of ways certain events can happen, and this is not always easy. However, powerful mathematical tools can assist us in this counting task. The development of these tools is the subject matter of the next section.

4-1   Multiplication Principle, Permutations, and Combinations

- Multiplication Principle
- Factorial
- Permutations
- Combinations

■ Multiplication Principle

The best way to start this discussion is with an example.

Example 1   Suppose we spin a spinner that can land on four possible numbers, 1, 2, 3, or 4. We then flip a coin that can turn up either heads (H) or tails (T). What are the possible combined outcomes?

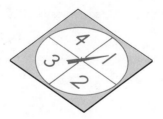

Solution   To solve this problem, let us use a **tree diagram:**

SPINNER OUTCOMES	COIN OUTCOMES	COMBINED OUTCOMES
1	H	(1, H)
	T	(1, T)
2	H	(2, H)
	T	(2, T)
3	H	(3, H)
	T	(3, T)
4	H	(4, H)
	T	(4, T)

Start

Thus, there are eight possible combined outcomes (there are four places the spinner can stop followed by two ways the coin can land). The order in the ordered pair representing a combined outcome is important: the first element in the ordered pair represents a spinner outcome and the second element a coin outcome.

Problem 1   Use a tree diagram to determine the possible combined outcomes of flipping a coin followed by spinning the dial in Example 1.

Now suppose you asked, "From the twenty-six letters in the alphabet, how many ways can three letters appear in a row on a license plate if no letter is repeated?" To try to count the possibilities using a tree diagram would be extremely tedious, to say the least. The following **multiplication principle** (for counting) will enable us to solve this problem easily; in addition, it forms the basis for several other counting devices that are developed later in this section:

Multiplication Principle

1. If two operations O_1 and O_2 are performed in order, with N_1 possible outcomes for the first operation and N_2 possible outcomes for the second operation, then there are

   $$N_1 \cdot N_2$$

   possible combined outcomes of the first operation followed by the second.
2. In general, if n operations $O_1, O_2, \ldots, O_n$ are performed in order, with possible number of outcomes $N_1, N_2, \ldots, N_n$, respectively, then there are

   $$N_1 \cdot N_2 \cdot \cdots \cdot N_n$$

   possible combined outcomes of the operations performed in the given order.

In Example 1, we see that there are four possible outcomes of spinning the dial (first operation) and two possible outcomes of flipping the coin (second operation); hence, by the multiplication principle, there are $4 \cdot 2 = 8$ possible combined outcomes. Use the multiplication principle to solve Problem 1. [*Answer:* $2 \cdot 4 = 8$.]

To answer the license plate question: There are twenty-six ways the first letter can be chosen; after a first letter is chosen, there are twenty-five ways a second letter can be chosen; and after two letters are chosen, there are twenty-four ways a third letter can be chosen. Hence, using the multiplica-

tion principle, there are $26 \cdot 25 \cdot 24 = 15{,}600$ possible ways three letters can be chosen from the alphabet without repeats.

Example 2   Many colleges and universities are now using computer-assisted testing procedures. Suppose a screening test is to consist of five questions, and a computer stores five comparable questions for the first test question, eight for the second, six for the third, five for the fourth, and ten for the fifth. How many different five-question tests can the computer select? (Two tests are considered different if they differ in one or more questions.)

Solution O_1: Selecting the first question

N_1: 5 ways

O_2: Selecting the second question

N_2: 8 ways

O_3: Selecting the third question

N_3: 6 ways

O_4: Selecting the fourth question

N_4: 5 ways

O_5: Selecting the fifth question

N_5: 10 ways

Thus, the computer can generate

$$5 \cdot 8 \cdot 6 \cdot 5 \cdot 10 = 12{,}000 \text{ different tests}$$

Problem 2   Each question on a multiple-choice test has five choices. If there are five such questions on a test, how many different response sheets are possible if only one choice is marked for each question?

Example 3   How many three-letter code words are possible using the first eight letters of the alphabet if:

(A)   No letter can be repeated?   (B)   Letters can be repeated?
(C)   Adjacent letters cannot be alike?

Solutions   To form three-letter code words from the eight letters available, we select a letter for the first position, one for the second position, and one for the third position. Altogether, there are three operations.

(A) O_1: Selecting the first letter

N_1: 8 ways

O_2: Selecting the second letter

N_2: 7 ways (since one letter has been used)

O_3: Selecting the third letter

N_3: 6 ways (since two letters have been used)

Thus, there are

$$8 \cdot 7 \cdot 6 = 336 \text{ possible code words}$$

(possible combined operations).

(B) O_1: Selecting the first letter
   N_1: 8 ways
   O_2: Selecting the second letter
   N_2: 8 ways (repeats are allowed)
   O_3: Selecting the third letter
   N_3: 8 ways (repeats are allowed)

Thus, there are

$$8 \cdot 8 \cdot 8 = 8^3 = 512 \text{ possible code words}$$

(C) O_1: Selecting the first letter
   N_1: 8 ways
   O_2: Selecting the second letter
   N_2: 7 ways (cannot be the same as the first)
   O_3: Selecting the third letter
   N_3: 7 ways (cannot be the same as the second letter, but can be the same as the first)

Thus, there are

$$8 \cdot 7 \cdot 7 = 392 \text{ possible code words}$$

Problem 3   How many four-letter code words are possible using the first ten letters of the alphabet under the three different conditions stated in Example 3?

The multiplication principle can be used to develop two additional devices for counting that are extremely useful in more complicated counting problems. Both of these devices use a function called a *factorial function*, which we introduce first.

■ Factorial

When using the multiplication principle, we encountered expressions of the form

$$5 \cdot 4 \cdot 3 \cdot 2 \cdot 1 \qquad 50 \cdot 49 \cdot 48 \cdot 47 \cdot 46$$

where each natural number factor is decreased by one as we move from left to right. Forms of this type are encountered with such great frequency in certain types of counting problems that it is useful to express them in a concise notation. The product of the first n natural numbers is called **n factorial** and is denoted by $n!$. Also, we define **zero factorial** to be 1.

Symbolically,

Factorial

For n a natural number,

$$n! = n(n-1)(n-2) \cdot \cdots \cdot 2 \cdot 1$$

$$0! = 1$$

$$n! = n \cdot (n-1)!$$

[*Note:* n! appears on many hand calculators.]

Example 4   (A) $5! = 5 \cdot 4 \cdot 3 \cdot 2 \cdot 1 = 120$

(B) $\dfrac{7!}{6!} = \dfrac{7 \cdot \cancel{6!}}{\cancel{6!}} = 7$

(C) $\dfrac{8!}{5!} = \dfrac{8 \cdot 7 \cdot 6 \cdot \cancel{5!}}{\cancel{5!}} = 8 \cdot 7 \cdot 6 = 336$

(D) $\dfrac{52!}{5!47!} = \dfrac{52 \cdot 51 \cdot 50 \cdot 49 \cdot 48 \cdot \cancel{47!}}{5 \cdot 4 \cdot 3 \cdot 2 \cdot 1 \cdot \cancel{47!}} = 2{,}598{,}960$

Problem 4   Find: (A) 6!   (B) $\dfrac{10!}{9!}$ (C) $\dfrac{10!}{7!}$ (D) $\dfrac{5!}{0!3!}$ (E) $\dfrac{20!}{3!17!}$

It is interesting and useful to note that n! grows very rapidly. Compare the following:

$$5! = 120$$

$$10! = 3{,}628{,}800$$

$$15! = 1{,}307{,}674{,}000{,}000$$

Try 69!, 70!, and 71! on your calculator.

■ Permutations

Suppose four pictures are to be arranged from left to right on one wall of an art gallery. How many ordered arrangements are possible? Using the multiplication principle, there are four ways of selecting the first picture; after the first picture is selected, there are three ways of selecting the second picture; after the first two pictures are selected, there are two ways of selecting the third picture; and after the first three pictures are selected, there is only one way to select the fourth. Thus, the number of ordered arrangements possible for the four pictures is

$$4 \cdot 3 \cdot 2 \cdot 1 = 4! \qquad \text{or} \qquad 24$$

In general, we refer to a particular ordered arrangement or ordering of n objects as a **permutation** of the n objects. How many orderings (permutations) of n objects are there? From the reasoning above, there are n ways in which the first object can be chosen, there are $n - 1$ ways in which the second object can be chosen, and so on. Using the multiplication principle, we have

---

Permutations of n Objects

Number of permutations of n objects $= n(n - 1) \cdot \cdots \cdot 2 \cdot 1 = n!$

Now suppose the museum director decides to use only two of the four available pictures on the wall arranged from left to right. How many ordered arrangements of two pictures can be formed from the four? There are four ways the first picture can be selected; after selecting the first picture, there are three ways the second picture can be selected. Thus, the number of ordered arrangements of two pictures from four pictures, denoted by $P_{4,2}$ is given by

$$P_{4,2} = 4 \cdot 3$$

or in terms of factorials, multiplying $4 \cdot 3$ by $2!/2!$, we have

$$P_{4,2} = 4 \cdot 3 = \frac{4 \cdot 3 \cdot 2!}{2!} = \frac{4!}{2!}$$

This last form gives $P_{4,2}$ in terms of factorials, which is useful in some cases.

A **permutation of a set of n objects taken r at a time** is a listing of the r objects in a specific order. Thus, reasoning in the same way as in the example, we find that the **number of permutations of n objects taken r at a time**, $0 \le r \le n$, denoted by $P_{n,r}$, is given by

$$P_{n,r} = n(n - 1)(n - 2) \cdot \cdots \cdot (n - r + 1)$$

Multiplying the right side by 1 in the form $(n - r)!/(n - r)!$, we obtain a factorial form for $P_{n,r}$:

$$P_{n,r} = n(n - 1)(n - 2) \cdot \cdots \cdot (n - r + 1) \frac{(n - r)!}{(n - r)!}$$

But

$$n(n - 1)(n - 2) \cdot \cdots \cdot (n - r + 1)(n - r)! = n!$$

Hence,

Permutation of *n* Objects Taken *r* at a Time

The number of permutations of n objects taken r at a time is given by*

$$P_{n,r} = n(n-1)(n-2) \cdot \cdots \cdot (n-r+1) \qquad r \text{ factors}$$

or

$$P_{n,r} = \frac{n!}{(n-r)!} \qquad 0 \le r \le n$$

[Note: $P_{n,n} = \dfrac{n!}{(n-n)!} = \dfrac{n!}{0!} = n!$ permutations of n objects.]

Example 5 From a committee of eight people, in how many ways can we choose a chairperson and a vice-chairperson, assuming one person cannot hold more than one position?

Solution We are actually asking for the number of permutations of eight objects taken two at a time; that is, $P_{8,2}$:

$$P_{8,2} = \frac{8!}{(8-2)!} = \frac{8!}{6!} = \frac{8 \cdot 7 \cdot 6!}{6!} = 56$$

Problem 5 From a committee of ten people, in how many ways can we choose a chairperson, vice-chairperson, and a secretary, assuming one person cannot hold more than one position?

As we mentioned earlier, many hand calculators have an n! button, and some even have a $P_{n,r}$ button. The use of such a calculator will greatly facilitate many of the calculations in this and the following sections.

Example 6 Find the number of permutations of twenty-five objects taken eight at a time. Compute the anwer to four significant digits using a calculator.

Solution $P_{25,8} = \dfrac{25!}{(25-8)!} = \dfrac{25!}{17!} = 4.361 \times 10^{10}$

Problem 6 Find the number of permutations of thirty objects taken four at a time. Compute the answer exactly using a calculator.

* In place of the symbol $P_{n,r}$, one will also see P_r^n, $_nP_r$, and $P(n, r)$.

■ Combinations

Now suppose that an art museum owns eight paintings by a given artist and another art museum wishes to borrow three of these paintings for a special show. How many ways can three paintings be selected for shipment out of the eight available? Here the order does not matter. What we are actually interested in is how many three-object subsets can be formed from a set of eight objects. We call such a subset a **combination** of eight objects taken three at a time. The total number of such subsets (combinations) is denoted by the symbol

$$C_{8,3} \quad \text{or} \quad \binom{8}{3}$$

To find the number of combinations of eight objects taken three at a time, $C_{8,3}$, we make use of the formula for $P_{n,r}$ developed above and the multiplication principle. We know that the number of permutations of eight objects taken three at a time is given by $P_{8,3}$, and we have a formula for computing this. Now suppose we think of $P_{8,3}$ in terms of two operations:

O_1: Selecting a subset of three objects (paintings)

N_1: $C_{8,3}$ ways

O_2: Arranging the subset in a given order

N_2: 3! ways

The combined operation, O_1 followed by O_2, produces a permutation of eight objects taken three at a time. Thus,

$$P_{8,3} = C_{8,3} \cdot 3!$$

To find $C_{8,3}$, the number of combinations of eight objects taken three at a time, we replace $P_{8,3}$ with $8!/(8-3)!$ and solve for $C_{8,3}$.

$$\frac{8!}{(8-3)!} = C_{8,3} \cdot 3!$$

$$C_{8,3} = \frac{8!}{3!(8-3)!} = \frac{8 \cdot 7 \cdot 6 \cdot \cancel{5!}}{3 \cdot 2 \cdot 1 \cdot \cancel{5!}} = 56$$

Thus, the museum can make fifty-six choices (different shipments) in selecting three paintings from the eight available.

A **combination of a set of n objects taken r at a time** (order is not important) is an r-element subset of the n objects. Reasoning in the same way as in the example, the number of **combinations of n objects taken r at a time,** $0 \leq r \leq n$, denoted by $C_{n,r}$, can be obtained by solving for $C_{n,r}$ in the relationship:

$$P_{n,r} = C_{n,r} \cdot r!$$

$$C_{n,r} = \frac{P_{n,r}}{r!}$$

$$= \frac{n!}{r!(n-r)!} \qquad \text{Since } P_{n,r} = \frac{n!}{(n-r)!}$$

In summary,

Combinations of n Objects Taken r at a Time

The number of combinations of n objects taken r at a time is given by*

$$C_{n,r} = \binom{n}{r} = \frac{P_{n,r}}{r!} = \frac{n!}{r!(n-r)!} \qquad 0 \leqslant r \leqslant n$$

If n and r are other than small numbers, a calculator with an $n!$ button will simplify the computation, and one with a $C_{n,r}$ button will simplify the computation even further.

Example 7　From a committee of eight people, in how many ways can we choose a subcommittee of two people?

Solution　Notice how this example differs from Example 5, where we asked in how many ways can we choose a chairperson and a vice-chairperson from a committee of eight people. In Example 5, ordering matters; in choosing a two-person subcommittee the ordering does not matter. Thus, we are actually asking how many combinations of eight objects taken two at a time there are. The number is given by

$$C_{8,2} = \binom{8}{2} = \frac{8!}{2!(8-2)!} = \frac{8 \cdot 7 \cdot \cancel{6!}}{2 \cdot 1 \cdot \cancel{6!}} = 28$$

Problem 7　How many three-person subcommittees can be chosen from a committee of eight people?

Example 8　Find the number of combinations of twenty-five objects taken eight at a time. Compute the answer to four significant digits using a calculator.

Solution　$$C_{25,8} = \binom{25}{8} = \frac{25!}{8!(25-8)!} = \frac{25!}{8!17!} = 1.082 \times 10^6$$

Compare this result with that obtained in Example 6.

---

* In place of the symbols $C_{n,r}$ and $\binom{n}{r}$, one will also see C_r^n, $_nC_r$, and $C(n, r)$.

Problem 8   Find the number of combinations of thirty objects taken four at a time. Compute the answer exactly using a calculator.

Remember

In a permutation, order counts.

In a combination, order does not count.

To decide between permutations and combinations, decide whether rearranging the collection or listing produces a different object. If so, use permutations; if not use combinations.

Example 9   How many 5-card hands will have 3 aces and 2 kings?

Solution   Operation 1.   Choosing 3 aces out of 4 possible (order is not important) $(C_{4,3})$

Operation 2.   Choosing 2 kings out of 4 possible (order is not important) $(C_{4,2})$

Using the multiplication principle, we have:

Number of hands $= C_{4,3} \cdot C_{4,2} = (4)(6) = 24$

Problem 9   How many 5-card hands will have 3 hearts and 2 spades?

Example 10   Serial numbers for a product are to be made using two letters followed by three numbers. If the letters are to be taken from the first eight letters of the alphabet with no repeats and the numbers from the ten digits (0–9) with no repeats, how many serial numbers are possible?

Solution   Operation 1.   Choosing two letters out of eight available (order is important) $P_{8,2}$

Operation 2.   Choosing three numbers out of ten available (order is important) $P_{10,3}$

Using the multiplication principle, we have:

Number of serial numbers $= P_{8,2} \cdot P_{10,3} = 40{,}320$

Problem 10   Repeat Example 10 under the same conditions, except the serial numbers are now to have three letters followed by two digits (no repeats).

Example 11   A company has seven senior and five junior officers. An ad hoc legislative committee is to be formed. In how many ways can a four-officer committee be formed so that it is composed of:

(A)   Any four officers?
(B)   Four senior officers?
(C)   Three senior officers and one junior officer?
(D)   Two senior and two junior officers?
(E)   At least two senior officers?

Solutions   (A)   Since there are a total of twelve officers in the company, the number of different four-member committees is

$$C_{12,4} = \frac{12!}{4!(12-4)!} = \frac{12!}{4!8!} = 495$$

(B)   If only senior officers can be on the committee, the number of different committees is

$$C_{7,4} = \frac{7!}{4!(7-4)!} = \frac{7!}{4!3!} = 35$$

(C)   The three senior officers can be selected in $C_{7,3}$ ways, and the one junior officer can be selected in $C_{5,1}$ ways. Applying the multiplication principle, the number of ways that three senior officers and one junior officer can be selected is

$$C_{7,3} \cdot C_{5,1} = \frac{7!}{3!(7-3)!} \cdot \frac{5!}{1!(5-1)!} = \frac{7!5!}{3!4!1!4!} = 175$$

(D) $$C_{7,2} \cdot C_{5,2} = \frac{7!}{2!(7-2)!} \cdot \frac{5!}{2!(5-2)!} = \frac{7!5!}{2!5!2!3!} = 210$$

(E)   The committees with at least two senior officers can be divided into three disjoint collections:

1.   Committees with four senior and zero junior officers
2.   Committees with three senior officers and one junior officer
3.   Committees with two senior and two junior officers

The number of committees of types 1, 2, and 3 were computed in parts B, C, and D, respectively. The total number of committees of all three types is the sum of these quantities

Type 1   Type 2   Type 3

$$C_{7,4} + C_{7,3}C_{5,1} + C_{7,2}C_{5,2} = 35 + 175 + 210 = 420$$

Problem 11   Given the information in Example 11, answer the following questions:

(A)   How many committees with one senior and three junior officers can be formed?

(B) How many committees with four junior officers can be formed?
(C) How many committees with at least two junior officers can be formed?

Answers to Matched Problems

1.

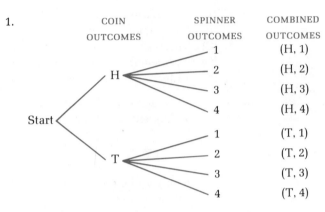

COIN OUTCOMES	SPINNER OUTCOMES	COMBINED OUTCOMES
H	1	(H, 1)
	2	(H, 2)
	3	(H, 3)
	4	(H, 4)
T	1	(T, 1)
	2	(T, 2)
	3	(T, 3)
	4	(T, 4)

2. 5^5 or 3,125

3. (A) $10 \cdot 9 \cdot 8 \cdot 7 = 5,040$ (B) $10 \cdot 10 \cdot 10 \cdot 10 = 10,000$
   (C) $10 \cdot 9 \cdot 9 \cdot 9 = 7,290$

4. (A) 720   (B) 10   (C) 720   (D) 20   (E) 1,140

5. $P_{10,3} = \dfrac{10!}{(10-3)!} = 720$ 6. $P_{30,4} = \dfrac{30!}{(30-4)!} = 657,720$

7. $C_{8,3} = \dfrac{8!}{3!(8-3)!} = 56$ 8. $C_{30,4} = \dfrac{30!}{4!(30-4)!} = 27,405$

9. $C_{13,3} \cdot C_{13,2} = 22,308$ 10. $P_{8,3} \cdot P_{10,2} = 30,240$

11. (A) $C_{7,1}C_{5,3} = 70$ (B) $C_{5,4} = 5$
    (C) $C_{7,2}C_{5,2} + C_{7,1}C_{5,3} + C_{5,4} = 285$

Exercise 4-1

A   *Evaluate.*

1. $4!$ 2. $6!$ 3. $\dfrac{9!}{8!}$ 4. $\dfrac{14!}{13!}$

5. $\dfrac{11!}{8!}$ 6. $\dfrac{14!}{12!}$ 7. $\dfrac{5!}{2!3!}$ 8. $\dfrac{6!}{4!2!}$

9. $\dfrac{7!}{4!(7-4)!}$ 10. $\dfrac{8!}{3!(8-3)!}$ 11. $\dfrac{7!}{7!(7-7)!}$ 12. $\dfrac{8!}{0!(8-0)!}$

13. $P_{5,3}$ 14. $P_{4,2}$ 15. $P_{52,4}$ 16. $P_{52,2}$
17. $C_{5,3}$ 18. $C_{4,2}$ 19. $C_{52,4}$ 20. $C_{52,2}$

21. A particular new car model is available with five choices of color, three choices of transmission, four types of interior, and two types of engine. How many different variations of this model car are possible?

22. A deli serves meat sandwiches with the following options: three kinds of bread, five kinds of meat, and lettuce or sprouts. How many different sandwiches are possible, assuming one item is used out of each category?

23. In a horse race, how many different finishes among the first three places are possible for a ten-horse race? (Exclude ties.)

24. In a long distance foot race, how many different finishes among the first five places are possible for a fifty-person race? (Exclude ties.)

25. How many ways can a three-person subcommittee be selected from a committee of seven people? How many ways can a president, vice president, and secretary be chosen from a committee of seven people?

26. Nine cards are numbered with the nine digits from 1 to 9. A 3-card hand is dealt, 1 card at a time. How many hands are possible where:

    (A) Order is taken into consideration?
    (B) Order is not taken into consideration?

27. There are ten teams in a conference. If each team is to play every other team exactly once, how many games must be scheduled?

28. Given seven points, no three of which are on a straight line, how many lines can be drawn joining two points at a time?

B

29. How many four-letter code words are possible from the first six letters of the alphabet with no letter repeated? Allowing letters to repeat?

30. How many five-letter code words are possible from the first seven letters of the alphabet with no letters repeated? Allowing letters to repeat?

31. A combination lock has five wheels, each labeled with the ten digits from 0 to 9. How many five-number opening combinations are possible, assuming no digit is repeated? Assuming digits can be repeated?

32. A small combination lock on a suitcase has three wheels, each labeled with digits from 0 to 9. How many three-number combinations are possible, assuming no digit is repeated? Assuming digits can be repeated?

33. From a standard 52-card deck, how many 5-card hands will have all hearts?

34. From a standard 52-card deck, how many 5-card hands will have all face cards? All face cards, but no kings?

35. How many different license plates are possible if each contains three letters followed by three digits? How many of these license plates contain no repeated letters and no repeated digits? [*Digits*: 0, 1, 2, 3, 4, 5, 6, 7, 8, 9.]

36. How many five-digit ZIP code numbers are possible? How many of these numbers contain no repeated digits?

37. From a standard 52-card deck, how many 7-card hands have exactly 5 spades and 2 hearts?

38. From a standard 52-card deck, how many 5-card hands will have 2 clubs and 3 hearts?

39. A catering service offers eight appetizers, ten main courses, and seven desserts. A banquet chairperson is to select three appetizers, four main courses, and two desserts for a banquet. How many ways can this be done?

40. Three departments have twelve, fifteen, and eighteen members, respectively. If each department is to select a delegate and an alternate to represent the department at a conference, how many ways can this be done?

C 41. A sporting goods store has twelve pairs of ski gloves of the same size, but of different brands, all in a large bin. In how many ways can a left-hand glove and a right-hand glove be selected that do not match?

42. A sporting goods store has six pairs of running shoes of the same size, but different styles. In how many ways can a left shoe and a right shoe be selected that do not match?

43. Eight distinct points are selected on the circumference of a circle.

   (A) How many chords can be drawn by joining the points in all possible ways?
   (B) How many triangles can be drawn using these eight points as vertices?
   (C) How many quadrilaterals can be drawn using these eight points as vertices?

44. Five distinct points are selected on the circumference of a circle.

   (A) How many chords can be drawn by joining the points in all possible ways?
   (B) How many triangles can be drawn using these five points as vertices?

45. How many ways can two people be seated in a row of five chairs? Three people? Four people? Five people?

46. Each of two countries sends five delegates to a negotiating conference. A rectangular table is used with five chairs on each long side. If each country is assigned a long side of the table (operation 1), how many seating arrangements are possible?

47. A basketball team has five distinct positions. Out of eight players, how many starting teams are possible if:

   (A) The distinct positions are taken into consideration?
   (B) The distinct positions are not taken into consideration?

(C) The distinct positions are not taken into consideration, but either Mike or Ken (but not both) must start?

48. How many four-person committees are possible from a group of nine people if:

(A) There are no restrictions?
(B) Both Jim and Mary must be on the committee?
(C) Either Jim or Mary (but not both) must be on the committee?

Applications

Business & Economics

49. *Management selection.* A management selection service classifies its applicants (using tests and interviews) as high-IQ, middle-IQ, or low-IQ and as aggressive or passive. How many combined classifications are possible?

(A) Solve by using a tree diagram.
(B) Solve by using the multiplication principle.

50. *Management selection.* A corporation plans to fill two different vice-president positions, V_1 and V_2, from administrative officers in two of its manufacturing plants. Plant A has six officers and plant B has eight. How many ways can these two positions be filled if the V_1 position is to be filled from plant A and the V_2 position from plant B? How many ways can the two positions be filled if the selection is made without regard to plant?

51. *Transportation.* A sales representative who lives in city A wishes to start from home and fly to three different cities, B, C, and D. If there are two choices of local transportation (drive his private car to and from the airport or use a taxi for both trips), and if all cities are interconnected by airlines, how many travel plans can be constructed to visit each city exactly once and return home?

52. *Transportation.* A manufacturing company in city A wishes to truck its product to four different cities, B, C, D, and E. If the cities are all interconnected by roads, how many different route plans can be constructed so that a single truck, starting from A, will visit each city exactly once, then return home?

53. *Personnel selection.* Six female and five male applicants have been successfully screened for five positions. In how many ways can the following compositions be selected?

(A) Three females and two males
(B) Four females and one male
(C) Five females

    (D)   Five people regardless of sex

    (E)   At least four females

54. *Committee selection.* A four-person grievance committee is to be selected out of two departments, *A* and *B*, with fifteen and twenty people, respectively. In how many ways can the following committees be selected?

    (A)   Three from *A* and one from *B*

    (B)   Two from *A* and two from *B*

    (C)   All from *A*

    (D)   Four people regardless of department

    (E)   At least three from department *A*

Life Sciences   55. *Medicine.* A medical researcher classifies subjects according to male or female, smoker or nonsmoker, and underweight, average weight, or overweight. How many combined classifications are possible?

    (A)   Solve using a tree diagram.

    (B)   Solve using the multiplication principle.

56. *Family planning.* A couple is planning to have three children. How many boy-girl combinations are possible? Distinguish between combined outcomes such as (B, B, G), (B, G, B), and (G, B, B).

    (A)   Solve by using a tree diagram.

    (B)   Solve by using the multiplication principle.

57. *Medicine.* There are eight standard classifications of blood type. An examination for prospective laboratory technicians consists of having the candidate determine the type of three blood samples. How many different examinations can be given if no two of the samples provided for the candidate have the same type? If two or more samples can have the same type?

58. *Medical research.* Because of limited funds, five research centers are to be chosen out of eight suitable ones for a study on heart disease. How many choices are possible?

Social Sciences   59. *Politics.* A nominating convention is to select a president and vice-president from among four candidates. Campaign buttons, listing a president and a vice-president, are to be designed for each possible outcome before the convention. How many different kinds of buttons should be designed?

60. *Politics.* In how many different ways can six candidates for an office be listed on a ballot?

4-2 Experiments, Sample Spaces, and Probability of an Event

- Experiments
- Sample Spaces
- Events
- Probability of an Event
- Equally Likely Assumption

■ Experiments

Certain experiments in science produce the same results when performed repeatedly under exactly the same conditions. For example, when all other conditions are held constant, a given liquid will always freeze at the same temperature. Experiments of this type are called **deterministic**—the conditions of the experiment determine the outcome. There are also experiments that do not yield the same results no matter how carefully they are repeated under the same conditions. These experiments are called **random experiments.** Familiar examples of the latter are flipping coins, rolling dice, observing the sex of a newborn child, or observing the frequency of death in a certain age group. Probability theory is a branch of mathematics that has been developed to deal with outcomes of random experiments, both real and conceptual. In the work that follows, the word *experiment* will be used to mean a random experiment.

■ Sample Spaces

Consider the experiment "A driver of a car has an accident." What can be observed about this accident? In determining rates, an insurance company might be interested in the driver's age, sex, address, seatbelt use, intoxication level; vehicle type; weather; time; and so on. The list of possible outcomes (observations) appears endless. In general, there is no unique method of analyzing all possible outcomes of an experiment. Therefore, before conducting an experiment (making observations), it is important to decide just what outcomes are of interest.

In the accident experiment, suppose we limit our interest to questions concerning the age of accident drivers with legal licenses (16 years or older in most states). Having decided what to observe, we make a list of outcomes of the experiment, called **simple outcomes,** such that in each trial of the experiment (each accident involving a legal driver), one and only one of the results on the list will occur. The set of simple outcomes for the experiment is called a **sample space** for the experiment. (The elements in the sample space are also called **sample points.**) In the accident experiment,

$$U = \{16, 17, 18, \ldots, n\} \qquad n \text{ is the oldest legal driver}$$

is an appropriate sample space for our interests (18, for example, represents the outcome "the driver of the accident vehicle is 18 years old").

Now consider the nonsimple outcome "The accident driver is a teenager." Since this outcome will occur if any of the simple outcomes 16, 17, 18, or 19 occur, it is referred to as a *compound outcome*. In general, *C* is a **compound outcome** relative to a sample space *S* if there exist at least two simple outcomes in *S* that imply the occurrence of *C*. Of course, none of the outcomes in a sample space are compound outcomes relative to that space (Why?). Is the outcome "The accident driver was a senior citizen (65 or older)" a simple outcome or a compound outcome?

Suppose we are interested in the sex of the accident driver as well as the age. Then we must refine the sample space *U* given above. A suitable new sample space for the experiment "An accident involving a legal driver," reflecting our additional interest, is

$$V = \{16F, 16M, 17F, 17M, \ldots, nF, nM\}$$

where, for example, 43M is the outcome "The accident driver is a 43 year old male." Each simple outcome in the original sample space *U* is now a compound outcome in the new sample space *V*; that is, we will know that 43 has occurred if either 43F or 43M has occurred (think about this).

Important Remark

There is no one correct sample space for a given experiment. We do require, however, that a set of outcomes satisfies both conditions in the definition above before it can be called a sample space. When specifying a sample space for an experiment, we include as much detail as is necessary to answer *all* questions of interest regarding the outcomes of the experiment. If in doubt, include more sample points rather than fewer.

Example 12 A nickel and a dime are tossed. How shall we identify a sample space for this experiment? There are a number of possibilities, depending on our interest. We shall consider three.

(A) If we are interested in whether each coin falls heads (H) or tails (T), then, using a tree diagram, we can easily determine an appropriate sample space for the experiment:

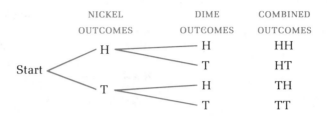

Thus,

$$S_1 = \{HH, HT, TH, TT\}$$

and there are four sample points in the sample space.

(B)   If we are only interested in the number of heads that appear on a single toss of the two coins, then we can let

$$S_2 = \{0, 1, 2\}$$

and there are three sample points in the sample space.

(C)   If we are interested in whether the coins match (M) or do not match (D), then we can let

$$S_3 = \{M, D\}$$

and there are only two sample points in the sample space.

In Example 12, sample space S_1 contains more information than either S_2 or S_3. If we know which outcome has occurred in S_1, then we know which outcome has occurred in S_2 and S_3. However, the reverse is not true. In this sense, we say that **S_1 is a more fundamental sample space than either S_2 or S_3.**

Problem 12   An experiment consists of recording the boy–girl composition of two-child families.

(A)   What is an appropriate sample space if we are interested in the sex of each child in the order of their births? Draw a tree diagram.

(B)   What is an appropriate sample space if we are only interested in the number of girls in a family?

(C)   What is an appropriate sample space if we are only interested in whether the sexes are alike (A) or different (D)?

(D)   What is an appropriate sample space for all three interests expressed above?

A sample space may be **finite** or **infinite.** For example, a sample space for a single roll of a die might be

$$S = \{1, 2, 3, 4, 5, 6\}$$

This is a finite sample space, since there are only a finite number of outcomes of the experiment.

On the other hand, if we are interested in the number of rolls it takes for the die to turn up 5 for the first time, then an appropriate sample space would be the set of natural numbers

$$N = \{1, 2, 3, 4, \ldots \}$$

which is infinite. In this book, unless stated to the contrary, we will restrict our attention to finite sample spaces.

■ Events

We have now completed a first step in constructing a mathematical model for probability studies. That is, we have introduced a sample space, a set of sample points, as the mathematical counterpart of an experiment. The sample space becomes the universal set for all discussion pertaining to the experiment.

Now let us return to the two-coin problem in Example 12 and the sample space

$$S_1 = \{HH, HT, TH, TT\}$$

Suppose we are interested in the compound outcome "Exactly one head is up." Looking at S_1, we find that it will occur if either of the two simple outcomes HT or TH occurs. Thus, to say that the compound outcome "Exactly one head is up" occurs is the same as saying the experiment has an outcome in the set

$$E = \{HT, TH\}$$

which is a subset of the sample space S_1. We will call the subset E an *event.*

Event

In general, given a sample space S for an experiment, we define an **event E** to be any subset of S. We say that **an event E occurs** if any of the simple outcomes in E occurs. If an event E has only one element in it, it is called a **simple event;** if it has more than one element, it is called a **compound event.**

A second step in constructing a mathematical model for probability studies has now been completed by introducing an event as a subset of a sample space. In the coin example above, the event E, a subset of S_1, is the mathematical counterpart of the experimental outcome "Exactly one head is up" in the toss of a nickel and a dime.

Let us now consider a more complex experiment.

Example 13

Consider an experiment of rolling two dice. A convenient sample space that will enable us to answer many questions about interesting events is shown in Figure 1. Let S be the set of all ordered pairs in the table. The sample point (3, 2) is to be distinguished from the sample point (2, 3); the former indicates a 3 turned up on the first die and a 2 on the second, while the latter indicates that a 2 turned up on the first die and a 3 on the second.

SECOND DIE

	⚀	⚁	⚂	⚃	⚄	⚅
⚀	(1, 1)	(1, 2)	(1, 3)	(1, 4)	(1, 5)	(1, 6)
⚁	(2, 1)	(2, 2)	(2, 3)	(2, 4)	(2, 5)	(2, 6)
⚂	(3, 1)	(3, 2)	(3, 3)	(3, 4)	(3, 5)	(3, 6)
⚃	(4, 1)	(4, 2)	(4, 3)	(4, 4)	(4, 5)	(4, 6)
⚄	(5, 1)	(5, 2)	(5, 3)	(5, 4)	(5, 5)	(5, 6)
⚅	(6, 1)	(6, 2)	(6, 3)	(6, 4)	(6, 5)	(6, 6)

FIRST DIE

Figure 1

Write down the event (subset of the sample space S) that corresponds to each of the following outcomes:

(A) A 7 turns up.   (B) An 11 turns up.
(C) A sum less than 4 turns up.   (D) A 12 turns up.

Solutions

(A) By "A 7 turns up," we mean that the sum of all dots on both turned-up faces is 7. This compound outcome corresponds to the event:

{(6, 1), (5, 2), (4, 3), (3, 4), (5, 2), (1, 6)}

Notice that there are 6 ways in which a 7 can be obtained out of the 36 simple outcomes in the sample space.

(B) "An 11 turns up" corresponds to the event

{(6, 5), (5, 6)}

(C) "A sum less than 4 turns up" corresponds to the event

{(1, 1), (2, 1), (1, 2)}

(D) "A 12 turns up" corresponds to the event

{(6, 6)}

which is a simple event.

Problem 13   Using the sample space in Example 13 (Figure 1), write down the events corresponding to the following outcomes:

(A) A 5 turns up.   (B) A prime number* greater than 7 turns up.

Informal Use of the Word *Event*

Informally, to facilitate discussion, we will often use *event* and *outcome of an experiment* interchangeably. Thus, in Example 13 we might use "the event 'An 11 turns up' " in place of "the outcome 'An 11 turns up,' " or even write

$E =$ An 11 turns up $= \{(6, 5), (5, 6)\}$

Technically speaking, as we said earlier, an event is the mathematical counterpart of an outcome of an experiment. Formally, we have

Real World	**Mathematical Model**
Experiment (real or conceptual)	Sample space (set S)
Outcome (simple or compound)	Event (subset of S) (simple or compound)

▪ Probability of an Event

The next step in developing our mathematical model for probability studies is the introduction of a *probability function*. This is a function that assigns to an arbitrary event associated with a sample space a real number between 0 and 1, inclusive. Since an arbitrary event relative to a sample space S can be thought of as the union of simple events in S, we start by discussing ways in which probabilities are assigned to simple events in S. We will then use these results as building blocks in assigning probabilities for compound events.

---

* Recall that a *prime number* is a natural number greater than 1 that cannot be divided by any natural number other than itself or 1.

Probabilities for Simple Events

Given a sample space

$$S = \{e_1, e_2, \ldots, e_n\}$$

to each simple event* e_i we assign a real number, denoted by $P(e_i)$, that is called the **probability of the event e_i.** These numbers can be assigned in an arbitrary manner as long as the following two conditions are satisfied:

1. If e_i is a simple event, then $0 \leq P(e_i) \leq 1$.
2. $P(e_1) + P(e_2) + \cdots + P(e_n) = 1$; that is, the sum of the probabilities of all simple events in the sample space is 1.

Any probability assignment that meets conditions 1 and 2 is said to be an **acceptable probability assignment.**

How specific acceptable probabilities are assigned to simple events is a question our mathematical theory does not answer. These assignments, however, are generally based on expected or actual long-run relative frequencies of the occurrences of the various simple events for a given experiment. Such assignments will be called *suitable* or *reasonable*.

Example 14　Let an experiment be the flipping of a single coin, and let us choose a sample space S to be

$$S = \{H, T\}$$

Psychologically, if a coin appears to be "fair," we are inclined to assign probabilities to the simple events in S as follows:

$$P(H) = \tfrac{1}{2} \quad \text{and} \quad P(T) = \tfrac{1}{2}$$

thinking (since there are two ways a coin can land) that in the long run a head will turn up half the time and a tail will turn up half the time. These probability assignments are acceptable, since both conditions for acceptable probability assignments are satisfied:

1. $0 \leq P(H) \leq 1, \quad 0 \leq P(T) \leq 1$
2. $P(H) + P(T) = \tfrac{1}{2} + \tfrac{1}{2} = 1$

But there are other acceptable assignments. Maybe after flipping a coin 1,000 times, we find that the head turns up 376 times and the tail 624 times.

---

* Technically, we should write $\{e_i\}$, since there is a logical distinction between an element of a set and a subset consisting only of that element. But we will just keep this in mind and drop the braces for simple events to simplify the notation.

With this result, we might suspect that the coin is not fair and assign simple events in S the probabilities

$$P(H) = .376 \quad \text{and} \quad P(T) = .624$$

This is also an acceptable assignment. Which of the following are acceptable assignments?

(A) $P(H) = \frac{7}{8}$ and $P(T) = \frac{1}{8}$
(B) $P(H) = 1$ and $P(T) = 0$
(C) $P(H) = .6$ and $P(T) = .8$

Assignments A and B are acceptable, but C is not. The latter has a sum of 1.4, which violates condition 2.

It is important to keep in mind that out of the infinitely many possible acceptable probability assignments to simple events in a sample space, we are generally inclined to choose one assignment over another based on feelings, reasoning, or experimental results. In Example 14, we would probably choose

$$P(H) = .376 \quad \text{and} \quad P(T) = .624$$

if, in 1,000 tosses of a coin, a head turned up 376 times and a tail turned up 624 times. On the other hand, if we just pull a coin out of a pocket and flip it to see who pays for lunch, then we would probably be happy with

$$P(H) = \frac{1}{2} \quad \text{and} \quad P(T) = \frac{1}{2}$$

In neither case would we be happy with

$$P(H) = 1 \quad \text{and} \quad P(T) = 0$$

even though it is also an acceptable assignment.

Problem 14
A blank six-sided die (not necessarily fair) is marked with a 1 on two sides, a 2 on two sides, and a 3 on the two remaining sides. If we choose a sample space for a single roll of the die to be

$$S = \{1, 2, 3\}$$

which of the following probability assignments to the simple events in S are acceptable? Which would appear to be the most suitable if the die is fair?

(A) $P(1) = 1, \quad P(2) = -1, \quad P(3) = 1$
(B) $P(1) = \frac{1}{3}, \quad P(2) = \frac{2}{3}, \quad P(3) = 0$
(C) $P(1) = \frac{1}{3}, \quad P(2) = \frac{1}{3}, \quad P(3) = \frac{1}{3}$
(D) $P(1) = .35, \quad P(2) = .32, \quad P(3) = .33$

Given an acceptable probability assignment for simple events in a sample space S, how do we define the probability of an arbitrary event associated with S?

> **Probability of an Event _E_**
>
> Given an acceptable probability assignment for the simple events in a sample space S, we define the **probability of an arbitrary event _E_,** denoted by $P(E)$, as follows:
>
> 1. If E is the empty set, then $P(E) = 0$.
> 2. If E is a simple event, then $P(E)$ has already been assigned.
> 3. If E is the union of two or more simple events, then $P(E)$ is the sum of the probabilities of the simple events whose union is E.
> 4. If $E = S$, then $P(E) = P(S) = 1$ (this is a special case of 3).

Example 15   Let us return to Example 12, the tossing of a nickel and dime, with sample space

$$S = \{HH, HT, TH, TT\}$$

Since there are four simple outcomes and the coins are assumed to be fair, it would appear that each outcome would occur in the long run 25% of the time. Let us assign the same probability of $\frac{1}{4}$ to each simple event in S:

Simple Event e_i	HH	HT	TH	TT
$P(e_i)$	$\frac{1}{4}$	$\frac{1}{4}$	$\frac{1}{4}$	$\frac{1}{4}$

This is an acceptable assignment and is a reasonable assignment for ideal coins or coins close to ideal (perfectly balanced).

(A)   What is the probability of getting one head (and one tail)?
(B)   What is the probability of getting at least one head?
(C)   What is the probability of getting three heads?

Solutions   (A) E_1 = Getting one head

$$= \{HT, TH\} = \{HT\} \cup \{TH\}$$

$$P(E_1) = P(HT) + P(TH) = \tfrac{1}{4} + \tfrac{1}{4} = \tfrac{1}{2}$$

(B) E_2 = Getting at least one head

$$= \{HH, HT, TH\} = \{HH\} \cup \{HT\} \cup \{TH\}$$

$$P(E_2) = P(HH) + P(HT) + P(TH)$$

$$= \tfrac{1}{4} + \tfrac{1}{4} + \tfrac{1}{4} = \tfrac{3}{4}$$

(C) E_3 = Getting three heads $= \varnothing$

$$P(\varnothing) = 0$$

Let us summarize the key steps for finding probabilities of events:

Steps for Finding Probabilities of Events

1. Set up an appropriate sample space S for the experiment.
2. Assign acceptable probabilities to the simple events of S.
3. To obtain the probability of an arbitrary event E, add the probabilities of the simple events whose union is E.
4. If it is easier to find $P(E')$, where E' is the complement of E relative to S, then we can use $P(E) = 1 - P(E')$. (More will be said about this later in the chapter.)

The function P defined in steps 2 and 3 is called a **probability function** with domain all possible events (subsets) in the sample space S and range a set of real numbers between 0 and 1, inclusive.

Problem 15

Suppose in Example 15 after flipping the nickel and dime 1,000 times, we find that HH turns up 273 times, HT 206 times, TH 312 times, and TT 209 times. On the basis of this evidence, we assign probabilities to simple events in S as follows:

Simple Event e_i	HH	HT	TH	TT
$P(e_i)$	.273	.206	.312	.209

This is an acceptable probability assignment. What are the probabilities of the following events?

(A) $E_1 = $ Getting at least one tail   (B) $E_2 = $ Getting two tails
(C) $E_3 = $ Getting either a head or a tail

Example 15 and Problem 15 illustrate two important ways in which acceptable and reasonable probability assignments are made for simple events in a sample space S.

1. *Theoretical.* The internal structure of an experiment is analyzed and assignments are made through a deductive process by using certain basic assumptions. (No coins are flipped or dice rolled ahead of time.) These assignments are used as an approximation of the actual probabilities. This is what we did in Example 15 above.
2. *Empirical.* Nothing is assumed about the internal structure of the

experiment; instead, we take a sample of all possible outcomes and use the relative frequency (percentage) of each simple event in the total sample as approximations of the actual probabilities.* This is what we did in Problem 15 above.

Each approach has its advantages in certain situations. For the rest of this section, we will emphasize the theoretical approach. In the next section, we will consider the empirical approach in more detail.

■ Equally Likely Assumption

In tossing a nickel and dime (Example 15), we assigned the same probability, $\frac{1}{4}$, to each simple event in the sample space

S = {HH, HT, TH, TT}

By assigning the same probability to each simple event in S, we are actually making the assumption that each simple event is as likely to occur as any other. We refer to this as an **equally likely assumption.**

In general,

Probability of a Simple Event (Under Equally Likely Assumption)

If, in a sample space

$$S = \{e_1, e_2, \ldots, e_n\}$$

with n elements, we assume each simple event is as likely to occur as any other, then we assign the probability $1/n$ to each; that is,

$$P(e_i) = \frac{1}{n}$$

Under the equally likely assumption, we can develop a very useful formula for finding probabilities of arbitrary events associated with S. Consider the following example.

If a single die is rolled and we assume each face is as likely to come up as any other, then for the sample space

S = {1, 2, 3, 4, 5, 6}

we assign $\frac{1}{6}$ to each simple event, since there are six simple events. The

---

* The **actual probability of an event** is generally defined as the single fixed number (if it exists) that the relative frequency of the occurrence of the event approaches as an experiment is repeated without end.

probability of

$$E = \text{Rolling a prime number}$$
$$= \{2, 3, 5\} = \{2\} \cup \{3\} \cup \{5\}$$

is

$$P(E) = P(2) + P(3) + P(5)$$
$$= \tfrac{1}{6} + \tfrac{1}{6} + \tfrac{1}{6} = \tfrac{3}{6} = \tfrac{1}{2}$$

Notice the following:

$$\frac{3}{6} = \frac{\text{Number of elements in } E}{\text{Number of elements in } S}$$

Thus, under the assumption that each simple event is as likely to occur as any other, the computation of the probability of the occurrence of any event E in S is relatively easy. We simply count the number of elements in E and divide by the number of elements in the sample space S:

Probability of an Arbitrary Event E (Under Equally Likely Assumption)

If we assume each simple event in S is as likely to occur as any other, then the probability of an arbitrary event E in S is given by

$$P(E) = \frac{\text{Number of elements in } E}{\text{Number of elements in } S} = \frac{n(E)}{n(S)}$$

Example 16

If in rolling two dice we assume each simple event in the sample space shown in Figure 1 (page 343) is as likely as any other, find the probabilities of the following events (each event refers to the sum of the dots facing up on both dice):

(A) $E_1 = $ A 7 turns up   (B) $E_2 = $ An 11 turns up
(C) $E_3 = $ A sum less than 4 turns up   (D) $E_4 = $ A 12 turns up

Solutions

Referring to Figure 1 (page 343), we see that

(A) $P(E_1) = \dfrac{n(E_1)}{n(S)} = \dfrac{6}{36} = \dfrac{1}{6}$

(B) $P(E_2) = \dfrac{n(E_2)}{n(S)} = \dfrac{2}{36} = \dfrac{1}{18}$

(C) $P(E_3) = \dfrac{n(E_3)}{n(S)} = \dfrac{3}{36} = \dfrac{1}{12}$

(D) $P(E_4) = \dfrac{n(E_4)}{n(S)} = \dfrac{1}{36}$

Problem 16   Under the conditions in Example 16, find the probabilities of the following events (each event refers to the sum of the dots facing up on both dice):

(A) E_5 = A 5 turns up
(B) E_6 = A prime number greater than 7 turns up

Example 17   The following questions pertain to the composition of a three-child family, excluding multiple births.

(A) Under the assumption that a girl is as likely as a boy at each birth, select a sample space S such that all simple events can be assumed equally likely to occur.
(B) What is the probability of having three girls?
(C) What is the probability of having two boys and a girl in that order?
(D) What is the probability of having two boys and a girl in any order?

Solutions   (A) A tree diagram is helpful in selecting a sample space S:

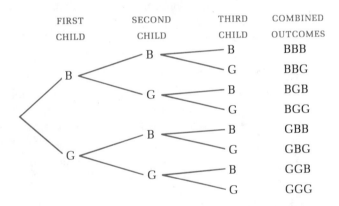

| FIRST CHILD | SECOND CHILD | THIRD CHILD | COMBINED OUTCOMES |

Under the assumption that a boy is as likely as a girl at each birth, each branch at the end is as likely as any other; hence, each combined outcome is as likely as any other. Thus, we let

$$S = \{BBB, BBG, BGB, BGG, GBB, GBG, GGB, GGG\}$$

(B) The event of having three girls is the simple event

$$E = \{GGG\}$$

Thus,

$$P(E) = \frac{n(E)}{n(S)} = \frac{1}{8}$$

(C) The event of having two boys and a girl in that order is the simple event

$$E = \{BBG\}$$

Thus,

$$P(E) = \frac{n(E)}{n(S)} = \frac{1}{8}$$

(D)   The event of having two boys and a girl in any order is

$$E = \{BBG, BGB, GBB\}$$

Thus,

$$P(E) = \frac{n(E)}{n(S)} = \frac{3}{8}$$

Problem 17   Using the sample space in Example 17, find the probability of having:

(A)   Three boys   (B)   At least two girls

We now turn to some examples that make use of the counting techniques developed in the last section.

Example 18   In drawing 5 cards from a 52-card deck without replacement (without replacing a drawn card before selecting the next card), what is the probability of getting 5 spades?

Solution   Let the sample space S be the set of all 5-card hands from a 52-card deck. Since the order in a hand does not matter, $n(S) = C_{52,5}$. The event $E =$ the set of all 5-card hands from 13 spades. Again, the order does not matter and $n(E) = C_{13,5}$. Thus, assuming each 5 card hand is as likely as any other,

$$P(E) = \frac{n(E)}{n(S)} = \frac{C_{13,5}}{C_{52,5}} = \frac{13!/(5!8!)}{52!/(5!47!)} = \frac{13!}{5!8!} \cdot \frac{5!47!}{52!} \approx .0005$$

Problem 18   In drawing 7 cards from a 52-card deck without replacement, what is the probability of getting 7 hearts?

Example 19   The board of regents of a university is made up of twelve men and sixteen women. If a committee of six is chosen at random, what is the probability that it will contain three men and three women?

Solution   Let $S =$ The set of all six-person committees out of twenty-eight people:

$$n(S) = C_{28,6}$$

$E =$ The set of all six-person committees with three men and three women. Using the multiplication principle,

$$n(E) = C_{12,3} C_{16,3}$$

Thus,

$$P(E) = \frac{n(E)}{n(S)} = \frac{C_{12,3} C_{16,3}}{C_{28,6}} \approx .327$$

Problem 19   What is the probability that the committee in Example 19 will have four men and two women?

We should point out that there are many counting problems for which it is not possible to produce a simple formula that will yield the number of possible cases. In cases of this type, we usually revert back to tree diagrams and count branches.

Answers to
Matched Problems

12. (A)

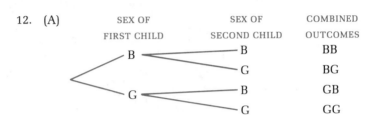

	SEX OF FIRST CHILD	SEX OF SECOND CHILD	COMBINED OUTCOMES
	B	B	BB
		G	BG
	G	B	GB
		G	GG

Thus, $S_1 = \{BB, BG, GB, GG\}$.

(B) $S_2 = \{0, 1, 2\}$ (C) $S_3 = \{A, D\}$

(D) The sample space in part A.

13. (A) (4, 1), (3, 2), (2, 3), (1, 4)   (B) (6, 5), (5,6)

14. (A) Not acceptable   (B) Acceptable
    (C) Acceptable   (D) Acceptable

C appears most suitable if the die is fair

15. (A) .727   (B) .209   (C) 1

16. (A) $P(E_5) = \frac{1}{9}$ (B) $P(E_6) = \frac{1}{18}$

17. (A) $\frac{1}{8}$ (B) $\frac{1}{2}$ 18. $\dfrac{C_{13,7}}{C_{52,7}} \approx .000013$ 19. $\dfrac{C_{12,4}C_{16,2}}{C_{28,6}} \approx .158$

Exercise 4-2

A   1. How would you interpret $P(E) = 1$?
         2. How would you interpret $P(E) = 0$?

An experiment consists of a coin being tossed three times in succession. Answer the questions in Problems 3–6 regarding this experiment.

3. Find a sample space composed of equally likely simple events. (See Example 17.)

4. Let $E =$ Getting exactly two heads. Write E as a subset of the sample space in Problem 3 and find $P(E)$.

5. Let $E =$ Getting at least two heads. Write E as a subset of the sample space in Problem 3 and find $P(E)$.

6. Let $E =$ Getting at least one tail. Write E as a subset of the sample space in Problem 3 and find $P(E)$.

7. A spinner can land on four different colors: red (R), green (G), yellow (Y), and blue (B). If we do not assume each color is as likely to turn up as any other, which of the probability assignments below have to be rejected, and why?

   (A) $P(R) = .15$, $P(G) = -.35$, $P(Y) = .50$, $P(B) = .70$
   (B) $P(R) = .32$, $P(G) = .28$, $P(Y) = .24$, $P(B) = .30$
   (C) $P(R) = .26$, $P(G) = .14$, $P(Y) = .30$, $P(B) = .30$

8. Using the probability assignments in Problem 7C, what is the probability that the spinner will not land on blue?

9. Using the probability assignments in Problem 7C, what is the probability that the spinner will land on red or yellow?

10. Using the probability assignments in Problem 7C, what is the probability that the spinner will not land on red or yellow?

B   11. A small combination lock on a suitcase has three wheels, each labeled with the ten digits from 0 to 9. If an opening combination is a particular sequence of three digits with no repeats, what is the probability of a person guessing the right combination?

12. A combination lock has 5 wheels, each labeled with the ten digits from 0 to 9. If an opening combination is a particular sequence of five digits with no repeats, what is the probability of a person guessing the right combination?

An experiment consists of dealing 5 cards from a standard 52-card deck. In Problems 13–16, what is the probability of being dealt:

13. 5 black cards   14. 5 hearts
15. 5 face cards, including aces   16. 5 nonface cards, including aces

17. If four-digit numbers less than 5,000 are randomly formed from the digits 1, 3, 5, 7, and 9, what is the probability of forming a number divisible by 5? (Digits may be repeated; for example, 1,355 is acceptable.)

18. If four-letter code words are generated at random using the letters A, B, C, D, E, and F, what is the probability of forming a word without a vowel in it? (Letters may be repeated.)

19. Five thank-you notes are written and five envelopes are addressed. Accidentally, the notes are randomly inserted into the envelopes and mailed without checking the addresses. What is the probability that all notes will be inserted into the correct envelopes?

20. Six people check their coats in a checkroom. If all claim checks are lost and the six coats are randomly returned, what is the probability that all people will get their own coats back?

An experiment consists of rolling two fair dice and adding the dots on the two sides facing up. Using the sample space shown in Figure 1 and assuming each simple event is as likely as any other, find the probability of the sum of the dots in Problems 21–36:

21. Being 2
22. Being 10
23. Being 6
24. Being 8
25. Being less than 5
26. Being greater than 8
27. Not being 7 or 11
28. Not being 2, 4, or 6
29. Being 1
30. Not being 13
31. Being divisible by 3
32. Being divisible by 4
33. Being 7 or 11 (a natural)
34. Being 2, 3, or 12 (craps)
35. Being divisible by 2 or 3
36. Being divisible by 2 and 3

An experiment consists of tossing three fair (not weighted) coins, except one of the three coins has a head on both sides. Compute the probability of obtaining the indicated results in Problems 37–42.

37. 1 head
38. 2 heads
39. 3 heads
40. 0 heads
41. More than 1 head
42. More than 1 tail

C   *An experiment consists of rolling two fair (not weighted) dice and adding the dots on the two sides facing up. Each die has the number 1 on two opposite faces, the number 2 on two opposite faces, and the number 3 on two opposite faces. Compute the probability of obtaining the indicated sums in Problems 43–50.*

43. 2
44. 3
45. 4
46. 5
47. 6
48. 7
49. An odd sum
50. An even sum

An experiment consists of dealing 5 cards from a standard 52-card deck. In Problems 51–58 what is the probability of being dealt:

51. 5 cards, jacks through aces?
52. 5 cards, 2 through 10?
53. 4 aces?
54. Four of a kind?
55. Straight flush, ace high?
56. Straight flush, starting with 2?
57. 2 aces and 3 queens?
58. 2 kings and 3 aces?

Applications

Business & Economics

59. *Consumer testing.* Twelve popular brands of beer are to be used in a blind taste study for consumer recognition.

   (A) If four distinct brands are chosen at random from the twelve and if a consumer is not allowed to repeat any answers, what is the probability that all four brands could be identified by just guessing?

   (B) If repeats are allowed in the four brands chosen at random from the twelve and if the consumer is allowed to repeat answers, what is the probability of correct identification of all four by just guessing?

60. *Consumer testing.* Six popular brands of cola are to be used in a blind taste study for consumer recognition.

   (A) If three distinct brands are chosen at random from the six and if a consumer is not allowed to repeat any answers, what is the probability that all three brands could be identified by just guessing?
   (B) If repeats are allowed in the three brands chosen at random from the six and if the consumer is allowed to repeat answers, what is the probability of correct identification of all three by just guessing?

61. *Product sampling.* One hundred blank video cassettes, including five defectives, are sent to a retailer. The retailer will select six at random and will return the whole shipment if one or more of the sample are found defective. What is the probability that the shipment will be returned?

62. *Product sampling.* Twenty-five computer controlled toys, including two defectives, are shipped to a department store. The store will select three at random and will return the whole shipment if one or more of the sample are found defective. What is the probability that the shipment will be returned?

63. *Personnel selection.* Six female and five male applicants have been successfully screened for five positions. If the five positions are selected at random from the eleven finalists, what is the probability of selecting:

   (A) Three females and two males?
   (B) Four females and one male?
   (C) Five females?
   (D) At least four females?

64. *Committee selection.* A four-person grievance committee is to be composed of employees in two departments *A* and *B* with fifteen and twenty employees, respectively. If the four people are selected at random from the thirty-five people, what is the probability of selecting:

   (A) Three from *A* and one from *B*?
   (B) Two from *A* and two from *B*?
   (C) All from *A*?
   (D) At least three from *A*?

Life Sciences   65. *Medicine.* A prospective laboratory technician is to be tested on identifying blood types from eight standard classifications.

(A) If three distinct samples are chosen at random from the eight types and if the examinee is not allowed to repeat any answers, what is the probability that all three could be correctly identified by just guessing?

(B) If repeats are allowed in the three blood types chosen at random from the eight and if the examinee is allowed to repeat answers, what is the probability of correct identification of all three by just guessing?

66. *Medical research.* Because of limited funds, five research centers are to be chosen out of eight suitable ones for a study on heart disease. If the selection is made at random, what is the probability that five particular regions will be chosen?

Social Sciences   **67.** *Membership selection.* A town council has eleven members, six Democrats and five Republicans.

(A) If the president and vice-president are selected at random, what is the probability that they are both Democrats?

(B) If a three-person committee is selected at random, what is the probability that a majority is Republicans?

4-3 Empirical Probability

- Theoretical versus Empirical Probability
- Statistics versus Probability Theory
- Law of Large Numbers

■ Theoretical versus Empirical Probability

In the last section we indicated that acceptable and reasonable probability assignments are made for events in a sample space in two common ways, theoretical and empirical. Let us look at another example and compare the two approaches.

There are 20,000 students registered in a state university. Students are legally either state residents, out-of-state residents, or foreign residents. What is the probability that a student chosen at random is a state resident? An out-of-state resident? A foreign resident? How do we proceed to find these probabilities?

Theoretical Approach

Suppose resident information is available in the registrar's office and can be obtained from a computer printout. Requesting the printout, we find

State residents (E_1)	12,000
Out-of-state residents (E_2)	5,000
Foreign residents (E_3)	3,000
	20,000 $= N$

Looking at the total structure, we reason as follows: We choose the total register of registered students with resident status indicated as our sample space S. We assume one student is as likely to be chosen as another in a random sample of one. Thus, we assign the probability $\frac{1}{20,000}$ to each simple event in S. This is an acceptable assignment. Under the equally likely assumption,

$$P(E_1) = \frac{n(E_1)}{n(S)} = \frac{12,000}{20,000} = .60$$

$$P(E_2) = \frac{n(E_2)}{n(S)} = \frac{5,000}{20,000} = .25$$

$$P(E_3) = \frac{n(E_3)}{n(S)} = \frac{3,000}{20,000} = .15$$

Our approach here is analogous to that used in assigning a probability of $\frac{1}{4}$ to the drawing of a heart in a single draw of one card from a 52 card deck.

Empirical Approach

Suppose residency status was not recorded during registration and the information is not available through the registrar. Not having the time, inclination, or money to interview each student, we choose a random sample of 200 students and find:

State residents	128
Out-of-state residents	47
Foreign residents	25
	200 $= n$

It would be reasonable to say that

$$P(E_1) \approx \frac{128}{200} = .640$$

$$P(E_2) \approx \frac{47}{200} = .235$$

$$P(E_3) \approx \frac{25}{200} = .125$$

As we increase the sample size, our confidence in the probability assignments would likely increase. We refer to these probability assignments as

approximate empirical probabilities and use them to approximate the actual probabilities for the total population.

In general, if we conduct an experiment n times and an event E occurs with frequency $f(E)$, then the ratio $f(E)/n$ is called the **relative frequency** of the occurrence of event E in n trials. We define the **empirical probability** of E, denoted by $P(E)$, by the number (if it exists) that the relative frequency $f(E)/n$ approaches as n gets larger and larger. Of course, for any particular n, the relative frequency $f(E)/n$ is generally only approximately equal to $P(E)$. However, as n increases in size, we would expect the approximation to improve.

Empirical Probability Approximation

$$P(E) \approx \frac{\text{Frequency of occurrence of } E}{\text{Total number of trials}} = \frac{f(E)}{n}$$

(The larger n is, the better the approximation.)

If equally likely assumptions used to obtain theoretical probability assignments are actually warranted, then we would also expect corresponding approximate empirical probabilities to approach the theoretical ones as the number of trials n of actual experiments becomes very large.

Example 20   Two coins are tossed 1,000 times with the following frequencies of outcomes:

2 heads	200
1 head	560
0 heads	240

(A)   Compute the approximate empirical probability for each type of outcome.

(B)   Compute the theoretical probabilities for each type of outcome.

Solutions   (A) $P(2 \text{ heads}) \approx \dfrac{200}{1,000} = .20$ (B)   (See Example 15.)

$P(1 \text{ head}) \approx \dfrac{560}{1,000} = .56$ $P(2 \text{ heads}) = .25$

$P(1 \text{ head}) = .50$

$P(0 \text{ heads}) \approx \dfrac{240}{1,000} = .24$ $P(0 \text{ heads}) = .25$

Problem 20   One die is rolled 1,000 times with the following frequencies of outcomes:

1	180	4	138
2	140	5	175
3	152	6	215

(A) Calculate approximate empirical probabilities for each indicated outcome.

(B) Do the indicated outcomes seem equally likely?

(C) Assuming the indicated outcomes are equally likely, compute their theoretical probabilities.

Example 21   An insurance company selected 1,000 drivers at random in a particular city to determine a relationship between age and accidents. The data obtained are listed in Table 1. Compute the following approximate empirical probabilities for a driver chosen at random in the city:

(A) Of being under 20 years old **and** having three accidents in one year (E_1)

(B) Of being 30–39 years old **and** having one or more accidents in one year (E_2)

(C) Of having no accidents in one year (E_3)

(D) Of being under 20 years old **or** having three accidents in one year (E_4)

Table 1

| Age | Accidents in One Year | | | | |
	0	1	2	3	Over 3
Under 20	50	62	53	35	20
20–29	64	93	67	40	36
30–39	82	68	32	14	4
40–49	38	32	20	7	3
Over 49	43	50	35	28	24

Solutions   (A) $P(E_1) \approx \dfrac{35}{1,000} = .035$

(B) $P(E_2) \approx \dfrac{68 + 32 + 14 + 4}{1,000} = .118$

(C) $P(E_3) \approx \dfrac{50 + 64 + 82 + 38 + 43}{1,000} = .277$

(D) $P(E_4) \approx \dfrac{50 + 62 + 53 + 35 + 20 + 40 + 14 + 7 + 28}{1,000} = .309$

Notice that in this type of problem, which is typical of many realistic problems, approximate empirical probabilities are the only type we can compute.

Problem 21   Referring to the results of the survey in Example 21, compute each of the following approximate empirical probabilities for a driver chosen at random in the city:

(A) Of being under 20 years old with no accidents in one year (E_1)

(B) Of being 20–29 years old and having fewer than two accidents in one year (E_2)

(C) Of not being over 49 years old (E_3)

Approximate empirical probabilities are often used to test theoretical probabilities. As we said before, equally likely assumptions may not be justified in reality. In addition to this use, there are many situations in which it is either very difficult or impossible to compute the theoretical probabilities for given events. For example, insurance companies use past experience to establish approximate empirical probabilities to predict the future, baseball teams use batting averages (approximate empirical probabilities based on past experience) to predict the future performance of a player, and pollsters use approximate empirical probabilities to predict outcomes of elections.

■ Statistics versus Probability Theory

We are now entering the area of mathematical statistics, a subject that we will not pursue too far in this book. Mathematical statistics is a branch of mathematics that draws inferences about certain characteristics of a total population, called **population parameters,** based on corresponding characteristics of a random sample from the population. In general, a **population** is the set containing every element we are describing (all people in a school, all flashbulbs produced by a given company using a particular type of manufacturing process, all flips of a certain coin, or all rolls of a certain die). A **sample** is a subset of a population. The population size, if finite, is denoted by N; the sample size is denoted by n. [Except when the sample is a census (the whole population), n is less than N.]

Because samples are used to draw inferences about the total population, it is desirable that a sample be **representative** of the population, that is, that various population characteristics are proportionately represented in the sample. **Random samples** are those in which each element of the population has the same probability of being chosen for the sample. Much statistical theory is based on random samples.

Statistics starts with a known sample and proceeds to describe certain characteristics of the total population that are not known. [For example, in Example 21 the insurance company used the approximate empirical probability .035 (computed from the sample) as an approximation for the actual probability of a person drawn at random from the *total* population being under 20 years old and having three accidents in one year.]

Probability theory, on the other hand, starts with a known composition of a population and from this deduces the probable composition of a sample. [For example, knowing the composition of a standard deck of 52 cards, we can (assuming each 5 card hand has the same probability of being dealt as any other) deduce that the probability of being dealt a flush (5 cards of the same suit) is given by $4C_{13,5}/C_{52,5} = .00198.$] In short, statistics proceeds from a sample to the population, while probability theory proceeds from a population to a sample.

■ Law of Large Numbers

How does the approximate empirical probability of an event determined from a sample relate to the actual probability of the event relative to the total population? In mathematical statistics an important theorem, called the **law of large numbers** (or the **law of averages**), is proved. Informally, it states that the approximate empirical probability can be made as close to the actual probability as we please by making the sample sufficiently large.

For example, if we roll a fair die a large number of times, we would expect to get each number about (not exactly) $\frac{1}{6}$ of the time. The law of large numbers states (informally) the greater the number of times we roll a fair die, the closer the relative frequency of the occurrence of a given number will be to $\frac{1}{6}$ [or if the die is not fair (and no die can be absolutely fair), then the closer the relative frequency of the occurrence of a given number will be to the actual probability of the occurrence of that number].

Answers to Matched Problems

20. (A) $P(1) \approx .180$, $P(2) \approx .140$, $P(3) \approx .152$, $P(4) \approx .138$, $P(5) \approx .175$, $P(6) \approx .215$
    (B) No   (C) $\frac{1}{6} \approx .167$ for each

21. (A) $P(E_1) \approx .05$ (B) $P(E_2) \approx .157$
    (C) $P(E_3) \approx .82$ or $P(E_3) = 1 - P(E_3') = 1 - .18 = .82$

Exercise 4-3

A

1. A ski jumper has jumped over 300 feet in 25 out of 250 jumps. What is the approximate empirical probability of the next jump being over 300 feet?

2. In a city there are 4,000 youths between 16 and 20 years old who drive cars. If 560 of them were involved in accidents last year, what is the approximate empirical probability of a youth in this age group being involved in an accident this year?

3. Out of 420 times at bat, a baseball player gets 189 hits. What is the approximate empirical probability that the player will get a hit next time at bat?

4. In a medical experiment, a new drug is found to help 2,400 out of 3,000 people. If a doctor prescribes the drug for a particular patient, what is the approximate empirical probability that the patient will be helped?

5. A thumbtack is tossed 1,000 times with the following outcome frequencies:

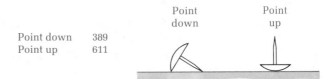

Point down	389
Point up	611

Compute the approximate empirical probability for each outcome. Does each outcome appear to be equally likely?

6. Toss a thumbtack 100 times and let it fall to the floor. Count the number of times it lands point down. What is the approximate empirical probability of the tack landing point down? Point up? (Actually, you can toss ten tacks at a time and count the total number pointing down in ten throws.)

B 7. A random sample of 10,000 two-child families excluding those with twins produced the following frequencies:

2,351 families with two girls

5,435 families with one girl

2,214 families with no girls

(A) Compute the approximate empirical probability for each outcome.

(B) Compute the theoretical probability for each outcome assuming a boy is as likely as a girl at each birth.

8. If we multiply the probability of the occurrence of an event E by the total number of trials n, we obtain the **expected frequency** of the occurrence of E in n trials. Using the theoretical probabilities found in Problem 7B, compute the expected frequency of each outcome in Problem 7 from the sample of 10,000.

9. Three coins are flipped 1,000 times with the following frequencies of outcomes:

3 heads	132
2 heads	368
1 head	380
0 heads	120

(A) Compute the approximate empirical probabilities for each outcome.

(B) Compute the theoretical probability for each outcome, assuming fair coins.

(C) Using the theoretical probabilities computed in part B, compute the expected frequency for each outcome. (See Problem 8 above for a definition of expected frequency.)

10. Toss three coins fifty times and compute the approximate empirical probability for three heads, two heads, one head, and no heads, respectively.

C   11. If four fair coins are tossed eighty times, what is the expected frequency of four heads turning up? Three heads? Two heads? One head? No heads? (See Problem 8 for a definition of expected frequency.)

12. Actually toss four coins eighty times and tabulate the frequencies of the outcomes indicated in Problem 11. What are the approximate empirical probabilities for these outcomes?

Applications

Business & Economics   13. *Market analysis.* A company selected 1,000 households at random and surveyed them to determine a relationship between income level and the number of television sets in a home.

Yearly Income	Televisions per Household				
	0	1	2	3	Above 3
Less than $6,000	0	40	51	11	0
$6,000–10,000	0	70	80	15	1
$10,000–20,000	2	112	130	80	12
$20,000–30,000	10	90	80	60	21
More than $30,000	30	32	28	25	20

Compute the approximate empirical probabilities:

(A) Of a household earning $6,000–10,000 per year **and** owning three television sets

(B) Of a household earning $10,000–20,000 per year **and** owning more than one television

(C) Of a household earning more than $30,000 per year **or** owning more than three television sets

(D) Of a household not owning zero television sets

14. *Market analysis.* Compute approximate empirical probabilities (from the sample results in Problem 13):

(A) Of a household earning $20,000–30,000 per year **and** owning no television sets.

(B) Of a household earning $6,000–20,000 per year **and** owning more than two television sets.

(C) Of a household earning less than $10,000 per year **or** owning two television sets.

(D) Of a household not owning more than three television sets.

Life Sciences

15. *Genetics.* A particular type of flowering plant has the following possible colors:

Genes	Flowers
RR	Red
RW or WR	Pink
WW	White

If two pink plants are crossed, the theoretical probabilities associated with each possible flower color are determined by the table:

		Pink-Flowered Plant	
		R	W
Pink-Flowered	R	RR	RW
Plant	W	WR	WW

$P(\text{Red}) = \frac{1}{4}$
$P(\text{Pink}) = \frac{1}{2}$
$P(\text{White}) = \frac{1}{4}$

In an experiment, 1,000 crosses were made with pink flowered plants with the following results:

Red   300
Pink   440
White 260

(A) What is the approximate empirical probability for each color?

(B) What is the expected number of plants with each color in the experiment, based on the theoretical probabilities?

Social Sciences

16. *Sociology.* One thousand women between the ages of 50 and 60 who had been married at least once were chosen at random. They were surveyed to determine a relationship between the age at which they were first married and the total number of marriages they had had to date.

First Marriage Age	Number of Marriages				
	1	2	3	4	Above 4
Under 18	44	88	25	12	7
18–20	82	70	30	14	8
21–25	130	110	30	10	4
26–30	95	84	12	6	3
Over 30	56	48	25	5	2

Compute the approximate empirical probabilities:

(A) Of a woman being 21–25 years old on her first marriage **and** having a total of three marriages

(B) Of a woman being 18–20 years old on her first marriage **and** having more than one marriage

(C) Of a woman being under 18 on her first marriage **or** having two marriages

(D) Of a woman not being over 30 on her first marriage

4-4   Random Variable, Probability Distribution, and Expectation

- Random Variable
- Probability Distribution of a Random Variable
- Expected Value of a Random Variable
- Decision-Making and Expected Value

■ Random Variable

When performing a random experiment, a sample space S is selected in such a way that all probability problems of interest relative to the experiment can be solved. In many situations we may not be interested in each simple event in the sample space S but in some numerical value associated with the event. For example, if three coins are tossed, we may be interested in the number of heads that turn up rather than in the particular pattern that turns up. Or, in selecting a random sample of students, we may be interested in the proportion that are women rather than which particular students are women. In the same way, a craps player is usually interested in the sum of the dots on the showing faces rather than the pattern of dots on each face.

In each of these examples, we have a rule that assigns to each simple event in S a single real number. Mathematically speaking, we are dealing with a function (see Section 0-5). Historically, this particular type of function has been called a "random variable."

Random Variable

A **random variable** is a function that assigns a numerical value to each simple event in a sample space S.

The term *random variable* is an unfortunate choice, since it is neither random nor a variable—it is a function with a numerical value and it is defined on a sample space. But the terminology has stuck and is now standard, so we shall have to live with it. Capital letters, such as X, are used to represent random variables.

Let us return to the experiment of tossing three coins. A sample space S of equally likely simple events is indicated in the first column of Table 2. The second column indicates the number of heads corresponding to a simple event. The last column indicates the probability of each simple event occurring (each simple event occurs with a probability of $\frac{1}{8}$, since each is equally likely and there are eight of them). The random variable X (a function) associates exactly one of the numbers 0, 1, 2, or 3 with each simple event. For example, $X(e_1) = 0$, $X(e_2) = 1$, $X(e_3) = 1$, and so on.

Table 2 Tossing Three Coins

S		Number of Heads $X(e_i)$	Probability $P(e_i)$
e_1:	TTT	0	$\frac{1}{8}$
e_2:	TTH	1	$\frac{1}{8}$
e_3:	THT	1	$\frac{1}{8}$
e_4:	HTT	1	$\frac{1}{8}$
e_5:	THH	2	$\frac{1}{8}$
e_6:	HTH	2	$\frac{1}{8}$
e_7:	HHT	2	$\frac{1}{8}$
e_8:	HHH	3	$\frac{1}{8}$

■ Probability Distribution of a Random Variable

We are interested in the probability of the occurrence of each image value of X; that is, in the probability of the occurrence of zero heads, one head, two heads, or three heads in the single toss of three coins. We indicate this probability by

$p(x)$ where $x \in \{0, 1, 2, 3\}$

The function p is called the **probability function* of the random variable X.** What is $p(2)$, the probability of getting exactly two heads on the single toss of three coins? "Exactly two heads occur" is the event

$E = \{THH, HTH, HHT\}$

Thus,

$$p(2) = \frac{n(E)}{n(s)} = \frac{3}{8}$$

---

* Formally, the probability function p of the random variable X is defined by $p(x) = P(\{e_i \in S | X(e_i) = x\})$, which, because of its cumbersome nature, is usually simplified to $p(x) = P(X = x)$ or, simply, $p(x)$. We will use the simplified notation.

Proceeding similarly for $p(0)$, $p(1)$, and $p(3)$, we obtain the results in Table 3. This table is called a **probability distribution for the random variable X.** Probability distributions are also represented graphically, as in Figure 2.

Table 3 Probability Distribution

Number of Heads				
x	0	1	2	3
Probability $p(x)$	$\frac{1}{8}$	$\frac{3}{8}$	$\frac{3}{8}$	$\frac{1}{8}$

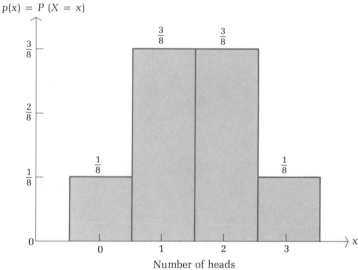

Figure 2 Probability distribution

Note from Table 3 or Figure 2 that

1. $0 \leqslant p(x) \leqslant 1$, $x \in \{0, 1, 2, 3\}$
2. $p(0) + p(1) + p(2) + p(3) = \frac{1}{8} + \frac{3}{8} + \frac{3}{8} + \frac{1}{8} = 1$

These are general properties that any probability distribution of a random variable X associated with a finite sample space must have.

Probability Distribution of a Random Variable X

A probability function $P(X = x) = p(x)$ is a **probability distribution of the random variable X** if

1. $0 \leqslant p(x) \leqslant 1$, $x \in \{x_1, x_2, \ldots, x_n\}$
2. $p(x_1) + p(x_2) + \cdots + p(x_n) = 1$

where $\{x_1, x_2, \ldots, x_n\}$ are the (range) values of X. (see Fig. 3)

■ Expected Value of a Random Variable

Suppose the experiment of tossing three coins was repeated a large number of times. What would be the average number of heads per toss (the total number of heads in all tosses divided by the total number of tosses)?

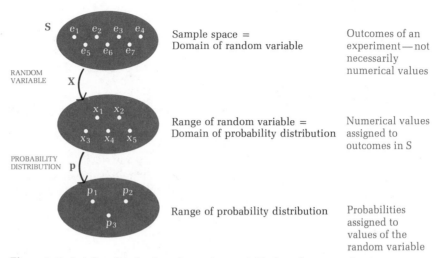

Figure 3   Probability distribution of a random variable for a finite sample space

Consulting the probability distribution in Table 3 or Figure 2, we see that we would expect to toss zero heads $\frac{1}{8}$ of the time, one head $\frac{3}{8}$ of the time, two heads $\frac{3}{8}$ of the time, and three heads $\frac{1}{8}$ of the time. Thus, in the long run, we would expect the average number of heads per toss of the three coins, or the *expected value* $E(X)$, to be given by

$$E(X) = 0(\tfrac{1}{8}) + 1(\tfrac{3}{8}) + 2(\tfrac{3}{8}) + 3(\tfrac{1}{8}) = \tfrac{12}{8} = 1.5$$

It is important to note that the expected value is not a value that will necessarily occur in a single experiment (1.5 heads cannot occur in the toss of three coins), but it is an average of what occurs over a large number of experiments. Sometimes we will toss more than 1.5 heads and sometimes less, but if the experiment is repeated many times, the average number of heads per experiment should approach 1.5.

We now make the above discussion precise through the following definition of expected value:

Expected Value of a Random Variable X

Given the probability distribution for the random variable X

x_i	x_1	x_2	$\cdots$	x_m
p_i	p_1	p_2	$\cdots$	p_m

where $p_i = p(x_i)$, we define the **expected value of X**, denoted by $E(X)$, by the formula

$$E(X) = x_1 p_1 + x_2 p_2 + \cdots + x_m p_m$$

We again emphasize that the expected value is not something to be expected to happen in a single experiment; it is a long-run average of repeated experiments—it is the weighted average of the possible outcomes, each weighted by its probability.

Steps for Computing the Expected Value of a Random Variable X

1. Form the probability distribution of the random variable X.
2. Multiply each image value of X, x_i, by its corresponding probability of occurrence p_i; then add the results.

Example 22

What is the expected value (long-run average) of the number of dots facing up for the roll of a single die?

Solution

If we choose

$$S = \{1, 2, 3, 4, 5, 6\}$$

as our sample space, then each simple event is a numerical outcome reflecting our interest, and each is equally likely. The random variable X in this case is just the identity function (each number is associated with itself). Thus, the probability distribution for X is

x_i	1	2	3	4	5	6
p_i	$\frac{1}{6}$	$\frac{1}{6}$	$\frac{1}{6}$	$\frac{1}{6}$	$\frac{1}{6}$	$\frac{1}{6}$

Hence,

$$E(X) = 1(\tfrac{1}{6}) + 2(\tfrac{1}{6}) + 3(\tfrac{1}{6}) + 4(\tfrac{1}{6}) + 5(\tfrac{1}{6}) + 6(\tfrac{1}{6})$$
$$= \tfrac{21}{6} = 3.5$$

Problem 22

Suppose the die in Example 22 is not fair and we obtain (empirically) the following probability distribution for X:

x_i	1	2	3	4	5	6
p_i	.14	.13	.18	.20	.11	.24

[Note: Sum $= 1$.]

What is the expected value of X?

Example 23

A carton of twenty calculator batteries contains two dead ones. A random sample of three are selected from the twenty and tested. Let X be the random variable associated with the number of dead batteries found in a sample.

(A) Find the probability distribution of X.
(B) Find the expected number of dead batteries in a sample.

Solutions

(A) The number of ways of selecting a sample of 3 from 20 (order is not important) is $C_{20,3}$. This is the number of simple events in the experiment, each as likely as the other. A sample will have either 0, 1, or 2 dead batteries. These are the values of the random variable in which we are interested. The probability distribution is computed as follows:

$$p(0) = \frac{C_{18,3}}{C_{20,3}} \approx .716$$

$$p(1) = \frac{C_{2,1}C_{18,2}}{C_{20,3}} \approx .268$$

$$p(2) = \frac{C_{2,2}C_{18,1}}{C_{20,3}} \approx .016$$

We summarize the above results in a convenient table:

x_i	0	1	2
p_i	.716	.268	.016

[Note: $.716 + .268 + .016 = 1$.]

(B) The expected number of dead batteries in a sample is readily computed as follows:

$$E(X) = (0)(.716) + (1)(.268) + (2)(.016) = .3$$

The expected value is not one of the random variable values; rather, it is a number that the average number of dead batteries in a sample would approach as the experiment is repeated without end.

Problem 23

Repeat Example 23 using a random sample of four instead of three.

Example 24

A spinner device is numbered from 0 to 5, and each of the six numbers is as likely to come up as any other. A player who bets $1 on any given number wins $4 (and gets the bet back) if the pointer comes to rest on the chosen number; otherwise, the $1 bet is lost. What is the expected value of the game (long-run average gain or loss per game)?

Solution   The sample space of equally likely events is

$$S = \{0, 1, 2, 3, 4, 5\}$$

Each sample point occurs with a probability of $\frac{1}{6}$. The random variable X assigns \$4 to the winning number and $-$\$1 to each of the remaining numbers. Thus, the probability distribution for X, called a **payoff table,** is

Payoff Table
(Probability
Distribution for X)

x_i	\$4	$-$\$1
p_i	$\frac{1}{6}$	$\frac{5}{6}$

The probability of winning \$4 is $\frac{1}{6}$ and of losing \$1 is $\frac{5}{6}$. We can now compute the expected value of the game:

$$E(X) = \$4(\tfrac{1}{6}) + (-\$1)(\tfrac{5}{6}) = -\$\tfrac{1}{6} \approx -\$0.1667 \approx -17¢ \text{ per game}$$

Thus, in the long run the player will lose an average of about 17¢ per game.

In general, a game is said to be **fair** if $E(X) = 0$. The game in Example 24 is not fair—the "house" has an advantage, on the average, of about 17¢ per game.

Problem 24   Repeat Example 24 with the player winning \$5 instead of \$4 if the chosen number turns up. The loss is still \$1 if any other number turns up. Is this now a fair game?

Example 25   Suppose you are interested in insuring a car stereo system for \$500 against theft. An insurance company charges a premium of \$60 for coverage for one year, claiming an empirically determined probability of .1 that the system will be stolen some time during the year. What is your expected return from the insurance company if you take out this insurance?

Solution   This is actually a game of chance in which your stake is \$60. You have a .1 chance of receiving \$440 from the insurance company (\$500 minus your stake of \$60) and a .9 chance of losing your stake of \$60. What is the expected value of this "game"? We form a payoff table (the probability distribution for X):

Payoff Table

x_i	\$440	$-$\$60
p_i	.1	.9

Then we compute the expected value as follows:

$$E(X) = (\$440)(.1) + (-\$60)(.9) = -\$10$$

This means that if you insure with this company over many years and the circumstances remain the same, you would have an average net loss to the insurance company of $10 per year.

Problem 25   Find the expected value in Example 25 from the insurance company's point of view.

■ Decision-Making and Expected Value

We conclude this section with some examples in decision-making.

Example 26   An outdoor concert featuring a very popular musical group is scheduled for a Sunday afternoon in a large open stadium. The promoter, worrying about being rained out, contacts a long-range weather forecaster who predicts the chance of rain on that Sunday to be .24. If it does not rain, the promoter is certain to net $100,000; if it does rain, the promoter estimates that the net will be only $10,000. An insurance company agrees to insure the concert for $100,000 against rain at a premium of $20,000. Should the promoter buy the insurance?

Solution   The promoter has a choice between two courses of action: A_1—insure and A_2—do not insure. As an aid in making a decision, the expected value is computed for each course of action. Probability distributions are indicated in the following payoff table (read vertically):

Payoff Table

p_i	A_1—Insure x_i	A_2—Do Not Insure x_i
.24 (rain)	$90,000	$10,000
.76 (no rain)	$80,000	$100,000

Note that the $90,000 entry comes from the insurance company's payoff ($100,000) minus the premium ($20,000) plus gate receipts ($10,000). The reasons for the other entries should be clear. The expected value for each course of action is computed as follows:

$$A_1\text{—insure} \quad E(X) = x_1 p_1 + x_2 p_2$$
$$= (\$90,000)(.24) + (\$80,000)(.76)$$
$$= \$82,400$$

A_2—do not insure $E(X) = (\$10,000)(.24) + (\$100,000)(.76)$
$$= \$78,400$$

It appears that the promoter's best course of action is to buy the insurance at $20,000.

Problem 26   In Example 26, what is the insurance company's expected value if it writes the policy?

Example 27   A truck rental company rents vans for $25 a day. Each van that the company makes available for rental costs them $15 a day in plant, interest, and maintenance costs, whether or not it is rented that day. By examining their past records, the company has determined that the daily demand for van rentals is always between ten and fourteen vans, inclusive. They have also assigned probabilities to each possible daily demand, which are listed in the table. How many vans should the company have available for rental in order to maximize its expected daily profit? What is the maximum expected daily profit?

Daily Demand	10	11	12	13	14
Probability	.1	.2	.2	.3	.2

Solution   The company must decide on one of five possible courses of action: having 10, 11, 12, 13, or 14 vans available for rental. We must determine the expected daily profit for each choice.

Choice 1   *10 vans available for rental.* The daily cost of providing 10 vans is

$C(10) = (10)(\$15)$
$$= \$150$$

Since the daily demand is always at least 10, all 10 vans will be rented and the daily revenue is

$R(10) = (10)(\$25)$
$$= \$250$$

The daily profit in this case is

$$P(10) = R(10) - C(10)$$
$$= \$250 - \$150$$
$$= \$100$$

This is also the expected daily profit for this choice.

Choice 2   *11 vans available for rental.* The daily cost of providing 11 vans is

$$C(11) = (11)(\$15)$$
$$= \$165$$

The daily revenue and profit will now depend on the number of customers that want to rent vans. If 10 customers want to rent vans, the revenue and profit are

$$R(10) = (10)(\$25) \qquad P(10) = R(10) - C(11)$$
$$= \$250 \qquad\qquad = \$250 - \$165$$
$$= \$85$$

If 11 customers want to rent vans, the revenue and profit are

$$R(11) = (11)(\$25) \qquad P(11) = R(11) - C(11)$$
$$= \$275 \qquad\qquad = \$275 - \$165$$
$$= \$110$$

What happens if 12, 13, or 14 customers want to rent vans? Since the company has already decided to have 11 vans available for rental, the additional customers will be turned away and the daily profit remains at $110. The probability distribution for this choice is

	11 Vans Available for Rental				
Daily Demand	10	11	12	13	14
Probability	.1	.2	.2	.3	.2
Daily Profit	$85	$110	$110	$110	$110

The expected daily profit is

$$E(X) = (\$85)(.1) + (\$110)(.2) + (\$110)(.2) + (\$110)(.3) + (\$110)(.2)$$
$$= \$107.50$$

Proceeding as in choice 2 leads to the probability distributions and expected profits for the remaining three choices.

Choice 3   *12 vans available for rental.*

	12 Vans Available for Rental				
Daily Demand	10	11	12	13	14
Probability	.1	.2	.2	.3	.2
Daily Profit	$70	$95	$120	$120	$120

$$E(X) = (\$70)(.1) + (\$95)(.2) + (\$120)(.2) + (\$120)(.3) + (\$120)(.2)$$
$$= \$110$$

Choice 4   *13 vans available for rental.*

	13 Vans Available for Rental				
Daily Demand	10	11	12	13	14
Probability	.1	.2	.2	.3	.2
Daily Profit	$55	$80	$105	$130	$130

$$E(X) = (\$55)(.1) + (\$80)(.2) + (\$105)(.2) + (\$130)(.3) + (\$130)(.2)$$
$$= \$107.50$$

Choice 5   *14 vans available for rental.*

	14 Vans Available for Rental				
Daily Demand	10	11	12	13	14
Probability	.1	.2	.2	.3	.2
Daily Profit	$40	$65	$90	$115	$140

$$E(X) = (\$40)(.1) + (\$65)(.2) + (\$90)(.2) + (\$115)(.3) + (\$140)(.2)$$
$$= \$97.50$$

Conclusion   The five possible decisions and their corresponding expected profits are

Number of Vans Available for Rental	Expected Daily Profit	
10	$100	
11	$107.50	
12	$110	← Maximum expected daily profit
13	$107.50	
14	$ 95.50	

The maximum daily expected profit is $110, which occurs when the company makes 12 vans available for rental.

Problem 27   Repeat Example 27 if the probability distribution for the daily demand is

Daily Demand	10	11	12	13	14
Probability	.3	.3	.2	.1	.1

Answers to   22. $E(X) = 3.73$

Matched Problems   23. (A)

x_i	0	1	2
p_i	.632	.337	.032

(B) .4

24. $E(X) = \$0$; the game is fair

25. $E(X) = (-\$440)(.1) + (\$60)(.9) = \$10$;   this amount, of course, is necessary to cover expenses and profit

26. $E(X) = (-\$80,000)(.24) + (\$20,000)(.76) = -\$4,000$;   this means the insurance company had other information regarding the weather than the promoter; otherwise, the company would not have written this policy

27.

Number of Vans Available for Rental	Expected Daily Profit
10	$100
11	$102.50
12	$ 97.50
13	$ 87.50
14	$ 75

17.

The maximum daily profit is $102.50 when eleven vans are available for rental.

18.

Exercise 4-4

Where possible, construct a probability distribution or payoff table for a suitable random variable X; then complete the problem.

A   1. If the probability distribution for the random variable X is

x_i	−3	0	4
p_i	.3	.5	.2

what is the expected value of X?

2. If the probability distribution for the random variable X is

x_i	-2	-1	0	1	2
p_i	.1	.2	.4	.2	.1

what is the expected value of X?

3. In tossing two fair coins, what is the expected number of heads?

4. In a two-child family, excluding multiple births and assuming a boy is as likely as a girl at each birth, what is the expected number of boys?

5. A fair coin is flipped. If a head turns up, you win $1. If a tail turns up, you lose $1. What is the expected value of the game? Is the game fair?

6. Repeat Problem 5, assuming an unfair coin with the probability of a head being .55 and a tail .45.

B

7. After paying $4 to play, a single fair die is rolled and you are paid back the number of dollars corresponding to the number of dots facing up. For example, if a 5 turns up, $5 is returned to you for a net gain or payoff of $1; if a 1 turns up, $1 is returned for a net gain or payoff of $-$3; and so on. What is the expected value of the game? Is the game fair?

8. Repeat Problem 7 with the same game costing $3.50 for each play.

9. Two coins are flipped. You win $2 if either two heads or two tails turn up; you lose $3 if a head and a tail turn up. What is the expected value of the game?

10. In Problem 9 how much *should* you lose if a head and a tail turn up for the game to be fair?

11. A friend offers the following game: She wins $1 from you if on four rolls of a single die at least one 6 turns up; otherwise, you win $1 from her. What is the expected value of the game to you? To her?

12. On three rolls of a single die, you will lose $10 if at least one 5 turns up and win $7 otherwise. What is the expected value of the game?

13. A pair of dice is rolled once. Suppose you lose $10 if a 7 turns up and win $11 if 11 or 12 turns up. How much should you win or lose if any other number turns up in order for the game to be fair?

14. A coin is tossed three times. Suppose you lose $3 if three heads appear, lose $2 if two heads appear, and win $3 if no heads appear. How much should you win or lose if one head appears in order for the game to be fair?

15. Suppose the payoff table for two courses of action, A_1 or A_2, is given as follows:

p_i	A_1 x_i	A_2 x_i
.1	−$200	−$100
.2	$100	$200
.4	$400	$300
.3	$100	$200

Which of the two courses, A_1 or A_2, will produce the largest expected value? What is it?

16. The payoff table for three possible courses of action is given as follows:

p_i	A_1 x_i	A_2 x_i	A_3 x_i
.2	$ 500	$ 400	$ 300
.4	1,200	1,100	1,000
.3	1,200	1,800	1,700
.1	1,200	1,800	2,400

Which of the three courses, A_1, A_2, or A_3, will produce the largest expected value? What is it?

17. Roulette wheels in Nevada generally have 38 equally spaced slots numbered 00, 0, 1, 2, . . . , 36. A player who bets $1 on any given number wins $35 (and gets the bet back) if the ball comes to rest on the chosen number; otherwise, the $1 bet is lost. What is the expected value of this game?

18. In roulette (see Problem 17) the numbers from 1 to 36 are evenly divided between red and black. A player who bets $1 on black wins $1 (and gets the bet back) if the ball comes to rest on black; otherwise (if the ball lands on red, 0, or 00), the $1 bet is lost. What is the expected value of the game?

C 19. Five thousand tickets are sold at $1 each for a charity raffle. Tickets are to be drawn at random and monetary prizes awarded as follows: one prize of $500, three prizes of $100, five prizes of $20, and twenty prizes of $5. What is the expected value of this raffle if you buy one ticket?

20. A player rolls two dice and receives a number of dollars equal to the number of dots showing on both faces. Assuming the dice are fair, what should the player pay each time for the game to be fair?

21. A box of ten flashbulbs contains three defective bulbs. A random sample of two is selected and tested. Let X be the random variable associated with the number of defective bulbs in the sample.

(A) Find the probability distribution of *X*.

(B) Find the expected number of defective bulbs in a sample.

22. A box of eight flashbulbs contains three defective bulbs. A random sample of two is selected and tested. Let *X* be the random variable associated with the number of defective bulbs in a sample.

    (A) Find the probability distribution of *X*.

    (B) Find the expected number of defective bulbs in a sample.

23. One thousand raffle tickets are sold at $1 each. Three tickets will be drawn at random (without replacement) and each will pay $200. Suppose you buy five tickets.

    (A) Create a payoff table for 0, 1, 2, and 3 winning tickets among the five tickets you purchased. (If you don't have any winning tickets, you lose $5; if you have one winning ticket you net $195, since your initial $5 will not be returned to you; and so on.)

    (B) What is the expected value of the raffle (to you)?

24. Repeat the preceding problem with the purchase of ten tickets instead of five.

Applications

Business & Economics

25. *Insurance.* The annual premium for a $5,000 insurance policy against the theft of a painting is $150. If the (empirical) probability that the painting will be stolen during the year is .01, what is your expected return from the insurance company if you take out this insurance?

26. *Insurance.* Repeat Problem 25 from the point of view of the insurance company.

27. *Decision analysis.* An oil company, after careful testing and analysis, is considering drilling in two different sites. It is estimated that site *A* will net $30 million if successful (probability .2) and lose $3 million if not (probability .8); site *B* will net $70 million if successful (probability .1) and lose $4 million if not (probability .9). Which site should the company choose according to the expected return from each site?

28. *Decision analysis.* Repeat Problem 27, assuming additional analysis caused the estimated probability of success in field *B* to be changed from .1 to .11.

29. *Decision analysis.* An office rental company rents completely equipped office suites on a daily basis at major airports. They are contemplating a new facility and wish to determine how many units to build. From past records they know they will rent at least nine units and at most twelve units per day. Each unit rents for $200 per day and costs $140 per day. If daily demands and associated probabilities are

listed in the following table, how many office suites should the company build to maximize the expected daily profit?

Daily Demand	9	10	11	12
Probability	.2	.3	.4	.1

30. *Decision analysis.* Repeat Problem 29 using

Daily Demand	9	10	11	12
Probability	.1	.1	.4	.4

Life Sciences

31. *Genetics.* Suppose that, at each birth, having a girl is not as likely as having a boy, and that the probability assignments for the number of boys in a three-child family is approximated empirically from past records to be:

Number of Boys x_i	p_i
0	.12
1	.36
2	.38
3	.14

What is the expected number of boys in a three-child family?

32. *Genetics.* A pink-flowering plant is of genotype RW. If two such plants are crossed, we obtain a red plant (RR) with probability .25, a pink plant (RW or WR) with probability .50, a white plant (WW) with probability .25:

Number of W Genes Present x_i	p_i
0	.25
1	.50
2	.25

What is the expected number of W genes present in a crossing of this type?

Social Sciences

33. *Politics.* A money drive is organized by a campaign committee for a candidate running for public office. Two approaches are considered:

A_1—A general mailing with a followup mailing

A_2—Door-to-door solicitation with followup telephone calls

From campaign records of previous committees, average donations and their corresponding probabilities are estimated to be

A_1		A_2	
x_i (return per person)	p_i	x_i (return per person)	p_i
$10	.3	$15	.3
5	.2	3	.1
0	.5	0	.6
	1.0		1.0

Which course of action should be taken according to the expected return?

4-5   Chapter Review

Important Terms and Symbols

4-1 *Multiplication principle, permutations, and combinations.* Tree diagram, multiplication principle, *n* factorial, zero factorial, permutation, permutation of *n* objects, permutation of *n* objects taken *r* at a time, combination, combination of *n* objects taken *r* at a time

$$n! = n(n-1)(n-2) \cdot \cdots \cdot 2 \cdot 1, \qquad 0! = 1,$$

$$P_{n,r} = \frac{n!}{(n-r)!}, \quad C_{n,r} = \binom{n}{r} = \frac{P_{n,r}}{r!} = \frac{n!}{r!(n-r)!}$$

4-2 *Experiments, sample spaces, and probability of an event.* Deterministic experiment, random experiment, sample space, sample point, simple outcome, compound outcome, finite sample space, infinite sample space, event, simple event, compound event, probability of an event, acceptable probability assignment, probability function, equally likely assumptions, $P(E)$

4-3 *Empirical probability.* Approximate empirical probability, empirical probability, relative frequency, population parameters, population, sample, representative sample, random sample, law of large numbers (or law of averages), expected frequency, $P(E)$, $f(E)/n$

4-4 *Random variable, probability distribution, and expectation.* Random variable, probability function of a random variable X, probability distribution for a random variable, expected value of a random variable, payoff table, fair game,

$$E(X) = x_1 p_1 + x_2 p_2 + \cdots + x_n p_n$$

Exercise 4-5   Chapter Review

Work through all the problems in this chapter review and check your answers in the back of the book. (Answers to all review problems are there.) Where weaknesses show up, review appropriate sections in the text.

A 1. A single die is rolled and a coin is flipped. How many combined outcomes are possible? Solve:

    (A)   By using a tree diagram

    (B)   By using the multiplication principle

2. Evaluate $C_{6,2}$ and $P_{6,2}$.

3. How many seating arrangements are possible with six people and six chairs in a row? Solve by using the multiplication principle.

4. Solve Problem 3 using permutations or combinations, whichever is applicable.

5. In a single deal of 5 cards from a standard 52-card deck, what is the probability of being dealt 5 clubs?

6. Betty and Bill are members of a fifteen-person ski club. If the president and treasurer are selected by lottery, what is the probability that Betty will be president and Bill will be treasurer? (A person cannot hold more than one office.)

7. Each letter of the first ten letters of the alphabet is printed on one of ten different cards. What is the probability of drawing the code word *dig* by drawing *d* on the first draw, *i* on the second draw, and *g* on the third draw? What is the probability of being dealt a three-card hand containing the letters *d*, *i*, and *g* in any order?

8. A drug has side effects for 50 out of 1,000 people in a test. What is the approximate empirical probability that a person using the drug will have side effects?

9. A spinning device has five numbers, 1, 2, 3, 4, and 5, each as likely to turn up as the other. A person pays \$3 and then receives back the dollar amount corresponding to the number turning up on a single spin. What is the expected value of the game? Is the game fair?

B 10. A person tells you that the following approximate empirical probabilities apply to the sample space $\{e_1, e_2, e_3, e_4\}$: $P(e_1) \approx .1$, $P(e_2) \approx -.2$, $P(e_3) \approx .6$, $P(e_4) \approx 2$. There are three reasons why P cannot be a probability function. Name them.

11. Six distinct points are selected on the circumference of a circle. How many triangles can be formed using these points as vertices?

12. How many three-letter code words are possible using the first eight letters of the alphabet if no letter can be repeated? If letters can be repeated? If adjacent letters cannot be alike?

13. Solve the following problems using $P_{n,r}$ or $C_{n,r}$:

(A) How many three-digit opening combinations are possible on a combination lock with six digits if the digits cannot be repeated?

(B) Five tennis players have made the finals. If each of the five players is to play every other player exactly once, how many games must be scheduled?

14. Two coins are flipped 1,000 times with the following frequencies:

2 heads   210
1 head   480
0 heads   310

(A) Compute the empirical probability for each outcome.
(B) Compute the theoretical probability for each outcome.
(C) Using the theoretical probabilities computed in part B, compute the expected frequency of each outcome, assuming fair coins.

15. From a standard deck of 52 cards, what is the probability of obtaining a 5-card hand:

(A) Of all diamonds?   (B) Of 3 diamonds and 2 spades?

Write answers in terms of $C_{n,r}$ or $P_{n,r}$; do not evaluate.

16. A group of ten people includes one married couple. If four people are selected at random, what is the probability that the married couple is selected?

17. A player tosses two coins and receives $5 if two heads turn up, loses $4 if one head turns up, and wins $2 if no heads turn up. (Would you play this game?) Compute the expected value of the game. Is the game fair?

18. A spinning device has three numbers, 1, 2, and 3, each as likely to turn up as the other. If the device is spun twice, what is the probability that:

(A) The same number turns up both times?
(B) The sum of the numbers turning up is 5?

19. An experiment consists of rolling a pair of fair dice. Let X be the random variable associated with the sum of the values that turn up.

(A) Find the probability distribution for X.
(B) Find the expected value of X.

C 20. How many different five-child families are possible where the sex of each child in the order of their birth is taken into consideration [that is, birth sequences such as (B, G, G, B, B) and (G, B, G, B, B) produce different families]? How many families are possible if the order pattern is not taken into account?

21. If three people are selected from a group of seven men and three women, what is the probability that at least one woman is selected?

22. A software development department consists of six women and four men.

(A) How many ways can they select a chief programmer, a backup programmer, and a programming librarian?

(B) If the positions in part A are selected by lottery, what is the probability that women are selected for all three positions?

(C) How many ways can they select a team of three programmers to work on a particular project?

(D) If the selections in part C are made by lottery, what is the probability that a majority of the team members will be women?

23. How many ways can two people be seated in a row of four chairs?

24. Three fair coins are tossed 1,000 times with the following frequencies of outcomes:

Number of Heads	0	1	2	3
Frequency	120	360	350	170

(A) What is the approximate empirical probability of obtaining two heads?

(B) What is the theoretical probability of obtaining two heads?

(C) What is the expected frequency of obtaining two heads?

25. You bet a friend $1 that you will get one or more double sixes on twenty-four rolls of a pair of fair dice. What is your expectation for this game? What is your friend's expectation? Is the game fair?

26. Two fair (not weighted) dice are each numbered with a 3 on one side, a 2 on two sides, and a 1 on three sides. The dice are rolled and the numbers on the two up faces are added. If X is the random variable associated with the sample space $S = \{2, 3, 4, 5, 6\}$:

(A) Find the probability distribution of X.

(B) Find the expected value of X.

27. If in the preceding problem you pay $3.50 to play the game (the dice are rolled once) and you are returned the dollar amount corresponding to the sum on the faces, what is the expected value of the game? Is the game fair?

Applications

28. *Transportation.* A distribution center A wishes to distribute its products to five different retail stores, $B, C, D, E,$ and F, in a city. How many different route plans can be constructed so that a single truck, starting from A, will deliver to each store exactly once, then return to the center?

29. *Market analysis.* From a survey of 100 students in a school, it was found that 70 played video games at home, 60 played video games in an arcade, and 40 played video games both at home and in arcades. If a student in the school is selected at random, what is the (empirical) probability that:

    (A)   The student plays video games at home or in arcades?
    (B)   The student plays video games only at home?

30. *Market analysis.* From a survey of 100 residents of a city, it was found that 40 read the daily morning paper, 70 read the daily evening paper, and 30 read both papers. What is the (empirical) probability that a resident selected at random:

    (A)   Reads a daily paper?
    (B)   Does not read a daily paper?
    (C)   Reads exactly one daily paper?

31. *Market analysis.* A record company selected 1,000 persons at random and surveyed them to determine a relationship between age of purchaser and annual record album purchases.

		Albums Purchased Annually				
		0	1	2	Above 2	Total
Age	Under 12	60	70	30	10	170
	12–18	30	100	100	60	290
	19–25	70	110	120	30	330
	Over 25	100	50	40	20	210
	Total	260	330	290	120	1,000

Find the empirical probability that a person selected at random:

(A)   Is over 25 and buys two albums annually
(B)   Is 12–18 years old and buys more than one album annually
(C)   Is 12–18 years old or buys more than one album annually

32. *Decision analysis.* A company sales manager, after careful analysis, presents two sales plans. It is estimated that plan *A* will net $10 million if successful (probability .8) and lose $2 million if not (probability .2); plan *B* will net $12 million if successful (probability .7) and lose $2 million if not (probability .3). What is the expected return for each plan? Which plan should be chosen based on the expected return?

33. *Decision analysis.* A meat market is trying to decide how many truckloads of fresh turkeys to order for Thanksgiving. Each truckload of turkeys costs them $2,000 and sells for $6,000. The probabilities of selling one, two, or three truckloads are listed in the table on the next page. How many truckloads should they order to maximize their expected profit?

Number of Truckloads Sold	1	2	3
Probability	.2	.4	.4

34. *Insurance.* A $300 bicycle is insured against theft for an annual premium of $30. If the probability that the bicycle will be stolen during the year is .08 (empirically determined), what is the expected value of the policy?

35. *Quality control.* Twelve precision parts, including two that are substandard, are sent to an assembly plant. The plant will select four at random and will return the whole shipment if one or more of the sample are found substandard. What is the probability that the shipment will be returned?

36. *Quality control.* A dozen computer circuit boards, including two that are defective, are sent to a computer service center. A random sample of three is selected and tested. Let X be the random variable associated with the number of circuit boards in a sample that is defective.

   (A) Find the probability distribution of X.
   (B) Find the expected number of defective boards in a sample.

Additional Topics in Probability

CHAPTER 5	Contents

5-1 Union, Intersection, and Complement of Events; Odds

- Union and Intersection
- Complement of an Event
- Odds
- Applications to Empirical Probability

Recall that in Section 4-2 we said that given a sample space

$$S = \{e_1, e_2, \ldots, e_n\}$$

any function P defined on S such that

$$0 \le P(e_i) \le 1 \qquad i = 1, 2, \ldots, n$$

and

$$P(e_1) + P(e_2) + \cdots + P(e_n) = 1$$

is called a *probability function*. In addition, we said that any subset of S is called an *event E*, and we defined the probability of E to be the sum of the probabilities of the simple events in E.

Union and Intersection

Since events are subsets of a sample space, the union and intersection of events are simply the union and intersection of sets as defined in Section 0-1.

In this section we will concentrate on the union of events and only consider simple cases of intersection. The latter will be investigated in more detail in the next section.

Union and Intersection of Events

If A and B are two events in a sample space S, then the **union** of A and B, denoted by $A \cup B$, and the **intersection** of A and B, denoted by $A \cap B$, are defined as follows:

$$A \cup B = \{e \in S | e \in A \text{ or } e \in B\}$$
$$A \cap B = \{e \in S | e \in A \text{ and } e \in B\}$$

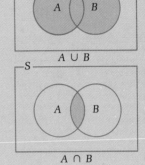

Furthermore, we define

The event A or B to be $A \cup B$

The event A and B to be $A \cap B$

Example 1

Consider the sample space of equally likely events for the rolling of a single fair die

$$S = \{1, 2, 3, 4, 5, 6\}$$

(A)   What is the probability of rolling a number that is odd **and** exactly divisible by 3?

(B)   What is the probability of rolling a number that is odd **or** exactly divisible by 3?

Solutions

(A)   Let A be the event of rolling an odd number, B the event of rolling a number divisible by 3, and F the event of rolling a number that is odd **and** divisible by 3. Then

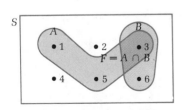

$$A = \{1, 3, 5\} \qquad B = \{3, 6\} \quad F = A \cap B = \{3\}$$

Thus, the probability of rolling a number that is odd **and** exactly divisible by 3 is

$$P(F) = P(A \cap B) = \frac{n(A \cap B)}{n(S)} = \frac{1}{6}$$

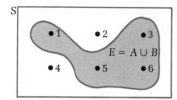

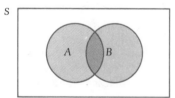

Figure 1 Mutually exclusive $A \cap B = \varnothing$

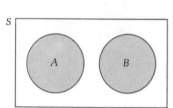

Figure 2 Not mutually exclusive $A \cap B \neq \varnothing$

(B) Let A and B be the same events as in part B and let E be the event of rolling a number that is odd **or** divisible by 3. Then,

$$A = \{1, 3, 5\} \qquad B = \{3, 6\} \quad E = A \cup B = \{1, 3, 5, 6\}$$

Thus, the probability of rolling a number that is odd **or** exactly divisible by 3 is

$$P(E) = P(A \cup B) = \frac{n(A \cup B)}{n(E)} = \frac{4}{6} = \frac{2}{3}$$

Problem 1 Use the sample space in Example 1 to answer the following:

(A) What is the probability of rolling an odd number **and** a prime number?

(B) What is the probability of rolling an odd number **or** a prime number?

Suppose

$$E = A \cup B$$

Can we find $P(E)$ in terms of A and B? The answer is almost yes, but we must be careful. It would be nice if

$$P(A \cup B) = P(A) + P(B) \tag{1}$$

This turns out to be true if events A and B are **mutually exclusive (disjoint)**; that is, if $A \cap B = \varnothing$ (Fig. 1). In this case, $P(A \cup B)$ is the sum of all of the probabilities of simple events in A added to the sum of all the probabilities of simple events in B. But what happens if events A and B are not mutually exclusive; that is, if $A \cap B \neq \varnothing$ (see Fig. 2)? If we simply add the probabilities of the elements in A to the probabilities of the elements in B, we would be adding some of the probabilities twice, namely those for elements that are in both A and B. To compensate for this double counting, we subtract $P(A \cap B)$ from equation (1) to obtain

$$P(A \cup B) = P(A) + P(B) - P(A \cap B) \tag{2}$$

We notice that (2) holds for both cases, $A \cap B \neq \varnothing$ and $A \cap B = \varnothing$, since (2) reduces to (1) for the latter case $[P(A \cap B) = P(\varnothing) = 0]$. It is better to use (2) if there is any doubt that A and B are mutually exclusive (disjoint). We summarize this discussion in the box for convenient reference.

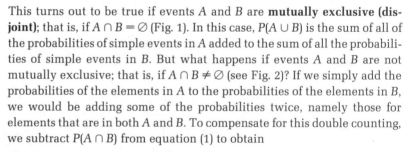

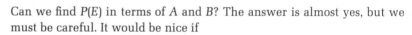

Probability of a Union of Two Events

For any events A and B

$$P(A \cup B) = P(A) + P(B) - P(A \cap B) \tag{2}$$

If A and B are mutually exclusive, then

$$P(A \cup B) = P(A) + P(B) \tag{1}$$

Example 2 Suppose two fair dice are rolled:

(A) What is the probability that a 7 or 11 turns up?
(B) What is the probability that both dice turn up the same or that a sum less than 5 turns up?

Solutions (A) If A is the event that a 7 turns up and B is the event that an 11 turns up, then (see Fig. 3) the event that a 7 or 11 turns up is $A \cup B$ where

$$A = \{(1, 6), (2, 5), (3, 4), (4, 3), (5, 2), (6, 1)\}$$

and

$$B = \{(5, 6), (6, 5)\}$$

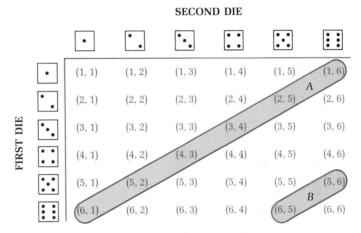

SECOND DIE

Figure 3

Since events A and B are mutually exclusive, we can use equation (1) to calculate $P(A \cup B)$:

$$P(A \cup B) = P(A) + P(B)$$

$$= \tfrac{6}{36} + \tfrac{2}{36} \qquad \text{In this equally likely sample space,}$$

$$= \tfrac{8}{36} \qquad\qquad n(A) = 6,\ n(B) = 2,\ \text{and}\ n(S) = 36$$

$$= \tfrac{2}{9}$$

(B) If A is the event that both dice turn up the same and B is the event that the sum is less than 5, then (see Fig. 4 on the next page) the event that both dice turn up the same or the sum is less than 5 is $A \cup B$, where

$$A = \{(1, 1), (2, 2), (3, 3), (4, 4), (5, 5), (6, 6)\}$$
$$B = \{(1, 1), (1, 2), (1, 3), (2, 1), (2, 2), (3, 1)\}$$

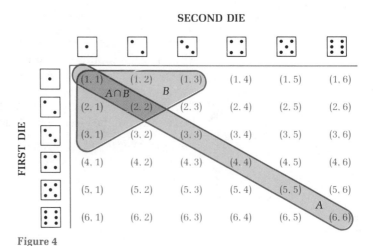

Figure 4

Since $A \cap B = \{(1, 1), (2, 2)\}$, A and B are not mutually exclusive and we use equation (2) to calculate $P(A \cup B)$:

$$P(A \cup B) = P(A) + P(B) - P(A \cap B)$$

$$= \tfrac{6}{36} + \tfrac{6}{36} - \tfrac{2}{36}$$

$$= \tfrac{10}{36}$$

$$= \tfrac{5}{18}$$

Problem 2   Use the sample space in Example 2 to answer the following:

(A)   What is the probability that a sum of 2 or a sum of 3 turns up?

(B)   What is the probability that both dice turn up the same or that a sum greater than 8 turns up?

You no doubt noticed in Example 2 that we actually did not have to use either formula (1) or (2). We could have proceeded as in Example 1 and simply counted sample points in $A \cup B$. The following example illustrates the use of formula (2) in a situation where visual representation of sample points is not practical.

Example 3   What is the probability that a number selected at random from the first 500 positive integers is (exactly) divisible by 3 or 4?

Solution   Let A be the event that a drawn integer is divisible by 3 and B the event that a drawn integer is divisible by 4. Note that events A and B are not mutually exclusive (Why?). Since each of the positive integers from 1 to 500 is likely to be drawn as any other, we can use $n(A)$, $n(B)$, and $n(A \cap B)$ to determine $P(A \cup B)$, where (think about this):

$$n(A) = \text{(the largest integer less than or equal to } 500/3) = 166$$
$$n(B) = \text{(the largest integer less than or equal to } 500/4) = 125$$
$$n(A \cap B) = \text{(the largest integer less than or equal to } 500/12) = 41$$

[*Note:* A positive integer is divisible by 3 and 4 if and only if it is divisible by 12, the least common multiple of 3 and 4.]

Now we can compute $P(A \cup B)$:

$$P(A \cup B) = P(A) + P(B) - P(A \cap B)$$
$$= \frac{n(A)}{n(S)} + \frac{n(B)}{n(S)} - \frac{n(A \cap B)}{n(S)}$$
$$= \frac{166}{500} + \frac{125}{500} - \frac{41}{500} = \frac{250}{500} = .5$$

Problem 3   What is the probability that a number selected at random from the first 140 positive integers is (exactly) divisible by 4 or 6?

■ Complement of an Event

Suppose we divide a finite sample space

$$S = \{e_1, \ldots, e_n\}$$

into two subsets E and E' such that

$$E \cap E' = \varnothing$$

that is, E and E' are mutually exclusive, and

$$E \cup E' = S$$

Then E' is called the **complement of E** relative to S. Thus, E' contains all the elements of S that are not in E (Fig. 5). Furthermore,

$$P(S) = P(E \cup E')$$
$$= P(E) + P(E') = 1$$

Hence,

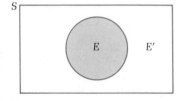

Figure 5

Complements

$$P(E) = 1 - P(E')$$
$$P(E') = 1 - P(E)$$

(3)

If the probability of rain is .67, then the probability of no rain is $1 - .67 = .33$; if the probability of striking oil is .01, then the probability of not striking oil is .99. If the probability of having at least one boy in a two-child family is .75, what is the probability of having two girls? (Answer: .25.)

In looking for $P(E)$ (as was stated in Section 4-2), there are situations in which it is easier to find $P(E')$ first, then use equations (3) to find $P(E)$. The next two examples illustrate two such situations.

Example 4   A shipment of forty-five precision parts, including nine that are defective, are sent to an assembly plant. The quality control division selects ten at random for testing and rejects the whole shipment if one or more in the sample are found defective. What is the probability that the shipment will be rejected?

Solution   If E is the event that 1 or more parts in a random sample of 10 are defective, then E', the complement of E, is the event that no parts in a random sample of 10 are defective. It is easier to compute $P(E')$ than to compute $P(E)$ directly (try the latter to see why). Once $P(E')$ is found, we will use $P(E) = 1 - P(E')$ to find $P(E)$.

The sample space S for this experiment is the set of all 10 element subsets from the set of 45 parts shipped. Thus, since there are $45 - 9 = 36$ nondefective parts,

$$P(E') = \frac{n(E')}{n(S)} = \frac{C_{36,10}}{C_{45,10}} \approx .08$$

and

$$P(E) = 1 - P(E') \approx 1 - .08 = .92$$

Problem 4   A shipment of forty precision parts, including eight that are defective, are sent to an assembly plant. The quality control division selects ten at random for testing and rejects the whole shipment if one or more in the sample are found defective. What is the probability that the shipment will be rejected?

Example 5
Birthday Problem   In a group of n people, what is the probability that at least two people have the same birthday (the same month and day excluding leap years)? (Make a guess for a class of forty people, and check your guess with the conclusion of this example.)

Solution   If we form a list of the birthdays of all the people in the group, then we have a simple event in the sample space

$S =$ Set of all lists of n birthdays

For any person in the group, we will assume that any birthday is as likely as any other, so that the simple events in S are equally likely. How many simple events are in the set S? Since any person could have any one of 365 birthdays (excluding leap years), the multiplication principle implies that the number of simple events in S is

1st person	2nd person	3rd person		nth person

$$n(S) = 365 \cdot 365 \cdot 365 \cdots \cdots 365$$

$$= 365^n$$

Now, let E be the event that at least two people in the group have the same birthday. Then E' is the event that no two people have the same birthday. The fundamental principle of counting can be used to determine the number of simple events in E':

1st person	2nd person	3rd person		nth person

$$n(E') = 365 \cdot 364 \cdot 363 \cdots \cdots (366 - n)$$

$$= \frac{[365 \cdot 364 \cdot 363 \cdots \cdots (366 - n)](365 - n)!}{(365 - n)!}$$

Multiply numerator and denominator by $(365 - n)!$

$$= \frac{365!}{(365 - n)!}$$

Since we have assumed that S is an equally likely sample space,

$$P(E') = \frac{n(E')}{n(S)} = \frac{\dfrac{365!}{(365 - n)!}}{365^n} = \frac{365!}{365^n(365 - n)!}$$

Thus,

$$P(E) = 1 - P(E')$$

$$= 1 - \frac{365!}{365^n(365 - n)!} \tag{4}$$

Equation (4) is valid for any n satisfying $1 \leqslant n \leqslant 365$. [What is $P(E)$ if $n > 365$?] For example, in a group of six people,

$$P(E) = 1 - \frac{365!}{(365)^6 359!}$$

$$= 1 - \frac{365 \cdot 364 \cdot 363 \cdot 362 \cdot 361 \cdot 360 \cdot 359!}{365 \cdot 365 \cdot 365 \cdot 365 \cdot 365 \cdot 365 \cdot 359!}$$

$$= .04$$

It is interesting to note that as the size of the group increases, $P(E)$ increases more rapidly than you might expect. Table 1 on the next page gives the value of $P(E)$ for selected values of n. Notice that for a group of only twenty-three people, the probability that two or more have the same birthday is greater than $\frac{1}{2}$.

Table 1   The Birthday Problem

Number of People in Group n	Probability That Two or More Have Same Birthday $P(E)$
5	.027
10	.117
15	.253
20	.411
23	**.507**
30	.706
40	.891
50	.970
60	.994
70	.999

Problem 5   Use equation (4) to evaluate $P(E)$ for $n = 4$.

■ Odds

When the probability of an event E is known it is often customary, particularly in gaming situations, to speak of *odds* for (or against) the event E, rather than the *probability* of the event E. The relationships between these two designations are simple.

From Probability to Odds

If $P(E)$ is the probability of the event E, then we define:

(A)   Odds for $E = \dfrac{P(E)}{1 - P(E)} = \dfrac{P(E)}{P(E')}$ $\qquad P(E) \neq 1$

(B)   Odds against $E = \dfrac{P(E')}{P(E)}$ $\qquad P(E) \neq 0$

[*Note:*   When possible, odds are expressed as ratios of whole numbers.]

Example 6   If you roll a fair die once, the probability of rolling a 4 is $\frac{1}{6}$, whereas the odds in favor of rolling a 4 are

$$\frac{P(E)}{P(E')} = \frac{\frac{1}{6}}{\frac{5}{6}} = \frac{1}{5} \qquad \text{Which is read "1 to 5" and is also written "1:5"}$$

and

$$\text{odds against rolling a } 4 = \frac{5}{1}$$

In terms of a fair game, if you bet $1 on a 4 turning up, you would lose $1 to the house if any number other than 4 turns up and would be paid $5 by the house (and your bet of $1 returned) if a 4 turns up. (An experienced gambler would say that the house pays 5 to 1 on a 4 turning up on a single roll of a die.) Note that, under these rules, the expected value of the game is:

$$E(X) = x_1 p_1 + x_2 p_2$$
$$= (\$5)(\tfrac{1}{6}) + (-\$1)(\tfrac{5}{6}) = 0$$

The game is fair (and you would not likely see it in a casino).

Problem 6 (A) What are the odds for rolling an 8 in a single roll of two fair dice?
(B) If you bet $5 that an 8 will turn up, what should the house pay (and return your $5 bet) for the game to be fair?

Now we will go in the other direction: If we are given the odds for an event, what is the probability of the event? (The verification of the following formula is left to Problem 53 in Exercise 5-1.)

From Odds to Probability

If the odds for event E are a/b, then the probability of E is

$$P(E) = \frac{a}{a+b}$$

Example 7 If in repeated rolls of two fair dice the odds for rolling a 5 before rolling a 7 are 2 to 3, then the probability of rolling a 5 before rolling a 7 is

$$P(E) = \frac{a}{a+b} = \frac{2}{2+3} = \frac{2}{5}$$

Problem 7 If in repeated rolls of two fair dice the odds against rolling a 6 before rolling a 7 are 6 to 5, then what is the probability of rolling a 6 before rolling a 7? (Be careful! Read the problem again.)

■ Applications to Empirical Probability

The following examples illustrate the application of the concepts discussed in this section to problems involving data from surveys of a randomly selected sample from a total population. In this situation, the distinction between theoretical and empirical probabilities is a subtle one. If we use the data to assign probabilities to events in the sample population, we are dealing with theoretical probabilities. If we use the same data to assign probabilities to events in the total population, then we are working with empirical probabilities. (See the discussion at the beginning of Section 4-3.) Fortunately, the procedures for computing the probabilities are the same in either case, and all we must do is be careful to use the correct terminology. In the following discussions, we will use *empirical probability* to mean the probability of an event determined by a sample that is used to approximate the probability of the corresponding event in the total population.

Example 8   From a survey involving 1,000 people in a certain city, it was found that 500 people had tried a certain brand of diet cola, 600 had tried a certain brand of regular cola, and 200 had tried both brands. If a resident of the city is selected at random, what is the (empirical) probability that:

(A)   He or she has tried the diet or the regular cola? What are the (empirical) odds for this event?

(B)   He or she has tried one of the colas but not both? What are the (empirical) odds against this event?

Solutions   Let D be the event that a person has tried the diet cola and R the event that a person has tried the regular cola. The events D and R can be used to partition the residents of the city into four mutually exclusive subsets (a collection of subsets is mutually exclusive if the intersection of any two of them is the empty set):

$D \cap R$ = Set of people who have tried both colas

$D \cap R'$ = Set of people who have tried the diet cola but not the regular cola

$D' \cap R$ = Set of people who have tried the regular cola but not the diet cola

$D' \cap R'$ = Set of people who have not tried either cola

These sets are displayed in the Venn diagram in Figure 6.

The sample population of 1,000 residents is also partitioned into four mutually exclusive sets, with $n(D) = 500$, $n(R) = 600$, and $n(D \cap R) = 200$. By using a Venn diagram (Fig. 7), we can determine the number of sample points in the sets $D \cap R'$, $D' \cap R$, and $D' \cap R'$ (see Example 5 in Section 0-1).

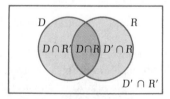

Figure 6 Total population

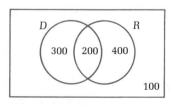

Figure 7 Sample population

These frequencies can be conveniently displayed in a table:

		Regular R	No Regular R'	Total
Diet	D	200	300	500
No Diet	D'	400	100	500
	Total	600	400	1,000

Assuming that each sample point is equally likely, we form a probability table by dividing each entry in this table by 1,000, the total number surveyed. These are theoretical probabilities for the sample population, which we can use as empirical probabilities to approximate the corresponding probabilities for the total population.

		Regular R	No Regular R'	Total
Diet	D	.2	.3	.5
No Diet	D'	.4	.1	.5
	Total	.6	.4	1.0

Now we are ready to compute the required probabilities.

(A) The event that a person has tried the diet or the regular cola is $E = D \cup R$. We compute $P(E)$ two ways:

Method 1. *Direct.*

$$P(E) = P(D \cup R)$$
$$= P(D) + P(R) - P(D \cap R)$$
$$= .5 + .6 - .2 = .9$$

Method 2. *Using the complement of E.*

$$P(E) = 1 - P(E')$$
$$= 1 - P(D' \cap R') \qquad E' = (D \cup R)' = D' \cap R' \text{ (See Fig. 6.)}$$
$$= 1 - .1 = .9$$

In either case,

$$\text{Odds for } E = \frac{P(E)}{P(E')} = \frac{.9}{.1} = \frac{9}{1}$$

(B) The event that a person has tried one cola but not both is the event that the person has tried diet and not regular cola or has tried regular and not diet cola. In terms of sets, this is event $E = (D \cap R') \cup (D' \cap R)$. Since $D \cap R'$ and $D' \cap R$ are mutually exclusive (look at the Venn diagrams in Fig. 6),

$$P(E) = P[(D \cap R') \cup (D' \cap R)]$$
$$= P(D \cap R') + P(D' \cap R)$$
$$= .3 + .4 = .7$$

$$\text{Odds against } E = \frac{P(E')}{P(E)} = \frac{.3}{.7} = \frac{3}{7}$$

Problem 8   If a person is selected at random from the city in Example 8, what is the (empirical) probability that:

(A) He or she has not tried either cola? What are the (empirical) odds for this event?

(B) He or she has tried the diet cola or has not tried the regular cola? What are the (empirical) odds against this event?

Answers to   1. (A) $\frac{1}{3}$ (B) $\frac{2}{3}$ 2. (A) $\frac{1}{12}$ (B) $\frac{7}{18}$
Matched Problems   3. $\frac{47}{140} \approx .336$ 4. .92   5. .016
6. (A) $5:31$ (B) \$31   7. (A) $\frac{5}{11} \approx .455$
8. (A) $P(D' \cap R') = .1$; Odds for $D' \cap R' = \frac{1}{9}$
(B) $P(D \cup R') = .6$; Odds against $D \cup R' = \frac{2}{3}$

Exercise 5-1

A   1. If a manufactured item has the probability of .003 of failing within 90 days, what is the probability that the item will not fail in that time period?

2. If in a particular cross of two plants the probability that the flowers will be red is .25, what is the probability that they will not be red?

A spinner is numbered from 1 through 10, and each number is as likely to occur as any other. Use equation (1) or (2), indicating which is used, to compute the probability that in a single spin the dial will stop at:

3. A number less than 3 or larger than 7
4. A 2 or a number larger than 6
5. An even number or a number divisible by 3
6. An odd number or a number divisible by 3

Problems 7–18 refer to the Venn diagram for events A and B in an equally likely sample space S

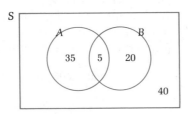

Find each of the following probabilities:

7. $P(A)$	**8.** $P(A')$	**9.** $P(B)$	**10.** $P(B')$
11. $P(A \cap B)$	**12.** $P(A \cap B')$	**13.** $P(A' \cap B)$	**14.** $P(A' \cap B')$
15. $P(A \cup B)$	**16.** $P(A \cup B')$	**17.** $P(A' \cup B)$	**18.** $P(A' \cup B')$

In Problems 19–22, use the equally likely sample space in Example 2 and equation (1) or (2), indicating which is used, to compute the probability of the following events:

19. A sum of 5 or 6

20. A sum of 9 or 10

21. The number on the first die is a 1 or the number on the second die is a 1.

22. The number on the first die is a 1 or the number on the second die is less than 3.

23. Given the following probabilities for an event E, find the odds for and against E: (A) $\frac{3}{8}$ (B) $\frac{1}{4}$ (C) .4 (D) .55

24. Given the following probabilities for an event E, find the odds for and against E: (A) $\frac{3}{5}$ (B) $\frac{1}{7}$ (C) .6 (D) .35

25. Compute the probability of event E if the odds in favor of E are: (A) $\frac{3}{8}$ (B) $\frac{11}{7}$ (C) $\frac{4}{1}$ (D) $\frac{49}{51}$

26. Compute the probability of event E if the odds in favor of E are: (A) $\frac{5}{9}$ (B) $\frac{4}{3}$ (C) $\frac{3}{7}$ (D) $\frac{23}{77}$

B   *In Problems 27–30, compute the odds in favor of obtaining:*

27. A head in a single toss of a coin

28. A number divisible by 3 in a single roll of a die

29. At least one head when a single coin is tossed three times

30. One head when a single coin is tossed twice

In Problems 31–34, compute the odds against obtaining:

31. A number greater than 4 in a single roll of a die

32. Two heads when a single coin is tossed twice

33. A 3 or an even number in a single roll of a die

34. An odd number or a number divisible by 3 in a single roll of a die

35. (A) What are the odds for rolling a 5 in a single roll of two fair dice?
    (B) If you bet $1 that a 5 will turn up, what should the house pay (and return your $1 bet) for the game to be fair?
36. (A) What are the odds for rolling a 10 in a single roll of two fair dice?
    (B) If you bet $1 that a 10 will turn up, what should the house pay (and return your $1 bet) for the game to be fair?

A pair of dice are rolled 1,000 times with the following frequencies of outcomes:

Sum	2	3	4	5	6	7	8	9	10	11	12
Frequency	10	30	50	70	110	150	170	140	120	80	70

Use these frequencies to calculate the approximate empirical probabilities and odds for the events in Problems 37 and 38.

37. (A) The sum is less than 4 or greater than 9.
    (B) The sum is even or exactly divisible by 5.
38. (A) The sum is a prime number or is exactly divisible by 4.
    (B) The sum is an odd number or exactly divisible by 3.

In Problems 39–42, a single card is drawn from a 52-card deck. What is the probability of and odds for each event:

39. A face card or a club is drawn?
40. A king or a heart is drawn?
41. A black card or an ace is drawn?
42. A heart or a number less than 7 (count an ace as 1) is drawn?
43. What is the probability of getting at least one diamond in a 5-card hand dealt from a 52-card deck?
44. What is the probability of getting at least one black card in a 7-card hand dealt from a 52-card deck?
45. What is the probability that a number selected at random from the first 1,000 positive integers is (exactly) divisible by 6 or 8?
46. What is the probability that a number selected at random from the first 600 positive integers is (exactly) divisible by 6 or 9?
47. Five integers are selected at random from the first fifty positive integers, without replacement. What is the probability that there is at least one number divisible by 3 among the five drawn?
48. Four integers are selected at random from the first sixty positive integers, without replacement. What is the probability that there is at least one number divisible by 7 among the four drawn?
49. On a Nevada type roulette wheel (with a 0 and 00), the true odds for landing on red are 9 to 10. What is the probability (to 4 decimal places) of landing on red? If the house pays $1 for a $1 winning bet on red (and

returns the $1 bet), what is the expected value of the game? (Moral: Nobody said that casinos play fair.)

50. In a game of craps, if a shooter gets an 8 on the first roll, then in order to win, the shooter, on subsequent rolls of the dice, must roll an 8 before a 7. The shooter loses if a 7 turns up. If the true odds in obtaining an 8 before a 7 are 5 to 6, what is the probability of getting an 8 before a 7? If the house pays $1 for a $1 winning side bet on 8 (and returns the $1 bet) what is the expected value of the side bet game? (Now you know why casinos make so much money.)

C   51. In a group of n people (n ≤ 12), what is the probability that at least two of them have the same birth month? (Assume any birth month is as likely as any other.)

52. In a group of n people (n ≤ 100), each person is asked to select a number between 1 and 100, write the number on a slip of paper, and place the slip in a hat. What is the probability that at least two of the slips in the hat have the same number written on them?

53. If the odds in favor of an event E occurring are a to b, show that

$$P(E) = \frac{a}{a+b}$$

[Hint: Solve the equation $P(E)/P(E') = a/b$ for $P(E)$.]

54. If $P(E) = c/d$, show that the odds in favor of E occurring are c to d − c.

■ Applications

Business & Economics   55. *Market research.* From a survey involving 1,000 students at a large university, a market research company found that 750 students owned stereos, 450 owned cars, and 350 owned cars and stereos. If a student at the university is selected at random, what is the (empirical) probability that:

(A)   The student owns either a car or a stereo?
(B)   The student owns neither a car nor a stereo?

56. *Market research.* If a student at the university in Problem 55 is selected at random, what is the (empirical) probability that:

(A)   The student does not own a car?
(B)   The student owns a car but not a stereo?

57. *Insurance.* By examining the past driving records of drivers in a certain city, an insurance company has determined the (empirical) probabilities in the table on the next page.

		Miles Driven per Year			
		Less than 10,000, M_1	10,000 to 15,000 Inclusive, M_2	More than 15,000, M_3	Total
Accident	A	.05	.1	.15	.3
No Accident	A'	.15	.2	.35	.7
	Total	.2	.3	.5	1.0

If a driver in this city is selected at random, what is the probability that:

(A) He or she drives less than 10,000 miles per year or has an accident?

(B) He or she drives 10,000 or more miles per year and has no accidents?

58. *Insurance.* Use the (empirical) probabilities in Problem 57 to find the probability that a driver in the city selected at random:

(A) Drives more than 15,000 miles per year or has an accident

(B) Drives 15,000 or fewer miles per year and has an accident

59. *Manufacturing.* Manufacturers of a portable computer provide a 90-day limited warranty covering only the keyboard and the disk drive. Their records indicate that during the warranty period, 6% of their computers are returned because they have defective keyboards, 5% are returned because they have defective disk drives, and 1% are returned because both the keyboard and the disk drive are defective. What is the (empirical) probability that a computer will not be returned during the warranty period?

60. *Product testing.* In order to test a new car, an automobile manufacturer wants to select four employees to test drive the car for one year. If twelve management and eight union employees volunteer to be test drivers and the selection is made at random, what is the probability that at least one union employee is selected?

61. *Quality control.* A shipment of sixty inexpensive digital watches, including nine that are defective, are sent to a department store. The receiving department selects ten at random for testing and rejects the whole shipment if one or more in the sample are found defective. What is the probability that the shipment will be rejected?

62. *Quality control.* An automated manufacturing process produces forty computer circuit boards, including seven that are defective. The quality control department selects ten at random (from the forty produced) for testing and will shut down the plant for trouble shooting if one or more in the sample are found defective. What is the probability that the plant will be shut down?

Life Sciences
63. *Medicine.* In order to test a new drug for adverse reactions, the drug was administered to 1,000 test subjects with the following results: 60 subjects reported that their only adverse reaction was a loss of appetite, 90 subjects reported that their only adverse reaction was a loss of sleep, and 800 subjects reported no adverse reactions at all. If this drug is released for general use, what is the (empirical) probability that a person using the drug will suffer both a loss of appetite and a loss of sleep?

64. *Medicine.* Thirty animals are to be used in a medical experiment on diet deficiency: three male and seven female rhesus monkeys, six male and four female chimpanzees, and two male and eight female dogs. If one animal is selected at random, what is the probability of getting:

(A) A chimpanzee or a dog?
(B) A chimpanzee or a male?
(C) An animal other than a female monkey?

Social Sciences
Problems 65 and 66 refer to the data in the table that was obtained from a random survey of 1,000 residents of a state. The participants were asked their political affiliations and their preferences in an upcoming gubernatorial election.

		Democrat D	Republican R	Unaffiliated U	Total
Candidate A	A	200	100	85	385
Candidate B	B	250	230	50	530
No Preference	N	50	20	15	85
	Total	500	350	150	1,000

65. *Politics.* If a resident of the state is selected at random, what is the (empirical) probability that the resident is:

(A) Not affiliated with a political party or has no preference? What are the odds for this event?
(B) Affiliated with a political party and prefers candidate *A*? What are the odds against this event?

66. *Politics.* If a resident of the state is selected at random, what is the (empirical) probability that the resident is:

(A) A Democrat or prefers candidate *B*? What are the odds for this event?
(B) Not a Democrat and has no preference? What are the odds against this event?

67. *Sociology.* A group of five Blacks, five Asians, five Latinos, and five Whites were used in a study on racial influence in small group dynamics. If three people are chosen at random, what is the probability that at least one is Black?

5-2 Conditional Probability, Intersection, and Independence

- Conditional Probability
- Intersection of Events—Product Rule
- Probability Trees
- Independent Events

In Section 5-1 we asked if the probability of the union of two events could be expressed in terms of the probabilities of the individual events, and we found the answer to be a qualified yes. Now we ask the same question for the intersection of two events; that is, can the probability of the intersection of two events be represented in terms of the probabilities of the individual events? The answer again is a qualified yes. But before we find out how and under what conditions, we must investigate a related concept called *conditional probability*.

■ Conditional Probability

The probability of an event may change if we are told of the occurrence of another event. For example, if an adult is selected at random from all adults in the United States, the probability of that person having lung cancer would not be too high. However, if we are told that the person is also a heavy smoker, then we would certainly want to revise the probability upward.

In general, the probability of the occurrence of an event A, given the occurrence of another event B, is called a **conditional probability** and is denoted by $P(A|B)$.

In the above illustration, events A and B would be

A = An adult has lung cancer

B = An adult is a heavy smoker

And $P(A|B)$ would represent the probability of an adult having lung cancer, given that he or she is a heavy smoker.

Our objective now is to try to formulate a precise definition of $P(A|B)$. It is helpful to start with a relatively simple problem, solve it intuitively, and then generalize from this experience.

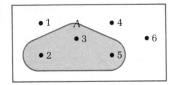

Figure 8

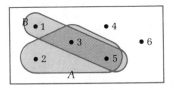

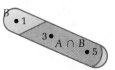

B is new sample space

Figure 9

What is the probability of rolling a prime number (2, 3, or 5) in a single roll of a fair die? Let

$$S = \{1, 2, 3, 4, 5, 6\}$$

Then the event of rolling a prime number is (see Fig. 8)

$$A = \{2, 3, 5\}$$

Thus, since we assume each simple event in the sample space is equally likely,

$$P(A) = \frac{n(A)}{n(S)} = \frac{3}{6} = \frac{1}{2}$$

Now suppose you are asked, "What is the probability of rolling a prime number, given that an odd number has turned up?" The additional knowledge that another event has occurred, namely,

$$B = \text{An odd number turns up}$$

puts the problem in a new light. We are now interested only in the part of event A (rolling a prime number) that is in event B (rolling an odd number). Event B, since we know it has occurred, becomes the new sample space. The Venn diagrams in Figure 9 illustrate the various relationships. Thus, the probability of A given B is the number of A elements in B divided by the total number of elements in B. Symbolically,

$$P(A|B) = \frac{n(A \cap B)}{n(B)} = \frac{2}{3}$$

Dividing the numerator and denominator of $n(A \cap B)/n(B)$ by $n(S)$, the number of elements in the original sample space, we can express $P(A|B)$ in terms of $P(A \cap B)$ and $P(B)$:*

$$P(A|B) = \frac{n(A \cap B)}{n(B)} = \frac{\dfrac{n(A \cap B)}{n(S)}}{\dfrac{n(B)}{n(S)}} = \frac{P(A \cap B)}{P(B)}$$

Using the right side to compute $P(A|B)$ for the example above, we obtain the same result, as we should:

$$P(A|B) = \frac{P(A \cap B)}{P(B)} = \frac{\frac{2}{6}}{\frac{3}{6}} = \frac{2}{3}$$

It is this latter form for $P(A|B)$ that we will use to generalize the concept of conditional probability to arbitrary sample spaces (spaces where simple events are not necessarily equally likely).

* Note that $P(A|B)$ is a probability based on the new sample space B, while $P(A \cap B)$ and $P(B)$ are both probabilities based on the original sample space S.

> **Conditional Probability**
>
> For events A and B in an arbitrary sample space S, we define the conditional probability of A given B by
>
> $$P(A|B) = \frac{P(A \cap B)}{P(B)} \qquad P(B) \neq 0 \tag{1}$$

Example 9   A pointer is spun once on the circular spinner below. The probability assigned to the pointer landing on a given integer (from 1 to 6) is the ratio of the area of the corresponding circular sector to the area of the whole circle (see table):

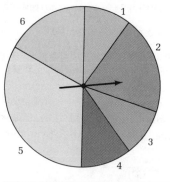

e_i	1	2	3	4	5	6
p_i	.1	.2	.1	.1	.3	.2

(A) What is the probability of the pointer landing on a prime number?

(B) What is the probability of the pointer landing on a prime number, given that it landed on an odd number?

Solutions   Let the events E and F be defined as follows:

E = The pointer lands on a prime number = {2, 3, 5}

F = The pointer lands on an odd number = {1, 3, 5}

(A) $P(E) = p(2) + p(3) + p(5)$

$\qquad = .2 + .1 + .3 = .6$

(B) First note that $E \cap F = \{3, 5\}$.

$$P(E|F) = \frac{P(E \cap F)}{P(F)} = \frac{p(3) + p(5)}{p(1) + p(3) + p(5)}$$

$$= \frac{.1 + .3}{.1 + .1 + .3} = \frac{.4}{.5} = .8$$

Problem 9 Refer to the pointer in Example 9:

(A) What is the probability of the pointer landing on a number greater than 4?

(B) What is the probability of the pointer landing on a number greater than 4, given that it landed on an even number?

Example 10 Suppose past records in a large city produced the following probability data on a driver being in an accident on the last day of a Memorial Day weekend:

		Rain R	No Rain R′	Total
Accident	A	.025	.015	.040
No Accident	A′	.335	.625	.960
	Total	.360	.640	1.000

(A) The probability of an accident (rain or shine) is

$$P(A) = .040$$

(B) The probability of an accident and rain is

$$P(A \cap R) = .025$$

(C) The probability of rain is

$$P(R) = .360$$

(D) The probability of an accident, given rain is [using equation (1)]

$$P(A|R) = \frac{P(A \cap R)}{P(R)} = \frac{.025}{.360} = .069$$

Compare this result with part A.

Problem 10 Referring to the table in Example 10, determine the following:

(A) The probability of no rain
(B) The probability of an accident and no rain
(C) The probability of an accident, given no rain [use formula (1) and the results of parts A and B]

■ Intersection of Events — Product Rule

We now return to the original problem of this section; that is, representing the probability of an intersection of two events in terms of the probabilities of the individual events. If $P(A) \neq 0$ and $P(B) \neq 0$, then using (1) we can write:

$$P(A|B) = \frac{P(A \cap B)}{P(B)} \quad \text{and} \quad P(B|A) = \frac{P(B \cap A)}{P(A)}$$

Solving the first equation for $P(A \cap B)$ and the second equation for $P(B \cap A)$, we have

$$P(A \cap B) = P(B)P(A|B) \quad \text{and} \quad P(B \cap A) = P(A)P(B|A)$$

Since $A \cap B = B \cap A$ for any sets A and B, it follows that

$$P(A \cap B) = P(B)P(A|B) = P(A)P(B|A)$$

In summary we have the *product rule*:

Product Rule

For events A and B with nonzero probabilities in a sample space S,

$$P(A \cap B) = P(A)P(B|A) = P(B)P(A|B) \qquad (2)$$

Example 11   If 60% of a department store's customers are female and 75% of the female customers have charge accounts at the store, what is the probability that a customer selected at random is a female and has a charge account?

Solution   Let

F = Female customer

C = Customer with a charge account

If 60% of the customers are female, then the probability that a customer selected at random is a female is

$$P(F) = .60$$

Since 75% of the female customers have charge accounts, the probability that a customer has a charge account, given that the customer is a female, is

$$P(C|F) = .75$$

Using equation (2), the probability that a customer is a female and has a charge account is

$$P(F \cap C) = P(F)P(C|F) = (.60)(.75) = .45$$

Problem 11   If 80% of the male customers of the department store in Example 11 have charge accounts, what is the probability that a customer selected at random is a male and has a charge account?

■ Probability Trees

We used tree diagrams in Section 4-1 to help us count the number of combined outcomes in a sequence of experiments. In much the same way we will now use probability trees to help us compute the probabilities of combined outcomes in a sequence of experiments. An example will help make the process of forming and using probability trees clear.

Example 12   Two balls are drawn in succession, without replacement, from a box containing three red and two white balls. What is the probability of drawing a white ball on the second draw?

Solution   We start with a tree diagram showing the combined outcomes of the two experiments (first draw and second draw):

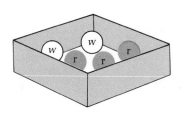

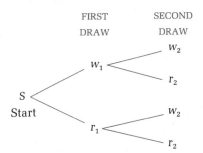

We now assign a probability to each branch on the tree. For example, we assign the probability $\frac{2}{5}$ to the branch sw_1, since this is the probability of drawing a white ball on the first draw (there are two white balls and three red balls in the box). What probability should be assigned to the branch w_1w_2? This is the conditional probability $P(w_2|w_1)$; that is, the probability of drawing a white ball on the second draw given that a white ball was drawn on the first draw and not replaced. Since the box now contains one white ball and three red balls, the probability is $\frac{1}{4}$. Continuing in the same way, we assign probabilities to the other branches of the tree and obtain the following probability tree:

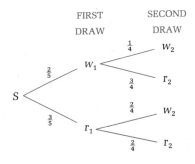

What is the probability of the combined outcome $w_1 \cap w_2$; that is, of drawing a white ball on the first draw and a white ball on the second draw?

Using the product rule (2), we have

$$P(w_1 \cap w_2) = P(w_1)P(w_2|w_1)$$
$$= \left(\tfrac{2}{5}\right)\left(\tfrac{1}{4}\right) = \tfrac{1}{10}$$

The combined outcome $w_1 \cap w_2$ corresponds to the unique path sw_1w_2 in the tree diagram, and we see that the probability of reaching w_2 along this path is just the product of the probabilities assigned to the branches on the path. Reasoning in the same way, we obtain the probability of each remaining combined outcome by multiplying the probabilities assigned to the branches on the path corresponding to the given combined outcome. These probabilities are often written at the end of the paths to which they correspond.

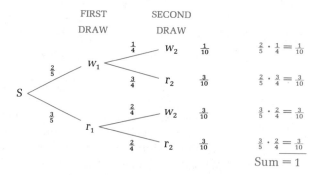

Now it is an easy matter to complete the problem. A white ball drawn on the second draw corresponds to either the combined outcome $w_1 \cap w_2$ or $r_1 \cap w_2$ occurring. Thus, since these combined outcomes are mutually exclusive:

$$P(w_2) = P(w_1 \cap w_2) + P(r_1 \cap w_2)$$
$$= \tfrac{1}{10} + \tfrac{3}{10} = \tfrac{4}{10} = \tfrac{2}{5}$$

which is just the sum of the probabilities listed at the end of the two paths terminating in w_2.

Problem 12   Two balls are drawn in succession without replacement from a box containing four red and two white balls. What is the probability of drawing a red ball on the second draw?

The sequence of two experiments in Example 12 is an example of a *stochastic process*. In general, a **stochastic process** involves a sequence of experiments where the outcome of each experiment is not certain. Our interest is in making predictions about the process as a whole. The analysis in Example 12 generalizes to stochastic processes involving any finite sequence of experiments. We summarize the procedures used in Example 12 for general application:

Constructing Probability Trees

1. Draw a tree diagram corresponding to all combined outcomes of the sequence of experiments.
2. Assign a probability to each tree branch. (This is the probability of the occurrence of the event on the right end of the branch subject to the occurrence of all events on the path leading to the event on the right end of the branch. The probability of the occurrence of a combined outcome that corresponds to a path through the tree is the product of all branch probabilities on the path.*)
3. Use the results in steps 1 and 2 to answer various questions related to the sequence of experiments as a whole.

Example 13

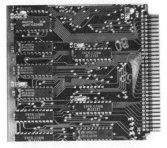

A large computer company A subcontracts the manufacturing of its circuit boards to two companies, 40% to company B and 60% to company C. Company B in turn subcontracts 70% of the orders it receives from company A to company D and the remaining 30% to company E, both subsidiaries of company B. When the boards are completed by companies D, E, and C, they are shipped to company A to be used in various computer models. It has been found that 1.5%, 1%, and .5% of the boards from D, E, and C, respectively, prove defective during the 90 day warranty period after a computer is first sold. What is the probability that a given board in a computer will be defective during the 90 day warranty period?

Solution   Draw a tree diagram and assign probabilities to each branch.

---

* If we form a sample space S such that each simple event in S corresponds to one path through the tree, and if the probability assigned to each simple event in S is the product of the branch probabilities on the corresponding path, then it can be shown that this is not only an acceptable assignment (all probabilities for the simple events in S are nonnegative and their sum is 1—see Example 12), but it is the only assignment consistent with the method used to assign branch probabilities within the tree.

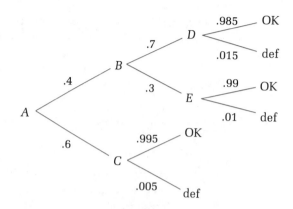

There are three paths leading to def (the board will be defective within the 90 day warranty period). We multiply the branch probabilities on each path and add the three products:

P(the board will be defective during the 90 day warranty period)

$$= (.4)(.7)(.015) + (.4)(.3)(.01) + (.6)(.005)$$

$$= .0084$$

Problem 13   In Example 13, what is the probability that a circuit board in a completed computer came from E or C?

■ Independent Events

Suppose events A and B are subsets of a sample space S with $P(A) \neq 0$ and $P(B) \neq 0$. Both $P(A|B)$ and $P(A)$ are probabilities of the event A, the first with respect to a new sample space B and the second with respect to the original sample space S [Note: $P(A)$ is simply an abbreviation for $P(A|S)$]. In general, $P(A|B)$ and $P(A)$ are not equal. However, there is an important class of events for which they are. If

$$P(A|B) = P(A) \tag{3}$$

then the knowledge of B occurring does not change the probability of A, and we say that A *is independent of* B. Similarly, if

$$P(B|A) = P(B) \tag{4}$$

we say that B *is independent of* A. Substituting (3) and (4) into the product rule (2)

$$P(A \cap B) = P(A)P(B|A) = P(B)P(A|B)$$

we obtain

$$P(A \cap B) = P(A)P(B)$$

which leads us to the following general definition of the independence of two events:

Independence

If A and B are any events in a sample space S, we say that **A and B are independent** if and only if

$$P(A \cap B) = P(A)P(B) \tag{5}$$

Otherwise, A and B are said to be **dependent.**

It is important to note that the general definition of independence allows either event A or event B (or both) to have 0 probability—a situation we rarely encounter in practice, but an important consideration in a more advanced treatment of the subject. Equations (3), (4), and (5) are equivalent (in that they are either all true or all false) whenever events A and B have nonzero probabilities.

The definition of independence is used in two ways: (A) if we know two events are independent, then we can use (5) in place of the product rule (2) to find the probability of the intersection of the two events* and (B) if we do not know whether two events are independent or dependent, we can use (5) to decide which.

In practice, one often has correct feelings about independence. For example, if one tosses a coin twice, the second toss is independent of the first (a coin has no memory); if a card is drawn from a deck twice, with replacement, the second draw is independent of the first (the deck has no memory); if one rolls a pair of dice twice, the second roll is independent of the first (dice have no memory); and so on. However, there are pairs of events that are not obviously independent or dependent, so we need equation (5) in the definition to decide which. Example 14 considers two events that are obviously independent and Example 15 considers events whose independence or dependence is not obvious.

Example 14   In two tosses of a single fair coin show that the events "a head on the first toss" and "a head on the second toss" are independent.

Solution   Consider the sample space of equally likely outcomes for the tossing of a fair coin twice

$$S = \{HH, HT, TH, TT\}$$

---

* It is important to keep in mind that equation (5) is a special case of the product rule (2); that is, (2) applies to both dependent and independent events, while (5) only applies to independent events. If independence is in doubt, use the product rule (2).

and the two events

A = A head on the first toss = {HH, HT}

B = A head on the second toss = {HH, TH}

Then,

$P(A) = \frac{2}{4} = \frac{1}{2}$

$P(B) = \frac{2}{4} = \frac{1}{2}$

$P(A \cap B) = \frac{1}{4}$

Thus,

$P(A \cap B) = \frac{1}{4} = \frac{1}{2} \cdot \frac{1}{2} = P(A)P(B)$

and the two events are independent. (The theory agrees with our intuition —a comforting thought.)

Problem 14   In Example 14 compute $P(B|A)$ and compare with $P(B)$.

Example 15   A single card is drawn from a standard 52-card deck. Test the events in parts A and B for independence (try guessing the answer of each before looking at the solution):

(A) E = The drawn card is a spade.
F = The drawn card is a face card.
(B) G = The drawn card is a club.
H = The drawn card is a heart.

Solutions   (A)   To test E and F for independence, we compute $P(E \cap F)$ and $P(E)P(F)$. If they are equal, then events E and F are independent; if they are not equal, then events E and F are dependent.

$$P(E \cap F) = \frac{3}{52}$$

$$P(E)P(F) = \left(\frac{13}{52}\right)\left(\frac{12}{52}\right) = \frac{3}{52}$$

Events E and F are independent. (Did you guess this?)
(B)   Proceeding as in part A, we see that

$$P(G \cap H) = P(\varnothing) = 0$$

$$P(G)P(H) = \left(\frac{13}{52}\right)\left(\frac{13}{52}\right) = \frac{1}{16}$$

Events G and H are dependent. (Did you guess this?)

Students often confuse *mutually exclusive (disjoint) events* with *independent events*. One does not necessarily imply the other. In fact, it is not difficult to show (Problem 45, Exercise 5-2) that any two mutually exclusive events A and B, with nonzero probabilities, are always dependent!

Problem 15   A single card is drawn from a standard 52-card deck. Test the events in parts A and B for independence:

(A) E = The drawn card is a red card.
F = The drawn card's number is divisible by 5 (face cards are not assigned values).

(B) G = The drawn card is a King.
H = The drawn card is a Queen.

Example 16   Using the data from Example 10, test the indicated events for independence:

(A)   Events A and R.   (B)   Events A and R'.

		Rain	**No Rain**	
		R	R'	Total
Accident	A	.025	.015	.040
No Accident	A'	.335	.625	.960
	Total	.360	.640	1.000

Solutions   (A) $P(A \cap R) = .025$
$P(A)P(R) = (.040)(.360) = .0144$
Events A and R are dependent.

(B) $P(A \cap R') = .015$
$P(A)P(R') = (.040)(.640) = .0256$
Events A and R' are dependent.

Problem 16   Referring to the table in Example 16, test for independence:

(A)   Events A' and R (B)   Events A' and R'

The notion of independence can be extended to more than two events:

Independent Set of Events

A **finite set of events** is said to be **independent** if for each subset, say $\{E_1, E_2, \ldots, E_n\}$, we have

$$P(E_1 \cap E_2 \cap \cdots \cap E_n) = P(E_1)P(E_2) \cdots P(E_n) \qquad (6)$$

As was stated earlier, in some experiments it is clear that certain events are independent (e.g., the repeated toss of a coin; the repeated roll of two dice; the repeated draw, with replacement, of an object from a set of objects; the repeated spin of a wheel; etc.) Equation (6) is a useful tool in computing probabilities related to experiments of this type.

Example 17   A space shuttle has four independent computer control systems. If the probability of failure (during flight) of any one system is .001, what is the probability of failure of all four systems?

Solution   Let E_1 = failure of system 1
E_2 = failure of system 2
E_3 = failure of system 3
E_4 = failure of system 4
then, since events E_1, E_2, E_3, and E_4 are given to be independent,

$$P(E_1 \cap E_2 \cap E_3 \cap E_4) = P(E_1)P(E_2)P(E_3)P(E_4)$$
$$= (.001)^4$$
$$= .000\ 000\ 000\ 001$$

Problem 17   A single die is rolled six times. What is the probability of getting the sequence, 1, 2, 3, 4, 5, 6?

Answers to
Matched Problems

9. (A) .5   (B) .4
10. (A) $P(R') = .640$ (B) $P(A \cap R') = .015$
    (C) $P(A|R') = \dfrac{P(A \cap R')}{P(R)} = .023$
11. $P(M \cap C) = P(M)P(C|M) = .32$
12. $\frac{2}{3}$
13. .72
14. $P(B|A) = \dfrac{P(A \cap B)}{P(A)} = \dfrac{\frac{1}{4}}{\frac{1}{2}} = \dfrac{1}{2} = P(B)$
15. (A) E and F are independent   (B) G and H are dependent
16. (A) A' and R are dependent   (B) A' and R' are dependent
17. $(\frac{1}{6})^6 \approx .000\ 021\ 4$

Exercise 5-2

A   Given the following probabilities for events in a sample space S, solve Problems 1–16 relative to these probabilities:

	A	B	C	Total
D	.10	.04	.06	.20
E	.40	.26	.14	.80
Total	.50	.30	.20	1.00

Read the following directly out of the table:

1. $P(A)$ **2.** $P(C)$ **3.** $P(D)$ **4.** $P(E)$

5. $P(A \cap D)$ **6.** $P(A \cap E)$ **7.** $P(C \cap D)$ **8.** $P(C \cap E)$

Compute the following using equation (1) and appropriate table values:

9. $P(A|D)$ **10.** $P(A|E)$ **11.** $P(C|D)$ **12.** $P(C|E)$

Test the following pairs of events for independence:

13. A and D **14.** A and E **15.** C and D **16.** C and E

17. A fair coin is tossed eight times.

  (A) What is the probability of tossing a head on the eighth toss, given that the preceding seven tosses were heads?

  (B) What is the probability of getting eight heads or eight tails?

18. A fair die is rolled five times.

  (A) What is the probability of getting a 6 on the fifth roll, given that a 6 turned up on the preceding four rolls?

  (B) What is the probability that the same number turns up every time?

19. A pointer is spun once on a circular spinner (see figure). The probability assigned to the pointer landing on a given integer (from 1 to 5) is the ratio of the area of the corresponding circular sector to the area of the whole circle:

e_i	1	2	3	4	5
p_i	.3	.1	.2	.3	.1

Given the events:

  E = The pointer lands on an even number.

  F = The pointer lands on a number less than 4.

  (A) Find $P(F|E)$.

  (B) Test events E and F for independence.

20. Repeat the preceding example with the events:

E = The pointer lands on an odd number.

F = The pointer lands on a prime number.

Compute the indicated probabilities in Problems 21 and 22 by referring to the probability tree:

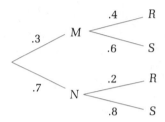

21. (A) $P(M \cap S)$ (B) $P(R)$
22. (A) $P(N \cap R)$ (B) $P(S)$

B 23. A fair coin is tossed twice. Given S = {HH, HT, TH, TT} as the sample space of equally likely sample points and given the events

E_1 = A head on the first toss

E_2 = A tail on the first toss

E_3 = A tail on the second toss

(A) Are E_1 and E_3 independent?
(B) Are E_1 and E_3 mutually exclusive?

24. For the events in Problem 23:

(A) Are E_2 and E_3 independent?
(B) Are E_2 and E_3 mutually exclusive?
(C) Are E_1 and E_2 mutually exclusive?

25. In two throws of a fair die, what is the probability that you will get an even number on each throw? An even number on the first or second throw?

26. In two throws of a fair die, what is the probability that you will get at least five points on each throw? At least five points on the first or second throw?

27. Two cards are drawn in succession from a 52-card deck. What is the probability that the first card is a club and the second card is a heart:

(A) If the cards are drawn without replacement?
(B) If the cards are drawn with replacement?

28. Two cards are drawn in succession from a 52-card deck. What is the probability that the both cards are red:

(A) If the cards are drawn without replacement?
(B) If the cards are drawn with replacement?

29. A card is drawn at random from a 52-card deck. Events G and H are:

    G = The drawn card is black.

    H = The drawn card is divisible by 3 (face cards are not valued).

    (A) Find $P(H|G)$.   (B) Test H and G for independence.

30. A card is drawn at random from a 52-card deck. Events M and N are:

    M = The drawn card is a diamond.
    N = The drawn card is even (face cards are not valued).

    (A) Find $P(N|M)$.   (B) Test M and N for independence.

31. Let A be the event that all of a family's children are the same sex and let B be the event that the family has at most one boy. Assuming the probability of having a girl is the same as the probability of having a boy (both .5), test events A and B for independence if:

    (A) The family has two children
    (B) The family has three children

32. An experiment consists of tossing n coins. Let A be the event that at least two heads turn up and B be the event that all the coins turn up the same. Test A and B for independence if:

    (A) Two coins are tossed   (B) Three coins are tossed

Problems 33–36 refer to the following experiment: Two balls are drawn in succession out of a box containing two red and five white balls.

33. Construct a probability tree for this experiment and find the probability of each of the events, $R_1 \cap R_2$, $R_1 \cap W_2$, $W_1 \cap R_2$, and $W_1 \cap W_2$, given that the first ball drawn was:

    (A) Replaced before the second draw
    (B) Not replaced before the second draw

34. Find the probability that the second ball was red, given that the first ball was:

    (A) Replaced before the second draw
    (B) Not replaced before the second draw

35. Find the probability that at least one ball was red, given that the first ball was:

    (A) Replaced before the second draw
    (B) Not replaced before the second draw

36. Find the probability that both balls were the same color, given that the first ball was:

    (A) Replaced before the second draw
    (B) Not replaced before the second draw

37. Find the probability of drawing exactly one ace if 2 cards are drawn from a 52-card deck and the first card is:

    (A) Replaced before the second card is drawn
    (B) Not replaced before the second card is drawn

38. Find the probability of drawing exactly one heart if 2 cards are drawn from a 52 card deck and the first card is:

    (A) Replaced before the second card is drawn
    (B) Not replaced before the second card is drawn

C
39. A box contains two red, three white, and four green balls. Two balls are drawn out of the box in succession without replacement. What is the probability that both balls are the same color?

40. For the experiment in Problem 39, what is the probability that no white balls are drawn?

41. An urn contains two one-dollar bills, one five-dollar bill, and one ten-dollar bill. A player draws bills one at a time without replacement from the urn until a ten-dollar bill is drawn. Then the game stops. All bills are kept by the player.

    (A) What is the probability of winning $16?
    (B) What is the probability of winning all bills in the urn?
    (C) What is the probability of the game stopping at the second draw?
    (D) What should the player pay to play the game if the game is to be fair?

42. Ann and Barbara are playing a tennis match. The first player to win two sets wins the match. For any given set, the probability that Ann wins that set is $\frac{2}{3}$. Find the probability that:

    (A) Ann wins the match
    (B) Three sets are played
    (C) The player who wins the first set goes on to win the match

43. Show that $P(A|A) = 1$, when $P(A) \neq 0$.
44. Show that $P(A|B) + P(A'|B) = 1$.
45. Show that A and B are dependent if A and B are mutually exclusive and $P(A) \neq 0$, $P(B) \neq 0$.
46. Show that $P(A|B) = 1$ if $B \subset A$ and $P(B) \neq 0$.

Applications

Business & Economics   47. *Labor relations.* In a study to determine employee voting patterns in a recent strike election, 1,000 employees were selected at random and the following tabulation was made.

| To Strike | Salary Classification | | | Total |
	Hourly (H)	Salary (S)	Salary + Bonus (B)	
Yes (Y)	400	180	20	600
No (N)	150	120	130	400
Total	550	300	150	1,000

(A) Convert this table to a probability table by dividing each entry by 1,000.

(B) What is the probability of an employee voting to strike, given the person is paid hourly?

(C) What is the probability of an employee voting to strike, given the person receives a salary plus bonus?

(D) What is the probability of an employee being on straight salary (S)? Of being on straight salary given he or she voted in favor of striking?

(E) What is the probability of an employee being paid hourly? Of being paid hourly given he or she voted in favor of striking?

(F) What is the probability of an employee being in a salary plus bonus position and voting against striking?

(G) Are events S and Y independent?

(H) Are events H and Y independent?

(I) Are events B and N independent?

48. *Quality control.* An automobile manufacturer produces 37% of its cars at plant A. If 5% of the cars manufactured at plant A have defective emission control devices, what is the probability that one of this manufacturer's cars was manufactured at plant A and has a defective emission control device?

49. *Bonus incentives.* If a salesperson has gross sales of over $300,000 in a year, he or she is eligible to play the company's bonus game: A black box contains one twenty-dollar bill, two five-dollar bills, and one one-dollar bill. Bills are drawn out of the box one at a time without replacement until a twenty-dollar bill is drawn. Then the game stops. The salesperson's bonus is 1,000 times the value of the bills drawn.

(A) What is the probability of winning a $26,000 bonus?

(B) What is the probability of winning the maximum bonus, $31,000, by drawing out all bills in the box?

(C) What is the probability of the game stopping at the third draw?

(D) If the salesperson does not like to gamble and requests the expected value of the game for a bonus, what would the bonus be?

50. *Personnel selection.* To transfer into a particular technical department, a company requires an employee to pass a screening test. A maximum of three attempts are allowed at six month intervals between trials. From past records it is found that 40% pass on the first trial; of those that fail the first trial and take the test a second time, 60% pass; and of those that fail on the second trial and take the test a third time, 20% pass. For an employee wishing to transfer:

(A)   What is the probability of passing the test on the first or second try?

(B)   What is the probability of failing on the first two trials and passing on the third?

(C)   What is the probability of failing on all three attempts?

Life Sciences   51.   *Medicine.* In order to test a new drug for adverse reactions, the drug was administered to 1,000 test subjects with the following results: 60 subjects reported that their only adverse reaction was a loss of appetite, 90 subjects reported that their only adverse reaction was a loss of sleep, and 800 students reported no adverse reactions at all.

(A)   If a randomly selected test subject suffered a loss of appetite, what is the probability that the subject also suffered a loss of sleep?

(B)   If a randomly selected test subject suffered a loss of sleep, what is the probability that the subject also suffered a loss of appetite?

(C)   If a randomly selected test subject did not suffer a loss of appetite, what is the probability that the subject suffered a loss of sleep?

(D)   If a randomly selected test subject did not suffer a loss of sleep, what is the probability that the subject suffered a loss of appetite?

52.   *Genetics.* In a study to determine frequency and dependency of color-blindness relative to females and males, 1,000 people were chosen at random and the following results were recorded:

		Female F	Male F'	Total
Color-Blind	C	2	24	26
Normal	C'	518	456	974
	Total	520	480	1,000

(A)   Convert this table to a probability table by dividing each entry by 1,000.

(B)   What is the probability that a person is a woman, given that the person is color-blind?

(C)   What is the probability that a person is color-blind, given that the person is a male?

(D)   Are the events color-blindness and male independent?

(E)   Are the events color-blindness and female independent?

Social Sciences   **53.** *Psychology.* In a study to determine the frequency and dependency of IQ ranges relative to males and females, 1,000 people were chosen at random and the following results were recorded:

		IQ			
		Below 90 (A)	90–120 (B)	Above 120 (C)	Total
Female	F	130	286	104	520
Male	F′	120	264	96	480
	Total	250	550	200	1,000

(A) Convert this table to a probability table by dividing each entry by 1,000.

(B) What is the probability of a person having an IQ below 90, given that the person is a female? A male?

(C) What is the probability of a person having an IQ above 120, given that the person is a female? A male?

(D) What is the probability of a person having an IQ below 90?

(E) What is the probability of a person having an IQ between 90 and 120? Of a person having an IQ between 90 and 120, given that the person is a male?

(F) What is the probability of a person being female and having an IQ above 120?

(G) Are any of the events A, B, or C dependent relative to F or $F′$?

54. *Voting patterns.* A survey of the residents of a precinct in a large city revealed that 55% of the residents were members of the Democratic party and that 60% of the Democratic party members voted in the last election. What is the probability that a person selected at random from the residents of this precinct is a member of the Democratic party and voted in the last election?

5-3 Bayes' Formula

In the last section we discussed the conditional probability of the occurrence of an event, given the occurrence of an earlier event (see Example 9). Now we are going to reverse the problem and try to find the probability of an earlier event conditioned on the occurrence of a later event. As you will see before the discussion is over, a number of practical problems are of this form. First, let us consider a relatively simple problem that will provide the basis for a generalization.

Example 18   One urn has three red and two white balls; a second urn has one red and three white balls. A single fair die is rolled and if 1 or 2 comes up, a ball is drawn out of the first urn; otherwise, a ball is drawn out of the second urn. If the drawn ball is red, what is the probability that it came out of the first urn? Out of the second urn?

Solution   We form a probability tree, letting U_1 represent urn 1, U_2 urn 2, R a red ball, and W a white ball. Then, on the various outcome branches we assign appropriate probabilities. For example, $P(U_1) = \frac{1}{3}$, $P(R|U_1) = \frac{3}{5}$, and so on:

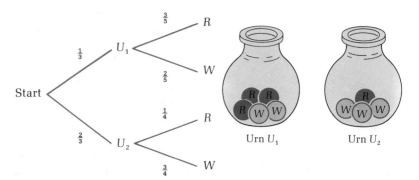

Now we are interested in finding $P(U_1|R)$; that is, the probability that the ball came out of urn 1, given the drawn ball is red. Using equation (1) from the last section, we can write

$$P(U_1|R) = \frac{P(U_1 \cap R)}{P(R)} \tag{1}$$

If we look at the tree diagram, we can see that R is at the end of two different branches; thus,

$$P(R) = P(U_1 \cap R) + P(U_2 \cap R) \tag{2}$$

After substituting equation (2) into equation (1), we get

$$P(U_1|R) = \frac{P(U_1 \cap R)}{P(U_1 \cap R) + P(U_2 \cap R)}$$

$$= \frac{P(U_1)P(R|U_1)}{P(U_1)P(R|U_1) + P(U_2)P(R|U_2)}$$

$$= \frac{P(R|U_1)P(U_1)}{P(R|U_1)P(U_1) + P(R|U_2)P(U_2)} \tag{3}$$

Don't panic! Formula (3) is a lot simpler to use than it looks. You don't need to memorize it; you simply need to understand its form relative to the probability tree above. Referring to the probability tree, we see that

$$P(R|U_1)P(U_1) = \text{Product of branch probabilities leading to } R \text{ through } U_1$$
$$\text{(we usually start at } R \text{ and work back through } U_1)$$

$$= (\tfrac{3}{5})(\tfrac{1}{3})$$

$P(R|U_2)P(U_2) =$ Product of branch probabilities leading to R through U_2
(we usually start at R and work back through U_2)

$$= \left(\tfrac{1}{4}\right)\left(\tfrac{2}{3}\right)$$

Equation (3) can now be interpreted in terms of the probability tree as follows:

$$P(U_1|R) = \frac{\text{Product of branch probabilities leading to R through } U_1}{\text{Sum of all branch products leading to R}}$$

$$= \frac{\left(\tfrac{3}{5}\right)\left(\tfrac{1}{3}\right)}{\left(\tfrac{3}{5}\right)\left(\tfrac{1}{3}\right) + \left(\tfrac{1}{4}\right)\left(\tfrac{2}{3}\right)} = \frac{6}{11} \approx .55$$

Similarly,

$$P(U_2|R) = \frac{\text{Product of branch probabilities leading to R through } U_2}{\text{Sum of all branch products leading to R}}$$

$$= \frac{\left(\tfrac{1}{4}\right)\left(\tfrac{2}{3}\right)}{\left(\tfrac{3}{5}\right)\left(\tfrac{1}{3}\right) + \left(\tfrac{1}{4}\right)\left(\tfrac{2}{3}\right)} = \frac{5}{11} \approx .45$$

[*Note:* We also could have obtained $P(U_2|R)$ by subtracting $P(U_1|R)$ from 1. Why?]

Problem 18   Repeat Example 18, but find $P(U_1|W)$ and $P(U_2|W)$.

In generalizing the results in Example 18, it is helpful to look at its structure in terms of the Venn diagram shown in Figure 10. We note that U_1 and U_2 are mutually exclusive (disjoint) and their union forms S. The following two equations can now be interpreted in terms of this diagram:

$$P(U_1|R) = \frac{P(U_1 \cap R)}{P(R)} = \frac{P(U_1 \cap R)}{P(U_1 \cap R) + P(U_2 \cap R)}$$

$$P(U_2|R) = \frac{P(U_2 \cap R)}{P(R)} = \frac{P(U_2 \cap R)}{P(U_1 \cap R) + P(U_2 \cap R)}$$

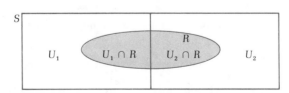

Figure 10

Look over the equations and the diagram carefully.

Of course, there is no reason to stop here. Suppose U_1, U_2, and U_3 are three mutually exclusive events whose union is the whole sample space S.

Then, for an arbitrary event E in S, with $P(E) \neq 0$, the corresponding Venn diagram looks like Figure 11, and

$$P(U_1|E) = \frac{P(U_1 \cap E)}{P(E)} = \frac{P(U_1 \cap E)}{P(U_1 \cap E) + P(U_2 \cap E) + P(U_3 \cap E)}$$

Similar results hold for U_2 and U_3.

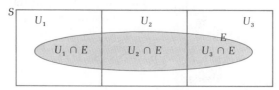

Figure 11

Reasoning in the same way, we arrive at the following famous theorem, which was first stated by the Presbyterian minister Thomas Bayes (1702–1763):

Theorem 1

Bayes' Formula

Let $U_1, U_2, \ldots, U_n$ be n mutually exclusive events whose union is the sample space S. Let E be an arbitrary event in S such that $P(E) \neq 0$. Then

$$P(U_1|E) = \frac{P(U_1 \cap E)}{P(E)}$$

$$= \frac{P(U_1 \cap E)}{P(U_1 \cap E) + P(U_2 \cap E) + \cdots + P(U_n \cap E)}$$

$$= \frac{P(E|U_1)P(E)}{P(E|U_1)P(E) + P(E|U_2)P(E) + \cdots + P(E|U_n)P(E)}$$

Similar results hold for $U_2, U_3, \ldots, U_n$.

You do not need to memorize Bayes' formula. In practice it is often easier to draw a probability tree and use:

Bayes' Formula and Probability Trees

$$P(U_1|E) = \frac{\text{Product of branch probabilities leading to } E \text{ through } U_1}{\text{Sum of all branch products leading to } E}$$

Similar results hold for $U_2, U_3, \ldots, U_n$.

Example 19   A new, inexpensive skin test is devised for detecting tuberculosis. To evaluate the test before it is put into use, a medical researcher randomly selects 1,000 people. Using precise but more expensive methods already available, it is found that 8% of the 1,000 people tested have tuberculosis. Now each of the 1,000 subjects is given the new skin test and the following results are recorded: The test indicates tuberculosis in 96% of those who have it and in 2% of those who do not. Based on these results, what is the probability of a randomly chosen person having tuberculosis, given that the skin test indicates the disease?

Solution   Now we will see the power of Bayes' formula in an important application. To start, we form a tree diagram and place appropriate probabilities on each branch:

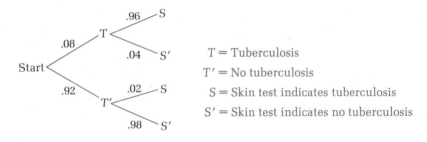

T = Tuberculosis

T' = No tuberculosis

S = Skin test indicates tuberculosis

S' = Skin test indicates no tuberculosis

We are interested in finding $P(T|S)$; that is, the probability of a person having tuberculosis given that the skin test indicates the disease. Bayes' formula for this case is

$$P(T|S) = \frac{\text{Product of branch probabilities leading to } S \text{ through } T}{\text{Sum of all branch products leading to } S}$$

Substituting appropriate values from the probability tree, we obtain

$$P(T|S) = \frac{(.08)(.96)}{(.08)(.96) + (.92)(.02)}$$

$$= .81$$

Of course,

$$P(T'|S) = .19 \qquad \text{Why?}$$

Another important question that needs to be answered is indicated in Problem 19.

Problem 19   What is the probability that a person has tuberculosis given that the test indicates no tuberculosis is present?

Example 20   A company produces 1,000 refrigerators a week at three plants. Plant A produces 350 refrigerators a week, plant B produces 250 refrigerators a week, and plant C produces 400 refrigerators a week. Production records indicate that 5% of the refrigerators produced at plant A will be defective,

3% of those produced at plant B will be defective, and 7% of those produced at plant C will be defective. All the refrigerators are shipped to a central warehouse. If a refrigerator at the warehouse is found to be defective, what is the probability that it was produced at plant A?

Solution   We begin by constructing a tree diagram:

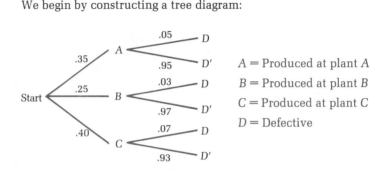

A = Produced at plant A
B = Produced at plant B
C = Produced at plant C
D = Defective

The probability that a defective refrigerator was produced at plant A is $P(A|D)$. Bayes' formula for this case is

$$P(A|D) = \frac{\text{Product of branch probabilities leading to } D \text{ through } A}{\text{Sum of all branch products leading to } D}$$

Using the values from the probability tree, we have

$$P(A|D) = \frac{(.35)(.05)}{(.35)(.05) + (.25)(.03) + (.4)(.07)}$$

$$\approx .33$$

Problem 20   In Example 20, what is the probability that a defective refrigerator in the warehouse was produced at plant B? At plant C?

Answers to   18. $P(U_1|W) = \frac{4}{19} \approx .21$; $P(U_2|W) = \frac{15}{19} \approx .79$ 19.   .004
Matched Problems   20. $P(B|D) \approx .14$; $P(C|D) \approx .53$

Exercise 5-3

A   *Find the probabilities in Problems 1–6 by referring to the following tree diagram:*

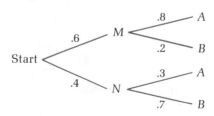

1. $P(M \cap A) = P(M)P(A|M)$
2. $P(N \cap B) = P(N)P(B|N)$
3. $P(A) = P(M \cap A) + P(N \cap A)$
4. $P(B) = P(M \cap B) + P(N \cap B)$
5. $P(M|A) = \dfrac{P(M \cap A)}{P(M \cap A) + P(N \cap A)}$
6. $P(N|B) = \dfrac{P(N \cap B)}{P(N \cap B) + P(M \cap B)}$

Find the probabilities in Problems 7–10 by referring to the following Venn diagram and using Bayes' formula (assume that the simple events in S are equally likely):

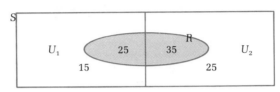

7. $P(U_1|R)$ 8. $P(U_2|R)$ 9. $P(U_1|R')$ 10. $P(U_2|R')$

B   Find the probabilities in Problems 11–16 by referring to the following tree diagram and using Bayes' formula:

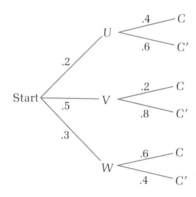

11. $P(U|C)$ 12. $P(V|C')$ 13. $P(W|C)$
14. $P(U|C')$ 15. $P(V|C)$ 16. $P(W|C')$

Find the probabilities in Problems 17–22 by referring to the following Venn diagram and using Bayes' formula (assume that the simple events in S are equally likely):

17. $P(U_1|R)$ 18. $P(U_2|R')$ 19. $P(U_3|R)$
20. $P(U_1|R')$ 21. $P(U_2|R)$ 22. $P(U_3|R')$

In Problems 23–24, use the probabilities on the tree diagram on the left to find the probability of each branch of the tree diagram on the right.

23.

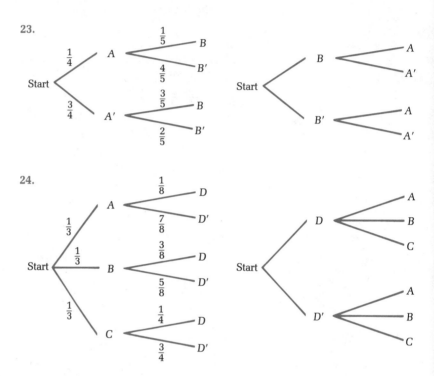

24.

One of two urns is chosen at random with one as likely to be chosen as the other. Then a ball is withdrawn from the chosen urn. Urn 1 contains one white and four red balls, and urn 2 has three white and two red balls.

25. If a white ball is drawn, what is the probability that it came from urn 1?

26. If a white ball is drawn, what is the probability that it came from urn 2?

27. If a red ball is drawn, what is the probability that it came from urn 2?

28. If a red ball is drawn, what is the probability that it came from urn 1?

An urn contains four red and five white balls. Two balls are drawn in succession without replacement.

29. If the second ball is white, what is the probability that the first ball was white?

30. If the second ball is red, what is the probability that the first ball was red?

Urn 1 contains seven red and three white balls. Urn 2 contains four red and five white balls. A ball is drawn from urn 1 and placed in urn 2. Then a ball is drawn from urn 2.

31. If the ball drawn from urn 2 is red, what is the probability that the ball drawn from urn 1 was red?

32. If the ball drawn from urn 2 is white, what is the probability that the ball drawn from urn 1 was white?

C 33. If 2 cards are drawn in succession from a 52 card deck without replacement and the second card is a heart, what is the probability that the first card is a heart?

34. A box contains ten balls numbered 1 through 10. Two balls are drawn in succession without replacement. If the second ball drawn has the number 4 on it, what is the probability that the first ball had a smaller number on it? An even number on it?

35. Show that $P(U_1|R) + P(U_1'|R) = 1$.

36. If U_1 and U_2 are two mutually exclusive events whose union is the equally likely sample space S and if E is an arbitrary event in S such that $P(E) \neq 0$, show that

$$P(U_1|E) = \frac{n(U_1 \cap E)}{n(U_1 \cap E) + n(U_2 \cap E)}$$

■

Applications

In the following applications, the word "probability" is often understood to mean "approximate empirical probability."

Business & Economics 37. *Employee screening.* The management of a company finds that 30% of the secretaries hired are unsatisfactory. The personnel director is instructed to devise a test that will improve the situation. One hundred employed secretaries are chosen at random and are given a newly constructed test. Out of these, 90% of the successful secretaries pass the test and 20% of the unsuccessful secretaries pass. Based on these results, if a person applies for a secretarial job, takes the test, and passes it, what is the probability that he or she is a good secretary? If the applicant fails the test, what is the probability that he or she is a good secretary?

38. *Employee rating.* A company has rated 75% of its employees as satisfactory and 25% as unsatisfactory. Personnel records indicate that 80% of the satisfactory workers had previous work experience, while only 40% of the unsatisfactory workers had any previous work experience. If a person with previous work experience is hired, what is the probability that this person will be a satisfactory employee? If a

person with no previous work experience is hired, what is the probability that this person will be a satisfactory employee?

39. *Manufacturing.* A manufacturer obtains clock–radios from three different subcontractors: 20% from *A*, 40% from *B*, and 40% from *C*. The defective rates for these subcontractors are 1%, 3%, and 2%, respectively. If a defective clock–radio is returned by a customer, what is the probability that it came from subcontractor *A*? From *B*? From *C*?

40. *Marketing.* A computer store sells three types of microcomputers, brand *A*, brand *B*, and brand *C*. Of the computers they sell, 60% are brand *A*, 25% are brand *B*, and 15% are brand *C*. They have found that 20% of the brand *A* computers, 15% of the brand *B* computers, and 5% of the brand *C* computers are returned for service during the warranty period. If a computer is returned for service during the warranty period, what is the probability that it is a brand *A* computer? A brand *B* computer? A brand *C* computer?

Life Sciences

41. *Cancer screening.* A new, simple test has been developed to detect a particular type of cancer. The test must be evaluated before it is put into use. A medical researcher selects a random sample of 1,000 adults and finds (by other means) that 2% have this type of cancer. Each of the 1,000 adults is given the test, and it is found that the test indicates cancer in 98% of those who have it and in 1% of those who do not. Based on these results, what is the probability of a randomly chosen person having cancer given that the test indicates cancer? Of a person having cancer given that the test does not indicate cancer?

42. *Pregnancy testing.* A new pregnancy test was given to 100 pregnant women and 100 nonpregnant women. The test indicated pregnancy in 92 of the 100 pregnant women and in 12 of the 100 nonpregnant women. If a randomly selected woman takes this test and the test indicates that she is pregnant, what is the probability that she is pregnant? If the test indicates that she is not pregnant, what is the probability that she is not pregnant?

43. *Medical research.* In a random sample of 1,000 people, it is found that 7% have a liver ailment. Of those who have a liver ailment, 40% are heavy drinkers, 50% are moderate drinkers, and 10% are nondrinkers. Of those who do not have a liver ailment, 10% are heavy drinkers, 70% are moderate drinkers, and 20% are nondrinkers. If a person is chosen at random and it is found that he or she is a heavy drinker, what is the probability of that person having a liver ailment? What is the probability for a nondrinker?

44. *Tuberculosis screening.* A test for tuberculosis was given to 1,000 subjects, 8% of whom were known to have tuberculosis. For the subjects who had tuberculosis, the test indicated tuberculosis in 90% of the subjects, was inconclusive for 7%, and indicated no tuberculosis in 3%. For the subjects who did not have tuberculosis, the test indicated tuberculosis in 5% of the subjects, was inconclusive for 10%, and indicated no tuberculosis in the remaining 85%. What is the probability of a randomly selected person having tuberculosis given that the test indicates tuberculosis? Of not having tuberculosis given that the test was inconclusive?

Social Sciences

45. *Police science.* A new lie-detector test has been devised and must be tested before it is put into use. One hundred people are selected at random, and each person draws and keeps a card from a box of 100 cards. Half the cards instruct the person to lie and the others instruct the person to tell the truth. The test indicates lying in 80% of those who lied and in 5% of those who did not. What is the probability that a randomly chosen subject will have lied given that the test indicates lying? That the subject will not have lied given that the test indicates lying?

46. *Politics.* In a given county, records show that of the registered voters, 45% are Democrats, 35% are Republicans, and 20% are independents. In an election, 70% of the Democrats, 40% of the Republicans, and 80% of the independents voted in favor of a parks and recreation bond proposal. If a registered voter chosen at random is found to have voted in favor of the bond, what is the probability that the voter is a Republican? An independent? A Democrat?

5-4 Markov Chains

In this section we are going to be interested in physical *systems* and their possible *states*. To understand what this means, consider the following examples:

1. A stock listed on the New York Stock Exchange either increases, decreases, or does not change in price each day the exchange is open. The stock can be thought of as a physical system with three possible states: increase, decrease, or no change.

2. A commuter, relative to a rapid transit system, can be thought of as a physical system with two states, a user or a nonuser.

3. A voting precinct casts a simple majority vote during each congressional election for a Republican candidate, a Democratic candidate, or a third-party candidate. The precinct, relative to all congressional elections past, present, and future, constitutes a physical system that can be thought of as being in one (and only one) of three states after each election: Republican, Democratic, or other.

If a system evolves from one state to another in such a way that we are only able to assign probabilities other than 0 or 1 to the occurrences of future states, then the progression of the system through a sequence of states is called a **stochastic process.** We will now consider a simple example of a stochastic process in detail, and out of it will arise further definitions and methodology.

A toothpaste company makes a major breakthrough in improving its product (brand A) and launches an aggressive sales campaign. After acquiring 10% of the market, the company hires a market research firm to help estimate the percentage of the market it might expect to have in the future. The research firm finds after extensive surveys that if a person uses brand A, then the probability is .8 that the person will buy it again when he or she runs out of toothpaste. On the other hand, a person using another brand will switch to brand A with a probability of .6 when he or she runs out of toothpaste. This information is conveniently represented in a **transition probability matrix:**

$$
\begin{array}{cc}
 & \text{Next state} \\
\end{array}
$$

$$
\text{Current state} \quad
\begin{array}{c}
 \\
A \\
A'
\end{array}
\begin{array}{cc}
A & A' \\
\begin{bmatrix} .8 & .2 \\ .6 & .4 \end{bmatrix}
\end{array}
\quad
\begin{array}{l}
A = \text{Uses brand } A \\
A' = \text{Uses another brand}
\end{array}
\tag{1}
$$

Each entry in the matrix is the probability of moving from a given state to another state. For example, the probability of a person who is now using brand A switching to another brand is .2, the probability of a person using another brand switching to brand A is .6, and so on.

We would like to know the probability of a randomly chosen person buying brand A now, buying it on the next purchase, buying it on the third purchase, buying it on the fourth purchase, and, in general, what happens in the long run.

Since the company now has 10% of the market, the probability of a randomly chosen person purchasing brand A (being in state A) at the start is .1 and of the person not purchasing brand A (being in state A') at the start is .9. Thus, we say that a person's **initial state** is A with probability .1 and A' with probability .9. We represent these probabilities in an **initial-state probability matrix:**

$$
\begin{array}{cc}
A & A' \\
[.1 & .9\,]
\end{array}
\tag{2}
$$

This matrix gives us the probabilities of a randomly chosen person being in state A or A' on the first purchase. The probabilities must add up to 1. (Why?)

What are the probabilities of a person being in state A or A' on the second purchase? Let us look at a probability tree:

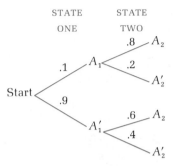

[Note: A_2 represents state A on the second purchase, A_1' represents state A' on the first purchase, and so on.]

Proceeding as in the previous sections, we can read the required probabilities directly from the tree:

$$P(A_2) = P(A_1 \cap A_2) + P(A_1' \cap A_2)$$
$$= P(A_1)P(A_2|A_1) + P(A_1')P(A_2|A_1')$$
$$= (.1)(.8) + (.9)(.6) = .62$$
$$P(A_2') = P(A_1 \cap A_2') + P(A_1' \cap A_2')$$
$$= P(A_1)P(A_2'|A_1) + P(A_1')P(A_2'|A_1')$$
$$= (.1)(.2) + (.9)(.4) = .38$$

[Note: $P(A_2) + P(A_2') = 1$, as it should.]

Thus, the **second-state matrix** is

$$\begin{matrix} A_2 & A_2' \\ [.62 & .38] \end{matrix} \tag{3}$$

This matrix gives us the probabilities of a randomly chosen person being in state A or A' on the second purchase.

Now, if you were asked to find the probabilities of a person being in state A or state A' after the tenth successive purchase, you might start to draw additional branches on the probability tree, but you would soon become discouraged—and for good reason, because for each successive purchase the number of branches doubles. By the tenth purchase there would be $2^{10} = 1,024$ branches! Fortunately, we can convert the summing of branch products to matrix multiplication. In particular, if we multiply the initial-state matrix (2) by the transition matrix (1), we will obtain the second-state matrix (3):

$$\begin{matrix} A & A' \\ [.1 & .9] \end{matrix} \begin{bmatrix} .8 & .2 \\ .6 & .4 \end{bmatrix} = [\{(.1)(.8) + (.9)(.6)\} \quad \{(.1)(.2) + (.9)(.4)\}] = \begin{matrix} A & A' \\ [.62 & .38] \end{matrix}$$

Initial state   Transition matrix   Compare with the tree computations above

As you might guess, we can get the third-state (third purchase) matrix by multiplying the second-state matrix by the transition matrix:

$$
\begin{array}{cc} A & A' \\ [.62 & .38] \end{array}
\begin{bmatrix} .8 & .2 \\ .6 & .4 \end{bmatrix}
= \begin{array}{cc} A & A' \\ [.724 & .276] \end{array}
$$

Second
state
          Transition
          matrix
                              Third
                              state

Continuing this process several more steps leads to an interesting observation:

$$
\begin{array}{cc} A & A' \\ [.724 & .276] \end{array}
\begin{bmatrix} .8 & .2 \\ .6 & .4 \end{bmatrix}
= \begin{array}{cc} A & A' \\ [.745 & .255] \end{array}
$$

Third
state
                              Fourth
                              state

$$
[.745 \quad .255]
\begin{bmatrix} .8 & .2 \\ .6 & .4 \end{bmatrix}
= [.7490 \quad .2510]
$$

Fourth
state
                              Fifth
                              state

$$
[.749 \quad .251]
\begin{bmatrix} .8 & .2 \\ .6 & .4 \end{bmatrix}
= [.7498 \quad .2502] \approx [.75 \quad .25]
$$

Fifth
state
                              Sixth
                              state

It appears that the state matrices are getting closer and closer to [.75   .25] as we proceed to higher states. Let us multiply this last matrix (the matrix the other state matrices are approaching) by the transition matrix:

$$
[.75 \quad .25]
\begin{bmatrix} .8 & .2 \\ .6 & .4 \end{bmatrix}
= [.75 \quad .25]
$$

No change occurs! The matrix [.75   .25] is called a **steady-state matrix**. If we reach this state or are very close to it, the system is said to be in **equilibrium**—further states either will not change or will not change very much. In terms of the example, this means that in the long run a person will purchase brand A with a probability of .75; that is, the company can expect to capture 75% of the market assuming the transition matrix does not change.

Does this steady-state solution to the problem depend on the initial-state matrix? The answer is no. If the company had started with only 5% of the market instead of 10%, the initial-state matrix would be

$$
\begin{array}{cc} A & A' \\ [.05 & .95] \end{array}
$$

Proceeding as above (a good exercise for the reader), you will find that the state matrices will still approach [.75   .25] as you go to higher states.

In general, Q is a **steady-state matrix** relative to the transition matrix P if the elements of Q are nonnegative and have a sum of 1 (they represent a probability distribution for the possible states) and if, starting with an arbitrary initial-state matrix (probabilities must add up to 1), the future state matrices can be made as close to Q as we wish by going to high enough states. The system approaches an equilibrium state as the states approach Q. This is why Q is called the steady-state matrix.

The steady-state matrix is important in many applications. If it exists, it tells how a stochastic process finally settles down after many states or trials.

How do we know when Q exists? And if Q exists, how can we find it? It can be proved that if P is **regular** (some power of P has only positive elements), then a steady-state matrix Q exists and satisfies

$$QP = Q \tag{4}$$

We can find the steady-state matrix Q directly (if it exists), by solving the matrix equation (4) for Q, given a regular transition matrix P. Let us do this for the toothpaste example discussed above. (Note that P is regular so that Q exists.) Let

$$Q = [m \quad n]$$

and write

$$[m \quad n] \begin{bmatrix} .8 & .2 \\ .6 & .4 \end{bmatrix} = [m \quad n]$$

After multiplying the left side, we obtain

$$[(.8m + .6n) \quad (.2m + .4n)] = [m \quad n]$$

which is equivalent to the system

$$.8m + .6n = m \quad \text{or} \quad -.2m + .6n = 0$$
$$.2m + .4n = n \qquad\qquad .2m - .6n = 0$$

In addition, since $[m \quad n]$ is a state (probability) matrix,

$$m + n = 1$$

We now have a system of three equations and two unknowns:

$$m + n = 1$$
$$-.2m + .6n = 0$$
$$.2m - .6n = 0$$

This system can be solved by using matrix methods or elimination to obtain

$$m = .75 \quad \text{and} \quad n = .25$$

Thus,

$$Q = [.75 \quad .25]$$

is the steady-state solution, which means that after a sufficient number of successive purchases, a person will choose brand A with a probability very close to .75; that is, the company will have close to 75% of the market in the long run (assuming the transition matrix P does not change).

The sequence of trials with the constant transition matrix P described above is a special kind of stochastic process called a *Markov chain* or *process*. In general, a **Markov chain** is a sequence of experiments, trials, or observations such that the probabilities for the next state are completely determined by the present state. In short, a Markov process has no memory. Andrei Markov (1856–1922) was a prominent Russian mathematician who is credited with supplying much of the foundation work in stochastic processes.

A **state matrix** for a Markov chain is a matrix of the form $[p_1 \quad p_2 \quad \cdots \quad p_n]$, where each entry indicates the probability of a system being in the state corresponding to the position of the entry and

$$p_1 + p_2 + \cdots + p_n = 1$$

A **transition matrix** for a Markov chain is a square matrix such that each entry indicates the probability of a system moving from a given state to another state on the next observation or trial. The sum of the entries in each row must be 1. (Why?) A transition matrix for a Markov chain is **regular** if some power of the matrix has only positive elements. All of the transition matrices we consider will be regular and, consequently, will have steady-state matrices.

Example 21   An insurance company found in a particular community (on the average over a ten-year period) that 20% of the drivers involved in an accident one year were also involved in an accident the following year, while only 10% of the drivers not involved in an accident one year were involved in an accident the following year. Use these percentages as approximate empirical probabilities for the following:

(A) Find the transition matrix.

(B) If 8% of the drivers in the community are involved in an accident this year, what is the probability that a driver chosen at random from the community will be involved in an accident next year? Year after next?

(C) Find the steady-state solution.

Solutions   (A)

$$\begin{array}{c} & \text{Next year} \\ & \begin{array}{cc} A & A' \end{array} \quad A = \text{accident} \\ \begin{array}{c} \text{This} \\ \text{year} \end{array} \begin{array}{c} A \\ A' \end{array} \left[\begin{array}{cc} .2 & .8 \\ .1 & .9 \end{array} \right] \end{array}$$

(B) The initial state matrix is

$$A \quad A'$$
$$[.08 \quad .92]$$

Thus,

$$A \quad A' \quad\quad\quad\quad A \quad A'$$
$$[.08 \quad .92] \begin{bmatrix} .2 & .8 \\ .1 & .9 \end{bmatrix} = [.108 \quad .892]$$

This year   Next year

$$[.108 \quad .892] \begin{bmatrix} .2 & .8 \\ .1 & .9 \end{bmatrix} = [.1108 \quad .8892]$$

Next year   Year after next

The probability of a driver chosen at random from the community having an accident next year is .108 and having an accident year after next is .1108 (that is, it is expected that 10.8% of the drivers in the community will have an accident next year and 11.08% will have an accident the year after).

(C) To find the steady-state solution, we solve the system

$$[m \quad n] \begin{bmatrix} .2 & .8 \\ .1 & .9 \end{bmatrix} = [m \quad n] \quad\quad \text{and} \quad\quad m + n = 1$$

which is equivalent to

$$.2m + .1n = m \quad\quad \text{or} \quad\quad -.8m + .1n = 0$$
$$.8m + .9n = n \quad\quad\quad\quad\quad .8m - .1n = 0$$
$$m + \; n = 1 \quad\quad\quad\quad\quad m + \; n = 1$$

Solving the system, we obtain

$$m \approx .111 \quad\quad \text{and} \quad\quad n \approx .889$$

The steady-state solution is approximately [.111 .889], which means, in the long run, assuming that the transition matrix does not change, about 11% of the drivers in the community will have an accident during any given year.

Problem 21 Repeat Example 21 assuming the insurance company found that 12% of the drivers involved in an accident one year were also involved in an accident the following year, while only 5% of the drivers not involved in an accident one year were involved in an accident the following year.

Answers to Matched Problems

21. (A)

		Next year	
		A	A'
This year	A	.12	.88
	A'	.05	.95

(B) Next year: .0556
Year after next: .053892

(C) Approximately
[.054 .946]

Exercise 5-4

A   *The transition matrix for a Markov process is*

State

$$
\begin{array}{c}
 & \begin{array}{cc} A & B \end{array} \\
\text{State} \quad \begin{array}{c} A \\ B \end{array} & \begin{bmatrix} .8 & .2 \\ .4 & .6 \end{bmatrix} = P
\end{array}
$$

and four initial-state matrices are $M = [1 \quad 0]$, $N = [0 \quad 1]$, $R = [.5 \quad .5]$, and $T = [.3 \quad .7]$. Perform each of the indicated matrix multiplications.

1. *MP, and interpret with the aid of a tree diagram.*
2. *NP, and interpret with the aid of a tree diagram.*
3. *(MP)P, and explain what it represents.*
4. *(NP)P, and explain what it represents.*
5. *RP, and interpret with the aid of a tree diagram.*
6. *TP, and interpret with the aid of a tree diagram.*
7. *(RP)P, and explain what it represents.*
8. *(TP)P, and explain what it represents.*

B   9. Find the values of a, b, and c that will make the following matrix a transition matrix for a Markov chain:

$$
P = \begin{bmatrix} .2 & a & .3 \\ b & .7 & .1 \\ 0 & 0 & c \end{bmatrix}
$$

10. Explain why the following matrix cannot be a transition matrix for a Markov chain (three reasons):

$$
\begin{bmatrix} .6 & .4 & .2 \\ -.2 & 0 & 1 \end{bmatrix}
$$

Find the steady-state matrix for each transition matrix.

11. $\begin{bmatrix} .2 & .8 \\ .7 & .3 \end{bmatrix}$ 12. $\begin{bmatrix} .6 & .4 \\ .2 & .8 \end{bmatrix}$ 13. $\begin{bmatrix} .5 & .5 \\ .3 & .7 \end{bmatrix}$ 14. $\begin{bmatrix} .3 & .7 \\ .6 & .4 \end{bmatrix}$

C   *Find the steady-state matrix for each transition matrix.*

15. $\begin{bmatrix} .5 & .5 & 0 \\ .25 & .5 & .25 \\ 0 & .5 & .5 \end{bmatrix}$ 16. $\begin{bmatrix} .4 & .6 & 0 \\ .3 & .2 & .5 \\ 0 & .6 & .4 \end{bmatrix}$

Applications

Business & Economics

17. *Scheduling.* An outdoor restaurant in a summer resort only closes on days that it rains. From past records it is found that from May through September, when it rains one day, then the probability of rain for the next day is .4; when it does not rain one day, then the probability of rain the next day is .06.

(A) Write the appropriate transition matrix.
(B) If it rains on Thursday, what is the probability that the restaurant will be closed on Saturday? On Sunday?
(C) Find the steady-state solution.
(D) What is the expected percentage of time the restaurant will be closed during the summer?

18. *Scheduling.* Repeat the preceding problem if the probability of rain following a rainy day is .6 and the probability of rain following a nonrainy day is .1.

19. *Advertising.* A vigorous television advertising campaign is conducted during the football season to promote a well-known brand X shaving cream. For each of several weeks, a survey is made and it is found that each week 80% of those using brand X continue to use it and 20% switch. It is also found that of those not using brand X, 20% switch to brand X while the other 80% continue using another brand.

(A) Write the transition matrix, assuming the transition percentages continue to hold for succeeding weeks.
(B) If 20% of the people are using brand X at the start of the advertising campaign, what percentage will be using brand X one week later? Two weeks later?
(C) What portion of the market will be using brand X near the end of the season, assuming the transition matrix remains the same? (Find the steady-state matrix.)

20. *Car rental.* A car rental agency has rental and return facilities at both Kennedy and LaGuardia airports, two of the principal airports in the New York City area. Assume a car rental at either airport must be returned to one or the other airport. If a car is rented at LaGuardia, the probability that it will be returned there is .8; if a car is rented at Kennedy, the probability that it will be returned there is .7. Assume the company rents all of its 100 cars each day and each car is rented (and returned) only once a day. If we start with 50 cars at each airport:

(A) What is the expected distribution the next day?
(B) What is the expected distribution 2 days later?
(C) What is the expected steady-state distribution?

Life Sciences

21. *Genetics.* A given plant species has red, pink, or white flowers according to the genotypes RR, RW, and WW, respectively. If each of these genotypes is crossed with a pink-flowering plant (genotype RW), then the transition matrix is

Next generation

		Red	Pink	White
This generation	Red	.5	.5	0
	Pink	.25	.5	.25
	White	0	.5	.5

Assuming the plants of each generation are crossed only with pink plants to produce the next generation, show that regardless of the makeup of the first generation, the genotype composition will eventually stabilize at 25% red, 50% pink, and 25% white. (Find the steady-state matrix.)

22. *Gene mutation.* Suppose a gene in a chromosome is of type A or type B. Assume that the probability that a gene of type A will mutate to type B in one generation is 10^{-4} and that a gene of type B will mutate to type A is 10^{-6}.

(A) What is the transition matrix?

(B) After many generations, what is the probability that the gene will be of type A? Of type B? (Find the steady-state matrix.)

Social Sciences

23. *Rapid transit.* A new rapid transit system has just started operating. In the first month of operation, it is found that 25% of the commuters are using the system, while 75% still travel by automobile. The following transition matrix was determined from records of other rapid transit systems:

Next month

		Rapid transit	Automobile
Current month	Rapid transit	.8	.2
	Automobile	.3	.7

(A) What is the initial-state matrix?

(B) What percentage of the commuters will be using the new system after one month? After two months?

(C) Find the percentage of commuters using each type of transportation after it has been in service for a long time.

24. *Politics—filibuster.* The Senate is in the middle of a floor debate and a filibuster is threatened. Senator Hanks, who is still vacillating, has a probability of .1 of changing his mind during the next five minutes. If this pattern continues for each five minutes that the debate continues, and if a 24 hour filibuster takes place before a vote is taken, what is the probability that Senator Hanks will cast a yes vote? A no vote?

(A) First, complete the following transition matrix:

Next 5 minutes

$$
\begin{array}{c}
\text{Current} \\
\text{5 minutes}
\end{array}
\begin{array}{c}
\\
\text{Yes} \\
\text{No}
\end{array}
\begin{array}{cc}
\text{Yes} & \text{No} \\
\begin{bmatrix} .9 & .1 \\ & \end{bmatrix}
\end{array}
$$

(B) Find the steady-state matrix and answer the two questions.

(C) What is the steady-state matrix if the probability of Senator Hanks changing his mind (.1) is replaced with an arbitrary probability p?

5-5 Chapter Review

Important Terms and Symbols

5-1 *Union, intersection, and complement of events; odds.* Event A **or** event B, event A **and** event B, mutually exclusive, complement of an event, odds, $A \cup B$, $A \cap B$, $P(A \cup B) = P(A) + P(B) - P(A \cap B)$, $P(A \cup B) = P(A) + P(B)$ if $A \cap B = \varnothing$, A', $P(A') = 1 - P(A)$, $P(E)/P(E')$ (odds for E)

5-2 *Conditional probability, independent events, and intersection.* Conditional probability of A given B, independent events, dependent events,

$$P(A|B) = \frac{P(A \cap B)}{P(B)} \quad \text{when} \quad P(B) \neq 0$$

$P(A \cap B) = P(A)P(B|A)$, $\qquad P(A \cap B) = P(A)P(B)$ if and only if A and B are independent

5-3 *Bayes' formula.*

$$P(U_1|E) = \frac{P(E|U_1)P(E)}{P(E|U_1)P(E) + P(E|U_2)P(E) + \cdots + P(E|U_n)P(E)}$$

$$= \frac{\text{Product of branch probabilities leading to } E \text{ through } U_1}{\text{Sum of all branch products leading to } E}$$

Similar results hold for $U_2, U_3, \ldots, U_n$.

5-4 *Markov chains.* Stochastic process, transition probability matrix, initial state, initial-state matrix, second-state matrix, equilibrium, steady-state matrix, regular transition matrix, Markov chain, transition matrix for a Markov chain, state matrix for a Markov chain

Exercise 5-5 Chapter Review

Work through all the problems in this chapter review and check your answers in the back of the book. (Answers to all review problems are there.) Where weaknesses show up, review appropriate sections in the text.

A

1. If A and B are events in a sample space S and $P(A) = .3$, $P(B) = .4$, and $P(A \cap B) = .1$, find:

   (A) $P(A')$ (B) $P(A \cup B)$

2. A spinner lands on R with probability .3, on G with probability .5, and on B with probability .2. Find the probability and odds for the spinner landing on either R or G.

3. If in repeated rolls of two fair dice the odds for rolling an 8 before rolling a 7 are 5 to 6, then what is the probability of rolling an 8 before rolling a 7?

Answer Problems 4–12 using the following table of probabilities:

	X	Y	Z	Total
S	.10	.25	.15	.50
T	.05	.20	.02	.27
R	.05	.15	.03	.23
Total	.20	.60	.20	1.00

4. Find $P(T)$.
6. Find $P(T \cap Z)$.
8. Find $P(R|Z)$.
10. Find $P(T|Z)$.
12. Are S and X independent?

5. Find $P(Z)$.
7. Find $P(R \cap Z)$.
9. Find $P(Z|R)$.
11. Are T and Z independent?

Answer Problems 13–20 using the following probability tree:

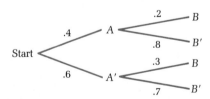

13. $P(A)$
17. $P(A' \cap B)$

14. $P(B|A)$
18. $P(B)$

15. $P(B|A')$
19. $P(A|B)$

16. $P(A \cap B)$
20. $P(A|B')$

21. Multiply: $[.3 \quad .7] \begin{bmatrix} .2 & .8 \\ .7 & .3 \end{bmatrix}$

22. Find the values of a, b, and c that will make the following matrix a transition matrix for a Markov chain:

$$T = \begin{bmatrix} .7 & .3 & a \\ .2 & b & .2 \\ 0 & c & .9 \end{bmatrix}$$

B 23. In a single draw from a 52-card deck, what is the probability and odds for drawing:

(A) A jack or a queen?   (B) A jack or a spade?
(C) A card other than an ace?

24. (A) What are the odds for rolling a sum of 5 on the single roll of two fair dice?
(B) If you bet \$1 that a sum of 5 will turn up, what should the house pay (and return your \$1 bet) for the game to be fair?

25. A pair of dice are rolled. The sample space is chosen as the set of all ordered pairs of integers taken from {1, 2, 3, 4, 5, 6}. What is the event A that corresponds to the sum being divisible by 4? What is the event B that corresponds to the sum being divisible by 6? What are $P(A)$, $P(B)$, $P(A \cap B)$, and $P(A \cup B)$?

26. A pointer is spun on a circular spinner. The probabilities of the pointer landing on the integers from 1 to 5 are:

e_i	1	2	3	4	5
p_i	.2	.1	.3	.3	.1

(A) What is the probability of the pointer landing on an odd number?
(B) What is the probability of the pointer landing on a number less than 4, given that it landed on an odd number?

27. A card is drawn at random from a 52-card deck. If E is the event "the drawn card is red" and F is the event "the drawn card is an ace," then

(A) Find $P(F|E)$.   (B) Test E and F for independence.

In Problems 28–32, urn U_1 contains two white balls and three red balls; urn U_2 contains two white balls and one red ball.

28. Two balls are drawn out of urn U_1 in succession. What is the probability of drawing a white ball followed by a red ball if the first ball is:

(A) Replaced?   (B) Not replaced?

29. Which of the two parts in Problem 28 involve dependent events?

30. In Problem 28, what is the expected number of red balls if the first ball is:

    (A) Replaced?   (B) Not replaced?

31. An urn is selected at random by flipping a fair coin; then a ball is drawn from the urn. Compute:

    (A) $P(R|U_1)$ (B) $P(R|U_2)$ (C) $P(R)$
    (D) $P(U_1|R)$ (E) $P(U_2|W)$ (F) $P(U_1 \cap R)$

32. In Problem 31, are selecting urn U_1 and drawing a red ball independent events?

33. What is the probability that a number selected at random from the first 200 positive integers is (exactly) divisible by 3 or 5?

34. Three integers are selected at random, without replacement, from the first thirty positive integers. What is the probability that there is at least one number divisible by 4 among the three drawn?

C *Two cards are drawn in succession without replacement from a 52-card deck. In Problems 35 and 36, compute the indicated probabilities.*

35. The second card is a heart given the first card is a heart.
36. The first card is a heart given the second card is a heart.
37. Three white balls and one black ball are placed in a box. Balls are drawn in succession without replacement until a black ball is drawn, and then the game is over. You win if the black ball is drawn on the fourth draw.

    (A) What are the probability and odds for winning?
    (B) If you bet $1, what should the house pay you for winning (and return your $1 bet) if the game is to be fair?

38. If each of five people is asked to identify his or her favorite book from a list of ten best-sellers, what is the probability that at least two of them identify the same book?

◼︎

Applications

39. *Quality control.* A shipment of thirty parts, including five that are defective, are sent to an assembly plant. The quality control division of the plant selects ten at random for testing and rejects the whole shipment if one or more in the sample are found defective. What is the probability that the shipment will be rejected?

40. *Product switching.* A company's brand (X) has 20% of the market. A market research firm finds that if a person uses brand X, the probability is .6 that he or she will buy it the next time. On the other hand, if a person does not use X (represented by X'), the probability is .5 that he or she will switch to X next time.

(A) Write the transition probability matrix.

(B) Write the initial-state matrix.

(C) Find the second-state matrix.

(D) Find the steady-state matrix.

(E) Approximately what percentage of the market will brand X have in the long run if the transition matrix does not change?

41. *Market research.* A market research firm has determined that 40% of the people in a certain area have seen the advertising for a new product and that 85% of those who have seen the advertising have purchased the product. What is the probability that a person in this area has seen the advertising and purchased the product?

42. *Medicine — cardiogram test.* By testing a large number of individuals, it has been determined that 82% of the population have normal hearts, 11% have some minor heart problems, and 7% have severe heart problems. Ninety-five percent of the persons with normal hearts, 30% of those with minor problems, and 5% of those with severe problems will pass a cardiogram test. What is the probability that a person who passes the cardiogram test has a normal heart?

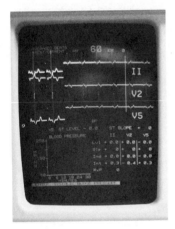

43. *Genetics.* Six men in 100 and one woman in 100 are color-blind. A person is selected at random and is found to be color-blind. What is the probability that this person is a man? (Assume the total population contains the same number of women as men.)

44. *Politics (Markov chain problem).* Assume that the probabilities that a child of conservative parents will be conservative is .70 and that a child of liberal parents will be conservative is .20. Also assume that conservatives marry conservatives and liberals marry liberals.

(A) What is the probability that a conservative couple will have a liberal grandchild?

(B) What is the probability that a conservative couple will have a liberal great-grandchild?

(C) What percentage of the population will eventually be liberal under these assumptions?

Data Description and Probability Distributions

CHAPTER 6	Contents

In this chapter we will take a look at ways of describing data sets using graphs, tables, averages, and so on. In addition, we will develop the idea of probability distributions associated with both actual and theoretical data sets.

6-1   Graphing Qualitative Data

- Bar Graphs
- Broken-Line Graphs
- Pie Graphs

Data are generally of either a **qualitative** nature or a **quantitative** nature. For example, if we were interested in the population size for each country in the world, every person would be assigned to a country (qualitative category) and counted. On the other hand, if we were interested in the number of people in the world in various height ranges (quantitative categories), we would measure the height of every person and assign him or her to an appropriate height (numerical) category.

In this section we will look at some of the techniques used to graph qualitative data, and in the next section we will consider quantitative data.

■ Bar Graphs

Bar graphs are widely used because of their ease of construction and their effectiveness as a visual aid in comparing and interpreting sets of data. Consider the data in Tables 1 and 2. Bar graphs are well suited to describe these data sets. Vertical bars are usually used for time series, such as the data in Table 1. Horizontal bars are generally used for the type of data contained in Table 2 because of the ease of labeling categories. To increase clarity, a space of one-half the width of a bar is left between bars. Bar graphs for Tables 1 and 2 are illustrated in Figures 1 and 2.

Table 1

Gross National Product

Year	Billions of 1975 Dollars, United States
1960	$ 500
1965	700
1970	1,000
1975	1,400

Table 2

Gross National Product

Country or Region	Billions of Dollars, 1975
United States	$1,400
European community	1,200
Japan	450
Canada	200

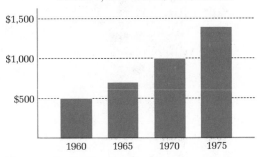

GROSS NATIONAL PRODUCT
Billions of 1975 dollars, United States

Figure 1 Vertical bar graph

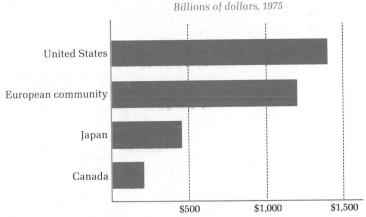

GROSS NATIONAL PRODUCT
Billions of dollars, 1975

Figure 2 Horizontal bar graph

Remember, graphs are visual aids and as such should be prepared with care. The object is to provide a viewer with the maximum amount of information, while minimizing the effort required to obtain the information. Two additional variations on bar graphs are illustrated in Figures 3 and 4 on the next page.

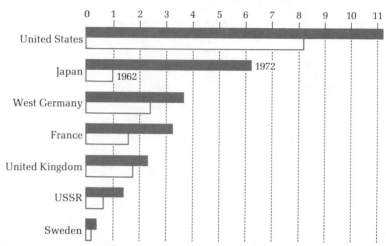

Figure 3 Double bar graph

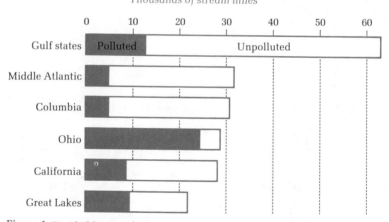

Figure 4 Divided bar graph

■ Broken-Line Graphs

A **broken-line graph** can be obtained from a vertical bar graph by joining the midpoints of the tops of consecutive bars with straight lines. For example, using Figure 1 we obtain the broken-line graph in Figure 5.

Broken-line graphs are particularly useful when we want to emphasize the change in one or more variables relative to time. Figures 6 and 7 illustrate two additional variations of broken-line graphs.

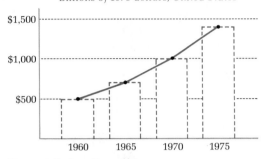

Figure 5 Broken-line graph

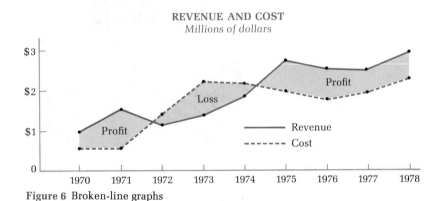

Figure 6 Broken-line graphs

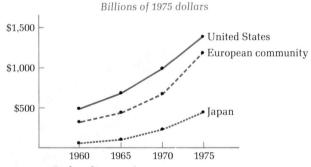

Figure 7 Broken-line graphs

■ Pie Graphs

A **pie graph** is generally used to show how a whole is divided among several categories. The amount going to each category is expressed as a percentage, and then a circle is divided into segments (pieces of pie) proportional to the percentages of each category. The central angle of a segment is the percentage of 360° corresponding to the percentage of a matching category. (See Figs. 8 and 9.) In constructing pie graphs, we use relatively few categories, arrange the segments in ascending or descending order of size around the circle, and label each part clearly.

HOUSEHOLD OWNERSHIP OF CARS, 1972
66.5 million households

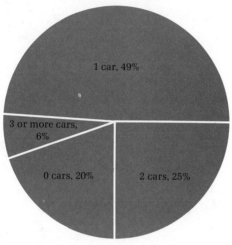

Figure 8

VOTING DISTRIBUTION, 1974
Voting-age population

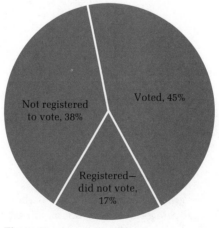

Figure 9

Exercise 6-1

Applications

Business & Economics

1. Graph the data in the following table using a bar graph:

Percentage of Civilian Labor Force Aged 18–64 with One or More Years of College

1940	1950	1960	1970
12%	16%	20%	27%

2. Graph the data in the following table using a double bar graph (see Fig. 3):

Country	Fatalities per Million Miles of Automobile Travel	
	1970	1971
Belgium	26	20
France	16	17
Japan	16	13
Germany	12	11
United Kingdom	6	7
United States	5	5

3. Graph the data in the following table using a broken-line graph for each country (see Fig. 7):

Country	Unemployment Rate				
	1971	1972	1973	1974	1975
United States	5.9%	5.7%	4.9%	5.0%	8.2%
Germany	0.9	1.0	1.2	2.0	4.5
Japan	1.2	1.2	1.1	1.1	2.0

4. Graph the data in the following table using a pie graph:

Percentage of Households in 1972 Owning Cars

0 cars	1 car	2 cars	3 or more cars
20%	49%	25%	6%

Life Sciences   5. Graph the data in the following table using a bar graph:

Year	Air Pollution Emissions in United States Millions of Tons
1940	160
1950	190
1960	220
1970	270

6. Graph the data in the following table using a double bar graph (see Fig. 3):

Year	World Population (Billions) Developed Countries	Undeveloped Countries
1950	0.8	1.8
1975	1.2	2.9
2000	1.4	5.2

7. Graph the data in Problem 5 using a broken-line graph.
8. Graph the data in the following table using a pie graph:

Source	Percentage of Air Pollution Emissions, 1970
Transportation	55%
Stationary fuel use	17
Industrial processes	13
Solid waste disposal	4
Miscellaneous	11
	100%

Social Sciences   9. Graph the data in the following table using a bar graph:

Country	Immigration to the United States, 1972
Mexico	62,000
Philippines	25,000
Italy	21,000
China	21,000
Cuba	19,000
Great Britain	9,000
Germany	6,000

10. Graph the data in the following table using a double bar graph (see Fig. 3):

| Country | Women in Work Force Aged 15–69 | |
	1950	1970
United States	37%	48%
Canada	33	43
Finland	57	58
England	48	49
France	41	40

11. Graph the data in the following table using a broken-line graph:

Year	Illegitimate Births per 1,000 Live Births in United States
1940	38
1945	42
1950	40
1955	46
1960	52
1965	77
1970	100

12. Graph the data in the following table using one pie graph for males and one pie graph for females:

| Marital Status | Youths Aged 18–24, 1970 | |
	Male	Female
Married	32%	50%
Single	68	50
	100%	100%

6-2 Graphing Quantitative Data

- Frequency Distributions
- Histograms
- Frequency Polygon
- Cumulative Frequency Table and Polygon

Sets of data that are numerical in nature—bond yields, price–earnings ratios, weights, ages, test scores, and so on—are called *quantitative data.*

In this section we will consider how large sets of quantitative data can be made more comprehensible through special tables and graphs.

■ Frequency Distributions

A random sample of 100 people was taken from the entering freshman class at a large university, and their Scholastic Aptitude Test scores in mathematics (SAT-M) were recorded (see Table 3). The mass of raw data in Table 3 certainly does not elicit much interest or exhibit much useful information. The data must be organized in some way so that it is comprehensible. This is generally done by constructing a **frequency table.** We choose five to twenty intervals of convenient length to cover the data range—the more data, the greater the number of intervals—and tally the data relative to these intervals. The **data range** in Table 3 is $787 - 340 = 447$ (found by subtracting the smallest value in the data from the largest). If we choose ten intervals, each of length 50, we will be able to cover all the scores. Table 4 shows the result of this type of tally.

Table 3 Scholastic Aptitude Test Scores (Mathematics) of 100 Entering Freshmen

762	451	602	440	570	553	367	520	454	653
433	508	520	603	532	673	480	592	565	662
712	415	595	580	643	542	470	743	608	503
566	493	635	780	537	622	463	613	502	577
618	581	644	605	588	695	517	537	552	682
340	537	370	745	605	673	487	412	613	470
548	627	576	637	787	507	566	628	676	750
442	591	735	523	518	612	589	648	662	512
663	588	627	584	672	533	738	455	512	622
544	462	730	576	588	705	695	541	537	563

At first it might seem appropriate to start at 300 and form the class intervals: 300–350, 350–400, 400–450, and so on. But if we do this, where will we place 350 or 400? We could, of course, adopt a convention of placing a score falling on an upper boundary of a class in the next higher class (and some people do exactly this); however, to avoid confusion, we will always use one decimal place more for class boundaries than appears in the raw data. Thus, in this case, we chose the class intervals 299.5–349.5, 349.5–399.5, and so on, so that each score could be assigned to one and only one class interval.

The number of measurements that fall within a given class interval is called the **class frequency,** and the set of all such frequencies associated with their corresponding classes is called a **frequency distribution.** Thus, Table 4 represents a frequency distribution of the set of raw scores in Table 3. If we divide each frequency by the total number of items in the original

Table 4 Frequency Table

Class Interval	Tally	Frequency	Relative Frequency
299.5 – 349.5	|	1	.01
349.5 – 399.5	||	2	.02
399.5 – 449.5	⊬⊬⊬	5	.05
449.5 – 499.5	⊬⊬⊬ ⊬⊬⊬	10	.10
499.5 – 549.5	⊬⊬⊬ ⊬⊬⊬ ⊬⊬⊬ ⊬⊬⊬ |	21	.21
549.5 – 599.5	⊬⊬⊬ ⊬⊬⊬ ⊬⊬⊬ ⊬⊬⊬	20	.20
599.5 – 649.5	⊬⊬⊬ ⊬⊬⊬ ⊬⊬⊬ ||||	19	.19
649.5 – 699.5	⊬⊬⊬ ⊬⊬⊬ |	11	.11
699.5 – 749.5	⊬⊬⊬ ||	7	.07
749.5 – 799.5	||||	4	.04
		100	1.00

data set (in our case 100), we obtain the **relative frequency** of the data falling in each class interval, that is, the percentage of the whole that falls in each class interval (see the last column in Table 4).

The relative frequencies can also be interpreted as probabilities associated with the experiment:

A score is drawn at random out of the 100 in the sample

An appropriate sample space for this experiment would be the set of simple outcomes

e_1 = A score falls in the first class interval

e_2 = A score falls in the second class interval

.

.

.

e_{10} = A score falls in the tenth class interval

The set of relative frequencies interpreted as indicated is called a **probability distribution.**

Example 1 Referring to the probability distribution just described and Table 4, determine the probability that:

(A) A randomly drawn score is between 499.5 and 549.5

(B) A randomly drawn score is between 449.5 and 649.5

Solutions (A) Since the relative frequency associated with the class interval 499.5 – 549.5 is .21, the probability that a randomly drawn score (from the sample of 100) falls in this interval is .21.

(B) Since a score falling in the interval 449.5 – 649.5 is a compound event, we simply add the probabilities for the simple events whose union is this compound event. Thus, we add the probabilities corresponding to each class interval from 449.5 to 649.5 to obtain

$$.10 + .21 + .20 + .19 = .70$$

Problem 1 Repeat Example 1 for the following intervals:

(A) 649.5–699.5   (B) 299.5–499.5

Now, of course, what we are really interested in is whether the probability distribution for the sample of 100 SAT-M scores has anything to do with the total population of entering freshmen in the university in question. This is a problem for the important branch of mathematics called *statistics*, which deals with the process of making judgments about a total population based on random samples drawn from that population (recall our discussion in Section 4-3). Our studies in probability play an important role in this inferential process. However, we will not go into inferential statistics here. Intuitively, we would expect that the closer the sample size is to the total population, the more closely the probability distribution for the sample will approximate that for the total population (see the law of large numbers in Section 4-3). That is about all we can say at the moment.

■ Histograms

A **histogram** is a special kind of vertical bar graph. In fact, if you rotate Table 4 counterclockwise 90°, the tally marks in the table take on the appearance of a bar graph. Histograms have no space between the bars, class boundaries are located on the horizontal axis, and frequencies are

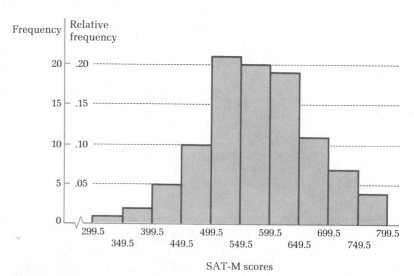

Figure 10 Histogram

associated with the vertical axis. Figure 10 is a histogram for the frequency distribution in Table 4. Note that we have included both frequencies and relative frequencies on the vertical scale. You can include either one or the other, or both, depending on what needs to be emphasized. The histogram is the most common graphical representation of frequency distributions.

■ Frequency Polygon

A **frequency polygon** is a broken-line graph where successive midpoints of the tops of the bars in a histogram are joined by straight lines. To draw a frequency polygon for a frequency distribution, you do not need to draw a histogram first; you can just locate the midpoints and join them with straight lines. Figure 11 is a frequency polygon for the frequency distribu-

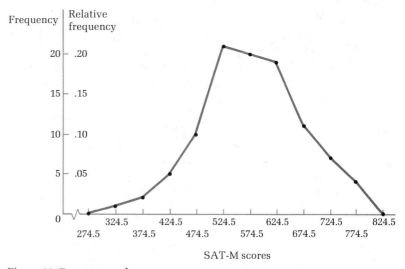

Figure 11 Frequency polygon

tion in Table 4. If the amount of data becomes very large and we substantially increase the number of classes, the frequency polygon will take on the appearance of a smooth curve called a **frequency curve.**

■ Cumulative Frequency Table and Polygon

If we are interested in how many or what percentage of a total sample lies above or below a particular measurement, a **cumulative frequency table** and **polygon** are useful. Using the frequency distribution in Table 4, we accumulate the frequencies by starting with the first class and adding frequencies as we move down the column. The results are shown in Table 5. (How is the last column formed?)

Table 5 Cumulative Frequency Distribution

Class Interval	Frequency	Cumulative Frequency	Relative Cumulative Frequency
299.5 – 349.5	1	1	.01
349.5 – 399.5	2	3	.03
399.5 – 449.5	5	8	.08
449.5 – 499.5	10	18	.18
499.5 – 549.5	21	39	.39
549.5 – 599.5	20	59	.59
599.5 – 649.5	19	78	.78
649.5 – 699.5	11	89	.89
699.5 – 749.5	7	96	.96
749.5 – 799.5	4	100	1.00

To form a *cumulative frequency polygon*, or **ogive** as it is also called, the cumulative frequency is plotted over the upper boundary of the corresponding class. Figure 12 is the cumulative frequency polygon for the cumulative frequency distribution in Table 5. Notice that we can easily see that 78% of the people scored below 649.5, while only 18% scored below 499.5. We can also conclude that the probability of a randomly selected score from the sample of 100 lying below 649.5 is .78 and above 649.5 is $1.00 - .78 = .22$.

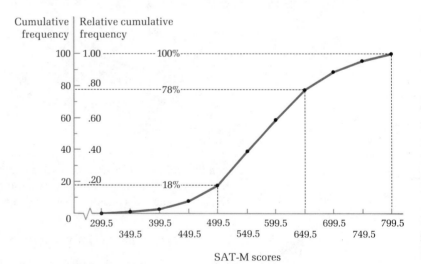

Figure 12 Cumulative frequency polygon (ogive)

Answers to Matched Problems

1. (A) .11
   (B) .18

Exercise 6-2

Applications

Business & Economics

1. *Common stocks.* The following table shows price–earnings ratios of 100 common stocks chosen at random from the New York Stock Exchange:

Price–Earnings Ratios

7	11	6	6	10	6	31	28	13	19
6	18	9	7	5	5	9	8	10	6
10	3	4	6	7	9	9	19	7	9
17	33	17	12	7	5	7	10	7	9
18	17	4	6	11	13	7	6	10	7
7	9	8	15	16	11	10	7	5	14
12	10	6	7	7	13	10	5	6	4
10	6	7	11	19	17	6	9	6	5
6	13	4	7	6	12	9	14	9	7
18	5	12	8	8	8	13	9	13	15

(A) Construct a frequency and relative frequency table using a class interval of 5 starting at −0.5.
(B) Construct a histogram.
(C) Construct a frequency polygon.
(D) Construct a cumulative frequency and relative cumulative frequency table. What is the probability of a price–earnings ratio drawn at random from the sample lying between 4.5 and 14.5?
(E) Construct a cumulative frequency polygon.

Life Sciences

2. *Mouse weights.* One hundred healthy mice were weighed at the beginning of an experiment with the following results:

Mouse Weights in Grams

51	54	47	53	59	46	50	50	56	46
48	50	45	49	52	55	42	57	45	51
53	55	51	47	53	53	49	51	43	48
44	48	54	46	49	51	52	50	55	51
50	53	45	49	57	54	53	49	46	48
52	48	50	52	47	50	44	46	47	49
49	51	57	49	51	42	49	53	44	52
53	55	48	52	44	46	54	54	57	55
48	50	50	55	52	48	47	52	55	50
59	52	47	46	56	54	51	56	54	55

(A) Construct a frequency and relative frequency table using a class interval of 2 starting at 41.5.
(B) Construct a histogram.
(C) Construct a frequency polygon.
(D) Construct a cumulative frequency and relative cumulative frequency table. What is the probability of a mouse weight drawn at random from the sample lying between 45.5 and 53.5?
(E) Construct a cumulative frequency polygon.

Social Sciences

3. *Grade-point averages.* One hundred seniors were chosen at random from a graduating class at a university and their grade-point averages recorded:

Grade-Point Averages (GPA)

2.1	2.0	2.7	2.6	2.1	3.5	3.1	2.1	2.2	2.9
2.3	2.5	3.1	2.2	2.2	2.0	2.3	2.5	2.1	2.4
2.7	2.9	2.1	2.2	2.5	2.3	2.1	2.1	3.3	2.1
2.2	2.2	2.5	2.3	2.7	2.4	2.8	3.1	2.0	2.3
2.6	3.2	2.2	2.5	3.6	2.3	2.4	3.7	2.5	2.4
3.5	2.4	2.3	3.9	2.9	2.7	2.6	2.1	2.4	2.0
2.4	3.3	3.1	2.8	2.3	2.5	2.1	3.0	2.6	2.3
2.1	2.6	2.2	3.2	2.7	2.8	3.4	2.7	3.6	2.1
2.7	2.8	3.5	2.4	2.3	2.0	2.1	3.1	2.8	2.1
3.8	2.5	2.7	2.1	2.2	2.4	2.9	3.3	2.0	2.6

(A) Construct a frequency and relative frequency table using a class interval of 0.2 starting at 1.95.
(B) Construct a histogram.
(C) Construct a frequency polygon.
(D) Construct a cumulative frequency and relative cumulative frequency table. What is the probability of a GPA drawn at random from the sample being over 2.95?
(E) Construct a cumulative frequency polygon.

6-3 Measures of Central Tendency

- Mean
- Median
- Mode

In the last section, we found that graphic techniques contributed substantially to our comprehension of large masses of raw data. In this and the next section, we will discuss several important numerical measures that are used to describe sets of data. These numerical descriptions are generally of two types:

1. Measures that indicate the approximate center of a distribution, called *measures of central tendency*
2. Measures that indicate the amount of scatter about a central point, called *measures of dispersion*

In this section we will look at three widely used measures of central tendency, and in the next section we will consider measures of dispersion.

■ Mean

When we speak of the average yield of municipal bonds, the average number of smog-free days in a year, or the average SAT score for students at a university, most people would interpret these averages to be **arithmetic means.** To obtain an arithmetic mean, or simply a **mean,** for a set of quantitative data, we sum all the measurements and divide the sum by the total number of measurements in the set. The result is a single number that in a sense represents the entire set. The mean involves all the measurements, is easy to compute, and enters readily into other formulas. Because of these desirable properties, the mean is the most widely used measure of central tendency.

Before considering examples, let us formulate the concept symbolically using the **summation symbol** Σ. If

$$x_1, x_2, \ldots, x_n$$

represents a set of n numbers, then the sum

$$x_1 + x_2 + \cdots + x_n$$

is compactly and conveniently represented by

$$\sum x$$

Now, if we denote the mean of $x_1, x_2, \ldots, x_n$ by $\bar{x}$, then it is given by

---

Mean (Ungrouped Data)

$$\bar{x} = \frac{\sum x}{n} = \frac{x_1 + x_2 + \cdots + x_n}{n} \qquad (1)$$

Example 2   Find the mean for 3, 5, 1, 8, 6, 5, 4, and 6.

Solution $\bar{x} = \dfrac{\sum x}{n} = \dfrac{3 + 5 + 1 + 8 + 6 + 5 + 4 + 6}{8} = \dfrac{38}{8} = 4.75$

Problem 2 Find the mean for 3.2, 4.5, 2.8, 5.0, and 3.6.

If data have been grouped in a frequency table, such as Table 4 in the last section, then an alternate formula for the mean is generally used. If x_k is the midpoint of the kth class interval and f_k is the kth class frequency, then the mean for the grouped data is given by

> **Mean (Grouped Data)**
>
> $$\bar{x} = \frac{\sum xf}{N} = \frac{x_1f_1 + x_2f_2 + \cdots + x_nf_n}{N} \qquad N = \sum f \qquad (2)$$

Note that N is the total number of measurements in the entire data set—not the number of classes! The mean computed by (2) is a **weighted average** of the midpoints of the class intervals, and in general it will be close to but not exactly the same as the mean computed by (1) for ungrouped data.

Example 3 Find the mean for the data summarized in Table 4 of the last section.

Solution We repeat Table 4 here, adding columns for the class midpoints x and the products xf (Table 6). Thus, the average SAT-M score for the sample of 100 entering freshmen is

$$\bar{x} = \frac{\sum xf}{N} = \frac{57,900}{100} = 579$$

Table 6 Scholastic Aptitude Test Scores (Mathematics)

Class Interval	Midpoint x	Frequency f	Product xf
299.5 – 349.5	324.5	1	324.5
349.5 – 399.5	374.5	2	749.0
399.5 – 449.5	424.5	5	2,122.5
449.5 – 499.5	474.5	10	4,745.0
499.5 – 549.5	524.5	21	11,014.5
549.5 – 599.5	574.5	20	11,490.0
599.5 – 649.5	624.5	19	11,865.5
649.5 – 699.5	674.5	11	7,419.5
699.5 – 749.5	724.5	7	5,071.5
749.5 – 799.5	774.5	4	3,098.0
		$N = \sum f = 100$	$\sum xf = 57,900.0$

If the histogram for the data in Table 6 (Fig. 10 in the last section) was drawn on a piece of wood of uniform thickness and the wood cut around

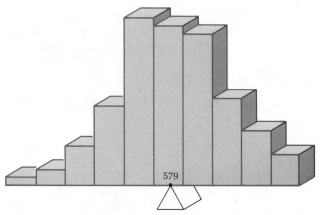

Figure 13 The balance point on the histogram is $\overline{x} = 579$.

the outside of the figure, then the resulting object would balance on a wedge placed at the mean $\overline{x} = 579$ (see Fig. 13).

Problem 3   Compute the mean for the grouped data listed in Table 7.

Table 7

Class Interval	Frequency
0.5–5.5	6
5.5–10.5	20
10.5–15.5	18
15.5–20.5	4

The Greek letter μ (read "mu") is generally used to represent the actual (or theoretical) **population mean,** one of a number of **population parameters** (measures of particular population characteristics). The sample mean $\overline{x}$ is used to approximate the population mean μ. Informally, the **law of large numbers** states that we can make $\overline{x}$ as close to μ as we like by computing $\overline{x}$ for a sufficiently large random sample.

■ Median

The mean can occasionally be misleading as a measure of central tendency. Suppose the annual salaries of seven people in a small company are $8,500, $10,000, $14,000, $9,000, $9,000, $60,000, and $12,000. The mean salary is

$$\overline{x} = \frac{\sum x}{n} = \frac{\$122,500}{7} = \$17,500$$

The one large salary distorts the results—six of the seven salaries are below the average!

A measure of central tendency that is not influenced by extreme values is the **median.** The median is simply the middle measurement when all measurements are arranged in increasing or decreasing order.

Example 4   Find the median salary in the above list of seven salaries.

Solution   Arrange the salaries in increasing order and choose the middle one:

Salary

$ 8,500	
9,000	
9,000	
10,000	← Median ($10,000)
12,000	
14,000	← Mean ($17,500)
60,000	

In this case, the median is a better measure of central tendency than the mean.

To find the median when there are an even number of measurements, we arrange the measurements in increasing or decreasing order and then take the average of the middle two.

Problem 4   Add the salary $50,000 to those in Example 4 and compute the median and mean for these eight salaries.

The median is most often used with small sets of data, since it is easily determined and is not influenced by extreme values. There are methods of estimating the median when data are summarized in a frequency table; however, we will not discuss this, since the mean is the measure of central tendency most frequently used for data presented in this form.

■ Mode

A third measure of central tendency is the **mode,** the most frequently occurring value in a data set. There may be a unique mode, several modes, or essentially no modes.

Example 5

Data Set	Mode	Median	Mean
4, 5, 5, 5, 6, 6, 7, 8, 12	5	6	6.44
1, 2, 3, 3, 3, 5, 6, 7, 7, 7, 23	3, 7	5	6.09
1, 3, 5, 6, 7, 9, 11, 15, 16	None	7	8.11

The second data set is referred to as **bimodal,** since there are two modes.

Problem 5   Compute the mode, median, and mean for each data set:

Data Set	Mode	Median	Mean
2, 1, 2, 1, 1, 5, 1, 9, 4			
2, 5, 1, 4, 9, 8, 7			
8, 2, 6, 8, 3, 3, 1, 5, 1, 8, 3			

As with the median, the mode is not influenced by extreme values. If in the second data set in Example 5 we replace 23 by 8, the modes remain 3 and 7 and the median 5, but the mean changes to 4.73.

The mode can also be used for qualitative attributes; that is, attributes that are not numerical. The mean and median are not suitable in this case. For example, the mode can be used to give an indication of a favorite brand of ice cream or the worst movie of the year. Figure 14 shows the results of a random survey of one thousand people on entree preferences when eating dinner out. According to this survey, we would say that the modal preference is beef. Note that the mode is the only measure of central tendency (location) that can be used for this type of data; the mean and median make no sense.

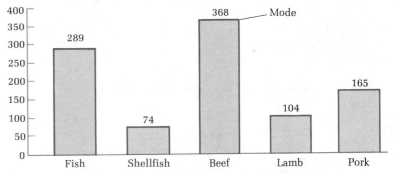

Figure 14 The modal preference for an entree is beef.

In actual practice, the mean is used the most, the median next, and the mode a distant third.

Answers to Matched Problems

2. $\bar{x} \approx 3.8$ 3. $\bar{x} \approx 10.1$

4.   Median $= \$11,000$; mean $= \$21,562.50$

5.   First, arrange each set of data in ascending order.

Data Set	Mode	Median	Mean
1, 1, 1, 1, 2, 2, 4, 5, 9	1	2	2.89
1, 2, 4, 5, 7, 8, 9	None	5	5.14
1, 1, 2, 3, 3, 3, 5, 6, 8, 8, 8	3, 8	3	4.36

Exercise 6-3

A *Find the mean, median, and mode for the following data sets of ungrouped data:*

1. 1, 2, 2, 3, 3, 3, 3, 4, 4, 5

2. 1, 1, 1, 1, 2, 3, 4, 5, 5, 5

Find the mean, median, or mode, whichever are applicable, in Problems 3 and 4.

3.

Flavor	Number Preferring
Vanilla	139
Chocolate	376
Strawberry	89
Pistachio	105
Cherry	63
Almond Mocha	228

4.

Car Color	Number Preferring
Red	1,324
White	3,084
Black	1,617
Blue	2,303
Brown	2,718
Gold	1,992

Find the mean for each set of grouped data.

5.

Interval	Frequency
0.5–2.5	2
2.5–4.5	5
4.5–6.5	7
6.5–8.5	1

6.

Interval	Frequency
0.5–2.5	5
2.5–4.5	1
4.5–6.5	2
6.5–8.5	7

Applications

Business & Economics

7. Find the mean, median, and mode for the data in the table.

Number of New One-Family Homes

Year	Number
1967	430,000
1968	430,000
1969	410,000
1970	430,000
1971	600,000
1972	650,000
1973	550,000

8. Find the mean for the data in the table.

Price–Earnings Ratios of 100 Randomly Chosen Stocks from the New York Stock Exchange

Interval	Frequency
−0.5–4.5	5
4.5–9.5	54
9.5–14.5	25
14.5–19.5	13
19.5–24.5	0
24.5–29.5	1
29.5–34.5	2

Life Sciences

9. Find the mean, median, and mode for the data in the table.

Water Pollution, 1971

Major Watersheds	Polluted Miles
Northeast	5,500
Middle Atlantic	5,500
Southeast	4,500
Great Lakes	8,000
Ohio	24,000
Missouri	2,000
Gulf states	12,000
Columbia	5,500
California	8,000

10. Find the mean for the data in the table.

Mouse Weights in Grams

Interval	Frequency
41.5 – 43.5	3
43.5 – 45.5	7
45.5 – 47.5	13
47.5 – 49.5	17
49.5 – 51.5	19
51.5 – 53.5	17
53.5 – 55.5	15
55.5 – 57.5	7
57.5 – 59.5	2

Social Sciences

11. Find the mean, median, and mode for the data in the table.

Immigration to the
United States, 1972

Country	Number
China	21,000
Cuba	19,000
Korea	18,000
India	17,000
Italy	21,000
Jamaica	13,000
Mexico	62,000
Philippines	25,000

12. Find the mean for the data in the table.

Graduating Class
Grade-Point Averages

Interval	Frequency
1.95 – 2.15	21
2.15 – 2.35	19
2.35 – 2.55	17
2.55 – 2.75	14
2.75 – 2.95	9
2.95 – 3.15	6
3.15 – 3.35	5
3.35 – 3.55	4
3.55 – 3.75	3
3.75 – 3.95	2

6-4 Measures of Dispersion

- Range
- Standard Deviation — Ungrouped Data
- Standard Deviation — Grouped Data
- Significance of Standard Deviation

A measure of central tendency gives us a typical value that can be used to describe a whole set of data, but this measure does not tell us whether the data are tightly clustered or widely dispersed. We will now consider two measures of variation, *range* and *standard deviation*, that will give some indication of data scatter.

■ Range

A measure of dispersion or scatter that is easy to compute and is easily understood is the range. The **range for a set of ungrouped data** is the difference between the largest and the smallest values in the data set. **For a frequency distribution, the range is** the difference between the upper boundary of the highest class and the lower boundary of the lowest class.

Considering the histograms in Figure 15, we see that the range adds only a little information about the amount of variation in a data set. The graphs clearly show that even though each data set has the same mean and range, all three sets differ in the amount of scatter or variation of the data relative to the mean. The data set in part A is tightly clustered about the mean; the data set in part B is dispersed away from the mean; and the data set in part C is uniformly distributed over its range.

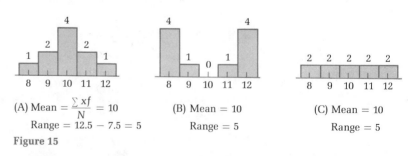

(A) Mean $= \dfrac{\sum xf}{N} = 10$

Range $= 12.5 - 7.5 = 5$

(B) Mean $= 10$

Range $= 5$

(C) Mean $= 10$

Range $= 5$

Figure 15

Since the range depends only on the extreme values of the data, it does not give us any information about the dispersion of the data between these extremes. We need a measure of dispersion that gives us some idea of how the data are clustered or scattered relative to the mean. The standard deviation is such a measure.

■ Standard Deviation — Ungrouped Data

We will develop the concept of standard deviation, a measure of variation, through a simple example.

Suppose a random sample of five stamped parts are selected from a production process and are found to have lengths (in inches) of

5.2,   5.3,   5.2,   5.5,   5.3

Computing the sample mean, we obtain

$$\bar{x} = \frac{\sum x}{n} = \frac{5.2 + 5.3 + 5.2 + 5.5 + 5.3}{5} = 5.3 \text{ inches}$$

How much variation exists between the sample mean and all other elements in the sample? As a first attempt at measuring the variation, let us represent the **deviation** of a measurement from the mean by $(x - \bar{x})$. Table 8 lists each deviation.

Table 8

x	$(x - \bar{x})$
5.2	−0.1
5.3	0.0
5.2	−0.1
5.5	0.2
5.3	0.0

What kind of a formula can we form, using these deviations, that will give us a good measure of variation? It appears that the average of the deviations might be a good measure. But look what happens when we add the second column in Table 8. We get zero! It turns out that this will always happen for any data set. Now what? We could take the average of the absolute values of the variations. This has actually been used as a measure of variation, but there are problems in its use in statistical inference. Instead, to get around the sign problem, we will take the average of the squares of the variations:

$$\frac{\sum (x - \bar{x})^2}{n} \tag{1}$$

Formally,

> **Variance**
>
> The **variance** of a data set $x_1, x_2, \ldots, x_n$ is the average of the squares of the deviations of each element relative to the mean.

Calculating the variance, using the entries in Table 8, we have

$$\frac{\sum (x - 5.3)^2}{5} = 0.012 \text{ square inch}$$

We still have a problem in that the units in the variance are in square inches and not in inches (the units of the original data set). To obtain the units of the original data set, we take the square root of the variance and call the result the *standard deviation* of the data set:

$$\sqrt{\frac{\sum (x - 5.3)^2}{5}} \approx 0.11 \text{ inch}$$

The sample variance is usually denoted by s^2 and the population variance by σ^2 (σ is the Greek letter "sigma"). In a more advanced treatment of the subject, it can be shown that for small samples, our formula for variance

$$\frac{\sum (x - \overline{x})^2}{n}$$

tends to underestimate the population variance σ^2. The following formula provides a better estimate:

> **Variance Formula (Ungrouped Data)**
>
> $$s^2 = \frac{\sum (x - \overline{x})^2}{n - 1} \tag{2}$$

The only difference between formulas (2) and (1) is that n in (1) is replaced by $n - 1$ in (2). For large n, formulas (1) and (2) produce nearly the same result.

The formula for **standard deviation** (the positive square root of the variance) is similarly modified, and we have

---

Standard Deviation Formula (Ungrouped Data)

$$s = \sqrt{\frac{\sum (x - \bar{x})^2}{n - 1}}$$

x = A measurement

$\bar{x}$ = Mean

n = Total number of measurements

(3)

Computing the standard deviation for the original data set (Table 8), we obtain

$$s = \sqrt{\frac{\sum (x - 5.3)^2}{5 - 1}} \approx 0.12 \text{ inch}$$

Example 6   Find the standard deviation for the data set 1, 3, 5, 4, 3.

Solution   To find the standard deviation for the data set, we can utilize a table or use a calculator. Most will prefer the latter. Here is what we compute:

$$\bar{x} = \frac{1 + 3 + 5 + 4 + 3}{5} = 3.2$$

$$s = \sqrt{\frac{(1 - 3.2)^2 + (3 - 3.2)^2 + (5 - 3.2)^2 + (4 - 3.2)^2 + (3 - 3.2)^2}{5 - 1}}$$

$$\approx 1.48$$

Problem 6   Find the standard deviation for the data set:

1.2, 1.4, 1.7, 1.3, 1.5

The **law of large numbers** informally states that we can make a **sample standard deviation s** as close to the **population standard deviation σ** as we like by making the sample sufficiently large.

■ Standard Deviation — Grouped Data

Formula (3) for the standard deviation of ungrouped data is extended to grouped data as follows:

Standard Deviation Formula (Grouped Data)

$$s = \sqrt{\frac{\sum (x - \bar{x})^2 f}{N - 1}}$$

$x = $ A class midpoint

$f = $ A corresponding class frequency **(4)**

$\bar{x} = $ Mean

$N = \sum f = $ Total number of measurements

Example 7   Find the standard deviation for each set of grouped data.

(A)

$$\text{Mean} = \frac{\sum xf}{N} = 10$$

(B)

$$\text{Mean} = 10$$

Solutions   (A)

$$s = \sqrt{\frac{(8 - 10)^2(1) + (9 - 10)^2(2) + (10 - 10)^2(4) + (11 - 10)^2(2) + (12 - 10)^2(1)}{10 - 1}}$$

$$= \sqrt{\frac{12}{9}} \approx 1.2$$

(B)

$$s = \sqrt{\frac{(8 - 10)^2(4) + (9 - 10)^2(1) + (10 - 10)^2(0) + (11 - 10)^2(1) + (12 - 10)^2(4)}{10 - 1}}$$

$$= \sqrt{\frac{34}{9}} \approx 1.9$$

Comparing the results of parts A and B, we find that the larger standard deviation is associated with the data that deviate furthest from the mean.

Problem 7   Find the standard deviation for the grouped data in the figure:

$$\text{Mean} = 10$$

■ Significance of Standard Deviation

The standard deviation can give us additional information about a frequency distribution of a set of raw data. Suppose we draw a smooth curve through the midpoints of the tops of the rectangles, forming a histogram for a fairly large frequency distribution (see Fig. 16). If the resulting curve is approximately bell-shaped, then it can be shown that approximately 68% of the data will lie in the interval from $\overline{x} - s$ to $\overline{x} + s$, about 95% of the data will lie in the interval from $\overline{x} - 2s$ to $\overline{x} + 2s$, and almost all the data will lie in the interval from $\overline{x} - 3s$ to $\overline{x} + 3s$. We will have much more to say about this in Section 6-6.

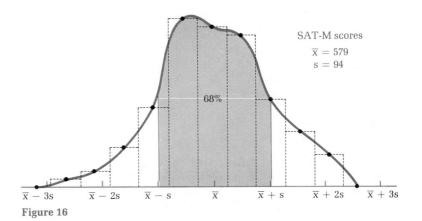

SAT-M scores
$\overline{x} = 579$
$s = 94$

68%

$\overline{x} - 3s$ $\overline{x} - 2s$ $\overline{x} - s$ $\overline{x}$ $\overline{x} + s$ $\overline{x} + 2s$ $\overline{x} + 3s$

Figure 16

Answers to Matched Problems

6. $s \approx 0.19$

7. $s \approx 1.5$ (a value between those found in Example 7, as we would hope)

Exercise 6-4

A *Find the standard deviation for each of the following sets of ungrouped data using formula (3).*

1. 1, 2, 2, 3, 3, 3, 3, 4, 4, 5   2. 1, 1, 1, 1, 2, 3, 4, 5, 5, 5

B *Find the standard deviation for each set of grouped data using formula (4).*

3.

Interval	Frequency
0.5–3.5	2
3.5–6.5	5
6.5–9.5	7
9.5–12.5	1

4.

Interval	Frequency
0.5–3.5	5
3.5–6.5	1
6.5–9.5	2
9.5–12.5	7

■

Applications

6-5 Bernoulli Trials and Binomial Distributions

- Bernoulli Trials
- Binomial Formula (Brief Review)
- Binomial Distribution
- Application

In Section 6-2 we discussed frequency and relative frequency distributions, which were represented by tables and histograms (see Fig. 10 on page 464). Frequency distributions and their corresponding probability distributions based on actual observations are *empirical* in nature. But there are many situations in which it is of interest (and possible) to determine the kind of relative frequency distribution we might expect before any data have actually been collected. What we have in mind is a **theoretical** or **hypothetical probability distribution;** that is, a probability distribution based on assumptions and theory rather than actual observations or measurements. Theoretical probability distributions are used to approximate properties of real-world distributions, assuming the theoretical and empirical distributions are closely matched.

There are many interesting theoretical probability distributions. One of particular interest because of its widespread use is the binomial distribution. The reason for the name "binomial distribution" is that the distribution is closely related to the binomial expansion of $(p + q)^n$, n a natural number. We start the discussion with a particular type of experiment called a *Bernoulli experiment* or *trial*.

■ Bernoulli Trials

If we toss a coin, either a head occurs or it does not. If we roll a die, either a 3 shows or it fails to show. If you are vaccinated for smallpox, either you contract smallpox or you do not. What do all these situations have in common? All can be classified as experiments with two possible outcomes, each the complement of the other. An experiment for which there are only two possible outcomes, E or E', is called a **Bernoulli experiment** or **trial,** after Jacob Bernoulli (1654–1705), a Swiss scientist and mathematician who was one of the first people to study systematically the probability problems related to a two-outcome experiment.

In a Bernoulli experiment or trial, it is customary to refer to one of the two outcomes as a success S and to the other as a failure F. If we designate the probability of success by

$$P(S) = p$$

then the probability of failure will be

$$P(F) = 1 - p = q \qquad \text{Note:} \quad p + q = 1$$

Example 8   We roll a fair die and ask for the probability of a 6 turning up. This can be viewed as a Bernoulli trial by identifying a success with a 6 turning up and a failure with any of the other numbers turning up. Thus,

$$p = \tfrac{1}{6} \quad \text{and} \quad q = 1 - \tfrac{1}{6} = \tfrac{5}{6}$$

Problem 8   Identify p and q for a single roll of a fair die where a success is a number divisible by 3 turning up.

Now, suppose a Bernoulli trial is repeated a number of times. It becomes of interest to try to determine the probability of a given number of successes out of the given number of trials. For example, we might be interested in the probability of obtaining exactly three 5's in six rolls of a fair die or the probability that eight people will not catch influenza out of the ten who have been inoculated.

Suppose a Bernoulli trial is repeated five times so that each trial is completely *independent* of any other and p is the probability of success on each trial. Then the probability of the outcome SSFFS would be

$$P(SSFFS) = P(S)P(S)P(F)P(F)P(S) \qquad \text{See Section 5-2}$$
$$= ppqqp$$
$$= p^3 q^2$$

In general, we define a *sequence of Bernoulli trials* as follows:

Bernoulli Trials

A sequence of experiments is called a **sequence of Bernoulli trials** or a **binomial experiment** if:

1. Only two outcomes are possible on each trial.
2. The probability of success p for each trial is a constant (probability of failure is then $q = 1 - p$).
3. All trials are independent.

The reason for calling *a sequence of Bernoulli trials* a *binomial experiment* will be made clear shortly.

Example 9   If we roll a fair die five times and identify a success in a single roll with a 1 turning up, what is the probability of the sequence *SFFSS* occurring?

Solution $p = \frac{1}{6}$ $q = 1 - p = \frac{5}{6}$

$P(SFFSS) = pqqpp$

$\qquad\qquad = p^3 q^2$

$\qquad\qquad = (\frac{1}{6})^3 (\frac{5}{6})^2 \approx .003$

Problem 9   In Example 9, find the probability of the outcome *FSSSF*.

If we roll a fair die five times, what is the probability of obtaining exactly three 1's? Notice how this problem differs from Example 9. In that example we looked at only one way three 1's can occur. Then in Problem 9 we saw another way. Thus, exactly three 1's may occur in the following two sequences (among others):

SFFSS   *FSSSF*

We found that the probability of each sequence occurring is the same, namely,

$(\frac{1}{6})^3 (\frac{5}{6})^2$

How many more sequences will produce exactly three 1's? To answer this question, think of the number of ways the following five blank positions can be filled with three S's and two F's:

b_1 b_2 b_3 b_4 b_5

□ □ □ □ □

A given sequence is determined, of course, once the S's are located. Thus, we are interested in the number of ways three blank positions can be selected for the S's out of the five available blank positions b_1, b_2, b_3, b_4, and b_5. This problem should sound familiar—it is just the problem of finding the number of combinations of five objects taken three at a time; that is, $C_{5,3}$. Thus, the number of different sequences of successes and failures that produce exactly three successes (exactly three 1's) is

$$C_{5,3} = \frac{5!}{3!2!} = 10$$

Since the probability of each sequence is the same,

$$p^3q^2 = (\tfrac{1}{6})^3(\tfrac{5}{6})^2$$

and there are ten mutually exclusive sequences that produce exactly three 1's, then

$$P(\text{Exactly three successes}) = C_{5,3}(\tfrac{1}{6})^3(\tfrac{5}{6})^2$$

$$= \frac{5!}{3!2!}(\tfrac{1}{6})^3(\tfrac{5}{6})^2 \approx .032$$

Reasoning in essentially the same way, the following important theorem can be proved:

Theorem 1

Probability of x Successes in n Bernoulli Trials

The probability of exactly x successes in n independent repeated Bernoulli trials, with the probability of success of each trial p, is

$$P(x \text{ successes}) = C_{n,x}p^xq^{n-x} \tag{1}$$

Example 10 If a fair die is rolled five times, what is the probability of rolling:

(A) Exactly two 3's? (B) At least two 3's?

Solutions (A) Use formula (1) with $n = 5$, $x = 2$, and $p = \tfrac{1}{6}$:

$$P(x = 2) = C_{5,2}(\tfrac{1}{6})^2(\tfrac{5}{6})^3$$

$$= \frac{5!}{2!3!}(\tfrac{1}{6})^2(\tfrac{5}{6})^3 \approx .161$$

(B) Notice how this problem differs from part A. Here we have

$$P(x \geqslant 2) = P(x = 2) + P(x = 3) + P(x = 4) + P(x = 5)$$

It is actually easier to compute the probability of the complement of this event, $P(x < 2)$, and use

$$P(x \geqslant 2) = 1 - P(x < 2)$$

where

$$P(x < 2) = P(x = 0) + P(x = 1)$$

We now compute $P(x = 0)$ and $P(x = 1)$:

$$P(x = 0) = C_{5,0}(\tfrac{1}{6})^0(\tfrac{5}{6})^5$$
$$= (\tfrac{5}{6})^5 \approx .402$$
$$P(x = 1) = C_{5,1}(\tfrac{1}{6})^1(\tfrac{5}{6})^4$$

$$= \frac{5!}{1!4!}(\tfrac{1}{6})^1(\tfrac{5}{6})^4 \approx .402$$

Thus,

$$P(x < 2) = .402 + .402 = .804$$

and

$$P(x \geqslant 2) = 1 - .804 = .196$$

Problem 10   Using the same die experiment as in Example 10, what is the probability of rolling:

(A)   Exactly one 3?   (B)   At least one 3?

■ Binomial Formula (Brief Review)

Before extending Bernoulli trials to binomial distributions it is worthwhile to briefly review the binomial formula. (A more detailed discussion of this formula can be found in Appendix A.) To start, let us calculate directly the first five natural number powers of $(a + b)^n$:

$$(a + b)^1 = a + b$$
$$(a + b)^2 = a^2 + 2ab + b^2$$
$$(a + b)^3 = a^3 + 3a^2b + 3ab^2 + b^3$$
$$(a + b)^4 = a^4 + 4a^3b + 6a^2b^2 + 4ab^3 + b^4$$
$$(a + b)^5 = a^5 + 5a^4b + 10a^3b^2 + 10a^2b^3 + 5ab^4 + b^5$$

In general, it can be shown that a binomial expansion is given by the well-known binomial formula:

Binomial Formula

For n a natural number,

$$(a + b)^n = C_{n,0}a^n + C_{n,1}a^{n-1}b + C_{n,2}a^{n-2}b^2 + \cdots + C_{n,n}b^n$$

Example 11   Use the binomial formula to expand $(p + q)^3$.

Solution $(p + q)^3 = C_{3,0}p^3 + C_{3,1}p^2q + C_{3,2}pq^2 + C_{3,3}q^3$

$\qquad\qquad = p^3 + 3p^2q + 3pq^2 + q^3$

Problem 11   Use the binomial formula to expand $(p + q)^4$.

■ Binomial Distribution

We now generalize the discussion of Bernoulli trials to *binomial distributions*. We start by considering a sequence of three Bernoulli trials. Let the random variable (see Section 4-4)X_3 represent the number of successes in three trials, 0, 1, 2, or 3. We are interested in the probability distribution for this random variable.

Which outcomes of an experiment consisting of a sequence of three Bernoulli trials lead to the random variable values 0, 1, 2, and 3, and what are the probabilities associated with these values? Table 9 answers these questions completely.

Table 9

Simple Event	Probability of Simple Event	X_3 x successes in 3 trials	$P(X_3 = x)$
SSS	$ppp = p^3$	3	p^3
SSF	$ppq = p^2q$		
SFS	$pqp = p^2q$	2	$3p^2q$
FSS	$qpp = p^2q$		
SFF	$pqq = pq^2$		
FSF	$qpq = pq^2$	1	$3pq^2$
FFS	$qqp = pq^2$		
FFF	$qqq = q^3$	0	q^3

The terms in the last column are the terms in the binomial expansion of $(p + q)^3$; see Example 11. The last two columns in Table 9 provide a probability distribution for the random variable X_3. Note that both conditions for a probability distribution (see Section 4-4) are met:

1. $0 \le P(X_3 = x) \le 1$, $x \in \{0, 1, 2, 3\}$
2. $1 = 1^3 = (p + q)^3$ Recall that $p + q = 1$
$\qquad = C_{3,0}p^3 + C_{3,1}p^2q + C_{3,2}pq^2 + C_{3,3}q^3$
$\qquad = p^3 + 3p^2q + 3pq^2 + q^3$
$\qquad = P(X_3 = 3) + P(X_3 = 2) + P(X_3 = 1) + P(X_3 = 0)$

Reasoning in the same way for the general case, we see why the probability distribution of a random variable associated with the number of successes in a sequence of n Bernoulli trials is called a **binomial distribution** —the probability of each number is a term in the binomial expansion of $(p + q)^n$. For this reason, a sequence of Bernoulli trials is often referred to as a **binomial experiment.** In terms of a formula which we already discussed from another point of view (see Theorem 1), we have

---

Binomial Distribution

$P(X_n = x)^* = P(x \text{ successes in } n \text{ trials})$
$$= C_{n,x}p^x q^{n-x} \qquad x \in \{0, 1, 2, \ldots, n\}$$

Example 12 Suppose a fair die is rolled three times and a success on a single roll is considered to be rolling a number divisible by 3.

(A) Write the probability function for the binomial distribution.
(B) Construct a table for this binomial distribution.
(C) Draw a histogram for this theoretical distribution.

Solutions (A) $p = \frac{1}{3}$ Since there are two numbers out of six that are divisible by 3

$q = 1 - p = \frac{2}{3}$

$n = 3$

Hence,

$$P(x) = P(x \text{ successes in 3 trials}) = C_{3,x}(\tfrac{1}{3})^x(\tfrac{2}{3})^{3-x}$$

(B)

x	$P(x)$	
0	$C_{3,0}(\tfrac{1}{3})^0(\tfrac{2}{3})^3$	$\approx .30$
1	$C_{3,1}(\tfrac{1}{3})^1(\tfrac{2}{3})^2$	$\approx .44$
2	$C_{3,2}(\tfrac{1}{3})^2(\tfrac{2}{3})^1$	$\approx .22$
3	$C_{3,3}(\tfrac{1}{3})^3(\tfrac{2}{3})^0$	$\approx .04$
		1.00

---

* Informally, we will write $P(x)$ in place of $P(X_n = x)$.

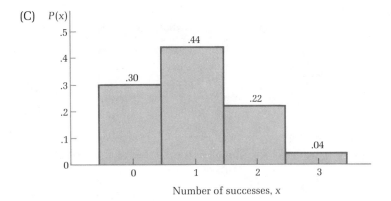

If we actually performed the binomial experiment described in Example 12 a large number of times with a fair die, we would find that we would roll no number divisible by 3 in three rolls of a die about 30% of the time, one number divisible by 3 in three rolls about 44% of the time, two numbers divisible by 3 in three rolls about 22% of the time, and three numbers divisible by 3 in three rolls only 4% of the time. Note that the sum of all the probabilities is 1, as it should be.

Problem 12   Repeat Example 12 where the binomial experiment consists of two rolls of a die instead of three rolls.

We close our discussion of binomial distributions by stating (without proof) formulas for the mean and standard deviation of the random variable associated with the distribution. These are theoretical results that apply to the total population; hence, they are denoted by the Greek letters μ and σ, respectively.

Mean and Standard Deviation (Random Variable in a Binomial Distribution)

$$\text{Mean:}\quad \mu = np$$
$$\text{Standard deviation:}\quad \sigma = \sqrt{npq}$$

Example 13   Compute the mean and standard deviation for the random variable in Example 12.

Solution $n = 3 \qquad p = \frac{1}{3} \qquad q = 1 - \frac{1}{3} = \frac{2}{3}$

$\mu = np = 3(\frac{1}{3}) = 1 \qquad \sigma = \sqrt{npq} = \sqrt{3(\frac{1}{3})(\frac{2}{3})} \approx .82$

Problem 13   Compute the mean and standard deviation for the random variable in Problem 12 above.

■ Application

Binomial experiments are associated with a wide variety of practical problems: industrial sampling, drug testing, genetics, epidemics, medical diagnosis, opinion polls, analysis of social phenomena, qualifying tests, and so on. Several types of applications are included in Exercise 6-5. We will now consider one application in detail.

Example 14   The probability of recovering after a particular type of operation is .5. Let us investigate the binomial distribution involving eight patients undergoing this operation.

(A) Write the function defining this distribution.
(B) Construct a table for the distribution.
(C) Construct a histogram for the distribution.
(D) Find the mean and standard deviation for the distribution.

Solutions   (A) $p = .5$ $q = 1 - p = .5$ $n = 8$

Hence, letting a recovery be a success,

$$P(x) = P(\text{Exactly } x \text{ successes in 8 trials}) = C_{8,x}(.5)^x(.5)^{8-x}$$
$$= C_{8,x}(.5)^8$$

(B)

x	P(x)
0	$C_{8,0}(.5)^8 \approx .004$
1	$C_{8,1}(.5)^8 \approx .031$
2	$C_{8,2}(.5)^8 \approx .109$
3	$C_{8,3}(.5)^8 \approx .219$
4	$C_{8,4}(.5)^8 \approx .273$
5	$C_{8,5}(.5)^8 \approx .219$
6	$C_{8,6}(.5)^8 \approx .109$
7	$C_{8,7}(.5)^8 \approx .031$
8	$C_{8,8}(.5)^8 \approx .004$
	$.999 \approx 1$

(C)

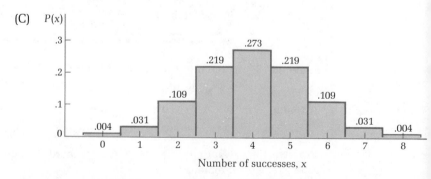

Number of successes, x

(D) $\mu = np = 8(.5) = 4$ $\sigma = \sqrt{npq} = \sqrt{8(.5)(.5)} \approx 1.41$

Problem 14 Repeat Example 14 for four patients.

Answers to Matched Problems

8. $p = \frac{1}{3}, q = \frac{2}{3}$ 9. $p^3 q^2 = (\frac{1}{6})^3 (\frac{5}{6})^2 \approx .003$

10. (A) .402   (B) $1 - P(x = 0) = 1 - .402 = .598$

11. $C_{4,0} p^4 + C_{4,1} p^3 q + C_{4,2} p^2 q^2 + C_{4,3} pq^3 + C_{4,4} q^4$

   $= p^4 + 4p^3 q + 6p^2 q^2 + 4pq^3 + q^4$

12. (A) $P(x \text{ successes in 2 trials}) = C_{2,x} (\frac{1}{3})^x (\frac{2}{3})^{2-x} \qquad x \in \{0, 1, 2\}$

(B)

x	P(x)
0	$\frac{4}{9} \approx .44$
1	$\frac{4}{9} \approx .44$
2	$\frac{1}{9} \approx .12$

(C)
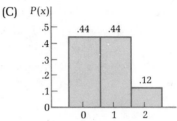

Number of successes, x

13. $\mu \approx .67; \sigma \approx .67$

14. (A) $P(\text{Exactly } x \text{ successes in 4 trials}) = C_{4,x} (.5)^4$

(B)

x	P(x)
0	.06
1	.25
2	.38
3	.25
4	.06
	1.00

(C)
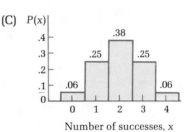

Number of successes, x

(D) $\mu = 2; \quad \sigma = 1$

Exercise 6-5

A *Evaluate* $C_{n,x} p^x q^{n-x}$ *for the following values of n, x, and p:*

1. $n = 3, \quad x = 2, \quad p = \frac{1}{2}$
2. $n = 3, \quad x = 1, \quad p = \frac{1}{2}$
3. $n = 3, \quad x = 0, \quad p = \frac{1}{2}$
4. $n = 3, \quad x = 3, \quad p = \frac{1}{2}$
5. $n = 5, \quad x = 3, \quad p = .4$
6. $n = 5, \quad x = 0, \quad p = .4$

A fair coin is tossed three times. What is the probability of obtaining:

7. Exactly two heads?   8. Exactly one head?

9. No heads?

10. Three heads?

11. At least two heads?

12. At least one head?

Construct a histogram for each of the binomial distributions in Problems 13–16. Compute the mean and standard deviation for each distribution.

13. $P(x) = C_{2,x}(.3)^x(.7)^{2-x}$

14. $P(x) = C_{2,x}(.7)^x(.3)^{2-x}$

15. $P(x) = C_{4,x}(.5)^x(.5)^{4-x}$

16. $P(x) = C_{6,x}(.5)^x(.5)^{6-x}$

B   *A fair die is rolled four times. What is the probability of rolling:*

17. Exactly three 2's?

18. Exactly two 3's?

19. No 1's?

20. All 4's?

21. At least one 6?

22. At least one 4?

23. If a baseball player has a batting average of .350, what is the probability that the player will get:

    (A) Exactly two hits   (B) At least two hits

    in the next four times at bat?

24. If a ten-question, true-false test is given, what is the probability of scoring:

    (A) Exactly 70% just by guessing?
    (B) 70% or better just by guessing?

Construct a histogram for each of the binomial distributions in Problems 25–28. Compute the mean and standard deviation for each distribution.

25. $P(x) = C_{6,x}(.4)^x(.6)^{6-x}$

26. $P(x) = C_{6,x}(.6)^x(.4)^{6-x}$

27. $P(x) = C_{8,x}(.3)^x(.7)^{8-x}$

28. $P(x) = C_{8,x}(.7)^x(.3)^{8-x}$

C   *In Problems 29 and 30 a coin is loaded so that the probability of a head occurring on a single toss is $\frac{3}{4}$. In five tosses of the coin, what is the probability of getting:*

29. All heads or all tails?

30. Exactly two heads or exactly two tails?

31. Toss a coin three times or toss three coins simultaneously, and record the number of heads. Repeat the binomial experiment 100 times and compare your relative frequency distribution with the theoretical probability distribution.

32. Roll a die three times or roll three dice simultaneously, and record the number of 5's that occur. Repeat the binomial experiment 100 times and compare your relative frequency distribution with the theoretical probability distribution.

Applications

Business & Economics

33. *Management training.* Each year a company selects a number of employees for a management training program given by a nearby university. On the average, 70% of those sent complete the program. Out of seven people sent by the company, what is the probability that:

(A) Exactly five complete the program?

(B) Five or more complete the program?

34. *Employee turnover.* If the probability of a new employee in a fastfood chain still being with the company at the end of one year is .6, what is the probability that out of eight newly hired people:

(A) Five will still be with the company after one year?

(B) Five or more will still be with the company after one year?

35. *Quality control.* A manufacturing process produces, on the average, six defective items out of 100. To control quality, each day a sample of ten completed items is selected at random and is inspected. If the sample produces more than two defective items, then the whole day's output is inspected and the manufacturing process is reviewed. What is the probability of this happening, assuming that the process is still producing 6% defective items?

36. *Guarantees.* A manufacturing process produces, on the average, 3% defective items. The company ships ten items in each box and wishes to guarantee no more than one defective item per box. If this guarantee accompanies each box, what is the probability that the box will fail to satisfy the guarantee?

37. *Quality control.* A manufacturing process produces on the average 5 defective items out of 100. To control quality, each day a random sample of six completed items is selected and inspected. If a success on a single trial (inspection of one item) is finding the item defective, then the inspection of each of the 6 items in the sample constitutes a binomial experiment, which has a binomial distribution.

(A) Write the function defining the distribution.

(B) Construct a table for the distribution.

(C) Draw a histogram.

(D) Compute the mean and standard deviation.

38. *Management training.* Each year a company selects five employees for a management training program given at a nearby university. On the average, 40% of those sent complete the course in the top 10% of their class. If we consider an employee finishing in the top 10% of the class a success in a binomial experiment, then for the five employees entering the program there exists a binomial distribution involving P(x successes out of 5).

(A) Write the function defining the distribution.
(B) Construct a table for the distribution.
(C) Draw a histogram.
(D) Compute the mean and standard deviation.

Life Sciences

39. *Medical diagnosis.* A person with tuberculosis is given a chest x ray. Four tuberculosis x-ray specialists examine each x ray independently. If each specialist can detect tuberculosis 80% of the time when it is present, what is the probability that at least one of the specialists will detect tuberculosis in this person?

40. *Harmful side effects of drugs.* A pharmaceutical laboratory claims that a drug it produces causes serious side effects in twenty people out of 1,000 on the average. To check this claim, a hospital administers the drug to ten randomly chosen people and finds that three suffer from serious side effects. If the laboratory's claims are correct, what is the probability of the hospital obtaining the results that they did?

41. *Genetics.* The probability that brown-eyed parents, both with the recessive gene for blue, will have a child with brown eyes is .75. If such parents have five children, what is the probability that they will have:

(A) All blue-eyed children?
(B) Exactly three children with brown eyes?
(C) At least three children with brown eyes?

42. *Gene mutations.* The probability of gene mutation under a given level of radiation is 3×10^{-5}. What is the probability of the occurrence of at least one gene mutation if 10^5 genes are exposed to this level of radiation?

43. *Epidemics.* If the probability of a person contracting influenza on exposure is .6, consider the binomial distribution for a family of six that has been exposed.

(A) Write the function defining the distribution.
(B) Construct a table for the distribution.
(C) Draw a histogram.
(D) Compute the mean and standard deviation.

44. *Side effects of drugs.* The probability that a given drug will produce a serious side effect in a person using the drug is .02. In the binomial distribution for 450 people using the drug, what are the mean and standard deviation?

Social Sciences   45. *Testing.* A multiple-choice test is given with five choices for each of ten questions. What is the probability of passing the test with a grade of 70% or better just by guessing?

46. *Opinion polls.* An opinion poll based on a small sample can be unrepresentative of the population. To see why, let us assume that 40% of the electorate favors a certain candidate. If a random sample of seven is asked their preference, what is the probability that a majority will favor the candidate?

47. *Testing.* A multiple-choice test is given with five choices for each of five questions. Answering each of the five questions by guessing constitutes a binomial experiment with an associated binomial distribution.

(A) Write the function defining the distribution.
(B) Construct a table for the distribution.
(C) Draw a histogram.
(D) Compute the mean and standard deviation.

48. *Sociology.* The probability that a marriage will end in divorce within 10 years is .4. What are the mean and standard deviation for the binomial distribution involving 1,000 marriages?

49. *Sociology.* If the probability is .60 that a marriage will end in divorce within 20 years after its start, what is the probability that out of six couples just married, in the next 20 years:

(A) None will be divorced?
(B) All will be divorced?
(C) Exactly two will be divorced?
(D) At least two will be divorced?

6-6   Normal Distributions

- Normal Distribution
- Areas under Normal Curves
- Approximating a Binomial Distribution with a Normal Distribution

■ Normal Distribution

If we take the histogram for a binomial distribution, say, the one we drew for Example 14 in Section 6-5 ($n = 8$, $p = .5$), and join the midpoints of the tops of each rectangle with a smooth curve, we obtain the bell-shaped curve in Figure 17.

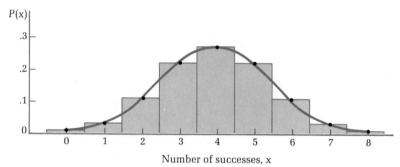

Figure 17 The binomial distribution and a bell-shaped curve

The mathematical foundation for this type of curve was established by Abraham De Moivre (1667–1754), Pierre Laplace (1749–1827), and Karl Gauss (1777–1855). The bell-shaped curves studied by these famous mathematicians are called **normal curves** or **normal probability distributions,**

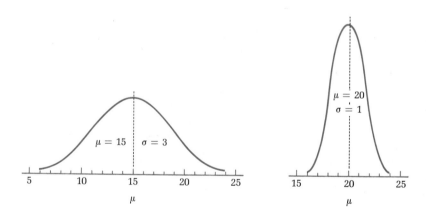

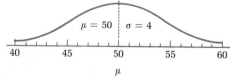

Figure 18 Normal probability distributions

and their equations* are completely determined by the mean μ and standard deviation σ of the distribution. Figure 18 illustrates three normal curves with different means and standard deviations.

Up until now we have dealt with **discrete random variables,** that is, random variables that assume a finite or a "countably infinite" number of values (we have only dealt with the finite case). Random variables associated with normal distributions are continuous in nature; that is, they assume all values over an interval on a real number line. These are called **continuous random variables.** Random variables associated with people's heights, light bulb lives, or the length of time between breakdowns of an office copier are continuous. The following is a list of some of the important properties of normal curves (normal probability distributions of a continuous random variable):

Normal Curve Properties

1. Normal curves are bell-shaped and are symmetrical with respect to a vertical line.
2. The mean is at the point where the axis of symmetry intersects the horizontal axis.
3. The shape of a normal curve is completely determined by its mean and standard deviation—a small standard deviation indicates a tight clustering about the mean and thus a tall, narrow curve; a large standard deviation indicates a large deviation from the mean and thus a broad, flat curve (see Fig. 18).
4. Irrespective of the shape, the area between the curve and the x axis is always 1.
5. Irrespective of the shape, 68.27% of the area will lie within an interval of one standard deviation on either side of the mean, 95.45% within two standard deviations on either side, and 99.73% within three standard deviations on either side (see Fig. 19 on the next page).

The normal probability distribution is the most important of all theoretical distributions. It is at the heart of a great deal of statistical theory, and it is also a useful tool in its own right for solving practical problems. Not only does a normal curve provide a good approximation for a binomial distribution for large n, but it also approximates many other relative frequency

---

* The equation for a normal curve is fairly complicated:

$$f(x) = \frac{1}{\sigma\sqrt{2\pi}}\, e^{-(x-\mu)^2/2\sigma^2}$$

where $\pi \approx 3.1416$ and $e \approx 2.7183$.

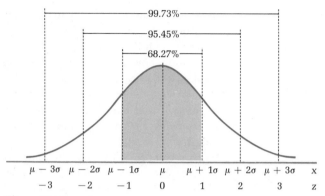

Figure 19 Normal curve areas

distributions. For example, normal curves often provide good approxima-tions for the relative frequency distributions for heights and weights of people, measurements of manufactured parts, scores on IQ tests, college entrance examinations, civil service tests, and measurements of errors in laboratory experiments.

■ Areas under Normal Curves

In order to use normal curves in practical problems, we must be able to determine areas under different parts of a curve. Fortunately, we can use the same approach and table for all normal curves, irrespective of their shapes, that is, irrespective of the values of μ and σ. It is a remarkable fact that the area under a normal curve between a mean μ and a given number of standard deviations to the right (or left) of μ is the same regardless of the shape of the normal curve (see Fig. 20). Thus, if **z represents the number of standard deviations that a measurement x is from a mean μ** (see Figs. 19

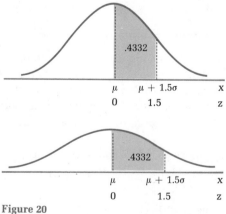

Figure 20

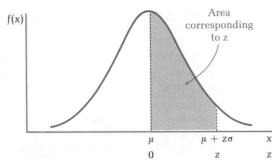

Figure 21 Areas and z values

through 21), then we need only one table that gives areas in terms of these z values. Table IV in Appendix B is such a table.

Example 15 Scholastic Aptitude Test scores have a mean of 500 and a standard deviation of 100, and their relative frequencies can be closely approximated by a normal curve. What percentage of the students taking the test can be expected to score between 500 and 670?

Solution To answer this question, we first determine how many standard deviations 670 is from 500, the mean. This is easily done by dividing the distance between 500 and 670 by 100. Thus,

$$z = \frac{670 - 500}{100} = \frac{170}{100} = 1.70$$

That is, 670 is 1.7 standard deviations from 500, the mean. Referring to Table IV, we see that .4554 corresponds to z = 1.70. And since the total area under a normal curve is 1, we conclude that 45.54% of the students will score between 500 and 670 (see Fig. 22).

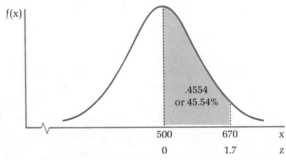

Figure 22 Scholastic Aptitude Test scores—positive z

Problem 15   What percentage of the students can be expected to score between 500 and 750?

In general, to find how many standard deviations a measurement x is from a mean μ, first determine the distance between x and μ and then divide by σ:

$$z = \frac{\text{Distance between } x \text{ and } \mu}{\text{Standard deviation}} = \frac{x - \mu}{\sigma}$$

Example 16   From all high school students taking SATs, what is the probability of a student chosen at random scoring between 380 and 500? To answer this, we first find z:

$$z = \frac{x - \mu}{\sigma} = \frac{380 - 500}{100} = -1.20$$

It is usually a good idea to draw a rough sketch of a normal curve and insert relevant data (see Fig. 23).

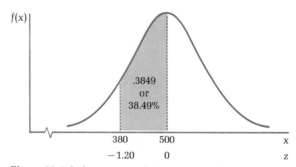

Figure 23 Scholastic Aptitude Test scores — negative z

Table IV in Appendix B does not include negative values for z, but because normal curves are symmetrical with respect to a vertical line through the mean, we simply use the absolute value (positive value) of z for the table. Thus, the area corresponding to $z = -1.20$ is the same as the area corresponding to $z = 1.20$, which is .3849. And since the area under the whole normal curve is 1, we conclude that the probability of a student scoring between 380 and 500 is .3849.

Problem 16   What is the probability of a student scoring between 400 and 500?

■ Approximating a Binomial Distribution
with a Normal Distribution

You no doubt found in some of the exercises in the last section that when a binomial random variable assumes a large number of values (that is, when n is large), the use of the probability distribution formula

$$P(x \text{ successes in } n \text{ trials}) = C_{n,x}p^x q^{n-x}$$

became very tedious. It would be very helpful if there was an easily computed approximation of this distribution for large n. Such a distribution is found in the form of an appropriately selected normal distribution.

To clarify ideas and relationships, let us consider an example of a binomial distribution with a relatively small n value. Then we will consider an example with a large n value.

Example 17   A credit card company claims that their card is used by 40% of the people buying gasoline in a particular city. A random sample of twenty gasoline purchasers is made. If the company's claim is correct, what is the probability that:

(A)   From six to twelve people in the sample use the card?
(B)   Fewer than four people in the sample use the card?

Solutions   Before we start, it is useful to look at a histogram of the binomial distribution with a normal distribution fitted to it using the same mean and standard deviation. The mean and standard deviation of the binomial distribution are:

$$\mu = np = (20)(.4) = 8 \qquad n = \text{sample size}$$
$$\sigma = \sqrt{npq} = \sqrt{(20)(.4)(.6)} \approx 2.19 \qquad p = .4 \text{ (from the 40\% claim)}$$

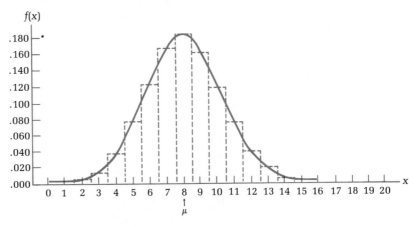

(A)   To approximate the probability that 6 to 12 people in the sample use the credit card, we find the area under the normal curve from 5.5 to

12.5. We use 5.5 rather than 6, because the rectangle in the histogram corresponding to 6 extends from 5.5 to 6.5. And, reasoning in the same way, we use 12.5 instead of 12. To use Table IV, we split the area into two parts: A_1 to the left of the mean and A_2 to the right of the mean. A sketch is helpful:

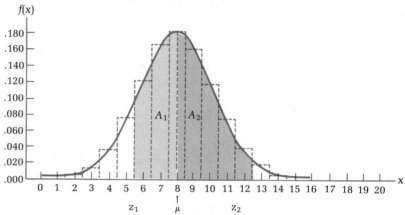

Areas A_1 and A_2 are found as follows:

$$z_1 = \frac{x - \mu}{\sigma} = \frac{5.5 - 8}{2.19} \approx -1.14 \qquad A_1 = .3729$$

$$z_2 = \frac{x - \mu}{\sigma} = \frac{12.5 - 8}{2.19} \approx 2.05 \qquad A_2 = .4798$$

Thus, the approximate probability that the sample will contain between 6 and 12 users of the credit card is .85 (assuming the firm's claim is correct).

(B)   To use the normal curve to approximate the probability that the sample contains fewer than 4 users of the credit card, we must find the area A_1 under the normal curve to the left of 3.5. Again, a sketch is useful:

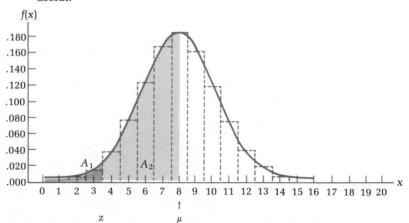

Since the total area under either half of the normal curve is .5, we first use Table IV to find the area A_2 under the normal curve from 3.5 to the mean 8, then subtract A_2 from .5.

$$z = \frac{x - \mu}{\sigma} = \frac{3.5 - 8}{2.19} \approx -2.05 \qquad A_2 = .4798$$

$$A_1 = .5 - A_2 = .5 - .4798 = .0202$$

Thus, the approximate probability that the sample contains fewer than 4 users of the credit card is approximately .02 (assuming the company's claim is correct).

Problem 17 In Example 17 use the normal curve to approximate the probability that in the sample there are:

(A) From five to nine users of the credit card.
(B) More than ten users of the card.

You no doubt are wondering how large n should be before a normal distribution provides an adequate approximation for a binomial distribution. Without getting too involved, the following rule-of-thumb provides a good test:

Rule-of-Thumb Test

Only use a normal distribution to approximate a binomial distribution if the interval $[\mu - 3\sigma, \mu + 3\sigma]$ lies entirely in the interval from 0 to n.

Note that in Example 17 the interval $[\mu - 3\sigma, \mu + 3\sigma] = [1.43, 14.57]$ lies entirely within the interval from 1 to 20; hence, the use of the normal distribution was justified.

Example 18 A company manufactures 50,000 ballpoint pens each day. The manufacturing process produces fifty defective pens per 1,000 on the average. A random sample of 400 pens is selected from each day's production and tested. What is the probability that the sample contains:

(A) At least fourteen and no more than twenty-five defective pens?
(B) Thirty-three or more defective pens?

Solutions Is it appropriate to use a normal distribution to approximate this binomial distribution? The answer is "yes," since the rule-of-thumb test passes with ease:

$$\mu = np = 400(.05) = 20$$
$$\sigma = \sqrt{npq} = \sqrt{400(.05)(.95)} \approx 4.36$$
$$[\mu - 3\sigma, \mu + 3\sigma] = [6.92,\ 33.08]$$

This interval is within the interval from 0 to 500.

(A)   To find the approximate probability of the number of defective pens in a sample being at least 14 and not more than 25, we find the area under the normal curve from 13.5 to 25.5. To use Table IV, we split the area into an area to the left of the mean and an area to the right of the mean (see the figure):

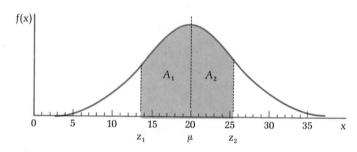

$$z_1 = \frac{x - \mu}{\sigma} = \frac{13.5 - 20}{4.36} \approx -1.49 \qquad A_1 = .4319$$

$$z_2 = \frac{x - \mu}{\sigma} = \frac{25.5 - 20}{4.36} \approx 1.26 \qquad A_2 = .3962$$

Total area $= A_1 + A_2 = .8281$

Thus, the approximate probability of the number of defective pens in the sample being at least 14 and not more than 25 is .83.

(B)

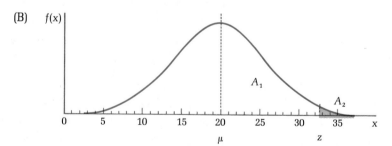

Since the total area under a normal curve from the mean on is .5, we find the area A_1 from Table IV and subtract it from .5 to obtain A_2.

$$z = \frac{x - \mu}{\sigma} = \frac{32.5 - 20}{4.36} \approx 2.87$$

$$A_1 = .4980$$

$$A_2 = .5 - A_1 = .5 - .4980 = .002$$

Thus, the approximate probability of finding 33 or more defective pens in the sample is .002. If a random sample of 400 included more than 33 defective pens, then the management would conclude that either a rare event has happened and the manufacturing process is still producing only 50 defective pens per 1,000 on the average, or something is wrong with the manufacturing process and it is producing more than 50 defective pens per 1,000 on the average. The company might very well have a policy of checking the manufacturing process whenever 33 or more defective pens are found in a sample rather than believing a rare event has happened and that the manufacturing process is still all right.

Problem 18   Suppose in Example 18 that the manufacturing process produces forty defective pens per 1,000 on the average. What is the approximate probability that in the sample of pens there are:

(A)   At least ten and no more than twenty defective pens?
(B)   Twenty-seven or more defective pens?

Answers to   15.   49.38%   16.   .3413
Matched Problems   17.   (A)   .70   (B)   .13   18.   (A)   .83   (B)   .004

Exercise 6-6

A   *Given a normal distribution with mean 50 and standard deviation 10, find the number of standard deviations each of the measurements in Problems 1–8 is from the mean. Express the answer as a positive number.*

1.   65   2.   75   3.   83   4.   79
5.   45   6.   38   7.   42   8.   26

Using the normal distribution described for Problems 1–8 and Table IV, find the area under the normal curve from the mean to the indicated measurement in Problems 9–16.

9.   65   10.   75   11.   83   12.   79
13.   45   14.   38   15.   42   16.   26

B   *Given a normal distribution with mean 70 and standard deviation 8, find the area under the normal curve above the intervals in Problems 17–24.*

17.   60–80   18.   50–90   19.   62–74
20.   66–78   21.   88 or larger   22.   90 or larger
23.   60 or smaller   24.   56 or smaller

In Problems 25–32, use the rule-of-thumb test to check whether a normal distribution (with the same mean and standard deviation as the binomial distribution) is a suitable approximation for the binomial distribution with:

25. $n = 15$, $p = .7$

26. $n = 12$, $p = .6$

27. $n = 15$, $p = .4$

28. $n = 20$, $p = .6$

29. $n = 100$, $p = .05$

30. $n = 200$, $p = .03$

31. $n = 500$, $p = .05$

32. $n = 400$, $p = .08$

A binomial experiment consists of 500 trials with the probability of success for each trial .4. What is the probability of obtaining the number of successes indicated in Problems 33–40? Approximate these probabilities to two decimal places using a normal curve. (This binomial experiment easily passes the rule-of-thumb test, as you can check. When computing the probabilities, adjust the intervals as in Examples 17 and 18.)

33. 185–220

34. 190–205

35. 210–220

36. 175–185

37. 225 or more

38. 212 or more

39. 175 or less

40. 188 or less

Applications

In problems involving random samples of a population, use normal distributions to approximate the appropriate binomial distributions. In all other problems, assume normal distributions.

Business & Economics

41. *Sales.* Salespeople for a business machine company have average annual sales of $200,000, with a standard deviation of $20,000. What percentage of the salespeople would be expected to make annual sales of $240,000 or more?

42. *Guarantees.* The average lifetime for a car battery of a certain brand is 170 weeks, with a standard deviation of 10. If the company guarantees the battery for 3 years, what percentage of the batteries sold would be expected to be returned before the end of the warranty period?

43. *Quality control.* A manufacturing process produces a critical part of average length 100 millimeters, with a standard deviation of 2 millimeters. All parts deviating by more than 5 millimeters from the mean must be rejected. What percentage of the parts must be rejected on the average?

44. *Quality control.* An automated manufacturing process produces a component with an average width of 7.55 centimeters, with a standard deviation of 0.02 centimeter. All components deviating by more than 0.05 centimeter from the mean must be rejected. What percentage of the parts must be rejected on the average?

45. *Marketing claims.* A company claims that 60% of the households in a given community use their product. A competitor surveys the community, using a random sample of forty households, and finds only fifteen households out of the forty in the sample using the product. If the company's claim is correct, what is the probability of fifteen or fewer households using the product in a sample of forty? Conclusion?

46. *Labor relations.* A union representative claims 60% of the union membership will vote in favor of a particular settlement. A random sample of 100 members is polled, and out of these forty-seven favor the settlement. What is the approximate probability of forty-seven or less in a sample of 100 favoring the settlement when 60% of all the membership favor the settlement? Conclusion?

Life Sciences

47. *Medicine.* The average healing time of a certain type of incision is 240 hours, with standard deviation of twenty hours. What percentage of the people having this incision would heal in eight days or less?

48. *Agriculture.* The average height of a hay crop is 38 inches, with a standard deviation of 1.5 inches. What percentage of the crop will be 40 inches or more?

49. *Genetics.* In a two-child family, the probability that both children are girls is approximately .25. In a random sample of 1,000 two-child families, what is the approximate probability that 220 or fewer will have two girls?

50. *Genetics.* In Problem 49, what is the approximate probability of the number of families with two girls in the sample being at least 225 and not more than 275?

Social Sciences

51. *Testing.* Scholastic Aptitude Tests are scaled so that the mean score is 500 and the standard deviation is 100. What percentage of the students taking this test should score 700 or more?

52. *Politics.* Candidate Harkins claims a private poll shows that she will receive 52% of the vote for governor. Her opponent, Mankey, secures the services of another pollster, who finds that 470 out of a random sample of 1,000 registered voters favor Harkins. If Harkins' claim is correct, what is the probability that only 470 or fewer will favor her in a random sample of 1,000? Conclusion?

53. *Grading on a curve.* An instructor grades on a curve by assuming the grades on a test are normally distributed. If the average grade is 70 and the standard deviation is 8, find the test scores for each grade interval if the instructor wishes to assign grades as follows: 10% A's, 20% B's, 40% C's, 20% D's, and 10% F's.

54. *Psychology.* A test devised to measure aggressive–passive personalities was standardized on a large group of people. The scores were normally distributed with a mean of 50 and a standard deviation of 10. If we want to designate the highest 10% as aggressive, the next 20% as moderately aggressive, the middle 40% as average, the next 20% as moderately passive, and the lowest 10% as passive, what ranges of scores will be covered by these five designations?

6-7   Chapter Review

Important Terms and Symbols

6-1 *Graphing qualitative data.* Qualitative data, quantitative data, bar graphs, broken-line graphs, pie graphs

6-2 *Graphing quantitative data.* Quantitative data, frequency table, data range, class frequency, frequency distribution, relative frequency, probability distribution, histogram, frequency polygon, frequency curve, cumulative frequency table, cumulative frequency polygon, ogive

6-3 *Measures of central tendency.* Arithmetic mean (or mean), summation symbol, mean (ungrouped data), mean (grouped data), weighted average, population mean, population parameter, law of large numbers, median, mode, bimodal, Σ, $\bar{x} = (\Sigma x)/n$ (mean of ungrouped data), $\bar{x} = (\Sigma xf)/N$, where $N = \Sigma f$ (mean of grouped data), μ

6-4 *Measures of dispersion.* Range, deviation, variance, standard deviation, population standard deviation, law of large numbers, s, σ,

$$s = \sqrt{\frac{\Sigma(x - \bar{x})^2}{n - 1}},$$ where n = sample size (standard deviation of ungrouped data),

$$s = \sqrt{\frac{\Sigma(x - \bar{x})^2 f}{N - 1}},$$ where $N = \Sigma f$ (standard deviation of grouped data)

6-5 *Bernoulli trials and binomial distributions.* Bernoulli trial, sequence of Bernoulli trials (or binomial experiment), binomial formula, binomial distribution, $P(x$ successes in n trials$) = C_{n,x} p^x q^{n-x}$, $x \in \{0, 1, \ldots, n\}$, Mean $= \mu = np$, Standard deviation $= \sigma = \sqrt{npq}$

6-6 *Normal distributions.* Normal curves, normal probability distributions, discrete random variable, continuous random variable, z value, rule-of-thumb test, $z = \dfrac{x - \mu}{\sigma}$

Exercise 6-7   Chapter Review

Work through all the problems in this chapter review and check your answers in the back of the book. (Answers to all review problems are there.) Where weaknesses show up, review appropriate sections in the text.

A   1.   Graph the following data using a bar graph and a broken-line graph:

Imports as a Percentage of Total New Car Sales in the United States

1955	1960	1965	1970	1975
1%	7.5%	6.5%	15%	16%

2. Graph the data in the following table using a pie graph:

United States Population Distribution, 1970

White	Black	Spanish-speaking	Other
83%	11%	5%	1%

3. (A) Draw a histogram for the binomial distribution

$$P(x) = C_{3,x}(.4)^x(.6)^{3-x}$$

(B) What are the mean and standard deviation?

4. For the set of data 1, 1, 2, 2, 2, 3, 3, 4, 4, 5, find the:

(A) Mean   (B) Median   (C) Mode
(D) Standard deviation

5. If a normal distribution has a mean of 100 and a standard deviation of 10, then:

(A) How many standard deviations is 118 from the mean?
(B) What is the area under the normal curve between the mean and 118?

B   6. Given the following scores on a quiz:

Quiz Scores

14	13	16	15	17
19	15	14	17	15
15	13	12	14	14
12	14	13	11	15
16	14	16	17	14

(A) Construct a frequency table using a class interval of width 2 starting at 9.5.
(B) Construct a histogram.
(C) Construct a frequency polygon.

(D)   Construct a cumulative frequency and relative cumulative frequency table.

(E)   Construct a cumulative frequency polygon.

7.   For the following set of grouped data:

Interval	Frequency
0.5–3.5	1
3.5–6.5	5
6.5–9.5	7
9.5–12.5	2

(A)   Find the mean.   (B)   Find the standard deviation.

8.   (A)   Construct a histogram for the binomial distribution

$$P(x) = C_{6,x}(.5)^x(.5)^{6-x}$$

(B)   What are the mean and standard deviation?

9.   What are the mean and standard deviation for a binomial distribution with $p = .6$ and $n = 1,000$?

10.   If the probability of success in a single trial of a binomial experiment with 1,000 trials is .6, what is the probability of obtaining at least 550 and no more than 650 successes in 1,000 trials? [*Hint:* Approximate with a normal distribution.]

11.   Given a normal distribution with mean 50 and standard deviation 6, find the area under the normal curve:

(A)   Between 41 and 62   (B)   From 59 on

C   12.   For the data in Problem 6 above, find the mean and standard deviation using the data:

(A)   Without grouping

(B)   Grouped with class interval of width 2 starting at 9.5

13.   A fair die is rolled five times. What is the probability of rolling:

(A)   Exactly three 6's?   (B)   At least three 6's?

14.   Two dice are rolled three times. What is the probability of getting at least one 7?

Applications

15.   *Retail sales.* The daily record of bad checks received by a large department store over a ten-day period was 15, 12, 17, 5, 5, 8, 13, 5, 16, and 4. Find the:

(A) Mean   (B) Median
(C) Mode   (D) Standard deviation

16. *Preference Survey.* Find the mean, median, or mode, whichever are
applicable, for the following fast food service survey:

Drink Ordered with Meal	Number
Coffee	435
Tea	137
Milk	298
Soft Drink	522
Milk Shake	392

17. *Plant safety.* The weekly record of reported accidents in a large auto
assembly plant over a 35-week period is listed below.

34	33	36	35	37	31	37
39	34	35	37	35	32	35
33	35	32	34	32	32	39
34	31	35	33	31	38	34
36	34	37	34	36	39	34

(A) Construct a frequency and relative frequency table using class
intervals of width 2 and starting at 29.5.
(B) Construct a histogram and frequency polygon.
(C) Find the mean and standard deviation for the grouped data.

18. *Personnel screening.* The scores on a screening test for new technicians are normally distributed with mean 100 and standard deviation
10. Find the approximate percent of applicants taking the test scoring:

(A) Between 92 and 108
(B) 115 or higher

19. *Market research.* A newspaper publisher claims that 70% of the people in a community read their newspaper. Doubting the assertion, a
competitor randomly surveys 200 people in the community. Based on
the publisher's claim (and assuming a binomial distribution):

(A) Compute the mean and standard deviation of the binomial distribution.
(B) Determine whether the rule-of-thumb test warrants the use of a
normal distribution to approximate this binomial distribution.

(C)   Calculate the approximate probability of finding at least 130 and no more than 155 readers in the sample.

(D)   Determine the approximate probability of finding 125 or fewer readers in the sample.

20.   *Health care.* A small town has three doctors on call for emergency service. The probability that any one doctor will be available when called is .90. What is the probability that at least one doctor will be available for an emergency call?

The Derivative

7

CHAPTER 7   Contents

How do algebra and calculus differ? The two words *static* and *dynamic* probably come as close as any in expressing the difference between the two disciplines. In algebra, we solve equations for a particular value of a variable—a static notion. In calculus, we are interested in how a change in one variable affects another variable—a dynamic notion.

Figure 1 illustrates three basic problems in calculus. It may surprise you to learn that all three problems—as different as they appear—are mathematically related. The solutions to these problems and the discovery of their relationship required the creation of a new kind of mathematics. Isaac Newton (1642–1727) of England and Gottfried Wilhelm von Leibniz (1646–1716) of Germany simultaneously and independently developed this new mathematics, called **the calculus**—it was an idea whose time had come.

In addition to solving the problems described in Figure 1, calculus will enable us to solve many important problems. Until fairly recently, calculus was used primarily in the physical sciences, but now people in many other disciplines are finding it a useful tool.

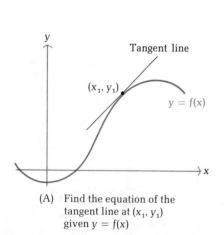

(A) Find the equation of the tangent line at (x_1, y_1) given $y = f(x)$

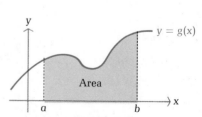

(B) Find the instantaneous velocity of a falling object

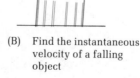

(C) Find the indicated area bounded by $y = g(x)$, $x = a$, $x = b$, and the x axis

Figure 1

514

7-1   Limits

Basic to the study of calculus is the concept of *limit*. This concept helps us to describe, in a precise way, the behavior of $f(x)$ when x is close to but not equal to a particular value c. And as we will soon see, it is fundamental to the two main topics of calculus—*the derivative* and the *integral*. In our discussion, we will concentrate on concept development and understanding rather than on the formal details.

■ Introduction

We introduce the concept of limit through a problem that goes back to early Grecian times. The problem concerns estimating the circumference of a circle using perimeters of regular polygons inscribed in the circle. Figure 2 illustrates three-sided, six-sided, and twelve-sided regular polygons inscribed in a circle. It appears that if we continue to double the number of sides of an inscribed regular polygon, we can make the perimeter as close to the circumference of the circle as we like. We say that the circumference C of the circle is the *limit* of the perimeter of the inscribed regular polygon as the number of sides increases without bound. Archimedes, a Greek mathematician and inventor (287–212 B.C.), approximated the value of π as the limit of perimeters of inscribed regular polygons in a circle with diameter $D = 1$. (Recall that $C = \pi D$. If $D = 1$, then $\pi = C$.)

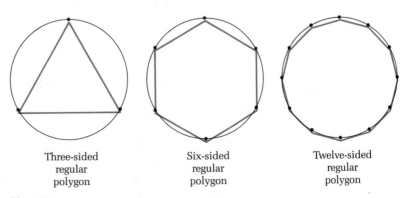

| Three-sided regular polygon | Six-sided regular polygon | Twelve-sided regular polygon |

Figure 2

We now turn to another geometric example related to circles. A line that intersects a circle in one and only one point is called a **tangent line** (see Fig. 3A). One of the basic problems of calculus is the generalization of the concept of a tangent line to the graph of an arbitrary function, as illustrated in Figure 1A. The key to this generalization is the relationship between the slope of the tangent line and the slopes of secant lines. Recall that a **secant line** is a line that intersects a circle in two points. If P is a fixed point on the circle and Q is any other point on the circle, then as Q moves closer to P, the secant lines seem to approach the tangent line (see Fig. 3B). It seems reasonable to assume that the slopes of the secant lines will be approaching the slope of the tangent line.

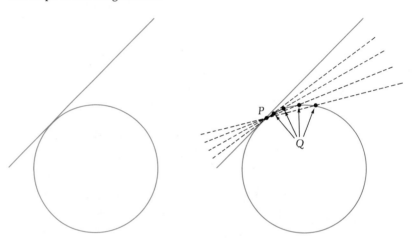

(A) Tangent line for a circle

(B) Secant lines approach the tangent line as Q approaches P

Figure 3

Now consider the graph of $f(x) = x^2$, a parabola, and the line through the (fixed) point $(2, 4)$ and another arbitrary point (x, x^2) on the graph (see Fig. 4A). As with circles, a line through two points on a graph is called a *secant line*. The formula for the slope of the line passing through (x_1, y_1) and (x_2, y_2) is

$$m = \frac{y_2 - y_1}{x_2 - x_1} \qquad x_1 \neq x_2 \qquad \text{See Section 0-4.}$$

Thus, the slope of the secant line through $(2, 4)$ and (x, x^2) is given by

$$\text{Slope of secant line} = m_s = \frac{x^2 - 4}{x - 2}$$

As x approaches 2 (from either side of 2), the secant lines seem to be approaching the line graphed in Figure 4B, which we will call the *tangent line*. For now, we assume that m_s, the slope of the secant line, approaches the slope of the tangent line as x approaches 2. (Precise definitions of tangent line and slope of the tangent line will be given in Section 7-3.) How

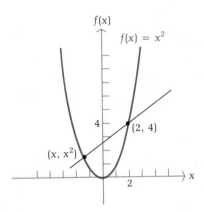

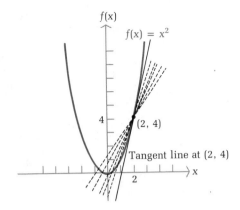

(A) Secant line through (2, 4) and (x, x²)

(B) The (dashed) secant lines are approaching the (solid) tangent line.

Figure 4

can we find the slope of this tangent line? If we substitute $x = 2$ in the formula for m_s, we get

$$m_s = \frac{2^2 - 4}{2 - 2} = \frac{0}{0} = ?$$

Since division by 0 is not permitted, the expression $\frac{0}{0}$ is meaningless and m_s is not defined at $x = 2$. Thus, we cannot find the slope of the tangent line by evaluating the formula for m_s at $x = 2$. But this formula is defined for all other values of x, and in particular for values of x that are very close to 2.

What happens to m_s when x approaches 2 from either side of 2? Let us investigate this question using a calculator experiment. Table 1 shows the secant line slopes m_s for values of x approaching 2 from the left and for values of x approaching 2 from the right. It appears that m_s approaches 4 ($m_s \to 4$) as x approaches 2 ($x \to 2$) from either side of 2, and the closer x is to 2, the closer m_s will be to 4. We say that 4 is the "limit of m_s as x approaches 2" and write

$$\lim_{x \to 2} \frac{x^2 - 4}{x - 2} = 4$$

As x approaches 2, $(x^2 - 4)/(x - 2)$ approaches 4, and it is this number 4 that we call the *limit*, even though $(x^2 - 4)/(x - 2)$ is not defined at $x = 2$.

In Figure 4B we associate 4 with the slope of the tangent line to the graph at (2, 4).

Table 1

	x approaches 2 from the left $\to$ 2 $\leftarrow$ x approaches 2 from the right									
x	1.5	1.8	1.9	1.99	1.999 $\to$ 2 $\leftarrow$ 2.001	2.01	2.1	2.2	2.5
m_s	3.5	3.8	3.9	3.99	3.999 $\to$? $\leftarrow$ 4.001	4.01	4.1	4.2	4.5

■ Definition of Limit

Finding slopes of tangent lines is not the only problem involving limits we will encounter. In general, we will be concerned with finding **the limit of a function f as x approaches a number c.** We now state an informal definition of this concept. A precise definition will not be needed for our discussion, but one is given in the footnote.*

Limit (Informal Definition)

We write

$$\lim_{x \to c} f(x) = L$$

if the functional value $f(x)$ is close to the single real number L whenever x is close to but not equal to c (on either side of c).

Example 1   Graph $f(x) = x^2 + 2$ and use the graph to find $\lim_{x \to 1} f(x)$.

Solution   The graph of f is a parabola opening upwards with vertex (0, 2), as shown in the figure. For each number x, the functional value $f(x)$ represents the

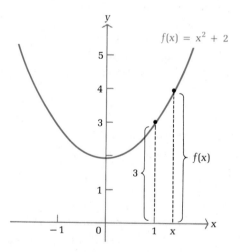

* To make the informal definition of limit precise, the use of the word *close* must be made more precise. This is done as follows: We write $\lim_{x \to c} f(x) = L$ if for each $e > 0$, there exists a $d > 0$ such that $|f(x) - L| < e$ whenever $0 < |x - c| < d$. This definition is used to establish particular limits and to prove many useful properties of limits that will be helpful to us in finding particular limits. [Even though intuitive notions of limit existed for a long time, it was not until the nineteenth century that a precise definition was given by the German mathematician, Karl Weierstrass (1815–1897).]

vertical distance from the x axis to the point $(x, f(x))$ on the graph of f. If x is close to 1, the graph shows that this vertical distance is close to the vertical distance from the x axis to the point $(1, 3)$. Thus, we conclude that $\lim_{x \to 1} f(x) = 3$.

Problem 1   Graph $f(x) = 2x + 1$ and use the graph to find $\lim_{x \to 2} f(x)$.

Example 2   Graph $f(x) = |x|/x$ and use the graph to find:

     (A) $\lim_{x \to 2} f(x)$ (B) $\lim_{x \to 0} f(x)$

Solutions   We start by sketching a graph of f:

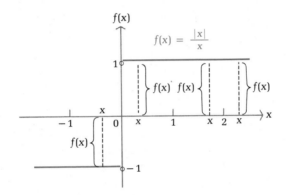

For $x > 0$, $f(x) = |x|/x = x/x = 1$.
For $x < 0$, $f(x) = |x|/x = -x/x = -1$.
For $x = 0$, $f(x)$ is undefined.

     (A)   If x is close to 2 (on either side of 2), then $f(x) = 1$. Thus, $\lim_{x \to 2} f(x) = 1$.

     (B)   If x is close to 0 and greater than 0, then $f(x) = 1$, but if x is close to 0 and less than 0, then $f(x) = -1$. Since the functional values $f(x)$ are not close to a single number L for x close to 0 on both sides of 0, we conclude that $\lim_{x \to 0} f(x)$ does not exist.

Problem 2   Graph $f(x) = x + |x|/x$ and use the graph to find:

     (A) $\lim_{x \to 2} f(x)$ (B) $\lim_{x \to 0} f(x)$

Example 3   Let $f(x) = 1/(x + 1)$. Use a table of values to find $\lim_{x \to -1} f(x)$.

Solution   Notice that f is not defined at $x = -1$ (division by 0 is not permitted). We construct a table of values of $f(x)$ for x near -1 on both sides of -1:

Table 2

	x approaches −1 from the left →−1← x approaches −1 from the right								
x	−1.1	−1.01	−1.001	−1.0001	→−1←	−0.9999	−0.999	−0.99	−0.9
f(x)	−10	−100	−1,000	−10,000	→ ? ←	10,000	1,000	100	10

As x approaches −1 from either side, the values of $f(x)$ are becoming larger and larger in absolute value. Since the functional values are not approaching a number L, we conclude that $\lim_{x \to -1} f(x)$ does not exist. This behavior is illustrated graphically by drawing a dashed vertical line through $x = -1$. This line is called a *vertical asymptote* for the graph of function f (see the figure).

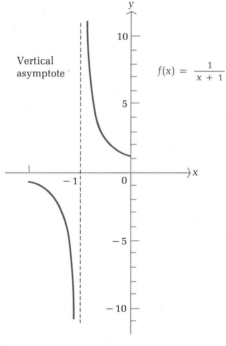

$$\lim_{x \to -1} \frac{1}{x + 1} \text{ does not exist}$$

Problem 3   Let $f(x) = 1/(2 - x)$. Use a table of values to find $\lim_{x \to 2} f(x)$. (Do not graph f.)

■ Properties of Limits

We now turn to some basic properties of limits that will enable us to evaluate limits of a rather large class of functions without resorting to tables, figures, or graphs. We state some important properties without proof in Theorem 1.

Theorem 1

Properties of Limits

If k and c are constants, n is a positive integer, and

$$\lim_{x \to c} f(x) = A \qquad \lim_{x \to c} g(x) = B$$

then:

1. $\lim_{x \to c} k = k$

2. $\lim_{x \to c} kf(x) = k \lim_{x \to c} f(x) = kA$

3. $\lim_{x \to c} [f(x) \pm g(x)] = \lim_{x \to c} f(x) \pm \lim_{x \to c} g(x) = A \pm B$

4. If P is a polynomial function,* then $\lim_{x \to c} P(x) = P(c)$

5. $\lim_{x \to c} [f(x) \cdot g(x)] = [\lim_{x \to c} f(x)][\lim_{x \to c} g(x)] = AB$

6. $\lim_{x \to c} \dfrac{f(x)}{g(x)} = \dfrac{\lim_{x \to c} f(x)}{\lim_{x \to c} g(x)} = \dfrac{A}{B} \qquad B \neq 0$

7. $\lim_{x \to c} \sqrt[n]{f(x)} = \sqrt[n]{\lim_{x \to c} f(x)} = \sqrt[n]{A}$

    (x is restricted to avoid even roots of negative numbers)

Example 4   Use the properties of limits to evaluate each limit.

(A) $\lim_{x \to 2} (3x^5 - 2x^2 + 3x - 1)$ Use property 4, since $P(x) = 3x^5 - 2x^2 + 3x - 1$ is a polynomial function.

$$= 3(2)^5 - 2(2)^2 + 3(2) - 1$$

$$= 93$$

(B) $\lim_{x \to 4} \sqrt{x^2 - 4} = \sqrt{\lim_{x \to 4} (x^2 - 4)}$ Use properties 7 and 4. Note that $x^2 - 4$ is positive for x near 4.

$$= \sqrt{4^2 - 4}$$

$$= \sqrt{12} = 2\sqrt{3}$$

* A **polynomial function** is any function that can be specified by an equation of the form

$$P(x) = a_n x^n + a_{n-1} x^{n-1} + \cdots + a_1 x + a_0$$

where the coefficients $a_0, a_1, \ldots, a_n$ are real numbers and n is a nonnegative integer. [*Examples:* $P(x) = 2x - 3$, $P(x) = 5$, $P(x) = 4x^5 - 2x^3 + 3x^2 - x + 1$.]

(C) $\lim\limits_{x \to -1} \dfrac{x^2+1}{x+4} = \dfrac{\lim\limits_{x \to -1} (x^2+1)}{\lim\limits_{x \to -1} (x+4)}$ Use properties 6 and 4. Note that $\lim_{x \to -1}(x+4) = 3 \neq 0$.

$$= \frac{(-1)^2+1}{(-1)+4} = \frac{2}{3}$$

Problem 4

Use properties of limits to evaluate each limit.

(A) $\lim\limits_{x \to -2} (2x^4 - 3x^3 + 5)$ (B) $\lim\limits_{x \to 3} \sqrt{x^2 - 1}$ (C) $\lim\limits_{x \to 0} \dfrac{x^2+5}{x+3}$

Example 5

Use properties of limits and algebraic manipulations to find each limit, if it exists.

(A) $\lim\limits_{x \to 3} \dfrac{x^2-x-6}{x-3}$ (B) $\lim\limits_{x \to -1} \dfrac{x-1}{x^2-1}$ (C) $\lim\limits_{x \to 9} \dfrac{\sqrt{x}-3}{x-9}$

Solutions

(A) We cannot use property 6, since $\lim_{x \to 3}(x-3) = 0$. We factor the numerator to see if we can simplify the function:

$$\frac{x^2-x-6}{x-3} = \frac{\overset{1}{\cancel{(x-3)}}(x+2)}{\underset{1}{\cancel{(x-3)}}} = x+2 \qquad x \neq 3 \tag{1}$$

The left and right sides of (1) are equal for all values of x except $x=3$. Since the limit process involves functional values for x near 3 but not equal to 3, we can write

$$\lim\limits_{x \to 3} \frac{x^2-x-6}{x-3} = \lim\limits_{x \to 3} (x+2) \qquad \text{Use property 4.}$$

$$= 5$$

In practice, the algebraic manipulations and the limit evaluation are often combined. The solution to this problem can be written more compactly as

$$\lim\limits_{x \to 3} \frac{x^2-x-6}{x-3} = \lim\limits_{x \to 3} \frac{\overset{1}{\cancel{(x-3)}}(x+2)}{\underset{1}{\cancel{(x-3)}}} = \lim\limits_{x \to 3} (x+2) = 5 \tag{2}$$

Notice that in (2) we do not have to explicitly state that $x \neq 3$. It is understood that the limit operation is concerned with the functional values for x near 3 but not equal to 3. On the other hand, the restriction $x \neq 3$ is essential in (1). It is incorrect to write

$$\frac{x^2-x-6}{x-3} = x+2$$

without stating that $x \neq 3$.

(B)   Since property 6 does not apply, we proceed as in part A.

$$\lim_{x \to -1} \frac{x-1}{x^2-1} = \lim_{x \to -1} \frac{\overset{1}{\cancel{(x-1)}}}{\cancel{(x-1)}(x+1)}$$

$$= \lim_{x \to -1} \frac{1}{x+1}$$

Does not exist

The values of $1/(x+1)$ become arbitrarily large in absolute value as x approaches -1. See Example 3.

(C) $\displaystyle\lim_{x \to 9} \frac{\sqrt{x}-3}{x-9} = \lim_{x \to 9} \frac{(\sqrt{x}-3)}{(x-9)} \cdot \frac{(\sqrt{x}+3)}{(\sqrt{x}+3)}$

Property 6 does not apply. We rationalize the numerator, then use properties 6, 1, and 7.

$$= \lim_{x \to 9} \frac{\overset{1}{\cancel{(x-9)}}}{\cancel{(x-9)}(\sqrt{x}+3)}$$

$$= \lim_{x \to 9} \frac{1}{\sqrt{x}+3}$$

$$= \frac{1}{\sqrt{9}+3} = \frac{1}{6}$$

Problem 5   Use properties of limits and algebraic manipulations to find each limit, if it exists.

(A) $\displaystyle\lim_{x \to 3} \frac{x^2-2x-3}{x-3}$ (B) $\displaystyle\lim_{x \to 2} \frac{2+x}{4-x^2}$ (C) $\displaystyle\lim_{x \to 1} \frac{\sqrt{x}-1}{x-1}$

■ Limits at Infinity

It is also of interest to determine what happens to the functional values $f(x)$ as x assumes large positive values and large negative values. We begin by considering an example.

Example 6   Consider the function $f(x) = 2x^2/(1+x^2)$, which is defined for all real numbers. What happens to the functional value $f(x)$ as x assumes larger and larger positive values?

Solution   Let us investigate this question using a calculator. Table 3 shows the values of $f(x)$ for increasingly large values of x.

Table 3

	x assumes larger and larger positive values						
x	0	5	10	20	50	100	500	1,000
$f(x)$	0	1.92	1.98	1.995	1.9992	1.9998	1.999992	1.999998

The calculations shown here suggest that as the values of x continue to increase, the functional value $f(x)$ approaches the number 2. It seems that we can make the functional value $f(x)$ come as close to 2 as we like by taking a sufficiently large value of x. If we use the symbol "$x \to \infty$" to indicate that x is increasing with no upper limit on its size, then we can write

$$\lim_{x \to \infty} \frac{2x^2}{1 + x^2} = 2$$

It is important to understand that the symbol "∞" does not represent an actual number that x is approaching, but is used to indicate only that the value of x is increasing with no upper limit on its size. In particular, the statement "$x = \infty$" is meaningless since ∞ is not a symbol for a real number. We will also use the statement "$x \to -\infty$" to indicate that the value of x is decreasing with no lower limit on its size. Since for the function in this example $f(-x) = f(x)$, the values in Table 3 also suggest that

$$\lim_{x \to -\infty} \frac{2x^2}{1 + x^2} = 2$$

Examining the graph of this function (see Figure 5) provides us with a geometric interpretation of these two limit statements. The graph of f is approaching the horizontal line with equation $y = 2$ as $x \to \infty$ and as $x \to -\infty$. The line $y = 2$ is called a **horizontal asymptote** for the graph of f.

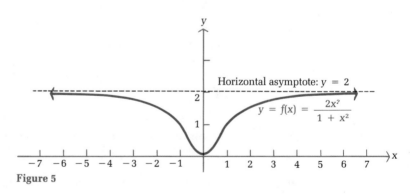

Figure 5

Problem 6   Construct a table such as Table 3 in order to estimate (do not graph):

$$\lim_{x \to \infty} \frac{2}{1 + x^2}$$

We now state an informal definition of **the limit of a function f as x approaches ∞ or $-\infty$.**

Limits at Infinity

We write

$$\lim_{x \to \infty} f(x) = L$$

if the functional value $f(x)$ is close to the single real number L whenever x is a very large positive number. We write

$$\lim_{x \to -\infty} f(x) = M$$

if the functional value $f(x)$ is close to the single real number M whenever x is a negative number with very large absolute value.

How can we evaluate limits of the form $\lim_{x \to \infty} f(x)$ and $\lim_{x \to -\infty} f(x)$ without drawing figures or performing calculator experiments? Fortunately, all the limit properties listed in Theorem 1, except property 4,* are valid if we replace the statement $x \to c$ with the statement $x \to \infty$ (or $x \to -\infty$). These properties, together with Theorem 2, will enable us to evaluate limits at infinity for many functions.

Theorem 2

If p is a positive number, then

$$\lim_{x \to \infty} \frac{1}{x^p} = 0$$

and

$$\lim_{x \to -\infty} \frac{1}{x^p} = 0$$

provided that x^p names a real number for negative values of x.

Figure 6 (at the top of the next page) illustrates the theorem for several values of p.

---

* Limit property 4, $\lim_{x \to c} P(x) = P(c)$, does not make sense if c is replaced with ∞. Remember, ∞ is not a number and it is impossible to evaluate a function at ∞.

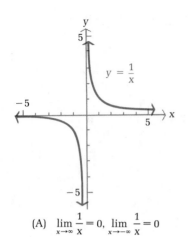

(A) $\lim\limits_{x\to\infty}\dfrac{1}{x}=0,\ \lim\limits_{x\to-\infty}\dfrac{1}{x}=0$

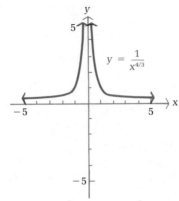

(B) $\lim\limits_{x\to\infty}\dfrac{1}{x^{4/3}}=0,\ \lim\limits_{x\to-\infty}\dfrac{1}{x^{4/3}}=0$

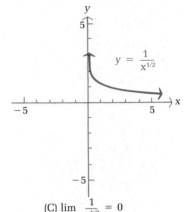

(C) $\lim\limits_{x\to\infty}\dfrac{1}{x^{1/2}}=0$

$x^{1/2}$ is not defined for negative values of x

Figure 6 $\lim\limits_{x\to\infty}\dfrac{1}{x^p}$

Example 7 Find each limit.

(A) $\lim\limits_{x\to\infty}\dfrac{5x+4}{2x+3}$ (B) $\lim\limits_{x\to-\infty}\dfrac{4x^2+3x+2}{2x^3+5}$ (C) $\lim\limits_{x\to\infty}\dfrac{3x^4+6x}{x^2+4}$

Solutions (A) $\lim\limits_{x\to\infty}\dfrac{5x+4}{2x+3}$

$$=\lim\limits_{x\to\infty}\dfrac{\dfrac{5x+4}{x}}{\dfrac{2x+3}{x}}$$

$$=\lim\limits_{x\to\infty}\dfrac{5+\dfrac{4}{x}}{2+\dfrac{3}{x}}=\dfrac{5+0}{2+0}=\dfrac{5}{2}$$

$\neq\dfrac{\lim_{x\to\infty}5x+4}{\lim_{x\to\infty}2x+3}$ since $\lim\limits_{x\to\infty}(5x+4)$ and $\lim\limits_{x\to\infty}(2x+3)$ do not exist

We divide numerator and denominator by x in order to express the fraction in a form where the limits of the numerator and denominator do exist.

Use limit properties 6 and 3 and Theorem 2.

(B) $\lim\limits_{x\to-\infty}\dfrac{4x^2+3x+2}{2x^3+5}$

$$=\lim\limits_{x\to-\infty}\dfrac{\dfrac{4}{x}+\dfrac{3}{x^2}+\dfrac{2}{x^3}}{2+\dfrac{5}{x^3}}$$

$$=\dfrac{0+0+0}{2+0}=\dfrac{0}{2}=0$$

Divide numerator and denominator by x^3, the highest power of x that occurs in the numerator or the denominator, simplify, and proceed as before.

Use limit properties 6 and 3 and Theorem 2.

(C) $\lim\limits_{x\to\infty} \dfrac{3x^4 + 6x}{x^2 + 4}$

This time, divide numerator and denominator by x^4.

$$= \lim\limits_{x\to\infty} \dfrac{3 + \dfrac{6}{x^3}}{\dfrac{1}{x^2} + \dfrac{4}{x^4}}$$

Since the numerator of this fraction approaches 3 and the denominator approaches 0, the fraction can be made as large as you like; hence, the limit does not exist.

Does not exist

Problem 7 Find each limit.

(A) $\lim\limits_{x\to\infty} \dfrac{2x - 4}{3x + 5}$ (B) $\lim\limits_{x\to\infty} \dfrac{3x^3 + 4}{2x^2 + 6}$ (C) $\lim\limits_{x\to\infty} \dfrac{2x + 1}{x^2 + 4}$

The methods used to evaluate the limits in Example 7 can be applied to any rational function.* The results are summarized in Theorem 3.

Theorem 3

Limits at Infinity for Rational Functions

If

$$f(x) = \frac{p(x)}{q(x)}$$

where

$$p(x) = a_n x^n + a_{n-1} x^{n-1} + \cdots + a_0 \qquad a_n \neq 0$$

and

$$q(x) = b_m x^m + b_{m-1} x^{m-1} + \cdots + b_0 \qquad b_m \neq 0$$

then

$$\lim\limits_{x\to\pm\infty} f(x) = \begin{cases} 0 & \text{if } n < m \quad (3) \\ \dfrac{a_n}{b_m} & \text{if } n = m \quad (4) \\ \text{Does not exist} & \text{if } n > m \quad (5) \end{cases}$$

[Note: If $n > m$, then the limit fails to exist because $f(x)$ is unbounded as $x \to \infty$ and as $x \to -\infty$.]

* A **rational function** is any function that can be specified by an equation of the form

$$R(x) = \frac{P(x)}{Q(x)}$$

where $P(x)$ and $Q(x)$ are polynomials.

Examples: $R(x) = \dfrac{x}{x - 3}$, $R(x) = \dfrac{x^2 - 3x + 1}{2x^3 - 3x^2 + 5}$, $R(x) = \dfrac{5}{x^3 - 9}$

Thus, we see that the limit at infinity of a rational function can be determined by simply comparing the degree of the numerator and the degree of the denominator. Notice that the value of the limit is the same, whether $x \to \infty$ or $x \to -\infty$. This implies that a rational function can have at most one horizontal asymptote.

Example 8   Use equations (3), (4), and (5) in Theorem 3 to find each limit.

(A) $\displaystyle \lim_{x \to \pm\infty} \frac{5x^2 + 3}{3x^2 + 4}$

(B) $\displaystyle \lim_{x \to \pm\infty} \frac{2x^5 + 7}{6x^3 + 4}$

(C) $\displaystyle \lim_{x \to \pm\infty} \frac{3x^4 + 9}{8x^6 + 5}$

Solutions   (A) $\displaystyle \lim_{x \to \pm\infty} \frac{5x^2 + 3}{3x^2 + 4} = \frac{5}{3}$

Use (4): $n = m = 2$, $a_n = 5$, $b_m = 3$

(B) $\displaystyle \lim_{x \to \pm\infty} \frac{2x^5 + 7}{6x^3 + 4}$ Does not exist

Use (5): $n = 5$, $m = 3$, $n > m$

(C) $\displaystyle \lim_{x \to \pm\infty} \frac{3x^4 + 9}{8x^6 + 5} = 0$

Use (3): $n = 4$, $m = 6$, $n < m$

Problem 8   Use equations (3), (4), and (5) in Theorem 3 to find each limit.

(A) $\displaystyle \lim_{x \to \pm\infty} \frac{4x^3 + 5}{2x^4 + 4}$

(B) $\displaystyle \lim_{x \to \pm\infty} \frac{x^6 + 2}{x^5 + 4}$

(C) $\displaystyle \lim_{x \to \pm\infty} \frac{4x^2 + 7}{9x^2 + 11}$

Answers to Matched Problems

1.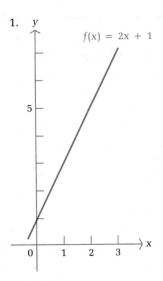

$$\lim_{x \to 2} f(x) = 5$$

2.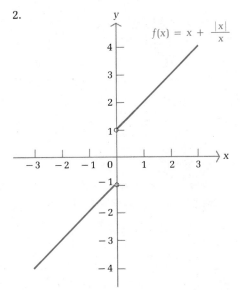

(A) $\lim_{x \to 2} f(x) = 3$ (B) $\lim_{x \to 0} f(x)$ does not exist

3. Does not exist   4. (A) 61   (B) $\sqrt{8}$ (C) $\frac{5}{3}$

5. (A) 4   (B) Does not exist   (C) $\frac{1}{2}$ 6. 0

7. (A) $\frac{2}{3}$ (B) Does not exist   (C) 0

8. (A) 0   (B) Does not exist   (C) $\frac{4}{9}$

Exercise 7-1

A   1. Use the graph of function g to estimate each limit, if it exists.

(A) $\lim\limits_{x \to -2} g(x)$ (B) $\lim\limits_{x \to 0} g(x)$ (C) $\lim\limits_{x \to 1} g(x)$ (D) $\lim\limits_{x \to 3} g(x)$

2. Use the graph of function f to estimate each limit, if it exists.

(A) $\lim\limits_{x \to 1} f(x)$ (B) $\lim\limits_{x \to 2} f(x)$ (C) $\lim\limits_{x \to 4} f(x)$ (D) $\lim\limits_{x \to 5} f(x)$

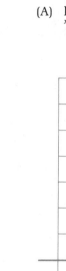

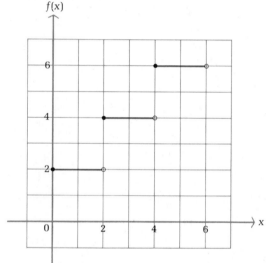

Find each limit.

3. $\lim\limits_{x \to 5} (2x^2 - 3)$

4. $\lim\limits_{x \to 2} (x^2 - 8x + 2)$

5. $\lim\limits_{x \to 4} (x^2 - 5x)$

6. $\lim\limits_{x \to -2} (3x^3 - 9)$

7. $\lim\limits_{x \to 2} \dfrac{5x}{2 + x^2}$

8. $\lim\limits_{x \to 10} \dfrac{2x + 5}{3x - 5}$

9. $\lim\limits_{x \to 2} (x + 1)^3 (2x - 1)^2$

10. $\lim\limits_{x \to 3} (x + 2)^2 (2x - 4)$

Use a calculator to complete the following table for each function in Problems 11–14:

x	0.9	0.99	0.999	→1←	1.001	1.01	1.1
f(x)				→?←			

Use the completed table to estimate $\lim_{x \to 1} f(x)$, if it exists.

11. $f(x) = \dfrac{x^2 - 1}{(x - 1)^2}$

12. $f(x) = \dfrac{x^2 - 1}{x - 1}$

13. $f(x) = \dfrac{|x - 1|}{x - 1}$

14. $f(x) = \dfrac{x^2 - 1}{|x - 1|}$

Use a calculator to complete the following table for each function in Problems 15–18:

x	10	100	1,000	10,000	$\to \infty$
$f(x)$					$\to$?

Use the completed table to estimate $\lim_{x \to \infty} f(x)$, if it exists.

15. $f(x) = \dfrac{1}{x + 1}$

16. $f(x) = \dfrac{x}{x + 1}$

17. $f(x) = \dfrac{x^2}{x + 1}$

18. $f(x) = \dfrac{x + 1}{x^2}$

B   19. Use the graph of function f to estimate each limit, if it exists.

(A) $\lim\limits_{x \to -\infty} f(x)$ (B) $\lim\limits_{x \to -1} f(x)$

(C) $\lim\limits_{x \to 1} f(x)$ (D) $\lim\limits_{x \to \infty} f(x)$

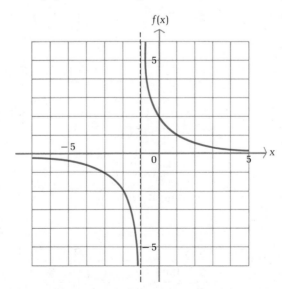

20. Use the graph of function g to estimate each limit, if it exists.

(A) $\lim\limits_{x \to -\infty} g(x)$ (B) $\lim\limits_{x \to -1} g(x)$ (C) $\lim\limits_{x \to 1} g(x)$ (D) $\lim\limits_{x \to \infty} g(x)$

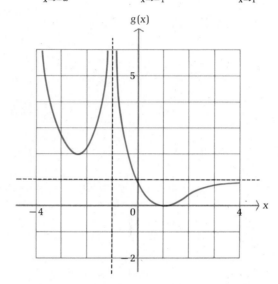

Find each limit, if it exists. (Use algebraic manipulations where necessary.)

21. $\lim\limits_{x \to 0} \dfrac{x^2 - 3x}{x}$

22. $\lim\limits_{x \to 0} \dfrac{2x^2 + 5x}{x}$

23. $\lim\limits_{x \to 5} \dfrac{x^2 - 25}{x - 5}$

24. $\lim\limits_{x \to 4} \dfrac{x^2 - 16}{x - 4}$

25. $\lim\limits_{x \to -5} \dfrac{x^2 - 25}{x - 5}$

26. $\lim\limits_{x \to -4} \dfrac{x^2 - 16}{x - 4}$

27. $\lim\limits_{x \to -2} \dfrac{x^2 - x - 6}{x + 2}$

28. $\lim\limits_{x \to -4} \dfrac{2x^2 + 7x - 4}{x + 4}$

29. $\lim\limits_{x \to 3} \dfrac{x^2 - x - 6}{x^2 - 9}$

30. $\lim\limits_{x \to 2} \dfrac{x^2 + 2x - 8}{x^2 - 2x}$

31. $\lim\limits_{x \to 1} \dfrac{2x^3 - 3x + 2}{x^2 + x}$

32. $\lim\limits_{x \to 2} \dfrac{x^3 - x^2 + 1}{x - x^2}$

33. $\lim\limits_{x \to 3} \left(\dfrac{x}{x + 3} + \dfrac{x - 3}{x^2 - 9} \right)$

34. $\lim\limits_{x \to 2} \left(\dfrac{1}{x + 2} + \dfrac{x - 2}{x^2 - 4} \right)$

35. $\lim\limits_{x \to 0} \dfrac{(2 + x)^2 - 4}{x}$

36. $\lim\limits_{x \to 0} \dfrac{(3 + x)^2 - 9}{x}$

37. $\lim\limits_{x \to \infty} \dfrac{2x + 4}{x}$

38. $\lim\limits_{x \to \infty} \dfrac{3x^2 + 5}{x^2}$

39. $\lim\limits_{x \to \infty} \left(4 + \dfrac{2}{x} - \dfrac{3}{x^2} \right)$

40. $\lim\limits_{x \to -\infty} \left(3 - \dfrac{5}{x^3} + \dfrac{2}{x^4} \right)$

41. $\lim\limits_{x\to\infty} \dfrac{2x^3}{3x^3+5}$

42. $\lim\limits_{x\to\infty} \dfrac{4x^4}{9x^4+10}$

43. $\lim\limits_{x\to-\infty} \dfrac{2x^3}{4x^4+7}$

44. $\lim\limits_{x\to-\infty} \dfrac{3x^2}{x+2}$

45. $\lim\limits_{x\to\infty} \dfrac{3x^3+5}{4x^2+2}$

46. $\lim\limits_{x\to\infty} \dfrac{7x^2}{x^5+7}$

In Problems 47–50, graph the function f and use the graph to estimate each limit, if it exists.

47. $f(x) = \begin{cases} 1 & -1 \leqslant x < 1 \\ 2 & 1 \leqslant x < 3 \\ 3 & 3 \leqslant x \leqslant 5 \end{cases}$

   (A) $\lim\limits_{x\to 1} f(x)$ (B) $\lim\limits_{x\to 2} f(x)$ (C) $\lim\limits_{x\to 3} f(x)$

48. $f(x) = \begin{cases} 1 & -1 \leqslant x < 1 \\ x & 1 \leqslant x < 3 \\ 3 & 3 \leqslant x \leqslant 5 \end{cases}$

   (A) $\lim\limits_{x\to 1} f(x)$ (B) $\lim\limits_{x\to 2} f(x)$ (C) $\lim\limits_{x\to 3} f(x)$

49. $f(x) = \begin{cases} 2 & x \leqslant -1 \\ x^2 & -1 < x < 1 \\ 1 & x \geqslant 1 \end{cases}$

   (A) $\lim\limits_{x\to -1} f(x)$ (B) $\lim\limits_{x\to 0} f(x)$ (C) $\lim\limits_{x\to 1} f(x)$

50. $f(x) = \begin{cases} -x-1 & x \leqslant -1 \\ 1-x^2 & -1 < x < 1 \\ x-1 & x \geqslant 1 \end{cases}$

   (A) $\lim\limits_{x\to -1} f(x)$ (B) $\lim\limits_{x\to 0} f(x)$ (C) $\lim\limits_{x\to 1} f(x)$

C   Find each limit. [Note: $a^3 - b^3 = (a-b)(a^2+ab+b^2)$ and $a^3 + b^3 = (a+b)(a^2-ab+b^2)$.]

51. $\lim\limits_{x\to 4} \sqrt[3]{x^2-3x}$

52. $\lim\limits_{x\to 2} \sqrt{x^2+2x}$

53. $\lim\limits_{x\to 4} \dfrac{\sqrt{x}-2}{x^2-4}$

54. $\lim\limits_{x\to 25} \dfrac{5-\sqrt{x}}{x+25}$

55. $\lim\limits_{x\to 4} \dfrac{\sqrt{x}-2}{x-4}$

56. $\lim\limits_{x\to 0} \dfrac{\sqrt{x+4}-2}{x}$

57. $\lim\limits_{x \to 9} \dfrac{x + 3}{\sqrt{x} - 3}$

58. $\lim\limits_{x \to 25} \dfrac{x + 5}{\sqrt{x} - 5}$

59. $\lim\limits_{x \to 16} \dfrac{x - 16}{\sqrt{x} - 4}$

60. $\lim\limits_{x \to 36} \dfrac{x - 36}{\sqrt{x} - 6}$

61. $\lim\limits_{x \to 2} \dfrac{x^3 - 8}{x - 2}$

62. $\lim\limits_{x \to 1} \dfrac{x^2 - 1}{x^3 - 1}$

63. $\lim\limits_{x \to -2} \dfrac{x + 2}{x^3 + 8}$

64. $\lim\limits_{x \to -1} \dfrac{x^3 + 1}{(x - 1)^2}$

65. $\lim\limits_{x \to 0} \dfrac{(a + x)^2 - a^2}{x}$, a any real number

66. $\lim\limits_{x \to 0} \dfrac{(a + x)^3 - a^3}{x}$, a any real number

67. $\lim\limits_{x \to 0} \dfrac{\sqrt{a + x} - \sqrt{a}}{x}$, $a > 0$

68. $\lim\limits_{x \to 0} \dfrac{\dfrac{1}{a + x} - \dfrac{1}{a}}{x}$, $a \neq 0$

Applications

Business & Economics

69. *Average cost.* The cost equation for manufacturing a particular compact disk album is

$$C(x) = 20{,}000 + 3x$$

where x is the number of disks produced. The average cost per disk, denoted by $\overline{C}(x)$, is found by dividing $C(x)$ by x:

$$\overline{C}(x) = \frac{C(x)}{x} = \frac{20{,}000 + 3x}{x}$$

If only ten disks were manufactured, for example, the average cost per disk would be $2,003. Find:

(A) $\overline{C}(1{,}000)$

(B) $\overline{C}(100{,}000)$

(C) $\lim\limits_{x \to 10{,}000} \overline{C}(x)$

(D) $\lim\limits_{x \to \infty} \overline{C}(x)$

70. *Employee training.* A company producing computer components has established that on the average, a new employee can assemble N(t) components per day after *t* days of on-the-job training, as given by

$$N(t) = \frac{100t}{t + 9}$$

Find:

(A) N(1)   (B) N(11)   (C) $\lim_{t \to 11} N(t)$ (D) $\lim_{t \to \infty} N(t)$

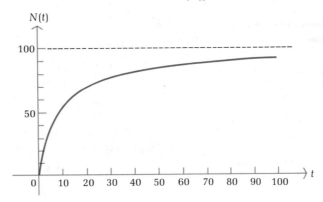

71. *Compound interest.* If $100 is invested at 8% compounded n times per year, then the amount in the account A(n) at the end of one year is given by

$$A(n) = 100 \left(1 + \frac{0.08}{n} \right)^n$$

(A) Use a calculator with a y^x button to complete the following table (each entry to the nearest cent):

Compounded	n	A(n)
Annually	1	$108.00
Semiannually	2	$108.16
Quarterly	4	$108.24
Monthly	12	
Weekly	52	
Daily	365	
Hourly	8,760	

(B) Using the results of part A, guess the following limit:

$$\lim_{n \to \infty} A(n) = ?$$

(This example leads to the important concept of compounding continuously, which will be discussed in detail in Section 9-1.)

72. *Pollution.* In Silicon Valley, California, a number of computer related manufacturing firms were found to be contaminating underground water supplies with toxic chemicals stored in leaking underground containers. A water quality control agency ordered the companies to take immediate corrective action and to contribute to a monetary pool for testing and cleanup of the underground contamination. Suppose the required monetary pool (in millions of dollars) for the testing and cleanup is estimated by

$$P(x) = \frac{2x}{1-x}$$

where x is the percentage (expressed as a decimal fraction) of the total contaminant removed.

(A) Complete the table in the margin.

(B) Find $\lim_{x \to 0.80} P(x)$.

(C) What happens to the required monetary pool as the desired percentage of contaminant removed approaches 100% (x approaches 1 from the left)?

Percentage Removed	Pool Required
0.50 (50%)	$2 million
0.60 (60%)	$3 million
0.70 (70%)	
0.80 (80%)	
0.90 (90%)	
0.95 (95%)	
0.99 (99%)	

Life Sciences

73. *Medicine.* A drug is injected into the bloodstream of a patient through her right arm. The concentration of the drug in the bloodstream of the left arm t hours after the injection is given by

$$C(t) = \frac{0.14t}{t^2 + 1}$$

Find:

(A) C(0.5)   (B) C(1)   (C) $\lim_{t \to 1} C(t)$ (D) $\lim_{t \to \infty} C(t)$

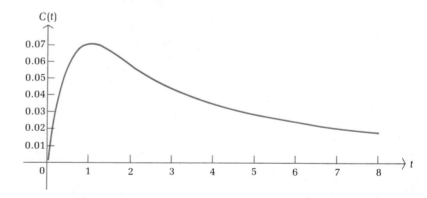

74. *Physiology.* In a study on the speed of muscle contraction in frogs under various loads, researchers W. O. Fems and J. Marsh found that the speed of contraction decreases with increasing loads. More precisely, they found that the relationship between speed of contraction S (in centimeters/second) and load w (in grams) is given approximately by

$$S(w) = \frac{26 + 0.06w}{w} \qquad w > 5$$

Find:

(A) $S(10)$ (B) $S(50)$ (C) $\lim_{w \to 50} S(w)$ (D) $\lim_{w \to \infty} S(w)$

Social Sciences

75. *Psychology—Learning theory.* In 1917, L. L. Thurstone, a pioneer in quantitative learning theory, proposed the function

$$f(x) = \frac{a(x + c)}{(x + c) + b}$$

to describe the number of successful acts per unit time that a person could accomplish after x practice sessions. Suppose for a particular person enrolling in a typing school

$$f(x) = \frac{60(x + 1)}{x + 5}$$

where $f(x)$ is the number of words per minute that the person is able to type after x weeks of lessons. Find:

(A) $f(3)$ (B) $f(10)$ (C) $\lim_{x \to 10} f(x)$ (D) $\lim_{x \to \infty} f(x)$

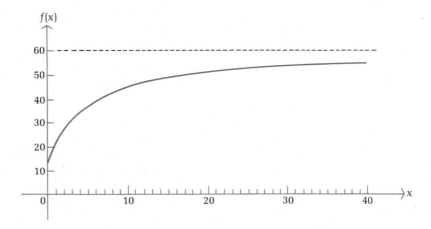

76. *Psychology—Retention.* An experiment on retention is conducted in a psychology class. Each student in the class is given one day to memorize the same list of thirty special characters. The lists are turned in at the end of the day, and for each succeeding day for thirty days each student is asked to turn in a list of as many of the symbols as can be recalled. Averages are taken and it is found that

$$N(t) = \frac{5t + 20}{t} \qquad t \geq 1$$

provides a good approximation of the average number of symbols, $N(t)$, retained after t days. Find:

(A) $N(2)$ (B) $N(10)$ (C) $\lim_{t \to 10} N(t)$ (D) $\lim_{t \to \infty} N(t)$

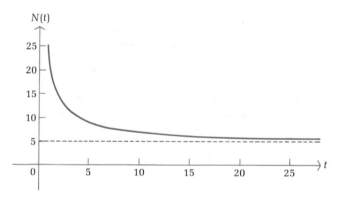

7-2   Continuity

■ Introduction
■ Definition of Continuity
■ Properties of Continuity
■ Solving Nonlinear Inequalities Using Continuity Properties

■ Introduction

In this section we will use the limit concept to describe an important property possessed by many functions. We begin by discussing an example.

Most daily newspapers include hourly temperatures in the weather report. Table 4 lists hourly temperatures from midnight to noon. We can represent the temperature at any time during this 12 hour period by plotting these points and connecting them with a smooth curve, as illustrated in Figure 7.

Table 4

Time	Temperature (°F)
12 midnight	30
1 AM	29
2 AM	25
3 AM	25
4 AM	27
5 AM	22
6 AM	20
7 AM	28
8 AM	30
9 AM	32
10 AM	38
11 AM	40
12 noon	48

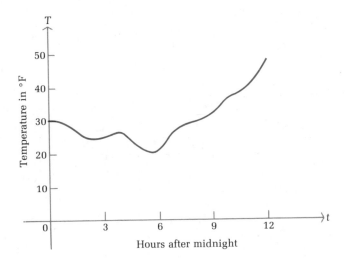

Figure 7

Notice that this curve can be drawn without lifting a pen off the paper. Informally, we say that this is a *continuous* curve. We drew the curve in this manner because our intuition tells us that temperature varies continuously with time. That is, if the temperature is 29°F at 1 AM and 25°F at 2 AM, then the temperature must have gradually and continuously changed from 29°F to 25°F during that hour.

Most graphs of natural phenomena (temperature, growth, decay, and so on) vary continuously with time, whereas many graphs in business and economics do not. The next example illustrates a graph that is not continuous.

A national delivery service uses weight of a package to determine the charge for delivery. The charge is $11.50 for the first pound (or any fraction thereof) and $1 for each additional pound (or fraction thereof). If $C(x)$ is the charge for delivering a package weighing x pounds, then

$$C(x) = \begin{cases} 11.50 & \text{for} \quad 0 < x \leqslant 1 \\ 12.50 & \text{for} \quad 1 < x \leqslant 2 \\ 13.50 & \text{for} \quad 2 < x \leqslant 3 \\ \text{and so on} \end{cases}$$

The function C is graphed for $0 < x \leqslant 3$ in Figure 8. Notice that it is not possible to draw the graph of C without lifting a pen off the paper. There are breaks in the graph at $x = 1$ and at $x = 2$. We say that the graph of C is *discontinuous* at $x = 1$ and $x = 2$. The graph of C is continuous on the intervals $(0, 1)$, $(1, 2)$, and $(2, 3)$.

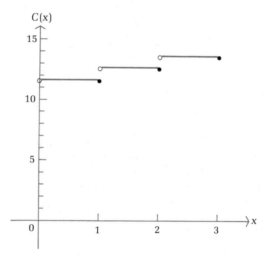

Figure 8

■ Definition of Continuity

If we have a graph of a function, then it is usually easy to identify points of discontinuity. If a function is defined by an equation, how can we identify points of discontinuity without looking at its graph? Figure 9 and Table 5 suggest some procedures as well as a formal definition of continuity in terms of limits. Study the figure and table carefully before proceeding further.

The function shown in Figure 9 is not the type of function that you are likely to encounter with great frequency. It was designed to illustrate most of the kinds of points of discontinuity exhibited by various types of func-

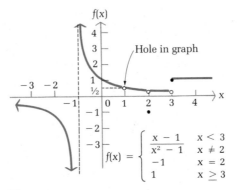

$$f(x) = \begin{cases} \dfrac{x - 1}{x^2 - 1} & x < 3 \quad x \neq 2 \\ -1 & x = 2 \\ 1 & x \geq 3 \end{cases}$$

Figure 9

Table 5

c	$\lim_{x \to c} f(x)$	$f(c)$	Graph
-2	-1	-1	No break in graph
-1	Does not exist	Does not exist	Break in graph
0	1	1	No break in graph
1	$1/2$	Does not exist	Break in graph
2	$1/3$	-1	Break in graph
3	Does not exist	1	Break in graph
4	1	1	No break in graph

tions. Looking at Table 5, we are led to the following precise definition of continuity:

Continuity

A function f is **continuous at the point** $x = c$ if

1. $\lim\limits_{x \to c} f(x)$ exists.

2. $f(c)$ exists.

3. $\lim\limits_{x \to c} f(x) = f(c)$.

A function is **continuous on the open interval** (a, b) if it is continuous at each point on the interval.

If one or more of the three conditions in the definition fails, then a function is **discontinuous** at $x = c$. Note that at least one of the three conditions fails at $x = -1, 1, 2,$ and 3 in Figure 9 (determine which for each number).

Example 9 Using the definition of continuity, discuss the continuity of each function at the indicated value of c.

(A) $f(x) = \dfrac{x^2 - 4}{x - 2}$

at $c = 1$ and $c = 2$

(B) $f(x) = \begin{cases} x^2 & x < 0 \\ 1 & x \geqslant 0 \end{cases}$

at $c = 0$

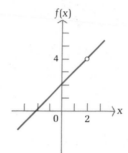

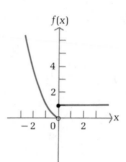

(C) $f(x) = \begin{cases} 4 - x^2 & x \neq 1 \\ 2 & x = 1 \end{cases}$

at $c = 1$

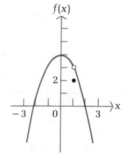

Solutions
(A) $\lim_{x \to 1} f(x) = 3 = f(1)$; thus, all three conditions in the definition are satisfied and f is continuous at $x = 1$. $\lim_{x \to 2} f(x) = 4$, but $f(2)$ is not defined. Condition 2 in the definition is not satisfied and f is not continuous at $x = 2$.

(B) $f(0) = 1$ [thus, $f(0)$ is defined], but $\lim_{x \to 0} f(x)$ does not exist. Condition 1 in the definition is not satisfied and f is not continuous at $x = 0$.

(C) $\lim_{x \to 1} f(x) = 3$ and $f(1) = 2$. But $\lim_{x \to 1} f(x) \neq f(1)$. Condition 3 in the definition is not satisfied and f is not continuous at $x = 1$.

Problem 9 Using the definition of continuity, discuss the continuity of each function at the indicated value of c.

(A) $f(x) = \begin{cases} x^2 - 4 & x \neq 1 \\ 2 & x = 1 \end{cases}$

at $c = 1$

(B) $f(x) = \dfrac{x^2 - 1}{x + 1}$

at $c = -1$ and $c = 1$

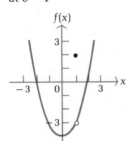

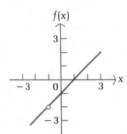

(C) $f(x) = \begin{cases} -x & x < 0 \\ 2 - x & x \geq 0 \end{cases}$

at $c = 0$

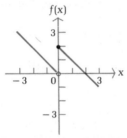

■ Properties of Continuity

Functions have continuity properties similar to limit properties. For example, **the sum, difference, product, and quotient of two continuous functions are continuous, except for values of x that make a denominator 0.** These properties, along with Theorem 4, enable us to determine intervals of continuity for some important classes of functions without having to look at their graphs or use the three conditions in the definition.

Theorem 4

(A) Polynomial functions are continuous for all values of x.

(B) Rational functions are continuous for all values of x except those that make a denominator 0.

(C) If n is an odd positive integer greater than 1, then $\sqrt[n]{f(x)}$ is continuous wherever $f(x)$ is continuous.

(D) If n is an even positive integer, then $\sqrt[n]{f(x)}$ is continuous wherever $f(x)$ is continuous and positive.

Example 10   Using Theorem 4, determine where each function is continuous.

(A) $f(x) = x^2 - 2x + 1$ (B) $f(x) = \dfrac{x}{(x+2)(x-3)}$

(C) $f(x) = \sqrt[3]{x^2 - 4}$ (D) $f(x) = \sqrt{x - 2}$

Solutions   (A) Since f is a polynomial function, f is continuous for all x.
(B) Since f is a rational function, f is continuous for all x except -2 and 3 (values of x that make the denominator 0). Using interval notation, f is continuous on $(-\infty, -2)$, $(-2, 3)$, and $(3, \infty)$.
(C) The polynomial function $x^2 - 4$ is continuous for all x. Since $n = 3$ is odd, f is continuous for all x.
(D) The polynomial function $x - 2$ is continuous for all x and positive for $x > 2$. Since $n = 2$ is even, f is continuous for $x > 2$ or on the interval $(2, \infty)$.

Problem 10   Using Theorem 4, determine where each function is continuous.

(A) $f(x) = x^4 + 2x^2 + 1$ (B) $f(x) = \dfrac{x^2}{(x+1)(x-4)}$

(C) $f(x) = \sqrt{4 - x}$ (D) $f(x) = \sqrt[3]{x^3 + 1}$

■ Solving Nonlinear Inequalities Using Continuity Properties

We will soon see that it is useful to be able to solve nonlinear inequalities of the form

$$(x + 1)(x - 2) > 0 \quad \text{and} \quad \frac{(x^2 - 1)}{(x - 3)} < 0$$

Theorem 5 states a property of continuous functions that can be of great use in solving such inequalities.

Theorem 5

> If f is continuous on (a, b) and $f(x) \neq 0$ for any x in (a, b), then either $f(x) > 0$ for all x in (a, b) or $f(x) < 0$ for all x in (a, b).

In other words, if f is continuous and $f(x) \neq 0$ on (a, b), then $f(x)$ cannot change sign on (a, b). To see why this is the case, suppose that there exist numbers x_1 and x_2 in (a, b) such that $f(x_1)$ and $f(x_2)$ do not have the same sign. For purposes of illustration, we assume that $a < x_1 < x_2 < b$, $f(x_1) < 0$, $f(x_2) > 0$ and graph this information in Figure 10A.

f(x) graph (A) with points (x₂, f(x₂)) above axis and (x₁, f(x₁)) below axis, axis marked a, x₁, x₂, b

f(x) graph (B) with curve from (x₁, f(x₁)) to (x₂, f(x₂)), axis marked a, x₁, x₂, b

(A)   (B)

Figure 10

Since we are given that $f(x)$ is not zero on (a, b), its graph must not cross the x axis. Try to draw a continuous curve from $(x_1, f(x_1))$ to $(x_2, f(x_2))$ without crossing the x axis (see Fig. 10B). It can't be done! Thus, if we know that f is continuous and $f(x) \neq 0$ on (a, b), then it is impossible to find numbers x_1 and x_2 in (a, b) such that $f(x_1)$ and $f(x_2)$ have opposite signs; that is, $f(x)$ must either be positive for all x in (a, b) or negative for all x in (a, b).

The next example illustrates the application of Theorem 5 to the solution of nonlinear inequalities.

Example 11   Solve $\dfrac{x + 1}{x - 2} > 0$.

Solution   We start by using the left side of the inequality to form the function f:

$$f(x) = \frac{x + 1}{x - 2}$$

The function f is discontinuous at $x = 2$, and $f(x) = 0$ for $x = -1$ (a fraction is 0 when the numerator is 0 and the denominator is not 0). We plot $x = 2$ and $x = -1$ on a real number line:

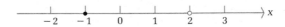

[Note: The dot at 2 is open; the function is not defined at $x = 2$.] The numbers 2 and -1 divide the real line into three intervals: $(-\infty, -1)$, $(-1, 2)$, and $(2, \infty)$. The function f is continuous and nonzero on each of these intervals. From Theorem 5 we know that $f(x)$ does not change sign on any of these intervals. Thus, we can find the sign of $f(x)$ on each of these intervals by selecting a **test number** in each interval and evaluating $f(x)$ at that number. Since any number in each subinterval will do, choose test numbers that are easy to evaluate. We choose -2, 0, and 3:

x	−2	0	3	Test numbers
f(x)	$\frac{1}{4}$	$-\frac{1}{2}$	4	
	+	−	+	

The sign of $f(x)$ at each test number determines the sign of $f(x)$ over the interval containing that test number. Using this information, we construct a **sign chart** for $f(x)$:

Using this sign chart, we can easily write the solution for the nonlinear inequality at the beginning of this discussion: $f(x) > 0$ for

$x < -1$ or $x > 2$	Inequality notation
$(-\infty, -1) \cup (2, \infty)$	Interval notation

Most of the inequalities we will encounter will involve strict inequalities ($>$ or $<$). If it is necessary to solve inequalities of the $\geq$ or $\leq$ form, simply include the end point of any interval if it is a zero of f [that is, if it is a value of x such that $f(x) = 0$]. Referring to the sign chart above, the solution of the inequality

$$\frac{x+1}{x-2} \geq 0 \quad \text{is} \qquad \begin{array}{ll} x \leq -1 \ \ \text{or} \ \ x > 2 & \text{Inequality notation} \\ (-\infty, -1] \cup (2, \infty) & \text{Interval notation} \end{array}$$

We summarize the procedure for constructing sign charts in the box below.

Constructing Sign Charts

Given a function f:

Step 1. Find all numbers where f is discontinuous.

Step 2. Find all numbers where $f(x) = 0$.

Step 3. Plot the numbers found in steps 1 and 2 on a number line, dividing the number line into intervals.

Step 4. Select a test number in each interval found in step 3 and evaluate $f(x)$ at each number.

Step 5. Construct a sign chart using the real number line in step 3 and the results of step 4. This will show the sign of $f(x)$ on each interval.

Problem 11 Solve $\dfrac{x^2 - 1}{x - 3} < 0$.

Example 12
Profit Analysis

The marketing research and financial departments of a company estimate that at a price of p dollars per unit, the weekly cost C and revenue R (in thousands of dollars) will be given by the equations

$$C = 14 - p \qquad \text{Cost equation}$$
$$R = 8p - p^2 \qquad \text{Revenue equation}$$

Find the prices for which the company has a profit.

Solution

A profit will result if revenue is greater than cost; that is, if

$$R > C$$
$$8p - p^2 > 14 - p$$
$$-p^2 + 9p - 14 > 0 \qquad \text{Multiply both sides by } -1 \text{ (inequality sign}$$
$$p^2 - 9p + 14 < 0 \qquad \text{reverses). Factor left side.}$$
$$(p - 2)(p - 7) < 0$$

We form a function f using the left side of the inequality,

$$f(p) = (p - 2)(p - 7)$$

and construct a sign chart for $f(p)$.

Step 1. Find all numbers where f is discontinuous. There are no points of discontinuity (f is a polynomial function that is continuous for all p).

Step 2. Find all numbers where $f(p) = 0$:

$$f(p) = 0$$
$$(p - 2)(p - 7) = 0$$
$$p = 2, 7$$

Step 3. Plot the numbers found in steps 1 and 2 on a number line:

Step 4. Evaluate $f(p)$ for a test number in each interval:

p	0	5	8	Test numbers
$f(p)$	14	−6	6	
	+	−	+	

Step 5. Form a sign chart for f using the results of steps 3 and 4:

Thus, a profit will result for $f(p) < 0$; that is, for any price between $2 and $7. (The break-even prices are $2 and $7; losses will occur for prices less than $2 or greater than $7. Later we will show how to find a price that will result in the maximum profit.)

Problem 12   Repeat Example 12 for

$$C = 8 - p \qquad \text{Cost equation}$$
$$R = 5p - p^2 \qquad \text{Revenue equation}$$

Answers to   9. (A) f is not continuous at $x = 1$; condition 3 is not satisfied.
Matched Problems   (B) f is not continuous at $x = -1$; condition 2 is not satisfied. f is continuous at $x = 1$.
                 (C) f is not continuous at $x = 0$; condition 1 is not satisfied.
            10. (A) For all x (B) $(-\infty, -1)$, $(-1, 4)$, and $(4, \infty)$ (C) $(-\infty, 4)$
                 (D) For all x
            11. $-\infty < x < -1$ or $1 < x < 3$, $(-\infty, -1) \cup (1, 3)$
            12. The company makes a profit for $2 < p < 4$.

Exercise 7-2

A   *Problems 1–6 refer to the function f in the following graph. Use the graph to estimate limits.*

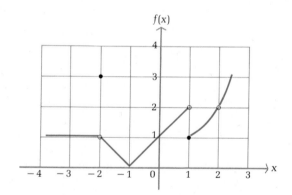

1. (A) $\lim\limits_{x \to 0} f(x)$ (B) $f(0) = ?$ (C) Is f continuous at $x = 0$?

2. (A) $\lim\limits_{x \to -1} f(x)$ (B) $f(-1) = ?$ (C) Is f continuous at $x = -1$?

3. (A) $\lim\limits_{x \to 1} f(x)$ (B) $f(1) = ?$ (C) Is f continuous at $x = 1$?

4. (A) $\lim\limits_{x \to 2} f(x)$ (B) $f(2) = ?$ (C) Is f continuous at $x = 2$?

5. (A) $\lim\limits_{x \to -2} f(x)$ (B) $f(-2) = ?$ (C) Is f continuous at $x = -2$?

6. (A) $\lim\limits_{x \to 0.5} f(x)$ (B) $f(0.5) = ?$ (C) Is f continuous at $x = 0.5$?

Use Theorem 4 to determine where each function is continuous. Express the answer in interval notation.

7. $f(x) = 2x - 3$ 8. $g(x) = 3 - 5x$

9. $h(x) = \dfrac{2}{x - 5}$ 10. $k(x) = \dfrac{x}{x + 3}$

11. $g(x) = \dfrac{x - 5}{(x - 3)(x + 2)}$ 12. $F(x) = \dfrac{1}{x(x + 7)}$

Solve each inequality. Express the answer in inequality notation.

13. $x^2 - x - 12 < 0$ 14. $x^2 - 2x - 8 < 0$

15. $x^2 + 21 > 10x$ 16. $x^2 + 7x + 10 > 0$

17. $x^2 \leq 8x$ 18. $x^2 + 6x \geq 0$

B   *Problems 19–24 refer to the function f in the following graph. Use the definition of continuity to discuss the continuity of f at the indicated value of c.*

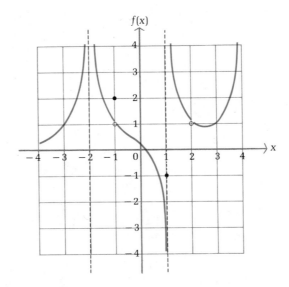

19. $c = -3$ 20. $c = -2$ 21. $c = -1$

22. $c = 1$ 23. $c = 2$ 24. $c = 3$

In Problems 25–30, graph f and locate all points of discontinuity.

25. $f(x) = \begin{cases} 1 + x & x \le 1 \\ 5 - x & x > 1 \end{cases}$

26. $f(x) = \begin{cases} x^2 & x \le 1 \\ 2x & x > 1 \end{cases}$

27. $f(x) = \begin{cases} 1 + x & x \le 2 \\ 5 - x & x > 2 \end{cases}$

28. $f(x) = \begin{cases} x^2 & x \le 2 \\ 2x & x > 2 \end{cases}$

29. $f(x) = \begin{cases} -x & x < 0 \\ 1 & x = 0 \\ x & x > 0 \end{cases}$

30. $f(x) = \begin{cases} 1 & x < 0 \\ 0 & x = 0 \\ 1 + x & x > 0 \end{cases}$

Use Theorem 4 to determine where each function is continuous. Express the answer in interval notation.

31. $F(x) = 2x^8 - 3x^4 + 5$

32. $h(x) = \dfrac{x^4 - 3x + 5}{x^2 + 2x}$

33. $g(x) = \sqrt{x - 5}$

34. $f(x) = \sqrt{3 - x}$

35. $K(x) = \sqrt[3]{x - 5}$

36. $H(x) = \sqrt[3]{3 - x}$

37. $f(x) = \dfrac{x^2 - 1}{x^2 - 3x + 2}$

38. $k(x) = \dfrac{x^2 - 4}{x^2 + x - 2}$

Solve each inequality. Express the answer in inequality notation.

39. $(x - 1)(x - 3)(x - 5) > 0$

40. $(x - 2)(x - 4)(x - 6) < 0$

41. $(x - 4)^3(x + 5)^2 < 0$

42. $(x + 2)^2(x - 3)^3 > 0$

43. $\dfrac{x - 2}{x + 4} \le 0$

44. $\dfrac{x + 3}{x - 1} \ge 0$

45. $\dfrac{x^2 + 5x}{x - 3} \ge 0$

46. $\dfrac{x - 4}{x^2 + 2x} \le 0$

47. $\dfrac{(x + 4)^3}{(1 - x)^2} < 0$

48. $\dfrac{(3 - x)^2}{(x + 5)^3} > 0$

49. $\dfrac{x^3(x + 3)}{(2x - 3)^2} \ge 0$

50. $\dfrac{x(x - 4)^2}{(2x + 5)^3} \le 0$

C   Use Theorem 4 to determine where each function is continuous. Express the answer in interval notation.

51. $f(x) = \sqrt{4 - x^2}$

52. $g(x) = \sqrt{x^2 - 9}$

53. $h(x) = \sqrt{x^3 + x^2 - 6x}$

54. $k(x) = \sqrt{8x - 2x^2 - x^3}$

55. $F(x) = \sqrt{\dfrac{1 + x}{1 - x}}$

56. $G(x) = \sqrt{\dfrac{2 - x}{x + 3}}$

In Problems 57–60, the function f is not defined at the indicated value of c. Graph f and determine whether f(c) can be assigned a value that will make f continuous at c.

57. $f(x) = \dfrac{x}{|x|}$, $c = 0$

58. $f(x) = \dfrac{x^2}{|x|}$, $c = 0$

59. $f(x) = \dfrac{x^2 - 1}{x - 1}$, $c = 1$

60. $f(x) = \dfrac{x(x - 1)}{|x - 1|}$, $c = 1$

Applications

Business & Economics

61. *Postal rates.* First-class postage in 1986 was $0.22 for the first ounce (or any fraction thereof) and $0.17 for each additional ounce (or fraction thereof) up to 12 ounces. If $P(x)$ is the amount of postage for a letter weighing x ounces, then we can write

$$P(x) = \begin{cases} \$0.22 & \text{for} \quad 0 < x \leqslant 1 \\ \$0.39 & \text{for} \quad 1 < x \leqslant 2 \\ \$0.56 & \text{for} \quad 2 < x \leqslant 3 \\ \text{and so on} \end{cases}$$

(A) Graph P for $0 < x \leqslant 5$.
(B) Find $\lim_{x \to 4.5} P(x)$ and $P(4.5)$.
(C) Find $\lim_{x \to 4} P(x)$ and $P(4)$.
(D) Is P continuous at $x = 4.5$? At $x = 4$?

62. *Telephone rates.* A person placing a station-to-station call on Saturday from San Francisco to New York is charged $0.30 for the first minute (or any fraction thereof) and $0.20 for each additional minute (or fraction thereof). If the length of a call is x minutes, then the long-distance charge $R(x)$ is

$$R(x) = \begin{cases} \$0.30 & \text{for} \quad 0 < x \leqslant 1 \\ \$0.50 & \text{for} \quad 1 < x \leqslant 2 \\ \$0.70 & \text{for} \quad 2 < x \leqslant 3 \\ \text{and so on} \end{cases}$$

(A) Graph R for $0 < x \leqslant 6$.
(B) Find $\lim_{x \to 2.5} R(x)$ and $R(2.5)$.
(C) Find $\lim_{x \to 2} R(x)$ and $R(2)$.
(D) Is R continuous at $x = 2.5$? At $x = 2$?

63. *Income.* A personal computer salesperson receives a base salary of $1,000 per month and a commission of 5% of all sales over $10,000 during the month. If the monthly sales are $20,000 or more, the salesperson is given an additional $500 bonus. Let $E(s)$ represent the person's earnings during the month as a function of the monthly sales s.

(A) Graph $E(s)$ for $0 \leqslant s \leqslant 30,000$.

(B) Find $\lim_{s \to 10,000} E(s)$ and $E(10,000)$.

(C) Find $\lim_{s \to 20,000} E(s)$ and $E(20,000)$.

(D) Is E continuous at $s = 10,000$? At $s = 20,000$?

64. *Equipment rental.* An office equipment rental and leasing company rents electric typewriters for $10 per day (and any fraction thereof) or for $50 per 7 day week. Let $C(x)$ be the cost of renting a typewriter for x days.

(A) Graph $C(x)$ for $0 \leqslant x \leqslant 10$.

(B) Find $\lim_{x \to 4.5} C(x)$ and $C(4.5)$.

(C) Find $\lim_{x \to 8} C(x)$ and $C(8)$.

(D) Is C continuous at $x = 4.5$? At $x = 8$?

65. *Profit/loss analysis.* At a price of p dollars per unit the financial department in a company estimates that the weekly cost C and revenue R (in thousands of dollars) will be given by the equations

$C = 28 - 2p$ Cost equation

$R = 9p - p^2$ Revenue equation

Find the prices for which the company has a loss. A profit.

66. *Profit/loss analysis.* At a price of p dollars per unit the financial department in a company estimates that the weekly cost C and revenue R (in thousands of dollars) will be given by the equations

$C = 27 - 2p$ Cost equation

$R = 10p - p^2$ Revenue equation

Find the prices for which the company has a loss. A profit.

Life Sciences   67. *Animal supply.* A medical laboratory raises its own rabbits. The number of rabbits $N(t)$ available at any time t depends on the number of births and deaths. When a birth or death occurs, the function N generally has a discontinuity, as shown in the figure.

(A) Where is the function N discontinuous?

(B) $\lim_{t \to t_5} N(t) = ?$, $N(t_5) = ?$

(C) $\lim_{t \to t_3} N(t) = ?$, $N(t_3) = ?$

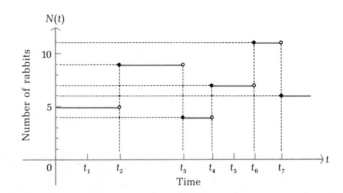

Social Sciences   **68.** *Learning.* The graph shown here might represent the history of a particular person learning the material on limits and continuity in this book. At time t_2, the student's mind goes blank during a quiz. At time t_4, the instructor explains a concept particularly well, and suddenly, a big jump in understanding takes place.

(A)   Where is the function p discontinuous?
(B) $\lim_{t \to t_1} p(t) = ?$, $p(t_1) = ?$
(C) $\lim_{t \to t_2} p(t) = ?$, $p(t_2) = ?$
(D) $\lim_{t \to t_4} p(t) = ?$, $p(t_4) = ?$

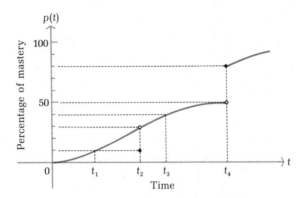

7-3   Increments, Tangent Lines, and Rates of Change

- Increments
- Slope and Tangent Line
- Average and Instantaneous Rates of Change

We will now use the concept of limit to solve two of the three basic problems of calculus stated at the beginning of this chapter. The parts of Figure 1 that we will concentrate on are repeated in Figure 11 (on the next page).

■ Increments

Before pursuing these problems, we digress for a moment to introduce *increment* notation. If we are given a function defined by $y = f(x)$ and the independent variable x changes from x_1 to x_2, then the dependent variable y will change from $y_1 = f(x_1)$ to $y_2 = f(x_2)$ (see Figure 12 on the next page). Mathematically, the change in x and the corresponding change in y, called **increments in x and y,** respectively, are denoted by Δx and Δy (read "delta x" and "delta y").

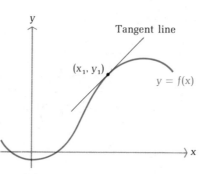

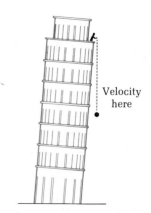

(A)   Find the equation of the
      tangent line at (x_1, y_1)
      given $y = f(x)$

(B)   Find the instantaneous
      velocity of a falling
      object

Figure 11

Increments

For $y = f(x)$ (see Figure 12)

$$\Delta x = x_2 - x_1$$
$$x_2 = x_1 + \Delta x$$
$$\Delta y = y_2 - y_1$$
$$= f(x_2) - f(x_1)$$
$$= f(x_1 + \Delta x) - f(x_1)$$

Δy represents the change in y corresponding to a Δx change in x.

[Note: Δy depends on the function f, the input x, and the increment Δx.]

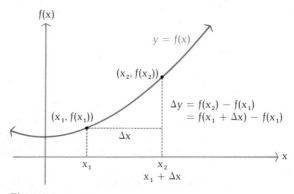

Figure 12

Example 13   Given the function

$$f(x) = \frac{x^2}{2}$$

(A)   Find Δx, Δy, and $\Delta y / \Delta x$ for $x_1 = 1$ and $x_2 = 2$.
(B)   Find

$$\frac{f(x_1 + \Delta x) - f(x_1)}{\Delta x}$$

for $x_1 = 1$ and $\Delta x = 2$.

Solutions   (A) $\Delta x = x_2 - x_1 = 2 - 1 = 1$

$\Delta y = f(x_2) - f(x_1)$

$$= f(2) - f(1) = \frac{4}{2} - \frac{1}{2} = \frac{3}{2}$$

$$\frac{\Delta y}{\Delta x} = \frac{f(x_2) - f(x_1)}{x_2 - x_1} = \frac{\frac{3}{2}}{1} = \frac{3}{2}$$

(B) $$\frac{f(x_1 + \Delta x) - f(x_1)}{\Delta x} = \frac{f(1 + 2) - f(1)}{2}$$

$$= \frac{f(3) - f(1)}{2} = \frac{\frac{9}{2} - \frac{1}{2}}{2} = \frac{4}{2} = 2$$

Problem 13   Given the function $f(x) = x^2 + 1$:

(A)   Find Δx, Δy, and $\Delta y / \Delta x$ for $x_1 = 2$ and $x_2 = 3$.
(B)   Find

$$\frac{f(x_1 + \Delta x) - f(x_1)}{\Delta x}$$

for $x_1 = 1$ and $\Delta x = 2$.

■ Slope and Tangent Line

From plane geometry, we know that a tangent to a circle is a line that passes through one and only one point on the circle, but how do we define and find a tangent line to a graph of a function at a point? The concept of the slope of a straight line (see Section 0-4) will play a central role in the process. If we pass a straight line through two points on the graph of $y = f(x)$, as in Figure 13 on the next page, we obtain a secant line. Given the coordinates of the two points, we can find the slope of the secant line using the point–slope formula from Section 0-4. (This is exactly what we did in Figure 4 in Section 7-1 to motivate the concept of limit.)

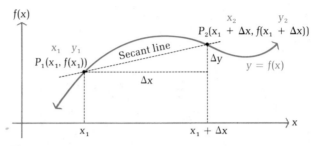

Figure 13

$$\text{Secant line slope} = \frac{y_2 - y_1}{x_2 - x_1} = \frac{f(x_1 + \Delta x) - f(x_1)}{\Delta x} = \frac{\Delta y}{\Delta x}$$

As we let Δx tend to 0, P_2 will approach P_1, and it appears that the secant lines will approach a limiting position and the secant slopes will approach a limiting value (see Figure 14). If they do, then we will call the line that the secant lines approach the *tangent line to the graph* at $(x_1, f(x_1))$, and the limiting slope will be the slope of the tangent line. This leads to the following definition of a tangent line:

Tangent Line

Given the graph of $y = f(x)$, then the **tangent line** at $(x_1, f(x_1))$ is the line that passes through this point with slope

$$\text{Tangent line slope} = \lim_{\Delta x \to 0} \frac{f(x_1 + \Delta x) - f(x_1)}{\Delta x} \tag{1}$$

if the limit exists. The slope of the tangent line is also referred to as the **slope of the graph** at $(x_1, f(x_1))$. [Actually, in much of the work that follows, our main interest will be in the *slope* of the graph of $y = f(x)$ at $(x_1, f(x_1))$ rather than in the tangent line itself.]

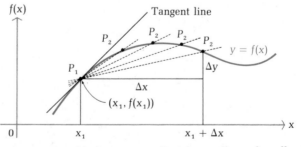

Figure 14 Dotted lines are secant lines for smaller and smaller Δx.

Example 14

Given $f(x) = x^2$, find the slope and equation of the tangent line at $x = 1$. Sketch the graph of f, the tangent line at $(1, f(1))$, and the secant line passing through $(1, f(1))$ and $(2, f(2))$.

Solution

First, we find the slope of the tangent line using equation (1):

$$\frac{f(1 + \Delta x) - f(1)}{\Delta x} = \frac{(1 + \Delta x)^2 - 1^2}{\Delta x}$$

We are computing the slope of a secant line passing through $(1, f(1))$ and $(1 + \Delta x, f(1 + \Delta x))$— see Figure 13.

$$= \frac{1 + 2\Delta x + (\Delta x)^2 - 1}{\Delta x}$$

$$= \frac{2\Delta x + (\Delta x)^2}{\Delta x}$$

$$= \frac{\Delta x(2 + \Delta x)}{\Delta x} = 2 + \Delta x \qquad \Delta x \neq 0$$

$$\textbf{Tangent line slope} = \lim_{\Delta x \to 0} \frac{f(1 + \Delta x) - f(1)}{\Delta x}$$

This is also the slope of the graph of $f(x) = x^2$ at $(1, f(1))$.

$$= \lim_{\Delta x \to 0} (2 + \Delta x) = 2$$

Next, we find the point on the graph of f corresponding to $x = 1$:

$$f(1) = 1^2 = 1$$

$$(1, f(1)) = (1, 1) \qquad \text{Point on the graph of } f$$

Now we use the point–slope formula for the equation of a line to find the **equation of the tangent line:**

$$(x_1, y_1) = (1, 1) \qquad \text{Point}$$

$$m = 2 \qquad \text{Slope}$$

$$y - y_1 = m(x - x_1) \qquad \text{Point–slope formula}$$

$$y - 1 = 2(x - 1)$$

$$y - 1 = 2x - 2 \quad \text{or} \quad y = 2x - 1 \qquad \text{Tangent line equation}$$

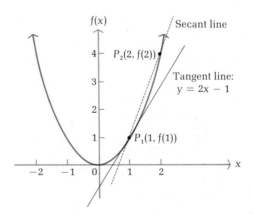

Problem 14 Find the equation of the tangent line for the graph of $f(x) = x^2$ at $x = 2$. Write the answer in the form $y = mx + b$.

■ Average and Instantaneous Rates of Change

We now show how increments and limits can be used to analyze rate problems. In the process, we will solve the second basic calculus problem we stated at the beginning of the chapter.

Example 15
Velocity

A small steel ball dropped from a tower will fall a distance of y feet in x seconds, as given approximately by the formula (from physics) $y = f(x) = 16x^2$. Let us determine the ball's position on a coordinate line at various times (see Figure 15). Our ultimate objective is to find the ball's *velocity* at a given instant, say, at the end of 2 seconds.

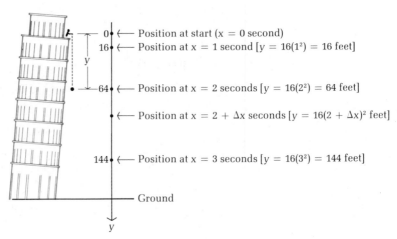

0 ← Position at start ($x = 0$ second)
16 ← Position at $x = 1$ second [$y = 16(1^2) = 16$ feet]
64 ← Position at $x = 2$ seconds [$y = 16(2^2) = 64$ feet]
← Position at $x = 2 + \Delta x$ seconds [$y = 16(2 + \Delta x)^2$ feet]
144 ← Position at $x = 3$ seconds [$y = 16(3^2) = 144$ feet]
Ground

y

Figure 15 *Note:* Positive y direction is down.

(A) Find x_2 and Δy for $x_1 = 2$ and $\Delta x = 1$.
(B) Find the average velocity for the time change in part A.
(C) Find an expression for the average velocity from $x = 2$ to $x = 2 + \Delta x$, where Δx represents a small but arbitrary change in time and $\Delta x \neq 0$ (see Figure 15).
(D) Find $\lim_{\Delta x \to 0} (\Delta y / \Delta x)$ using $\Delta y / \Delta x$ from part C.

Solutions (A) $x_2 = x_1 + \Delta x = 2 + 1 = 3$

$$\Delta y = f(x_1 + \Delta x) - f(x_1)$$

$$= f(3) - f(2)$$

$$= 16(3^2) - 16(2^2)$$

$$= 144 - 64 = 80 \text{ feet} \qquad \text{Distance fallen from end of 2 seconds to end of 3 seconds (see Figure 15)}$$

(B)   Recall the formula $d = rt$, which can be written in the form

$$r = \frac{d}{t} = \frac{\text{Total distance}}{\text{Elapsed time}} = \text{Average rate}$$

For example, if a person drives from San Francisco to Los Angeles—a distance of about 420 miles—in 10 hours, then the average rate is

$$r = \frac{d}{t} = \frac{420}{10} = 42 \text{ miles per hour}$$

Sometimes the person will be traveling faster and sometimes slower, but the *average rate* is 42 miles per hour. In our present problem, it is clear from Figure 15 that the ball is *accelerating* (falling faster and faster), but we can compute an average rate, or average velocity, just as we did for the trip from San Francisco to Los Angeles:

$$\textbf{Average velocity} = \frac{\text{Total distance}}{\text{Elapsed time}}$$

$$= \frac{\Delta y}{\Delta x} = \frac{f(3) - f(2)}{1} = \frac{80}{1} = 80 \text{ feet per second}$$

Thus, the average velocity from the end of 2 seconds to the end of 3 seconds is 80 feet per second.

(C) $\text{Average velocity} = \dfrac{\Delta y}{\Delta x} = \dfrac{f(2 + \Delta x) - f(2)}{\Delta x} \qquad \Delta x \neq 0$

$$= \frac{16(2 + \Delta x)^2 - 16(2^2)}{\Delta x}$$

$$= \frac{16[4 + 4\Delta x + (\Delta x)^2] - 64}{\Delta x}$$

$$= \frac{64 + 64\Delta x + 16(\Delta x)^2 - 64}{\Delta x}$$

$$= \frac{64\Delta x + 16(\Delta x)^2}{\Delta x} = \frac{\Delta x(64 + 16\Delta x)}{\Delta x}$$

$$= 64 + 16\Delta x \qquad \Delta x \neq 0$$

Note that if $\Delta x = 1$, the average velocity is 80 feet per second; if $\Delta x = 0.5$, then the average velocity is 72 feet per second; if $\Delta x = 0.01$, then the average velocity is 64.16 feet per second; and so on. The smaller Δx gets, the closer the average velocity gets to 64 feet per second.

(D) $\displaystyle \lim_{x \to 0} \frac{\Delta y}{\Delta x} = \lim_{\Delta x \to 0} \frac{f(2 + \Delta x) - f(2)}{\Delta x}$

$\displaystyle \qquad\qquad = \lim_{\Delta x \to 0} \,(64 + 16\Delta x)$

$\qquad\qquad = 64$ feet per second

We call 64 feet per second the **instantaneous velocity** at $x = 2$ seconds, and we have solved the second basic problem stated at the beginning of this chapter!

The discussion in Example 15 leads to the following general definitions of average rate and instantaneous rate:

Average and Instantaneous Rates

For $y = f(x)$

$$\textbf{Average rate} = \frac{\Delta y}{\Delta x} = \frac{f(x_2) - f(x_1)}{x_2 - x_1} = \frac{f(x_1 + \Delta x) - f(x_1)}{\Delta x}$$

$$\textbf{Instantaneous rate} = \lim_{\Delta x \to 0} \frac{\Delta y}{\Delta x} = \lim_{\Delta x \to 0} \frac{f(x_1 + \Delta x) - f(x_1)}{\Delta x}$$

if the limit exists

The ratio $[f(x_1 + \Delta x) - f(x_1)]/\Delta x$ is also called the **difference quotient**.

Problem 15   For the falling steel ball in Example 15, find:

(A)   The average velocity from $x = 1$ to $x = 2$.
(B)   The average velocity from $x = 1$ to $x = 1 + \Delta x$.
(C)   The instantaneous velocity at $x = 1$.

Now we consider a slightly different type of rate problem, but we will use the same approach as in Example 15.

Example 16
Advertising

An advertising agency for a chain of pizzerias has determined that the relationship between the number of pizzas N sold each day and the num-

ber of television ads x shown each day is

$$N(x) = 100 + 100x - x^2$$

Thus, showing 20 ads would result in sales of $N(20) = 1,700$ pizzas and showing 30 ads would result in sales of $N(30) = 2,200$ pizzas.

(A)   What is the average rate of change in the number of pizzas sold from 20 daily ads to 30 daily ads?

(B)   What is the average rate of change in the number of pizzas sold from 20 daily ads to $20 + \Delta x$ daily ads?

(C)   What value does $\Delta N/\Delta x$ in part B approach as Δx tends to 0?

Solutions   (A) $\dfrac{\Delta N}{\Delta x} = \dfrac{N(30) - N(20)}{30 - 20} = \dfrac{2,200 - 1,700}{10}$

$$= 50 \text{ pizzas per ad}$$

(B) $\dfrac{\Delta N}{\Delta x} = \dfrac{N(20 + \Delta x) - N(20)}{\Delta x}$

$$= \dfrac{[100 + 100(20 + \Delta x) - (20 + \Delta x)^2] - 1,700}{\Delta x}$$

$$= \dfrac{100 + 2,000 + 100\Delta x - 400 - 40\Delta x - (\Delta x)^2 - 1,700}{\Delta x}$$

$$= \dfrac{60\Delta x - (\Delta x)^2}{\Delta x} = \dfrac{\Delta x(60 - \Delta x)}{\Delta x} = 60 - \Delta x \qquad \Delta x \neq 0$$

(C) $\displaystyle\lim_{\Delta x \to 0} \dfrac{\Delta N}{\Delta x} = \lim_{\Delta x \to 0} (60 - \Delta x) = 60$ pizzas per ad

Thus, the instantaneous rate of change of N with respect to x at $x = 20$ is 60 pizzas per ad.*

Problem 16   For Example 16, find:

(A)   The average rate of change in number of pizzas from 30 ads to 40 ads.

(B)   The average rate of change in number of pizzas from 30 ads to $30 + \Delta x$ ads.

(C)   The limiting value of $\Delta N/\Delta x$ in part B as Δx tends to 0.

---

* Technically, the function $N(x)$ is defined only for n a nonnegative integer (it is not possible to show 3.7 or $\sqrt{23}$ ads per day). However, to find the instantaneous rate of change of N with respect to x at $x = 20$, we must assume that N is defined for an interval of real numbers containing the number 20. When applying calculus techniques to real-world problems, it is common practice to automatically extend the domain of a function from a discrete set of integers to a set of real numbers. Thus, we assume that the domain of $N(x)$ is the set of all real numbers $x \geq 0$ and not just $x = 0$, 1, 2, 3, ...

13. (A) $\Delta x = 1$, $\Delta y = 5$, $\Delta y / \Delta x = 5$ (B) 4
14. $y = 4x - 4$
15. (A) 48 feet per second   (B) $32 + 16\Delta x$
    (C) 32 feet per second
16. (A) 30 pizzas per ad   (B) $40 - \Delta x$
    (C) 40 pizzas per ad

Exercise 7-3

In Problems 1–14, find the indicated quantities for $y = f(x) = 3x^2$.

A

1. Δx, Δy, and $\Delta y / \Delta x$, given $x_1 = 1$ and $x_2 = 4$
2. Δx, Δy, and $\Delta y / \Delta x$, given $x_1 = 2$ and $x_2 = 5$
3. $\dfrac{f(x_1 + \Delta x) - f(x_1)}{\Delta x}$, given $x_1 = 1$ and $\Delta x = 2$
4. $\dfrac{f(x_1 + \Delta x) - f(x_1)}{\Delta x}$, given $x_1 = 2$ and $\Delta x = 1$
5. $\dfrac{y_2 - y_1}{x_2 - x_1}$, given $x_1 = 1$ and $x_2 = 3$
6. $\dfrac{y_2 - y_1}{x_2 - x_1}$, given $x_1 = 2$ and $x_2 = 3$
7. $\dfrac{\Delta y}{\Delta x}$, given $x_1 = 1$ and $x_2 = 3$
8. $\dfrac{\Delta y}{\Delta x}$, given $x_1 = 2$ and $x_2 = 3$

B

9. The average rate of change of y, for x changing from 1 to 4
10. The average rate of change of y, for x changing from 2 to 5

11. (A) $\dfrac{f(2 + \Delta x) - f(2)}{\Delta x}$ (simplify)

   (B) What does the ratio in part A approach as Δx approaches 0?

12. (A) $\dfrac{f(3 + \Delta x) - f(3)}{\Delta x}$ (simplify)

   (B) What does the ratio in part A approach as Δx approaches 0?

13. (A) $\dfrac{f(4 + \Delta x) - f(4)}{\Delta x}$ (simplify)

   (B) What does the ratio in part A approach as Δx approaches 0?

14. (A) $\dfrac{f(5 + \Delta x) - f(5)}{\Delta x}$ (simplify)

   (B) What does the ratio in part A approach as Δx approaches 0?

Suppose an object moves along the y axis so that its location is $y = f(x) = x^2 + x$ at time x (y is in meters and x is in seconds). Find:

15. (A) The average velocity (the average rate of change of y) for x changing from 1 to 3 seconds
    (B) The average velocity for x changing from 1 to $(1 + \Delta x)$ seconds
    (C) The instantaneous velocity at $x = 1$

16. (A) The average velocity (the average rate of change of y) for x changing from 2 to 4 seconds
    (B) The average velocity for x changing from 2 to $(2 + \Delta x)$ seconds
    (C) The instantaneous velocity at $x = 2$

In Problems 17 and 18, find each of the following for the graph of $y = f(x) = x^2 + x$:

17. (A) The slope of the secant line joining $(1, f(1))$ and $(3, f(3))$
    (B) The slope of the secant line joining $(1, f(1))$ and $(1 + \Delta x, f(1 + \Delta x))$
    (C) The slope of the tangent line at $(1, f(1))$
    (D) The equation of the tangent line at $(1, f(1))$

18. (A) The slope of the secant line joining $(2, f(2))$ and $(4, f(4))$
    (B) The slope of the secant line joining $(2, f(2))$ and $(2 + \Delta x, f(2 + \Delta x))$
    (C) The slope of the tangent line at $(2, f(2))$
    (D) The equation of the tangent line at $(2, f(2))$

C

19. If an object moves on the x axis so that it is at $x = f(t) = t^2 - t$ at time t (t measured in seconds and x measured in meters), find the instantaneous velocity of the object at $t = 2$.

20. Find the equation of the tangent line for the graph of $y = x^2 - x$ at $x = 2$.

■

Applications

Business & Economics

21. *Income.* The per capita income in the United States from 1969 to 1973 is given approximately in the table. Find the average rate of change of per capita income for a time change from:

    (A) 1969 to 1971   (B) 1971 to 1973

Year	1969	1970	1971	1972	1973
Income	$3,700	$3,900	$4,100	$4,500	$5,000

22. *Demand function.* Suppose in a given grocery store people are willing to buy $D(x)$ pounds of chocolate candy per day at $\$x$ per pound, as given by the demand function

$$D(x) = 100 - x^2 \qquad \$1 \leqslant x \leqslant \$10$$

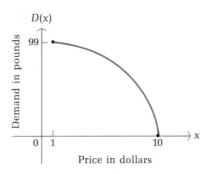

Note that as price goes up, demand goes down (see the figure).

(A) Find the average rate of change in demand for a price change from $2 to $5; that is, find $\Delta y / \Delta x$ for $x_1 = 2$ and $x_2 = 5$.

(B) Simplify:

$$\frac{D(2 + \Delta x) - D(2)}{\Delta x}$$

(C) What does the ratio in part B approach as Δx approaches 0? [This is called the instantaneous rate of change of $D(x)$ with respect to x at $x = 2$.]

23. *Advertising.* A discount appliance store uses television ads to promote weekend specials on clothes dryers. Suppose that the store can sell $N(x)$ dryers by showing x ads where

$$N(x) = 5 + 40x - x^2$$

(A) Find the average rate of change in the number of dryers sold from 5 ads to 10 ads.

(B) Find the average rate of change in the number of dryers sold from 5 ads to $5 + \Delta x$ ads.

(C) Find the limiting value of $\Delta N / \Delta x$ in part B as Δx tends to 0. (This is the instantaneous rate of change of N with respect to x at $x = 5$.)

24. *Depreciation.* Office equipment was purchased for $20,000 and is assumed to have a scrap value of $2,000 after 10 years. If its value is depreciated linearly (for tax purposes) from $20,000 to $2,000, then the value $V(t)$ after t years is given by

$$V(t) = 20,000 - 1,800t \qquad 0 \leqslant t \leqslant 10$$

(A) Find the average rate of change in the value of the equipment from 2 years to 6 years.

(B) Find the average rate of change in the value of the equipment from 3 years to 5 years.

(C) Find the average rate of change in the value of the equipment from t_1 years to t_2 years.

Life Sciences   25. *Medicine.* The area of a small (healing) wound in square millimeters, where time is measured in days, is given in the table.

Area	400	360	180	120	90	72	60
Days	0	1	2	3	4	5	6

Find the average rate of change of area for the time change from:

(A) 0 to 2 days   (B) 4 to 6 days

26. *Weight–height.* A formula relating the approximate weight of an average person and his or her height is

$$W(h) = 0.0005h^3$$

where $W(h)$ is in pounds and h is in inches.

(A) Find the average rate of change of weight for a height change from 60 to 70 inches.

(B) Simplify:

$$\frac{W(60 + \Delta h) - W(60)}{\Delta h}$$

(C) What does the ratio in part B approach as Δh approaches 0? [This is called the instantaneous rate of change of $W(h)$ with respect to h at $h = 60$.]

Social Sciences   27. *Illegitimate births.* The approximate numbers of illegitimate births per 1,000 live births in the United States from 1940 to 1970 are given in the table. Find the average rate of change of illegitimate births per 1,000 live births for the time change from:

(A) 1940 to 1945   (B) 1965 to 1970

Year	1940	1945	1950	1955	1960	1965	1970
Illegitimate Births per 1,000 Live Births	38	41	40	47	54	80	120

28. *Learning.* A certain person learning to type has an achievement record given approximately by the function

$$N(t) = 60 \left(1 - \frac{2}{t} \right) \qquad 3 \leqslant t \leqslant 10$$

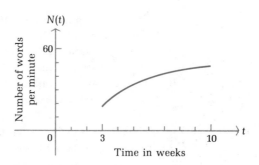

where $N(t)$ is in number of words per minute and t is in weeks. Find the average rate of change of the number of words per minute for the change in time from:

(A)   4 to 6 weeks   (B)   8 to 10 weeks

7-4   The Derivative

- The Derivative
- Tangent Lines
- Nonexistence of the Derivative
- Instantaneous Rates of Change
- Marginal Cost
- Summary

■ The Derivative

In the last section we found that the special limit

$$\lim_{\Delta x \to 0} \frac{f(x_1 + \Delta x) - f(x_1)}{\Delta x} \tag{1}$$

if it exists, gives us the slope of the tangent line to the graph of $y = f(x)$ at $(x_1, f(x_1))$. It also gives us the instantaneous rate of change of y per unit change in x at $x = x_1$. Formula (1) is of such basic importance to calculus and to the applications of calculus that we will give it a name and study it in detail. To keep formula (1) simple and general, we will drop the subscript on x_1 and think of the ratio

$$\frac{f(x + \Delta x) - f(x)}{\Delta x}$$

as a function of Δx, with x held fixed as we let Δx tend to 0. We are now ready to define one of the basic concepts in calculus, the *derivative*:

Derivative

For $y = f(x)$ we define the **derivative of f at x,** denoted by $f'(x)$, to be

$$f'(x) = \lim_{\Delta x \to 0} \frac{f(x + \Delta x) - f(x)}{\Delta x} \qquad \text{if the limit exists}$$

If $f'(x)$ exists, then f is said to be a **differentiable function** at x.

The process of finding the derivative of a function is called **differentiation.** That is, the derivative of a function is obtained by **differentiating** the function. Differentiating a function f creates a new function f' that gives, among other things, the instantaneous rate of change of $y = f(x)$ and the slope of the tangent line to the graph of $y = f(x)$ for each x. The domain of f' is a subset of the domain of f, which will become clearer as we progress through this section.

Example 17 Find $f'(x)$, the derivative of f at x, for $f(x) = 4x - x^2$.

Solution To find $f'(x)$, we find

$$\lim_{\Delta x \to 0} \frac{f(x + \Delta x) - f(x)}{\Delta x}$$

To make the computation easier, we introduce a two-step process:

Step 1. Find $[f(x + \Delta x) - f(x)]/\Delta x$ and simplify.

$$\frac{f(x + \Delta x) - f(x)}{\Delta x} = \frac{[4(x + \Delta x) - (x + \Delta x)^2] - (4x - x^2)}{\Delta x}$$

$$= \frac{4x + 4\Delta x - x^2 - 2x\Delta x - (\Delta x)^2 - 4x + x^2}{\Delta x}$$

$$= \frac{4\Delta x - 2x\Delta x - (\Delta x)^2}{\Delta x}$$

$$= \frac{\Delta x}{\Delta x}(4 - 2x - \Delta x)$$

$$= 4 - 2x - \Delta x \qquad \Delta x \neq 0$$

Step 2. Find the limit of the result of step 1.

$$f'(x) = \lim_{\Delta x \to 0} \frac{f(x + \Delta x) - f(x)}{\Delta x} = \lim_{\Delta x \to 0}(4 - 2x - \Delta x)$$

$$= 4 - 2x$$

Thus, if $f(x) = 4x - x^2$, then $f'(x) = 4 - 2x$.

Problem 17   Find $f'(x)$, the derivative of f at x, for $f(x) = 8x - 2x^2$.

Now that we are performing more complicated algebraic operations involving the symbol Δx, it is important to remember that Δx is a single symbol representing the change in x, not the product of Δ and x. In particular,

$$(\Delta x)x \neq \Delta x^2 \quad \text{and} \quad (\Delta x)^2 \neq \Delta^2 x^2$$

Example 18   Find $f'(x)$, the derivative of f at x, for $f(x) = \sqrt{x} + 2$.

Solution   To find $f'(x)$, we find

$$\lim_{\Delta x \to 0} \frac{f(x + \Delta x) - f(x)}{\Delta x}$$

We use the two-step process presented in Example 17.

Step 1.   Find $[f(x + \Delta x) - f(x)]/\Delta x$ and simplify.

$$\frac{f(x + \Delta x) - f(x)}{\Delta x} = \frac{(\sqrt{x + \Delta x} + 2) - (\sqrt{x} + 2)}{\Delta x}$$

$$= \frac{\sqrt{x + \Delta x} + 2 - \sqrt{x} - 2}{\Delta x}$$

$$= \frac{\sqrt{x + \Delta x} - \sqrt{x}}{\Delta x}$$

Trying to apply the quotient property of limits, we find that $\lim_{\Delta x \to 0} \Delta x = 0$; hence, we cannot use it. We try rationalizing the numerator:

$$\frac{\sqrt{x + \Delta x} - \sqrt{x}}{\Delta x} \cdot \frac{\sqrt{x + \Delta x} + \sqrt{x}}{\sqrt{x + \Delta x} + \sqrt{x}} = \frac{x + \Delta x - x}{\Delta x(\sqrt{x + \Delta x} + \sqrt{x})}$$

$$= \frac{\Delta x}{\Delta x(\sqrt{x + \Delta x} + \sqrt{x})}$$

$$= \frac{1}{\sqrt{x + \Delta x} + \sqrt{x}} \quad \Delta x \neq 0$$

Step 2.   Find the limit of the result of step 1.

$$f'(x) = \lim_{\Delta x \to 0} \frac{\sqrt{x + \Delta x} - \sqrt{x}}{\Delta x}$$

$$= \lim_{\Delta x \to 0} \frac{1}{\sqrt{x + \Delta x} + \sqrt{x}}$$

$$= \frac{1}{\sqrt{x} + \sqrt{x}} = \frac{1}{2\sqrt{x}}$$

Thus, if $f(x) = \sqrt{x} + 2$, then $f'(x) = 1/(2\sqrt{x})$. [*Note:* The domain of $f(x) = \sqrt{x} + 2$ is $[0, \infty)$. Since $f'(0)$ is undefined, the domain of $f'(x) = 1/(2\sqrt{x})$ is $(0, \infty)$, a subset of the original domain.]

Problem 18   Find $f'(x)$, the derivative of f at x, for $f(x) = x^{-1}$.

■ Tangent Lines

In the last section we defined the slope of the tangent line to the graph of $y = f(x)$ at $(x_1, f(x_1))$ to be

$$\lim_{\Delta x \to 0} \frac{f(x_1 + \Delta x) - f(x_1)}{\Delta x}$$

if the limit exists. This, of course, is $f'(x_1)$, the derivative of f at $x = x_1$. To find the equation of a tangent line to the graph of $y = f(x)$ at $(x_1, f(x_1))$, we use the point–slope form for the equation of a line, $y - y_1 = m(x - x_1)$, and the facts that $m = f'(x_1)$ and $y_1 = f(x_1)$ to obtain:

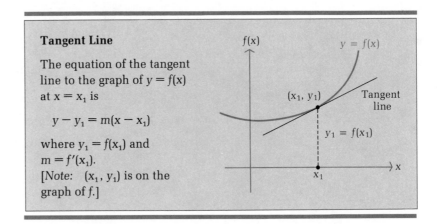

Tangent Line

The equation of the tangent line to the graph of $y = f(x)$ at $x = x_1$ is

$$y - y_1 = m(x - x_1)$$

where $y_1 = f(x_1)$ and $m = f'(x_1)$.
[*Note:* (x_1, y_1) is on the graph of f.]

More generally,

$$f'(x) = \lim_{\Delta x \to 0} \frac{f(x + \Delta x) - f(x)}{\Delta x}$$

gives us the slope of the graph of f at *any* point $(x, f(x))$ on the graph of f for which the limit exists.

Example 19   In Example 17 we started with the function specified by $f(x) = 4x - x^2$ and found the derivative of f at x to be $f'(x) = 4 - 2x$. Thus, the slope of the graph of f at any point $(x, f(x))$ on the graph of f is

$$f'(x) = 4 - 2x$$

We will use this derivative in the following problems.

(A)   Find the slopes of the graph of f at $x = 0$, 2, and 3.
(B)   Find the equations of the tangent lines at $x = 0$, 2, and 3.
(C)   Sketch the tangent lines to the graph of $y = 4x - x^2$ at $x = 0$, 2, and 3.

Solutions   (A)   Using $f'(x) = 4 - 2x$, we have:

$$f'(0) = 4 - 2(0) = 4$$
$$f'(2) = 4 - 2(2) = 0$$
$$f'(3) = 4 - 2(3) = -2$$

(B)   Tangent line at $x = 0$:

$$y - y_1 = m(x - x_1) \qquad y_1 = f(x_1) = f(0) = 4(0) - (0)^2 = 0$$
$$m = f'(x_1) = f'(0) = 4 \text{ (see part A)}$$

$$y - 0 = 4(x - 0)$$
$$y = 4x \qquad \text{Tangent line at } x = 0$$

Tangent line at $x = 2$:

$$y - y_1 = m(x - x_1) \qquad y_1 = f(x_1) = f(2) = 4(2) - (2)^2 = 4$$
$$m = f'(x_1) = f'(2) = 0 \text{ (see part A)}$$

$$y - 4 = 0(x - 2)$$
$$y = 4 \qquad \text{Tangent line at } x = 2$$

Tangent line at $x = 3$:

$$y - y_1 = m(x - x_1) \qquad y_1 = f(x_1) = f(3) = 4(3) - (3)^2 = 3$$
$$m = f'(x_1) = f'(3) = -2 \text{ (see part A)}$$

$$y - 3 = -2(x - 3)$$
$$y = -2x + 9 \qquad \text{Tangent line at } x = 3$$

(C)

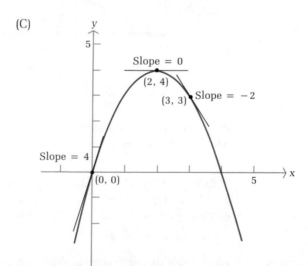

Problem 19 In Problem 17 we started with the function specified by $f(x) = 8x - 2x^2$ and found the derivative of f at x to be $f'(x) = 8 - 4x$.

(A) Find the slopes of the graph of f at $x = 1, 2,$ and 4.
(B) Find the equations of the tangent lines at $x = 1, 2,$ and 4.
(C) Sketch the tangent lines to the graph of $y = 8x - 2x^2$ at $x = 1, 2,$ and 4.

■ Nonexistence of the Derivative

The existence of a derivative at $x = a$ depends on the existence of a limit at $x = a$; that is, on the existence of

$$f'(a) = \lim_{\Delta x \to 0} \frac{f(a + \Delta x) - f(a)}{\Delta x} \tag{2}$$

If the limit does not exist at $x = a$, we say that the function f is **nondifferentiable at $x = a$ or $f'(a)$ does not exist.**

How can we recognize the points on the graph of f where $f'(a)$ does not exist? It is impossible to describe all the ways that the limit in (2) can fail to exist. However, we can illustrate some common situations where $f'(a)$ does fail to exist:

1. If f is not continuous at $x = a$, then $f'(a)$ does not exist (see Fig. 16A). It can be shown that **if f is differentiable at $x = a$, then f must be continuous at $x = a$.**
2. If the graph of f has a sharp corner at $x = a$, then $f'(a)$ does not exist and the graph has no tangent line at $x = a$ (see Fig. 16B).
3. If the graph of f has a vertical tangent line at $x = a$, then $f'(a)$ does not exist (see Figs. 16C and 16D).

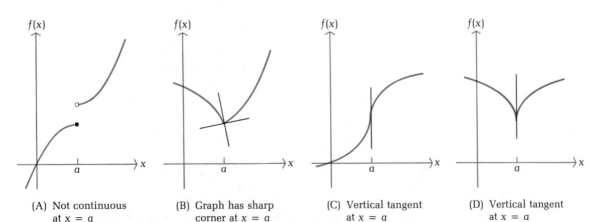

(A) Not continuous at $x = a$

(B) Graph has sharp corner at $x = a$

(C) Vertical tangent at $x = a$

(D) Vertical tangent at $x = a$

Figure 16 The function f is nondifferentiable at $x = a$.

If f is differentiable on the interval (a, b), then none of the situations in Figure 16 can occur. Thus, **the graph of a differentiable function is a continuous curve with no corners and no vertical tangent lines.**

■ Instantaneous Rates of Change

From the definition of instantaneous rate of change of $f(x)$ at x given in Section 7-3, we see that the instantaneous rate of change is simply the derivative of f at x—that is, $f'(x)$.

Example 20
Velocity

Refer to Example 15 in Section 7-3. Find a function that will give the instantaneous velocity, v, of the falling steel ball at any time x. Find the velocity at $x = 2$, 3, and 5 seconds.

Solution

Recall that the distance y (in feet) that the ball falls in x seconds is given by

$$y = f(x) = 16x^2$$

The instantaneous velocity function is $v = f'(x)$; thus,

$$v = f'(x) = \lim_{\Delta x \to 0} \frac{f(x + \Delta x) - f(x)}{\Delta x}$$

We will find $f'(x)$ using the two-step process described in Example 17.

Step 1.   Find $[f(x + \Delta x) - f(x)]/\Delta x$ and simplify.

$$\frac{f(x + \Delta x) - f(x)}{\Delta x} = \frac{[16(x + \Delta x)^2] - (16x^2)}{\Delta x}$$

$$= \frac{16x^2 + 32x\Delta x + 16(\Delta x)^2 - 16x^2}{\Delta x}$$

$$= \frac{32x\Delta x + 16(\Delta x)^2}{\Delta x}$$

$$= \frac{\Delta x}{\Delta x}(32x + 16\Delta x) = 32x + 16\Delta x \qquad \Delta x \neq 0$$

Step 2.   Find the limit of the result of step 1.

$$\lim_{\Delta x \to 0} \frac{f(x + \Delta x) - f(x)}{\Delta x} = \lim_{\Delta x \to 0} (32x + 16\Delta x)$$

$$= 32x$$

Thus,

$$v = f'(x) = 32x$$

The instantaneous velocities at $x = 2$, 3, and 5 seconds are

$f'(2) = 32(2) = 64$ feet per second

$f'(3) = 32(3) = 96$ feet per second

$f'(5) = 32(5) = 160$ feet per second

An instantaneous rate of 64 feet per second at the end of 2 seconds means that *if* the rate were to remain constant for the next second, the object would fall an additional 64 feet. If the object is accelerating or decelerating (that is, if the rate does not remain constant), then the instantaneous rate is an approximation of what actually happens during the next second.

Problem 20 A steel ball falls so that its distance y (in feet) at time x (in seconds) is given by $y = f(x) = 16x^2 - 4x$.

(A) Find a function that will give the instantaneous velocity v at time x.

(B) Find the velocity at $x = 2$, 4, and 6 seconds.

■ Marginal Cost

In business and economics one is often interested in the rate at which something is taking place. A manufacturer, for example, is not only interested in the total cost $C(x)$ at certain production levels x, but is also interested in the rate of change of costs at various production levels.

In economics the word **marginal** refers to a rate of change; that is, to a derivative. Thus, if

$C(x) =$ Total cost of producing x units during some unit of time

then

$C'(x) =$ Marginal cost

$\quad =$ Rate of change in cost per unit change in production at an output level of x units

Just as with instantaneous velocity, $C'(x)$ is an instantaneous rate. It indicates the change in cost for a 1 unit change in production at a production level of x units *if* the rate were to remain constant for the next unit change in production. If the rate does *not* remain constant, then the instantaneous rate is an approximation of what actually happens during the next unit change in production. Example 21 should help to clarify these ideas.

Example 21
Marginal Cost
Suppose the total cost $C(x)$ in thousands of dollars for manufacturing x sailboats per week is given by the function shown in the figure at the top of the next page.

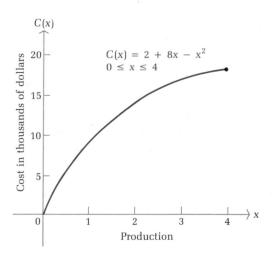

Find:

(A)   The marginal cost at x

(B)   The marginal cost at x = 1, 2, and 3 unit levels of production

Solutions   (A)   Marginal cost at x is

$$C'(x) = \lim_{\Delta x \to 0} \frac{C(x + \Delta x) - C(x)}{\Delta x}$$

which we find using the two-step process discussed in Example 17 (steps omitted here).

Marginal cost = $C'(x) = 8 - 2x$

(B)   Marginal costs at x = 1, 2, and 3 unit levels of production are:

$C'(1) = 8 - 2(1) = 6$ \$6,000 per unit increase in production
$C'(2) = 8 - 2(2) = 4$ \$4,000 per unit increase in production
$C'(3) = 8 - 2(3) = 2$ \$2,000 per unit increase in production

Notice that, as production goes up, the marginal cost goes down, as we might expect.

Let us now look at the marginal cost at the 1 unit level of production and interpret the result geometrically:

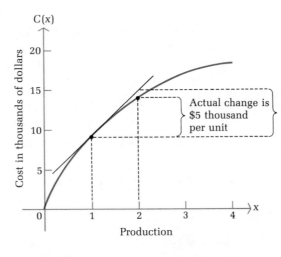

Approximate change using $C'(1)$ is $6 thousand per unit (which is slope of tangent line at $x = 1$). Using the tangent assumes a constant rate of change.

Actual change is $5 thousand per unit

Problem 21 Repeat Example 21 with the cost function $C(x) = 3 + 10x - x^2$, $0 \leqslant x \leqslant 4$.

We will have more to say about marginal analysis in Section 7-8.

■ Summary

The concept of the derivative is a very powerful mathematical idea, and its applications are many and varied. In the next three sections we will develop formulas and general properties of derivatives that will enable us to find the derivatives of many functions without having to go through the (two-step) limiting process each time.

Answers to Matched Problems

17. $f'(x) = 8 - 4x$ 18. $f'(x) = -1/x^2$ or $-x^{-2}$

19. (A) $f'(1) = 4, f'(2) = 0, f'(4) = -8$

(B) At $x = 1$, $y = 4x + 2$; at $x = 2$, $y = 8$; at $x = 4$, $y = -8x + 32$

(C)

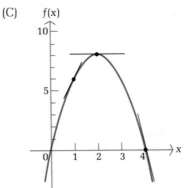

20. (A) $v = f'(x) = 32x - 4$
    (B) $f'(2) = 60$ feet per second, $f'(4) = 124$ feet per second, $f'(6) = 188$ feet per second
21. (A) Marginal cost $= C'(x) = 10 - 2x$
    (B) Marginal costs at 1, 2, and 3 unit levels of production are:

$C'(1) = 8$	\$8,000 per unit increase
$C'(2) = 6$	\$6,000 per unit increase
$C'(3) = 4$	\$4,000 per unit increase

Exercise 7-4

A Problems 1–8 refer to the function f in the following graph. Use the graph to determine if $f'(x)$ exists at the indicated value of x.

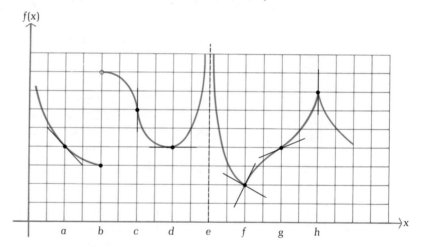

1. $x = a$		2. $x = b$		3. $x = c$		4. $x = d$	
5. $x = e$		6. $x = f$		7. $x = g$		8. $x = h$	

In Problems 9–18, find $f'(x)$ for each indicated function; then find $f'(1)$, $f'(2)$, and $f'(3)$.

9. $f(x) = 2x - 3$ 10. $f(x) = 4x + 3$
11. $f(x) = 6x - x^2$ 12. $f(x) = 8x - x^2$

B 13. $f(x) = \dfrac{1}{x+1}$ 14. $f(x) = \dfrac{1}{x-5}$

15. $f(x) = \sqrt{x} - 3$ 16. $f(x) = 2 - \sqrt{x}$

17. $f(x) = x^{-2}$ 18. $f(x) = \dfrac{1}{x^2}$

19. If an object moves along a line so that it is at $y = f(x) = 4x^2 - 2x$ at time x (in seconds), find the instantaneous velocity function $v = f'(x)$ and find the velocity at times 1, 3, and 5 seconds (y is measured in feet).

20. Repeat Problem 19 with $f(x) = 8x^2 - 4x$.

21. Given $y = f(x) = x^2$, $-3 \leqslant x \leqslant 3$:

(A) Find $f'(x)$.
(B) Find the slope of the tangent line to the graph of $y = x^2$ at $x = -2$, 0, and 2.
(C) Find the equations of the tangents at $x = -2$, 0, and 2.
(D) Sketch the tangent lines on the graph at $x = -2$, 0, and 2.

22. Repeat Problem 21 for $y = f(x) = x^2 + 1$, $-3 \leqslant x \leqslant 3$.

C 23. For $f(x) = x^3 + 2x$, find:

(A) $f'(x)$ (B) $f'(1)$ and $f'(3)$

24. For $f(x) = x^2 - 3x^3$, find:

(A) $f'(x)$ (B) $f'(1)$ and $f'(2)$

In Problems 25 and 26, sketch the graph of f and determine where f is nondifferentiable.

25. $f(x) = \begin{cases} 2x & x < 1 \\ 2 & x \geqslant 1 \end{cases}$

26. $f(x) = \begin{cases} 2x & x < 2 \\ 6 - x & x \geqslant 2 \end{cases}$

In Problems 27–32, determine whether f is differentiable at x = 0 by considering

$$\lim_{\Delta x \to 0} \frac{f(\Delta x) - f(0)}{\Delta x}$$

27. $f(x) = |x|$
28. $f(x) = x + |x|$
29. $f(x) = x|x|$
30. $f(x) = x^{2/3}$
31. $f(x) = x^{1/3}$
32. $f(x) = x^3|x|$

Applications

Business & Economics

33. *Marginal cost.* The total cost per day, $C(x)$ (in hundreds of dollars), for manufacturing x windsurfers is given by

$$C(x) = 3 + 10x - x^2 \qquad 0 \leqslant x \leqslant 5$$

(A) Find the marginal cost at x.
(B) Find the marginal cost at $x = 1, 3$, and 4 unit levels of production.

34. *Marginal cost.* Repeat Problem 33 for $C(x) = 5 + 12x - x^2$, $0 \leqslant x \leqslant 5$.

Life Sciences   **35.** *Negative growth.* A colony of bacteria was treated with a poison, and the number of survivors $N(t)$, in thousands, after t hours was found to be given approximately by

$$N(t) = t^2 - 8t + 16 \qquad 0 \leqslant t \leqslant 4$$

(A)   Find $N'(t)$.
(B)   Find the rate of change of the colony at $t = 1$, 2, and 3.

Social Sciences   **36.** *Learning.* A private foreign language school found that the average person learned $N(t)$ basic phrases in t continuous hours, as given approximately by

$$N(t) = 14t - t^2 \qquad 0 \leqslant t \leqslant 7$$

(A)   Find $N'(t)$.
(B)   Find the rate of learning at $t = 1$, 3, and 6 hours.

7-5   Derivatives of Constants, Power Forms, and Sums

- Derivative of a Constant
- Power Rule
- Derivative of a Constant Times a Function
- Derivatives of Sums and Differences
- Applications

In the last section we defined the derivative of f at x as

$$f'(x) = \lim_{\Delta x \to 0} \frac{f(x + \Delta x) - f(x)}{\Delta x}$$

(if the limit exists) and we used this definition and a two-step process to find the derivatives of a number of functions. In this and the next two sections we will develop some rules based on this definition that will enable us to determine the derivatives of a rather large class of functions without having to go through the two-step process each time.

Before starting on these rules, we list some symbols that are widely used to represent derivatives:

> **Derivative Notation**
>
> Given $y = f(x)$, then
>
> $$f'(x) \qquad y' \qquad \frac{dy}{dx} \qquad D_x f(x)$$
>
> all represent the derivative of f at x.

Each of these symbols for derivatives has its particular advantage in certain situations. All of them will become familiar to you after a little experience.

■ Derivative of a Constant

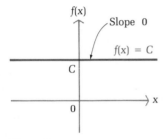

Figure 17

Suppose

$$f(x) = C \qquad C \text{ a constant} \qquad \text{A constant function}$$

Geometrically, the graph of $f(x) = C$ is a horizontal straight line with slope 0 (see Figure 17); hence, we would expect $D_x C = 0$. We will show that this is actually the case using the definition of the derivative and the two-step process introduced in the last section. We want to find

$$f'(x) = \lim_{\Delta x \to 0} \frac{f(x + \Delta x) - f(x)}{\Delta x} \qquad \text{Definition of } f'(x)$$

Step 1. $\dfrac{f(x + \Delta x) - f(x)}{\Delta x} = \dfrac{C - C}{\Delta x} = \dfrac{0}{\Delta x} = 0 \qquad \Delta x \neq 0$

Step 2. $\lim\limits_{\Delta x \to 0} 0 = 0$

Thus,

$$D_x C = 0$$

And we conclude that **the derivative of any constant is 0.**

> **Derivative of a Constant**
>
> If $y = f(x) = C$, then
>
> $$f'(x) = 0$$
>
> Also, $y' = 0$, $dy/dx = 0$, and $D_x C = 0$.
>
> *Note:* When we write $D_x C = 0$, we mean $D_x f(x) = 0$, where $f(x) = C$.

Example 22   (A) If $f(x) = 3$, then $f'(x) = 0$.   (B) If $y = -1.4$, then $y' = 0$.
(C) If $y = \pi$, then $dy/dx = 0$.   (D) $D_x(23) = 0$

Problem 22   Find:

(A) $f'(x)$ for $f(x) = -24$ (B) y' for $y = 12$
(C) dy/dx for $y = -\sqrt{7}$ (D) $D_x(-\pi)$

■ Power Rule

Using the definition of derivative and the two-step process introduced in the last section, we can show that:

If $f(x) = x$,   then $f'(x) = 1$
If $f(x) = x^2$,   then $f'(x) = 2x$
If $f(x) = x^3$,   then $f'(x) = 3x^2$
If $f(x) = x^4$,   then $f'(x) = 4x^3$

In general, for any positive integer n:

$$\text{If}\quad f(x) = x^n, \quad \text{then}\quad f'(x) = nx^{n-1} \tag{1}$$

In fact, more advanced techniques can be used to show that (1) holds for *any* real number n. We will assume this general result for the remainder of this book.

Power Rule

If $y = f(x) = x^n$, where n is a real number, then

$$f'(x) = nx^{n-1}$$

Example 23   (A) If $f(x) = x^5$, then $f'(x) = 5x^{5-1} = 5x^4$.
(B) If $y = x^{25}$, then $y' = 25x^{25-1} = 25x^{24}$.
(C) If $y = x^{-3}$, then $dy/dx = -3x^{-3-1} = -3x^{-4}$.
(D) $D_x x^{5/3} = \frac{5}{3}x^{(5/3)-1} = \frac{5}{3}x^{2/3}$

Problem 23   Find:

(A) $f'(x)$ for $f(x) = x^6$ (B) y' for $y = x^{30}$
(C) dy/dx for $y = x^{-2}$ (D) $D_x x^{3/2}$

In some cases, properties of exponents must be used to rewrite an expression before the power rule is applied.

Example 24   (A)   If $f(x) = 1/x^4$, then we can write $f(x) = x^{-4}$ and

$$f'(x) = -4x^{-4-1} = -4x^{-5} \quad \text{or} \quad \frac{-4}{x^5}$$

(B)   If $y = \sqrt{x}$, then we can write $y = x^{1/2}$ and

$$y' = \frac{1}{2} x^{(1/2)-1} = \frac{1}{2} x^{-1/2} \quad \text{or} \quad \frac{1}{2\sqrt{x}}$$

(C) $D_x \dfrac{1}{\sqrt[3]{x}} = D_x x^{-1/3} = -\dfrac{1}{3} x^{(-1/3)-1} = -\dfrac{1}{3} x^{-4/3} \quad \text{or} \quad \dfrac{-1}{3\sqrt[3]{x^4}}$

Problem 24   Find:

(A) $f'(x)$ for $f(x) = 1/x$ (B) y' for $y = \sqrt[3]{x^2}$ (C) $D_x(1/\sqrt{x})$

■ Derivative of a Constant Times a Function

Let $f(x) = 16x^2 = 16u(x)$, where $u(x) = x^2$. Using the power rule, we have

$$u'(x) = 2x$$

From Example 20 in the last section, $f'(x) = 32x$, which can be written in the form

$$f'(x) = 32x = 16(2x) = 16u'(x)$$

Using the definition of derivative and the two-step process introduced in the last section, we can show that, in general, if $f(x) = ku(x)$, where k is a constant and $u'(x)$ exists, then $f'(x)$ exists and $f'(x) = ku'(x)$. Thus, **the derivative of a constant times a differentiable function is the constant times the derivative of the function.**

Constant Times a Function Rule

If $y = f(x) = ku(x)$, then

$$f'(x) = ku'(x)$$

Also, $y' = ku'$, $dy/dx = k\,du/dx$, and $D_x ku(x) = kD_x u(x)$.

Example 25   (A)   If $f(x) = 3x^2$, then $f'(x) = 3 \cdot 2x^{2-1} = 6x$.

(B)   If $y = \dfrac{x^3}{6} = \dfrac{1}{6} x^3$, then $\dfrac{dy}{dx} = \dfrac{1}{6} \cdot 3x^{3-1} = \dfrac{1}{2} x^2$.

(C) If $y = \dfrac{1}{2x^4} = \dfrac{1}{2}x^{-4}$, then $y' = \dfrac{1}{2}(-4x^{-4-1}) = -2x^{-5}$ or $\dfrac{-2}{x^5}$.

(D) $D_x \dfrac{4}{\sqrt{x^3}} = D_x \dfrac{4}{x^{3/2}} = D_x\, 4x^{-3/2} = 4\left[-\dfrac{3}{2}x^{(-3/2)-1}\right]$

$$= -6x^{-5/2} \quad \text{or} \quad -\dfrac{6}{\sqrt{x^5}}$$

Problem 25   Find:

(A) $f'(x)$ for $f(x) = 4x^5$ (B) $\dfrac{dy}{dx}$ for $y = \dfrac{x^4}{12}$

(C) y' for $y = \dfrac{1}{3x^3}$ (D) $D_x \dfrac{9}{\sqrt[3]{x}}$

■ Derivatives of Sums and Differences

Let $f(x) = 4x - x^2 = u(x) - v(x)$, where $u(x) = 4x$ and $v(x) = x^2$. Using the power rule and the constant times a function rule, we have

  $u'(x) = 4$ and $v'(x) = 2x$

From Example 17 in the last section, $f'(x) = 4 - 2x$, which can be written in the form

  $f'(x) = 4 - 2x = u'(x) - v'(x)$

In general, we can show that if $f(x) = u(x) \pm v(x)$ and $u'(x)$ and $v'(x)$ exist, then $f'(x)$ exists and $f'(x) = u'(x) \pm v'(x)$. Thus, **the derivative of the sum of two differentiable functions is the sum of the derivatives and the derivative of the difference of two differentiable functions is the difference of the derivatives.** Together, we then have the sum and difference rule for differentiation.

Sum and Difference Rule

If $y = f(x) = u(x) \pm v(x)$, then

  $f'(x) = u'(x) \pm v'(x)$

[*Note:* This rule generalizes to the sum and difference of any given number of functions.]

With this and the other rules stated previously, we will be able to compute the derivatives of all polynomials and a variety of other functions.

Example 26

(A) If $f(x) = 3x^2 + 2x$, then $f'(x) = (3x^2)' + (2x)' = 6x + 2$.

(B) If $y = 4 + 2x^3 - 3x^{-1}$, then $y' = (4)' + (2x^3)' - (3x^{-1})' = 6x^2 + 3x^{-2}$.

(C) If $y = \sqrt[3]{x} - 3x$, then $\dfrac{dy}{dx} = \dfrac{d}{dx}x^{1/3} - \dfrac{d}{dx}3x = \dfrac{1}{3}x^{-2/3} - 3$.

(D) $D_x\left(\dfrac{5}{3x^2} - \dfrac{2}{x^4} + \dfrac{x^3}{9}\right) = D_x\dfrac{5}{3}x^{-2} - D_x 2x^{-4} + D_x\dfrac{1}{9}x^3$

$= \dfrac{5}{3}(-2)x^{-3} - 2(-4)x^{-5} + \dfrac{1}{9}\cdot 3x^2 = -\dfrac{10}{3x^3} + \dfrac{8}{x^5} + \dfrac{1}{3}x^2.$

Problem 26

Find:

(A) $f'(x)$ for $f(x) = 3x^4 - 2x^3 + x^2 - 5x + 7$

(B) y' for $y = 3 - 7x^{-2}$

(C) $\dfrac{dy}{dx}$ for $y = 5x^3 - \sqrt[4]{x}$

(D) $D_x\left(-\dfrac{3}{4x} + \dfrac{4}{x^3} - \dfrac{x^4}{8}\right)$

■ Applications

Example 27
Instantaneous Velocity

An object moves along the y axis (marked in feet) so that its position at time x in seconds is

$f(x) = x^3 - 6x^2 + 9x$

(A) Find the instantaneous velocity function v.

(B) Find the velocity at $x = 2$ and $x = 5$ seconds.

(C) Find the time(s) when the velocity is 0.

Solutions

(A) $v = f'(x) = (x^3)' - (6x^2)' + (9x)' = 3x^2 - 12x + 9$

(B) $f'(2) = 3(2)^2 - 12(2) + 9 = -3$ feet per second

$f'(5) = 3(5)^2 - 12(5) + 9 = 24$ feet per second

(C) $v = f'(x) = 3x^2 - 12x + 9 = 0$

$3(x^2 - 4x + 3) = 0$

$3(x - 1)(x - 3) = 0$

$x = 1, 3$

Thus, $v = 0$ at $x = 1$ and $x = 3$ seconds.

Problem 27

Repeat Example 27 for $f(x) = x^3 - 15x^2 + 72x$.

Example 28   Let $f(x) = x^4 - 8x^2 + 10$.

Tangents
(A) Find $f'(x)$.
(B) Find the equation of the tangent line at $x = 1$.
(C) Find the values of x where the tangent line is horizontal.

Solutions   (A) $f'(x) = \boxed{(x^4)' - (8x^2)' + (10)'}$

$$= 4x^3 - 16x$$

(B) $y - y_1 = m(x - x_1)$ $y_1 = f(x_1) = f(1) = (1)^4 - 8(1)^2 + 10 = 3$
 $m = f'(x_1) = f'(1) = 4(1)^3 - 16(1) = -12$

$$y - 3 = -12(x - 1)$$
$$y = -12x + 15 \qquad \text{Tangent line at } x = 1$$

(C) Since a horizontal line has 0 slope, we must solve $f'(x) = 0$ for x:

$$f'(x) = 4x^3 - 16x = 0$$
$$4x(x^2 - 4) = 0$$
$$4x(x - 2)(x + 2) = 0$$
$$x = 0, 2, -2$$

Thus, the tangent line to the graph of f will be horizontal at $x = -2$, $x = 0$, and $x = 2$. (In the next chapter, we will see how this information is used to help sketch the graph of f.)

Problem 28   Repeat Example 28 for $f(x) = x^4 - 4x^3 + 7$

Example 29   The total cost $C(x)$ in thousands of dollars for manufacturing x sailboats is
Marginal Cost   given by

$$C(x) = 2 + 8x - x^2 \qquad 0 \leqslant x \leqslant 4$$

(A) The marginal cost at a production level of x is

$$C'(x) \boxed{= (2)' + (8x)' - (x^2)'} = 8 - 2x$$

(B) The marginal cost at $x = 1$ is

$$C'(1) = 8 - 2(1) = 6 \qquad \text{\$6,000 per unit increase in production}$$

(C) The marginal cost at $x = 3$ is

$$C'(3) = 8 - 2(3) = 2 \qquad \text{\$2,000 per unit increase in production}$$

Problem 29   Repeat Example 29 with the cost function $C(x) = 3 + 10x - x^2$, $0 \leqslant x \leqslant 4$.

Answers to   22. All are 0.
Matched Problems   23. (A) $6x^5$ (B) $30x^{29}$ (C) $-2x^{-3}$ (D) $\frac{3}{2}x^{1/2}$
 24. (A) $-x^{-2}$ or $-1/x^2$ (B) $\frac{2}{3}x^{-1/3}$ or $2/(3\sqrt[3]{x})$
 (C) $-\frac{1}{2}x^{-3/2}$ or $-1/(2\sqrt{x^3})$

25. (A) $20x^4$ (B) $x^3/3$ (C) $-x^{-4}$ or $-1/x^4$
    (D) $-3x^{-4/3}$ or $-3/\sqrt[3]{x^4}$
26. (A) $12x^3 - 6x^2 + 2x - 5$ (B) $14x^{-3}$
    (C) $15x^2 - \frac{1}{4}x^{-3/4}$ (D) $3/(4x^2) - (12/x^4) - (x^3/2)$
27. (A) $v = 3x^2 - 30x + 72$
    (B) $f'(2) = 24$ feet per second; $f'(5) = -3$ feet per second
    (C) $x = 4$ seconds or $x = 6$ seconds
28. (A) $f'(x) = 4x^3 - 12x^2$ (B) $y = -8x + 12$ (C) $x = 0$ or $x = 3$
29. (A) Marginal cost $= C'(x) = 10 - 2x$
    (B) $C'(1) = 8$ $8,000 per unit increase in production
    (C) $C'(3) = 4$ $4,000 per unit increase in production

Exercise 7-5

Find each of the following:

A 1. $f'(x)$ for $f(x) = 12$

2. $\dfrac{dy}{dx}$ for $y = -\sqrt{3}$

3. $D_x 23$

4. y' for $y = \pi$

5. $\dfrac{dy}{dx}$ for $y = x^{12}$

6. $D_x x^5$

7. $f'(x)$ for $f(x) = x$

8. y' for $y = x^7$

9. y' for $y = x^{-7}$

10. $f'(x)$ for $f(x) = x^{-11}$

11. $\dfrac{dy}{dx}$ for $y = x^{5/2}$

12. $D_x x^{7/3}$

13. $D_x \dfrac{1}{x^5}$

14. $f'(x)$ for $f(x) = \dfrac{1}{x^9}$

15. $f'(x)$ for $f(x) = 2x^4$

16. $\dfrac{dy}{dx}$ for $y = -3x$

17. $D_x \left(\dfrac{1}{3} x^6 \right)$

18. y' for $y = \dfrac{1}{2} x^4$

19. $\dfrac{dy}{dx}$ for $y = \dfrac{x^5}{15}$

20. $f'(x)$ for $f(x) = \dfrac{x^6}{24}$

B 21. $D_x(2x^{-5})$

22. y' for $y = -4x^{-1}$

23. $f'(x)$ for $f(x) = \dfrac{4}{x^4}$

24. $\dfrac{dy}{dx}$ for $y = \dfrac{-3}{x^6}$

25. $D_x \dfrac{-1}{2x^2}$

26. y' for $y = \dfrac{1}{6x^3}$

27. $f'(x)$ for $f(x) = -3x^{1/3}$

28. $\dfrac{dy}{dx}$ for $y = -8x^{1/4}$

29. $D_x(2x^2 - 3x + 4)$

30. y' for $y = 3x^2 + 4x - 7$

31. $\dfrac{dy}{dx}$ for $y = 3x^5 - 2x^3 + 5$

32. $f'(x)$ for $y = 2x^3 - 6x + 5$

33. $D_x(3x^{-4} + 2x^{-2})$

34. y' for $y = 2x^{-3} - 4x^{-1}$

35. $\dfrac{dy}{dx}$ for $y = \dfrac{1}{2x} - \dfrac{2}{3x^3}$

36. $f'(x)$ for $f(x) = \dfrac{3}{4x^3} + \dfrac{1}{2x^5}$

37. $D_x(3x^{2/3} - 5x^{1/3})$

38. $D_x(8x^{3/4} + 4x^{-1/4})$

39. $D_x\left(\dfrac{3}{x^{3/5}} - \dfrac{6}{x^{1/2}}\right)$

40. $D_y\left(\dfrac{5}{y^{1/5}} - \dfrac{8}{y^{3/2}}\right)$

41. $D_x\dfrac{1}{\sqrt[3]{x}}$

42. y' for $y = \dfrac{10}{\sqrt[5]{x}}$

43. $\dfrac{dy}{dx}$ for $y = \dfrac{12}{\sqrt{x}} - 3x^{-2} + x$

44. $f'(x)$ for $f(x) = 2x^{-3} - \dfrac{6}{\sqrt[3]{x^2}} + 7$

45. Given the equation $y = f(x) = 6x - x^2$, find:

   (A) $f'(x)$
   (B) The equation of the lines tangent to the graph at $x = 2$ and at $x = 4$

46. Repeat Problem 45 for $y = f(x) = 2x^2 + 8x$.
47. Repeat Problem 45 for $y = f(x) = x^3 - 3x^2 + 2$.
48. Repeat Problem 45 for $y = f(x) = 2x^3 - 3x^2 - 5$.
49. If an object moves along the y axis (marked in feet) so that its position at time x in seconds is given by $y = f(x) = 176x - 16x^2$, find:

   (A) The instantaneous velocity function $v = f'(x)$
   (B) The velocity at $x = 0$, 3, and 6 seconds
   (C) The time(s) when $v = 0$

50. Repeat Problem 49 for $y = f(x) = 80x - 10x^2$.
51. Repeat Problem 49 for $y = f(x) = x^3 - 9x^2 + 15x$.
52. Repeat Problem 49 for $y = f(x) = x^3 - 9x^2 + 24x$.
53. Given the equation $y = f(x) = x^3 + 6x^2 - 15x$, find:

   (A) $f'(x)$
   (B) The values of x where the tangent line is horizontal

54. Repeat Problem 53 for $y = f(x) = x^3 - 9x^2 + 27x - 9$.
55. Repeat Problem 53 for $y = f(x) = 3x^4 - 4x^3 + 2$.
56. Repeat Problem 53 for $y = f(x) = x^4 - 32x^2 + 10$.

Find each of the following:

C 57. $f'(x)$ for $f(x) = \dfrac{10x + 20}{x}$

58. $\dfrac{dy}{dx}$ for $y = \dfrac{x^2 + 25}{x^2}$

59. $D_x\dfrac{x^4 - 3x^3 + 5}{x^2}$

60. y' for $y = \dfrac{2x^5 - 4x^3 + 2x}{x^3}$

In Problems 61–64, use the definition of derivative and the two-step process to verify each statement.

61. $D_x x^3 = 3x^2$

62. $D_x x^4 = 4x^3$

63. $D_x[kf(x)] = kD_x f(x)$

64. $D_x[u(x) + v(x)] = u'(x) + v'(x)$

Applications

Business & Economics

65. *Advertising.* Using past records it is estimated that a company will sell $N(x)$ units of a product after spending x thousand on advertising, as given by

$$N(x) = 60x - x^2 \qquad 5 \leqslant x \leqslant 30$$

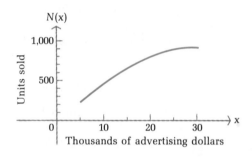

(A) Find $N'(x)$, the rate of change of sales per unit change in money spent on advertising at the x thousand level.

(B) Find $N'(10)$ and $N'(20)$ and interpret.

66. *Marginal average cost.* (This topic is treated in detail in Section 7-8.) Economists often work with average costs—cost per unit output—rather than total costs. We would expect higher average costs, because of plant inefficiency, at low output levels and also at output levels near plant capacity. Therefore, we would expect the graph of an average cost function to be U-shaped. Suppose that for a given firm the total cost of producing x thousand units is given by

$$C(x) = x^3 - 6x^2 + 12x$$

Then the average cost $\overline{C}(x)$ is given by

$$\overline{C}(x) = \frac{C(x)}{x} = x^2 - 6x + 12$$

(A) Find the marginal average cost $\overline{C}'(x)$.

(B) Find the marginal average cost at $x = 2$, 3, and 4, and interpret.

Life Sciences

67. *Medicine.* A person x inches tall has a pulse rate of y beats per minute, as given approximately by

$$y = 590x^{-1/2} \qquad 30 \leqslant x \leqslant 75$$

What is the instantaneous rate of change of pulse rate at the:

(A)   36 inch level?   (B)   64 inch level?

68. *Ecology.* A coal-burning electrical generating plant emits sulfur dioxide into the surrounding air. The concentration $C(x)$ in parts per million is given approximately by

$$C(x) = \frac{0.1}{x^2}$$

where x is the distance from the plant in miles. Find the (instantaneous) rate of change of concentration at:

(A) $x = 1$ mile   (B) $x = 2$ miles

Social Sciences

69. *Learning.* Suppose a person learns y items in x hours, as given by

$$y = 50\sqrt{x} \qquad 0 \leqslant x \leqslant 9$$

Find the rate of learning at the end of:

(A)   1 hour   (B)   9 hours

70. *Learning.* If a person learns y items in x hours, as given by

$$y = 21\sqrt[3]{x^2} \qquad 0 \leqslant x \leqslant 8$$

find the rate of learning at the end of:

(A)   1 hour   (B)   8 hours

7-6   Derivatives of Products and Quotients

■ Derivatives of Products
■ Derivatives of Quotients

The derivative rules discussed in the last section added substantially to our ability to compute and apply derivatives to many practical problems. In this and the next section we will add a few more rules that will increase this ability even further.

■ Derivatives of Products

In the last section we found that the derivative of a sum is the sum of the derivatives. Is the derivative of a product the product of the derivatives? Let us take a look at a simple example. Consider

$$f(x) = u(x)v(x) = (x^2 - 3x)(2x^3 - 1) \tag{1}$$

where $u(x) = x^2 - 3x$ and $v(x) = 2x^3 - 1$. The product of the derivatives is

$$u'(x)v'(x) = (2x - 3)6x^2 = 12x^3 - 18x^2 \tag{2}$$

To see if this is equal to the derivative of the product, we multiply the right side of (1) and use derivative formulas from the last section:

$$f(x) = (x^2 - 3x)(2x^3 - 1) = 2x^5 - 6x^4 - x^2 + 3x$$

Thus,

$$f'(x) = 10x^4 - 24x^3 - 2x + 3 \tag{3}$$

Since (2) and (3) are not equal, we conclude that the derivative of a product is *not* the product of the derivatives. There is a product rule for derivatives, but it is slightly more complicated than you might expect.

Using the definition of derivative and the two-step process, we can show that **the derivative of a product is the first times the derivative of the second plus the second times the derivative of the first.**

Product Rule

If $y = f(x) = u(x)v(x)$, then

$$f'(x) = u(x)v'(x) + v(x)u'(x)$$

Also,

$$y' = uv' + vu'$$
$$\frac{dy}{dx} = u\frac{dv}{dx} + v\frac{du}{dx}$$
$$D_x[u(x)v(x)] = u(x)D_xv(x) + v(x)D_xu(x)$$

Example 30 Find $f'(x)$ for $f(x) = 2x^2(3x^4 - 2)$ two ways.

Solution Method I. Use the product rule:

$$\begin{aligned}
f'(x) &= 2x^2(3x^4 - 2)' + (3x^4 - 2)(2x^2)' \\
&= 2x^2(12x^3) + (3x^4 - 2)(4x) \\
&= 24x^5 + 12x^5 - 8x \\
&= 36x^5 - 8x
\end{aligned}$$

First times derivative of second plus second times derivative of first

Method II.   Multiply first; then take derivatives:

$$f(x) = 2x^2(3x^4 - 2) = 6x^6 - 4x^2$$
$$f'(x) = 36x^5 - 8x$$

Problem 30   Find $f'(x)$ two ways for $f(x) = 3x^3(2x^2 - 3x + 1)$.

At this point, all the products we will encounter can be differentiated by either of the methods illustrated in Example 30. In the next and later sections, we will see that there are situations where the product rule must be used. Unless instructed otherwise, you should use the product rule to differentiate all products in this section to gain experience with the use of this important differentiation rule.

Example 31   Let $f(x) = (2x - 9)(x^2 + 6)$.

(A)   Find the equation of the line tangent to the graph of $f(x)$ at $x = 3$.
(B)   Find the values of x where the tangent line is horizontal.

Solutions   (A)   First find $f'(x)$:

$$f'(x) = (2x - 9)(x^2 + 6)' + (x^2 + 6)(2x - 9)'$$
$$= (2x - 9)(2x) + (x^2 + 6)(2)$$

Now find the equation of the tangent line at $x = 3$.

$$y - y_1 = m(x - x_1) \qquad y_1 = f(x_1) = f(3) = -45$$
$$m = f'(x_1) = f'(3) = 12$$

$$y - (-45) = 12(x - 3)$$
$$y = 12x - 81 \qquad \text{Tangent line at } x = 3$$

(B)   The tangent line is horizontal at values of x such that $f'(x) = 0$, so

$$f'(x) = (2x - 9)2x + (x^2 + 6)2 = 0$$
$$6x^2 - 18x + 12 = 0$$
$$x^2 - 3x + 2 = 0$$
$$(x - 1)(x - 2) = 0$$
$$x = 1, 2$$

The tangent line is horizontal at $x = 1$ and at $x = 2$.

Problem 31   Repeat Example 31 for $f(x) = (2x + 9)(x^2 - 12)$.

As Example 31 illustrates, the way we write $f'(x)$ depends on what we want to do with it. If we are interested only in evaluating $f'(x)$ at specified values of x, the form in part A is sufficient. However, if we want to solve $f'(x) = 0$, we must multiply and collect like terms, as we did in part B.

■ Derivatives of Quotients

As is the case with a product, the derivative of a quotient is *not* the quotient of the derivatives.

Let

$$f(x) = \frac{u(x)}{v(x)} \qquad \text{where} \qquad u'(x) \text{ and } v'(x) \text{ exist}$$

Starting with the definition of a derivative, you can show that

$$f'(x) = \frac{v(x)u'(x) - u(x)v'(x)}{[v(x)]^2}$$

Thus, **the derivative of a quotient is the denominator times the derivative of the numerator minus the numerator times the derivative of the denominator, all over the denominator squared.**

Quotient Rule

If

$$y = f(x) = \frac{u(x)}{v(x)}$$

then

$$f'(x) = \frac{v(x)u'(x) - u(x)v'(x)}{[v(x)]^2}$$

Also,

$$y' = \frac{vu' - uv'}{v^2}$$

$$\frac{dy}{dx} = \frac{v(du/dx) - u(dv/dx)}{v^2}$$

$$D_x \frac{u(x)}{v(x)} = \frac{v(x)D_x u(x) - u(x)D_x v(x)}{[v(x)]^2}$$

Example 32   (A) If

$$f(x) = \frac{x^2}{2x - 1}$$

find $f'(x)$.

(B) Find

$$D_x \frac{x^2 - x}{x^3 + 1}$$

(C) Find

$$D_x \frac{x^2 - 3}{x^2}$$

by using the quotient rule and also by splitting the fraction into two fractions.

Solutions   (A) $f'(x) = \dfrac{(2x - 1)(x^2)' - x^2(2x - 1)'}{(2x - 1)^2}$ The denominator times the derivative of the numerator minus the numerator times the derivative of the denominator, all over the square of the denominator

$$= \frac{(2x - 1)(2x) - x^2(2)}{(2x - 1)^2}$$

$$= \frac{4x^2 - 2x - 2x^2}{(2x - 1)^2}$$

$$= \frac{2x^2 - 2x}{(2x - 1)^2}$$

(B) $D_x \dfrac{x^2 - x}{x^3 + 1} = \dfrac{(x^3 + 1)D_x(x^2 - x) - (x^2 - x)D_x(x^3 + 1)}{(x^3 + 1)^2}$

$$= \frac{(x^3 + 1)(2x - 1) - (x^2 - x)(3x^2)}{(x^3 + 1)^2}$$

$$= \frac{2x^4 - x^3 + 2x - 1 - 3x^4 + 3x^3}{(x^3 + 1)^2}$$

$$= \frac{-x^4 + 2x^3 + 2x - 1}{(x^3 + 1)^2}$$

(C) Method I. Use the quotient rule:

$$D_x \frac{x^2 - 3}{x^2} = \frac{x^2 D_x(x^2 - 3) - (x^2 - 3)D_x x^2}{(x^2)^2}$$

$$= \frac{x^2(2x) - (x^2 - 3)2x}{x^4}$$

$$= \frac{2x^3 - 2x^3 + 6x}{x^4} = \frac{6x}{x^4} = \frac{6}{x^3}$$

Method II. Split into two fractions:

$$\frac{x^2 - 3}{x^2} = \frac{x^2}{x^2} - \frac{3}{x^2} = 1 - 3x^{-2}$$

$$D_x(1 - 3x^{-2}) = 0 - 3(-2)x^{-3} = \frac{6}{x^3}$$

Comparing methods I and II, we see that it may sometimes pay to change an expression algebraically before blindly using a differentiation formula.

Problem 32   Find:

(A) $f'(x)$ for $f(x) = \dfrac{2x}{x^2 + 3}$

(B) y' for $y = \dfrac{x^3 - 3x}{x^2 - 4}$

(C) $D_x \dfrac{2 + x^3}{x^3}$ two ways

Example 33
Sales Analysis

When a successful home video game is first introduced, the monthly sales generally increase rapidly for a period of time, and then begin to decrease. Suppose that the monthly sales $S(t)$ (in thousands of games) t months after the game is introduced are given by

$$S(t) = \frac{200t}{t^2 + 100}$$

(A)   Find $S'(t)$.
(B)   Find $S(5)$ and $S'(5)$ and interpret.
(C)   Find $S(30)$ and $S'(30)$ and interpret.

Solutions   (A) $S'(t) = \dfrac{(t^2 + 100)(200t)' - 200t(t^2 + 100)'}{(t^2 + 100)^2}$

$$= \frac{(t^2 + 100)200 - 200t(2t)}{(t^2 + 100)^2}$$

$$= \frac{200t^2 + 20{,}000 - 400t^2}{(t^2 + 100)^2}$$

$$= \frac{20{,}000 - 200t^2}{(t^2 + 100)^2}$$

(B) $S(5) = \dfrac{200(5)}{5^2 + 100} = 8$ and $S'(5) = \dfrac{20{,}000 - 200(5)^2}{(5^2 + 100)^2} = 0.96$

The sales for the fifth month are 8,000 units. At this point in time, sales are increasing at the rate of 0.96(1000) = 960 units per month.

(C) $S(30) = \dfrac{200(30)}{30^2 + 100} = 6$ and $S'(30) = \dfrac{20{,}000 - 200(30)^2}{(30^2 + 100)^2} = -0.16$

The sales for the thirtieth month are 6,000 units. At this point in time, sales are decreasing at the rate of 0.16(1,000) = 160 units per month.

The function $S(t)$ in Example 33 is graphed in Figure 18. Notice that the maximum monthly sales seem to occur during the tenth month. In the next chapter, we will see how the derivative $S'(t)$ is used to help sketch the graph of $S(t)$ and to find the maximum monthly sales.

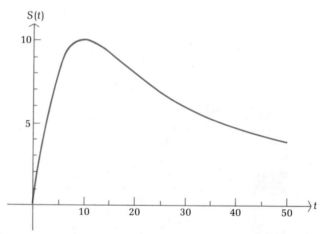

Figure 18

Problem 33

Refer to Example 33. Suppose that the monthly sales $S(t)$ (in thousands of games) t months after the game is introduced are given by

$$S(t) = \frac{200t}{t^2 + 64}$$

(A) Find $S'(t)$.
(B) Find $S(4)$ and $S'(4)$ and interpret.
(C) Find $S(24)$ and $S'(24)$ and interpret.

Answers to Matched Problems

30. $30x^4 - 36x^3 + 9x^2$ 31. (A) $y = 84x - 297$ (B) $x = -4; x = 1$

32. (A) $\dfrac{(x^2 + 3)2 - (2x)(2x)}{(x^2 + 3)^2} = \dfrac{6 - 2x^2}{(x^2 + 3)^2}$

(B) $\dfrac{(x^2 - 4)(3x^2 - 3) - (x^3 - 3x)(2x)}{(x^2 - 4)^2} = \dfrac{x^4 - 9x^2 + 12}{(x^2 - 4)^2}$

(C) $-\dfrac{6}{x^4}$

33. (A) $S'(t) = \dfrac{12{,}800 - 200t^2}{(t^2 + 64)^2}$

(B) $S(4) = 10$; $S'(4) = 1.5$; at $t = 4$ months, monthly sales are 10,000 and increasing at 1,500 games per month.

(C) $S(24) = 7.5$; $S'(24) = -0.25$; at $t = 24$ months, monthly sales are 7,500 and decreasing at 250 games per month.

Exercise 7-6

A   For $f(x)$ as given, find $f'(x)$ and simplify.

1. $f(x) = 2x^3(x^2 - 2)$

2. $f(x) = 5x^2(x^3 + 2)$

3. $f(x) = (x - 3)(2x - 1)$

4. $f(x) = (3x + 2)(4x - 5)$

5. $f(x) = \dfrac{x}{x - 3}$

6. $f(x) = \dfrac{3x}{2x + 1}$

7. $f(x) = \dfrac{2x + 3}{x - 2}$

8. $f(x) = \dfrac{3x - 4}{2x + 3}$

9. $f(x) = (x^2 + 1)(2x - 3)$

10. $f(x) = (3x + 5)(x^2 - 3)$

11. $f(x) = \dfrac{x^2 + 1}{2x - 3}$

12. $f(x) = \dfrac{3x + 5}{x^2 - 3}$

13. $f(x) = (x^2 + 2)(x^2 - 3)$

14. $f(x) = (x^2 - 4)(x^2 + 5)$

15. $f(x) = \dfrac{x^2 + 2}{x^2 - 3}$

16. $f(x) = \dfrac{x^2 - 4}{x^2 + 5}$

B   Find each of the following and simplify:

17. $f'(x)$ for $f(x) = (2x + 1)(x^2 - 3x)$

18. y' for $y = (x^3 + 2x^2)(3x - 1)$

19. $\dfrac{dy}{dx}$ for $y = (2x - x^2)(5x + 2)$

20. $D_x[(3 - x^3)(x^2 - x)]$

21. y' for $y = \dfrac{5x - 3}{x^2 + 2x}$

22. $f'(x)$ for $f(x) = \dfrac{3x^2}{2x - 1}$

23. $D_x \dfrac{x^2 - 3x + 1}{x^2 - 1}$

24. $\dfrac{dy}{dx}$ for $y = \dfrac{x^4 - x^3}{3x - 1}$

In Problems 25–28, find $f'(x)$ and find the equation of the line tangent to the graph of f at $x = 2$.

25. $f(x) = (1 + 3x)(5 - 2x)$

26. $f(x) = (7 - 3x)(1 + 2x)$

27. $f(x) = \dfrac{x - 8}{3x - 4}$

28. $f(x) = \dfrac{2x - 5}{2x - 3}$

In Problems 29–32, find $f'(x)$ and find the values of x where $f'(x) = 0$.

29. $f(x) = (2x - 15)(x^2 + 18)$

30. $f(x) = (2x - 3)(x^2 - 6)$

31. $f(x) = \dfrac{x}{x^2 + 1}$

32. $f(x) = \dfrac{x}{x^2 + 9}$

In Problems 33–36, find $f'(x)$ two ways: by using the product or quotient rule and by simplifying first.

33. $f(x) = x^3(x^4 - 1)$

34. $f(x) = x^4(x^3 - 1)$

35. $f(x) = \dfrac{x^3 + 9}{x^3}$

36. $f(x) = \dfrac{x^4 + 4}{x^4}$

C   Find each of the following. Do not simplify.

37. $f'(x)$ for $f(x) = (2x^4 - 3x^3 + x)(x^2 - x + 5)$

38. $\dfrac{dy}{dx}$ for $y = (x^2 - 3x + 1)(x^3 + 2x^2 - x)$

39. $D_x \dfrac{3x^2 - 2x + 3}{4x^2 + 5x - 1}$

40. y' for $y = \dfrac{x^3 - 3x + 4}{2x^2 + 3x - 2}$

41. $\dfrac{dy}{dx}$ for $y = 9x^{1/3}(x^3 + 5)$

42. $D_x[(4x^{1/2} - 1)(3x^{1/3} + 2)]$

43. $f'(x)$ for $f(x) = \dfrac{6\sqrt[3]{x}}{x^2 - 3}$

44. y' for $y = \dfrac{2\sqrt{x}}{x^2 - 3x + 1}$

45. $D_x \dfrac{x^3 - 2x^2}{\sqrt[3]{x^2}}$

46. $\dfrac{dy}{dx}$ for $y = \dfrac{x^2 - 3x + 1}{\sqrt[4]{x}}$

47. $f'(x)$ for $f(x) = \dfrac{(2x^2 - 1)(x^2 + 3)}{x^2 + 1}$

48. y' for $y = \dfrac{2x - 1}{(x^3 + 2)(x^2 - 3)}$

Applications

Business & Economics   **49.** *Sales analysis.* The monthly sales S (in thousands) for a record album are given by

$$S(t) = \frac{200t}{t^2 + 36}$$

where t is the number of months since the release of the album.

(A)   Find $S'(t)$, the rate of change of monthly sales with respect to time.

(B)   Find $S(2)$ and $S'(2)$ and interpret.

(C)   Find $S(8)$ and $S'(8)$ and interpret.

50. *Sales analysis.* A communications company has installed a cable television system in a city. The total number N (in thousands) of subscribers t months after the installation of the system is given by

$$N(t) = \frac{200t}{t + 5}$$

(A)   Find $N'(t)$, the rate of change of total number of subscribers with respect to time.

(B)   Find $N(5)$ and $N'(5)$ and interpret.

(C)   Find $N(15)$ and $N'(15)$ and interpret.

51. *Price–demand function.* According to classical economic theory, the demand $d(x)$ for a commodity in a free market decreases as the price x increases. Suppose that the number $d(x)$ of transistor radios people are willing to buy per week in a given city at a price $x is given by

$$d(x) = \frac{50{,}000}{x^2 + 10x + 25} \qquad \$4 \leq x \leq \$15$$

(A)   Find $d'(x)$, the rate of change of demand with respect to price change.

(B)   Find $d'(5)$ and $d'(10)$ and interpret.

52. *Employee training.* A company producing computer components has established that on the average a new employee can assemble N(t) components per day after t days of on-the-job training, as given by

$$N(t) = \frac{100t}{t + 9}$$

(A)   Find $N'(t)$, the rate of change of units assembled with respect to time.

(B)   Find $N'(1)$ and $N'(11)$ and interpret.

Life Sciences   **53.** *Medicine.* A drug is injected into the bloodstream of a patient through her right arm. The concentration of the drug in the bloodstream of the left arm t hours after the injection is given by

$$C(t) = \frac{0.14t}{t^2 + 1}$$

(A)   Find $C'(t)$, the rate of change of drug concentration with respect to time.

(B)   Find $C'(0.5)$ and $C'(3)$ and interpret.

54.   *Drug sensitivity.* One hour after x milligrams of a particular drug are given to a person, the change in body temperature $T(x)$ in degrees Fahrenheit is given approximately by

$$T(x) = x^2 \left(1 - \frac{x}{9}\right) \qquad 0 \leqslant x \leqslant 7$$

The rate at which T changes with respect to the size of the dosage x, $T'(x)$, is called the *sensitivity* of the body to the dosage.

(A)   Find $T'(x)$, using the product rule.
(B)   Find $T'(1)$, $T'(3)$, and $T'(6)$.

Social Sciences   55.   *Learning.* In the early days of quantitative learning theory (around 1917), L. L. Thurstone found that a given person successfully accomplished $N(x)$ acts after x practice acts, as given by

$$N(x) = \frac{100x + 200}{x + 32}$$

(A)   Find the rate of change of learning, $N'(x)$, with respect to the number of practice acts x.
(B)   Find $N'(4)$ and $N'(68)$.

7-7   General Power Rule

■ General Power Rule
■ Combining Rules of Differentiation

■ General Power Rule

We have already made extensive use of the power rule:

$$D_x x^n = n x^{n-1} \qquad n \text{ any real number} \tag{1}$$

Now we want to generalize this rule so that we can differentiate functions of the form $[u(x)]^n$. Is (1) still valid if we replace x with a function $u(x)$? We begin by considering a simple example. Let $u(x) = 2x$ and $n = 4$. Then

$$[u(x)]^n = (2x)^4 = 2^4 x^4 = 16x^4$$

and

$$D_x[u(x)]^n = D_x 16x^4 = 64x^3 \tag{2}$$

But

$$n[u(x)]^{n-1} = 4(2x)^3 = 32x^3 \tag{3}$$

Comparing (2) and (3), we see that

$$D_x[u(x)]^n \neq n[u(x)]^{n-1}$$

for this particular choice of $u(x)$ and n. (In fact, it can be shown that the only time this last equation is valid is if $u(x) = x$.) Thus, we cannot generalize the power rule by simply substituting $u(x)$ for x in (1).

How can we find a formula for $D_x[u(x)]^n$ where $u(x)$ is an arbitrary differentiable function? Let us first find $D_x[u(x)]^2$ and $D_x[u(x)]^3$ to see if a general pattern emerges. Since $[u(x)]^2 = u(x)u(x)$, we use the product rule with $v(x) = u(x)$ to write

$$D_x[u(x)]^2 = D_x u(x)u(x) = u(x)u'(x) + u'(x)u(x)$$
$$= 2u(x)u'(x) \qquad (4)$$

Since $[u(x)]^3 = [u(x)]^2 u(x)$, we now use the product rule with $v(x) = [u(x)]^2$ and (4) to write

$$D_x[u(x)]^3 = D_x[u(x)]^2 u(x) = [u(x)]^2 D_x u(x) + u(x)D_x[u(x)]^2$$
$$= [u(x)]^2 u'(x) + u(x)[2u(x)u'(x)]$$
$$= 3[u(x)]^2 u'(x)$$

Continuing in this fashion, it can be shown that

$$D_x[u(x)]^n = n[u(x)]^{n-1}u'(x) \qquad n \text{ a positive integer} \qquad (5)$$

Using more advanced techniques, the formula in (5) can be established for all real numbers n. Thus, we have the *general power rule*.

General Power Rule

If n is any real number, then

$$D_x[u(x)]^n = n[u(x)]^{n-1}u'(x)$$

provided $u'(x)$ exists. This rule is often written more compactly as

$$D_x u^n = u^{n-1}\frac{du}{dx} \qquad u = u(x)$$

Example 34   Find $f'(x)$:

(A) $f(x) = (3x + 1)^4$ (B) $f(x) = (x^3 + 4)^7$

(C) $f(x) = \dfrac{1}{(x^2 + x + 4)^3}$ (D) $f(x) = \sqrt{3 - x}$

Solutions   (A) $f(x) = (3x + 1)^4$ Let $u = 3x + 1$, $n = 4$.

$f'(x) = 4(3x + 1)^3 D_x(3x + 1)$ $nu^{n-1} \dfrac{du}{dx}$

$= 4(3x + 1)^3 3$ $\dfrac{du}{dx} = 3$

$= 12(3x + 1)^3$

(B) $f(x) = (x^3 + 4)^7$ Let $u = (x^3 + 4)$, $n = 7$.

$f'(x) = 7(x^3 + 4)^6 D_x(x^3 + 4)$ $nu^{n-1} \dfrac{du}{dx}$

$= 7(x^3 + 4)^6 3x^2$ $\dfrac{du}{dx} = 3x^2$

$= 21x^2(x^3 + 4)^6$

(C) $f(x) = \dfrac{1}{(x^2 + x + 4)^3} = (x^2 + x + 4)^{-3}$ Let $u = x^2 + x + 4$, $n = -3$.

$f'(x) = -3(x^2 + x + 4)^{-4} D_x(x^2 + x + 4)$ $nu^{n-1} \dfrac{du}{dx}$

$= -3(x^2 + x + 4)^{-4}(2x + 1)$ $\dfrac{du}{dx} = 2x + 1$

$= \dfrac{-3(2x + 1)}{(x^2 + x + 4)^4}$

(D) $f(x) = \sqrt{3 - x} = (3 - x)^{1/2}$ Let $u = 3 - x$, $n = \frac{1}{2}$.

$f'(x) = \dfrac{1}{2}(3 - x)^{-1/2} D_x(3 - x)$ $nu^{n-1} \dfrac{du}{dx}$

$= \dfrac{1}{2}(3 - x)^{-1/2}(-1)$ $\dfrac{du}{dx} = -1$

$= -\dfrac{1}{2(3 - x)^{1/2}}$ or $-\dfrac{1}{2\sqrt{3 - x}}$

Problem 34   Find $f'(x)$:

(A) $f(x) = (5x + 2)^3$ (B) $f(x) = (x^4 - 5)^5$

(C) $f(x) = \dfrac{1}{(x^2 + 4)^2}$ (D) $f(x) = \sqrt{4 - x}$

Notice that we used two steps to differentiate each function in Example 34: First, we applied the general power rule; then we found du/dx. As you gain experience with the general power rule, you may want to combine these two steps. If you do this, be certain to multiply by du/dx. For example,

$D_x(x^5 + 1)^4 = 4(x^5 + 1)^3 5x^4$ Correct

$\cancel{D_x(x^5 + 1)^4 = 4(x^5 + 1)^3}$ Incorrect, $du/dx = 5x^4$ is missing

If we let $u(x) = x$, then $du/dx = 1$ and the general power rule reduces to the (ordinary) power rule discussed in Section 7-5. Compare the following:

$D_x x^n = n x^{n-1}$ Yes — power rule

$D_x u^n = n u^{n-1} \dfrac{du}{dx}$ Yes — general power rule

$D_x u^n = n u^{n-1}$ No, unless $u(x) = x$ and $du/dx = 1$

■ Combining Rules of Differentiation

The following examples illustrate the use of the general power rule in combination with other rules of differentiation.

Example 35   Find the line tangent to the graph of f at $x = 2$ for

$$f(x) = x^2 \sqrt{2x + 12}$$

Solution $f(x) = x^2 \sqrt{2x + 12}$

$\qquad = x^2 (2x + 12)^{1/2}$ Apply the product rule with $u = x^2$ and $v = (2x + 12)^{1/2}$.

$f'(x) = x^2 D_x (2x + 12)^{1/2}$ Use the general power rule to
$\qquad + (2x + 12)^{1/2} D_x x^2$ differentiate $(2x + 12)^{1/2}$ and the
$\qquad = x^2 \frac{1}{2}(2x + 12)^{-1/2}(2)$ ordinary power rule to differentiate x^2.
$\qquad + (2x + 12)^{1/2}(2x)$

$$\qquad = \frac{x^2}{\sqrt{2x + 12}} + 2x \sqrt{2x + 12}$$

$$f'(2) = \frac{4}{\sqrt{16}} + 4\sqrt{16} = 1 + 16 = 17$$

$$f(2) = 4\sqrt{16} = 16$$

$(x_1, y_1) = (2, f(2)) = (2, 16)$ Point
$\qquad\qquad m = f'(2) = 17$ Slope
$\qquad\qquad y - 16 = 17(x - 2)$
$\qquad\qquad\qquad y = 17x - 18$ Tangent line

Problem 35   Find the line tangent to the graph of f at $x = 3$ for

$$f(x) = x\sqrt{15 - 2x}$$

Example 36   Find the values of x where the tangent line is horizontal for

$$f(x) = \frac{x^3}{(2 - 3x)^5}$$

Solution   Use the quotient rule with $u = x^3$ and $v = (2 - 3x)^5$

$$f'(x) = \frac{(2 - 3x)^5 D_x x^3 - x^3 D_x (2 - 3x)^5}{[(2 - 3x)^5]^2}$$

Use the ordinary power rule to differentiate x^3 and the general power rule to differentiate $(2 - 3x)^5$.

$$= \frac{(2 - 3x)^5 3x^2 - x^3 5(2 - 3x)^4(-3)}{(2 - 3x)^{10}}$$

$$= \frac{(2 - 3x)^4 3x^2[(2 - 3x) + 5x]}{(2 - 3x)^{10}}$$

$$= \frac{3x^2(2 + 2x)}{(2 - 3x)^6} = \frac{6x^2(x + 1)}{(2 - 3x)^6}$$

Since a fraction is 0 when the numerator is zero and the denominator is not, we see that $f'(x) = 0$ at $x = -1$ and $x = 0$. Thus, the graph of f will have horizontal tangent lines at $x = -1$ and $x = 0$.

Problem 36   Find the values of x where the tangent line is horizontal for

$$f(x) = \frac{x^3}{(3x - 2)^2}$$

Example 37   Starting with the function f in Example 36, write f as a product and then differentiate.

Solution
$$f(x) = \frac{x^3}{(2 - 3x)^5} = x^3(2 - 3x)^{-5}$$

$$f'(x) = x^3 D_x(2 - 3x)^{-5} + (2 - 3x)^{-5} D_x x^3$$

$$= x^3(-5)(2 - 3x)^{-6}(-3) + (2 - 3x)^{-5} 3x^2$$

$$= 15x^3(2 - 3x)^{-6} + 3x^2(2 - 3x)^{-5}$$

At this point, we have an unsimplified form for $f'(x)$. This may be satisfactory for some purposes, but not for others. For example, if we need to solve the equation $f'(x) = 0$, we must perform the following algebraic simplifications.

$$f'(x) = \frac{15x^3}{(2 - 3x)^6} + \frac{3x^2}{(2 - 3x)^5}$$

$$= \frac{15x^3}{(2 - 3x)^6} + \frac{3x^2(2 - 3x)}{(2 - 3x)^6}$$

$$= \frac{15x^3 + 3x^2(2 - 3x)}{(2 - 3x)^6}$$

$$= \frac{3x^2(5x + 2 - 3x)}{(2 - 3x)^6}$$

$$= \frac{3x^2(2 + 2x)}{(2 - 3x)^6} = \frac{6x^2(1 + x)}{(2 - 3x)^6}$$

Problem 37   Refer to the function f in Problem 36. Write f as a product and then differentiate. Do not simplify.

As Example 37 illustrates, any quotient can be converted to a product and differentiated by the product rule. However, if the derivative must be simplified, it is usually easier to use the quotient rule. (Compare the algebraic simplifications in Example 37 with those in Example 36.) There is one special case where using negative exponents is the preferred method —a fraction whose numerator is a constant.

Example 38   Find $f'(x)$ two ways for $f(x) = \dfrac{4}{(x^2 + 9)^3}$.

Solution   Method I: Use the quotient rule:

$$f'(x) = \frac{(x^2 + 9)^3 D_x 4 - 4D_x(x^2 + 9)^3}{[(x^2 + 9)^3]^2}$$

$$= \frac{(x^2 + 9)^3(0) - 4[3(x^2 + 9)^2(2x)]}{(x^2 + 9)^6}$$

$$= \frac{-24x(x^2 + 9)^2}{(x^2 + 9)^6} = \frac{-24x}{(x^2 + 9)^4}$$

Method II: Rewrite, then use the general power rule:

$$f(x) = \frac{4}{(x^2 + 9)^3} = 4(x^2 + 9)^{-3}$$

$$f'(x) = 4(-3)(x^2 + 9)^{-4}(2x)$$

$$= \frac{-24x}{(x^2 + 9)^4}$$

Which method do you prefer?

Problem 38   Find $f'(x)$ two ways for $f(x) = \dfrac{5}{(x^3 + 1)^2}$.

Answers to
Matched Problems

34. (A) $15(5x + 2)^2$ (B) $20x^3(x^4 - 5)^4$
    (C) $-4x/(x^2 + 4)^3$ (D) $-1/(2\sqrt{4 - x})$
35. $y = 2x + 3$ 36. $x = 0, x = 2$
37. $-6x^3(3x - 2)^{-3} + 3x^2(3x - 2)^{-2}$
38. $-30x^2/(x^3 + 1)^3$

Exercise 7-7

A   *Find $f'(x)$ using the general power rule.*

1. $f(x) = (2x + 5)^3$ 2. $f(x) = (3x - 7)^5$
3. $f(x) = (5 - 2x)^4$ 4. $f(x) = (9 - 5x)^2$

5. $f(x) = (3x^2 + 5)^5$

6. $f(x) = (5x^2 - 3)^6$

7. $f(x) = (x^3 - 2x^2 + 2)^8$

8. $f(x) = (2x^2 + x + 1)^7$

9. $f(x) = (2x - 5)^{1/2}$

10. $f(x) = (4x + 3)^{1/2}$

11. $f(x) = (x^4 + 1)^{-2}$

12. $f(x) = (x^5 + 2)^{-3}$

B   *Find dy/dx using the general power rule.*

13. $y = 3(x^2 - 2)^4$

14. $y = 2(x^3 + 6)^5$

15. $y = 2(x^2 + 3x)^{-3}$

16. $y = 3(x^3 + x^2)^{-2}$

17. $y = \sqrt{x^2 + 8}$

18. $y = \sqrt[3]{3x - 7}$

19. $y = \sqrt[3]{3x + 4}$

20. $y = \sqrt{2x - 5}$

21. $y = (x^2 - 4x + 2)^{1/2}$

22. $y = (2x^2 + 2x - 3)^{1/2}$

23. $y = \dfrac{1}{2x + 4}$

24. $y = \dfrac{1}{3x - 7}$

25. $y = \dfrac{1}{(x^3 + 4)^5}$

26. $y = \dfrac{1}{(x^2 - 3)^6}$

27. $y = \dfrac{1}{4x^2 - 4x + 1}$

28. $y = \dfrac{1}{2x^2 - 3x + 1}$

29. $y = \dfrac{4}{\sqrt{x^2 - 3x}}$

30. $y = \dfrac{3}{\sqrt[3]{x - x^2}}$

In Problems 31–36, find f'(x) and find the equation of the line tangent to the graph of f at the indicated value of x.

31. $f(x) = x(4 - x)^3$, $x = 2$

32. $f(x) = x^2(1 - x)^4$, $x = 2$

33. $f(x) = \dfrac{x}{(2x - 5)^3}$, $x = 3$

34. $f(x) = \dfrac{x^4}{(3x - 8)^2}$, $x = 4$

35. $f(x) = x\sqrt{2x + 2}$, $x = 1$

36. $f(x) = x\sqrt{x - 6}$, $x = 7$

In Problems 37–42, find f'(x) and find the values of x where the tangent line is horizontal.

37. $f(x) = x^2(x - 5)^3$

38. $f(x) = x^3(x - 7)^4$

39. $f(x) = \dfrac{x}{(2x + 5)^2}$

40. $f(x) = \dfrac{x - 1}{(x - 3)^3}$

41. $f(x) = \sqrt{x^2 - 8x + 20}$

42. $f(x) = \sqrt{x^2 + 4x + 5}$

C   *Find each derivative and simplify.*

43. $D_x[3x(x^2 + 1)^3]$

44. $D_x[2x^2(x^3 - 3)^4]$

45. $D_x \dfrac{(x^3 - 7)^4}{2x^3}$

46. $D_x \dfrac{3x^2}{(x^2 + 5)^3}$

47. $D_x[(2x - 3)^2(2x^2 + 1)^3]$

48. $D_x[(x^2 - 1)^3(x^2 - 2)^2]$

49. $D_x[4x^2\sqrt{x^2 - 1}]$

50. $D_x[3x\sqrt{2x^2 + 3}]$

51. $D_x \dfrac{2x}{\sqrt{x-3}}$

52. $D_x \dfrac{x^2}{\sqrt{x^2+1}}$

53. $D_x \sqrt{(2x-1)^3(x^2+3)^4}$

54. $D_x \sqrt{\dfrac{4x+1}{2x^2+1}}$

Applications

Business & Economics

55. *Marginal average cost.* A manufacturer of skis finds that the average cost $\overline{C}(x)$ per pair of skis at an output level of x thousand skis is

$$\overline{C}(x) = (2x-8)^2 + 25$$

(A) Find the marginal average cost $\overline{C}'(x)$ using the general power rule.

(B) Find $\overline{C}'(2)$, $\overline{C}'(4)$, and $\overline{C}'(6)$.

56. *Compound interest.* If \$100 is invested at an interest rate of i compounded semiannually, the amount in the account at the end of 5 years is given by

$$A = 100\left(1 + \frac{1}{2}i\right)^{10}$$

Find dA/di.

Life Sciences

57. *Bacteria growth.* The number y of bacteria in a certain colony after x days is given approximately by

$$y = (3 \times 10^6)\left(1 - \frac{1}{\sqrt[3]{(x^2-1)^2}}\right)$$

Find dy/dx.

58. *Pollution.* A small lake in a resort area became contaminated with harmful bacteria because of excessive septic tank seepage. After treating the lake with a bactericide, the Department of Public Health estimated the bacteria concentration (number per cubic centimeter) after t days to be given by

$$C(t) = 500(8-t)^2 \qquad 0 \le t \le 7$$

(A) Find $C'(t)$ using the general power rule.

(B) Find $C'(1)$ and $C'(6)$, and interpret.

Social Sciences

59. *Learning.* In 1930, L. L. Thurstone developed the following formula to indicate how learning time T depends on the length of a list n:

$$T = f(n) = \frac{c}{k}\, n\sqrt{n-a}$$

where a, c, and k are empirical constants. Suppose for a particular person, time T in minutes for learning a list of length n is

$$T = f(n) = 2n\sqrt{n-2}$$

(A) Find dT/dn, the rate of change in time with respect to n.
(B) Find $f'(11)$ and $f'(27)$, and interpret.

7-8 Marginal Analysis in Business and Economics

- Marginal Cost, Revenue, and Profit
- Application
- Marginal Average Cost, Revenue, and Profit

■ Marginal Cost, Revenue, and Profit

One important use of calculus in business and economics is in marginal analysis. We introduced the concept of marginal cost earlier. There is no reason to stop there. Economists also talk about **marginal revenue** and **marginal profit.** Recall that the word *marginal* refers to a rate of change — that is, a derivative. Thus, we define the following:

Marginal Cost, Revenue, and Profit

If x is the number of units of product produced in some time interval, then

$$\text{Total cost} = C(x)$$
$$\text{Marginal cost} = C'(x)$$
$$\text{Total revenue} = R(x)$$
$$\text{Marginal revenue} = R'(x)$$
$$\text{Total profit} = P(x) = R(x) - C(x)$$
$$\text{Marginal profit} = P'(x) = R'(x) - C'(x)$$
$$= (\text{Marginal revenue}) - (\text{Marginal cost})$$

Marginal functions have several important economic interpretations. We will discuss these interpretations in terms of the marginal cost function. Similar statements can be made for marginal revenue and marginal profit.

We have already seen that marginal cost is the rate of change of total cost per unit change in production at a given level of production. As Figure 19 illustrates, this implies that **the marginal cost approximates the change in total cost that results from a unit change in production.**

Since $C(x)$ is the total cost of producing x units and $C(x + 1)$ is the total cost of producing $x + 1$ units, the change in total cost

$$\Delta C = \begin{pmatrix} \text{Cost for} \\ x + 1 \text{ units} \end{pmatrix} - \begin{pmatrix} \text{Cost for} \\ x \text{ units} \end{pmatrix}$$
$$\Delta C = \quad C(x + 1) \quad - \quad C(x)$$

is also the cost of producing the $(x + 1)$st item. Thus, **the marginal cost $C'(x)$ also approximates the cost of producing the $(x + 1)$st item.**

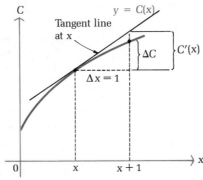

If $\Delta x = 1$, then
$$\Delta C = C(x + 1) - C(x)$$
= Exact change in total cost per unit change in production at a production level of x units

Marginal cost
$C'(x)$ = Slope of tangent line
= Approximate change in total cost C per unit change in production at a production level of x units

Figure 19 $C'(x) \approx \Delta C = C(x + 1) - C(x)$

Example 39
Marginal Cost

A small machine shop manufactures drill bits used in the petroleum industry. The shop manager estimates that the total daily cost in dollars of producing x bits is

$$C(x) = 1{,}000 + 25x - \frac{x^2}{10}$$

(A) Find $C'(10)$ and interpret.
(B) Find $C(11) - C(10)$ and interpret.

Solutions

(A) $C'(x) = 25 - \dfrac{x}{5}$ Marginal cost function

$C'(10) = 25 - 2$ Marginal cost at a production level of 10 bits

= 23

At a production level of 10 bits, a unit increase in production will increase total production costs by approximately $23. Also, the cost of producing the 11th bit is approximately $23.

(B) $C(10) = \$1,240$ Total cost of producing 10 bits

$C(11) = \$1,262.90$ Total cost of producing 11 bits

$\Delta C = C(11) - C(10) = \$22.90$

At a production level of 10 bits, a unit increase in production will increase total production costs by exactly $22.90. Also, the cost of producing the 11th bit is exactly $22.90.

Problem 39   Refer to the total cost function in Example 39.

(A) Find $C'(20)$ and interpret.

(B) Find $C(21) - C(20)$ and interpret.

■ Application

We now present an example in market research to show how marginal cost, revenue, and profit are tied together.

Example 40
Production Strategy

The market research department of a company recommends that the company manufacture and market a new transistor radio. After suitable test marketing, the research department presents the following **demand equation:**

$$x = 10,000 - 1,000p \qquad x \text{ is demand at } \$p \text{ per radio} \tag{1}$$

or

$$p = 10 - \frac{x}{1,000} \tag{2}$$

where x is the number of radios retailers are likely to buy per week at $p per radio. Equation (2) is simply equation (1) solved for p in terms of x. Notice that as price goes up, demand goes down.

The financial department provides the following **cost equation:**

$$C(x) = 7,000 + 2x \tag{3}$$

where $7,000 is the estimated fixed costs (tooling and overhead) and $2 is the estimated variable costs (cost per unit for materials, labor, marketing, transportation, storage, etc.).

The **marginal cost** is

$$C'(x) = 2$$

Since this is a constant, it costs an additional $2 to produce one more radio at all production levels.

The **revenue** (the amount of money R received by the company for manufacturing and selling x units at $p per unit) is

$$R = \text{(Number of units sold)(Price per unit)} = xp$$

In general, the revenue R can be expressed in terms of p by using equation (1) or in terms of x by using equation (2). In marginal analysis (problems involving marginal cost, marginal revenue, or marginal profit), cost, revenue, and profit must be expressed in terms of the number of units x. Thus, the **revenue equation** in terms of x is

$$R(x) = xp = x\left(10 - \frac{x}{1,000}\right) \qquad \text{Using equation (2)} \qquad (4)$$

$$= 10x - \frac{x^2}{1,000}$$

The **marginal revenue** is

$$R'(x) = 10 - \frac{x}{500}$$

For production levels of $x = 2,000$, $5,000$, and $7,000$, we have

$$R'(2,000) = 6 \qquad R'(5,000) = 0 \qquad R'(7,000) = -4$$

This means that at production levels of 2,000, 5,000, and 7,000, the respective approximate changes in revenue per unit change in production are $6, $0, and −$4. That is, at the 2,000 output level revenue increases as production increases; at the 5,000 output level revenue does not change with a "small" change in production; and at the 7,000 output level revenue decreases with an increase in production.

When we graph $R(x)$ and $C(x)$ in the same coordinate system, we obtain Figure 20.

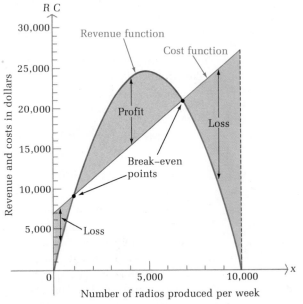

Figure 20

The break-even points (the points where revenue equals cost) are obtained as follows:

$$C(x) = R(x)$$

$$7{,}000 + 2x = 10x - \frac{x^2}{1{,}000}$$

$$\frac{x^2}{1{,}000} - 8x + 7{,}000 = 0$$

$$x^2 - 8{,}000x + 7{,}000{,}000 = 0 \qquad \text{Solve using the quadratic formula.}$$
$$\text{(See Section 0-3.)}$$

$$x = \frac{8{,}000 \pm \sqrt{8{,}000^2 - 4(7{,}000{,}000)}}{2}$$

$$= \frac{8{,}000 \pm \sqrt{36{,}000{,}000}}{2}$$

$$= \frac{8{,}000 \pm 6{,}000}{2}$$

$$= 1{,}000, \quad 7{,}000$$

$$R(1{,}000) = 10(1{,}000) - \frac{1{,}000^2}{1{,}000} = 9{,}000$$

$$C(1{,}000) = 7{,}000 + 2(1{,}000) = 9{,}000$$

$$R(7{,}000) = 10(7{,}000) - \frac{7{,}000^2}{1{,}000} = 21{,}000$$

$$C(7{,}000) = 7{,}000 + 2(7{,}000) = 21{,}000$$

Thus, the break-even points are (1,000, 9,000) and (7,000, 21,000). The **profit equation** is

$$P(x) = R(x) - C(x)$$

$$= \left(10x - \frac{x^2}{1{,}000}\right) - (7{,}000 + 2x)$$

$$= -\frac{x^2}{1{,}000} + 8x - 7{,}000$$

The graph in Figure 20 also provides some useful information concerning the profit equation. At a production level of 1,000 or 7,000, revenue equals cost; hence, profit is 0 and the company will break even. For any production level between 1,000 and 7,000, revenue is greater than cost; hence, $P(x)$ is positive and the company will make a profit. For production levels less than 1,000 or greater than 7,000, revenue is less than cost; hence, $P(x)$ is negative and the company will have a loss.

The **marginal profit** is

$$P'(x) = -\frac{x}{500} + 8$$

For production levels of 1,000, 4,000, and 6,000, we have

$$P'(1,000) = 6 \qquad P'(4,000) = 0 \qquad P'(6,000) = -4$$

This means that at production levels of 1,000, 4,000, and 6,000, the respective approximate changes in profit per unit change in production are $6, $0, and −$4. That is, at the 1,000 output level profit will be increased if production is increased; at the 4,000 output level profit does not change for "small" changes in production; and at the 6,000 output level profits will decrease if production is increased. It seems the best production level to produce a maximum profit is 4,000. [In the next chapter we will develop a systematic procedure for finding the production level (and, using the demand equation, the selling price) that will maximize profit.] This example warrants careful study, since a number of important ideas in economics and calculus are involved.

Problem 40 Refer to the revenue and profit equations in Example 40.

(A) Find $R'(3,000)$ and $R'(6,000)$ and interpret.

(B) Find $P'(2,000)$ and $P'(7,000)$ and interpret.

■ Marginal Average Cost, Revenue, and Profit

Sometimes it is desirable to carry out marginal analysis relative to **average cost (cost per unit), average revenue (revenue per unit), and average profit (profit per unit).** The relevant definitions are summarized in the following box:

Marginal Average Cost, Revenue, and Profit

If x is the number of units of a product produced in some time interval, then

$$\text{Average cost} = \overline{C}(x) = \frac{C(x)}{x} \qquad \text{Cost per unit}$$

$$\text{Marginal average cost} = \overline{C}'(x) = D_x\overline{C}(x)$$

$$\text{Average revenue} = \overline{R}(x) = \frac{R(x)}{x} \qquad \text{Revenue per unit}$$

$$\text{Marginal average revenue} = \overline{R}'(x) = D_x\overline{R}(x)$$

$$\text{Average profit} = \overline{P}(x) = \frac{P(x)}{x} \qquad \text{Profit per unit}$$

$$\text{Marginal average profit} = \overline{P}'(x) = D_x\overline{P}(x)$$

As was the case with marginal cost, **the marginal average cost approximates the change in average cost that results from a unit increase in production.** Similar statements can be made for marginal average revenue and marginal average profit.

Example 41   Referring to Example 39, we have

$$C(x) = 1,000 + 25x - \frac{x^2}{10}$$ Total cost function

$$\overline{C}(x) = \frac{C(x)}{x} = \frac{1,000}{x} + 25 - \frac{x}{10}$$ Average cost function

$$\overline{C}'(x) = D_x\overline{C}(x) = -\frac{1,000}{x^2} - \frac{1}{10}$$ Marginal average cost function

$$\overline{C}(10) = \frac{1,000}{10} + 25 - \frac{10}{10}$$ Average cost per unit if 10 units are produced

$$= \$124$$

$$\overline{C}'(10) = -\frac{1,000}{100} - \frac{1}{10}$$ A unit increase in production will decrease the average cost per unit by approximately $10.10 at a production level of 10 units.

$$= -\$10.10$$

Problem 41   Let $C(x) = 7,000 + 2x$ be the cost function considered in Example 40.

(A)   Find $\overline{C}(x)$ and $\overline{C}'(x)$.
(B)   Find $\overline{C}(1,000)$ and $\overline{C}'(1,000)$ and interpret.

Answers to
Matched Problems

39. (A) $C'(20) = 21$. At a production level of 20 bits, a unit increase in production will increase total production costs by approximately $21. Also, the cost of producing the 21st bit is approximately $21.
     (B) $C(21) - C(20) = 20.90$. At a production level of 20 bits, a unit increase in production will increase total production costs by exactly $20.90. Also, the cost of producing the 21st bit is exactly $20.90.

40. (A) $R'(3,000) = 4$. At a production level of 3,000, a unit increase in production will increase revenue by approximately $4. $R'(6,000) = -2$. At a production level of 6,000, a unit increase in production will decrease revenue by approximately $2.
     (B) $P'(2,000) = 4$. At a production level of 2,000, a unit increase in production will increase profit by approximately $4. $P'(7,000) = -6$. At a production level of 7,000, a unit increase in production will decrease profit by approximately $6.

41. (A) $\overline{C}(x) = \frac{7,000}{x} + 2$, $\overline{C}'(x) = -\frac{7,000}{x^2}$

(B) $\overline{C}(1,000) = 9$. At a production level of 1,000, the average cost per unit is \$9. $\overline{C}'(1,000) = -0.007$. At a production level of 1,000, a unit increase in production will decrease the average cost per unit by approximately 0.7¢.

Exercise 7-8

Applications

1. *Cost analysis.* The total cost in dollars of producing x food processors is

$$C(x) = 2,000 + 50x - \frac{x^2}{2}$$

   (A) Find the exact cost of producing the 21st food processor.
   (B) Use the marginal cost to approximate the cost of producing the 21st food processor.

2. *Cost analysis.* The total cost in dollars of producing x electric guitars is

$$C(x) = 1,000 + 100x - \frac{x^2}{4}$$

   (A) Find the exact cost of producing the 51st guitar.
   (B) Use the marginal cost to approximate the cost of producing the 51st guitar.

3. *Cost analysis.* The total cost in dollars of manufacturing x auto body frames is

$$C(x) = 60,000 + 300x$$

   (A) Find the average cost per unit if 500 frames are produced.
   (B) Find the marginal average cost at a production level of 500 units and interpret.

4. *Cost analysis.* The total cost in dollars of printing x dictionaries is

$$C(x) = 20,000 + 10x$$

   (A) Find the average cost per unit if 1,000 dictionaries are produced.
   (B) Find the marginal average cost at a production level of 1,000 units and interpret.

5. *Revenue analysis.* The total revenue in dollars from the sale of x clock

radios is

$$R(x) = 100x - \frac{x^2}{40}$$

Evaluate the marginal revenue at the given values of x and interpret the results.

(A)   x = 1,600   (B)   x = 2,500

6. *Revenue analysis.* The total revenue in dollars from the sale of x steam irons is

$$R(x) = 50x - \frac{x^2}{20}$$

Evaluate the marginal revenue at the given values of x and interpret the results.

(A)   x = 400   (B)   x = 650

7. *Profit analysis.* The total profit in dollars from the sale of x skateboards is

$$P(x) = 30x - \frac{x^2}{2} - 250$$

(A)   Find the exact profit from the sale of the 26th skateboard.
(B)   Use the marginal profit to approximate the profit from the sale of the 26th skateboard.

8. *Profit analysis.* The total profit in dollars from the sale of x portable stereos is

$$P(x) = 22x - \frac{x^2}{10} - 400$$

(A)   Find the exact profit from the sale of the 41st stereo.
(B)   Use the marginal profit to approximate the profit from the sale of the 41st stereo.

9. *Profit analysis.* The total profit in dollars from the sale of x video cassettes is

$$P(x) = 5x - \frac{x^2}{200} - 450$$

Evaluate the marginal profit at the given values of x and interpret the results.

(A)   x = 450   (B)   x = 750

10. *Profit analysis.* The total profit in dollars from the sale of x cameras is

$$P(x) = 12x - \frac{x^2}{50} - 1,000$$

Evaluate the marginal profit at the given values of x and interpret the results.

(A) x = 200   (B) x = 350

11. *Profit analysis.* Refer to the profit equation in Problem 9.

(A) Find the average profit per unit if 150 cassettes are produced.
(B) Find the marginal average profit at a production level of 150 units and interpret.

12. *Profit analysis.* Refer to the profit equation in Problem 10.

(A) Find the average profit per unit if 200 cameras are produced.
(B) Find the marginal average profit at a production level of 200 units and interpret.

13. *Revenue, cost, and profit.* In Example 40, suppose we have the demand equation

$$x = 6,000 - 30p \qquad \text{or} \qquad p = 200 - \frac{x}{30}$$

and the cost equation

$$C(x) = 72,000 + 60x$$

(A) Find the marginal cost.
(B) Find the revenue equation in terms of x.
(C) Find the marginal revenue.
(D) Find $R'(1,500)$ and $R'(4,500)$, and interpret.
(E) Graph the cost function and the revenue function on the same coordinate system for $0 \leqslant x \leqslant 6,000$. Find the break-even points, and indicate regions of loss and profit.
(F) Find the profit equation in terms of x.
(G) Find the marginal profit.
(H) Find $P'(1,500)$ and $P'(3,000)$, and interpret.

14. *Revenue, cost, and profit.* In Example 40, suppose we have the demand equation

$$x = 9,000 - 30p \qquad \text{or} \qquad p = 300 - \frac{x}{30}$$

and the cost equation

$$C(x) = 150,000 + 30x$$

(A) Find the marginal cost.
(B) Find the revenue equation in terms of x.
(C) Find the marginal revenue.
(D) Find $R'(3,000)$ and $R'(6,000)$, and interpret.

(E) Graph the cost function and the revenue function on the same coordinate system for $0 \leq x \leq 9{,}000$. Find the break-even points, and indicate regions of loss and profit.

(F) Find the profit equation in terms of x.

(G) Find the marginal profit.

(H) Find $P'(1{,}500)$ and $P'(4{,}500)$, and interpret.

15. *Revenue, cost, and profit.* A company is planning to manufacture and market a new two-slice electric toaster. After conducting extensive market surveys, the research department provides the following estimates: a weekly demand of 200 toasters at a price of $16 per toaster and a weekly demand of 300 toasters at a price of $14 per toaster. The financial department estimates that weekly fixed costs will be $1,400 and the variable costs (cost per unit) will be $4.

(A) Assume that the demand equation is a linear equation of the form $p = mx + b$ and use the research department's estimates to find m and b.

(B) Find the revenue equation in terms of x.

(C) Assume that the cost equation is a linear equation of the form $C(x) = mx + b$ and use the financial department's estimates to find m and b.

(D) Graph the cost function and the revenue function on the same coordinate system for $0 \leq x \leq 1{,}000$. Find the break-even points and indicate regions of loss and profit.

(E) Find the profit equation in terms of x.

(F) Evaluate the marginal profit at $x = 250$ and $x = 475$, and interpret the results.

16. *Revenue, cost, and profit.* The company in Problem 15 is also planning to manufacture and market a four-slice toaster. For this toaster, the research department's estimates are a weekly demand of 300 toasters at a price of $25 per toaster and a weekly demand of 400 toasters at a price of $20. The financial department's estimates are fixed weekly costs of $5,000 and variable costs of $5 per toaster. Assume the demand and cost equations are linear. (See Problem 15, parts A and C.)

(A) Use the research department's estimates to find the demand equation.

(B) Find the revenue equation in terms of x.

(C) Use the financial department's estimates to find the cost equation in terms of x.

(D) Graph the cost function and the revenue function on the same coordinate system for $0 \leq x \leq 800$. Find the break-even points and indicate regions of loss and profit.

(E) Find the profit equation in terms of x.

(F) Evaluate the marginal profit at $x = 325$ and $x = 425$, and interpret the results.

<hr>

7-9 Chapter Review

<hr>

Important Terms and
Symbols

7-1 *Limits.* Tangent line, secant line, limit of $f(x)$ as x approaches c, vertical asymptote, polynomial function, limit of $f(x)$ as x approaches infinity, horizontal asymptote, rational function, $\lim_{x \to c} f(x)$, $\lim_{x \to \pm\infty} f(x)$

7-2 *Continuity.* Continuous curve, discontinuous curve, continuity at a point, continuity on an open interval, discontinuity at a point, continuity properties, solving nonlinear inequalities, test number, sign chart

7-3 *Increments, tangent lines, and rates of change.* Increments, slope, tangent line, slope of graph at a point, average rate of change, instantaneous rate of change, difference quotient, average velocity, instantaneous velocity, Δx, Δy, average rate $= \Delta y / \Delta x$, instantaneous rate $= \lim_{\Delta x \to 0} \Delta y / \Delta x$

7-4 *The derivative.* The derivative of f at x, tangent line, differentiable function, nonexistence of the derivative, nondifferentiable at $x = a$, instantaneous rates of change, marginal cost, $f'(x)$

7-5 *Derivatives of constants, power forms, and sums.* Derivative notation, derivative of a constant, power rule, derivative of a constant times a function, derivatives of sums and differences, $f'(x)$, y', dy/dx, $D_x f(x)$

7-6 *Derivatives of products and quotients.* Derivatives of products, product rule, derivatives of quotients, quotient rule

7-7 *General power rule.* General power rule, combining rules of differentiation

7-8 *Marginal analysis in business and economics.* Demand equation, cost equation, marginal cost, revenue equation, marginal revenue, break-even points, profit equation, marginal profit, average cost, marginal average cost, average revenue, marginal average revenue, average profit, marginal average profit, $C'(x)$, $\overline{C}'(x)$, $R'(x)$, $\overline{R}'(x)$, $P'(x)$, $\overline{P}'(x)$

Summary of Rules
of Differentiation

$$D_x C = 0$$

$$D_x x^n = n x^{n-1}$$

$$D_x k f(x) = k f'(x)$$

$$D_x [u(x) \pm v(x)] = u'(x) \pm v'(x)$$

$$D_x [u(x) v(x)] = u(x) v'(x) + v(x) u'(x)$$

$$D_x \frac{u(x)}{v(x)} = \frac{v(x) u'(x) - u(x) v'(x)}{[v(x)]^2}$$

$$D_x [u(x)]^n = n [u(x)]^{n-1} u'(x)$$

Exercise 7-9   Chapter Review

Work through all the problems in this chapter review and check your answers in the back of the book. (Answers to all review problems are there.) Where weaknesses show up, review appropriate sections in the text.

A   *In Problems 1–10 find $f'(x)$ for $f(x)$ as given.*

1. $f(x) = 3x^4 - 2x^2 + 1$

2. $f(x) = 2x^{1/2} - 3x$

3. $f(x) = 5$

4. $f(x) = \dfrac{1}{2x^2} + \dfrac{x^2}{2}$

5. $f(x) = (2x - 1)(3x + 2)$

6. $f(x) = (x^2 - 1)(x^3 - 3)$

7. $f(x) = \dfrac{2x}{x^2 + 2}$

8. $f(x) = \dfrac{1}{3x + 2}$

9. $f(x) = (2x - 3)^3$

10. $f(x) = (x^2 + 2)^{-2}$

B   *In Problems 11–18 find the indicated derivatives.*

11. $\dfrac{dy}{dx}$ for $y = 3x^4 - 2x^{-3} + 5$

12. y' for $y = (2x^2 - 3x + 2)(x^2 + 2x - 1)$

13. $f'(x)$ for $f(x) = \dfrac{2x - 3}{(x - 1)^2}$

14. y' for $y = 2\sqrt{x} + \dfrac{4}{\sqrt{x}}$

15. $D_x[(x^2 - 1)(2x + 1)^2]$

16. $D_x \sqrt[3]{x^3 - 5}$

17. $\dfrac{dy}{dx}$ for $y = \dfrac{3x^2 + 4}{x^2}$

18. $D_x \dfrac{(x^2 + 2)^4}{2x - 3}$

19.   For $y = f(x) = x^2 + 4$, find:

   (A)   The slope of the graph at $x = 1$
   (B)   The equation of the tangent line at $x = 1$ in the form $y = mx + b$

20.   Repeat Problem 19 for $f(x) = x^3(x + 1)^2$.

In Problems 21–24, find the values of x where the tangent line is horizontal.

21. $f(x) = 10x - x^2$

22. $f(x) = (x + 3)(x^2 - 45)$

23. $f(x) = \dfrac{x}{x^2 + 4}$

24. $f(x) = x^2(2x - 15)^3$

25. If an object moves along the y axis (scale in feet) so that it is at $y = f(x) = 16x^2 - 4x$ at time x (in seconds), find:

    (A) The instantaneous velocity function
    (B) The velocity at time x = 3 seconds

26. An object moves along the y axis (scale in feet) so that at time x (in seconds) it is at $y = f(x) = 96x - 16x^2$. Find:

    (A) The instantaneous velocity function
    (B) The time(s) when the velocity is 0

Solve each inequality. Express the answer in inequality notation.

27. $x^2 - x - 12 < 0$ 28. $x^2 - 2x - 8 \geq 0$

29. $x^2 + 25 \geq 10x$ 30. $\dfrac{x - 5}{x^2 + 3x} \leq 0$

31. $\dfrac{x(x - 2)^2}{(x - 5)^3} < 0$ 32. $(x + 2)^3(x - 1)^2(x - 3) > 0$

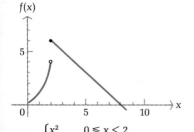

f(x)

$f(x) = \begin{cases} x^2 & 0 \leq x < 2 \\ 8 - x & x \geq 2 \end{cases}$

Problems 33 and 34 refer to the function f described in the figure.

33. (A) $\lim\limits_{x \to 2} f(x) = ?$ (B) $f(2) = ?$

    (C) Is f continuous at x = 2?

34. (A) $\lim\limits_{x \to 5} f(x) = ?$ (B) $f(5) = ?$

    (C) Is f continuous at x = 5?

In Problems 35–40, determine where f is continuous. Express the answer in interval notation.

35. $f(x) = 2x^2 - 3x + 1$ 36. $f(x) = \dfrac{1}{x + 5}$

37. $f(x) = \dfrac{x - 3}{x^2 - x - 6}$ 38. $f(x) = \sqrt{x - 3}$

39. $f(x) = \sqrt[3]{1 - x^2}$ 40. $f(x) = \sqrt{20 + x - x^2}$

In Problems 41–52, find each limit if it exists.

41. $\lim\limits_{x \to 3} \dfrac{2x - 3}{x + 5}$ 42. $\lim\limits_{x \to 3} (2x^2 - x + 1)$

43. $\lim\limits_{x \to 0} \dfrac{2x}{3x^2 - 2x}$

44. $\lim\limits_{\Delta x \to 0} \dfrac{f(2 + \Delta x) - f(2)}{\Delta x}$ for $f(x) = x^2 + 4$

45. $\lim\limits_{x \to 3} \dfrac{x-3}{x^2-9}$

46. $\lim\limits_{x \to -3} \dfrac{x-3}{x^2-9}$

47. $\lim\limits_{x \to 7} \dfrac{\sqrt{x}-\sqrt{7}}{x-7}$

48. $\lim\limits_{x \to -2} \sqrt{\dfrac{x^2+4}{2-x}}$

49. $\lim\limits_{x \to \infty} \left(3 + \dfrac{1}{x^{1/3}} + \dfrac{2}{x^3}\right)$

50. $\lim\limits_{x \to \infty} \dfrac{2x^2+3}{3x^2+2}$

51. $\lim\limits_{x \to \infty} \dfrac{2x+3}{3x^2+2}$

52. $\lim\limits_{x \to \infty} \dfrac{2x^2+3}{3x+2}$

In Problems 53 and 54, use the definition of the derivative to find $f'(x)$.

53. $f(x) = x^2 - x$

54. $f(x) = \sqrt{x} - 3$

C   Problems 55–58 refer to the function f in the figure. Determine if f is differentiable at the indicated value of x.

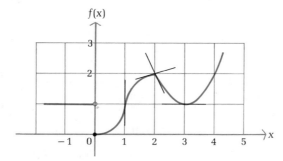

55. $x = 0$ 56. $x = 1$ 57. $x = 2$ 58. $x = 3$

In Problems 59 and 60, graph f and find all discontinuities.

59. $f(x) = \begin{cases} 4 - x^2 & x < 0 \\ 2 + x^2 & x \geqslant 0 \end{cases}$

60. $f(x) = \begin{cases} 4 - x^2 & x < 1 \\ 2 + x^2 & x \geqslant 1 \end{cases}$

Problems 61–63 refer to

$$f(x) = \dfrac{2x^2 - 3x - 2}{3x^2 - 4x - 4}$$

61. (A) $\lim\limits_{x \to 2} f(x) = ?$ (B) $f(2) = ?$ (C) Is f continuous at $x = 2$?

62. (A) $\lim\limits_{x \to 0} f(x) = ?$ (B) $f(0) = ?$ (C) Is f continuous at $x = 0$?

63. Find all points of discontinuity for f.

In Problems 64–67, find $f'(x)$ and simplify.

64. $f(x) = (x - 4)^4(x + 3)^3$

65. $f(x) = \dfrac{x^5}{(2x+1)^4}$

66. $f(x) = \dfrac{\sqrt{x^2 - 1}}{x}$

67. $f(x) = \dfrac{x}{\sqrt{x^2 + 4}}$

■

Applications

Business & Economics

68. *Profit/loss analysis.* Let

$$p = 14 - x \quad \text{and} \quad C = 2x + 20 \qquad 0 \leqslant x \leqslant 14$$

be the demand equation and the cost equation, respectively, for a certain commodity.

(A) Express the cost C in terms of the price p.
(B) Express the revenue R in terms of the price p.
(C) Solve the inequality $R > C$ to find the range of prices that will result in a profit.

69. *Marginal analysis.* Let

$$p = 20 - x \quad \text{and} \quad C(x) = 2x + 56 \qquad 0 \leqslant x \leqslant 20$$

be the demand equation and the cost function, respectively, for a certain commodity.

(A) Find the marginal cost, average cost, and marginal average cost functions.
(B) Express the revenue in terms of x and find the marginal revenue, average revenue, and marginal average revenue functions.
(C) Find the profit, marginal profit, average profit, and marginal average profit functions.
(D) Find the break-even point(s).
(E) Evaluate the marginal profit at $x = 7$, 9, and 11, and interpret.
(F) Graph $R = R(x)$ and $C = C(x)$ on the same axes and locate regions of profit and loss.

70. *Employee training.* A company producing computer components has established that on the average, a new employee can assemble $N(t)$ components per day after t days of on-the-job training, as given by

$$N(t) = \frac{40t}{t + 2}$$

(A) Find the average rate of change of $N(t)$ from 3 days to 6 days.
(B) Find the instantaneous rate of change of $N(t)$ at 3 days.
(C) Find $\lim_{t \to \infty} N(t)$.

Life Sciences

71. *Pollution.* A sewage treatment plant disposes of its effluent through a pipeline that extends 1 mile toward the center of a large lake. The concentration of effluent $C(x)$, in parts per million, x meters from the end of the pipe is given approximately by

$$C(x) = 500(x + 1)^{-2}$$

What is the instantaneous rate of change of concentration at 9 meters? At 99 meters?

Social Sciences   72. *Learning.* If a person learns N items in t hours, as given by

$$N(t) = 20\sqrt{t}$$

find the rate of learning after:

(A) 1 hour   (B) 4 hours

Additional Derivative Topics

Contents

8-1 First Derivative and Graphs

- Increasing and Decreasing Functions
- Critical Values and Local Extrema
- First-Derivative Test

Since the derivative is associated with the slope of the graph of a function at a point, we might expect that it is also associated with other properties of a graph. As we will see in this and the next section, the derivative can tell us a great deal about the shape of the graph of a function. In addition, this investigation will lead to methods for finding absolute maximum and minimum values for functions that do not require graphing. Companies can use these methods to find production levels that will minimize cost or maximize profit. Pharmacologists can use them to find levels of drug dosages that will produce maximum sensitivity to a drug. And so on.

A brief review of Section 7-2, where we discussed the use of continuity and sign charts in solving inequalities, will prove useful in this section.

■ Increasing and Decreasing Functions

Graphs of functions generally have rising or falling sections as we move from left to right. It would be an aid to graphing if we could figure out where these sections occur. Suppose the graph of a function f is as indicated in Figure 1. As we move from left to right, we see that on the interval (a, b) the graph of f is rising, $f(x)$ is increasing,* and the slope of the graph is positive $[f'(x) > 0]$. On the other hand, on the interval (b, c) the graph of f is falling, $f(x)$ is decreasing, and the slope of the graph is negative $[f'(x) < 0]$. At $x = b$ the graph of f changes direction (from rising to falling), $f(x)$ changes from increasing to decreasing, the slope of the graph is 0 $[f'(b) = 0]$, and the tangent line is horizontal.

In general, we can prove that if $f'(x) > 0$ (is positive) on the interval (a, b),

---

* Formally, we say that $f(x)$ is *increasing* on an interval (a, b) if $f(x_2) > f(x_1)$ whenever $a < x_1 < x_2 < b$; f is decreasing on (a, b) if $f(x_2) < f(x_1)$ whenever $a < x_1 < x_2 < b$.

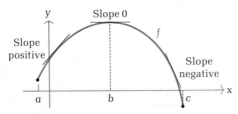

Figure 1

then $f(x)$ increases ($\nearrow$) and the graph of f rises as we move from left to right over the interval; if $f'(x) < 0$ (is negative) on an interval (a, b), then $f(x)$ decreases ($\searrow$) and the graph of f falls as we move from left to right over the interval. We summarize these important results in the box.

Increasing and Decreasing Functions

For the interval (a, b):

$f'(x)$	$f(x)$	Graph of f	Examples
$+$	Increases $\nearrow$	Rises $\nearrow$	
$-$	Decreases $\searrow$	Falls $\searrow$	

Example 1   Given $f(x) = 8x - x^2$:

(A)   Which values of x correspond to horizontal tangent lines?

(B)   For which values of x is $f(x)$ increasing? Decreasing?

(C)   Sketch a graph of f. Add horizontal tangent lines.

Solutions   (A) $f'(x) = 8 - 2x = 0$

$$x = 4$$

Thus, a horizontal tangent line exists at $x = 4$ only.

(B)   Construct a sign chart for $f'(x)$ to determine which values of x make $f'(x) > 0$ and which values make $f'(x) < 0$. (Solving inequalities by use of continuity and sign charts was discussed in Section 7-2.)

Sign chart for $f'(x) = 8 - 2x$:

	Test Numbers	
	x	$f'(x)$
	3	2 (+)
	5	-2 (−)

Thus, $f(x)$ is increasing on $(-\infty, 4)$ and decreasing on $(4, \infty)$.

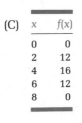

(C)

x	f(x)
0	0
2	12
4	16
6	12
8	0

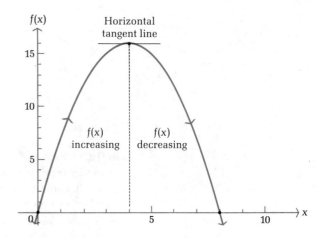

Problem 1   Repeat Example 1 for $f(x) = x^2 - 6x + 10$.

Example 2   Determine the intervals where f is increasing and those where f is decreasing for:

(A) $f(x) = 1 + x^3$ (B) $f(x) = (1 - x)^{1/3}$ (C) $f(x) = \dfrac{1}{x - 2}$

Solutions   (A) $f(x) = 1 + x^3$
$$f'(x) = 3x^2 = 0$$
$$x = 0$$

Sign chart for $f'(x) = 3x^2$:

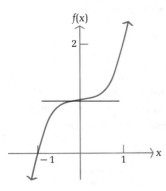

$f'(x)$ $+ + + + \ 0 \ + + + +$

$\xrightarrow{\hspace{4cm}} x$

              0

$f(x)$ Increasing | Increasing

Test Numbers

x	f'(x)
-1	3 (+)
1	3 (+)

The sign chart indicates that $f(x)$ is increasing on $(-\infty, 0)$ and $(0, \infty)$. Since f is continuous at $x = 0$, it follows that $f(x)$ is increasing for all x. Thus, **a continuous function can be increasing (or decreasing) on an interval containing values of x where $f'(x) = 0$.** The graph of f is shown in the margin.

(B) $f(x) = (1 - x)^{1/3}$

$$f'(x) = -\frac{1}{3}(1 - x)^{-2/3} = \frac{-1}{3(1 - x)^{2/3}}$$

To construct a sign chart for a fraction, we plot the zeros of both the numerator and the denominator on a number line. In this case, the numerator is a constant, so the only point plotted is $x = 1$. We use the abbreviation ND to emphasize that $f'(x)$ is not defined at $x = 1$.

Sign chart for $f'(x) = -1/[3(1 - x)^{2/3}]$:

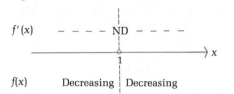

Test Numbers

x	$f'(x)$
0	$-\frac{1}{3}\,(-)$
2	$-\frac{1}{3}\,(-)$

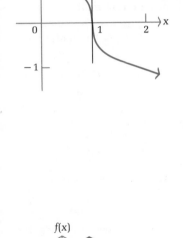

The sign chart indicates that f is decreasing on $(-\infty, 1)$ and $(1, \infty)$. Since f is continuous at $x = 1$, it follows that $f(x)$ is decreasing for all x. Thus, **a continuous function can be decreasing (or increasing) on an interval containing values of x where $f'(x)$ does not exist.** The graph of f is shown in the margin. Notice that the undefined derivative at $x = 1$ results in a vertical tangent line at $x = 1$. In general, **a vertical tangent will occur at $x = c$ if f is continuous at $x = c$ and $|f'(x)|$ becomes larger and larger as x approaches c.**

(C) $f(x) = \dfrac{1}{x - 2}$

$f'(x) = \dfrac{-1}{(x - 2)^2}$

Sign chart for $f'(x) = -1/(x - 2)^2$:

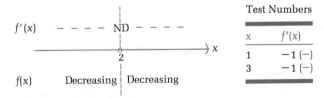

Test Numbers

x	$f'(x)$
1	$-1\,(-)$
3	$-1\,(-)$

Thus, f is decreasing on $(-\infty, 2)$ and $(2, \infty)$. Since f is not continuous at $x = 2$, we cannot conclude that $f(x)$ is decreasing for all x, or even for all x except $x = 2$. (See the graph of f in the margin.) **The values where a function is increasing or decreasing must always be expressed in terms of open intervals that are subsets of the domain of the function.**

Problem 2 Determine the intervals where f is increasing and those where f is decreasing for:

(A) $f(x) = 1 - x^3$ (B) $f(x) = (1 + x)^{1/3}$ (C) $f(x) = \dfrac{1}{x}$

■ Critical Values and Local Extrema

When the graph of a continuous function changes from rising to falling, a high point or *local maximum* occurs, and when the graph changes from falling to rising, a low point or *local minimum* occurs. In Figure 2, high points occur at c_3 and c_6, and low points occur at c_2 and c_4. In general, we call $f(c)$ a **local maximum** if there exists an interval (m, n) containing c such that

$$f(x) \leqslant f(c)$$

for all x in (m, n). The quantity $f(c)$ is called a **local minimum** if there exists an interval (m, n) containing c such that

$$f(x) \geqslant f(c)$$

for all x in (m, n). The quantity $f(c)$ is called a **local extremum** if it is either a local maximum or a local minimum. Thus, in Figure 2 we see that local maxima occur at c_3 and c_6, local minima occur at c_2 and c_4, and all four of these points produce local extrema.

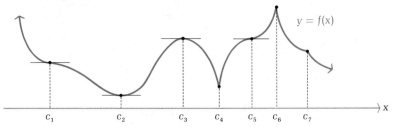

Figure 2

How can we locate local maxima and minima if we are given the equation for a function and not its graph? Figure 2 suggests an approach. It appears that local maxima and minima occur among those values of x such that $f'(x) = 0$ or $f'(x)$ does not exist; that is, among the values c_1, c_2, c_3, c_4, c_5, c_6, and c_7. [Recall from Section 7-4 that $f'(x)$ is not defined at points on the graph of f where there is a sharp corner or a vertical tangent line.] The values of x in the domain of f where $f'(x) = 0$ or $f'(x)$ does not exist are called the **critical values** of f. It is possible to prove the following theorem:

Theorem 1

Existence of Local Extrema

If f is continuous on the interval (a, b) and $f(c)$ is a local extremum, then either $f'(c) = 0$ or $f'(c)$ does not exist (is not defined).

Theorem 1 implies that a local extremum can occur only at a critical value, but it does not imply that every critical value produces a local extremum. In Figure 2, c_1 and c_5 are critical values (the slope is 0), but the function does not have a local maximum or local minimum at either of these values.

Our strategy for finding local extrema is now clear. We find all critical values for f and test each one to see if it produces a local maximum, a local minimum, or neither.

■ First-Derivative Test

If $f'(x)$ exists on both sides of a critical value c, then the sign of $f'(x)$ can be used to determine if the point $(c, f(c))$ is a local maximum, a local minimum, or neither. The various possibilities are summarized in the box below and illustrated in Figure 3 on the next page.

First-Derivative Test for Local Extrema

Let c be a critical value of f [$f(c)$ is defined and either $f'(c) = 0$ or $f'(c)$ is not defined]. Construct a sign chart for $f'(x)$ close to and on either side of c.

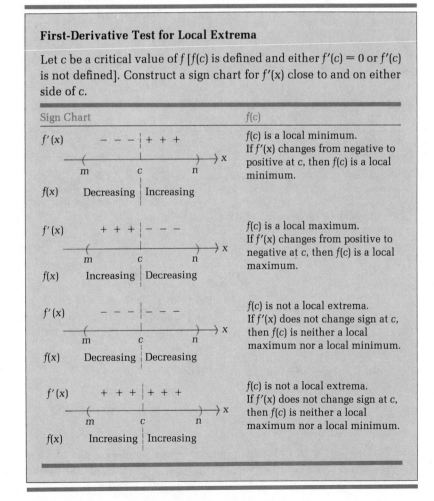

Sign Chart	$f(c)$
$f'(x)$ $\quad - - - \mid + + +$ $m \quad c \quad n$ $f(x)$ Decreasing $\mid$ Increasing	$f(c)$ is a local minimum. If $f'(x)$ changes from negative to positive at c, then $f(c)$ is a local minimum.
$f'(x)$ $\quad + + + \mid - - -$ $m \quad c \quad n$ $f(x)$ Increasing $\mid$ Decreasing	$f(c)$ is a local maximum. If $f'(x)$ changes from positive to negative at c, then $f(c)$ is a local maximum.
$f'(x)$ $\quad - - - \mid - - -$ $m \quad c \quad n$ $f(x)$ Decreasing $\mid$ Decreasing	$f(c)$ is not a local extrema. If $f'(x)$ does not change sign at c, then $f(c)$ is neither a local maximum nor a local minimum.
$f'(x)$ $\quad + + + \mid + + +$ $m \quad c \quad n$ $f(x)$ Increasing $\mid$ Increasing	$f(c)$ is not a local extrema. If $f'(x)$ does not change sign at c, then $f(c)$ is neither a local maximum nor a local minimum.

f'(c) = 0
Horizontal tangent

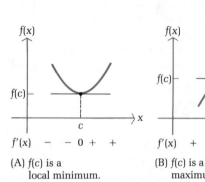

$f(x)$

$f(c)$

c

$f'(x)$ −   − 0 +   +

(A) $f(c)$ is a
local minimum.

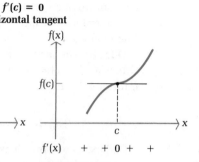

$f(x)$

$f(c)$

c

$f'(x)$ +   + 0 −   −

(B) $f(c)$ is a local
maximum.

$f(x)$

$f(c)$

c

$f'(x)$ +   + 0 +   +

(C) $f(c)$ is neither
a local maximum
nor a local minimum.

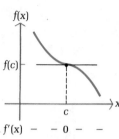

$f(x)$

$f(c)$

c

$f'(x)$ −   − 0 −   −

(D) $f(c)$ is neither a
local maximum nor
a local minimum.

f'(c) is not defined
but f(c) is defined

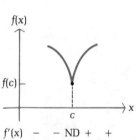

$f(x)$

$f(c)$

c

$f'(x)$ −   − ND +   +

(E) $f(c)$ is a local
minimum.

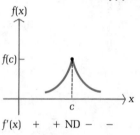

$f(x)$

$f(c)$

c

$f'(x)$ +   + ND −   −

(F) $f(c)$ is a local
maximum.

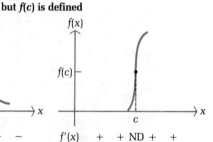

$f(x)$

$f(c)$

c

$f'(x)$ +   + ND +   +

(G) $f(c)$ is neither a
local maximum nor
a local minimum.

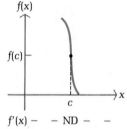

$f(x)$

$f(c)$

c

$f'(x)$ −   − ND −   −

(H) $f(c)$ is neither a
local maximum nor
a local minimum.

Figure 3 Local extrema

Example 3   Given $f(x) = x^3 - 6x^2 + 9x + 1$:

(A)   Find the critical values of f.
(B)   Find the local maxima and minima.
(C)   Sketch the graph of f.

Solutions   (A) $f'(x) = 3x^2 - 12x + 9 = 0$

$$3(x^2 - 4x + 3) = 0$$

$$3(x - 1)(x - 3) = 0$$

$$x = 1 \quad \text{or} \quad x = 3$$

The critical values are $x = 1$ and $x = 3$.

(B)   The easiest way to apply the first-derivative test is to construct a sign chart for $f'(x)$ for all x.

Sign chart for $f'(x) = 3(x - 1)(x - 3)$:

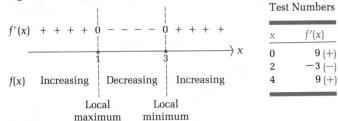

Test Numbers

x	$f'(x)$
0	9 (+)
2	−3 (−)
4	9 (+)

The sign chart indicates that f increases on $(-\infty, 1)$, has a local maximum at $x = 1$, decreases on $(1, 3)$, has a local minimum at $x = 3$, and increases on $(3, \infty)$. These facts are summarized in the following table:

x	$f'(x)$	$f(x)$	Graph of f
$x < 1$	+	Increasing	Rising
$x = 1$	0	Local maximum	Horizontal tangent
$1 < x < 3$	−	Decreasing	Falling
$x = 3$	0	Local minimum	Horizontal tangent
$3 < x$	+	Increasing	Rising

(C)   We sketch a graph of f using the information from part B and point-by-point plotting.

x	$f(x)$
0	1
1	5
2	3
3	1
4	5

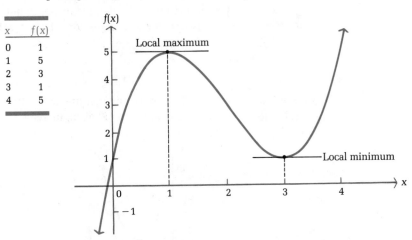

Problem 3   Given $f(x) = x^3 - 9x^2 + 24x - 10$:

(A)   Find the critical values of f.

(B)   Find the local maxima and minima.

(C)   Sketch a graph of f.

In Example 3, the function f had local extrema at both of its critical values. However, as was noted earlier, not every critical value of a function will produce a local extremum. For example, consider the function discussed in Example 2B:

$$f(x) = (1 - x)^{1/3} \quad \text{and} \quad f'(x) = \frac{-1}{3(1 - x)^{2/3}}$$

Since $f(1)$ exists and $f'(1)$ does not exist, $x = 1$ is a critical value for this function. However, the sign chart for $f'(x)$ shows that $f'(x)$ does not change sign at $x = 1$:

$f'(x)$ — — — — ND — — — —

→ x

1

$f(x)$ Decreasing Decreasing

Thus, f does not have a local maximum or a local minimum at $x = 1$.

Finally, it is important to remember that a critical value must be in the domain of the function. Refer to the function discussed in Example 2C:

$$f(x) = \frac{1}{x - 2} \quad \text{and} \quad f'(x) = \frac{-1}{(x - 2)^2}$$

The derivative is not defined at $x = 2$, but neither is the function. Thus, $x = 2$ is not a critical value for f. In fact, this function does not have any critical values.

Answers to Matched Problems

1. (A) Horizontal tangent line at $x = 3$
   (B) Decreasing on $(-\infty, 3)$, increasing on $(3, \infty)$
   (C) $f(x)$

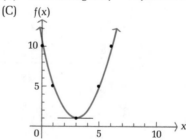

2. (A) Decreasing for all x (B) Increasing for all x
   (C) Decreasing on $(-\infty, 0)$ and $(0, \infty)$
3. (A) Critical values: $x = 2$, $x = 4$
   (B) Local maximum at $x = 2$, local minimum at $x = 4$

(C) $f(x)$

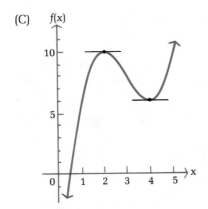

Exercise 8-1

A   Problems 1–6 refer to the following graph of $y = f(x)$:

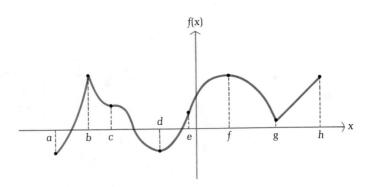

1. Identify the intervals over which $f(x)$ is increasing.

2. Identify the intervals over which $f(x)$ is decreasing.

3. Identify the points where $f'(x) = 0$.

4. Identify the points where $f'(x)$ does not exist.

5. Identify the points where f has a local maximum.

6. Identify the points where f has a local minimum.

B   Find the intervals where $f(x)$ is increasing, the intervals where $f(x)$ is decreasing, and the local extrema.

7. $f(x) = x^2 - 16x + 12$

8. $f(x) = x^2 + 6x + 7$

9. $f(x) = 4 + 10x - x^2$

10. $f(x) = 5 + 8x - 2x^2$

11. $f(x) = 2x^3 + 4$

12. $f(x) = 2 - 3x^3$

13. $f(x) = 2 - 6x - 2x^3$

14. $f(x) = x^3 + 9x + 7$

15. $f(x) = x^3 - 12x + 8$

16. $f(x) = 3x - x^3$

17. $f(x) = x^3 - 3x^2 - 24x + 7$

18. $f(x) = x^3 + 3x^2 - 9x + 5$

19. $f(x) = 2x^2 - x^4$

20. $f(x) = x^4 - 8x^2 + 3$

Find the intervals where f(x) is increasing, the intervals where f(x) is decreasing, and sketch the graph. Add horizontal tangent lines.

21. $f(x) = 4 + 8x - x^2$

22. $f(x) = 2x^2 - 8x + 9$

23. $f(x) = x^3 - 3x + 1$

24. $f(x) = x^3 - 12x + 2$

25. $f(x) = 10 - 12x + 6x^2 - x^3$

26. $f(x) = x^3 + 3x^2 + 3x$

C   *Find the critical values, the intervals where f(x) is increasing, the intervals where f(x) is decreasing, and the local extrema. Do not graph.*

27. $f(x) = \dfrac{x - 1}{x + 2}$

28. $f(x) = \dfrac{x + 2}{x - 3}$

29. $f(x) = x + \dfrac{4}{x}$

30. $f(x) = \dfrac{9}{x} + x$

31. $f(x) = 1 + \dfrac{1}{x} + \dfrac{1}{x^2}$

32. $f(x) = 3 - \dfrac{4}{x} - \dfrac{2}{x^2}$

33. $f(x) = \dfrac{x^2}{x - 2}$

34. $f(x) = \dfrac{x^2}{x + 1}$

35. $f(x) = x^4(x - 6)^2$

36. $f(x) = x^3(x - 5)^2$

37. $f(x) = 3(x - 2)^{2/3} + 4$

38. $f(x) = 6(4 - x)^{2/3} + 4$

39. $f(x) = 2\sqrt{x} - x, \quad x > 0$

40. $f(x) = x - 4\sqrt{x}, \quad x > 0$

Applications

Business & Economics

41. *Average cost.* A manufacturer has the following costs in producing x toasters in one day, $0 < x < 150$: fixed costs, $320; unit production cost, $20 per toaster; equipment maintenance and repairs, $x^2/20$ dollars. Thus, the cost of manufacturing x toasters in one day is given by

$$C(x) = \frac{x^2}{20} + 20x + 320 \qquad 0 < x < 150$$

and the average cost per toaster is given by

$$\overline{C}(x) = \frac{C(x)}{x} = \frac{x}{20} + 20 + \frac{320}{x} \qquad 0 < x < 150$$

Find the critical values for $\overline{C}(x)$, the intervals where the average cost per toaster is decreasing, the intervals where the average cost per toaster is increasing, and the local extrema. Do not graph.

42. *Average cost.* A manufacturer has the following costs in producing x blenders in one day, $0 < x < 200$: fixed costs, \$450; unit production cost, \$60 per blender; equipment maintenance and repairs, $x^2/18$ dollars.

   (A) What is the average cost $\overline{C}(x)$ per blender if x blenders are produced in one day?

   (B) Find the critical values for $\overline{C}(x)$, the intervals where the average cost per blender is decreasing, the intervals where the average cost per blender is increasing, and the local extrema. Do not graph.

43. *Marginal analysis.* Show that profit will be increasing over production intervals (a, b) for which marginal revenue is greater than marginal cost. [*Hint:* $P(x) = R(x) - C(x)$.]

44. *Marginal analysis.* Show that profit will be decreasing over production intervals (a, b) for which marginal revenue is less than marginal cost.

Life Sciences

45. *Medicine.* A drug is injected into the bloodstream of a patient through the right arm. The concentration of the drug in the bloodstream of the left arm t hours after the injection is approximated by

$$C(t) = \frac{0.14t}{t^2 + 1} \qquad 0 < t < 24$$

   Find the critical values for $C(t)$, the intervals where the concentration of the drug is increasing, the intervals where the concentration of the drug is decreasing, and the local extrema. Do not graph.

46. *Medicine.* The concentration $C(t)$ in milligrams per cubic centimeter of a particular drug in a patient's bloodstream is given by

$$C(t) = \frac{0.16t}{t^2 + 4t + 4} \qquad 0 < t < 12$$

   where t is the number of hours after the drug is taken orally. Find the critical values for $C(t)$, the intervals where the concentration of the drug is increasing, the intervals where the concentration of the drug is decreasing, and the local extrema. Do not graph.

Social Sciences

47. *Politics.* Public awareness of a Congressional candidate before and after a successful campaign was approximated by

$$P(t) = \frac{8.4t}{t^2 + 49} + 0.1 \qquad 0 < t < 24$$

   where t is time in months after the campaign started and $P(t)$ is the fraction of people in the Congressional district who could recall the candidate's (and later, Congressman's) name. Find the critical values for $P(t)$, the time intervals where the fraction is increasing, the time intervals where the fraction is decreasing, and the local extrema. Do not graph.

8-2 Second Derivative and Graphs

- Concavity
- Inflection Points
- Second-Derivative Test
- Application

In the preceding section we saw that the derivative can be used to determine when a graph is rising and falling. Now we want to see what the second derivative (the derivative of the derivative) can tell us about the shape of a graph.

■ Concavity

Consider the functions

$$f(x) = x^2 \quad \text{and} \quad g(x) = \sqrt{x}$$

for x in the interval $(0, \infty)$. Since

$$f'(x) = 2x > 0 \quad \text{for } 0 < x < \infty$$

and

$$g'(x) = \frac{1}{2\sqrt{x}} > 0 \quad \text{for } 0 < x < \infty$$

both functions are increasing on $(0, \infty)$.

Notice the different shapes of the graphs of f and g (see Figure 4). Even though the graph of each function is rising and each graph starts at $(0, 0)$ and goes through $(1, 1)$, the graphs are quite dissimilar. The graph of f opens upward while the graph of g opens downward. We say that the graph of f is *concave upward* and the graph of g is *concave downward*. It will help us draw graphs if we can determine the concavity of the graph before we draw it. How can we find a mathematical formulation of concavity?

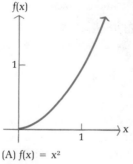

(A) $f(x) = x^2$

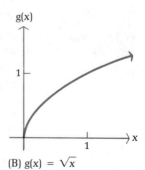

(B) $g(x) = \sqrt{x}$

Figure 4

It will be instructive to examine the slopes of f and g at various points on their graphs (see Figure 5). There are two observations we can make about each graph. Looking at the graph of f in Figure 5A, we see that $f'(x)$ (the slope of the tangent line) is *increasing* and that the graph lies *above* each tangent line. Looking at Figure 5B, we see that $g'(x)$ is *decreasing* and that the graph lies *below* each tangent line. With these ideas in mind, we state the general definition of concavity: The graph of a function f is **concave upward on the interval (a, b)** if $f'(x)$ is *increasing* on (a, b) and is **concave downward on the interval (a, b)** if $f'(x)$ is *decreasing* on (a, b). Geometrically, the graph is concave upward on (a, b) if it lies above its tangent lines in (a, b) and is concave downward on (a, b) if it lies below its tangent lines in (a, b).

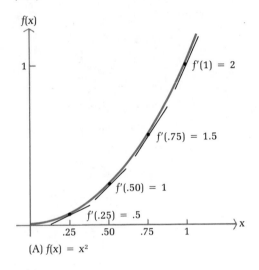

(A) $f(x) = x^2$

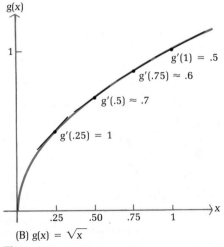

(B) $g(x) = \sqrt{x}$

Figure 5

How can we determine when $f'(x)$ is increasing or decreasing? In the last section we used the derivative of a function to determine when that function is increasing or decreasing. Thus, to determine when the function $f'(x)$ is increasing or decreasing, we use the derivative of $f'(x)$. The derivative of the derivative of a function is called the *second derivative* of the function. Various notations for the second derivative are given in the following box:

Second Derivative

For $y = f(x)$, the **second derivative** of f is

$$f''(x) = D_x f'(x)$$

Other notations for $f''(x)$ are

$$\frac{d^2y}{dx^2} \qquad y'' \qquad D_x^2 f(x)$$

Returning to the functions f and g discussed at the beginning of this section, we have

$$f(x) = x^2 \qquad\qquad g(x) = \sqrt{x} = x^{1/2}$$

$$f'(x) = 2x \qquad\qquad g'(x) = \frac{1}{2}x^{-1/2} = \frac{1}{2\sqrt{x}}$$

$$f''(x) = D_x 2x \qquad\qquad g''(x) = D_x \frac{1}{2}x^{-1/2}$$

$$= 2 \qquad\qquad\qquad = \frac{1}{4}x^{-3/2} = -\frac{1}{4\sqrt{x^3}}$$

For $x > 0$ we see that $f''(x) > 0$; thus, $f'(x)$ is increasing and the graph of f is concave upward (see Fig. 5A). For $x > 0$ we also see that $g''(x) < 0$; thus, $g'(x)$ is decreasing and the graph of g is concave downward (see Fig. 5B). These ideas are summarized in the following box:

Concavity

For the interval (a, b)

$f''(x)$	$f'(x)$	Graph of $y = f(x)$	Example
$+$	Increasing	Concave upward	$\smile$
$-$	Decreasing	Concave downward	$\frown$

Be careful not to confuse concavity with falling and rising. As Figure 6 illustrates, a graph that is concave upward on an interval may be falling, rising, or both falling and rising on that interval. A similar statement holds for a graph that is concave downward.

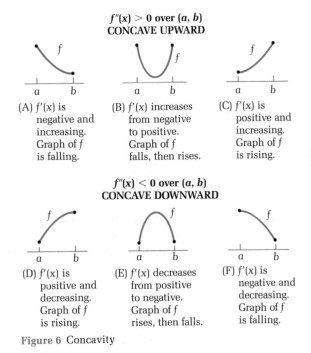

$f''(x) > 0$ over (a, b)
CONCAVE UPWARD

(A) $f'(x)$ is negative and increasing. Graph of f is falling.

(B) $f'(x)$ increases from negative to positive. Graph of f falls, then rises.

(C) $f'(x)$ is positive and increasing. Graph of f is rising.

$f''(x) < 0$ over (a, b)
CONCAVE DOWNWARD

(D) $f'(x)$ is positive and decreasing. Graph of f is rising.

(E) $f'(x)$ decreases from positive to negative. Graph of f rises, then falls.

(F) $f'(x)$ is negative and decreasing. Graph of f is falling.

Figure 6 Concavity

Example 4   Let $f(x) = x^3$. Find the intervals where the graph of f is concave upward and the intervals where the graph of f is concave downward. Sketch a graph of f.

Solution   To determine concavity, we must determine the sign of $f''(x)$.

$$f(x) = x^3$$
$$f'(x) = 3x^2$$
$$f''(x) = 6x$$

Sign chart for $f''(x) = 6x$:

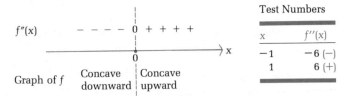

Thus, the graph of f is concave downward on $(-\infty, 0)$ and concave upward on $(0, \infty)$. The graph of f (without going through other graphing details) is shown in the figure.

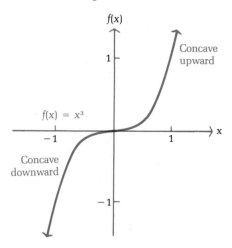

Problem 4   Repeat Example 4 for $f(x) = 1 - x^3$.

The graph in Example 4 changes from concave downward to concave upward at the point $(0, 0)$. This point is called an *inflection point*.

■ Inflection Points

In general, an **inflection point** is a point on the graph of a function where the concavity changes (from upward to downward or from downward to upward). In order for the concavity to change at a point, $f''(x)$ must change sign at that point. Reasoning as we did in the previous section, we conclude that the inflection points must occur at points where $f''(x) = 0$ or $f''(x)$ does not exist [but $f(x)$ must exist]. Figure 7 illustrates several typical cases.

If $f'(c)$ exists and $f''(x)$ changes sign at $x = c$, then the tangent line at an inflection point $(c, f(c))$ will always lie below the graph on the side that is concave upward and above the graph on the side that is concave downward (see Figs. 7A, B, and C).

Example 5   Find the inflection points of $f(x) = x^3 - 6x^2 + 9x + 1$.

Solution   Since inflection points occur at values of x where $f''(x)$ changes sign, we construct a sign chart for $f''(x)$.

$$f(x) = x^3 - 6x^2 + 9x + 1$$
$$f'(x) = 3x^2 - 12x + 9$$
$$f''(x) = 6x - 12 = 6(x - 2)$$

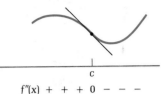

$f''(x)$ + + + 0 − − −

(A) $f'(c) > 0$

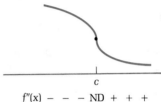

$f''(x)$ + + + 0 − − −

(B) $f'(c) < 0$

$f''(x)$ + + + 0 − − −

(C) $f'(c) = 0$

$f''(x)$ − − − ND + + +

(D) $f'(c)$ is not defined

Figure 7 Inflection points

Sign chart for $f''(x) = 6(x - 2)$:

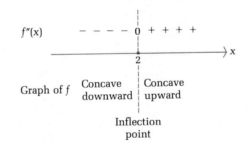

Test Numbers	
x	$f''(x)$
1	−6 (−)
3	6 (+)

$f''(x)$ − − − − 0 + + + +

Graph of f Concave downward   Concave upward

Inflection point

From the sign chart, we see that the graph of f has an inflection point at $x = 2$. The graph of f is shown in the figure. (See Example 3 in Section 8-1.)

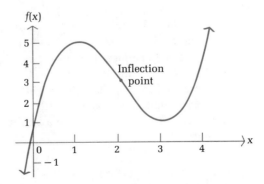

Problem 5   Find the inflection points of $f(x) = x^3 - 9x^2 + 24x - 10$. (See Problem 3 in Section 8-1 for the graph of f.)

It is important to remember that the values of x where $f''(x) = 0$ [or $f''(x)$ does not exist] are only candidates for inflection points. The second derivative must change sign at $x = c$ in order for the graph of f to have an inflection point at $x = c$. For example, consider

$$f(x) = x^4, \quad f'(x) = 4x^3, \quad \text{and} \quad f''(x) = 12x^2$$

The second derivative is 0 at $x = 0$, but $f''(x) > 0$ for all other values of x. Since $f''(x)$ does not change sign at $x = 0$, the graph of f does not have an inflection point at $x = 0$, as illustrated in Figure 8.

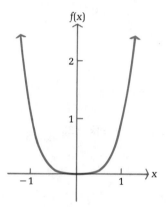

Figure 8 $f(x) = x^4$

■ Second-Derivative Test

Now we want to see how the second derivative can be used to find local extrema. Suppose f is a function satisfying $f'(c) = 0$ and $f''(c) > 0$. First, note that if $f''(c) > 0$, then it follows from the properties of limits* that $f''(x) > 0$ in some interval (m, n) containing c. Thus, the graph of f must be concave upward in this interval. But this implies that $f'(x)$ is increasing in this interval. Since $f'(c) = 0$, $f'(x)$ must change from negative to positive at $x = c$ and $f(c)$ is a local minimum (see Figure 9). Reasoning in the same fashion, we conclude that if $f'(c) = 0$ and $f''(c) < 0$, then $f(c)$ is a local maximum. Of course, it is possible that both $f'(c) = 0$ and $f''(c) = 0$. In this case the second derivative cannot be used to determine the shape of the graph around $x = c$; $f(c)$ may be a local minimum, a local maximum, or neither.

---

* Actually, we are assuming that $f''(x)$ is continuous in an interval containing c. It is very unlikely that we will encounter a function for which $f''(c)$ exists, but $f''(x)$ is not continuous in an interval containing c.

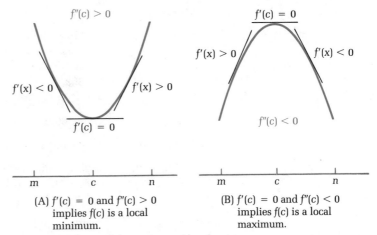

(A) $f'(c) = 0$ and $f''(c) > 0$ implies $f(c)$ is a local minimum.

(B) $f'(c) = 0$ and $f''(c) < 0$ implies $f(c)$ is a local maximum.

Figure 9 The second derivative and local extrema

The sign of the second derivative thus provides a simple test for identifying local maxima and minima. This test is most useful when we do not want to draw the graph of the function. If we are interested in drawing the graph and have already constructed the sign chart for $f'(x)$, then the first-derivative test can be used to identify the local extrema.

Second-Derivative Test for Local Maxima and Minima

Let c be a critical value for $f(x)$.

$f'(c)$	$f''(c)$	$f(c)$	Example
0	+	Local minimum	
0	−	Local maximum	
0	0	Test fails	

Example 6 Find the local maxima and minima of each function. Use the second-derivative test when it applies.

(A) $f(x) = x^3 - 6x^2 + 9x + 1$ (B) $f(x) = \frac{1}{6}x^6 - 4x^5 + 25x^4$

Solutions (A) Take first and second derivatives and find critical values:

$$f(x) = x^3 - 6x^2 + 9x + 1$$
$$f'(x) = 3x^2 - 12x + 9 = 3(x - 1)(x - 3)$$
$$f''(x) = 6x - 12 = 6(x - 2)$$

Critical values are $x = 1, 3$.

$$f''(1) = -6 < 0 \qquad f \text{ has a local maximum at } x = 1.$$
$$f''(3) = 6 > 0 \qquad f \text{ has a local minimum at } x = 3.$$

(B) $\qquad f(x) = \frac{1}{6}x^6 - 4x^5 + 25x^4$

$\qquad f'(x) = x^5 - 20x^4 + 100x^3 = x^3(x - 10)^2$

$\qquad f''(x) = 5x^4 - 80x^3 + 300x^2$

Critical values are $x = 0$ and $x = 10$.

$$f''(0) = 0 \qquad \text{The second-derivative test fails at both critical}$$
$$f''(10) = 0 \qquad \text{values, so the first-derivative test must be used.}$$

Sign chart for $f'(x) = x^3(x - 10)^2$:

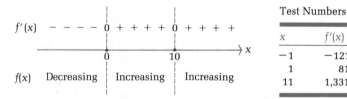

Test Numbers	
x	$f'(x)$
-1	$-121 \; (-)$
1	$81 \; (+)$
11	$1{,}331 \; (+)$

From the sign chart, we see that $f(x)$ has a local minimum at $x = 0$ and does not have a local extremum at $x = 10$.

Problem 6   Find the local maxima and minima of each function. Use the second-derivative test when it applies.

(A) $f(x) = x^3 - 9x^2 + 24x - 10$ (B) $f(x) = 10x^6 - 24x^5 + 15x^4$

A common error is to assume that $f''(c) = 0$ implies that $f(c)$ is not a local extreme point. As Example 6B illustrates, if $f''(c) = 0$, then $f(c)$ may or may not be a local extreme point. The first-derivative test *must* be used whenever $f''(c) = 0$ [or $f''(c)$ does not exist].

■ Application

Example 7
Maximum Rate of Change

Using past records, a company estimates that it will sell $N(x)$ units of a product after spending $\$x$ thousand on advertising, as given by

$$N(x) = 2{,}000 - 2x^3 + 60x^2 - 450x \qquad 5 \leqslant x \leqslant 15$$

When is the rate of change of sales per unit (thousand dollars) change in advertising increasing? Decreasing? What is the maximum rate of change? Graph N and N′ on the same axes and interpret.

Solution The rate of change of sales per unit (thousand dollars) change in advertising expenditure is

$$N'(x) = -6x^2 + 120x - 450 = -6(x - 5)(x - 15)$$

To determine when this rate is increasing and decreasing, we find N″(x), the derivative of N′(x):

$$N''(x) = -12x + 120 = 12(10 - x)$$

The information obtained by analyzing the signs of N′(x) and N″(x) is summarized in the table (sign charts are omitted).

x	N″(x)	N′(x)	N′(x)	N(x)
5 < x < 10	+	+	Increasing	Increasing, concave upward
x = 10	0	+	Local maximum	Inflection point
10 < x < 15	−	+	Decreasing	Increasing, concave downward

Thus, we see that N′(x), the rate of change of sales, is increasing on (5, 10) and decreasing on (10, 15). Both N and N′ are graphed in the figure. An examination of the graph of N′(x) shows that the maximum rate of change is N′(10) = 150. Notice that N′(x) has a local maximum and N(x) has an inflection point at x = 10. This value of x is referred to as the **point of diminishing returns** since the rate of change of sales begins to decrease at this point.

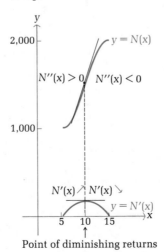

Point of diminishing returns

Problem 7   Repeat Example 7 for

$$N(x) = 5,000 - x^3 + 60x^2 - 900x \qquad 10 \leqslant x \leqslant 30$$

Answers to
Matched Problems

4.   Concave upward on $(-\infty, 0)$; concave downward on $(0, \infty)$

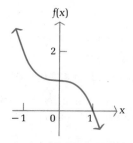

5.   Inflection point at $x = 3$

6.   (A) $f(2)$ is a local maximum; $f(4)$ is a local minimum
       (B) $f(0)$ is a local minimum; no local extremum at $x = 1$

7. $N'(x)$ is increasing on $(10, 20)$, decreasing on $(20, 30)$; maximum rate
      of change is $N'(20) = 300$; $x = 20$ is point of diminishing returns

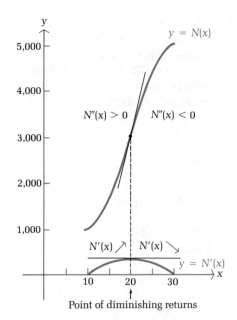

Exercise 8-2

A   Problems 1–4 refer to the following graph of $y = f(x)$:

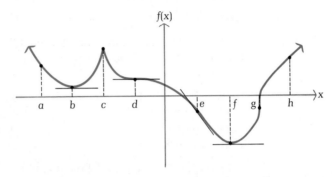

1. Identify intervals over which the graph of f is concave upward.
2. Identify intervals over which the graph of f is concave downward.
3. Identify inflection points.
4. Identify local extrema.

Find the indicated derivative for each function.

5. $f''(x)$ for $f(x) = x^3 - 2x^2 - 1$
6. $g''(x)$ for $g(x) = x^4 - 3x^2 + 5$
7. d^2y/dx^2 for $y = 2x^5 - 3$
8. d^2y/dx^2 for $y = 3x^4 - 7x$
9. $D_x^2(1 - 2x + x^3)$
10. $D_x^2(3x^2 - x^3)$
11. y'' for $y = (x^2 - 1)^3$
12. y'' for $y = (x^2 + 4)^4$
13. $f''(x)$ for $f(x) = 3x^{-1} + 2x^{-2} + 5$
14. $f''(x)$ for $f(x) = x^2 - x^{1/3}$

B   Find all local maxima and minima using the second-derivative test whenever it applies (do not graph). If the second-derivative test fails, use the first-derivative test.

15. $f(x) = 2x^2 - 8x + 6$ 16. $f(x) = 6x - x^2 + 4$
17. $f(x) = 2x^3 - 3x^2 - 12x - 5$ 18. $f(x) = 2x^3 + 3x^2 - 12x - 1$
19. $f(x) = 3 - x^3 + 3x^2 - 3x$ 20. $f(x) = x^3 + 6x^2 + 12x + 2$
21. $f(x) = x^4 - 8x^2 + 10$ 22. $f(x) = x^4 - 18x^2 + 50$
23. $f(x) = x^6 + 3x^4 + 2$ 24. $f(x) = 4 - x^6 - 6x^4$

25. $f(x) = x + \dfrac{16}{x}$ 26. $f(x) = x + \dfrac{25}{x}$

Find the intervals where the graph of f is concave upward, the intervals where the graph is concave downward, and the inflection points.

27. $f(x) = x^2 - 4x + 5$

28. $f(x) = 9 + 3x - 4x^2$

29. $f(x) = x^3 - 18x^2 + 10x - 11$

30. $f(x) = x^3 + 24x^2 + 15x - 12$

31. $f(x) = x^4 - 24x^2 + 10x - 5$

32. $f(x) = x^4 + 6x^2 + 9x + 11$

33. $f(x) = -x^4 + 4x^3 + 3x + 7$

34. $f(x) = -x^4 - 2x^3 + 12x^2 + 15$

Find local maxima, local minima, and inflection points. Sketch the graph of each function. Include tangent lines at each local extreme point and inflection point.

35. $f(x) = x^3 - 6x^2 + 16$

36. $f(x) = x^3 - 9x^2 + 15x + 10$

37. $f(x) = x^3 + x + 2$

38. $f(x) = 1 - 3x - x^3$

39. $f(x) = (2 - x)^3 + 1$

40. $f(x) = (1 + x)^3 - 1$

41. $f(x) = x^3 - 12x$

42. $f(x) = 27x - x^3$

C   *Find the inflection points. Do not graph.*

43. $f(x) = \dfrac{1}{x^2 + 12}$

44. $f(x) = \dfrac{x^2}{x^2 + 12}$

45. $f(x) = \dfrac{x}{x^2 + 12}$

46. $f(x) = \dfrac{x^3}{x^2 + 12}$

Applications

Business & Economics

47. *Revenue.* The marketing research department for a computer company used a large city to test market their new product. They found that a relationship between price p (dollars per unit) and the demand x (units per week) was given approximately by

$$p = 1{,}296 - 0.12x^2 \qquad 0 < x < 80$$

Thus, the weekly revenue can be approximated by

$$R(x) = xp = 1{,}296x - 0.12x^3 \qquad 0 < x < 80$$

(A) Find the local extrema for the revenue function.

(B) Over which intervals is the graph of the revenue function concave upward? Concave downward?

48. *Profit.* If the cost equation for the company in the preceding problem is

$$C(x) = 830 + 396x$$

(A) Find the local extrema for the profit function.

(B) Over which intervals is the graph of the profit function concave upward? Concave downward?

49. *Advertising.* A company estimates that it will sell $N(x)$ units of a

product after spending $x thousand on advertising, as given by

$$N(x) = -3x^3 + 225x^2 - 3{,}600x + 17{,}000 \qquad 10 \leqslant x \leqslant 40$$

(A) When is the rate of change of sales $N'(x)$ increasing? Decreasing?
(B) Find the inflection points for the graph of N.
(C) Graph N and N' on the same axes.
(D) What is the maximum rate of change of sales?

50. *Advertising.* A company estimates that it will sell $N(x)$ units of a product after spending $x thousand on advertising, as given by

$$N(x) = -2x^3 + 90x^2 - 750x + 2{,}000 \qquad 5 \leqslant x \leqslant 25$$

(A) When is the rate of change of sales $N'(x)$ increasing? Decreasing?
(B) Find the inflection points for the graph of N.
(C) Graph N and N' on the same axes.
(D) What is the maximum rate of change of sales?

Life Sciences   51. *Population growth — bacteria.* A drug that stimulates reproduction is introduced into a colony of bacteria. After t minutes, the number of bacteria is given approximately by

$$N(t) = 1{,}000 + 30t^2 - t^3 \qquad 0 \leqslant t \leqslant 20$$

(A) When is the rate of growth $N'(t)$ increasing? Decreasing?
(B) Find the inflection points for the graph of N.
(C) Sketch the graph of N and N' on the same axes.
(D) What is the maximum rate of growth?

52. *Drug sensitivity.* One hour after x milligrams of a particular drug are given to a person, the change in body temperature $T(x)$ in degrees Fahrenheit is given by

$$T(x) = x^2 \left(1 - \frac{x}{9} \right) \qquad 0 \leqslant x \leqslant 6$$

The rate at which $T(x)$ changes with respect to the size of the dosage x, $T'(x)$, is called the *sensitivity* of the body to the dosage.

(A) When is $T'(x)$ increasing? Decreasing?
(B) Where does the graph of T have inflection points?
(C) Sketch the graph of T and T' on the same axes.
(D) What is the maximum value of $T'(x)$?

Social Sciences   53. *Learning.* The time T in minutes it takes a person to learn a list of length n is

$$T(n) = \frac{2}{25} n^3 - \frac{6}{5} n^2 + 6n \qquad 0 \leqslant n$$

(A) When is the rate of change of T with respect to the length of the list increasing? Decreasing?

(B)   Where does the graph of T have inflection points? Graph T and T' on the same axes.

(C)   What is the minimum value of $T'(n)$?

8-3   Optimization; Absolute Maxima and Minima

■ Absolute Maxima and Minima
■ Applications

We are now ready to consider one of the most important applications of the derivative, namely, the use of derivatives to find the *absolute maximum* or *minimum* value of a function. As we mentioned earlier, an economist may be interested in the price or production level of a commodity that will bring a maximum profit; a doctor may be interested in the time it takes for a drug to reach its maximum concentration in the bloodstream after an injection; and a city planner might be interested in the location of heavy industry in a city to produce minimum pollution in residential and business areas. Before we launch an attack on problems of this type, we have to say a few words about the procedures needed to find absolute maximum and absolute minimum values of functions. We have most of the tools we need from the previous sections.

■ Absolute Maxima and Minima

First, what do we mean by *absolute maximum* and *absolute minimum*? We say that $f(c)$ is an **absolute maximum** of f if

$$f(c) \geq f(x)$$

for all x in the domain of f. Similarly, $f(c)$ is called an **absolute minimum** of f if

$$f(c) \leq f(x)$$

for all x in the domain of f. Figure 10 illustrates several typical examples.

In many practical problems, the domain of a function is restricted because of practical or physical considerations. If the domain is restricted to some closed interval, as is often the case, then Theorem 2 can be proved.

Theorem 2

A function f continuous on a closed interval $[a, b]$ assumes both an absolute maximum and an absolute minimum on that interval.

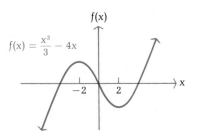

$$f(x) = \frac{x^3}{3} - 4x$$

(A) No absolute maximum or minimum
One local maximum at $x = -2$
One local minimum at $x = 2$

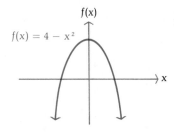

$$f(x) = 4 - x^2$$

(B) Absolute maximum at $x = 0$
No absolute minimum

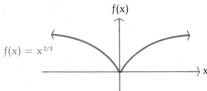

$$f(x) = x^{2/3}$$

(C) Absolute minimum at $x = 0$
No absolute maximum

Figure 10

It is important to understand that the absolute maximum and minimum depend on both the function f and the interval $[a, b]$ (see Fig. 11, on the next page). However, in all four cases illustrated in Figure 11, the absolute maximum and the absolute minimum both occur at a critical value or an end point. It can be proved that absolute extrema (if they exist) must always occur at critical values or end points. Thus, to find the absolute maximum or minimum value of a continuous function on a closed interval, we simply identify the end points and the critical values in the interval, evaluate each, and then choose the largest and smallest values out of this group.

Steps in Finding Absolute Maximum and Minimum Values of Continuous Functions

1. Check to make certain that f is continuous over $[a, b]$.
2. Find the critical values in the interval (a, b).
3. Evaluate f at the end points and at the critical values found in step 2.
4. The absolute maximum $f(x)$ on $[a, b]$ is the largest of the values found in step 3.
5. The absolute minimum $f(x)$ on $[a, b]$ is the smallest of the values found in step 3.

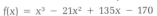

$f(x) = x^3 - 21x^2 + 135x - 170$

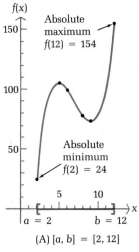

(A) $[a, b] = [2, 12]$

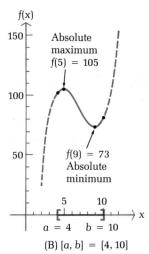

(B) $[a, b] = [4, 10]$

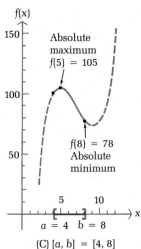

(C) $[a, b] = [4, 8]$

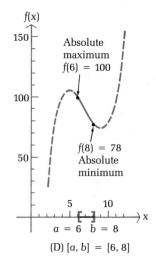

(D) $[a, b] = [6, 8]$

Figure 11 Absolute extrema on a closed interval

Example 8   Find the absolute maximum and absolute minimum values of

$$f(x) = x^3 + 3x^2 - 9x - 7$$

on each of the following intervals:

(A) $[-6, 4]$ (B) $[-4, 2]$ (C) $[-2, 2]$

Solutions   (A)   The function is continuous for all values of x.

$$f'(x) = 3x^2 + 6x - 9 = 3(x - 1)(x + 3)$$

Thus, $x = -3$ and $x = 1$ are critical values in the interval $(-6, 4)$. Evaluate f at the end points and critical values, $-6, -3, 1$, and 4, and choose the maximum and minimum from these:

$$f(-6) = -61 \quad \text{Absolute minimum}$$
$$f(-3) = 20$$
$$f(1) = -12$$
$$f(4) = 69 \quad \text{Absolute maximum}$$

(B)   Interval: $[-4, 2]$

x	$f(x)$	
-4	13	
-3	20	Absolute maximum
1	-12	Absolute minimum
2	-5	

(C)   Interval: $[-2, 2]$

x	$f(x)$	
-2	15	Absolute maximum
1	-12	Absolute minimum
2	-5	

The critical value $x = -3$ is not included in this table because it is not in the interval $[-2, 2]$.

Problem 8   Find the absolute maximum and absolute minimum values of

$$f(x) = x^3 - 12x$$

on each of the following intervals:

(A) $[-5, 5]$ (B) $[-3, 3]$ (C) $[-3, 1]$

Now suppose we want to find the absolute maximum or minimum value of a function that is continuous on an interval that is not closed. Since Theorem 2 no longer applies, we cannot be certain that the absolute maximum or minimum value exists. Figure 12 (on the next page) illustrates several ways that functions can fail to have absolute extrema.

In general, the best procedure to follow when the interval is not a closed interval (that is, is not of the form $[a, b]$) is to sketch the graph of the function. However, there is one special case that occurs frequently in applications and that can be analyzed without drawing a graph. It often happens that f is continuous on an interval I and has only one critical value c in the interval I (here I can be any type of interval—open, closed, or

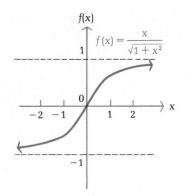

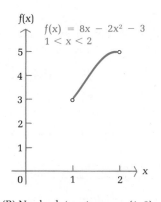

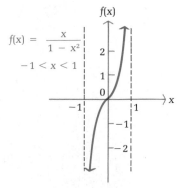

(A) No absolute extrema on $(-\infty, \infty)$:
$-1 < f(x) < 1$ for all x
$[f(x) \neq 1$ or -1 for any $x]$

(B) No absolute extrema on $(1, 2)$:
$3 < f(x) < 5$ for $x \in (1, 2)$
$[f(x) \neq 3$ or 5 for any $x \in (1, 2)]$

(C) No absolute extrema on $(-1, 1)$:
Graph has vertical
asymptotes at $x = -1$ and $x = 1$.

Figure 12 Functions with no absolute extrema

half-closed). If this is the case and if $f''(c)$ exists, then we have the second-derivative test for absolute extrema given in the box below.

Second-Derivative Test for Absolute Maximum and Minimum When f Is Continuous on an Interval I and c Is the Only Critical Value in I

$f'(c)$	$f''(c)$	$f(c)$	Example
0	+	Absolute minimum	
0	−	Absolute maximum	
0	0	Test fails	

Example 9 Find the absolute minimum value of

$$f(x) = x + \frac{4}{x}$$

on the interval $(0, \infty)$.

Solution $\quad f'(x) = 1 - \frac{4}{x^2} = \frac{x^2 - 4}{x^2} = \frac{(x-2)(x+2)}{x^2} \qquad f''(x) = \frac{8}{x^3}$

The only critical value in the interval $(0, \infty)$ is $x = 2$. Since $f''(2) = 1 > 0$, $f(2) = 4$ is the absolute minimum value of f on $(0, \infty)$.

Problem 9   Find the absolute maximum value of

$$f(x) = 12 - x - \frac{9}{x}$$

on the interval $(0, \infty)$.

■ Applications

Now we want to solve some applied problems that involve absolute extrema. Before beginning, we outline in the next box the steps to follow in solving this type of problem. The first step is the most difficult one. The techniques used to construct the model are best illustrated through a series of examples.

A Strategy for Solving Applied Optimization Problems

Step 1.   Introduce variables and construct a mathematical model of the form

Maximize (or minimize) $f(x)$ on the interval I

Step 2.   Find the absolute maximum (or minimum) value of $f(x)$ on the interval I and the value(s) of x where this occurs.

Step 3.   Use the solution to the mathematical model to answer the questions asked in the application.

Example 10
Cost–Demand

A company manufactures and sells x transistor radios per week. If the weekly cost and demand equations are

$$C(x) = 5,000 + 2x$$

$$p = 10 - \frac{x}{1,000} \qquad 0 \leqslant x \leqslant 8,000$$

find for each week:

(A)   The maximum revenue
(B)   The maximum profit, the production level that will realize the maximum profit, and the price that the company should charge for each radio

Solutions   (A)   The revenue received for selling x radios at $p per radio is

$$R(x) = xp$$

$$= x\left(10 - \frac{x}{1,000}\right)$$

$$= 10x - \frac{x^2}{1,000}$$

Thus, the mathematical model is

$$\text{Maximize} \quad R(x) = 10x - \frac{x^2}{1,000} \qquad 0 \leqslant x \leqslant 8,000$$

$$R'(x) = 10 - \frac{x}{500}$$

$$10 - \frac{x}{500} = 0$$

$$x = 5,000 \qquad \text{Only critical value}$$

Use the second-derivative test for absolute extrema:

$$R''(x) = -\frac{1}{500} < 0 \qquad \text{for all } x$$

Thus, the maximum revenue is

$$\text{Max } R(x) = R(5,000) = \$25,000$$

(B)   Profit = Revenue − Cost

$$P(x) = R(x) - C(x)$$

$$= 10x - \frac{x^2}{1,000} - 5,000 - 2x$$

$$= 8x - \frac{x^2}{1,000} - 5,000$$

The mathematical model is

$$\text{Maximize} \quad P(x) = 8x - \frac{x^2}{1,000} - 5,000 \qquad 0 \leqslant x \leqslant 8,000$$

$$P'(x) = 8 - \frac{x}{500}$$

$$8 - \frac{x}{500} = 0$$

$$x = 4,000$$

$$P''(x) = -\frac{1}{500} < 0 \qquad \text{for all } x$$

Since $x = 4,000$ is the only critical value and $P''(x) < 0$,

$$\text{Max } P(x) = P(4,000) = \$11,000$$

Using the price–demand equation with $x = 4,000$, we find

$$p = 10 - \frac{4,000}{1,000} = \$6$$

Thus, a maximum profit of $11,000 per week is realized when 4,000 radios are produced weekly and sold for $6 each. Notice that this is not the same level of production that produces the maximum revenue.

All the results in this example are illustrated in Figure 13. We also note that profit is maximum when

$$P'(x) = R'(x) - C'(x) = 0$$

that is, when the marginal revenue is equal to the marginal cost (the rate of increase in revenue is the same as the rate of increase in cost at the 4,000 output level—notice that the slopes of the two curves are the same at this point).

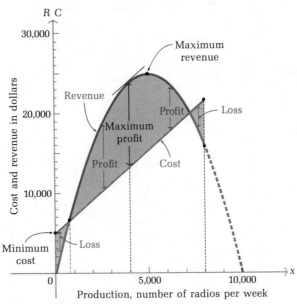

Figure 13

Problem 10   Repeat Example 10 for

$$C(x) = 90,000 + 30x$$

$$p = 300 - \frac{x}{30} \qquad 0 \le x \le 9,000$$

Example 11   In Example 10 the government has decided to tax the company $2 for each
Profit   radio produced. Taking into account this additional cost, how many radios
should the company manufacture each week in order to maximize its
weekly profit? What is the maximum weekly profit? How much should it
charge for the radios?

Solution   The tax of $2 per unit changes the company's cost equation:

$$C(x) = \text{Original cost} + \text{Tax}$$
$$= 5,000 + 2x + 2x$$
$$= 5,000 + 4x$$

The new profit function is

$$P(x) = R(x) - C(x)$$
$$= 10x - \frac{x^2}{1,000} - 5,000 - 4x$$
$$= 6x - \frac{x^2}{1,000} - 5,000$$

Thus, we must solve the following:

$$\text{Maximize} \quad P(x) = 6x - \frac{x^2}{1,000} - 5,000 \qquad 0 \leqslant x \leqslant 8,000$$

$$P'(x) = 6 - \frac{x}{500}$$

$$6 - \frac{x}{500} = 0$$

$$x = 3,000$$

$$P''(x) = -\frac{1}{500} < 0$$

$$\text{Max } P(x) = P(3,000) = \$4,000$$

Using the price–demand equation with $x = 3,000$, we find

$$p = 10 - \frac{3,000}{1,000} = \$7$$

Thus, the company's maximum profit is $4,000 when 3,000 radios are
produced and sold weekly at a price of $7.

Even though the tax caused the company's cost to increase by $2 per
radio, the price that the company should charge to maximize its profit
increases by only $1. The company must absorb the other $1 with a
resulting decrease of $7,000 in maximum profit.

Problem 11 Repeat Example 11 if

$$C(x) = 90{,}000 + 30x$$

$$p = 300 - \frac{x}{30} \qquad 0 \leqslant x \leqslant 9{,}000$$

and the government decides to tax the company $20 for each unit produced. Compare the results with the results in Problem 10B.

Example 12
Maximize Yield

A walnut grower estimates from past records that if twenty trees are planted per acre, each tree will average 60 pounds of nuts per year. If for each additional tree planted per acre (up to fifteen) the average yield per tree drops 2 pounds, how many trees should be planted to maximize the yield per acre? What is the maximum yield?

Solution

Let x be the number of additional trees planted per acre. Then

$$20 + x = \text{Total number of trees per acre}$$

$$60 - 2x = \text{Yield per tree}$$

Yield per acre = (Total number of trees per acre)(Yield per tree)

$$Y(x) = (20 + x)(60 - 2x)$$

$$= 1{,}200 + 20x - 2x^2 \qquad 0 \leqslant x \leqslant 15$$

Thus, we must solve the following:

Maximize $Y(x) = 1{,}200 + 20x - 2x^2 \qquad 0 \leqslant x \leqslant 15$

$$Y'(x) = 20 - 4x$$

$$20 - 4x = 0$$

$$x = 5$$

$$Y''(x) = -4 < 0 \qquad \text{for all } x$$

Hence,

Max $Y(x) = Y(5) = 1{,}250$ pounds per acre

Thus, a maximum yield of 1,250 pounds of nuts per acre is realized if twenty-five trees are planted per acre.

Problem 12 Repeat Example 12 starting with thirty trees per acre and a reduction of 1 pound per tree for each additional tree planted.

Example 13
Maximize Area

A farmer wants to construct a rectangular pen next to a barn 60 feet long, using all of the barn as part of one side of the pen. Find the dimensions of the pen with the largest area that the farmer can build if:

(A) 160 feet of fencing material is available
(B) 250 feet of fencing material is available

Solutions   (A)   We begin by constructing and labeling a figure:

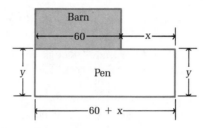

The area of the pen is

$$A = (x + 60)y$$

Before we can maximize the area, we must determine a relationship between x and y in order to express A as a function of one variable. In this case, x and y are related to the total amount of available fencing material:

$$x + y + 60 + x + y = 160$$
$$2x + 2y = 100$$
$$y = 50 - x$$

Thus,

$$A(x) = (x + 60)(50 - x)$$

Now we need to determine the permissible values of x. Since the farmer wants to use all of the barn as part of one side of the pen, x cannot be negative. Since y is the other dimension of the pen, y cannot be negative. Thus,

$$y = 50 - x \geqslant 0$$
$$50 \geqslant x$$

Thus, we must solve the following:

$$\text{Maximize} \quad A(x) = (x + 60)(50 - x) \qquad 0 \leqslant x \leqslant 50$$
$$A(x) = 3{,}000 - 10x - x^2$$
$$A'(x) = -10 - 2x$$
$$-10 - 2x = 0$$
$$x = -5$$

Since $x = -5$ is not in the interval $[0, 50]$, there are no critical points in the interval. $A(x)$ is continuous on $[0, 50]$, so the absolute maximum must occur at one of the end points.

$A(0) = 3,000$ Maximum area

$A(50) = 0$

If $x = 0$, then $y = 50$. Thus, the dimensions of the pen with largest area are 60 feet by 50 feet.

(B)   If there is 250 feet of fencing material available, then

$$x + y + x + 60 + y = 250$$

$$2x + 2y = 190$$

$$y = 95 - x$$

The model becomes

Maximize $A(x) = (x + 60)(95 - x)$ $0 \leqslant x \leqslant 100$

$$A(x) = 5,700 + 35x - x^2$$

$$A'(x) = 35 - 2x$$

$$35 - 2x = 0$$

$$x = \tfrac{35}{2} = 17.5$$ The only critical value

$$A''(x) = -2 < 0$$

$$\text{Max } A(x) = A(17.5) = 6,006.25$$

$$y = 95 - 17.5 = 77.5$$

This time the dimensions of the pen with the largest area are 77.5 feet by 77.5 feet.

Problem 13   Repeat Example 13 if the barn is 80 feet long.

Example 14
Inventory Control

A record company anticipates that there will be a demand for 20,000 copies of a certain album during the following year. It costs the company $0.50 to store a record for one year. Each time it must press additional records, it costs $200 to set up the equipment. How many records should the company press during each production run in order to minimize its total storage and set-up costs?

Solution

This type of problem is called an **inventory control problem.** One of the basic assumptions made in such problems is that the demand is uniform. For example, if there are 250 working days in a year, then the daily demand would be $20,000/250 = 800$ records. The company could decide to produce all 20,000 records at the beginning of the year. This would certainly minimize the set-up costs, but would result in very large storage costs. At the other extreme, it could produce 800 records each day. This would minimize the storage costs, but would result in very large set-up costs. Somewhere between these two extremes is the optimal solution that will minimize the total storage and set-up costs. Let

$x =$ Number of records pressed during each production run

$y =$ Number of production runs

It is easy to see that the total set-up cost for the year is $200y$, but what is the total storage cost? If the demand is uniform, then the number of records in storage between production runs will decrease from x to 0 and the average number in storage each day is $x/2$. This result is illustrated in the following figure:

Number of records in storage

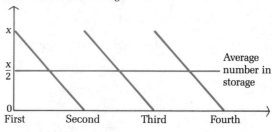

Production run

Since it costs \$0.50 to store one record for a year, the total storage cost is $0.5(x/2) = 0.25x$ and the total cost is

Total cost = Set-up cost + Storage cost

$$C = 200y + 0.25x$$

If the company produces x records in each of y production runs, then the total number of records produced is xy. Thus,

$$xy = 20,000$$

$$y = \frac{20,000}{x}$$

Certainly, x must be at least 1 and cannot exceed 20,000. Thus, we must solve the following:

$$\text{Minimize} \quad C(x) = 200\left(\frac{20,000}{x}\right) + 0.25x \quad 1 \leqslant x \leqslant 20,000$$

$$C(x) = \frac{4,000,000}{x} + 0.25x$$

$$C'(x) = -\frac{4,000,000}{x^2} + 0.25$$

$$-\frac{4,000,000}{x^2} + 0.25 = 0$$

$$x^2 = \frac{4,000,000}{0.25}$$

$$x^2 = 16,000,000$$

$$x = 4,000 \qquad -4,000 \text{ is not a critical value}$$
$$\text{since } 1 \leqslant x \leqslant 20,000$$

$$C''(x) = \frac{8,000,000}{x^3} > 0 \qquad \text{for } x \in (1, 20,000)$$

Thus,

$$\text{Min } C(x) = C(4,000) = 2,000$$

$$y = \frac{20,000}{4,000} = 5$$

The company will minimize its total cost by pressing 4,000 records five times during the year.

Problem 14   Repeat Example 14 if it costs $250 to set up a production run and $0.40 to store one record for a year.

Answers to
Matched Problems

8. (A)   Absolute maximum: $f(5) = 65$; absolute minimum: $f(-5) = -65$
   (B)   Absolute maximum: $f(-2) = 16$; absolute minimum: $f(2) = -16$
   (C)   Absolute maximum: $f(-2) = 16$; absolute minimum: $f(1) = -11$
9. $f(3) = 6$
10. (A)   Max $R(x) = R(4,500) = \$675,000$
    (B)   Max $P(x) = P(4,050) = \$456,750$; $p = \$165$
11.   Max $P(x) = P(3,750) = \$378,750$; $p = \$175$; price increases $10, profit decreases $78,000
12.   Max $Y(x) = Y(15) = 2,025$ pounds per acre
13. (A)   80 feet by 40 feet   (B)   82.5 feet by 82.5 feet
14.   Press 5,000 records four times during the year

Exercise 8-3

A   *Find the absolute maximum and absolute minimum, if either exists, for each function.*

1. $f(x) = x^2 - 4x + 5$ 2. $f(x) = x^2 + 6x + 7$
3. $f(x) = 10 + 8x - x^2$ 4. $f(x) = 6 - 8x - x^2$
5. $f(x) = 1 - x^3$ 6. $f(x) = 1 - x^4$

B   *Find the indicated extrema of each function.*

7.   Absolute maximum value of $f(x) = 24 - 2x - \dfrac{8}{x}$, $x > 0$

8. Absolute minimum value of $f(x) = 3x + \dfrac{27}{x}, \quad x > 0$

9. Absolute minimum value of $f(x) = 5 + 3x + \dfrac{12}{x^2}, \quad x > 0$

10. Absolute maximum value of $f(x) = 10 - 2x - \dfrac{27}{x^2}, \quad x > 0$

Find the absolute maximum and minimum, if either exists, of each function on the indicated intervals.

11. $f(x) = x^3 - 6x^2 + 9x - 6$

    (A) $[-1, 5]$ (B) $[-1, 3]$ (C) $[2, 5]$

12. $f(x) = 2x^3 - 3x^2 - 12x + 24$

    (A) $[-3, 4]$ (B) $[-2, 3]$ (C) $[-2, 1]$

13. $f(x) = (x - 1)(x - 5)^3 + 1$

    (A) $[0, 3]$ (B) $[1, 7]$ (C) $[3, 6]$

14. $f(x) = x^4 - 8x^2 + 16$

    (A) $[-1, 3]$ (B) $[0, 2]$ (C) $[-3, 4]$

Preliminary word problems:

C

15. How would you divide a 10 inch line so that the product of the two lengths is a maximum?

16. What quantity should be added to 5 and subtracted from 5 in order to produce the maximum product of the results?

17. Find two numbers whose difference is 30 and whose product is a minimum.

18. Find two positive numbers whose sum is 60 and whose product is a maximum.

19. Find the dimensions of a rectangle with perimeter 100 centimeters that has maximum area. Find the maximum area.

20. Find the dimensions of a rectangle of area 225 square centimeters that has the least perimeter. What is the perimeter?

Applications

Business & Economics

21. *Average costs.* If the average manufacturing cost (in dollars) per pair of sunglasses is given by

$$\overline{C}(x) = x^2 - 6x + 12 \qquad 0 \leqslant x \leqslant 6$$

where x is the number (in thousands) of pairs manufactured, how many pairs of glasses should be manufactured to minimize the average cost per pair? What is the minimum average cost per pair?

22. *Maximum revenue and profit.* A company manufactures and sells x television sets per month. The monthly cost and demand equations are

    $$C(x) = 72,000 + 60x$$

    $$p = 200 - \frac{x}{30} \qquad 0 \leqslant x \leqslant 6,000$$

    (A) Find the maximum revenue.

    (B) Find the maximum profit, the production level that will realize the maximum profit, and the price the company should charge for each television set.

    (C) If the government decides to tax the company $5 for each set it produces, how many sets should the company manufacture each month in order to maximize its profit? What is the maximum profit? What should the company charge for each set?

23. *Car rental.* A car rental agency rents 200 cars per day at a rate of $30 per day. For each $1 increase in rate, five fewer cars are rented. At what rate should the cars be rented to produce the maximum income? What is the maximum income?

24. *Rental income.* A 300 room hotel in Las Vegas is filled to capacity every night at $80 a room. For each $1 increase in rent, three fewer rooms are rented. If each rented room costs $10 to service per day, how much should the management charge for each room to maximize gross profit? What is the maximum gross profit?

25. *Agriculture.* A commercial cherry grower estimates from past records that if thirty trees are planted per acre, each tree will yield an average of 50 pounds of cherries per season. If for each additional tree planted per acre (up to twenty) the average yield per tree is reduced by 1 pound, how many trees should be planted per acre to obtain the maximum yield per acre? What is the maximum yield?

26. *Agriculture.* A commercial pear grower must decide on the optimum time to have fruit picked and sold. If the pears are picked now, they will bring 30¢ per pound, with each tree yielding an average of 60 pounds of salable pears. If the average yield per tree increases 6 pounds per tree per week for the next 4 weeks, but the price drops 2¢ per pound per week, when should the pears be picked to realize the maximum return per tree? What is the maximum return?

27. *Manufacturing.* A candy box is to be made out of a piece of cardboard that measures 8 by 12 inches. Squares of equal size will be cut out of each corner, and then the ends and sides will be folded up to form a rectangular box. What size square should be cut from each corner to obtain a maximum volume?

28. *Packaging.* A parcel delivery service will deliver a package only if the length plus girth (distance around) does not exceed 108 inches.

(A)   Find the dimensions of a rectangular box with square ends that satisfies the delivery service's restriction and has maximum volume. What is the maximum volume?

(B)   Find the dimensions (radius and height) of a cylindrical container that meets the delivery service's requirement and has maximum volume. What is the maximum volume?

29.   *Construction costs.* A fence is to be built to enclose a rectangular area of 800 square feet. The fence along three sides is to be made of material that costs $2 per foot. The material for the fourth side costs $6 per foot. Find the dimensions of the rectangle that will allow the most economical fence to be built.

30.   *Construction costs.* The owner of a retail lumber store wants to construct a fence to enclose an outdoor storage area adjacent to the store as indicated in the accompanying figure. Find the dimensions that will enclose the largest area if:

(A)   240 feet of fencing material is used.

(B)   400 feet of fencing material is used.

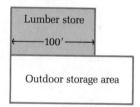

31.   *Inventory control.* A publishing company sells 50,000 copies of a certain book each year. It costs the company $1.00 to store a book for one year. Each time it must print additional copies, it costs the company $1,000 to set up the presses. How many books should the company produce during each printing in order to minimize its total storage and set-up costs?

32.   *Operational costs.* The cost per hour for fuel for running a train is $v^2/4$ dollars, where v is the speed in miles per hour. (Note that the cost goes up as the square of the speed.) Other costs, including labor, are $300 per hour. How fast should the train travel on a 360 mile trip to minimize the total cost for the trip?

33.   *Construction costs.* A freshwater pipeline is to be run from a source on the edge of a lake to a small resort community on an island 5 miles off-shore, as indicated in the figure at the top of the next page.

(A)   If it costs 1.4 times as much to lay the pipe in the lake as it does on land, what should x be (in miles) to minimize the total cost of the project?

(B)   If it costs only 1.1 times as much to lay the pipe in the lake as it does on land, what should x be to minimize the total cost of the project? [*Note:*   Compare with Problem 38.]

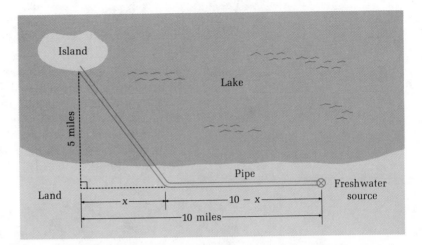

34. *Manufacturing costs.* A manufacturer wants to produce cans that will hold 12 ounces (approximately 22 cubic inches) in the form of a right circular cylinder. Find the dimensions (radius of an end and height) of the can that will use the smallest amount of material. Assume the circular ends are cut out of squares, with the corner portions wasted, and the sides are made from rectangles, with no waste.

Life Sciences

35. *Bacteria control.* A recreational swimming lake is treated periodically to control harmful bacteria growth. Suppose t days after a treatment, the concentration of bacteria per cubic centimeter is given by

$$C(t) = 30t^2 - 240t + 500 \qquad 0 \leqslant t \leqslant 8$$

How many days after a treatment will the concentration be minimal? What is the minimum concentration?

36. *Drug concentration.* The concentration $C(t)$ in milligrams per cubic centimeter of a particular drug in a patient's bloodstream is given by

$$C(t) = \frac{0.16t}{t^2 + 4t + 4}$$

where t is the number of hours after the drug is taken. How many hours after the drug is given will the concentration be maximum? What is the maximum concentration?

37. *Laboratory management.* A laboratory uses 500 white mice each year for experimental purposes. It costs $4.00 to feed a mouse for one year. Each time mice are ordered from a supplier, there is a service charge of $10 for processing the order. How many mice should be ordered each time in order to minimize the total cost of feeding the mice and of placing the orders for the mice?

38. *Bird flights.* Some birds tend to avoid flights over large bodies of water during daylight hours. It is speculated that more energy is required to fly over water than land because air generally rises over land and falls over water during the day. Suppose an adult bird with these tenden-

cies is taken from its nesting area on the edge of a large lake to an island 5 miles off-shore and is then released (see the accompanying figure).

(A)   If it takes 1.4 times as much energy to fly over water as land, how far up-shore (x, in miles) should the bird head in order to minimize the total energy expended in returning to the nesting area?

(B)   If it takes only 1.1 times as much energy to fly over water as land, how far up-shore should the bird head in order to minimize the total energy expended in returning to the nesting area? [*Note:* Compare with Problem 33.]

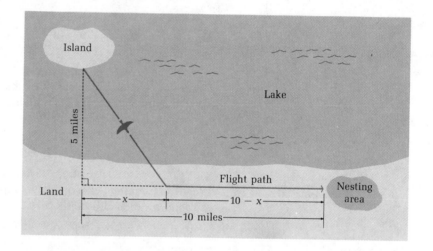

39.   *Botany.* If it is known from past experiments that the height in feet of a given plant after t months is given approximately by

$$H(t) = 4t^{1/2} - 2t \qquad 0 \leqslant t \leqslant 2$$

how long, on the average, will it take a plant to reach its maximum height? What is the maximum height?

40.   *Pollution.* Two heavy industrial areas are located 10 miles apart, as indicated in the figure at the top of the next page. If the concentration of particulate matter in parts per million decreases as the reciprocal of the square of the distance from the source, and area A_1 emits eight times the particulate matter as A_2, then the concentration of particulate matter at any point between the two areas is given by

$$C(x) = \frac{8k}{x^2} + \frac{k}{(10 - x)^2} \qquad 0.5 \leqslant x \leqslant 9.5, \quad k > 0$$

How far from A_1 will the concentration of particulate matter be at a minimum?

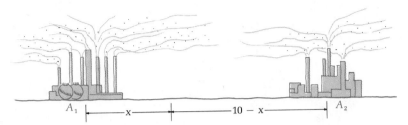

Social Sciences

41. *Politics.* In a newly incorporated city it is estimated that the voting population (in thousands) will increase according to

$$N(t) = 30 + 12t^2 - t^3 \qquad 0 \leqslant t \leqslant 8$$

where t is time in years. When will the rate of increase be most rapid?

42. *Learning.* A large grocery chain found that, on the average, a checker can memorize $P\%$ of a given price list in x continuous hours, as given approximately by

$$P(x) = 96x - 24x^2 \qquad 0 \leqslant x \leqslant 3$$

How long should a checker plan to take to memorize the maximum percentage? What is the maximum?

8-4 Curve Sketching Techniques: Unified and Extended

- Asymptotes
- Graphing Strategy
- Using the Strategy
- Application

In this section we will apply, in a systematic way, all the graphing concepts discussed in Sections 8-1 and 8-2. Before outlining a graphing strategy and considering the graphs of specific functions, we need to discuss one additional graphing concept, *asymptotes.*

■ Asymptotes

Horizontal and vertical asymptotes were introduced in Section 7-1. To review these concepts, consider the function f whose graph is shown in Figure 14 (on the next page). The lines $y = L$ and $y = M$ are horizontal asymptotes since $\lim_{x \to \infty} f(x) = L$ and $\lim_{x \to -\infty} f(x) = M$. The lines $x = a$ and $x = b$ are vertical asymptotes since the values of $f(x)$ become very large in absolute value for x near a and x near b.

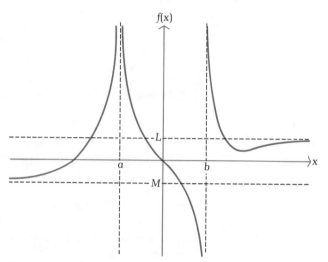

Figure 14

How can we find the asymptotes of a function before we draw its graph? Horizontal asymptotes are located by evaluating

$$\lim_{x \to \infty} f(x) \quad \text{and} \quad \lim_{x \to -\infty} f(x) \tag{1}$$

If f is a rational function (a ratio of polynomials), and either of the limits in (1) exists, then the other also exists and has the same value (see Theorem 3 in Section 7-1). Thus, **a rational function has at most one horizontal asymptote.** (Notice that this implies that the function graphed in Figure 14 is not a rational function, since it has two horizontal asymptotes.)

Theorem 3 provides a simple method for locating vertical asymptotes.

Theorem 3

> Let $f(x) = p(x)/q(x)$, where both $p(x)$ and $q(x)$ are continuous at $x = c$. If $q(c) = 0$ and $p(c) \neq 0$, then the line $x = c$ is a vertical asymptote for the graph of f.

Since polynomial functions are continuous for all values of x, Theorem 3 can be applied to any rational function. Thus, **a rational function has vertical asymptotes at all values of x where the denominator equals 0, provided that the numerator is nonzero at that value of x.**

The next example shows how Theorem 3 and the limit techniques discussed in Section 7-1 can be used to locate asymptotes. Later in this section, we will discuss graphing techniques for functions with asymptotes.

Example 15   Find horizontal and vertical asymptotes for:

(A) $f(x) = \dfrac{6x + 5}{2x - 4}$

(B) $f(x) = \dfrac{x}{x^2 + 1}$

(C) $f(x) = \dfrac{x^2 - 4}{x}$

Solutions   (A) $\displaystyle\lim_{x \to \infty} \dfrac{6x + 5}{2x - 4} = \dfrac{6}{2} = 3$ Theorem 3 in Section 7-1

Thus, the line $y = 3$ is a horizontal asymptote. Now let $q(x) = 2x - 4$ and $p(x) = 6x + 5$. Since $q(2) = 0$ and $p(2) = 17 \neq 0$, Theorem 3 (on the facing page) implies that the line $x = 2$ is a vertical asymptote.

(B) $\displaystyle\lim_{x \to \infty} \dfrac{x}{x^2 + 1} = 0$ Theorem 3 in Section 7-1

Thus, the line $y = 0$ (the x axis) is a horizontal asymptote. Since the denominator is never 0, there are no vertical asymptotes.

(C) $\displaystyle\lim_{x \to \infty} \dfrac{x^2 - 4}{x}$ does not exist   Theorem 3 in Section 7-1

Thus, there is no horizontal asymptote. Let $q(x) = x$ and $p(x) = x^2 - 4$. Since $q(0) = 0$ and $p(0) = -4 \neq 0$, the line $x = 0$ (the y axis) is a vertical asymptote.

Problem 15   Find horizontal and vertical asymptotes for:

(A) $f(x) = \dfrac{3x + 5}{x + 2}$

(B) $f(x) = \dfrac{x + 1}{x^2}$

(C) $f(x) = \dfrac{x^3}{x^2 + 4}$

■ Graphing Strategy

We now have powerful tools to determine the shape of a graph of a function, even before we plot any points. We can accurately sketch the graphs of many functions using these tools and point-by-point plotting as necessary (often, very little point-by-point plotting is necessary). We organize these tools in the graphing strategy summarized in the box on the next page.

A Graphing Strategy

[*Omit any of the following steps if procedures involved are too difficult or impossible (what may seem too difficult now, with a little practice, will become less so).*]

Step 1. Use the first derivative. Construct a sign chart for $f'(x)$, determine the intervals where $f(x)$ is increasing and decreasing, and find local maxima and minima.

Step 2. Use the second derivative. Construct a sign chart for $f''(x)$, determine the intervals where the graph of f is concave upward and downward, and find any inflection points.

Step 3. Find horizontal and vertical asymptotes. Find any horizontal asymptotes by calculating $\lim_{x \to \pm\infty} f(x)$. Find any vertical asymptotes by using Theorem 3.

Step 4. Find intercepts. Find the y intercept by evaluating $f(0)$, if it exists. Find x intercepts by solving the equation $f(x) = 0$ for x, if possible. This equation may be too difficult to solve and the x intercepts are omitted.

Step 5. Sketch the graph of f. Draw asymptotes and locate intercepts, local maxima and minima, and inflection points. Sketch in what you know from steps 1–4. Use point-by-point plotting to complete the graph in regions of uncertainty.

■ Using the Strategy

Several examples will illustrate the use of the graphing strategy.

Example 16   Graph $f(x) = x^4 - 2x^3 + 2$ using the graphing strategy.

Solution   Step 1. Use the first derivative:

$$f'(x) = 4x^3 - 6x^2 = 4x^2(x - \tfrac{3}{2})$$

Sign chart for $f'(x) = 4x^2(x - \tfrac{3}{2})$:

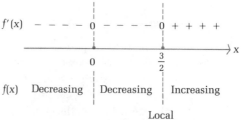

Test Numbers

x	$f'(x)$
-1	$-10 \ (-)$
1	$-2 \ (-)$
2	$8 \ (+)$

Thus, $f(x)$ is decreasing on $(-\infty, \frac{3}{2})$, increasing on $(\frac{3}{2}, \infty)$, and has a local minimum at $x = \frac{3}{2}$.

Step 2. Use the second derivative:

$$f''(x) = 12x^2 - 12x = 12x(x-1)$$

Sign chart for $f''(x) = 12x(x-1)$:

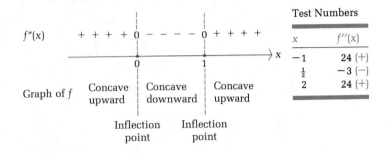

x	f''(x)
−1	24 (+)
$\frac{1}{2}$	−3 (−)
2	24 (+)

Thus, the graph of f is concave upward on $(-\infty, 0)$ and $(1, \infty)$, concave downward on $(0, 1)$, and has inflection points at $x = 0$ and $x = 1$.

Step 3. Find horizontal and vertical asymptotes. Since $f(x)$ is a polynomial, there are no asymptotes.

Step 4. Find intercepts. The y intercept is $f(0) = 2$. Since the equation $f(x) = 0$ cannot be solved easily, we do not try to find x intercepts.

Step 5. Sketch the graph of f:

x	f(x)
0	2
1	1
$\frac{3}{2}$	$\frac{5}{16}$

Problem 16   Graph $f(x) = x^4 + 4x^3 + 10$ using the graphing strategy.

Example 17   Graph

$$f(x) = \frac{x-1}{x-2}$$

using the graphing strategy.

Solution   **Step 1.**   Use the first derivative:

$$f'(x) = \frac{(x-2)(1) - (x-1)(1)}{(x-2)^2} = \frac{-1}{(x-2)^2}$$

Sign chart for $f'(x) = -1/(x-2)^2$:

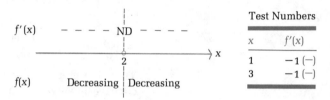

	Test Numbers
x	$f'(x)$
1	$-1\,(-)$
3	$-1\,(-)$

Thus, $f(x)$ is decreasing on $(-\infty, 2)$ and $(2, \infty)$. There are no local extrema.

Step 2.   Use the second derivative:

$$f''(x) = \frac{2}{(x-2)^3}$$

Sign chart for $f''(x) = 2/(x-2)^3$:

	Test Numbers
x	$f''(x)$
1	$-2(-)$
3	$2(+)$

Thus, the graph of f is concave downward on $(-\infty, 2)$ and concave upward on $(2, \infty)$. Since $f(2)$ is not defined, there is no inflection point at $x = 2$, even though $f''(x)$ changes sign at $x = 2$.

Step 3.   Find horizontal and vertical asymptotes:

$$\lim_{x \to \infty} \frac{x-1}{x-2} = \frac{1}{1} = 1$$

Thus, $y = 1$ is a horizontal asymptote. Let $p(x) = x - 1$ and $q(x) = x - 2$. Since $q(2) = 0$ and $p(2) = 1 \neq 0$, $x = 2$ is a vertical asymptote.

Step 4. Find intercepts. The y intercept is

$$y = f(0) = \frac{0 - 1}{0 - 2} = \frac{1}{2}$$

Since a fraction is 0 when its numerator is 0, the x intercept is $x = 1$.

Step 5. Sketch the graph of f. Draw the asymptotes and plot points. (For functions with asymptotes, plotting additional points is often helpful.) Then sketch the graph.

x	$f(x)$
-2	$\frac{3}{4}$
0	$\frac{1}{2}$
1	0
$\frac{3}{2}$	-1
$\frac{5}{2}$	3
3	2
4	$\frac{3}{2}$

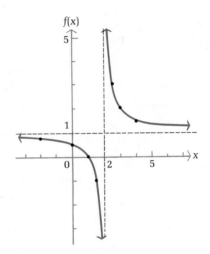

Problem 17 Graph

$$f(x) = \frac{2x}{1 - x}$$

using the graphing strategy.

▪ Application

Example 18
Average Cost

Given the cost function $C(x) = 5{,}000 + \frac{1}{2}x^2$, where x is the number of units produced, graph the average cost function and the marginal cost function on the same set of coordinate axes.

Solution Let

$$\overline{C}(x) = \frac{C(x)}{x} = \frac{5{,}000}{x} + \frac{1}{2}x \qquad x > 0$$

and use the graphing strategy.

Step 1. Use the first derivative:

$$\overline{C}'(x) = -\frac{5,000}{x^2} + \frac{1}{2} = \frac{x^2 - 10,000}{2x^2}$$

Sign chart for $\overline{C}'(x) = (x^2 - 10,000)/(2x^2)$:

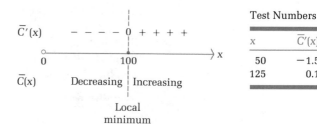

Thus, $\overline{C}(x)$ is decreasing on (0, 100), increasing on (100, ∞), and has a local minimum at $x = 100$.

Step 2. Use the second derivative:

$$\overline{C}''(x) = \frac{10,000}{x^3} > 0 \qquad x > 0$$

Thus, the graph of $\overline{C}(x)$ is concave upward on (0, ∞).

Step 3. Find horizontal and vertical asymptotes. To determine asymptotes, we first write $\overline{C}(x)$ as a single fraction:

$$\overline{C}(x) = \frac{5,000}{x} + \frac{1}{2}x = \frac{10,000 + x^2}{2x}$$

Let $q(x) = 2x$ and $p(x) = 10,000 + x^2$. Since $q(0) = 0$ and $p(0) = 10,000 \neq 0$, $x = 0$ is a vertical asymptote.

$$\lim_{x \to \infty} \frac{10,000 + x^2}{2x} \qquad \text{does not exist} \qquad \text{Theorem 3, Section 7-1}$$

Thus, there is no horizontal asymptote. However, consider the following limit:

$$\lim_{x \to \infty} \left[\overline{C}(x) - \frac{1}{2}x \right] = \lim_{x \to \infty} \frac{5,000}{x} = 0$$

This implies that the graph of $\overline{C}(x)$ approaches the line $y = \frac{1}{2}x$ as x approaches ∞. This line is called an **oblique asymptote** for the graph of $\overline{C}(x)$.

Step 4. Find intercepts. Since $x > 0$, there is no y intercept. Since $p(x)$ is never 0, there are no x intercepts.

Step 5. Sketch the graph of $\overline{C}$. The graph of $\overline{C}$ is shown in the figure. The marginal cost function is $C'(x) = x$. The graph of this linear function is also shown in the figure. This graph illustrates an important principle in economics: The minimal average cost occurs when the average cost is equal to the marginal cost.

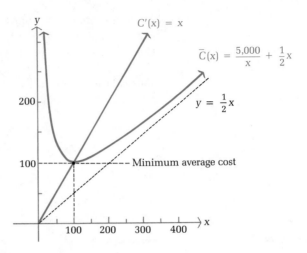

Problem 18 Given the cost function $C(x) = 1,600 + \frac{1}{4}x^2$:

(A) Find the minimum average cost.

(B) Find the marginal cost function.

(C) Graph the average cost function and the marginal cost function on the same axes. Include any oblique asymptotes.

Answers to 15. (A) Horizontal asymptote: $y = 3$; vertical asymptote: $x = -2$
Matched Problems   (B) Horizontal asymptote: $y = 0$ (x axis); vertical asymptote: $x = 0$ (y axis)
                           (C) No horizontal asymptote; no vertical asymptotes

16. Increasing on $(-3, \infty)$
     Decreasing on $(-\infty, -3)$
     Local minimum at $x = -3$
     Concave upward on $(-\infty, -2)$ and $(0, \infty)$
     Concave downward on $(-2, 0)$
     Inflection points at $x = -2$ and $x = 0$
     y intercept: $f(0) = 10$

x	$f(x)$
-3	-17
-2	-6
0	10

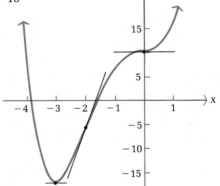

17. Increasing on $(-\infty, 1)$ and $(1, \infty)$
Concave upward on $(-\infty, 1)$
Concave downward on $(1, \infty)$
Horizontal asymptote: $y = -2$
Vertical asymptote: $x = 1$
x (and y) intercept: $f(0) = 0$

x	$f(x)$
-1	-1
0	0
$\frac{1}{2}$	2
$\frac{3}{2}$	-6
2	-4
5	$-\frac{5}{2}$

18. (A) Minimal average cost is 40 at $x = 80$

(B) $C'(x) = \frac{1}{2}x$

(C)

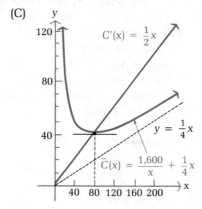

Exercise 8-4

A   Problems 1–10 refer to the following graph of $y = f(x)$:

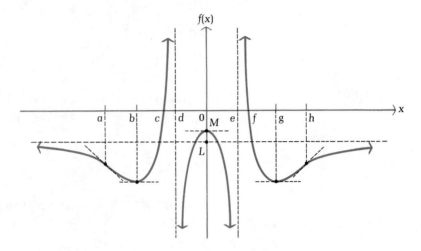

1. Identify the intervals over which $f(x)$ is increasing.
2. Identify the intervals over which $f(x)$ is decreasing.
3. Identify the points where $f(x)$ has a local maximum.
4. Identify the points where $f(x)$ has a local minimum.
5. Identify the intervals over which the graph of f is concave upward.
6. Identify the intervals over which the graph of f is concave downward.
7. Identify the inflection points.
8. Identify the horizontal asymptotes.
9. Identify the vertical asymptotes.
10. Identify the x and y intercepts.

B   Find the horizontal and vertical asymptotes.

11. $f(x) = \dfrac{2x}{x + 2}$

12. $f(x) = \dfrac{3x + 2}{x - 4}$

13. $f(x) = \dfrac{x^2 + 1}{x^2 - 1}$

14. $f(x) = \dfrac{x^2 - 1}{x^2 + 2}$

15. $f(x) = \dfrac{x^3}{x^2 + 6}$

16. $f(x) = \dfrac{x}{x^2 - 4}$

17. $f(x) = \dfrac{x}{x^2 + 4}$

18. $f(x) = \dfrac{x^2 + 9}{x}$

19. $f(x) = \dfrac{x^2}{x - 3}$

20. $f(x) = \dfrac{x + 5}{x^2}$

Sketch a graph of y = f(x) using the graphing strategy.

21. $f(x) = x^2 - 6x + 5$

22. $f(x) = 3 + 2x - x^2$

23. $f(x) = x^3 - 6x^2$

24. $f(x) = 3x^2 - x^3$

25. $f(x) = (x + 4)(x - 2)^2$

26. $f(x) = (2 - x)(x + 1)^2$

27. $f(x) = 8x^3 - 2x^4$

28. $f(x) = x^4 - 4x^3$

29. $f(x) = \dfrac{x + 3}{x - 3}$

30. $f(x) = \dfrac{2x - 4}{x + 2}$

31. $f(x) = \dfrac{x}{x - 2}$

32. $f(x) = \dfrac{2 + x}{3 - x}$

C   In Problems 33 and 34, show that the line $y = x$ is an oblique asymptote for the graph of $y = f(x)$ and then use the graphing strategy to sketch a graph of $y = f(x)$.

33. $f(x) = x + \dfrac{1}{x}$

34. $f(x) = x - \dfrac{1}{x}$

Sketch a graph of y = f(x) using the graphing strategy.

35. $f(x) = x^3 - x$

36. $f(x) = x^3 + x$

37. $f(x) = (x^2 + 3)(9 - x^2)$

38. $f(x) = (x^2 + 3)(x^2 - 1)$

39. $f(x) = (x^2 - 4)^2$

40. $f(x) = (x^2 - 1)(x^2 - 5)$

41. $f(x) = 2x^6 - 3x^5$

42. $f(x) = 3x^5 - 5x^4$

43. $f(x) = \dfrac{x}{x^2 - 4}$

44. $f(x) = \dfrac{1}{x^2 - 4}$

45. $f(x) = \dfrac{1}{1 + x^2}$

46. $f(x) = \dfrac{x^2}{1 + x^2}$

◼

Applications

Business & Economics

47. *Revenue.* The marketing research department for a computer company used a large city to test market their new product. They found that a relationship between price p (dollars per unit) and the demand x (units per week) was given approximately by

$$p = 1{,}296 - 0.12x^2 \qquad 0 < x < 80$$

Thus, the weekly revenue can be approximated by

$$R(x) = xp = 1{,}296x - 0.12x^3 \qquad 0 < x < 80$$

Graph the revenue function R.

48. *Profit.* If the cost equation for the company in the preceding problem is

$$C(x) = 830 + 396x$$

(A) Write an equation for the profit $P(x)$.

(B) Graph the profit function P.

49. *Pollution.* In Silicon Valley (California), a number of computer related manufacturing firms were found to be contaminating underground water supplies with toxic chemicals stored in leaking underground containers. A water quality control agency ordered the companies to take immediate corrective action and to contribute to a monetary pool for testing and cleanup of the underground contamination. Suppose the required monetary pool (in millions of dollars) for the testing and cleanup is estimated to be given by

$$P(x) = \frac{2x}{1 - x} \qquad 0 \leq x < 1$$

where x is the percentage (expressed as a decimal fraction) of the total contaminant removed.

(A) Where is $P(x)$ increasing? Decreasing?

(B) Where is the graph of P concave upward? Downward?

(C) Find the horizontal and vertical asymptotes.

(D) Find the x and y intercepts.

(E) Sketch a graph of P.

50. *Employee training.* A company producing computer components has established that on the average a new employee can assemble $N(t)$ components per day after t days of on-the-job training, as given by

$$N(t) = \frac{100t}{t + 9} \qquad t \geq 0$$

(A) Where is $N(t)$ increasing? Decreasing?

(B) Where is the graph of N concave upward? Downward?

(C) Find the horizontal and vertical asymptotes.

(D) Find the intercepts.

(E) Sketch a graph of N.

51. *Replacement time.* An office copier has an initial price of $3,200. A maintenance/service contract costs $300 for the first year and increases $100 per year thereafter. It can be shown that the total cost of the copier after n years is given by

$$C(n) = 3{,}200 + 250n + 50n^2$$

(A) Write an expression for the average cost per year, $\overline{C}(n)$, for n years.

(B) When is the average cost per year minimum? (This is frequently referred to as the **replacement time** for this piece of equipment.)

(C) Graph the average cost function found in part A.

52. *Construction costs.* The management of a manufacturing plant wishes to add a fenced-in rectangular storage yard of 20,000 square feet, using the plant building as one side of the yard. If x is the distance from the building to the fence parallel to the building, then show that the length of the fence required for the yard is given by

$$L(x) = 2x + \frac{20{,}000}{x} \qquad x > 0$$

(A) What are the dimensions of the rectangle requiring the least amount of fencing?

(B) Graph L.

53. *Average and marginal costs.* The cost of producing x units of a certain product is given by

$$C(x) = 1{,}000 + 5x + \tfrac{1}{10}x^2$$

(A) Find the minimum average cost.

(B) Sketch the graph of the average cost function and the marginal cost function on the same set of coordinate axes. Include any oblique asymptotes.

54. Repeat Problem 53 for $C(x) = 500 + 2x + \tfrac{1}{5}x^2$.

Life Sciences

55. *Medicine.* A drug is injected into the bloodstream of a patient through her right arm. The concentration of the drug in the bloodstream of the left arm *t* hours after the injection is given by

$$C(t) = \frac{0.14t}{t^2 + 1}$$

Graph C.

56. *Physiology.* In a study on the speed of muscle contraction in frogs under various loads, researchers W. O. Fems and J. Marsh found that the speed of contraction decreases with increasing loads. More precisely, they found that the relationship between speed of contraction S (in centimeters per second) and load w (in grams) is given approximately by

$$S(w) = \frac{26 + 0.06w}{w} \qquad w \geqslant 5$$

Graph S.

Social Sciences

57. *Psychology — retention.* An experiment on retention is conducted in a psychology class. Each student in the class is given one day to memorize the same list of thirty special characters. The lists are turned in at the end of the day, and for each succeeding day for thirty days each student is asked to turn in a list of as many of the symbols as can be recalled. Averages are taken and it is found that

$$N(t) = \frac{5t + 20}{t} \qquad t \geq 1$$

provides a good approximation of the average number of symbols, $N(t)$, retained after t days. Graph N.

8-5 Differentials

- The Differential
- Approximations Using Differentials
- Applications

■ The Differential

In Chapter 7 we introduced the concept of increment. Recall that for a function defined by

$$y = f(x)$$

we said that Δx represents a change in the independent variable x; that is,

$$\Delta x = x_2 - x_1 \qquad \text{or} \qquad x_2 = x_1 + \Delta x$$

And Δy represents the corresponding change in the dependent variable y; that is,

$$\Delta y = f(x_1 + \Delta x) - f(x_1)$$

We then defined the derivative of f at x_1 to be

$$\frac{dy}{dx} = \lim_{\Delta x \to 0} \frac{\Delta y}{\Delta x}$$

If the limit exists, then it follows that

$$\frac{\Delta y}{\Delta x} \approx \frac{dy}{dx} \quad \text{for small } \Delta x$$

or

$$\Delta y \approx \frac{dy}{dx} \Delta x \tag{1}$$

We used dy/dx as an alternate symbol for $f'(x)$. We will now give dy and dx special meaning, and we will show how dy can be used to approximate Δy. This turns out to be quite useful, since a number of practical problems require the computation of Δy, and we will be able to use the more readily computed dy. The symbols dy and dx are called **differentials** and are defined in the box on the next page.

> **Differentials**
>
> If $y = f(x)$ defines a differentiable function, then:
>
> 1. The **differential dx** of the independent variable x is an arbitrary real number.
> 2. The **differential dy** of the dependent variable y is defined as the product of $f'(x)$ and dx; that is,
>
> $$dy = f'(x)\, dx \tag{2}$$
>
> The differential dy is actually a function involving two independent variables, x and dx—a change in either one or both will affect dy.

Example 19   Find dy for $f(x) = x^2 + 3x$. Evaluate dy for $x = 2$ and $dx = 0.1$, for $x = 3$ and $dx = 0.1$, and for $x = 1$ and $dx = 0.02$.

Solution $dy = f'(x)\, dx$

$\qquad = (2x + 3)\, dx$

When $x = 2$ and $dx = 0.1$,

$\quad dy = [2(2) + 3]0.1 = 0.7$

When $x = 3$ and $dx = 0.1$,

$\quad dy = [2(3) + 3]0.1 = 0.9$

When $x = 1$ and $dx = 0.02$,

$\quad dy = [2(1) + 3]0.02 = 0.1$

Problem 19   Find dy for $f(x) = \sqrt{x} + 3$. Evaluate dy for $x = 4$ and $dx = 0.1$, for $x = 9$ and $dx = 0.12$, and for $x = 1$ and $dx = 0.01$.

We now have two interpretations of the symbol dy/dx. Referring to the function $y = f(x) = x^2 + 3x$ in Example 19 with $x = 2$ and $dx = 0.1$, we have

$$\frac{dy}{dx} = f'(2) = 7 \qquad \text{Derivative}$$

and

$$\frac{dy}{dx} = \frac{0.7}{0.1} = 7 \qquad \text{Ratio of differentials}$$

Since differentials are defined in terms of derivatives, the derivative rules discussed in Chapter 7 lead to the differential rules in the box.

> **Differential Rules**
>
> If u and v are differentiable functions and c is a constant, then:
>
> 1. $dc = 0$
> 2. $du^n = nu^{n-1} du$
> 3. $d(u \pm v) = du \pm dv$
> 4. $d(uv) = u\, dv + v\, du$
> 5. $d\left(\dfrac{u}{v}\right) = \dfrac{v\, du - u\, dv}{v^2}$

Example 20   (A) Find dy for $y = \dfrac{x^2}{4 + x^2}$.   (B) Find du for $u = (7 + x^3)^5$.

Solutions   (A) $dy = \dfrac{(4 + x^2)\, d(x^2) - x^2\, d(4 + x^2)}{(4 + x^2)^2}$

$$= \dfrac{(4 + x^2)2x\, dx - x^2 2x\, dx}{(4 + x^2)^2}$$

$$= \dfrac{8x\, dx}{(4 + x^2)^2}$$

(B) $du = 5(7 + x^3)^4\, d(7 + x^3)$

$$= 5(7 + x^3)^4 3x^2\, dx$$

$$= 15x^2(7 + x^3)^4\, dx$$

Problem 20   (A) Find dy for $y = x^2(2x - 5)^3$.   (B) Find du for $u = \dfrac{1}{4x + x^2}$.

■ Approximations Using Differentials

The differential of a function $y = f(x)$ can be used to approximate the change in y and the values of $f(x)$. If we let $dx = \Delta x$, then from (1) and (2) we have

$$\Delta y \approx \frac{dy}{dx}\, \Delta x = f'(x)\, dx = dy$$

Thus, dy can be used to approximate Δy. To interpret this result geometrically, we need to recall a basic property of slope. The vertical change in a line is equal to the product of the slope and the horizontal change, as shown in Figure 15 (on the next page).

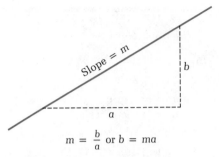

$$m = \frac{b}{a} \text{ or } b = ma$$

Figure 15

Now consider the line tangent to the graph of $y = f(x)$, as shown in Figure 16. Since $f'(x)$ is the slope of the tangent line and dx is the horizontal change in the tangent line, it follows that the vertical change in the tangent line is given by $dy = f'(x)\, dx$, as indicated in Figure 16.

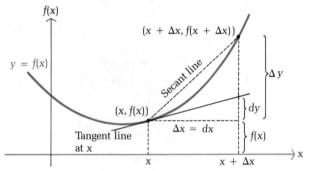

Figure 16

To see how differentials can be used to approximate the values of a function, we write

$$\Delta y \approx dy$$
$$f(x + \Delta x) - f(x) \approx f'(x)\, dx$$
$$f(x + \Delta x) \approx f(x) + f'(x)\, dx$$

These relationships are summarized in the following box.

Differential Approximation

If $f'(x)$ exists and $dx = \Delta x$, then for small Δx

$$\Delta y \approx dy$$

and

$$f(x + \Delta x) \approx f(x) + f'(x)\, dx$$

We will use these relationships in the examples that follow. (Before proceeding, however, it should be mentioned that even though differentials can be used to approximate certain quantities, the error can be substantial in certain cases.)

Example 21   Find Δy and dy for $f(x) = 6x - x^2$ when $x = 2$ and $\Delta x = dx = 0.1$.

Solution
$$\Delta y = f(x + \Delta x) - f(x)$$
$$= f(2.1) - f(2)$$
$$= [6(2.1) - (2.1)^2] - [6(2) - 2^2]$$
$$= 8.19 - 8$$
$$= 0.19$$

$$dy = f'(x)\, dx$$
$$= (6 - 2x)\, dx$$
$$= [6 - 2(2)](0.1)$$
$$= 0.2$$

Notice that dy and Δy differ by only 0.01 in this case.

Problem 21   Repeat Example 21 for $x = 4$ and $\Delta x = dx = 0.2$.

Example 22   Use differentials to approximate $\sqrt[3]{27.54}$.

Solution   Even though the problem is trivial using a hand calculator, its solution using differentials will help increase the understanding of this concept. Form the function

$$y = f(x) = \sqrt[3]{x} = x^{1/3}$$

and note that we can compute $f(27)$ and $f'(27)$ exactly. Thus, if we let $x = 27$ and $dx = \Delta x = 0.54$ and use

$$f(x + \Delta x) = f(x) + \Delta y$$
$$\approx f(x) + dy$$
$$= f(x) + f'(x)\, dx$$

we will obtain an approximation for $f(27.54) = \sqrt[3]{27.54}$ that is easy to compute.

$$f(x + \Delta x) \approx f(x) + f'(x)\, dx$$

$$(x + \Delta x)^{1/3} \approx x^{1/3} + \frac{1}{3x^{2/3}}\, dx$$

$$(27 + 0.54)^{1/3} \approx 27^{1/3} + \frac{1}{3(27)^{2/3}}\,(0.54)$$

Thus,

$$\sqrt[3]{27.54} \approx 3 + \frac{0.54}{27} = 3.02 \qquad \text{(Calculator value} = 3.0199)$$

Problem 22   Use differentials to approximate $\sqrt{36.72}$.

▪ Applications

Example 23
Weight–Height

A formula relating the approximate weight, W (in pounds), of an average person and their height, h (in inches), is

$$W = 0.0005h^3 \qquad 30 \leqslant h \leqslant 74$$

What is the approximate change in weight for a height increase from 40 to 42 inches?

Solution

We are actually interested in finding ΔW, the change in weight brought about by the change in height from 40 to 42 inches ($\Delta h = 2$). We will use the differential dW to approximate ΔW, since Δh is small. The problem is now to find dW for $h = 40$ and $dh = \Delta h = 2$.

$$W(h) = 0.0005h^3$$

$$\begin{aligned} dW &= W'(h)\, dh \\ &= 0.0015h^2\, dh \\ &= 0.0015(40)^2(2) \\ &= 4.8 \text{ pounds} \end{aligned}$$

Thus, a child growing from 40 inches to 42 inches would expect to increase in weight by approximately 4.8 pounds. Notice that using the differential is somewhat easier than finding $\Delta W = W(42) - W(40)$.

Problem 23   Refer to Example 23. Approximate the change in weight resulting from a height increase from 70 to 72 inches.

Example 24
Cost–Revenue

A company manufactures and sells x transistor radios per week. If the weekly cost and revenue equations are

$$C(x) = 5,000 + 2x$$
$$R(x) = 10x - \frac{x^2}{1,000} \qquad 0 \leqslant x \leqslant 8,000$$

find the approximate changes in revenue and profit if production is increased from 2,000 to 2,010 units per week.

Solution

We will approximate ΔR and ΔP with dR and dP, respectively, using $x = 2,000$ and $dx = \Delta x = 2,010 - 2,000 = 10$.

$$R(x) = 10x - \frac{x^2}{1,000}$$

$$dR = R'(x)\, dx$$

$$= \left(10 - \frac{x}{500}\right) dx$$

$$= \left(10 - \frac{2,000}{500}\right) 10$$

$$= \$60 \text{ per week}$$

$$P(x) = R(x) - C(x)$$

$$= 10x - \frac{x^2}{1,000} - 5,000 - 2x$$

$$= 8x - \frac{x^2}{1,000} - 5,000$$

$$dP = P'(x)\, dx$$

$$= \left(8 - \frac{x}{500}\right) dx$$

$$= \left(8 - \frac{2,000}{500}\right) 10$$

$$= \$40 \text{ per week}$$

Problem 24 Repeat Example 24 with production increasing from 6,000 to 6,010.

Comparing the results in Example 24 and Problem 24, we see that an increase in production results in a revenue and profit increase at the 2,000 production level, but a revenue and profit loss at the 6,000 production level.

Answers to Matched Problems

19. $dy = \dfrac{1}{2\sqrt{x}}\, dx$; 0.025, 0.02, 0.005

20. (A) $dy = 2x(2x - 5)^3\, dx + 6x^2(2x - 5)^2\, dx$

(B) $du = -\dfrac{(4 + 2x)\, dx}{(4x + x^2)^2}$

21. $\Delta y = -0.44$, $dy = -0.4$ 22. 6.06   23. 14.7 pounds
24. $dR = -\$20$ per week, $dP = -\$40$ per week

Exercise 8-5

A   Find dy for each function.

1. $y = 30 + 12x^2 - x^3$

2. $y = 200x - \dfrac{x^2}{30}$

3. $y = x^2 \left(1 - \dfrac{x}{9}\right)$

4. $y = x^3(60 - x)$

5. $y = f(x) = \dfrac{590}{\sqrt{x}}$

6. $y = 52\sqrt{x}$

7. $y = 75 \left(1 - \dfrac{2}{x}\right)$

8. $y = 100 \left(x - \dfrac{4}{x^2}\right)$

B   9. $y = (2x + 1)^3$

10. $y = (3x + 5)^5$

11. $y = \dfrac{x}{x^2 + 9}$

12. $y = \dfrac{x^2}{(x + 1)^2}$

Evaluate dy and Δy for each function at the indicated values.

13. $y = f(x) = x^2 - 3x + 2$, $x = 5$, $\Delta x = dx = 0.2$
14. $y = f(x) = 30 + 12x^2 - x^3$, $x = 2$, $\Delta x = dx = 0.1$

15. $y = f(x) = 75 \left(1 - \dfrac{2}{x}\right)$, $x = 5$, $dx = \Delta x = 0.5$

16. $y = f(x) = 100 \left(x - \dfrac{4}{x^2}\right)$, $x = 2$, $\Delta x = dx = 0.1$

Use differentials to approximate the indicated roots.

17. $\sqrt[4]{17}$

18. $\sqrt{83}$

19. $\sqrt[3]{28}$

20. $\sqrt[5]{34}$

21. A cube with sides 10 inches long is covered with a 0.2 inch thick coat of fiberglass. Use differentials to estimate the volume of the fiberglass shell.

22. A sphere with a radius of 5 centimeters is coated with ice 0.1 centimeter thick. Use differentials to estimate the volume of the ice [recall that $V = \frac{4}{3}\pi r^3$, $\pi \approx 3.14$].

C   23. Find dy if $y = \sqrt[3]{3x^2 - 2x + 1}$.
24. Find dy if $y = (2x^2 - 4)\sqrt{x + 2}$.
25. Find dy and Δy for $y = 52\sqrt{x}$, $x = 4$, and $\Delta x = dx = 0.3$.
26. Find dy and Δy for $y = 590/\sqrt{x}$, $x = 64$, and $\Delta x = dx = 1$.

Applications

Use differential approximations in the following problems.

Business & Economics   27. *Advertising.* Using past records, it is estimated that a company will sell N units of a product after spending x thousand dollars in advertising, as given by

$$N = 60x - x^2 \qquad 5 \leqslant x \leqslant 30$$

Approximately what increase in sales will result by increasing the advertising budget from \$10,000 to \$11,000? From \$20,000 to \$21,000?

28. *Price–demand.* Suppose in a grocery chain the daily demand in pounds for chocolate candy at $x per pound is given by

$$D = 1,000 - 40x^2 \qquad 1 \le x \le 5$$

If the price is increased from $3.00 per pound to $3.20 per pound, what is the approximate change in demand?

29. *Average cost.* For a company that manufactures tennis rackets, the average cost per racket, $\overline{C}$, is found to be

$$\overline{C} = x^2 - 20x + 110 \qquad 6 \le x \le 14$$

where x is the number of rackets produced per hour. What will the approximate change in cost per racket be if production is increased from seven per hour to eight per hour? From twelve per hour to thirteen per hour?

30. *Revenue and profit.* A company manufactures and sells x televisions per month. If the cost and revenue equations are

$$C(x) = 72,000 + 60x$$
$$R(x) = 200x - \frac{x^2}{30} \qquad 0 \le x \le 6,000$$

what will the approximate changes in revenue and profit be if production is increased from 1,500 to 1,501? From 4,500 to 4,501?

Life Sciences

31. *Pulse rate.* The average pulse rate y in beats per minute of a healthy person x inches tall is given approximately by

$$y = \frac{590}{\sqrt{x}} \qquad 30 \le x \le 75$$

Approximately how will the pulse rate change for a height change from 36 to 37 inches? From 64 to 65 inches?

32. *Measurement.* An egg of a particular bird is very nearly spherical. If the radius to the inside of the shell is 5 millimeters and the radius to the outside of the shell is 5.3 millimeters, approximately what is the volume of the shell? [Remember that $V = \frac{4}{3}\pi r^3$ and use $\pi \approx 3.14$.]

33. *Medicine.* A drug is given to a patient to dilate her arteries. If the radius of an artery is increased from 2 to 2.1 millimeters, approximately how much is a cross-sectional area increased? (Assume the cross-section of the artery is circular; $A = \pi r^2$ and $\pi \approx 3.14$.)

34. *Drug sensitivity.* One hour after x milligrams of a particular drug are given to a person, the change in body temperature T in degrees Fahrenheit is given by

$$T = x^2 \left(1 - \frac{x}{9}\right) \qquad 0 \le x \le 6$$

Approximate the changes in body temperature produced by the following changes in drug dosages:

(A)   From 2 to 2.1 milligrams
(B)   From 3 to 3.1 milligrams
(C)   From 4 to 4.1 milligrams

Social Sciences

35. *Learning.* A particular person learning to type has an achievement record given approximately by

$$N = 75\left(1 - \frac{2}{t}\right) \qquad 3 \leqslant t \leqslant 20$$

where N is the number of words per minute typed after t weeks of practice. What is the approximate improvement from 5 to 5.5 weeks of practice?

36. *Learning.* If a person learns y items in x hours, as given approximately by

$$y = 52\sqrt{x} \qquad 0 \leqslant x \leqslant 9$$

what is the approximate increase in the number of items learned when x changes from 1 to 1.1 hours? From 4 to 4.1 hours?

37. *Politics.* In a newly incorporated city it is estimated that the voting population (in thousands) will increase according to

$$N(t) = 30 + 12t^2 - t^3 \qquad 0 \leqslant t \leqslant 8$$

where t is time in years. Find the approximate change in votes for the following time changes:

(A)   From 1 to 1.1 years
(B)   From 4 to 4.1 years
(C)   From 7 to 7.1 years

8-6   Chapter Review

Important Terms and Symbols

8-1   *First derivative and graphs.* Increasing function, decreasing function, rising, falling, critical value, local extrema, local maximum, local minimum, first-derivative test for local extrema

8-2   *Second derivative and graphs.* Concave upward, concave downward, second derivative, concavity and the second derivative, inflection point, second-derivative test for local maxima and minima, $f''(x)$, d^2y/dx^2, y'', $D_x^2 f(x)$

8-3   *Optimization; absolute maxima and minima.* Absolute maxima, absolute minima, absolute extrema of a function continuous on a closed interval, second-derivative test for absolute maximum and minimum

8-4   *Curve sketching techniques: unified and extended.* Locating asymptotes, graphing strategy, increasing, decreasing, local maxima and minima, concave upward, concave downward, inflection point, horizontal asymptote, vertical asymptote, y intercept, x intercept, oblique asymptote

8-5   *Differentials.* Differential dx, differential $dy = f'(x)\,dx$, differential approximation, $\Delta y \approx dy$, $f(x + \Delta x) \approx f(x) + f'(x)\,dx$, differential rules, $dc = 0$, $du^n = nu^{n-1}\,du$, $d(u \pm v) = du \pm dv$,

$$d(uv) = u\,dv + v\,du, \quad d\left(\frac{u}{v}\right) = \frac{v\,du - u\,dv}{v^2}$$

Exercise 8-6   Chapter Review

Work through all the problems in this chapter review and check your answers in the back of the book. (Answers to all review problems are there.) Where weaknesses show up, review appropriate sections in the text.

A   Problems 1–8 refer to the following graph of $y = f(x)$:

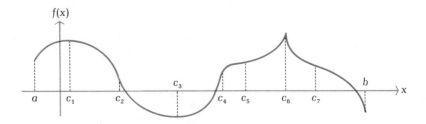

Identify the points or intervals on the x axis that produce the indicated behavior.

1. $f(x)$ is increasing
2. $f'(x) < 0$
3. Graph of f is concave downward
4. Local minima
5. Absolute maxima
6. $f'(x)$ appears to be 0
7. $f'(x)$ does not exist
8. Inflection points
9. Find $f''(x)$ for $f(x) = x^4 + 5x^3$.
10. Find y'' for $y = 3x + 4/x$.
11. Find dy for $y = f(x) = x^3 + 4x$.
12. Find dy for $y = f(x) = (3x^2 - 7)^3$.

B   Problems 13–18 refer to the function $y = f(x) = x^3 + 3x^2 - 24x - 3$.

13. Identify critical values.
14. Find intervals over which $f(x)$ is increasing. Decreasing.

15. Find local maxima and minima.
16. Find intervals over which the graph of f is concave upward. Concave downward.
17. Identify inflection points.
18. Graph f.

Problems 19–23 refer to the function $y = f(x) = \dfrac{3x}{x+2}$.

19. Find horizontal asymptotes.
20. Find vertical asymptotes.
21. Find intervals over which $f(x)$ is increasing. Decreasing.
22. Find intervals over which the graph of f is concave upward. Concave downward.
23. Graph f.
24. Find the absolute maximum and minimum for

$$y = f(x) = x^3 - 12x + 12 \qquad -3 \leqslant x \leqslant 5$$

25. Find the absolute minimum for

$$y = f(x) = x^2 + \frac{16}{x^2} \qquad x > 0$$

Find horizontal and vertical asymptotes.

26. $f(x) = \dfrac{x}{x^2 + 9}$ 27. $f(x) = \dfrac{x^3}{x^2 - 9}$
28. Find dy and Δy for $f(x) = x^3 - 2x + 1$, $x = 5$, and $\Delta x = dx = 0.1$.
29. Approximate $\sqrt{17}$ using differentials.

C   30. Find the absolute maximum for $f'(x)$ if

$$f(x) = 6x^2 - x^3 + 8$$

Graph f and f' on the same axes.
31. Find two positive numbers whose product is 400 and whose sum is a minimum. What is the minimum sum?
32. Sketch the graph of $f(x) = (x-1)^3(x+3)$ using the graphing strategy discussed in Section 8-4.
33. Find dy and Δy for $y = (2/\sqrt{x}) + 8$, $x = 16$, and $\Delta x = dx = 0.2$.

Applications

Business & Economics   34. *Profit.* The profit for a company manufacturing and selling x units per month is given by

$$P(x) = 150x - \frac{x^2}{40} - 50{,}000 \qquad 0 \leqslant x \leqslant 5{,}000$$

What production level will produce the maximum profit? What is the maximum profit?

35. *Average cost.* The total cost of producing x units per month is given by

    $$C(x) = 4{,}000 + 10x + \tfrac{1}{10}x^2$$

    Find the minimum average cost. Graph the average cost and the marginal cost functions on the same axes. Include any oblique asymptotes.

36. *Rental income.* A 200 room hotel in Fresno is filled to capacity every night at a rate of $40 per room. For each $1 increase in the nightly rate, four fewer rooms are rented. If each rented room costs $8 a day to service, how much should the management charge per room in order to maximize gross profit? What is the maximum gross profit?

37. *Inventory control.* A computer store sells 7,200 boxes of floppy discs annually. It costs the store $0.20 to store a box of discs for one year. Each time it reorders discs, the store must pay a $5.00 service charge for processing the order. How many times during the year should the store order discs in order to minimize the total storage and reorder costs?

38. *Rate of change of revenue.* A company is manufacturing a new video game and can sell all it manufactures. The revenue (in dollars) is given by

    $$R = 36x - \frac{x^2}{20}$$

    where the production output in one day is x games. Use dR to approximate the change in revenue if production is increased from 250 to 260 games per day.

Life Sciences

39. *Bacteria control.* If t days after a treatment the bacteria count per cubic centimeter in a body of water is given by

    $$C(t) = 20t^2 - 120t + 800 \qquad 0 \leqslant t \leqslant 9$$

    in how many days will the count be a minimum?

Social Sciences

40. *Politics.* In a new suburb it is estimated that the number of registered voters will grow according to

    $$N = 10 + 6t^2 - t^3 \qquad 0 \leqslant t \leqslant 5$$

    where t is time in years and N is in thousands. When will the rate of increase be maximum?

Exponential and Logarithmic Functions

Contents

We now know how to differentiate algebraic functions—that is, functions that can be defined using the algebraic operations of addition, subtraction, multiplication, division, powers, and roots. In this chapter we will discuss differentiation of forms that involve the exponential and logarithmic functions discussed in Sections 0-6 and 0-7. (You might want to review some of the properties of these functions before proceeding further.) We begin with a discussion of the irrational number e.

9-1 The Constant e and Continuous Compound Interest

- The Constant e
- Continuous Compound Interest

■ The Constant e

The special irrational number e is a particularly suitable base for both exponential and logarithmic functions. The reasons for choosing this number as a base will become clear as we develop differentiation formulas for the exponential function e^x and the natural logarithmic function ln x.

In precalculus treatments, the number e is informally defined as an irrational number that can be approximated by the expression $[1 + (1/n)]^n$ by taking n sufficiently large. Now we will use the limit concept to formally define e as either of the following two limits:

The Number e

$$e = \lim_{n \to \infty} \left(1 + \frac{1}{n}\right)^n$$

or, alternately,

$$e = \lim_{s \to 0} (1 + s)^{1/s}$$

$$e = 2.718\ 281\ 8\ \ldots$$

We will use both these forms. [Note: If $s = 1/n$, then as $n \to \infty$, $s \to 0$.]

The proof that the indicated limits exist and represent an irrational number between 2 and 3 is not easy and is omitted here. Many people reason (incorrectly) that the limits are 1, since "$(1 + s)$ approaches 1 as $s \to 0$, and 1 to any power is 1." A little experimentation with a pocket calculator can convince you otherwise. Consider the table of values for s and $f(s) = (1 + s)^{1/s}$ and the graph shown in Figure 1 for s close to 0.

s approaches 0 from the left $\to 0 \leftarrow$ s approaches 0 from the right

s	-0.5	-0.2	-0.1	$-0.01 \to 0 \leftarrow 0.01$		0.1	0.2	0.5
$(1 + s)^{1/s}$	4.000 0	3.051 8	2.868 0	$2.732\ 0 \to e \leftarrow 2.704\ 8$		2.593 7	2.488 3	2.250 0

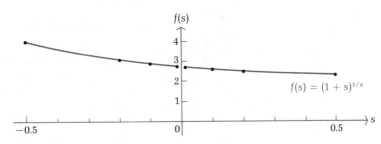

Figure 1

Compute some of the table values with a calculator yourself and also try several values of s even closer to 0. Note that the function is discontinuous at $s = 0$.

Exactly who discovered e is still being debated. It is named after the great mathematician Leonhard Euler (1707–1783), who computed e to twenty-three decimal places using $[1 + (1/n)]^n$.

■ Continuous Compound Interest

Now we will see how e appears quite naturally in the important application of compound interest. Let us start with simple interest, move on to compound interest, and then to continuous compound interest.

If a principal P is borrowed at an annual rate of 100r%, then after t years at simple interest the borrower will owe the lender an amount A given by

$$A = P + Prt = P(1 + rt) \qquad \text{Simple interest} \tag{1}$$

On the other hand, if interest is compounded n times a year, then the borrower will owe the lender an amount A given by

$$A = P\left(1 + \frac{r}{n}\right)^{nt} \qquad \text{Compound interest} \tag{2}$$

where r/n is the interest rate per compounding period and nt is the number of compounding periods. Suppose P, r, and t in (2) are held fixed and n is increased. Will the amount A increase without bound or will it tend to some limiting value?

Let us perform a calculator experiment before we attack the general limit problem. If $P = \$100$, $r = 0.06$, and $t = 2$ years, then

$$A = 100\left(1 + \frac{0.06}{n}\right)^{2n}$$

We compute A for several values of n in Table 1. The biggest gain appears in the first step; then the gains slow down as n increases. In fact, it appears that A might be tending to something close to $\$112.75$ as n gets larger and larger.

Table 1

Compounding Frequency	n	$A = 100\left(1 + \dfrac{0.06}{n}\right)^{2n}$
Annually	1	$112.3600
Semiannually	2	112.5509
Quarterly	4	112.6493
Weekly	52	112.7419
Daily	365	112.7486
Hourly	8,760	112.7491

Now we turn back to the general problem for a moment. Keeping P, r, and t fixed in equation (2), we compute the following limit and observe an interesting and useful result:

$$\lim_{n \to \infty} P\left(1 + \frac{r}{n}\right)^{nt} = P \lim_{n \to \infty} \left(1 + \frac{r}{n}\right)^{(n/r)rt} \qquad \text{Insert } r/r \text{ in the exponent}$$
$$\text{and let } s = r/n.$$

$$= P[\lim_{s \to 0} (1 + s)^{1/s}]^{rt} \qquad \lim_{s \to 0} (1 + s)^{1/s} = e$$

$$= Pe^{rt}$$

The resulting formula is called the **continuous compound interest formula,** a very important and widely used formula in business and economics.

Continuous Compound Interest

$$A = Pe^{rt}$$

where

$P = $ Principal

$r = $ Annual nominal interest rate compounded continuously

$t = $ Time in years

$A = $ Amount at time t

Example 1   If $100 is invested at an annual nominal rate of 6%, compounded continuously, what amount will be in the account after 2 years?

Solution $A = Pe^{rt}$

$\quad\quad = 100e^{(0.06)(2)}$ 6% is equivalent to $r = 0.06$.

$\quad\quad \approx \$112.7497$

(Compare this result with the values calculated in Table 1.)

Problem 1   What amount (to the nearest cent) will an account have after 5 years if $100 is invested at an annual nominal rate of 8%, compounded annually? Semiannually? Continuously?

Example 2   If $100 is invested at 12%, compounded continuously,* graph the amount in the account relative to time for a period of 10 years.

Solution   We want to graph

$$A = 100e^{0.12t} \quad\quad 0 \le t \le 10$$

We construct a table of values using a calculator or Table I of Appendix B, graph the points from the table, and join the points with a smooth curve.

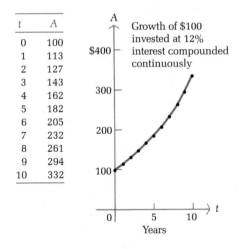

t	A
0	100
1	113
2	127
3	143
4	162
5	182
6	205
7	232
8	261
9	294
10	332

Growth of $100 invested at 12% interest compounded continuously

Problem 2   If $5,000 is invested at 20%, compounded continuously, graph the amount in the account relative to time for a period of 10 years.

---

* Following common usage, we will often write the form "at 12%, compounded continuously," understanding that this means "at an annual nominal rate of 12%, compounded continuously."

Example 3   How long will it take money to double if it is invested at 18%, compounded continuously?

Solution   Starting with the continuous compound interest formula $A = Pe^{rt}$, we must solve for t given $A = 2P$ and $r = 0.18$.

$2P = Pe^{0.18t}$	Divide both sides by P.
$e^{0.18t} = 2$	Take natural logs of both sides.
$\ln e^{0.18t} = \ln 2$	Recall that $\log_b b^x = x$.
$0.18t = \ln 2$	
$t = \dfrac{\ln 2}{0.18}$	
$t = 3.85$ years	

Problem 3   How long will it take money to triple if it is invested at 12%, compounded continuously?

Answers to   1. $146.93; $148.02; $149.18
Matched Problems   2. $A = 5{,}000e^{0.2t}$

t	A
0	5,000
1	6,107
2	7,459
3	9,111
4	11,128
5	13,591
6	16,601
7	20,276
8	24,765
9	30,248
10	36,945

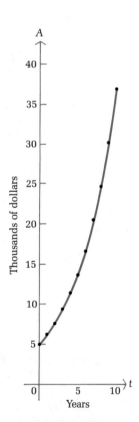

3. 9.16 years

Exercise 9-1

A   *Use a calculator or table to evaluate A to the nearest cent in Problems 1–2.*

1. $A = \$1,000e^{0.1t}$ for $t = 2, 5,$ and 8
2. $A = \$5,000e^{0.08t}$ for $t = 1, 4,$ and 10

B   *In Problems 3–8 solve for t or r to two decimal places.*

3. $2 = e^{0.06t}$ 4. $2 = e^{0.03t}$
5. $3 = e^{0.1t}$ 6. $3 = e^{0.25t}$
7. $2 = e^{5r}$ 8. $3 = e^{10r}$

C   *In Problems 9 and 10 complete each table to five decimal places using a hand calculator.*

9.

n	$(1 + 1/n)^n$
10	2.593 74
100	
1,000	
10,000	
100,000	
1,000,000	
10,000,000	
↓	↓
∞	$e = 2.718\ 281\ 8\ \ldots$

10.

s	$(1 + s)^{1/s}$
0.01	2.704 81
−0.01	
0.001	
−0.001	
0.000 1	
−0.000 1	
0.000 01	
−0.000 01	
↓	↓
0	$e = 2.718\ 281\ 8\ \ldots$

Applications

Business & Economics

11. *Continuous compound interest.* If $20,000 is invested at an annual nominal rate of 12%, compounded continuously, how much will it be worth in 8.5 years?

12. *Continuous compound interest.* Assume $1 had been invested at an annual nominal rate of 4%, compounded continuously, at the birth of Christ. What would be the value of the account in solid gold earths in the year 2000? (Assume that the earth weighs approximately 2.11×10^{26} ounces and that gold will be worth $1,000 an ounce in the year 2000). What would be the value of the account in dollars at simple interest?

13. *Present value.* A note will pay $20,000 at maturity 10 years from now. How much should you be willing to pay for the note now if money is worth 7%, compounded continuously?

14. *Present value.* A note will pay $50,000 at maturity 5 years from now. How much should you be willing to pay for the note now if money is worth 8%, compounded continuously?

15. *Continuous compound interest.* An investor buys stock for $20,000. Four years later the stock is sold for $30,000. If interest is compounded continuously, what annual nominal rate of interest did the original $20,000 investment earn?

16. *Continuous compound interest.* A family paid $40,000 cash for a house. Ten years later, they sell the house for $100,000. If interest is compounded continuously, what annual nominal rate of interest did the original $40,000 investment earn?

17. *Present value.* Solving $A = Pe^{rt}$ for P, we obtain

$$P = Ae^{-rt}$$

which is the present value of the amount A due in t years if money is worth $100r\%$, compounded continuously.

(A) Graph $P = 10,000e^{-0.08t}$, $0 \le t \le 50$.
(B) $\lim_{x \to \infty} 10,000e^{-0.08t} = ?$ (Guess, using part A.)

(*Conclusion:* The further out that amount A is due, the smaller its present value, as we would expect.)

18. *Present value.* Referring to the preceding problem, in how many years will the $10,000 have to be due in order for its present value to be $5,000?

19. *Doubling time.* How long will it take money to double if invested at 25%, compounded continuously?

20. *Doubling time.* How long will it take money to double if invested at 5%, compounded continuously?

21. *Doubling rate.* At what nominal rate compounded continuously must money be invested to double in 5 years?

22. *Doubling rate.* At what nominal rate compounded continuously must money be invested to double in 3 years?

23. *Doubling time.* It is instructive to look at doubling times for money invested at various nominal rates of interest compounded continuously. Show that doubling time t at $100r\%$ interest compounded continuously is given by

$$t = \frac{\ln 2}{r}$$

24. *Doubling time.* Graph the doubling time equation from Problem 23 for $0 < r < 1.00$. Identify vertical and horizontal asymptotes.

Life Sciences   25. *World population.* A mathematical model for world population growth over short periods of time is given by

$$P = P_0 e^{rt}$$

where

$P_0 =$ Population at time $t = 0$

$r =$ Continuous compound rate of growth

t = Time

P = Population at time t

How long will it take the earth's population to double if it continues to grow at its current continuous compound rate of 2% per year?

26. *World population.* Repeat Problem 25 under the assumption that the world population is growing at a continuous compound rate of 1% per year.

27. *Population growth.* Some underdeveloped nations have population doubling times of 20 years. At what continuous compound rate is the population growing? (Use the population growth model in Problem 25.)

28. *Population growth.* Some developed nations have population doubling times of 120 years. At what continuous compound rate is the population growing? (Use the population growth model in Problem 25.)

29. *Radioactive decay.* A mathematical model for the decay of radioactive substances is given by

$$Q = Q_0 e^{rt}$$

where

Q_0 = Amount of the substance at time $t = 0$

r = Continuous compound rate of decay

t = Time

Q = Amount of the substance at time t

If the continuous compound rate of decay of radium per year is $r = -0.000\ 433\ 2$, how long will it take an amount of radium to decay to half the original amount? (This period of time is called the half-life of the substance.)

30. *Radioactive decay.* The continuous compound rate of decay of carbon-14 per year is $r = -0.000\ 123\ 8$. How long will it take an amount of carbon-14 to decay to half the original amount? (Use the radioactive decay model in Problem 29.)

31. *Radioactive decay.* A cesium isotope has a half-life of 30 years. What is the continuous compound rate of decay? (Use the radioactive decay model in Problem 29.)

32. *Radioactive decay.* A strontium isotope has a half-life of 90 years. What is the continuous compound rate of decay? (Use the radioactive decay model in Problem 29.)

Social Sciences

33. *World population.* If the world population is now 4 billion (4×10^9) people and if it continues to grow at a continuous compound rate of 2% per year, how long will it be before there is only 1 square yard of land per person? (The earth has approximately 1.68×10^{14} square yards of land.)

9-2 Derivatives of Logarithmic and Exponential Functions

- Derivative Formulas
- Common Error
- Graphing Techniques
- Application

■ Derivative Formulas

We are now ready to derive a formula for the derivative of

$$f(x) = \ln x = \log_e x \qquad x > 0$$

using the definition of the derivative

$$f'(x) = \lim_{\Delta x \to 0} \frac{f(x + \Delta x) - f(x)}{\Delta x}$$

and the two-step process discussed in Section 7-4.

Step 1. Simplify the difference quotient first:

$$\frac{f(x + \Delta x) - f(x)}{\Delta x} = \frac{\ln(x + \Delta x) - \ln x}{\Delta x}$$

$$= \frac{1}{\Delta x}[\ln(x + \Delta x) - \ln x]$$

$$= \frac{1}{\Delta x} \ln \frac{x + \Delta x}{x} \qquad \text{Property of logs}$$

$$= \frac{1}{x}\left(\frac{x}{\Delta x}\right) \ln\left(1 + \frac{\Delta x}{x}\right) \qquad \text{Multiply by } \frac{x}{x} = 1.$$

$$= \frac{1}{x} \ln\left(1 + \frac{\Delta x}{x}\right)^{x/\Delta x} \qquad \text{Property of logs}$$

Step 2. Find the limit. Let $s = \Delta x / x$. For x fixed, if $\Delta x \to 0$, then $s \to 0$.
Thus,

$$D_x \ln x = \lim_{\Delta x \to 0} \frac{f(x + \Delta x) - f(x)}{\Delta x}$$

$$= \lim_{\Delta x \to 0} \frac{1}{x} \ln\left(1 + \frac{\Delta x}{x}\right)^{x/\Delta x} \qquad \text{Let } s = \frac{\Delta x}{x}.$$

$$= \lim_{s \to 0} \frac{1}{x} \ln(1 + s)^{1/s}$$

$$= \frac{1}{x} \ln[\lim_{s \to 0}(1 + s)^{1/s}] \qquad \begin{array}{l}\text{Properties of limits and} \\ \text{continuity of log} \\ \text{functions}\end{array}$$

$$D_x \ln x = \frac{1}{x} \ln e \qquad\qquad \text{Definition of } e$$

$$= \frac{1}{x} \qquad\qquad \ln e = \log_e e = 1$$

Thus,

$$D_x \ln x = \frac{1}{x}$$

If we apply the two-step process to the exponential function $f(x) = e^x$, we can show that (see Problems 51 and 52 at the end of this section)

$$D_x e^x = e^x$$

Thus, **the derivative of the exponential function is the function itself.** (This important property is the reason that, out of all the possible exponential functions, the exponential function to the base e is often referred to as *the* exponential function.)

These two new and important derivative formulas are restated in the box:

Derivatives of the Natural Logarithmic and Exponential Functions

$$D_x \ln x = \frac{1}{x} \qquad\qquad D_x e^x = e^x$$

These new derivative formulas can be combined with the rules of differentiation discussed in Chapter 7 to differentiate a wide variety of functions.

Example 4 Find $f'(x)$ for:

(A) $f(x) = 2e^x + 3 \ln x$ (B) $f(x) = \dfrac{e^x}{x^3}$

(C) $f(x) = (\ln x)^4$ (D) $f(x) = \ln x^4$

Solutions (A) $f'(x) = \boxed{2D_x e^x + 3D_x \ln x}$

$$= 2e^x + 3\left(\frac{1}{x}\right) = 2e^x + \frac{3}{x}$$

(B) $f'(x) = \boxed{\dfrac{x^3 D_x e^x - e^x D_x x^3}{(x^3)^2}}$ Quotient rule

$$= \frac{x^3 e^x - e^x 3x^2}{x^6} = \frac{x^2 e^x(x-3)}{x^6} = \frac{e^x(x-3)}{x^4}$$

(C) $D_x(\ln x)^4 = 4(\ln x)^3 D_x \ln x$ Power rule for functions

$$= 4(\ln x)^3 \left(\frac{1}{x}\right) = \frac{4(\ln x)^3}{x}$$

(D) $D_x \ln x^4 = D_x 4 \ln x$ Property of logarithms

$$= 4\left(\frac{1}{x}\right) = \frac{4}{x}$$

Problem 4   Find $f'(x)$ for:

(A) $f(x) = 4 \ln x - 5e^x$ (B) $f(x) = x^2 e^x$

(C) $f(x) = \ln x^3$ (D) $f(x) = (\ln x)^3$

▪ Common Error

$$\cancel{D_x e^x = x e^{x-1}}$$

The power rule cannot be used to differentiate the exponential function. The power rule applies to exponential forms x^n where the exponent is a constant and the base is a variable. In the exponential form e^x, the base is a constant and the exponent is a variable.

▪ Graphing Techniques

Using the techniques discussed in Chapter 8, we can use first and second derivatives to give us useful information about the graphs of $y = \ln x$ and $y = e^x$. Using the derivative formulas given previously, we have the following:

$\ln x$		e^x	
$y = \ln x$	$x > 0$	$y = e^x$	$-\infty < x < \infty$
$y' = 1/x > 0$	$x > 0$	$y' = e^x > 0$	$-\infty < x < \infty$
$y'' = -1/x^2 < 0$	$x > 0$	$y'' = e^x > 0$	$-\infty < x < \infty$

Thus, we see that both functions are increasing throughout their respective domains, the graph of $y = \ln x$ is always concave downward, and the graph of $y = e^x$ is always concave upward. It can be shown that the y axis is a vertical asymptote for the graph of $y = \ln x$ and the x axis is a horizontal asymptote for the graph of $y = e^x$ ($\lim_{x \to -\infty} e^x = 0$). Both equations are graphed in Figure 2.

Notice that if we fold the page along the line $y = x$, the two graphs match exactly (see Section 0-7). Also notice that both graphs are unbounded as $x \to \infty$. Comparing each graph with the graph of $y = x$ (the dashed line), we

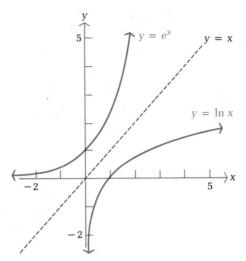

Figure 2

conclude that e^x grows more rapidly than x and ln x grows more slowly than x. In fact, the following limits can be established:

$$\lim_{x \to \infty} \frac{x^n}{e^x} = 0, \quad n > 0 \qquad \text{and} \qquad \lim_{x \to \infty} \frac{\ln x}{x^n} = 0, \quad n > 0$$

These limits indicate that e^x grows more rapidly than any positive power of x and ln x grows more slowly than any positive power of x.

Now let's apply graphing techniques to a slightly more complicated function.

Example 5   Sketch the graph of $f(x) = xe^x$.

Solution   Step 1.   Use the first derivative:

$$f'(x) = xD_xe^x + e^xD_xx$$
$$= xe^x + e^x$$
$$= e^x(x + 1)$$

Since e^x is never 0 (see Figure 2), the only critical value is $x = -1$.

Sign chart for $f'(x) = e^x(x + 1)$:

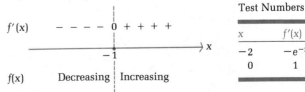

Thus, $f(x)$ decreases on $(-\infty, -1)$, has a local minimum at $x = -1$, and increases on $(-1, \infty)$. Since $e^x > 0$ for all x (see Figure 2), we do not have to evaluate e^{-2} to conclude that $-e^{-2} < 0$.

Step 2. Use the second derivative:

$$f''(x) = e^x D_x(x + 1) + (x + 1)D_x e^x$$
$$= e^x + (x + 1)e^x$$
$$= e^x(x + 2)$$

Sign chart for $f''(x) = e^x(x + 2)$:

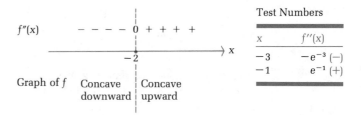

	Test Numbers	
x	$f''(x)$	
-3	$-e^{-3}$	$(-)$
-1	e^{-1}	$(+)$

Thus, the graph of f is concave downward on $(-\infty, -2)$, has an inflection point at $x = -2$, and is concave upward on $(-2, \infty)$.

Step 3. Find intercepts. The y (and x) intercept is $f(0) = 0$. Since e^x is never 0, there are no other x intercepts.

Step 4. Investigate behavior as $x \to \infty$ and $x \to -\infty$. We have not developed limit techniques for functions of this type, but the following tables of values are sufficient to determine the nature of the graph as $x \to \infty$ and $x \to -\infty$:

x	1	5	10	$\to \infty$
$f(x)$	2.72	742.07	220,264.66	$\to \infty$

x	-1	-5	-10	$\to -\infty$
$f(x)$	-0.37	-0.03	$-0.000\ 45$	$\to 0$

Step 5.   Sketch a graph of f, using the information from steps 1–4.

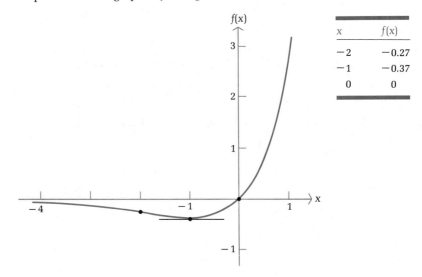

x	$f(x)$
-2	-0.27
-1	-0.37
0	0

Problem 5   Sketch the graph of $f(x) = x \ln x$.

Application

Example 6
Maximum Profit

The market research department of a pet store chain test marketed their aquarium pumps (as well as other items) in several pet stores in a test city. They found that the weekly demand for aquarium pumps is given approximately by

$$p = 12 - 2 \ln x \qquad 0 < x < 90$$

where x is the number of pumps sold each week and p is the price of one pump. If each pump costs the chain \$3, how should it be priced in order to maximize the weekly profit?

Solution   Although we want to find the price that maximizes the weekly profit, it will be easier to first find the number of pumps that will maximize the weekly profit. The revenue equation is

$$R(x) = xp = 12x - 2x \ln x$$

The cost equation is

$$C(x) = 3x$$

and the profit equation is

$$P(x) = R(x) - C(x)$$
$$= 12x - 2x \ln x - 3x$$
$$= 9x - 2x \ln x$$

Thus, we must solve the following:

Maximize $P(x) = 9x - 2x \ln x$ $0 < x < 90$

$$P'(x) = 9 - 2x\left(\frac{1}{x}\right) - 2 \ln x$$
$$= 7 - 2 \ln x = 0$$
$$2 \ln x = 7$$
$$\ln x = 3.5$$
$$x = e^{3.5}$$

$$P''(x) = -2\left(\frac{1}{x}\right) = -\frac{2}{x}$$

Since $x = e^{3.5}$ is the only critical value and $P''(e^{3.5}) < 0$, the maximum weekly profit occurs when $x = e^{3.5} \approx 33$ and $p = 12 - 2 \ln e^{3.5} = \$5$.

Problem 6   Repeat Example 6 if each pump costs the chain \$3.50.

Answers to
Matched Problems

4. (A) $4/x - 5e^x$ (B) $xe^x(x+2)$ (C) $3/x$ (D) $3(\ln x)^2/x$
5. Increasing on (e^{-1}, ∞)
   Decreasing on $(0, e^{-1})$
   Local minimum at $x = e^{-1}$
   Concave upward on $(0, \infty)$
   $f(1) = 0$

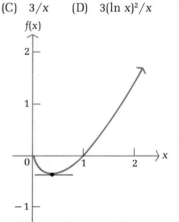

x	5	10	100	$\rightarrow \infty$
$f(x)$	8.05	23.03	460.52	$\rightarrow \infty$

x	0.1	0.01	0.001	0.000 1	$\rightarrow 0$
$f(x)$	-0.23	-0.046	$-0.006\ 9$	$-0.000\ 92$	$\rightarrow 0$

6. Maximum profit occurs for $x = e^{3.25} \approx 26$ and $p = \$5.50$

Exercise 9-2

A Find $f'(x)$.

1. $f(x) = 6e^x - 7 \ln x$
2. $f(x) = 4e^x + 5 \ln x$
3. $f(x) = 2x^e + 3e^x$
4. $f(x) = 4e^x - ex^e$
5. $f(x) = \ln x^5$
6. $f(x) = (\ln x)^5$
7. $f(x) = (\ln x)^2$
8. $f(x) = \ln x^2$

B
9. $f(x) = x^4 \ln x$
10. $f(x) = x^3 \ln x$
11. $f(x) = x^3 e^x$
12. $f(x) = x^4 e^x$

13. $f(x) = \dfrac{e^x}{x^2 + 9}$

14. $f(x) = \dfrac{e^x}{x^2 + 4}$

15. $f(x) = \dfrac{\ln x}{x^4}$

16. $f(x) = \dfrac{\ln x}{x^3}$

17. $f(x) = (x + 2)^3 \ln x$
18. $f(x) = (x - 1)^2 \ln x$
19. $f(x) = (x + 1)^3 e^x$
20. $f(x) = (x - 2)^3 e^x$

21. $f(x) = \dfrac{x^2 + 1}{e^x}$

22. $f(x) = \dfrac{x + 1}{e^x}$

23. $f(x) = x(\ln x)^3$
24. $f(x) = x(\ln x)^2$
25. $f(x) = (4 - 5e^x)^3$
26. $f(x) = (5 - \ln x)^4$
27. $f(x) = \sqrt{1 + \ln x}$
28. $f(x) = \sqrt{1 + e^x}$
29. $f(x) = xe^x - e^x$
30. $f(x) = x \ln x - x$
31. $f(x) = 2x^2 \ln x - x^2$
32. $f(x) = x^2 e^x - 2xe^x + 2e^x$

Find the equation of the line tangent to the graph of $y = f(x)$ at the indicated value of x.

33. $f(x) = e^x; \quad x = 1$
34. $f(x) = e^x; \quad x = 2$
35. $f(x) = \ln x; \quad x = e$
36. $f(x) = \ln x; \quad x = 1$

C Find the indicated extremum of each function for $x > 0$.

37. Absolute maximum value of $f(x) = 4x - x \ln x$
38. Absolute minimum value of $f(x) = x \ln x - 3x$

39. Absolute minimum value of $f(x) = \dfrac{e^x}{x}$

40. Absolute maximum value of $f(x) = \dfrac{x^2}{e^x}$

41. Absolute maximum value of $f(x) = \dfrac{1 + 2 \ln x}{x}$

42. Absolute minimum value of $f(x) = \dfrac{1 - 5 \ln x}{x}$

Sketch the graph of $y = f(x)$.

43. $f(x) = 1 - e^x$

44. $f(x) = 1 - \ln x$

45. $f(x) = x - \ln x$

46. $f(x) = e^x - x$

47. $f(x) = (3 - x)e^x$

48. $f(x) = (x - 2)e^x$

49. $f(x) = x^2 \ln x$

50. $f(x) = \dfrac{\ln x}{x}$

Problems 51 and 52 refer to the function $f(x) = e^x$.

51. Show that

$$\lim_{\Delta x \to 0} \frac{f(x + \Delta x) - f(x)}{\Delta x} = e^x \lim_{\Delta x \to 0} \frac{e^{\Delta x} - 1}{\Delta x}$$

52. Use a calculator to estimate

$$\lim_{\Delta x \to 0} \frac{e^{\Delta x} - 1}{\Delta x}$$

and then use the result in Problem 51 to show that $f'(x) = e^x$.

Applications

Business & Economics

53. *Maximum profit.* A national food service runs food concessions for sporting events throughout the country. Their marketing research department chose a particular baseball/football stadium to test market a new jumbo hot dog. It was found that the demand for the new hot dog is given approximately by

$$p = 5 - \ln x \qquad 5 \leqslant x \leqslant 50$$

where x is the number of hot dogs (in thousands) that can be sold during one game at a price of $\$p$. If the concessionaire pays $\$1$ for each hot dog, how should the hot dogs be priced to maximize the profit per game?

54. *Maximum profit.* On a national tour of a rock band, the demand for tee shirts is given by

$$p = 15 - 4 \ln x \qquad 5 \leqslant x \leqslant 40$$

where x is the number of shirts (in thousands) that can be sold during a single concert at a price of $\$p$. If the shirts cost the band $\$5$ each, how should they be priced in order to maximize the profit per concert?

55. *Minimum average cost.* The cost of producing x units of a product is given by

$$C(x) = 600 + 100x - 100 \ln x \qquad x \geqslant 1$$

Find the minimal average cost.

56. *Minimum average cost.* The cost of producing x units of a product is

given by

$$C(x) = 1,000 + 200x - 200 \ln x \qquad x \geqslant 1$$

Find the minimal average cost.

57. *Maximizing revenue.* A cosmetic company is planning the introduction and promotion of a new lipstick line. The marketing research department, after test marketing the new line in a large carefully selected city, found that the demand in that city is given approximately by

$$p = 10e^{-x} \qquad 0 \leqslant x \leqslant 2$$

where x thousand lipsticks were sold per week at a price of p dollars each.

(A) At what price will the weekly revenue $R(x) = xp$ be maximum? What is the maximum weekly revenue in the test city?

(B) Graph R for $0 \leqslant x \leqslant 2$.

58. *Maximizing revenue.* Repeat the preceding problem using the demand equation $p = 12e^{-x}$, $0 \leqslant x \leqslant 2$.

Life Sciences

59. *Blood pressure.* An experiment was set up to find a relationship between weight and systolic blood pressure in normal children. Using hospital records for 5,000 normal children, it was found that the systolic blood pressure was given approximately by

$$P(x) = 17.5(1 + \ln x) \qquad 10 \leqslant x \leqslant 100$$

where P(x) is measured in millimeters of mercury and x is measured in pounds. What is the rate of change of blood pressure with respect to weight at the 40 pound weight level? At the 90 pound weight level?

60. *Blood pressure.* Graph the systolic blood pressure equation in the preceding problem.

61. *Drug concentration.* The concentration of a drug in the blood stream t hours after injection is given approximately by

$$C(t) = 4.35e^{-t} \qquad 0 \leqslant t \leqslant 5$$

where C(t) is concentration in milligrams per milliliter.

(A) What is the rate of change of concentration after 1 hour? After 4 hours?

(B) Graph C.

62. *Water pollution.* The use of iodine crystals is a popular way of making small quantities of nondrinkable water drinkable. Crystals placed in a 1 ounce bottle of water will dissolve until the solution is saturated. After saturation, one-half of this solution is poured into a quart container of questionable water, then after about an hour the questionable water is usually drinkable. The half empty 1 ounce bottle is then refilled to be used again in the same way. Suppose the concentration of iodine in the 1 ounce bottle t minutes after the crystals are introduced can be approximated by

$$C(t) = 250(1 - e^{-t}) \qquad t \geqslant 0$$

where $C(t)$ is the concentration of iodine in micrograms per milliliter.

(A) What is the rate of change of the concentration after 1 minute? After 4 minutes?

(B) Graph C for $0 \leqslant t \leqslant 5$.

Social Sciences

63. *Psychology—stimulus/response.* In psychology the Weber-Fechner Law for stimulus response is

$$R = k \ln\left(\frac{S}{S_0}\right)$$

where R is the response, S is the stimulus, and S_0 is the lowest level of stimulus that can be detected. Find dR/dS.

64. *Psychology–learning.* A mathematical model for the average of a group of people learning to type is given by

$$N(t) = 10 + 6 \ln t \qquad t \geqslant 1$$

where $N(t)$ is the number of words per minute typed after t hours of instruction and practice (2 hours per day, 5 days per week). What is the rate of learning after 10 hours of instruction and practice? After 100 hours?

9-3 Chain Rule

- Composite Functions
- Chain Rule
- Generalized Derivative Rules
- Other Logarithmic and Exponential Functions

Suppose you were asked to find the derivative of

$$h(x) = \ln(2x + 1)$$

We have developed formulas for computing the derivatives of the natural logarithm function and polynomial functions separately, but not in the indicated combination. In this section we will discuss one of the most important derivative rules of all—the **chain rule.** This rule will enable us to determine the derivatives of some fairly complicated functions in terms of derivatives of more elementary functions. The chain rule is used to compute derivatives of functions that are compositions of more elementary functions whose derivatives are known.

■ Composite Functions

Let us look at the given function h more closely:

$h(x) = \ln(2x + 1)$

The function h is a combination of the natural logarithm function and a linear function. To see this more clearly, let

$y = f(u) = \ln u$

$u = g(x) = 2x + 1$

Then we can express y as a function of x as follows:

$y = f(u) = f[g(x)] = \ln(2x + 1) = h(x)$

The function h is said to be the *composite* of the two simpler functions f and g. (Loosely speaking, we can think of h as a function of a function.) In general:

Composite Functions

A function h is a **composite** of functions f and g if

$h(x) = f[g(x)]$

The domain of h is the set of all numbers x such that x is in the domain of g and $g(x)$ is in the domain of f.

Example 7　Let $f(u) = e^u$ and $g(x) = 3x^2 + 1$. Find:

(A)　$f[g(x)]$　　(B)　$g[f(u)]$

Solutions　(A)　$f[g(x)] = e^{g(x)} = e^{3x^2+1}$
　　　　　(B)　$g[f(u)] = 3[f(u)]^2 + 1 = 3[e^u]^2 + 1 = 3e^{2u} + 1$

Problem 7　Let $f(u) = \ln u$ and $g(x) = 2x^3 + 4$. Find:

(A)　$f[g(x)]$　　(B)　$g[f(u)]$

Example 8　Write each function as a composition of the natural logarithm or exponential function and a polynomial.

(A)　$y = \ln(x^3 - 2x^2 + 1)$　　(B)　$y = e^{x^2+4}$

Solutions   (A)   Let

$$y = f(u) = \ln u$$
$$u = g(x) = x^3 - 2x^2 + 1$$

Check $$y = f[g(x)] = \ln[g(x)] = \ln(x^3 - 2x^2 + 1)$$

(B)   Let

$$y = f(u) = e^u$$
$$u = g(x) = x^2 + 4$$

Check $$y = f[g(x)] = e^{g(x)} = e^{x^2 + 4}$$

Problem 8   Repeat Example 8 for:

(A) $y = e^{2x^3 + 7}$ (B) $y = \ln(x^4 + 10)$

▪ Chain Rule

The word "chain" comes from the fact that a function formed by composition (such as those in Example 7) involves a "chain" of functions — that is, "a function of a function." We now introduce the *chain rule*, which will enable us to compute the derivative of a composite function in terms of the derivatives of the functions making up the composition.

Suppose

$$y = h(x) = f[g(x)]$$

is a composite of f and g where

$$y = f(u) \quad \text{and} \quad u = g(x)$$

We would like to express the derivative dy/dx in terms of the derivatives of f and g. From the definition of a derivative we have

$$\frac{dy}{dx} = \lim_{\Delta x \to 0} \frac{h(x + \Delta x) - h(x)}{\Delta x}$$

$$= \lim_{\Delta x \to 0} \frac{\Delta y}{\Delta x} \tag{1}$$

Noting that

$$\frac{\Delta y}{\Delta x} = \frac{\Delta y}{\Delta u} \frac{\Delta u}{\Delta x} \tag{2}$$

we might be tempted to substitute (2) into (1) to obtain

$$\frac{dy}{dx} = \lim_{\Delta x \to 0} \frac{\Delta y}{\Delta u} \frac{\Delta u}{\Delta x}$$

and reason that $\Delta u \to 0$ as $\Delta x \to 0$ so that

$$\frac{dy}{dx} = \left(\lim_{\Delta u \to 0} \frac{\Delta y}{\Delta u}\right)\left(\lim_{\Delta x \to 0} \frac{\Delta u}{\Delta x}\right)$$

$$= \frac{dy}{du}\frac{du}{dx}$$

The result is correct under rather general conditions, and is called the *chain rule*, but our "derivation" is superficial, because it ignores a number of hidden problems. Since a formal proof of the **chain rule** is beyond the scope of this book, we simply state it as follows:

Chain Rule

If $y = f(u)$ and $u = g(x)$, define the composite function

$$y = h(x) = f[g(x)]$$

Then

$$\frac{dy}{dx} = \frac{dy}{du}\frac{du}{dx} \qquad \text{provided } \frac{dy}{du} \text{ and } \frac{du}{dx} \text{ exist}$$

Example 9   Find dy/dx, given:

(A) $y = \ln(x^2 - 4x + 2)$ (B) $y = e^{2x^3+5}$

Solutions   (A) Let $y = \ln u$ and $u = x^2 - 4x + 2$. Then

$$\frac{dy}{dx} = \frac{dy}{du}\frac{du}{dx} \quad {}^*$$

$$= \frac{1}{u}(2x - 4)$$

$$= \frac{1}{x^2 - 4x + 2}(2x - 4) \qquad \text{Since } u = x^2 - 4x + 2$$

$$= \frac{2x - 4}{x^2 - 4x + 2}$$

(B) Let $y = e^u$ and $u = 2x^3 + 5$. Then

$$\frac{dy}{dx} = \frac{dy}{du}\frac{du}{dx}$$

$$= e^u(6x^2)$$

$$= 6x^2 e^{2x^3+5} \qquad \text{Since } u = 2x^3 + 5$$

* After some experience with the chain rule, the steps in the dashed boxes are usually done mentally.

Problem 9 Find dy/dx, given:

(A) $y = e^{3x^4+6}$ (B) $y = \ln(x^2 + 9x + 4)$

The chain rule can be extended to compositions of three or more functions. For example, if $y = f(w)$, $w = g(u)$, and $u = h(x)$ then

$$\frac{dy}{dx} = \frac{dy}{dw} \frac{dw}{du} \frac{du}{dx}$$

Example 10 For $y = h(x) = e^{1+(\ln x)^2}$, find dy/dx.

Solution Note that h is of the form $y = e^w$ where $w = 1 + u^2$ and $u = \ln x$. Thus,

$$\frac{dy}{dx} = \frac{dy}{dw} \frac{dw}{du} \frac{du}{dx}$$

$$= e^w (2u) \left(\frac{1}{x}\right)$$

$$= e^{1+u^2} (2u) \left(\frac{1}{x}\right) \qquad \text{Since } w = 1 + u^2$$

$$= e^{1+(\ln x)^2} (2 \ln x) \left(\frac{1}{x}\right) \qquad \text{Since } u = \ln x$$

$$= \frac{2}{x} (\ln x) e^{1+(\ln x)^2}$$

Problem 10 For $y = h(x) = [\ln(1 + e^x)]^3$, find dy/dx.

■ Generalized Derivative Rules

In practice, it is not necessary to introduce additional variables when using the chain rule, as we did in Examples 9 and 10. Instead, the chain rule can be used to extend the derivative rules for specific functions to general derivative rules for compositions. This is what we did in Section 7-7 when we discussed the general power rule. In fact, the general power rule is a consequence of the chain rule. To see this, let $y = [f(x)]^n$ and $u = f(x)$. Applying the chain rule to $y = u^n$, we have

$$\frac{dy}{dx} = \frac{dy}{du} \frac{du}{dx} = nu^{n-1} f'(x) = n[f(x)]^{n-1} f'(x)$$

The same technique can be applied to functions of the form $y = e^{f(x)}$ and $y = \ln[f(x)]$ (see Problems 59 and 60 at the end of this section). The results are summarized in the following box:

> **General Derivative Rules**
>
> $$D_x[f(x)]^n = n[f(x)]^{n-1}f'(x) \tag{3}$$
>
> $$D_x \ln[f(x)] = \frac{1}{f(x)} f'(x) \tag{4}$$
>
> $$D_x e^{f(x)} = e^{f(x)}f'(x) \tag{5}$$

For power, natural logarithm, or exponential forms, we can either use the chain rule discussed earlier or these special differentiation formulas based on the chain rule. Use whichever is easier for you. In Example 11, we will use the general derivative rules.

Example 11 (A) $D_x e^{2x} = e^{2x}D_x 2x$ Using (5)

$$= e^{2x}(2) = 2e^{2x}$$

(B) $D_x \ln(x^2 + 9) = \dfrac{1}{x^2 + 9}D_x(x^2 + 9)$ Using (4)

$$= \frac{1}{x^2 + 9}2x = \frac{2x}{x^2 + 9}$$

(C) $D_x(1 + e^{x^2})^3 = 3(1 + e^{x^2})^2 D_x(1 + e^{x^2})$ Using (3)

$$= 3(1 + e^{x^2})^2 e^{x^2}D_x x^2 \qquad \text{Using (5)}$$

$$= 3(1 + e^{x^2})^2 e^{x^2}(2x)$$

$$= 6xe^{x^2}(1 + e^{x^2})^2$$

Problem 11 Find:

(A) $D_x \ln(x^3 + 2x)$ (B) $D_x e^{3x^2 + 2}$ (C) $D_x(2 + e^{-x^2})^4$

■ Other Logarithmic and Exponential Functions

In most applications involving logarithmic or exponential functions, the number e is the preferred base. However, there are situations where it is convenient to use a base other than e. Derivatives of $y = \log_b x$ and $y = b^x$ can be obtained by expressing these functions in terms of the natural logarithmic and exponential functions. We begin by finding a relationship between $\log_b x$ and $\ln x$ for any base b, $b > 0$ and $b \neq 1$.

$y = \log_b x$	Change to exponential form.
$b^y = x$	Take the natural log of both sides.
$\ln b^y = \ln x$	Recall that $\ln b^y = y \ln b$.
$y \ln b = \ln x$	Solve for y.
$y = \dfrac{1}{\ln b} \ln x$	

Thus,

$$\log_b x = \frac{1}{\ln b} \ln x \qquad \text{Change of base formula*} \tag{6}$$

Differentiating both sides of (6), we have

$$D_x \log_b x = \frac{1}{\ln b} D_x \ln x = \frac{1}{\ln b} \frac{1}{x}$$

Example 12 Find $f'(x)$ for:

(A) $f(x) = \log_2 x$ (B) $f(x) = \log(1 + x^3)$

Solutions (A) $f(x) = \log_2 x = \frac{1}{\ln 2} \ln x$ Using (6)

$$f'(x) = \frac{1}{\ln 2} \frac{1}{x}$$

(B) $f(x) = \log(1 + x^3)$ Recall that $\log r = \log_{10} r$.

$$= \frac{1}{\ln 10} \ln(1 + x^3)$$ Using (6)

$$f'(x) = \frac{1}{\ln 10} \frac{1}{1 + x^3} 3x^2 = \frac{1}{\ln 10} \frac{3x^2}{1 + x^3}$$

Problem 12 Find $f'(x)$ for:

(A) $f(x) = \log x$ (B) $f(x) = \log_3(x + x^2)$

Now we want to find a relationship between b^x and e^x for any base b, $b > 0$ and $b \neq 1$.

$$y = b^x \qquad \text{Take the natural log of both sides.}$$
$$\ln y = \ln b^x$$
$$= x \ln b \qquad \text{Change to exponential form.}$$
$$y = e^{x \ln b}$$

Thus,

$$b^x = e^{x \ln b} \tag{7}$$

Differentiating both sides of (7), we have

$$D_x b^x = e^{x \ln b} \ln b = b^x \ln b$$

Example 13 Find $f'(x)$ for:

(A) $f(x) = 2^x$ (B) $f(x) = 10^{x^5 + x}$

---

* Equation (6) is a special case of the **change of base** formula for logarithms (which can be derived in the same way): $\log_b x = \log_a x / \log_a b$.

Solutions

(A) $f(x) = 2^x = e^{x \ln 2}$ Using (7)

$f'(x) = e^{x \ln 2} \ln 2 = 2^x \ln 2$

(B) $f(x) = 10^{x^5+x} = e^{(x^5+x) \ln 10}$ Using (7)

$f'(x) = e^{(x^5+x) \ln 10}(5x^4 + 1) \ln 10$

$= 10^{x^5+x}(5x^4 + 1) \ln 10$

Problem 13   Find $f'(x)$ for:

(A) $f(x) = 5^x$ (B) $f(x) = 4^{x^2+3x}$

Answers to
Matched Problems

7.   (A) $f[g(x)] = \ln(2x^3 + 4)$ (B) $g[f(u)] = 2(\ln u)^3 + 4$
8.   (A) $y = f(u) = e^u$ and $u = g(x) = 2x^3 + 7$
     (B) $y = f(u) = \ln u$ and $u = g(x) = x^4 + 10$

9.   (A) $12x^3 e^{3x^4+6}$ (B) $\dfrac{2x + 9}{x^2 + 9x + 4}$

10. $\dfrac{dy}{dx} = \dfrac{3e^x[\ln(1 + e^x)]^2}{1 + e^x}$

11.   (A) $\dfrac{3x^2 + 2}{x^3 + 2x}$ (B) $6xe^{3x^2+2}$ (C) $-8xe^{-x^2}(2 + e^{-x^2})^3$

12.   (A) $\dfrac{1}{\ln 10} \dfrac{1}{x}$ (B) $\dfrac{1}{\ln 3} \dfrac{1 + 2x}{x + x^2}$

13.   (A) $5^x \ln 5$ (B) $4^{x^2+3x}(2x + 3) \ln 4$

Exercise 9-3

A   *Write each composite function in the form $y = f(u)$ and $u = g(x)$.*

1. $y = (2x + 5)^3$
2. $y = (3x - 7)^5$
3. $y = \ln(2x^2 + 7)$
4. $y = \ln(x^2 - 2x + 5)$
5. $y = e^{x^2-2}$
6. $y = e^{3x^3+5x}$

Express y in terms of x. Use the chain rule to find dy/dx and then express dy/dx in terms of x.

7. $y = u^2$, $u = 2 + e^x$
8. $y = u^3$, $u = 3 - \ln x$
9. $y = e^u$, $u = 2 - x^4$
10. $y = e^u$, $u = x^6 + 5x^2$
11. $y = \ln u$, $u = 4x^5 - 7$
12. $y = \ln u$, $u = 2 + 3x^4$

Find each derivative.

13. $D_x \ln(x - 3)$
14. $D_w \ln(w + 100)$
15. $D_t \ln(3 - 2t)$
16. $D_y \ln(4 - 5y)$

17. $D_x 3e^{2x}$

18. $D_y 2e^{3y}$

19. $D_t 2e^{-4t}$

20. $D_r 6e^{-3r}$

B

21. $D_x 100e^{-0.03x}$

22. $D_t 1{,}000e^{0.06t}$

23. $D_x \ln(x+1)^4$

24. $D_x \ln(x+1)^{-3}$

25. $D_x(2e^{2x} - 3e^x + 5)$

26. $D_t(1 + e^{-t} - e^{-2t})$

27. $D_x e^{3x^2 - 2x}$

28. $D_x e^{x^3 - 3x^2 + 1}$

29. $D_t \ln(t^2 + 3t)$

30. $D_x \ln(x^3 - 3x^2)$

31. $D_x \ln(x^2 + 1)^{1/2}$

32. $D_x \ln(x^4 + 5)^{3/2}$

33. $D_t[\ln(t^2 + 1)]^4$

34. $D_w[\ln(w^3 - 1)]^2$

35. $D_x(e^{2x} - 1)^4$

36. $D_x(e^{x^2} + 3)^5$

37. $D_x \dfrac{e^{2x}}{x^2 + 1}$

38. $D_x \dfrac{e^{x+1}}{x + 1}$

39. $D_x(x^2 + 1)e^{-x}$

40. $D_x(1 - x)e^{2x}$

41. $D_x e^{-x} \ln x$

42. $D_x \dfrac{\ln x}{e^x + 1}$

43. $D_x \dfrac{1}{\ln(1 + x^2)}$

44. $D_x \dfrac{1}{\ln(1 - x^3)}$

45. $D_x \sqrt[3]{\ln(1 - x^2)}$

46. $D_t \sqrt[5]{\ln(1 - t^5)}$

C   *Sketch the graph of $y = f(x)$.*

47. $f(x) = 1 - e^{-x}$

48. $f(x) = 2 - 3e^{-2x}$

49. $f(x) = \ln(1 - x)$

50. $f(x) = \ln(2x + 4)$

51. $f(x) = e^{-(1/2)x^2}$

52. $f(x) = \ln(x^2 + 4)$

Express y in terms of x. Use the chain rule to find dy/dx. Express dy/dx in terms of x.

53. $y = 1 + w^2$, $w = \ln u$, $u = 2 + e^x$

54. $y = \ln w$, $w = 1 + e^u$, $u = x^2$

Find each derivative.

55. $D_x \log_2(3x^2 - 1)$

56. $D_x \log(x^3 - 1)$

57. $D_x 10^{x^2 + x}$

58. $D_x 8^{1 - 2x^2}$

59. Use the chain rule to derive the formula

$$D_x \ln[f(x)] = \frac{1}{f(x)} f'(x)$$

60. Use the chain rule to derive the formula

$$D_x e^{f(x)} = e^{f(x)} f'(x)$$

Applications

Business & Economics   61. *Maximum revenue.* Suppose the price–demand equation for x units of a commodity is determined from empirical data to be

$$p = 100e^{-0.05x}$$

where x units are sold per day at a price of $p each. Find the production level and price that maximizes revenue. What is the maximum revenue?

62. *Maximum revenue.* Repeat the preceding problem using the price-demand equation

$$p = 10e^{-0.04x}$$

63. *Salvage value.* The salvage value S, in dollars, of a company airplane after t years is estimated to be given by

$$S(t) = 300,000e^{-0.1t}$$

What is the rate of depreciation in dollars per year after 1 year? 5 years? 10 years?

64. *Resale value.* The resale value R, in dollars, of a company car after t years is estimated to be given by

$$R(t) = 20,000e^{-0.15t}$$

What is the rate of depreciation in dollars per year after 1 year? 2 years? 3 years?

65. *Promotion and maximum profit.* A recording company has produced a new compact disc featuring a very popular recording group. Before launching a national sales campaign, the marketing research department chose to test market the disc in a bellwether city. Their interest is in determining the length of a sales campaign that will maximize total profits. From empirical data, the research department estimates that the proportion of a target group of 50,000 persons buying the disc after t days of television promotion is given by $1 - e^{-0.03t}$. If a $4 profit is realized on each disc sold, then the total revenue after t days of promotion will be approximated by

$$R(t) = (4)(50,000)(1 - e^{-0.03t}) \qquad t \geq 0$$

Television promotion costs are

$$C(t) = 4,000 + 3,000t \qquad t \geq 0$$

(A) How many days of television promotion should be used to maximize total profit? What is the maximum total profit? What percentage of the target market will have purchased the disc when the maximum profit is reached?

(B) Graph the profit function.

66. *Promotion and maximum profit.* Repeat the preceding problem using the revenue equation

$$R(t) = (3)(60,000)(1 - e^{-0.04t})$$

Life Sciences

67. *Blood pressure and age.* A research group using hospital records developed the following approximate mathematical model relating systolic blood pressure and age:

$$P(x) = 40 + 25 \ln(x + 1) \qquad 0 \le x \le 65$$

where $P(x)$ is pressure measured in millimeters of mercury and x is age in years. What is the rate of change of pressure at the end of 10 years? At the end of 30 years? At the end of 60 years?

68. *Biology.* A yeast culture at room temperature (68°F) is placed in a refrigerator maintaining a constant temperature of 38°F. After t hours the temperature T of the culture is given approximately by

$$T = 30e^{-0.58t} + 38 \qquad t \ge 0$$

What is the rate of change of temperature of the culture at the end of 1 hour? At the end of 4 hours?

69. *Bacterial growth.* A single cholera bacterium divides every 0.5 hour to produce two complete cholera bacteria. If we start with a colony of 5,000 bacteria, then after t hours there will be

$$A(t) = 5,000 \cdot 2^{2t}$$

bacteria. Find $A'(t)$, $A'(1)$, and $A'(5)$ and interpret.

70. *Bacterial growth.* Repeat the preceding problem for a starting colony of 1,000 bacteria where a single bacterium divides every 0.25 hour.

Social Sciences

71. *Sociology.* Daniel Lowenthal, a sociologist at Columbia University, made a 5 year study on the sale of popular records relative to their position in the top 20. He found that the average number of sales $N(n)$ of the nth ranking record was given approximately by

$$N(n) = N_1 e^{-0.09(n-1)} \qquad 1 \le n \le 20$$

where N_1 was the number of sales of the number one record on the list at a given time. Graph N for $N_1 = 1,000,000$ records.

72. *Political science.* Thomas W. Casstevens, a political scientist at Oakland University, has studied legislative turnover. He (with others) found that the number $N(t)$ of continuously serving members of an elected legislative body remaining t years after an election is given approximately by a function of the form

$$N(t) = N_0 e^{-ct}$$

In particular, for the 1965 election for the U.S. House of Representatives, it was found that

$$N(t) = 434e^{-0.0866t}$$

What is the rate of change after 2 years? After 10 years?

9-4   Chapter Review

Important Terms and Symbols

9-1   *The constant e and continuous compound interest.* Definition of e, continuous compound interest

9-2   *Derivatives of logarithmic and exponential functions.* Derivative formulas for the natural logarithmic and exponential functions, graph properties of $y = \ln x$ and $y = e^x$

9-3   *Chain rule.* Composite functions, chain rule, general derivative formulas, derivative formulas for $y = \log_b x$ and $y = b^x$

Additional Rules of Differentiation

$$D_x \ln x = \frac{1}{x}$$

$$D_x e^x = e^x$$

$$D_x \ln[f(x)] = \frac{1}{f(x)} f'(x)$$

$$D_x e^{f(x)} = e^{f(x)} f'(x)$$

$$D_x \log_b x = D_x \frac{1}{\ln b} \ln x = \frac{1}{\ln b} \frac{1}{x}$$

$$D_x b^x = D_x e^{x \ln b} = e^{x \ln b} \ln b = b^x \ln b$$

$$\frac{dy}{dx} = \frac{dy}{du} \frac{du}{dx}, \quad \frac{dy}{dx} = \frac{dy}{dw} \frac{dw}{du} \frac{du}{dx}, \quad \text{and so on}$$

Exercise 9-4   Chapter Review

Work through all the problems in this chapter review and check your answers in the back of the book. (Answers to all review problems are there.) Where weaknesses show up, review appropriate sections in the text.

A   1.   Use a calculator to evaluate $A = 2{,}000e^{0.09t}$ to the nearest cent for $t = 5$, 10, and 20.

Find the indicated derivatives in Problems 2–4.

2. $D_x(2 \ln x + 3e^x)$ 3. $D_x e^{2x-3}$

4. y' for $y = \ln(2x + 7)$

5.   Let $y = \ln u$ and $u = 3 + e^x$.

   (A)   Express y in terms of x.

   (B)   Use the chain rule to find dy/dx and then express dy/dx in terms of x.

B   6.   Graph $y = 100e^{-0.1x}$.

Find the indicated derivatives in Problems 7–12.

7. $D_z[(\ln z)^7 + \ln z^7]$

8. $D_x x^6 \ln x$

9. $D_x \dfrac{e^x}{x^6}$

10. y' for $y = \ln(2x^3 - 3x)$

11. $f'(x)$ for $f(x) = e^{x^3 - x^2}$

12. dy/dx for $y = e^{-2x} \ln 5x$

13. Find the equation of the line tangent to the graph of $y = f(x) = 1 + e^{-x}$ at $x = 0$. At $x = -1$.

C   *In Problems 14 and 15, find the absolute maximum value of $f(x)$ for $x > 0$.*

14. $f(x) = 11x - 2x \ln x$

15. $f(x) = 10xe^{-2x}$

Sketch the graph of $y = f(x)$ in Problems 16 and 17.

16. $f(x) = 5 - 5e^{-x}$

17. $f(x) = x^3 \ln x$

18. Let $y = w^3$, $w = \ln u$, and $u = 4 - e^x$.

(A) Express y in terms of x.

(B) Use the chain rule to find dy/dx and then express dy/dx in terms of x.

Find the indicated derivatives in Problems 19–21.

19. y' for $y = 5^{x^2 - 1}$

20. $D_x \log_5(x^2 - x)$

21. $D_x \sqrt{\ln(x^2 + x)}$

Applications

Business & Economics

22. *Doubling time.* How long will it take money to double if it is invested at 5% interest compounded

(A) Annually?   (B) Continuously?

23. *Continuous compound interest.* If $100 is invested at 10% interest compounded continuously, the amount (in dollars) at the end of t years is given by

$$A = 100e^{0.1t}$$

Find $A'(t)$, $A'(1)$, and $A'(10)$.

24. *Marginal analysis.* If the price–demand equation for x units of a commodity is

$$p(x) = 1,000e^{-0.02x}$$

find the marginal revenue equation.

25. *Maximum revenue.* For the price–demand equation in the preceding problem, find the production level and price per unit that produces the maximum revenue. What is the maximum revenue?

26. *Maximum revenue.* Graph the revenue function from the preceding two problems for $0 \leqslant x \leqslant 100$.

27. *Minimal average cost.* The cost of producing x units of a product is given by

$$C(x) = 200 + 50x - 50 \ln x \qquad x \geqslant 1$$

Find the minimal average cost.

Life Sciences

28. *Drug concentration.* The concentration of a drug in the bloodstream t hours after injection is given approximately by

$$C(t) = 5e^{-0.3t}$$

where $C(t)$ is concentration in milligrams per milliliter. What is the rate of change of concentration after 1 hour? After 5 hours?

Social Sciences

29. *Psychology — learning.* In a computer assembly plant, a new employee on the average is able to assemble

$$N(t) = 10(1 - e^{-0.4t})$$

units after t days of on-the-job training.

(A) What is the rate of learning after 1 day? After 5 days?

(B) Graph N for $0 \leqslant t \leqslant 10$.

Integration

CHAPTER 10   Contents

The last three chapters dealt with differential calculus. We now begin the development of the second main part of calculus, called *integral calculus*. Two types of integrals will be introduced, the *indefinite integral* and the *definite integral*; each is quite different from the other. But through the remarkable *fundamental theorem of calculus*, we will show that not only are the two integral forms intimately related, but both are intimately related to differentiation.

10-1 Antiderivatives and Indefinite Integrals

- Antiderivatives
- Indefinite Integrals
- Indefinite Integrals Involving Algebraic Functions
- Indefinite Integrals Involving Exponential and Logarithmic Functions
- Applications

■ Antiderivatives

Many operations in mathematics have reverses—compare addition and subtraction, multiplication and division, and powers and roots. The function $f(x) = \frac{1}{3}x^3$ has the derivative $f'(x) = x^2$. Reversing this process is referred to as *antidifferentiation*. Thus,

$$\frac{x^3}{3} \quad \text{is an antiderivative of} \quad x^2$$

since

$$D_x\left(\frac{x^3}{3}\right) = x^2$$

In general, we say that $F(x)$ is an **antiderivative** of $f(x)$ if

$$F'(x) = f(x)$$

Note that

$$D_x\left(\frac{x^3}{3} + 2\right) = x^2 \qquad D_x\left(\frac{x^3}{3} - \pi\right) = x^2 \qquad D_x\left(\frac{x^3}{3} + \sqrt{5}\right) = x^2$$

Hence,

$$\frac{x^3}{3} + 2 \qquad \frac{x^3}{3} - \pi \qquad \frac{x^3}{3} + \sqrt{5}$$

are also antiderivatives of x^2, since each has x^2 as a derivative. In fact, it appears that

$$\frac{x^3}{3} + C$$

for any real number C, is an antiderivative of x^2, since

$$D_x\left(\frac{x^3}{3} + C\right) = x^2$$

Thus, antidifferentiation of a given function does not, in general, lead to a unique function, but to a whole set of functions.

Does the expression

$$\frac{x^3}{3} + C$$

with C any real number, include all antiderivatives of x^2? Theorem 1 (which we state without proof) indicates that the answer is yes.

Theorem 1

> If F and G are differentiable functions on the interval (a, b) and $F'(x) = G'(x)$, then $F(x) = G(x) + k$ for some constant k.

■ Indefinite Integrals

In words, Theorem 1 states that **if the derivatives of two functions are equal, then the functions differ by at most a constant.** We use the symbol

$$\int f(x)\, dx$$

called the **indefinite integral,** to represent all antiderivatives of $f(x)$, and we write

$$\int f(x)\, dx = F(x) + C \qquad \text{where } F'(x) = f(x)$$

that is, if $F(x)$ is any antiderivative of $f(x)$. The symbol $\int$ is called an **integral sign** and $f(x)$ is called the **integrand.** (We will have more to say about the symbol dx later.) The arbitrary constant C is called the **constant of integration.**

▪ Indefinite Integrals Involving Algebraic Functions

Just as with differentiation, we can develop formulas and special properties that will enable us to find indefinite integrals of many frequently encountered functions. To start, we list some formulas that can be established using the definitions of antiderivative and indefinite integral, and the many properties of derivatives considered in Chapter 7.

Indefinite Integral Formulas and Properties

For k and C constants:

1. $\displaystyle\int k\,dx = kx + C$

2. $\displaystyle\int x^n\,dx = \frac{x^{n+1}}{n+1} + C \qquad n \neq -1$

3. $\displaystyle\int kf(x)\,dx = k\int f(x)\,dx$

4. $\displaystyle\int [f(x) \pm g(x)]\,dx = \int f(x)\,dx \pm \int g(x)\,dx$

We will establish formula 2 and property 3 here (the others may be shown to be true in a similar manner). To establish formula 2, we simply differentiate the right side to obtain the integrand on the left side. Thus,

$$D_x\left(\frac{x^{n+1}}{n+1} + C\right) = \frac{(n+1)x^n}{n+1} + 0 = x^n \qquad n \neq -1$$

(The case when $n = -1$ will be considered later in this section.) To establish property 3, let F be a function such that $F'(x) = f(x)$. Then

$$k\int f(x)\,dx = k\int F'(x)\,dx = k[F(x) + C_1] = kF(x) + kC_1$$

and since $(kF(x))' = kF'(x) = kf(x)$, we have

$$\int kf(x)\,dx = \int kF'(x)\,dx = kF(x) + C_2$$

But $kF(x) + kC_1$ and $kF(x) + C_2$ describe the same set of functions, since C_1 and C_2 are arbitrary real numbers. It is important to remember that property 3 states that a constant factor can be moved across an integral sign; a variable factor cannot be moved across an integral sign.

Correct

$$\int 5x^{1/2}\,dx = 5\int x^{1/2}\,dx$$

Incorrect

$$\int xx^{1/2}\,dx = x\int x^{1/2}\,dx$$

Now let us put the formulas and properties to use.

Example 1 (A) $\displaystyle\int 5\,dx = 5x + C$

(B) $\displaystyle\int x^4\,dx = \frac{x^{4+1}}{4+1} + C = \frac{x^5}{5} + C$

(C) $\displaystyle\int 5x^7\,dx = 5\int x^7\,dx = 5\,\frac{x^8}{8} + C = \frac{5}{8}x^8 + C$

(D) $\displaystyle\int (4x^3 + 2x - 1)\,dx$

$$= \int 4x^3\,dx + \int 2x\,dx - \int dx$$

$$= 4\int x^3\,dx + 2\int x\,dx - \int dx$$

$$= \frac{4x^4}{4} + \frac{2x^2}{2} - x + C$$

$$= x^4 + x^2 - x + C$$

Property 4 can be extended to the sum and difference of an arbitrary number of functions.

(E) $\displaystyle\int \frac{3\,dx}{x^2} = \int 3x^{-2}\,dx = \frac{3x^{-2+1}}{-2+1} + C = -3x^{-1} + C$

(F) $\displaystyle\int 5\sqrt[3]{x^2}\,dx = 5\int x^{2/3}\,dx = 5\,\frac{x^{(2/3)+1}}{\frac{2}{3}+1} + C$

$$= 5\,\frac{x^{5/3}}{\frac{5}{3}} + C = 3x^{5/3} + C$$

To check any of these, we differentiate the final result to obtain the integrand in the original indefinite integral. When you evaluate an indefinite integral, do not forget to include the arbitrary constant C.

Problem 1 Find each of the following:

(A) $\displaystyle\int dx$

(B) $\displaystyle\int 3x^4\,dx$

(C) $\displaystyle\int (2x^5 - 3x^2 + 1)\,dx$

(D) $\displaystyle\int 4\sqrt[5]{x^3}\,dx$

(E) $\displaystyle\int \left(2x^{2/3} - \frac{3}{x^4}\right)dx$

Example 2   (A) $\displaystyle\int \frac{x^3 - 3}{x^2}\, dx \;=\; \int \left(\frac{x^3}{x^2} - \frac{3}{x^2}\right) dx$

$$= \int (x - 3x^{-2})\, dx$$

$$= \int x\, dx - 3 \int x^{-2}\, dx$$

$$= \frac{x^{1+1}}{1+1} - 3\frac{x^{-2+1}}{-2+1} + C$$

$$= \tfrac{1}{2}x^2 + 3x^{-1} + C$$

(B) $\displaystyle\int \left(\frac{2}{\sqrt[3]{x}} - 6\sqrt{x}\right) dx = \int (2x^{-1/3} - 6x^{1/2})\, dx$

$$= 2 \int x^{-1/3}\, dx - 6 \int x^{1/2}\, dx$$

$$= 2\frac{x^{(-1/3)+1}}{-\tfrac{1}{3}+1} - 6\frac{x^{(1/2)+1}}{\tfrac{1}{2}+1} + C$$

$$= 2\frac{x^{2/3}}{\tfrac{2}{3}} - 6\frac{x^{3/2}}{\tfrac{3}{2}} + C$$

$$= 3x^{2/3} - 4x^{3/2} + C$$

Problem 2   Find each indefinite integral.

(A) $\displaystyle\int \frac{x^4 - 8x^3}{x^2}\, dx$ (B) $\displaystyle\int \left(8\sqrt[3]{x} - \frac{6}{\sqrt{x}}\right) dx$

■ Indefinite Integrals Involving Exponential and Logarithmic Functions

Formula 5 (in the next box) follows immediately from the derivative formula for the exponential function discussed in the last chapter. Because of the absolute value, formula 6 does not follow directly from the derivative formula for the natural logarithm function. Let us show that

$$D_x \ln|x| = \frac{1}{x} \qquad x \neq 0$$

We consider two cases:

Case 1. $x > 0$

$$D_x \ln|x| = D_x \ln x \qquad \text{Since } |x| = x \text{ for } x > 0$$

$$= \frac{1}{x}$$

Indefinite Integral Formulas

5. $\displaystyle\int e^x \, dx = e^x + C$

6. $\displaystyle\int \frac{dx}{x} = \ln|x| + C \qquad x \neq 0$

Case 2. $x < 0$

$$D_x \ln|x| = D_x \ln(-x) \qquad \text{Since } |x| = -x \text{ for } x < 0$$

$$= \frac{1}{-x} D_x(-x)$$

$$= \frac{-1}{-x} = \frac{1}{x}$$

Thus,

$$D_x \ln|x| = \frac{1}{x} \qquad x \neq 0$$

Hence,

$$\int \frac{1}{x} \, dx = \ln|x| + C \qquad x \neq 0$$

What about the indefinite integral of $\ln x$? We postpone a discussion of $\int \ln x \, dx$ until Section 11-3, where we will be able to find it using a technique called *integration by parts*.

Example 3 $\displaystyle\int \left(2e^x + \frac{3}{x}\right) dx = 2 \int e^x \, dx + 3 \int \frac{1}{x} \, dx$

$$= 2e^x + 3 \ln|x| + C$$

Problem 3   Find $\displaystyle\int \left(\frac{5}{x} - 4e^x\right) dx$.

Let us now consider some applications of the indefinite integral to see why we are interested in finding antiderivatives of functions.

■ Applications

Example 4
Curves
Find the equation of the curve that passes through (2, 5) if its slope is given by $dy/dx = 2x$ at any point x.

Solution   We are interested in finding a function $y = f(x)$ such that

$$\frac{dy}{dx} = 2x \tag{1}$$

and

$$y = 5 \quad \text{when } x = 2 \tag{2}$$

If

$$\frac{dy}{dx} = 2x$$

then

$$y = \int 2x \, dx$$
$$= x^2 + C \tag{3}$$

Since $y = 5$ when $x = 2$, we determine the *particular* value of C so that

$$5 = 2^2 + C$$

Thus,

$$C = 1$$

and

$$y = x^2 + 1$$

is the particular antiderivative out of all those possible from (3) that satisfies both (1) and (2). See Figure 1.

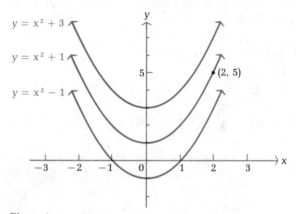

Figure 1 $y = x^2 + C$

Problem 4   Find the equation of the curve that passes through (2, 6) if the slope of the curve at any point x is given by $dy/dx = 3x^2$.

In certain situations it is easier to determine the rate at which something happens than how much of it has happened in a given length of time (e.g., population growth rates, business growth rates, rate of healing of a wound, rates of learning or forgetting). If a rate function (derivative) is given and we know the value of the dependent variable for a given value of the indepen- dent variable, then—if the rate function is not too complicated—we can often find the original function by integration.

Example 5
Cost Function

If the marginal cost of producing x units is given by

$$C'(x) = 0.3x^2 + 2x$$

and the fixed cost is $2,000, find the cost function $C(x)$ and the cost of producing twenty units.

Solution

Recall that marginal cost is the derivative of the cost function and that fixed cost is cost at a zero production level. Thus, the mathematical problem is to find $C(x)$ given

$$C'(x) = 0.3x^2 + 2x \qquad C(0) = 2,000$$

We now find the indefinite integral of $0.3x^2 + 2x$ and determine the arbi- trary integration constant using $C(0) = 2,000$.

$$C'(x) = 0.3x^2 + 2x$$

$$C(x) = \int (0.3x^2 + 2x) \, dx$$

$$= 0.1x^3 + x^2 + K \qquad \text{Since } C \text{ represents the cost, we use } K \text{ for the constant of integration.}$$

But

$$C(0) = (0.1)0^3 + 0^2 + K = 2,000$$

Thus,

$$K = 2,000$$

and the particular cost function is

$$C(x) = 0.1x^3 + x^2 + 2,000$$

We now find $C(20)$, the cost of producing twenty units:

$$C(20) = (0.1)20^3 + 20^2 + 2,000$$

$$= \$3,200$$

Problem 5

Find the revenue function $R(x)$ when the marginal revenue is

$$R'(x) = 400 - 0.4x$$

and no revenue results at a zero production level. What is the revenue at a production level of 1,000 units?

1. (A) $x + C$ (B) $\frac{3}{5}x^5 + C$ (C) $(x^6/3) - x^3 + x + C$
   (D) $\frac{5}{2}x^{8/5} + C$ (E) $\frac{6}{5}x^{5/3} + x^{-3} + C$
2. (A) $\frac{1}{3}x^3 - 4x^2 + C$ (B) $6x^{4/3} - 12x^{1/2} + C$
3. $5\ln|x| - 4e^x + C$ 4. $y = x^3 - 2$
5. $R(x) = 400x - 0.2x^2$; $R(1,000) = \$200,000$

Exercise 10-1

A   Find each indefinite integral. (Check by differentiating.)

1. $\displaystyle\int 7 \, dx$

2. $\displaystyle\int \pi \, dx$

3. $\displaystyle\int x^6 \, dx$

4. $\displaystyle\int x^3 \, dx$

5. $\displaystyle\int 8t^3 \, dt$

6. $\displaystyle\int 10t^4 \, dt$

7. $\displaystyle\int (2u + 1) \, du$

8. $\displaystyle\int (1 - 2u) \, du$

9. $\displaystyle\int (3x^2 + 2x - 5) \, dx$

10. $\displaystyle\int (2 + 4x - 6x^2) \, dx$

11. $\displaystyle\int (s^4 - 8s^5) \, ds$

12. $\displaystyle\int (t^5 + 6t^3) \, dt$

13. $\displaystyle\int 3e^t \, dt$

14. $\displaystyle\int 2e^t \, dt$

15. $\displaystyle\int 2z^{-1} \, dz$

16. $\displaystyle\int \frac{3}{s} \, ds$

Find all the antiderivatives for each derivative.

17. $\dfrac{dy}{dx} = 200x^4$

18. $\dfrac{dx}{dt} = 42t^5$

19. $\dfrac{dP}{dx} = 24 - 6x$

20. $\dfrac{dy}{dx} = 3x^2 - 4x^3$

21. $\dfrac{dy}{du} = 2u^5 - 3u^2 - 1$

22. $\dfrac{dA}{dt} = 3 - 12t^3 - 9t^5$

23. $\dfrac{dy}{dx} = e^x + 3$

24. $\dfrac{dy}{dx} = x - e^x$

25. $\dfrac{dx}{dt} = 5t^{-1} + 1$

26. $\dfrac{du}{dv} = \dfrac{4}{v} + \dfrac{v}{4}$

B Find each indefinite integral. (Check by differentiation.)

27. $\displaystyle\int 6x^{1/2}\,dx$

28. $\displaystyle\int 8t^{1/3}\,dt$

29. $\displaystyle\int 8x^{-3}\,dx$

30. $\displaystyle\int 12u^{-4}\,du$

31. $\displaystyle\int \frac{du}{\sqrt{u}}$

32. $\displaystyle\int \frac{dt}{\sqrt[3]{t}}$

33. $\displaystyle\int \frac{dx}{4x^3}$

34. $\displaystyle\int \frac{6\,dm}{m^2}$

35. $\displaystyle\int \frac{du}{2u^5}$

36. $\displaystyle\int \frac{dy}{3y^4}$

37. $\displaystyle\int \left(3x^2 - \frac{2}{x^2}\right)dx$

38. $\displaystyle\int \left(4x^3 + \frac{2}{x^3}\right)dx$

39. $\displaystyle\int \left(10x^4 - \frac{8}{x^5} - 2\right)dx$

40. $\displaystyle\int \left(\frac{6}{x^4} - \frac{2}{x^3} + 1\right)dx$

41. $\displaystyle\int \left(3\sqrt{x} + \frac{2}{\sqrt{x}}\right)dx$

42. $\displaystyle\int \left(\frac{2}{\sqrt[3]{x}} - \sqrt[3]{x^2}\right)dx$

43. $\displaystyle\int \left(\sqrt[3]{x^2} - \frac{4}{x^3}\right)dx$

44. $\displaystyle\int \left(\frac{12}{x^5} - \frac{1}{\sqrt[3]{x^2}}\right)dx$

45. $\displaystyle\int \frac{e^x - 3x}{4}\,dx$

46. $\displaystyle\int \frac{e^x - 3x^2}{2}\,dx$

47. $\displaystyle\int (2z^{-3} + z^{-2} + z^{-1})\,dz$

48. $\displaystyle\int (3x^{-2} - x^{-1})\,dx$

In Problems 49–58, find the particular antiderivative of each derivative that satisfies the given condition.

49. $\dfrac{dy}{dx} = 2x - 3, \quad y(0) = 5$

50. $\dfrac{dy}{dx} = 5 - 4x, \quad y(0) = 20$

51. $C'(x) = 6x^2 - 4x, \quad C(0) = 3{,}000$

52. $R'(x) = 600 - 0.6x, \quad R(0) = 0$

53. $\dfrac{dx}{dt} = \dfrac{20}{\sqrt{t}}, \quad x(1) = 40$

54. $\dfrac{dR}{dt} = \dfrac{100}{t^2}, \quad R(1) = 400$

55. $\dfrac{dy}{dx} = 2x^{-2} + 3x^{-1} - 1, \quad y(1) = 0$

56. $\dfrac{dy}{dx} = 3x^{-1} + x^{-2}, \quad y(1) = 1$

57. $\dfrac{dx}{dt} = 4e^t - 2, \quad x(0) = 1$

58. $\dfrac{dy}{dt} = 5e^t - 4, \quad y(0) = -1$

59. Find the equation of the curve that passes through (2, 3) if its slope is given by

$$\frac{dy}{dx} = 4x - 3$$

for each x.

60. Find the equation of the curve that passes through (1, 3) if its slope is given by

$$\frac{dy}{dx} = 12x^2 - 12x$$

for each x.

C *Find each indefinite integral.*

61. $\displaystyle\int \frac{2x^4 - x}{x^3} \, dx$

62. $\displaystyle\int \frac{x^{-1} - x^4}{x^2} \, dx$

63. $\displaystyle\int \frac{x^5 - 2x}{x^4} \, dx$

64. $\displaystyle\int \frac{1 - 3x^4}{x^2} \, dx$

65. $\displaystyle\int \frac{x^2 e^x - 2x}{x^2} \, dx$

66. $\displaystyle\int \frac{1 - xe^x}{x} \, dx$

Find the antiderivative of each of the derivatives that satisfies the given condition.

67. $\dfrac{dM}{dt} = \dfrac{t^2 - 1}{t^2}, \quad M(4) = 5$

68. $\dfrac{dR}{dx} = \dfrac{1 - x^4}{x^3}, \quad R(1) = 4$

69. $\dfrac{dy}{dx} = \dfrac{5x + 2}{\sqrt[3]{x}}, \quad y(1) = 0$

70. $\dfrac{dx}{dt} = \dfrac{\sqrt{t^3} - t}{\sqrt{t^3}}, \quad x(9) = 4$

71. $p'(x) = -\dfrac{10}{x^2}, \quad p(1) = 20$

72. $p'(x) = \dfrac{10}{x^3}, \quad p(1) = 15$

Applications

Business & Economics

73. *Profit function.* If the marginal profit for producing x units is given by

$$P'(x) = 50 - 0.04x \qquad P(0) = 0$$

where P(x) is the profit in dollars, find the profit function P and the profit on 100 units of production.

74. *Natural resources.* The world demand for wood is increasing. In 1975 the demand was 12.6 billion cubic feet, and the rate of increase in demand is given approximately by

$$d'(t) = 0.009t$$

where t is time in years after 1975 (data from the U.S. Department of Agriculture and Forest Service). Noting that $d(0) = 12.6$, find $d(t)$. Also find $d(25)$, the demand in the year 2000.

75. *Revenue function.* The marginal revenue for producing x digital sports watches is given by

$$R'(x) = 100 - \tfrac{1}{5}x \qquad R(0) = 0$$

where $R(x)$ is the revenue in dollars. Find the revenue function and the price–demand equation. What is the price when the demand is 700 units?

76. *Cost function.* The marginal average cost for producing x digital sports watches is given by

$$\overline{C}'(x) = -\frac{1,000}{x^2} \qquad \overline{C}(100) = 25$$

where $\overline{C}(x)$ is the average cost in dollars. Find the average cost function and the cost function. What are the fixed costs?

77. *Labor costs and learning.* A defense contractor is starting production on a new missile control system. On the basis of data collected while assembling the first 16 control systems, the production manager obtained the following function describing the rate of labor use:

$$g(x) = 2,400x^{-1/2}$$

where $g(x)$ is the number of labor-hours required to assemble the xth unit of the control system. For example, after assembling 16 units, the rate of assembly is 600 labor-hours per unit, and after assembling 25 units, the rate of assembly is 480 labor-hours per unit. The more units assembled, the more efficient the process because of learning. If 19,200 labor-hours are required to assemble the first 16 units, how many labor-hours, $L(x)$, will be required to assemble the first x units? The first 25 units?

78. *Labor costs and learning.* If the rate of labor use in Problem 77 is

$$g(x) = 2,000x^{-1/3}$$

and if the first 8 control units require 12,000 labor-hours, how many labor-hours, $L(x)$, will be required for the first x control units? The first 27 control units?

Life Sciences **79.** *Weight–height.* The rate of change of an average person's weight with respect to their height h (in inches) is given approximately by

$$\frac{dW}{dh} = 0.0015h^2$$

Find $W(h)$ if $W(60) = 108$ pounds. Also find the average weight for a person who is 5 feet 10 inches tall.

80. *Wound healing.* If the area of a healing wound changes at a rate given approximately by

$$\frac{dA}{dt} = -4t^{-3} \qquad 1 \leqslant t \leqslant 10$$

where t is in days and $A(1) = 2$ square centimeters, what will the area of the wound be in 10 days?

Social Sciences
81. *Urban growth.* A suburban area of Chicago incorporated into a city. The growth rate t in years after incorporation is estimated to be

$$\frac{dN}{dt} = 400 + 600\sqrt{t} \qquad 0 \leqslant t \leqslant 9$$

If the current population is 5,000, what will the population be 9 years from now?

82. *Learning.* A beginning high school language class was chosen for an experiment in learning. Using a list of 50 words, the experiment involved measuring the rate of vocabulary memorization at different times during a continuous 5 hour study session. It was found that the average rate of learning for the whole class was inversely proportional to the time spent studying and was given approximately by

$$V'(t) = \frac{15}{t} \qquad 1 \leqslant t \leqslant 5$$

If the average number of words memorized after 1 hour of study was 15 words, what was the average number of words learned after t hours of study, $1 \leqslant t \leqslant 5$? After 4 hours of study? (Round answer to the nearest whole number.)

10-2 Integration by Substitution

- General Integral Formulas
- Integration by Substitution
- Application
- Common Errors

■ General Integral Formulas

In Section 9-3, we saw that the chain rule extends the derivative formulas for x^n, e^x, and $\ln x$ to derivative formulas for $[f(x)]^n$, $e^{f(x)}$, and $\ln[f(x)]$. The chain rule can also be used to extend the integral formulas discussed in Section 10-1. The general formulas are summarized in the following box:

General Integral Formulas

1. $\displaystyle \int [f(x)]^n f'(x)\, dx = \frac{[f(x)]^{n+1}}{n+1} + C \qquad n \neq -1$

2. $\displaystyle \int e^{f(x)} f'(x)\, dx = e^{f(x)} + C$

3. $\displaystyle \int \frac{1}{f(x)} f'(x)\, dx = \ln|f(x)| + C$

Each of these formulas can be verified by using the chain rule to show that the derivative of the function on the right is the integrand on the left. For example,

$$D_x[e^{f(x)} + C] = e^{f(x)} f'(x)$$

verifies formula 2.

Example 6 (A) $\displaystyle \int (3x+4)^{10} 3\, dx = \frac{(3x+4)^{11}}{11} + C \qquad$ Formula 1 with $f(x) = 3x+4$ and $f'(x) = 3$

Check $\displaystyle D_x \frac{(3x+4)^{11}}{11} = 11 \frac{(3x+4)^{10}}{11} D_x(3x+4) = (3x+4)^{10} 3$

(B) $\displaystyle \int e^{x^2} 2x\, dx = e^{x^2} + C \qquad$ Formula 2 with $f(x) = x^2$ and $f'(x) = 2x$

Check $\displaystyle D_x e^{x^2} = e^{x^2} D_x x^2 = e^{x^2} 2x$

(C) $\displaystyle \int \frac{1}{1+x^3} 3x^2\, dx = \ln|1+x^3| + C \qquad$ Formula 3 with $f(x) = 1+x^3$ and $f'(x) = 3x^2$

Check $\displaystyle D_x \ln|1+x^3| = \frac{1}{1+x^3} D_x(1+x^3) = \frac{1}{1+x^3} 3x^2$

Problem 6 Find each indefinite integral.

(A) $\displaystyle \int (2x^3 - 3)^{20} 6x^2\, dx$ (B) $\displaystyle \int e^{5x} 5\, dx$ (C) $\displaystyle \int \frac{1}{4+x^2} 2x\, dx$

■ Integration by Substitution

The key step in using formulas 1, 2, and 3 is recognizing the form of the integrand. Some people find it difficult to identify $f(x)$ and $f'(x)$ in these formulas and prefer to use a *substitution* to simplify the integrand. The

method of substitution, which we now discuss, becomes increasingly useful as one progresses in studies of integration.

Example 7   Find $\int (x^2 + 2x + 5)^5(2x + 2)\, dx$.

Solution   If

$$u = x^2 + 2x + 5$$

then the differential of u is (see Section 8-5)

$$du = (2x + 2)\, dx$$

Notice that du is one of the factors in the integrand. Substitute u for $x^2 + 2x + 5$ and du for $(2x + 2)\, dx$ to obtain

$$\int (x^2 + 2x + 5)^5(2x + 2)\, dx = \int u^5\, du$$

$$= \frac{u^6}{6} + C$$

$$= \tfrac{1}{6}(x^2 + 2x + 5)^6 + C \qquad \text{Since } u = x^2 + 2x + 5$$

Check $D_x \tfrac{1}{6}(x^2 + 2x + 5)^6 = \tfrac{1}{6}(6)(x^2 + 2x + 5)^5 D_x(x^2 + 2x + 5)$
$$= (x^2 + 2x + 5)^5(2x + 2)$$

Problem 7   Find $\int (x^2 - 3x + 7)^4(2x - 3)\, dx$ by substitution.

Substituting $u = f(x)$ and $du = f'(x)\, dx$ in formulas 1, 2, and 3 produces the formulas in the next box. These formulas are valid if u is an independent variable or if u is a function and du is the differential of u.

Integration Formulas

4. $\displaystyle \int u^n\, du = \frac{u^{n+1}}{n + 1} + C \qquad n \neq -1$

5. $\displaystyle \int e^u\, du = e^u + C$

6. $\displaystyle \int \frac{1}{u}\, du = \ln|u| + C$

In some cases, the integrand will have to be modified before making a substitution and using one of the integration formulas. Example 8 illustrates this process.

Example 8   Integrate:

(A) $\displaystyle \int \frac{1}{4x + 7}\, dx$ (B) $\displaystyle \int xe^{-x^2}\, dx$ (C) $\displaystyle \int 4x^2 \sqrt{x^3 + 5}\, dx$

Solutions   (A) If $u = 4x + 7$, then $du = 4\,dx$. We are missing a factor of 4 in the integrand to match formula 6 exactly. Recalling that a constant factor can be moved across an integral sign, we proceed as follows:

$$\int \frac{1}{4x+7}\,dx = \int \frac{1}{4x+7}\frac{4}{4}\,dx$$

$$= \frac{1}{4}\int \frac{1}{4x+7}4\,dx \qquad \text{Substitute } u = 4x + 7$$
$$\text{and } du = 4\,dx.$$

$$= \frac{1}{4}\int \frac{1}{u}\,du \qquad \text{Use formula 6.}$$

$$= \tfrac{1}{4}\ln|u| + C$$

$$= \tfrac{1}{4}\ln|4x+7| + C \qquad \text{Since } u = 4x + 7$$

Check $D_x \dfrac{1}{4}\ln|4x+7| = \dfrac{1}{4}\dfrac{1}{4x+7}D_x(4x+7) = \dfrac{1}{4}\dfrac{1}{4x+7}(4) = \dfrac{1}{4x+7}$

(B) If $u = -x^2$, then $du = -2x\,dx$. Proceed as in part A:

$$\int xe^{-x^2}\,dx = \int e^{-x^2}\frac{-2}{-2}x\,dx$$

$$= -\frac{1}{2}\int e^{-x^2}(-2x)\,dx \qquad \text{Substitute } u = -x^2$$
$$\text{and } du = -2x\,dx.$$

$$= -\frac{1}{2}\int e^u\,du \qquad \text{Use formula 5.}$$

$$= -\tfrac{1}{2}e^u + C$$

$$= -\tfrac{1}{2}e^{-x^2} + C \qquad \text{Since } u = -x^2$$

Check $D_x(-\tfrac{1}{2}e^{-x^2}) = -\tfrac{1}{2}e^{-x^2}D_x(-x^2) = -\tfrac{1}{2}e^{-x^2}(-2x) = xe^{-x^2}$

(C) $\displaystyle\int 4x^2\sqrt{x^3+5}\,dx = 4\int \sqrt{x^3+5}\,x^2\,dx$ Move the 4 across the integral sign and proceed as before.

$$= 4\int \sqrt{x^3+5}\,\frac{3}{3}x^2\,dx$$

$$= \frac{4}{3}\int \sqrt{x^3+5}\,3x^2\,dx \qquad \text{Substitute } u = x^3 + 5$$
$$\text{and } du = 3x^2.$$

$$= \frac{4}{3}\int \sqrt{u}\,du$$

$$= \frac{4}{3}\int u^{1/2}\,du \qquad \text{Use formula 4.}$$

$$= \frac{4}{3}\frac{u^{3/2}}{\frac{3}{2}} + C$$

$$= \tfrac{8}{9}u^{3/2} + C$$

$$= \tfrac{8}{9}(x^3+5)^{3/2} + C \qquad \text{Since } u = x^3 + 5$$

Check $D_x[\frac{8}{9}(x^3 + 5)^{3/2}] = \frac{4}{3}(x^3 + 5)^{1/2}D_x(x^3 + 5)$
$$= \frac{4}{3}(x^3 + 5)^{1/2}3x^2 = 4x^2\sqrt{x^3 + 5}$$

Problem 8   Integrate:

(A) $\displaystyle\int e^{-3x}\,dx$ (B) $\displaystyle\int \frac{x}{x^2 - 9}\,dx$ (C) $\displaystyle\int 5x^2(x^3 + 4)^{-2}\,dx$

■ Application

Example 9
Price–Demand

The market research department for a supermarket chain has determined that for one store the marginal price $p'(x)$ at x tubes per week for a certain brand of toothpaste is given by

$$p'(x) = -0.015e^{-0.01x}$$

Find the price–demand equation if the weekly demand is 50 when the price of a tube is $2.35. Find the weekly demand when the price of a tube is $1.89.

Solution

$$p(x) = \int -0.015e^{-0.01x}\,dx$$

$$= -0.015\int e^{-0.01x}\,dx$$

$$= -0.015\int e^{-0.01x}\frac{-0.01}{-0.01}\,dx$$

$$= \frac{-0.015}{-0.01}\int e^{-0.01x}(-0.01)\,dx \qquad \text{Substitute } u = -0.01x \text{ and } du = -0.01\,dx.$$

$$= 1.5\int e^u\,du$$

$$= 1.5e^u + C$$

$$= 1.5e^{-0.01x} + C \qquad \text{Since } u = -0.01x$$

We find C by noting that

$$p(50) = 1.5e^{-0.01(50)} + C = \$2.35$$

$$C = \$2.35 - 1.5e^{-0.5} \qquad \text{Use a calculator or a table.}$$

$$C = \$2.35 - 0.91$$

$$C = \$1.44$$

Thus,

$$p(x) = 1.5e^{-0.01x} + 1.44$$

To find the demand when the price is $1.89, we solve $p(x) = \$1.89$ for x:

$$1.5e^{-0.01x} + 1.44 = 1.89$$

$$1.5e^{-0.01x} = 0.45$$

$$e^{-0.01x} = 0.3$$

$$-0.01x = \ln 0.3$$

$$x = -100 \ln 0.3 \approx 120 \text{ tubes}$$

Problem 9 The marginal price $p'(x)$ at a supply level of x tubes per week for a certain brand of toothpaste is given by

$$p'(x) = 0.001e^{0.01x}$$

Find the price–supply equation if the supplier is willing to supply 100 tubes per week at a price of \$1.65 each. How many tubes would the supplier be willing to supply at a price of \$1.98 each?

■ Common Errors

1. $\displaystyle \int 2(x^2 - 3)^{3/2} \, dx = \int (x^2 - 3)^{3/2} 2 \, \frac{x}{x} \, dx$

$$= \frac{1}{x} \int (x^2 - 3)^{3/2}(2x) \, dx$$

A variable cannot be moved across an integral sign! This integral requires techniques that are beyond the scope of this book.

2. $\displaystyle \int \frac{2x^2}{(x^2 - 3)^2} \, dx = \int (x^2 - 3)^{-2} 2x^2 \, dx$

$$= x \int (x^2 - 3)^{-2}(2x) \, dx$$

No, for the same reason as in illustration 1.

3. $\displaystyle \int \frac{1}{x^2 + 9} \, dx = \int \frac{1}{u} \, dx \qquad u = x^2 + 9$

$$= \ln |u|$$

An integrand must be expressed entirely in terms of u and du before formulas 4, 5, and 6 on page 746 can be used.

A constant factor can be moved back and forth across an integral sign, but a variable factor cannot.

Yes	*No*
$\displaystyle \int kf(x) \, dx = k \int f(x) \, dx$	$\displaystyle \int f(x)g(x) \, dx = f(x) \int g(x) \, dx$
(k a constant factor)	[$f(x)$ a variable factor]

6. (A) $\frac{1}{21}(2x^3 - 3)^{21} + C$ (B) $e^{5x} + C$
   (C) $\ln|4 + x^2| + C$ or $\ln(4 + x^2) + C$, since $4 + x^2 > 0$
7. $\frac{1}{5}(x^2 - 3x + 7)^5 + C$
8. (A) $-\frac{1}{3}e^{-3x} + C$ (B) $\frac{1}{2}\ln|x^2 - 9| + C$ (C) $-\frac{2}{3}(x^3 + 4)^{-1} + C$
9. $p(x) = 0.1e^{0.01x} + 1.38$; 179 tubes

Exercise 10-2

A   *Find each indefinite integral and check the result by differentiating.*

1. $\displaystyle\int (x^2 - 4)^5 2x \, dx$

2. $\displaystyle\int (x^3 + 1)^4 3x^2 \, dx$

3. $\displaystyle\int e^{4x} 4 \, dx$

4. $\displaystyle\int e^{-3x}(-3) \, dx$

5. $\displaystyle\int \frac{1}{2t + 3} 2 \, dt$

6. $\displaystyle\int \frac{1}{5t - 7} 5 \, dt$

B   7. $\displaystyle\int (3x - 2)^7 \, dx$

8. $\displaystyle\int (5x + 3)^9 \, dx$

9. $\displaystyle\int (x^2 + 3)^7 x \, dx$

10. $\displaystyle\int (x^3 - 5)^4 x^2 \, dx$

11. $\displaystyle\int 10e^{-0.5t} \, dt$

12. $\displaystyle\int 4e^{0.01t} \, dt$

13. $\displaystyle\int \frac{1}{10x + 7} \, dx$

14. $\displaystyle\int \frac{1}{100 - 3x} \, dx$

15. $\displaystyle\int xe^{2x^2} \, dx$

16. $\displaystyle\int x^2 e^{4x^3} \, dx$

17. $\displaystyle\int \frac{x^2}{x^3 + 4} \, dx$

18. $\displaystyle\int \frac{x}{x^2 - 2} \, dx$

19. $\displaystyle\int \frac{t}{(3t^2 + 1)^4} \, dt$

20. $\displaystyle\int \frac{t^2}{(t^3 - 2)^5} \, dt$

21. $\displaystyle\int \frac{x^2}{(4 - x^3)^2} \, dx$

22. $\displaystyle\int \frac{x}{(5 - 2x^2)^5} \, dx$

23. $\displaystyle\int e^{2x}(1 + e^{2x})^3 \, dx$

24. $\displaystyle\int e^{-x}(1 - e^{-x})^4 \, dx$

25. $\displaystyle\int \frac{1 + x}{4 + 2x + x^2} \, dx$

26. $\displaystyle\int \frac{x^2 - 1}{x^3 - 3x + 7} \, dx$

27. $\displaystyle\int (2x + 1)e^{x^2 + x + 1} \, dx$

28. $\displaystyle\int (x^2 + 2x)e^{x^3 + 3x^2} \, dx$

29. $\displaystyle\int (e^x - 2x)^3(e^x - 2)\, dx$

30. $\displaystyle\int (x^2 - e^x)^4(2x - e^x)\, dx$

31. $\displaystyle\int \frac{x^3 + x}{(x^4 + 2x^2 + 1)^4}\, dx$

32. $\displaystyle\int \frac{x^2 - 1}{(x^3 - 3x + 7)^2}\, dx$

C 33. $\displaystyle\int x\sqrt{3x^2 + 7}\, dx$

34. $\displaystyle\int x^2\sqrt{2x^3 + 1}\, dx$

35. $\displaystyle\int \frac{x^3}{\sqrt{2x^4 + 3}}\, dx$

36. $\displaystyle\int \frac{x^2}{\sqrt{4x^3 - 1}}\, dx$

37. $\displaystyle\int \frac{(\ln x)^3}{x}\, dx$

38. $\displaystyle\int \frac{e^x}{1 + e^x}\, dx$

39. $\displaystyle\int \frac{1}{x^2}\, e^{-1/x}\, dx$

40. $\displaystyle\int \frac{1}{x \ln x}\, dx$

Find the antiderivative of each derivative.

41. $\dfrac{dx}{dt} = 7t^2(t^3 + 5)^6$

42. $\dfrac{dm}{dn} = 10n(n^2 - 8)^7$

43. $\dfrac{dy}{dt} = \dfrac{3t}{\sqrt{t^2 - 4}}$

44. $\dfrac{dy}{dx} = \dfrac{5x^2}{(x^3 - 7)^4}$

45. $\dfrac{dp}{dx} = \dfrac{e^x + e^{-x}}{(e^x - e^{-x})^2}$

46. $\dfrac{dm}{dt} = \dfrac{\ln(t - 5)}{t - 5}$

■ Applications
_____

Business & Economics

47. *Price–demand equation.* The marginal price for a weekly demand of x bottles of baby shampoo in a drug store is given by

$$p'(x) = \frac{-6,000}{(3x + 50)^2}$$

Find the price–demand equation if the weekly demand is 150 when the price of a bottle of shampoo is $4. What is the weekly demand when the price is $2.50?

48. *Price–supply equation.* The marginal price at a supply level of x bottles of baby shampoo per week is given by

$$p'(x) = \frac{300}{(3x + 25)^2}$$

Find the price–supply equation if the distributor of the shampoo is willing to supply 75 bottles a week at a price of $1.60 per bottle. How many bottles would the supplier be willing to supply at a price of $1.75 per bottle?

49. *Cost function.* The weekly marginal cost of producing x pairs of tennis

shoes is given by

$$C'(x) = 12 + \frac{500}{x + 1}$$

where $C(x)$ is cost in dollars. If the fixed costs are $2,000 per week, find the cost function. What is the average cost per pair of shoes if 1,000 pairs of shoes are produced each week?

50. *Revenue function.* The weekly marginal revenue from the sale of x pairs of tennis shoes is given by

$$R'(x) = 40 - 0.02x + \frac{200}{x + 1} \qquad R(0) = 0$$

where $R(x)$ is revenue in dollars. Find the revenue function. Find the revenue from the sale of 1,000 pairs of shoes.

51. *Marketing.* An automobile company is ready to introduce a new line of cars with a national sales campaign. After test marketing the line in a carefully selected city, the marketing research department estimates that sales (in millions of dollars) will increase at the monthly rate of

$$S'(t) = 10 - 10e^{-0.1t} \qquad 0 \leqslant t \leqslant 24$$

t months after the national campaign has started. What will be the total sales, $S(t)$, t months after the beginning of the national campaign if we assume zero sales at the beginning of the campaign? What is the estimated total sales for the first 12 months of the campaign?

52. *Marketing.* Repeat Problem 51 if the monthly rate of increase in sales is found to be approximated by

$$S'(t) = 20 - 20e^{-0.05t} \qquad 0 \leqslant t \leqslant 24$$

53. *Oil production.* Using data from the first 3 years' production as well as geological studies, the management of an oil company estimates that oil will be pumped from a producing field at a rate given by

$$R(t) = \frac{100}{t + 1} + 5 \qquad 0 \leqslant t \leqslant 20$$

where $R(t)$ is the rate of production in thousands of barrels per year t years after pumping begins. How many barrels of oil, $Q(t)$, will the field produce the first t years if $Q(0) = 0$? How many barrels will be produced the first 9 years?

54. *Oil production.* In Problem 53, if the rate is found to be

$$R(t) = \frac{120t}{t^2 + 1} + 3 \qquad 0 \leqslant t \leqslant 20$$

how many barrels of oil, $Q(t)$, will the field produce the first t years if $Q(0) = 0$? How many barrels will be produced the first 5 years?

Life Sciences

55. *Biology.* A yeast culture is growing at the rate of $W'(t) = 0.2e^{0.1t}$ grams per hour. If the starting culture weighs 2 grams, what will be the weight of the culture, $W(t)$, after t hours? After 8 hours?

56. *Medicine.* The rate of healing for a skin wound (in square centimeters per day) is approximated by $A'(t) = -0.9e^{0.1t}$. If the initial wound has an area of 9 square centimeters, what will its area, $A(t)$, be after t days? After 5 days?

57. *Pollution.* A contaminated lake is treated with a bactericide. The rate of decrease in harmful bacteria t days after the treatment is given by

$$\frac{dN}{dt} = -\frac{2{,}000t}{1 + t^2} \qquad 0 \le t \le 10$$

where $N(t)$ is the number of bacteria per milliliter of water. If the initial count was 5,000 bacteria per milliliter, find $N(t)$ and then find the bacteria count after 10 days.

58. *Pollution.* An oil tanker aground on a reef is losing oil and producing an oil slick that is radiating outward at a rate given approximately by

$$\frac{dR}{dt} = \frac{60}{\sqrt{t + 9}} \qquad t \ge 0$$

where R is the radius in feet of the circular slick after t minutes. Find the radius of the slick after 16 minutes if the radius is 0 when $t = 0$.

Social Sciences

59. *Learning.* In a particular business college, it was found that an average student enrolled in an advanced typing class progressed at a rate of $N'(t) = 6e^{-0.1t}$ words per minute per week, t weeks after enrolling in a 15 week course. If at the beginning of the course a student could type 40 words per minute, how many words per minute, $N(t)$, would the student be expected to type t weeks into the course? After completing the course?

60. *Learning.* In the same business college, it was also found that an average student enrolled in a beginning shorthand class progressed at a rate of $N'(t) = 12e^{-0.06t}$ words per minute per week, t weeks after enrolling in a 15 week course. If at the beginning of the course a student could take dictation in shorthand at 0 words per minute, how many words per minute, $N(t)$, would the student be expected to handle t weeks into the course? After completing the course?

61. *College enrollment.* The projected rate of increase in enrollment in a new college is estimated by

$$\frac{dE}{dt} = 5{,}000(t + 1)^{-3/2} \qquad t \ge 0$$

where $E(t)$ is the projected enrollment in t years. If enrollment is 2,000 when $t = 0$, find the projected enrollment 15 years from now.

10-3 Differential Equations—Growth and Decay

- Differential Equations
- Continuous Compound Interest Revisited
- Exponential Growth Law
- Population Growth, Radioactive Decay, Learning
- A Comparison of Exponential Growth Phenomena

■ Differential Equations

In the last section we considered equations of the form

$$\frac{dy}{dx} = 6x^2 - 4x \qquad p'(x) = -400e^{-0.04x}$$

These are examples of differential equations. In general an equation is a **differential equation** if it involves an unknown function (often denoted by y) and one or more of its derivatives. Other examples of differential equations are

$$\frac{dy}{dx} = ky \qquad y'' - xy' + x^2 = 5$$

Finding solutions to different types of differential equations (functions that satisfy the equation) is the subject matter for whole books and courses on the subject. Here we will consider only a few very special but very important types of equations that have immediate and significant application. We start by considering the problem of continuous compound interest from another point of view, which will enable us to generalize the concept and apply the results to problems from a number of different fields.

■ Continuous Compound Interest Revisited

Let P be the initial amount of money deposited in an account and let A be the amount in the account at any time t. Instead of assuming that the money in the account earns a particular rate of interest, suppose we say that *the rate of growth of the amount of money in the account at any time t is proportional to the amount present at that time.* Since dA/dt is the rate of growth of A with respect to t, we have

$$\frac{dA}{dt} = rA \qquad A(0) = P \qquad A, P > 0 \tag{1}$$

where r is an appropriate constant. We would like to find a function $A = A(t)$ that satisfies these conditions. Multiplying both sides of equation

(1) by $1/A$, we obtain

$$\frac{1}{A}\frac{dA}{dt} = r$$

Now we integrate each side with respect to t,

$$\int \frac{1}{A}\frac{dA}{dt}\,dt = \int r\,dt \qquad \text{Use formula 3 in Section 10-2}$$
$$\text{to evaluate the left side.}$$

$$\ln|A| = rt + C \qquad |A| = A \quad \text{since } A > 0$$
$$\ln A = rt + C$$

and convert this last equation into the equivalent exponential form

$$A = e^{rt+C} \qquad \text{From Section 0-7, } y = \ln x \text{ if and}$$
$$\text{only if } x = e^y.$$

$$= e^C e^{rt} \qquad \text{Property of exponents: } b^m b^n = b^{m+n}$$

Since $A(0) = P$, we evaluate $A(t) = e^C e^{rt}$ at $t = 0$ and set it equal to P:

$$A(0) = e^C e^0 = e^C = P$$

Hence, $e^C = P$, and we can rewrite $A = e^C e^{rt}$ in the form

$$A = Pe^{rt}$$

This is the same continuous compound interest formula obtained in Section 9-1, where the principal P is invested at an annual nominal rate of $100r\%$ compounded continuously for t years.

■ Exponential Growth Law

In general, if the rate of change with respect to time of a quantity Q is proportional to the amount present and $Q(0) = Q_0$, then proceeding in exactly the same way as above, we obtain the following:

Exponential Growth Law

If $\dfrac{dQ}{dt} = rQ$ and $Q(0) = Q_0$, then $Q = Q_0 e^{rt}$.

$Q_0 = $ Amount at $t = 0$

$r = $ Continuous compound growth rate

$t = $ Time

$Q = $ Quantity at time t

The constant r in the exponential growth law is sometimes called the **growth constant** or even the **growth rate.** This last term can be misleading, since the rate of growth of Q with respect to time is dQ/dt, not r. Notice that if $r < 0$, then $dQ/dt < 0$ and Q is decreasing. This type of growth is called **exponential decay.**

Once we know that the rate of growth of something is proportional to the amount present, then we know it has exponential growth and we can use the results summarized in the box without having to solve the involved differential equation each time. The exponential growth law applies not only to money invested at interest compounded continuously, but also to many other types of problems—population growth, radioactive decay, natural resource depletion, and so on.

■ Population Growth, Radioactive Decay, Learning

The world population is growing at an ever-increasing rate, as illustrated in Figure 2. **Population growth** over certain periods of time can often be approximated by the exponential growth law described above.

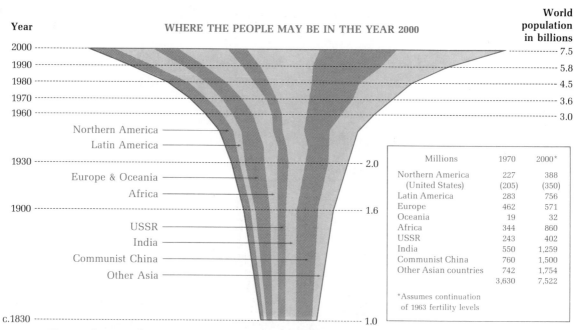

Figure 2 The population explosion. *Source:* United States State Department

Example 10
Population Growth

India had a population of 500 million people in 1966 ($t = 0$) and a growth rate of 3% per year (which we will assume is compounded continuously). If

P is the population in millions *t* years after 1966, and the same growth rate continues, then

$$\frac{dP}{dt} = 0.03P \qquad P(0) = 500$$

Thus, using the exponential growth law, we obtain

$$P = 500e^{0.03t}$$

With this result, we can estimate the population of India in 1986 ($t = 20$) to be

$$P(20) = 500e^{0.03(20)}$$

$$\approx 911 \text{ million people}$$

Problem 10   Assuming the same continuous compound growth rate, what will India's population be in the year 2001?

Example 11   If the exponential growth law applies to Russia's population growth, at
Population Growth   what continuous compound growth rate will the population double over the next 100 years?

Solution   The problem is to find *r*, given $P = 2P_0$ and $t = 100$:

$$P = P_0 e^{rt}$$
$$2P_0 = P_0 e^{100r}$$
$$2 = e^{100r} \qquad\qquad \text{Take ln of both sides and reverse equation.}$$
$$100r = \ln 2$$
$$r = \frac{\ln 2}{100}$$
$$\approx 0.0069 \quad \text{or} \quad 0.69\%$$

Problem 11   If the exponential growth law applies to population growth in Mexico, find the doubling time of the population if it continues to grow at 3.2% per year compounded continuously.

We now turn to another type of exponential growth — **radioactive decay.** In 1946, Willard Libby (who later received a Nobel Prize in chemistry) found that as long as a plant or animal is alive, radioactive carbon-14 is maintained at a constant level in its tissues. Once the plant or animal is dead, however, the radioactive carbon-14 diminishes by radioactive decay at a rate proportional to the amount present. Thus,

$$\frac{dQ}{dt} = rQ \qquad Q(0) = Q_0$$

and we have another example of the exponential growth law. The continuous compound rate of decay for radioactive carbon-14 is found to be 0.000 123 8; thus, $r = -0.000\ 123\ 8$, since decay implies a negative continuous compound growth rate.

Example 12
Archaeology

A piece of human bone was found at an archaeological site in Africa. If 10% of the original amount of radioactive carbon-14 was present, estimate the age of the bone.

Solution

Using the exponential growth law for

$$\frac{dQ}{dt} = -0.000\ 123\ 8Q \qquad Q(0) = Q_0$$

we find that

$$Q = Q_0 e^{-0.0001238t}$$

and our problem is to find t so that $Q = 0.1Q_0$ (the amount of carbon-14 present now is 10% of the amount present, Q_0, at the death of the person). Thus,

$$0.1Q_0 = Q_0 e^{-0.0001238t}$$
$$0.1 = e^{-0.0001238t}$$
$$\ln 0.1 = \ln e^{-0.0001238t}$$
$$t = \frac{\ln 0.1}{-0.0001238} \approx 18,600 \text{ years}$$

Problem 12

Estimate the age of the bone in Example 12 if 50% of the original amount of carbon-14 is present.

In learning certain skills such as typing and swimming, a mathematical model often used is one that assumes there is a maximum skill attainable, say M, and the rate of improving is proportional to the difference between that achieved, y, and that attainable, M. Mathematically,

$$\frac{dy}{dt} = k(M - y) \qquad y(0) = 0$$

We solve this using the same technique that was used to obtain the exponential growth law. First, multiply both sides of the first equation by $1/(M - y)$ to obtain

$$\frac{1}{M - y}\frac{dy}{dt} = k$$

and then integrate both sides:

$$\int \frac{1}{M-y} \frac{dy}{dt}\, dt = \int k\, dt$$

$$-\int \frac{1}{M-y} \left(-\frac{dy}{dt}\right) dt = \int k\, dt \qquad \text{Use formula 3 in Section 10-2 to evaluate the left side.}$$

$$-\ln(M-y) = kt + C \qquad \text{No absolute value signs required. (Why?)}$$

Change this last equation to equivalent exponential form:

$$M - y = e^{-kt-C}$$

$$M - y = e^{-C}e^{-kt}$$

$$y = M - e^{-C}e^{-kt}$$

Now $y(0) = 0$; hence,

$$y(0) = M - e^{-C}e^0 = 0$$

Solving for e^{-C}, we obtain

$$e^{-C} = M$$

and our final solution is

$$y = M - Me^{-kt} = M(1 - e^{-kt})$$

Example 13
Learning

For a particular person who is learning to swim, it is found that the distance y (in feet) the person is able to swim in 1 minute after t hours of practice is given approximately by

$$y = 50(1 - e^{-0.04t})$$

What is the rate of improvement after 10 hours of practice?

Solution

$$y = 50 - 50e^{-0.04t}$$

$$y'(t) = 2e^{-0.04t}$$

$$y'(10) = 2e^{-0.04(10)} \approx 1.34 \text{ feet per hour of practice}$$

Problem 13   In Example 13, what is the rate of improvement after 50 hours of practice?

■ A Comparison of Exponential Growth Phenomena

The graphs and equations given in Table 1 (on the next page) compare several widely used growth models. These are divided basically into two groups: unlimited growth and limited growth. Following each graph and equation is a short, incomplete list of areas in which the models are used. This only touches on a subject that has been extensively developed and which you are likely to encounter in greater depth in the future.

Table 1 Exponential Growth

Description	Model	Solution	Graph	Uses
Unlimited growth Rate of growth is proportional to the amount present.	$\dfrac{dy}{dt} = ky$ $k, t > 0$ $y(0) = c$	$y = ce^{kt}$		· Short-term population growth (people, bacteria, etc.) · Growth of money at continuous compound interest · Price–supply curves · Depletion of natural resources
Exponential decay Rate of growth is proportional to the amount present.	$\dfrac{dy}{dt} = -ky$ $k, t > 0$ $y(0) = c$	$y = ce^{-kt}$		· Radioactive decay · Light absorption in water · Price–demand curves · Atmospheric pressure (t is altitude)
Limited growth Rate of growth is proportional to the difference between the amount present and a fixed limit.	$\dfrac{dy}{dt} = k(M - y)$ $k, t > 0$ $y(0) = 0$	$y = c(1 - e^{-kt})$		· Learning · Sales fads (e.g., skateboards) · Depreciation of equipment · Company growth
Logistic growth Rate of growth is proportional to the amount present and to the difference between the amount present and a fixed amount.	$\dfrac{dy}{dt} = ky(M - y)$ $k, t > 0$ $y(0) = \dfrac{M}{1 + c}$	$y = \dfrac{M}{1 + ce^{-kMt}}$		· Learning · Long-term population growth · Epidemics · Sales of new products · Company growth

Answers to Matched Problems

10. 1,429 million people   11. Approx. 22 years
12. Approx. 5,600 years   13. Approx. 0.27 foot per hour

Exercise 10-3

Applications

Business & Economics

1. *Continuous compound interest.* Find the amount A in an account after t years if

   $$\frac{dA}{dt} = 0.08A \quad \text{and} \quad A(0) = 1{,}000$$

2. *Continuous compound interest.* Find the amount A in an account after t years if

   $$\frac{dA}{dt} = 0.12A \quad \text{and} \quad A(0) = 5{,}250$$

3. *Continuous compound interest.* Find the amount A in an account after t years if

   $$\frac{dA}{dt} = rA \qquad A(0) = 8{,}000 \quad A(2) = 9{,}020$$

4. *Continuous compound interest.* Find the amount A in an account after t years if

   $$\frac{dA}{dt} = rA \qquad A(0) = 5{,}000 \quad A(5) = 7{,}460$$

5. *Price-demand.* If the marginal price dp/dx at x units of demand per week is proportional to the price p, and if at \$100 there is no weekly demand [$p(0) = 100$], and if at \$77.88 there is a weekly demand of 5 units [$p(5) = 77.88$], find the price–demand equation.

6. *Price–supply.* If the marginal price dp/dx at x units of supply per day is proportional to the price p, and if at a price of \$10 there is no daily supply [$p(0) = 10$], and if at a price of \$12.84 there is a daily supply of 50 units [$p(50) = 12.84$], find the price–supply equation.

7. *Advertising.* A company is trying to expose a new product to as many people as possible through television advertising. Suppose the rate of exposure to new people is proportional to the number of those who have not seen the product out of L possible viewers. If no one is aware of the product at the start of the campaign and after 10 days 40% of L are aware of the product, solve

   $$\frac{dN}{dt} = k(L - N) \qquad N(0) = 0 \quad N(10) = 0.4L$$

   for $N = N(t)$, the number of people who are aware of the product after t days of advertising.

8. *Advertising.* Repeat Problem 7 for

$$\frac{dN}{dt} = k(L - N) \qquad N(0) = 0 \quad N(10) = 0.1L$$

Life Sciences

9. *Ecology.* For relatively clear bodies of water, light intensity is reduced according to

$$\frac{dI}{dx} = -kI \qquad I(0) = I_0$$

where I is the intensity of light at x feet below the surface. For the Sargasso Sea off the West Indies, $k = 0.009\ 42$. Find I in terms of x and find the depth at which the light is reduced to half of that at the surface.

10. *Blood pressure.* It can be shown under certain assumptions that blood pressure P in the largest artery in the human body (the aorta) changes between beats with respect to time t according to

$$\frac{dP}{dt} = -aP \qquad P(0) = P_0$$

where a is a constant. Find $P = P(t)$ that satisfies both conditions.

11. *Drug concentrations.* A single injection of a drug is administered to a patient. The amount Q in the body then decreases at a rate proportional to the amount present, and for this particular drug the rate is 4% per hour. Thus,

$$\frac{dQ}{dt} = -0.04Q \qquad Q(0) = Q_0$$

where t is time in hours. If the initial injection is 3 milliliters $[Q(0) = 3]$, find $Q = Q(t)$ that satisfies both conditions. How many milliliters of the drug are still in the body after 10 hours?

12. *Simple epidemic.* A community of 1,000 individuals is assumed to be homogeneously mixed. One individual who has just returned from another community has influenza. Assume the home community has not had influenza shots and all are susceptible. One mathematical model for an influenza epidemic assumes that influenza tends to spread at a rate in direct proportion to the number who have it, N, and to the number who have not contracted it, in this case, $1,000 - N$. Mathematically,

$$\frac{dN}{dt} = kN(1,000 - N) \qquad N(0) = 1$$

where N is the number of people who have contracted influenza after t days. For $k = 0.0004$, it can be shown that $N(t)$ is given by

$$N(t) = \frac{1,000}{1 + 999e^{-0.4t}}$$

See Table 1 (logistic growth) for the characteristic graph.

(A) How many people have contracted influenza after 10 days? After 20 days?

(B) How many days will it take until half the community has contracted influenza?

(C) Find $\lim_{t \to \infty} N(t)$.

Social Sciences

13. *Archaeology.* A skull from an ancient tomb was discovered and was found to have 5% of the original amount of radioactive carbon-14 present. Estimate the age of the skull. (See Example 12.)

14. *Learning.* For a particular person learning to type, it was found that the number of words per minute, N, the person was able to type after t hours of practice was given approximately by

$$N = 100(1 - e^{-0.02t})$$

See Table 1 (limited growth) for a characteristic graph. What is the rate of improvement after 10 hours of practice? After 40 hours of practice?

15. *Small group analysis.* In a study on small group dynamics, sociologists Stephan and Mischler found that, when the members of a discussion group of ten were ranked according to the number of times each participated, the number of times $N(k)$ the kth-ranked person participated was given approximately by

$$N(k) = N_1 e^{-0.11(k-1)} \qquad 1 \leqslant k \leqslant 10$$

where N_1 is the number of times the first-ranked person participated in the discussion. If, in a particular discussion group of ten people, $N_1 = 180$, estimate how many times the sixth-ranked person participated. The tenth-ranked person.

16. *Perception.* One of the oldest laws in mathematical psychology is the Weber–Fechner law (discovered in the middle of the nineteenth century). It concerns a person's sensed perception of various strengths of stimulation involving weights, sound, light, shock, taste, and so on. One form of the law states that the rate of change of sensed sensation S with respect to stimulus R is inversely proportional to the strength of the stimulus R. Thus,

$$\frac{dS}{dR} = \frac{k}{R}$$

where k is a constant. If we let R_0 be the threshold level at which the stimulus R can be detected (the least amount of sound, light, weight, and so on that can be detected), then it is appropriate to write

$$S(R_0) = 0$$

Find a function S in terms of R that satisfies the above conditions.

17. *Rumor spread.* A group of 400 parents, relatives, and friends are waiting anxiously at Kennedy Airport for a student charter to return

after a year in Europe. It is stormy and the plane is late. A particular parent thought he had heard that the plane's radio had gone out and related this news to some friends, who in turn passed it on to others, and so on. Sociologists have studied rumor propagation and have found that a rumor tends to spread at a rate in direct proportion to the number who have heard it, x, and to the number who have not, $P - x$, where P is the total population. Mathematically, for our case, $P = 400$ and

$$\frac{dx}{dt} = 0.001x(400 - x) \qquad x(0) = 1$$

where t is time in minutes. From this, it can be shown that

$$x(t) = \frac{400}{1 + 399e^{-0.4t}}$$

See Table 1 (logistic growth) for a characteristic graph.

(A) How many people have heard the rumor after 5 minutes? 20 minutes?

(B) Find $\lim_{t \to \infty} x(t)$.

10-4 Definite Integral

- Definite Integral
- Properties
- Definite Integrals and Substitution
- Applications
- Common Errors

■ Definite Integral

We start this discussion with a simple example, out of which will evolve a new integral form, called the *definite integral*. Our approach in this section will be intuitive and informal; these concepts will be made more precise in Section 11-1.

Suppose a manufacturing company's marginal cost equation for a given product is given by

$$C'(x) = 2 - 0.2x \qquad 0 \leqslant x \leqslant 8$$

where the marginal cost is in thousands of dollars and production is x units per day. What is the total change in cost per day going from a production level of 2 units per day to 6 units per day? If $C = C(x)$ is the cost function, then

$$\left(\begin{array}{l} \text{Total net change in cost} \\ \text{between } x = 2 \text{ and } x = 6 \end{array} \right) = C(6) - C(2) = C(x)|_2^6 \qquad (1)$$

The special symbol $C(x)|_2^6$ is a convenient way of representing the center expression that will prove useful to us later.

To evaluate (1), we need to find the antiderivative of $C'(x)$; that is,

$$C(x) = \int (2 - 0.2x)\, dx = 2x - 0.1x^2 + K \tag{2}$$

Thus, we are within a constant of knowing the original cost function. However, we do not need to know the constant K to solve the original problem (1). We compute $C(6) - C(2)$ for $C(x)$ found in (2):

$$C(6) - C(2) = [2(6) - 0.1(6)^2 + K] - [2(2) - 0.1(2)^2 + K]$$
$$= 12 - 3.6 + K - 4 + 0.4 - K$$
$$= \$4.8 \text{ thousand per day increase in costs for a production}$$
$$\text{increase from 2 to 6 units per day}$$

The unknown constant K canceled out! Thus, we conclude that any antiderivative of $C'(x) = 2 - 0.2x$ will do, since antiderivatives of a given function can differ by at most a constant (see Section 10-1). Thus, we really do not have to find the constant in the original cost function to solve the problem.

Since $C(x)$ is an antiderivative of $C'(x)$, the above discussion suggests the following notation:

$$C(6) - C(2) = C(x)|_2^6 = \int_2^6 C'(x)\, dx \tag{3}$$

The integral form on the right in (3) is called a *definite integral*—it represents the number found by evaluating an antiderivative of the integrand at 6 and 2 and taking the difference as indicated.

Definite Integral

The **definite integral** of a continuous function f over an interval from $x = a$ to $x = b$ is the net change of an antiderivative of f over the interval. Symbolically, if $F(x)$ is an antiderivative of $f(x)$, then

$$\int_a^b f(x)\, dx = F(x)|_a^b = F(b) - F(a) \qquad \text{where} \quad F'(x) = f(x)$$

Integrand: $f(x)$ **Upper limit:** b **Lower limit:** a

In Section 11-1 we will formally define a definite integral as a limit of a special sum. Then the relationship in the box turns out to be the most important theorem in calculus—the fundamental theorem of calculus. Our intent in this and the next section is to give you some intuitive experience with the definite integral concept and its use. You will then be better able to understand a formal definition and to appreciate the significance of the fundamental theorem.

Example 14   Evaluate $\int_{-1}^{2} (3x^2 - 2x)\, dx$.

Solution   We choose the simplest antiderivative of $(3x^2 - 2x)$, namely $(x^3 - x^2)$, since any antiderivative will do (see discussion at beginning of section).

$$\int_{-1}^{2} (3x^2 - 2x)\, dx = (x^3 - x^2)|_{-1}^{2}$$

$$= (2^3 - 2^2) - [(-1)^3 - (-1)^2] \qquad \text{Be careful of}$$
$$= 4 - (-2) = 6 \qquad\qquad\qquad \text{sign errors here.}$$

Problem 14   Evaluate $\int_{-2}^{2} (2x - 1)\, dx$.

Remark

Do not confuse a definite integral with an indefinite integral. The definite integral $\int_{a}^{b} f(x)\, dx$ is a real number; the indefinite integral $\int f(x)\, dx$ is a whole set of functions—all the antiderivatives of $f(x)$.

■ Properties

In the next box we state several useful properties of the definite integral. You will note that some of these parallel the properties for the indefinite integral listed in Section 10-1.

Definite Integral Properties

1. $\int_{a}^{a} f(x)\, dx = 0$

2. $\int_{a}^{b} f(x)\, dx = -\int_{b}^{a} f(x)\, dx$

3. $\int_{a}^{b} Kf(x)\, dx = K \int_{a}^{b} f(x)\, dx \qquad K$ a constant

4. $\int_{a}^{b} [f(x) \pm g(x)]\, dx = \int_{a}^{b} f(x)\, dx \pm \int_{a}^{b} g(x)\, dx$

5. $\int_{a}^{b} f(x)\, dx = \int_{a}^{c} f(x)\, dx + \int_{c}^{b} f(x)\, dx$

These properties are justified as follows: If $F'(x) = f(x)$, then

1. $\displaystyle\int_a^a f(x)\,dx = F(x)|_a^a = F(a) - F(a) = 0$

2. $\displaystyle\int_a^b f(x)\,dx = F(x)|_a^b = F(b) - F(a) = -[F(a) - F(b)] = -\int_b^a f(x)\,dx$

3. $\displaystyle\int_a^b Kf(x)\,dx = KF(x)|_a^b = KF(b) - KF(a) = K[F(b) - F(a)]$

$$= K\int_a^b f(x)\,dx$$

and so on.

Example 15 Evaluate $\displaystyle\int_1^2 \left(2x + 3e^x - \frac{4}{x}\right)dx$.

Solution
$$\int_1^2 \left(2x + 3e^x - \frac{4}{x}\right)dx = 2\int_1^2 x\,dx + 3\int_1^2 e^x\,dx - 4\int_1^2 \frac{1}{x}\,dx$$
$$= 2\frac{x^2}{2}\Big|_1^2 + 3e^x\Big|_1^2 - 4\ln|x|\Big|_1^2$$
$$= (2^2 - 1^2) + (3e^2 - 3e^1) - (4\ln 2 - 4\ln 1)$$
$$= 3 + 3e^2 - 3e - 4\ln 2 \approx 14.24$$

Problem 15 Evaluate $\displaystyle\int_1^3 \left(4x - 2e^x + \frac{5}{x}\right)dx$.

▪ Definite Integrals and Substitution

The evaluation of a definite integral is a two-step process: First find an antiderivative and then find the net change in that antiderivative. The next example illustrates several different ways these steps can be performed when substitution is involved.

Example 16 Evaluate:

(A) $\displaystyle\int_2^4 e^{-0.5x}\,dx$ (B) $\displaystyle\int_1^2 (2x-1)^3\,dx$ (C) $\displaystyle\int_0^5 \frac{x}{x^2+10}\,dx$

Solutions (A) First find an antiderivative:

$$\int e^{-0.5x}\,dx = \int e^{-0.5x}\frac{-0.5}{-0.5}\,dx$$
$$= \frac{1}{-0.5}\int e^{-0.5x}(-0.5)\,dx \qquad \text{Substitute } u = -0.5x$$
$$\qquad\qquad\qquad\qquad\qquad \text{and } du = -0.5\,dx.$$
$$= -2\int e^u\,du$$

$$\int e^{-0.5x} \, dx = -2e^u + C$$
$$= -2e^{-0.5x} + C \qquad \text{Since } u = -0.5x$$

Now find the net change in an antiderivative:

$$\int_2^4 e^{-0.5x} \, dx = -2e^{-0.5x} \Big|_2^4 \qquad \text{Choose } C = 0.$$
$$= [-2e^{-0.5(4)}] - [-2e^{-0.5(2)}]$$
$$= -2e^{-2} + 2e^{-1} \approx 0.465$$

(B) Perform the substitution mentally:

$$\int_1^2 (2x - 1)^3 \, dx = \frac{1}{2} \int_1^2 (2x - 1)^3 2 \, dx \qquad \begin{array}{l} \text{The integrand} \\ \text{has the form} \\ u^3 \, du. \text{ The anti-} \\ \text{derivative is} \\ u^4/4 = (2x - 1)^4/4. \end{array}$$
$$= \frac{1}{2} \frac{(2x - 1)^4}{4} \Big|_1^2$$
$$= \frac{(2 \cdot 2 - 1)^4}{8} - \frac{(2 \cdot 1 - 1)^4}{8}$$
$$= \frac{3^4}{8} - \frac{1^4}{8} = \frac{81}{8} - \frac{1}{8} = \frac{80}{8} = 10$$

(C) Substitute directly in the definite integral, changing the limits of integration:

$$\int_0^5 \frac{x}{x^2 + 10} \, dx = \frac{1}{2} \int_0^5 \frac{1}{x^2 + 10} 2x \, dx \qquad \begin{array}{l} \text{If } u = x^2 + 10, \text{ then} \\ x = 0 \text{ implies } u = 10 \\ \text{and } x = 5 \text{ implies} \\ u = 35. \end{array}$$
$$= \frac{1}{2} \int_{10}^{35} \frac{1}{u} \, du$$
$$= \frac{1}{2} \ln|u| \Big|_{10}^{35}$$
$$= \tfrac{1}{2} \ln 35 - \tfrac{1}{2} \ln 10 \approx 0.626$$

Problem 16   Evaluate:

(A) $\displaystyle\int_{10}^{30} e^{-0.1x} \, dx$ (B) $\displaystyle\int_0^1 \frac{1}{2x + 4} \, dx$ (C) $\displaystyle\int_{-1}^2 x^2(1 + x^3)^2 \, dx$

■ Applications

Example 17
Pollution
A large factory on the Mississippi River discharges pollutants into the river at a rate that is estimated by a water quality control agency to be

$$P'(t) = R(t) = t\sqrt{t^2 + 1} \qquad 0 \leq t \leq 5$$

where $P(t)$ is the total number of tons of pollutants discharged into the river after t years of operation. What quantity of pollutants will be discharged into the river during the first 3 years of operation?

Solution

$$P(3) - P(0) = \int_0^3 t\sqrt{t^2 + 1}\ dt$$

$$= \int_0^3 (t^2 + 1)^{1/2} t\ dt$$

$$= \frac{1}{2} \int_0^3 (t^2 + 1)^{1/2} 2t\ dt$$

$$= \frac{1}{2} \cdot \frac{(t^2 + 1)^{3/2}}{\frac{3}{2}} \Big|_0^3$$

$$= \frac{1}{3} (t^2 + 1)^{3/2} \Big|_0^3$$

$$= \frac{1}{3} (3^2 + 1)^{3/2} - \frac{1}{3} (0^2 + 1)^{3/2}$$

$$= \frac{1}{3} (10^{3/2} - 1) \approx 10.2 \text{ tons}$$

Problem 17 Repeat Example 17 for the time interval from 3 to 5 years.

Example 18
Useful Life

An amusement company maintains records for each video game it installs in an arcade. Suppose that $C(t)$ and $R(t)$ represent the total accumulated costs and revenues (in thousands of dollars), respectively, t years after a particular game has been installed and that

$$C'(t) = 2$$
$$R'(t) = 9e^{-0.5t}$$

The value of t for which $C'(t) = R'(t)$ is called the **useful life** of the game.

(A) Find the useful life of the game to the nearest year.
(B) Find the total profit accumulated during the useful life of the game.

Solutions (A) $R'(t) = C'(t)$

$$9e^{-0.5t} = 2$$

$$e^{-0.5t} = \tfrac{2}{9}$$

$$-0.5t = \ln \tfrac{2}{9}$$

$$t = -2 \ln \tfrac{2}{9} \approx 3 \text{ years}$$

Thus, the game has a useful life of 3 years.

(B) The total profit accumulated during the useful life of the game is

$$P(3) - P(0) = \int_0^3 P'(t)\, dt$$

$$= \int_0^3 [R'(t) - C'(t)]\, dt$$

$$= \int_0^3 (9e^{-0.5t} - 2)\, dt$$

$$= (-18e^{-0.5t} - 2t)\Big|_0^3$$

$$= (-18e^{-1.5} - 6) - (-18e^0 - 0)$$

$$= 12 - 18e^{-1.5} \approx 7.984 \text{ or } \$7{,}984$$

Problem 18 Repeat Example 18 if $C'(t) = 1$ and $R'(t) = 7.5e^{-0.5t}$.

■ Common Errors

1. $\displaystyle\int_0^2 e^x\, dx = e^x\Big|_0^2 = \cancel{e^2}$

Do not forget to evaluate the antiderivative at both the upper and lower limits of integration and do not assume that the antiderivative is 0 just because the lower limit is 0. The correct procedure for this problem is

$$\int_0^2 e^x\, dx = e^x\Big|_0^2 = e^2 - e^0 = e^2 - 1$$

2. $\displaystyle\int_0^5 \frac{x}{x^2 + 10}\, dx = \frac{1}{2}\int_{\cancel{0}}^{\cancel{5}} \frac{1}{u}\, du \qquad \begin{aligned} u &= x^2 + 10 \\ du &= 2x\, dx \end{aligned}$

If a substitution is made in a definite integral, the limits of integration also must be changed. The new limits are determined by the particular substitution used in the integral. (See Example 16C for the correct procedure for this integral.)

Answers to
Matched Problems

14. -4 15. $16 + 2e - 2e^3 + 5 \ln 3 \approx -13.241$
16. (A) $10(e^{-1} - e^{-3}) \approx 3.181$ (B) $(\ln 6 - \ln 4)/2 \approx 0.203$
     (C) 81
17. $\frac{1}{3}(26^{3/2} - 10^{3/2}) \approx 33.7$ tons
18. (A) $-2 \ln(\frac{2}{15}) \approx 4$ years   (B) $11 - 15e^{-2} \approx 8.970$ or $\$8{,}970$

Exercise 10-4

Evaluate.

A 1. $\displaystyle\int_2^3 2x\, dx$ 2. $\displaystyle\int_1^2 3x^2\, dx$

3. $\displaystyle\int_3^4 5\,dx$

4. $\displaystyle\int_{12}^{20} dx$

5. $\displaystyle\int_1^3 (2x - 3)\,dx$

6. $\displaystyle\int_1^3 (6x + 5)\,dx$

7. $\displaystyle\int_0^4 (3x^2 - 4)\,dx$

8. $\displaystyle\int_0^2 (6x^2 - 2x)\,dx$

9. $\displaystyle\int_{-3}^4 (4 - x^2)\,dx$

10. $\displaystyle\int_{-1}^2 (x^2 - 4x)\,dx$

11. $\displaystyle\int_0^1 24x^{11}\,dx$

12. $\displaystyle\int_0^2 30x^5\,dx$

13. $\displaystyle\int_0^1 e^{2x}\,dx$

14. $\displaystyle\int_{-1}^1 e^{5x}\,dx$

15. $\displaystyle\int_1^{3.5} 2x^{-1}\,dx$

16. $\displaystyle\int_1^2 \frac{dx}{x}$

B   17. $\displaystyle\int_1^2 (2x^{-2} - 3)\,dx$

18. $\displaystyle\int_1^2 (5 - 16x^{-3})\,dx$

19. $\displaystyle\int_1^4 3\sqrt{x}\,dx$

20. $\displaystyle\int_4^{25} \frac{2}{\sqrt{x}}\,dx$

21. $\displaystyle\int_2^3 12(x^2 - 4)^5 x\,dx$

22. $\displaystyle\int_0^1 32(x^2 + 1)^7 x\,dx$

23. $\displaystyle\int_3^9 \frac{1}{x - 1}\,dx$

24. $\displaystyle\int_2^8 \frac{1}{x + 1}\,dx$

25. $\displaystyle\int_0^1 (e^{2x} - 2x)^2(e^{2x} - 1)\,dx$

26. $\displaystyle\int_0^1 \frac{2e^{4x} - 3}{e^{2x}}\,dx$

27. $\displaystyle\int_{-2}^{-1} (x^{-1} + 2x)\,dx$

28. $\displaystyle\int_{-3}^{-1} (-3x^{-2} + x^{-1})\,dx$

C   29. $\displaystyle\int_2^3 x\sqrt{2x^2 - 3}\,dx$

30. $\displaystyle\int_0^1 x\sqrt{3x^2 + 2}\,dx$

31. $\displaystyle\int_0^1 \frac{x - 1}{x^2 - 2x + 3}\,dx$

32. $\displaystyle\int_1^2 \frac{x + 1}{2x^2 + 4x + 4}\,dx$

33. $\displaystyle\int_{-1}^1 \frac{e^{-x} - e^x}{(e^{-x} + e^x)^2}\,dx$

34. $\displaystyle\int_6^7 \frac{\ln(t - 5)}{t - 5}\,dt$

Applications

Business & Economics

35. *Salvage value.* A new piece of industrial equipment will depreciate in value rapidly at first, then less rapidly as time goes on. Suppose the rate (in dollars per year) at which the book value of a new milling machine changes is given approximately by

$$V'(t) = f(t) = 500(t - 12) \qquad 0 \leqslant t \leqslant 10$$

where $V(t)$ is the value of the machine after t years. What is the total loss in value of the machine in the first 5 years? In the second 5 years? Set up appropriate integrals and solve.

36. *Maintenance costs.* Maintenance costs for an apartment house generally increase as the building gets older. From past records, a managerial service determines that the rate of increase in maintenance costs (in dollars per year) for a particular apartment complex is given approximately by

$$M'(x) = f(x) = 90x^2 + 5,000$$

where x is the age of the apartment in years and $M(x)$ is the total (accumulated) cost of maintenance for x years. Write a definite integral that will give the total maintenance costs from 2 to 7 years after the apartment house was built, and evaluate it.

37. *Useful life.* The total accumulated costs $C(t)$ and revenues $R(t)$ (in thousands of dollars), respectively, for a coin-operated photocopying machine satisfy

$$C'(t) = \tfrac{1}{11}t \quad \text{and} \quad R'(t) = 5te^{-t^2}$$

where t is time in years. Find the useful life of the machine to the nearest year. What is the total profit accumulated during the useful life of the machine?

38. *Useful life.* The total accumulated costs $C(t)$ and revenues $R(t)$ (in thousands of dollars), respectively, for a coal mine satisfy

$$C'(t) = 3 \quad \text{and} \quad R'(t) = 15e^{-0.1t}$$

where t is the number of years the mine has been in operation. Find the useful life of the mine to the nearest year. What is the total profit accumulated during the useful life of the mine?

39. *Labor costs and learning.* A defense contractor is starting production on a new missile control system. On the basis of data collected while assembling the first 16 control systems, the production manager obtained the following function for rate of labor use:

$$g(x) = 2,400x^{-1/2}$$

where $g(x)$ is the number of labor-hours required to assemble the xth unit of a control system. Approximately how many labor-hours will be required to assemble the 17th through the 25th control units? [*Hint:* Let $a = 16$ and $b = 25$.]

40. *Labor costs and learning.* If the rate of labor use in Problem 39 is

$$g(x) = 2,000x^{-1/3}$$

approximately how many labor-hours will be required to assemble the 9th through the 27th control units? [*Hint:* Let $a = 8$ and $b = 27$.]

41. *Oil production.* Using data from the first 3 years' production as well as geological studies, the management of an oil company estimates that oil will be pumped from a producing field at a rate given by

$$R(t) = \frac{100}{t+1} + 5 \qquad 0 \le t \le 20$$

where $R(t)$ is the rate of production in thousands of barrels per year t years after pumping begins. Approximately how many barrels of oil will the field produce during the first 10 years of production? From the end of the 10th year to the end of the 20th year of production?

42. *Oil production.* In Problem 41, if the rate is found to be

$$R(t) = \frac{120t}{t^2+1} + 3 \qquad 0 \le t \le 20$$

approximately how many barrels of oil will the field produce during the first 5 years of production? The second 5 years of production?

43. *Marketing.* An automobile company is ready to introduce a new line of cars with a national sales campaign. After test marketing the line in a carefully selected city, the marketing research department estimates that sales (in millions of dollars) will increase at the monthly rate of

$$S'(t) = 10 - 10e^{-0.1t} \qquad 0 \le t \le 24$$

t months after the national campaign is started. What will be the approximate total sales during the first 12 months of the campaign? The second 12 months of the campaign?

44. *Marketing.* Repeat Problem 43 if the monthly rate of increase in sales is found to be approximated by

$$S'(t) = 20 - 20e^{-0.05t} \qquad 0 \le t \le 24$$

Life Sciences

45. *Natural resource depletion.* The instantaneous rate of change of demand for wood in the United States since 1970 ($t = 0$) in billions of cubic feet per year is estimated to be given by

$$Q'(t) = 12 + 0.006t^2 \qquad 0 \le t \le 50$$

where $Q(t)$ is the total amount of wood consumed in billions of cubic feet t years after 1970. How many billions of cubic feet of wood will be consumed from 1980 to 1990?

46. *Natural resource depletion.* Repeat Problem 45 for the time interval from 1990 to 2000.

47. *Biology.* A yeast culture weighing 2 grams is removed from a refrigerator unit and is expected to grow at the rate of $W'(t) = 0.2e^{0.1t}$ grams per hour at a higher controlled temperature. How much will the weight of the culture increase during the first 8 hours of growth? How much will the weight of the culture increase from the end of the 8th hour to the end of the 16th hour of growth?

48. *Medicine.* The rate of healing for a skin wound (in square centimeters per day) is approximated by $A'(t) = -0.9e^{-0.1t}$. The initial wound has an area of 9 square centimeters. How much will the area change during the first 5 days? The second 5 days?

Social Sciences

49. *Learning.* In a particular business college, it was found that an average student enrolled in an advanced typing class progressed at a rate of $N'(t) = 6e^{-0.1t}$ words per minute per week, t weeks after enrolling in a 15 week course. At the beginning of the course an average student could type 40 words per minute. How much improvement would be expected during the first 5 weeks of the course? The second 5 weeks of the course? The last 5 weeks of the course?

50. *Learning.* In the same business college, it was also found that an average student enrolled in a beginning shorthand class progressed at a rate of $N'(t) = 12e^{-0.06t}$ words per minute per week, t weeks after enrolling in a 15 week course. At the beginning of the course none of the students could take any dictation by shorthand. How much improvement would be expected during the first 5 weeks of the course? The second 5 weeks of the course? The last 5 weeks of the course?

10-5 Area and the Definite Integral

- Area under a Curve
- Area between a Curve and the x Axis
- Area between Two Curves
- Application: Distribution of Income

■ Area under a Curve

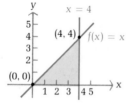

Figure 3

Consider the graph of $f(x) = x$ from $x = 0$ to $x = 4$ (Fig. 3). We can easily compute the area of the triangle bounded by $f(x) = x$, the x axis ($y = 0$), and the line $x = 4$, using the formula for the area of a triangle:

$$A = \frac{bh}{2} = \frac{4 \cdot 4}{2} = 8$$

Let us integrate $f(x) = x$ from $x = 0$ to $x = 4$:

$$\int_0^4 x\, dx = \frac{x^2}{2} \Big|_0^4 = \frac{4^2}{2} - \frac{0^2}{2} = 8$$

We get the same result! It turns out that this is not a coincidence. In general, we can prove the following:

Area under a Curve

If f is continuous and $f(x) \geq 0$ over the interval $[a, b]$, then the area bounded by $y = f(x)$, the x axis $(y = 0)$, and the vertical lines $x = a$ and $x = b$ is given exactly by

$$A = \int_a^b f(x)\, dx$$

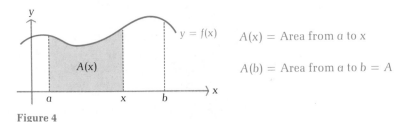

Let us see why the definite integral gives us the area exactly. Let $A(x)$ be the area under the graph of $y = f(x)$ from a to x, as indicated in Figure 4.

$A(x) = $ Area from a to x

$A(b) = $ Area from a to $b = A$

Figure 4

If we can show that $A(x)$ is an antiderivative of $f(x)$, then we can write

$$\int_a^b f(x)\, dx = A(x)\big|_a^b = A(b) - A(a)$$

$$= \left(\begin{array}{c} \text{Area from} \\ x = a \text{ to } x = b \end{array}\right) - \left(\begin{array}{c} \text{Area from} \\ x = a \text{ to } x = a \end{array}\right)$$

$$= A - 0 = A$$

To show that $A(x)$ is an antiderivative of $f(x)$—that is, $A'(x) = f(x)$—we use the definition of a derivative (Section 7-4) and write

$$A'(x) = \lim_{\Delta x \to 0} \frac{A(x + \Delta x) - A(x)}{\Delta x}$$

Geometrically, $A(x + \Delta x) - A(x)$ is the area from x to $x + \Delta x$ (see Fig. 5 on the next page). This area is given approximately by the area of the rectangle $\Delta x \cdot f(x)$, and the smaller Δx is, the better the approximation. Using

$$A(x + \Delta x) - A(x) \approx \Delta x \cdot f(x)$$

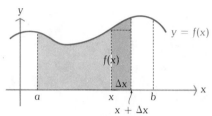

Figure 5

and dividing both sides by Δx, we obtain

$$\frac{A(x + \Delta x) - A(x)}{\Delta x} \approx f(x)$$

Now, if we let $\Delta x \to 0$, then the left side has $A'(x)$ as a limit, which is equal to the right side. Hence,

$$A'(x) = f(x)$$

that is, $A(x)$ is an antiderivative of $f(x)$. Thus,

$$\int_a^b f(x)\,dx = A(x)|_a^b = A(b) - A(a) = A - 0 = A$$

This is a remarkable result: The area under the graph of $y = f(x)$, $f(x) \geqslant 0$, can be obtained simply by evaluating the antiderivative of $f(x)$ at the end points of the interval $[a, b]$. We have now solved, at least in part, the third basic problem of calculus stated in Section 7-1.

Example 19   Find the area bounded by $f(x) = 6x - x^2$ and $y = 0$ for $1 \leqslant x \leqslant 4$.

Solution   We sketch a graph of the region first:

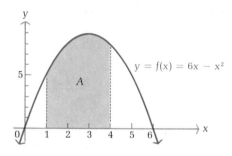

$$A = \int_1^4 (6x - x^2)\,dx = \left(3x^2 - \frac{x^3}{3}\right)\Big|_1^4$$

$$= \left[3(4)^2 - \frac{4^3}{3}\right] - \left[3(1)^2 - \frac{1^3}{3}\right]$$

$$= 48 - \frac{64}{3} - 3 + \frac{1}{3}$$

$$= 48 - 21 - 3 = 24$$

Problem 19   Find the area bounded by $f(x) = x^2 + 1$ and $y = 0$ for $-1 \leqslant x \leqslant 3$.

■ Area between a Curve and the x Axis

The condition $f(x) \geqslant 0$ is essential to the relationship between an area under a graph and the definite integral. How can we find the area between the graph of f and the x axis if $f(x) \leqslant 0$ on $[a, b]$ or if $f(x)$ is both positive and negative on $[a, b]$? To begin, suppose $f(x) \leqslant 0$ and A is the area between the graph of f and the x axis for $a \leqslant x \leqslant b$, as illustrated in Figure 6A. If we let $g(x) = -f(x)$, then A is also the area between the graph of g and the x axis for $a \leqslant x \leqslant b$ (see Fig. 6B). Since $g(x) \geqslant 0$ for $a \leqslant x \leqslant b$, we can use the definite integral of g to find A:

$$A = \int_a^b g(x)\, dx = \int_a^b [-f(x)]\, dx$$

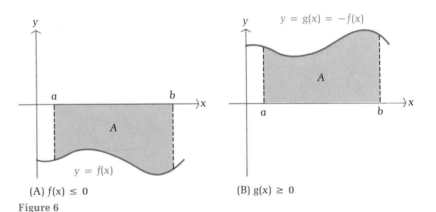

(A) $f(x) \leq 0$ (B) $g(x) \geq 0$

Figure 6

Thus, **the area between the graph of a negative function and the x axis is equal to the definite integral of the negative of the function.** Finally, if $f(x)$ is positive for some values of x and negative for others, the area between the graph of f and the x axis can be obtained by dividing $[a, b]$ into intervals over which f is always positive or always negative.

Example 20   Find the area between the graph of $f(x) = x^2 - 2x$ and the x axis over the indicated intervals:

(A) $[1, 2]$ (B) $[-1, 1]$

Solutions   We begin by sketching the graph of f. (The solution of every area problem should begin with a sketch.)

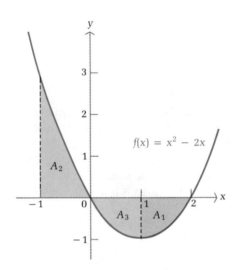

(A) From the graph we see that $f(x) \leqslant 0$ for $1 \leqslant x \leqslant 2$, so we integrate $-f(x)$:

$$A_1 = \int_1^2 [-f(x)]\, dx$$

$$= \int_1^2 (2x - x^2)\, dx$$

$$= \left(x^2 - \frac{x^3}{3} \right) \Big|_1^2$$

$$= \left[(2)^2 - \frac{(2)^3}{3} \right] - \left[(1)^2 - \frac{(1)^3}{3} \right]$$

$$= 4 - \tfrac{8}{3} - 1 + \tfrac{1}{3} = \tfrac{2}{3}$$

(B) Since the graph shows that $f(x) \geqslant 0$ on $[-1, 0]$ and $f(x) \leqslant 0$ on $[0, 1]$, the computation of this area will require two integrals:

$$A = A_2 + A_3$$

$$= \int_{-1}^0 f(x)\, dx + \int_0^1 [-f(x)]\, dx$$

$$= \int_{-1}^0 (x^2 - 2x)\, dx + \int_0^1 (2x - x^2)\, dx$$

$$= \left(\frac{x^3}{3} - x^2 \right) \Big|_{-1}^0 + \left(x^2 - \frac{x^3}{3} \right) \Big|_0^1$$

$$= \tfrac{4}{3} + \tfrac{2}{3} = 2$$

Problem 20   Find the area between the graph of $f(x) = x^2 - 9$ and the x axis over the indicated intervals:

(A) [0, 2]   (B) [2, 4]

■ Area between Two Curves

Consider the area bounded by $y = f(x)$ and $y = g(x)$, $f(x) \geq g(x) \geq 0$, for $a \leq x \leq b$, as indicated in Figure 7.

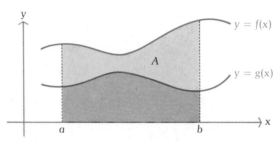

Figure 7

$$\begin{pmatrix} \text{Area } A \text{ between} \\ f(x) \text{ and } g(x) \end{pmatrix}$$

$$= \begin{pmatrix} \text{Area under} \\ f(x) \end{pmatrix} - \begin{pmatrix} \text{Area under} \\ g(x) \end{pmatrix}$$

Areas are from $x = a$ to $x = b$ above the x axis.

$$= \int_a^b f(x)\, dx - \int_a^b g(x)\, dx$$

Use definite integral property 4 (Section 10-4).

$$= \int_a^b [f(x) - g(x)]\, dx$$

It can be shown that the above result does not require $f(x)$ or $g(x)$ to remain positive over the interval $[a, b]$. A more general result is stated in the box:

Area between Two Curves

If f and g are continuous and $f(x) \geq g(x)$ over the interval $[a, b]$, then the area bounded by $y = f(x)$ and $y = g(x)$ for $a \leq x \leq b$ is given exactly by

$$A = \int_a^b [f(x) - g(x)]\, dx$$

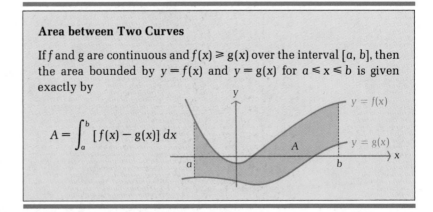

Example 21   Find the area bounded by $f(x) = \frac{1}{2}x + 3$, $g(x) = -x^2 + 1$, $x = -2$, and $x = 1$.

Solution   We first sketch the area, then set up and evaluate an appropriate definite integral:

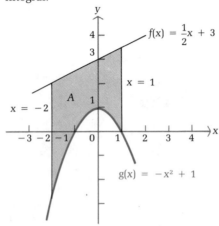

We observe from the graph that $f(x) \geq g(x)$ for $-2 \leq x \leq 1$, so

$$A = \int_{-2}^{1} [f(x) - g(x)] \, dx = \int_{-2}^{1} \left[\left(\frac{x}{2} + 3 \right) - (-x^2 + 1) \right] dx$$

$$= \int_{-2}^{1} \left(x^2 + \frac{x}{2} + 2 \right) dx$$

$$= \left(\frac{x^3}{3} + \frac{x^2}{4} + 2x \right) \Big|_{-2}^{1} = \left(\frac{1}{3} + \frac{1}{4} + 2 \right) - \left(\frac{-8}{3} + \frac{4}{4} - 4 \right) = \frac{33}{4}$$

Problem 21   Find the area bounded by $f(x) = x^2 - 1$, $g(x) = -\frac{1}{2}x - 3$, $x = -1$, and $x = 2$.

Example 22   Find the area bounded by $f(x) = 5 - x^2$ and $g(x) = 2 - 2x$.

Solution

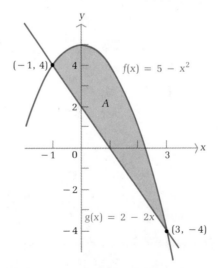

The graph of f is a parabola and the graph of g is a line, as shown in the figure. To find the points of intersection (hence the upper and lower limits of integration), we solve $y = 5 - x^2$ and $y = 2 - 2x$ simultaneously by setting $5 - x^2$ equal to $2 - 2x$ (substitution method):

$$5 - x^2 = 2 - 2x$$
$$x^2 - 2x - 3 = 0$$
$$x = -1, 3$$

The figure shows that $f(x) \geqslant g(x)$ over the interval $[-1, 3]$, so

$$A = \int_{-1}^{3} [f(x) - g(x)] \, dx = \int_{-1}^{3} [5 - x^2 - (2 - 2x)] \, dx$$

$$= \int_{-1}^{3} (3 + 2x - x^2) \, dx$$

$$= \left(3x + x^2 - \frac{x^3}{3} \right) \Big|_{-1}^{3}$$

$$= \left[3(3) + (3)^2 - \frac{(3)^3}{3} \right] - \left[3(-1) + (-1)^2 - \frac{(-1)^3}{3} \right]$$

$$= 9 + 9 - 9 + 3 - 1 - \tfrac{1}{3} = \tfrac{32}{3}$$

Problem 22   Find the area bounded by $f(x) = 6 - x^2$ and $g(x) = x$.

■ Application: Distribution of Income

Economists use a cumulative distribution called a **Lorenz curve** to describe the distribution of income between different households in a given country. A typical Lorenz curve is shown in Figure 8. The points on this curve are determined by ranking all households by income and then computing

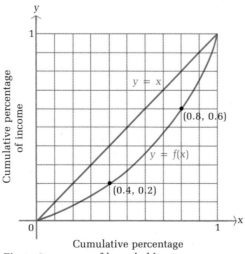

Figure 8   Cumulative percentage of households

the percentage of households whose income is less than or equal to a given percentage of the total income for the country. For example, the point (0.4, 0.2) on the Lorenz curve in Figure 8 indicates that the bottom 40% of the households receive 20% of the income, the point (0.8, 0.6) indicates that the bottom 80% of the households receive 60% of the income, and so on. **Absolute equality** of income distribution would occur if every household received the same income. This is represented by the line $y = x$ in Figure 8. The area between the Lorenz curve and the line $y = x$ is used to indicate how much the income distribution for a given country differs from absolute equality. More precisely, the **coefficient of inequality** of income distribution is defined to be the ratio of the area between the Lorenz curve and the line $y = x$ to the area under the line $y = x$. Since the area under the line $y = x$ from $x = 0$ to $x = 1$ is $\frac{1}{2}$, it follows that *the coefficient of inequality is simply twice the area between the two curves.*

If we are given a function f whose graph is a Lorenz curve, then we can use a definite integral to find the coefficient of inequality.

Coefficient of Inequality for a Lorenz Curve

If $y = f(x)$ is the equation of a Lorenz curve, then

$$\text{Coefficient of inequality} = 2 \int_0^1 [x - f(x)] \, dx$$

Example 23   Find the coefficient of inequality for the Lorenz curve given by $f(x) = \frac{3}{5}x^2 + \frac{2}{5}x$.

Solution

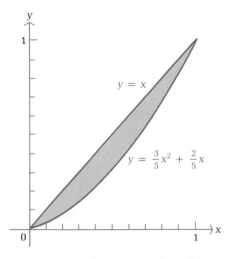

$$2 \int_0^1 [x - f(x)] \, dx = 2 \int_0^1 \left[x - \left(\frac{3}{5}x^2 + \frac{2}{5}x \right) \right] dx$$

$$= 2 \int_0^1 \left(\frac{3}{5}x - \frac{3}{5}x^2 \right) dx$$

$$= 2 \left(\frac{3}{10}x^2 - \frac{1}{5}x^3 \right) \Big|_0^1$$

$$= 2(\tfrac{3}{10} - \tfrac{1}{5}) = \tfrac{1}{5}$$

Thus, the coefficient of inequality is $\frac{1}{5}$ or 0.2. This number provides a relative measure of the income distribution in the country. For example, if the coefficient of inequality for a second country is 0.3, then we would conclude that income is less equally distributed in this second country.

Problem 23   Find the coefficient of inequality for the Lorenz curve given by $f(x) = \frac{9}{10}x^2 + \frac{1}{10}x$.

Answers to Matched Problems

19. $A = \int_{-1}^{3} (x^2 + 1) \, dx = \frac{40}{3}$
20. (A) $A = \int_0^2 (9 - x^2) \, dx = \frac{46}{3}$
      (B) $A = \int_2^3 (9 - x^2) \, dx + \int_3^4 (x^2 - 9) \, dx = 6$
21. $A = \int_{-1}^{2} [(x^2 - 1) - (-x/2 - 3)] \, dx = \frac{39}{4}$
22. $A = \int_{-3}^{2} [(6 - x^2) - x] \, dx = \frac{125}{6}$ 23. 0.3

Exercise 10-5

Find the area bounded by the graphs of the indicated equations.

A

1. $y = 2x + 4,\quad y = 0,\quad 1 \le x \le 3$
2. $y = -2x + 6,\quad y = 0,\quad 0 \le x \le 2$
3. $y = 3x^2,\quad y = 0,\quad 1 \le x \le 2$
4. $y = 4x^3,\quad y = 0,\quad 1 \le x \le 2$
5. $y = x^2 + 2,\quad y = 0,\quad -1 \le x \le 0$
6. $y = 3x^2 + 1,\quad y = 0,\quad -2 \le x \le 0$
7. $y = 4 - x^2,\quad y = 0,\quad -1 \le x \le 2$
8. $y = 12 - 3x^2,\quad y = 0,\quad -2 \le x \le 1$
9. $y = e^x,\quad y = 0,\quad -1 \le x \le 2$
10. $y = e^{-x},\quad y = 0,\quad -2 \le x \le 1$

11. $y = \dfrac{1}{t},\quad y = 0,\quad 0.5 \le t \le 1$

12. $y = \dfrac{1}{t},\quad y = 0,\quad 0.1 \le t \le 1$

B

13. $y = 12,\quad y = -2x + 8,\quad -1 \le x \le 2$
14. $y = 3,\quad y = 2x + 6,\quad -1 \le x \le 2$

15. $y = 3x^2$, $y = 12$
16. $y = x^2$, $y = 9$
17. $y = 4 - x^2$, $y = -5$
18. $y = x^2 - 1$, $y = 3$
19. $y = x^2 + 1$, $y = 2x - 2$, $-1 \le x \le 2$
20. $y = x^2 - 1$, $y = x - 2$, $-2 \le x \le 1$
21. $y = -x$, $y = 0$, $-2 \le x \le 1$
22. $y = -x + 1$, $y = 0$, $-1 \le x \le 2$

23. $y = e^{0.5x}$, $y = \dfrac{-1}{x}$, $1 \le x \le 2$

24. $y = \dfrac{1}{x}$, $y = -e^x$, $0.5 \le x \le 1$

C

25. $y = x^2 - 4$, $y = 0$, $0 \le x \le 3$
26. $y = 4\sqrt[3]{x}$, $y = 0$, $-1 \le x \le 8$
27. $y = x^2 + 2x + 3$, $y = 2x + 4$
28. $y = 8 + 4x - x^2$, $y = x^2 - 2x$
29. $y = x^2 - 4x - 10$, $y = 14 - 2x - x^2$
30. $y = 6 + 6x - x^2$, $y = 13 - 2x$
31. $y = x^3$, $y = 4x$
32. $y = x^3 + 1$, $y = x + 1$

Applications

Business & Economics

33. *Oil production.* Using data from the first 3 years' production as well as geological studies, the management of an oil company estimates that oil will be pumped from a producing field at a rate given by

$$R(t) = \frac{100}{t + 10} + 10 \qquad 0 \le t \le 15$$

where $R(t)$ is the rate of production in thousands of barrels per year t years after pumping begins. Find the area between the graph of R and the t axis over the interval $[5, 10]$ and interpret.

34. *Oil production.* In Problem 33, if the rate is found to be

$$R(t) = \frac{100t}{t^2 + 25} + 4 \qquad 0 \le t \le 25$$

find the area between the graph of R and the t axis over the interval $[5, 15]$ and interpret.

35. *Useful life.* An amusement company maintains records for each video game it installs in an arcade. Suppose that $C(t)$ and $R(t)$ represent the total accumulated costs and revenues (in thousands of dollars), respectively, t years after a particular game has been installed. If

$$C'(t) = 2 \quad \text{and} \quad R'(t) = 9e^{-0.3t}$$

find the area between the graphs of C' and R' over the interval on the t axis from 0 to the useful life of the game and interpret.

36. *Useful life.* Repeat Problem 35 if

$$C'(t) = 2t \quad \text{and} \quad R'(t) = 5te^{-0.1t^2}$$

37. *Income distribution.* The income distribution for a certain country is represented by the Lorenz curve with the equation

$$f(x) = \tfrac{9}{25}x^2 + \tfrac{16}{25}x$$

(A) What is the percentage of total income received by the bottom 25% of the households? By the bottom 50% of the households?
(B) Find the coefficient of inequality.

38. *Income distribution.* Repeat Problem 37 for

$$f(x) = \tfrac{3}{25}x^2 + \tfrac{22}{25}x$$

39. *Distribution of wealth.* Lorenz curves can be used to provide a relative measure of the distribution of the total assets of a country. A report by the U.S. Congressional Joint Economic Committee stated that in 1963, the bottom 90% of the households in the United States controlled 35% of the country's assets. Show that the Lorenz curve given by

$$y = f(x) = x^{9.964}$$

passes through the point (0.9, 0.35). Find the coefficient of inequality.

40. *Distribution of wealth.* The congressional report discussed in Problem 39 also stated that by 1983, the percentage of total assets controlled by the bottom 90% of the households in the United States had declined to 28%. Show that the Lorenz curve given by

$$y = f(x) = x^{12.082}$$

passes through the point (0.9, 0.28). Find the coefficient of inequality.

Life Sciences

41. *Biology.* A yeast culture is growing at a rate of $W'(t) = 0.3e^{0.1t}$ grams per hour. Find the area between the graph of W' and the t axis over the interval [0, 10] and interpret.

42. *Natural resource depletion.* The instantaneous rate of change of the demand for lumber in the United States since 1970 ($t = 0$) in billions of cubic feet per year is estimated to be given by

$$Q'(t) = 12 + 0.006t^2 \qquad 0 \leqslant t \leqslant 50$$

Find the area between the graph of Q' and the t axis over the interval [15, 20] and interpret.

Social Sciences

43. *Learning.* A beginning high school language class was chosen for an experiment on learning. Using a list of 50 words, the experiment involved measuring the rate of vocabulary memorization at different times during a continuous 5 hour study session. It was found that the average rate of learning for the whole class was inversely proportional to the time spent studying and was given approximately by

$$V'(t) = \frac{15}{t} \qquad 1 \le t \le 5$$

Find the area between the graph of V' and the t axis over the interval $[2, 4]$ and interpret.

10-6 Chapter Review

Important Terms and Symbols

10-1 *Antiderivatives and indefinite integrals.* Antiderivative, indefinite integral, integral sign, integrand, constant of integration, $\int f(x)\, dx$

10-2 *Integration by substitution.* General integral formulas, method of substitution

10-3 *Differential equations — growth and decay.* Differential equation, continuous compound interest, exponential growth law, $dQ/dt = rQ$, $Q = Q_0 e^{rt}$

10-4 *Definite integral.* Definite integral, integrand, upper limit, lower limit, $\int_a^b f(x)\, dx$

10-5 *Area and the definite integral.* Area under a curve, area between a curve and the x axis, area between two curves, distribution of income

Integration Formulas

$$\int k\, dx = kx + C$$

$$\int kf(x)\, dx = k \int f(x)\, dx$$

$$\int [f(x) \pm g(x)]\, dx = \int f(x)\, dx \pm \int g(x)\, dx$$

$$\int u^n\, du = \frac{u^{n+1}}{n+1} + C \qquad n \ne -1$$

$$\int e^u\, du = e^u + C$$

$$\int \frac{1}{u}\, du = \ln|u| + C$$

Exercise 10-6 Chapter Review

Work through all the problems in this chapter review and check your answers in the back of the book. (Answers to all review problems are there.) Where weaknesses show up, review appropriate sections in the text.

A Find each integral in Problems 1–6.

1. $\displaystyle\int (3t^2 - 2t)\, dt$

2. $\displaystyle\int_2^5 (2x - 3)\, dx$

3. $\displaystyle\int (3t^{-2} - 3)\, dt$

4. $\displaystyle\int_1^4 x\, dx$

5. $\displaystyle\int e^{-0.5x}\, dx$

6. $\displaystyle\int_1^5 \frac{2}{u}\, du$

7. Find a function $y = f(x)$ that satisfies both conditions:

$$\frac{dy}{dx} = 3x^2 - 2 \qquad f(0) = 4$$

8. Find the area bounded by the graphs of $y = 3x^2 + 1$, $y = 0$, $x = -1$, and $x = 2$.

B Find each integral in Problems 9–14.

9. $\displaystyle\int \sqrt[3]{6x - 5}\, dx$

10. $\displaystyle\int_0^1 10(2x - 1)^4\, dx$

11. $\displaystyle\int \left(\frac{2}{x^2} - 2xe^{x^2}\right) dx$

12. $\displaystyle\int_0^4 \sqrt{x^2 + 4}\, x\, dx$

13. $\displaystyle\int (e^{-2x} + x^{-1})\, dx$

14. $\displaystyle\int_0^{10} 10e^{-0.02x}\, dx$

15. Find a function $y = f(x)$ that satisfies both conditions:

$$\frac{dy}{dx} = 3x^{-1} - x^{-2} \qquad f(1) = 5$$

16. Find the equation of the curve that passes through $(2, 10)$ if its slope is given by

$$\frac{dy}{dx} = 6x + 1$$

for each x.

C 17. Find the area bounded by the graphs of $y = x^2 - 4$, $y = 0$, $x = -2$, and $x = 4$.

Find each integral in Problems 18–23.

18. $\displaystyle\int_0^3 \frac{x}{1 + x^2}\, dx$

19. $\displaystyle\int_0^3 \frac{x}{(1 + x^2)^2}\, dx$

20. $\displaystyle\int x^3(2x^4 + 5)^5\, dx$

21. $\displaystyle\int \frac{e^{-x}}{e^{-x} + 3}\, dx$

22. $\displaystyle\int \frac{e^x}{(e^x + 2)^2}\, dx$

23. $\displaystyle\int \frac{(\ln x)^2}{x}\, dx$

24. Find a function $y = f(x)$ that satisfies both conditions:

$$\frac{dy}{dx} = 9x^2 e^{x^3} \qquad f(0) = 2$$

25. Solve the differential equation:

$$\frac{dN}{dt} = 0.06N \qquad N(0) = 800 \qquad N > 0$$

26. Find the area bounded by the graphs of $y = 6 - x^2$, $y = x^2 - 2$, $x = 0$, and $x = 3$. Be careful!

■	Applications

Business & Economics

27. *Profit function.* If the marginal profit for producing x units per day is given by

$$P'(x) = 100 - 0.02x \qquad P(0) = 0$$

where $P(x)$ is the profit in dollars, find the profit function P and the profit on ten units of production per day.

28. *Resource depletion.* An oil well starts out producing oil at the rate of 60,000 barrels of oil per year, but the production rate is expected to decrease by 4,000 barrels per year. Thus, if $P(t)$ is the total production (in thousands of barrels) in t years, then

$$P'(t) = f(t) = 60 - 4t \qquad 0 \leqslant t \leqslant 15$$

Write a definite integral that will give the total production after 15 years of operation. Evaluate it.

29. *Profit and production.* The weekly marginal profit for an output of x units is given approximately by

$$P'(x) = 150 - \frac{x}{10} \qquad 0 \leqslant x \leqslant 40$$

What is the total change in profit for a production change from ten units per week to forty units? Set up a definite integral and evaluate it.

30. *Useful life.* The total accumulated costs $C(t)$ and revenues $R(t)$ (in thousands of dollars), respectively, for a coal mine satisfy

$$C'(t) = 3 \quad \text{and} \quad R'(t) = 20e^{-0.1t}$$

where t is the number of years the mine has been in operation. Find the useful life of the mine to the nearest year. What is the total profit accumulated during the useful life of the mine?

31. *Marketing.* The marketing research department for an automobile company estimates that sales (in millions of dollars) will increase at

the monthly rate of

$$S'(t) = 15 - 15e^{-0.03t} \qquad 0 \leqslant t \leqslant 24$$

t months after the beginning of a national sales campaign. What will be the approximate total sales the first 12 months of the campaign?

32. *Income distribution.* Find the coefficient of inequality for the income distribution represented by the Lorenz curve with the equation

$$f(x) = \tfrac{1}{2}x + \tfrac{1}{2}x^2$$

Life Sciences

33. *Wound healing.* The area of a small, healing surface wound changes at a rate given approximately by

$$\frac{dA}{dt} = -5t^{-2} \qquad 1 \leqslant t \leqslant 5$$

where t is in days and $A(1) = 5$ square centimeters. What will the area of the wound be in 5 days?

34. *Pollution.* An environmental protection agency estimates that the rate of seepage of toxic chemicals from a waste dump in gallons per year is given by

$$R(t) = \frac{1{,}000}{(1 + t)^2}$$

where t is time in years since the discovery of the seepage. Find the total amount of toxic chemicals that seep from the dump during the first 4 years after the seepage is discovered.

35. *Population.* The population of the United States in 1980 was approximately 226 million. The continuous compound growth rate for the decade from 1970 to 1980 was 1.1%. (Data from the 1980 census.)

(A) If the population continues to grow at the same continuous compound growth rate, what will be the population in 1990?

(B) How long will it take the population to double at this continuous compound growth rate?

Social Sciences

36. *Archaeology.* The continuous compound rate of decay for carbon-14 is $r = -0.000\ 123\ 8$. A piece of animal bone found at an archaeological site contains 4% of the original amount of carbon-14. Estimate the age of the bone.

37. *Learning.* In a particular business college, it was found that an average student enrolled in a typing class progressed at a rate of $N'(t) = 7e^{-0.1t}$ words per minute t weeks after enrolling in a 15 week course. If at the beginning of the course a student could type 25 words per minute, how many words per minute, $N(t)$, would the student be expected to type t weeks into the course? After completing the course?

Additional Integration Topics 11

CHAPTER 11   Contents

11-1   Definite Integral as a Limit of a Sum

- Rectangle Rule for Approximating Definite Integrals
- Definite Integral as a Limit of a Sum
- Recognizing a Definite Integral
- Average Value of a Continuous Function

Up to this point, in order to evaluate a definite integral

$$\int_a^b f(x)\, dx$$

we need to find an antiderivative of the function f so that we can write

$$\int_a^b f(x)\, dx = F(x)\,\Big|_a^b = F(b) - F(a) \qquad F'(x) = f(x)$$

But suppose we cannot find an antiderivative of f (it may not even exist in a convenient or closed form). For example, how would you evaluate the following?

$$\int_2^8 \sqrt{x^3 + 1}\, dx \qquad \int_1^5 \left(\frac{x}{x+1}\right)^3 dx \qquad \int_0^5 e^{-x^2} dx$$

We now introduce the *rectangle rule* for approximating definite integrals, and out of this discussion will evolve a new way of looking at definite integrals.

■ Rectangle Rule for Approximating Definite Integrals

In Section 10-5 we saw that any definite integral of a positive continuous function f over an interval $[a, b]$ can always be interpreted as the area bounded by $y = f(x)$, $y = 0$, $x = a$, and $x = b$ (see Fig. 1). What we need is a way of approximating such areas, given $y = f(x)$ and an interval $[a, b]$.

$$A = \int_a^b f(x)\,dx$$

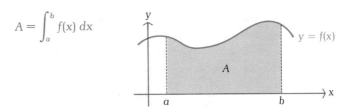

Figure 1

Let us start with a concrete example and generalize from the experience. We will start with a simple definite integral we can evaluate exactly:

$$\int_1^5 (x^2 + 3)\,dx = \left(\frac{x^3}{3} + 3x\right)\Big|_1^5$$

$$= \left[\frac{5^3}{3} + 3(5)\right] - \left[\frac{1^3}{3} + 3(1)\right]$$

$$= \left(\frac{125}{3} + 15\right) - \left(\frac{1}{3} + 3\right)$$

$$= \frac{160}{3} = 53\tfrac{1}{3}$$

This integral represents the area bounded by $y = x^2 + 3$, $y = 0$, $x = 1$, and $x = 5$, as indicated in Figure 2.

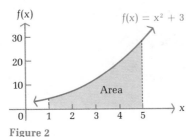

Figure 2

Since areas of rectangles are easy to compute, we cover the area in Figure 2 with rectangles (see Fig. 3) so that the top of each rectangle has a point in

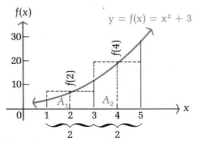

Figure 3

common with the graph of $y = f(x)$. As our first approximation, we divide the interval $[1, 5]$ into two equal subintervals, each with length $(b - a)/2 = (5 - 1)/2 = 2$, and use the midpoint of each subinterval to compute the altitude of the rectangle sitting on top of that subinterval (see Fig. 3).

$$\int_1^5 (x^2 + 3) \, dx \approx A_1 + A_2$$
$$= f(2) \cdot 2 + f(4) \cdot 2$$
$$= 2[f(2) + f(4)]$$
$$= 2(7 + 19) = 52$$

This approximation is less than 3% off of the exact area we found above $(53\frac{1}{3})$.

Now let us divide the interval $[1, 5]$ into four equal subintervals, each of length $(b - a)/4 = (5 - 1)/4 = 1$, and use the midpoint* of each subinterval to compute the altitude of the rectangle corresponding to that subinterval (see Fig. 4).

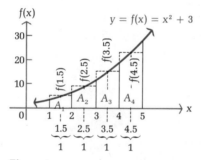

Figure 4

$$\int_1^5 (x^2 + 3) \, dx \approx A_1 + A_2 + A_3 + A_4$$
$$= f(1.5) \cdot 1 + f(2.5) \cdot 1 + f(3.5) \cdot 1 + f(4.5) \cdot 1$$
$$= f(1.5) + f(2.5) + f(3.5) + f(4.5)$$
$$= 5.25 + 9.25 + 15.25 + 23.25$$
$$= 53$$

Now we are less than 1% off of the exact area $(53\frac{1}{3})$.

---

* We actually do not need to choose the midpoint of each subinterval; any point from each subinterval will do. The midpoint is often a convenient point to choose, because then the rectangle tops are usually above part of the graph and below part of the graph. This tends to cancel some of the error that occurs.

We would expect the approximations to continue to improve as we use more and more rectangles with smaller and smaller bases. We now state the *rectangle rule* for approximating definite integrals of a continuous function f over the interval from $x = a$ to $x = b$.

Rectangle Rule

Divide the interval from $x = a$ to $x = b$ into n equal subintervals of length $\Delta x = (b - a)/n$. Let c_k be any point in the kth subinterval. Then

$$\int_a^b f(x)\, dx \approx f(c_1)\Delta x + f(c_2)\Delta x + \cdots + f(c_n)\Delta x$$

$$= \Delta x[f(c_1) + f(c_2) + \cdots + f(c_n)]$$

The rectangle rule is valid for any continuous function f. However, if f is not positive on $[a, b]$, then neither the definite integral nor the approximating sum represent areas.

Example 1   Use the rectangle rule to approximate

$$\int_2^{10} \frac{x}{x + 1}\, dx$$

using $n = 4$ and c_k the midpoint of each subinterval. Compute the approximation to three decimal places.

Solution   Step 1.   Find Δx, the length of each subinterval:

$$\Delta x = \frac{b - a}{n} = \frac{10 - 2}{4} = \frac{8}{4} = 2$$

Step 2.   Use the midpoint of each subinterval for c_k:

Subintervals: [2, 4],   [4, 6],   [6, 8],   [8, 10]

Midpoints: $c_1 = 3$, $c_2 = 5$, $c_3 = 7$, $c_4 = 9$

Step 3.   Use the rectangle rule with $n = 4$:

$$\int_a^b f(x)\, dx \approx f(c_1)\Delta x + f(c_2)\Delta x + f(c_3)\Delta x + f(c_4)\Delta x$$

$$= \Delta x[f(c_1) + f(c_2) + f(c_3) + f(c_4)]$$
$$= 2[f(3) + f(5) + f(7) + f(9)]$$
$$= 2(0.750 + 0.833 + 0.875 + 0.900)$$
$$= 2(3.358) = 6.716 \qquad \text{To 3 decimal places}$$

Problem 1   Use the rectangle rule to approximate

$$\int_2^{14} \frac{x}{x-1}\, dx$$

using $n = 4$ and c_k the midpoint of each subinterval. Compute the approximation to two decimal places.

One important application of the rectangle rule is the approximation of definite integrals involving **tabular functions**—that is, functions defined by tables rather than by formulas. The following example illustrates this approach.

Example 2
Real Estate   A developer is interested in estimating the area of the irregularly shaped property shown in Figure 5A. A surveyor used the straight horizontal road at the bottom of the property as the x axis and measured the vertical distance across the property at 400 foot intervals, starting at 200 (see Fig. 5B). These distances can be viewed as the values of the continuous function f whose graph forms the top of the property. Use the rectangle rule to approximate the area of the property.

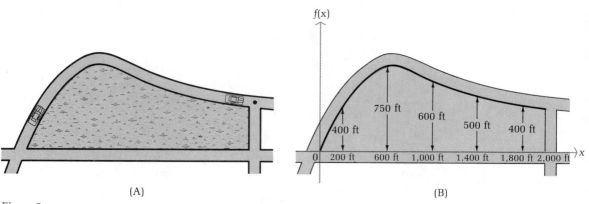

(A)   (B)

Figure 5

Solution   List the values of the function f in a table:

x	200	600	1,000	1,400	1,800
$f(x)$	400	750	600	500	400

The area of the property is given by

$$A = \int_0^{2,000} f(x)\, dx$$

Using the rectangle rule with $n = 5$ and $\Delta x = 400$, and the values of f in the table, we have

$$A \approx \Delta x[f(200) + f(600) + f(1{,}000) + f(1{,}400) + f(1{,}800)]$$
$$= 400[400 + 750 + 600 + 500 + 400]$$
$$= 1{,}060{,}000 \text{ square feet}$$

Problem 2   To obtain a more accurate approximation of the area of the property shown in Figure 5A, the surveyor measured the vertical distances at 200 foot intervals, starting at 100. The results are listed in the table. Use these values and the rectangle rule with $n = 10$ and $\Delta x = 200$ to approximate the area of the property.

x	100	300	500	700	900	1,100	1,300	1,500	1,700	1,900
$f(x)$	· 225	500	700	725	650	575	525	475	425	375

■ Definite Integral as a Limit of a Sum

In using the rectangle rule to approximate a definite integral, one might expect

$$\lim_{\Delta x \to 0} [f(c_1)\Delta x + f(c_2)\Delta x + \cdots + f(c_n)\Delta x] = \int_a^b f(x)\, dx$$

This idea motivates the formal definition of a definite integral that we referred to in Section 10-4.

Definition of a Definite Integral

Let f be a continuous function defined on the closed interval $[a, b]$, and let

1. $a = x_0 \leq x_1 \leq \cdots \leq x_{n-1} \leq x_n = b$
2. $\Delta x_k = x_k - x_{k-1}$ for $k = 1, 2, \ldots, n$
3. $\Delta x_k \to 0$ as $n \to \infty$
4. $x_{k-1} \leq c_k \leq x_k$ for $k = 1, 2, \ldots, n$

Then

$$\int_a^b f(x)\, dx = \lim_{n \to \infty} [f(c_1)\Delta x_1 + f(c_2)\Delta x_2 + \cdots + f(c_n)\Delta x_n]$$

is called a **definite integral**.

In the definition of a definite integral, we divide the closed interval $[a, b]$ into n subintervals of arbitrary lengths in such a way that the length of each subinterval $\Delta x_k = x_k - x_{k-1}$ tends to 0 as n increases without bound. From each of the n subintervals we then select a point c_k and form the sum

$$f(c_1)\Delta x_1 + f(c_2)\Delta x_2 + \cdots + f(c_n)\Delta x_n$$

which is called a **Riemann sum** [named after the celebrated German mathematician Georg Riemann (1826–1866)].

Under the conditions stated in the definition, it can be shown that the limit of the Riemann sum always exists and it is a real number. The limit is independent of the nature of the subdivisions of $[a, b]$ as long as condition 3 holds, and it is independent of the choice of the c_k as long as condition 4 holds.

In a more formal treatment of the subject, we would then prove the remarkable **fundamental theorem of calculus,** which shows that the limit in the definition of a definite integral can be determined exactly by evaluating an antiderivative of $f(x)$, if it exists, at the end points of the interval $[a, b]$ and taking the difference.

Theorem 1

Fundamental Theorem of Calculus

Under the conditions stated in the definition of a definite integral

(Definition)

$$\int_a^b f(x)\,dx = \lim_{n \to \infty} [f(c_1)\Delta x_1 + f(c_2)\Delta x_2 + \cdots + f(c_n)\Delta x_n]$$

(Theorem)

$$= F(b) - F(a) \qquad \text{where } F'(x) = f(x)$$

Now we are free to evaluate a definite integral by using the fundamental theorem if an antiderivative of $f(x)$ can be found; otherwise, we can approximate it using the formal definition in the form of the rectangle rule.

■ Recognizing a Definite Integral

Recall that the derivative of a function f was defined by

$$f'(x) = \lim_{\Delta x \to 0} \frac{f(x + \Delta x) - f(x)}{\Delta x}$$

a form that is generally not easy to compute directly, but is easy to recognize in certain practical problems (slope, instantaneous velocity, rates of change, etc.). Once it is recognized that we are dealing with a derivative, we then proceed to try to compute it using derivative formulas and rules.

Similarly, evaluating a definite integral using the definition

$$\int_a^b f(x)\,dx = \lim_{n\to\infty}\,[f(c_1)\Delta x_1 + f(c_2)\Delta x_2 + \cdots + f(c_n)\Delta x_n] \tag{1}$$

is generally not easy; but the form on the right occurs naturally in many practical problems. We can use the fundamental theorem to evaluate the integral (once it is recognized) if an antiderivative can be found; otherwise, we will approximate it using the rectangle rule. We will now illustrate these points by finding the average value of a continuous function.

■ Average Value of a Continuous Function

Suppose the temperature T (in degrees Fahrenheit) in the middle of a small shallow lake from 8 AM ($t = 0$) to 6 PM ($t = 10$) during the month of May is given approximately as shown in Figure 6.

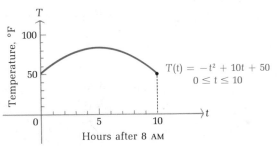

Figure 6

How can we compute the average temperature from 8 AM to 6 PM? We know that the average of a finite number of values

$$a_1, a_2, \ldots, a_n$$

is given by

$$\text{Average} = \frac{a_1 + a_2 + \cdots + a_n}{n}$$

But how can we handle a continuous function with infinitely many values? It would seem reasonable to divide the time interval $[0, 10]$ into n equal subintervals, compute the temperature at a point in each subinterval, and then use the average of these values as an approximation of the average value of the continuous function $T = T(t)$ over $[0, 10]$. We would expect the approximations to improve as n increases. In fact, we would be inclined to define the limit of the average for n values as $n \to \infty$ as *the average value of T* over $[0, 10]$, if the limit exists. This is exactly what we will do:

$$\left(\begin{array}{c}\text{Average temperature}\\ \text{for } n \text{ values}\end{array}\right) = \frac{1}{n}[T(t_1) + T(t_2) + \cdots + T(t_n)] \qquad (2)$$

where t_k is a point in the kth subinterval. We will call the limit of (2) as $n \to \infty$ the *average temperature over the time interval* [0, 10].

Form (2) looks sort of like form (1), but we are missing the Δt_k. We take care of this by multiplying (2) by $(b - a)/(b - a)$, which will change the form of (2) without changing its value:

$$\frac{b - a}{b - a} \cdot \frac{1}{n}[T(t_1) + T(t_2) + \cdots + T(t_n)]$$

$$= \frac{1}{b - a} \cdot \frac{b - a}{n}[T(t_1) + T(t_2) + \cdots + T(t_n)]$$

$$= \frac{1}{b - a} \cdot \left[T(t_1)\frac{b - a}{n} + T(t_2)\frac{b - a}{n} + \cdots + T(t_n)\frac{b - a}{n}\right]$$

$$= \frac{1}{b - a}[T(t_1)\Delta t + T(t_2)\Delta t + \cdots + T(t_n)\Delta t]$$

Thus,

$$\left(\begin{array}{c}\text{Average temperature}\\ \text{over } [a, b] = [0, 10]\end{array}\right)$$

$$= \lim_{n \to \infty} \frac{1}{b - a}[T(t_1)\Delta t + T(t_2)\Delta t + \cdots + T(t_n)\Delta t]$$

$$= \frac{1}{b - a}\left\{\lim_{n \to \infty} [T(t_1)\Delta t + T(t_2)\Delta t + \cdots + T(t_n)\Delta t]\right\}$$

Now the part in the braces is of form (1)—that is, a definite integral. Thus,

$$\left(\begin{array}{c}\text{Average temperature}\\ \text{over } [a, b] = [0, 10]\end{array}\right)$$

$$= \frac{1}{b - a}\int_a^b T(t)\, dt$$

$$= \frac{1}{10 - 0}\int_0^{10} (-t^2 + 10t + 50)\, dt \qquad \text{We now evaluate the definite}$$

$$= \frac{1}{10}\left(-\frac{t^3}{3} + 5t^2 + 50t\right)\bigg|_0^{10} \qquad \begin{array}{l}\text{integral using the fundamental}\\ \text{theorem.}\end{array}$$

$$= \frac{200}{3} \approx 67°\text{F}$$

In general, proceeding as above for an arbitrary continuous function f over an interval $[a, b]$, we obtain the general formula:

Average Value of a Continuous Function f over $[a, b]$

$$\frac{1}{b-a} \int_a^b f(x)\, dx$$

Example 3   Find the average value of $f(x) = x - 3x^2$ over the interval $[-1, 2]$.

Solution

$$\frac{1}{b-a} \int_a^b f(x)\, dx = \frac{1}{2-(-1)} \int_{-1}^2 (x - 3x^2)\, dx$$

$$= \frac{1}{3} \left(\frac{x^2}{2} - x^3 \right) \bigg|_{-1}^2 = -\frac{5}{2}$$

Problem 3   Find the average value of $g(t) = 6t^2 - 2t$ over the interval $[-2, 3]$.

Example 4
Average Price

Given the demand function

$$p = D(x) = 100e^{-0.05x}$$

find the average price (in dollars) over the demand interval $[40, 60]$.

Solution   Average price $= \dfrac{1}{b-a} \displaystyle\int_a^b D(x)\, dx$

$$= \frac{1}{60 - 40} \int_{40}^{60} 100e^{-0.05x}\, dx$$

$$= \frac{100}{20} \int_{40}^{60} e^{-0.05x}\, dx$$

$$= -\frac{5}{0.05} e^{-0.05x} \bigg|_{40}^{60}$$

$$= 100(e^{-2} - e^{-3}) \approx \$8.55$$

Problem 4   Given the supply equation

$$p = S(x) = 10e^{0.05x}$$

find the average price (in dollars) over the supply interval $[20, 30]$.

Example 5
Advertising

A metropolitan newspaper currently has a daily circulation of 50,000 papers (weekdays and Sunday). The management of the paper decides to initiate an aggressive advertising campaign to increase circulation. Suppose that the daily circulation (in thousands of papers) t days after the beginning of the campaign is given by

$$S(t) = 100 - 50e^{-0.01t}$$

What is the average daily circulation during the first 30 days of the campaign? During the second 30 days of the campaign?

Solution

$$\left(\begin{matrix}\text{Average daily circulation} \\ \text{over } [a,\, b] = [0,\, 30]\end{matrix}\right)$$

$$= \frac{1}{b-a} \int_a^b S(t)\, dt$$

$$= \frac{1}{30} \int_0^{30} (100 - 50e^{-0.01t})\, dt$$

$$= \frac{1}{30} (100t + 5{,}000e^{-0.01t}) \Big|_0^{30}$$

$$= \tfrac{1}{30}(3{,}000 + 5{,}000e^{-0.3} - 5{,}000)$$

$$\approx 56.8 \text{ or } 56{,}800 \text{ papers}$$

$$\left(\begin{matrix}\text{Average daily circulation} \\ \text{over } [a,\, b] = [30,\, 60]\end{matrix}\right)$$

$$= \frac{1}{60-30} \int_{30}^{60} (100 - 50e^{-0.01t})\, dt$$

$$= \frac{1}{30} (100t + 5{,}000e^{-0.01t}) \Big|_{30}^{60}$$

$$= \tfrac{1}{30}(6{,}000 + 5{,}000e^{-0.6} - 3{,}000 - 5{,}000e^{-0.3})$$

$$\approx 68.0 \text{ or } 68{,}000 \text{ papers}$$

Problem 5   Refer to Example 5. Satisfied with the increase in circulation, management decides to terminate the advertising campaign. Suppose that the daily circulation (in thousands of papers) t days after the end of the advertising campaign is given by

$$S(t) = 65 + 8e^{-0.02t}$$

What is the average daily circulation during the first 30 days after the end of the campaign? During the second 30 days after the end of the campaign?

Answers to
Matched Problems

1. 14.36   2. 1,035,000 square feet

3. 13   4. $35.27

5. $\dfrac{2{,}350 - 400e^{-0.6}}{30} \approx 71.0$ or 71,000 papers;

$\dfrac{1{,}950 - 400e^{-1.2} + 400e^{-0.6}}{30} \approx 68.3$ or 68,300 papers

Exercise 11-1

For Problems 1–8:

(A) Use the rectangle rule to approximate each definite integral for the indicated number of subintervals n. Choose c_k as the midpoint of each subinterval.

(B) Evaluate each integral exactly using an antiderivative.

A

1. $\int_1^5 3x^2\, dx, \quad n = 2$

2. $\int_2^6 x^2\, dx, \quad n = 2$

3. $\int_1^5 3x^2\, dx, \quad n = 4$

4. $\int_2^6 x^2\, dx, \quad n = 4$

B

5. $\int_0^4 (4 - x^2)\, dx, \quad n = 2$

6. $\int_0^4 (3x^2 - 12)\, dx, \quad n = 2$

7. $\int_0^4 (4 - x^2)\, dx, \quad n = 4$

8. $\int_0^4 (3x^2 - 12)\, dx, \quad n = 4$

In Problems 9–12, use the rectangle rule with n = 4 and the values of f in the given table to approximate the indicated definite integral. Choose c_k as the midpoint of each interval.

9. $\int_0^8 f(x)\, dx$

10. $\int_1^9 f(x)\, dx$

x	1	3	5	7
f(x)	4.5	3.2	2.4	1.6

x	2	4	6	8
f(x)	3.2	4.5	7.9	9.4

11. $\int_1^5 f(x)\, dx$

12. $\int_0^4 f(x)\, dx$

x	1.5	2.5	3.5	4.5
f(x)	12.5	16.7	15.4	10.7

x	0.5	1.5	2.5	3.5
f(x)	9.4	14.7	11.5	6.4

Find the average value of each function over the indicated interval.

13. $f(x) = 500 - 50x, \quad [0, 10]$

14. $g(x) = 2x + 7, \quad [0, 5]$

15. $f(t) = 3t^2 - 2t, \quad [-1, 2]$

16. $g(t) = 4t - 3t^2, \quad [-2, 2]$

17. $f(x) = \sqrt[3]{x}, \quad [1, 8]$

18. $g(x) = \sqrt{x + 1}, \quad [3, 8]$

19. $f(x) = 4e^{-0.2x}, \quad [0, 10]$

20. $f(x) = 64e^{0.08x}, \quad [0, 10]$

Use the rectangle rule to approximate (to three decimal places) each quantity in Problems 21–24. Use n = 4 and choose c_k as the midpoint of each subinterval.

21. The average value of $f(x) = (x + 1)/(x^2 + 1)$ for $[-1, 1]$

22. The average value of $f(x) = x/(x + 1)$ for $[0, 4]$
23. The area under the graph of $f(x) = \ln(1 + x^3)$ from $x = 0$ to $x = 2$
24. The area under the graph of $f(x) = 1/(2 + x^3)$ from $x = -1$ to $x = 1$

C   In Problems 25–28, use the rectangle rule to approximate (to three decimal places) each definite integral for the indicated number of subintervals n. Choose c_k as the midpoint of each subinterval.

25. $\displaystyle\int_0^1 e^{-x^2}\, dx, \quad n = 5$

26. $\displaystyle\int_0^1 e^{x^2}\, dx, \quad n = 5$

27. $\displaystyle\int_0^1 e^{-x^2}\, dx, \quad n = 10$

28. $\displaystyle\int_0^1 e^{x^2}\, dx, \quad n = 10$

29. Find the average value of $f'(x)$ over the interval $[a, b]$ for any differentiable function f.

30. Show that the average value of $f(x) = Ax + B$ over the interval $[a, b]$ is

$$f\left(\frac{a + b}{2}\right)$$

Applications

Business & Economics

31. *Inventory.* A store orders 600 units of a product every 3 months. If the product is steadily depleted to zero by the end of each 3 months, the inventory on hand, I, at any time t during the year is illustrated as follows:

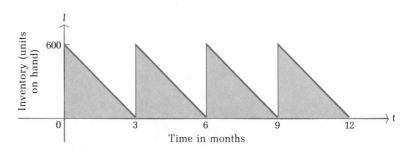

(A) Write an inventory function (assume it is continuous) for the first 3 months. [The graph is a straight line joining (0, 600) and (3, 0).]

(B) What is the average number of units on hand for a 3 month period?

32. Repeat Problem 31 with an order of 1,200 units every 4 months.

33. *Cash reserves.* Suppose cash reserves (in thousands of dollars) are approximated by

$$C(x) = 1 + 12x - x^2 \qquad 0 \leqslant x \leqslant 12$$

where x is the number of months after the first of the year. What is the average cash reserve for the first quarter?

34. Repeat Problem 33 for the second quarter.

35. *Average cost.* The total cost in dollars of manufacturing x auto body frames is

$$C(x) = 60,000 + 300x$$

(A) Find the average cost per unit if 500 frames are produced. [*Hint:* Recall that $\overline{C}(x)$ is the average cost per unit.]

(B) Find the average value of the cost function over the interval $[0, 500]$.

36. *Average cost.* The total cost in dollars of printing x dictionaries is

$$C(x) = 20,000 + 10x$$

(A) Find the average cost per unit if 1,000 dictionaries are produced.

(B) Find the average value of the cost function over the interval $[0, 1,000]$.

37. *Continuous compound interest.* If $100 is deposited in an account that earns interest at an annual nominal rate of 8% compounded continuously, find the amount in the account after 5 years and the average amount in the account during this 5 year period. (Continuous compound interest is discussed in Section 9-1.)

38. *Continuous compound interest.* If $500 is deposited in an account that earns interest at an annual nominal rate of 12% compounded continuously, find the amount in the account after 10 years and the average amount in the account during this 10 year period.

39. *Supply function.* Given the supply function

$$p = S(x) = 10(e^{0.02x} - 1)$$

find the average price (in dollars) over the supply interval $[20, 30]$.

40. *Demand function.* Given the demand function

$$p = D(x) = \frac{1,000}{x}$$

find the average price (in dollars) over the demand range $[400, 600]$.

41. *Advertising.* The number of hamburgers (in thousands) sold each day by a chain of restaurants t days after the beginning of an advertising campaign is given by

$$S(t) = 20 - 10e^{-0.1t}$$

What is the average number of hamburgers sold each day during the first week of the advertising campaign? During the second week of the campaign?

42. *Advertising.* The number of hamburgers (in thousands) sold each day by a chain of restaurants t days after the end of an advertising campaign is given by

$$S(t) = 10 + 8e^{-0.2t}$$

What is the average number of hamburgers sold each day during the first week after the end of the advertising campaign? During the second week after the end of the campaign?

43. *Real estate.* A surveyor produced the table below by measuring the vertical distance (in feet) across a piece of real estate at 600 foot intervals, starting at 300 (see the figure). Use these values and the rectangle rule to estimate the area of the property.

x	300	900	1,500	2,100
$f(x)$	900	1,700	1,700	900

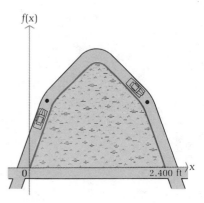

44. *Real estate.* Repeat Problem 43 for the following table of measurements:

x	200	600	1,000	1,400	1,800	2,200
$f(x)$	600	1,400	1,800	1,800	1,400	600

Life Sciences

45. *Temperature.* If the temperature $C(t)$ in an artificial habitat was made to change according to

$$C(t) = t^3 - 2t + 10 \qquad 0 \le t \le 2$$

(in degrees Celsius) over a 2 hour period, what is the average temperature over this period?

46. *Medicine.* A drug is injected into the bloodstream of a patient through her right arm. The concentration of the drug in the bloodstream of the left arm t hours after the injection is given by

$$C(t) = \frac{0.14t}{t^2 + 1}$$

What is the average concentration of the drug in the bloodstream of the left arm during the first hour after the injection? During the first 2 hours after the injection?

Social Sciences

47. *Politics.* Public awareness of a Congressional candidate before and after a successful campaign was approximated by

$$P(t) = \frac{8.4t}{t^2 + 49} + 0.1 \qquad 0 \le t \le 24$$

where t is time in months after the campaign started and $P(t)$ is the fraction of people in the Congressional district who could recall the candidate's name. What is the average fraction of people who could recall the candidate's name during the first 7 months after the campaign began? During the first 2 years after the campaign began?

48. *Population composition.* Because of various factors (such as birth rate expansion, then contraction; family flights from urban areas; etc.), the number of children in a large city was found to increase and then decrease rather drastically. If the number of children over a 6 year period was found to be given approximately by

$$N(t) = -\tfrac{1}{4}t^2 + t + 4 \qquad 0 \le t \le 6$$

what was the average number of children in the city over the 6 year time period? [Assume $N = N(t)$ is continuous.]

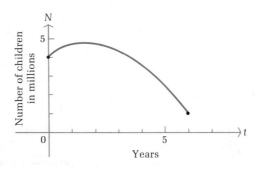

11-2 Applications in Business and Economics

- Continuous Income Stream
- Present Value of a Continuous Income Stream
- Consumers' and Producers' Surplus

■ Continuous Income Stream

We start this discussion with an example.

Example 6

The rate of change of the income produced by a vending machine (in dollars per year) is given by

$$f(t) = 1,000e^{0.04t}$$

where t is time in years since the installation of the machine. Find the total income produced by the machine during the first 5 years of operation.

Solution

Since we have been given the rate of change of income, we can find the total income by using a definite integral:

$$\text{Total income} = \int_0^5 1{,}000e^{0.04t}\, dt$$

$$= 25{,}000e^{0.04t}\Big|_0^5$$

$$= 25{,}000e^{0.04(5)} - 25{,}000e^{0.04(0)}$$

$$= 30{,}535 - 25{,}000 \qquad \text{Rounded to the nearest dollar}$$

$$= \$5{,}535$$

Thus, the vending machine produces a total income of $5,535 during the first 5 years of operation.

Problem 6

Refer to Example 6. Find the total income produced during the second 5 years of operation.

In reality, income from a vending machine is not received as a single payment at the end of the 5 year period. Instead, the income is collected on a regular basis, perhaps daily or weekly. In problems of this type, it is convenient to assume that income is actually received in a **continuous stream.** That is, we assume that income is a continuous function of time. The rate of change of income is called the **rate of flow** of the continuous income stream. In general, we have:

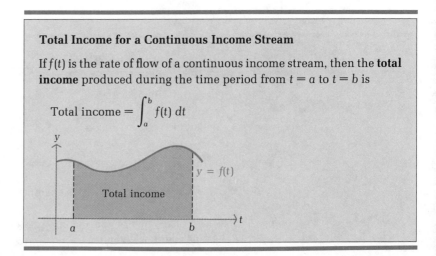

Total Income for a Continuous Income Stream

If $f(t)$ is the rate of flow of a continuous income stream, then the **total income** produced during the time period from $t = a$ to $t = b$ is

$$\text{Total income} = \int_a^b f(t)\, dt$$

■ Present Value of a Continuous Income Stream

In Section 9-1, we discussed continuous compound interest. Recall that if P dollars are invested at an annual nominal rate of $100r\%$, compounded continuously, then the amount A after t years is

$$A = Pe^{rt}$$

Solving this equation for P, we have

$$P = Ae^{-rt}$$

which is referred to as the present value of A. That is, P is the amount that would have to be invested at time $t = 0$ (the present) in order to receive A dollars t years from now (the future) at $100r\%$ compounded continuously. For example, if a bond pays $10,000 in 5 years and money is worth 12% compounded continuously, then the present value is (to the nearest dollar)

$$P = 10,000e^{-0.12(5)} = \$5,488$$

Thus, it is easy to compute the present value of an investment that returns a single payment. Now we want to consider investments that return payments to the investor on a regular basis.

In order to generalize the concept of present value to continuous income streams, we assume that the income produced is instantaneously invested at an annual rate of $100r\%$, compounded continuously. (In general, the value of money is determined by the currently available interest rate.) Suppose $f(t)$ is the rate of flow of a continuous income stream. To find the present value of this continuous income stream at $100r\%$, compounded continuously for T years, we begin by dividing the interval $[0, T]$ into n equal subintervals of length Δt and choose an arbitrary point c_k in each subinterval, as illustrated in Figure 7. The total income produced during the time period from $t = t_{k-1}$ to $t = t_k$ is equal to the area under the graph of $f(t)$ over this subinterval and is approximately equal to $f(c_k)\Delta t$, the area of the shaded rectangle in Figure 7.

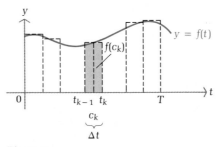

Figure 7

Using the present value formula $P = Ae^{-rt}$ with $A = f(c_k)\Delta t$ and $t = c_k$, the present value of the income received during the time period from

$t = t_{k-1}$ to $t = t_k$ is approximately equal to

$$f(c_k)\Delta t e^{-rc_k}$$

The total present value for the time period from $t = 0$ to $t = T$ is approximately equal to

$$f(c_1)\Delta t e^{-rc_1} + f(c_2)\Delta t e^{-rc_2} + \cdots + f(c_n)\Delta t e^{-rc_n}$$

which has the form of a Riemann sum. And in the limit we have a definite integral. (See the definition of definite integral in Section 11-1.) Thus, we have:

Present Value of a Continuous Income Stream

If $f(t)$ is the rate of flow of a continuous income stream, then the **present value,** PV, at $100r\%$ compounded continuously for T years is

$$PV = \int_0^T f(t)e^{-rt}\,dt$$

Example 7 Let $f(t) = 1{,}000e^{0.04t}$ be the rate of flow of the income produced by the vending machine in Example 6.

(A) Find the present value of this income stream at 12% compounded continuously for 5 years.

(B) Find the amount (income plus interest) produced by the vending machine over this 5 year period.

(C) Find the interest earned during this 5 year period.

Solutions (A) $PV = \displaystyle\int_0^T f(t)e^{-rt}\,dt$

$$= \int_0^5 1{,}000e^{0.04t}e^{-0.12t}\,dt$$

$$= 1{,}000\int_0^5 e^{-0.08t}\,dt$$

$$= -12{,}500e^{-0.08t}\Big|_0^5$$

$$= -12{,}500e^{-0.4} + 12{,}500$$

$$= \$4{,}121$$

(B) The total amount produced by a continuous income stream is the same as the amount that would result if the present value were deposited in an account earning 12% interest compounded continuously for 5 years. Using the present value in the formula for continuous compound interest, we have

$$A = PVe^{rt} = 4{,}121e^{0.12(5)} = \$7{,}509$$

(C) In Example 6, we saw that the income produced by this vending machine was $5,535. Since the amount is the total of all money produced (income plus interest), the difference between the amount and the income is interest. Thus,

$$7{,}509 - 5{,}535 = \$1{,}974$$

is the interest earned by the income produced during the 5 year period.

Problem 7 Repeat Example 7 if the interest rate is 9% compounded continuously.

■ Consumers' and Producers' Surplus

Let $p = D(x)$ be the price–demand equation for a product, let $\bar{p}$ be the current price, and let $\bar{x}$ be the corresponding demand.* The demand curve in Figure 8 shows that some of these $\bar{x}$ units could have been sold at a higher price. The consumers who would have been willing to pay higher prices have saved money. We want to determine the amount of money saved by these consumers.

To do this, consider the interval $[c_k, c_k + \Delta x]$ where $c_k < \bar{x}$. If the price remained constant over this interval, then the savings on each unit would

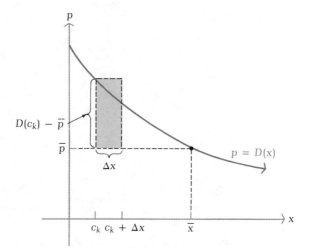

Figure 8

* Unless otherwise specified, we will assume that price is in dollars and demand is in number of units.

be the difference between $D(c_k)$, the price consumers are willing to pay, and $\bar{p}$, the price they actually pay. The total savings to consumers over this interval is approximately equal to

$$[D(c_k) - \bar{p}]\Delta x$$

which is the area of the shaded rectangle shown in Figure 8. If we divide the interval $[0, \bar{x}]$ into n equal subintervals, then the total savings to consumers is approximately equal to

$$[D(c_1) - \bar{p}]\Delta x + [D(c_2) - \bar{p}]\Delta x + \cdots + [D(c_n) - \bar{p}]\Delta x$$

which we recognize as a Riemann sum for the integral

$$\int_0^{\bar{x}} [D(x) - \bar{p}]\, dx$$

Thus, we define the *consumers' surplus* to be this integral.

Consumers' Surplus

If $(\bar{x}, \bar{p})$ is a point on the graph of the price–demand equation $p = D(x)$, then the **consumers' surplus, CS,** at a price level of $\bar{p}$ is

$$CS = \int_0^{\bar{x}} [D(x) - \bar{p}]\, dx$$

which is the area between $p = \bar{p}$ and $p = D(x)$ from $x = 0$ to $x = \bar{x}$.

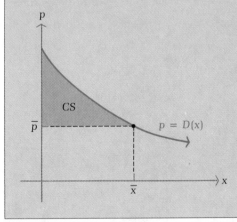

Example 8   Find the consumers' surplus at a price level of \$8 for the price–demand equation

$$p = D(x) = 20 - \frac{1}{20}x$$

Solution Step 1. Find $\bar{x}$, the demand when the price is $\bar{p} = 8$:

$$\bar{p} = 20 - \frac{1}{20}\bar{x}$$

$$8 = 20 - \frac{1}{20}\bar{x}$$

$$\frac{1}{20}\bar{x} = 12$$

$$\bar{x} = 240$$

Step 2. Sketch a graph:

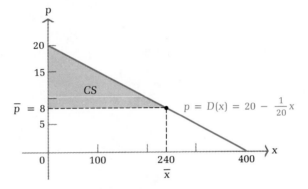

Step 3. Find the consumers' surplus (the shaded area in the graph):

$$CS = \int_0^{\bar{x}} [D(x) - \bar{p}]\, dx$$

$$= \int_0^{240} \left(20 - \frac{1}{20}x - 8\right) dx$$

$$= \int_0^{240} \left(12 - \frac{1}{20}x\right) dx$$

$$= \left(12x - \frac{1}{40}x^2\right)\Big|_0^{240}$$

$$= 2{,}880 - 1{,}440 = \$1{,}440$$

Problem 8 Repeat Example 8 for a price level of $4.

If $p = S(x)$ is the price–supply equation for a product, $\bar{p}$ is the current price, and $\bar{x}$ is the current supply, then there are suppliers that would be willing to supply some units at a lower price. The additional money that these suppliers gain from the higher price is called the *producers' surplus* and can be expressed in terms of a definite integral (proceeding as we did for the consumers' surplus).

Producers' Surplus

If $(\bar{x}, \bar{p})$ is a point on the graph of the price–supply equation $p = S(x)$, then the **producers' surplus,** PS, at a price level of $\bar{p}$ is

$$PS = \int_0^{\bar{x}} [\bar{p} - S(x)] \, dx$$

which is the area between $p = \bar{p}$ and $p = S(x)$ from $x = 0$ to $x = \bar{x}$.

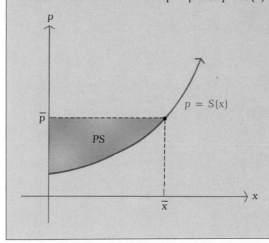

Example 9   Find the producers' surplus at a price level of $20 for the price–supply equation

$$p = S(x) = 2 + \frac{1}{5,000} x^2$$

Solution   Step 1.   Find $\bar{x}$, the supply when the price is $\bar{p} = 20$:

$$\bar{p} = 2 + \frac{1}{5,000} \bar{x}^2$$

$$20 = 2 + \frac{1}{5,000} \bar{x}^2$$

$$\frac{1}{5,000} \bar{x}^2 = 18$$

$$\bar{x}^2 = 90,000$$

$$\bar{x} = 300 \qquad \text{There is only one solution since } \bar{x} \geqslant 0.$$

Step 2.   Sketch a graph:

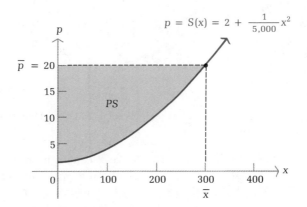

$$p = S(x) = 2 + \frac{1}{5,000}x^2$$

Step 3. Find the producers' surplus (the shaded area in the graph):

$$PS = \int_0^{\bar{x}} [\bar{p} - S(x)]\, dx$$

$$= \int_0^{300} \left[20 - \left(2 + \frac{1}{5,000}x^2 \right) \right] dx$$

$$= \int_0^{300} \left(18 - \frac{1}{5,000}x^2 \right) dx$$

$$= \left(18x - \frac{1}{15,000}x^3 \right) \Big|_0^{300}$$

$$= 5,400 - 1,800 = \$3,600$$

Problem 9 Repeat Example 9 for a price level of $4.

In a competitive market, the price of a product is determined by the relationship between supply and demand. If $p = D(x)$ and $p = S(x)$ are the price–demand and price–supply equations, respectively, for a product, then the price at which supply equals demand $[S(x) = D(x)]$ is called the **equilibrium price.** If the price stabilizes at the equilibrium price, then both consumers and producers benefit.

Example 10 Find the equilibrium price and then find the consumers' surplus and the producers' surplus at the equilibrium price level if

$$p = D(x) = 20 - \frac{1}{20}x \quad \text{and} \quad p = S(x) = 2 + \frac{1}{5,000}x^2$$

Solution **Step 1.** Find the equilibrium point. Set $D(x)$ equal to $S(x)$ and solve:

$$D(x) = S(x)$$

$$20 - \frac{1}{20}x = 2 + \frac{1}{5,000}x^2$$

$$\frac{1}{5,000}x^2 + \frac{1}{20}x - 18 = 0$$

$$x^2 + 250x - 90,000 = 0$$

$$x = 200, -450$$

Since x cannot be negative, the only solution is $x = 200$. The equilibrium price can be determined by using $D(x)$ or $S(x)$. We will use both to check our work:

$$\bar{p} = D(200) \qquad\qquad \bar{p} = S(200)$$

$$= 20 - \frac{1}{20}(200) = 10 \qquad = 2 + \frac{1}{5,000}(200)^2 = 10$$

Thus, the equilibrium price is $\bar{p} = 10$, and the corresponding demand and supply is $\bar{x} = 200$.

Step 2.   Sketch a graph:

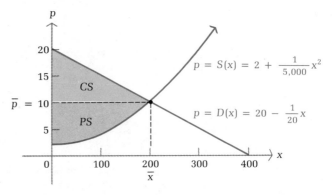

Step 3.   Find the consumers' surplus:

$$CS = \int_0^{\bar{x}} [D(x) - \bar{p}] \, dx$$

$$= \int_0^{200} \left(20 - \frac{1}{20}x - 10\right) dx$$

$$= \int_0^{200} \left(10 - \frac{1}{20}x\right) dx$$

$$= \left(10x - \frac{1}{40}x^2\right) \bigg|_0^{200}$$

$$= 2,000 - 1,000 = \$1,000$$

Step 4.   Find the producers' surplus:

$$PS = \int_0^{\bar{x}} [\bar{p} - S(x)]\, dx$$

$$= \int_0^{200} \left[10 - \left(2 + \frac{1}{5,000} x^2 \right) \right] dx$$

$$= \int_0^{200} \left(8 - \frac{1}{5,000} x^2 \right) dx$$

$$= \left(8x - \frac{1}{15,000} x^3 \right) \Big|_0^{200}$$

$$= 1,600 - \frac{1,600}{3} \approx \$1,067 \qquad \text{Rounded to the nearest dollar}$$

Problem 10   Repeat Example 10 for

$$p = D(x) = 25 - \frac{1}{1,000} x^2 \quad \text{and} \quad p = S(x) = 5 + \frac{1}{10} x$$

Answers to   6. $6,761   7. (A) $4,424   (B) $6,938   (C) $1,403
Matched Problems   8. $2,560   9. $133   10. $\bar{p} = 15$; $CS = \$667$; $PS = \$500$

Exercise 11-2

Applications

Business & Economics

1. Find the total income produced by a continuous income stream in the first 5 years if the rate of flow is $f(t) = 2,500$.
2. Repeat Problem 1 if the rate of flow is $f(t) = 3,000$.
3. Find the total income produced by a continuous income stream in the first 3 years if the rate of flow is $f(t) = 400e^{0.05t}$.
4. Repeat Problem 3 if the rate of flow is $f(t) = 600e^{-0.06t}$.
5. Find the present value at 8% interest compounded continuously for 10 years for the continuous income stream with rate of flow $f(t) = 800$.
6. Repeat Problem 5 if the rate of flow is $f(t) = 1,200$.
7. Find the present value at 10% interest compounded continuously for 4 years for the continuous income stream with rate of flow $f(t) = 1,500e^{-0.02t}$.
8. Repeat Problem 7 if the rate of flow is $f(t) = 2,000e^{0.06t}$.
9. Find the consumers' surplus at a price level of $\bar{p} = 150$ for the price–demand equation $p = D(x) = 400 - \frac{1}{20}x$.
10. Find the consumers' surplus at a price level of $\bar{p} = 120$ for the price–demand equation $p = D(x) = 200 - \frac{1}{50}x$.

11. Find the producers' surplus at a price level of $\bar{p} = 65$ for the price-supply equation

$$p = S(x) = 10 + \frac{1}{10}x + \frac{1}{3,600}x^2$$

12. Find the producers' surplus at a price level of $\bar{p} = 55$ for the price-supply equation

$$p = S(x) = 15 + \frac{1}{10}x + \frac{3}{1,000}x^2$$

13. Find the equilibrium price, and then find the consumers' surplus and the producers' surplus for

$$p = D(x) = 50 - \frac{1}{10}x \quad \text{and} \quad p = S(x) = 11 + \frac{1}{20}x$$

14. Repeat Problem 13 for

$$p = D(x) = 20 - \frac{1}{600}x^2 \quad \text{and} \quad p = S(x) = 2 + \frac{1}{300}x^2$$

15. Find the equilibrium price (rounded to the nearest dollar), and then find the consumers' surplus and the producers' surplus for

$$p = D(x) = 80e^{-0.001x} \quad \text{and} \quad p = S(x) = 30e^{0.001x}$$

16. Repeat Problem 15 for

$$p = D(x) = 185e^{-0.005x} \quad \text{and} \quad p = S(x) = 25e^{0.005x}$$

17. Find the amount (income plus interest) produced by a continuous income stream at 14% compounded continuously for 2 years if the rate of flow is $f(t) = 1,000$.

18. Repeat Problem 17 if the rate of flow is $f(t) = 1,000e^{0.04t}$.

19. Find the interest earned at 12% compounded continuously for 3 years by a continuous income stream with rate of flow $f(t) = 2,000e^{0.07t}$.

20. Repeat Problem 19 if the rate of flow is $f(t) = 2,000$.

21. An investor is presented with a choice of two investments, an established clothing store and a new computer store. Each choice requires the same initial investment and each produces a continuous income stream at 10% compounded continuously. The rate of flow of income from the clothing store is $f(t) = 12,000$ and the rate of flow of income from the computer store is $g(t) = 10,000e^{0.05t}$. Compare the present values of these investments to determine which is the better choice over the next 5 years.

22. Refer to Problem 21. Which investment is the better choice over the next 10 years?

Problems 23 and 24 refer to a continuous income stream with rate of flow
$f(t) = k$, *where* k *is a constant.*

23. Find the present value at $100r\%$ compounded continuously for T years.

24. Find the amount after T years at $100r\%$ compounded continuously.

11-3 Integration by Parts

In Section 10-1 we said that we would return to the indefinite integral

$$\int \ln x \, dx$$

later, since none of the integration techniques considered up to that time could be used to find an antiderivative for $\ln x$. We will now develop a very useful technique, called *integration by parts*, that will not only enable us to find the above integral, but also many others, including integrals such as

$$\int x \ln x \, dx \quad \text{and} \quad \int xe^x \, dx$$

The integration by parts technique is also used to derive many integration formulas that are tabulated in mathematical handbooks.

The method of integration by parts is based on the product formula for derivatives. If f and g are differentiable functions, then

$$D_x[f(x)g(x)] = f(x)g'(x) + g(x)f'(x)$$

which can be written in the equivalent form

$$f(x)g'(x) = D_x[f(x)g(x)] - g(x)f'(x)$$

Integrating both sides, we obtain

$$\int f(x)g'(x) \, dx = \int D_x[f(x)g(x)] \, dx - \int g(x)f'(x) \, dx$$

The first integral to the right of the equal sign is $f(x)g(x) + C$. (Why?) We will leave out the constant of integration for now, since we can add it after integrating the second integral to the right of the equal sign. So we have

$$\int f(x)g'(x) \, dx = f(x)g(x) - \int g(x)f'(x) \, dx$$

This last form can be transformed into a more convenient form by letting $u = f(x)$ and $v = g(x)$; then $du = f'(x) \, dx$ and $dv = g'(x) \, dx$. Making these substitutions, we obtain the **integration by parts formula:**

Integration by Parts Formula

$$\int u\ dv = uv - \int v\ du$$

This formula can be very useful when the integral on the left is difficult to integrate using standard formulas. If u and dv are chosen with care, then the integral on the right side may be easier to integrate than the one on the left. Several examples will demonstrate the use of the formula.

Example 11   Find $\int x \ln x\ dx$, $x > 0$, using integration by parts.

Solution   First, write the integration by parts formula

$$\int u\ dv = uv - \int v\ du$$

Then try to identify u and dv in $\int x \ln x\ dx$ (this is the key step) so that when $\int u\ dv$ is written in the form $uv - \int v\ du$, the new integral will be easier to integrate.

Suppose we choose

$$u = x \qquad \text{and} \qquad dv = \ln x\ dx$$

Then

$$du = dx \qquad v = ?$$

We do not know an antiderivative of $\ln x$ yet, so we change our choice for u and dv to

$$u = \ln x \qquad dv = x\ dx$$

Then

$$du = \frac{1}{x}\ dx \qquad v = \frac{x^2}{2}$$

Any constant may be added to v (we choose 0 for simplicity). There are cases where it is convenient to add a constant other than 0, but in most cases 0 will do. The general arbitrary constant of integration will be added at the end of the process.

Using the chosen u, du, dv, and v in the integration by parts formula, we obtain

$$\int u \quad dv = u \quad v \quad - \int v \quad du$$

$$\int (\ln x)x\,dx = (\ln x)\left(\frac{x^2}{2}\right) - \int \left(\frac{x^2}{2}\right)\frac{1}{x}\,dx$$

$$= \frac{x^2}{2}\ln x - \int \frac{x}{2}\,dx$$ This new integral is easy to integrate.

$$= \frac{x^2}{2}\ln x - \frac{x^2}{4} + C$$

To check this result, show that

$$D_x\left(\frac{x^2}{2}\ln x - \frac{x^2}{4} + C\right) = x \ln x$$

which is the integrand in the original integral.

Problem 11   Find $\int x \ln 2x\,dx$.

Example 12   Find $\int xe^x\,dx$.

Solution   We write the integration by parts formula

$$\int u\,dv = uv - \int v\,du$$

and choose

$$u = e^x \qquad dv = x\,dx$$

Then

$$du = e^x\,dx \qquad v = \frac{x^2}{2}$$

and

$$\int u \quad dv = u \quad v \quad - \int v \cdot du$$

$$\int e^x x\,dx = e^x\left(\frac{x^2}{2}\right) - \int \left(\frac{x^2}{2}\right)e^x\,dx$$

$$= \frac{x^2}{2}e^x - \frac{1}{2}\int x^2 e^x\,dx$$ This new integral is more complicated than the original one.

This time the integration by parts formula leads to a new integral that is more complicated than the one we started with. This does not mean that there is an error in our calculations or in the formula. It simply means that our first choice for u and dv did not change the original problem into one that we can solve. Thus, we must make a different selection. Suppose we choose

$$u = x \qquad dv = e^x \, dx$$

Then

$$du = dx \qquad v = e^x$$

and

$$\int u \, dv = u v - \int v \, du$$

$$\int x e^x \, dx = x e^x - \int e^x \, dx \qquad \text{This integral is one we can evaluate.}$$

$$= x e^x - e^x + C$$

Check this result by differentiation.

Problem 12   Find $\int x e^{2x} \, dx$.

Integration by Parts: Selection of u and dv

1. It must be possible to integrate dv (preferably by using standard formulas or simple substitutions).
2. The new integral, $\int v \, du$, should be simpler than the original integral, $\int u \, dv$.
3. For integrals involving $x^p (\ln x)^q$, try

    $$u = (\ln x)^q \qquad dv = x^p \, dx$$

4. For integrals involving $x^p e^{ax}$, try

    $$u = x^p \qquad dv = e^{ax} \, dx$$

5. For integrals involving $x^p (ax + b)^q$, try

    $$u = x^p \qquad dv = (ax + b)^q \, dx$$

Example 13   Find $\displaystyle \int x(x + 5)^9 \, dx$.

Solution   Following suggestion 5 in the box, we choose

$$u = x \qquad dv = (x + 5)^9 \, dx$$

Then

$$du = dx \qquad v = \frac{(x + 5)^{10}}{10}$$

and

$$\int x(x+5)^9 \, dx = x\frac{(x+5)^{10}}{10} - \int \frac{(x+5)^{10}}{10} \, dx$$

$$= \frac{1}{10}x(x+5)^{10} - \frac{1}{110}(x+5)^{11} + C$$

Problem 13 Find $\int x(x-4)^8 \, dx$.

Example 14 Find $\int x^2 e^{-x} \, dx$.

Solution Following suggestion 4 in the box, we choose

$$u = x^2 \qquad dv = e^{-x} \, dx$$

Then

$$du = 2x \, dx \qquad v = -e^{-x}$$

and

$$\int x^2 e^{-x} \, dx = x^2(-e^{-x}) - \int (-e^{-x})2x \, dx$$

$$= -x^2 e^{-x} + 2\int xe^{-x} \, dx \tag{1}$$

The new integral is not one we can evaluate by standard formulas, but it is simpler than the original integral. Applying the integration by parts formula to it will produce an even simpler integral. For the integral $\int xe^{-x} \, dx$, we choose

$$u = x \qquad dv = e^{-x} \, dx$$

Then

$$du = dx \qquad v = -e^{-x}$$

and

$$\int xe^{-x} \, dx = x(-e^{-x}) - \int (-e^{-x}) \, dx$$

$$= -xe^{-x} + \int e^{-x} \, dx$$

$$= -xe^{-x} - e^{-x} \tag{2}$$

Substituting (2) into (1) and adding a constant of integration, we have

$$\int x^2 e^{-x} \, dx = -x^2 e^{-x} + 2(-xe^{-x} - e^{-x}) + C$$

$$= -x^2 e^{-x} - 2xe^{-x} - 2e^{-x} + C$$

Problem 14   Find $\int x^2 e^{2x}\, dx$.

Example 15   Find $\int_1^e \ln x\, dx$.

Solution   First, find $\int \ln x\, dx$; then return to the definite integral. Following suggestion 3 in the box (with $p = 0$), we choose

$$u = \ln x \qquad dv = dx$$

Then

$$du = \frac{1}{x}\, dx \qquad v = x$$

Hence,

$$\int \ln x\, dx = (\ln x)(x) - \int (x)\frac{1}{x}\, dx$$
$$= x \ln x - x + C$$

Thus,

$$\int_1^e \ln x\, dx = (x \ln x - x)\Big|_1^e$$
$$= (e \ln e - e) - (1 \ln 1 - 1)$$
$$= (e - e) - (0 - 1)$$
$$= 1$$

Problem 15   Find $\int_1^2 \ln 3x\, dx$.

Answers to   11. $\dfrac{x^2}{2} \ln 2x - \dfrac{x^2}{4} + C$ 12. $\dfrac{x}{2}e^{2x} - \dfrac{1}{4}e^{2x} + C$
Matched Problems

13. $\dfrac{1}{9}x(x-4)^9 - \dfrac{1}{90}(x-4)^{10} + C$ 14. $\dfrac{x^2}{2}e^{2x} - \dfrac{x}{2}e^{2x} + \dfrac{1}{4}e^{2x} + C$

15. $2 \ln 6 - \ln 3 - 1 \approx 1.4849$

Exercise 11-3

A   *Integrate using integration by parts. Assume $x > 0$ whenever the natural log
function is involved.*

1. $\displaystyle\int xe^{3x}\, dx$ 2. $\displaystyle\int xe^{4x}\, dx$

3. $\displaystyle\int x^2 \ln x\, dx$ 4. $\displaystyle\int x^3 \ln x\, dx$

5. $\displaystyle\int x(x-6)^7\, dx$ 6. $\displaystyle\int x(x+9)^6\, dx$

B Problems 7–24 are mixed—some require integration by parts and others can be solved using techniques we have considered earlier. Integrate as indicated, assuming x > 0 whenever the natural log function is involved.

7. $\displaystyle\int xe^{-x}\,dx$

8. $\displaystyle\int (x-1)e^{-x}\,dx$

9. $\displaystyle\int xe^{x^2}\,dx$

10. $\displaystyle\int xe^{-x^2}\,dx$

11. $\displaystyle\int x(2x-1)^5\,dx$

12. $\displaystyle\int (2x-1)^5\,dx$

13. $\displaystyle\int (3x+2)^6\,dx$

14. $\displaystyle\int x(3x+2)^6\,dx$

15. $\displaystyle\int_0^1 (x-3)e^x\,dx$

16. $\displaystyle\int_0^2 (x+5)e^x\,dx$

17. $\displaystyle\int_1^3 \ln 2x\,dx$

18. $\displaystyle\int_2^3 \ln 7x\,dx$

19. $\displaystyle\int \frac{2x}{x^2+1}\,dx$

20. $\displaystyle\int \frac{x^2}{x^3+5}\,dx$

21. $\displaystyle\int \frac{\ln x}{x}\,dx$

22. $\displaystyle\int \frac{e^x}{e^x+1}\,dx$

23. $\displaystyle\int \sqrt{x}\,\ln x\,dx$

24. $\displaystyle\int \frac{\ln x}{\sqrt{x}}\,dx$

C Some of these problems may require using the integration by parts formula more than once. Assume x > 0 whenever the natural log function is involved.

25. $\displaystyle\int x^2 e^x\,dx$

26. $\displaystyle\int x^3 e^x\,dx$

27. $\displaystyle\int xe^{ax}\,dx, \quad a\neq 0$

28. $\displaystyle\int \ln(ax)\,dx, \quad a>0$

29. $\displaystyle\int_1^e \frac{\ln x}{x^2}\,dx$

30. $\displaystyle\int_1^2 x^3 e^{x^2}\,dx$

31. $\displaystyle\int x^2(x+1)^7\,dx$

32. $\displaystyle\int x(x-7)^{-4}\,dx$

33. $\displaystyle\int x(x+6)^{-3}\,dx$

34. $\displaystyle\int x^2(x+2)^6\,dx$

35. $\displaystyle\int (\ln x)^2\,dx$

36. $\displaystyle\int x(\ln x)^2\,dx$

37. $\displaystyle\int (\ln x)^3\,dx$

38. $\displaystyle\int x(\ln x)^3\,dx$

39. $\displaystyle\int x\sqrt{x+4}\,dx$

40. $\displaystyle\int \frac{x}{\sqrt{x-2}}\,dx$

Find the area bounded by the graphs of the indicated equations.

41. $y = x - \ln x$, $y = 0$, $x = 1$, $x = e$
42. $y = 1 - \ln x$, $y = 0$, $x = 1$, $x = 4$
43. $y = (x - 2)e^x$, $y = 0$, $x = 0$, $x = 3$
44. $y = (3 - x)e^x$, $y = 0$, $x = 0$, $x = 3$

Applications

Business & Economics

45. *Profit.* If the rate of change of profit in millions of dollars per year is given by

$$P'(t) = 2t - te^{-t}$$

where t is time in years and the profit at time 0 is 0, find $P = P(t)$.

46. *Production.* An oil field is estimated to produce oil at a rate of $R(t)$ thousand barrels per month t months from now, as given by

$$R(t) = 10te^{-0.1t}$$

Estimate the total production in the first year of operation by use of an appropriate definite integral.

47. *Continuous income stream.* Find the present value at 8% compounded continuously for 5 years for the continuous income stream with rate of flow

$$f(t) = 1{,}000 - 200t$$

48. *Continuous income stream.* Find the amount (income plus interest) at 10% compounded continuously for 4 years for the continuous income stream with rate of flow

$$f(t) = 4{,}000 - 250t^2$$

49. *Income distribution.* Find the coefficient of inequality for the Lorenz curve with equation

$$y = \frac{1}{16}x(x + 1)^4$$

50. *Producers' surplus.* Find the producers' surplus at a price level of $\overline{p} = 26$ for the price–supply equation

$$p = S(x) = 5\ln(x + 1)$$

[*Hint:* To find an antiderivative of $\ln(x + 1)$, first substitute $t = x + 1$, then use integration by parts.]

Life Sciences

51. *Pollution.* The concentration of particulate matter in parts per million t hours after a factory ceases operation for the day is given by

$$C(t) = \frac{20 \ln(t + 1)}{(t + 1)^2}$$

Find the average concentration for the time period from $t = 0$ to $t = 5$.

52. *Medicine.* After a person takes a pill, the drug contained in the pill is assimilated into the bloodstream. The rate of assimilation t minutes after taking the pill is

$$R(t) = te^{-0.2t}$$

Find the total amount of the drug that is assimilated into the bloodstream during the first 10 minutes after the pill is taken.

Social Sciences

53. *Politics.* The number of voters (in thousands) in a certain city is given by

$$N(t) = 20 + 4t - 5te^{-0.1t}$$

where t is the time in years. Find the average number of voters during the time period from $t = 0$ to $t = 5$.

11-4 Improper Integrals

- Improper Integrals
- Application: Capital Value
- Probability Density Functions

■ Improper Integrals

We are now going to consider an integral form that has wide application in probability studies as well as other areas. Earlier, when we introduced the idea of a definite integral,

$$\int_a^b f(x)\, dx \tag{1}$$

we required f to be continuous over a closed interval $[a, b]$. Now we are going to extend the meaning of (1) so that the interval $[a, b]$ may become infinite in length.

Let us investigate a particular example that will motivate several general definitions. What would be a reasonable interpretation for the following expression?

$$\int_1^\infty \frac{dx}{x^2}$$

Sketching a graph of $f(x) = 1/x^2$, $x \geq 1$ (see Fig. 9 on the next page), we note that for any fixed $b > 1$, $\int_1^b f(x)\, dx$ is the area between the curve $y = 1/x^2$, the x axis, $x = 1$, and $x = b$.

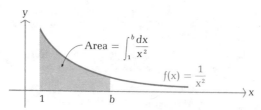

Figure 9

Let us see what happens when we let $b \to \infty$; that is, when we compute the following limit:

$$\lim_{b \to \infty} \int_1^b \frac{dx}{x^2} = \lim_{b \to \infty} \left[(-x^{-1}) \Big|_1^b \right]$$

$$= \lim_{b \to \infty} \left(-\frac{1}{b} + 1 \right) = 1$$

Did you expect this result? No matter how large b is taken, the area under the curve from $x = 1$ to $x = b$ never exceeds 1, and in the limit it is 1. This suggests that we write

$$\int_1^\infty \frac{dx}{x^2} = \lim_{b \to \infty} \int_1^b \frac{dx}{x^2} = 1$$

This integral is an example of an *improper integral*. In general, the forms

$$\int_{-\infty}^b f(x)\, dx \qquad \int_a^\infty f(x)\, dx \qquad \int_{-\infty}^\infty f(x)\, dx$$

where f is continuous over the indicated interval, are called **improper integrals.** (There are also other types of improper integrals that will not be considered here. These involve certain types of points of discontinuity within the interval of integration.) Each type of improper integral above is formally defined in the box:

Improper Integrals

If f is continuous over the indicated interval and the limit exists, then:

1. $$\int_a^\infty f(x)\, dx = \lim_{b \to \infty} \int_a^b f(x)\, dx$$

2. $$\int_{-\infty}^b f(x)\, dx = \lim_{a \to -\infty} \int_a^b f(x)\, dx$$

3. $$\int_{-\infty}^\infty f(x)\, dx = \int_{-\infty}^c f(x)\, dx + \int_c^\infty f(x)\, dx$$

where c is any point on $(-\infty, \infty)$, provided *both* improper integrals on the right exist.

If the indicated limit exists, then the improper integral is said to exist or **converge;** if the limit does not exist, then the improper integral is said not to exist or to **diverge** (and no value is assigned to it).

Example 16   Evaluate $\int_2^\infty dx/x$ if it converges.

Solution
$$\int_2^\infty \frac{dx}{x} = \lim_{b\to\infty} \int_2^b \frac{dx}{x}$$
$$= \lim_{b\to\infty} \left[(\ln x)\Big|_2^b \right]$$
$$= \lim_{b\to\infty} (\ln b - \ln 2)$$

Since $\ln b \to \infty$ as $b \to \infty$, the limit does not exist. Hence, the improper integral diverges.

Problem 16   Evaluate $\int_3^\infty dx/(x-1)^2$ if it converges.

Example 17   Evaluate $\int_{-\infty}^2 e^x\, dx$ if it converges.

Solution
$$\int_{-\infty}^2 e^x\, dx = \lim_{a\to-\infty} \int_a^2 e^x\, dx$$
$$= \lim_{a\to-\infty} (e^x|_a^2)$$
$$= \lim_{a\to-\infty} (e^2 - e^a) = e^2 - 0 = e^2 \qquad \text{The integral converges.}$$

Problem 17   Evaluate $\int_{-\infty}^{-1} x^{-2}\, dx$ if it converges.

Example 18   Evaluate
$$\int_{-\infty}^\infty \frac{2x}{(1+x^2)^2}\, dx$$
if it converges.

Solution
$$\int_{-\infty}^\infty \frac{2x}{(1+x^2)^2}\, dx = \int_{-\infty}^0 (1+x^2)^{-2}2x\, dx + \int_0^\infty (1+x^2)^{-2}2x\, dx$$
$$= \lim_{a\to-\infty} \int_a^0 (1+x^2)^{-2}2x\, dx + \lim_{b\to\infty} \int_0^b (1+x^2)^{-2}2x\, dx$$
$$= \lim_{a\to-\infty} \left[\frac{(1+x^2)^{-1}}{-1}\bigg|_a^0 \right] + \lim_{b\to\infty} \left[\frac{(1+x^2)^{-1}}{-1}\bigg|_0^b \right]$$
$$= \lim_{a\to-\infty} \left[-1 + \frac{1}{1+a^2} \right] + \lim_{b\to\infty} \left[-\frac{1}{1+b^2} + 1 \right]$$
$$= -1 + 1 = 0 \qquad \text{The integral converges.}$$

Problem 18   Evaluate $\int_{-\infty}^\infty dx/e^x$ if it converges.

Example 19
Oil Production

It is estimated that an oil well will produce oil at a rate of $R(t)$ thousand barrels per month t months from now, as given by

$$R(t) = 50e^{-0.05t} - 50e^{-0.1t}$$

Estimate the total amount of oil produced by this well.

Solution   The total amount of oil produced in T months of operation is

$$\int_0^T R(t) \, dt$$

At some point in time, the monthly production rate will become so low that it will no longer be economically feasible to operate the well. However, for the purpose of estimating the total production, it is convenient to assume that the well is operated indefinitely. Thus, the total amount of oil produced is

$$\int_0^\infty R(t) \, dt = \lim_{T \to \infty} \int_0^T R(t) \, dt$$

$$= \lim_{T \to \infty} \int_0^T (50e^{-0.05t} - 50e^{-0.1t}) \, dt$$

$$= \lim_{T \to \infty} \left[(-1{,}000e^{-0.05t} + 500e^{-0.1t}) \Big|_0^T \right]$$

$$= \lim_{T \to \infty} (-1{,}000e^{-0.05T} + 500e^{-0.1T} + 500)$$

$$= 500 \text{ thousand barrels}$$

Problem 19   Find the total amount of oil produced by a well whose monthly production rate (in thousands of barrels) is given by

$$R(t) = 100e^{-0.1t} - 25e^{-0.2t}$$

■ Application: Capital Value

If $f(t)$ is the rate of flow of a continuous income stream at an annual nominal rate of $100r\%$, compounded continuously, then the **capital value** of the income stream is the present value over the time interval $[0, \infty)$. That is,

$$\text{Capital value} = \int_0^\infty f(t)e^{-rt} \, dt$$

Example 20   A family has leased the oil rights of a property to a petroleum company in return for a perpetual annual payment of $1,200. Find the capital value of this lease at 10% compounded continuously.

Solution   The annual payments from the oil company produce a continuous income stream with rate of flow $f(t) = 1{,}200$ that continues indefinitely. (It is common practice to treat a sequence of equal periodic payments as a continuous income stream with a constant rate of flow, even if the income is received only at the end of each period.) Thus, the capital value is

$$\int_0^\infty f(t)e^{-rt}\,dt = \int_0^\infty 1{,}200e^{-0.1t}\,dt$$

$$= \lim_{T\to\infty} \int_0^T 1{,}200e^{-0.1t}\,dt$$

$$= \lim_{T\to\infty} \left[-12{,}000e^{-0.1t}\,\Big|_0^T \right]$$

$$= \lim_{T\to\infty} (-12{,}000e^{-0.1T} + 12{,}000) = \$12{,}000$$

Problem 20 Repeat Example 20 if the interest rate is 8%, compounded continuously.

■ Probability Density Functions

We will now take a brief look at the use of improper integrals relative to probability density functions. The approach will be intuitive and informal.

Suppose an experiment is designed in such a way that any real number x on the interval [a, b] is a possible outcome. For example, x may represent an IQ score, the height of a person in inches, or the life of a light bulb in hours.

In certain situations it is possible to find a function f with x as an independent variable that can be used to determine the probability that x will assume a value on a given subinterval of $(-\infty, \infty)$. Such a function, called a **probability density function,** must satisfy the following three conditions (see Fig. 10):

1. $f(x) \geq 0$ for all $x \in (-\infty, \infty)$
2. $\int_{-\infty}^{\infty} f(x)\,dx = 1$
3. If $[c, d]$ is a subinterval of $(-\infty, \infty)$, then

$$\text{Probability}(c \leq x \leq d) = \int_c^d f(x)\,dx$$

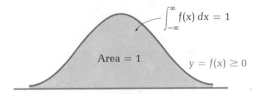

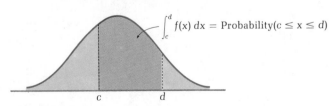

Figure 10

Example 21
Finish Time

A sailing club has a race over the same course twice a month. The races always start at 12 noon on Sunday, and the boats finish according to the probability density function (where x is hours after noon):

$$f(x) = \begin{cases} -\dfrac{x}{2} + 2 & 2 \leqslant x \leqslant 4 \\ 0 & \text{otherwise} \end{cases}$$

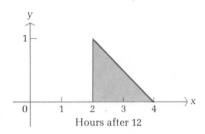

Hours after 12

Note that

$$f(x) \geqslant 0$$

and

$$\int_{-\infty}^{\infty} f(x)\, dx = \int_{2}^{4} \left(-\frac{x}{2} + 2\right) dx = \left(-\frac{x^2}{4} + 2x\right)\bigg|_{2}^{4} = 1$$

The probability that a boat selected at random from the sailing fleet will finish between 2 and 3 hours after the start is given by

$$\text{Probability}(2 \leqslant x \leqslant 3) = \int_{2}^{3} \left(-\frac{x}{2} + 2\right) dx$$

$$= \left(-\frac{x^2}{4} + 2x\right)\bigg|_{2}^{3} = .75$$

which is the area under the curve from x = 2 to x = 3.

Problem 21

In Example 21, find the probability that a boat selected at random from the fleet will finish between 2:30 and 3:30 PM.

Example 22
Duration of
Telephone Calls

Suppose the length of telephone calls (in minutes) in a public telephone booth has the probability density function

$$f(t) = \begin{cases} \dfrac{1}{4} e^{-t/4} & t \geqslant 0 \\ 0 & \text{otherwise} \end{cases}$$

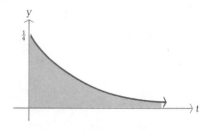

(A) Compute $\int_{-\infty}^{\infty} f(t)\, dt$.

(B) Determine the probability that a call selected at random will last between 2 and 3 minutes.

Solutions   (A) $\displaystyle \int_{-\infty}^{\infty} f(t)\, dt = \int_{-\infty}^{0} f(t)\, dt + \int_{0}^{\infty} f(t)\, dt$

$$= 0 + \int_{0}^{\infty} \frac{1}{4} e^{-t/4}\, dt$$

$$= \lim_{b \to \infty} \int_{0}^{b} \frac{1}{4} e^{-t/4}\, dt$$

$$= \lim_{b \to \infty} \left(-e^{-t/4} \Big|_{0}^{b} \right)$$

$$= \lim_{b \to \infty} \left(-e^{-b/4} + e^{0} \right)$$

$$= \lim_{b \to \infty} \left(-\frac{1}{e^{b/4}} + 1 \right)$$

$$= 0 + 1 = 1$$

(B)   Probability$(2 \leqslant t \leqslant 3) = \displaystyle \int_{2}^{3} \frac{1}{4} e^{-t/4}\, dt$

$$= \left(-e^{-t/4} \right) \Big|_{2}^{3}$$

$$= -e^{-3/4} + e^{-1/2} \approx .13$$

Problem 22   In Example 22, find the probability that a call selected at random will last longer than 4 minutes.

The most important probability density function is the **normal probability density function** defined below and graphed in Figure 11.

$$f(x) = \frac{1}{\sigma \sqrt{2\pi}} e^{-(x-\mu)^2/2\sigma^2} \qquad \begin{array}{l} \mu \text{ is the mean} \\ \sigma \text{ is the standard deviation} \end{array}$$

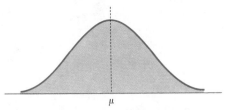

Figure 11 Normal curve

It can be shown, but not easily, that

$$\frac{1}{\sigma \sqrt{2\pi}} \int_{-\infty}^{\infty} e^{-(x-\mu)^2/2\sigma^2}\, dx = 1$$

Since $\int e^{-x^2}$ is nonintegrable in terms of elementary functions (that is, the antiderivative cannot be expressed as a finite combination of simple functions), probabilities such as

$$\text{Probability}(c \le x \le d) = \frac{1}{\sigma\sqrt{2\pi}} \int_c^d e^{-(x-\mu)^2/2\sigma^2} \, dx$$

are generally determined by making an appropriate substitution in the integrand and then using a table of areas under the standard normal curve (that is, the normal curve with $\mu = 0$ and $\sigma = 1$). Such tables are readily available in most mathematical handbooks. A table can be constructed by using the rectangle rule discussed in Section 11-1; however, digital computers that use refined techniques are generally used for this purpose. Some hand calculators have the capability of computing normal curve areas directly.

Answers to   16. $\frac{1}{2}$ 17. 1   18. Diverges   19. 875 thousand barrels
Matched Problems   20. $15,000   21. .5   22. $e^{-1} \approx .37$

Exercise 11-4

Find the value of each improper integral that converges.

A   1. $\displaystyle\int_1^\infty \frac{dx}{x^4}$ 2. $\displaystyle\int_1^\infty \frac{dx}{x^3}$

3. $\displaystyle\int_0^\infty e^{-x/2} \, dx$ 4. $\displaystyle\int_0^\infty e^{-x} \, dx$

B   5. $\displaystyle\int_1^\infty \frac{dx}{\sqrt{x}}$ 6. $\displaystyle\int_1^\infty \frac{dx}{\sqrt[3]{x}}$

7. $\displaystyle\int_0^\infty \frac{dx}{(x+1)^2}$ 8. $\displaystyle\int_0^\infty \frac{dx}{(x+1)^3}$

9. $\displaystyle\int_0^\infty \frac{dx}{(x+1)^{2/3}}$ 10. $\displaystyle\int_0^\infty \frac{dx}{\sqrt{x+1}}$

11. $\displaystyle\int_1^\infty \frac{dx}{x^{0.99}}$ 12. $\displaystyle\int_1^\infty \frac{dx}{x^{1.01}}$

13. $0.3 \displaystyle\int_0^\infty e^{-0.3x} \, dx$ 14. $0.01 \displaystyle\int_0^\infty e^{-0.1x} \, dx$

15. In Example 21, find the probability that a randomly selected boat will finish before 3:30 PM.

16. In Example 21, find the probability that a randomly selected boat will finish after 2:30 PM.

17. In Example 22, find the probability that a telephone call selected at random will last longer than 1 minute.

18. In Example 22, find the probability that a telephone call selected at random will last less than 3 minutes.

C Find the value of each improper integral that converges. Note that $\lim_{x \to \infty} x^n e^{-x} = 0$ and $\lim_{x \to \infty} x^{-n} \ln x = 0$ for all positive integers n.

19. $\displaystyle\int_0^\infty \frac{1}{k} e^{-x/k}\,dx,\ k > 0$

20. $\displaystyle\int_0^\infty x e^{-x}\,dx$

21. $\displaystyle\int_{-\infty}^0 \frac{dx}{\sqrt{1-x}}$

22. $\displaystyle\int_{-\infty}^\infty x e^{-x^2}\,dx$

23. $\displaystyle\int_0^\infty (e^{-x} - e^{-2x})\,dx$

24. $\displaystyle\int_0^\infty x^2 e^{-x}\,dx$

25. $\displaystyle\int_1^\infty \frac{\ln x}{x}\,dx$

26. $\displaystyle\int_1^\infty \frac{\ln x}{x^2}\,dx$

■

Applications

Business & Economics

Note that $\lim_{t \to \infty} t^n e^{-kt} = 0$ for $n > 0$ and $k > 0$. Limits of this form will occur in several of the following applications.

27. *Capital value.* The perpetual annual rent for a property is $6,000. Find the capital value at 12% compounded continuously.

28. *Capital value.* The perpetual annual rent for a property is $10,000. Find the capital value at 5% compounded continuously.

29. *Capital value.* A trust fund produces a perpetual stream of income with rate of flow

$$f(t) = 1{,}500 e^{0.04t}$$

Find the capital value at 9% compounded continuously.

30. *Capital value.* A trust fund produces a perpetual stream of income with rate of flow

$$f(t) = 1{,}000t$$

Find the capital value at 10% compounded continuously.

31. *Production.* The rate of production of a natural gas well in millions of cubic feet per month is given by

$$R(t) = te^{-0.4t}$$

Assuming that the well is operated indefinitely, find the total production.

32. *Production.* Repeat Problem 31 for $R(t) = t^2 e^{-0.4t}$.

33. *Consumption.* The daily per capita use of water (in hundreds of gallons) for domestic purposes has a probability density function of the form

$$g(x) = \begin{cases} .05e^{-.05x} & x \geqslant 0 \\ 0 & \text{otherwise} \end{cases}$$

Find the probability that a person chosen at random will use at least 300 gallons of water per day.

34. *Warranty.* A manufacturer guarantees a product for 1 year. The time for failure of a new product after it is sold is given by the probability density function

$$f(t) = \begin{cases} .01e^{-.01t} & t \geqslant 0 \\ 0 & \text{otherwise} \end{cases}$$

where t is time in months. What is the probability that a buyer chosen at random will have a product failure during the warranty period?

Life Sciences

35. *Pollution.* It has been estimated that the rate of seepage of toxic chemicals from a waste dump is $R(t)$ gallons per year t years from now, where

$$R(t) = \frac{500}{(1 + t)^2}$$

Assuming that this seepage continues indefinitely, find the total amount of toxic chemicals that seep from the dump.

36. *Drug assimilation.* When a person takes a drug, the body does not assimilate all of the drug. One way to determine the amount of the drug that is assimilated is to measure the rate at which the drug is eliminated from the body. If the rate of elimination of the drug (in milliliters per minute) is given by

$$R(t) = te^{-0.2t}$$

where t is the time in minutes since the drug was administered, how much of the drug is eliminated from the body?

37. *Medicine.* If the length of stay for people in a hospital has a probability density function

$$g(t) = \begin{cases} .2e^{-.2t} & t \geqslant 0 \\ 0 & \text{otherwise} \end{cases}$$

where t is time in days, find the probability that a patient chosen at random will stay in the hospital less than 5 days.

38. *Medicine.* For a particular disease, the length of time in days for recovery has a probability density function of the form

$$R(t) = \begin{cases} .03e^{-.03t} & t \geqslant 0 \\ 0 & \text{otherwise} \end{cases}$$

For a randomly selected person who contracts this disease, what is the probability that he or she will take at least 7 days to recover?

Social Sciences 39. *Politics.* In a particular election, the length of time each voter spent on campaigning for a candidate or issue was found to have a probability density function

$$F(x) = \begin{cases} \dfrac{1}{(x+1)^2} & x \geqslant 0 \\ 0 & \text{otherwise} \end{cases}$$

where x is time in minutes. For a voter chosen at random, what is the probability of his or her spending at least 9 minutes on the campaign?

40. *Psychology.* In an experiment on conditioning, pigeons were required to recognize on a light display one pattern of dots out of five possible patterns to receive a food pellet. After the ninth successful trial, it was found that the probability density function for the length of time in seconds until success on the tenth trial is given by

$$f(t) = \begin{cases} e^{-t} & t \geqslant 0 \\ 0 & \text{otherwise} \end{cases}$$

What is the probability that a pigeon selected at random from those having successfully completed nine trials will take 2 or more seconds to complete the tenth trial successfully?

11-5 Chapter Review

Important Terms
and Symbols

11-1 *Definite integral as a limit of a sum.* Rectangle rule, tabular function, definite integral (as a limit of a Riemann sum), fundamental theorem of calculus, average value of a continuous function

11-2 *Applications in business and economics.* Continuous income stream, rate of flow, total income, consumers' surplus, producers' surplus, equilibrium price

11-3 *Integration by parts.* $\int u \, dv = uv - \int v \, du$

11-4 *Improper integrals.* Improper integral, converge, diverge, capital value, probability density function, normal probability density function,
$\int_a^\infty f(x) \, dx = \lim_{b \to \infty} \int_a^b f(x) \, dx, \quad \int_{-\infty}^b f(x) \, dx = \lim_{a \to -\infty} \int_a^b f(x) \, dx,$
$\int_{-\infty}^\infty f(x) \, dx = \int_{-\infty}^c f(x) \, dx + \int_c^\infty f(x) \, dx$

Exercise 11-5   Chapter Review

Work through all the problems in this chapter review and check your answers in the back of the book. (Answers to all review problems are there.) Where weaknesses show up, review appropriate sections in the text.

A   *Evaluate the indicated integrals.*

1. $\displaystyle\int xe^{4x}\,dx$

2. $\displaystyle\int x\ln x\,dx$

3. $\displaystyle\int x(x+7)^5\,dx$

4. $\displaystyle\int_0^\infty e^{-2x}\,dx$

5. $\displaystyle\int_0^\infty \frac{1}{x+1}\,dx$

6. $\displaystyle\int_1^\infty \frac{16}{x^3}\,dx$

7. Approximate $\int_1^5 (x^2+1)\,dx$ using the rectangle rule with $n=2$ and c_k as the midpoint of each subinterval.

8. Use the table of values below and the rectangle rule with $n=4$ and c_k as the midpoint of each subinterval to approximate $\int_1^{17} f(x)\,dx$.

x	3	7	11	15
$f(x)$	1.2	3.4	2.6	0.5

9. Find the average value of $f(x)=6x^2+2x$ over the interval $[-1,2]$.

B   *Evaluate the indicated integrals.*

10. $\displaystyle\int_0^1 xe^x\,dx$

11. $\displaystyle\int_{-\infty}^0 e^x\,dx$

12. $\displaystyle\int_{-1}^1 x(x+1)^3\,dx$

13. $\displaystyle\int te^{-0.5t}\,dt$

14. $\displaystyle\int x^2\ln x\,dx$

15. $\displaystyle\int_0^\infty \frac{1}{(x+3)^2}\,dx$

16. Find the area bounded by the graphs of $y=\ln x$, $y=0$, and $x=e$.
17. Approximate $\int_0^1 e^{2x^2}\,dx$ to three decimal places using the rectangle rule with $n=5$ and c_k as the midpoint of each subinterval.
18. Find the average value of $f(x)=3x^{1/2}$ over the interval $[1,9]$.

C   *Evaluate the indicated integrals.*

19. $\displaystyle\int \frac{(\ln x)^2}{x}\,dx$

20. $\displaystyle\int x(\ln x)^2\,dx$

21. $\displaystyle\int xe^{-2x^2}\,dx$

22. $\displaystyle\int x^2 e^{-2x}\,dx$

23. $\displaystyle\int x^2(x-1)^4\,dx$

24. $\displaystyle\int_{-\infty}^{\infty}\frac{x}{(1+x^2)^3}\,dx$

25. $\displaystyle\int_0^{\infty}(x+1)e^{-x}\,dx$ [Hint: Recall that $\lim\limits_{x\to\infty} x^n e^{-x}=0,\;\;n>0.$]

26. $\displaystyle\int_1^{\infty}\frac{\ln x}{x^3}\,dx$ $\left[\text{Hint:}\;\; \text{Recall that } \lim\limits_{x\to\infty}\frac{\ln x}{x^n}=0,\;\;n>0.\right]$

Applications

Business & Economics

27. *Inventory.* Suppose the inventory of a certain item t months after the first of the year is given approximately by

$$I(t)=10+36t-3t^2 \qquad 0\leqslant t\leqslant 12$$

What is the average inventory for the second quarter of the year?

28. *Supply function.* Given the supply function

$$p=S(x)=8(e^{0.05x}-1)$$

find the average price (in dollars) over the supply interval [40, 50].

29. *Continuous income stream.* Find the present value at 15% compounded continuously for 4 years for the continuous income stream with rate of flow

$$f(t)=2{,}500e^{0.05t}$$

Find the amount, the total income, and the interest earned during this 4 year period.

30. *Capital value.* The perpetual annual rent for a property is $2,400. Find the capital value at 12% compounded continuously.

31. *Consumers' and producers' surplus.* Given the price–demand and price–supply equations

$$p=D(x)=70-\frac{1}{5}x \qquad p=S(x)=13+\frac{3}{2{,}500}x^2$$

(A)   Find the consumers' surplus at a price level of $\bar p=50$.
(B)   Find the producers' surplus at a price level of $\bar p=25$.
(C)   Find the equilibrium price, and then find the consumers' surplus and the producers' surplus at the equilibrium price level.

32. *Production.* An oil field is estimated to produce oil at the rate of $R(t)$ thousand barrels per month t months from now, as given by

$$R(t)=25te^{-0.05t}$$

How much oil is produced during the first 2 years of operation? If the well is operated indefinitely, what is the total amount of oil produced? [Recall that $\lim\limits_{t\to\infty} t^n e^{-kt}=0$ for $n>0$ and $k>0$.]

33. *Parts testing.* If in testing printed circuits for hand calculators, failures occur relative to time in hours according to the probability density function

$$F(t) = \begin{cases} .02e^{-.02t} & t \geq 0 \\ 0 & \text{otherwise} \end{cases}$$

what is the probability that a circuit chosen at random will fail in the first hour of testing?

Life Sciences
34. *Drug assimilation.* The rate at which the body eliminates a drug (in milliliters per hour) is given by

$$R(t) = 20t(t + 1)^{-3}$$

where t is the number of hours since the drug was administered. How much of the drug is eliminated in the first hour after it was administered? What is the total amount of the drug that is eliminated by the body?

35. *Medicine.* For a particular doctor, the length of time in hours spent with a patient per office visit has the probability density function

$$f(t) = \begin{cases} \dfrac{\frac{4}{3}}{(t + 1)^2} & 0 \leq t \leq 3 \\ 0 & \text{otherwise} \end{cases}$$

What is the probability that the doctor will spend more than 1 hour with a randomly selected patient?

Social Sciences
36. *Politics.* The rate of change of the voting population of a city, $N'(t)$, with respect to time t in years is estimated to be

$$N'(t) = \frac{100t}{(1 + t^2)^2}$$

where $N(t)$ is in thousands. If $N(0)$ is the current voting population, how much will this population increase during the next 3 years? If the population continues to grow at this rate indefinitely, what is the total increase in the voting population?

37. *Psychology.* Rats were trained to go through a maze by rewarding them with a food pellet upon successful completion. After the seventh successful run, it was found that the probability density function for length of time in minutes until success on the eighth trial is given by

$$f(t) = \begin{cases} .5e^{-.5t} & t \geq 0 \\ 0 & \text{otherwise} \end{cases}$$

What is the probability that a rat selected at random after seven successful runs will take 2 or more minutes to complete the eighth run successfully?

Multivariable Calculus

CHAPTER 12   Contents

12-1   Functions of Several Variables

- Functions of Two or More Independent Variables
- Examples of Functions of Several Variables
- Three-Dimensional Coordinate Systems

■ Functions of Two or More Independent Variables

In Section 0-5 we introduced the concept of a function with one independent variable. Now we will broaden the concept to include functions with more than one independent variable. We start with an example.

A small manufacturing company produces a standard type of surfboard and no other products. If fixed costs are $500 per week and variable costs are $70 per board produced, then the weekly cost function is given by

$$C(x) = 500 + 70x \tag{1}$$

where x is the number of boards produced per week. The cost function is a function of a single independent variable x. For each value of x from the domain of C there exists exactly one value of $C(x)$ in the range of C.

Now, suppose the company decides to add a high-performance competition board to its line. If the fixed costs for the competition board are $200 per week and the variable costs are $100 per board, then the cost function (1) must be modified to

$$C(x, y) = 700 + 70x + 100y \tag{2}$$

where $C(x, y)$ is the cost for weekly output of x standard boards and y competition boards. Equation (2) is an example of a function with two independent variables, x and y. Of course, as the company expands its product line even further, its weekly cost function must be modified to include more and more independent variables, one for each new product produced.

In general, an equation of the form

$$z = f(x, y)$$

will describe a **function of two independent variables** if for each ordered pair (x, y) from the domain of f there is one and only one value of z determined by $f(x, y)$ in the range of f. Unless otherwise stated, we will assume that the domain of a function specified by an equation of the form $z = f(x, y)$ is the set of all ordered pairs of real numbers (x, y) such that $f(x, y)$ is also a real number. It should be noted, however, that certain conditions in practical problems often lead to further restrictions of the domain of a function.

We can similarly define functions of three independent variables, $w = f(x, y, z)$; of four independent variables, $u = f(w, x, y, z)$; and so on. In this chapter, we will primarily concern ourselves with functions with two independent variables.

Example 1   For $C(x, y) = 700 + 70x + 100y$, find $C(10, 5)$.

Solution $C(10, 5) = 700 + 70(10) + 100(5)$
$$= \$1,900$$

Problem 1   Find $C(20, 10)$ for the cost function in Example 1.

Example 2   For $f(x, y, z) = 2x^2 - 3xy + 3z + 1$, find $f(3, 0, -1)$.

Solution $f(3, 0, -1) = 2(3)^2 - 3(3)(0) + 3(-1) + 1$
$$= 18 - 0 - 3 + 1$$
$$= 16$$

Problem 2   Find $f(-2, 2, 3)$ for f in Example 2.

Example 3
Revenue, Cost, and Profit
Functions

The surfboard company discussed previously has determined that the demand equations for the two types of boards they produce are given by

$$p = 210 - 4x + y$$
$$q = 300 + x - 12y$$

where p is the price of the standard board, q is the price of the competition board, x is the weekly demand for standard boards, and y is the weekly demand for competition boards.

(A)   Find the weekly revenue function $R(x, y)$ and evaluate $R(20, 10)$.
(B)   If the weekly cost function is

$$C(x, y) = 700 + 70x + 100y$$

find the weekly profit function $P(x, y)$ and evaluate $P(20, 10)$.

Solutions (A) Revenue = $\left(\begin{array}{c}\text{Demand for}\\\text{standard}\\\text{boards}\end{array}\right)\times\left(\begin{array}{c}\text{Price of a}\\\text{standard}\\\text{board}\end{array}\right)$

$+\left(\begin{array}{c}\text{Demand for}\\\text{competition}\\\text{boards}\end{array}\right)\times\left(\begin{array}{c}\text{Price of a}\\\text{competition}\\\text{board}\end{array}\right)$

$R(x, y) = xp + yq$

$= x(210 - 4x + y) + y(300 + x - 12y)$

$= 210x + 300y - 4x^2 + 2xy - 12y^2$

$R(20, 10) = 210(20) + 300(10) - 4(20)^2 + 2(20)(10) - 12(10)^2$

$= \$4,800$

(B) Profit = Revenue − Cost

$P(x, y) = R(x, y) - C(x, y)$

$= 210x + 300y - 4x^2 + 2xy - 12y^2 - 700 - 70x - 100y$

$= 140x + 200y - 4x^2 + 2xy - 12y^2 - 700$

$P(20, 10) = 140(20) + 200(10) - 4(20)^2 + 2(20)(10) - 12(10)^2 - 700$

$= \$1,700$

Problem 3 Repeat Example 3 if the demand and cost equations are given by

$p = 220 - 6x + y$

$q = 300 + 3x - 10y$

$C(x, y) = 40x + 80y + 1,000$

■ Examples of Functions of Several Variables

A number of concepts we have already considered can be thought of in terms of functions of two or more variables. We list a few of these below.

Area of a rectangle $A(x, y) = xy$

$A = $ Area

Volume of a box $V(x, y, z) = xyz$

$V = $ Volume

Volume of a right circular cylinder $V(r, h) = \pi r^2 h$

Simple interest	$A(P, r, t) = P(1 + rt)$	A = Amount
		P = Principal
		r = Annual rate
		t = Time in years
Compound interest	$A(P, r, t, n) = P\left(1 + \dfrac{r}{n}\right)^{nt}$	A = Amount
		P = Principal
		r = Annual rate
		t = Time in years
		n = Compound periods per year
IQ	$Q(M, C) = \dfrac{M}{C}(100)$	Q = IQ = Intelligence quotient
		M = MA = Mental age
		C = CA = Chronological age
Resistance for blood flow in a vessel	$R(L, r) = k\dfrac{L}{r^4}$	R = Resistance
		L = Length of vessel
		r = Radius of vessel
		k = Constant

Example 4
Package Design

A company uses a box with a square base and an open top for one of its products (see the figure). If x is the length in inches of each side of the base and y is the height in inches, find the total amount of material $M(x, y)$ required to construct one of these boxes and evaluate $M(5, 10)$.

Solution

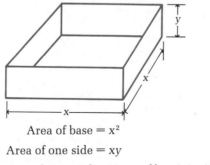

Area of base = x^2

Area of one side = xy

Total material = (Area of base) + 4(Area of one side)

$$M(x, y) = x^2 + 4xy$$
$$M(5, 10) = 5^2 + 4(5)(10)$$
$$= 225 \text{ square inches}$$

Problem 4 For the box in Example 4, find the volume $V(x, y)$ and evaluate $V(5, 10)$.

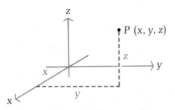

Figure 1 Rectangular coordinate system

■ Three-Dimensional Coordinate Systems

We now take a brief look at some graphs of functions of two independent variables. Since functions of the form $z = f(x, y)$ involve two independent variables, x and y, and one dependent variable, z, we need a three-dimensional coordinate system for their graphs. We take three mutually perpendicular number lines intersecting at their origins to form a rectangular coordinate system in three-dimensional space (see Fig. 1). In such a system, every ordered triplet of numbers (x, y, z) can be associated with a unique point, and conversely.

Example 5   Locate $(-3, 5, 2)$ in a rectangular coordinate system.

Solution

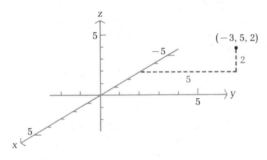

Problem 5   Find the coordinates of the corners A, C, G, and D of the rectangular box shown in the figure.

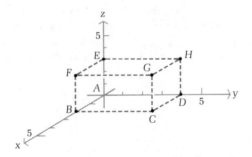

What does the graph of $z = x^2 + y^2$ look like? If we let $x = 0$ and graph $z = 0^2 + y^2 = y^2$ in the yz plane, we obtain a parabola; if we let $y = 0$ and graph $z = x^2 + 0^2 = x^2$ in the xz plane, we obtain another parabola. It can be shown that the graph of $z = x^2 + y^2$ is just one of these parabolas rotated around the z axis (see Fig. 2). This cup-shaped figure is a *surface* and is called a **paraboloid.**

In general, the graph of any function of the form $z = f(x, y)$ is called a **surface.** The graph of such a function is the graph of all ordered triplets of numbers (x, y, z) that satisfy the equation. Graphing functions of two independent variables is often a very difficult task, and the general process will not be dealt with in this book. We present only a few simple graphs to suggest extensions of earlier geometric interpretations of the derivative and local maxima and minima to functions of two variables. Note that $z = f(x, y) = x^2 + y^2$ appears (see Fig. 2) to have a local minimum at $(x, y) = (0, 0)$. Figure 3 shows a local maximum at $(x, y) = (0, 0)$.

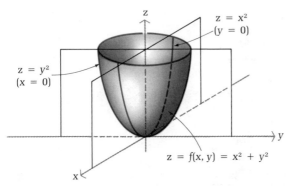

Figure 2 Paraboloid

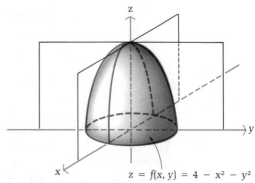

Figure 3 Local maximum: $f(0, 0) = 4$

Figure 4 shows a point at $(x, y) = (0, 0)$, called a **saddle point,** which is neither a local minimum nor a local maximum. More will be said about local maxima and minima in Section 12-3.

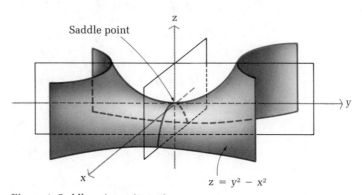

Figure 4 Saddle point at $(0, 0, 0)$

Answers to
Matched Problems

1. $3,100   2.   30
3. (A) $R(x, y) = 220x + 300y - 6x^2 + 4xy - 10y^2$; $R(20, 10) = \$4,800$
    (B) $P(x, y) = 180x + 220y - 6x^2 + 4xy - 10y^2 - 1,000$;
          $P(20, 10) = \$2,200$
4. $V(x, y) = x^2y$; $V(5, 10) = 250$ cubic inches
5. $A(0, 0, 0)$; $C(2, 4, 0)$; $G(2, 4, 3)$; $D(0, 4, 0)$

Exercise 12-1

A   For the functions

$$f(x, y) = 10 + 2x - 3y \qquad g(x, y) = x^2 - 3y^2$$

find each of the following:

1. $f(0, 0)$ 2. $f(2, 1)$ 3. $f(-3, 1)$ 4. $f(2, -7)$
5. $g(0, 0)$ 6. $g(0, -1)$ 7. $g(2, -1)$ 8. $g(-1, 2)$

B   Find each of the following:

9. $A(2, 3)$ for $A(x, y) = xy$

10. $V(2, 4, 3)$ for $V(x, y, z) = xyz$

11. $Q(12, 8)$ for $Q(M, C) = \dfrac{M}{C}(100)$

12. $T(50, 17)$ for $T(V, x) = \dfrac{33V}{x + 33}$

13. $V(2, 4)$ for $V(r, h) = \pi r^2 h$

14. $S(4, 2)$ for $S(x, y) = 5x^2y^3$

15. $R(1, 2)$ for $R(x, y) = -5x^2 + 6xy - 4y^2 + 200x + 300y$

16. $P(2, 2)$ for $P(x, y) = -x^2 + 2xy - 2y^2 - 4x + 12y + 5$

17. $R(6, 0.5)$ for $R(L, r) = 0.002\dfrac{L}{r^4}$

18. $L(2,000, 50)$ for $L(w, v) = (1.25 \times 10^{-5})wv^2$

19. $A(100, 0.06, 3)$ for $A(P, r, t) = P + Prt$

20. $A(10, 0.04, 3, 2)$ for $A(P, r, t, n) = P\left(1 + \dfrac{r}{n}\right)^{tn}$

21. $A(100, 0.08, 10)$ for $A(P, r, t) = Pe^{rt}$

22. $A(1,000, 0.06, 8)$ for $A(P, r, t) = Pe^{rt}$

C   23.   For the function $f(x, y) = x^2 + 2y^2$, find:

$$\frac{f(x + \Delta x, y) - f(x, y)}{\Delta x}$$

24.   For the function $f(x, y) = x^2 + 2y^2$, find:

$$\frac{f(x, y + \Delta y) - f(x, y)}{\Delta y}$$

25.   For the function $f(x, y) = 2xy^2$, find:

$$\frac{f(x + \Delta x, y) - f(x, y)}{\Delta x}$$

26. For the function $f(x, y) = 2xy^2$, find:

$$\frac{f(x, y + \Delta y) - f(x, y)}{\Delta y}$$

27. Find the coordinates of E and F in the figure for Problem 5 in the text.
28. Find the coordinates of B and H in the figure for Problem 5 in the text.

Applications

Business & Economics

29. *Cost function.* A small manufacturing company produces two models of a surfboard: a standard model and a competition model. If the standard model is produced at a variable cost of $70 each, the competition model at a variable cost of $100 each, and the total fixed costs per month are $2,000, then the monthly cost function is given by

$$C(x, y) = 2,000 + 70x + 100y$$

where x and y are the numbers of standard and competition models produced per month, respectively. Find $C(20, 10)$, $C(50, 5)$, and $C(30, 30)$.

30. *Advertising and sales.* A company spends x thousand dollars per week on newspaper advertising and y thousand dollars per week on television advertising. Its weekly sales were found to be given by

$$S(x, y) = 5x^2y^3$$

Find $S(3, 2)$ and $S(2, 3)$.

31. *Revenue function.* A supermarket sells two brands of coffee: brand A at p per pound and brand B at q per pound. The daily demand equations for brands A and B are, respectively,

$$x = 200 - 5p + 4q$$
$$y = 300 + 2p - 4q$$

(both in pounds). Find the daily revenue function $R(p, q)$. Evaluate $R(2, 3)$ and $R(3, 2)$.

32. *Revenue, cost, and profit functions.* A company manufactures ten-speed and three-speed bicycles. The weekly demand and cost equations are

$$p = 230 - 9x + y$$
$$q = 130 + x - 4y$$
$$C(x, y) = 200 + 80x + 30y$$

where p is the price of a ten-speed bicycle, q is the price of a three-speed bicycle, x is the weekly demand for ten-speed bicycles, y is the weekly demand for three-speed bicycles, and $C(x, y)$ is the cost function. Find the weekly revenue function $R(x, y)$ and the weekly profit function $P(x, y)$. Evaluate $R(10, 15)$ and $P(10, 15)$.

33. *Future value.* At the end of each year $2,000 is invested into an IRA account earning 9% compounded annually. How much will be in the account at the end of 30 years? Use the annuity formula

$$F(P, i, n) = P\frac{(1 + i)^n - 1}{i}$$

where

    $P = \text{PMT} = \text{Periodic payment}$

    $i = \text{Rate per period}$

    $n = \text{Number of payments (periods)}$

    $F = \text{FV} = \text{Amount or future value}$

34. *Package design.* The packaging department in a company has been asked to design a rectangular box with no top and a partition down the middle (see the accompanying figure). If x, y, and z are the dimensions in inches, find the total amount of material $M(x, y, z)$ used in constructing one of these boxes and evaluate $M(10, 12, 6)$.

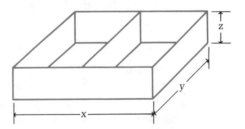

Life Sciences

35. *Marine biology.* In using scuba diving gear, a marine biologist estimates the time of a dive according to the equation

$$T(V, x) = \frac{33V}{x + 33}$$

where

    $T = \text{Time of dive in minutes}$

    $V = \text{Volume of air, at sea level pressure, compressed into tanks}$

    $x = \text{Depth of dive in feet}$

Find $T(70, 47)$ and $T(60, 27)$.

36. *Blood flow.* Poiseuille's law states that the resistance, R, for blood flowing in a blood vessel varies directly as the length of the vessel, L, and inversely as the fourth power of its radius, r. Stated as

an equation,

$$R(L, r) = k\frac{L}{r^4} \qquad k \text{ a constant}$$

Find $R(8, 1)$ and $R(4, 0.2)$.

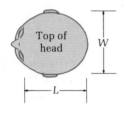

37. *Physical anthropology.* Anthropologists, in their study of race and human genetic groupings, often use an index called the *cephalic index*. The cephalic index, C, varies directly as the width, W, of the head, and inversely as the length, L, of the head (both viewed from the top). In terms of an equation,

$$C(W, L) = 100\frac{W}{L}$$

where

W = Width in inches

L = Length in inches

Find $C(6, 8)$ and $C(8.1, 9)$.

Social Sciences

38. *Safety research.* Under ideal conditions, if a person driving a car slams on the brakes and skids to a stop, the length of the skid marks is given by the formula

$$L(w, v) = kwv^2$$

where

k = Constant

w = Weight of car in pounds

v = Speed of car in miles per hour

For $k = 0.000\ 013\ 3$, find $L(2,000, 40)$ and $L(3,000, 60)$.

39. *Psychology.* Intelligence quotient (IQ) is defined to be the ratio of the mental age (MA), as determined by certain tests, and the chronological age (CA), multiplied by 100. Stated as an equation,

$$Q(M, C) = \frac{M}{C} \cdot 100$$

where

Q = IQ

M = MA

C = CA

Find $Q(12, 10)$ and $Q(10, 12)$.

12-2   Partial Derivatives

- Partial Derivatives
- Second-Order Partial Derivatives

■ Partial Derivatives

We know how to differentiate many kinds of functions of one independent variable and how to interpret the results. What about functions with two or more independent variables? Let us return to the surfboard example considered at the beginning of the chapter.

For the company producing only the standard board, the cost function was

$$C(x) = 500 + 70x$$

Differentiating with respect to x, we obtain the marginal cost function

$$C'(x) = 70$$

Since the marginal cost is constant, $70 is the change in cost for one unit increase in production at any output level.

For the company producing two boards, a standard model and a competition model, the cost function was

$$C(x, y) = 700 + 70x + 100y$$

Now suppose we differentiate with respect to x, holding y fixed, and denote this by $C_x(x, y)$; or we differentiate with respect to y, holding x fixed, and denote this by $C_y(x, y)$. Differentiating in this way, we obtain

$$C_x(x, y) = 70 \qquad C_y(x, y) = 100$$

Both these are called **partial derivatives** and, in this example, both represent marginal costs. The first is the change in cost due to one unit increase in production of the standard board with the production of the competition model held fixed. The second is the change in cost due to one unit increase in production of the competition board with the production of the standard board held fixed.

In general, if $z = f(x, y)$, then the **partial derivative of f with respect to x,** denoted by $\partial z/\partial x$, f_x, $f_x(x, y)$, is defined by

$$\frac{\partial z}{\partial x} = \lim_{\Delta x \to 0} \frac{f(x + \Delta x, y) - f(x, y)}{\Delta x}$$

provided the limit exists. This is the ordinary derivative of f with respect to x, holding y constant. Thus, we are able to continue to use all the derivative rules and properties discussed in Chapters 7, 8, and 9 for partials.

Similarly, the **partial derivative of f with respect to y,** denoted by $\partial z/\partial y$, f_y, or $f_y(x, y)$, is defined by

$$\frac{\partial z}{\partial y} = \lim_{\Delta y \to 0} \frac{f(x, y + \Delta y) - f(x, y)}{\Delta y}$$

which is the ordinary derivative with respect to y, holding x constant.

Parallel definitions and interpretations hold for functions with three or more independent variables.

Example 6   For $z = f(x, y) = 2x^2 - 3x^2y + 5y + 1$, find:

(A) $\dfrac{\partial z}{\partial x}$ (B) $f_x(2, 3)$

Solutions   (A) $z = 2x^2 - 3x^2y + 5y + 1$

Differentiating with respect to x, holding y constant (that is, treating y as a constant), we obtain

$$\frac{\partial z}{\partial x} = 4x - 6xy$$

(B) $f(x, y) = 2x^2 - 3x^2y + 5y + 1$

First differentiate with respect to x (part A) to obtain

$$f_x(x, y) = 4x - 6xy$$

Then evaluate at $(2, 3)$. Thus,

$$f_x(2, 3) = 4(2) - 6(2)(3) = -28$$

Problem 6   For f in Example 6, find:

(A) $\dfrac{\partial z}{\partial y}$ (B) $f_y(2, 3)$

Example 7   For $z = f(x, y) = e^{x^2+y^2}$, find:

(A) $\dfrac{\partial z}{\partial x}$ (B) $f_y(2, 1)$

Solutions   (A)   Using the chain rule [thinking of $z = e^u$, $u = u(x)$; y is held constant], we obtain

$$\frac{\partial z}{\partial x} = e^{x^2+y^2} \frac{\partial(x^2 + y^2)}{\partial x}$$

$$= 2xe^{x^2+y^2}$$

(B) $f_y(x, y) = 2ye^{x^2+y^2}$

$$f_y(2, 1) = 2(1)e^{2^2+1^2}$$

$$= 2e^5$$

Problem 7   For $z = f(x, y) = (x^2 + 2xy)^5$, find:

(A) $\dfrac{\partial z}{\partial y}$ (B) $f_x(1, 0)$

Example 8   The profit function for the surfboard company in Example 3 in Section 12-1
Profit   was

$$P(x, y) = 140x + 200y - 4x^2 + 2xy - 12y^2 - 700$$

Find $P_x(15, 10)$ and $P_x(30, 10)$, and interpret.

Solution
$$P_x(x, y) = 140 - 8x + 2y$$
$$P_x(15, 10) = 140 - 8(15) + 2(10) = 40$$
$$P_x(30, 10) = 140 - 8(30) + 2(10) = -80$$

At a production level of 15 standard and 10 competition boards per week, increasing the production of standard boards by 1 and holding the production of competition boards fixed at 10 will increase profit by approximately $40. At a production level of 30 standard and 10 competition boards per week, increasing the production of standard boards by 1 unit and holding the production of competition boards fixed at 10 will decrease profit by approximately $80.

Problem 8   For the profit function in Example 8, find $P_y(25, 10)$ and $P_y(25, 15)$, and interpret.

Partials have simple geometric interpretations, as indicated in Figure 5. If we hold x fixed, say $x = a$, then $f_y(a, y)$ is the slope of the curve obtained by intersecting the plane $x = a$ with the surface $z = f(x, y)$. A similar interpretation is given to $f_x(x, b)$.

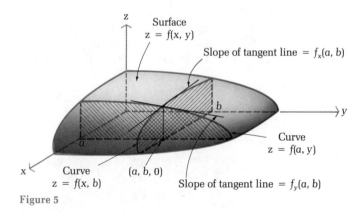

Figure 5

■ Second-Order Partial Derivatives

Just as there are second-order ordinary derivatives, there are second-order partials, and we will be using some of these in the next section when we discuss local maxima and minima. The following second-order partials will be useful:

Second-Order Partials

If $z = f(x, y)$, then

$$\frac{\partial^2 z}{\partial x^2} = \frac{\partial}{\partial x}\left(\frac{\partial z}{\partial x}\right) = f_{xx}(x, y) = f_{xx}$$

$$\frac{\partial^2 z}{\partial x\, \partial y} = \frac{\partial}{\partial x}\left(\frac{\partial z}{\partial y}\right) = f_{yx}(x, y) = f_{yx}$$

$$\frac{\partial^2 z}{\partial y\, \partial x} = \frac{\partial}{\partial y}\left(\frac{\partial z}{\partial x}\right) = f_{xy}(x, y) = f_{xy}$$

$$\frac{\partial^2 z}{\partial y^2} = \frac{\partial}{\partial y}\left(\frac{\partial z}{\partial y}\right) = f_{yy}(x, y) = f_{yy}$$

In the mixed partial $\partial^2 z/(\partial x\, \partial y) = f_{yx}$, we start with $z = f(x, y)$ and first differentiate with respect to y (holding x constant). Then we differentiate with respect to x (holding y constant). What is the order of differentiation for $\partial^2 z/(\partial y\, \partial x) = f_{xy}$? It can be shown that for the functions we will consider, $f_{xy}(x, y) = f_{yx}(x, y)$.

Example 9 For $z = f(x, y) = 3x^2 - 2xy^3 + 1$, find:

(A) $\dfrac{\partial^2 z}{\partial x\, \partial y}, \dfrac{\partial^2 z}{\partial y\, \partial x}$ (B) $\dfrac{\partial^2 z}{\partial x^2}$ (C) $f_{yx}(2, 1)$

Solutions (A) First differentiate with respect to y and then with respect to x:

$$\frac{\partial z}{\partial y} = -6xy^2 \qquad \frac{\partial^2 z}{\partial x\, \partial y} = \frac{\partial}{\partial x}\left(\frac{\partial z}{\partial y}\right) = \frac{\partial}{\partial x}(-6xy^2) = -6y^2$$

First differentiate with respect to x and then with respect to y:

$$\frac{\partial z}{\partial x} = 6x - 2y^3 \qquad \frac{\partial^2 z}{\partial y\, \partial x} = \frac{\partial}{\partial y}\left(\frac{\partial z}{\partial x}\right) = \frac{\partial}{\partial y}(6x - 2y^3) = -6y^2$$

(B) Differentiate with respect to x twice:

$$\frac{\partial z}{\partial x} = 6x - 2y^3 \qquad \frac{\partial^2 z}{\partial x^2} = \frac{\partial}{\partial x}\left(\frac{\partial z}{\partial x}\right) = 6$$

(C)   First find $f_{yx}(x, y)$. Then evaluate at (2, 1). Again, remember that f_{yx} means to differentiate with respect to y first and then with respect to x. Thus,

$$f_y(x, y) = -6xy^2$$
$$f_{yx}(x, y) = -6y^2$$

and

$$f_{yx}(2, 1) = -6(1)^2 = -6$$

Problem 9   For the function in Example 9, find:

(A) $\dfrac{\partial^2 z}{\partial y\, \partial x}$ (B) $\dfrac{\partial^2 z}{\partial y^2}$ (C) $f_{xy}(2, 3)$ (D) $f_{yx}(2, 3)$

Answers to Matched Problems

6. (A) $\dfrac{\partial z}{\partial y} = -3x^2 + 5$ (B) $f_y(2, 3) = -7$

7. (A) $10x(x^2 + 2xy)^4$ (B) 10

8. $P_y(25, 10) = 10$: At a production level of $x = 25$ and $y = 10$, increasing y by 1 unit and holding x fixed at 25 will increase profit by approximately $10; $P_y(25, 15) = -110$: At a production level of $x = 25$ and $y = 15$, increasing y by 1 unit and holding x fixed at 25 will decrease profit by approximately $110.

9. (A) $-6y^2$ (B) $-12xy$ (C) -54 (D) -54

Exercise 12-2

A   For $z = f(x, y) = 10 + 3x + 2y$, find each of the following:

1. $\dfrac{\partial z}{\partial x}$
2. $\dfrac{\partial z}{\partial y}$
3. $f_y(1, 2)$
4. $f_x(1, 2)$

For $z = f(x, y) = 3x^2 - 2xy^2 + 1$, find each of the following:

5. $\dfrac{\partial z}{\partial y}$
6. $\dfrac{\partial z}{\partial x}$
7. $f_x(2, 3)$
8. $f_y(2, 3)$

For $S(x, y) = 5x^2y^3$, find each of the following:

9. $S_x(x, y)$
10. $S_y(x, y)$
11. $S_y(2, 1)$
12. $S_x(2, 1)$

B For $C(x, y) = x^2 - 2xy + 2y^2 + 6x - 9y + 5$, find each of the following:

13. $C_x(x, y)$ 14. $C_y(x, y)$

15. $C_x(2, 2)$ 16. $C_y(2, 2)$

17. $C_{xy}(x, y)$ 18. $C_{yx}(x, y)$

19. $C_{xx}(x, y)$ 20. $C_{yy}(x, y)$

For $z = f(x, y) = e^{2x+3y}$, find each of the following:

21. $\dfrac{\partial z}{\partial x}$ 22. $\dfrac{\partial z}{\partial y}$

23. $\dfrac{\partial^2 z}{\partial x\, \partial y}$ 24. $\dfrac{\partial^2 z}{\partial y\, \partial x}$

25. $f_{xy}(1, 0)$ 26. $f_{yx}(0, 1)$

27. $f_{xx}(0, 1)$ 28. $f_{yy}(1, 0)$

Find $f_x(x, y)$ and $f_y(x, y)$ for each function f given by:

29. $f(x, y) = (x^2 - y^3)^3$ 30. $f(x, y) = \sqrt{2x - y^2}$

31. $f(x, y) = (3x^2y - 1)^4$ 32. $f(x, y) = (3 + 2xy^2)^3$

33. $f(x, y) = \ln(x^2 + y^2)$ 34. $f(x, y) = \ln(2x - 3y)$

35. $f(x, y) = y^2 e^{xy^2}$ 36. $f(x, y) = x^3 e^{x^2y}$

37. $f(x, y) = \dfrac{x^2 - y^2}{x^2 + y^2}$ 38. $f(x, y) = \dfrac{2x^2y}{x^2 + y^2}$

Find $f_{xx}(x, y)$, $f_{xy}(x, y)$, $f_{yx}(x, y)$, and $f_{yy}(x, y)$ for each function f given by:

39. $f(x, y) = x^2y^2 + x^3 + y$ 40. $f(x, y) = x^3y^3 + x + y^2$

41. $f(x, y) = \dfrac{x}{y} - \dfrac{y}{x}$ 42. $f(x, y) = \dfrac{x^2}{y} - \dfrac{y^2}{x}$

43. $f(x, y) = xe^{xy}$ 44. $f(x, y) = x \ln(xy)$

C 45. For

$$P(x, y) = -x^2 + 2xy - 2y^2 - 4x + 12y - 5$$

find values of x and y such that

$$P_x(x, y) = 0 \quad \text{and} \quad P_y(x, y) = 0$$

simultaneously.

46. For

$$C(x, y) = 2x^2 + 2xy + 3y^2 - 16x - 18y + 54$$

find values of x and y such that

$$C_x(x, y) = 0 \quad \text{and} \quad C_y(x, y) = 0$$

simultaneously.

In Problems 47–48, show that the function f satisfies $f_{xx}(x, y) + f_{yy}(x, y) = 0$.

47. $f(x, y) = \ln(x^2 + y^2)$

48. $f(x, y) = x^3 - 3xy^2$

49. For $f(x, y) = x^2 + 2y^2$, find:

   (A) $\displaystyle \lim_{\Delta x \to 0} \frac{f(x + \Delta x, y) - f(x, y)}{\Delta x}$ (B) $\displaystyle \lim_{\Delta y \to 0} \frac{f(x, y + \Delta y) - f(x, y)}{\Delta y}$

50. For $f(x, y) = 2xy^2$, find:

   (A) $\displaystyle \lim_{\Delta x \to 0} \frac{f(x + \Delta x, y) - f(x, y)}{\Delta x}$ (B) $\displaystyle \lim_{\Delta y \to 0} \frac{f(x, y + \Delta y) - f(x, y)}{\Delta y}$

Applications

Business & Economics

51. *Profit function.* A firm produces two types of calculators, x thousand of type A and y thousand of type B per year. The revenue and cost functions for the year are (in thousands of dollars)

$$R(x, y) = 14x + 20y$$
$$C(x, y) = x^2 - 2xy + 2y^2 + 12x + 16y + 5$$

Find $P_x(1, 2)$ and $P_y(1, 2)$, and interpret.

52. *Advertising and sales.* A company spends x thousand dollars per week on newspaper advertising and y thousand dollars per week on television advertising. Its weekly sales were found to be given by

$$S(x, y) = 5x^2y^3$$

Find $S_x(3, 2)$ and $S_y(3, 2)$, and interpret.

53. *Demand equations.* A supermarket sells two brands of coffee, brand A at \$p per pound and brand B at \$q per pound. The daily demand equations for brands A and B are, respectively,

$$x = 200 - 5p + 4q$$
$$y = 300 + 2p - 4q$$

Find $\partial x / \partial p$ and $\partial y / \partial p$, and interpret.

54. *Revenue and profit functions.* A company manufactures ten-speed and three-speed bicycles. The weekly demand and cost functions are

$$p = 230 - 9x + y$$
$$q = 130 + x - 4y$$
$$C(x, y) = 200 + 80x + 30y$$

where \$p is the price of a ten-speed bicycle, \$q is the price of a three-speed bicycle, x is the weekly demand for ten-speed bicycles, y is the weekly demand for three-speed bicycles, and $C(x, y)$ is the cost function. Find $R_x(10, 5)$ and $P_x(10, 5)$, and interpret.

Problems 55 and 56 refer to the **Cobb–Douglas production function**

$$f(x, y) = kx^m y^n$$

where k, m, and n are positive constants with m + n = 1. The function f measures the number of units of a finished product produced from the use of x units of labor and y units of capital (for equipment such as tools, machinery, buildings, and so on). The partial derivative $f_x(x, y)$ approximates the change in productivity per unit change in labor units and is called **marginal productivity of labor.** The partial derivative $f_y(x, y)$ approximates the change in productivity per unit change in capital units and is called **marginal productivity of capital.**

55. *Productivity.* The productivity of a third-world country is given approximately by the function

$$f(x, y) = 10x^{0.75}y^{0.25}$$

with the utilization of x units of labor and y units of capital.

(A) Find $f_x(x, y)$ and $f_y(x, y)$.
(B) If the country is now using 625 units of labor and 81 units of capital, find the marginal productivity of labor and the marginal productivity of capital.
(C) For the greatest increase in the country's productivity, should the government encourage increased use of labor or increased use of capital?

56. *Productivity.* The productivity of an automobile manufacturing company is given approximately by the function

$$f(x, y) = 50\sqrt{xy} = 50x^{0.5}y^{0.5}$$

with the utilization of x units of labor and y units of capital.

(A) Find $f_x(x, y)$ and $f_y(x, y)$.
(B) If the company is now using 256 units of labor and 144 units of capital, find the marginal productivity of labor and the marginal productivity of capital.
(C) For the greatest increase in the company's productivity, should the management encourage increased use of labor or increased use of capital?

Problems 57–60 refer to the following: If a decrease in demand for one product results in an increase in demand for another product, then the two products are said to be **competitive** or **substitute products.** (Real whipping cream and imitation whipping cream are examples of competitive or substitute products.) If a decrease in demand for one product results in a decrease in demand for another product, then the two products are said to be **complementary products.** (Fishing boats and outboard motors are examples of *complementary products.)* Partial derivatives can be used to test whether two products are competitive, complementary, or neither. We start with demand functions for two products where the demand for either depends on the prices for both:

$x = f(p, q)$ *Demand function for product A*

$y = g(p, q)$ *Demand function for product B*

The variables x and y represent the number of units demanded of products A and B, respectively, at a price p for 1 unit of product A and a price q for 1 unit of product B. Normally, if the price of A increases while the price of B is held constant, then the demand for A will decrease; that is, $f_p(p, q) < 0$. Then, if A and B are competitive products, the demand for B will increase; that is, $g_p(p, q) > 0$. Similarly, if the price of B increases while the price of A is held constant, then the demand for B will decrease; that is, $g_q(p, q) < 0$. And if A and B are competitive products, then the demand for A will increase; that is, $f_q(p, q) > 0$. Reasoning similarly for complementary products, we arrive at the following test:

Test for Competitive and Complementary Products

Partials	Products *A* and *B*
$f_q(p, q) > 0$ and $g_p(p, q) > 0$	Competitive (Substitute)
$f_q(p, q) < 0$ and $g_p(p, q) < 0$	Complementary
$f_q(p, q) \geq 0$ and $g_p(p, q) \leq 0$	Neither
$f_q(p, q) \leq 0$ and $g_p(p, q) \geq 0$	Neither

57. *Product demand.* The weekly demand equations for the sale of butter and margarine in a supermarket are

$$x = f(p, q) = 8{,}000 - 0.09p^2 + 0.08q^2 \quad \text{Butter}$$
$$y = g(p, q) = 15{,}000 + 0.04p^2 - 0.3q^2 \quad \text{Margarine}$$

Determine whether the products are competitive, complementary, or neither.

58. *Product demand.* The daily demand equations for the sale of brand *A* coffee and brand *B* coffee in a supermarket are

$$x = f(p, q) = 200 - 5p + 4q \quad \text{Brand A coffee}$$
$$y = g(p, q) = 300 + 2p - 4q \quad \text{Brand B coffee}$$

Determine whether the two products are competitive, complementary, or neither.

59. *Product demand.* The monthly demand equations for the sale of skis and ski boots in a sporting goods store are

$$x = f(p, q) = 800 - 0.004p^2 - 0.003q^2 \quad \text{Skis}$$
$$y = g(p, q) = 600 - 0.003p^2 - 0.002q^2 \quad \text{Ski boots}$$

Determine whether the products are competitive, complementary, or neither.

60. *Product demand.* The monthly demand equations for the sale of tennis rackets and tennis balls in a sporting goods store are

$$x = f(p, q) = \quad 500 - 0.5p - \quad q^2 \qquad \text{Tennis rackets}$$
$$y = g(p, q) = 10{,}000 - \quad 8p - 100q^2 \qquad \text{Tennis balls (cans)}$$

Determine whether the products are competitive, complementary, or neither.

Life Sciences 61. *Medicine.* The following empirical formula relates the surface area A (in square inches) of an average human body to its weight w (in pounds) and its height h (in inches):

$$A = f(w, h) = 15.64 w^{0.425} h^{0.725}$$

Knowing the surface area of a human body is useful, for example, in studies pertaining to hypothermia (heat loss due to exposure).

(A) Find $f_w(w, h)$ and $f_h(w, h)$.

(B) For a 65 pound child who is 57 inches tall, find $f_w(65, 57)$ and $f_h(65, 57)$ and interpret.

62. *Blood flow.* Poiseuille's law states that the resistance, R, for blood flowing in a blood vessel varies directly as the length of the vessel, L, and inversely as the fourth power of its radius, r. Stated as an equation,

$$R(L, r) = k \frac{L}{r^4} \qquad k \text{ a constant}$$

Find $R_L(4, 0.2)$ and $R_r(4, 0.2)$, and interpret.

Social Sciences 63. *Physical anthropology.* Anthropologists, in their study of race and human genetic groupings, often use an index called the *cephalic index.* The cephalic index, C, varies directly as the width, W, of the head, and inversely as the length, L, of the head (both viewed from the top). In terms of an equation,

$$C(W, L) = 100 \frac{W}{L}$$

where

$W =$ Width in inches

$L =$ Length in inches

Find $C_W(6, 8)$ and $C_L(6, 8)$, and interpret.

64. *Safety research.* Under ideal conditions, if a person driving a car slams on the brakes and skids to a stop, the length of the skid marks is given

by the formula

$$L(w, v) = kwv^2$$

where

k = Constant

w = Weight of car in pounds

v = Speed of car in miles per hour

For $k = 0.000\ 013\ 3$, find $L_w(2,500, 60)$ and $L_v(2,500, 60)$, and interpret.

12-3   Maxima and Minima

We are now ready to undertake a brief but useful analysis of local maxima and minima for functions of the type $z = f(x, y)$. Basically, we are going to extend the second-derivative test developed for functions of a single independent variable. To start, we assume that all second-order partials exist for the function f in some circular region in the xy plane. This guarantees that the surface $z = f(x, y)$ has no sharp points, breaks, or ruptures. In other words, we are dealing only with smooth surfaces with no edges (like the edge of a box); or breaks (like an earthquake fault); or sharp points (like the bottom point of a golf tee). See Figure 6.

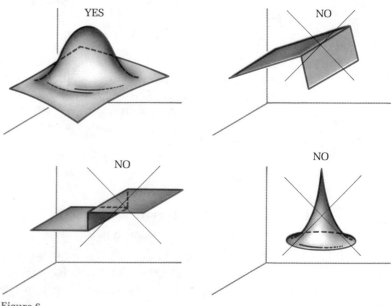

Figure 6

In addition, we will not concern ourselves with boundary points or absolute maxima–minima theory. In spite of these restrictions, the procedure we are now going to describe will help us solve a large number of useful problems.

What does it mean for $f(a, b)$ to be a local maximum or a local minimum? We say that $f(a, b)$ **is a local maximum** if there exists a circular region in the domain of f with (a, b) as the center, such that

$$f(a, b) \geq f(x, y)$$

for all (x, y) in the region. Similarly, we say that $f(a, b)$ **is a local minimum** if there exists a circular region in the domain of f with (a, b) as the center, such that

$$f(a, b) \leq f(x, y)$$

for all (x, y) in the region. Figure 7A illustrates a local maximum, Figure 7B a local minimum, and Figure 7C a saddle point, which is neither a local maximum nor a local minimum.

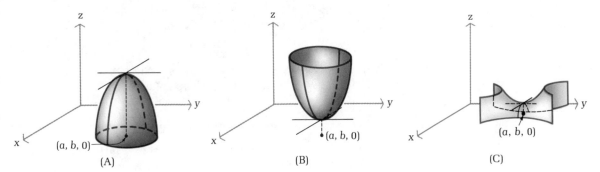

Figure 7

What happens to $f_x(a, b)$ and $f_y(a, b)$ if $f(a, b)$ is a local minimum or a local maximum and the partials of f exist in a circular region containing (a, b)? Figure 7 suggests that $f_x(a, b) = 0$ and $f_y(a, b) = 0$, since the tangents to the indicated curves are horizontal. Theorem 1 indicates that our intuitive reasoning is correct.

Theorem 1

> Let $f(a, b)$ be an extreme (a local maximum or a local minimum) for the function f. If both f_x and f_y exist at (a, b), then
>
> $$f_x(a, b) = 0 \quad \text{and} \quad f_y(a, b) = 0 \qquad (1)$$

The converse of this theorem is false; that is, if $f_x(a, b) = 0$ and $f_y(a, b) = 0$, then $f(a, b)$ may or may not be a local extreme—the point $(a, b, f(a, b))$ may be a saddle point, for example (see Fig. 7C).

Theorem 1 gives us what are called *necessary* (but not *sufficient*) conditions for $f(a, b)$ to be a local extreme. We thus find all points (a, b) such that $f_x(a, b) = 0$ and $f_y(a, b) = 0$ and test these further to determine whether $f(a, b)$ is a local extreme or a saddle point. Points (a, b) such that (1) holds are called **critical points.** The next theorem, using second-derivative tests, gives us *sufficient* conditions for a local point to produce a local extreme or a saddle point. As was the case with Theorem 1, we state this theorem without proof.

Theorem 2

Second-Derivative Test for Local Extrema

If:

1. $z = f(x, y)$
2. $f_x(a, b) = 0$ and $f_y(a, b) = 0$ [(a, b) is a critical point]
3. All second-order partials of f exist in some circular region containing (a, b) as a center
4. $A = f_{xx}(a, b), \quad B = f_{xy}(a, b), \quad C = f_{yy}(a, b)$

Then:

1. If $AC - B^2 > 0$ and $A < 0$, then $f(a, b)$ is a local maximum.
2. If $AC - B^2 > 0$ and $A > 0$, then $f(a, b)$ is a local minimum.
3. If $AC - B^2 < 0$, then f has a saddle point at (a, b).
4. If $AC - B^2 = 0$, the test fails.

To illustrate the use of Theorem 2, we will first find the local extrema for a very simple function whose solution is almost obvious: $z = f(x, y) = x^2 + y^2 + 2$. From the function f itself and its graph (Fig. 8), it is clear that a local minimum is found at $(0, 0)$. Let us see how Theorem 2 confirms this observation.

Step 1.   Find critical points. Find (x, y) such that $f_x(x, y) = 0$ and $f_y(x, y) = 0$ simultaneously:

$$f_x(x, y) = 2x = 0$$
$$x = 0$$
$$f_y(x, y) = 2y = 0$$
$$y = 0$$

The only critical point is $(a, b) = (0, 0)$.

Step 2.   Compute $A = f_{xx}(0, 0)$, $B = f_{xy}(0, 0)$, and $C = f_{yy}(0, 0)$:

$$f_{xx}(x, y) = 2, \quad \text{thus} \quad A = f_{xx}(0, 0) = 2$$
$$f_{xy}(x, y) = 0, \quad \text{thus} \quad B = f_{xy}(0, 0) = 0$$
$$f_{yy}(x, y) = 2, \quad \text{thus} \quad C = f_{yy}(0, 0) = 2$$

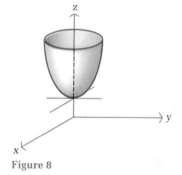

Figure 8

Step 3.   Evaluate $AC - B^2$ and try to classify the critical point $(0, 0)$ using Theorem 2:

$$AC - B^2 = 2 \cdot 2 - 0^2 = 4 > 0 \qquad \text{and} \qquad A = 2 > 0$$

Therefore, case 2 in Theorem 2 holds. That is, $f(0, 0) = 2$ is a local minimum.

We will now use Theorem 2 in the following examples to analyze extrema without the aid of graphs.

Example 10   Use Theorem 2 to find local extrema for

$$f(x, y) = -x^2 - y^2 + 6x + 8y - 21$$

Solution   Step 1.   Find critical points. Find (x, y) such that $f_x(x, y) = 0$ and $f_y(x, y) = 0$ simultaneously:

$$f_x(x, y) = -2x + 6 = 0$$
$$x = 3$$
$$f_y(x, y) = -2y + 8 = 0$$
$$y = 4$$

The only critical point is $(a, b) = (3, 4)$.

Step 2.   Compute $A = f_{xx}(3, 4)$, $B = f_{xy}(3, 4)$, and $C = f_{yy}(3, 4)$:

$$f_{xx}(x, y) = -2, \quad \text{thus} \quad A = f_{xx}(3, 4) = -2$$
$$f_{xy}(x, y) = 0, \quad \text{thus} \quad B = f_{xy}(3, 4) = 0$$
$$f_{yy}(x, y) = -2, \quad \text{thus} \quad C = f_{yy}(3, 4) = -2$$

Step 3.   Evaluate $AC - B^2$ and try to classify the critical point $(3, 4)$ using Theorem 2:

$$AC - B^2 = (-2)(-2) - (0)^2 = 4 > 0 \qquad \text{and} \qquad A = -2 < 0$$

Therefore, case 1 in Theorem 2 holds. That is, $f(3, 4) = 4$ is a local maximum.

Problem 10   Use Theorem 2 to find local extrema for

$$f(x, y) = x^2 + y^2 - 10x - 2y + 36$$

Example 11   Use Theorem 2 to find local extrema for

$$f(x, y) = x^3 + y^3 - 6xy$$

Solution   Step 1. Find critical points for $f(x, y) = x^3 + y^3 - 6xy$:

$$f_x(x, y) = 3x^2 - 6y = 0 \qquad \text{Solve for } y.$$

$$6y = 3x^2$$

$$y = \frac{1}{2}x^2 \tag{2}$$

$$f_y(x, y) = 3y^2 - 6x = 0$$

$$3y^2 = 6x \qquad \text{Use (2) to eliminate } y.$$

$$3\left(\frac{1}{2}x^2\right)^2 = 6x$$

$$\frac{3}{4}x^4 = 6x \qquad \text{Solve for } x.$$

$$3x^4 - 24x = 0$$

$$3x(x^3 - 8) = 0$$

$$x = 0 \quad \text{or} \quad x = 2$$

$$y = 0 \qquad\qquad y = \frac{1}{2}(2)^2 = 2$$

The critical points are (0, 0) and (2, 2). Since there are two critical points, steps 2 and 3 must be performed twice.

Test (0, 0)   Step 2. Compute $A = f_{xx}(0, 0)$, $B = f_{xy}(0, 0)$, and $C = f_{yy}(0, 0)$:

$$f_{xx}(x, y) = 6x, \quad \text{thus} \quad A = f_{xx}(0, 0) = \ \ 0$$
$$f_{xy}(x, y) = -6, \quad \text{thus} \quad B = f_{xy}(0, 0) = -6$$
$$f_{yy}(x, y) = 6y, \quad \text{thus} \quad C = f_{yy}(0, 0) = \ \ 0$$

Step 3. Evaluate $AC - B^2$ and try to classify the critical point (0, 0) using Theorem 2:

$$AC - B^2 = (0)(0) - (-6)^2 = -36 < 0$$

Therefore, case 3 in Theorem 2 applies. That is, f has a saddle point at (0, 0).

Now we will consider the second critical point, (2, 2).

Test (2, 2)   Step 2. Compute $A = f_{xx}(2, 2)$, $B = f_{xy}(2, 2)$, and $C = f_{yy}(2, 2)$:

$$f_{xx}(x, y) = 6x, \quad \text{thus} \quad A = f_{xx}(2, 2) = \ 12$$
$$f_{xy}(x, y) = -6, \quad \text{thus} \quad B = f_{xy}(2, 2) = -6$$
$$f_{yy}(x, y) = 6y, \quad \text{thus} \quad C = f_{yy}(2, 2) = \ 12$$

Step 3. Evaluate $AC - B^2$ and try to classify the critical point (2, 2) using Theorem 2:

$$AC - B^2 = (12)(12) - (-6)^2 = 108 > 0 \quad \text{and} \quad A = 12 > 0$$

Thus, case 2 in Theorem 2 applies and $f(2, 2) = -8$ is a local minimum.

Problem 11   Use Theorem 2 to find local extrema for

$$f(x, y) = x^3 + y^2 - 6xy$$

Example 12   Suppose the surfboard company discussed earlier has developed the yearly
Profit   profit equation

$$P(x, y) = -2x^2 + 2xy - y^2 + 10x - 4y + 107$$

where x is the number (in thousands) of standard surfboards produced per year, y is the number (in thousands) of competition surfboards produced per year, and P is profit (in thousands of dollars). How many of each type of board should be produced per year to realize a maximum profit? What is the maximum profit?

Solution   Step 1.   Find critical points:

$$P_x(x, y) = -4x + 2y + 10 = 0$$
$$P_y(x, y) = 2x - 2y - 4 = 0$$

Solving this system, we obtain (3, 1) as the only critical point.

Step 2.   Compute $A = P_{xx}(3, 1)$, $B = P_{xy}(3, 1)$, and $C = P_{yy}(3, 1)$:

$$P_{xx}(x, y) = -4, \quad \text{thus} \quad A = P_{xx}(3, 1) = -4$$
$$P_{xy}(x, y) = 2, \quad \text{thus} \quad B = P_{xy}(3, 1) = 2$$
$$P_{yy}(x, y) = -2, \quad \text{thus} \quad C = P_{yy}(3, 1) = -2$$

Step 3.   Evaluate $AC - B^2$ and try to classify the critical point (3, 1) using Theorem 2:

$$AC - B^2 = (-4)(-2) - (2)^2 = 8 - 4 = 4 > 0$$
$$A = -4 < 0$$

Therefore, case 1 in Theorem 2 applies. That is, $P(3, 1) = \$120{,}000$ is a local maximum. This is obtained by producing 3,000 standard boards and 1,000 competition boards per year.

Problem 12   Repeat Example 12 with

$$P(x, y) = -2x^2 + 4xy - 3y^2 + 4x - 2y + 77$$

Example 13   The packaging department in a company has been asked to design a
Package Design   rectangular box with no top and a partition down the middle. The box must have a volume of 48 cubic inches. Find the dimensions that will minimize the amount of material used to construct the box.

Solution

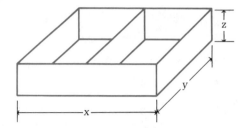

The amount of material used in constructing this box is

$$
M = \underset{\substack{\text{Base}}}{\underset{\substack{\text{and}}}{xy}} + \underset{\substack{\text{Front}\\ \text{and}\\ \text{back}}}{2xz} + \underset{\substack{\text{Sides}\\ \text{and}\\ \text{partition}}}{3yz} \tag{3}
$$

The volume of the box is

$$
V = xyz = 48 \tag{4}
$$

Since Theorem 2 applies only to functions with two independent variables, we must use (4) to eliminate one of the variables in (3).

$$
M = xy + 2xz + 3yz \qquad\qquad \text{Substitute } z = \frac{48}{xy}
$$

$$
= xy + 2x\left(\frac{48}{xy}\right) + 3y\left(\frac{48}{xy}\right)
$$

$$
= xy + \frac{96}{y} + \frac{144}{x}
$$

Thus, we must find the minimum value of

$$
M(x, y) = xy + \frac{96}{y} + \frac{144}{x}
$$

Step 1. Find critical points:

$$
M_x(x, y) = y - \frac{144}{x^2} = 0
$$

$$
y = \frac{144}{x^2} \tag{5}
$$

$$
M_y(x, y) = x - \frac{96}{y^2} = 0
$$

$$
x = \frac{96}{y^2} \qquad\qquad \text{Solve for } y^2.
$$

$$
y^2 = \frac{96}{x} \qquad\qquad \text{Use (5) to eliminate } y \text{ and solve for } x.
$$

$$\left(\frac{144}{x^2}\right)^2 = \frac{96}{x}$$

$$\frac{20{,}736}{x^4} = \frac{96}{x}$$

$$x^3 = \frac{20{,}736}{96} = 216$$

$$x = 6 \qquad \text{Use (5) to find } y.$$

$$y = \frac{144}{36} = 4$$

Step 2. Compute $A = M_{xx}(6, 4)$, $B = M_{xy}(6, 4)$, and $C = M_{yy}(6, 4)$:

$$M_{xx}(x, y) = \frac{288}{x^3}, \quad \text{thus} \quad A = M_{xx}(6, 4) = \frac{288}{216} = \frac{4}{3}$$

$$M_{xy} = \quad 1, \quad \text{thus} \quad B = M_{xy}(6, 4) = \quad 1$$

$$M_{yy}(x, y) = \frac{192}{y^3}, \quad \text{thus} \quad C = M_{yy}(6, 4) = \frac{192}{64} = 3$$

Step 3. Evaluate $AC - B^2$ and try to classify the critical point $(6, 4)$ using Theorem 2:

$$AC - B^2 = \left(\frac{4}{3}\right)(3) - (1)^2 = 3 > 0 \quad \text{and} \quad A = \frac{4}{3} > 0$$

Therefore, case 2 in Theorem 2 applies; $M(x, y)$ has a local minimum at $(6, 4)$. If $x = 6$ and $y = 4$, then

$$z = \frac{48}{xy} = \frac{48}{6(4)} = 2$$

Thus, the dimensions that will require the minimum amount of material are 6 inches by 4 inches by 2 inches.

Problem 13 If the box in Example 13 must have a volume of 384 cubic inches, find the dimensions that will require the least amount of material.

Answers to Matched Problems

10. $f(5, 1) = 10$ is a local minimum
11. f has a saddle point at $(0, 0)$; $f(6, 18) = -108$ is a local minimum
12. Local maximum for $x = 2$ and $y = 1$; $P(2, 1) = \$80{,}000$
13. 12 inches by 8 inches by 4 inches

Exercise 12-3

Find local extrema using Theorem 2.

A
1. $f(x, y) = 6 - x^2 - 4x - y^2$
2. $f(x, y) = 3 - x^2 - y^2 + 6y$

3. $f(x, y) = x^2 + y^2 + 2x - 6y + 14$
4. $f(x, y) = x^2 + y^2 - 4x + 6y + 23$

B

5. $f(x, y) = xy + 2x - 3y - 2$
6. $f(x, y) = x^2 - y^2 + 2x + 6y - 4$
7. $f(x, y) = -3x^2 + 2xy - 2y^2 + 14x + 2y + 10$
8. $f(x, y) = -x^2 + xy - 2y^2 + x + 10y - 5$
9. $f(x, y) = 2x^2 - 2xy + 3y^2 - 4x - 8y + 20$
10. $f(x, y) = 2x^2 - xy + y^2 - x - 5y + 8$

C

11. $f(x, y) = e^{xy}$
12. $f(x, y) = x^2y - xy^2$
13. $f(x, y) = x^3 + y^3 - 3xy$
14. $f(x, y) = 2y^3 - 6xy - x^2$
15. $f(x, y) = 2x^4 + y^2 - 12xy$
16. $f(x, y) = 16xy - x^4 - 2y^2$
17. $f(x, y) = x^3 - 3xy^2 + 6y^2$
18. $f(x, y) = 2x^2 - 2x^2y + 6y^3$

Applications

Business & Economics

19. *Product mix for maximum profit.* A firm produces two types of calculators, x thousand of type A and y thousand of type B per year. If the revenue and cost equations for the year are (in millions of dollars)

$$R(x, y) = 2x + 3y$$
$$C(x, y) = x^2 - 2xy + 2y^2 + 6x - 9y + 5$$

find how many of each type of calculator should be produced per year to maximize profit. What is the maximum profit?

20. *Automation–labor mix for minimum cost.* The annual labor and automated equipment cost (in millions of dollars) for a company's production of television sets is given by

$$C(x, y) = 2x^2 + 2xy + 3y^2 - 16x - 18y + 54$$

where x is the amount spent per year on labor and y is the amount spent per year on automated equipment (both in millions of dollars). Determine how much should be spent on each per year to minimize this cost. What is the minimum cost?

21. *Maximizing profit.* A department store sells two brands of inexpensive calculators. The store pays $6 for each brand *A* calculator and $8 for each brand *B* calculator. The research department has estimated the following weekly demand equations for these two competitive products:

$$x = 116 - 30p + 20q \quad \text{Demand equation for brand } A$$
$$y = 144 + 16p - 24q \quad \text{Demand equation for brand } B$$

where *p* is the selling price for brand *A* and *q* is the selling price for brand *B*.

(A) Determine the demands x and y when $p = \$10$ and $q = \$12$; when $p = \$11$ and $q = \$11$.

(B) How should the store price each calculator to maximize weekly profits? What is the maximum weekly profit? [*Hint:* $C = 6x + 8y$, $R = px + qy$, and $P = R - C$.]

22. *Maximizing profit.* A store sells two brands of color print film. The store pays $2 for each roll of brand A film and $3 for each roll of brand B film. A consulting firm has estimated the following daily demand equations for these two competitive products:

$$x = 75 - 40p + 25q \qquad \text{Demand equation for brand } A$$

$$y = 80 + 20p - 30q \qquad \text{Demand equation for brand } B$$

where p is the selling price for brand A and q is the selling price for brand B.

(A) Determine the demands x and y when $p = \$4$ and $q = \$5$; when $p = \$4$ and $q = \$4$.

(B) How should the store price each brand of film to maximize daily profits? What is the maximum daily profit? [*Hint:* $C = 2x + 3y$, $R = px + qy$, and $P = R - C$.]

23. *Minimizing cost.* A satellite television reception station is to be located at $P(x, y)$ so that the sum of the squares of the distances from P to the three towns A, B, and C is minimum (see the figure). Find the coordinates of P. This location will minimize the cost of providing satellite cable television for all three towns.

24. *Minimizing cost.* Repeat Problem 23 replacing the coordinates of B with B(6, 9) and the coordinates of C with C(9, 0).

25. *Minimum material.* A rectangular box with no top and two parallel partitions (see accompanying figure) is to be made to hold 64 cubic inches. Find the dimensions that will require the least amount of material.

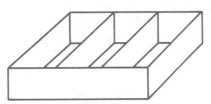

26. *Minimum material.* A rectangular box with no top and two intersecting partitions (see accompanying figure) is to be made to hold 72 cubic inches. What should its dimensions be in order to use the least amount of material in its construction?

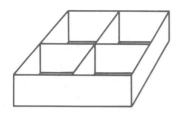

27. *Maximum volume.* A mailing service states that a rectangular package shall have the sum of the length and girth not to exceed 120 inches (see the figure). What are the dimensions of the largest (in volume) mailing carton that can be constructed meeting these restrictions?

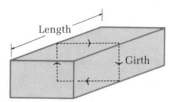

28. *Maximum shipping volume.* A shipping box is reinforced with steel bands in all three directions, as indicated in the figure. A total of 150 inches of steel tape are to be used, with 6 inches of waste because of a 2 inch overlap in each direction. Find the dimensions of the box with maximum volume that can be taped as indicated.

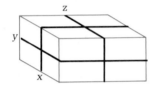

12-4 Maxima and Minima Using Lagrange Multipliers (Optional)

- Functions of Two Independent Variables
- Functions of Three Independent Variables

■ Functions of Two Independent Variables

We will now consider a particularly powerful method of solving a certain class of maxima–minima problems. The method is due to Joseph Louis Lagrange (1736–1813), an eminent eighteenth century French mathematician, and it is called the **method of Lagrange multipliers.** We introduce the method through an example; then we will formalize the discussion in the form of a theorem.

A rancher wants to construct two feeding pens of the same size along an existing fence (see Fig. 9). If 720 feet of fencing are available, how long should x and y be in order to obtain the maximum total area? What is the maximum area?

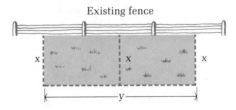

Figure 9

The total area is given by

$$f(x, y) = xy$$

which can be made as large as we like providing there are no restrictions on x and y. But there are restrictions on x and y, since we have only 720 feet of fencing. That is, x and y must be chosen so that

$$3x + y = 720$$

This restriction on x and y, also called a **constraint,** leads to the following maxima–minima problem:

Maximize $f(x, y) = xy$ (1)

Subject to $3x + y = 720$ or $3x + y - 720 = 0$ (2)

This problem is a special case of a general class of problems of the form

Maximize (or minimize) $z = f(x, y)$ (3)

Subject to $g(x, y) = 0$ (4)

Of course, we could try to solve (4) for y in terms of x, or for x in terms of y, then substitute the result into (3), and use methods developed in Section 8-3 for functions of a single variable. But what if (4) were more complicated than (2), and solving for one variable in terms of the other was either very difficult or impossible? In the method of Lagrange multipliers we work with g(x, y) directly and avoid having to solve (4) for one variable in terms of the other. In addition, the method generalizes to functions of arbitrarily many variables subject to one or more constraints.

Now, to the method. We form a new function F, using functions f and g in (3) and (4), as follows:

$$F(x, y, \lambda) = f(x, y) + \lambda g(x, y)$$ (5)

where λ (lambda) is called a **Lagrange multiplier.** Theorem 3 forms the basis for the method.

Theorem 3

The relative maxima and minima of the function $z = f(x, y)$ subject to the constraint $g(x, y) = 0$ will be among those points (x_0, y_0) for which (x_0, y_0, λ_0) is a solution to the system

$$F_x(x, y, \lambda) = 0$$
$$F_y(x, y, \lambda) = 0$$
$$F_\lambda(x, y, \lambda) = 0$$

where $F(x, y, \lambda) = f(x, y) + \lambda g(x, y)$, provided all the partial derivatives exist.

We now solve the fence problem using the method of Lagrange multipliers.

Step 1.   Formulate the problem in the form of equations (3) and (4):

Maximize $f(x, y) = xy$

Subject to $g(x, y) = 3x + y - 720 = 0$

Step 2.   Form the function F, introducing the Lagrange multiplier λ:

$$F(x, y, \lambda) = f(x, y) + \lambda g(x, y)$$
$$= xy + \lambda(3x + y - 720)$$

Step 3.   Solve the system $F_x = 0$, $F_y = 0$, $F_\lambda = 0$. (Solutions are called **critical points** for F.)

$$F_x = y + 3\lambda = 0$$
$$F_y = x + \lambda = 0$$
$$F_\lambda = 3x + y - 720 = 0$$

From the first two equations, we see that

$$y = -3\lambda$$
$$x = -\lambda$$

Substitute these values for x and y into the third equation and solve for λ.

$$-3\lambda - 3\lambda = 720$$
$$-6\lambda = 720$$
$$\lambda = -120$$

Thus,

$$y = -3(-120) = 360 \text{ feet}$$
$$x = -(-120) = 120 \text{ feet}$$

Step 4.   Test the critical points for maxima and minima. The function F has only one critical point at $(120, 360, -120)$, and since $f(x, y) = xy$ has a minimum at $(0, 0)$, we conclude that $(120, 360)$ produces a maximum for f. Hence,

Max $f(x, y) = f(120, 360)$

$$= (120)(360) = 43,200 \text{ square feet}$$

The key steps in applying the method of Lagrange multipliers are listed in the following box:

Method of Lagrange Multipliers—Key Steps

1. Formulate the problem in the form

    Maximize (or minimize) $z = f(x, y)$

    Subject to $g(x, y) = 0$

2. Form the function F:

    $F(x, y, \lambda) = f(x, y) + \lambda g(x, y)$

3. Find the critical points for F; that is, solve the system

    $F_x(x, y, \lambda) = 0$
    $F_y(x, y, \lambda) = 0$
    $F_\lambda(x, y, \lambda) = 0$

4. Evaluate $z = f(x, y)$ at each point (x_0, y_0) such that (x_0, y_0, λ_0) satisfies the system in step 3. The maximum or minimum value of $f(x, y)$ will be among these values in the problems we consider.

Example 14   Minimize $f(x, y) = x^2 + y^2$ subject to $x + y = 10$.

Solution   Step 1.   Minimize $f(x, y) = x^2 + y^2$

Subject to $g(x, y) = x + y - 10 = 0$

Step 2. $F(x, y, \lambda) = x^2 + y^2 + \lambda(x + y - 10)$

Step 3. $F_x = 2x + \lambda = 0$
           $F_y = 2y + \lambda = 0$
           $F_\lambda = x + y - 10 = 0$

From the first two equations,

$$x = -\frac{\lambda}{2} \qquad y = -\frac{\lambda}{2}$$

Substituting these into the third equation, we obtain

$$-\frac{\lambda}{2} - \frac{\lambda}{2} = 10$$

$$-\lambda = 10$$

$$\lambda = -10$$

The critical point is $(5, 5, -10)$.

Step 4. $f(5, 5) = 5^2 + 5^2 = 50$

Checking other points on the line $x + y = 10$ near $(5, 5)$, we see that this is a minimum. (See Fig. 10 on the next page.)

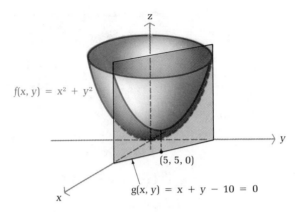

$f(x, y) = x^2 + y^2$

$(5, 5, 0)$

$g(x, y) = x + y - 10 = 0$

Figure 10

Problem 14   Maximize $f(x, y) = 25 - x^2 - y^2$ subject to $x + y = 4$. (See Fig. 11.)

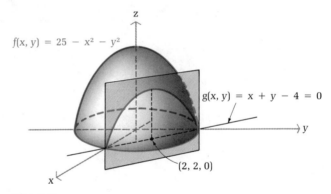

$f(x, y) = 25 - x^2 - y^2$

$g(x, y) = x + y - 4 = 0$

$(2, 2, 0)$

Figure 11

■ Functions of Three Independent Variables

We have indicated that the method of Lagrange multipliers can be extended to functions with arbitrarily many independent variables with one or more constraints. We state a theorem for functions with three independent variables and one constraint and consider an example that will demonstrate the advantage of the method of Lagrange multipliers over the method used in Section 12-3.

<table>
<tr><td>Theorem 4</td><td>

The relative maxima and minima of the function $w = f(x, y, z)$ subject to the constraint $g(x, y, z) = 0$ will be among the set of points (x_0, y_0, z_0) for which $(x_0, y_0, z_0, \lambda_0)$ is a solution to the system

$F_x(x, y, z, \lambda) = 0$

$F_y(x, y, z, \lambda) = 0$

$F_z(x, y, z, \lambda) = 0$

$F_\lambda(x, y, z, \lambda) = 0$

where $F(x, y, z, \lambda) = f(x, y, z) + \lambda g(x, y, z)$, provided all the partial derivatives exist.

</td></tr>
</table>

Example 15
Package Design

A rectangular box with an open top and one partition is to be constructed from 162 square inches of cardboard. Find the dimensions that will result in a box with the largest possible volume.

Solution

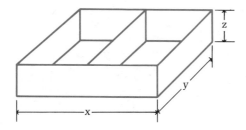

We must maximize

$V(x, y, z) = xyz$

subject to the constraint that the amount of material used is 162 square inches. Thus, x, y, and z must satisfy

$xy + 2xz + 3yz = 162$

Step 1. Maximize $V(x, y, z) = xyz$

Subject to $g(x, y, z) = xy + 2xz + 3yz - 162 = 0$

Step 2. $F(x, y, z, \lambda) = xyz + \lambda(xy + 2xz + 3yz - 162)$

Step 3. $F_x = yz + \lambda(y + 2z) = 0$

$F_y = xz + \lambda(x + 3z) = 0$

$F_z = xy + \lambda(2x + 3y) = 0$

$F_\lambda = xy + 2xz + 3yz - 162 = 0$

From the first two equations, we can write

$$\lambda = \frac{-yz}{y + 2z} \qquad \lambda = \frac{-xz}{x + 3z}$$

Eliminating λ, we have

$$\frac{-yz}{y + 2z} = \frac{-xz}{x + 3z}$$

$$-xyz - 3yz^2 = -xyz - 2xz^2$$

$$3yz^2 = 2xz^2 \qquad \text{We can assume } z \neq 0.$$

$$3y = 2x$$

$$x = \frac{3}{2}y$$

From the second and third equations,

$$\lambda = \frac{-xz}{x + 3z} \qquad \lambda = \frac{-xy}{2x + 3y}$$

Eliminating λ, we have

$$\frac{-xz}{x + 3z} = \frac{-xy}{2x + 3y}$$

$$-2x^2z - 3xyz = -x^2y - 3xyz \qquad \text{We can assume } x \neq 0.$$

$$2x^2z = x^2y$$

$$2z = y$$

$$z = \frac{1}{2}y$$

Substituting $x = \frac{3}{2}y$ and $z = \frac{1}{2}y$ in the fourth equation, we have

$$\left(\frac{3}{2}y\right)y + 2\left(\frac{3}{2}y\right)\left(\frac{1}{2}y\right) + 3y\left(\frac{1}{2}y\right) - 162 = 0$$

$$\frac{3}{2}y^2 + \frac{3}{2}y^2 + \frac{3}{2}y^2 = 162$$

$$y^2 = 36 \qquad \text{We can assume}$$

$$y = 6 \qquad \qquad y > 0.$$

$$x = \frac{3}{2}(6) = 9 \qquad \text{Using } x = \frac{3}{2}y$$

$$z = \frac{1}{2}(6) = 3 \qquad \text{Using } z = \frac{1}{2}y$$

Since (9, 6, 3) is the only critical point with x, y, and z all positive, the dimensions of the box with maximum volume are 9 inches by 6 inches by 3 inches.

Problem 15   Find the dimensions of the box of the type described in Example 15 with the largest volume that can be constructed from 288 square inches of cardboard.

Suppose we had decided to solve Example 15 by the method used in Section 12-3. First we would have to solve the material constraint for one of the variables, say z:

$$z = \frac{162 - xy}{2x + 3y}$$

Then we would eliminate z in the volume function and maximize

$$V(x, y) = xy\frac{162 - xy}{2x + 3y}$$

Using the method of Lagrange multipliers allows us to avoid the formidable task of finding the partial derivatives of V.

Answers to   14. Max $f(x, y) = f(2, 2) = 17$ (see Fig. 11)
Matched Problems   15. 12 inches by 8 inches by 4 inches

Exercise 12-4

Use the method of Lagrange multipliers in the following problems:

A   1. Maximize $f(x, y) = 2xy$ 2. Minimize $f(x, y) = 6xy$
        Subject to $x + y = 6$ Subject to $y - x = 6$
     3. Minimize $f(x, y) = x^2 + y^2$
        Subject to $3x + 4y = 25$
     4. Maximize $f(x, y) = 25 - x^2 - y^2$
        Subject to $2x + y = 10$

B   5. Find the maximum and minimum of $f(x, y) = 2xy$ subject to $x^2 + y^2 = 18$.
     6. Find the maximum and minimum of $f(x, y) = x^2 - y^2$ subject to $x^2 + y^2 = 25$.
     7. Maximize the product of two numbers if their sum must be 10.
     8. Minimize the product of two numbers if their difference must be 10.

C   9. Minimize $f(x, y, z) = x^2 + y^2 + z^2$
        Subject to $2x - y + 3z = -28$
    10. Maximize $f(x, y, z) = xyz$
        Subject to $2x + y + 2z = 120$
    11. Maximize and minimize $f(x, y, z) = x + y + z$
        Subject to $x^2 + y^2 + z^2 = 12$

12. Maximize and minimize $f(x, y, z) = 2x + 4y + 4z$
    Subject to $x^2 + y^2 + z^2 = 9$

Applications

Business & Economics

13. *Budgeting for least cost.* A manufacturing company produces two models of a television set, x units of model A and y units of model B per week, at a cost in dollars of

    $$C(x, y) = 6x^2 + 12y^2$$

    If it is necessary (because of shipping considerations) that

    $$x + y = 90$$

    how many of each type of set should be manufactured per week to minimize cost? What is the minimum cost?

14. *Budgeting for maximum production.* A manufacturing firm has budgeted $60,000 per month for labor and materials. If x thousand dollars is spent on labor and y thousand dollars is spent on materials, and if the monthly output in units is given by

    $$N(x, y) = 4xy - 8x$$

    how should the $60,000 be allocated to labor and materials in order to maximize N? What is the maximum N?

15. *Productivity.* A consulting firm for a manufacturing company arrived at the following Cobb–Douglas production function for a particular product:

    $$N(x, y) = 50x^{0.8}y^{0.2}$$

    where x is the number of units of labor and y is the number of units of capital required to produce N(x, y) units of the product. If $400,000 is budgeted for production of the product, each unit of labor costs $40, and each unit of capital costs $80, determine the number of labor units and capital units required to maximize production.

16. *Productivity.* The research department for a manufacturing company arrived at the following Cobb–Douglas production function for a particular product:

    $$N(x, y) = 10x^{0.6}y^{0.4}$$

    where x is the number of units of labor and y is the number of units of capital required to produce N(x, y) units of the product. If $300,000 is budgeted for production of the product, each unit of labor costs $30, and each unit of capital costs $60, determine the number of labor units and capital units required to maximize production.

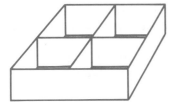

17. *Maximum volume.* A rectangular box with no top and two intersecting partitions is to be constructed from 192 square inches of cardboard (see accompanying figure). Find the dimensions that will maximize the volume.

18. *Maximum volume.* A mailing service states that a rectangular package shall have the sum of the length and girth not to exceed 120 inches (see the figure). What are the dimensions of the largest (in volume) mailing carton that can be constructed meeting these restrictions?

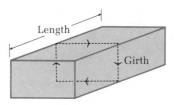

Life Sciences

19. *Agriculture.* Three pens of the same size are to be built along an existing fence (see the figure). If 400 feet of fencing are available, what length should x and y be to produce the maximum total area? What is the maximum area?

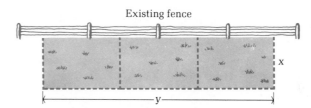

20. *Diet and minimum cost.* A group of guinea pigs is to receive 25,600 calories per week. Two available foods produce 200xy calories for a mixture of x kilograms of type M food and y kilograms of type N food. If type M costs $1 per kilogram and type N costs $2 per kilogram, how much of each type of food should be used to minimize weekly food costs? What is the minimum cost? [*Note:* x ≥ 0, y ≥ 0]

12-5 Method of Least Squares

- Least Squares Approximation
- Applications

■ Least Squares Approximation

In this section we will use the optimization techniques discussed in Section 12-3 to find the equation of a line which is a "best" approximation to a set of points in a rectangular coordinate system. This very popular method is known as **least squares approximation** or **linear regression.** Let us begin by considering a specific case.

A manufacturer wants to approximate the cost function for a product. The value of the cost function has been determined for certain levels of production, as listed in the table:

Number of Units x, in hundreds	Cost y, in thousands of dollars
2	4
5	6
6	7
9	8

Although these points do not all lie on a line (see Fig. 12), they are very close to being linear. The manufacturer would like to approximate the cost function by a linear function; that is, determine values m and d so that the line

$$y = mx + d$$

is, in some sense, the "best" approximation to the cost function.

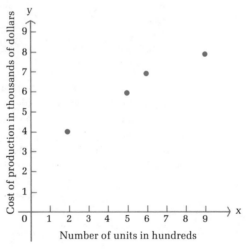

Figure 12

What do we mean by "best"? Since the line $y = mx + d$ will not go through all four points, it is reasonable to examine the differences between the y coordinates of the points listed in the table and the y coordinates of the corresponding points on the line. Each of these differences is called the **residual** at that point (see Fig. 13). For example, at $x = 2$ the point from the table is (2, 4) and the point on the line is (2, $2m + d$), so the residual is

$$4 - (2m + d) = 4 - 2m - d$$

All the residuals are listed in the table below:

x	y	$mx + d$	Residual
2	4	$2m + d$	$4 - 2m - d$
5	6	$5m + d$	$6 - 5m - d$
6	7	$6m + d$	$7 - 6m - d$
9	8	$9m + d$	$8 - 9m - d$

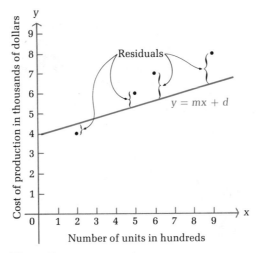

Figure 13

Our criterion for the "best" approximation is the following: Determine the values of m and d that *minimize* the sum of the squares of the residuals. The resulting line is called the **least squares line** or the **regression line.** To this end, we minimize

$$F(m, d) = (4 - 2m - d)^2 + (6 - 5m - d)^2 + (7 - 6m - d)^2 + (8 - 9m - d)^2$$

Step 1.   Find critical points:

$$F_m(m, d) = 2(4 - 2m - d)(-2) + 2(6 - 5m - d)(-5)$$
$$+ 2(7 - 6m - d)(-6) + 2(8 - 9m - d)(-9)$$
$$= -304 + 292m + 44d = 0$$

$$F_d(m, d) = 2(4 - 2m - d)(-1) + 2(6 - 5m - d)(-1)$$
$$+ 2(7 - 6m - d)(-1) + 2(8 - 9m - d)(-1)$$
$$= -50 + 44m + 8d = 0$$

Solving the system

$$-304 + 292m + 44d = 0$$

$$-50 + 44m + 8d = 0$$

we obtain $(m, d) = (0.58, 3.06)$ as the only critical point.

Step 2. Compute $A = F_{mm}(m, d)$, $B = F_{md}(m, d)$, and $C = F_{dd}(m, d)$:

$$F_{mm}(m, d) = 292, \quad \text{thus} \quad A = F_{mm}(0.58, 3.06) = 292$$

$$F_{md}(m, d) = 44, \quad \text{thus} \quad B = F_{md}(0.58, 3.06) = 44$$

$$F_{dd}(m, d) = 8, \quad \text{thus} \quad C = F_{dd}(0.58, 3.06) = 8$$

Step 3. Evaluate $AC - B^2$ and try to classify the critical point (m, d) using Theorem 2 in Section 12-3:

$$AC - B^2 = (292)(8) - (44)^2 = 400 > 0$$

$$A = 292 > 0$$

Therefore, case 2 in Theorem 2 applies, and $F(m, d)$ has a local minimum at the critical point $(0.58, 3.06)$.

Thus, the least squares line for the given data is

$$y = 0.58x + 3.06 \qquad \text{Least squares line}$$

Note that the sum of the squares of the residuals is minimized for this choice of m and d (see Fig. 14).

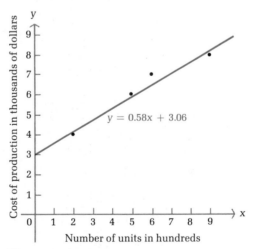

Figure 14

This linear function can now be used by the manufacturer to estimate any of the quantities normally associated with the cost function—such as costs, marginal costs, average costs, and so on. For example, the cost of producing 2,000 units is approximately

$$y = (0.58)(20) + 3.06 = 14.66 \quad \text{or} \quad \$14,660$$

The marginal cost function is

$$\frac{dy}{dx} = 0.58$$

The average cost function is

$$\overline{y} = \frac{0.58x + 3.06}{x}$$

In general, if we are given a set of n points $(x_1, y_1), (x_2, y_2), \ldots, (x_n, y_n)$, then it can be shown that the coefficients m and d of the least squares line $y = mx + d$ must satisfy the system of equations

$$\left(\sum_{k=1}^{n} x_k\right) m + nd = \sum_{k=1}^{n} y_k \tag{1}$$

$$\left(\sum_{k=1}^{n} x_k^2\right) m + \left(\sum_{k=1}^{n} x_k\right) d = \sum_{k=1}^{n} x_k y_k \tag{2}$$

Using the notation

$$\overline{x} = \frac{1}{n} \sum_{k=1}^{n} x_k \qquad \text{Average of the } x \text{ coordinates}$$

$$\overline{y} = \frac{1}{n} \sum_{k=1}^{n} y_k \qquad \text{Average of the } y \text{ coordinates}$$

to simplify the form of equations (1) and (2) and solving for m and d produces the formulas given in the box.

Least Squares Approximation

For a set of n points $(x_1, y_1), (x_2, y_2), \ldots, (x_n, y_n)$, the coefficients m and d of the least squares line

$$y = mx + d$$

are given by the formulas

$$m = \frac{\sum_{k=1}^{n} x_k y_k - n\overline{x}\,\overline{y}}{\sum_{k=1}^{n} x_k^2 - n\overline{x}^2} \tag{3}$$

$$d = \overline{y} - \overline{x}m \tag{4}$$

where

$$\overline{x} = \frac{1}{n} \sum_{k=1}^{n} x_k \qquad \text{Average of the } x \text{ coordinates}$$

$$\overline{y} = \frac{1}{n} \sum_{k=1}^{n} y_k \qquad \text{Average of the } y \text{ coordinates}$$

Since the value of m is used in equation (4) to compute the value of d, the value of m must always be computed first. Notice that equation (4) implies that the point $(\bar{x}, \bar{y})$ is always on the least squares line.

■ Applications

Example 16
Educational Testing

The table lists the midterm and final examination scores for ten students in a calculus course.

Midterm	Final	Midterm	Final
49	61	78	77
53	47	83	81
67	72	85	79
71	76	91	93
74	68	99	99

(A) Find the least squares line for the data given in the table.
(B) Use the least squares line to predict the final examination score for a student who scored 95 on the midterm examination.
(C) Graph the data and the least squares line on the same set of axes.

Solutions

(A) A table is a convenient way to compute all the sums in the formulas for m and d:

	x_k	y_k	$x_k y_k$	x_k^2
	49	61	2,989	2,401
	53	47	2,491	2,809
	67	72	4,824	4,489
	71	76	5,396	5,041
	74	68	5,032	5,476
	78	77	6,006	6,084
	83	81	6,723	6,889
	85	79	6,715	7,225
	91	93	8,463	8,281
	99	99	9,801	9,801
Totals	750	753	58,440	58,496

Thus,

$$\bar{x} = \frac{1}{10} \sum_{k=1}^{10} x_k = \frac{1}{10}(750) = 75.0$$

$$\bar{y} = \frac{1}{10} \sum_{k=1}^{10} y_k = \frac{1}{10}(753) = 75.3$$

$$\sum_{k=1}^{10} x_k y_k = 58,440$$

$$\sum_{k=1}^{10} x_k^2 = 58,496$$

Substituting the appropriate values in equation (3),

$$m = \frac{\sum\limits_{k=1}^{n} x_k y_k - n\bar{x}\bar{y}}{\sum\limits_{k=1}^{n} x_k^2 - n\bar{x}^2}$$

$$= \frac{58{,}440 - 10(75.0)(75.3)}{58{,}496 - 10(75.0)^2} = \frac{1{,}965}{2{,}246} \approx 0.875$$

Then, using equation (4),

$$d = \bar{y} - \bar{x}m$$

$$\approx 75.3 - (75.0)(0.875) \approx 9.68$$

The least squares line is given (approximately) by

$$y = 0.875x + 9.68$$

(B)   If $x = 95$, then the predicted score on the final examination is

$$y = 0.875(95) + 9.68$$

$$\approx 93 \qquad \text{Assuming that the score}$$
$$\text{must be an integer}$$

(C)

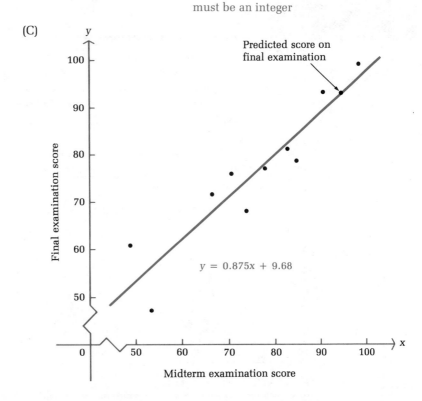

Problem 16   Repeat Example 16 for the following scores:

Midterm	Final	Midterm	Final
54	50	84	80
60	66	88	95
75	80	89	85
76	68	97	94
78	71	99	86

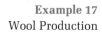

Example 17
Wool Production

Table 1 lists the annual production of wool throughout the world for the years 1970–1980. Use the data in the table to predict the worldwide wool production for 1981.

Table 1
World Wool Production

Year	Millions of Pounds	Year	Millions of Pounds
1970	6,107	1976	5,827
1971	5,972	1977	5,838
1972	5,560	1978	5,983
1973	5,474	1979	6,168
1974	5,769	1980	6,285
1975	5,911		

Solution   Solving this problem by hand is certainly possible, but would require considerable effort. Instead, we used a computer to perform the necessary computations. (The program we used can be found in the computer supplement for this text. See the Preface.) The computer output is listed in Table 2.

Table 2

Input to Program	Output from Program
11 DATA POINTS HAVE BEEN ENTERED.	<------- LEAST SQUARES LINE ------->
DO YOU WANT TO SEE THE POINTS (Y/N)?Y	SLOPE: M = 33.9
	Y INTERCEPT: D = 5729.96
DATA POINTS	EQUATION: Y = 33.9 X + 5729.96
------------------	--
0 6107	
1 5972	TO COMPUTE AN ESTIMATED VALUE OF Y,
2 5560	ENTER AN X VALUE. ENTER 999 TO STOP.
3 5474	?11
4 5769	
5 5911	X = 11 Y = 6102.85
6 5827	
7 5838	ENTER AN X VALUE. ENTER 999 TO STOP.
8 5983	?999
9 6168	
10 6285	

PRESS RETURN TO CONTINUE?	

Notice that we used x = 0 for 1970, x = 1 for 1971, and so on. Examining the computer output in Table 2, we see that the least squares line is

y = 33.9x + 5,729.96

and the estimated worldwide wool production in 1981 is 6,102.85 million pounds.

Problem 17   Use the least squares line in Example 17 to estimate the worldwide wool production in 1982.

Answers to   16.   (A)   y = 0.85x + 9.47   (B)   90.2
Matched Problems   (C)

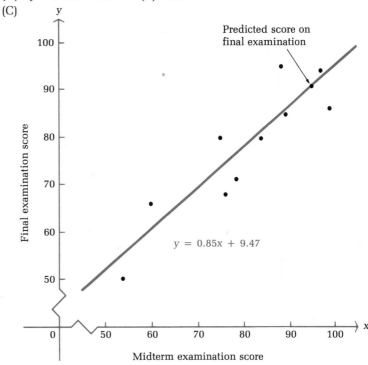

17.   6,136.76 million pounds

Exercise 12-5

A   *Find the least squares line. Graph the data and the least squares line.*

1.	x	y
	1	1
	2	3
	3	4
	4	3

2.	x	y
	1	−2
	2	−1
	3	3
	4	5

3.	x	y
	1	8
	2	5
	3	4
	4	0

4.	x	y
	1	20
	2	14
	3	11
	4	3

5.	x	y
	1	3
	2	4
	3	5
	4	6

6.	x	y
	1	2
	2	3
	3	3
	4	2

B   *Find the least squares line and use it to estimate y for the indicated value of x.*

7.	x	y
	0	10
	5	22
	10	31
	*15	46
	20	51

Estimate y when x = 25.

8.	x	y
	-5	60
	0	50
	5	30
	10	20
	15	15

Estimate y when x = 20.

9.	x	y
	-1	14
	1	12
	3	8
	5	6
	7	5

Estimate y when x = 2.

10.	x	y
	2	-4
	6	0
	10	8
	14	12
	18	14

Estimate y for x = 15.

11.	x	y
	0.5	25
	2	22
	3.5	21
	5	21
	6.5	18
	9.5	12
	11	11
	12.5	8
	14	5
	15.5	1

Estimate y for x = 8.

12.	x	y
	0	-15
	2	-9
	4	-7
	6	-7
	8	-1
	12	11
	14	13
	16	19
	18	25
	20	33

Estimate y for x = 10.

C   **13.**   The method of least squares can be generalized to curves other than straight lines. To find the coefficients of the parabola

$$y = ax^2 + bx + c$$

that is the "best" fit for the points (1, 2), (2, 1), (3, 1), and (4, 3), minimize the sum of the squares of the residuals

$$F(a, b, c) = (a + b + c - 2)^2 + (4a + 2b + c - 1)^2$$
$$+ (9a + 3b + c - 1)^2 + (16a + 4b + c - 3)^2$$

by solving the system

$$F_a(a, b, c) = 0 \qquad F_b(a, b, c) = 0 \qquad F_c(a, b, c) = 0$$

for a, b, and c. Graph the points and the parabola.

14.   Repeat Problem 13 for the points $(-1, -2)$, $(0, 1)$, $(1, 2)$, and $(2, 0)$.

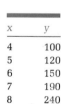

Applications

Business & Economics

15.   *Cost.* The cost y in thousands of dollars for producing x units of a product at various times in the past is given in the table.

x	y
10	5
12	6
15	7
18	8
20	9

(A)   Find the least squares line for the data.

(B)   Use the least squares line to estimate the cost of producing 25 units.

16.   *Advertising and sales.* A company spends x thousand dollars on advertising each month and has y thousand dollars in monthly sales. The data in the table were obtained by examining the past history of the company.

x	y
4	100
5	120
6	150
7	190
8	240

(A)   Find the least squares line for the data.

(B)   Use the least squares line to estimate the sales if $10,000 is spent on advertising.

17.   *Maximizing profit.* The marketing research department for a drug store chain chose two summer resort areas to test market a new sun screen lotion packaged in 4 ounce plastic bottles. After a summer of varying the selling price and recording the monthly demand, the research department arrived at the given demand table, where y is the number of bottles purchased per month (in thousands) at x dollars per bottle.

x	y
5.0	2.0
5.5	1.8
6.0	1.4
6.5	1.2
7.0	1.1

(A)   Find a demand equation using the method of least squares.

(B)   If each bottle of sun screen costs the drug store chain $4, how should it be priced to achieve a maximum monthly profit? [*Hint:*   Use the result of part A, with $C = 4y$, $R = xy$, and $P = R - C$.]

18. *Maximizing profit.* A marketing research consultant for a supermarket chain chose a large city to test market a new brand of mixed nuts packaged in 8 ounce cans. After a year of varying the selling price and recording the monthly demand, the consultant arrived at the given demand table, where y is the number of cans purchased per month (in thousands) at x dollars per can.

x	y
4.0	4.2
4.5	3.5
5.0	2.7
5.5	1.5
6.0	0.7

(A) Find a demand equation using the method of least squares.

(B) If each can of nuts costs the supermarket chain $3, how should it be priced to achieve a maximum monthly profit?

Life Sciences

19. *Medicine.* If a person dives into cold water, a neural reflex response automatically shuts off blood circulation to the skin and muscles and reduces the pulse rate. A medical research team conducted an experiment using a group of ten 2-year-olds. A child's face was placed momentarily in cold water and the corresponding reduction in pulse rate recorded. The average reduction in heart rate for each temperature was summarized in the following table:

Water Temperature	Pulse Rate Reduction
50	15
55	13
60	10
65	6
70	2

(A) If T is water temperature in degrees Fahrenheit and P is pulse rate reduction in beats per minute, use the method of least squares to find a linear equation relating T and P.

(B) Use the equation found in part A to find P when $T = 57$.

20. *Biology.* In biology there is an approximate rule, called the *bioclimatic rule for temperate climates*, that has been known for a couple of hundred years. This rule states that in spring and early summer, periodic phenomena such as blossoming of flowers, appearance of insects, and ripening of fruit usually come about 4 days later for each 500 feet of altitude. Stated as a formula,

$$d = 8h \qquad 0 \leqslant h \leqslant 4$$

h	d
0	0
1	7
2	18
3	28
4	33

where d is the change in days and h is the altitude in thousands of feet. To test this rule, an experiment was set up to record the difference in blossoming time of the same type of apple tree at different altitudes. A summary of the results is given in the table in the margin.

(A) Use the method of least squares to find a linear equation relating h and d. Does the bioclimatic rule, $d = 8h$, appear to be approximately correct?

(B) How much longer will it take this type of apple tree to blossom at 3.5 thousand feet than at sea level? [Use the linear equation found in part A.]

Social Sciences

21. *Political science.* Association of economic class and party affiliation did not start with Roosevelt's New Deal; it goes back to the time of Andrew Jackson (1767–1845). Paul Lazarsfeld of Columbia University published an article in the November 1950 issue of *Scientific American* in which he discusses statistical investigations of the relationships between economic class and party affiliation. The data in the table are taken from this article.

Ward	Average Assessed Value per Person (in $100) 1836	Percent Democratic Votes 1836
12	1.7	51
3	2.1	49
1	2.3	53
5	2.4	36
2	3.6	65
11	3.7	35
10	4.7	29
4	6.2	40
6	7.1	34
9	7.4	29
8	8.7	20
7	11.9	23

(A) If A represents the average assessed value per person in a given ward in 1836 and D represents the percentage of people in that ward voting Democratic in 1836, use the method of least squares to find a linear equation relating A and D.

(B) If the average assessed value per person in a ward had been $300, what is the predicted percentage of people in that ward that would have voted Democratic?

22. *Education.* The table lists the high school grade-point averages of ten students and their college grade-point averages after one semester of college.

High School GPA	College GPA
2.0	1.5
2.2	1.5
2.4	1.6
2.7	1.8
2.9	2.1
3.0	2.3
3.1	2.5
3.3	2.9
3.4	3.2
3.7	3.5

(A) Find the least squares line for the data.
(B) Estimate the college GPA for a student with a high school GPA of 3.5.
(C) Estimate the high school GPA necessary for a college GPA of 2.7.

12-6 Double Integrals over Rectangular Regions

- Introduction
- Definition of the Double Integral
- Average Value over Rectangular Regions
- Volume and Double Integrals

■ Introduction

We have generalized the concept of differentiation to functions with two or more independent variables. How can we do the same with integration and how can we interpret the results? Let us first look at the operation of antidifferentiation. We can antidifferentiate a function of two or more variables with respect to one of the variables by treating all the other variables as though they were constants. Thus, this operation is the reverse operation of partial differentiation, just as ordinary antidifferentiation is the reverse operation of ordinary differentiation. We write $\int f(x, y)\, dx$ to indicate that we are to antidifferentiate $f(x, y)$ with respect to x, holding y fixed; we write $\int f(x, y)\, dy$ to indicate that we are to antidifferentiate $f(x, y)$ with respect to y, holding x fixed.

Example 18   Evaluate:

(A) $\displaystyle\int (6xy^2 + 3x^2)\, dy$ (B) $\displaystyle\int (6xy^2 + 3x^2)\, dx$

Solutions   (A)   Treating x as a constant and using the properties of antidifferentiation from Section 10-1, we have

$$\int (6xy^2 + 3x^2)\, dy = \int 6xy^2\, dy + \int 3x^2\, dy$$

$$= 6x \int y^2\, dy + 3x^2 \int dy$$

$$= 6x \left(\frac{y^3}{3}\right) + 3x^2(y) + C(x)$$

$$= 2xy^3 + 3x^2y + C(x)$$

The *dy* tells us we are looking for the antiderivative of $(6xy^2 + 3x^2)$ with respect to y only, holding x constant.

Notice that the constant of integration can actually be *any function of x alone*, since, for any such function, $\partial/\partial y\, [C(x)] = 0$. We can verify that our answer is correct by using partial differentiation:

$$\frac{\partial}{\partial y}\, [2xy^3 + 3x^2y + C(x)] = 6xy^2 + 3x^2 + 0$$

$$= 6xy^2 + 3x^2$$

(B)   Now we treat y as a constant:

$$\int (6xy^2 + 3x^2)\, dx = \int 6xy^2\, dx + \int 3x^2\, dx$$

$$= 6y^2 \int x\, dx + 3 \int x^2\, dx$$

$$= 6y^2 \left(\frac{x^2}{2}\right) + 3 \left(\frac{x^3}{3}\right) + E(y)$$

$$= 3x^2y^2 + x^3 + E(y)$$

This time the antiderivative contains an arbitrary function E(y) of y alone.

Check $$\frac{\partial}{\partial x}\, [3x^2y^2 + x^3 + E(y)] = 6xy^2 + 3x^2 + 0$$

$$= 6xy^2 + 3x^2$$

Problem 18   Evaluate:

(A) $\displaystyle\int (4xy + 12x^2y^3)\, dy$ (B) $\displaystyle\int (4xy + 12x^2y^3)\, dx$

Now that we have extended the concept of antidifferentiation to functions with two variables, we can also evaluate definite integrals of the form

$$\int_a^b f(x, y)\, dx \qquad \text{or} \qquad \int_c^d f(x, y)\, dy$$

Example 19   Evaluate, substituting the limits of integration in y if dy is used and in x if dx is used:

(A) $\displaystyle\int_0^2 (6xy^2 + 3x^2)\, dy$

(B) $\displaystyle\int_0^1 (6xy^2 + 3x^2)\, dx$

Solutions   (A)   From Example 18A, we know that $\int (6xy^2 + 3x^2)\, dy = 2xy^3 + 3x^2y + C(x)$. According to the definition of the definite integral for a function of one variable, we can use any antiderivative to evaluate the definite integral. Thus, choosing $C(x) = 0$, we have

$$\int_0^2 (6xy^2 + 3x^2)\, dy = (2xy^3 + 3x^2y)\Big|_{y=0}^{y=2}$$
$$= [2x(2)^3 + 3x^2(2)] - [2x(0)^3 + 3x^2(0)]$$
$$= 16x + 6x^2$$

(B)   From Example 18B, we know that $\int (6xy^2 + 3x^2)\, dx = 3x^2y^2 + x^3 + E(y)$. Thus, choosing $E(y) = 0$, we have

$$\int_0^1 (6xy^2 + 3x^2)\, dx = (3x^2y^2 + x^3)\Big|_{x=0}^{x=1}$$
$$= [3y^2(1)^2 + (1)^3] - [3y^2(0)^2 + (0)^3]$$
$$= 3y^2 + 1$$

Problem 19   Evaluate:

(A) $\displaystyle\int_0^1 (4xy + 12x^2y^3)\, dy$

(B) $\displaystyle\int_0^3 (4xy + 12x^2y^3)\, dx$

Notice that integrating and evaluating a definite integral, with integrand $f(x, y)$, with respect to y produces a function of x alone (or a constant). Likewise, integrating and evaluating a definite integral, with integrand $f(x, y)$, with respect to x produces a function of y alone (or a constant). Each of these results, involving at most one variable, can now be used as an integrand in a second definite integral.

Example 20   Evaluate:

(A) $\displaystyle\int_0^1\left[\int_0^2 (6xy^2 + 3x^2)\,dy\right]dx$

(B) $\displaystyle\int_0^2\left[\int_0^1 (6xy^2 + 3x^2)\,dx\right]dy$

Solutions   (A) Example 19A showed that

$$\int_0^2 (6xy^2 + 3x^2)\,dy = 16x + 6x^2$$

Thus,

$$\int_0^1\left[\int_0^2 (6xy^2 + 3x^2)\,dy\right]dx = \int_0^1 (16x + 6x^2)\,dx$$

$$= (8x^2 + 2x^3)\Big|_{x=0}^{x=1}$$

$$= [8(1)^2 + 2(1)^3] - [8(0)^2 + 2(0)^3]$$

$$= 10$$

(B) Example 19B showed that

$$\int_0^1 (6xy^2 + 3x^2)\,dx = 3y^2 + 1$$

Thus,

$$\int_0^2\left[\int_0^1 (6xy^2 + 3x^2)\,dx\right]dy = \int_0^2 (3y^2 + 1)\,dy$$

$$= (y^3 + y)\Big|_{y=0}^{y=2}$$

$$= [(2)^3 + 2] - [(0)^3 + 0]$$

$$= 10$$

Problem 20   Evaluate:

(A) $\displaystyle\int_0^3\left[\int_0^1 (4xy + 12x^2y^3)\,dy\right]dx$

(B) $\displaystyle\int_0^1\left[\int_0^3 (4xy + 12x^2y^3)\,dx\right]dy$

■ Definition of the Double Integral

Notice that the answers in Examples 20A and 20B are identical. This is not an accident. In fact, it is this property that enables us to define the **double integral.** (See the box at the top of the next page.)

Double Integral

The double integral of a function $f(x, y)$ over a rectangle $R = \{(x, y)|a \leq x \leq b, \quad c \leq y \leq d\}$ is

$$\iint\limits_{R} f(x, y)\, dA$$

$$= \int_{a}^{b}\left[\int_{c}^{d} f(x, y)\, dy\right] dx$$

$$= \int_{c}^{d}\left[\int_{a}^{b} f(x, y)\, dx\right] dy$$

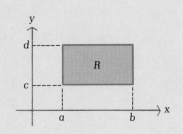

In the double integral $\iint_{R} f(x, y)\, dA, f(x, y)$ is called the **integrand** and R is called the **region of integration.** The expression dA indicates that this is an integral over a two-dimensional region. The integrals

$$\int_{a}^{b}\left[\int_{c}^{d} f(x, y)\, dy\right] dx \qquad \text{and} \qquad \int_{c}^{d}\left[\int_{a}^{b} f(x, y)\, dx\right] dy$$

are referred to as **iterated integrals** (the brackets are often omitted), and the order in which dx and dy are written indicates the order of integration. This is not the most general definition of the double integral over a rectangular region; however, it is equivalent to the general definition for all the functions we will consider.

Example 21   Evaluate $\iint_{R} (x + y)\, dA$ over $R = \{(x, y)|1 \leq x \leq 3, \quad -1 \leq y \leq 2\}$.

Solution   We can choose either order of iteration. As a check, we will evaluate the integral both ways:

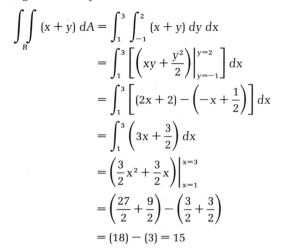

$$\iint\limits_{R} (x + y)\, dA = \int_{1}^{3}\int_{-1}^{2} (x + y)\, dy\, dx$$

$$= \int_{1}^{3}\left[\left(xy + \frac{y^2}{2}\right)\bigg|_{y=-1}^{y=2}\right] dx$$

$$= \int_{1}^{3}\left[(2x + 2) - \left(-x + \frac{1}{2}\right)\right] dx$$

$$= \int_{1}^{3}\left(3x + \frac{3}{2}\right) dx$$

$$= \left(\frac{3}{2}x^2 + \frac{3}{2}x\right)\bigg|_{x=1}^{x=3}$$

$$= \left(\frac{27}{2} + \frac{9}{2}\right) - \left(\frac{3}{2} + \frac{3}{2}\right)$$

$$= (18) - (3) = 15$$

$$\iint\limits_R (x + y)\, dA = \int_{-1}^{2} \int_{1}^{3} (x + y)\, dx\, dy$$

$$= \int_{-1}^{2} \left[\left(\frac{x^2}{2} + xy \right) \Big|_{x=1}^{x=3} \right] dy$$

$$= \int_{-1}^{2} \left[\left(\frac{9}{2} + 3y \right) - \left(\frac{1}{2} + y \right) \right] dy$$

$$= \int_{-1}^{2} (4 + 2y)\, dy$$

$$= (4y + y^2) \Big|_{y=-1}^{y=2}$$

$$= (8 + 4) - (-4 + 1)$$

$$= (12) - (-3) = 15$$

Problem 21   Evaluate both ways:

$$\iint\limits_R (2x - y)\, dA \quad \text{over } R = \{(x, y) | -1 \leqslant x \leqslant 5, \quad 2 \leqslant y \leqslant 4\}$$

Example 22   Evaluate:

$$\iint\limits_R 2xe^{x^2+y}\, dA \quad \text{over } R = \{(x, y) | 0 \leqslant x \leqslant 1, \quad -1 \leqslant y \leqslant 1\}$$

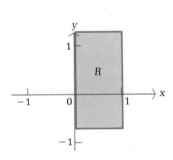

Solution

$$\iint\limits_R 2xe^{x^2+y}\, dA = \int_{-1}^{1} \int_{0}^{1} 2xe^{x^2+y}\, dx\, dy$$

$$= \int_{-1}^{1} \left[(e^{x^2+y}) \Big|_{x=0}^{x=1} \right] dy$$

$$= \int_{-1}^{1} (e^{1+y} - e^y)\, dy$$

$$= (e^{1+y} - e^y) \Big|_{y=-1}^{y=1}$$

$$= (e^2 - e) - (e^0 - e^{-1})$$

$$= e^2 - e - 1 + e^{-1}$$

Problem 22   Evaluate:

$$\iint\limits_R \frac{x}{y^2} e^{x/y}\, dA \quad \text{over } R = \{(x, y) | 0 \leqslant x \leqslant 1, \quad 1 \leqslant y \leqslant 2\}$$

■ Average Value over Rectangular Regions

In Section 11-1 the average value of a function $f(x)$ over an interval $[a, b]$ was defined as

$$\frac{1}{b-a} \int_a^b f(x) \, dx$$

This definition is easily extended to functions of two variables over rectangular regions, as shown in the box. Notice that the denominator in the expression given in the box, $(b - a)(d - c)$, is simply the area of the rectangle R.

Average Value over Rectangular Regions

The **average value** of the function $f(x, y)$ over the rectangle $R = \{(x, y)|a \leqslant x \leqslant b, \ \ c \leqslant y \leqslant d\}$ is

$$\frac{1}{(b-a)(d-c)} \iint\limits_R f(x, y) \, dA$$

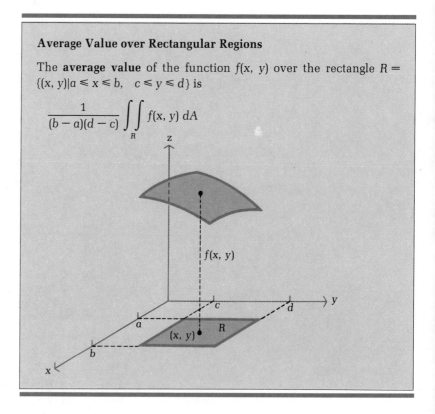

Example 23   Find the average value of $f(x, y) = 4 - \frac{1}{2}x - \frac{1}{2}y$ over the rectangle $R = \{(x, y)|0 \leqslant x \leqslant 2, \ \ 0 \leqslant y \leqslant 2\}$.

Solution

$$\frac{1}{(b-a)(d-c)} \iint_R f(x, y)\, dA = \frac{1}{(2-0)(2-0)} \iint_R \left(4 - \frac{1}{2}x - \frac{1}{2}y\right) dA$$

$$= \frac{1}{4} \int_0^2 \int_0^2 \left(4 - \frac{1}{2}x - \frac{1}{2}y\right) dy\, dx$$

$$= \frac{1}{4} \int_0^2 \left[\left(4y - \frac{1}{2}xy - \frac{1}{4}y^2\right)\Big|_{y=0}^{y=2}\right] dx$$

$$= \frac{1}{4} \int_0^2 (7 - x)\, dx$$

$$= \frac{1}{4} \left(7x - \frac{1}{2}x^2\right)\Big|_{x=0}^{x=2}$$

$$= \frac{1}{4}(12) = 3$$

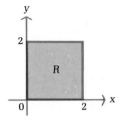

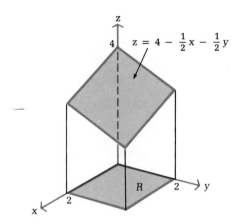

$$z = 4 - \frac{1}{2}x - \frac{1}{2}y$$

Problem 23   Find the average value of $f(x, y) = x + 2y$ over the rectangle $R = \{(x, y) | 0 \leqslant x \leqslant 2, \quad 0 \leqslant y \leqslant 1\}$.

■ Volume and Double Integrals

One application of the definite integral of a function with one variable is the calculation of areas, so it is not surprising that the definite integral of a function of two variables can be used to calculate volumes of solids.

Volume under a Surface

If $f(x, y) \geq 0$ over a rectangle R, $R = \{(x, y) | a \leq x \leq b, \ c \leq y \leq d\}$, then the volume of the solid formed by graphing f over the rectangle R is given by

$$V = \iint\limits_{R} f(x, y) \, dA$$

A proof of the statement in the box is left to a more advanced text.

Example 24   Find the volume of the solid under the graph of $f(x, y) = 1 + x^2 + y^2$ over the rectangle $R = \{(x, y) | 0 \leq x \leq 1, \ 0 \leq y \leq 1\}$.

Solution

$$V = \iint\limits_{R} (1 + x^2 + y^2) \, dA$$

$$= \int_0^1 \int_0^1 (1 + x^2 + y^2) \, dx \, dy$$

$$= \int_0^1 \left[\left(x + \frac{1}{3}x^3 + xy^2 \right) \Big|_{x=0}^{x=1} \right] dy$$

$$= \int_0^1 \left(\frac{4}{3} + y^2 \right) dy$$

$$= \left(\frac{4}{3}y + \frac{1}{3}y^3 \right) \Big|_{y=0}^{y=1} = \frac{5}{3} \text{ cubic units}$$

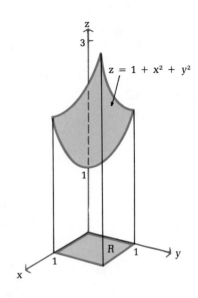

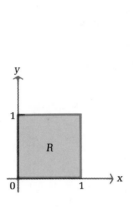

Problem 24   Find the volume of the solid under the graph of $f(x, y) = 1 + x + y$ over the rectangle $R = \{(x, y)|0 \leqslant x \leqslant 1, \ 0 \leqslant y \leqslant 2\}$.

Answers to   18. (A) $2xy^2 + 3x^2y^4 + C(x)$ (B) $2x^2y + 4x^3y^3 + E(y)$
Matched Problems   19. (A) $2x + 3x^2$ (B) $18y + 108y^3$ 20. (A) 36   (B) 36
21. 12   22. $e - 2e^{1/2} + 1$ 23. 2   24. 5 cubic units

Exercise 12-6

A   *Find each antiderivative. Then use the antiderivative to evaluate the definite integral.*

1. (A) $\displaystyle\int 12x^2y^3 \, dy$ (B) $\displaystyle\int_0^1 12x^2y^3 \, dy$

2. (A) $\displaystyle\int 12x^2y^3 \, dx$ (B) $\displaystyle\int_{-1}^2 12x^2y^3 \, dx$

3. (A) $\displaystyle\int (4x + 6y + 5) \, dx$ (B) $\displaystyle\int_{-2}^3 (4x + 6y + 5) \, dx$

4. (A) $\displaystyle\int (4x + 6y + 5) \, dy$ (B) $\displaystyle\int_1^4 (4x + 6y + 5) \, dy$

5. (A) $\displaystyle\int \frac{x}{\sqrt{y + x^2}} \, dx$ (B) $\displaystyle\int_0^2 \frac{x}{\sqrt{y + x^2}} \, dx$

6. (A) $\displaystyle\int \frac{x}{\sqrt{y + x^2}}\, dy$ (B) $\displaystyle\int_1^5 \frac{x}{\sqrt{y + x^2}}\, dy$

B   *Evaluate each iterated integral. (See the indicated problem for the evaluation of the inner integral.)*

7. $\displaystyle\int_{-1}^2 \int_0^1 12x^2y^3\, dy\, dx$ 8. $\displaystyle\int_0^1 \int_{-1}^2 12x^2y^3\, dx\, dy$

     (see Problem 1)   (see Problem 2)

9. $\displaystyle\int_1^4 \int_{-2}^3 (4x + 6y + 5)\, dx\, dy$ 10. $\displaystyle\int_{-2}^3 \int_1^4 (4x + 6y + 5)\, dy\, dx$

     (see Problem 3)   (see Problem 4)

11. $\displaystyle\int_1^5 \int_0^2 \frac{x}{\sqrt{y + x^2}}\, dx\, dy$ 12. $\displaystyle\int_0^2 \int_1^5 \frac{x}{\sqrt{y + x^2}}\, dy\, dx$

     (see Problem 5)   (see Problem 6)

Use both orders of iteration to evaluate each double integral.

13. $\displaystyle\iint_R xy\, dA;\quad R = \{(x, y)|0 \leqslant x \leqslant 2,\ \ 0 \leqslant y \leqslant 4\}$

14. $\displaystyle\iint_R \sqrt{xy}\, dA;\quad R = \{(x, y)|1 \leqslant x \leqslant 4,\ \ 1 \leqslant y \leqslant 9\}$

15. $\displaystyle\iint_R (x + y)^5\, dA;\quad R = \{(x, y)|-1 \leqslant x \leqslant 1,\ \ 1 \leqslant y \leqslant 2\}$

16. $\displaystyle\iint_R xe^y\, dA;\quad R = \{(x, y)|-2 \leqslant x \leqslant 3,\ \ 0 \leqslant y \leqslant 2\}$

Find the average value of each function over the given rectangle.

17. $f(x, y) = (x + y)^2;\quad R = \{(x, y)|1 \leqslant x \leqslant 5,\ -1 \leqslant y \leqslant 1\}$
18. $f(x, y) = x^2 + y^2;\quad R = \{(x, y)|-1 \leqslant x \leqslant 2,\ 1 \leqslant y \leqslant 4\}$

19. $f(x, y) = \dfrac{x}{y};\quad R = \{(x, y)|1 \leqslant x \leqslant 4,\ \ 2 \leqslant y \leqslant 7\}$

20. $f(x, y) = x^2y^3;\quad R = \{(x, y)|-1 \leqslant x \leqslant 1,\ \ 0 \leqslant y \leqslant 2\}$

Find the volume of the solid under the graph of each function over the given rectangle.

21. $f(x, y) = 2 - x^2 - y^2;\quad R = \{(x, y)|0 \leqslant x \leqslant 1,\ \ 0 \leqslant y \leqslant 1\}$
22. $f(x, y) = 5 - x;\quad R = \{(x, y)|0 \leqslant x \leqslant 5,\ \ 0 \leqslant y \leqslant 5\}$
23. $f(x, y) = 4 - y^2;\quad R = \{(x, y)|0 \leqslant x \leqslant 2,\ \ 0 \leqslant y \leqslant 2\}$
24. $f(x, y) = e^{-x-y};\quad R = \{(x, y)|0 \leqslant x \leqslant 1,\ \ 0 \leqslant y \leqslant 1\}$

C   *Evaluate each double integral. Select the order of integration carefully—*
each problem is easy to do one way and difficult the other.

25. $\displaystyle\iint\limits_R xe^{xy}\, dA; \quad R = \{(x, y)|0 \leqslant x \leqslant 1, \quad 1 \leqslant y \leqslant 2\}$

26. $\displaystyle\iint\limits_R xye^{x^2y}\, dA; \quad R = \{(x, y)|0 \leqslant x \leqslant 1, \quad 1 \leqslant y \leqslant 2\}$

27. $\displaystyle\iint\limits_R \frac{2y + 3xy^2}{1 + x^2}\, dA; \quad R = \{(x, y)|0 \leqslant x \leqslant 1, \quad -1 \leqslant y \leqslant 1\}$

28. $\displaystyle\iint\limits_R \frac{2x + 2y}{1 + 4y + y^2}\, dA; \quad R = \{(x, y)|1 \leqslant x \leqslant 3, \quad 0 \leqslant y \leqslant 1\}$

Applications

Business & Economics

29.   *Economics–multiplier principle.* Suppose Congress enacts a one-time-only 10% tax rebate that is expected to infuse y billion dollars, $5 \leqslant y \leqslant 7$, into the economy. If every individual and corporation is expected to spend a proportion x, $0.6 \leqslant x \leqslant 0.8$, of each dollar received, then by the **multiplier principle** in economics (using the sum of an infinite geometric progression—see Appendix A), the total amount of spending S (in billions of dollars) generated by this tax rebate is given by

$$S(x, y) = \frac{y}{1 - x}$$

What is the average total amount of spending for the indicated ranges of the values of x and y? Set up a double integral and evaluate.

30.   *Economics—multiplier principle.* Repeat Problem 29 if $6 \leqslant y \leqslant 10$ and $0.7 \leqslant x \leqslant 0.9$.

31.   *Economics—Cobb–Douglas production function.* If an industry invests x thousand labor-hours, $10 \leqslant x \leqslant 20$, and y million dollars, $1 \leqslant y \leqslant 2$, in the production of N thousand units of a certain item, then N is given by

$$N(x, y) = x^{0.75}y^{0.25}$$

What is the average number of units produced for the indicated ranges of x and y? Set up a double integral and evaluate.

32.   *Economics—Cobb–Douglas production function.* Repeat Problem 31 for

$$N(x, y) = x^{0.5}y^{0.5}$$

where $10 \leqslant x \leqslant 30$ and $1 \leqslant y \leqslant 3$.

Life Sciences

33. *Population distribution.* In order to study the population distribution of a certain species of insects, a biologist has constructed an artificial habitat in the shape of a rectangle 16 feet long and 12 feet wide. The only food available to the insects in this habitat is located at its center. The biologist has determined that the concentration C of insects per square foot at a point d units from the food supply (see the figure) is given approximately by

$$C = 10 - \tfrac{1}{10}d^2$$

What is the average concentration of insects throughout the habitat? Express C as a function of x and y, set up a double integral, and evaluate.

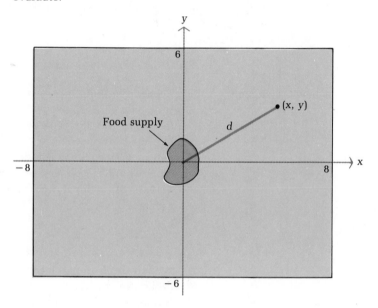

34. *Population distribution.* Repeat Problem 33 for a square habitat that measures 12 feet on each side, where the insect concentration is given by

$$C = 8 - \tfrac{1}{10}d^2$$

35. *Pollution.* A heavy industrial plant located in the center of a small town emits particulate matter into the atmosphere. Suppose the concentration of particulate matter in parts per million at a point d miles from the plant is given by

$$C = 100 - 15d^2$$

If the boundaries of the town form a rectangle 4 miles long and 2 miles wide, what is the average concentration of particulate matter throughout the city? Express C as a function of x and y, set up a double integral, and evaluate.

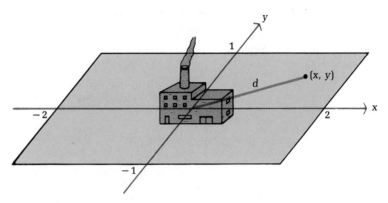

36. *Pollution.* Repeat Problem 35 if the boundaries of the town form a rectangle 8 miles long and 4 miles wide and the concentration of particulate matter is given by

$$C = 100 - 3d^2$$

Social Sciences

37. *Safety research.* Under ideal conditions, if a person driving a car slams on the brakes and skids to a stop, the length of the skid marks (in feet) is given by the formula

$$L = 0.000\ 013\ 3xy^2$$

where x is the weight of the car in pounds and y is the speed of the car in miles per hour. What is the average length of the skid marks for cars weighing between 2,000 and 3,000 pounds and traveling at speeds between 50 and 60 miles per hour? Set up a double integral and evaluate.

38. *Safety research.* Repeat Problem 37 for cars weighing between 2,000 and 2,500 pounds and traveling at speeds between 40 and 50 miles per hour.

39. *Psychology.* The intelligence quotient Q for an individual with mental age x and chronological age y is given by

$$Q(x, y) = 100\frac{x}{y}$$

In a group of sixth graders, the mental age varies between 8 and 16 years and the chronological age varies between 10 and 12 years. What is the average intelligence quotient for this group? Set up a double integral and evaluate.

40. *Psychology.* Repeat Problem 39 for a group with mental ages between 6 and 14 years and chronological ages between 8 and 10 years.

12-7   Chapter Review

Important Terms
and Symbols

12-1 *Functions of several variables.* Functions of two independent variables, functions of several independent variables, surface, paraboloid, saddle point, $z = f(x, y)$, $w = f(x, y, z)$

12-2 *Partial derivatives.* Partial derivative of f with respect to x, partial derivative of f with respect to y, second-order partials,

$$\frac{\partial z}{\partial x}, \quad \frac{\partial z}{\partial y}, \quad f_x(x, y), \quad f_y(x, y), \quad \frac{\partial^2 z}{\partial x^2} = f_{xx}(x, y), \quad \frac{\partial^2 z}{\partial x\, \partial y} = f_{yx}(x, y),$$

$$\frac{\partial^2 z}{\partial y\, \partial x} = f_{xy}(x, y), \quad \frac{\partial^2 z}{\partial y^2} = f_{yy}(x, y)$$

12-3 *Maxima and minima.* Local maximum, local minimum, critical point, second-derivative test

12-4 *Maxima and minima using Lagrange multipliers (optional).* Constraint, Lagrange multiplier, method of Lagrange multipliers for functions of two variables, method of Lagrange multipliers for functions of three variables

12-5 *Method of least squares.* Least squares approximation, linear regression, residual, least squares line, regression line, estimation, approximation

12-6 *Double integrals over rectangular regions.* Double integral, iterated integral, average value over rectangular regions, volume under a surface, $\iint_R f(x, y)\, dA = \int_a^b \left[\int_c^d f(x, y)\, dy \right] dx = \int_c^d \left[\int_a^b f(x, y)\, dx \right] dy$

Exercise 12-7   Chapter Review

Work through all the problems in this chapter review and check your answers in the back of the book. (Answers to all review problems are there.) Where weaknesses show up, review appropriate sections in the text.

A   1. For $f(x, y) = 2{,}000 + 40x + 70y$, find $f(5, 10)$, $f_x(x, y)$, and $f_y(x, y)$.

2. For $z = x^3 y^2$, find $\partial^2 z / \partial x^2$ and $\partial^2 z / \partial x\, \partial y$.

3. Evaluate: $\displaystyle \int (6xy^2 + 4y)\, dy$ 4. Evaluate: $\displaystyle \int (6xy^2 + 4y)\, dx$

5. Evaluate: $\displaystyle \int_0^1 \int_0^1 4xy\, dy\, dx$

B   6. For $f(x, y) = 3x^2 - 2xy + y^2 - 2x + 3y - 7$, find $f(2, 3)$, $f_y(x, y)$, and $f_y(2, 3)$.

7. For $f(x, y) = -4x^2 + 4xy - 3y^2 + 4x + 10y + 81$, find

$$[f_{xx}(2, 3)][f_{yy}(2, 3)] - [f_{xy}(2, 3)]^2$$

x	y
2	12
4	10
6	7
8	3

8. Use the least squares line for the data in the table to estimate y when $x = 10$.

9. For $R = \{(x, y)|-1 \leqslant x \leqslant 1, \ 1 \leqslant y \leqslant 2\}$, evaluate the following two ways:

$$\iint\limits_{R} (4x + 6y) \, dA$$

C 10. For $f(x, y) = e^{x^2 + 2y}$, find f_x, f_y, and f_{xy}.

11. For $f(x, y) = (x^2 + y^2)^5$, find f_x and f_{xy}.

12. Find all critical points and test for extrema for

$$f(x, y) = x^3 - 12x + y^2 - 6y$$

13. Find the least squares line for the data in the table:

x	y	x	y
10	50	60	80
20	45	70	85
30	50	80	90
40	55	90	90
50	65	100	110

14. Find the average value of $f(x, y) = x^{2/3}y^{1/3}$ over the rectangle

$$R = \{(x, y)|-8 \leqslant x \leqslant 8, \quad 0 \leqslant y \leqslant 27\}$$

15. Find the volume of the solid under the graph of

$$z = 3x^2 + 3y^2$$

over the rectangle

$$R = \{(x, y)|0 \leqslant x \leqslant 1, \quad -1 \leqslant y \leqslant 1\}$$

Applications

Business & Economics

16. *Maximizing profit.* A company produces x units of product A and y units of product B (both in hundreds per month). The monthly profit equation (in thousands of dollars) is found to be

$$P(x, y) = -4x^2 + 4xy - 3y^2 + 4x + 10y + 81$$

(A) Find $P_x(1, 3)$ and interpret.

(B) How many of each product should be produced each month to maximize profit? What is the maximum profit?

17. *Minimizing material.* A rectangular box with no top and six compart-ments (see the figure) is to have a volume of 96 cubic inches. Find the dimensions that will require the least amount of material.

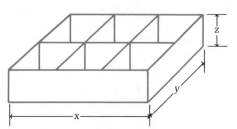

Year	Profit
1	2
2	2.5
3	3.1
4	4.2
5	4.3

18. *Profit.* A company's annual profit (in millions of dollars) over a 5 year period is given in the table. Use the least squares line to estimate the profit for the sixth year.

19. *Economics—Cobb–Douglas production function.* The Cobb–Douglas production function for an industry is

$$N(x, y) = x^{0.8}y^{0.2}$$

where x is the number of labor-hours (in thousands) and y is the amount of money (in millions) invested in the production of N thou-sand units of a certain item. If $10 \le x \le 12$ and $1 \le y \le 3$, find the average number of units produced. Set up a definite integral and evaluate.

Life Sciences

20. *Marine biology.* The function used for timing dives with scuba gear is

$$T(V, x) = \frac{33V}{x + 33}$$

where T is the time of the dive in minutes, V is the volume of air (at sea level pressure) compressed into tanks, and x is the depth of the dive in feet. Find $T_x(70, 17)$ and interpret.

21. *Pollution.* A heavy industrial plant located in the center of a small town emits particulate matter into the atmosphere. Suppose the con-centration of particulate matter in parts per million at a point d miles from the plant is given by

$$C = 100 - 24d^2$$

If the boundaries of the town form a square 4 miles long and 4 miles wide, what is the average concentration of particulate matter throughout the city? Express C as a function of x and y, set up a double integral, and evaluate.

Social Sciences

22. *Sociology.* Joseph Cavanaugh, a sociologist, found that the number of long-distance telephone calls, n, between two cities in a given period of time varied (approximately) jointly as the populations P_1 and P_2 of the two cities, and varied inversely as the distance, d, between the two cities. In terms of an equation for a time period of 1 week,

$$n(P_1, P_2, d) = 0.001 \frac{P_1 P_2}{d}$$

Find $n(100{,}000, 50{,}000, 100)$.

23. *Education.* At the beginning of the semester, students in a foreign language course are given a proficiency exam. The same exam is given at the end of the semester. The results for five students are given in the table. Use the least squares line to estimate the score on the second exam for a student who scored 40 on the first exam.

First Exam	Second Exam
30	60
50	75
60	80
70	85
90	90

Special Topics

A

APPENDIX A   Contents

A-1   Integer Exponents and Square Root Radicals

- Integer Exponents
- Scientific Notation
- Square Root Radicals

■ Integer Exponents

Table 1 lists definitions for **integer exponents.**

Table 1 Definition of a^n

Given: n is an integer and a is a real number

1. For n a positive integer,

   $$a^n = a \cdot a \cdot \cdots \cdot a \qquad n \text{ factors of } a \qquad\qquad 5^4 = 5 \cdot 5 \cdot 5 \cdot 5$$

2. For $n = 0$,

   $$a^0 = 1 \qquad a \neq 0 \qquad\qquad 12^0 = 1$$

   0^0 is not defined.

3. For n a negative integer,

   $$a^n = \frac{1}{a^{-n}} \qquad a \neq 0 \qquad\qquad a^{-3} = \frac{1}{a^{-(-3)}} = \frac{1}{a^3}$$

   [If n is negative, then $(-n)$ is positive.]
   Note: It can be shown that for *all* integers n,

   $$a^{-n} = \frac{1}{a^n} \quad \text{and} \quad a^n = \frac{1}{a^{-n}} \qquad a \neq 0 \qquad a^5 = \frac{1}{a^{-5}}, \ \ a^{-5} = \frac{1}{a^5}$$

Table 2 lists integer exponent properties that are very useful in manipulating integer exponent forms.

Table 2 Exponent Properties

Given: n and m are integers and a and b are real numbers

1. $a^m a^n = a^{m+n}$ $\qquad\qquad\qquad$ $a^8 a^{-3} = a^{8+(-3)} = a^5$
2. $(a^n)^m = a^{mn}$ $\qquad\qquad\qquad\quad$ $(a^{-2})^3 = a^{3(-2)} = a^{-6}$
3. $(ab)^m = a^m b^m$ $\qquad\qquad\qquad$ $(ab)^{-2} = a^{-2} b^{-2}$
4. $\left(\dfrac{a}{b}\right)^m = \dfrac{a^m}{b^m}$ $\quad b \neq 0$ $\qquad\quad$ $\left(\dfrac{a}{b}\right)^5 = \dfrac{a^5}{b^5}$
5. $\dfrac{a^m}{a^n} = a^{m-n} = \dfrac{1}{a^{n-m}}$ $\quad a \neq 0$ $\quad$ $\dfrac{a^{-3}}{a^7} = \dfrac{1}{a^{7-(-3)}} = \dfrac{1}{a^{10}}$

Exponent and radical forms are frequently encountered in algebraic applications. You should sharpen your skills in using these forms by reviewing the basic definitions, properties, and exercises that follow.

Example 1   Simplify and express the answers using positive exponents only.

(A) $(2x^3)(3x^5)$ $\boxed{= 2 \cdot 3x^{3+5}}$ $= 6x^8$ $\qquad$ (B) $x^5 x^{-9} = x^{-4} = \dfrac{1}{x^4}$

(C) $\dfrac{x^5}{x^7}$ $\boxed{= x^{5-7}}$ $= x^{-2} = \dfrac{1}{x^2}$ $\qquad$ (D) $\dfrac{x^{-3}}{y^{-4}} = \dfrac{y^4}{x^3}$

$\qquad$ or $\quad \dfrac{x^5}{x^7}$ $\boxed{= \dfrac{1}{x^{7-5}}}$ $= \dfrac{1}{x^2}$

(E) $(u^{-3}v^2)^{-2}$ $\boxed{= (u^{-3})^{-2}(v^2)^{-2}}$ $= u^6 v^{-4} = \dfrac{u^6}{v^4}$

(F) $\left(\dfrac{y^{-5}}{y^{-2}}\right)^{-2}$ $\boxed{= \dfrac{(y^{-5})^{-2}}{(y^{-2})^{-2}}}$ $= \dfrac{y^{10}}{y^4} = y^6$

(G) $\dfrac{4m^{-3}n^{-5}}{6m^{-4}n^3}$ $\boxed{= \dfrac{2m^{-3-(-4)}}{3n^{3-(-5)}}}$ $= \dfrac{2m}{3n^8}$

(H) $\left(\dfrac{2x^{-3}x^3}{n^{-2}}\right)^{-3} = \left(\dfrac{2x^0}{n^{-2}}\right)^{-3} = \left(\dfrac{2}{n^{-2}}\right)^{-3} = \dfrac{2^{-3}}{n^6} = \dfrac{1}{2^3 n^6} = \dfrac{1}{8n^6}$

Problem 1   Simplify and express the answers using positive exponents only.

(A) $(3y^4)(2y^3)$ $\qquad$ (B) $m^2 m^{-6}$ $\qquad$ (C) $(u^3 v^{-2})^{-2}$

(D) $\left(\dfrac{y^{-6}}{y^{-2}}\right)^{-1}$ $\qquad$ (E) $\dfrac{8x^{-2}y^{-4}}{6x^{-5}y^2}$ $\qquad$ (F) $\left(\dfrac{3m^{-3}}{2x^2 x^{-2}}\right)^{-2}$

■ Scientific Notation

Writing and working with very large or very small numbers in standard decimal notation is often awkward, even with electronic hand calculators. It is often convenient to represent numbers of this type in **scientific notation;** that is, as the product of a number between 1 and 10 and a power of 10.

Example 2

Decimal Fractions and Scientific Notation

$$7 = 7 \times 10^0 \qquad\qquad 0.5 = 5 \times 10^{-1}$$
$$67 = 6.7 \times 10 \qquad\qquad 0.45 = 4.5 \times 10^{-1}$$
$$580 = 5.8 \times 10^2 \qquad\qquad 0.003\ 2 = 3.2 \times 10^{-3}$$
$$43{,}000 = 4.3 \times 10^4 \qquad 0.000\ 045 = 4.5 \times 10^{-5}$$
$$73{,}400{,}000 = 7.34 \times 10^7 \qquad 0.000\ 000\ 391 = 3.91 \times 10^{-7}$$

Note that the power of 10 used corresponds to the number of places we move the decimal to form a number between 1 and 10. The power is positive if the decimal is moved to the left and negative if it is moved to the right. Positive exponents are associated with numbers greater than or equal to 10; negative exponents are associated with positive numbers less than 1.

Problem 2   Write each number in scientific notation.

(A)   370   (B)   47,300,000,000   (C)   0.047   (D)   0.000 000 089

■ Square Root Radicals

To start, we define a **square root** of a number:

Definition of Square Root

x is a square root of y if $x^2 = y$.

2 is a square root of 4 since $2^2 = 4$.

-2 is a square root of 4 since $(-2)^2 = 4$.

How many square roots of a real number are there? The following theorem, which we state without proof, answers the question.

Theorem 1

(A)   Every positive real number has exactly two real square roots, each the negative of the other.

(B)   Negative real numbers have no real number square roots (since no real number squared can be negative — think about this).

(C)   The square root of 0 is 0.

Square Root Notation

For a a positive number.

$\sqrt{a}$ is the positive square root of a.

$-\sqrt{a}$ is the negative square root of a.

[Note: $\sqrt{-a}$ is not a real number.]

Example 3   (A) $\sqrt{4} = 2$ (B) $-\sqrt{4} = -2$
(C) $\sqrt{-4}$ is not a real number.   (D) $\sqrt{0} = 0$

Problem 3   Evaluate, if possible.

(A) $\sqrt{9}$ (B) $-\sqrt{9}$ (C) $\sqrt{-9}$ (D) $\sqrt{0}$

It can be shown that if a is a positive integer that is not the square of an integer, then

$-\sqrt{a}$ and $\sqrt{a}$

are irrational numbers. Thus,

$-\sqrt{7}$ and $\sqrt{7}$

name irrational numbers that are, respectively, the negative and positive square roots of 7.

Properties of Radicals

For a and b nonnegative real numbers.

1. $\sqrt{a^2} = a$
2. $\sqrt{a}\sqrt{b} = \sqrt{ab}$
3. $\dfrac{\sqrt{a}}{\sqrt{b}} = \sqrt{\dfrac{a}{b}}$

To see that property 2 holds, let $N = \sqrt{a}$ and $M = \sqrt{b}$, then $N^2 = a$ and $M^2 = b$. Hence,

$$\sqrt{a}\,\sqrt{b} = NM = \sqrt{(NM)^2} = \sqrt{N^2 M^2} = \sqrt{ab}$$

Note how properties of exponents are used. The proof of the quotient part is left as an exercise.

Example 4

(A) $\sqrt{5}\,\sqrt{10} = \sqrt{5 \cdot 10} = \sqrt{50} = \sqrt{25 \cdot 2} = \sqrt{25}\,\sqrt{2} = 5\sqrt{2}$

(B) $\dfrac{\sqrt{32}}{\sqrt{8}} = \sqrt{\dfrac{32}{8}} = \sqrt{4} = 2$

(C) $\sqrt{\dfrac{7}{4}} = \dfrac{\sqrt{7}}{\sqrt{4}} = \dfrac{\sqrt{7}}{2}$ or $\dfrac{1}{2}\sqrt{7}$

Problem 4

Simplify as in Example 4.

(A) $\sqrt{3}\,\sqrt{6}$ (B) $\dfrac{\sqrt{18}}{\sqrt{2}}$ (C) $\sqrt{\dfrac{11}{9}}$

The foregoing definitions and theorems allow us to change algebraic expressions containing radicals to a variety of equivalent forms. One form that is often useful is called the *simplest radical form*.

Definition of the Simplest Radical Form

An algebraic expression that contains square root radicals is in **simplest radical form** if all three of the following conditions are satisfied:

1. No radicand (the expression within the radical sign) when expressed in completely factored form contains a factor raised to a power greater than 1. ($\sqrt{x^3}$ violates this condition.)

2. No radical appears in a denominator. $\left(\dfrac{3}{\sqrt{5}} \text{ violates this condition.}\right)$

3. No fraction appears within a radical. $\left(\sqrt{\dfrac{2}{3}} \text{ violates this condition.}\right)$

It should be understood that forms other than the simplest radical form may be more useful on occasion. The situation dictates what form to choose.

Example 5

Change to simplest radical form—all variables represent nonnegative real numbers.

(A) $\sqrt{8x^3}$ (B) $\dfrac{3x}{\sqrt{3}}$ (C) $\sqrt{\dfrac{3x}{8}}$

Solutions   (A) $\sqrt{8x^3}$ violates condition 1. Separate $8x^3$ into a perfect square part, (2^2x^2), and what is left over, $(2x)$, then use multiplication property 2.

$$\sqrt{8x^3} = \sqrt{(2^2x^2)(2x)}$$
$$= \sqrt{2^2x^2}\,\sqrt{2x}$$
$$= 2x\sqrt{2x}$$

(B) $3x/\sqrt{3}$ has a radical in the denominator; hence, it violates condition 2. To remove the radical from the denominator, we multiply the numerator and denominator by $\sqrt{3}$ to obtain $\sqrt{3^2}$ in the denominator (this is called **rationalizing a denominator**):

$$\frac{3x}{\sqrt{3}} = \frac{3x}{\sqrt{3}} \cdot \frac{\sqrt{3}}{\sqrt{3}}$$
$$= \frac{3x\sqrt{3}}{\sqrt{3^2}}$$
$$= \frac{3x\sqrt{3}}{3} = x\sqrt{3}$$

(C) $\sqrt{3x/8}$ has a fraction within the radical; hence it violates condition 3. To remove the fraction from the radical, we multiply the numerator and denominator of $3x/8$ by 2 to make the denominator a perfect square:

$$\sqrt{\frac{3x}{8}} = \sqrt{\frac{3x \cdot 2}{8 \cdot 2}}$$
$$= \sqrt{\frac{6x}{16}}$$
$$= \frac{\sqrt{6x}}{\sqrt{16}} = \frac{\sqrt{6x}}{4}$$

Problem 5   Change to simplest radical form. All variables represent positive real numbers.

(A) $\sqrt{18y^3}$ (B) $\dfrac{4xy}{\sqrt{2x}}$ (C) $\sqrt{\dfrac{5y}{18x}}$

Answers to
Matched Problems

1. (A) $6y^7$ (B) $1/m^4$ (C) v^4/u^6
   (D) y^4 (E) $4x^3/3y^6$ (F) $4m^6/9$
2. (A) 3.7×10^2 (B) 4.73×10^{10}
   (C) 4.7×10^{-2} (D) 8.9×10^{-8}
3. (A) 3   (B) -3
   (C) Not a real number   (D) 0
4. (A) $3\sqrt{2}$ (B) 3   (C) $\sqrt{11}/3$ or $\frac{1}{3}\sqrt{11}$
5. (A) $3y\sqrt{2y}$ (B) $2y\sqrt{2x}$ (C) $\dfrac{\sqrt{10xy}}{6x}$ or $\dfrac{1}{6x}\sqrt{10xy}$

Exercise A-1

A *Simplify and express answers using positive exponents only. Variables are restricted to avoid division by zero.*

1. $2x^{-9}$

2. $3y^{-5}$

3. $\dfrac{3}{2w^{-7}}$

4. $\dfrac{5}{4x^{-9}}$

5. $2x^{-8}x^5$

6. $3c^{-9}c^4$

7. $\dfrac{w^{-8}}{w^{-3}}$

8. $\dfrac{m^{-11}}{m^{-5}}$

9. $5v^8v^{-8}$

10. $7d^{-4}d^4$

11. $(a^{-3})^2$

12. $(b^4)^{-3}$

13. $(x^6y^{-3})^{-2}$

14. $(a^{-3}b^4)^{-3}$

Express in simplest radical form. All variables represent positive real numbers.

15. $\sqrt{x^2}$

16. $\sqrt{m^2}$

17. $\sqrt{a^5}$

18. $\sqrt{m^7}$

19. $\sqrt{18x^4}$

20. $\sqrt{8x^3}$

21. $\dfrac{1}{\sqrt{m}}$

22. $\dfrac{1}{\sqrt{A}}$

23. $\sqrt{\dfrac{2}{3}}$

24. $\sqrt{\dfrac{3}{5}}$

25. $\sqrt{\dfrac{2}{x}}$

26. $\sqrt{\dfrac{3}{y}}$

Write in scientific notation.

27. 82,300,000,000

28. 5,380,000

29. 0.783

30. 0.019

31. 0.000 034

32. 0.000 000 007 832

B *Simplify and express answers using positive exponents only.*

33. $(22 + 31)^0$

34. $(2x^3y^4)^0$

35. $\dfrac{10^{-3} \cdot 10^4}{10^{-11} \cdot 10^{-2}}$

36. $\dfrac{10^{-17} \cdot 10^{-5}}{10^{-3} \cdot 10^{-14}}$

37. $(5x^2y^{-3})^{-2}$

38. $(2m^{-3}n^2)^{-3}$

39. $\dfrac{8 \times 10^{-3}}{2 \times 10^{-5}}$

40. $\dfrac{18 \times 10^{12}}{6 \times 10^{-4}}$

41. $\dfrac{8x^{-3}y^{-1}}{6x^2y^{-4}}$

42. $\dfrac{9m^{-4}n^3}{12m^{-1}n^{-1}}$

43. $\left(\dfrac{6xy^{-2}}{3x^{-1}y^2}\right)^{-3}$

44. $\left(\dfrac{2x^{-3}y^2}{4xy^{-1}}\right)^{-2}$

Simplify and express answers in simplest radical form. All variables represent positive real numbers.

45. $\sqrt{18x^8y^5z^2}$

46. $\sqrt{8p^3q^6r^5}$

47. $\dfrac{12}{\sqrt{3x}}$

48. $\dfrac{10}{\sqrt{2y}}$

49. $\sqrt{\dfrac{6x}{7y}}$

50. $\sqrt{\dfrac{3m}{2n}}$

51. $\sqrt{\dfrac{4a^3}{3b}}$

52. $\sqrt{\dfrac{9m^5}{2n}}$

53. $\sqrt{18m^3n^4}\,\sqrt{2m^3n^2}$

54. $\sqrt{10x^3y}\,\sqrt{5xy}$

55. $\dfrac{\sqrt{4a^3}}{\sqrt{3b}}$

56. $\dfrac{\sqrt{9m^5}}{\sqrt{2n}}$

Convert each numeral to scientific notation and simplify. Express the answer in scientific notation and in standard decimal form. (Answers cannot have more significant digits than the number with the least number of significant digits in the problem.)

57. $\dfrac{9,600,000,000}{(1,600,000)(0.000\ 000\ 25)}$

58. $\dfrac{(60,000)(0.000\ 003)}{(0.000\ 4)(1,500,000)}$

59. $\dfrac{(1,250,000)(0.000\ 38)}{0.042\ 3}$

60. $\dfrac{(0.000\ 000\ 82)(230,000)}{(430,000)(0.008\ 2)}$

C *Simplify and write answers using positive exponents only.*

61. $\left[\left(\dfrac{x^{-2}y^3t}{x^{-3}y^{-2}t^2}\right)^2\right]^{-1}$

62. $\left[\left(\dfrac{u^3v^{-1}w^{-2}}{u^{-2}v^{-2}w}\right)^{-2}\right]^2$

63. $\left(\dfrac{2^2x^2y^0}{8x^{-1}}\right)^{-2}\left(\dfrac{x^{-3}}{x^{-5}}\right)^3$

64. $\left(\dfrac{3^3x^0y^{-2}}{2^3x^3y^{-5}}\right)^{-1}\left(\dfrac{3^3x^{-1}y}{2^2x^2y^{-2}}\right)^2$

Express in simplest radical form. All variables are restricted to avoid division by zero and square roots of negative numbers.

65. $\dfrac{\sqrt{2x}\,\sqrt{5}}{\sqrt{20x}}$

66. $\dfrac{\sqrt{x}\,\sqrt{8y}}{\sqrt{12y}}$

67. $\dfrac{2}{\sqrt{x-2}}$

68. $\sqrt{\dfrac{1}{x-5}}$

A-2 Rational Exponents and Radicals

- nth Roots of Real Numbers
- Rational Exponents and Radicals
- Properties of Radicals

A brief review of the material on integer exponents and square root radicals (Section A-1) might prove helpful before beginning this section.

■ nth Roots of Real Numbers

Recall from Section A-1 that r is a **square root** of b if $r^2 = b$. There is no reason to stop there. We may also say that r is a **cube root** of b if $r^3 = b$.

In general:

For any natural number n:

  r is an **nth root** of b if $r^n = b$

How many real square roots of 16 exist? Of 7? Of -4? How many real fourth roots of 7 exist? Of -7? How many real cube roots of -8 exist? Of 11? Theorem 2 (which we state without proof) answers these questions completely.

Theorem 2   Number of Real nth Roots of a Real Number b

	n even	**n odd**
b positive	Two real nth roots	One real nth root
	-2 and 2 are both 4th roots of 16	2 is the only real cube root of 8
b negative	No real nth root	One real nth root
	-4 has no real square roots	-2 is the only real cube root of -8
b zero	One real nth root	One real nth root
	The nth root of 0 is 0 for any natural number n	

On the basis of Theorem 2, we conclude that

   7   has two real square roots, two real 4th roots, and so on.

  10   has one real cube root, one real 5th root, and so on.

-13 has one real cube root, one real 5th root, and so on.

  -8 has no real square roots, no real 4th roots, and so on.

■ Rational Exponents and Radicals

We now turn to the question of what symbols to use to represent the various kinds of real nth roots. For a natural number n greater than 1 we use

  $b^{1/n}$ or $\sqrt[n]{b}$

to represent one of the **real nth roots of b.** Which one? The symbols represent the real nth root of b if n is odd and the positive real nth root of b if b is positive and n is even. The symbol $\sqrt[n]{b}$ is called an **nth root radical.** The number n is the **index** of the radical and the number b is called the **radicand.** Note that we write $\sqrt{b}$ to indicate $\sqrt[2]{b}$.

Example 6   (A) $4^{1/2} = \sqrt{4} = 2$ $(\sqrt{4} \neq \pm 2)$ (B) $-4^{1/2} = -\sqrt{4} = -2$
(C) $(-4)^{1/2}$ and $\sqrt{-4}$ are not real numbers
(D) $8^{1/3} = \sqrt[3]{8} = 2$ (E) $(-8)^{1/3} = \sqrt[3]{-8} = -2$

Problem 6   Evaluate each of the following:

(A) $16^{1/2}$ (B) $-\sqrt{16}$ (C) $\sqrt[3]{-27}$
(D) $(-9)^{1/2}$ (E) $(\sqrt[4]{81})^3$

For m and n natural numbers without common prime factors,* b a real number, and b nonnegative when n is even, we define $b^{m/n}$ as follows (both definitions are equivalent under the indicated restrictions):

$$b^{m/n} = \begin{cases} (b^{1/n})^m = (\sqrt[n]{b})^m \\ (b^m)^{1/n} = (\sqrt[n]{b^m}) \end{cases}$$

Thus,

$$8^{2/3} = (8^{1/3})^2 = 2^2 = 4 \quad \text{or} \quad 8^{2/3} = (8^2)^{1/3} = 64^{1/3} = 4$$

We complete the definition of rational exponents with

$$b^{-m/n} = \frac{1}{b^{m/n}} \quad (b \neq 0)$$

All the properties listed for integer exponents in Section A-1 also hold for rational exponents, provided b is nonnegative when n is even. Unless stated to the contrary, all variables in the rest of the discussion represent positive real numbers.

Example 7   Change rational exponent form to radical form.

(A) $x^{1/7} = \sqrt[7]{x}$

(B) $(3u^2v^3)^{3/5} = \sqrt[5]{(3u^2v^3)^3}$ or $(\sqrt[5]{3u^2v^3})^3$ (The first is usually preferred.)

(C) $y^{-2/3} = \dfrac{1}{y^{2/3}} = \dfrac{1}{\sqrt[3]{y^2}}$ or $\sqrt[3]{y^{-2}}$ or $\sqrt[3]{\dfrac{1}{y^2}}$

* Prime factors will be discussed in detail in Section A-3.

Change radical form to rational exponent form.

(D) $\sqrt[5]{6} = 6^{1/5}$ (E) $-\sqrt[3]{x^2} = -x^{2/3}$

(F) $\sqrt{x^2 + y^2} = (x^2 + y^2)^{1/2}$ Note that $(x^2 + y^2)^{1/2} \neq x + y$. Why?

Problem 7   Convert to radical form.

(A) $u^{1/5}$ (B) $(6x^2y^5)^{2/9}$ (C) $(3xy)^{-3/5}$

Convert to rational exponent form.

(D) $\sqrt[4]{9u}$ (E) $-\sqrt[7]{(2x)^4}$ (F) $\sqrt[3]{x^3 + y^3}$

Example 8   Simplify each and express answers using positive exponents only. If rational exponents appear in final answers, convert to radical form.

(A) $(3x^{1/3})(2x^{1/2}) = 6x^{1/3+1/2} = 6x^{5/6} = 6\sqrt[6]{x^5}$

(B) $(-8)^{5/3} = [(-8)^{1/3}]^5 = (-2)^5 = -32$

(C) $(2x^{1/3}y^{-2/3})^3 = 8xy^{-2} = \dfrac{8x}{y^2}$

(D) $\left(\dfrac{4x^{1/3}}{x^{1/2}}\right)^{1/2} = \dfrac{4^{1/2}x^{1/6}}{x^{1/4}} = \dfrac{2}{x^{1/4-1/6}} = \dfrac{2}{x^{1/12}} = \dfrac{2}{\sqrt[12]{x}}$

Problem 8   Simplify each and express answers using positive exponents only. If rational exponents appear in final answers, convert to radical form.

(A) $9^{3/2}$ (B) $(-27)^{4/3}$ (C) $(5y^{1/4})(2y^{1/3})$

(D) $(2x^{-3/4}y^{1/4})^4$ (E) $\left(\dfrac{8x^{1/2}}{x^{2/3}}\right)^{1/3}$

■ Properties of Radicals

Changing or simplifying radical expressions is aided by the introduction of several properties of radicals that follow directly from properties of exponents considered earlier.

Properties of Radicals

If c, n, and m are natural numbers greater than or equal to 2, and if x and y are positive real numbers, then

1. $\sqrt[n]{x^n} = x$ $\sqrt[3]{x^3} = x$

2. $\sqrt[n]{xy} = \sqrt[n]{x}\,\sqrt[n]{y}$ $\sqrt[5]{xy} = \sqrt[5]{x}\,\sqrt[5]{y}$

3. $\sqrt[n]{\dfrac{x}{y}} = \dfrac{\sqrt[n]{x}}{\sqrt[n]{y}}$ $\sqrt[4]{\dfrac{x}{y}} = \dfrac{\sqrt[4]{x}}{\sqrt[4]{y}}$

4. $\sqrt[cn]{x^{cm}} = \sqrt[n]{x^m}$ $\sqrt[12]{x^8} = \sqrt[4\cdot3]{x^{4\cdot2}} = \sqrt[3]{x^2}$

The properties of radicals provide us with the means of changing algebraic expressions containing radicals into a variety of equivalent forms. One particularly useful form is the simplest radical form. An algebraic expression that contains radicals is said to be in the **simplest radical form** if all four of the following conditions are satisfied:

Simplest Radical Form

1. A radicand contains no factor to a power greater than or equal to the index of the radical.

   $\sqrt[3]{x^5}$ violates this condition.

2. The power of the radicand and the index of the radical have no common factor other than 1.

   $\sqrt[6]{x^4}$ violates this condition.

3. No radical appears in a denominator.

   $y/\sqrt[3]{x}$ violates this condition.

4. No fraction appears within a radical.

   $\sqrt[4]{\dfrac{3}{5}}$ violates this condition.

Example 9   Write in simplest radical form.

(A) $\sqrt[3]{x^3y^6} = \sqrt[3]{(xy^2)^3} = xy^2$

   or $\sqrt[3]{x^3y^6} = (x^3y^6)^{1/3} \;\boxed{= x^{3/3}y^{6/3}}\; = xy^2$

(B) $\sqrt[3]{32x^8y^3} = \sqrt[3]{(2^3x^6y^3)(4x^2)} \;\boxed{= \sqrt[3]{2^3x^6y^3}\,\sqrt[3]{4x^2}}$

   $\qquad\qquad = 2x^2y\sqrt[3]{4x^2}$

(C) $\dfrac{6x^2}{\sqrt[3]{9x}} = \dfrac{6x^2}{\sqrt[3]{9x}} \cdot \dfrac{\sqrt[3]{3x^2}}{\sqrt[3]{3x^2}} \;\boxed{= \dfrac{6x^2\sqrt[3]{3x^2}}{\sqrt[3]{3^3x^3}}}$

   $\qquad = \dfrac{6x^2\sqrt[3]{3x^2}}{3x} = 2x\sqrt[3]{3x^2}$

(D) $6\sqrt[4]{\dfrac{3}{4x^3}} = 6\sqrt[4]{\dfrac{3}{2^2x^3} \cdot \dfrac{2^2x}{2^2x}} = 6\sqrt[4]{\dfrac{12x}{2^4x^4}}$

   $\qquad\qquad \boxed{= 6\,\dfrac{\sqrt[4]{12x}}{\sqrt[4]{2^4x^4}}} = 6\,\dfrac{\sqrt[4]{12x}}{2x} = \dfrac{3\sqrt[4]{12x}}{x}$

(E) $\sqrt[6]{16x^4y^2} = \sqrt[6]{(4x^2y)^2}$
$$= \sqrt[2\cdot 3]{(4x^2y)^{2\cdot 1}}$$
$$= \sqrt[3]{4x^2y}$$

Note that in Examples 9C and 9D, we **rationalized the denominators;** that is, we performed operations to remove radicals from the denominators. This is a useful operation in some problems.

Problem 9   Write in simplest radical form.

(A) $\sqrt{12x^5y^6}$ (B) $\sqrt[3]{-27x^7y^5}$ (C) $\dfrac{8y^3}{\sqrt[4]{2y}}$

(D) $4x^2\sqrt[5]{\dfrac{y^2}{2x^3}}$ (E) $\sqrt[9]{8x^6y^3}$

Answers to
Matched Problems

6. (A) 4   (B) -4 (C) -3 (D) Not a real number
 (E) 27
7. (A) $\sqrt[5]{u}$ (B) $\sqrt[9]{(6x^2y^5)^2}$ or $(\sqrt[9]{6x^2y^5})^2$ (C) $1/\sqrt[5]{(3xy)^3}$
 (D) $(9u)^{1/4}$ (E) $-(2x)^{4/7}$ (F) $(x^3+y^3)^{1/3}$ (not $x+y$)
8. (A) 27   (B) 81   (C) $10y^{7/12} = 10\sqrt[12]{y^7}$ (D) $16y/x^3$
 (E) $2/x^{1/18} = 2/\sqrt[18]{x}$
9. (A) $2x^2y^3\sqrt{3x}$ (B) $-3x^2y\sqrt[3]{xy^2}$ (C) $4y^2\sqrt[4]{8y^3}$
 (D) $2x\sqrt[5]{16x^2y^2}$ (E) $\sqrt[3]{2x^2y}$

Exercise A-2

A   *Change to radical form; do not simplify.*

1. $6x^{3/5}$ 2. $7y^{2/5}$ 3. $(4xy^3)^{2/5}$
4. $(7x^2y)^{5/7}$ 5. $(x^2+y^2)^{1/2}$ 6. $x^{1/2}+y^{1/2}$

Change to rational exponent form; do not simplify.

7. $5\sqrt[4]{x^3}$ 8. $7m\sqrt[5]{n^2}$ 9. $\sqrt[5]{(2x^2y)^3}$
10. $\sqrt[9]{(3m^4n)^2}$ 11. $\sqrt[3]{x}+\sqrt[3]{y}$ 12. $\sqrt[3]{x^2+y^3}$

Find rational number representations for each if they exist.

13. $25^{1/2}$ 14. $64^{1/3}$ 15. $16^{3/2}$
16. $16^{3/4}$ 17. $-36^{1/2}$ 18. $-32^{3/5}$
19. $(-36)^{1/2}$ 20. $(-32)^{3/5}$ 21. $(\frac{4}{25})^{3/2}$
22. $(\frac{8}{27})^{2/3}$ 23. $9^{-3/2}$ 24. $8^{-2/3}$

Simplify each expression and write answer using positive exponents only. All variables represent positive real numbers.

25. $x^{4/5}x^{-2/5}$

26. $y^{-3/7}y^{4/7}$

27. $\dfrac{m^{2/3}}{m^{-1/3}}$

28. $\dfrac{x^{1/4}}{x^{3/4}}$

29. $(8x^3y^{-6})^{1/3}$

30. $(4u^{-2}v^4)^{1/2}$

B   **31.** $\left(\dfrac{4x^{-2}}{y^4}\right)^{-1/2}$

32. $\left(\dfrac{w^4}{9x^{-2}}\right)^{-1/2}$

33. $\dfrac{8x^{-1/3}}{12x^{1/4}}$

34. $\dfrac{6a^{3/4}}{15a^{-1/3}}$

35. $\left(\dfrac{8x^{-4}y^3}{27x^2y^{-3}}\right)^{1/3}$

36. $\left(\dfrac{25x^5y^{-1}}{16x^{-3}y^{-5}}\right)^{1/2}$

Write in simplest radical form.

37. $\sqrt[3]{16m^4n^6}$

38. $\sqrt[3]{27x^7y^3}$

39. $\sqrt[4]{32m^9n^7}$

40. $\sqrt[5]{64u^{17}v^9}$

41. $\dfrac{x}{\sqrt[3]{x}}$

42. $\dfrac{u^2}{\sqrt[3]{u^2}}$

43. $\dfrac{4a^3b^2}{\sqrt[3]{2ab^2}}$

44. $\dfrac{8x^3y^5}{\sqrt[3]{4x^2y}}$

45. $\sqrt[4]{\dfrac{3x^3}{4}}$

46. $\sqrt[5]{\dfrac{3x^2}{2}}$

47. $\sqrt[12]{(x-3)^9}$

48. $\sqrt[8]{(t+1)^6}$

C   **49.** $\sqrt{x}\,\sqrt[3]{x^2}$

50. $\sqrt[3]{x}\,\sqrt{x}$

51. $\dfrac{\sqrt{x}}{\sqrt[3]{x^2}}$

52. $\dfrac{\sqrt{x}}{\sqrt[3]{x}}$

A-3   Algebraic Expressions: Basic Operations

- Algebraic Expressions and Polynomials
- Addition and Subtraction
- Multiplication
- Factoring

■ Algebraic Expressions and Polynomials

Algebraic expressions are formed by using constants and variables* with the algebraic operations of addition, subtraction, multiplication, division,

---

* A **constant** is any symbol that is used to represent exactly one real number. For example, 4, $\sqrt{2}$, and π are all constants. A **variable** is a symbol used as a placeholder for any number in a given set of real numbers. This set is called the **replacement set** for the variable.

and the taking of roots. The following are examples of algebraic expressions:

$$\sqrt[3]{x^3 - 2x + 1} \qquad \frac{x - 5}{x^2 + 2x - 5} \qquad (3x^{-5} - 2x^{-3})^{2/3}$$

An algebraic expression that involves only the operations of addition, subtraction, and multiplication on variables and constants (such as $x^3 - 2x^2 + 5x - 1$) is called a **polynomial.** In general,

---

Polynomial in x

A **polynomial in x** is an algebraic expression of the form

$$a_n x^n + a_{n-1} x^{n-1} + \cdots + a_1 x + a_0$$

where the coefficients $a_0, a_1, \ldots, a_n$ are real numbers and n is a nonnegative integer.

Of course, we may consider polynomials in more than one variable. A polynomial in the two variables x and y is an algebraic expression formed by adding terms of the form $ax^m y^n$, where a is a real number and m and n are nonnegative integers. For example,

$$3x^3 - \sqrt{2}x^2 y + xy - \frac{1}{2} xy^2 + y^3 + 2x - 3$$

is a polynomial in two variables. Polynomials in three or more variables are defined in a similar way.

Polynomial forms are encountered frequently in mathematics, and it is useful to classify them according to their degree. If a term in a polynomial has only one variable as a factor, then the **degree of that term** is the power of the variable. If a term has two or more variables as factors, then the **degree of the term** is the sum of the powers of the variables. The **degree of a polynomial** is the degree of the nonzero term with the highest degree in the polynomial. Any nonzero constant is defined to be a **polynomial of degree 0.** The number 0 is also a polynomial, but is not assigned a degree.

Example 10   (A)   Polynomials in one variable:

$$x^2 - 3x + 2 \qquad 6x^3 - \sqrt{2}x - \frac{1}{3}$$

(B)   Polynomials in several variables:

$$3x^2 - 2xy + y^2 \qquad 4x^3 y^2 - \sqrt{3}xy^2 z^5$$

(C)   Nonpolynomials:

$$\sqrt{2x} - \frac{3}{x} + 5 \qquad \frac{x^2 - 3x + 2}{x - 3} \qquad \sqrt{x^2 - 3x + 1}$$

(D)   The degree of the first term in $6x^3 - \sqrt{2}x - \frac{1}{3}$ is 3; the second term, 1; the third term, 0; and the whole polynomial, 3.

(E)   The degree of the first term in $4x^3y^2 - \sqrt{3}xy^2$ is 5; the second, 3; and the whole polynomial, 5.

Problem 10   (A)   Which of the following are polynomials?

$$3x^2 - 2x + 1 \qquad \sqrt{x - 3} \qquad x^2 - 2xy + y^2 \qquad \frac{x - 1}{x^2 + 2}$$

(B)   Given the polynomial $3x^5 - 6x^3 + 5$, what is the degree of the first term? The second term? The whole polynomial?

(C)   Given the polynomial $6x^4y^2 - 3xy^3$, what is the degree of the first term? The second term? The whole polynomial?

The rules behind manipulating algebraic expressions have their basis in the operational properties of real numbers. We list a few of these properties here for ready reference. Let R be the set of real numbers and let x, y, z be arbitrary elements of R; then

Commutative Properties

$$x + y = y + x$$
$$xy = yx$$

Associative Properties

$$(x + y) + z = x + (y + z)$$
$$(xy)z = x(yz)$$

Distributive Properties

$$x(y + z) = xy + xz$$
$$(y + z)x = yx + zx$$

Subtraction

$$x - y = x + (-y)$$

These properties are either used or assumed almost any time you work with algebraic expressions.

■ Addition and Subtraction

Example 11   (A)   Add $5x^3 - 2x^2 + x - 3$ and $7x^3 + 5x^2 + 9$.

(B)   Subtract $5x^3 - 2x^2 + x - 3$ from $7x^3 + 5x^2 + 9$.

Solutions   (A) $(5x^3 - 2x^2 + x - 3) + (7x^3 + 5x^2 + 9)$

$$= 1(5x^3 - 2x^2 + x - 3) + 1(7x^3 + 5x^2 + 9)$$

$$= 5x^3 - 2x^2 + x - 3 + 7x^3 + 5x^2 + 9$$

$$= 5x^3 + 7x^3 + 5x^2 - 2x^2 + x + 6$$
$$= (5 + 7)x^3 + (5 - 2)x^2 + x + 6$$

$$= 12x^3 + 3x^2 + x + 6$$

(B) $(7x^3 + 5x^2 + 9) - (5x^3 - 2x^2 + x - 3)$

$$= 1(7x^3 + 5x^2 + 9) + (-1)(5x^3 - 2x^2 + x - 3)$$

$$= 7x^3 + 5x^2 + 9 - 5x^3 + 2x^2 - x + 3$$

$$= 7x^3 - 5x^3 + 5x^2 + 2x^2 - x + 12$$
$$= (7 - 5)x^3 + (5 + 2)x^2 - x + 12$$

$$= 2x^3 + 7x^2 - x + 12$$

Problem 11 Given the polynomials $x^3 - 7x + 2$ and $4x^3 - x^2 + x - 1$.

(A) Add the two polynomials.
(B) Subtract the first polynomial from the second.

Example 12 (A) Add $3\sqrt{x} + 5\sqrt{y} + 2$ and $\sqrt{x} + \sqrt[3]{y} - 4$.
(B) Subtract $4x^{2/3} - x^{1/3} + 2$ from $3x^{2/3} + 2x^{1/3} - 8$.

Solutions (A) $(3\sqrt{x} + 5\sqrt{y} + 2) + (\sqrt{x} + \sqrt[3]{y} - 4)$ These are not
$$= 3\sqrt{x} + 5\sqrt{y} + 2 + \sqrt{x} + \sqrt[3]{y} - 4$$ polynomials.

$$= 3\sqrt{x} + \sqrt{x} + 5\sqrt{y} + \sqrt[3]{y} - 2$$
$$= (3 + 1)\sqrt{x} + 5\sqrt{y} + \sqrt[3]{y} - 2$$

$$= 4\sqrt{x} + 5\sqrt{y} + \sqrt[3]{y} - 2$$

(B) $(3x^{2/3} + 2x^{1/3} - 8) - (4x^{2/3} - x^{1/3} + 2)$ These are not
$$= 3x^{2/3} + 2x^{1/3} - 8 - 4x^{2/3} + x^{1/3} - 2$$ polynomials.

$$= 3x^{2/3} - 4x^{2/3} + 2x^{1/3} + x^{1/3} - 10$$
$$= (3 - 4)x^{2/3} + (2 + 1)x^{1/3} - 10$$

$$= -x^{2/3} + 3x^{1/3} - 10$$

Problem 12 (A) Add $(2\sqrt[4]{m} + 3\sqrt{pq} - 3)$ and $(\sqrt[3]{m} - \sqrt{pq} + 5)$.
(B) Subtract the first algebraic expression from the second in part A.

■ Multiplication

Multiplication of algebraic expressions requires extensive use of the properties for real numbers, especially the distributive properties.

Example 13 Multiply $(2x - 3)(3x^2 - 2x + 3)$.

Solution $(2x - 3)(3x^2 - 2x + 3)$ or $3x^2 - 2x + 3$

$$= 2x(3x^2 - 2x + 3) - 3(3x^2 - 2x + 3)$$

$$= 6x^3 - 4x^2 + 6x - 9x^2 + 6x - 9$$

$$= 6x^3 - 13x^2 + 12x - 9$$

$$\frac{2x - 3}{6x^3 - 4x^2 + 6x}$$
$$\frac{- 9x^2 + 6x - 9}{6x^3 - 13x^2 + 12x - 9}$$

Problem 13   Multiply $(2x - 3)(2x^2 + 3x - 2)$.

Certain types of products occur so frequently it is useful to note the following formulas for them:

Special Products

$$(ax + b)(cx + d) = acx^2 + (ad + bc)x + bd$$

$$(a - b)(a + b) = a^2 - b^2$$

$$(a + b)^2 = a^2 + 2ab + b^2$$

$$(a - b)^2 = a^2 - 2ab + b^2$$

Example 14   (A) $(2x - 3y)(5x + 2y) = 10x^2 - 11xy - 6y^2$

(B) $(\sqrt{2} - \sqrt{3})(\sqrt{2} + \sqrt{3}) = (\sqrt{2})^2 - (\sqrt{3})^2$

$$= 2 - 3 = -1$$

(C) $(3x^{1/2} - 2y^{1/2})^2 = 9x - 12x^{1/2}y^{1/2} + 4y$

(D) $(3\sqrt{x} + 2\sqrt{y})(2\sqrt{x} - \sqrt{y}) = 6x + \sqrt{xy} - 2y$

Problem 14   Multiply and simplify.

(A) $(5u + 3v)(4u - v)$ (B) $(\sqrt{x} - \sqrt{y})(\sqrt{x} + \sqrt{y})$

(C) $(2^{1/2} - 3^{1/2})^2$ (D) $(4\sqrt{a} - \sqrt{b})(3\sqrt{a} + 2\sqrt{b})$

■ Factoring

If a number is written as the product of other numbers, then each number in the product is called a **factor** of the original number. Similarly, if an algebraic expression is written as the product of other algebraic expressions, then each algebraic expression in the product is called a **factor** of the original algebraic expression. For example,

$30 = 2 \cdot 3 \cdot 5$ 2, 3, and 5 are factors of 30

$x^2 - 4 = (x - 2)(x + 2)$ $(x - 2)$ and $(x + 2)$ are factors of $x^2 - 4$

The process of writing a number or algebraic expression as the product of other numbers or algebraic expressions is called **factoring.** We start our discussion of factoring with the positive integers.

An integer such as 30 can be represented in a factored form in many ways. The products

$$6 \cdot 5 \qquad (\tfrac{1}{2})(10)(6) \qquad 15 \cdot 2 \qquad \sqrt{15} \cdot \sqrt{60} \qquad 2 \cdot 3 \cdot 5$$

all yield 30. A particularly useful way of factoring positive integers greater than 1 is in terms of prime numbers.

Prime and Composite Numbers

A positive integer greater than 1 is **prime** if its only positive integer factors are itself and 1. A positive integer greater than 1 that is not prime is called a **composite** number. The integer 1 is neither prime nor composite.

Prime numbers: 2, 3, 5, 7, 11, 13, . . .
Composite numbers: 4, 6, 8, 9, 10, 12, . . .

A composite integer greater than 1 is said to be **factored completely** if it is represented as a product of prime factors. The only factoring of 30 that meets this condition is $30 = 2 \cdot 3 \cdot 5$.

Example 15   Write 60 in a completely factored form.

Solution
$$60 = 6 \cdot 10 = 2 \cdot 3 \cdot 2 \cdot 5 = 2^2 \cdot 3 \cdot 5$$

or $\quad 60 = 5 \cdot 12 = 5 \cdot 4 \cdot 3 = 2^2 \cdot 3 \cdot 5$

or $\quad 60 = 2 \cdot 30 = 2 \cdot 2 \cdot 15 = 2^2 \cdot 3 \cdot 5$

Notice in Example 15 that we obtain the same prime factors for 60, regardless of how we progress through the factoring process. This illustrates the following basic property of integers:

Fundamental Theorem of Arithmetic

Each positive integer greater than 1 is either prime or has, except for the order of factors, a unique set of prime factors.

Problem 15   Write 180 in a completely factored form.

We can also talk about writing polynomials in a completely factored form. The following polynomials are written in a factored form:

$$x^2 - 9 = (x - 3)(x + 3)$$

$$2x^3 - 4x = 2x(x - \sqrt{2})(x + \sqrt{2})$$

$$2x^4 - 15x^2 - 27 = (x^2 - 9)(2x^2 + 3)$$

$$x^2 + 3x + \frac{9}{4} = \left(x + \frac{3}{2}\right)^2$$

But which are in a completely factored form? Paralleling our discussion with prime numbers, we define a **prime polynomial** as follows:

Prime Polynomials

A polynomial is said to be **prime** relative to a given set of numbers if:

1. It has coefficients from that set.
2. It cannot be written as a product of two polynomials of positive degree having coefficients from that set.

For example, $x^2 - 2$ is a prime polynomial relative to the integers, but is not prime relative to the real numbers [since $x^2 - 2 = (x - \sqrt{2})(x + \sqrt{2})$]. A nonprime polynomial is said to be **factored completely** relative to a given set of numbers if it is represented as a product of prime polynomials relative to that set of numbers.

Writing polynomials in a completely factored form is often a difficult task. But accomplishing it can lead to the simplification of certain algebraic expressions and to solutions of certain types of equations.

Example 16   Take out all factors common to all terms.

(A) $2x^3y - 8x^2y^2 - 6xy^3$ (B) $2x(3x - 2) - 7(3x - 2)$

Solutions   (A) $2x^3y - 8x^2y^2 - 6xy^3$ $= (2xy)x^2 - (2xy)4xy - (2xy)3y^2$

$= (2xy)(x^2 - 4xy - 3y^2)$

(B) $2x(3x - 2) - 7(3x - 2)$ $= 2x(3x - 2) - 7(3x - 2)$

$= (2x - 7)(3x - 2)$

Problem 16   Take out all factors common to all terms.

(A) $3x^3y - 6x^2y^2 - 3xy^3$ (B) $3y(2y + 5) + 2(2y + 5)$

The factoring formulas given in the box show us how to factor certain polynomial forms that occur often.

Special Factoring Formulas

1. $u^2 + (a + b)u + ab = (u + a)(u + b)$
2. $acu^2 + (ad + bc)u + bd = (au + b)(cu + d)$
3. $a^2u^2 + 2abuv + b^2v^2 = (au + bv)^2$ Perfect square
4. $u^2 - v^2 = (u - v)(u + v)$ Difference of two squares
5. $u^3 - v^3 = (u - v)(u^2 + uv + v^2)$ Difference of two cubes
6. $u^3 + v^3 = (u + v)(u^2 - uv + v^2)$ Sum of two cubes

These formulas can be established by multiplying the factors on the right.

Example 17   Factor completely in the integers.

(A) $x^2 - 5x - 6$ (B) $6x^2 - 5x - 4$ (C) $x^2 + 6xy + 9y^2$
(D) $9x^2 - 4y^2$ (E) $8m^3 - 1$ (F) $x^3 + y^3z^3$

Solutions   (A) $x^2 - 5x - 6 = (x - 6)(x + 1)$
(B) $6x^2 - 5x - 4 = (3x - 4)(2x + 1)$
(C) $x^2 + 6xy + 9y^2 = (x + 3y)^2$
(D) $9x^2 - 4y^2 = (3x - 2y)(3x + 2y)$

(E) $8m^3 - 1 = (2m)^3 - 1^3$

$= (2m - 1)[(2m)^2 + (2m)(1) + 1^2]$

$= (2m - 1)(4m^2 + 2m + 1)$

(F) $x^3 + y^3z^3 = x^3 + (yz)^3$

$= (x + yz)(x^2 - xyz + y^2z^2)$

Problem 17   Factor completely in the integers.

(A) $x^2 + 7x - 8$ (B) $4m^2 - 4mn - 3n^2$ (C) $4m^2 - 12mn + 9n^2$
(D) $x^2 - 16y^2$ (E) $z^3 - 1$ (F) $m^3 + n^3$

We now complete this section by considering factoring that involves combinations of the techniques discussed previously. Generally speaking, *when factoring a polynomial, we first take out all factors common to all terms (if any are present), then apply the special factoring formulas until all factors are prime.*

Example 18   Factor completely relative to the integers.

     (A) $18x^3 - 8x$ (B) $3x^4y^2 + 12x^2y^4$ (C) $4m^3n - 2m^2n^2 + 2mn^3$

     (D) $2t^4 - 16t$ (E) $2y^4 - 5y^2 - 12$

Solutions   (A) $18x^3 - 8x = 2x(9x^2 - 4)$

$$= 2x(3x - 2)(3x + 2)$$

     (B) $3x^4y^2 + 12x^2y^4$ $(x^2 + 4y^2)$ is prime relative

$$= 3x^2y^2(x^2 + 4y^2) \qquad \text{to the integers.}$$

     (C) $4m^3n - 2m^2n^2 + 2mn^3 = 2mn(2m^2 - mn + n^2)$

     (D) $2t^4 - 16t = 2t(t^3 - 8)$

$$= 2t(t - 2)(t^2 + 2t + 4)$$

     (E) $2y^4 - 5y^2 - 12 = (2y^2 + 3)(y^2 - 4)$

$$= (2y^2 + 3)(y - 2)(y + 2)$$

Problem 18   Factor completely relative to the integers.

     (A) $3x^3 - 48x$ (B) $18m^2n + 2mn^3$ (C) $3u^4 - 3u^3v - 9u^2v^2$

     (D) $3m^4 - 24mn^3$ (E) $3x^4 - 5x^2 + 2$

Remark: It should be noted that if one writes down a polynomial with random integer coefficients, then the resulting polynomial is more likely to be prime than not prime; that is, it most likely will not have polynomial factors of positive degree relative to the integers. But if it does, the results may be very useful, as we pointed out earlier.

Answers to Matched Problems

10. (A) $3x^2 - 2x + 1$, $x^2 - 2xy + y^2$ (B)   5, 3, 5   (C)   6, 4, 6
11. (A) $5x^3 - x^2 - 6x + 1$ (B) $3x^3 - x^2 + 8x - 3$
12. (A) $2\sqrt[4]{m} + \sqrt[3]{m} + 2\sqrt{pq} + 2$ (B) $-2\sqrt[4]{m} + \sqrt[3]{m} - 4\sqrt{pq} + 8$
13. $4x^3 - 13x + 6$
14. (A) $20u^2 + 7uv - 3v^2$ (B) $x - y$
     (C) $5 - 2 \cdot 2^{1/2} \cdot 3^{1/2}$ or $5 - 2(6)^{1/2}$
     (D) $12a + 5\sqrt{ab} - 2b$
15. $2^2 \cdot 3^2 \cdot 5$
16. (A) $3xy(x^2 - 2xy - y^2)$ (B) $(3y + 2)(2y + 5)$
17. (A) $(x + 8)(x - 1)$ (B) $(2m - 3n)(2m + n)$ (C) $(2m - 3n)^2$
     (D) $(x - 4y)(x + 4y)$ (E) $(z - 1)(z^2 + z + 1)$
     (F) $(m + n)(m^2 - mn + n^2)$
18. (A) $3x(x - 4)(x + 4)$ (B) $2mn(9m^2 + n^2)$
     (C) $3u^2(u^2 - uv - 3v^2)$ (D) $3m(m - 2n)(m^2 + 2mn + 4n^2)$
     (E) $(3x^2 - 2)(x - 1)(x + 1)$

Exercise A-3

Unless stated to the contrary, express all answers with positive exponents.

A *Consider the polynomials* $2x^3 - 3x^2 + x + 5$, $2x^2 + x - 1$, *and* $3x - 2$.

1. What is the degree of the first polynomial?
2. What is the degree of the second?
3. Add the first and second polynomials.
4. Add the second and third.
5. Subtract the second polynomial from the first.
6. Subtract the third from the second.
7. Multiply the first and third polynomials.
8. Multiply the second and third.

In Problems 9–18, perform the indicated operations and simplify.

9. $2(x - 3) - (4x + 5)$
10. $4(w + 1) - (2w - 3)$
11. $4m - 3[4 - 2(m - 1)]$
12. $3y - 2[6 - 3(y + 2)]$
13. $(4a - b)(2a + b)$
14. $(3m + 2n)(2m - 3n)$
15. $(3x - 2y)(3x + 2y)$
16. $(4m + 3n)(4m - 3n)$
17. $(4x - y)^2$
18. $(3u + 4v)^2$

Factor completely relative to the integers. Specify which polynomials are already prime (relative to the integers).

19. $x^2 - 9x + 14$
20. $y^2 + 7y + 12$
21. $w^2 + 3w - 40$
22. $x^2 - 4x - 21$
23. $2x^2 + 5x - 3$
24. $3y^2 - y - 2$
25. $x^2 - 4xy - 12y^2$
26. $u^2 - 2uv - 15v^2$
27. $x^2 + x - 4$
28. $m^2 - 6m - 3$
29. $A^2 - 36B^2$
30. $9m^2 - 1$
31. $25m^2 - 16n^2$
32. $w^2x^2 - y^2$
33. $x^2 + 10xy + 25y^2$
34. $9m^2 - 6mn + n^2$
35. $u^2 + 81$
36. $y^2 + 16$
37. $6x^2 + 48x + 72$
38. $4z^2 - 28z + 48$

B *In Problems 39–62, perform the indicated operations and simplify. All variables involved with radicals or fractional exponents represent positive real numbers.*

39. $2x(x - 3y) - y(x + 2y)$
40. $3u(2u + v) - v(u - 3v)$
41. $2\{x + 2[x - (x + 5)] + 1\}$
42. $u - \{u - [u - (u - 1)]\}$
43. $2(x - 2y)(x + y)$
44. $3(u + 3v)(u - v)$
45. $(a + b)(a^2 - ab + b^2)$
46. $(a - b)(a^2 + ab + b^2)$
47. $(2x^2 + x - 2)(x^2 - 3x + 5)$
48. $(x^2 - 2xy + y^2)(x^2 + 2xy + y^2)$
49. $(2x - 1)^2 - (3x + 2)(3x - 2)$
50. $(3a - b)(3a + b) - (2a - 3b)^2$

51. $(2m - n)^3$
52. $(x - 2y)^3$
53. $\sqrt{x}(\sqrt{x} - 3)$
54. $\sqrt{w}(5 - \sqrt{w})$
55. $(\sqrt{m} + 2)(\sqrt{m} - 2)$
56. $(4 - \sqrt{y})(4 + \sqrt{y})$
57. $(\sqrt{c} - \sqrt{d})(\sqrt{c} + \sqrt{d})$
58. $(x^{1/2} + y^{1/2})(x^{1/2} - y^{1/2})$
59. $(x^{1/2} + y^{1/2})^2$
60. $(\sqrt{y} + \sqrt{z})^2$
61. $(2x^{1/2} + 3)(x^{1/2} - 5)$
62. $(3u^{1/2} - 2)(2u^{1/2} + 4)$

In Problems 63–78, factor completely relative to the integers. Specify which polynomials are already prime (relative to the integers).

63. $2x^2 - 7xy + 6y^2$
64. $3x^2 - 11xy + 6y^2$
65. $3m^2 + 17m - 6$
66. $5z^2 - 18z - 8$
67. $2y^3 - 22y^2 + 48y$
68. $2x^4 - 24x^3 + 40x^2$
69. $6s^2 + 7st - 3t^2$
70. $6m^2 - mn - 12n^2$
71. $x^3y - 9xy^3$
72. $4u^3v - uv^3$
73. $m^3 + n^3$
74. $r^3 - t^3$
75. $3x^2 - 2xy - 4y^2$
76. $5u^2 + 4uv - 2v^2$
77. $m^4 - n^4$
78. $y^4 - 3y^2 - 4$

C *In Problems 79–84, perform the indicated operations and simplify. All variables represent positive real numbers.*

79. $2\sqrt[3]{a} + 3\sqrt[3]{a} - \sqrt[4]{a}$
80. $4\sqrt[3]{y} - \sqrt[3]{y} + 2\sqrt{y}$
81. $2x^{1/2}(3x^{2/3} - x^6)$
82. $3m^{3/4}(4m^{1/4} - 2m^8)$
83. $(\sqrt{x + h} - \sqrt{x})(\sqrt{x + h} + \sqrt{x})$
84. $[(u + k)^{1/2} - u^{1/2}][(u + k)^{1/2} + u^{1/2}]$

A-4 Algebraic Fractions

- Fundamental Principle of Fractions
- Multiplication and Division
- Addition and Subtraction

Algebraic fractions represent quotients, and for those replacements of the variables by real numbers that result in the quotient of real numbers (division by 0 excluded), the properties of real fractions apply. We will review the use of these properties in this section. Note the following:

1. $\dfrac{1}{x}$, $\dfrac{1}{\sqrt{x}}$, and $\dfrac{x - 1}{x^{2/3}}$ are undefined for $x = 0$

2. $\dfrac{1}{x - 3}$, $\dfrac{1}{\sqrt{x - 3}}$, and $\dfrac{x - 1}{(x - 3)^{2/3}}$ are undefined for $x = 3$

3. $\dfrac{u - 1}{u^2 + u - 2} = \dfrac{u - 1}{(u - 1)(u + 2)}$ is undefined for $u = -2, 1$

We will not always explicitly state restrictions of the type just indicated, but it is important to remember that operations on algebraic fractions are valid only for values of the variables for which *all* fractions are defined.

■ Fundamental Principle of Fractions

A property of real fractions that is used frequently when working with algebraic fractions is the **fundamental principle of fractions.**

Fundamental Principle of Fractions

For real numbers a, b, and k:

$$\frac{ak}{bk} = \frac{a}{b} \qquad (b, k \neq 0)$$

Using the principle from left to right to eliminate all common factors from a numerator and denominator of a given fraction is referred to as **reducing a fraction to lowest terms.** We are actually dividing the numerator and denominator by the same nonzero common factor. Using the principle from right to left — that is, multiplying a numerator and denominator by the same nonzero factor — is referred to as **raising a fraction to higher terms.** We will use the principle in both directions in the material that follows.

A particular type of algebraic fraction, the quotient of two polynomials, is called a **rational expression.** We say that a rational expression is **reduced to lowest terms** if the numerator and denominator do not have any prime factors in common. (Unless stated to the contrary, "prime" will mean "prime relative to the integers.")

Example 19   Reduce to lowest terms:

(A) $\dfrac{x^2 - 6x + 9}{x^2 - 9} = \dfrac{(x-3)^2}{(x-3)(x+3)}$ Factor numerator and denominator completely. Divide numerator and
$= \dfrac{x-3}{x+3}$ denominator by $(x-3)$, a valid operation as long as $x \neq 3$. Of course, $x \neq -3$, as well.

(B) $\dfrac{x^3 - 1}{x^2 - 1} = \dfrac{(x-1)(x^2+x+1)}{(x-1)(x+1)} = \dfrac{x^2+x+1}{x+1}$

(C) $\dfrac{x^{2/3} - 1}{x^{1/3} + 1} = \dfrac{(x^{1/3} - 1)\overset{1}{\cancel{(x^{1/3} + 1)}}}{\underset{1}{\cancel{(x^{1/3} + 1)}}} = x^{1/3} - 1$

Note: Throughout our work with fractions, we will always assume without specific statement for each case that variables are restricted in order to avoid division by 0.

Problem 19   Reduce to lowest terms:

(A) $\dfrac{6x^2 + x - 2}{2x^2 + x - 1}$ (B) $\dfrac{x^4 - 8x}{3x^3 - 2x^2 - 8x}$ (C) $\dfrac{u^{2/5} - 3}{u^{4/5} - 9}$

■ Multiplication and Division

Since in algebraic fractions we will restrict variable replacements to real numbers that produce real fractions, multiplication and division of algebraic fractions follow the rules for multiplication and division of fractions in real numbers. That is (excluding division by 0):

Multiplication and Division

$$\frac{a}{b} \cdot \frac{c}{d} = \frac{ac}{bd}$$

$$\frac{a}{b} \div \frac{c}{d} = \frac{a}{b} \cdot \frac{d}{c}$$

Example 20   (A) $\dfrac{10x^3y}{3xy + 9y} \cdot \dfrac{x^2 - 9}{4x^2 - 12x}$

$$= \frac{\overset{5x^2}{\cancel{10x^3y}}}{\underset{3\cdot 1}{\cancel{3y(x+3)}}} \cdot \frac{\overset{1 \cdot 1}{\cancel{(x-3)}\cancel{(x+3)}}}{\underset{2 \cdot 1}{4x\cancel{(x-3)}}}$$

$$= \frac{5x^2}{6}$$

(B) $\dfrac{4 - 2x}{4} \div (x - 2)$ $x - 2$ is the same as $\dfrac{x-2}{1}$

$$= \frac{\overset{1}{\cancel{2}(2 - x)}}{\underset{2}{\cancel{4}}} \cdot \frac{1}{x - 2}$$

$$= \frac{2 - x}{2(x - 2)} = \frac{\overset{1}{-\cancel{(x-2)}}}{2\cancel{(x-2)}}$$ $b - a = -(a - b)$, a useful change in
$$\underset{1}{\phantom{= \frac{2-x}{2(x-2)}}}$$ some problems

$$= -\frac{1}{2}$$

(C) $\dfrac{2x^3 - 2x^2y + 2xy^2}{x^3y - xy^3} \div \dfrac{x^3 + y^3}{x^2 + 2xy + y^2}$

$$= \frac{\overset{2}{\cancel{2x(x^2 - xy + y^2)}}}{\underset{y}{\cancel{xy(x + y)(x - y)}}} \cdot \frac{\overset{1}{\cancel{(x + y)^2}}}{\underset{1}{\cancel{(x + y)(x^2 - xy + y^2)}}}$$

$$= \frac{2}{y(x - y)}$$

Problem 20   Perform the indicated operations and reduce to lowest terms.

(A) $\dfrac{12x^2y^3}{2xy^2 + 6xy} \cdot \dfrac{y^2 + 6y + 9}{3y^3 + 9y^2}$ (B) $(4 - x) \div \dfrac{x^2 - 16}{5}$

(C) $\dfrac{m^3 + n^3}{2m^2 + mn - n^2} \div \dfrac{m^3n - m^2n^2 + mn^3}{2m^3n^2 - m^2n^3}$

We will now use the fundamental principle of fractions to rationalize denominators and numerators in fractional expressions involving radicals.

Example 21   (A) Rationalize the denominator: $\dfrac{\sqrt{x} - \sqrt{y}}{\sqrt{x} + \sqrt{y}}$

(B) Rationalize the numerator: $\dfrac{\sqrt{x + h} - \sqrt{x}}{h}$

Solutions   (A) $\dfrac{\sqrt{x} - \sqrt{y}}{\sqrt{x} + \sqrt{y}} = \dfrac{(\sqrt{x} - \sqrt{y})}{(\sqrt{x} + \sqrt{y})} \cdot \dfrac{(\sqrt{x} - \sqrt{y})}{(\sqrt{x} - \sqrt{y})}$ Multiplying numerator and denominator by $(\sqrt{x} - \sqrt{y})$ eliminates radicals from the denominator since $(a + b)(a - b) = a^2 - b^2$.

$\qquad = \dfrac{x - 2\sqrt{xy} + y}{x - y}$

(B) $\dfrac{\sqrt{x + h} - \sqrt{x}}{h} = \dfrac{(\sqrt{x + h} - \sqrt{x})}{h} \cdot \dfrac{(\sqrt{x + h} + \sqrt{x})}{(\sqrt{x + h} + \sqrt{x})}$

$\qquad = \dfrac{x + h - x}{h(\sqrt{x + h} + \sqrt{x})}$

$\qquad = \dfrac{h}{h(\sqrt{x + h} + \sqrt{x})} = \dfrac{1}{\sqrt{x + h} + \sqrt{x}}$

Problem 21   (A) Rationalize the denominator: $\dfrac{\sqrt{m} + \sqrt{n}}{\sqrt{m} - \sqrt{n}}$

(B) Rationalize the numerator: $\dfrac{\sqrt{3 + h} - \sqrt{3}}{h}$

■ Addition and Subtraction

Since in algebraic fractions we will restrict variable replacements to real numbers that produce real fractions, addition and subtraction of algebraic fractions follow the rules for addition and subtraction of fractions in real numbers. That is (excluding division by 0):

Addition and Subtraction

$$\frac{a}{b} + \frac{c}{b} = \frac{a + c}{b}$$

$$\frac{a}{b} - \frac{c}{b} = \frac{a - c}{b}$$

Thus, we add algebraic fractions, if their denominators are the same, by adding or subtracting their numerators and placing the result over the common denominator. If the denominators are not the same, we raise the fractions to higher terms (using the fundamental principle of fractions to obtain common denominators) and then proceed as indicated in the box.

Even though any common denominator will do, the problem is generally less involved if the **least common denominator (LCD)** is used. Often the LCD is obvious, but if it is not, use the following procedure to find it:

The Least Common Denominator

The LCD of two or more rational expressions is found as follows:

1. Factor each denominator completely.
2. Form a product containing each different factor from all denominators to the highest power it occurs in any one denominator. This product is the LCD.

Example 22   Combine into single fractions and simplify.

(A) $\dfrac{x-4}{x+2} - \dfrac{x-2}{x+2} = \dfrac{x-4-(x-2)}{x+2} = \dfrac{x-4-x+2}{x+2} = \dfrac{-2}{x+2}$

(B) $\dfrac{1}{3y^2} - \dfrac{1}{6y} + 1 = \dfrac{2(1)}{2(3y^2)} - \dfrac{y(1)}{y(6y)} + \dfrac{6y^2}{6y^2}$

$$= \frac{2 - y + 6y^2}{6y^2} \qquad \text{LCD} = 6y^2$$

(C) $2 - \dfrac{x-2}{x+1} = \dfrac{2(x+1)}{x+1} - \dfrac{x-2}{x+1} = \dfrac{2(x+1) - (x-2)}{x+1}$

$\qquad\qquad = \dfrac{2x+2-x+2}{x+1} = \dfrac{x+4}{x+1} \qquad \text{LCD} = x+1$

(D) $\dfrac{3}{x^2-1} - \dfrac{2}{x^2+2x+1} = \dfrac{3}{(x-1)(x+1)} - \dfrac{2}{(x+1)^2}$

$\qquad\qquad = \dfrac{3(x+1)}{(x-1)(x+1)^2} - \dfrac{2(x-1)}{(x-1)(x+1)^2}$

$\qquad\qquad = \dfrac{3(x+1) - 2(x-1)}{(x-1)(x+1)^2} = \dfrac{3x+3-2x+2}{(x-1)(x+1)^2}$

$\qquad\qquad = \dfrac{x+5}{(x-1)(x+1)^2} \qquad \text{LCD} = (x-1)(x+1)^2$

Problem 22 Combine into single fractions and simplify.

(A) $\dfrac{x-2}{x-3} - \dfrac{x+2}{x-3}$ (B) $\dfrac{1}{y} + \dfrac{1}{4y^2} - 1$

(C) $u - \dfrac{u-1}{u-2}$ (D) $\dfrac{4}{x^2-4} - \dfrac{3}{x^2-x-2}$

Example 23 Combine into single fractions and simplify. Write answers using positive exponents only.

(A) $-6y^2(y-1)^{-3} + 6y(y-1)^{-2} = \dfrac{-6y^2}{(y-1)^3} + \dfrac{6y}{(y-1)^2}$

$\qquad\qquad = \dfrac{-6y^2 + 6y(y-1)}{(y-1)^3}$

$\qquad\qquad = \dfrac{-6y}{(y-1)^3}$

(B) $x^{1/2}2x + \tfrac{1}{2}x^{-1/2}(x^2-1) = 2x^{3/2} + \dfrac{x^2-1}{2x^{1/2}}$

$\qquad\qquad = \dfrac{2x^{1/2}2x^{3/2}}{2x^{1/2}} + \dfrac{x^2-1}{2x^{1/2}}$

$\qquad\qquad = \dfrac{4x^2 + x^2 - 1}{2x^{1/2}} = \dfrac{5x^2-1}{2x^{1/2}}$

(C) $\dfrac{x^{1/3} - \tfrac{1}{3}x^{-2/3}(x-1)}{x^{2/3}} = \dfrac{\dfrac{x^{1/3}}{1} - \dfrac{x-1}{3x^{2/3}}}{x^{2/3}}$

$\qquad\qquad = \dfrac{\dfrac{3x - (x-1)}{3x^{2/3}}}{x^{2/3}} = \dfrac{3x-x+1}{3x^{2/3}} \cdot \dfrac{1}{x^{2/3}}$

$\qquad\qquad = \dfrac{2x+1}{3x^{4/3}}$

Problem 23   Combine into single fractions and simplify. Write answers using positive exponents only.

(A) $-3n(n+3)^{-2} + 3(n+3)^{-1}$ (B) $2(x-1)^{1/2}x^2 + \frac{1}{2}(x-1)^{-1/2}x^3$

(C) $\dfrac{x^{1/2} - \frac{1}{2}x^{-1/2}(x+2)}{x}$

Answers to Matched Problems

19. (A) $\dfrac{3x+2}{x+1}$ (B) $\dfrac{x^2+2x+4}{3x+4}$ (C) $\dfrac{1}{u^{2/5}+3}$

20. (A) $2x$ (B) $\dfrac{-5}{x+4}$ (C) mn

21. (A) $\dfrac{m+2\sqrt{mn}+n}{m-n}$ (B) $\dfrac{1}{\sqrt{3+h}+\sqrt{3}}$

22. (A) $\dfrac{-4}{x-3}$ or $\dfrac{4}{3-x}$ (B) $\dfrac{1+4y-4y^2}{4y^2}$

   (C) $\dfrac{u^2-3u+1}{u-2}$ (D) $\dfrac{1}{(x+2)(x+1)}$

23. (A) $\dfrac{9}{(n+3)^2}$ (B) $\dfrac{5x^3-4x^2}{2(x-1)^{1/2}}$ (C) $\dfrac{x-2}{2x^{3/2}}$

Exercise A-4

A   *Perform the indicated operations and reduce to lowest terms.*

1. $\dfrac{3x^2y}{x-y} \div \dfrac{6xy}{x-y}$ 2. $\dfrac{x+3}{2x^2} \div \dfrac{x+3}{4x}$

3. $\dfrac{v-1}{v^2} - \dfrac{1}{v} + \dfrac{3}{v^3}$ 4. $\dfrac{2}{x} - \dfrac{x+1}{x^2} + \dfrac{5}{x^3}$

5. $\left(\dfrac{d^5}{3a} \div \dfrac{d^2}{6a^2}\right) \cdot \dfrac{a}{4d^3}$ 6. $\dfrac{d^5}{3a} \div \left(\dfrac{d^2}{6a^2} \cdot \dfrac{a}{4d^3}\right)$

7. $1 - \dfrac{1}{x-3}$ 8. $2 + \dfrac{3}{u+1}$

9. $\dfrac{2x^2+7x+3}{4x^2-1} \div (x+3)$ 10. $\dfrac{x^2-9}{x^2-3x} \div (x^2-x-12)$

B   11. $\dfrac{x^2-6x+9}{x^2-x-6} \div \dfrac{x^2+2x-15}{x^2+2x}$ 12. $\dfrac{m+n}{m^2-n^2} \div \dfrac{m^2-mn}{m^2-2mn+n^2}$

13. $\dfrac{3x+8}{4x^2} - \dfrac{2x-1}{x^3} - \dfrac{5}{8x}$ 14. $\dfrac{4m-3}{18m^3} + \dfrac{3}{4m} - \dfrac{2m-1}{6m^2}$

15. $\dfrac{1}{a^2 - b^2} + \dfrac{1}{a^2 + 2ab + b^2}$

16. $\dfrac{3}{x^2 - 1} + \dfrac{2}{x^2 - 2x + 1}$

17. $m - 3 - \dfrac{m - 1}{m - 2}$

18. $\dfrac{x + 1}{x - 1} + x + 1$

19. $\dfrac{2}{y + 3} - \dfrac{1}{y - 3} + \dfrac{2y}{y^2 - 9}$

20. $\dfrac{2x}{x^2 - y^2} + \dfrac{1}{x + y} - \dfrac{1}{x - y}$

21. $\dfrac{x^2 - 16}{2x^2 + 10x + 8} \div \dfrac{x^2 - 13x + 36}{x^3 + 1}$

22. $\dfrac{x^3 y - y^4}{xy^3 - y^4} \div \dfrac{x^2 + xy + y^2}{y^2}$

23. $\left(\dfrac{-b + \sqrt{b^2 - 4ac}}{2a}\right) \cdot \left(\dfrac{-b - \sqrt{b^2 - 4ac}}{2a}\right)$

24. $\dfrac{-b + \sqrt{b^2 - 4ac}}{2a} + \dfrac{-b - \sqrt{b^2 - 4ac}}{2a}$

Rationalize the denominators.

25. $\dfrac{3 - \sqrt{a}}{\sqrt{a} - 2}$

26. $\dfrac{2 + \sqrt{x}}{\sqrt{x} - 3}$

27. $\dfrac{x^2}{\sqrt{x^2 + 9} - 3}$

28. $\dfrac{-y^2}{2 - \sqrt{y^2 + 4}}$

Rationalize the numerators.

29. $\dfrac{\sqrt{t} - \sqrt{x}}{t - x}$

30. $\dfrac{\sqrt{x} - \sqrt{y}}{\sqrt{x} + \sqrt{y}}$

31. $\dfrac{\sqrt{x + h} - \sqrt{x}}{h}$

32. $\dfrac{\sqrt{2 + h} + \sqrt{2}}{h}$

Write as single fractions and simplify. Write answers using positive exponents only.

33. $-2x(x - 1)^{-2} + 2(x - 1)^{-1}$

34. $-4m(m + 3)^{-2} + 4(m + 3)^{-1}$

35. $15x^3(2 - 3x)^{-6} + 3x^2(2 - 3x)^{-5}$

36. $-10u^3(u + 2)^{-3} + 15u^2(u + 2)^{-2}$

C *Write as single fractions and simplify. Write answers using positive exponents only.*

37. $2x^{-1/3} + 1$

38. $1 - 3u^{-1/2}$

39. $(x + 1)^{-3/4} - (x + 1)^{1/4}$

40. $(u - 1)^{2/5} - u(u - 1)^{-3/5}$

41. $(x - 1)\tfrac{1}{4}x^{-1/4} + x^{3/4}$

42. $(x - 2)^{1/4} + \tfrac{1}{4}(x - 2)^{-3/4}x$

43. $\dfrac{u^{1/2}2u - (u^2 - 1)\tfrac{1}{2}u^{-1/2}}{u}$

44. $\dfrac{x^2 \tfrac{1}{3}(x - 1)^{-2/3} - 2x(x - 1)^{1/3}}{x^4}$

A-5 Arithmetic Progressions

- Arithmetic Progressions—Definitions
- Special Formulas
- Application

■ Arithmetic Progressions–Definitions

Consider the sequence of numbers

$$1, 4, 7, 10, 13, \ldots$$

Assuming the pattern continues, can you guess what the next two numbers are? If you guessed 16 and 19, you have observed that each number after the first can be obtained from the preceding one by adding 3 to it. This is an example of an *arithmetic progression*. In general,

---

Arithmetic Progression

A sequence of numbers

$$a_1, a_2, a_3, \ldots, a_n, \ldots$$

is called an **arithmetic progression** if there is a constant d, called the **common difference,** such that

$$a_n - a_{n-1} = d$$

That is,

$$a_n = a_{n-1} + d \quad \text{for every} \quad n > 1 \tag{1}$$

Example 24   Which sequence of numbers is an arithmetic progression and what is its common difference?

(A)   2, 4, 8, 10, . . .   (B)   3, 8, 13, 18, . . .

Solution   Sequence A does not have a common difference, since $4 - 2 = 2$ and $8 - 4 = 4$; hence, it is not an arithmetic progression. Sequence B is an arithmetic progression, since the difference between any two successive terms is 5, the common difference, and each number after the first one can be obtained by adding 5 to the preceding number.

Problem 24   Which sequence of numbers is an arithmetic progression, and what is its common difference?

(A)   15, 13, 11, 9, . . .   (B)   3, 9, 27, 81, . . .

■ Special Formulas

Arithmetic progressions have a number of convenient properties. For example, it is easy to derive formulas for the nth term in terms of n and the sum of any number of consecutive terms. To obtain a formula for the nth term of an arithmetic progression, we note that if a_1 is the first term and d is the common difference, then

$$a_2 = a_1 + d$$
$$a_3 = a_2 + d = (a_1 + d) + d = a_1 + 2d$$
$$a_4 = a_3 + d = (a_1 + 2d) + d = a_1 + 3d$$

This suggests that

$$a_n = a_1 + (n-1)d \qquad \text{for all} \quad n > 1 \qquad (2)$$

Example 25 Find the twenty-first term in the arithmetic progression 3, 8, 13, 18, . . .

Solution Find the common difference d and use formula (2):

$$d = 5, \qquad n = 21, \qquad a_1 = 3$$

Thus

$$a_{21} = 3 + (21 - 1)5$$
$$= 103$$

Problem 25 Find the fifty-first term in the arithmetic progression 15, 13, 11, 9, . . .

We now derive two simple and very useful formulas for the sum of n consecutive terms of an arithmetic progression. Let

$$S_n = a_1 + a_2 + \cdots + a_{n-1} + a_n$$

be the sum of n terms of an arithmetic progression with common difference d. Then,

$$S_n = a_1 + (a_1 + d) + \cdots + [a_1 + (n-2)d] + [a_1 + (n-1)d]$$

Reversing the order of the sum, we obtain

$$S_n = [a_1 + (n-1)d] + [a_1 + (n-2)d] + \cdots + (a_1 + d) + a_1$$

Something interesting happens if we combine these last two equations by addition (adding corresponding terms on the right sides):

$$2S_n = [2a_1 + (n-1)d] + [2a_1 + (n-1)d] + \cdots$$
$$+ [2a_1 + (n-1)d] + [2a_1 + (n-1)d]$$

All the terms on the right side are the same, and there are n of them. Thus,

$$2S_n = n[2a_1 + (n-1)d]$$

and

$$S_n = \frac{n}{2}[2a_1 + (n-1)d] \qquad (3)$$

Replacing

$$[a_1 + (n-1)d] \quad \text{in} \quad \frac{n}{2}[a_1 + a_1 + (n-1)d]$$

by a_n from equation (2), we can obtain a second useful formula for the sum:

$$S_n = \frac{n}{2}(a_1 + a_n) \qquad (4)$$

Example 26 Find the sum of the first 30 terms in the arithmetic progression 3, 8, 13, 18, . . .

Solution Use (3) with $n = 30$, $a_1 = 3$, and $d = 5$:

$$S_{30} = \frac{30}{2}[2 \cdot 3 + (30-1)5] = 2{,}265$$

Problem 26 Find the sum of the first 40 terms in the arithmetic progression 15, 13, 11, 9, . . .

Example 27 Find the sum of all the even numbers between 31 and 87.

Solution First, find n using (2):

$$a_n = a_1 + (n-1)d$$
$$86 = 32 + (n-1)2$$
$$n = 28$$

Now find S_{28} using (4):

$$S_n = \frac{n}{2}(a_1 + a_n)$$

$$S_{28} = \frac{28}{2}(32 + 86) = 1{,}652$$

Problem 27 Find the sum of all the odd numbers between 24 and 208.

■ Application

Example 28 A person borrows $3,600 and agrees to repay the loan in monthly install-ments over a 3 year period. The agreement is to pay 1% of the unpaid balance each month for using the money and $100 each month to reduce the loan. What is the total cost of the loan over the 3 year period?

Solution Let us look at the problem relative to a time line:

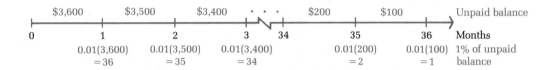

The total cost of the loan is

$$1 + 2 + \cdots + 34 + 35 + 36$$

The terms form an arithmetic progression with $n = 36$, $a_1 = 1$, and $a_{36} = 36$, so we can use (4):

$$S_n = \frac{n}{2}(a_1 + a_n)$$

$$S_{36} = \frac{36}{2}(1 + 36) = \$666$$

And we conclude that the total cost of the loan over the 3 year period is $666.

Problem 28 Repeat Example 28 with a loan of $6,000 over a 5 year period.

Answers to 24. Sequence A; $d = -2$ 25. -85 26. -960
Matched Problems 27. 10,672 28. $1,830

Exercise A-5

A 1. Determine which of the following are arithmetic progressions. Find the common difference d and the next two terms for those progres-sions.

(A) 5, 8, 11, . . . (B) 4, 8, 16, . . .
(C) $-2, -4, -8, \ldots$ (D) 8, $-2, -12, \ldots$

2. Repeat Problem 1 for:

   (A) $11, 16, 21, \ldots$ (B) $16, 8, 4, \ldots$
   (C) $2, -3, -8, \ldots$ (D) $-1, -2, -4, \ldots$

   Let $a_1, a_2, a_3, \ldots, a_n, \ldots$ be an arithmetic progression and S_n be the sum of the first n terms. In Problems 3–8 find the indicated quantities.

   3. $a_1 = 7$, $d = 4$, $a_2 = ?$, $a_3 = ?$
   4. $a_1 = -2$, $d = -3$, $a_2 = ?$, $a_3 = ?$

B

   5. $a_1 = 2$, $d = 4$, $a_{21} = ?$, $S_{31} = ?$
   6. $a_1 = 8$, $d = -10$, $a_{15} = ?$, $S_{23} = ?$
   7. $a_1 = 18$, $a_{20} = 75$, $S_{20} = ?$
   8. $a_1 = 203$, $a_{30} = 261$, $S_{30} = ?$
   9. Find $f(1) + f(2) + f(3) + \cdots + f(50)$ if $f(x) = 2x - 3$.
   10. Find $g(1) + g(2) + g(3) + \cdots + g(100)$ if $g(t) = 18 - 3t$.
   11. Find the sum of all the odd integers between 12 and 68.
   12. Find the sum of all the even integers between 23 and 97.

C

   13. Show that the sum of the first n odd positive integers is n^2, using appropriate formulas from this section.
   14. Show that the sum of the first n positive even integers is $n + n^2$, using formulas in this section.

Applications

Business & Economics

   15. You are confronted with two job offers. Firm A will start you at $24,000 per year and guarantees you a $900 raise each year for 10 years. Firm B will start you at $22,000 per year but guarantees you a $1,300 raise each year for 10 years. Over the 10 year period, what is the total amount each firm will pay you?
   16. In Problem 15, what would be your annual salary in each firm for the tenth year?
   17. *Loan repayment.* If you borrow $4,800 and repay the loan by paying $200 per month to reduce the loan and 1% of the unpaid balance each month for the use of the money, what is the total cost of the loan over 24 months?
   18. *Loan repayment.* Repeat Problem 17 replacing 1% with 1.5%.

A-6   Geometric Progressions

- Geometric Progressions—Definition
- Special Formulas
- Infinite Geometric Progressions

- Geometric Progressions — Definition

Consider the sequence of numbers

2, 6, 18, 54, . . .

Assuming the pattern continues, can you guess what the next two numbers are? If you guessed 162 and 486, you have observed that each number after the first can be obtained from the preceding one by multiplying it by 3. This is an example of a *geometric progression*. In general,

---

Geometric Progression

A sequence of numbers

$$a_1, a_2, a_3, . . . , a_n, . . .$$

is called a **geometric progression** if there exists a nonzero constant r, called a **common ratio,** such that

$$\frac{a_n}{a_{n-1}} = r$$

That is,

$$a_n = r a_{n-1} \qquad \text{for every} \quad n \geq 1 \tag{1}$$

Example 29 Which sequence of numbers is a geometric progression and what is its common ratio?

(A) 5, 3, 1, −1, . . .   (B) 1, 2, 4, 8, . . .

Solution Sequence A does not have a common ratio, since $3 \div 5 \neq 1 \div 3$; hence, it is not a geometric progression. Sequence B is a geometric progression, since the ratio of any two successive terms (the second divided by the first) is the constant 2, the common ratio, and each number after the first can be obtained by multiplying the preceding number by 2.

Problem 29 Which sequence of numbers is a geometric progression and what is its common ratio?

(A) 4, −2, 1, −$\frac{1}{2}$, . . .   (B) 2, 4, 6, 8, . . .

- Special Formulas

Like arithmetic progressions, geometric progressions have several useful properties. It is easy to derive formulas for the nth term in terms of n and for the sum of any number of consecutive terms. To obtain a formula for the nth term of a geometric progression, we note that if a_1 is the first term and r is the common ratio, then

$$a_2 = ra_1$$
$$a_3 = ra_2 = r(ra_1) \; = r^2 a_1 = a_1 r^2$$
$$a_4 = ra_3 = r(r^2 a_1) = r^3 a_1 = a_1 r^3$$

This suggests that

$$a_n = a_1 r^{n-1} \qquad \text{for all} \quad n > 1 \qquad\qquad (2)$$

Example 30   Find the eighth term in the geometric progression $\frac{1}{2}, \frac{1}{4}, \frac{1}{8}, \ldots$

Solution   Find the common ratio r and use formula (2):

$$r = \tfrac{1}{2}, \qquad n = 8, \qquad a_1 = \tfrac{1}{2}$$

Thus,

$$a_8 = (\tfrac{1}{2})(\tfrac{1}{2})^{8-1}$$
$$= \tfrac{1}{256}$$

Problem 30   Find the seventh term in the geometric progression $\frac{1}{32}, -\frac{1}{16}, \frac{1}{8}, \ldots$

Example 31   If the first and tenth terms of a geometric progression are 2 and 4, respectively, find the common ratio r.

Solution $$a_n = a_1 r^{n-1}$$
$$4 = 2 \cdot r^{10-1}$$
$$2 = r^9$$
$$r = 2^{1/9} \approx 1.08 \qquad \text{Use a calculator or logarithms}$$

Problem 31   If the first and eighth terms of a geometric progression are 1,000 and 2,000, respectively, find the common ratio r.

We now derive two very useful formulas for the sum of n consecutive terms of a geometric progression. Let

$$a_1, a_1 r, a_1 r^2, \ldots, a_1 r^{n-2}, a_1 r^{n-1}$$

be n terms of a geometric progression. Their sum is

$$S_n = a_1 + a_1 r + a_1 r^2 + \cdots + a_1 r^{n-2} + a_1 r^{n-1}$$

If we multiply both sides by r, we obtain

$$rS_n = a_1r + a_1r^2 + a_1r^3 + \cdots + a_1r^{n-1} + a_1r^n$$

Now combine these last two equations by subtraction to obtain

$$rS_n - S_n = (a_1r + a_1r^2 + a_1r^3 + \cdots + a_1r^{n-1} + a_1r^n)$$
$$- (a_1 + a_1r + a_1r^2 + \cdots + a_1r^{n-2} + a_1r^{n-1})$$
$$(r - 1)S_n = a_1r^n - a_1$$

Notice how many terms drop out on the right side. Hence,

$$S_n = \frac{a_1(r^n - 1)}{r - 1} \qquad r \neq 1 \tag{3}$$

Since $a_n = a_1r^{n-1}$, or $ra_n = a_1r^n$, formula (3) can also be written in the form

$$S_n = \frac{ra_n - a_1}{r - 1} \qquad r \neq 1 \tag{4}$$

Example 32   Find the sum of the first ten terms of the geometric progression 1, 1.05, 1.05^2, . . .

Solution   Use formula (3) with $a_1 = 1$, $r = 1.05$, and $n = 10$:

$$S_n = \frac{a_1(r^n - 1)}{r - 1}$$

$$S_{10} = \frac{1(1.05^{10} - 1)}{1.05 - 1}$$

$$\approx \frac{0.6289}{0.05} \approx 12.58$$

Problem 32   Find the sum of the first eight terms of the geometric progression 100, 100(1.08), $100(1.08)^2$, . . .

■ Infinite Geometric Progressions

Given a geometric progression, what happens to the sum S_n of the first n terms as n increases without stopping? To answer this question, let us write formula (3) in the form

$$S_n = \frac{a_1 r^n}{r-1} - \frac{a_1}{r-1}$$

It is possible to show that if $|r| < 1$ (that is, $-1 < r < 1$), then r^n will tend to zero as n increases. (See what happens, for example, if you let $r = \frac{1}{2}$ and then increase n.) Thus, the first term above will tend to zero and S_n can be made as close as we please to the second term, $-a_1/(r-1)$ [which can be written as $a_1/(1-r)$], by taking n sufficiently large. Thus, if the common ratio r is between -1 and 1, we define the sum of an infinite geometric progression to be

$$S_\infty = \frac{a_1}{1-r} \qquad |r| < 1 \qquad (5)$$

If $r \leqslant -1$ or $r \geqslant 1$, then an infinite geometric progression has no sum.

Example 33   The government has decided on a tax rebate program to stimulate the economy. Suppose you receive $600 and that you spend 80% of this, and that each of the people who receive what you spend also spend 80% of what they receive, and this process continues without end. According to the **multiplier doctrine** in economics, the effect of your $600 tax rebate on the economy is multiplied many times. What is the total amount spent if the process continues as indicated?

Solution   We need to find the sum of an infinite geometric progression with the first amount spent being $a_1 = (.08)(\$600) = \$480$ and $r = 0.8$. Using formula (5), we obtain

$$S_\infty = \frac{a_1}{1-r}$$

$$= \frac{\$480}{1-0.8}$$

$$= \$2,400$$

Thus, assuming the process continues as indicated, we would expect the $600 tax rebate to result in about $2,400 of spending.

Problem 33   Repeat Example 33 with a tax rebate of $1,000.

Answers to   29. Sequence A; $R = -\frac{1}{2}$ 30. 2   31. Approximately 1.104
Matched Problems   32. 1,063.66   33. $4,000

Exercise A-6

A

1. Determine which of the following are geometric progressions. Find the common ratio r and the next two terms for those that are:

   (A) $1, -2, 4, \ldots$ (B) $7, 6, 5, \ldots$ (C) $2, 1, \frac{1}{2}, \ldots$
   (D) $2, -4, 6, \ldots$

2. Repeat Problem 1 for:

   (A) $4, -1, -6, \ldots$ (B) $15, 5, \frac{5}{3}, \ldots$ (C) $\frac{1}{4}, -\frac{1}{2}, 1, \ldots$
   (D) $\frac{1}{2}, \frac{2}{3}, \frac{3}{4}, \ldots$

Let $a_1, a_2, a_3, \ldots, a_n, \ldots$ be a geometric progression and S_n be the sum of the first n terms. In Problems 3–12 find the indicated quantities. Use logarithms or a calculator as needed.

3. $a_1 = 3$, $r = -2$, $a_2 = ?$, $a_3 = ?$, $a_4 = ?$

4. $a_1 = 32$, $r = -\frac{1}{2}$, $a_2 = ?$, $a_3 = ?$, $a_4 = ?$

5. $a_1 = 1$, $a_7 = 729$, $r = -3$, $S_7 = ?$

6. $a_1 = 3$, $a_7 = 2,187$, $r = 3$, $S_7 = ?$

B

7. $a_1 = 100$, $r = 1.08$, $a_{10} = ?$

8. $a_1 = 240$, $r = 1.06$, $a_{12} = ?$

9. $a_1 = 100$, $a_9 = 200$, $r = ?$

10. $a_1 = 100$, $a_{10} = 300$, $r = ?$

11. $a_1 = 500$, $r = 0.6$, $S_{10} = ?$, $S_\infty = ?$

12. $a_1 = 8,000$, $r = 0.4$, $S_{10} = ?$, $S_\infty = ?$

13. Find the sum of each infinite geometric progression (if it exists).

    (A) $2, 4, 8, \ldots$ (B) $2, -\frac{1}{2}, \frac{1}{8}, \ldots$

14. Repeat Problem 13 for:

    (A) $16, 4, 1, \ldots$ (B) $1, -3, 9, \ldots$

C

15. Find $f(1) + f(2) + \cdots + f(10)$ if $f(x) = (\frac{1}{2})^x$.

16. Find $g(1) + g(2) + \cdots + g(10)$ if $g(x) = 2^x$.

■

Applications

Business & Economics

17. *Economy stimulation.* The government, through a subsidy program, distributes $5,000,000. If we assume each individual or agency spends 70% of what is received, and 70% of this is spent, and so on, how much total increase in spending results from this government action? (Let $a_1 = \$3,500,000$.)

18. *Economy stimulation.* Repeat Problem 17 using $10,000,000 as the amount distributed and 80%.

19. *Cost-of-living adjustment.* If the cost-of-living index increased 5% for each of the past 10 years and you had a salary agreement that increased your salary by the same percentage each year, what would your present salary be if you had a $20,000 per year salary 10 years ago? What would be your total earnings in the past 10 years? [*Hint:* $r = 1.05$.]

20. *Depreciation.* In *straight-line depreciation*, an asset less its salvage value at the end of its useful life is depreciated (for tax purposes) in equal annual amounts over its useful life. Thus, a $100,000 company airplane with a salvage value of $20,000 at the end of 10 years would be depreciated at $8,000 per year for each of the 10 years.

Since certain assets, such as airplanes, cars, and so on, depreciate more rapidly during the early years of their useful life, several methods of depreciation that take this into consideration are available to the taxpayer. One such method is called the *method of declining balance.* The rate used cannot exceed double that used for straight-line depreciation (ignoring salvage value) and is applied to the remaining value of an asset after the previous year's depreciation has been deducted. In our airplane example, the annual rate of straight-line depreciation over the 10 year period is 10%. Let us assume we can double this rate for the method of declining balance. At some point before the salvage value is reached (taxpayer's choice), we must switch over to the straight-line method to depreciate the final amount of the asset.

The table below illustrates the two methods of depreciation for the company airplane.

Year end	Straight-Line		Declining Balance		
	Amount depreciated	Asset value	Amount depreciated	Asset value	
0	$ 0	$100,000	$ 0	$100,000	
1	0.1(80,000) = 8,000	92,000	0.2(100,000) = 20,000	80,000	
2	0.1(80,000) = 8,000	84,000	0.2(80,000) = 16,000	64,000	
3	0.1(80,000) = 8,000	76,000	0.2(64,000) = 12,800	51,200	
·	·	·	·	·	
·	·	·	·	·	⎧ Shift to straight-
·	·	·	·	·	⎪ line, otherwise
7	0.1(80,000) = 8,000	44,000	0.2(26,214) = 5,243	20,972	⎨ next entry will
8	0.1(80,000) = 8,000	36,000	$\frac{972}{3}$ = 324	20,648	⎪ drop below
9	0.1(80,000) = 8,000	28,000	$\frac{972}{3}$ = 324	20,324	⎩ salvage value
10	0.1(80,000) = 8,000	20,000	$\frac{972}{3}$ = 324	20,000	

Arithmetic progression   Geometric progressions above dashed line

(A) For the declining balance, find the sum of the depreciation amounts above the dashed line using formula (4) and then add the entries below the line to this result.

(B) Repeat part A using formula (3).

(C) Find the asset value under declining balance at the end of the fifth year using formula (2).

(D) Find the asset value under straight-line at the end of the fifth year using formula (2) in the preceding section.

A-7 The Binomial Formula

■ Factorial
■ Binomial Theorem — Development

The binomial form

$$(a + b)^n$$

where n is a natural number, appears more frequently than you might expect. The coefficients in the expansion play an important role in probability studies. The binomial formula, which we will informally derive, enables us to expand $(a + b)^n$ directly for n any natural number. Since the formula involves **factorials,** we digress for a moment here to introduce this important concept.

■ Factorial

For n a natural number, **n factorial** — denoted by **$n!$** — is the product of the first n natural numbers. **Zero factorial** is defined to be one. Symbolically,

$$n! = n(n - 1) \cdot \cdots \cdot 2 \cdot 1$$
$$1! = 1$$
$$0! = 1$$

It is also useful to note that

$$n! = n \cdot (n-1)!$$

Example 34   Evaluate each.

(A) $5! = 5 \cdot 4 \cdot 3 \cdot 2 \cdot 1 = 120$ (B) $\dfrac{8!}{7!} = \dfrac{8 \cdot 7!}{7!} = 8$

(C) $\dfrac{10!}{7!} = \dfrac{10 \cdot 9 \cdot 8 \cdot 7!}{7!} = 720$

Problem 34   Evaluate each: (A) $4!$ (B) $\dfrac{7!}{6!}$ (C) $\dfrac{8!}{5!}$

A special formula involving factorials is

$$C_{n,r} = \dfrac{n!}{r!(n-r)!} \qquad n \geq r \geq 0$$

Example 35   (A) $C_{9,2} = \dfrac{9!}{2!(9-2)!} = \dfrac{9!}{2!7!} = \dfrac{9 \cdot 8 \cdot 7!}{2 \cdot 7!} = 36$

(B) $C_{5,5} = \dfrac{5!}{5!(5-5)!} = \dfrac{5!}{5!0!} = \dfrac{5!}{5!} = 1$

Problem 35   Find: (A) $C_{5,2}$ (B) $C_{6,0}$

■ Binomial Theorem — Development

Let us expand $(a+b)^n$ for several values of n to see if we can observe a pattern that leads to a general formula for the expansion for any natural number n:

$(a+b)^1 = a + b$

$(a+b)^2 = a^2 + 2ab + b^2$

$(a+b)^3 = a^3 + 3a^2b + 3ab^2 + b^3$

$(a+b)^4 = a^4 + 4a^3b + 6a^2b^2 + 4ab^3 + b^4$

$(a+b)^5 = a^5 + 5a^4b + 10a^3b^2 + 10a^2b^3 + 5ab^4 + b^5$

Observations

1. The expansion of $(a + b)^n$ has $(n + 1)$ terms.
2. The power of a decreases by 1 for each term as we move from left to right.
3. The power of b increases by 1 for each term as we move from left to right.
4. In each term the sum of the powers of a and b always equals n.
5. Starting with a given term, we can get the coefficient of the next term by multiplying the coefficient of the given term by the exponent of a and dividing by the number that represents the position of the term in the series of terms. For example, in the expansion of $(a + b)^4$, above, the coefficient of the third term is found from the second term by multiplying 4 and 3, and then dividing by 2 [that is, the coefficient of the third term $= (4 \cdot 3)/2 = 6$].

We now postulate these same properties for the general case:

$$(a + b)^n = a^n + \frac{n}{1} a^{n-1}b + \frac{n(n-1)}{1 \cdot 2} a^{n-2}b^2 + \frac{n(n-1)(n-2)}{1 \cdot 2 \cdot 3} a^{n-3}b^3 + \cdots + b^n$$

$$= \frac{n!}{0!(n-0)!} a^n + \frac{n!}{1!(n-1)!} a^{n-1}b + \frac{n!}{2!(n-2)!} a^{n-2}b^2 + \frac{n!}{3!(n-3)!} a^{n-3}b^3 + \cdots + \frac{n!}{n!(n-n)!} b^n$$

$$= C_{n,0}a_n + C_{n,1}a^{n-1}b + C_{n,2}a^{n-2}b^2 + C_{n,3}a^{n-3}b^3 + \cdots + C_{n,n}b^n$$

And we are led to the formula in the binomial theorem (a formal proof requires mathematical induction, which is beyond the scope of this book):

Binomial Theorem

For all natural numbers n,

$$(a + b)^n = C_{n,0}a_n + C_{n,1}a^{n-1}b + C_{n,2}a^{n-2}b^2$$
$$+ C_{n,3}a^{n-3}b^3 + \cdots + C_{n,n}b^n$$

Example 36   Use the binomial formula to expand $(u + v)^6$.

Solution $(u + v)^6 = C_{6,0}u^6 + C_{6,1}u^5v + C_{6,2}u^4v^2 + C_{6,3}u^3v^3 + C_{6,4}u^2v^4 + C_{6,5}uv^5 + C_{6,6}v^6$

$\qquad = u^6 + 6u^5v + 15u^4v^2 + 20u^3v^3 + 15u^2v^4 + 6uv^5 + v^6$

Problem 36   Use the binomial formula to expand $(x + 2)^5$.

Example 37   Use the binomial formula to find the sixth term in the expansion of $(x - 1)^{18}$.

Solution   Sixth term $= C_{18,5}x^{13}(-1)^5$

$$= \frac{18!}{5!(18 - 5)!} x^{13}(-1)$$

$$= -8{,}568x^{13}$$

Problem 37   Use the binomial formula to find the fourth term in the expansion of $(x - 2)^{20}$.

Answers to   34. (A) 24   (B) 7   (C) 336   35. (A) 10   (B) 1
Matched Problems   36. $x^5 + 5x^4 \cdot 2 + 10x^3 \cdot 2^2 + 10x^2 \cdot 2^3 + 5x \cdot 2^4 + 2^5$

$$= x^5 + 10x^4 + 40x^3 + 80x^2 + 80x + 32$$

37. $-9{,}120x^{17}$

Exercise A-7

A   *Evaluate.*

1. 6!   2. 7!   3. $\dfrac{10!}{9!}$ 4. $\dfrac{20!}{19!}$

5. $\dfrac{12!}{9!}$ 6. $\dfrac{10!}{6!}$ 7. $\dfrac{5!}{2!3!}$ 8. $\dfrac{7!}{3!4!}$

9. $\dfrac{6!}{5!(6 - 5)!}$ 10. $\dfrac{7!}{4!(7 - 4)!}$ 11. $\dfrac{20!}{3!17!}$ 12. $\dfrac{52!}{50!2!}$

B   *Evaluate.*

13. $C_{5,3}$ 14. $C_{7,3}$ 15. $C_{6,5}$ 16. $C_{7,4}$
17. $C_{5,0}$ 18. $C_{5,5}$ 19. $C_{18,15}$ 20. $C_{18,3}$

Expand each expression using the binomial formula.

21. $(a + b)^4$ 22. $(m + n)^5$ 23. $(x - 1)^6$
24. $(u - 2)^5$ 25. $(2a - b)^5$ 26. $(x - 2y)^5$

Find the indicated term in each expansion.

27. $(x - 1)^{18}$,   fifth term   28. $(x - 3)^{20}$,   third term
29. $(p + q)^{15}$,   seventh term   30. $(p + q)^{15}$,   thirteenth term
31. $(2x + y)^{12}$,   eleventh term   32. $(2x + y)^{12}$,   third term

C   33.   Show that: $C_{n,0} = C_{n,n}$

34.   Show that: $C_{n,r} = C_{n,n-r}$

35.   The triangle below is called **Pascal's triangle.** Can you guess what the next two rows at the bottom are? Compare these numbers with the coefficients of binomial expansions.

```
            1
         1     1
      1     2     1
   1     3     3     1
1     4     6     4     1
```

Tables

B

Table I Exponential Functions (e^x and e^{-x})

x	e^x	e^{-x}	x	e^x	e^{-x}	x	e^x	e^{-x}
0.00	1.0000	1.00 000	0.50	1.6487	0.60 653	1.00	2.7183	0.36 788
0.01	1.0101	0.99 005	0.51	1.6653	0.60 050	1.01	2.7456	0.36 422
0.02	1.0202	0.98 020	0.52	1.6820	0.59 452	1.02	2.7732	0.36 059
0.03	1.0305	0.97 045	0.53	1.6989	0.58 860	1.03	2.8011	0.35 701
0.04	1.0408	0.96 079	0.54	1.7160	0.58 275	1.04	2.8292	0.35 345
0.05	1.0513	0.95 123	0.55	1.7333	0.57 695	1.05	2.8577	0.34 994
0.06	1.0618	0.94 176	0.56	1.7507	0.57 121	1.06	2.8864	0.34 646
0.07	1.0725	0.93 239	0.57	1.7683	0.56 553	1.07	2.9154	0.34 301
0.08	1.0833	0.92 312	0.58	1.7860	0.55 990	1.08	2.9447	0.33 960
0.09	1.0942	0.91 393	0.59	1.8040	0.55 433	1.09	2.9743	0.33 622
0.10	1.1052	0.90 484	0.60	1.8221	0.54 881	1.10	3.0042	0.33 287
0.11	1.1163	0.89 583	0.61	1.8404	0.54 335	1.11	3.0344	0.32 956
0.12	1.1275	0.88 692	0.62	1.8589	0.53 794	1.12	3.0649	0.32 628
0.13	1.1388	0.87 810	0.63	1.8776	0.53 259	1.13	3.0957	0.32 303
0.14	1.1503	0.86 936	0.64	1.8965	0.52 729	1.14	3.1268	0.31 982
0.15	1.1618	0.86 071	0.65	1.9155	0.52 205	1.15	3.1582	0.31 664
0.16	1.1735	0.85 214	0.66	1.9348	0.51 685	1.16	3.1899	0.31 349
0.17	1.1853	0.84 366	0.67	1.9542	0.51 171	1.17	3.2220	0.31 037
0.18	1.1972	0.83 527	0.68	1.9739	0.50 662	1.18	3.2544	0.30 728
0.19	1.2092	0.82 696	0.69	1.9937	0.50 158	1.19	3.2871	0.30 422
0.20	1.2214	0.81 873	0.70	2.0138	0.49 659	1.20	3.3201	0.30 119
0.21	1.2337	0.81 058	0.71	2.0340	0.49 164	1.21	3.3535	0.29 820
0.22	1.2461	0.80 252	0.72	2.0544	0.48 675	1.22	3.3872	0.29 523
0.23	1.2586	0.79 453	0.73	2.0751	0.48 191	1.23	3.4212	0.29 229
0.24	1.2712	0.78 663	0.74	2.0959	0.47 711	1.24	3.4556	0.28 938
0.25	1.2840	0.77 880	0.75	2.1170	0.47 237	1.25	3.4903	0.28 650
0.26	1.2969	0.77 105	0.76	2.1383	0.46 767	1.26	3.5254	0.28 365
0.27	1.3100	0.76 338	0.77	2.1598	0.46 301	1.27	3.5609	0.28 083
0.28	1.3231	0.75 578	0.78	2.1815	0.45 841	1.28	3.5966	0.27 804
0.29	1.3364	0.74 826	0.79	2.2034	0.45 384	1.29	3.6328	0.27 527
0.30	1.3499	0.74 082	0.80	2.2255	0.44 933	1.30	3.6693	0.27 253
0.31	1.3634	0.73 345	0.81	2.2479	0.44 486	1.31	3.7062	0.26 982
0.32	1.3771	0.72 615	0.82	2.2705	0.44 043	1.32	3.7434	0.26 714
0.33	1.3910	0.71 892	0.83	2.2933	0.43 605	1.33	3.7810	0.26 448
0.34	1.4049	0.71 177	0.84	2.3164	0.43 171	1.34	3.8190	0.26 185
0.35	1.4191	0.70 469	0.85	2.3396	0.42 741	1.35	3.8574	0.25 924
0.36	1.4333	0.69 768	0.86	2.3632	0.42 316	1.36	3.8962	0.25 666
0.37	1.4477	0.69 073	0.87	2.3869	0.41 895	1.37	3.9354	0.25 411
0.38	1.4623	0.68 386	0.88	2.4109	0.41 478	1.38	3.9749	0.25 158
0.39	1.4770	0.67 706	0.89	2.4351	0.41 066	1.39	4.0149	0.24 908
0.40	1.4918	0.67 032	0.90	2.4596	0.40 657	1.40	4.0552	0.24 660
0.41	1.5068	0.66 365	0.91	2.4843	0.40 252	1.41	4.0960	0.24 414
0.42	1.5220	0.65 705	0.92	2.5093	0.39 852	1.42	4.1371	0.24 171
0.43	1.5373	0.65 051	0.93	2.5345	0.39 455	1.43	4.1787	0.23 931
0.44	1.5527	0.64 404	0.94	2.5600	0.39 063	1.44	4.2207	0.23 693
0.45	1.5683	0.63 763	0.95	2.5857	0.38 674	1.45	4.2631	0.23 457
0.46	1.5841	0.63 128	0.96	2.6117	0.38 289	1.46	4.3060	0.23 224
0.47	1.6000	0.62 500	0.97	2.6379	0.37 908	1.47	4.3492	0.22 993
0.48	1.6161	0.61 878	0.98	2.6645	0.37 531	1.48	4.3939	0.22 764
0.49	1.6323	0.61 263	0.99	2.6912	0.37 158	1.49	4.4371	0.22 537
0.50	1.6487	0.60 653	1.00	2.7183	0.36 788	1.50	4.4817	0.22 313

x	e^x	e^{-x}	x	e^x	e^{-x}	x	e^x	e^{-x}
1.50	4.4817	0.22 313	2.00	7.3891	0.13 534	2.50	12.182	0.082 085
1.51	4.5267	0.22 091	2.01	7.4633	0.13 399	2.51	12.305	0.081 268
1.52	4.5722	0.21 871	2.02	7.5383	0.13 266	2.52	12.429	0.080 460
1.53	4.6182	0.21 654	2.03	7.6141	0.13 134	2.53	12.554	0.079 659
1.54	4.6646	0.21 438	2.04	7.6906	0.13 003	2.54	12.680	0.078 866
1.55	4.7115	0.21 225	2.05	7.7679	0.12 873	2.55	12.807	0.078 082
1.56	4.7588	0.21 014	2.06	7.8460	0.12 745	2.56	12.936	0.077 305
1.57	4.8066	0.20 805	2.07	7.9248	0.12 619	2.57	13.066	0.076 536
1.58	4.8550	0.20 598	2.08	8.0045	0.12 493	2.58	13.197	0.075 774
1.59	4.9037	0.20 393	2.09	8.0849	0.12 369	2.59	13.330	0.075 020
1.60	4.9530	0.20 190	2.10	8.1662	0.12 246	2.60	13.464	0.074 274
1.61	5.0028	0.19 989	2.11	8.2482	0.12 124	2.61	13.599	0.073 535
1.62	5.0531	0.19 790	2.12	8.3311	0.12 003	2.62	13.736	0.072 803
1.63	5.1039	0.19 593	2.13	8.4149	0.11 884	2.63	13.874	0.072 078
1.64	5.1552	0.19 398	2.14	8.4994	0.11 765	2.64	14.013	0.071 361
1.65	5.2070	0.19 205	2.15	8.5849	0.11 648	2.65	14.154	0.070 651
1.66	5.2593	0.19 014	2.16	8.6711	0.11 533	2.66	14.296	0.069 948
1.67	5.3122	0.18 825	2.17	8.7583	0.11 418	2.67	14.440	0.069 252
1.68	5.3656	0.18 637	2.18	8.8463	0.11 304	2.68	14.585	0.068 563
1.69	5.4195	0.18 452	2.19	8.9352	0.11 192	2.69	14.732	0.067 881
1.70	5.4739	0.18 268	2.20	9.0250	0.11 080	2.70	14.880	0.067 206
1.71	5.5290	0.18 087	2.21	9.1157	0.10 970	2.71	15.029	0.066 537
1.72	5.5845	0.17 907	2.22	9.2073	0.10 861	2.72	15.180	0.065 875
1.73	5.6407	0.17 728	2.23	9.2999	0.10 753	2.73	15.333	0.065 219
1.74	5.6973	0.17 552	2.24	9.3933	0.10 646	2.74	15.487	0.064 570
1.75	5.7546	0.17 377	2.25	9.4877	0.10 540	2.75	15.643	0.063 928
1.76	5.8124	0.17 204	2.26	9.5831	0.10 435	2.76	15.800	0.063 292
1.77	5.8709	0.17 033	2.27	9.6794	0.10 331	2.77	15.959	0.062 662
1.78	5.9299	0.16 864	2.28	9.7767	0.10 228	2.78	16.119	0.062 039
1.79	5.9895	0.16 696	2.29	9.8749	0.10 127	2.79	16.281	0.061 421
1.80	6.0496	0.16 530	2.30	9.9742	0.10 026	2.80	16.445	0.060 810
1.81	6.1104	0.16 365	2.31	10.074	0.099 261	2.81	16.610	0.060 205
1.82	6.1719	0.16 203	2.32	10.176	0.098 274	2.82	16.777	0.059 606
1.83	6.2339	0.16 041	2.33	10.278	0.097 296	2.83	16.945	0.059 013
1.84	6.2965	0.15 882	2.34	10.381	0.096 328	2.84	17.116	0.058 426
1.85	6.3598	0.15 724	2.35	10.486	0.095 369	2.85	17.288	0.057 844
1.86	6.4237	0.15 567	2.36	10.591	0.094 420	2.86	17.462	0.057 269
1.87	6.4883	0.15 412	2.37	10.697	0.093 481	2.87	17.637	0.056 699
1.88	6.5535	0.15 259	2.38	10.805	0.092 551	2.88	17.814	0.056 135
1.89	6.6194	0.15 107	2.39	10.913	0.091 630	2.89	17.993	0.055 576
1.90	6.6859	0.14 957	2.40	11.023	0.090 718	2.90	18.174	0.055 023
1.91	6.7531	0.14 808	2.41	11.134	0.089 815	2.91	18.357	0.054 476
1.92	6.8210	0.14 661	2.42	11.246	0.088 922	2.92	18.541	0.053 934
1.93	6.8895	0.14 515	2.43	11.359	0.088 037	2.93	18.728	0.053 397
1.94	6.9588	0.14 370	2.44	11.473	0.087 161	2.94	18.916	0.052 866
1.95	7.0287	0.14 227	2.45	11.588	0.086 294	2.95	19.106	0.052 340
1.96	7.0993	0.14 086	2.46	11.705	0.085 435	2.96	19.298	0.051 819
1.97	7.1707	0.13 946	2.47	11.822	0.084 585	2.97	19.492	0.051 303
1.98	7.2427	0.13 807	2.48	11.941	0.083 743	2.98	19.688	0.050 793
1.99	7.3155	0.13 670	2.49	12.061	0.082 910	2.99	19.886	0.050 287
2.00	7.3891	0.13 534	2.50	12.182	0.082 085	3.00	20.086	0.049 787

x	e^x	e^{-x}	x	e^x	e^{-x}	x	e^x	e^{-x}
3.00	20.086	0.049 787	3.50	33.115	0.030 197	4.00	54.598	0.018 316
3.01	20.287	0.049 292	3.51	33.448	0.029 897	4.01	55.147	0.018 133
3.02	20.491	0.048 801	3.52	33.784	0.029 599	4.02	55.701	0.017 953
3.03	20.697	0.048 316	3.53	34.124	0.029 305	4.03	56.261	0.017 774
3.04	20.905	0.047 835	3.54	34.467	0.029 013	4.04	56.826	0.017 597
3.05	21.115	0.047 359	3.55	34.813	0.028 725	4.05	57.397	0.017 422
3.05	21.328	0.046 888	3.56	35.163	0.028 439	4.06	57.974	0.017 249
3.07	21.542	0.046 421	3.57	35.517	0.028 156	4.07	58.557	0.017 077
3.08	21.758	0.045 959	3.58	35.874	0.027 876	4.08	59.145	0.016 907
3.09	21.977	0.045 502	3.59	36.234	0.027 598	4.09	59.740	0.016 739
3.10	22.198	0.045 049	3.60	36.598	0.027 324	4.10	60.340	0.016 573
3.11	22.421	0.044 601	3.61	36.966	0.027 052	4.11	60.947	0.016 408
3.12	22.646	0.044 157	3.62	37.338	0.026 783	4.12	61.559	0.016 245
3.13	22.874	0.043 718	3.63	37.713	0.026 516	4.13	62.178	0.016 083
3.14	23.104	0.043 283	3.64	38.092	0.026 252	4.14	62.803	0.015 923
3.15	23.336	0.042 852	3.65	38.475	0.025 991	4.15	63.434	0.015 764
3.16	23.571	0.042 426	3.66	38.861	0.025 733	4.16	64.072	0.015 608
3.17	23.807	0.042 004	3.67	39.252	0.025 476	4.17	64.715	0.015 452
3.18	24.047	0.041 586	3.68	39.646	0.025 223	4.18	65.366	0.015 299
3.19	24.288	0.041 172	3.69	40.045	0.024 972	4.19	66.023	0.015 146
3.20	24.533	0.040 762	3.70	40.447	0.024 724	4.20	66.686	0.014 996
3.21	24.779	0.040 357	3.71	40.854	0.024 478	4.21	67.357	0.014 846
3.22	25.028	0.039 955	3.72	41.264	0.024 234	4.22	68.033	0.014 699
3.23	25.280	0.039 557	3.73	41.679	0.023 993	4.23	68.717	0.014 552
3.24	25.534	0.039 164	3.74	42.098	0.023 754	4.24	69.408	0.014 408
3.25	25.790	0.038 774	3.75	42.521	0.023 518	4.25	70.105	0.014 264
3.26	26.050	0.038 388	3.76	42.948	0.023 284	4.26	70.810	0.014 122
3.27	26.311	0.038 006	3.77	43.380	0.023 052	4.27	71.522	0.013 982
3.28	26.576	0.037 628	3.78	43.816	0.022 823	4.28	72.240	0.013 843
3.29	26.843	0.037 254	3.79	44.256	0.022 596	4.29	72.966	0.013 705
3.30	27.113	0.036 883	3.80	44.701	0.022 371	4.30	73.700	0.013 569
3.31	27.385	0.036 516	3.81	45.150	0.022 148	4.31	74.440	0.013 434
3.32	27.660	0.036 153	3.82	45.604	0.021 928	4.32	75.189	0.013 300
3.33	27.938	0.035 793	3.83	46.063	0.021 710	4.33	75.944	0.013 168
3.34	28.219	0.035 437	3.84	46.525	0.021 494	4.34	76.708	0.013 037
3.35	28.503	0.035 084	3.85	46.993	0.021 280	4.35	77.478	0.012 907
3.36	28.789	0.034 735	3.86	47.465	0.021 068	4.36	78.257	0.012 778
3.37	29.079	0.034 390	3.87	47.942	0.020 858	4.37	79.044	0.012 651
3.38	29.371	0.034 047	3.88	48.424	0.020 651	4.38	79.838	0.012 525
3.39	29.666	0.033 709	3.89	48.911	0.020 445	4.39	80.640	0.012 401
3.40	29.964	0.033 373	3.90	49.402	0.020 242	4.40	81.451	0.012 277
3.41	30.265	0.033 041	3.91	49.899	0.020 041	4.41	82.269	0.012 155
3.42	30.569	0.032 712	3.92	50.400	0.019 841	4.42	83.096	0.012 034
3.43	30.877	0.032 387	3.93	50.907	0.019 644	4.43	83.931	0.011 914
3.44	31.187	0.032 065	3.94	51.419	0.019 448	4.44	84.775	0.011 796
3.45	31.500	0.031 746	3.95	51.935	0.019 255	4.45	85.627	0.011 679
3.46	31.817	0.031 430	3.96	52.457	0.019 063	4.46	86.488	0.011 562
3.47	32.137	0.031 117	3.97	52.985	0.018 873	4.47	87.357	0.011 447
3.48	32.460	0.030 807	3.98	53.517	0.018 686	4.48	88.235	0.011 333
3.49	32.786	0.030 501	3.99	54.055	0.018 500	4.49	89.121	0.011 221
3.50	33.115	0.030 197	4.00	54.598	0.018 316	4.50	90.017	0.011 109

x	e^x	e^{-x}	x	e^x	e^{-x}	x	e^x	e^{-x}
4.50	90.017	0.011 109	5.00	148.41	0.006 7379	7.50	1,808.0	0.000 5531
4.51	90.922	0.010 998	5.05	156.02	0.006 4093	7.55	1,900.7	0.000 5261
4.52	91.836	0.010 889	5.10	164.02	0.006 0967	7.60	1,998.2	0.000 5005
4.53	92.759	0.010 781	5.15	172.43	0.005 7994	7.65	2,100.6	0.000 4760
4.54	93.691	0.010 673	5.20	181.27	0.005 5166	7.70	2,208.3	0.000 4528
4.55	94.632	0.010 567	5.25	190.57	0.005 2475	7.75	2,321.6	0.000 4307
4.56	95.583	0.010 462	5.30	200.34	0.004 9916	7.80	2,440.6	0.000 4097
4.57	96.544	0.010 358	5.35	210.61	0.004 7482	7.85	2,565.7	0.000 3898
4.58	97.514	0.010 255	5.40	221.41	0.004 5166	7.90	2,697.3	0.000 3707
4.59	98.494	0.010 153	5.45	232.76	0.004 2963	7.95	2,835.6	0.000 3527
4.60	99.484	0.010 052	5.50	244.69	0.004 0868	8.00	2,981.0	0.000 3355
4.61	100.48	0.009 9518	5.55	257.24	0.003 8875	8.05	3,133.8	0.000 3191
4.62	101.49	0.009 8528	5.60	270.43	0.003 6979	8.10	3,294.5	0.000 3035
4.63	102.51	0.009 7548	5.65	284.29	0.003 5175	8.15	3,463.4	0.000 2887
4.64	103.54	0.009 6577	5.70	298.87	0.003 3460	8.20	3,641.0	0.000 2747
4.65	104.58	0.009 5616	5.75	314.19	0.003 1828	8.25	3,827.6	0.000 2613
4.66	105.64	0.009 4665	5.80	330.30	0.003 0276	8.30	4,023.9	0.000 2485
4.67	106.70	0.009 3723	5.85	347.23	0.002 8799	8.35	4,230.2	0.000 2364
4.68	107.77	0.009 2790	5.90	365.04	0.002 7394	8.40	4,447.1	0.000 2249
4.69	108.85	0.009 1867	5.95	383.75	0.002 6058	8.45	4,675.1	0.000 2139
4.70	109.95	0.009 0953	6.00	403.43	0.002 4788	8.50	4,914.8	0.000 2035
4.71	111.05	0.009 0048	6.05	424.11	0.002 3579	8.55	5,166.8	0.000 1935
4.72	112.17	0.008 9152	6.10	445.86	0.002 2429	8.60	5,431.7	0.000 1841
4.73	113.30	0.008 8265	6.15	468.72	0.002 1335	8.65	5,710.1	0.000 1751
4.74	114.43	0.008 7386	6.20	492.75	0.002 2094	8.70	6,002.9	0.000 1666
4.75	115.58	0.008 6517	6.25	518.01	0.001 9305	8.75	6,310.7	0.000 1585
4.76	116.75	0.008 5656	6.30	544.57	0.001 8363	8.80	6,634.2	0.000 1507
4.77	117.92	0.008 4804	6.35	572.49	0.001 7467	8.85	6,974.4	0.000 1434
4.78	119.10	0.008 3960	6.40	601.85	0.001 6616	8.90	7,332.0	0.000 1364
4.79	120.30	0.008 3125	6.45	632.70	0.001 5805	8.95	7,707.9	0.000 1297
4.80	121.51	0.008 2297	6.50	665.14	0.001 5034	9.00	8,103.1	0.000 1234
4.81	122.73	0.008 1479	6.55	699.24	0.001 4301	9.05	8,518.5	0.000 1174
4.82	123.97	0.008 0668	6.60	735.10	0.001 3604	9.10	8,955.3	0.000 1117
4.83	125.21	0.007 9865	6.65	772.78	0.001 2940	9.15	9,414.4	0.000 1062
4.84	126.47	0.007 9071	6.70	812.41	0.001 2309	9.20	9,897.1	0.000 1010
4.85	127.74	0.007 8284	6.75	854.06	0.001 1709	9.25	10,405	0.000 0961
4.86	129.02	0.007 7505	6.80	897.85	0.001 1138	9.30	10,938	0.000 0914
4.87	130.32	0.007 6734	6.85	943.88	0.001 0595	9.35	11,499	0.000 0870
4.88	131.63	0.007 5970	6.90	992.27	0.001 0078	9.40	12,088	0.000 0827
4.89	132.95	0.007 5214	6.95	1,043.1	0.000 9586	9.45	12,708	0.000 0787
4.90	134.29	0.007 4466	7.00	1,096.6	0.000 9119	9.50	13,360	0.000 0749
4.91	135.64	0.007 3725	7.05	1,152.9	0.000 8674	9.55	14,045	0.000 0712
4.92	137.00	0.007 2991	7.10	1,212.0	0.000 8251	9.60	14,765	0.000 0677
4.93	138.38	0.007 2265	7.15	1,274.1	0.000 7849	9.65	15,522	0.000 0644
4.94	139.77	0.007 1546	7.20	1,339.4	0.000 7466	9.70	16,318	0.000 0613
4.95	141.17	0.007 0834	7.25	1,408.1	0.000 7102	9.75	17,154	0.000 0583
4.96	142.59	0.007 0129	7.30	1,480.3	0.000 6755	9.80	18,034	0.000 0555
4.97	144.03	0.006 9431	7.35	1,556.2	0.000 6426	9.85	18,958	0.000 0527
4.98	145.47	0.006 8741	7.40	1,636.0	0.000 6113	9.90	19,930	0.000 0502
4.99	146.94	0.006 8057	7.45	1,719.9	0.000 5814	9.95	20,952	0.000 0477
5.00	148.41	0.006 7379	7.50	1,808.0	0.000 5531	10.00	22,026	0.000 0454

N	0	1	2	3	4	5	6	7	8	9
1.0	0.0000	0.004321	0.008600	0.01284	0.01703	0.02119	0.02531	0.02938	0.03342	0.03743
1.1	0.04139	0.04532	0.04922	0.05308	0.05690	0.06070	0.06446	0.06819	0.07188	0.07555
1.2	0.07918	0.08279	0.08636	0.08991	0.09342	0.09691	0.1004	0.1038	0.1072	0.1106
1.3	0.1139	0.1173	0.1206	0.1239	0.1271	0.1303	0.1335	0.1367	0.1399	0.1430
1.4	0.1461	0.1492	0.1523	0.1553	0.1584	0.1614	0.1644	0.1673	0.1703	0.1732
1.5	0.1761	0.1790	0.1818	0.1847	0.1875	0.1903	0.1931	0.1959	0.1987	0.2014
1.6	0.2041	0.2068	0.2095	0.2122	0.2148	0.2175	0.2201	0.2227	0.2253	0.2279
1.7	0.2304	0.2330	0.2355	0.2380	0.2405	0.2430	0.2455	0.2480	0.2504	0.2529
1.8	0.2553	0.2577	0.2601	0.2625	0.2648	0.2673	0.2695	0.2718	0.2742	0.2765
1.9	0.2788	0.2810	0.2833	0.2856	0.2878	0.2900	0.2923	0.2945	0.2967	0.2989
2.0	0.3010	0.3032	0.3054	0.3075	0.3096	0.3118	0.3139	0.3160	0.3181	0.3201
2.1	0.3222	0.3243	0.3263	0.3284	0.3304	0.3324	0.3345	0.3365	0.3385	0.3404
2.2	0.3424	0.3444	0.3464	0.3483	0.3502	0.3522	0.3541	0.3560	0.3579	0.3598
2.3	0.3617	0.3636	0.3655	0.3674	0.3692	0.3711	0.3729	0.3747	0.3766	0.3784
2.4	0.3802	0.3820	0.3838	0.3856	0.3874	0.3892	0.3909	0.3927	0.3945	0.3962
2.5	0.3979	0.3997	0.4014	0.4031	0.4048	0.4065	0.4082	0.4099	0.4116	0.4133
2.6	0.4150	0.4166	0.4183	0.4200	0.4216	0.4232	0.4249	0.4265	0.4281	0.4298
2.7	0.4314	0.4330	0.4346	0.4362	0.4378	0.4393	0.4409	0.4425	0.4440	0.4456
2.8	0.4472	0.4487	0.4502	0.4518	0.4533	0.4548	0.4564	0.4579	0.4594	0.4609
2.9	0.4624	0.4639	0.4654	0.4669	0.4683	0.4698	0.4713	0.4728	0.4742	0.4757
3.0	0.4771	0.4786	0.4800	0.4814	0.4829	0.4843	0.4857	0.4871	0.4886	0.4900
3.1	0.4914	0.4928	0.4942	0.4955	0.4969	0.4983	0.4997	0.5011	0.5024	0.5038
3.2	0.5051	0.5065	0.5079	0.5092	0.5105	0.5119	0.5132	0.5145	0.5159	0.5172
3.3	0.5185	0.5198	0.5211	0.5224	0.5237	0.5250	0.5263	0.5276	0.5289	0.5302
3.4	0.5315	0.5328	0.5340	0.5353	0.5366	0.5378	0.5391	0.5403	0.5416	0.5428
3.5	0.5441	0.5453	0.5465	0.5478	0.5490	0.5502	0.5514	0.5527	0.5539	0.5551
3.6	0.5563	0.5575	0.5587	0.5599	0.5611	0.5623	0.5635	0.5647	0.5658	0.5670
3.7	0.5682	0.5694	0.5705	0.5717	0.5729	0.5740	0.5752	0.5763	0.5775	0.5786
3.8	0.5798	0.5809	0.5821	0.5832	0.5843	0.5855	0.5866	0.5877	0.5888	0.5899
3.9	0.5911	0.5922	0.5933	0.5944	0.5955	0.5966	0.5977	0.5988	0.5999	0.6010
4.0	0.6021	0.6031	0.6042	0.6053	0.6064	0.6075	0.6085	0.6096	0.6107	0.6117
4.1	0.6128	0.6138	0.6149	0.6160	0.6170	0.6180	0.6191	0.6201	0.6212	0.6222
4.2	0.6232	0.6243	0.6253	0.6263	0.6274	0.6284	0.6294	0.6304	0.6314	0.6325
4.3	0.6335	0.6345	0.6355	0.6365	0.6375	0.6385	0.6395	0.6405	0.6415	0.6425
4.4	0.6435	0.6444	0.6454	0.6464	0.6474	0.6484	0.6493	0.6503	0.6513	0.6522
4.5	0.6532	0.6542	0.6551	0.6561	0.6571	0.6580	0.6590	0.6599	0.6609	0.6618
4.6	0.6628	0.6637	0.6646	0.6656	0.6665	0.6675	0.6684	0.6693	0.6702	0.6712
4.7	0.6721	0.6730	0.6739	0.6749	0.6758	0.6767	0.6776	0.6785	0.6794	0.6803
4.8	0.6812	0.6821	0.6830	0.6839	0.6848	0.6857	0.6866	0.6875	0.6884	0.6893
4.9	0.6902	0.6911	0.6920	0.6928	0.6937	0.6946	0.6955	0.6964	0.6972	0.6981
5.0	0.6990	0.6998	0.7007	0.7016	0.7024	0.7033	0.7042	0.7050	0.7059	0.7067
5.1	0.7076	0.7084	0.7093	0.7101	0.7110	0.7118	0.7126	0.7135	0.7143	0.7152
5.2	0.7160	0.7168	0.7177	0.7185	0.7193	0.7202	0.7210	0.7218	0.7226	0.7235
5.3	0.7243	0.7251	0.7259	0.7267	0.7275	0.7284	0.7292	0.7300	0.7308	0.7316
5.4	0.7324	0.7332	0.7340	0.7348	0.7356	0.7364	0.7372	0.7380	0.7388	0.7396

N	0	1	2	3	4	5	6	7	8	9
5.5	0.7404	0.7412	0.7419	0.7427	0.7435	0.7443	0.7451	0.7459	0.7466	0.7474
5.6	0.7482	0.7490	0.7497	0.7505	0.7513	0.7520	0.7528	0.7536	0.7543	0.7551
5.7	0.7559	0.7566	0.7574	0.7582	0.7589	0.7597	0.7604	0.7612	0.7619	0.7627
5.8	0.7634	0.7642	0.7649	0.7657	0.7664	0.7672	0.7679	0.7686	0.7694	0.7701
5.9	0.7709	0.7716	0.7723	0.7731	0.7738	0.7745	0.7752	0.7760	0.7767	0.7774
6.0	0.7782	0.7789	0.7796	0.7803	0.7810	0.7818	0.7825	0.7832	0.7839	0.7846
6.1	0.7853	0.7860	0.7868	0.7875	0.7882	0.7889	0.7896	0.7903	0.7910	0.7917
6.2	0.7924	0.7931	0.7938	0.7945	0.7952	0.7959	0.7966	0.7973	0.7980	0.7987
6.3	0.7993	0.8000	0.8007	0.8014	0.8021	0.8028	0.8035	0.8041	0.8048	0.8055
6.4	0.8062	0.8069	0.8075	0.8082	0.8089	0.8096	0.8102	0.8109	0.8116	0.8122
6.5	0.8129	0.8136	0.8142	0.8149	0.8156	0.8162	0.8169	0.8176	0.8182	0.8189
6.6	0.8195	0.8202	0.8209	0.8215	0.8222	0.8228	0.8235	0.8241	0.8248	0.8254
6.7	0.8261	0.8267	0.8274	0.8280	0.8287	0.8293	0.8299	0.8306	0.8312	0.8319
6.8	0.8325	0.8331	0.8338	0.8344	0.8351	0.8357	0.8363	0.8370	0.8376	0.8382
6.9	0.8388	0.8395	0.8401	0.8407	0.8414	0.8420	0.8426	0.8432	0.8439	0.8445
7.0	0.8451	0.8457	0.8463	0.8470	0.8476	0.8482	0.8488	0.8494	0.8500	0.8506
7.1	0.8513	0.8519	0.8525	0.8531	0.8537	0.8543	0.8549	0.8555	0.8561	0.8567
7.2	0.8573	0.8579	0.8585	0.8591	0.8597	0.8603	0.8609	0.8615	0.8621	0.8627
7.3	0.8633	0.8639	0.8645	0.8651	0.8657	0.8663	0.8669	0.8675	0.8681	0.8686
7.4	0.8692	0.8698	0.8704	0.8710	0.8716	0.8722	0.8727	0.8733	0.8739	0.8745
7.5	0.8751	0.8756	0.8762	0.8768	0.8774	0.8779	0.8785	0.8791	0.8797	0.8802
7.6	0.8808	0.8814	0.8820	0.8825	0.8831	0.8837	0.8842	0.8848	0.8854	0.8859
7.7	0.8865	0.8871	0.8876	0.8882	0.8887	0.8893	0.8899	0.8904	0.8910	0.8915
7.8	0.8921	0.8927	0.8932	0.8938	0.8943	0.8949	0.8954	0.8960	0.8965	0.8971
7.9	0.8976	0.8982	0.8987	0.8993	0.8998	0.9004	0.9009	0.9015	0.9020	0.9025
8.0	0.9031	0.9036	0.9042	0.9047	0.9053	0.9058	0.9063	0.9069	0.9074	0.9079
8.1	0.9085	0.9090	0.9096	0.9101	0.9106	0.9112	0.9117	0.9122	0.9128	0.9133
8.2	0.9138	0.9143	0.9149	0.9154	0.9159	0.9165	0.9170	0.9175	0.9180	0.9186
8.3	0.9191	0.9196	0.9201	0.9206	0.9212	0.9217	0.9222	0.9227	0.9232	0.9238
8.4	0.9243	0.9248	0.9253	0.9258	0.9263	0.9269	0.9274	0.9279	0.9284	0.9289
8.5	0.9294	0.9299	0.9304	0.9309	0.9315	0.9320	0.9325	0.9330	0.9335	0.9340
8.6	0.9345	0.9350	0.9355	0.9360	0.9365	0.9370	0.9375	0.9380	0.9385	0.9390
8.7	0.9395	0.9400	0.9405	0.9410	0.9415	0.9420	0.9425	0.9430	0.9435	0.9440
8.8	0.9445	0.9450	0.9455	0.9460	0.9465	0.9469	0.9474	0.9479	0.9484	0.9489
8.9	0.9494	0.9499	0.9504	0.9509	0.9513	0.9518	0.9523	0.9528	0.9533	0.9538
9.0	0.9542	0.9547	0.9552	0.9557	0.9562	0.9566	0.9571	0.9576	0.9581	0.9586
9.1	0.9590	0.9595	0.9600	0.9605	0.9609	0.9614	0.9619	0.9624	0.9628	0.9633
9.2	0.9638	0.9643	0.9647	0.9652	0.9657	0.9661	0.9666	0.9671	0.9675	0.9680
9.3	0.9685	0.9689	0.9694	0.9699	0.9703	0.9708	0.9713	0.9717	0.9722	0.9727
9.4	0.9731	0.9736	0.9741	0.9745	0.9750	0.9754	0.9759	0.9763	0.9768	0.9773
9.5	0.9777	0.9782	0.9786	0.9791	0.9795	0.9800	0.9805	0.9809	0.9814	0.9818
9.6	0.9823	0.9827	0.9832	0.9836	0.9841	0.9845	0.9850	0.9854	0.9859	0.9863
9.7	0.9868	0.9872	0.9877	0.9881	0.9886	0.9890	0.9894	0.9899	0.9903	0.9908
9.8	0.9912	0.9917	0.9921	0.9926	0.9930	0.9934	0.9939	0.9943	0.9948	0.9952
9.9	0.9956	0.9961	0.9965	0.9969	0.9974	0.9978	0.9983	0.9987	0.9991	0.9996

Table III Natural Logarithms (ln $N = \log_e N$)

ln 10 = 2.3026	5 ln 10 = 11.5130	9 ln 10 = 20.7233
2 ln 10 = 4.6052	6 ln 10 = 13.8155	10 ln 10 = 23.0259
3 ln 10 = 6.9078	7 ln 10 = 16.1181	
4 ln 10 = 9.2103	8 ln 10 = 18.4207	

N	.00	.01	.02	.03	.04	.05	.06	.07	.08	.09
1.0	0.0000	0.0100	0.0198	0.0296	0.0392	0.0488	0.0583	0.0677	0.0770	0.0862
1.1	0.0953	0.1044	0.1133	0.1222	0.1310	0.1398	0.1484	0.1570	0.1655	0.1740
1.2	0.1823	0.1906	0.1989	0.2070	0.2151	0.2231	0.2311	0.2390	0.2469	0.2546
1.3	0.2624	0.2700	0.2776	0.2852	0.2927	0.3001	0.3075	0.3148	0.3221	0.3293
1.4	0.3365	0.3436	0.3507	0.3577	0.3646	0.3716	0.3784	0.3853	0.3920	0.3988
1.5	0.4055	0.4121	0.4187	0.4253	0.4318	0.4383	0.4447	0.4511	0.4574	0.4637
1.6	0.4700	0.4762	0.4824	0.4886	0.4947	0.5008	0.5068	0.5128	0.5188	0.5247
1.7	0.5306	0.5365	0.5423	0.5481	0.5539	0.5596	0.5653	0.5710	0.5766	0.5822
1.8	0.5878	0.5933	0.5988	0.6043	0.6098	0.6152	0.6206	0.6259	0.6313	0.6366
1.9	0.6419	0.6471	0.6523	0.6575	0.6627	0.6678	0.6729	0.6780	0.6831	0.6881
2.0	0.6931	0.6981	0.7031	0.7080	0.7129	0.7178	0.7227	0.7275	0.7324	0.7372
2.1	0.7419	0.7467	0.7514	0.7561	0.7608	0.7655	0.7701	0.7747	0.7793	0.7839
2.2	0.7885	0.7930	0.7975	0.8020	0.8065	0.8109	0.8154	0.8198	0.8242	0.8286
2.3	0.8329	0.8372	0.8416	0.8459	0.8502	0.8544	0.8587	0.8629	0.8671	0.8713
2.4	0.8755	0.8796	0.8838	0.8879	0.8920	0.8961	0.9002	0.9042	0.9083	0.9123
2.5	0.9163	0.9203	0.9243	0.9282	0.9322	0.9361	0.9400	0.9439	0.9478	0.9517
2.6	0.9555	0.9594	0.9632	0.9670	0.9708	0.9746	0.9783	0.9821	0.9858	0.9895
2.7	0.9933	0.9969	1.0006	1.0043	1.0080	1.0116	1.0152	1.0188	1.0225	1.0260
2.8	1.0296	1.0332	1.0367	1.0403	1.0438	1.0473	1.0508	1.0543	1.0578	1.0613
2.9	1.0647	1.0682	1.0716	1.0750	1.0784	1.0818	1.0852	1.0886	1.0919	1.0953
3.0	1.0986	1.1019	1.1053	1.1086	1.1119	1.1151	1.1184	1.1217	1.1249	1.1282
3.1	1.1314	1.1346	1.1378	1.1410	1.1442	1.1474	1.1506	1.1537	1.1569	1.1600
3.2	1.1632	1.1663	1.1694	1.1725	1.1756	1.1787	1.1817	1.1848	1.1878	1.1909
3.3	1.1939	1.1969	1.2000	1.2030	1.2060	1.2090	1.2119	1.2149	1.2179	1.2208
3.4	1.2238	1.2267	1.2296	1.2326	1.2355	1.2384	1.2413	1.2442	1.2470	1.2499
3.5	1.2528	1.2556	1.2585	1.2613	1.2641	1.2669	1.2698	1.2726	1.2754	1.2782
3.6	1.2809	1.2837	1.2865	1.2892	1.2920	1.2947	1.2975	1.3002	1.3029	1.3056
3.7	1.3083	1.3110	1.3137	1.3164	1.3191	1.3218	1.3244	1.3271	1.3297	1.3324
3.8	1.3350	1.3376	1.3403	1.3429	1.3455	1.3481	1.3507	1.3533	1.3558	1.3584
3.9	1.3610	1.3635	1.3661	1.3686	1.3712	1.3737	1.3762	1.3788	1.3813	1.3838
4.0	1.3863	1.3888	1.3913	1.3938	1.3962	1.3987	1.4012	1.4036	1.4061	1.4085
4.1	1.4110	1.4134	1.4159	1.4183	1.4207	1.4231	1.4255	1.4279	1.4303	1.4327
4.2	1.4351	1.4375	1.4398	1.4422	1.4446	1.4469	1.4493	1.4516	1.4540	1.4563
4.3	1.4586	1.4609	1.4633	1.4656	1.4679	1.4702	1.4725	1.4748	1.4770	1.4793
4.4	1.4816	1.4839	1.4861	1.4884	1.4907	1.4929	1.4951	1.4974	1.4996	1.5019
4.5	1.5041	1.5063	1.5085	1.5107	1.5129	1.5151	1.5173	1.5195	1.5217	1.5239
4.6	1.5261	1.5282	1.5304	1.5326	1.5347	1.5369	1.5390	1.5412	1.5433	1.5454
4.7	1.5476	1.5497	1.5518	1.5539	1.5560	1.5581	1.5602	1.5623	1.5644	1.5665
4.8	1.5686	1.5707	1.5728	1.5748	1.5769	1.5790	1.5810	1.5831	1.5851	1.5872
4.9	1.5892	1.5913	1.5933	1.5953	1.5974	1.5994	1.6014	1.6034	1.6054	1.6074
5.0	1.6094	1.6114	1.6134	1.6154	1.6174	1.6194	1.6214	1.6233	1.6253	1.6273
5.1	1.6292	1.6312	1.6332	1.6351	1.6371	1.6390	1.6409	1.6429	1.6448	1.6467
5.2	1.6487	1.6506	1.6525	1.6544	1.6563	1.6582	1.6601	1.6620	1.6639	1.6658
5.3	1.6677	1.6696	1.6715	1.6734	1.6752	1.6771	1.6790	1.6808	1.6827	1.6845
5.4	1.6864	1.6882	1.6901	1.6919	1.6938	1.6956	1.6974	1.6993	1.7011	1.7029

Note: $\ln 35{,}200 = \ln (3.52 \times 10^4)\ = \ln 3.52 + 4 \ln 10$

$\ln 0.00864 = \ln (8.64 \times 10^{-3}) = \ln 8.64 - 3 \ln 10$

N	.00	.01	.02	.03	.04	.05	.06	.07	.08	.09
5.5	1.7047	1.7066	1.7084	1.7102	1.7120	1.7138	1.7156	1.7174	1.7192	1.7210
5.6	1.7228	1.7246	1.7263	1.7281	1.7299	1.7317	1.7334	1.7352	1.7370	1.7387
5.7	1.7405	1.7422	1.7440	1.7457	1.7475	1.7492	1.7509	1.7527	1.7544	1.7561
5.8	1.7579	1.7596	1.7613	1.7630	1.7647	1.7664	1.7681	1.7699	1.7716	1.7733
5.9	1.7750	1.7766	1.7783	1.7800	1.7817	1.7834	1.7851	1.7867	1.7884	1.7901
6.0	1.7918	1.7934	1.7951	1.7967	1.7984	1.8001	1.8017	1.8034	1.8050	1.8066
6.1	1.8083	1.8099	1.8116	1.8132	1.8148	1.8165	1.8181	1.8197	1.8213	1.8229
6.2	1.8245	1.8262	1.8278	1.8294	1.8310	1.8326	1.8342	1.8358	1.8374	1.8390
6.3	1.8405	1.8421	1.8437	1.8453	1.8469	1.8485	1.8500	1.8516	1.8532	1.8547
6.4	1.8563	1.8579	1.8594	1.8610	1.8625	1.8641	1.8656	1.8672	1.8687	1.8703
6.5	1.8718	1.8733	1.8749	1.8764	1.8779	1.8795	1.8810	1.8825	1.8840	1.8856
6.6	1.8871	1.8886	1.8901	1.8916	1.8931	1.8946	1.8961	1.8976	1.8991	1.9006
6.7	1.9021	1.9036	1.9051	1.9066	1.9081	1.9095	1.9110	1.9125	1.9140	1.9155
6.8	1.9169	1.9184	1.9199	1.9213	1.9228	1.9242	1.9257	1.9272	1.9286	1.9301
6.9	1.9315	1.9330	1.9344	1.9359	1.9373	1.9387	1.9402	1.9416	1.9430	1.9445
7.0	1.9459	1.9473	1.9488	1.9502	1.9516	1.9530	1.9544	1.9559	1.9573	1.9587
7.1	1.9601	1.9615	1.9629	1.9643	1.9657	1.9671	1.9685	1.9699	1.9713	1.9727
7.2	1.9741	1.9755	1.9769	1.9782	1.9796	1.9810	1.9824	1.9838	1.9851	1.9865
7.3	1.9879	1.9892	1.9906	1.9920	1.9933	1.9947	1.9961	1.9974	1.9988	2.0001
7.4	2.0015	2.0028	2.0042	2.0055	2.0069	2.0082	2.0096	2.0109	2.0122	2.0136
7.5	2.0149	2.0162	2.0176	2.0189	2.0202	2.0215	2.0229	2.0242	2.0255	2.0268
7.6	2.0281	2.0295	2.0308	2.0321	2.0334	2.0347	2.0360	2.0373	2.0386	2.0399
7.7	2.0412	2.0425	2.0438	2.0451	2.0464	2.0477	2.0490	2.0503	2.0516	2.0528
7.8	2.0541	2.0554	2.0567	2.0580	2.0592	2.0605	2.0618	2.0631	2.0643	2.0656
7.9	2.0669	2.0681	2.0694	2.0707	2.0719	2.0732	2.0744	2.0757	2.0769	2.0782
8.0	2.0794	2.0807	2.0819	2.0832	2.0844	2.0857	2.0869	2.0882	2.0894	2.0906
8.1	2.0919	2.0931	2.0943	2.0956	2.0968	2.0980	2.0992	2.1005	2.1017	2.1029
8.2	2.1041	2.1054	2.1066	2.1078	2.1090	2.1102	2.1114	2.1126	2.1138	2.1150
8.3	2.1163	2.1175	2.1187	2.1199	2.1211	2.1223	2.1235	2.1247	2.1258	2.1270
8.4	2.1282	2.1294	2.1306	2.1318	2.1330	2.1342	2.1353	2.1365	2.1377	2.1389
8.5	2.1401	2.1412	2.1424	2.1436	2.1448	2.1459	2.1471	2.1483	2.1494	2.1506
8.6	2.1518	2.1529	2.1541	2.1552	2.1564	2.1576	2.1587	2.1599	2.1610	2.1622
8.7	2.1633	2.1645	2.1656	2.1668	2.1679	2.1691	2.1702	2.1713	2.1725	2.1736
8.8	2.1748	2.1759	2.1770	2.1782	2.1793	2.1804	2.1815	2.1827	2.1838	2.1849
8.9	2.1861	2.1872	2.1883	2.1894	2.1905	2.1917	2.1928	2.1939	2.1950	2.1961
9.0	2.1972	2.1983	2.1994	2.2006	2.2017	2.2028	2.2039	2.2050	2.2061	2.2072
9.1	2.2083	2.2094	2.2105	2.2116	2.2127	2.2138	2.2148	2.2159	2.2170	2.2181
9.2	2.2192	2.2203	2.2214	2.2225	2.2235	2.2246	2.2257	2.2268	2.2279	2.2289
9.3	2.2300	2.2311	2.2322	2.2332	2.2343	2.2354	2.2364	2.2375	2.2386	2.2396
9.4	2.2407	2.2418	2.2428	2.2439	2.2450	2.2460	2.2471	2.2481	2.2492	2.2502
9.5	2.2513	2.2523	2.2534	2.2544	2.2555	2.2565	2.2576	2.2586	2.2597	2.2607
9.6	2.2618	2.2628	2.2638	2.2649	2.2659	2.2670	2.2680	2.2690	2.2701	2.2711
9.7	2.2721	2.2732	2.2742	2.2752	2.2762	2.2773	2.2783	2.2793	2.2803	2.2814
9.8	2.2824	2.2834	2.2844	2.2854	2.2865	2.2875	2.2885	2.2895	2.2905	2.2915
9.9	2.2925	2.2935	2.2946	2.2956	2.2966	2.2976	2.2986	2.2996	2.3006	2.3016

Table IV Areas under the Standard Normal Curve

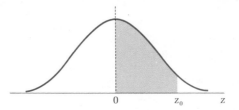

A represents the area between $z = 0$ and $z = z_0$, $z_0 \geq 0$

z	A	z	A	z	A	z	A
0.00	0.0000	0.30	0.1179	0.60	0.2258	0.90	0.3159
0.01	0.0040	0.31	0.1217	0.61	0.2291	0.91	0.3186
0.02	0.0080	0.32	0.1255	0.62	0.2324	0.92	0.3212
0.03	0.0120	0.33	0.1293	0.63	0.2357	0.93	0.3238
0.04	0.0160	0.34	0.1331	0.64	0.2389	0.94	0.3264
0.05	0.0199	0.35	0.1368	0.65	0.2422	0.95	0.3289
0.06	0.0239	0.36	0.1406	0.66	0.2454	0.96	0.3315
0.07	0.0279	0.37	0.1443	0.67	0.2486	0.97	0.3340
0.08	0.0319	0.38	0.1480	0.68	0.2518	0.98	0.3365
0.09	0.0359	0.39	0.1517	0.69	0.2549	0.99	0.3389
0.10	0.0398	0.40	0.1554	0.70	0.2580	1.00	0.3413
0.11	0.0438	0.41	0.1591	0.71	0.2612	1.01	0.3438
0.12	0.0478	0.42	0.1628	0.72	0.2642	1.02	0.3461
0.13	0.0517	0.43	0.1664	0.73	0.2673	1.03	0.3485
0.14	0.0557	0.44	0.1700	0.74	0.2704	1.04	0.3508
0.15	0.0596	0.45	0.1736	0.75	0.2734	1.05	0.3531
0.16	0.0636	0.46	0.1772	0.76	0.2764	1.06	0.3554
0.17	0.0675	0.47	0.1808	0.77	0.2794	1.07	0.3577
0.18	0.0714	0.48	0.1844	0.78	0.2823	1.08	0.3599
0.19	0.0754	0.49	0.1879	0.79	0.2852	1.09	0.3621
0.20	0.0793	0.50	0.1915	0.80	0.2881	1.10	0.3643
0.21	0.0832	0.51	0.1950	0.81	0.2910	1.11	0.3665
0.22	0.0871	0.52	0.1985	0.82	0.2939	1.12	0.3686
0.23	0.0910	0.53	0.2019	0.83	0.2967	1.13	0.3708
0.24	0.0948	0.54	0.2054	0.84	0.2996	1.14	0.3729
0.25	0.0987	0.55	0.2088	0.85	0.3023	1.15	0.3749
0.26	0.1026	0.56	0.2123	0.86	0.3051	1.16	0.3770
0.27	0.1064	0.57	0.2157	0.87	0.3079	1.17	0.3790
0.28	0.1103	0.58	0.2190	0.88	0.3106	1.18	0.3810
0.29	0.1141	0.59	0.2224	0.89	0.3133	1.19	0.3830

z	A	z	A	z	A	z	A
1.20	0.3849	1.55	0.4394	1.90	0.4713	2.25	0.4878
1.21	0.3869	1.56	0.4406	1.91	0.4719	2.26	0.4881
1.22	0.3888	1.57	0.4418	1.92	0.4726	2.27	0.4884
1.23	0.3907	1.58	0.4430	1.93	0.4732	2.28	0.4887
1.24	0.3925	1.59	0.4441	1.94	0.4738	2.29	0.4890
1.25	0.3944	1.60	0.4452	1.95	0.4744	2.30	0.4893
1.26	0.3962	1.61	0.4463	1.96	0.4750	2.31	0.4896
1.27	0.3980	1.62	0.4474	1.97	0.4756	2.32	0.4898
1.28	0.3997	1.63	0.4485	1.98	0.4762	2.33	0.4901
1.29	0.4015	1.64	0.4495	1.99	0.4767	2.34	0.4904
1.30	0.4032	1.65	0.4505	2.00	0.4773	2.35	0.4906
1.31	0.4049	1.66	0.4515	2.01	0.4778	2.36	0.4909
1.32	0.4066	1.67	0.4525	2.02	0.4783	2.37	0.4911
1.33	0.4082	1.68	0.4535	2.03	0.4788	2.38	0.4913
1.34	0.4099	1.69	0.4545	2.04	0.4793	2.39	0.4916
1.35	0.4115	1.70	0.4554	2.05	0.4798	2.40	0.4918
1.36	0.4131	1.71	0.4564	2.06	0.4803	2.41	0.4920
1.37	0.4147	1.72	0.4573	2.07	0.4808	2.42	0.4922
1.38	0.4162	1.73	0.4582	2.08	0.4812	2.43	0.4925
1.39	0.4177	1.74	0.4591	2.09	0.4817	2.44	0.4927
1.40	0.4192	1.75	0.4599	2.10	0.4821	2.45	0.4929
1.41	0.4207	1.76	0.4608	2.11	0.4826	2.46	0.4931
1.42	0.4222	1.77	0.4616	2.12	0.4830	2.47	0.4932
1.43	0.4236	1.78	0.4625	2.13	0.4834	2.48	0.4934
1.44	0.4251	1.79	0.4633	2.14	0.4838	2.49	0.4936
1.45	0.4265	1.80	0.4641	2.15	0.4842	2.50	0.4938
1.46	0.4279	1.81	0.4649	2.16	0.4846	2.51	0.4940
1.47	0.4292	1.82	0.4656	2.17	0.4850	2.52	0.4941
1.48	0.4306	1.83	0.4664	2.18	0.4854	2.53	0.4943
1.49	0.4319	1.84	0.4671	2.19	0.4857	2.54	0.4945
1.50	0.4332	1.85	0.4678	2.20	0.4861	2.55	0.4946
1.51	0.4345	1.86	0.4686	2.21	0.4865	2.56	0.4948
1.52	0.4357	1.87	0.4693	2.22	0.4868	2.57	0.4949
1.53	0.4370	1.88	0.4700	2.23	0.4871	2.58	0.4951
1.54	0.4382	1.89	0.4706	2.24	0.4875	2.59	0.4952

Table IV (Continued)

z	A	z	A	z	A	z	A
2.60	0.4953	2.95	0.4984	3.30	0.4995	3.65	0.4999
2.61	0.4955	2.96	0.4985	3.31	0.4995	3.66	0.4999
2.62	0.4956	2.97	0.4985	3.32	0.4996	3.67	0.4999
2.63	0.4957	2.98	0.4986	3.33	0.4996	3.68	0.4999
2.64	0.4959	2.99	0.4986	3.34	0.4996	3.69	0.4999
2.65	0.4960	3.00	0.4987	3.35	0.4996	3.70	0.4999
2.66	0.4961	3.01	0.4987	3.36	0.4996	3.71	0.4999
2.67	0.4962	3.02	0.4987	3.37	0.4996	3.72	0.4999
2.68	0.4963	3.03	0.4988	3.38	0.4996	3.73	0.4999
2.69	0.4964	3.04	0.4988	3.39	0.4997	3.74	0.4999
2.70	0.4965	3.05	0.4989	3.40	0.4997	3.75	0.4999
2.71	0.4966	3.06	0.4989	3.41	0.4997	3.76	0.4999
2.72	0.4967	3.07	0.4989	3.42	0.4997	3.77	0.4999
2.73	0.4968	3.08	0.4990	3.43	0.4997	3.78	0.4999
2.74	0.4969	3.09	0.4990	3.44	0.4997	3.79	0.4999
2.75	0.4970	3.10	0.4990	3.45	0.4997	3.80	0.4999
2.76	0.4971	3.11	0.4991	3.46	0.4997	3.81	0.4999
2.77	0.4972	3.12	0.4991	3.47	0.4997	3.82	0.4999
2.78	0.4973	3.13	0.4991	3.48	0.4998	3.83	0.4999
2.79	0.4974	3.14	0.4992	3.49	0.4998	3.84	0.4999
2.80	0.4974	3.15	0.4992	3.50	0.4998	3.85	0.4999
2.81	0.4975	3.16	0.4992	3.51	0.4998	3.86	0.4999
2.82	0.4976	3.17	0.4992	3.52	0.4998	3.87	0.5000
2.83	0.4977	3.18	0.4993	3.53	0.4998	3.88	0.5000
2.84	0.4977	3.19	0.4993	3.54	0.4998	3.89	0.5000
2.85	0.4978	3.20	0.4993	3.55	0.4998		
2.86	0.4979	3.21	0.4993	3.56	0.4998		
2.87	0.4980	3.22	0.4994	3.57	0.4998		
2.88	0.4980	3.23	0.4994	3.58	0.4998		
2.89	0.4981	3.24	0.4994	3.59	0.4998		
2.90	0.4981	3.25	0.4994	3.60	0.4998		
2.91	0.4982	3.26	0.4994	3.61	0.4999		
2.92	0.4983	3.27	0.4995	3.62	0.4999		
2.93	0.4983	3.28	0.4995	3.63	0.4999		
2.94	0.4984	3.29	0.4995	3.64	0.4999		

Table V Mathematics of Finance

			$i = 0.0025$ (¼%)				
n	$(1 + i)^n$	$s_{\overline{n}|i}$	$a_{\overline{n}|i}$	n	$(1 + i)^n$	$s_{\overline{n}|i}$	$a_{\overline{n}|i}$
1	1.002 500	1.000 000	0.997 506	51	1.135 804	54.321 654	47.826 604
2	1.005 006	2.002 500	1.992 525	52	1.138 644	55.457 459	48.704 842
3	1.007 519	3.007 506	2.985 062	53	1.141 490	56.596 102	49.580 890
4	1.010 038	4.015 025	3.975 124	54	1.144 344	57.737 593	50.454 753
5	1.012 563	5.025 063	4.962 718	55	1.147 205	58.881 936	51.326 437
6	1.015 094	6.037 625	5.947 848	56	1.150 073	60.029 141	52.195 947
7	1.017 632	7.052 719	6.930 522	57	1.152 948	61.179 214	53.063 288
8	1.020 176	8.070 351	7.910 745	58	1.155 830	62.332 162	53.928 467
9	1.022 726	9.090 527	8.888 524	59	1.158 720	63.487 993	54.791 489
10	1.025 283	10.113 253	9.863 864	60	1.161 617	64.646 713	55.652 358
11	1.027 846	11.138 536	10.836 772	61	1.164 521	65.808 329	56.511 080
12	1.030 416	12.166 383	11.807 254	62	1.167 432	66.972 850	57.367 661
13	1.032 992	13.196 799	12.775 316	63	1.170 351	68.140 282	58.222 106
14	1.035 574	14.229 791	13.740 963	64	1.173 277	69.310 633	59.074 420
15	1.038 163	15.265 365	14.704 203	65	1.176 210	70.483 910	59.924 608
16	1.040 759	16.303 529	15.665 040	66	1.179 150	71.660 119	60.772 676
17	1.043 361	17.344 287	16.623 481	67	1.182 098	72.839 270	61.618 630
18	1.045 969	18.387 648	17.579 533	68	1.185 053	74.021 368	62.462 474
19	1.048 584	19.433 617	18.533 200	69	1.188 016	75.206 421	63.304 213
20	1.051 205	20.482 201	19.484 488	70	1.190 986	76.394 437	64.143 853
21	1.053 834	21.533 407	20.433 405	71	1.193 964	77.585 423	64.981 400
22	1.056 468	22.587 240	21.379 955	72	1.196 948	78.779 387	65.816 858
23	1.059 109	23.643 708	22.324 145	73	1.199 941	79.976 335	66.650 232
24	1.061 757	24.702 818	23.265 980	74	1.202 941	81.176 276	67.481 528
25	1.064 411	25.764 575	24.205 466	75	1.205 948	82.379 217	68.310 751
26	1.067 072	26.828 986	25.142 609	76	1.208 963	83.585 165	69.137 907
27	1.069 740	27.896 059	26.077 416	77	1.211 985	84.794 128	69.962 999
28	1.072 414	28.965 799	27.009 891	78	1.215 015	86.006 113	70.786 034
29	1.075 096	30.038 213	27.940 041	79	1.218 053	87.221 129	71.607 017
30	1.077 783	31.113 309	28.867 871	80	1.221 098	88.439 181	72.425 952
31	1.080 478	32.191 092	29.793 388	81	1.224 151	89.660 279	73.242 845
32	1.083 179	33.271 570	30.716 596	82	1.227 211	90.884 430	74.057 700
33	1.085 887	34.354 749	31.637 503	83	1.230 279	92.111 641	74.870 524
34	1.088 602	35.440 636	32.556 112	84	1.233 355	93.341 920	75.681 321
35	1.091 323	36.529 237	33.472 431	85	1.236 438	94.575 275	76.490 095
36	1.094 051	37.620 560	34.386 465	86	1.239 529	95.811 713	77.296 853
37	1.096 787	38.714 612	35.298 220	87	1.242 628	97.051 242	78.101 599
38	1.099 528	39.811 398	36.207 700	88	1.245 735	98.293 871	78.904 339
39	1.102 277	40.910 927	37.114 913	89	1.248 849	99.539 605	79.705 076
40	1.105 033	42.013 204	38.019 863	90	1.251 971	100.788 454	80.503 816
41	1.107 796	43.118 237	38.922 557	91	1.255 101	102.040 425	81.300 565
42	1.110 565	44.226 033	39.822 999	92	1.258 239	103.295 526	82.095 327
43	1.113 341	45.336 598	40.721 196	93	1.261 384	104.553 765	82.888 106
44	1.116 125	46.449 939	41.617 154	94	1.264 538	105.815 150	83.678 909
45	1.118 915	47.566 064	42.510 876	95	1.267 699	107.079 688	84.467 740
46	1.121 712	48.684 979	43.402 370	96	1.270 868	108.347 387	85.254 603
47	1.124 517	49.806 692	44.291 641	97	1.274 046	109.618 255	86.039 504
48	1.127 328	50.931 208	45.178 695	98	1.277 231	110.892 301	86.822 448
49	1.130 146	52.058 536	46.063 536	99	1.280 424	112.169 532	87.603 440
50	1.132 972	53.188 683	46.946 170	100	1.283 625	113.449 956	88.382 483

Table V (Continued)

		$i = 0.005 \ (\tfrac{1}{2}\%)$					
n	$(1 + i)^n$	$s_{\overline{n}\mid i}$	$a_{\overline{n}\mid i}$	n	$(1 + i)^n$	$s_{\overline{n}\mid i}$	$a_{\overline{n}\mid i}$
1	1.005 000	1.000 000	0.995 025	51	1.289 642	57.928 389	44.918 195
2	1.010 025	2.005 000	1.985 099	52	1.296 090	59.218 031	45.689 747
3	1.015 075	3.015 025	2.970 248	53	1.302 571	60.514 121	46.457 459
4	1.020 151	4.030 100	3.950 496	54	1.309 083	61.816 692	47.221 353
5	1.025 251	5.050 250	4.925 866	55	1.315 629	63.125 775	47.981 445
6	1.030 378	6.075 502	5.896 384	56	1.322 207	64.441 404	48.737 757
7	1.035 529	7.105 879	6.862 074	57	1.328 818	65.763 611	49.490 305
8	1.040 707	8.141 409	7.822 959	58	1.335 462	67.092 429	50.239 110
9	1.045 911	9.182 116	8.779 064	59	1.342 139	68.427 891	50.984 189
10	1.051 140	10.228 026	9.730 412	60	1.348 850	69.770 031	51.725 561
11	1.056 396	11.279 167	10.677 027	61	1.355 594	71.118 881	52.463 245
12	1.061 678	12.335 562	11.618 932	62	1.362 372	72.474 475	53.197 258
13	1.066 986	13.397 240	12.556 151	63	1.369 184	73.836 847	53.927 620
14	1.072 321	14.464 226	13.488 708	64	1.376 030	75.206 032	54.654 348
15	1.077 683	15.536 548	14.416 625	65	1.382 910	76.582 062	55.377 461
16	1.083 071	16.614 230	15.339 925	66	1.389 825	77.964 972	56.096 976
17	1.088 487	17.697 301	16.258 632	67	1.396 774	79.354 797	56.812 912
18	1.093 929	18.785 788	17.172 768	68	1.403 758	80.751 571	57.525 285
19	1.099 399	19.879 717	18.082 356	69	1.410 777	82.155 329	58.234 115
20	1.104 896	20.979 115	18.987 419	70	1.417 831	83.566 105	58.939 418
21	1.110 420	22.084 011	19.887 979	71	1.424 920	84.983 936	59.641 212
22	1.115 972	23.194 431	20.784 059	72	1.432 044	86.408 856	60.339 514
23	1.121 552	24.310 403	21.675 681	73	1.439 204	87.840 900	61.034 342
24	1.127 160	25.431 955	22.562 866	74	1.446 401	89.280 104	61.725 714
25	1.132 796	26.559 115	23.445 638	75	1.453 633	90.726 505	62.413 645
26	1.138 460	27.691 911	24.324 018	76	1.460 901	92.180 138	63.098 155
27	1.144 152	28.830 370	25.198 028	77	1.468 205	93.641 038	63.779 258
28	1.149 873	29.974 522	26.067 689	78	1.475 546	95.109 243	64.456 974
29	1.155 622	31.124 395	26.933 024	79	1.482 924	96.584 790	65.131 317
30	1.161 400	32.280 017	27.794 054	80	1.490 339	98.067 714	65.802 305
31	1.167 207	33.441 417	28.650 800	81	1.497 790	99.558 052	66.469 956
32	1.173 043	34.608 624	29.503 284	82	1.505 279	101.055 842	67.134 284
33	1.178 908	35.781 667	30.351 526	83	1.512 806	102.561 122	67.795 308
34	1.184 803	36.960 575	31.195 548	84	1.520 370	104.073 927	68.453 042
35	1.190 727	38.145 378	32.035 371	85	1.527 971	105.594 297	69.107 505
36	1.196 681	39.336 105	32.871 016	86	1.535 611	107.122 268	69.758 711
37	1.202 664	40.532 785	33.702 504	87	1.543 289	108.657 880	70.406 678
38	1.208 677	41.735 449	34.529 854	88	1.551 006	110.201 169	71.051 421
39	1.214 721	42.944 127	35.353 089	89	1.558 761	111.752 175	71.692 956
40	1.220 794	44.158 847	36.172 228	90	1.566 555	113.310 936	72.331 300
41	1.226 898	45.379 642	36.987 291	91	1.574 387	114.877 490	72.966 467
42	1.233 033	46.606 540	37.798 300	92	1.582 259	116.451 878	73.598 475
43	1.239 198	47.839 572	38.605 274	93	1.590 171	118.034 137	74.227 338
44	1.245 394	49.078 770	39.408 232	94	1.598 121	119.624 308	74.853 073
45	1.251 621	50.324 164	40.207 196	95	1.606 112	121.222 430	75.475 694
46	1.257 879	51.575 785	41.002 185	96	1.614 143	122.828 542	76.095 218
47	1.264 168	52.833 664	41.793 219	97	1.622 213	124.442 684	76.711 660
48	1.270 489	54.097 832	42.580 318	98	1.630 324	126.064 898	77.325 035
49	1.276 842	55.368 321	43.363 500	99	1.638 476	127.695 222	77.935 358
50	1.283 226	56.645 163	44.142 786	100	1.646 668	129.333 698	78.542 645

			$i = 0.0075$ ($\frac{3}{4}\%$)				
n	$(1 + i)^n$	$s_{\overline{n}i}$	$a_{\overline{n}i}$	n	$(1 + i)^n$	$s_{\overline{n}i}$	$a_{\overline{n}i}$
1	1.007 500	1.000 000	0.992 556	51	1.463 854	61.847 214	42.249 575
2	1.015 056	2.007 500	1.977 723	52	1.474 833	63.311 068	42.927 618
3	1.022 669	3.022 556	2.955 556	53	1.485 894	64.785 901	43.600 614
4	1.030 339	4.045 225	3.926 110	54	1.497 038	66.271 796	44.268 599
5	1.038 067	5.075 565	4.889 440	55	1.508 266	67.768 834	44.931 612
6	1.045 852	6.113 631	5.845 598	56	1.519 578	69.277 100	45.589 689
7	1.053 696	7.159 484	6.794 638	57	1.530 975	70.796 679	46.242 868
8	1.061 599	8.213 180	7.736 613	58	1.542 457	72.327 659	46.891 184
9	1.069 561	9.274 779	8.671 576	59	1.554 026	73.870 111	47.534 674
10	1.077 583	10.344 339	9.599 580	60	1.565 681	75.424 137	48.173 374
11	1.085 664	11.421 922	10.520 675	61	1.577 424	76.989 818	48.807 319
12	1.093 807	12.507 586	11.434 913	62	1.589 254	78.567 242	49.436 545
13	1.102 010	13.601 393	12.342 345	63	1.601 174	80.156 496	50.061 086
14	1.110 276	14.703 404	13.243 022	64	1.613 183	81.757 670	50.680 979
15	1.118 603	15.813 679	14.136 995	65	1.625 281	83.370 852	51.296 257
16	1.126 992	16.932 282	15.024 313	66	1.637 471	84.996 134	51.906 955
17	1.135 445	18.059 274	15.905 025	67	1.649 752	86.633 605	52.513 107
18	1.143 960	19.194 718	16.779 181	68	1.662 125	88.283 356	53.114 746
19	1.152 540	20.338 679	17.646 830	69	1.674 591	89.945 482	53.711 907
20	1.161 184	21.491 219	18.508 020	70	1.687 151	91.620 073	54.304 622
21	1.169 893	22.652 403	19.362 799	71	1.699 804	93.307 223	54.892 925
22	1.178 667	23.822 296	20.211 215	72	1.712 553	95.007 028	55.476 849
23	1.187 507	25.000 963	21.053 315	73	1.725 397	96.719 580	56.056 426
24	1.196 414	26.188 471	21.889 146	74	1.738 337	98.444 977	56.631 688
25	1.205 387	27.384 884	22.718 755	75	1.751 375	100.183 314	57.202 668
26	1.214 427	28.590 271	23.542 189	76	1.764 510	101.934 689	57.769 397
27	1.223 535	29.804 698	24.359 493	77	1.777 744	103.699 199	58.331 908
28	1.232 712	31.028 233	25.170 713	78	1.791 077	105.476 943	58.890 231
29	1.241 957	32.260 945	25.975 893	79	1.804 510	107.268 021	59.444 398
30	1.251 272	33.502 902	26.775 080	80	1.818 044	109.072 531	59.994 440
31	1.260 656	34.754 174	27.568 318	81	1.831 679	110.890 575	60.540 387
32	1.270 111	36.014 830	28.355 650	82	1.845 417	112.722 254	61.082 270
33	1.279 637	37.284 941	29.137 122	83	1.859 258	114.567 671	61.620 119
34	1.289 234	38.564 578	29.912 776	84	1.873 202	116.426 928	62.153 965
35	1.298 904	39.853 813	30.682 656	85	1.887 251	118.300 130	62.683 836
36	1.308 645	41.152 716	31.446 805	86	1.901 405	120.187 381	63.209 763
37	1.318 460	42.461 361	32.205 266	87	1.915 666	122.088 787	63.731 774
38	1.328 349	43.779 822	32.958 080	88	1.930 033	124.004 453	64.249 900
39	1.338 311	45.108 170	33.705 290	89	1.944 509	125.934 486	64.764 169
40	1.348 349	46.446 482	34.446 938	90	1.959 092	127.878 995	65.274 609
41	1.358 461	47.794 830	35.183 065	91	1.973 786	129.838 087	65.781 250
42	1.368 650	49.153 291	35.913 713	92	1.988 589	131.811 873	66.284 119
43	1.378 915	50.521 941	36.638 921	93	2.003 503	133.800 462	66.783 245
44	1.389 256	51.900 856	37.358 730	94	2.018 530	135.803 965	67.278 655
45	1.399 676	53.290 112	38.073 181	95	2.033 669	137.822 495	67.770 377
46	1.410 173	54.689 788	38.782 314	96	2.048 921	139.856 164	68.258 439
47	1.420 750	56.099 961	39.486 168	97	2.064 288	141.905 085	68.742 867
48	1.431 405	57.520 711	40.184 782	98	2.079 770	143.969 373	69.223 689
49	1.442 141	58.952 116	40.878 195	99	2.095 369	146.049 143	69.700 932
50	1.452 957	60.394 257	41.566 447	100	2.111 084	148.144 512	70.174 623

Table V (Continued)

			$i = 0.01\ (1\%)$				
n	$(1 + i)^n$	$s_{\overline{n}|i}$	$a_{\overline{n}|i}$	n	$(1 + i)^n$	$s_{\overline{n}|i}$	$a_{\overline{n}|i}$
1	1.010 000	1.000 000	0.990 099	51	1.661 078	66.107 814	39.798 136
2	1.020 100	2.010 000	1.970 395	52	1.677 689	67.768 892	40.394 194
3	1.030 301	3.030 100	2.940 985	53	1.694 466	69.446 581	40.984 351
4	1.040 604	4.060 401	3.901 966	54	1.711 410	71.141 047	41.568 664
5	1.051 010	5.101 005	4.853 431	55	1.728 525	72.852 457	42.147 192
6	1.061 520	6.152 015	5.795 476	56	1.745 810	74.580 982	42.719 992
7	1.072 135	7.213 535	6.728 195	57	1.763 268	76.326 792	43.287 121
8	1.082 857	8.285 671	7.651 678	58	1.780 901	78.090 060	43.848 635
9	1.093 685	9.368 527	8.566 018	59	1.798 710	79.870 960	44.404 589
10	1.104 622	10.462 213	9.471 305	60	1.816 697	81.669 670	44.955 038
11	1.115 668	11.566 835	10.367 628	61	1.834 864	83.486 367	45.500 038
12	1.126 825	12.682 503	11.255 077	62	1.853 212	85.321 230	46.039 642
13	1.138 093	13.809 328	12.133 740	63	1.871 744	87.174 443	46.573 903
14	1.149 474	14.947 421	13.003 703	64	1.890 462	89.046 187	47.102 874
15	1.160 969	16.096 896	13.865 053	65	1.909 366	90.936 649	47.626 608
16	1.172 579	17.257 864	14.717 874	66	1.928 460	92.846 015	48.145 156
17	1.184 304	18.430 443	15.562 251	67	1.947 745	94.774 475	48.658 570
18	1.196 147	19.614 748	16.398 269	68	1.967 222	96.722 220	49.166 901
19	1.208 109	20.810 895	17.226 008	69	1.986 894	98.689 442	49.670 199
20	1.220 190	22.019 004	18.045 553	70	2.006 763	100.676 337	50.168 514
21	1.232 392	23.239 194	18.856 983	71	2.026 831	102.683 100	50.661 895
22	1.244 716	24.471 586	19.660 379	72	2.047 099	104.709 931	51.150 391
23	1.257 163	25.716 302	20.455 821	73	2.067 570	106.757 031	51.634 051
24	1.269 735	26.973 465	21.243 387	74	2.088 246	108.824 601	52.112 922
25	1.282 432	28.243 200	22.023 156	75	2.109 128	110.912 847	52.587 051
26	1.295 256	29.525 632	22.795 204	76	2.130 220	113.021 975	53.056 486
27	1.308 209	30.820 888	23.559 608	77	2.151 522	115.152 195	53.521 274
28	1.321 291	32.129 097	24.316 443	78	2.173 037	117.303 717	53.981 459
29	1.334 504	33.450 388	25.065 785	79	2.194 768	119.476 754	54.437 088
30	1.347 849	34.784 892	25.807 708	80	2.216 715	121.671 522	54.888 206
31	1.361 327	36.132 740	26.542 285	81	2.238 882	123.888 237	55.334 858
32	1.374 941	37.494 068	27.269 589	82	2.261 271	126.127 119	55.777 087
33	1.388 690	38.869 009	27.989 693	83	2.283 884	128.388 391	56.214 937
34	1.402 577	40.257 699	28.702 666	84	2.306 723	130.672 274	56.648 453
35	1.416 603	41.660 276	29.408 580	85	2.329 790	132.978 997	57.077 676
36	1.430 769	43.076 878	30.107 505	86	2.353 088	135.308 787	57.502 650
37	1.445 076	44.507 647	30.799 510	87	2.376 619	137.661 875	57.923 415
38	1.459 527	45.952 724	31.484 663	88	2.400 385	140.038 494	58.340 015
39	1.474 123	47.412 251	32.163 033	89	2.424 389	142.438 879	58.752 490
40	1.488 864	48.886 373	32.834 686	90	2.448 633	144.863 267	59.160 881
41	1.503 752	50.375 237	33.499 689	91	2.473 119	147.311 900	59.565 229
42	1.518 790	51.878 989	34.158 108	92	2.497 850	149.785 019	59.965 573
43	1.533 978	53.397 779	34.810 008	93	2.522 829	152.282 869	60.361 954
44	1.549 318	54.931 757	35.455 454	94	2.548 057	154.805 698	60.754 410
45	1.564 811	56.481 075	36.094 508	95	2.573 538	157.353 755	61.142 980
46	1.580 459	58.045 885	36.727 236	96	2.599 273	159.927 293	61.527 703
47	1.596 263	59.626 344	37.353 699	97	2.625 266	162.526 565	61.908 617
48	1.612 226	61.222 608	37.973 959	98	2.651 518	165.151 831	62.285 759
49	1.628 348	62.834 834	38.588 079	99	2.678 033	167.803 349	62.659 168
50	1.644 632	64.463 182	39.196 118	100	2.704 814	170.481 383	63.028 879

		$i = 0.0125\ (1\frac{1}{4}\%)$					
n	$(1 + i)^n$	$s_{\overline{n}i}$	$a_{\overline{n}i}$	n	$(1 + i)^n$	$s_{\overline{n}i}$	$a_{\overline{n}i}$
1	1.012 500	1.000 000	0.987 654	51	1.884 285	70.742 812	37.543 581
2	1.025 156	2.012 500	1.963 115	52	1.907 839	72.627 097	38.067 734
3	1.037 971	3.037 656	2.926 534	53	1.931 687	74.534 936	38.585 417
4	1.050 945	4.075 627	3.878 058	54	1.955 833	76.466 623	39.096 708
5	1.064 082	5.126 572	4.817 835	55	1.980 281	78.422 456	39.601 687
6	1.077 383	6.190 654	5.746 010	56	2.005 034	80.402 737	40.100 431
7	1.090 850	7.268 038	6.662 726	57	2.030 097	82.407 771	40.593 019
8	1.104 486	8.358 888	7.568 124	58	2.055 473	84.437 868	41.079 524
9	1.118 292	9.463 374	8.462 345	59	2.081 167	86.493 341	41.560 024
10	1.132 271	10.581 666	9.345 526	60	2.107 181	88.574 508	42.034 592
11	1.146 424	11.713 937	10.217 803	61	2.133 521	90.681 689	42.503 300
12	1.160 755	12.860 361	11.079 312	62	2.160 190	92.815 210	42.966 223
13	1.175 264	14.021 116	11.930 185	63	2.187 193	94.975 400	43.423 430
14	1.189 955	15.196 380	12.770 553	64	2.214 532	97.162 593	43.874 992
15	1.204 829	16.386 335	13.600 546	65	2.242 214	99.377 125	44.320 980
16	1.219 890	17.591 164	14.420 292	66	2.270 242	101.619 339	44.761 462
17	1.235 138	18.811 053	15.229 918	67	2.298 620	103.889 581	45.196 506
18	1.250 577	20.046 192	16.029 549	68	2.327 353	106.188 201	45.626 178
19	1.266 210	21.296 769	16.819 308	69	2.356 444	108.515 553	46.050 547
20	1.282 037	22.562 979	17.599 316	70	2.385 900	110.871 998	46.469 676
21	1.298 063	23.845 016	18.369 695	71	2.415 724	113.257 898	46.883 630
22	1.314 288	25.143 078	19.130 563	72	2.445 920	115.673 621	47.292 474
23	1.330 717	26.457 367	19.882 037	73	2.476 494	118.119 542	47.696 271
24	1.347 351	27.788 084	20.624 235	74	2.507 450	120.596 036	48.095 082
25	1.364 193	29.135 435	21.357 269	75	2.538 794	123.103 486	48.488 970
26	1.381 245	30.499 628	22.081 253	76	2.570 528	125.642 280	48.877 995
27	1.398 511	31.880 873	22.796 299	77	2.602 660	128.212 809	49.262 218
28	1.415 992	33.279 384	23.502 518	78	2.635 193	130.815 469	49.641 696
29	1.433 692	34.695 377	24.200 018	79	2.668 133	133.450 662	50.016 490
30	1.451 613	36.129 069	24.888 906	80	2.701 485	136.118 795	50.386 657
31	1.469 759	37.580 682	25.569 290	81	2.735 254	138.820 280	50.752 254
32	1.488 131	39.050 441	26.241 274	82	2.769 444	141.555 534	51.113 337
33	1.506 732	40.538 571	26.904 962	83	2.804 062	144.324 978	51.469 963
34	1.525 566	42.045 303	27.560 456	84	2.839 113	147.129 040	51.822 185
35	1.544 636	43.570 870	28.207 858	85	2.874 602	149.968 153	52.170 060
36	1.563 944	45.115 506	28.847 267	86	2.910 534	152.842 755	52.513 639
37	1.583 493	46.679 449	29.478 783	87	2.946 916	155.753 289	52.852 977
38	1.603 287	48.292 642	30.102 501	88	2.983 753	158.700 206	53.188 125
39	1.623 328	49.886 229	30.718 520	89	3.021 049	161.683 958	53.519 136
40	1.643 619	51.489 557	31.326 933	90	3.058 813	164.705 008	53.846 060
41	1.664 165	53.133 177	31.927 835	91	3.097 048	167.763 820	54.168 948
42	1.684 967	54.797 341	32.521 319	92	3.135 761	170.860 868	54.487 850
43	1.706 029	56.482 308	33.107 475	93	3.174 958	173.996 629	54.802 815
44	1.727 354	58.188 337	33.686 395	94	3.214 645	177.171 587	55.113 892
45	1.748 946	59.915 691	34.258 168	95	3.254 828	180.386 232	55.421 127
46	1.770 808	61.664 637	34.822 882	96	3.295 513	183.641 059	55.724 570
47	1.792 943	63.435 445	35.380 624	97	3.336 707	186.936 573	56.024 267
48	1.815 355	65.228 388	35.931 481	98	3.378 416	190.273 280	56.320 264
49	1.838 047	67.043 743	36.475 537	99	3.420 646	193.651 696	56.612 606
50	1.861 022	68.881 790	37.012 876	100	3.463 404	197.072 342	56.901 339

Table V (Continued)

n	$(1 + i)^n$	$s_{\overline{n}|i}$	$a_{\overline{n}|i}$	n	$(1 + i)^n$	$s_{\overline{n}|i}$	$a_{\overline{n}|i}$
1	1.015 000	1.000 000	0.985 222	51	2.136 821	75.788 070	35.467 673
2	1.030 225	2.015 000	1.955 883	52	2.168 873	77.924 892	35.928 742
3	1.045 678	3.045 225	2.912 200	53	2.201 406	80.093 765	36.382 997
4	1.061 364	4.090 903	3.854 385	54	2.234 428	82.295 171	36.830 539
5	1.077 284	5.152 267	4.782 645	55	2.267 944	84.529 599	37.271 467
6	1.093 443	6.229 551	5.697 187	56	2.301 963	86.797 543	37.705 879
7	1.109 845	7.322 994	6.598 214	57	2.336 493	89.099 506	38.133 871
8	1.126 493	8.432 839	7.485 925	58	2.371 540	91.435 999	38.555 538
9	1.143 390	9.559 332	8.360 517	59	2.407 113	93.807 539	38.970 973
10	1.160 541	10.702 722	9.222 185	60	2.443 220	96.214 652	39.380 269
11	1.177 949	11.863 262	10.071 118	61	2.479 868	98.657 871	39.783 516
12	1.195 618	13.041 211	10.907 505	62	2.517 066	101.137 740	40.180 804
13	1.213 552	14.236 830	11.731 532	63	2.554 822	103.654 806	40.572 221
14	1.231 756	15.450 382	12.543 382	64	2.593 144	106.209 628	40.957 853
15	1.250 232	16.682 138	13.343 233	65	2.632 042	108.802 772	41.337 786
16	1.268 986	17.932 370	14.131 264	66	2.671 522	111.434 814	41.712 105
17	1.288 020	19.201 355	14.907 649	67	2.711 595	114.106 336	42.080 891
18	1.307 341	20.489 376	15.672 561	68	2.752 269	116.817 931	42.444 228
19	1.326 951	21.796 716	16.426 168	69	2.793 553	119.570 200	42.802 195
20	1.346 855	23.123 667	17.168 639	70	2.835 456	122.363 753	43.154 872
21	1.367 058	24.470 522	17.900 137	71	2.877 988	125.199 209	43.502 337
22	1.387 564	25.837 580	18.620 824	72	2.921 158	128.077 197	43.844 667
23	1.408 377	27.225 144	19.330 861	73	2.964 975	130.998 355	44.181 938
24	1.429 503	28.633 521	20.030 405	74	3.009 450	133.963 331	44.514 224
25	1.450 945	30.063 024	20.719 611	75	3.054 592	136.972 781	44.841 600
26	1.472 710	31.513 969	21.398 632	76	3.100 411	140.027 372	45.164 138
27	1.494 800	32.986 678	22.067 617	77	3.146 917	143.127 783	45.481 910
28	1.517 222	34.481 479	22.726 717	78	3.194 120	146.274 700	45.794 985
29	1.539 981	35.998 701	23.376 076	79	3.242 032	149.468 820	46.103 433
30	1.563 080	37.538 681	24.015 838	80	3.290 663	152.710 852	46.407 323
31	1.586 526	39.101 762	24.646 146	81	3.340 023	156.001 515	46.706 723
32	1.610 324	40.688 288	25.267 139	82	3.390 123	159.341 536	47.001 697
33	1.634 479	42.298 612	25.878 954	83	3.440 975	162.731 661	47.292 313
34	1.658 996	43.933 092	26.481 728	84	3.492 590	166.172 636	47.578 633
35	1.683 881	45.592 088	27.075 595	85	3.544 978	169.665 226	47.860 722
36	1.709 140	47.275 969	27.660 684	86	3.598 153	173.210 204	48.138 643
37	1.734 777	48.985 109	28.237 127	87	3.652 125	176.808 357	48.412 456
38	1.760 798	50.719 885	28.805 052	88	3.706 907	180.460 482	48.682 222
39	1.787 210	52.480 684	29.364 583	89	3.762 511	184.167 390	48.948 002
40	1.814 018	54.267 894	29.915 845	90	3.818 949	187.929 900	49.209 855
41	1.841 229	56.081 912	30.458 961	91	3.876 233	191.748 849	49.467 837
42	1.868 847	57.923 141	30.994 050	92	3.934 376	195.625 082	49.722 007
43	1.896 880	59.791 988	31.521 232	93	3.993 392	199.559 458	49.972 421
44	1.925 333	61.688 868	32.040 622	94	4.053 293	203.552 850	50.219 134
45	1.954 213	63.614 201	32.552 337	95	4.114 092	207.606 142	50.462 201
46	1.983 526	65.568 414	33.056 490	96	4.175 804	211.720 235	50.701 675
47	2.013 279	67.551 940	33.553 192	97	4.238 441	215.896 038	50.937 611
48	2.043 478	69.565 219	34.042 554	98	4.302 017	220.134 479	51.170 060
49	2.074 130	71.608 698	34.524 683	99	4.366 547	224.436 496	51.399 074
50	2.105 242	73.682 828	34.999 688	100	4.432 046	228.803 043	51.624 704

		$i = 0.0175\ (1\frac{3}{4}\%)$					
n	$(1 + i)^n$	$s_{\overline{n}|i}$	$a_{\overline{n}|i}$	n	$(1 + i)^n$	$s_{\overline{n}|i}$	$a_{\overline{n}|i}$
1	1.017 500	1.000 000	0.982 801	51	2.422 453	81.283 014	33.554 014
2	1.035 306	2.017 500	1.948 699	52	2.464 846	83.705 466	33.959 719
3	1.053 424	3.052 806	2.897 984	53	2.507 980	86.170 312	34.358 446
4	1.071 859	4.106 230	3.830 943	54	2.551 870	88.678 292	34.750 316
5	1.090 617	5.178 089	4.747 855	55	2.596 528	91.230 163	35.135 446
6	1.109 702	6.268 706	5.648 998	56	2.641 967	93.826 690	35.513 951
7	1.129 122	7.378 408	6.534 641	57	2.688 202	96.468 658	35.885 947
8	1.148 882	8.507 530	7.405 053	58	2.735 245	99.156 859	36.251 545
9	1.168 987	9.656 412	8.260 494	59	2.783 112	101.892 104	36.610 855
10	1.189 444	10.825 399	9.101 223	60	2.831 816	104.675 216	36.963 986
11	1.210 260	12.014 844	9.927 492	61	2.881 373	107.507 032	37.311 042
12	1.231 439	13.225 104	10.739 550	62	2.931 797	110.388 405	37.652 130
13	1.252 990	14.456 543	11.537 641	63	2.983 104	113.320 202	37.987 351
14	1.274 917	15.709 533	12.322 006	64	3.034 308	116.303 306	38.316 807
15	1.297 228	16.984 449	13.092 880	65	3.088 426	119.338 614	38.640 597
16	1.319 929	18.281 677	13.850 497	66	3.142 473	122.427 039	38.958 817
17	1.343 028	19.601 607	14.595 083	67	3.197 466	125.569 513	39.271 565
18	1.366 531	20.944 635	15.326 863	68	3.253 422	128.766 979	39.578 934
19	1.390 445	22.311 166	16.046 057	69	3.310 357	132.020 401	39.881 016
20	1.414 778	23.701 611	16.752 881	70	3.368 288	135.330 758	40.177 903
21	1.439 537	25.116 389	17.447 549	71	3.427 233	138.699 047	40.469 683
22	1.464 729	26.555 926	18.130 269	72	3.487 210	142.126 280	40.756 445
23	1.490 361	28.020 655	18.801 248	73	3.548 236	145.613 490	41.038 276
24	1.516 443	29.511 016	19.460 686	74	3.610 330	149.161 726	41.315 259
25	1.542 981	31.027 459	20.108 782	75	3.673 511	152.772 056	41.587 478
26	1.569 983	32.570 440	20.745 732	76	3.737 797	156.445 567	41.855 015
27	1.597 457	34.140 422	21.371 726	77	3.803 209	160.183 364	42.117 951
28	1.625 413	35.737 880	21.986 955	78	3.869 765	163.986 573	42.376 364
29	1.653 858	37.363 293	22.591 602	79	3.937 486	167.856 338	42.630 334
30	1.682 800	39.017 150	23.185 849	80	4.006 392	171.793 824	42.879 935
31	1.712 249	40.699 950	23.769 876	81	4.076 504	175.800 216	43.125 243
32	1.742 213	42.412 200	24.343 859	82	4.147 843	179.876 720	43.366 332
33	1.772 702	44.154 413	24.907 970	83	4.220 430	184.024 563	43.603 275
34	1.803 725	45.927 115	25.462 378	84	4.294 287	188.244 992	43.836 142
35	1.835 290	47.730 840	26.007 251	85	4.369 437	192.539 280	44.065 005
36	1.867 407	49.566 129	26.542 753	86	4.445 903	196.908 717	44.289 931
37	1.900 087	51.433 537	27.069 045	87	4.523 706	201.354 620	44.510 989
38	1.933 338	53.333 624	27.586 285	88	4.602 871	205.878 326	44.728 244
39	1.967 172	55.266 962	28.094 629	89	4.683 421	210.481 196	44.941 764
40	2.001 597	57.234 134	28.594 230	90	4.765 381	215.164 617	45.151 610
41	2.036 625	59.235 731	29.085 238	91	4.848 775	219.929 998	44.357 848
42	2.072 266	61.272 357	29.567 801	92	4.933 629	224.778 773	45.560 539
43	2.108 531	63.344 623	30.042 065	93	5.019 967	229.712 401	45.759 743
44	2.145 430	65.453 154	30.508 172	94	5.107 816	234.732 368	45.955 521
45	2.182 975	67.598 584	30.966 263	95	5.197 203	239.840 185	46.147 933
46	2.221 177	69.781 559	31.416 474	96	5.288 154	245.037 388	46.337 035
47	2.260 048	72.002 736	31.858 943	97	5.380 697	250.325 542	46.522 884
48	2.299 599	74.262 784	32.293 801	98	5.474 859	255.706 239	46.705 537
49	2.339 842	76.562 383	32.721 181	99	5.570 669	261.181 099	46.885 049
50	2.380 789	78.902 225	33.141 209	100	5.668 156	266.751 768	47.061 473

Table V (Continued)

$i = 0.02\ (2\%)$							
n	$(1 + i)^n$	$s_{\overline{n}|i}$	$a_{\overline{n}|i}$	n	$(1 + i)^n$	$s_{\overline{n}|i}$	$a_{\overline{n}|i}$
1	1.020 000	1.000 000	0.980 392	51	2.745 420	87.270 989	31.787 849
2	1.040 400	2.020 000	1.941 561	52	2.800 328	90.016 409	32.144 950
3	1.061 208	3.060 400	2.883 883	53	2.856 335	92.816 737	32.495 049
4	1.082 432	4.121 608	3.807 729	54	2.913 461	95.673 072	32.838 283
5	1.104 081	5.204 040	4.713 460	55	2.971 731	98.586 534	33.174 788
6	1.126 162	6.308 121	5.601 431	56	3.031 165	101.558 264	33.504 694
7	1.148 686	7.434 283	6.471 991	57	3.091 789	104.589 430	33.828 131
8	1.171 659	8.582 969	7.325 481	58	3.153 624	107.681 218	34.145 226
9	1.195 093	9.754 628	8.162 237	59	3.216 697	110.834 843	34.456 104
10	1.218 994	10.949 721	8.982 585	60	3.281 031	114.051 539	34.760 887
11	1.243 374	12.168 715	9.786 848	61	3.346 651	117.332 570	35.059 693
12	1.268 242	13.412 090	10.575 341	62	3.413 584	120.679 222	35.352 640
13	1.293 607	14.680 331	11.348 374	63	3.481 856	124.092 806	35.639 843
14	1.319 479	15.973 938	12.106 249	64	3.551 493	127.574 662	35.921 415
15	1.345 868	17.293 417	12.849 264	65	3.622 523	131.126 155	36.197 466
16	1.372 786	18.639 285	13.577 709	66	3.694 974	134.748 679	36.468 103
17	1.400 241	20.012 071	14.291 872	67	3.768 873	138.443 652	36.733 435
18	1.428 246	21.412 312	14.992 031	68	3.844 251	142.212 525	36.993 564
19	1.456 811	22.840 559	15.678 462	69	3.921 136	146.056 776	37.248 592
20	1.485 947	24.297 370	16.351 433	70	3.999 558	149.977 911	37.498 619
21	1.515 666	25.783 317	17.011 209	71	4.079 549	153.977 469	37.743 744
22	1.545 980	27.298 984	17.658 048	72	4.161 140	158.057 019	37.984 063
23	1.576 899	28.844 963	18.292 204	73	4.244 363	162.218 159	38.219 670
24	1.608 437	30.421 862	18.913 926	74	4.329 250	166.462 522	38.450 657
25	1.640 606	32.030 300	19.523 456	75	4.415 835	170.791 773	38.677 114
26	1.673 418	33.670 906	20.121 036	76	4.504 152	175.207 608	38.899 132
27	1.706 886	35.344 324	20.706 898	77	4.594 235	179.711 760	39.116 796
28	1.741 024	37.051 210	21.281 272	78	4.686 120	184.305 996	39.330 192
29	1.775 845	38.792 235	21.844 385	79	4.779 842	188.992 115	39.539 404
30	1.811 362	40.568 079	22.396 456	80	4.875 439	193.771 958	39.744 514
31	1.847 589	42.379 441	22.937 702	81	4.972 948	198.647 397	39.945 602
32	1.884 541	44.227 030	23.468 335	82	5.072 407	203.620 345	40.142 747
33	1.922 231	46.111 570	23.988 564	83	5.173 855	208.692 752	40.336 026
34	1.960 676	48.033 802	24.498 592	84	5.277 332	213.866 607	40.525 516
35	1.999 890	49.994 478	24.998 619	85	5.382 879	219.143 939	40.711 290
36	2.039 887	51.994 367	25.488 842	86	5.490 536	224.526 818	40.893 422
37	2.080 685	54.034 255	25.969 453	87	5.600 347	230.017 354	41.071 982
38	2.122 299	56.114 940	26.440 641	88	5.712 354	235.617 701	41.247 041
39	2.164 745	58.237 238	26.902 589	89	5.826 601	241.330 055	41.418 668
40	2.208 040	60.401 983	27.355 479	90	5.943 133	247.156 656	41.586 929
41	2.252 200	62.610 023	27.799 489	91	6.061 996	253.099 789	41.751 891
42	2.297 244	64.862 223	28.234 794	92	6.183 236	259.161 785	41.913 619
43	2.343 189	67.159 468	28.661 562	93	6.306 900	265.345 021	42.072 175
44	2.390 053	69.502 657	29.079 963	94	6.433 038	271.651 921	42.227 623
45	2.437 854	71.892 710	29.490 159	95	6.561 699	278.084 960	42.380 023
46	2.486 611	74.330 564	29.892 314	96	6.692 933	284.646 659	42.529 434
47	2.536 344	76.817 176	30.286 582	97	6.826 792	291.339 592	42.675 916
48	2.587 070	79.353 519	30.673 120	98	6.963 328	298.166 384	42.819 525
49	2.638 812	81.940 590	31.052 078	99	7.102 594	305.129 712	42.960 319
50	2.691 588	84.579 401	31.423 606	100	7.244 646	312.232 306	43.098 352

		$i = 0.0225 (2\frac{1}{4}\%)$					
n	$(1 + i)^n$	$s_{\overline{n}i}$	$a_{\overline{n}i}$	n	$(1 + i)^n$	$s_{\overline{n}i}$	$a_{\overline{n}i}$
1	1.022 500	1.000 000	0.977 995	51	3.110 492	93.799 664	30.155 889
2	1.045 506	2.022 500	1.934 470	52	3.180 479	96.910 157	30.470 307
3	1.069 030	3.068 006	2.869 897	53	3.252 039	100.090 635	30.777 806
4	1.093 083	4.137 036	3.784 740	54	3.325 210	103.342 674	31.078 539
5	1.117 678	5.230 120	4.679 453	55	3.400 027	106.667 885	31.372 654
6	1.142 825	6.347 797	5.554 477	56	3.476 528	110.067 912	31.660 298
7	1.168 539	7.490 623	6.410 246	57	3.554 750	113.544 440	31.941 611
8	1.194 831	8.659 162	7.247 185	58	3.634 732	117.099 190	32.216 735
9	1.221 715	9.853 993	8.065 706	59	3.716 513	120.733 922	32.485 804
10	1.249 203	11.075 708	8.866 216	60	3.800 135	124.450 435	32.748 953
11	1.277 311	12.324 911	9.649 111	61	3.885 638	128.250 570	33.006 311
12	1.306 050	13.602 222	10.414 779	62	3.973 065	132.136 208	33.258 006
13	1.335 436	14.908 272	11.163 598	63	4.062 459	136.109 272	33.504 162
14	1.365 483	16.243 708	11.895 939	64	4.153 864	140.171 731	33.744 902
15	1.396 207	17.609 191	12.612 166	65	4.247 326	144.325 595	33.980 344
16	1.427 621	19.005 398	13.312 631	66	4.342 891	148.572 920	34.210 605
17	1.459 743	20.433 020	13.997 683	67	4.440 606	152.915 811	34.435 800
18	1.492 587	21.892 763	14.667 661	68	4.540 519	157.356 417	34.656 039
19	1.526 170	23.385 350	15.322 896	69	4.642 681	161.896 937	34.871 432
20	1.560 509	24.911 520	15.963 712	70	4.747 141	166.539 618	35.082 085
21	1.595 621	26.472 029	16.590 428	71	4.853 952	171.286 759	35.288 103
22	1.631 522	28.067 650	17.203 352	72	4.963 166	176.140 711	35.489 587
23	1.668 231	29.699 172	17.802 790	73	5.074 837	181.103 877	35.686 638
24	1.705 767	31.367 403	18.389 036	74	5.189 021	186.178 714	35.879 352
25	1.744 146	33.073 170	18.962 383	75	5.305 774	191.367 735	36.067 826
26	1.783 390	34.817 316	19.523 113	76	5.425 154	196.673 509	36.252 153
27	1.823 516	36.600 706	20.071 504	77	5.547 220	202.098 663	36.432 423
28	1.864 545	38.424 222	20.607 828	78	5.672 032	207.645 883	36.608 727
29	1.906 497	40.288 767	21.132 350	79	5.799 653	213.317 916	36.781 151
30	1.949 393	42.195 264	21.645 330	80	5.930 145	219.117 569	36.949 781
31	1.993 255	44.144 657	22.147 022	81	6.063 574	225.047 714	37.114 700
32	2.038 103	46.137 912	22.637 674	82	6.200 004	231.111 288	37.275 990
33	2.083 960	48.176 015	23.117 530	83	6.339 504	237.311 292	37.433 731
34	2.130 849	50.259 976	23.586 826	84	6.482 143	243.650 796	37.588 001
35	2.178 794	52.390 825	24.045 796	85	6.627 991	250.132 939	37.738 877
36	2.227 816	54.569 619	24.494 666	86	6.777 121	256.760 930	37.886 432
37	2.277 942	56.797 435	24.933 658	87	6.929 606	263.538 051	38.030 740
38	2.329 196	59.075 377	25.362 991	88	7.085 522	270.467 657	38.171 873
39	2.381 603	61.404 573	25.782 876	89	7.244 947	277.553 179	38.309 900
40	2.435 189	63.786 176	26.193 522	90	7.407 958	284.798 126	38.444 890
41	2.489 981	66.221 365	26.595 132	91	7.574 637	292.206 083	38.576 910
42	2.546 005	68.711 346	26.987 904	92	7.745 066	299.780 720	38.706 024
43	2.603 290	71.257 351	27.372 033	93	7.919 330	307.525 786	38.832 298
44	2.661 864	73.860 642	27.747 710	94	8.097 515	315.445 117	38.955 792
45	2.721 756	76.522 506	28.115 120	95	8.279 709	323.542 632	39.076 569
46	2.782 996	79.244 262	28.474 444	96	8.466 003	331.822 341	39.194 689
47	2.845 613	82.027 258	28.825 863	97	8.656 488	340.288 344	39.310 209
48	2.909 640	84.872 872	29.169 548	98	8.851 259	348.944 831	39.423 187
49	2.975 107	87.782 511	29.505 670	99	9.050 412	357.796 090	39.533 680
50	3.042 046	90.757 618	29.834 396	100	9.254 046	366.846 502	39.641 741

Table V (Continued)

n	$(1 + i)^n$	$s_{\overline{n}\rvert i}$	$a_{\overline{n}\rvert i}$	n	$(1 + i)^n$	$s_{\overline{n}\rvert i}$	$a_{\overline{n}\rvert i}$
			$i = 0.025\ (2\tfrac{1}{2}\%)$				
1	1.025 000	1.000 000	0.975 610	51	3.523 036	100.921 458	28.646 158
2	1.050 625	2.025 000	1.927 424	52	3.611 112	104.444 494	28.923 081
3	1.076 891	3.075 625	2.856 024	53	3.701 390	108.055 606	29.193 249
4	1.103 813	4.152 516	3.761 974	54	3.793 925	111.756 996	29.456 829
5	1.131 408	5.256 329	4.645 828	55	3.888 773	115.550 921	29.713 979
6	1.159 693	6.387 737	5.508 125	56	3.985 992	119.439 694	29.964 858
7	1.188 686	7.547 430	6.349 391	57	4.085 642	123.425 687	30.209 617
8	1.218 403	8.736 116	7.170 137	58	4.187 783	127.511 329	30.448 407
9	1.248 863	9.954 519	7.970 866	59	4.292 478	131.699 112	30.681 373
10	1.280 085	11.203 382	8.752 064	60	4.399 790	135.991 590	30.908 656
11	1.312 087	12.483 466	9.514 209	61	4.509 784	140.391 380	31.130 397
12	1.344 889	13.795 553	10.257 765	62	4.622 529	144.901 164	31.346 728
13	1.378 511	15.140 442	10.983 185	63	4.738 092	149.523 693	31.557 784
14	1.412 974	16.518 953	11.690 912	64	4.856 545	154.261 786	31.763 691
15	1.448 298	17.931 927	12.381 378	65	4.977 958	159.118 330	31.964 577
16	1.484 506	19.380 225	13.055 003	66	5.102 407	164.096 289	32.160 563
17	1.521 618	20.864 730	13.712 198	67	5.229 967	169.198 696	32.351 769
18	1.559 659	22.386 349	14.353 364	68	5.360 717	174.428 663	32.538 311
19	1.598 650	23.946 007	14.978 891	69	5.494 734	179.789 380	32.720 303
20	1.638 616	25.544 658	15.589 162	70	5.632 103	185.284 114	32.897 857
21	1.679 582	27.183 274	16.184 549	71	5.772 905	190.916 217	33.071 080
22	1.721 571	28.862 856	16.765 413	72	5.917 228	196.689 122	33.240 078
23	1.764 611	30.584 427	17.332 110	73	6.065 159	202.606 351	33.404 954
24	1.808 726	32.349 038	17.884 986	74	6.216 788	208.671 509	33.565 809
25	1.853 944	34.157 764	18.424 376	75	6.372 207	214.888 297	33.722 740
26	1.900 293	36.011 708	18.950 611	76	6.531 513	221.260 504	33.875 844
27	1.947 800	37.912 001	19.464 011	77	6.694 800	227.792 017	34.025 214
28	1.996 495	39.859 801	19.964 889	78	6.862 170	234.486 818	34.170 940
29	2.046 407	41.856 296	20.453 550	79	7.033 725	241.348 988	34.313 113
30	2.097 568	43.902 703	20.930 293	80	7.209 568	248.382 713	34.451 817
31	2.150 007	46.000 271	21.395 407	81	7.389 807	255.592 280	34.587 139
32	2.203 757	48.150 278	21.849 178	82	7.574 552	262.982 087	34.719 160
33	2.258 851	50.354 034	22.291 881	83	7.763 916	270.556 640	34.847 961
34	2.315 322	52.612 885	22.723 786	84	7.958 014	278.320 556	34.973 620
35	2.373 205	54.928 207	23.145 157	85	8.156 964	286.278 569	35.096 215
36	2.432 535	57.301 413	23.556 251	86	8.360 888	294.435 534	35.215 819
37	2.493 349	59.733 948	23.957 318	87	8.569 911	302.796 422	35.332 507
38	2.555 682	62.227 297	24.348 603	88	8.784 158	311.366 333	35.446 348
39	2.619 574	64.782 979	24.730 344	89	9.003 762	320.150 491	35.557 413
40	2.685 064	67.402 554	25.102 775	90	9.228 856	329.154 253	35.665 768
41	2.752 190	70.087 617	25.466 122	91	9.459 578	338.383 110	35.771 481
42	2.820 995	72.839 808	25.820 607	92	9.696 067	347.842 687	35.874 616
43	2.891 520	75.660 803	26.166 446	93	9.938 469	357.538 755	35.975 235
44	2.963 808	78.552 323	26.503 849	94	10.186 931	367.477 223	36.073 400
45	3.037 903	81.516 131	26.833 024	95	10.441 604	377.664 154	36.169 171
46	3.113 851	84.554 034	27.154 170	96	10.702 644	388.105 758	36.262 606
47	3.191 697	87.667 885	27.467 483	97	10.970 210	398.808 402	36.353 762
48	3.271 490	90.859 582	27.773 154	98	11.244 465	409.778 612	36.442 694
49	3.353 277	94.131 072	28.071 369	99	11.525 577	421.023 077	36.529 458
50	3.437 109	97.484 349	28.362 312	100	11.813 716	432.548 654	36.614 105

			$i = 0.03\ (3\%)$				
n	$(1+i)^n$	$s_{\overline{n}|i}$	$a_{\overline{n}|i}$	n	$(1+i)^n$	$s_{\overline{n}|i}$	$a_{\overline{n}|i}$
1	1.030 000	1.000 000	0.970 874	51	4.515 423	117.180 773	25.951 227
2	1.060 900	2.030 000	1.913 470	52	4.650 886	121.696 197	26.166 240
3	1.092 727	3.090 900	2.828 611	53	4.790 412	126.347 082	26.374 990
4	1.125 509	4.183 627	3.717 098	54	4.934 125	131.137 495	26.577 660
5	1.159 274	5.309 136	4.579 707	55	5.082 149	136.071 620	26.774 428
6	1.194 052	6.468 410	5.417 191	56	5.234 613	141.153 768	26.965 464
7	1.229 874	7.662 462	6.230 283	57	5.391 651	146.388 381	27.150 936
8	1.266 770	8.892 336	7.019 692	58	5.553 401	151.780 033	27.331 005
9	1.304 773	10.159 106	7.786 109	59	5.720 003	157.333 434	27.505 831
10	1.343 916	11.463 879	8.530 203	60	5.891 603	163.053 437	27.675 564
11	1.384 234	12.807 796	9.252 624	61	6.068 351	168.945 040	27.840 353
12	1.425 761	14.192 030	9.954 004	62	6.250 402	175.013 391	28.000 343
13	1.468 534	15.617 790	10.634 955	63	6.437 914	181.263 793	28.155 673
14	1.512 590	17.086 324	11.296 073	64	6.631 051	187.701 707	28.306 478
15	1.557 967	18.598 914	11.937 935	65	6.829 983	194.332 758	28.452 892
16	1.604 706	20.156 881	12.561 102	66	7.034 882	201.162 741	28.595 040
17	1.652 848	21.761 588	13.166 118	67	7.245 929	208.197 623	28.733 049
18	1.702 433	23.414 435	13.753 513	68	7.463 307	215.443 551	28.867 038
19	1.753 506	25.116 868	14.323 799	69	7.687 206	222.906 858	28.997 124
20	1.806 111	26.870 374	14.877 475	70	7.917 822	230.594 064	29.123 421
21	1.860 295	28.676 486	15.415 024	71	8.155 357	238.511 886	29.246 040
22	1.916 103	30.536 780	15.936 917	72	8.400 017	246.667 242	29.365 088
23	1.973 587	32.452 884	16.443 608	73	8.652 016	255.067 259	29.480 668
24	2.032 794	34.426 470	16.935 542	74	8.911 578	263.719 277	29.592 881
25	2.093 778	36.459 264	17.413 148	75	9.178 926	272.630 856	29.701 826
26	2.156 591	38.553 042	17.876 842	76	9.454 293	281.809 781	29.807 598
27	2.221 289	40.709 634	18.327 031	77	9.737 922	291.264 075	29.910 290
28	2.287 928	42.930 923	18.764 108	78	10.030 060	301.001 997	30.009 990
29	2.356 566	45.218 850	19.188 455	79	10.330 962	311.032 057	30.106 786
30	2.427 262	47.575 416	19.600 441	80	10.640 891	321.363 019	30.200 763
31	2.500 080	50.002 678	20.000 428	81	10.960 117	332.003 909	30.292 003
32	2.575 083	52.502 759	20.388 766	82	11.288 921	342.964 026	30.380 586
33	2.652 335	55.077 841	20.765 792	83	11.627 588	354.252 947	30.466 588
34	2.731 905	57.730 177	21.131 837	84	11.976 416	365.880 536	30.550 086
35	2.813 862	60.462 082	21.487 220	85	12.335 709	377.856 952	30.631 151
36	2.898 278	63.275 944	21.832 252	86	12.705 780	390.192 660	30.709 855
37	2.985 227	66.174 223	22.167 235	87	13.086 953	402.898 440	30.786 267
38	3.074 783	69.159 449	22.492 462	88	13.479 562	415.985 393	30.860 454
39	3.167 027	72.234 233	22.808 215	89	13.883 949	429.464 955	30.932 479
40	3.262 038	75.401 260	23.114 772	90	14.300 467	443.348 904	31.002 407
41	3.359 899	78.663 298	23.412 400	91	14.729 481	457.649 371	31.070 298
42	3.460 696	82.023 196	23.701 359	92	15.171 366	472.378 852	31.136 212
43	3.564 517	85.483 892	23.981 902	93	15.626 507	487.550 217	31.200 206
44	3.671 452	89.048 409	24.254 274	94	16.095 302	503.176 724	31.262 336
45	3.781 596	92.719 861	24.518 713	95	16.578 161	519.272 026	31.322 656
46	3.895 044	96.501 457	24.775 449	96	17.075 506	535.850 186	31.381 219
47	4.011 895	100.396 501	25.024 708	97	17.587 771	552.925 692	31.438 077
48	4.132 252	104.408 396	25.266 707	98	18.115 404	570.513 463	31.493 279
49	4.256 219	108.540 648	25.501 657	99	18.658 866	588.628 867	31.546 872
50	4.383 906	112.796 867	25.729 764	100	19.218 632	607.287 733	31.598 905

Table V (Continued)

Table V (Continued)

$i = 0.035\ (3\frac{1}{2}\%)$						
n	$(1+i)^n$	$s_{\overline{n}|i}$	$a_{\overline{n}|i}$	n	$(1+i)^n$	$s_{\overline{n}|i}$	$a_{\overline{n}|i}$

n	$(1+i)^n$	$s_{\overline{n}\rvert i}$	$a_{\overline{n}\rvert i}$	n	$(1+i)^n$	$s_{\overline{n}\rvert i}$	$a_{\overline{n}\rvert i}$
1	1.035 000	1.000 000	0.966 184	51	5.780 399	136.582 837	23.628 616
2	1.071 225	2.035 000	1.899 694	52	5.982 713	142.363 236	23.795 765
3	1.108 718	3.106 225	2.801 637	53	6.192 108	148.345 950	23.957 260
4	1.147 523	4.214 943	3.673 079	54	6.408 832	154.538 058	24.113 295
5	1.187 686	5.362 466	4.515 052	55	6.633 141	160.946 890	24.264 053
6	1.229 255	6.550 152	5.328 553	56	6.865 301	167.580 031	24.409 713
7	1.272 279	7.779 408	6.114 544	57	7.105 587	174.445 332	24.550 448
8	1.316 809	9.051 687	6.873 956	58	7.354 282	181.550 919	24.686 423
9	1.362 897	10.368 496	7.607 687	59	7.611 682	188.905 201	24.817 800
10	1.410 599	11.731 393	8.316 605	60	7.878 091	196.516 883	24.944 734
11	1.459 970	13.141 992	9.001 551	61	8.153 824	204.394 974	25.067 376
12	1.511 069	14.601 962	9.663 334	62	8.439 208	212.548 798	25.185 870
13	1.563 956	16.113 030	10.302 738	63	8.734 580	220.988 006	25.300 358
14	1.618 695	17.676 986	10.920 520	64	9.040 291	229.722 586	25.410 974
15	1.675 349	19.295 681	11.517 411	65	9.356 701	238.762 876	25.517 849
16	1.733 986	20.971 030	12.094 117	66	9.684 185	248.119 577	25.621 110
17	1.794 676	22.705 016	12.651 321	67	10.023 132	257.803 762	25.720 880
18	1.857 489	24.499 691	13.189 682	68	10.373 941	267.826 894	25.817 275
19	1.922 501	26.357 180	13.709 837	69	10.737 029	278.200 835	25.910 411
20	1.989 789	28.279 682	14.212 403	70	11.112 825	288.937 865	26.000 397
21	2.059 431	30.269 471	14.697 974	71	11.501 774	300.050 690	26.087 340
22	2.131 512	32.328 902	15.167 125	72	11.904 336	311.552 464	26.171 343
23	2.206 114	34.460 414	15.620 410	73	12.320 988	323.456 800	26.252 505
24	2.283 328	36.666 528	16.058 368	74	12.752 223	335.777 788	26.330 923
25	2.363 245	38.949 857	16.481 515	75	13.198 550	348.530 011	26.406 689
26	2.445 959	41.313 102	16.890 352	76	13.660 500	361.728 561	26.479 892
27	2.531 567	43.759 060	17.285 365	77	14.138 617	375.389 061	26.550 621
28	2.620 172	46.290 627	17.667 019	78	14.633 469	389.527 678	26.618 957
29	2.711 878	48.910 799	18.035 767	79	15.145 640	404.161 147	26.684 983
30	2.806 794	51.622 677	18.392 045	80	15.675 738	419.306 787	26.748 776
31	2.905 031	54.429 471	18.736 276	81	16.224 388	434.982 524	26.810 411
32	3.006 708	57.334 502	19.068 865	82	16.792 242	451.206 913	26.869 963
33	3.111 942	60.341 210	19.390 208	83	17.379 970	467.999 155	26.927 500
34	3.220 860	63.453 152	19.700 684	84	17.988 269	485.379 125	26.983 092
35	3.333 590	66.674 013	20.000 661	85	18.617 859	503.367 394	27.036 804
36	3.450 266	70.007 603	20.290 494	86	19.269 484	521.985 253	27.088 699
37	3.571 025	73.457 869	20.570 525	87	19.943 916	541.254 737	27.138 840
38	3.696 011	77.028 895	20.841 087	88	20.641 953	561.198 653	27.187 285
39	3.825 372	80.724 906	21.102 500	89	21.364 421	581.840 606	27.234 092
40	3.959 260	84.550 278	21.355 072	90	22.112 176	603.205 027	27.279 316
41	4.097 834	88.509 537	21.599 104	91	22.886 102	625.317 203	27.323 010
42	4.241 258	92.607 371	21.834 883	92	23.687 116	648.203 305	27.365 227
43	4.389 702	96.848 629	22.062 689	93	24.516 165	671.890 421	27.406 017
44	4.543 342	101.238 331	22.282 791	94	25.374 230	696.406 585	27.445 427
45	4.702 359	105.781 673	22.495 450	95	26.262 329	721.780 816	27.483 504
46	4.866 941	110.484 031	22.700 918	96	27.181 510	748.043 145	27.520 294
47	5.037 284	115.350 973	22.899 438	97	28.132 863	775.224 655	27.555 839
48	5.213 589	120.388 257	23.091 244	98	29.117 513	803.357 517	27.590 183
49	5.396 065	125.601 846	23.276 564	99	30.136 626	832.475 031	27.623 366
50	5.584 927	130.997 910	23.455 618	100	31.191 408	662.611 657	27.653 425

		$i = 0.04\ (4\%)$					
n	$(1+i)^n$	$s_{\overline{n}|i}$	$a_{\overline{n}|i}$	n	$(1+i)^n$	$s_{\overline{n}|i}$	$a_{\overline{n}|i}$
1	1.040 000	1.000 000	0.961 538	51	7.390 951	159.773 767	21.617 485
2	1.081 600	2.040 000	1.886 095	52	7.686 589	167.164 718	21.747 582
3	1.124 864	3.121 600	2.775 091	53	7.994 052	174.851 306	21.872 675
4	1.169 859	4.246 464	3.629 895	54	8.313 814	182.845 359	21.992 957
5	1.216 653	5.416 323	4.451 822	55	8.646 367	191.159 173	22.108 612
6	1.265 319	6.632 975	5.242 137	56	8.992 222	109.805 540	22.219 819
7	1.315 932	7.898 294	6.002 055	57	9.351 910	208.797 762	22.326 749
8	1.368 569	9.214 226	6.732 745	58	9.725 987	218.149 672	22.429 567
9	1.423 312	10.582 795	7.435 332	59	10.115 026	227.875 659	22.528 430
10	1.480 244	12.006 107	8.110 896	60	10.519 627	237.990 685	22.623 490
11	1.539 454	13.486 351	8.760 477	61	10.940 413	248.510 312	22.714 894
12	1.601 032	15.025 805	9.385 074	62	11.378 029	259.450 725	22.802 783
13	1.665 074	16.626 838	9.985 648	63	11.833 150	270.828 754	22.887 291
14	1.731 676	18.291 911	10.563 123	64	12.306 476	282.661 904	22.968 549
15	1.800 944	20.023 588	11.118 387	65	12.798 735	294.968 380	23.046 682
16	1.872 981	21.824 531	11.632 296	66	13.310 685	307.767 116	23.121 810
17	1.947 900	23.697 512	12.165 669	67	13.843 112	321.077 800	23.194 048
18	2.025 817	25.645 413	12.659 297	68	14.396 836	334.920 912	23.263 507
19	2.106 849	27.671 229	13.133 939	69	14.972 710	349.317 749	23.330 296
20	2.191 123	29.778 079	13.590 326	70	15.571 618	364.290 459	23.394 515
21	2.278 768	31.969 202	14.029 160	71	16.194 483	379.862 077	23.456 264
22	2.369 919	34.247 970	14.451 115	72	16.842 262	396.056 560	23.515 639
23	2.464 716	36.617 889	14.856 842	73	17.515 953	412.898 823	23.572 730
24	2.563 304	39.082 604	15.246 963	74	18.216 591	430.414 776	23.627 625
25	2.665 836	41.645 908	15.622 080	75	18.945 255	448.631 367	23.680 408
26	2.772 470	44.311 745	15.982 769	76	19.703 065	467.576 621	23.731 162
27	2.883 369	47.084 214	16.329 586	77	20.491 187	487.279 686	23.779 963
28	2.998 703	49.967 583	16.663 063	78	21.310 835	507.770 873	23.826 688
29	3.118 651	52.966 286	16.983 715	79	22.163 268	529.081 708	23.872 008
30	3.243 398	56.084 938	17.292 033	80	23.049 799	551.244 977	23.915 392
31	3.373 133	59.328 335	17.588 494	81	23.971 791	574.294 776	23.957 108
32	3.508 059	62.701 469	17.873 552	82	24.930 663	598.266 567	23.997 219
33	3.648 381	66.209 527	18.147 646	83	25.927 889	623.197 230	24.035 787
34	3.794 316	69.857 909	18.411 198	84	26.965 005	649.125 119	24.072 872
35	3.946 089	73.652 225	18.664 613	85	28.043 605	676.090 123	24.108 531
36	4.103 933	77.598 314	18.908 282	86	29.165 349	704.133 728	24.142 818
37	4.268 090	81.702 246	19.142 579	87	30.331 963	733.299 078	24.175 787
38	4.438 813	85.970 336	19.367 864	88	31.545 242	763.631 041	24.207 487
39	4.616 366	90.409 150	19.584 485	89	32.807 051	795.176 282	24.237 969
40	4.801 021	95.025 516	19.792 774	90	34.119 333	827.983 334	24.267 276
41	4.993 061	99.826 536	19.993 052	91	35.484 107	862.102 667	24.295 459
42	5.192 784	104.819 598	20.185 627	92	36.903 471	897.586 774	24.322 557
43	5.400 495	110.012 382	20.370 795	93	38.379 610	934.490 244	24.348 612
44	5.616 515	115.412 877	20.548 841	94	39.914 794	972.869 854	24.373 666
45	5.841 176	121.029 392	20.720 040	95	41.511 386	1012.784 648	24.397 756
46	6.074 823	126.870 568	20.884 654	96	43.171 841	1054.296 034	24.420 919
47	6.317 816	132.945 390	21.042 936	97	44.898 715	1097.467 876	24.443 191
48	6.570 528	139.263 206	21.195 131	98	46.694 664	1142.366 591	24.464 607
49	6.833 349	145.833 734	21.341 472	99	48.562 450	1189.061 254	24.485 199
50	7.106 683	152.667 084	21.482 185	100	50.504 948	1237.623 705	24.504 999

Table V (Continued)

$i = 0.045\ (4\frac{1}{2}\%)$							
n	$(1 + i)^n$	$s_{\overline{n}|i}$	$a_{\overline{n}|i}$	n	$(1 + i)^n$	$s_{\overline{n}|i}$	$a_{\overline{n}|i}$
1	1.045 000	1.000 000	0.956 938	51	9.439 105	187.535 665	19.867 950
2	1.092 025	2.045 000	1.872 668	52	9.863 865	196.974 770	19.969 330
3	1.141 166	3.137 025	2.748 964	53	10.307 739	206.838 634	20.066 345
4	1.192 519	4.278 191	3.587 526	54	10.771 587	217.146 373	20.159 181
5	1.246 182	5.470 710	4.389 977	55	11.256 308	227.917 959	20.248 021
6	1.302 260	6.716 892	5.157 872	56	11.762 842	239.174 268	20.333 034
7	1.360 862	8.019 152	5.892 701	57	12.292 170	250.937 110	20.414 387
8	1.422 101	9.380 014	6.595 886	58	12.845 318	263.229 280	20.492 236
9	1.486 095	10.802 114	7.268 790	59	13.423 357	276.074 597	20.566 733
10	1.552 969	12.288 209	7.912 718	60	14.027 408	289.497 954	20.638 022
11	1.622 853	13.841 179	8.528 917	61	14.658 641	303.525 362	20.706 241
12	1.695 881	15.464 032	9.118 581	62	15.318 280	318.184 031	20.771 523
13	1.772 196	17.159 913	9.682 852	63	16.007 603	333.502 283	20.833 993
14	1.851 945	18.932 109	10.222 825	64	16.727 945	349.509 868	20.893 773
15	1.935 282	20.784 054	10.739 546	65	17.480 702	366.237 831	20.950 979
16	2.022 370	22.719 337	11.234 015	66	18.267 334	383.718 533	21.005 722
17	2.113 377	24.741 707	11.707 191	67	19.089 364	401.985 867	21.058 107
18	2.208 479	26.855 084	12.159 992	68	19.948 385	421.075 231	21.108 236
19	2.307 860	29.063 562	12.593 294	69	20.846 063	441.023 617	21.156 207
20	2.411 714	31.371 423	13.007 936	70	21.784 136	461.869 680	21.202 112
21	2.520 241	33.783 137	13.404 724	71	22.764 422	483.653 815	21.246 040
22	2.633 652	36.303 378	13.784 425	72	23.788 821	506.418 237	21.288 077
23	2.752 166	38.937 030	14.147 775	73	24.859 318	530.207 057	21.328 303
24	2.876 014	41.689 196	14.495 478	74	25.977 987	555.066 375	21.366 797
25	3.005 434	44.565 210	14.828 209	75	27.146 996	581.044 362	21.403 634
26	3.140 679	47.570 645	15.146 611	76	28.368 611	608.191 358	21.438 884
27	3.282 010	50.711 324	15.451 303	77	29.645 199	636.559 969	21.472 616
28	3.429 700	53.993 333	15.742 874	78	30.979 233	666.205 168	21.504 896
29	3.584 036	57.423 033	16.021 889	79	32.373 298	697.184 401	21.535 785
30	3.745 318	61.007 070	16.288 889	80	33.830 096	729.557 699	21.565 345
31	3.913 857	64.752 388	16.544 391	81	35.352 451	763.387 795	21.593 632
32	4.089 981	68.666 245	16.788 891	82	36.943 311	798.740 246	21.620 700
33	4.274 030	72.756 226	17.022 862	83	38.605 760	835.683 557	21.646 603
34	4.466 362	77.030 256	17.246 758	84	40.343 019	874.289 317	21.671 390
35	4.667 348	81.496 618	17.461 012	85	42.158 455	914.632 336	21.695 110
36	4.877 378	86.163 966	17.666 041	86	44.055 586	956.790 791	21.717 809
37	5.096 860	91.041 344	17.862 240	87	46.038 087	1000.846 377	21.739 530
38	5.326 219	96.138 205	18.049 990	88	48.109 801	1046.884 464	21.760 316
39	5.565 899	101.464 424	18.229 656	89	50.274 742	1094.994 265	21.780 207
40	5.816 365	107.030 323	18.401 584	90	52.537 105	1145.269 007	21.799 241
41	6.078 101	112.846 688	18.566 109	91	54.901 275	1197.806 112	21.817 455
42	6.351 615	118.924 789	18.723 550	92	57.371 832	1252.707 387	21.834 885
43	6.637 438	125.276 404	18.874 210	93	59.953 565	1310.079 219	21.851 565
44	6.936 123	131.913 842	19.018 383	94	62.651 475	1370.032 784	21.867 526
45	7.248 248	138.849 965	19.156 347	95	65.470 792	1432.684 259	21.882 800
46	7.574 420	146.098 214	19.288 371	96	68.416 977	1498.155 051	21.897 417
47	7.915 268	153.672 633	19.414 709	97	71.495 741	1566.572 028	21.911 403
48	8.271 456	161.587 902	19.535 607	98	74.713 050	1638.067 770	21.924 788
49	8.643 671	169.859 357	19.651 298	99	78.075 137	1712.780 819	21.937 596
50	9.032 636	178.503 028	19.762 008	100	81.588 518	1790.855 956	21.949 853

	$i = 0.05\ (5\%)$				$i = 0.06\ (6\%)$		
n	$(1+i)^n$	$s_{\overline{n}|i}$	$a_{\overline{n}|i}$	n	$(1+i)^n$	$s_{\overline{n}|i}$	$a_{\overline{n}|i}$
1	1.050 000	1.000 000	0.952 381	1	1.060 000	1.000 000	0.943 396
2	1.102 500	2.050 000	1.859 410	2	1.123 600	2.060 000	1.833 393
3	1.157 625	3.152 500	2.723 248	3	1.191 016	3.183 600	2.673 012
4	1.215 506	4.310 125	3.545 951	4	1.262 477	4.374 616	3.465 106
5	1.276 282	5.525 631	4.329 477	5	1.338 226	5.637 093	4.212 364
6	1.340 096	6.801 913	5.075 692	6	1.418 519	6.975 319	4.917 324
7	1.407 100	8.142 008	5.786 373	7	1.503 630	8.393 838	5.582 381
8	1.477 455	9.549 109	6.463 213	8	1.593 848	9.897 468	6.209 794
9	1.551 328	11.026 564	7.107 822	9	1.689 479	11.491 316	6.801 692
10	1.628 895	12.577 893	7.721 735	10	1.790 848	13.180 795	7.360 087
11	1.710 339	14.206 787	8.306 414	11	1.898 299	14.971 643	7.886 875
12	1.795 856	15.917 127	8.863 252	12	2.012 196	16.869 941	8.383 844
13	1.885 649	17.712 983	9.393 573	13	2.132 928	18.882 138	8.852 683
14	1.979 932	19.598 632	9.898 641	14	2.260 904	21.015 066	9.294 984
15	2.078 928	21.578 564	10.379 658	15	2.396 558	23.275 970	9.712 249
16	2.182 875	23.657 492	10.837 770	16	2.540 352	25.672 528	10.105 895
17	2.292 018	25.040 366	11.274 066	17	2.692 773	28.212 880	10.477 260
18	2.406 619	28.132 385	11.689 587	18	2.854 339	30.905 653	10.827 603
19	2.526 950	30.539 004	12.085 321	19	3.025 600	33.759 992	11.158 116
20	2.653 298	33.065 954	12.462 210	20	3.207 135	36.785 591	11.469 921
21	2.785 963	35.719 252	12.821 153	21	3.399 564	39.992 727	11.764 077
22	2.925 261	38.505 214	13.163 003	22	3.603 537	43.392 290	12.041 582
23	3.071 524	41.430 475	13.488 574	23	3.819 750	46.995 828	12.303 379
24	3.225 100	44.501 999	13.798 642	24	4.048 935	50.815 577	12.550 358
25	3.386 355	47.727 099	14.093 945	25	4.291 871	54.864 512	12.783 356
26	3.555 673	51.113 454	14.375 185	26	4.549 383	59.156 383	13.003 166
27	3.733 456	54.669 126	14.643 034	27	4.822 346	63.705 766	13.210 534
28	3.920 129	58.402 583	14.898 127	28	5.111 687	68.528 112	13.406 164
29	4.116 136	62.322 712	15.141 074	29	5.418 388	73.639 798	13.590 721
30	4.321 942	66.438 848	15.372 451	30	5.743 491	79.058 186	13.764 831
31	4.538 039	70.760 790	15.592 810	31	6.088 101	84.801 677	13.929 086
32	4.764 941	75.298 829	15.802 677	32	6.453 387	90.889 778	14.084 043
33	5.003 189	80.063 771	16.002 549	33	6.840 590	97.343 165	14.230 230
34	5.253 348	85.066 959	16.192 904	34	7.251 025	104.183 755	14.368 141
35	5.516 015	90.320 307	16.374 194	35	7.686 087	111.434 780	14.498 246
36	5.791 816	95.836 323	16.546 852	36	8.147 252	119.120 867	14.620 987
37	6.081 407	101.628 139	16.711 287	37	8.636 087	127.268 119	14.736 780
38	6.385 477	107.709 546	16.867 893	38	9.154 252	135.904 206	14.846 019
39	6.704 751	114.095 023	17.017 041	39	9.703 507	145.058 458	14.949 075
40	7.039 989	120.799 774	17.159 086	40	10.285 718	154.761 966	15.046 297
41	7.391 988	127.839 763	17.294 368	41	10.902 861	165.047 684	15.138 016
42	7.761 588	135.231 751	17.423 208	42	11.557 033	175.950 545	15.224 543
43	8.149 667	142.993 339	17.545 912	43	12.250 455	187.507 577	15.306 173
44	8.557 150	151.143 006	17.662 773	44	12.985 482	199.758 032	15.383 182
45	8.985 008	159.700 156	17.774 070	45	13.764 611	212.743 514	15.455 832
46	9.434 258	168.685 164	17.880 066	46	14.590 487	226.508 125	15.524 370
47	9.905 971	178.119 422	17.981 016	47	15.465 917	241.098 612	15.589 028
48	10.401 270	188.025 393	18.077 158	48	16.393 872	256.564 529	15.650 027
49	10.921 333	198.426 663	18.168 722	49	17.377 504	272.958 401	15.707 572
50	11.467 400	209.347 996	18.255 925	50	18.420 154	290.335 905	15.761 861

Table V (Continued)

	$i = 0.07 \ (7\%)$				$i = 0.08 \ (8\%)$		
n	$(1 + i)^n$	$s_{\overline{n}|i}$	$a_{\overline{n}|i}$	n	$(1 + i)^n$	$s_{\overline{n}|i}$	$a_{\overline{n}|i}$
1	1.070 000	1.000 000	0.934 579	1	1.080 000	1.000 000	0.925 925
2	1.144 900	2.070 000	1.808 018	2	1.166 400	2.080 000	1.783 265
3	1.225 043	3.214 900	2.624 316	3	1.259 712	3.246 400	2.577 097
4	1.310 796	4.439 943	3.387 211	4	1.360 489	4.506 112	3.312 127
5	1.402 552	5.750 739	4.100 197	5	1.469 328	5.866 601	3.992 710
6	1.500 730	7.153 291	4.766 540	6	1.586 874	7.335 929	4.622 880
7	1.605 781	8.654 021	5.389 289	7	1.713 824	8.922 803	5.206 370
8	1.718 186	10.259 803	5.971 299	8	1.850 930	10.636 628	5.746 639
9	1.838 459	11.977 989	6.515 232	9	1.999 005	12.487 558	6.246 888
10	1.967 151	13.816 448	7.023 582	10	2.158 925	14.486 562	6.710 081
11	2.104 852	15.783 599	7.498 674	11	2.331 639	16.645 487	7.138 964
12	2.252 192	17.888 451	7.942 686	12	2.518 170	18.977 126	7.536 078
13	2.409 845	20.140 643	8.357 651	13	2.719 624	21.495 297	7.903 776
14	2.578 534	22.550 488	8.745 468	14	2.937 194	24.214 920	8.244 237
15	2.759 032	25.129 022	9.107 914	15	3.172 169	27.152 114	8.559 479
16	2.952 164	27.888 054	9.446 649	16	3.425 943	30.324 283	8.851 369
17	3.158 815	30.840 217	9.763 223	17	3.700 018	33.750 226	9.121 638
18	3.379 932	33.999 033	10.059 087	18	3.996 019	37.450 244	9.371 887
19	3.616 528	37.378 965	10.335 595	19	4.315 701	41.446 263	9.603 599
20	3.869 684	40.995 492	10.594 014	20	4.660 957	45.761 964	9.818 147
21	4.140 562	44.865 177	10.835 527	21	5.033 834	50.422 921	10.016 803
22	4.430 402	49.005 739	11.061 240	22	5.436 540	55.456 755	10.200 744
23	4.740 530	53.436 141	11.272 187	23	5.871 464	60.893 296	10.371 059
24	5.072 367	58.176 671	11.469 334	24	6.341 181	66.764 759	10.528 758
25	5.427 433	63.249 038	11.653 583	25	6.848 475	73.105 940	10.674 776
26	5.807 353	68.676 470	11.825 779	26	7.396 353	79.954 415	10.809 978
27	6.213 868	74.483 823	11.986 709	27	7.988 061	87.350 768	10.935 165
28	6.648 838	80.697 691	12.137 111	28	8.627 106	95.338 830	11.051 078
29	7.114 257	87.346 529	12.277 674	29	9.317 275	103.965 936	11.158 406
30	7.612 255	94.460 786	12.409 041	30	10.062 657	113.283 211	11.257 783
31	8.145 113	102.073 041	12.531 814	31	10.867 669	123.345 868	11.349 799
32	8.715 271	110.218 154	12.646 555	32	11.737 083	134.213 537	11.434 999
33	9.325 340	118.933 425	12.753 790	33	12.676 050	145.950 620	11.513 888
34	9.978 114	128.258 765	12.854 009	34	13.690 134	158.626 670	11.586 934
35	10.676 581	138.236 878	12.947 672	35	14.785 344	172.316 804	11.654 568
36	11.423 942	148.913 460	13.035 208	36	15.968 172	187.102 148	11.717 193
37	12.223 618	160.337 402	13.117 017	37	17.245 626	203.070 320	11.775 179
38	13.079 271	172.561 020	13.193 473	38	18.625 276	220.315 945	11.828 869
39	13.994 820	185.640 292	13.264 928	39	20.115 298	238.941 221	11.878 582
40	14.974 458	199.635 112	13.331 709	40	21.724 522	259.056 519	11.924 613
41	16.022 670	214.609 570	13.394 120	41	23.462 483	280.781 040	11.967 235
42	17.144 257	230.632 240	13.452 449	42	25.339 482	304.243 523	12.006 699
43	18.344 355	247.776 496	13.506 962	43	27.366 640	329.583 005	12.043 240
44	19.628 460	266.120 851	13.557 908	44	29.555 972	356.949 646	12.077 074
45	21.002 452	285.749 311	13.605 522	45	31.920 449	386.505 617	12.108 402
46	22.472 623	306.751 763	13.650 020	46	34.474 085	418.426 067	12.137 409
47	24.045 707	329.224 386	13.691 608	47	37.232 012	452.900 152	12.164 267
48	25.728 907	353.270 093	13.730 474	48	40.210 573	490.132 164	12.189 136
49	27.529 930	378.999 000	13.766 799	49	43.427 419	530.342 737	12.212 163
50	29.457 025	406.528 929	13.800 746	50	46.901 613	573.770 156	12.233 485

Answers

Chapter 0

Exercise 0-1

1. T **3.** T **5.** T **7.** T **9.** $\{1, 2, 3, 4, 5\}$ **11.** $\{3, 4\}$ **13.** $\varnothing$ **15.** $\{2\}$ **17.** $\{-7, 7\}$ **19.** $\{1, 3, 5, 7, 9\}$ **21.** $A' = \{1, 5\}$
23. 40 **25.** 60 **27.** 60 **29.** 20 **31.** 95 **33.** 40 **35.** (A) $\{1, 2, 3, 4, 6\}$ (B) $\{1, 2, 3, 4, 6\}$ **37.** $\{1, 2, 3, 4, 6\}$ **39.** Yes
41. Yes **43.** Yes **45.** (A) 2 (B) 4 (C) $8; 2^n$ **47.** 800 **49.** 200 **51.** 200 **53.** 800 **55.** 200 **57.** 200 **59.** 6
61. A+, AB+ **63.** A−, A+, B+, AB−, AB+, O+ **65.** O+, O− **67.** B−, B+
69. Everybody in the clique relates to each other.

Exercise 0-2

1. $m = 5$ **3.** $x < -9$ **5.** $x \leqslant 4$ **7.** $x < -3$ or $(-\infty, -3)$ 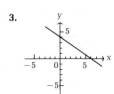 **9.** $-1 \leqslant x \leqslant 2$ or $[-1, 2]$ **11.** $y = 8$ **13.** $x > -6$ **15.** $y = 8$ **17.** $x = 10$ **19.** $y \geqslant 3$
21. $x = 36$ **23.** $m < 3$ **25.** $x = 10$ **27.** $3 \leqslant x < 7$ or $[3, 7)$ **29.** $-20 \leqslant C \leqslant 20$ or $[-20, 20]$
31. $y = \frac{3}{4}x - 3$ **33.** $y = -(A/B)x + (C/B) = (-Ax + C)/B$ **35.** $C = \frac{5}{9}(F - 32)$ **37.** $B = A/(m - n)$
39. $-2 < x \leqslant 1$ or $(-2, 1]$ **41.** 3,000 \$10 tickets, 5,000 \$6 tickets
43. \$7,200 at 10%, \$4,800 at 15% **45.** \$7,800 **47.** 5,000 **49.** 12.6 yr

Exercise 0-3

1. ± 2 **3.** $\pm\sqrt{11}$ **5.** $-2, 6$ **7.** $0, 2$ **9.** $3 \pm 2\sqrt{3}$ **11.** $-2 \pm \sqrt{2}$ **13.** $0, 2$ **15.** $\pm\frac{3}{2}$ **17.** $\frac{1}{2}, -3$ **19.** $(-1 \pm \sqrt{5})/2$
21. $(3 \pm \sqrt{3})/2$ **23.** No real solutions **25.** $-4 \pm \sqrt{11}$ **27.** $r = \sqrt{A/P} - 1$ **29.** \$2 **31.** 8 ft/sec; $4\sqrt{2}$ or 5.66 ft/sec

Exercise 0-4

1.

3.

5. Slope $= 2$; y intercept $= -3$
7. Slope $= -\frac{2}{3}$; y intercept $= 2$
9. $y = -2x + 4$
11. $y = -\frac{3}{5}x + 3$

A1

13.   **15.**   **17.**

19. $y = -3x + 5$, $m = -3$
21. $y = -\frac{2}{3}x + 4$, $m = -\frac{2}{3}$
23. $y + 1 = -3(x - 4)$, $y = -3x + 11$
25. $y + 5 = \frac{2}{3}(x + 6)$, $y = \frac{2}{3}x - 1$
27. $\frac{1}{3}$ **29.** $-\frac{1}{5}$

31. $(y - 3) = \frac{1}{3}(x - 1)$, $x - 3y = -8$ **33.** $(y + 2) = -\frac{1}{5}(x + 5)$, $x + 5y = -15$ **35.** $x = 3$, $y = -5$ **37.** $x = -1$, $y = -3$
39. $y = -\frac{1}{2}x + 4$ **41.** (A) $y = -\frac{1}{2}x + 1$ (B) $y = 2x + 6$ **43.** (A) $y = (\frac{1}{2})x$ (B) $y = -2x - 5$
45. 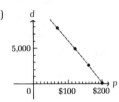 **47.** $x = 2$ **49.** $y = 3$ **51.** (A) \$130; \$220 (B)   (C) 6

53. (A) 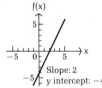 (B) $d = -60p + 12,000$ **55.** $0.2x + 0.1y = 20$

57. (A) 64 grams; 35 grams (B)   (C) $-\frac{1}{5}$

Exercise 0-5

1. Function **3.** Not a function **5.** Function **7.** Function **9.** Not a function **11.** Function **13.** 4 **15.** -5
17. -6 **19.** -2 **21.** -12 **23.** -1 **25.** -6 **27.** 12 **29.** $\frac{3}{4}$
31. 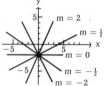 **33.** 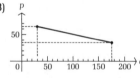 **35.**

37. 13 **39.** -3 **41.** 5 **43.** $\sqrt{2}$ **45.** $e^2 - e$ **47.** $\sqrt{u}$ **49.** $(2 + h)^2 - (2 + h) = h^2 + 3h + 2$

51. $2(a + h) + 1 = 2a + 2h + 1$ **53.** $\dfrac{[2(2 + h) + 1] - [2(2) + 1]}{h} = 2$ **55.** $\dfrac{[(2 + h)^2 - (2 + h)] - [2^2 - 2]}{h} = 3 + h$

57. All nonnegative real numbers **59.** All real numbers x except $x = -3, 5$ **61.** $x \geq -5$ or $[-5, \infty)$

63.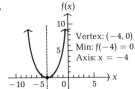

$f(x)$

Vertex: $(-4, 0)$
Min: $f(-4) = 0$
Axis: $x = -4$

65.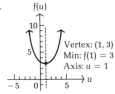

$f(u)$

Vertex: $(1, 3)$
Min: $f(1) = 3$
Axis: $u = 1$

67.

$h(x)$

Vertex: $(2, 6)$
Max: $h(2) = 6$
Axis: $x = 2$

69.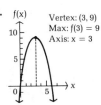

$f(x)$

Vertex: $(3, 9)$
Max: $f(3) = 9$
Axis: $x = 3$

71.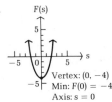

$F(s)$

Vertex: $(0, -4)$
Min: $F(0) = -4$
Axis: $s = 0$

73.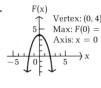

$F(x)$

Vertex: $(0, 4)$
Max: $F(0) = 4$
Axis: $x = 0$

75. (A) 1   (B) 0   (C) 2   (D) 6

77.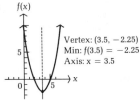

$f(x)$

Vertex: $(3.5, -2.25)$
Min: $f(3.5) = -2.25$
Axis: $x = 3.5$

79.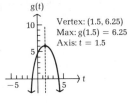

$g(t)$

Vertex: $(1.5, 6.25)$
Max: $g(1.5) = 6.25$
Axis: $t = 1.5$

81.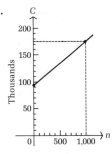

83. (A) $V(x) = x(8 - 2x)(12 - 2x)$ (B) Domain $= 0 < x < 4 = (0, 4)$ (C)

x	V(x)
1	60
2	64
3	36

85. (A) $C = 360,000 - 900p$ (B) $R = np = (9,000 - 30p)p = 9,000p - 30p^2$
(C)

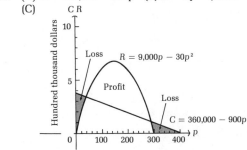

(D) $42, $288
(E) $150

87. (A) 1 pound; 3 pounds
(B)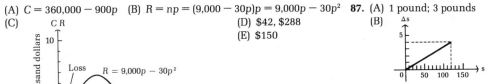
(C) $\frac{1}{30}$

Exercise 0-6

1.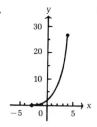
3.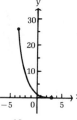
5.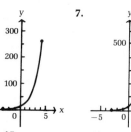
7.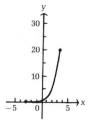
9.

11.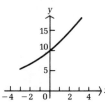
13.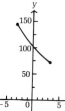
15.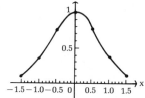
17.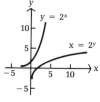

19.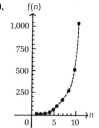
21.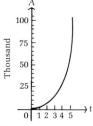
23.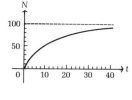

Exercise 0-7

1. $27 = 3^3$ **3.** $10^0 = 1$ **5.** $8 = 4^{3/2}$ **7.** $\log_7 49 = 2$ **9.** $\log_4 8 = 3/2$ **11.** $\log_b A = u$ **13.** 3 **15.** -3 **17.** 3
19. $\log_b P - \log_b Q$ **21.** $5 \log_b L$ **23.** $\log_b p - \log_b q - \log_b r - \log_b s$ **25.** $x = 9$ **27.** $y = 2$ **29.** $b = 10$ **31.** $x = 2$
33. $y = -2$ **35.** $b = 100$ **37.** $5 \log_b x - 3 \log_b y$ **39.** $\frac{1}{3} \log_b N$ **41.** $2 \log_b x + \frac{1}{3} \log_b y$ **43.** $\log_b 50 - 0.2t \log_b 2$
45. $\log_b P + t \log_b(1 + r)$ **47.** $\log_e 100 - 0.01t$ **49.** $x = 2$ **51.** $x = 8$ **53.** $x = 7$ **55.** No solution
57. 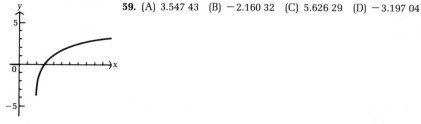   **59.** (A) 3.547 43 (B) -2.160 32 (C) 5.626 29 (D) -3.197 04

61. (A) 1,344 (B) 0.008 919 (C) 6,479 (D) 0.002 773 **63.** $\log_b 1 = 0, b > 0, b \neq 1$ **65.** $y = c10^{0.8x}$ **67.** 12 years
69. $n = \dfrac{\ln 3}{\ln(1 + i)}$ **73.** Approximately 538 years

Exercise 0-8   Chapter Review

1. (A) T (B) T (C) F (D) T **2.** u = 36 **3.** x < 4 or (−∞, 4)  **4.** x = 0, 5 **5.**

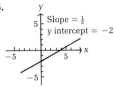

6. y = (x/2) + 1 **7.**

8. −2 **9.**

10. y = 10^x **11.** $\log_b w + \log_b x - \log_b y$

12. (A) {1, 2, 3, 4} (B) {2, 3} **13.** (A) {2, 4, 5, 6} (B) {5} (C) {8} (D) {2, 4} **14.** (A) F (B) T (C) T (D) T
15. (A) 28 (B) 5 (C) 4 (D) 10 **16.** (A) 90 (B) 45 **17.** x = 2 **18.** $x \geqslant \frac{9}{2}$ or $[\frac{9}{2}, \infty)$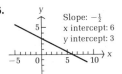

19. $2 \leqslant x < 12$ or [2, 12) **20.** $y = \frac{2}{3}x - 2$ **21.** y = 3/(x − 1) **22.** $x = \pm\sqrt{7}$ **23.** x = −4, 5

24. $x = (3 \pm \sqrt{17})/4$ **25.**

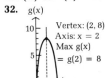

26. x + 2y = 4; slope = $-\frac{1}{2}$ **27.**

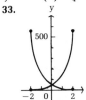

28. $y = -\frac{3}{2}x + 2$

29. (A) 22 (B) −36 (C) −91 (D) $-\frac{3}{4}$ **30.** (A) $\sqrt{8} = 2\sqrt{2}$ (B) $a + 2\sqrt{a}$ **31.** Domain f: R; Domain g: All R, except 2
32. **33.** **34.** **35.** (A) 3 (B) 4^{-3} or $\frac{1}{64}$ **36.** $\log_b 100 + t \log_b 1.06$

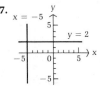

37. $x = \frac{1}{6}$ **38.** (A) −2.040 55 (B) 9.194 55 **39.** (A) 0.000 156 5 (B) 367,400 **40.** x = 7 **41.** Yes
42. $x = (-j \pm \sqrt{j^2 - 4k})/2$ **43.** x = 4 **44.** (A) x − 2y = 8 (B) 2x + y = 1

45. (A) All real numbers except 3 (B) All real numbers $\geqslant 1$ **46.** 2 **47.** t = 9.15 **48.** $y = ce^{-0.2x}$

49. (A) 900 (B) 350 **50.** $20,000 at 8%, $40,000 at 14% **51.** $x/800 = \frac{247}{89}$; x = $2,220.22 **52.** 10%

53. (A) V(t) = −1,250t + 12,000 (B) $5,750 **54.** (A) $R = \frac{8}{5}C$ (B) $168

55. (A) A(x) = x(20 − 2x) (B) Domain = (0, 10) (C)   **56.** 8 years **57.** 6.93 years

x	A(x)
2	32
4	48
5	50
6	48
8	32

Chapter 1

<hr>

Exercise 1-1

1. $x = 3, y = 2$ **3.** $x = 2, y = 4$ **5.** No solution (parallel lines) **7.** $x = 4, y = 5$ **9.** $x = 1, y = 4$ **11.** $u = 2, v = -3$
13. $m = 8, n = 6$ **15.** $x = 1, y = -5$ **17.** No solution (inconsistent) **19.** $x = -\frac{4}{3}, y = 1$
21. Infinitely many solutions (dependent) **23.** $x = 4,000, y = 280$ **25.** $x = 1.1, y = 0.3$ **27.** $x = 0, y = -2, z = 5$
29. $x = 2, y = 0, z = -1$ **31.** $a = -1, b = 2, c = 0$ **33.** $x = 0, y = 2. z = -3$ **35.** No solution (inconsistent)
37. (A) Equilibrium price = \$6.50, equilibrium quantity = 500
   (B)

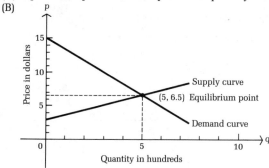

39. (A) For $x = 120$ units, $C = \$216,000 = R$
   (B)

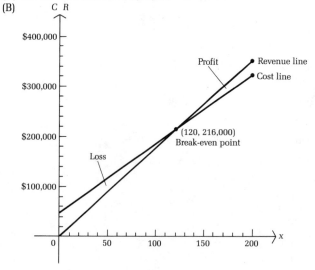

41. 50 one-person boats, 200 two-person boats, 100 four-person boats **43.** Mix A: 80 grams; mix B: 60 grams

45. (A)

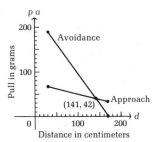

(B) $d = 141$ centimeters (approximately)   **(C)** Vacillate

Exercise 1-2

1. $\begin{bmatrix} 4 & -6 & | & -8 \\ 1 & -3 & | & 2 \end{bmatrix}$ **3.** $\begin{bmatrix} -4 & 12 & | & -8 \\ 4 & -6 & | & -8 \end{bmatrix}$ **5.** $\begin{bmatrix} 1 & -3 & | & 2 \\ 8 & -12 & | & -16 \end{bmatrix}$ **7.** $\begin{bmatrix} 1 & -3 & | & 2 \\ 0 & 6 & | & -16 \end{bmatrix}$ **9.** $\begin{bmatrix} 1 & -3 & | & 2 \\ 2 & 0 & | & -12 \end{bmatrix}$

11. $\begin{bmatrix} 1 & -3 & | & 2 \\ 3 & -3 & | & -10 \end{bmatrix}$ **13.** $x_1 = 3, x_2 = 2$ **15.** $x_1 = 3, x_2 = 1$ **17.** $x_1 = 2, x_2 = 1$ **19.** $x_1 = 2, x_2 = 4$ **21.** No solution

23. $x_1 = 1, x_2 = 4$ **25.** Infinitely many solutions: $x_2 = s, x_1 = 2s - 3$ for any real number s
27. Infinitely many solutions: $x_2 = s, x_1 = \frac{1}{2}s + \frac{1}{2}$ for any real number s **29.** $x_1 = 2, x_2 = -1$ **31.** $x_1 = 2, x_2 = -1$
33. $x_1 = 1.1, x_2 = 0.3$

Exercise 1-3

1. Yes   **3.** No   **5.** No   **7.** Yes   **9.** $x_1 = -2, x_2 = 3, x_3 = 0$ **11.** $x_1 = 2t + 3$ **13.** No solution
$x_2 = -t - 5$
$x_3 = t$
t any real number

15. $x_1 = 2s + 3t - 5$ **17.** $\begin{bmatrix} 1 & 0 & | & -7 \\ 0 & 1 & | & 3 \end{bmatrix}$ **19.** $\begin{bmatrix} 1 & 0 & 0 & | & -5 \\ 0 & 1 & 0 & | & 4 \\ 0 & 0 & 1 & | & -2 \end{bmatrix}$ **21.** $\begin{bmatrix} 1 & 0 & 2 & | & -\frac{5}{3} \\ 0 & 1 & -2 & | & \frac{1}{3} \\ 0 & 0 & 0 & | & 0 \end{bmatrix}$
$x_2 = s$
$x_3 = -3t + 2$
$x_4 = t$
s and t any real numbers
23. $x_1 = -2, x_2 = 3, x_3 = 1$ **25.** $x_1 = 0, x_2 = -2, x_3 = 2$ **27.** $x_1 = 2t + 3$ **29.** $x_1 = (-4t - 4)/7$
$x_2 = t - 2$ $x_2 = (5t + 5)/7$
$x_3 = t$ $x_3 = t$
t any real number t any real number

31. $x_1 = -1, x_2 = 2$ **33.** No solution   **35.** No solution   **37.** $x_1 = t - 1$ **39.** $x_1 = -2s + t + 1$
$x_2 = 2t + 2$ $x_2 = s$
$x_3 = t$ $x_3 = t$
t any real number s and t any real numbers

41. $x_1 = 0, x_2 = 2, x_3 = -3$ **43.** $x_1 = 1, x_2 = -2, x_3 = 1$ **45.** $x_1 = 2s - 3t + 3$
$x_2 = s + 2t + 2$
$x_3 = s$
$x_4 = t$
s and t any real numbers

47. 20 one-person boats, 220 two-person boats, 100 four-person boats
49. $(t - 80)$ one-person boats, $(-2t + 420)$ two-person boats, t four-person boats, $80 \le t \le 210$, t an integer
51. No solution; no production schedule will use all the labor-hours in all departments
53. Federal: \$370,500; state: \$123,500; local: \$58,500   **55.** 8 ounces food A, 2 ounces food B, 4 ounces food C
57. No solution   **59.** 8 ounces food A, $(-2t + 10)$ ounces food B, t ounces food C, $0 \le t \le 5$
61. $(10 - t)$ barrels of mix A, $(t - 5)$ barrels of mix B, $(25 - 2t)$ barrels of mix C, and t barrels of mix D where t is an integer, $5 \le t \le 10$
63. Company A: 10 hours; company B: 15 hours

Exercise 1-4

1. 2×2; 1×4 **3.** 2   **5.** $\begin{bmatrix} 0 & 0 \\ 0 & 0 \end{bmatrix}$ **7.** C, D **9.** A, B **11.** $\begin{bmatrix} -1 & 0 \\ 5 & -3 \end{bmatrix}$ **13.** $\begin{bmatrix} -2 \\ 3 \\ 0 \end{bmatrix}$ **15.** $\begin{bmatrix} -1 \\ 6 \\ 5 \end{bmatrix}$ **17.** $\begin{bmatrix} -15 & 5 \\ 10 & -15 \end{bmatrix}$

19. $\begin{bmatrix} 1 & 3 & -1 & 1 \\ -1 & -5 & 7 & 2 \\ 4 & 8 & 0 & -2 \end{bmatrix}$ **21.** $\begin{bmatrix} 5.4 & 0.7 & -1.8 \\ 7.6 & -4.0 & 7.9 \end{bmatrix}$ **23.** $\begin{bmatrix} 250 & 360 \\ 40 & 350 \end{bmatrix}$ **25.** $\begin{bmatrix} 2,280 & 3,460 \\ 1,380 & 2,310 \end{bmatrix}$

27. $a = -1, b = 1, c = 3, d = -5$ **29.** $x = 2, y = -3$ **31.** Guitar   Banjo
$$\begin{bmatrix} \$33 & \$26 \\ \$57 & \$77 \end{bmatrix} \begin{matrix} \text{Materials} \\ \text{Labor} \end{matrix}$$

33. $\begin{bmatrix} 135 & 282 & 50 \\ 55 & 258 & 155 \end{bmatrix}$; $\begin{bmatrix} 0.14 & 0.30 & 0.05 \\ 0.06 & 0.28 & 0.17 \end{bmatrix}$

Exercise 1-5

1. 10   **3.** -1 **5.** $[12 \quad 13]$ **7.** $\begin{bmatrix} 5 \\ -3 \end{bmatrix}$ **9.** $\begin{bmatrix} 2 & 4 \\ 1 & -5 \end{bmatrix}$ **11.** $\begin{bmatrix} 1 & -5 \\ -2 & -4 \end{bmatrix}$ **13.** $[-7]$ **15.** $\begin{bmatrix} -15 & 6 \\ -20 & 8 \end{bmatrix}$ **17.** 6   **19.** 15

21. $\begin{bmatrix} 0 & 9 \\ 5 & -4 \end{bmatrix}$ **23.** $\begin{bmatrix} 5 & 8 & -5 \\ -1 & -3 & 2 \\ -2 & 8 & -6 \end{bmatrix}$ **25.** $[11]$ **27.** $\begin{bmatrix} 3 & -2 & -4 \\ 6 & -4 & -8 \\ -9 & 6 & 12 \end{bmatrix}$ **29.** $\begin{bmatrix} 0 & 0 & -5 \\ -6 & 15 & 13 \\ 5 & -6 & -14 \end{bmatrix}$ **31.** $\begin{bmatrix} -3.73 & -5.28 \\ 18.47 & -36.27 \end{bmatrix}$

33. $AB = \begin{bmatrix} 5 & 7 \\ 2 & 3 \end{bmatrix}$, $BA = \begin{bmatrix} 1 & 3 \\ 2 & 7 \end{bmatrix}$ **35.** Both sides equal $\begin{bmatrix} 0 & 12 \\ 1 & 5 \end{bmatrix}$

37. (A) \$9 per boat   (B) $[1.5 \quad 1.2 \quad 0.4] \cdot \begin{bmatrix} 7 \\ 10 \\ 4 \end{bmatrix} = \$24.10$ (C) 3×2 (D)

	I	II	
	\$9.00	\$11.00	One-person
	\$14.10	\$17.20	Two-person
	\$19.80	\$24.10	Four-person

Labor costs per boat at each plant

39. (A) $\begin{matrix} A & B & C & D & E \end{matrix}$
$[16 \quad 9 \quad 11 \quad 11 \quad 10]$, which is the combined inventory in all three stores

$\quad\quad\quad\quad W \quad\quad\quad R$
(B) $[\$108,300 \quad \$141,340]$, which is the total wholesale and retail values of the total inventory in all three stores

41. (A) $2,025 (B) $[2{,}000 \quad 800 \quad 8{,}000] \cdot \begin{bmatrix} \$0.40 \\ \$0.75 \\ \$0.25 \end{bmatrix} = \$3{,}400$ (C) $\begin{bmatrix} \$2{,}025 \\ \$3{,}400 \end{bmatrix}$ Berkeley Oakland

Cost per town

(D) $\begin{matrix} \text{Telephone} & \text{House} & \text{Letter} \\ [3{,}000 & 1{,}300 & 13{,}000] \end{matrix}$

Number of each type of contact made

Exercise 1-6

1. $\begin{bmatrix} 2 & -3 \\ 4 & 5 \end{bmatrix}$ **3.** $\begin{bmatrix} -2 & 1 & 3 \\ 2 & 4 & -2 \\ 5 & 1 & 0 \end{bmatrix}$ **9.** $x_1 = -8, x_2 = 2$ **11.** $x_1 = 0, x_2 = 4$ **13.** $\begin{bmatrix} 3 & -2 \\ -1 & 1 \end{bmatrix}$ **15.** $\begin{bmatrix} 7 & -3 \\ -2 & 1 \end{bmatrix}$

17. $\begin{bmatrix} 7 & 6 & -3 \\ 2 & 2 & -1 \\ -6 & -5 & 3 \end{bmatrix}$ **19.** $\frac{1}{2}\begin{bmatrix} 3 & -1 & -1 \\ -1 & 1 & 1 \\ -3 & 1 & 3 \end{bmatrix}$ **21.** (A) $x_1 = -3, x_2 = 2$ **23.** (A) $x_1 = 17, x_2 = -5$
  (B) $x_1 = -1, x_2 = 2$ (B) $x_1 = 7, x_2 = -2$
  (C) $x_1 = -8, x_2 = 3$ (C) $x_1 = 24, x_2 = -7$

25. (A) $x_1 = 1, x_2 = 0, x_3 = 0$ **27.** (A) $x_1 = 1, x_2 = 1, x_3 = 3$ **29.** The inverse does not exist
  (B) $x_1 = -1, x_2 = 0, x_3 = 1$ (B) $x_1 = -1, x_2 = 1, x_3 = -1$
  (C) $x_1 = -1, x_2 = -1, x_3 = 1$ (C) $x_1 = 5, x_2 = -1, x_3 = -5$

31. $\begin{bmatrix} 1 & -\frac{1}{2} \\ -2 & \frac{3}{2} \end{bmatrix}$ **33.** $\begin{bmatrix} 1 & 2 & 2 \\ -2 & -3 & -4 \\ -1 & -2 & -1 \end{bmatrix}$ **35.** The inverse does not exist **37.** $\begin{bmatrix} 1 & 1 & -\frac{1}{2} \\ -2 & -\frac{3}{2} & 1 \\ -1 & -1 & \frac{3}{4} \end{bmatrix}$

41. Concert 1: 6,000 $4 tickets and 4,000 $8 tickets; Concert 2: 5,000 $4 tickets and 5,000 $8 tickets; Concert 3: 3,000 $4 tickets and 7,000 $8 tickets

43. Diet 1: 60 ounces mix *A* and 80 ounces mix *B*; Diet 2: 20 ounces mix *A* and 60 ounces mix *B*; Diet 3: 0 ounces mix *A* and 100 ounces mix *B*

Exercise 1-7

1. 40¢ from *A*, 20¢ from *E* **3.** $\begin{bmatrix} 0.6 & -0.2 \\ -0.2 & 0.9 \end{bmatrix}, \begin{bmatrix} 1.8 & 0.4 \\ 0.4 & 1.2 \end{bmatrix}$ **5.** $X = \begin{bmatrix} x_1 \\ x_2 \end{bmatrix} = \begin{bmatrix} 16.4 \\ 9.2 \end{bmatrix}$

7. 20¢ from *A*, 10¢ from *B*, and 10¢ from *C* **11.** Agriculture: $18 billion; building: $15.6 billion; energy: $22.4 billion

13. $\begin{bmatrix} 1.4 & 0.4 \\ 0.6 & 1.6 \end{bmatrix}, \begin{bmatrix} 24 \\ 46 \end{bmatrix}$ **15.** $\begin{bmatrix} 1.58 & 0.24 & 0.58 \\ 0.4 & 1.2 & 0.4 \\ 0.22 & 0.16 & 1.22 \end{bmatrix}, \begin{bmatrix} 38.6 \\ 18 \\ 17.4 \end{bmatrix}$ **17.** Coal: $28 billion; steel: $26 billion

19. Agriculture: $40.1 billion; manufacturing: $29.4 billion; energy: $34.4 billion

Exercise 1-8   Chapter Review

1. $x = 4, y = 4$ **2.** $x = 4, y = 4$ **3.** $\begin{bmatrix} 3 & 3 \\ 4 & 2 \end{bmatrix}$ **4.** Not defined **5.** $\begin{bmatrix} -3 & 0 \\ 1 & -1 \end{bmatrix}$ **6.** $\begin{bmatrix} 4 & 3 \\ 7 & 4 \end{bmatrix}$ **7.** Not defined **8.** $\begin{bmatrix} 5 \\ 5 \end{bmatrix}$

9. $\begin{bmatrix} 2 & 3 \\ 4 & 6 \end{bmatrix}$ **10.** 8 (a real number) **11.** Not defined **12.** $\begin{bmatrix} 3 & -2 \\ -4 & 3 \end{bmatrix}$ **13.** $x_1 = -1, x_2 = 3$ **14.** $x_1 = -1, x_2 = 3$

15. $x_1 = -1, x_2 = 3; x_1 = 1, x_2 = 2; x_1 = 8, x_2 = -10$ **16.** Not defined **17.** $\begin{bmatrix} 10 & -8 \\ 4 & 6 \end{bmatrix}$ **18.** $\begin{bmatrix} -2 & 8 \\ 8 & 6 \end{bmatrix}$

19. 9 (a real number) **20.** [9] (a matrix) **21.** $\begin{bmatrix} 10 & -5 & 1 \\ -1 & -4 & -5 \\ 1 & -7 & -2 \end{bmatrix}$ **22.** $\begin{bmatrix} -\frac{5}{2} & 2 & -\frac{1}{2} \\ 1 & -1 & 1 \\ \frac{1}{2} & 0 & -\frac{1}{2} \end{bmatrix}$ **23.** (A) $x_1 = 2, x_2 = 1, x_3 = -1$
(B) $x_1 = -5t - 12$
$x_2 = 3t + 7$
$x_3 = t$
t any real number

24. $x_1 = 2, x_2 = 1, x_3 = -1; x_1 = 1, x_2 = -2, x_3 = 1; x_1 = -1, x_2 = 2, x_3 = -2$ **25.** $\begin{bmatrix} -\frac{11}{12} & -\frac{1}{12} & 5 \\ \frac{10}{12} & \frac{2}{12} & -4 \\ \frac{1}{12} & -\frac{1}{12} & 0 \end{bmatrix}$

26. $x_1 = 1,000, x_2 = 4,000, x_3 = 2,000$ **27.** $x_1 = 1,000, x_2 = 4,000, x_3 = 2,000$ **28.** $0.01x_1 + 0.02x_2 = 4.5$
$0.02x_1 + 0.05x_2 = 10$
$x_1 = 250$ tons of ore A
$x_2 = 100$ tons of ore B

29. (A) $\overset{X}{\begin{bmatrix} x_1 \\ x_2 \end{bmatrix}} = \overset{A^{-1}}{\begin{bmatrix} 500 & -200 \\ -200 & 100 \end{bmatrix}} \begin{bmatrix} 4.5 \\ 10 \end{bmatrix} = \begin{bmatrix} 250 \\ 100 \end{bmatrix}$ (B) $\overset{X}{\begin{bmatrix} x_1 \\ x_2 \end{bmatrix}} = \overset{A^{-1}}{\begin{bmatrix} 500 & -200 \\ -200 & 100 \end{bmatrix}} \begin{bmatrix} 2.3 \\ 5 \end{bmatrix} = \begin{bmatrix} 150 \\ 40 \end{bmatrix}$
$x_1 = 250$ tons of ore A $x_1 = 150$ tons of ore A
$x_2 = 100$ tons of ore B $x_2 = 40$ tons of ore B

30. (A) $MN = \begin{array}{c} \\ \\ \end{array} \overset{\text{Supplier } A \quad \text{Supplier } B}{\begin{bmatrix} \$7,620 & \$7,530 \\ \$13,880 & \$13,930 \end{bmatrix}} \begin{array}{l} \text{Alloy 1} \\ \text{Alloy 2} \end{array}$ (B) $\overset{\text{Supplier } A \quad \text{Supplier } B}{[\$21,500 \quad \$21,460]}$
Cost of each alloy from   Total cost for both alloys
each supplier   from each supplier

31. (A) $[0.25 \quad 0.20 \quad 0.05] \cdot \begin{bmatrix} 15 \\ 12 \\ 4 \end{bmatrix} = \$6.35$ (B) $\overset{\text{Calif.} \quad \text{Texas}}{\begin{bmatrix} \$3.65 & \$3.00 \\ \$6.35 & \$5.20 \end{bmatrix}} \begin{array}{l} \text{Model } A \\ \text{Model } B \end{array}$
Total labor costs for each
model at each plant

32. $2,000 at 5%, $3,000 at 10% **33.** $2,000 at 5%, $3,000 at 10%

Chapter 2

Exercise 2-1

1.

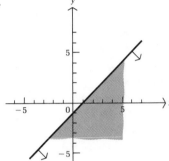

3.

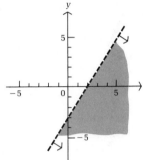

5.

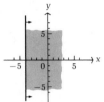

7.

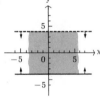

9.

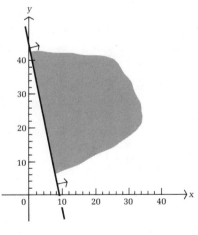

11.

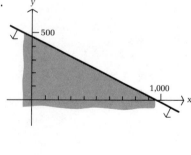

13.

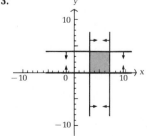

15.

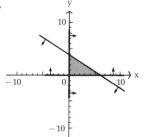

17.

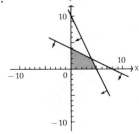

19.

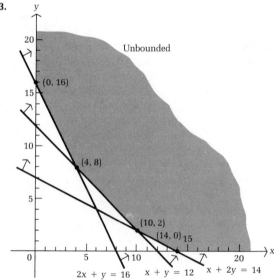

21.

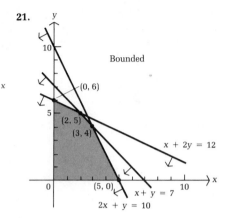

Bounded

(0, 6)

(2, 5)

(3, 4)

$x + 2y = 12$

(5, 0)

$x + y = 7$

$2x + y = 10$

23.

Unbounded

(0, 16)

(4, 8)

(10, 2)

(14, 0)

$2x + y = 16$ $x + y = 12$ $x + 2y = 14$

25.

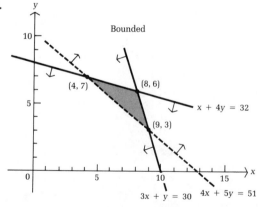

Bounded

(4, 7)

(8, 6)

$x + 4y = 32$

(9, 3)

$3x + y = 30$ $4x + 5y = 51$

27.

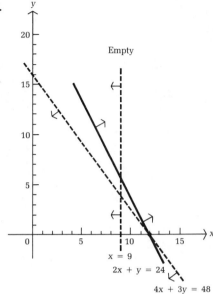

Empty

$x = 9$

$2x + y = 24$

$4x + 3y = 48$

29.

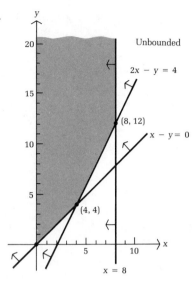

Unbounded

$2x - y = 4$

(8, 12)

$x - y = 0$

(4, 4)

$x = 8$

31.

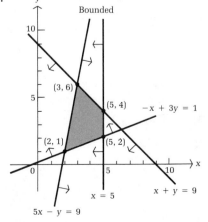

Bounded

(3, 6)

(5, 4)

$-x + 3y = 1$

(2, 1)

(5, 2)

$x = 5$

$x + y = 9$

$5x - y = 9$

33.

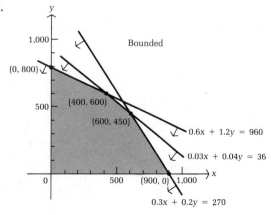

Bounded

1,000

(0, 800)

(400, 600)

500

(600, 450)

$0.6x + 1.2y = 960$

$0.03x + 0.04y = 36$

500   (900, 0) 1,000

$0.3x + 0.2y = 270$

35. $6x + 4y \leqslant 108$
$\quad\quad x + \ y \leqslant 24$
$\quad\quad\quad x \geqslant 0$
$\quad\quad\quad y \geqslant 0$

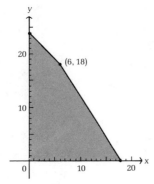

$(6, 18)$

37. $10x + 20y \leqslant 800$
$\quad\quad 20x + 10y \leqslant 640$
$\quad\quad\quad\quad x \geqslant 0$
$\quad\quad\quad\quad y \geqslant 0$

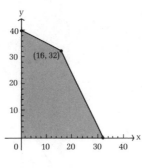

$(16, 32)$

Exercise 2-2

1. Max $P = 30$ at $x_1 = 4$ and $x_2 = 2$ **3.** Min $z = 14$ at $x_1 = 4$ and $x_2 = 2$; no maximum
5. Max $P = 260$ at $x_1 = 2$ and $x_2 = 5$ **7.** Min $z = 140$ at $x_1 = 14$ and $x_2 = 0$; no maximum
9. Min $P = 20$ at $x_1 = 0$ and $x_2 = 2$; Max $P = 150$ at $x_1 = 5$ and $x_2 = 0$ **11.** Feasible region empty, no optimal solutions
13. Min $P = 140$ at $x_1 = 3$ and $x_2 = 8$; Max $P = 260$ at $x_1 = 8$ and $x_2 = 10$, at $x_1 = 12$ and $x_2 = 2$, or at any point on the line segment from $(8, 10)$ to $(12, 2)$
15. Max $P = 26{,}000$ at $x_1 = 400$ and $x_2 = 600$ **17.** (A) $2a < b$ (B) $\frac{1}{3}a < b < 2a$ (C) $b < \frac{1}{3}a$ (D) $b = 2a$ (E) $b = \frac{1}{3}a$
19. 6 trick, 18 slalom; \$780   **21.** (A) Plant A: 5 days; Plant B; 4 days; minimum cost \$8,600
$\quad\quad\quad\quad\quad\quad\quad\quad\quad$ (B) Plant A: 10 days; Plant B: 0 days; minimum cost \$6,000
$\quad\quad\quad\quad\quad\quad\quad\quad\quad$ (C) Plant A: 0 days; Plant B: 10 days; minimum cost \$8,000
23. 7 buses, 15 vans; minimum cost \$9,900   **25.** 1,500 gallons by new process, none by old process; maximum profit \$300
27. (A) 150 bags Brand A, 100 bags Brand B; maximum nitrogen 1,500 pounds
$\quad\quad$ (B) 0 bags Brand A, 250 bags Brand B; minimum nitrogen 750 pounds
29. 20 cubic yards of A, 12 cubic yards of B; \$1,020   **31.** 48; 16 mice, 32 rats

Exercise 2-3

1.

	Nonbasic	Basic	Feasible?
(A)	x_1, x_2	s_1, s_2	Yes
(B)	x_1, s_1	x_2, s_2	Yes
(C)	x_1, s_2	x_2, s_1	No
(D)	x_2, s_1	x_1, s_2	No
(E)	x_2, s_2	x_1, s_1	Yes
(F)	s_1, s_2	x_1, x_2	Yes

3.

	x_1	x_2	s_1	s_2	Feasible?
(A)	0	0	50	40	Yes
(B)	0	50	0	-60	No
(C)	0	20	30	0	Yes
(D)	25	0	0	15	Yes
(E)	40	0	-30	0	No
(F)	20	10	0	0	Yes

5.

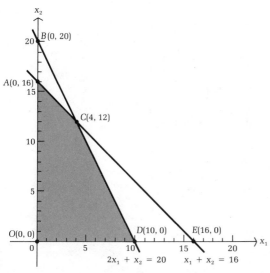

$$x_1 + x_2 + s_1 \quad\quad = 16$$
$$2x_1 + x_2 \quad\quad + s_2 = 20$$

x_1	x_2	s_1	s_2	Intersection Point	Feasible?
0	0	16	20	O	Yes
0	16	0	4	A	Yes
0	20	−4	0	B	No
16	0	0	−12	E	No
10	0	6	0	D	Yes
4	12	0	0	C	Yes

7.

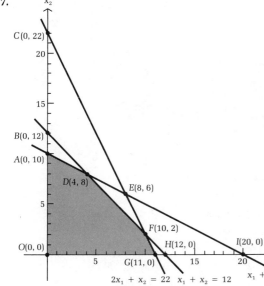

$$2x_1 + x_2 + s_1 \quad\quad\quad = 22$$
$$x_1 + x_2 \quad + s_2 \quad\quad = 12$$
$$x_1 + 2x_2 \quad\quad + s_3 = 20$$

x_1	x_2	s_1	s_2	s_3	Intersection Point	Feasible?
0	0	22	12	20	O	Yes
0	22	0	−10	−24	C	No
0	12	10	0	−4	B	No
0	10	12	2	0	A	Yes
11	0	0	1	9	G	Yes
12	0	−2	0	8	H	No
20	0	−18	−8	0	I	No
10	2	0	0	6	F	Yes
8	6	0	−2	0	E	No
4	8	6	0	0	D	Yes

Exercise 2-4

1. (A) Basic: x_2, s_1, P; nonbasic: x_1, s_2
(B) $x_1 = 0$, $x_2 = 12$, $s_1 = 15$, $s_2 = 0$ and $P = 20$
(C) Additional pivot required

3. (A) Basic: x_2, x_3, s_3, P; nonbasic: x_1, s_1, s_2
(B) $x_1 = 0$, $x_2 = 15$, $x_3 = 5$, $s_1 = 0$, $s_2 = 0$, $s_3 = 12$ and $P = 45$
(C) No solution

5. $\begin{bmatrix} 1 & 4 & 1 & 0 & 0 & | & 4 \\ 0 & -7 & -3 & 1 & 0 & | & 12 \\ 0 & 27 & 8 & 0 & 1 & | & 32 \end{bmatrix}$ **7.** $\begin{bmatrix} 1 & \frac{1}{2} & \frac{1}{2} & 0 & 0 & 0 & | & 2 \\ 0 & -\frac{3}{2} & -\frac{1}{2} & 1 & 0 & 0 & | & 2 \\ 0 & 0 & 2 & 0 & 1 & 0 & | & 2 \\ 0 & 2 & -1 & 0 & 0 & 1 & | & 13 \end{bmatrix}$

9. (A) $\begin{aligned} 2x_1 + x_2 + s_1 \quad\quad\quad &= 10 \\ x_1 + 2x_2 \quad + s_2 \quad &= 8 \\ -15x_1 - 10x_2 \quad\quad\quad + P &= 0 \end{aligned}$ (B) $\begin{bmatrix} ② & 1 & 1 & 0 & 0 & | & 10 \\ 1 & 2 & 0 & 1 & 0 & | & 8 \\ -15 & -10 & 0 & 0 & 1 & | & 0 \end{bmatrix}$

(C) Max $P = 80$ at $x_1 = 4$ and $x_2 = 2$

11. (A) $\begin{aligned} 2x_1 + x_2 + s_1 \quad\quad\quad &= 10 \\ x_1 + 2x_2 \quad + s_2 \quad &= 8 \\ -30x_1 - x_2 \quad\quad\quad + P &= 0 \end{aligned}$ (B) $\begin{bmatrix} ② & 1 & 1 & 0 & 0 & | & 10 \\ 1 & 2 & 0 & 1 & 0 & | & 8 \\ -30 & -1 & 0 & 0 & 1 & | & 0 \end{bmatrix}$

(C) Max $P = 150$ at $x_1 = 5$ and $x_2 = 0$

13. Max $P = 260$ at $x_1 = 2$ and $x_2 = 5$ **15.** No optimal solution exists   **17.** Max $P = 7$ at $x_1 = 3$ and $x_2 = 5$

19. Max $P = \frac{190}{3}$ at $x_1 = \frac{40}{3}$, $x_2 = 0$, and $x_3 = \frac{10}{3}$ **21.** Max $P = 17$ at $x_1 = 4$, $x_2 = 3$, and $x_3 = 0$

23. Max $P = 22$ at $x_1 = 1$, $x_2 = 6$, and $x_3 = 0$ **25.** Max $P = 26,000$ at $x_1 = 400$ and $x_2 = 600$

27. Max $P = 450$ at $x_1 = 0$, $x_2 = 180$, and $x_3 = 30$ **29.** Max $P = 88$ at $x_1 = 24$ and $x_2 = 8$

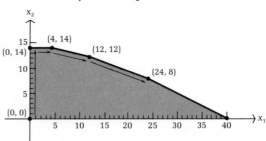

31. Let x_1 = Number of A components   Maximize $P = 7x_1 + 9x_2 + 10x_3$
x_2 = Number of B components   Subject to $2x_1 + x_2 + 2x_3 \leq 1,000$
x_3 = Number of C components $\quad\quad\quad\quad x_1 + 2x_2 + 2x_3 \leq 800$
$\quad\quad\quad\quad\quad\quad\quad\quad x_1, x_2, x_3 \geq 0$

400 A components, 200 B components, and 0 C components; maximum profit \$4,600

33. Let x_1 = Amount invested in government bonds   Maximize $P = 0.08x_1 + 0.13x_2 + 0.15x_3$
x_2 = Amount invested in mutual funds   Subject to $x_1 + x_2 + x_3 \leq 100,000$
x_3 = Amount invested in money market funds $\quad\quad\quad -x_1 + x_2 + x_3 \leq 0$
$\quad\quad\quad\quad\quad\quad\quad\quad x_1, x_2, x_3 \geq 0$

\$50,000 in government bonds, \$0 in mutual funds, and \$50,000 in money market funds; maximum return \$11,500

35. Let x_1 = Number of ads placed in daytime shows   Maximize $P = 14,000x_1 + 24,000x_2 + 18,000x_3$
x_2 = Number of ads placed in prime-time shows   Subject to $x_1 + x_2 + x_3 \leq 15$
x_3 = Number of ads placed in late-night shows $\quad 1,000x_1 + 2,000x_2 + 1,500x_3 \leq 20,000$
$\quad\quad\quad\quad\quad\quad\quad\quad x_1, x_2, x_3 \geq 0$

10 daytime ads, 5 prime-time ads, and 0 late-night ads; maximum number of potential customers 260,000

37. Let x_1 = Number of colonial houses

x_2 = Number of split-level houses

x_3 = Number of ranch houses

Maximize $P = 20{,}000x_1 + 18{,}000x_2 + 24{,}000x_3$

Subject to $\quad \frac{1}{2}x_1 + \quad \frac{1}{2}x_2 + \quad x_3 \leqslant \quad 30$

$60{,}000x_1 + 60{,}000x_2 + 80{,}000x_3 \leqslant 3{,}200{,}000$

$4{,}000x_1 + \ 3{,}000x_2 + \ 4{,}000x_3 \leqslant \ 180{,}000$

$x_1, x_2, x_3 \geqslant \ 0$

20 colonial, 20 split-level, and 10 ranch houses; maximum profit $1,000,000

39. Let x_1 = Number of boxes of Assortment I

x_2 = Number of boxes of Assortment II

x_3 = Number of boxes of Assortment III

Maximize $P = 4x_1 + 3x_2 + 5x_3$

Subject to $\quad 4x_1 + 12x_2 + 8x_3 \leqslant 4{,}800$

$4x_1 + \ 4x_2 + 8x_3 \leqslant 4{,}000$

$12x_1 + \ 4x_2 + 8x_3 \leqslant 5{,}600$

$x_1, x_2, x_3 \geqslant 0$

200 boxes of Assortment I, 100 boxes of Assortment II, and 350 boxes of Assortment III; maximum profit $2,850

41. Let x_1 = Number of grams of food A Maximize $P = 3x_1 + 3x_2 + 5x_3$

x_2 = Number of grams of food B Subject to $\ x_1 + 3x_2 + 2x_3 \leqslant 30$

x_3 = Number of grams of food C $\quad 2x_1 + \ x_2 + \ x_3 \leqslant 24$

$x_1, x_2, x_3 \geqslant 0$

6 grams of food A, 0 grams of food B, and 12 grams of food C; maximum protein 78 units

43. Let x_1 = Number of undergraduate students Maximize $P = 18x_1 + 25x_2 + 30x_3$

x_2 = Number of graduate students Subject to $\ x_1 + \ x_2 + \ x_3 \leqslant 20$

x_3 = Number of faculty members $\quad 60x_1 + 90x_2 + 120x_3 \leqslant 1{,}620$

$x_1, x_2, x_3 \geqslant 0$

6 undergraduate and 14 graduate students, 0 faculty members; maximum number of interviews 458

Exercise 2-5

1. (A) Maximize $P = 4y_1 + 5y_2$

Subject to $\quad y_1 + 2y_2 \leqslant 8$

$3y_1 + \ y_2 \leqslant 9$

$y_1, y_2 \geqslant 0$

(B) $\quad y_1 + 2y_2 + x_1 \qquad\quad = 8$

$3y_1 + \ y_2 \qquad + x_2 \qquad = 9$

$-4y_1 - 5y_2 \qquad\qquad\quad + P = 0$

(C)

$$\begin{array}{ccccc}
y_1 & y_2 & x_1 & x_2 & P \\
\end{array}$$

$$\left[\begin{array}{ccccc|c}
1 & 2 & 1 & 0 & 0 & 8 \\
3 & 1 & 0 & 1 & 0 & 9 \\
\hline
-4 & -5 & 0 & 0 & 1 & 0
\end{array}\right]$$

3. (A) Max $P = 121$ at $y_1 = 3$ and $y_2 = 5$

(B) Min $C = 121$ at $x_1 = 1$ and $x_2 = 2$

5. (A) Maximize $P = 13y_1 + 12y_2$

Subject to $4y_1 + 3y_2 \leqslant 9$

$y_1 + \ y_2 \leqslant 2$

$y_1, y_2 \geqslant 0$

(B) Min $C = 26$ at $x_1 = 0$ and $x_2 = 13$

7. (A) Maximize $P = 15y_1 + 8y_2$

Subject to $2y_1 + \ y_2 \leqslant 7$

$3y_1 + 2y_2 \leqslant 12$

$y_1, y_2 \geqslant 0$

(B) Min $C = 54$ at $x_1 = 6$ and $x_2 = 1$

9. (A) Maximize $P = 8y_1 + 4y_2$
Subject to $2y_1 - 2y_2 \leqslant 11$
$y_1 + 3y_2 \leqslant 4$
$y_1, y_2 \geqslant 0$
(B) Min $C = 32$ at $x_1 = 0$ and $x_2 = 8$

11. (A) Maximize $P = 6y_1 + 4y_2$
Subject to $-3y_1 + y_2 \leqslant 7$
$y_1 - 2y_2 \leqslant 9$
$y_1, y_2 \geqslant 0$
(B) No optimal solution exists

13. Min $C = 24$ at $x_1 = 8$ and $x_2 = 0$ **15.** Min $C = 20$ at $x_1 = 0$ and $x_2 = 4$ **17.** Min $C = 140$ at $x_1 = 14$ and $x_2 = 0$

19. Min $C = 44$ at $x_1 = 6$ and $x_2 = 2$ **21.** Min $C = 43$ at $x_1 = 0$, $x_2 = 1$, and $x_3 = 3$ **23.** No optimal solution exists

25. Min $C = 44$ at $x_1 = 0$, $x_2 = 3$, and $x_3 = 5$ **27.** Min $C = 166$ at $x_1 = 0$, $x_2 = 12$, $x_3 = 20$, and $x_4 = 3$

29. Let x_1 = Number of hours the Cedarburg plant is operated   Minimize $C = 70x_1 + 75x_2 + 90x_3$
x_2 = Number of hours the Grafton plant is operated   Subject to $20x_1 + 10x_2 + 20x_3 \geqslant 300$
x_3 = Number of hours the West Bend plant is operated $10x_1 + 20x_2 + 20x_3 \geqslant 200$
$x_1, x_2, x_3 \geqslant 0$

Cedarburg plant 10 hours per day, West Bend plant 5 hours per day, Grafton plant not used; $1,150

31. Let x_1 = Number of single-sided drives ordered from Associated Electronics
x_2 = Number of double-sided drives ordered from Associated Electronics
x_3 = Number of single-sided drives ordered from Digital Drives
x_4 = Number of double-sided drives ordered from Digital Drives
Minimize $C = 250x_1 + 350x_2 + 290x_3 + 320x_4$
Subject to $x_1 + x_2 \qquad \leqslant 1,000$
$x_3 + x_4 \leqslant 2,000$
$x_1 \quad + x_3 \qquad \geqslant 1,200$
$x_2 + \qquad x_4 \geqslant 1,600$
$x_1, x_2, x_3, x_4 \geqslant 0$

1,000 single-sided drives from Associated Electronics, 200 single-sided and 1,600 double-sided drives from Digital Drives; $820,000

33. Let x_1 = Number of ounces of food L Minimize $C = 20x_1 + 24x_2 + 18x_3$
x_2 = Number of ounces of food M Subject to $20x_1 + 10x_2 + 10x_3 \geqslant 300$
x_3 = Number of ounces of food N $10x_1 + 10x_2 + 10x_3 \geqslant 200$
$10x_1 + 20x_2 + 10x_3 \geqslant 240$
$x_1, x_2, x_3 \geqslant 0$

10 ounces of L, 4 ounces of M, 6 ounces of N; 404 units

35. Let x_1 = Number of students bused from North Division to Central   Minimize $C = 5x_1 + 2x_2 + 3x_3 + 4x_4$
x_2 = Number of students bused from North Division to Washington   Subject to $x_1 + x_2 \qquad\qquad \geqslant 300$
x_3 = Number of students bused from South Division to Central $x_3 + x_4 \geqslant 500$
x_4 = Number of students bused from South Division to Washington $x_1 \quad + x_3 \qquad \leqslant 400$
$x_2 \qquad + x_4 \leqslant 500$
$x_1, x_2, x_3, x_4 \geqslant 0$

300 students bused from North Division to Washington, 400 from South Division to Central High, and 100 from South Division to Washington; $2,200

Exercise 2-6

1. (A) Maximize $P = 5x_1 + 2x_2 - Ma_1$

Subject to $\quad x_1 + 2x_2 + s_1 \qquad\qquad = 12$

$\qquad\qquad x_1 + \; x_2 \qquad - s_2 + a_1 = 4$

$\qquad\qquad x_1, x_2, s_1, s_2, a_1 \geq 0$

(B)

	x_1	x_2	s_1	s_2	a_1	P	
	1	2	1	0	0	0	12
	1	1	0	-1	1	0	4
	$-M-5$	$-M-2$	0	M	0	1	$-4M$

(C) $x_1 = 12, x_2 = 0, s_1 = 0, s_2 = 8, a_1 = 0$, and $P = 60$ **(D)** Max $P = 60$ at $x_1 = 12$ and $x_2 = 0$

3. (A) Maximize $P = 3x_1 + 5x_2 - Ma_1$

Subject to $\quad 2x_1 + x_2 + s_1 \qquad = 8$

$\qquad\qquad x_1 + x_2 \qquad + a_1 = 6$

$\qquad\qquad x_1, x_2, s_1, a_1 \geq 0$

(B)

	x_1	x_2	s_1	a_1	P	
	2	1	1	0	0	8
	1	1	0	1	0	6
	$-M-3$	$-M-5$	0	0	1	$-6M$

(C) $x_1 = 0, x_2 = 6, s_1 = 2, a_1 = 0$, and $P = 30$ **(D)** Max $P = 30$ at $x_1 = 0$ and $x_2 = 6$

5. (A) Maximize $P = 4x_1 + 3x_2 - Ma_1$

Subject to $\quad -x_1 + 2x_2 + s_1 \qquad\qquad = 2$

$\qquad\qquad x_1 + \; x_2 \qquad - s_2 + a_1 = 4$

$\qquad\qquad x_1, x_2, s_1, s_2, a_1 \geq 0$

(B)

	x_1	x_2	s_1	s_2	a_1	P	
	-1	2	1	0	0	0	2
	1	1	0	-1	1	0	4
	$-M-4$	$-M-3$	0	M	0	1	$-4M$

(C) No optimal solution exists   **(D)** No optimal solution exists

7. (A) Maximize $P = 5x_1 + 10x_2 - Ma_1$

Subject to $\quad x_1 + \; x_2 + s_1 \qquad\qquad = 3$

$\qquad\qquad 2x_1 + 3x_2 \qquad - s_2 + a_1 = 12$

$\qquad\qquad x_1, x_2, s_1, s_2, a_1 \geq 0$

(B)

	x_1	x_2	s_1	s_2	a_1	P	
	1	1	1	0	0	0	3
	2	3	0	-1	1	0	12
	$-2M-5$	$-3M-10$	0	M	0	1	$-12M$

(C) $x_1 = 0, x_2 = 3, s_1 = 0, s_2 = 0, a_1 = 3$, and $P = -3M + 30$ **(D)** No optimal solution exists

9. Min $P = 12$ at $x_1 = 4$ and $x_2 = 6$; Max $P = 60$ at $x_1 = 10$ and $x_2 = 0$ **11.** Max $P = 44$ at $x_1 = 2$ and $x_2 = 8$

13. No optimal solution exists   **15.** Min $C = -9$ at $x_1 = 0, x_2 = \frac{7}{4}$, and $x_3 = \frac{3}{4}$

17. Max $P = 32$ at $x_1 = 0, x_2 = 4$, and $x_3 = 2$ **19.** Max $P = 65$ at $x_1 = \frac{35}{2}, x_2 = 0$, and $x_3 = \frac{15}{2}$

21. Max $P = 120$ at $x_1 = 20, x_2 = 0$, and $x_3 = 20$ **23.** Min $C = -30$ at $x_1 = 0, x_2 = \frac{3}{4}$, and $x_3 = 0$

25. Max $P = 17$ at $x_1 = \frac{49}{5}, x_2 = 0$, and $x_3 = \frac{22}{5}$ **27.** Min $C = \frac{135}{2}$ at $x_1 = \frac{15}{4}, x_2 = \frac{3}{4}$, and $x_3 = 0$

29. Max $P = 380$ at $x_1 = \frac{80}{3}, x_2 = \frac{20}{3}$, and $x_3 = 0$

31. Let $\;x_1 =$ Number of 16K modules manufactured daily

$\qquad\quad x_2 =$ Number of 64K modules manufactured daily

Maximize $\quad P = 18x_1 + 30x_2$

Subject to $\quad 10x_1 + 15x_2 \leq 1{,}500$

$\qquad\qquad 2x_1 + \; 4x_2 \leq 500$

$\qquad\qquad x_1 \qquad\qquad \geq 50$

$\qquad\qquad x_1, x_2 \geq 0$

Average daily production: 50 16K modules and $66\frac{2}{3}$ 64K modules; $2,900

33. Let $\;x_1 =$ Number of ads placed in the *Sentinel*

$\qquad\quad x_2 =$ Number of ads placed in the *Journal*

$\qquad\quad x_3 =$ Number of ads placed in the *Tribune*

Minimize $\quad C = 200x_1 + 200x_2 + 100x_3$

Subject to $\qquad\quad x_1 + \quad x_2 + \quad x_3 \leq 10$

$\qquad\qquad 2{,}000x_1 + 500x_2 + 1{,}500x_3 \geq 16{,}000$

$\qquad\qquad x_1, x_2, x_3 \geq 0$

2 ads in the *Sentinel*, 0 ads in the *Journal*, 8 ads in the *Tribune*; $1,200

35. Let $x_1 =$ Number of bottles of brand A Minimize $C = 0.6x_1 + 0.4x_2 + 0.9x_3$

  $x_2 =$ Number of bottles of brand B Subject to $10x_1 + 10x_2 + 20x_3 \geqslant 100$

  $x_3 =$ Number of bottles of brand C $2x_1 + 3x_2 + 4x_3 \leqslant 24$

 0 bottles of A, 4 bottles of B, 3 bottles of C; \$4.30 $x_1, x_2, x_3 \geqslant 0$

37. Let $x_1 =$ Number of cubic yards of mix A Maximize $P = 12x_1 + 16x_2 + 8x_3$

  $x_2 =$ Number of cubic yards of mix B Subject to $12x_1 + 8x_2 + 16x_3 \leqslant 700$

  $x_3 =$ Number of cubic yards of mix C $16x_1 + 8x_2 + 16x_3 \geqslant 800$

            $x_1, x_2, x_3 \geqslant 0$

 25 cubic yards of A, 50 cubic yards of B, 0 cubic yards of C; 1,100 pounds

39. Let $x_1 =$ Number of car frames produced at the Milwaukee plant

  $x_2 =$ Number of truck frames produced at the Milwaukee plant

  $x_3 =$ Number of car frames produced at the Racine plant

  $x_4 =$ Number of truck frames produced at the Racine plant

 Maximize $P = 50x_1 + 70x_2 + 50x_3 + 70x_4$

 Subject to $\begin{aligned} x_1 \quad\quad\; + \quad x_3 \quad\quad\;\; &\leqslant 250 \\ x_2 \quad\quad + \quad x_4 &\leqslant 350 \\ x_1 + \quad x_2 \quad\quad\quad\quad\;\; &\leqslant 300 \\ x_3 + \quad x_4 &\leqslant 200 \\ 150x_1 + 200x_2 \quad\quad\quad\quad &\leqslant 50{,}000 \\ 135x_3 + 180x_4 &\leqslant 35{,}000 \\ x_1, x_2, x_3, x_4 &\geqslant 0 \end{aligned}$

41. Let $x_1 =$ Number of barrels of A used in regular gasoline

  $x_2 =$ Number of barrels of A used in premium gasoline

  $x_3 =$ Number of barrels of B used in regular gasoline

  $x_4 =$ Number of barrels of B used in premium gasoline

  $x_5 =$ Number of barrels of C used in regular gasoline

  $x_6 =$ Number of barrels of C used in premium gasoline

 Maximize $P = 10x_1 + 18x_2 + 8x_3 + 16x_4 + 4x_5 + 12x_6$

 Subject to $\begin{aligned} x_1 + \quad x_2 \quad\quad\quad\quad\quad\quad\quad\quad\quad &\leqslant 40{,}000 \\ x_3 + \; x_4 \quad\quad\quad\quad\quad\quad &\leqslant 25{,}000 \\ x_5 + \quad x_6 &\leqslant 15{,}000 \\ x_1 \quad\quad + \; x_3 \quad\quad + \quad x_5 \quad\quad\quad\; &\geqslant 30{,}000 \\ x_2 \quad\quad + \; x_4 \quad\quad + \; x_6 &\geqslant 25{,}000 \\ -5x_1 \quad\quad + 5x_3 \quad\quad + 15x_5 \quad\quad\; &\geqslant 0 \\ -15x_2 \quad\quad - 5x_4 \quad\quad + 5x_6 &\geqslant 0 \\ x_1, x_2, x_3, x_4, x_5, x_6 &\geqslant 0 \end{aligned}$

43. Let $x_1 =$ Number of ounces of food L Minimize $C = 0.4x_1 + 0.6x_2 + 0.8x_3$

  $x_2 =$ Number of ounces of food M Subject to $30x_1 + 10x_2 + 30x_3 \geqslant 400$

  $x_3 =$ Number of ounces of food N $10x_1 + 10x_2 + 10x_3 \geqslant 200$

            $10x_1 + 30x_2 + 20x_3 \geqslant 300$

            $8x_1 + 4x_2 + 6x_3 \leqslant 150$

            $60x_1 + 40x_2 + 50x_3 \leqslant 900$

            $x_1, x_2, x_3 \geqslant 0$

45. Let x_1 = Number of students from town A enrolled in school I
 x_2 = Number of students from town A enrolled in school II
 x_3 = Number of students from town B enrolled in school I
 x_4 = Number of students from town B enrolled in school II
 x_5 = Number of students from town C enrolled in school I
 x_6 = Number of students from town C enrolled in school II

Minimize $C = 4x_1 + 8x_2 + 6x_3 + 4x_4 + 3x_5 + 9x_6$

$$
\begin{aligned}
\text{Subject to}\quad x_1 + x_2 \qquad\qquad\qquad\qquad\quad &= 500\\
x_3 + x_4 \qquad\qquad\qquad &= 1{,}200\\
x_5 + x_6 &= 1{,}800\\
x_1 \quad + x_3 \qquad + x_5 \qquad &\leq 2{,}000\\
x_2 \quad + x_4 \qquad + x_6 &\leq 2{,}000\\
x_1 \quad + x_3 \qquad + x_5 \qquad &\geq 1{,}400\\
x_2 \quad + x_4 \qquad + x_6 &\geq 1{,}400\\
x_1 \qquad\qquad\qquad\qquad &\leq 300\\
x_2 \qquad\qquad\qquad &\leq 300\\
x_3 \qquad\qquad &\leq 720\\
x_4 \qquad\quad &\leq 720\\
x_5 \quad &\leq 1{,}080\\
x_6 &\leq 1{,}080\\
x_1, x_2, x_3, x_4, x_5, x_6 &\geq 0
\end{aligned}
$$

Exercise 2-7   Chapter Review

1.

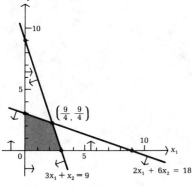

2. Max $P = 24$ at $x_1 = 4$ and $x_2 = 0$

3. $2x_1 + x_2 + s_1 \qquad = 8$
 $x_1 + 2x_2 \qquad + s_2 = 10$

4.

x_1	x_2	s_1	s_2	Feasible?
0	0	8	10	Yes
0	8	0	-6	No
0	5	3	0	Yes
4	0	0	6	Yes
10	0	-12	0	No
2	4	0	0	Yes

5.

$$
\begin{array}{ccccc|c}
x_1 & x_2 & s_1 & s_2 & P & \\
\hline
\boxed{2} & 1 & 1 & 0 & 0 & 8\\
1 & 2 & 0 & 1 & 0 & 10\\
\hdashline
-6 & -2 & 0 & 0 & 1 & 0
\end{array}
$$

6. Max $P = 24$ at $x_1 = 4$ and $x_2 = 0$

7. Basic: x_2, s_2, s_3, P; nonbasic x_1, x_3, s_1

$$
\begin{bmatrix}
0 & 1 & -2 & -3 & 0 & -1 & 0 & 10\\
0 & 0 & -\frac{7}{2} & -2 & 1 & -\frac{3}{2} & 0 & 15\\
1 & 0 & \frac{5}{2} & 1 & 0 & \frac{1}{2} & 0 & 5\\
\hdashline
0 & 0 & 15 & 11 & 0 & 4 & 1 & 90
\end{bmatrix}
$$

8. (A) $x_1 = 0$, $x_2 = 2$, $s_1 = 0$, $s_2 = 5$, $P = 12$; additional pivoting required **9.** Min $C = 40$ at $x_1 = 0$ and $x_2 = 20$
(B) $x_1 = 0$, $x_2 = 0$, $s_1 = 0$, $s_2 = 7$, $P = 22$; no optimal solution exists
(C) $x_1 = 6$, $x_2 = 0$, $s_1 = 15$, $s_2 = 0$, $P = 10$; optimal solution

10. Maximize $P = 15y_1 + 20y_2$
 Subject to $y_1 + 2y_2 \leqslant 5$
          $3y_1 + y_2 \leqslant 2$
          $y_1, y_2 \geqslant 0$

11. $y_1 + 2y_2 + x_1 \qquad = 5$
       $3y_1 + y_2 \qquad + x_2 \qquad = 2$
       $-15y_1 - 20y_2 \qquad\qquad + P = 0$

12.

$$
\begin{array}{ccccc}
y_1 & y_2 & x_1 & x_2 & P \\
\end{array}
$$
$$
\left[
\begin{array}{ccccc|c}
1 & 2 & 1 & 0 & 0 & 5 \\
3 & 1 & 0 & 1 & 0 & 2 \\
\hline
-15 & -20 & 0 & 0 & 1 & 0
\end{array}
\right]
$$

13. Max $P = 40$ at $y_1 = 0$ and $y_2 = 2$ **14.** Min $C = 40$ at $x_1 = 0$ and $x_2 = 20$ **15.** Max $P = 26$ at $x_1 = 2$ and $x_2 = 5$
16. Max $P = 26$ at $x_1 = 2$ and $x_2 = 5$ **17.** Min $C = 51$ at $x_1 = 9$ and $x_2 = 3$ **18.** Maximize $P = 10y_1 + 15y_2 + 3y_3$
                                      Subject to $y_1 + y_2 \qquad \leqslant 3$
                                            $y_1 + 2y_2 + y_3 \leqslant 8$
                                              $y_1, y_2, y_3 \geqslant 0$

19. Min $C = 51$ at $x_1 = 9$ and $x_2 = 3$ **23.** Min $C = 9{,}960$ at $x_1 = 0$, $x_2 = 240$, $x_3 = 400$, and $x_4 = 60$
20. No optimal solution exists
21. Max $P = 23$ at $x_1 = 4$, $x_2 = 1$, and $x_3 = 0$
22. Min $C = 14$ at $x_1 = 4$ and $x_2 = 2$

24. Let $x_1 =$ Number of regular sails   Maximize $P = 100x_1 + 200x_2$
       $x_2 =$ Number of competition sails   Subject to $2x_1 + 3x_2 \leqslant 150$
                                        $4x_1 + 9x_2 \leqslant 360$
                                          $x_1, x_2 \geqslant 0$

25. Let $x_1 =$ Number of motors shipped from factory A to plant X
       $x_2 =$ Number of motors shipped from factory A to plant Y
       $x_3 =$ Number of motors shipped from factory A to plant Z
       $x_4 =$ Number of motors shipped from factory B to plant X
       $x_5 =$ Number of motors shipped from factory B to plant Y
       $x_6 =$ Number of motors shipped from factory B to plant Z
 Minimize $C = 5x_1 + 8x_2 + 12x_3 + 9x_4 + 7x_5 + 6x_6$
 Subject to $x_1 + x_2 + x_3 \qquad\qquad \leqslant 1{,}500$
          $x_4 + x_5 + x_6 \leqslant 1{,}000$
      $x_1 \qquad + x_4 \qquad\qquad \geqslant 500$
        $x_2 \qquad + x_5 \qquad \geqslant 700$
          $x_3 \qquad + x_6 \geqslant 800$
       $x_1, x_2, x_3, x_4, x_5, x_6 \geqslant 0$

26. Let $x_1 =$ Number of grams of mix A Minimize $C = 0.02x_1 + 0.04x_2$
       $x_2 =$ Number of grams of mix B Subject to $3x_1 + 4x_2 \geqslant 300$
                                        $2x_1 + 5x_2 \geqslant 200$
                                        $6x_1 + 10x_2 \geqslant 900$
                                          $x_1, x_2 \geqslant 0$

Chapter 3

Exercise 3-1

1. $I = \$20$ **3.** $r = 0.08$ or 8% **5.** $A = \$112$ **7.** $P = \$888.89$ **9.** $r = I/Pt$ **11.** $P = A/(1 + rt)$ **13.** $140 **15.** $9.23
17. $7685.00 **19.** 10.125% **21.** 18% **23.** 36% **25.** 9.126% **27.** $9,693.91 **29.** 18% **31.** 21.335%

Exercise 3-2

1. $A = \$112.68$ **3.** $A = \$3,433.50$ **5.** $2,419.99 **7.** $P = \$7,351.04$
9. (A) $126.25; $26.25 (B) $126.90; $26.90 (C) $127.05; $27.05 **11.** (A) $7,147.51 (B) $10,217.39
13. (A) $6,755.64 (B) $4,563.87 **15.** (A) 10.38% (B) 12.68% **17.** 5 years 6 months **19.** $n \approx 11.9$
21. (A) 7 years (B) 6 years **23.** $22,702.60 **25.** $196,993.25 **27.** $14.26 per square foot per month **29.** 18 years
31. 9% compounded monthly, since its effective rate is 9.38%; the effective rate of 9.3% compounded annually is 9.3%
33. 2 years 10 months **35.** $328,791.70 **37.** 4.952 years; 4.959 years **39.** $5,935.34 **41.** 9.08%
43. (A) 8.60% (B) 8.60% (C) 8.57% **45.** 14.48%

Exercise 3-3

1. $FV = \$13,435.19$ **3.** $FV = \$60,401.98$ **5.** $PMT = \$123.47$ **7.** $PMT = \$310.62$ **9.** $n = 17$
11. Value: $30,200.99; interest: $10,200.99 **13.** $20,931.01 **15.** $331.46 **17.** $625.28
19. First year: $50.76; second year: $168.09; third year: $296.42 **21.** (A) $413,092 (B) $393,965
23. $177.46; $1,481.92 **25.** 3 years 5 months

Exercise 3-4

1. $PV = \$3,458.41$ **3.** $PV = \$4,606.09$ **5.** $PMT = \$199.29$ **7.** $PMT = \$586.01$ **9.** $n = 29$ **11.** $109,421.92
13. $14,064.67; $16,800.00 **15.** (A) $36.59 per month; $58.62 interest (B) $38.28 per month; $89.04 interest
17. $273.69 per month; $7,705.68 interest

19. Amortization Schedule

Payment Number	Payment	Interest	Unpaid Balance Reduction	Unpaid Balance
0				$5,000.00
1	$ 758.05	$ 225.00	$ 533.05	4,466.95
2	758.05	201.01	557.04	3,909.91
3	758.05	175.95	582.10	3,327.81
4	758.05	149.75	608.30	2,719.51
5	758.05	122.38	635.67	2,083.84
6	758.05	93.77	664.28	1,419.56
7	758.05	63.88	694.17	725.39
8	758.05	32.64	725.39	0.00
Total	$6,064.38	$1,064.38	$5,000.00	

21. First year interest = $625.01; second year interest = $400.91; third year interest = $148.46
23. $85,846.38; $128,153.62
25. $143.85 per month; $904.80
27. Monthly payment $R = \$841.39$
  (A) $70,952.33 (B) $55,909.02
  (C) $36,813.32
29. (A) Monthly payment $R = \$395.04$; total interest = $64,809.60
  (B) 114 months or 9.5 years; interest saved = $38,375.04
31. $29,799

Exercise 3-5   Chapter Review

1. $A = \$104.50$ **2.** $P = \$800$ **3.** $t = 0.75$ year or 9 months **4.** $r = 0.06$ or 6% **5.** $A = \$1,393.68$ **6.** $P = \$3,193.50$
7. $FV = \$69,770.03$ **8.** $PMT = \$115.00$ **9.** $PV = \$33,944.27$ **10.** $PMT = \$166.07$ **11.** $n \approx 16$ **12.** $n \approx 41$
13. $3,350.00; $350.00 **14.** $11.64 **15.** 15% **16.** 20% **17.** 28.8% **18.** 8.24% **19.** $4,744.73 **20.** $27,551
21. $9,422.24 **22.** $10,210 **23.** $6,268 **24.** 2 years 3 months **25.** 5 years 10 months; 3 years 11 months **26.** 9.38%
27. 9% compounded quarterly, since its effective rate is 9.31% while the effective rate of 9.25% compounded annually is 9.25%
28. $27,971.23; $8,771.23 **29.** $526.28 per month **30.** 43 **31.** $10,988.22; $12,000 **32.** $99.85 per month; $396.36 interest
33. Amortization Schedule

Payment Number	Payment	Interest	Unpaid Balance Reduction	Unpaid Balance
0				$1,000.00
1	$ 265.82	$25.00	$ 240.82	759.18
2	265.82	18.98	246.84	512.34
3	265.82	12.81	253.01	259.33
4	265.82	6.48	259.33	0.00
Total	$1,063.27	$63.27	$1,000.00	

34. $6,697.11
35. (A) $1,435.63 (B) $74,397.48 (C) $11,625.04
36. (A) $115,573.86 (B) $359.64 (C) $171,228.80
37. $164,402

38. 6.93 years; 7.27 years **39.** West Lake S & L: 9.800%; Security S & L: 9.794% **40.** $3,176.14 **41.** 8.37%
42. 10.45% compounded annually **43.** (A) $571,499 (B) $1,973,277 **44.** $55,347.48; $185,830.24
45. 1 year 1 month **46.** $10,318.91; $2,281.09 **47.** $175.28; $2,516.80 **48.** (A) $398,807 (B) $374,204
49. (A) $746.79 per month; $896.76 per month (B) $73,558.78; $41,482.19 **50.** $19,239

Chapter 4

Exercise 4-1

1. 24 **3.** 9 **5.** 990 **7.** 10 **9.** 35 **11.** 1 **13.** 60 **15.** 6,497,400 **17.** 10 **19.** 270,725 **21.** $5 \cdot 3 \cdot 4 \cdot 2 = 120$
23. $P_{10,3} = 10 \cdot 9 \cdot 8 = 720$ **25.** $C_{7,3} = 35; P_{7,3} = 210$ **27.** $C_{10,2} = 45$ **29.** $6 \cdot 5 \cdot 4 \cdot 3 = 360; 6 \cdot 6 \cdot 6 \cdot 6 = 1,296$
31. $P_{10,5} = 30,240; 10^5 = 100,000$ **33.** $C_{13,5} = 1,287$
35. $26 \cdot 26 \cdot 26 \cdot 10 \cdot 10 \cdot 10 = 17,576,000; 26 \cdot 25 \cdot 24 \cdot 10 \cdot 9 \cdot 8 = 11,232,000$ **37.** $C_{13,5}C_{13,2} = 100,386$
39. $C_{8,3}C_{10,4}C_{7,2} = 246,960$ **41.** $12 \cdot 11 = 132$ **43.** (A) $C_{8,2} = 28$ (B) $C_{8,3} = 56$ (C) $C_{8,4} = 70$
45. $P_{5,5}/P_{3,3} = 20, P_{5,5}/P_{2,2} = 60, P_{5,5} = 120, P_{5,5} = 120$ **47.** (A) $P_{8,5} = 6,720$ (B) $C_{8,5} = 56$ (C) $2 \cdot C_{6,4} = 30$
49. (A) Six combined outcomes: (B) $3 \cdot 2 = 6$ **51.** 12

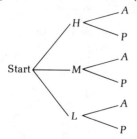

53. (A) $C_{6,3}C_{5,2} = 200$ (B) $C_{6,4}C_{5,1} = 75$ (C) $C_{6,5} = 6$ (D) $C_{11,5} = 462$ (E) $C_{6,4}C_{5,1} + C_{6,5} = 81$
55. (A) Twelve classifications: (B) $2 \cdot 2 \cdot 3 = 12$ **57.** 336; 512   **59.** $P_{4,2} = 12$

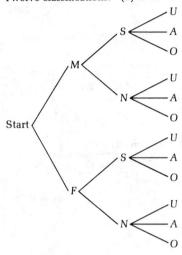

Exercise 4-2

1. Occurrence of E is certain   **3.** {(H, H, H), (H, H, T), (H, T, H), (H, T, T), (T, H, H), (T, H, T), (T, T, H), (T, T, T)}
5. $E = $ {(H, H, T), (H, T, H), (T, H, H), (H, H, H)}; $\frac{1}{2}$
7. (A) No probability can be negative   (B) $P(R) + P(G) + P(Y) + P(B) \neq 1$ **9.** $P(R) + P(Y) = .56$
11. $1/P_{10,3} \approx .0014$ **13.** $C_{26,5}/C_{52,5} \approx .025$ **15.** $C_{16,5}/C_{52,5} \approx .0017$ **17.** $(2 \cdot 5 \cdot 5 \cdot 1)/(2 \cdot 5 \cdot 5 \cdot 5) = .2$
19. $1/P_{5,5} = 1/5! = .008\ 33$ **21.** $\frac{1}{36}$ **23.** $\frac{5}{36}$ **25.** $\frac{1}{6}$ **27.** $\frac{7}{9}$ **29.** 0   **31.** $\frac{1}{3}$ **33.** $\frac{2}{9}$ **35.** $\frac{2}{3}$ **37.** $\frac{1}{4}$ **39.** $\frac{1}{4}$ **41.** $\frac{3}{4}$ **43.** $\frac{1}{9}$ **45.** $\frac{1}{3}$
47. $\frac{1}{9}$ **49.** $\frac{4}{9}$ **51.** $C_{16,5}/C_{52,5} \approx .001\ 68$ **53.** $48/C_{52,5} \approx .000\ 018\ 5$ **55.** $4/C_{52,5} \approx .000\ 001\ 5$
57. $C_{4,2}C_{4,3}/C_{52,5} \approx .000\ 009$ **59.** (A) $1/P_{12,4} \approx .000\ 084$ (B) $1/12^4 \approx .000\ 048$ **61.** $(1 - C_{95,6}/C_{100,6}) \approx .27$
63. (A) $C_{6,3}C_{5,2}/C_{11,5} \approx .433$ (B) $C_{6,4}C_{5,1}/C_{11,5} \approx .162$ (C) $C_{6,5}/C_{11,5} \approx .013$ (D) $[C_{6,4}C_{5,1} + C_{6,5}]/C_{11,5} \approx .175$
65. (A) $1/P_{8,3} \approx .0030$ (B) $1/8^3 \approx .0020$ **67.** (A) $P_{6,2}/P_{11,2} \approx .273$ (B) $[C_{5,3} + C_{6,1}C_{5,2}]/C_{11,3} \approx .424$

Exercise 4-3

1. .1   **3.** .45   **5.** P(Point down) = .389, P(Point up) = .611; no
7. (A) P(2 girls) ≈ .2351, P(1 girl) ≈ .5435, P(0 girls) ≈ .2214   (B) P(2 girls) = .25, P(1 girl) = .50
   (C) P(0 girls) = .25
9. (A) P(3 heads) ≈ .132, P(2 heads) ≈ .368, P(1 head) ≈ .38, P(0 heads) ≈ .12
   (B) P(3 heads) ≈ .125, P(2 heads) ≈ .375, P(1 head) ≈ .375, P(0 heads) ≈ .125
   (C) 3 heads, 125; 2 heads, 375; 1 head, 375; 0 heads, 125
11. 4 heads, 5; 3 heads, 20; 2 heads, 30; 1 head, 20; 0 heads, 5   **13.** (A) .015   (B) .222   (C) .169   (D) .958
15. (A) P(Red) = .3, P(Pink) = .44, P(White) = .26   (B) 250 red, 500 pink, 250 white

Exercise 4-4

1. $E(X) = -.1$ **3.** Probability distribution:

x_i	0	1	2
p_i	$\frac{1}{4}$	$\frac{1}{2}$	$\frac{1}{4}$

$E(X) = 1$

5. Payoff table:

x_i	\$1	$-$\$1
p_i	$\frac{1}{2}$	$\frac{1}{2}$

$E(X) = 0$; game is fair

7. Payoff table:

x_i	-$3	-$2	-$1	$0	$1	$2
p_i	$\frac{1}{6}$	$\frac{1}{6}$	$\frac{1}{6}$	$\frac{1}{6}$	$\frac{1}{6}$	$\frac{1}{6}$

$E(X) = -50¢$; game is not fair

9. -$0.50   **11.** -$0.036; $0.036   **13.** $1   **15.** A_2; $210

17. Payoff table

x_i	$35	-$1
p_i	$\frac{1}{38}$	$\frac{37}{38}$

$E(X) = -5.26¢$

19. Payoff table

x_i	$499	$99	$19	$4	-$1
p_i	.0002	.0006	.001	.004	.9942

$E(X) = -80¢$

21. (A)

x_i	0	1	2
p_i	.47	.46	.07

(B) .60

23. (A)

x_i	-$5	$195	$395	$595
p_i	.985	.0149	.000 059 9	.000 000 06

(B) $E(X) \approx -$2

25. Payoff table:

x_i	$4,850	-$150
p_i	.01	.99

$E(X) = -$100

27. Site A, with $E(X) = $3.6 million   **29.** 10, with $E(X) = $560   **31.** 1.54

33. A_2 is better since for A_1, $E(X) = $4, and for A_2, $E(X) = $4.80

Exercise 4-5   Chapter Review

1. (A) Twelve combined   (B) $6 \cdot 2 = 12$ **2.** 15, 30   **3.** $6 \cdot 5 \cdot 4 \cdot 3 \cdot 2 \cdot 1 = 720$
outcomes:

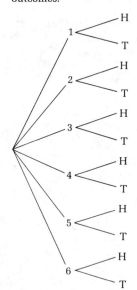

4. $P_{6,6} = 6! = 720$ **5.** $C_{13,5}/C_{52,5} \approx .0005$
6. $1/P_{15,2} \approx .0048$
7. $1/P_{10,3} \approx .0014$; $1/C_{10,3} \approx .0083$ **8.** .05
9. Payoff table:

x_i	-$2	-$1	$0	$1	$2
p_i	$\frac{1}{5}$	$\frac{1}{5}$	$\frac{1}{5}$	$\frac{1}{5}$	$\frac{1}{5}$

$E(X) = 0$; game is fair

10. (1) Probability of an event cannot be negative; (2) sum of probabilities of simple events must be 1; (3) probability of an event cannot be greater than 1

11. $C_{6,3} = 20$ **12.** 336; 512; 392   **13.** (A) $P_{6,3} = 120$ (B) $C_{5,2} = 10$

14. (A) P(2 heads) = .21, P(1 head) = .48, P(0 heads) = .31 **15.** (A) $C_{13,5}/C_{52,5}$ (B) $C_{13,3} \cdot C_{13,2}/C_{52,5}$
   (B) P(2 heads) = .25, P(1 head) = .50, P(0 heads) = .25
   (C) 2 heads, 250; 1 head, 500; 0 heads, 250

16. $C_{8,2}/C_{10,4} = \frac{2}{15}$ **17.** Payoff table:

x_i	\$5	−\$4	\$2
p_i	.25	.5	.25

$E(X) = -25¢$; game is not fair

18. (A) $\frac{1}{3}$ (B) $\frac{2}{9}$

19. (A)

x_i	2	3	4	5	6	7	8	9	10	11	12
p_i	$\frac{1}{36}$	$\frac{2}{36}$	$\frac{3}{36}$	$\frac{4}{36}$	$\frac{5}{36}$	$\frac{6}{36}$	$\frac{5}{36}$	$\frac{4}{36}$	$\frac{3}{36}$	$\frac{2}{36}$	$\frac{1}{36}$

(B) $E(X) = 7$

20. $2^5 = 32$; 6 **21.** $1 - C_{7,3}/C_{10,3} = \frac{17}{24}$
22. (A) $P_{10,3} = 720$ (B) $P_{6,3}/P_{10,3} = \frac{1}{6}$ (C) $C_{10,3} = 120$ (D) $(C_{6,3} + C_{6,2} \cdot C_{4,1})/C_{10,3} = \frac{2}{3}$
23. $P_{4,4}/P_{2,2} = 12$ **24.** (A) .350 (B) $\frac{3}{8} = .375$ (C) 375 **25.** −.0172; .0172; No

26. (A)

x_i	2	3	4	5	6
p_i	$\frac{9}{36}$	$\frac{12}{36}$	$\frac{10}{36}$	$\frac{4}{36}$	$\frac{1}{36}$

(B) $E(X) = 3\frac{1}{3} \approx 3.33$

27. $E(X) \approx -\$0.167$; No **28.** $P_{5,5} = 120$
29. (A) $P(H \cup A) = P(H) + P(A) - P(H \cap A) = .7 + .6 - .4 = .9$ (B) $P(H \cap A') = .3$
30. (A) $P(M \cup E) = .8$ (B) $P[(M \cup E)'] = .2$ (C) $P[(M \cap E') \cup (M' \cap E)] = .5$ **31.** (A) .04 (B) .16 (C) .54
32. A: $E(X) = \$7.6$ million; B: $E(X) = \$7.8$ million; plan B
33. 3 truckloads for an expected profit of \$7,200 **34.** Payoff table:

x_i	\$270	−\$30
p_i	.08	.92

$E(X) = -\$6$

35. $1 - (C_{10,4}/C_{12,4}) \approx .576$ **36.** (A)

x_i	0	1	2
p_i	$\frac{12}{22}$	$\frac{9}{22}$	$\frac{1}{22}$

(B) $E(X) = \frac{1}{2}$

Chapter 5

Exercise 5-1

1. .997 **3.** (1), $\frac{1}{2}$ **5.** (2), $\frac{7}{10}$ **7.** .4 **9.** .25 **11.** .05 **13.** .2 **15.** .6 **17.** .65 **19.** $\frac{1}{4}$ **21.** $\frac{11}{36}$
23. (A) $\frac{3}{5}; \frac{5}{3}$ (B) $\frac{1}{3}; \frac{3}{1}$ (C) $\frac{2}{3}; \frac{3}{2}$ (D) $\frac{11}{9}; \frac{9}{11}$ **25.** (A) $\frac{3}{11}$ (B) $\frac{11}{18}$ (C) $\frac{4}{5}$ or .8 (D) .49 **27.** 1 to 1
29. 7 to 1 **31.** 2 to 1 **33.** 1 to 2 **35.** (A) $\frac{1}{8}$ (B) \$8 **37.** (A) .31; $\frac{31}{69}$ (B) .6; $\frac{3}{2}$ **39.** $\frac{11}{26}; \frac{11}{15}$ **41.** $\frac{7}{13}; \frac{7}{6}$ **43.** .78
45. $\frac{250}{1,000} = .25$ **47.** $P(E) \approx 1 - .13 = .87$ **49.** $\frac{9}{19} \approx .4737$; $E(X) \approx -\$0.0526$ (The house edge is approximately 5.3%.)

51. $P(E) = 1 - \dfrac{12!}{(12 - n)!12^n}$ **55.** (A) $P(C \cup S) = P(C) + P(S) - P(C \cap S) = .45 + .75 - .35 = .85$ (B) $P(C' \cap S') = .15$

57. (A) $P(M_1 \cup A) = P(M_1) + P(A) - P(M_1 \cap A) = .2 + .3 - .05 = .45$
   (B) $P[(M_2 \cap A') \cup (M_3 \cap A')] = P(M_2 \cap A') + P(M_3 \cap A') = .2 + .35 = .55$
59. $P(K' \cap D') = .9$ **61.** .83 **63.** $P(A \cap S) = 50/1,000 = .05$ **65.** (A) $P(U \cup N) = .22; \frac{11}{39}$ (B) $P[(D \cap A) \cup (R \cap A)] = .3; \frac{7}{3}$
67. $1 - C_{15,3}/C_{20,3} \approx .6$

Exercise 5-2

1. .50 **3.** .20 **5.** .10 **7.** .06 **9.** .50 **11.** .30 **13.** Independent **15.** Dependent **17.** (A) $\frac{1}{2}$ (B) $2(\frac{1}{2})^8 \approx .007\ 81$
19. (A) $\frac{1}{4}$ (B) Dependent **21.** (A) .18 (B) .26 **23.** (A) Yes (B) No **25.** $(\frac{1}{2})(\frac{1}{2}) = \frac{1}{4}; \frac{1}{2} + \frac{1}{2} - \frac{1}{4} = \frac{3}{4}$
27. (A) $(\frac{1}{4})(\frac{13}{51}) \approx .0637$ (B) $(\frac{1}{4})(\frac{1}{4}) = .0625$ **29.** (A) $\frac{3}{13}$ (B) Independent
31. (A) Dependent (B) Independent
33.

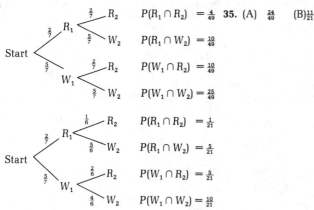

$P(R_1 \cap R_2) = \frac{4}{49}$ **35.** (A) $\frac{24}{49}$ (B)$\frac{11}{21}$

$P(R_1 \cap W_2) = \frac{10}{49}$

$P(W_1 \cap R_2) = \frac{10}{49}$

$P(W_1 \cap W_2) = \frac{25}{49}$

$P(R_1 \cap R_2) = \frac{1}{21}$

$P(R_1 \cap W_2) = \frac{5}{21}$

$P(W_1 \cap R_2) = \frac{5}{21}$

$P(W_1 \cap W_2) = \frac{10}{21}$

37. (A) $P(A_1 \cap A_2') + P(A_1' \cap A_2) = \frac{24}{169}$ (B) $P(A_1 \cap A_2') + P(A_1' \cap A_2) = \frac{32}{221}$ **39.** $\frac{5}{18}$
41. (A) .167 (B) .25 (C) .25 (D) \$13.50 **43.** $P(A|A) = P(A \cap A)/P(A) = P(A)/P(A) = 1$ **45.** $P(A)P(B) \neq 0 = P(A \cap B)$

47. (A)

	H	S	B	Total
Y	.400	.180	.020	.600
N	.150	.120	.130	.400
Total	.550	.300	.150	1.000

(B) $P(Y|H) = \dfrac{.400}{.550} \approx .727$ (C) $P(Y|B) = \dfrac{.020}{.150} \approx .133$

(D) $P(S) = .300; P(S|Y) = .300$
(E) $P(H) = .550; P(H|Y) \approx .667$
(F) $P(B \cap N) = .130$
(G) Yes (H) No (I) No

49. (A) .167 (B) .25 (C) .25 (D) \$25,500
51. (A) $P(S|A) = P(S \cap A)/P(A) = \frac{5}{11}$ (B) $P(A|S) = P(A \cap S)/P(A) = \frac{5}{14}$ (C) $P(S|A') = P(S \cap A')/P(A') = \frac{9}{89}$
   (D) $P(A|S') = P(A \cap S')/P(S') = \frac{3}{43}$

53. (A)

	A	B	C	Total
F	.130	.286	.104	.520
F'	.120	.264	.096	.480
Total	.250	.550	.200	1.000

(B) $P(A|F) = \dfrac{.130}{.520} = .250; P(A|F') = \dfrac{.120}{.480} = .250$

(C) $P(C|F) = \dfrac{.104}{.520} = .200; P(C|F') = \dfrac{.096}{.480} = .200$

(D) $P(A) = .250$
(E) $P(B) = .550; P(B|F') = .550$
(F) $P(F \cap C) = .104$
(G) No; A, B, and C are independent of F and F'

Exercise 5-3

1. $(.6)(.8) = .48$ **3.** $(.6)(.8) + (.4)(.3) = .60$ **5.** .80 **7.** .417 **9.** .375 **11.** .222 **13.** .50 **15.** .278 **17.** .125 **19.** .50
21. .375 **23.**

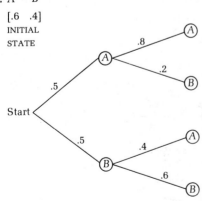

25. .25 **27.** .333 **29.** .50 **31.** .745 **33.** .235

35. $\dfrac{P(U_1 \cap R)}{P(R)} + \dfrac{P(U_1' \cap R)}{P(R)} = \dfrac{P(U_1 \cap R) + P(U_1' \cap R)}{P(R)} = \dfrac{P(R)}{P(R)} = 1$ **37.** .913; .225

39. .091, .545, .364 **41.** .667, .000 412 **43.** .231, .036 **45.** .941, .0588

Exercise 5-4

1. A B

$[.8 \quad .2]$

INITIAL
STATE

Start — 1 — (A) — .8 — (A)
(A) — .2 — (B)
Start — 0 — (B)

Starting in state A, at the second stage,
the probability of being in state A is .8
and in state B is .2.

3. A B

$[.72 \quad .28]$
Starting in state A, at the third stage, the
probability of being in state A is .72
and in state B is .28.

5. A B

$[.6 \quad .4]$

INITIAL
STATE

Start — .5 — (A) — .8 — (A)
(A) — .2 — (B)
Start — .5 — (B) — .4 — (A)
(B) — .6 — (B)

Starting with the initial-state
matrix R, at the second stage, the
probability of being in state A is .6
[because $(.5)(.8) + (.5)(.4) = .6$] and in state
B is .4 [because $(.5)(.2) + (.5)(.6) = .4$].

7. A B
$[.64 \quad .36]$
Starting in initial state R, at the third
stage, the probability of being in state A is
.64 and in state B is .36.

9. $a = .5, b = .2, c = 1$ **11.** $[.47 \quad .53]$ **13.** $[.375 \quad .625]$ **15.** $[.25 \quad .50 \quad .25]$
17. (A) $\begin{bmatrix} .4 & .6 \\ .06 & .94 \end{bmatrix}$ (B) Saturday: .20; Sunday: .13 (C) $[.09 \quad .91]$
(D) Closed 9% of the time

19. (A)
$$\begin{array}{cc} & X \quad X' \\ X & \begin{bmatrix} .8 & .2 \\ .2 & .8 \end{bmatrix} \\ X' & \end{array}$$
(B) 32%; 39% (C) 50% **21.** Steady-state matrix = [.25 .50 .25]

23. (A) [.25 .75] (B) 42.5%; 51.3% (C) 60% rapid transit, 40% automobile

Exercise 5-5 Chapter Review

1. (A) .7 (B) .6 **2.** $P(R \cup G) = .8$; odds for $R \cup G$ are 8 to 2 **3.** $\frac{5}{11} \approx .455$ **4.** .27 **5.** .20 **6.** .02 **7.** .03 **8.** .15
9. .130 4 **10.** .10 **11.** No, since $P(T|Z) \neq P(T)$ **12.** Yes, since $P(S \cap X) = P(S)P(X)$ **13.** .4 **14.** .2 **15.** .3 **16.** .08
17. .18 **18.** .26 **19.** .31 **20.** .43 **21.** [.55 .45] **22.** $a = 0, b = .6, c = .1$
23. (A) $\frac{2}{13}$; 2 to 11 (B) $\frac{4}{13}$; 4 to 9 (C) $\frac{12}{13}$; 12 to 1 **24.** (A) 1 to 8 (B) $8
25. $A = \{(1, 3), (2, 2), (3, 1), (2, 6), (3, 5), (4, 4), (5, 3), (6, 2), (6, 6)\};$
$B = \{(1, 5), (2, 4), (3, 3), (4, 2), (5, 1), (6, 6)\}; P(A) = \frac{1}{4}, P(B) = \frac{1}{6}, P(A \cap B) = \frac{1}{36},$
$P(A \cup B) = \frac{7}{18}$
26. (A) .6 (B) $\frac{5}{6}$ **27.** (A) $\frac{1}{13}$ (B) Independent **28.** (A) $\frac{6}{25}$ (B) $\frac{3}{10}$ **29.** Part B
30. (A) 1.2 (B) 1.2 **31.** (A) $\frac{3}{5}$ (B) $\frac{1}{3}$ (C) $\frac{7}{15}$ (D) $\frac{9}{14}$ (E) $\frac{5}{8}$ (F) $\frac{3}{10}$ **32.** No **33.** $\frac{93}{200} = .465$ **34.** .564 **35.** $\frac{12}{51} \approx .235$
36. $\frac{12}{51} \approx .235$ **37.** (A) $\frac{1}{4}$; 1 to 3 (B) $3 **38.** $1 - 10!/(5!10^5) \approx .70$ **39.** .891
40. (A)
$$\begin{array}{cc} & X \quad X' \\ X & \begin{bmatrix} .6 & .4 \\ .5 & .5 \end{bmatrix} \\ X' & \end{array}$$
(B) X X' [.2 .8] (C) [.52 .48] (D) [$\frac{5}{9}$ $\frac{4}{9}$] $\approx$ [.56 .44] (E) 56%

41. $P(A \cap P) = P(A)P(P|A) = .34$ **42.** .955 **43.** $\frac{6}{7} \approx .857$ **44.** (A) .45 (B) .525 (C) 60%

Chapter 6

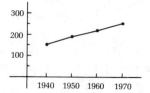

Exercise 6-1

1. Percentage of civilian labor force aged 18–64 with one or more years of college

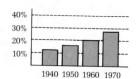

3. Unemployment rates

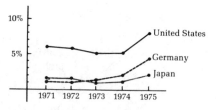

5. Millions of tons of air pollution emissions in the United States

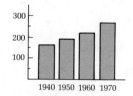

7. Millions of tons of air pollution emissions in the United States

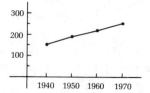

9. Immigration to the United States in 1972 (thousands)

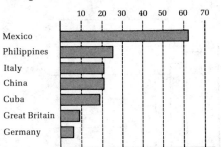

11. Illegitimate births per 1,000 live births in the United States

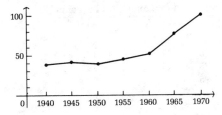

Exercise 6-2

1. (A)

Class Interval	Frequency	Relative Frequency
−0.5–4.5	5	.05
4.5–9.5	54	.54
9.5–14.5	25	.25
14.5–19.5	13	.13
19.5–24.5	0	.00
24.5–29.5	1	.01
29.5–34.5	2	.02
	100	1.00

(B)

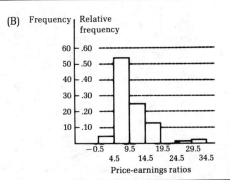

(C)

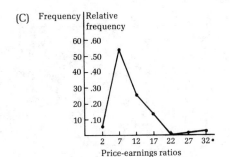

(D)

Class Interval	Frequency	Cumulative Frequency	Relative Cumulative Frequency
−0.5–4.5	5	5	.05
4.5–9.5	54	59	.59
9.5–14.5	25	84	.84
14.5–19.5	13	97	.97
19.5–24.5	0	97	.97
24.5–29.5	1	98	.98
29.5–34.5	2	100	1.00

P(PE ratio between 4.5 and 14.5) = .79

(E)

Cumulative frequency / Relative cumulative frequency

100 — 1.00 ---- 100%

75 — .75

50 — .50

25 — .25

2   7   12   17   22   27   32
Price-earnings ratios

3. (A)

Class Interval	Frequency	Relative Frequency
1.95–2.15	21	.21
2.15–2.35	19	.19
2.35–2.55	17	.17
2.55–2.75	14	.14
2.75–2.95	9	.09
2.95–3.15	6	.06
3.15–3.35	5	.05
3.35–3.55	4	.04
3.55–3.75	3	.03
3.75–3.95	2	.02
	100	1.00

(B)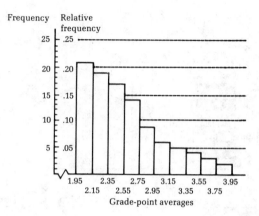

(C)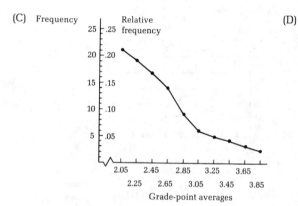

(D)

Class Interval	Frequency	Cumulative Frequency	Relative Cumulative Frequency
1.95–2.15	21	21	.21
2.15–2.35	19	40	.40
2.35–2.55	17	57	.57
2.55–2.75	14	71	.71
2.75–2.95	9	80	.80
2.95–3.15	6	86	.86
3.15–3.35	5	91	.91
3.35–3.55	4	95	.95
3.55–3.75	3	98	.98
3.75–3.95	2	100	1.00

$P(\text{GPA} > 2.95) = .2$

(E)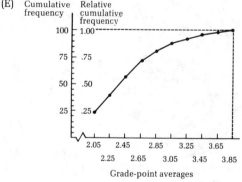

Exercise 6-3

1. Mean = 3; median = 3; mode = 3   **3.** Modal preference is chocolate   **5.** Mean = 4.4
7. Mean = 500,000; median = 430,000; mode = 430,000   **9.** Mean = 8,333; median = 5,500; mode = 5,500
11. Mean = 24,500; median = 20,000; mode = 21,000

Exercise 6-4

1. 1.15 **3.** 2.5 **5.** 98,150 **7.** 6,499 **9.** 15,547

Exercise 6-5

1. $\frac{3}{8} = .375$ **3.** $\frac{1}{8} = .125$ **5.** .230 **7.** $C_{3,2}(.5)^2(.5) = .375$ **9.** $C_{3,0}(.5)^0(.5)^3 = .125$ **11.** $C_{3,2}(.5)^2(.5) + C_{3,3}(.5)^3(.5)^0 = .500$
13. $\mu = .6, \sigma = .65$ **15.** $\mu = 2, \sigma = 1$

17. $C_{4,3}(\frac{1}{6})^3(\frac{5}{6}) \approx .0154$ **19.** $C_{4,0}(\frac{1}{6})^0(\frac{5}{6})^4 \approx .482$ **21.** $1 - [C_{4,0}(\frac{1}{6})^0(\frac{5}{6})^4] \approx .518$ **23.** (A) .311 (B) .437
25. $\mu = 2.4, \sigma = 1.2$ **27.** $\mu = 2.4, \sigma = 1.3$

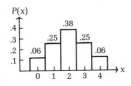

29. .238
31. The theoretical probability distribution is given by $P(x) = C_{3,x}(.5)^x(.5)^{3-x} = C_{3,x}(.5)^3$

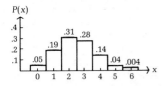

Frequency of Heads in 100 Tosses of Three Coins

Number of Heads	Theoretical Frequency	Actual Frequency
0	12.5	(List your experimental results here.)
1	37.5	
2	37.5	
3	12.5	

33. (A) .318 (B) .647 **35.** .0188
37. (A) $P(x) = C_{6,x}(.05)^x(.95)^{6-x}$

39. .998 **41.** (A) .001 (B) .264 (C) .897

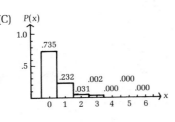

(B)

x	P(x)
0	.735
1	.232
2	.031
3	.002
4	.000
5	.000
6	.000

(C)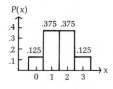

(D) $\mu = .30, \sigma = .53$

43. (A) $P(x) = C_{6,x}(.6)^x(.4)^{6-x}$

45. .000 864

(B)

x	P(x)
0	.004
1	.037
2	.138
3	.276
4	.311
5	.187
6	.047

(C)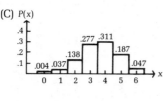

(D) $\mu = 3.6, \sigma = 1.2$

47. (A) $P(x) = C_{5,x}(.2)^x(.8)^{5-x}$

(B)

x	P(x)
0	.328
1	.410
2	.205
3	.051
4	.006
5	.000

(C)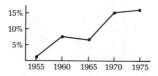

(D) $\mu = 1, \sigma = .89$

49. (A) .0041 (B) .0467 (C) .138 (D) .959

Exercise 6-6

1. 1.5 **3.** 3.3 **5.** 0.5 **7.** 0.8 **9.** .433 2 **11.** .499 5 **13.** .191 5 **15.** .288 1 **17.** .788 8 **19.** .532 8 **21.** .012 2 **23.** .105 6 **25.** No **27.** Yes **29.** No **31.** Yes **33.** .89 **35.** .16 **37.** .01 **39.** .01 **41.** 2.3% **43.** 1.2% **45.** .003; either a rare event has happened or the company's claim is false **47.** 0.82% **49.** .0158 **51.** 2.27% **53.** A's, 80.2 or greater; B's, 74.2–80.2; C's, 65.8–74.2; D's, 59.8–65.8; F's, 59.8 or lower

Exercise 6-7   Chapter Review

1. Imports as a percentage of total new car sales in the United States

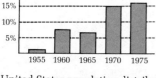

2. United States population distribution in 1970

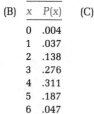

3. (A)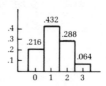

(B) $\mu = 1.2, \sigma = .85$

4. (A) 2.7 (B) 2.5 (C) 2 (D) 1.34
5. (A) 1.8 (B) .464 1

6. (A)

Class Interval	Frequency	Relative Frequency
9.5–11.5	1	.04
11.5–13.5	5	.20
13.5–15.5	12	.48
15.5–17.5	6	.24
17.5–19.5	1	.04
	25	1.00

(B) 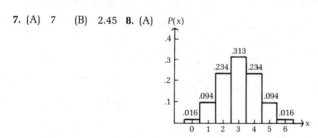   (C)

(D)

Class Interval	Frequency	Cumulative Frequency	Relative Cumulative Frequency
9.5–11.5	1	1	.04
11.5–13.5	5	6	.24
13.5–15.5	12	18	.72
15.5–17.5	6	24	.96
17.5–19.5	1	25	1.00

(E)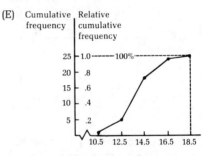

7. (A) 7   (B) 2.45   **8.** (A)   (B) $\mu = 3, \sigma = 1.22$

9. $\mu = 600, \sigma = 15.49$ **10.** .999   **11.** (A) .910 5   (B) .066 8   **12.** (A) $\bar{x} = 14.6, s = 1.83$ (B) $\bar{x} = 14.6, s = 1.78$
13. (A) .0322   (B) .0355   **14.** .421   **15.** (A) 10   (B) 10   (C) 5   (D) 5.14
16. Modal preference is soft drink

17. (A)

Interval	Frequency	Relative Frequency
29.5–31.5	3	.086
31.5–33.5	7	.2
33.5–35.5	14	.4
35.5–37.5	7	.2
37.5–39.5	4	.114
	35	1.00

(B)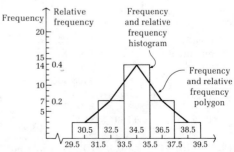

(C) $\bar{x} = 34.61, s = 2.22$

18. (A) 60.46   (B) 7.35   **19.** (A) $\mu = 140; \sigma = 6.48$ (B) Yes   (C) .939   (D) .0125   **20.** .999

Chapter 7

Exercise 7-1

1. (A) −5 (B) 3 (C) 4 (D) 0 **3.** 47 **5.** −4 **7.** $\frac{5}{3}$ **9.** 243

11.

x	0.9	0.99	0.999	→ 1 ←	1.001	1.01	1.1
$f(x)$	−19	−199	−1,999	→ ? ←	2,001	201	21

$\lim\limits_{x \to 1} f(x)$ does not exist

13.

x	0.9	0.99	0.999	→ 1 ←	1.001	1.01	1.1
$f(x)$	−1	−1	−1	→ ? ←	1	1	1

$\lim\limits_{x \to 1} f(x)$ does not exist

15.

x	10	100	1,000	10,000	→ ∞
$f(x)$	0.091	0.009 9	0.000 999	0.000 099 9	→ ?

$\lim\limits_{x \to \infty} f(x) = 0$

17.

x	10	100	1,000	10,000	→ ∞
$f(x)$	9.09	99.01	999.001	9,999.000 1	→ ?

$\lim\limits_{x \to \infty} f(x)$ does not exist

19. (A) 0 (B) Does not exist (C) 1 (D) 0 **21.** −3 **23.** 10 **25.** 0 **27.** −5 **29.** $\frac{5}{6}$ **31.** $\frac{1}{2}$ **33.** $\frac{2}{3}$ **35.** 4 **37.** 2 **39.** 4
41. $\frac{2}{3}$ **43.** 0 **45.** Does not exist
47. (A) Does not exist
(B) 2
(C) Does not exist

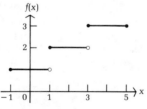

49. (A) Does not exist
(B) 0
(C) 1

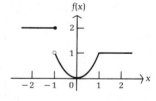

51. $\sqrt[3]{4}$ **53.** 0 **55.** $\frac{1}{4}$ **57.** Does not exist **59.** 8 **61.** 12 **63.** $\frac{1}{12}$ **65.** 2a **67.** $1/(2\sqrt{a})$
69. (A) $23 (B) $3.20 (C) $5 (D) $3

71. (A)

Compounded	n	A(n)
Annually	1	$108.00
Semiannually	2	$108.16
Quarterly	4	$108.24
Monthly	12	$108.30
Weekly	52	$108.32
Daily	365	$108.33
Hourly	8,760	$108.33

(B) $108.33

73. (A) 0.056 (B) 0.07 (C) 0.07 (D) 0 **75.** (A) 30 (B) 44 (C) 44 (D) 60

Exercise 7-2

1. (A) 1   (B) 1   (C) Yes   **3.** (A) Does not exist   (B) 1   (C) No   **5.** (A) 1   (B) 3   (C) No   **7.** $(-\infty, \infty)$
9. $(-\infty, 5)$, $(5, \infty)$ **11.** $(-\infty, -2)$, $(-2, 3)$, $(3, \infty)$ **13.** $-3 < x < 4$ **15.** $x < 3$ or $x > 7$ **17.** $0 \leqslant x \leqslant 8$ **19.** Continuous
21. Discontinuous: $\lim_{x \to -1} f(x) \neq f(-1)$ **23.** Discontinuous: f is not defined at $x = 2$
25. Discontinuous at $x = 1$ **27.** Continuous for all x **29.** Discontinuous at $x = 0$

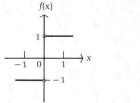   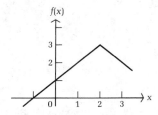   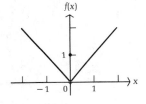

31. $(-\infty, \infty)$ **33.** $(5, \infty)$ **35.** $(-\infty, \infty)$ **37.** $(-\infty, 1)$, $(1, 2)$, $(2, \infty)$ **39.** $1 < x < 3$ or $x > 5$ **41.** $x < 4$ **43.** $-4 < x \leqslant 2$
45. $-5 \leqslant x \leqslant 0$ or $x > 3$ **47.** $x < -4$ **49.** $x \leqslant -3$, $0 \leqslant x < \frac{3}{2}$, or $x > \frac{3}{2}$ **51.** $(-2, 2)$ **53.** $(-3, 0)$, $(2, \infty)$ **55.** $(-1, 1)$
57. Not possible; $\lim_{x \to 0} f(x)$ does not exist   **59.** Define $f(1) = 2$

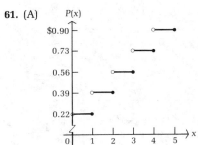   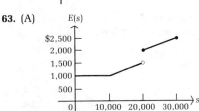

61. (A)
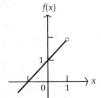

(B) $0.90, $0.90
(C) Does not exist; $0.73
(D) Yes, no

63. (A)

(B) $1,000, $1,000
(C) Does not exist, $2,000
(D) Yes, no

65. Loss: $0 \leqslant p < 4 or $p > 7; Profit: $4 < p < 7 **67.** (A) t_2, t_3, t_4, t_6, t_7 (B) 7, 7   (C) Does not exist; 4

Exercise 7-3

1. $\Delta x = 3$; $\Delta y = 45$; $\Delta y / \Delta x = 15$ **3.** 12   **5.** 12   **7.** 12   **9.** 15   **11.** (A) $12 + 3\Delta x$ (B) 12   **13.** (A) $24 + 3\Delta x$ (B) 24
15. (A) 5 meters per second   (B) $3 + \Delta x$ meters per second   (C) 3 meters per second
17. (A) 5   (B) $3 + \Delta x$ (C) 3   (D) $y = 3x - 1$ **19.** 3 meters per second   **21.** (A) $200 per year   (B) $450 per year
23. (A) 25 dryers per ad   (B) $30 - \Delta x$ (C) 30 dryers per ad
25. (A) -110 square millimeters per day   (B) -15 square millimeters per day
27. (A) 0.6 birth per year   (B) 8 births per year

Exercise 7-4

1. $f'(a)$ exists **3.** $f'(c)$ does not exist **5.** $f'(e)$ does not exist **7.** $f'(g)$ exists **9.** $f'(x) = 2$; $f'(1) = f'(2) = f'(3) = 2$
11. $f'(x) = 6 - 2x$; $f'(1) = 4$, $f'(2) = 2$, $f'(3) = 0$ **13.** $f'(x) = -1/(x + 1)^2$; $f'(1) = -\frac{1}{4}$, $f'(2) = -\frac{1}{9}$, $f'(3) = -\frac{1}{16}$
15. $f'(x) = 1/(2\sqrt{x})$; $f'(1) = \frac{1}{2}$, $f'(2) = 1/(2\sqrt{2})$, $f'(3) = 1/(2\sqrt{3})$ **17.** $f'(x) = -2/x^3$; $f'(1) = -2$, $f'(2) = -\frac{1}{4}$, $f'(3) = -\frac{2}{27}$
19. $v = f'(x) = 8x - 2$; $f'(1) = 6$ feet per second; $f'(3) = 22$ feet per second; $f'(5) = 38$ feet per second
21. (A) $m = f'(x) = 2x$ (B) $m_1 = f'(-2) = -4$; $m_2 = f'(0) = 0$; $m_3 = f'(2) = 4$ (C) $y = -4x - 4$; $y = 0$; $y = 4x - 4$
   (D)

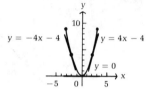

23. (A) $f'(x) = 3x^2 + 2$ (B) $f'(1) = 5$; $f'(3) = 29$ **25.** f is nondifferentiable at $x = 1$

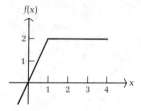

27. No **29.** Yes **31.** No
33. (A) $C'(x) = 10 - 2x$
   (B) $C'(1) = \$8$ hundred per unit increase; $C'(3) = \$4$ hundred per unit increase; $C'(4) = \$2$ hundred per unit
   increase
35. (A) $N'(t) = 2t - 8$
   (B) $N'(1) = -6$ thousand per hour; $N'(2) = -4$ thousand per hour; $N'(3) = -2$ thousand per hour [*Note:* A negative
   rate indicates the population is decreasing.]

Exercise 7-5

1. 0 **3.** 0 **5.** $12x^{11}$ **7.** 1 **9.** $-7x^{-8}$ **11.** $\frac{5}{2}x^{3/2}$ **13.** $-5x^{-6}$ **15.** $8x^3$ **17.** $2x^5$ **19.** $x^4/3$ **21.** $-10x^{-6}$ **23.** $-16x^{-5}$
25. x^{-3} **27.** $-x^{-2/3}$ **29.** $4x - 3$ **31.** $15x^4 - 6x^2$ **33.** $-12x^{-5} - 4x^{-3}$ **35.** $-\frac{1}{2}x^{-2} + 2x^{-4}$ **37.** $2x^{-1/3} - \frac{5}{3}x^{-2/3}$
39. $-\frac{8}{5}x^{-8/5} + 3x^{-3/2}$ **41.** $-\frac{1}{3}x^{-4/3}$ **43.** $-6x^{-3/2} + 6x^{-3} + 1$ **45.** $f'(x) = 6 - 2x$ (B) $y = 2x + 4$; $y = -2x + 16$
47. (A) $f'(x) = 3x^2 - 6x$ (B) $y = -2$; $y = 24x - 78$
49. (A) $v = 176 - 32x$ (B) 176 feet per second; 80 feet per second; -16 feet per second (C) $x = 5.5$ seconds
51. (A) $v = 3x^2 - 18x + 15$
   (B) 15 feet per second; -12 feet per second; 15 feet per second
   (C) $x = 1$ second; $x = 5$ seconds
53. (A) $f'(x) = 3x^2 + 12x - 15$ (B) $x = 1$; $x = -5$ **55.** (A) $f'(x) = 12x^3 - 12x^2$ (B) $x = 0$; $x = 1$ **57.** $-20x^{-2}$
59. $2x - 3 - 10x^{-3}$
65. (A) $N'(x) = 60 - 2x$
   (B) $N'(10) = 40$ (at the $\$10,000$ level of advertising, there would be an approximate increase of 40 units of sales per
   $\$1,000$ increase in advertising); $N'(20) = 20$ (at the $\$20,000$ level of advertising, there would be an approximate
   increase of only 20 units of sales per $\$1,000$ increase in advertising); the effect of advertising levels off as the
   amount spent increases.
67. (A) -1.37 beats per minute (B) -0.58 beat per minute **69.** (A) 25 items per hour (B) 8.33 items per hour

Exercise 7-6

1. $2x^3(2x) + (x^2 - 2)(6x^2) = 10x^4 - 12x^2$ **3.** $(x - 3)(2) + (2x - 1)(1) = 4x - 7$ **5.** $\dfrac{(x - 3)(1) - x(1)}{(x - 3)^2} = \dfrac{-3}{(x - 3)^2}$

7. $\dfrac{(x - 2)(2) - (2x + 3)(1)}{(x - 2)^2} = \dfrac{-7}{(x - 2)^2}$ **9.** $(x^2 + 1)(2) + (2x - 3)(2x) = 6x^2 - 6x + 2$

11. $\dfrac{(2x - 3)(2x) - (x^2 + 1)(2)}{(2x - 3)^2} = \dfrac{2x^2 - 6x - 2}{(2x - 3)^2}$ **13.** $2x(x^2 - 3) + 2x(x^2 + 2) = 4x^3 - 2x$

15. $\dfrac{(x^2 - 3)2x - (x^2 + 2)2x}{(x^2 - 3)^2} = \dfrac{-10x}{(x^2 - 3)^2}$ **17.** $(2x + 1)(2x - 3) + (x^2 - 3x)(2) = 6x^2 - 10x - 3$

19. $(2x - x^2)(5) + (5x + 2)(2 - 2x) = -15x^2 + 16x + 4$ **21.** $\dfrac{(x^2 + 2x)(5) - (5x - 3)(2x + 2)}{(x^2 + 2x)^2} = \dfrac{-5x^2 + 6x + 6}{(x^2 + 2x)^2}$

23. $\dfrac{(x^2 - 1)(2x - 3) - (x^2 - 3x + 1)(2x)}{(x^2 - 1)^2} = \dfrac{3x^2 - 4x + 3}{(x^2 - 1)^2}$ **25.** $f'(x) = (1 + 3x)(-2) + (5 - 2x)(3); \; y = -11x + 29$

27. $f'(x) = \dfrac{(3x - 4)(1) - (x - 8)(3)}{(3x - 4)^2}; \; y = 5x - 13$ **29.** $f'(x) = (2x - 15)(2x) + (x^2 + 18)(2) = 6(x - 2)(x - 3); \; x = 2, \, x = 3$

31. $f'(x) = \dfrac{(x^2 + 1)(1) - x(2x)}{(x^2 + 1)^2} = \dfrac{1 - x^2}{(x^2 + 1)^2}; \; x = -1, \, x = 1$ **33.** $7x^6 - 3x^2$ **35.** $-27x^{-4}$

37. $(2x^4 - 3x^3 + x)(2x - 1) + (x^2 - x + 5)(8x^3 - 9x^2 + 1)$ **39.** $\dfrac{(4x^2 + 5x - 1)(6x - 2) - (3x^2 - 2x + 3)(8x + 5)}{(4x^2 + 5x - 1)^2}$

41. $9x^{1/3}(3x^2) + (x^3 + 5)(3x^{-2/3})$ **43.** $\dfrac{(x^2 - 3)(2x^{-2/3}) - 6x^{1/3}(2x)}{(x^2 - 3)^2}$ **45.** $x^{-2/3}(3x^2 - 4x) + (x^3 - 2x^2)(-\tfrac{2}{3}x^{-5/3})$

47. $\dfrac{(x^2 + 1)[(2x^2 - 1)(2x) + (x^2 + 3)(4x)] - (2x^2 - 1)(x^2 + 3)(2x)}{(x^2 + 1)^2}$

49. (A) $S'(t) = \dfrac{7{,}200 - 200t^2}{(t^2 + 36)^2}$

(B) $S(2) = 10; S'(2) = 4$; at $t = 2$ months, monthly sales are 10,000 and increasing at 4,000 albums per month
(C) $S(8) = 16; S'(8) = -0.56$; at $t = 8$ months, monthly sales are 16,000 and decreasing at 560 albums per month

51. (A) $d'(x) = \dfrac{-50{,}000(2x + 10)}{(x^2 + 10x + 25)^2} = \dfrac{-100{,}000}{(x + 5)^3}$

(B) $d'(5) = -100$ radios per \$1 increase in price; $d'(10) = -30$ radios per \$1 increase in price

53. (A) $C'(t) = \dfrac{0.14 - 0.14t^2}{(t^2 + 1)^2}$

(B) $C'(0.5) = 0.0672$, concentration is increasing at 0.0672 unit per hour; $C'(3) = -0.0112$, concentration is decreasing at 0.0112 unit per hour

55. (A) $N'(x) = \dfrac{(x + 32)(100) - (100x + 200)}{(x + 32)^2} = \dfrac{3{,}000}{(x + 32)^2}$ (B) $N'(4) = 2.31; N'(68) = 0.30$

Exercise 7-7

1. $6(2x + 5)^2$ **3.** $-8(5 - 2x)^3$ **5.** $30x(3x^2 + 5)^4$ **7.** $8(x^3 - 2x^2 + 2)^7(3x^2 - 4x)$ **9.** $(2x - 5)^{-1/2}$ **11.** $-8x^3(x^4 + 1)^{-3}$
13. $24x(x^2 - 2)^3$ **15.** $-6(x^2 + 3x)^{-4}(2x + 3)$ **17.** $x(x^2 + 8)^{-1/2}$ **19.** $(3x + 4)^{-2/3}$

21. $\frac{1}{2}(x^2 - 4x + 2)^{-1/2}(2x - 4) = (x - 2)/(x^2 - 4x + 2)^{1/2}$ **23.** $(-1)(2x + 4)^{-2}(2) = -2/(2x + 4)^2$ **25.** $-15x^2(x^3 + 4)^{-6}$

27. $(-1)(4x^2 - 4x + 1)^{-2}(8x - 4) = -4/(2x - 1)^3$ **29.** $-2(x^2 - 3x)^{-3/2}(2x - 3) = \dfrac{-2(2x - 3)}{(x^2 - 3x)^{3/2}}$

31. $f'(x) = (4 - x)^3 - 3x(4 - x)^2; \ y = -16x + 48$ **33.** $f'(x) = \dfrac{(2x - 5)^3 - 6x(2x - 5)^2}{(2x - 5)^6}; \ y = -17x + 54$

35. $f'(x) = (2x + 2)^{1/2} + x(2x + 2)^{-1/2}; \ y = \frac{5}{2}x - \frac{1}{2}$
37. $f'(x) = 2x(x - 5)^3 + 3x^2(x - 5)^2 = 5x(x - 5)^2(x - 2); \ x = 0, \ x = 2, \ x = 5$

39. $f'(x) = \dfrac{(2x + 5)^2 - 4x(2x + 5)}{(2x + 5)^4} = \dfrac{5 - 2x}{(2x + 5)^3}; \ x = \frac{5}{2}$ **41.** $f'(x) = \dfrac{x - 4}{\sqrt{x^2 - 8x + 20}}; \ x = 4$

43. $18x^2(x^2 + 1)^2 + 3(x^2 + 1)^3 = 3(x^2 + 1)^2(7x^2 + 1)$ **45.** $\dfrac{2x^3 4(x^3 - 7)^3 3x^2 - (x^3 - 7)^4 6x^2}{4x^6} = \dfrac{3(x^3 - 7)^3(3x^3 + 7)}{2x^4}$

47. $(2x - 3)^2[3(2x^2 + 1)^2(4x)] + (2x^2 + 1)^3[2(2x - 3)(2)] = 4(2x^2 + 1)^2(2x - 3)(8x^2 - 9x + 1)$

49. $4x^2[\frac{1}{2}(x^2 - 1)^{-1/2}(2x)] + (x^2 - 1)^{1/2}(8x) = \dfrac{12x^3 - 8x}{\sqrt{x^2 - 1}}$ **51.** $\dfrac{(x - 3)^{1/2}(2) - 2x[\frac{1}{2}(x - 3)^{-1/2}]}{x - 3} = \dfrac{x - 6}{(x - 3)^{3/2}}$

53. $(2x - 1)^{1/2}(x^2 + 3)(11x^2 - 4x + 9)$
55. (A) $\overline{C}'(x) = 2(2x - 8)2 = 8x - 32$
   (B) $\overline{C}'(2) = -16; \overline{C}'(4) = 0; \overline{C}'(6) = 16.$ An increase in production at the 2,000 level will reduce costs; at the 4,000 level, no increase or decrease will occur; and at the 6,000 level, an increase in production will increase the costs.

57. $\dfrac{(4 \times 10^6)x}{(x^2 - 1)^{5/3}}$

59. (A) $f'(n) = n(n - 2)^{-1/2} + 2(n - 2)^{1/2} = \dfrac{3n - 4}{(n - 2)^{1/2}}$
   (B) $f'(11) = \frac{29}{3}$ (rate of learning is $\frac{29}{3}$ units per minute at the $n = 11$ level); $f'(27) = \frac{77}{5}$ (rate of learning is $\frac{77}{5}$ units per minute at the $n = 27$ level)

Exercise 7-8

1. (A) \$29.50   (B) \$30
3. (A) \$420
   (B) $\overline{C}'(500) = -0.24;$ at a production level of 500 units, a unit increase in production will decrease average cost by approximately 24¢.
5. (A) $R'(1,600) = 20;$ at a production level of 1,600 units, a unit increase in production will increase revenue by approximately \$20.
   (B) $R'(2,500) = -25;$ at a production level of 2,500 units, a unit increase in production will decrease revenue by approximately \$25.
7. (A) \$4.50   (B) \$5
9. (A) $P'(450) = 0.5;$ at a production level of 450 units, a unit increase in production will increase profit by approximately 50¢.
   (B) $P'(750) = -2.5;$ at a production level of 750 units, a unit increase in production will decrease profit by approximately \$2.50.
11. (A) \$1.25
   (B) $\overline{P}'(150) = 0.015;$ at a production level of 150 units, a unit increase in production will increase average profit by approximately 1.5¢.
13. (A) $C'(x) = 60$ (B) $R(x) = 200x - x^2/30$ (C) $R'(x) = 200 - x/15$
   (D) $R'(1,500) = 100;$ at a production level of 1,500 units, a unit increase in production will increase revenue by approximately \$100. $R'(4,500) = -100;$ at a production level of 4,500 units, a unit increase in production will decrease revenue by approximately \$100.

(E) Break-even points: (600, 108,000) and (3,600, 288,000)

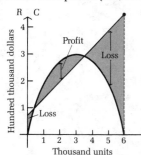

(F) $P(x) = -x^2/30 + 140x - 72,000$

(G) $P'(x) = -x/15 + 140$

(H) $P'(1,500) = 40$; at a production level of 1,500 units, a unit increase in production will increase profit by approximately \$40. $P'(3,000) = -60$; at a production level of 3,000 units, a unit increase in production will decrease profit by approximately \$60.

15. (A) $p = 20 - x/50$ (B) $R(x) = 20x - x^2/50$ (C) $C(x) = 4x + 1,400$
(D) Break-even points: (100, 1,800) and (700, 4,200)

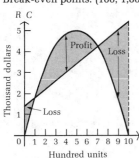

(E) $P(x) = 16x - x^2/50 - 1,400$

(F) $P'(250) = 6$; at a production level of 250 units, a unit increase in production will increase profit by approximately \$6. $P'(475) = -3$; at a production level of 475 units, a unit increase in production will decrease profit by approximately \$3.

Exercise 7-9 Chapter Review

1. $12x^3 - 4x$ **2.** $x^{-1/2} - 3 = \dfrac{1}{x^{1/2}} - 3$ **3.** 0 **4.** $-x^{-3} + x$ **5.** $(2x - 1)(3) + (3x + 2)(2) = 12x + 1$

6. $(x^2 - 1)(3x^2) + (x^3 - 3)(2x) = 5x^4 - 3x^2 - 6x$ **7.** $\dfrac{(x^2 + 2)2 - 2x(2x)}{(x^2 + 2)^2} = \dfrac{4 - 2x^2}{(x^2 + 2)^2}$ **8.** $(-1)(3x + 2)^{-2}3 = \dfrac{-3}{(3x + 2)^2}$

9. $3(2x - 3)^2 2 = 6(2x - 3)^2$ **10.** $-2(x^2 + 2)^{-3}2x = \dfrac{-4x}{(x^2 + 2)^3}$ **11.** $12x^3 + 6x^{-4}$

12. $(2x^2 - 3x + 2)(2x + 2) + (x^2 + 2x - 1)(4x - 3) = 8x^3 + 3x^2 - 12x + 7$ **13.** $\dfrac{(x - 1)^2 2 - (2x - 3)2(x - 1)}{(x - 1)^4} = \dfrac{4 - 2x}{(x - 1)^3}$

14. $x^{-1/2} - 2x^{-3/2} = \dfrac{1}{\sqrt{x}} - \dfrac{2}{\sqrt{x^3}}$ **15.** $(x^2 - 1)[2(2x + 1)2] + (2x + 1)^2(2x) = 2(2x + 1)(4x^2 + x - 2)$

16. $\dfrac{1}{3}(x^3 - 5)^{-2/3}3x^2 = \dfrac{x^2}{\sqrt[3]{(x^3 - 5)^2}}$ **17.** $-8x^{-3}$ **18.** $\dfrac{(2x - 3)4(x^2 + 2)^3 2x - (x^2 + 2)^4 2}{(2x - 3)^2} = \dfrac{2(x^2 + 2)^3(7x^2 - 12x - 2)}{(2x - 3)^2}$

19. (A) $m = f'(1) = 2$ (B) $y = 2x + 3$ **20.** (A) $m = f'(1) = 16$ (B) $y = 16x - 12$ **21.** $x = 5$ **22.** $x = -5, x = 3$
23. $x = -2, x = 2$ **24.** $x = 0, x = 3, x = \frac{15}{2}$ **25.** (A) $v = f'(x) = 32x - 4$ (B) $f'(3) = 92$ feet per second
26. (A) $v = f'(x) = 96 - 32x$ (B) $x = 3$ seconds **27.** $-3 < x < 4$ **28.** $x \leqslant -2$ or $x \geqslant 4$ **29.** $-\infty < x < \infty$
30. $x < -3$ or $0 < x \leqslant 5$ **31.** $0 < x < 2$ or $2 < x < 5$ **32.** $x < -2$ or $x > 3$ **33.** (A) Does not exist (B) 6 (C) No
34. (A) 3 (B) 3 (C) Yes **35.** $(-\infty, \infty)$ **36.** $(-\infty, -5), (-5, \infty)$ **37.** $(-\infty, -2), (-2, 3), (3, \infty)$ **38.** $(3, \infty)$ **39.** $(-\infty, \infty)$

40. $(-4, 5)$ **41.** $\dfrac{2(3) - 3}{3 + 5} = \dfrac{3}{8}$ **42.** $2(3^2) - 3 + 1 = 16$ **43.** -1 **44.** 4 **45.** $\dfrac{1}{6}$ **46.** Does not exist **47.** $\dfrac{1}{2\sqrt{7}}$ **48.** $\sqrt{2}$

49. 3 **50.** $\dfrac{2}{3}$ **51.** 0 **52.** Does not exist **53.** $2x - 1$ **54.** $\dfrac{1}{2\sqrt{x}}$ **55.** No **56.** No **57.** No **58.** Yes

59. Discontinuous at $x = 0$ **60.** Continuous for all x

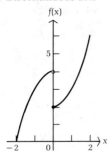

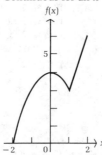

61. (A) $\frac{5}{8}$ (B) Does not exist   (C) No   **62.** (A) $\frac{1}{2}$ (B) $\frac{1}{2}$ (C) Yes   **63.** $x = -\frac{2}{3}, 2$ **64.** $7x(x-4)^3(x+3)^2$ **65.** $\dfrac{x^4(2x+5)}{(2x+1)^5}$

66. $\dfrac{1}{x^2\sqrt{x^2-1}}$ **67.** $\dfrac{4}{(x^2+4)^{3/2}}$ **68.** (A) $C = 48 - 2p$ (B) $R = 14p - p^2$ (C) $\$4 < p < \$12$

69. (A) $C'(x) = 2$; $\overline{C}(x) = 2 + 56x^{-1}$; $\overline{C}'(x) = -56x^{-2}$
  (B) $R(x) = xp = 20x - x^2$; $R'(x) = 20 - 2x$; $\overline{R}(x) = 20 - x$; $\overline{R}'(x) = -1$
  (C) $P(x) = R(x) - C(x) = 18x - x^2 - 56$; $P'(x) = 18 - 2x$; $\overline{P}(x) = 18 - x - 56x^{-1}$; $\overline{P}'(x) = -1 + 56x^{-2}$
  (D) Solving $R(x) = C(x)$, we find break-even points at $x = 4, 14$.
  (E) $P'(7) = 4$ (increasing production increases profit); $P'(9) = 0$ (stable); $P'(11) = -4$ (increasing production decreases profit)
  (F)

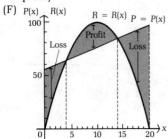

70. (A) 2 components per day   (B) 3.2 components per day   (C) 40 components per day
71. $C'(9) = -1$ part per million per meter; $C'(99) = -0.001$ part per million per meter
72. (A) 10 items per hour   (B) 5 items per hour

Chapter 8

Exercise 8-1

1. (a, b); (d, f); (g, h) **3.** c, d, f **5.** b, f **7.** Decreasing on $(-\infty, 8)$; increasing on $(8, \infty)$; local minimum at $x = 8$
9. Increasing on $(-\infty, 5)$; decreasing on $(5, \infty)$; local maximum at $x = 5$ **11.** Increasing for all x; no local extrema
13. Decreasing for all x; no local extrema
15. Increasing on $(-\infty, -2)$ and $(2, \infty)$; decreasing on $(-2, 2)$; local maximum at $x = -2$; local minimum at $x = 2$

17. Increasing on $(-\infty, -2)$ and $(4, \infty)$; decreasing on $(-2, 4)$; local maximum at $x = -2$; local minimum at $x = 4$

19. Increasing on $(-\infty, -1)$ and $(0, 1)$; decreasing on $(-1, 0)$ and $(1, \infty)$; local maxima at $x = -1$ and $x = 1$; local minimum at $x = 0$

21. Increasing on $(-\infty, 4)$
Decreasing on $(4, \infty)$
Horizontal tangent at $x = 4$

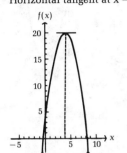

23. Increasing on $(-\infty, -1)$, $(1, \infty)$
Decreasing on $(-1, 1)$
Horizontal tangents at $x = -1, 1$

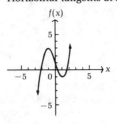

25. Decreasing for all x
Horizontal tangent at $x = 2$

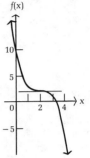

27. No critical values; increasing on $(-\infty, -2)$ and $(-2, \infty)$; no local extrema

29. Critical values: $x = -2$, $x = 2$; increasing on $(-\infty, -2)$ and $(2, \infty)$; decreasing on $(-2, 0)$ and $(0, 2)$; local maximum at $x = -2$; local minimum at $x = 2$

31. Critical value: $x = -2$; increasing on $(-2, 0)$; decreasing on $(-\infty, -2)$ and $(0, \infty)$; local minimum at $x = -2$

33. Critical values: $x = 0$, $x = 4$; increasing on $(-\infty, 0)$ and $(4, \infty)$; decreasing on $(0, 2)$ and $(2, 4)$; local maximum at $x = 0$; local minimum at $x = 4$

35. Critical values: $x = 0$, $x = 4$, $x = 6$; increasing on $(0, 4)$ and $(6, \infty)$; decreasing on $(-\infty, 0)$ and $(4, 6)$; local maximum at $x = 4$; local minima at $x = 0$ and $x = 6$

37. Critical value: $x = 2$; increasing on $(2, \infty)$; decreasing on $(-\infty, 2)$; local minimum at $x = 2$

39. Critical value: $x = 1$; increasing on $(0, 1)$; decreasing on $(1, \infty)$; local maximum at $x = 1$

41. Critical value: $x = 80$; decreasing for $0 < x < 80$; increasing for $80 < x < 150$; local minimum at $x = 80$

43. $P(x)$ is increasing over (a, b) if $P'(x) = R'(x) - C'(x) > 0$ over (a, b); that is, if $R'(x) > C'(x)$ over (a, b)

45. Critical value: $t = 1$; increasing for $0 < t < 1$; decreasing for $1 < t < 24$; local maximum at $t = 1$

47. Critical value: $t = 7$; increasing for $0 < t < 7$; decreasing for $7 < t < 24$; local maximum at $t = 7$

Exercise 8-2

1. (a, c), (c, d), (e, g) **3.** d, e, g **5.** $6x - 4$ **7.** $40x^3$ **9.** $6x$ **11.** $24x^2(x^2 - 1) + 6(x^2 - 1)^2 = 6(x^2 - 1)(5x^2 - 1)$

13. $6x^{-3} + 12x^{-4}$ **15.** $f(2) = -2$ is a local minimum   **17.** $f(-1) = 2$ is a local maximum; $f(2) = -25$ is a local minimum

19. No local extrema   **21.** $f(-2) = -6$ is a local minimum; $f(0) = 10$ is a local maximum; $f(2) = -6$ is a local minimum

23. $f(0) = 2$ is a local minimum   **25.** $f(-4) = -8$ is a local maximum; $f(4) = 8$ is a local minimum

27. Concave upward for all x; no inflection points

29. Concave upward on $(6, \infty)$; concave downward on $(-\infty, 6)$; inflection point at $x = 6$

31. Concave upward on $(-\infty, -2)$ and $(2, \infty)$; concave downward on $(-2, 2)$; inflection points at $x = -2$ and $x = 2$

33. Concave upward on $(0, 2)$; concave downward on $(-\infty, 0)$ and $(2, \infty)$; inflection points at $x = 0$ and $x = 2$

35. Local maximum at $x = 0$
Local minimum at $x = 4$
Inflection point at $x = 2$

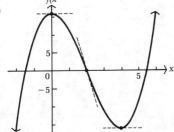

37. Inflection point at $x = 0$

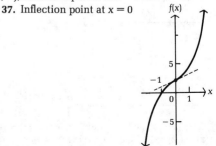

39. Inflection point at x = 0   f(x)

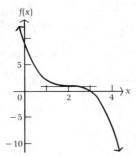

41. Local maximum at x = −2
Local minimum at x = 2
Inflection point at x = 0

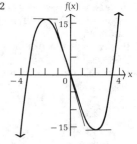

43. Inflection points at x = −2 and x = 2   **45.** Inflection points at x = −6, x = 0, and x = 6

47. (A) Local maximum at x = 60   (B) Concave downward on the whole interval (0, 80)

49. (A) Increasing on (10, 25); decreasing on (25, 40)
   (B) Inflection point at x = 25
   (C)

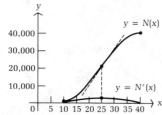

   (D) Max N'(x) = N'(25) = 2,025

51. (A) Increasing on (0, 10); decreasing on (10, 20)
   (B) Inflection point at t = 10
   (C)

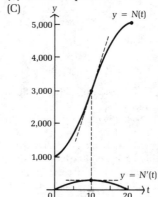

   (D) N'(10) = 300

53. (A) Increasing on (5, ∞); decreasing on (0, 5)
   (B) Inflection point at n = 5

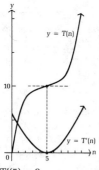

   (C) T'(5) = 0

Exercise 8-3

1. Min f(x) = f(2) = 1; no maximum   **3.** Max f(x) = f(4) = 26; no minimum   **5.** No absolute extrema exist
7. Max f(x) = f(2) = 16   **9.** Min f(x) = f(2) = 14

11. (A) Max $f(x) = f(5) = 14$; min $f(x) = f(-1) = -22$ (B) Max $f(x) = f(1) = -2$; min $f(x) = f(-1) = -22$
(C) Max $f(x) = f(5) = 14$; min $f(x) = f(3) = -6$
13. (A) Max $f(x) = f(0) = 126$; min $f(x) = f(2) = -26$ (B) Max $f(x) = f(7) = 49$; min $f(x) = f(2) = -26$
(C) Max $f(x) = f(6) = 6$; min $f(x) = f(3) = -15$
15. Exactly in half   **17.** 15 and -15 **19.** A square of side 25 cm; maximum area $= 625$ cm²
21. 3,000 pairs; \$3.00 per pair   **23.** \$35; \$6,125   **25.** 40 trees; 1,600 lb   **27.** $(10 - 2\sqrt{7})/3 = 1.57$ in. squares
29. 20 ft by 40 ft (with the expensive side being one of the short sides)   **31.** 10,000 books in 5 printings
33. (A) $x = 5.1$ mi   (B) $x = 10$ mi   **35.** 4 days; 20 bacteria per cm³   **37.** 50 mice per order   **39.** 1 month; 2 ft
41. 4 years from now

Exercise 8-4

1. (b, d), $(d, 0)$, (g, ∞) **3.** $x = 0$ **5.** (a, d), (e, h) **7.** $x = a$, $x = h$ **9.** $x = d$, $x = e$
11. Horizontal asymptote: $y = 2$; vertical asymptote: $x = -2$
13. Horizontal asymptote: $y = 1$; vertical asymptotes: $x = -1$ and $x = 1$ **15.** No horizontal or vertical asymptotes
17. Horizontal asymptote: $y = 0$; no vertical asymptotes   **19.** No horizontal asymptote; vertical asymptote: $x = 3$

21. Decreasing on $(-\infty, 3)$
Increasing on $(3, \infty)$
Local minimum at $x = 3$
Concave upward on $(-\infty, \infty)$
$f(1) = 0$; $f(5) = 0$; $f(0) = 5$

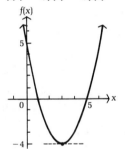

23. Increasing on $(-\infty, 0)$ and $(4, \infty)$
Decreasing on $(0, 4)$
Local maximum at $x = 0$
Local minimum at $x = 4$
Concave upward on $(2, \infty)$
Concave downward on $(-\infty, 2)$
Inflection point at $x = 2$
$f(0) = 0$; $f(6) = 0$

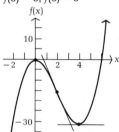

25. Increasing on $(-\infty, -2)$ and $(2, \infty)$
Decreasing on $(-2, 2)$
Local maximum at $x = -2$
Local minimum at $x = 2$
Concave upward on $(0, \infty)$
Concave downward on $(-\infty, 0)$
Inflection point at $x = 0$
$f(0) = 16$; $f(-4) = 0$; $f(2) = 0$

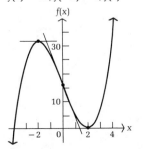

27. Increasing on $(-\infty, 3)$
Decreasing on $(3, \infty)$
Local maximum at $x = 3$
Concave upward on $(0, 2)$
Concave downward on $(-\infty, 0)$ and $(2, \infty)$
Inflection points at $x = 0$ and $x = 2$
$f(0) = 0$; $f(4) = 0$

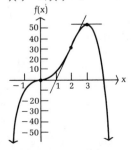

29. Decreasing on $(-\infty, 3)$ and $(3, \infty)$
Concave upward on $(3, \infty)$
Concave downward on $(-\infty, 3)$
Horizontal asymptote: $y = 1$
Vertical asymptote: $x = 3$
$f(0) = -1$; $f(-3) = 0$

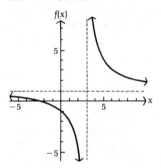

31. Decreasing on $(-\infty, 2)$ and $(2, \infty)$
Concave downward on $(-\infty, 2)$
Concave upward on $(2, \infty)$
Horizontal asymptote at $y = 1$
Vertical asymptote at $x = 2$
$f(0) = 0$

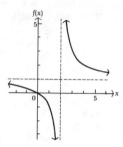

33. Increasing on $(-\infty, -1)$ and $(1, \infty)$
Decreasing on $(-1, 0)$ and $(0, 1)$
Local maximum at $x = -1$
Local minimum at $x = 1$
Concave upward on $(0, \infty)$
Concave downward on $(-\infty, 0)$
Vertical asymptote: $x = 0$

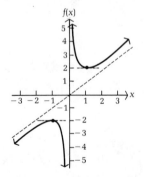

35. Increasing on $(-\infty, -\sqrt{3}/3)$ and $(\sqrt{3}/3, \infty)$
Decreasing on $(-\sqrt{3}/3, \sqrt{3}/3)$
Local maximum at $x = -\sqrt{3}/3$
Local minimum at $x = \sqrt{3}/3$
Concave downward on $(-\infty, 0)$
Concave upward on $(0, \infty)$
Inflection point at $x = 0$
$f(0) = 0$; $f(1) = 0$; $f(-1) = 0$

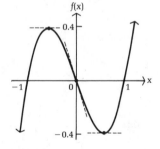

37. Increasing on $(-\infty, -\sqrt{3})$ and $(0, \sqrt{3})$
Decreasing on $(-\sqrt{3}, 0)$ and $(\sqrt{3}, \infty)$
Local maxima at $x = -\sqrt{3}$ and $x = \sqrt{3}$
Local minimum at $x = 0$
Concave upward on $(-1, 1)$
Concave downward on $(-\infty, -1)$ and $(1, \infty)$
$f(0) = 27$; $f(-3) = 0$; $f(3) = 0$

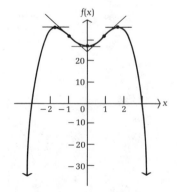

39. Decreasing on $(-\infty, -2)$ and $(0, 2)$
Increasing on $(-2, 0)$ and $(2, \infty)$
Local minima at $x = -2$ and $x = 2$
Local maximum at $x = 0$
Concave upward on $(-\infty, -2\sqrt{3}/3)$ and $(2\sqrt{3}/3, \infty)$
Concave downward on $(-2\sqrt{3}/3, 2\sqrt{3}/3)$
Inflection points at $x = -2\sqrt{3}/3$ and $x = 2\sqrt{3}/3$
$f(-2) = 0; f(2) = 0; f(0) = 16$

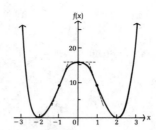

41. Decreasing on $(-\infty, 0)$ and $(0, 1.25)$
Increasing on $(1.25, \infty)$
Local minimum at $x = 1.25$
Concave upward on $(-\infty, 0)$ and $(1, \infty)$
Concave downward on $(0, 1)$
Inflection points at $x = 0$ and $x = 1$
$f(0) = 0; f(1.5) = 0$

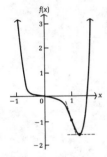

43. Decreasing on $(-\infty, -2)$, $(-2, 2)$, and $(2, \infty)$
Concave upward on $(-2, 0)$ and $(2, \infty)$
Concave downward on $(-\infty, -2)$ and $(0, 2)$
Inflection point at $x = 0$
Horizontal asymptote: $y = 0$
Vertical asymptotes: $x = -2$ and $x = 2$
$f(0) = 0$

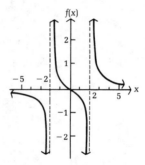

45. Increasing on $(-\infty, 0)$
Decreasing on $(0, \infty)$
Local maximum at $x = 0$
Concave upward on $(-\infty, -\sqrt{3}/3)$ and $(\sqrt{3}/3, \infty)$
Concave downward on $(-\sqrt{3}/3, \sqrt{3}/3)$
Inflection points at $x = -\sqrt{3}/3$ and $x = \sqrt{3}/3$
Horizontal asymptote: $y = 0$
$f(0) = 1$

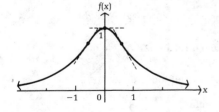

47.

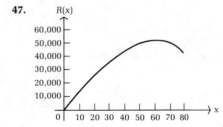

49. (A) Increasing on $(0, 1)$
    (B) Concave upward on $(0, 1)$
    (C) $x = 1$ is a vertical asymptote
    (D) The origin is both an x and a y intercept
    (E)

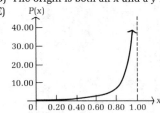

51. (A) $\bar{C}(n) = \dfrac{3{,}200}{n} + 250 + 50n$
    (B) 8 years
    (C)

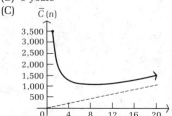

53. (A) 25 at $x = 100$
    (B)

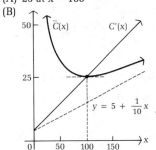
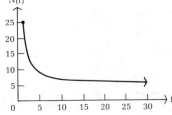

55.

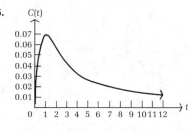

57.

Exercise 8-5

1. $dy = (24x - 3x^2)\, dx$ **3.** $dy = \left(2x - \dfrac{x^2}{3}\right) dx$ **5.** $dy = -\dfrac{295}{x^{3/2}}\, dx$ **7.** $dy = \dfrac{150}{x^2}\, dx$ **9.** $dy = 6(2x + 1)^2\, dx$

11. $dy = \dfrac{(9 - x^2)\, dx}{(x^2 + 9)^2}$ **13.** $dy = 1.4,\ \Delta y = 1.44$ **15.** $dy = 3,\ \Delta y = 2.73$ **17.** 2.03   **19.** 3.04   **21.** 120 in.³

23. $dy = \dfrac{6x - 2}{3(3x^2 - 2x + 1)^{2/3}}\, dx$ **25.** $dy = 3.9,\ \Delta y = 3.83$ **27.** 40 unit increase; 20 unit increase   **29.** $-\$6,\ \$4$

31. -1.37 per minute; -0.58 per minute   **33.** 1.26 mm²   **35.** 3 words per minute
37. (A) 2,100 increase   (B) 4,800 increase   (C) 2,100 increase

---

Exercise 8-6 Chapter Review

1. $(a, c_1),\ (c_3, c_5),\ (c_5, c_6)$ **2.** $(c_1, c_3),\ (c_6, b)$ **3.** $(a, c_2),\ (c_4, c_5),\ (c_7, b)$ **4.** c_3 **5.** c_6 **6.** c_1, c_3, c_5 **7.** c_6 **8.** c_2, c_4, c_5, c_7
9. $f''(x) = 12x^2 + 30x$ **10.** $y'' = 8/x^3$ **11.** $dy = (3x^2 + 4)\, dx$ **12.** $dy = 18x(3x^2 - 7)^2\, dx$ **13.** $-4, 2$

14. Increasing on $(-\infty, -4)$ and $(2, \infty)$; decreasing on $(-4, 2)$

15. Local maximum at $x = -4$; local minimum at $x = 2$

16. Concave upward on $(-1, \infty)$; concave downward on $(-\infty, -1)$

17. Inflection point at $x = -1$

18.

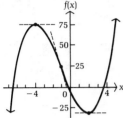

19. Horizontal asymptote at $y = 3$

20. Vertical asymptote at $x = -2$

21. Increasing on $(-\infty, -2)$ and $(-2, \infty)$

22. Concave upward on $(-\infty, -2)$; concave downward on $(-2, \infty)$

23.

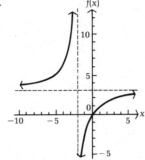

24. Min $f(x) = f(2) = -4$; max $f(x) = f(5) = 77$ **25.** Min $f(x) = f(2) = 8$

26. Horizontal asymptote: $y = 0$; no vertical asymptotes

27. No horizontal asymptotes; vertical asymptotes: $x = -3$ and $x = 3$ **28.** $dy = 7.3$, $\Delta y = 7.45$ **29.** 4.13

30. Max $f'(x) = f'(2) = 12$

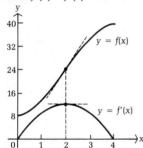

31. Each number is 20; minimum sum is 40

32. Increasing on $(-2, \infty)$
Decreasing on $(-\infty, -2)$
Local minimum at $x = -2$
Concave upward on $(-\infty, -1)$ and $(1, \infty)$
Concave downward on $(-1, 1)$
Inflection points at $x = -1$ and $x = 1$
$f(0) = -3$; $f(-3) = 0$; $f(1) = 0$

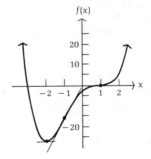

33. $dy = -0.0031$, $\Delta y = -0.0031$

34. Max $P(x) = P(3,000) = \$175,000$

35. Min $\overline{C}(x) = \overline{C}(200) = 50$

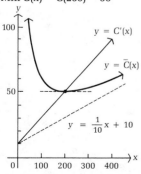

36. $49; $6,724

37. 12 orders per year

38. $110

39. 3 days

40. In 2 years

Chapter 9

Exercise 9-1

1. \$1,221.40; \$1,648.72; \$2,225.54 **3.** 11.55 **5.** 10.99 **7.** 0.14 **9.**

n	$(1 + 1/n)^n$
10	2.593 74
100	2.704 81
1,000	2.716 92
10,000	2.718 15
100,000	2.718 27
1,000,000	2.718 28
10,000,000	2.718 28
↓	↓
∞	$e = 2.718\ 281\ 8\ \ldots$

11. \$55,463.90

13. \$9,931.71 **15.** $r = \frac{1}{4} \ln 1.5 \approx 0.1014$ or 10.14%
17. (A)

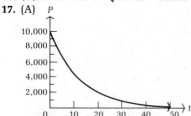

(B) $\lim_{x \to \infty} 10,000e^{-0.08t} = 0$ **19.** 2.77 years **21.** 13.86%

23. $A = Pe^{rt}; 2P = Pe^{rt}; e^{rt} = 2; \ln e^{rt} = \ln 2; rt = \ln 2; t = (\ln 2)/r$ **25.** 34.66 years **27.** 3.47%
29. $t = -(\ln 0.5)/0.000\ 433\ 2 \approx 1,600$ years **31.** $r = (\ln 0.5)/30 \approx -0.0231$ **33.** Approximately 538 years

Exercise 9-2

1. $6e^x - \dfrac{7}{x}$ **3.** $2exe^{-1} + 3e^x$ **5.** $\dfrac{5}{x}$ **7.** $\dfrac{2 \ln x}{x}$ **9.** $x^3 + 4x^3 \ln x = x^3(1 + 4 \ln x)$ **11.** $x^3e^x + 3x^2e^x = x^2e^x(x + 3)$

13. $\dfrac{(x^2 + 9)e^x - 2xe^x}{(x^2 + 9)^2} = \dfrac{e^x(x^2 - 2x + 9)}{(x^2 + 9)^2}$ **15.** $\dfrac{x^3 - 4x^3 \ln x}{x^8} = \dfrac{1 - 4 \ln x}{x^5}$

17. $3(x + 2)^2 \ln x + \dfrac{(x + 2)^3}{x} = (x + 2)^2 \left(3 \ln x + \dfrac{x + 2}{x} \right)$ **19.** $(x + 1)^3e^x + 3(x + 1)^2e^x = (x + 1)^2e^x(x + 4)$

21. $\dfrac{2xe^x - (x^2 + 1)e^x}{(e^x)^2} = \dfrac{2x - x^2 - 1}{e^x}$ **23.** $(\ln x)^3 + 3(\ln x)^2 = (\ln x)^2(\ln x + 3)$ **25.** $-15e^x(4 - 5e^x)^2$ **27.** $\dfrac{1}{2x \sqrt{1 + \ln x}}$

29. xe^x **31.** $4x \ln x$ **33.** $y = ex$ **35.** $y = \dfrac{1}{e}x$ **37.** Max $f(x) = f(e^3) = e^3 \approx 20.086$ **39.** Min $f(x) = f(1) = e \approx 2.718$

41. Max $f(x) = f(e^{1/2}) = 2e^{-1/2} \approx 1.213$

43. Decreasing on $(-\infty, \infty)$
Concave downward on $(-\infty, \infty)$
Horizontal asymptote: $y = 1$
$f(0) = 0$

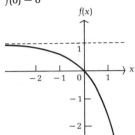

45. Increasing on $(1, \infty)$
Decreasing on $(0, 1)$
Local minimum at $x = 1$
Concave upward on $(0, \infty)$
Vertical asymptote: $x = 0$

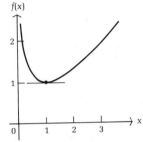

47. Increasing on $(-\infty, 2)$
Decreasing on $(2, \infty)$
Local maximum at $x = 2$
Concave upward on $(-\infty, 1)$
Concave downward on $(1, \infty)$
Inflection point at $x = 1$
Horizontal asymptote: $y = 0$
$f(0) = 3; f(3) = 0$

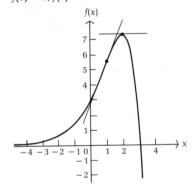

49. Increasing on $(e^{-1/2}, \infty)$
Decreasing on $(0, e^{-1/2})$
Local minimum at $x = e^{-1/2}$
Concave upward on $(e^{-3/2}, \infty)$
Concave downward on $(0, e^{-3/2})$
Inflection point at $x = e^{-3/2}$
$f(1) = 0$

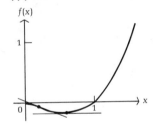

53. $p = \$2$ **55.** Min $\overline{C}(x) = \overline{C}(e^7) \approx \$99.91$
57. (A) At \$3.68 each, the maximum revenue will be \$3,678.79 per week (in the test city).
(B)

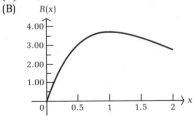

59. At the 40 lb weight level, blood pressure would increase at the rate of 0.44 in. of mercury per pound of weight gain.
At the 90 lb weight level, blood pressure would increase at the rate of 0.19 in. of mercury per pound of weight gain.

61. (A) After 1 hour, the concentration is decreasing at the rate of 1.60 mg/ml per hour; after 4 hours, the concentration is decreasing at the rate of 0.08 mg/ml per hour.

(B)

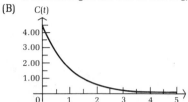

63. $dR/dS = k/S$

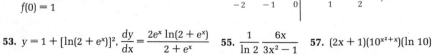

Exercise 9-3

1. $y = u^3$, $u = 2x + 5$ **3.** $y = \ln u$, $u = 2x^2 + 7$ **5.** $y = e^u$, $u = x^2 - 2$ **7.** $y = (2 + e^x)^2$, $dy/dx = 2e^x(2 + e^x)$

9. $y = e^{2-x^4}$, $dy/dx = -4x^3 e^{2-x^4}$ **11.** $y = \ln(4x^5 - 7)$, $\dfrac{dy}{dx} = \dfrac{20x^4}{4x^5 - 7}$ **13.** $\dfrac{1}{x - 3}$ **15.** $\dfrac{-2}{3 - 2t}$ **17.** $6e^{2x}$ **19.** $-8e^{-4t}$

21. $-3e^{-0.03x}$ **23.** $\dfrac{4}{x + 1}$ **25.** $4e^{2x} - 3e^x$ **27.** $(6x - 2)e^{3x^2 - 2x}$ **29.** $\dfrac{2t + 3}{t^2 + 3t}$ **31.** $\dfrac{x}{x^2 + 1}$

33. $\dfrac{4[\ln(t^2 + 1)]^3(2t)}{t^2 + 1} = \dfrac{8t[\ln(t^2 + 1)]^3}{t^2 + 1}$ **35.** $4(e^{2x} - 1)^3(2e^{2x}) = 8e^{2x}(e^{2x} - 1)^3$ **37.** $\dfrac{(x^2 + 1)(2e^{2x}) - e^{2x}(2x)}{(x^2 + 1)^2} = \dfrac{2e^{2x}(x^2 - x + 1)}{(x^2 + 1)^2}$

39. $(x^2 + 1)(-e^{-x}) + e^{-x}(2x) = e^{-x}(2x - x^2 - 1)$ **41.** $\dfrac{e^{-x}}{x} - e^{-x} \ln x$ **43.** $\dfrac{-2x}{(1 + x^2)[\ln(1 + x^2)]^2}$ **45.** $\dfrac{-2x}{3(1 - x^2)[\ln(1 - x^2)]^{2/3}}$

47. Increasing on $(-\infty, \infty)$
Concave downward on $(-\infty, \infty)$
Horizontal asymptote: $y = 1$
$f(0) = 0$

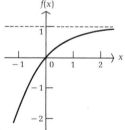

49. Decreasing on $(-\infty, 1)$
Concave downward on $(-\infty, 1)$
Vertical asymptote: $x = 1$
$f(0) = 0$

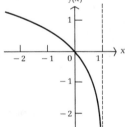

51. Increasing on $(-\infty, 0)$
Decreasing on $(0, \infty)$
Local maximum at $x = 0$
Concave upward on $(-\infty, -1)$ and $(1, \infty)$
Concave downward on $(-1, 1)$
Inflection points at $x = -1$ and $x = 1$
Horizontal asymptote: $y = 0$
$f(0) = 1$

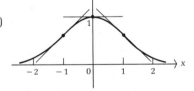

53. $y = 1 + [\ln(2 + e^x)]^2$, $\dfrac{dy}{dx} = \dfrac{2e^x \ln(2 + e^x)}{2 + e^x}$ **55.** $\dfrac{1}{\ln 2} \dfrac{6x}{3x^2 - 1}$ **57.** $(2x + 1)(10^{x^2 + x})(\ln 10)$

61. A maximum revenue of $735.76 is realized at a production level of 20 units at $36.79 each.
63. −$27,145 per year; −$18,196 per year; −$11,036 per year **65.** (A) 23 days; $26,685; about 50%

(B)

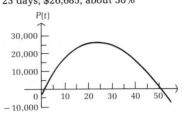

67. 2.27 mm of mercury per year; 0.81 mm of mercury per year; 0.41 mm of mercury per year
69. $A'(t) = 2(\ln 2)5,000e^{2t\ln 2} = 10,000(\ln 2)2^{2t}$; $A'(1) = 27,726$ bacteria per hour (rate of change at the end of the first hour); $A'(5) = 7,097,827$ bacteria per hour (rate of change at the end of the fifth hour)

71.

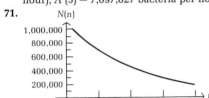

Exercise 9-4 Chapter Review

1. $3,136.62; $4,919.21; $12,099.29 **2.** $\dfrac{2}{x} + 3e^x$ **3.** $2e^{2x-3}$ **4.** $\dfrac{2}{2x+7}$ **5.** (A) $\ln(3 + e^x)$ (B) $\dfrac{e^x}{3 + e^x}$

6. Decreasing on $(-\infty, \infty)$
Concave upward on $(-\infty, \infty)$
Horizontal asymptote: $y = 0$
$y = 100$ when $x = 0$

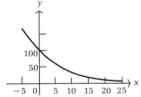

7. $\dfrac{7[(\ln z)^6 + 1]}{z}$

8. $x^5(1 + 6 \ln x)$

9. $\dfrac{e^x(x - 6)}{x^7}$

10. $\dfrac{6x^2 - 3}{2x^3 - 3x}$

11. $(3x^2 - 2x)e^{x^3-x^2}$

12. $\dfrac{e^{-2x}}{x - 2e^{-2x} \ln 5x}$

13. $y = -x + 2$; $y = -ex + 1$
14. Max $f(x) = f(e^{4.5}) = 2e^{4.5} \approx 180.03$
15. Max $f(x) = f(0.5) = 5e^{-1} \approx 1.84$

16. Increasing on $(-\infty, \infty)$
Concave downward on $(-\infty, \infty)$
Horizontal asymptote: $y = 5$
$f(0) = 0$

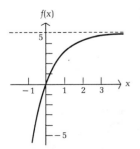

17. Increasing on $(e^{-1/3}, \infty)$
Decreasing on $(0, e^{-1/3})$
Local minimum at $x = e^{-1/3}$
Concave upward on $(e^{-5/6}, \infty)$
Concave downward on $(0, e^{-5/6})$
Inflection point at $x = e^{-5/6}$
$f(1) = 0$

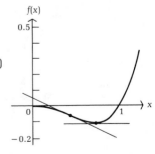

18. (A) $[\ln(4 - e^x)]^3$ (B) $\dfrac{-3e^x[\ln(4 - e^x)]^2}{4 - e^x}$ **19.** $2x(5^{x^2-1})(\ln 5)$ **20.** $\left(\dfrac{1}{\ln 5}\right)\dfrac{2x - 1}{x^2 - x}$ **21.** $\dfrac{2x + 1}{2(x^2 + x)\sqrt{\ln(x^2 + x)}}$

22. (A) 14.2 years (B) 13.9 years **23.** $A'(t) = 10e^{0.1t}$; $A'(1) = \$11.05$ per year; $A'(10) = \$27.18$ per year
24. $R'(x) = (1{,}000 - 20x)e^{-0.02x}$
25. A maximum revenue of $18,394 is realized at a production level of 50 units at $367.88 each.
26.

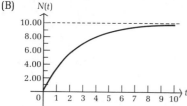

27. Min $\overline{C}(x) = \overline{C}(e^5) \approx \$49.66$

28. -1.111 mg/ml per hour; -0.335 mg/ml per hour
29. (A) Increasing at the rate of 2.68 units per day at the end of 1 day of training; increasing at the rate of 0.54 unit per day after 5 days of training

(B)

Chapter 10

Exercise 10-1

1. $7x + C$ **3.** $(x^7/7) + C$ **5.** $2t^4 + C$ **7.** $u^2 + u + C$ **9.** $x^3 + x^2 - 5x + C$ **11.** $(s^5/5) - \frac{4}{3}s^6 + C$ **13.** $3e^t + C$
15. $2 \ln|z| + C$ **17.** $y = 40x^5 + C$ **19.** $P = 24x - 3x^2 + C$ **21.** $y = \frac{1}{3}u^6 - u^3 - u + C$ **23.** $y = e^x + 3x + C$
25. $x = 5 \ln|t| + t + C$ **27.** $4x^{3/2} + C$ **29.** $-4x^{-2} + C$ **31.** $2\sqrt{u} + C$ **33.** $-(x^{-2}/8) + C$ **35.** $-(u^{-4}/8) + C$
37. $x^3 + 2x^{-1} + C$ **39.** $2x^5 + 2x^{-4} - 2x + C$ **41.** $2x^{3/2} + 4x^{1/2} + C$ **43.** $\frac{3}{5}x^{5/3} + 2x^{-2} + C$ **45.** $(e^x/4) - (3x^2/8) + C$
47. $-z^{-2} - z^{-1} + \ln|z| + C$ **49.** $y = x^2 - 3x + 5$ **51.** $C(x) = 2x^3 - 2x^2 + 3{,}000$ **53.** $x = 40\sqrt{t}$
55. $y = -2x^{-1} + 3 \ln|x| - x + 3$ **57.** $x = 4e^t - 2t - 3$ **59.** $y = 2x^2 - 3x + 1$ **61.** $x^2 + x^{-1} + C$ **63.** $\frac{1}{2}x^2 + x^{-2} + C$
65. $e^x - 2 \ln|x| + C$ **67.** $M = t + t^{-1} + \frac{3}{4}$ **69.** $y = 3x^{5/3} + 3x^{2/3} - 6$ **71.** $p(x) = 10x^{-1} + 10$
73. $P(x) = 50x - 0.02x^2$; $P(100) = \$4{,}800$ **75.** $R(x) = 100x - (x^2/10)$; $p = 100 - (x/10)$; $p = \$30$
77. $L(x) = 4{,}800x^{1/2}$; $L(25) = 24{,}000$ labor-hours **79.** $W(h) = 0.0005h^3$; $W(70) = 171.5$ lb **81.** 19,400

Exercise 10-2

1. $\frac{1}{6}(x^2 - 4)^6 + C$ **3.** $e^{4x} + C$ **5.** $\ln|2t + 3| + C$ **7.** $\frac{1}{24}(3x - 2)^8 + C$ **9.** $\frac{1}{16}(x^2 + 3)^8 + C$ **11.** $-20e^{-0.5t} + C$
13. $\frac{1}{10} \ln|10x + 7| + C$ **15.** $\frac{1}{4}e^{2x^2} + C$ **17.** $\frac{1}{3} \ln|x^3 + 4| + C$ **19.** $-\frac{1}{18}(3t^2 + 1)^{-3} + C$ **21.** $\frac{1}{3}(4 - x^3)^{-1} + C$

23. $\frac{1}{8}(1 + e^{2x})^4 + C$ **25.** $\frac{1}{2}\ln|4 + 2x + x^2| + C$ **27.** $e^{x^2+x+1} + C$ **29.** $\frac{1}{4}(e^x - 2x)^4 + C$ **31.** $-\frac{1}{12}(x^4 + 2x^2 + 1)^{-3} + C$
33. $\frac{1}{9}(3x^2 + 7)^{3/2} + C$ **35.** $\frac{1}{4}(2x^4 + 3)^{1/2} + C$ **37.** $\frac{1}{4}(\ln x)^4 + C$ **39.** $e^{-1/x} + C$ **41.** $x = \frac{1}{3}(t^3 + 5)^7 + C$
43. $y = 3(t^2 - 4)^{1/2} + C$ **45.** $p = -(e^x - e^{-x})^{-1} + C$ **47.** $p(x) = 2{,}000/(3x + 50)$; 250 bottles
49. $C(x) = 12x + 500 \ln(x + 1) + 2{,}000$; $\overline{C}(1{,}000) = \$17.45$
51. $S(t) = 10t + 100e^{-0.1t} - 100$, $0 \le t \le 24$; $S(12) \approx \$50$ million
53. $Q(t) = 100 \ln(t + 1) + 5t$, $0 \le t \le 20$; $Q(9) \approx 275$ thousand barrels **55.** $W(t) = 2e^{0.1t}$; $W(8) \approx 4.45$ g
57. $N(t) = 5{,}000 - 1{,}000 \ln(1 + t^2)$; $N(10) \approx 385$ bacteria per milliliter
59. $N(t) = 100 - 60e^{-0.1t}$, $0 \le t \le 15$; $N(15) \approx 87$ words per minute
61. $E(t) = 12{,}000 - 10{,}000(t + 1)^{-1/2}$; $E(15) = 9{,}500$ students

Exercise 10-3

1. $A = 1{,}000e^{0.08t}$ **3.** $A = 8{,}000e^{0.06t}$ **5.** $p(x) = 100e^{-0.05x}$ **7.** $N = L(1 - e^{-0.051t})$ **9.** $I = I_0 e^{-0.00942x}$; $x \approx 74$ feet
11. $Q = 3e^{-0.04t}$; $Q(10) = 2.01$ milliliters **13.** 24,200 years (approximately) **15.** 104 times; 67 times
17. (A) 7 people; 353 people **(B)** 400

Exercise 10-4

1. 5 **3.** 5 **5.** 2 **7.** 48 **9.** $-\frac{7}{3}$ **11.** 2 **13.** $\frac{1}{2}(e^2 - 1)$ **15.** $2 \ln 3.5$ **17.** -2 **19.** 14 **21.** $5^6 = 15{,}625$ **23.** $\ln 4$
25. $\frac{1}{6}[(e^2 - 2)^3] - 1$ **27.** $-3 - \ln 2$ **29.** $\frac{1}{6}(15^{3/2} - 5^{3/2})$ **31.** $\frac{1}{2}(\ln 2 - \ln 3)$ **33.** 0
35. $\int_0^5 500(t - 12)\,dt = -\$23{,}750$; $\int_5^{10} 500(t - 12)\,dt = -\$11{,}250$
37. Useful life $= \sqrt{\ln 55} \approx 2$ years; Total profit $= \frac{51}{22} - \frac{5}{2}e^{-4} \approx 2.272$ or \$2,272 **39.** 4,800 labor-hours
41. $100 \ln 11 + 50 \approx 290$ thousand barrels; $100 \ln 21 - 100 \ln 11 + 50 \approx 115$ thousand barrels
43. $20 + 100e^{-1.2} \approx \$50$ million; $120 + 100e^{-2.4} - 100e^{-1.2} \approx \$99$ million **45.** 134 billion ft^3
47. $2e^{0.8} - 2 \approx 2.45$ g; $2e^{1.6} - 2e^{0.8} \approx 5.45$ g
49. An increase of $60 - 60e^{-0.5} \approx 24$ words per minute; an increase of $60e^{-0.5} - 60e^{-1} \approx 14$ words per minute; an increase of $60e^{-1} - 60e^{-1.5} \approx 9$ words per minute

Exercise 10-5

1. 16 **3.** 7 **5.** $\frac{7}{3}$ **7.** 9 **9.** $e^2 - e^{-1}$ **11.** $-\ln 0.5$ **13.** 15 **15.** 32 **17.** 36 **19.** 9 **21.** $\frac{5}{2}$ **23.** $2e + \ln 2 - 2e^{0.5}$ **25.** $\frac{23}{3}$
27. $\frac{4}{3}$ **29.** $\frac{343}{3}$ **31.** 8
33. Total production from the end of the fifth year to the end of the tenth year is $50 + 100 \ln 20 - 100 \ln 15 \approx 79$ thousand barrels.
35. Total profit over the 5 year useful life of the game is $20 - 30e^{-1.5} \approx 13.306$ or \$13,306.
37. (A) 0.1825, 0.41 **(B)** $\frac{3}{25}$ **39.** $\frac{4.482}{5.482} \approx 0.82$ **41.** Total weight gain during the 10 hr is $3e - 3 \approx 5.15$ g.
43. Average number of words learned during the second 2 hr is $15 \ln 4 - 15 \ln 2 \approx 10$.

Exercise 10-6 Chapter Review

1. $t^3 - t^2 + C$ **2.** 12 **3.** $-3t^{-1} - 3t + C$ **4.** $\frac{15}{2}$ **5.** $-2e^{-0.5x} + C$ **6.** $2 \ln 5$ **7.** $y = f(x) = x^3 - 2x + 4$ **8.** 12
9. $\frac{1}{8}(6x - 5)^{4/3} + C$ **10.** 2 **11.** $-2x^{-1} - e^{x^2} + C$ **12.** $(20^{3/2} - 8)/3$ **13.** $-\frac{1}{2}e^{-2x} + \ln|x| + C$ **14.** $-500(e^{-0.2} - 1) \approx 90.63$
15. $y = f(x) = 3 \ln|x| + x^{-1} + 4$ **16.** $y = 3x^2 + x - 4$ **17.** $\frac{64}{3}$ **18.** $\frac{1}{2}\ln 10$ **19.** 0.45 **20.** $\frac{1}{48}(2x^4 + 5)^6 + C$
21. $-\ln(e^{-x} + 3) + C$ **22.** $-(e^x + 2)^{-1} + C$ **23.** $\frac{1}{3}(\ln x)^3 + C$ **24.** $y = 3e^{x^3} - 1$ **25.** $N = 800e^{0.06t}$ **26.** $\frac{46}{3}$

27. $P(x) = 100x - 0.01x^2$; $P(10) = \$999$ **28.** $\int_0^{15} (60 - 4t)\,dt = 450$ thousand barrels **29.** $\int_{10}^{40} \left(150 - \frac{x}{10}\right) dx = \$4{,}425$

30. Useful life $= 10 \ln \frac{20}{3} \approx 19$ years; total profit $= 143 - 200e^{-1.9} \approx 113.086$ or \$113,086

31. $500e^{-0.36} - 320 \approx \$29$ million **32.** $\frac{1}{6}$ **33.** 1 cm² **34.** 800 gal **35.** (A) $226e^{0.11} \approx 252$ million (B) $\dfrac{\ln 2}{0.011} \approx 63$ years

36. $\dfrac{-\ln 0.04}{0.000\ 123\ 8} \approx 26{,}000$ years **37.** $N(t) = 95 - 70e^{-0.1t}$; $N(15) \approx 79$ words per minute

Chapter 11

Exercise 11-1

1. (A) 120 (B) 124 **3.** (A) 123 (B) 124 **5.** (A) -4 (B) -5.33 **7.** (A) -5 (B) -5.33 **9.** 23.4 **11.** 55.3 **13.** 250
15. 2 **17.** $\frac{45}{28} \approx 1.61$ **19.** $2(1 - e^{-2}) \approx 1.73$ **21.** 0.791 **23.** 1.650 **25.** 0.748 **27.** 0.747 **29.** $[f(b) - f(a)]/(b - a)$
31. (A) $I = -200t + 600$ (B) $\frac{1}{3}\int_0^3 (-200t + 600)\,dt = 300$ **33.** \$16,000 **35.** (A) \$420 (B) \$135,000
37. \$149.18; \$122.96 **39.** $50e^{0.6} - 50e^{0.4} - 10 \approx \$6.51$
41. $(40 + 100e^{-0.7})/7 \approx 12.8$ or 12,800 hamburgers; $(140 + 100e^{-1.4} - 100e^{-0.7})/7 \approx 16.4$ or 16,400 hamburgers
43. 3,120,000 ft² **45.** 10°C **47.** $0.6 \ln 2 + 0.1 \approx 0.516$; $(4.2 \ln 625 + 2.4 - 4.2 \ln 49)/24 \approx 0.546$

Exercise 11-2

1. \$12,500 **3.** $8{,}000(e^{0.15} - 1) \approx \$1{,}295$ **5.** $10{,}000(1 - e^{-0.8}) \approx \$5{,}507$ **7.** $12{,}500(1 - e^{-0.48}) \approx \$4{,}765$ **9.** \$625,000
11. \$9,500 **13.** $\bar{p} = 24$; $CS = \$3{,}380$; $PS = \$1{,}690$
15. $\bar{p} \approx 49$; $CS = 55{,}990 - 80{,}000e^{-0.49} \approx \$6{,}980$; $PS = 54{,}010 - 30{,}000e^{0.49} \approx \$5{,}041$ **17.** \$2,308 **19.** \$1,310
21. Clothing store: $PV = 120{,}000(1 - e^{-0.5}) \approx \$47{,}216$; computer store: $PV = 200{,}000(1 - e^{-0.25}) \approx \$44{,}240$; the clothing store is the better choice.
23. $k(1 - e^{-rT})/r$

Exercise 11-3

1. $\frac{1}{3}xe^{3x} - \frac{1}{9}e^{3x} + C$ **3.** $\frac{x^3}{3}\ln x - \frac{x^3}{9} + C$ **5.** $\frac{1}{8}x(x - 6)^8 - \frac{1}{72}(x - 6)^9 + C$ **7.** $-xe^{-x} - e^{-x} + C$ **9.** $\frac{1}{2}e^{x^2} + C$

11. $\frac{1}{12}x(2x - 1)^6 - \frac{1}{168}(2x - 1)^7 + C$ **13.** $\frac{1}{21}(3x + 2)^7 + C$ **15.** $(xe^x - 4e^x)\Big|_0^1 = -3e + 4 \approx -4.1548$

17. $(x \ln 2x - x)\Big|_1^3 = (3 \ln 6 - 3) - (\ln 2 - 1) \approx 2.6821$ **19.** $\ln(x^2 + 1) + C$ **21.** $(\ln x)^2/2 + C$ **23.** $\frac{2}{3}x^{3/2}\ln x - \frac{4}{9}x^{3/2} + C$

25. $(x^2 - 2x + 2)e^x + C$ **27.** $\dfrac{xe^{ax}}{a} - \dfrac{e^{ax}}{a^2} + C$ **29.** $\left(-\dfrac{\ln x}{x} - \dfrac{1}{x}\right)\Big|_1^e = -\dfrac{2}{e} + 1 \approx 0.2642$

31. $\frac{1}{8}x^2(x + 1)^8 - \frac{1}{36}x(x + 1)^9 + \frac{1}{360}(x + 1)^{10} + C$ **33.** $-\frac{1}{2}x(x + 6)^{-2} - \frac{1}{2}(x + 6)^{-1} + C$ **35.** $x(\ln x)^2 - 2x \ln x + 2x + C$
37. $x(\ln x)^3 - 3x(\ln x)^2 + 6x \ln x - 6x + C$ **39.** $\frac{2}{3}x(x + 4)^{3/2} - \frac{4}{15}(x + 4)^{5/2} + C$ **41.** $(e^2 - 3)/2$ **43.** $2e^2 - 3$
45. $P(t) = t^2 + te^{-t} + e^{-t} - 1$ **47.** $31{,}250e^{-0.4} - 18{,}750 \approx \$2{,}198$ **49.** $\frac{37}{80} = 0.4625$
51. $(10 - 2 \ln 6)/3 \approx 2.1388$ parts per million **53.** 20,980

Exercise 11-4

1. $\frac{1}{3}$ **3.** 2 **5.** Diverges **7.** 1 **9.** Diverges **11.** Diverges **13.** 1 **15.** $\int_{2}^{3.5}\left(-\frac{x}{2}+2\right)dx \approx .94$ **17.** $\frac{1}{4}\int_{1}^{\infty}e^{-t/4}\,dt \approx .78$

19. 1 **21.** Diverges **23.** $\frac{1}{2}$ **25.** Diverges **27.** \$50,000 **29.** \$30,000 **31.** 6.25 million cubic feet

33. $.05\int_{3}^{\infty}e^{-.05x}\,dx \approx .86$ **35.** 500 gallons **37.** $.2\int_{0}^{5}e^{-.2t}\,dt \approx .63$ **39.** $\int_{9}^{\infty}\frac{dx}{(x+1)^2} = .1$

Exercise 11-5 Chapter Review

1. $\frac{1}{4}xe^{4x}-\frac{1}{16}e^{4x}+C$ **2.** $\frac{1}{2}x^2\ln x-\frac{1}{4}x^2+C$ **3.** $\frac{1}{6}x(x+7)^6-\frac{1}{42}(x+7)^7+C$ **4.** $\frac{1}{2}$ **5.** Diverges **6.** 8 **7.** 44 **8.** 30.8 **9.** 7
10. 1 **11.** 1 **12.** $\frac{12}{5}$ **13.** $-2te^{-0.5t}-4e^{-0.5t}+C$ **14.** $\frac{1}{3}x^3\ln x-\frac{1}{9}x^3+C$ **15.** $\frac{1}{3}$ **16.** 1 **17.** 2.317 **18.** $\frac{13}{2}$
19. $\frac{1}{3}(\ln x)^3+C$ **20.** $\frac{1}{2}x^2(\ln x)^2-\frac{1}{2}x^2\ln x+\frac{1}{4}x^2+C$ **21.** $-\frac{1}{4}e^{-2x^2}+C$ **22.** $-\frac{1}{2}x^2e^{-2x}-\frac{1}{2}xe^{-2x}-\frac{1}{4}e^{-2x}+C$
23. $\frac{1}{5}x^2(x-1)^5-\frac{1}{15}x(x-1)^6+\frac{1}{105}(x-1)^7+C$ **24.** 0 **25.** 2 **26.** $\frac{1}{4}$ **27.** 109 items **28.** $16e^{2.5}-16e^2-8 \approx \$68.70$
29. Present value $= 25,000(1-e^{-0.4}) \approx \$8,242$; amount $= \$15,018$; total income $= 50,000(e^{0.2}-1) \approx \$11,070$; interest $= \$3,948$
30. \$20,000 **31.** (A) \$1,000 (B) \$800 (C) $\bar{p} = 40$; $CS = \$2,250$; $PS = \$2,700$

32. 3,374 thousand barrels; 10,000 thousand barrels **33.** $.02\int_{0}^{1}e^{-.02t}\,dt \approx .02$ **34.** 2.5 milliliters; 10 milliliters

35. $\int_{1}^{\infty}f(t)\,dt = \int_{1}^{3}f(t)\,dt = \frac{1}{3}$ **36.** 45 thousand; 50 thousand **37.** $.5\int_{2}^{\infty}e^{-.5t}\,dt \approx .37$

Chapter 12

Exercise 12-1

1. 10 **3.** 1 **5.** 0 **7.** 1 **9.** 6 **11.** 150 **13.** 16π **15.** 791 **17.** 0.192 **19.** 118 **21.** $100e^{0.8} \approx 222.55$ **23.** $2x+\Delta x$
25. $2y^2$ **27.** $E(0, 0, 3)$; $F(2, 0, 3)$ **29.** \$4,400; \$6,000; \$7,100
31. $R(p, q) = -5p^2+6pq-4q^2+200p+300q$; $R(2, 3) = \$1,280$; $R(3, 2) = \$1,175$ **33.** \$272,615.08
35. $T(70, 47) \approx 29$ minutes; $T(60, 27) = 33$ minutes **37.** $C(6, 8) = 75$; $C(8.1, 9) = 90$ **39.** $Q(12, 10) = 120$; $Q(10, 12) \approx 83$

Exercise 12-2

1. 3 **3.** 2 **5.** $-4xy$ **7.** -6 **9.** $10xy^3$ **11.** 60 **13.** $2x-2y+6$ **15.** 6 **17.** -2 **19.** 2 **21.** $2e^{2x+3y}$ **23.** $6e^{2x+3y}$
25. $6e^2$ **27.** $4e^3$ **29.** $f_x(x, y) = 6x(x^2-y^3)^2$; $f_y(x, y) = -9y^2(x^2-y^3)^2$
31. $f_x(x, y) = 24xy(3x^2y-1)^3$; $f_y(x, y) = 12x^2(3x^2y-1)^3$ **33.** $f_x(x, y) = 2x/(x^2+y^2)$; $f_y(x, y) = 2y/(x^2+y^2)$
35. $f_x(x, y) = y^4e^{xy^2}$; $f_y(x, y) = 2xy^3e^{xy^2}+2ye^{xy^2}$ **37.** $f_x(x, y) = 4xy^2/(x^2+y^2)^2$; $f_y(x, y) = -4x^2y/(x^2+y^2)^2$
39. $f_{xx}(x, y) = 2y^2+6x$; $f_{xy}(x, y) = 4xy = f_{yx}(x, y)$; $f_{yy}(x, y) = 2x^2$
41. $f_{xx}(x, y) = -2y/x^3$; $f_{xy}(x, y) = (-1/y^2)+(1/x^2) = f_{yx}(x, y)$; $f_{yy}(x, y) = 2x/y^3$

43. $f_{xx}(x, y) = (2y + xy^2)e^{xy}$; $f_{xy}(x, y) = (2x + x^2y)e^{xy} = f_{yx}(x, y)$; $f_{yy}(x, y) = x^3e^{xy}$ **45.** $x = 2$ and $y = 4$
47. $f_{xx}(x, y) + f_{yy}(x, y) = (2y^2 - 2x^2)/(x^2 + y^2)^2 + (2x^2 - 2y^2)/(x^2 + y^2)^2 = 0$ **49.** (A) $2x$ (B) $4y$
51. $P_x(1, 2) = 4$: Profit will increase approximately $4 thousand per 1,000 increase in production of type A calculator at the (1, 2) output level; $P_y(1, 2) = -2$: Profit will decrease approximately $2 thousand per 1,000 increase in production of type B calculator at the (1, 2) output level
53. $\partial x/\partial p = -5$: A $1 increase in the price of brand A will decrease the demand for brand A by 5 pounds at any price level (p, q); $\partial y/\partial p = 2$: A $1 increase in the price of brand A will increase the demand for brand B by 2 pounds at any price level (p, q)
55. (A) $f_x(x, y) = 7.5x^{-0.25}y^{0.25}$; $f_y(x, y) = 2.5x^{0.75}y^{-0.75}$
(B) Marginal productivity of labor $= f_x(625, 81) = 4.50$, Marginal productivity of capital $= f_y(625, 81) = 11.57$
(C) Capital
57. Competitive **59.** Complementary
61. (A) $f_w(w, h) = 6.65w^{-0.575}h^{0.725}$; $f_h(w, h) = 11.34w^{0.425}h^{-0.275}$
(B) $f_w(65, 57) = 11.31$: For a 65 lb child 57 in. tall, the rate of change in surface area is 11.31 in.^{2} for each pound gained in weight (height is held fixed); $f_h(65, 57) = 21.99$: For a 65 lb child 57 in. tall, the rate of change in surface area is 21.99 in.^{2} for each inch gained in height (weight is held fixed).
63. $C_W(6, 8) = 12.5$: Index increases approximately 12.5 units for 1 in. increase in width of the head (length held fixed) when $W = 6$ and $L = 8$; $C_L(6, 8) = -9.38$: Index decreases approximately 9.38 units for 1 in. increase in length (width held fixed) when $W = 6$ and $L = 8$

Exercise 12-3

1. $f(-2, 0) = 10$ is a local maximum **3.** $f(-1, 3) = 4$ is a local minimum **5.** f has a saddle point at $(3, -2)$
7. $f(3, 2) = 33$ is a local maximum **9.** $f(2, 2) = 8$ is a local minimum **11.** f has a saddle point at $(0, 0)$
13. f has a saddle point at $(0, 0)$; $f(1, 1) = -1$ is a local minimum
15. f has a saddle point at $(0, 0)$; $f(3, 18) = -162$ and $f(-3, -18) = -162$ are local minima
17. The test fails at $(0, 0)$; f has saddle points at $(2, 2)$ and $(2, -2)$
19. 2,000 type A and 4,000 type B; Max $P = P(2, 4) = \$15$ million

21. (A)

p	q	x	y
$10	$12	56	16
$11	$11	6	56

(B) A maximum weekly profit of $288 is realized for $p = \$10$ and $q = \$12$.

23. $P(x, y) = P(4, 2)$ **25.** 8 by 4 by 2 in. **27.** 20 by 20 by 40 in.

Exercise 12-4

1. Max $f(x, y) = f(3, 3) = 18$ **3.** Min $f(x, y) = f(3, 4) = 25$
5. Max $f(x, y) = f(3, 3) = f(-3, -3) = 18$; min $f(x, y) = f(3, -3) = f(-3, 3) = -18$
7. Maximum product is 25 when each number is 5 **9.** Min $f(x, y, z) = f(-4, 2, -6) = 56$
11. Max $f(x, y, z) = f(2, 2, 2) = 6$; min $f(x, y, z) = f(-2, -2, -2) = -6$
13. 60 of model A and 30 of model B will yield a minimum cost of $32,400 per week
15. 8,000 labor units and 1,000 capital units **17.** 8 by 8 by $\frac{8}{3}$ in. **19.** $x = 50$ ft and $y = 200$ ft; maximum area is 10,000 ft^2

Exercise 12-5

1.
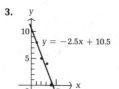
$y = 0.7x + 1$

3.
$y = -2.5x + 10.5$

5.

$y = x + 2$

7. $y = 2.12x + 10.8$; $y = 63.8$ when $x = 25$ **9.** $y = -1.2x + 12.6$; $y = 10.2$ when $x = 2$
11. $y = -1.53x + 26.67$; $y = 14.4$ when $x = 8$
13. $y = 0.75x^2 - 3.45x + 4.75$ **15.** (A) $y = 0.382x + 1.265$ (B) \$10,815

17. (A) $y = -0.48x + 4.38$ (B) \$6.56 per bottle
19. (A) $P = -0.66T + 48.8$ (B) 11.18 beats per minute
21. (A) $D = -3.1A + 54.6$ (B) 45%

Exercise 12-6

1. (A) $3x^2y^4 + C(x)$ (B) $3x^2$ **3.** (A) $2x^2 + 6xy + 5x + E(y)$ (B) $35 + 30y$ **5.** (A) $\sqrt{y + x^2} + E(y)$ (B) $\sqrt{y + 4} - \sqrt{y}$

7. 9 **9.** 330 **11.** $(56 - 20\sqrt{5})/3$ **13.** 16 **15.** 49 **17.** $\dfrac{1}{8}\displaystyle\int_1^5 \int_{-1}^1 (x + y)^2 \, dy \, dx = \dfrac{32}{3}$

19. $\dfrac{1}{15}\displaystyle\int_1^4 \int_2^7 \dfrac{x}{y} \, dy \, dx = \dfrac{1}{2}\ln\dfrac{7}{2} \approx 0.626\ 4$ **21.** $\tfrac{4}{3}$ **23.** $\tfrac{32}{3}$ **25.** $\displaystyle\int_0^1 \int_1^2 xe^{xy} \, dy \, dx = \dfrac{1}{2} + \dfrac{1}{2}e^2 - e$

27. $\displaystyle\int_0^1 \int_{-1}^1 \dfrac{2y + 3xy^2}{1 + x^2} \, dy \, dx = \ln 2$ **29.** $\dfrac{1}{0.4}\displaystyle\int_{0.6}^{0.8} \int_5^7 \dfrac{y}{1 - x} \, dy \, dx = 30 \ln 2 \approx \$20.8$ billion

31. $\dfrac{1}{10}\displaystyle\int_{10}^{20} \int_1^2 x^{0.75}y^{0.25} \, dy \, dx = \dfrac{8}{175}(2^{1.25} - 1)(20^{1.75} - 10^{1.75}) \approx 8.375$ or 8,375 items

33. $\dfrac{1}{192}\displaystyle\int_{-8}^8 \int_{-6}^6 \left[10 - \dfrac{1}{10}(x^2 + y^2) \right] dy \, dx = \dfrac{20}{3}$ insects per square foot

35. $\dfrac{1}{8}\displaystyle\int_{-2}^2 \int_{-1}^1 [100 - 15(x^2 + y^2)] \, dy \, dx = 75$ parts per million **37.** $\dfrac{1}{10,000}\displaystyle\int_{2,000}^{3,000} \int_{50}^{60} 0.000\ 013\ 3xy^2 \, dy \, dx \approx 100.86$ feet

39. $\dfrac{1}{16}\displaystyle\int_8^{16} \int_{10}^{12} 100\dfrac{x}{y} \, dy \, dx = 600 \ln 1.2 \approx 109.4$

Exercise 12-7 Chapter Review

1. $f(5, 10) = 2,900$; $f_x(x, y) = 40$; $f_y(x, y) = 70$ **2.** $\partial^2z/\partial x^2 = 6xy^2$; $\partial^2z/\partial x\,\partial y = 6x^2y$ **3.** $2xy^3 + 2y^2 + C(x)$
4. $3x^2y^2 + 4xy + E(y)$ **5.** 1 **6.** $f(2, 3) = 7$; $f_x(x, y) = -2x + 2y + 3$; $f_y(2, 3) = 5$ **7.** $(-8)(-6) - 4^2 = 32$
8. $y = -1.5x + 15.5$; $y = 0.5$ when $x = 10$ **9.** 18 **10.** $f_x(x, y) = 2xe^{x^2+2y}$; $f_y(x, y) = 2e^{x^2+2y}$; $f_{xy}(x, y) = 4xe^{x^2+2y}$
11. $f_x(x, y) = 10x(x^2 + y^2)^4$; $f_{xy}(x, y) = 80xy(x^2 + y^2)^3$
12. $f(2, 3) = -25$ is a local minimum; f has a saddle point at $(-2, 3)$ **13.** $y = \tfrac{116}{165}x + \tfrac{100}{3}$ **14.** $\tfrac{27}{5}$ **15.** 4 cubic units
16. (A) $P_x(1, 3) = 8$; profit will increase \$8,000 for 100 units increase in product A if production of product B is held
   fixed at an output level of $(1, 3)$
   (B) For 200 units of A and 300 units of B, $P(2, 3) = \$100$ thousand is a local maximum
17. 8 by 6 by 2 in. **18.** $y = 0.63x + 1.33$; profit in sixth year is \$5.11 million

19. $\dfrac{1}{4}\displaystyle\int_{10}^{12} \int_1^3 x^{0.8}y^{0.2} \, dy \, dx \approx 7.764$ or 7,764 units

20. $T_x(70, 17) = -0.924$ minute per foot increase in depth when $V = 70$ cubic feet and $x = 17$ feet **21.** 36 ppm
22. 50,000 **23.** $y = \tfrac{1}{2}x + 48$; $y = 68$ when $x = 40$

Appendix A

Exercise A-1

1. $2/x^9$ **3.** $3w^7/2$ **5.** $2/x^3$ **7.** $1/w^5$ **9.** 5 **11.** $1/a^6$ **13.** y^6/x^{12} **15.** x **17.** $a^2\sqrt{a}$ **19.** $3x^2\sqrt{2}$ **21.** $\sqrt{m}/m$
23. $\sqrt{6}/3$ **25.** $\sqrt{2x}/x$ **27.** 8.23×10^{10} **29.** 7.83×10^{-1} **31.** 3.4×10^{-5} **33.** 1 **35.** 10^{14} **37.** $y^6/(25x)^4$ **39.** 4×10^2
41. $4y^3/(3x)^5$ **43.** $y^{12}/(8x)^6$ **45.** $3x^4y^2z\sqrt{2y}$ **47.** $4\sqrt{3x}/x$ **49.** $\sqrt{42xy}/(7y)$ **51.** $2a\sqrt{3ab}/(3b)$ **53.** $6m^3n^3$
55. $2a\sqrt{3ab}/(3b)$ **57.** 2.4×10^{10}; 24,000,000,000 **59.** 1.1×10^4; 11,000 **61.** $t^2/(x^2y^{10})$ **63.** 4 **65.** $\sqrt{2}/2$
67. $2\sqrt{x} - 2/(x-2)$

Exercise A-2

1. $6\sqrt[5]{x^3}$ **3.** $\sqrt[5]{(4xy^3)^2}$ **5.** $\sqrt{x^2+y^2}$; not $x+y$ **7.** $5x^{3/4}$ **9.** $(2x^2y)^{3/5}$ **11.** $x^{1/3} + y^{1/3}$ **13.** 5 **15.** 64 **17.** -6
19. Not a rational number (not even a real number) **21.** $\frac{8}{125}$ **23.** $\frac{1}{27}$ **25.** $x^{2/5}$ **27.** m **29.** $2x/y^2$ **31.** $xy^2/2$
33. $2/(3x^{7/12})$ **35.** $2y^2/(3x^2)$ **37.** $2mn^2\sqrt[3]{2m}$ **39.** $2m^2n\sqrt[4]{2mn^3}$ **41.** $\sqrt[3]{x^2}$ **43.** $2a^2b\sqrt[3]{4a^2b}$ **45.** $\sqrt[4]{12x^3}/2$ **47.** $\sqrt[4]{(x-3)^3}$
49. $x\sqrt[6]{x}$ **51.** $\sqrt[6]{x^5}/x$

Exercise A-3

1. 3 **3.** $2x^3 - x^2 + 2x + 4$ **5.** $2x^3 - 5x^2 + 6$ **7.** $6x^4 - 13x^3 + 9x^2 + 13x - 10$ **9.** $-2x + 1$ **11.** $10m - 18$
13. $8a^2 + 2ab - b^2$ **15.** $9x^2 - 4y^2$ **17.** $16x^2 - 8xy + y^2$ **19.** $(x-7)(x-2)$ **21.** $(w+8)(w-5)$ **23.** $(2x-1)(x+3)$
25. $(x - 6y)(x + 2y)$ **27.** Prime **29.** $(A - 6B)(A + 6B)$ **31.** $(5m - 4n)(5m + 4n)$ **33.** $(x + 5y)^2$ **35.** Prime
37. $6(x + 2)(x + 6)$ **39.** $2x^2 - 7xy - 2y^2$ **41.** $2x - 18$ **43.** $2x^2 - 2xy - 8y^2$ **45.** $a^3 + b^3$
47. $2x^4 - 5x^3 + 5x^2 + 11x - 10$ **49.** $-5x^2 - 4x + 5$ **51.** $8m^3 - 12m^2n + 6mn^2 - n^3$ **53.** $x - 3\sqrt{x}$ **55.** $m - 4$
57. $c - d$ **59.** $x + 2x^{1/2}y^{1/2} + y$ **61.** $2x - 7x^{1/2} - 15$ **63.** $(2x - 3y)(x - 2y)$ **65.** $(3m - 1)(m + 6)$ **67.** $2y(y - 3)(y - 8)$
69. $(3s - t)(2s + 3t)$ **71.** $xy(x - 3y)(x + 3y)$ **73.** $(m + n)(m^2 - mn + n^2)$ **75.** Prime **77.** $(m - n)(m + n)(m^2 + n^2)$
79. $5\sqrt[3]{a} - \sqrt[4]{a}$ **81.** $6x - 2x^{19/3}$ **83.** h

Exercise A-4

1. $x/2$ **3.** $(3 - v)/v^2$ **5.** $a^2/2$ **7.** $(x - 4)/(x - 3)$ **9.** $1/(2x - 1)$ **11.** $x/(x + 5)$ **13.** $(x^2 + 8)/(8x^3)$
15. $2a/[(a + b)^2(a - b)]$ **17.** $(m^2 - 6m + 7)/(m - 2)$ **19.** $3/(y + 3)$ **21.** $(x^2 - x + 1)/[2(x - 9)]$ **23.** c/a
25. $(6 + \sqrt{a} - a)/(a - 4)$ **27.** $\sqrt{x^2 + 9} + 3$ **29.** $1/(\sqrt{t} + \sqrt{x})$ **31.** $1/(\sqrt{x + h} + \sqrt{x})$ **33.** $-2/(x - 1)^2$
35. $(6x^2 + 6x^3)/(2 - 3x)^6$ or $6x^2(1 + x)/(2 - 3x)^6$ **37.** $(2 + x^{1/3})/x^{1/3}$ **39.** $-x/(x + 1)^{3/4}$ **41.** $(5x - 1)/(4x^{1/4})$
43. $(3u^2 + 1)/(2u^{3/2})$

Exercise A-5

1. (A) $d = 3$; 14, 17 (B) Not an arithmetic progression (C) Not an arithmetic progression (D) $d = -10$; $-22, -32$
3. $a_2 = 11, a_3 = 15$ **5.** $a_{21} = 82, S_{31} = 1,922$ **7.** $S_{20} = 930$ **9.** 2,400 **11.** 1,120
13. Use $a_1 = 1$ and $d = 2$ in $S_n = (n/2)[2a_1 + (n - 1)d]$ **15.** Firm A: \$280,500; firm B: \$278,500
17. $\$48 + \$46 + \cdots + \$4 + \$2 = \$600$

Exercise A-6

1. (A) $r = -2$; $a_4 = -8$, $a_5 = 16$ (B) Not a geometric progression   (C) $r = \frac{1}{2}$, $a_4 = \frac{1}{4}$, $a_5 = \frac{1}{8}$
(D) Not a geometric progression
3. $a_2 = -6$, $a_3 = 12$, $a_4 = -24$ **5.** $S_7 = 547$ **7.** $a_{10} = 199.90$ **9.** $r = 1.09$ **11.** $S_{10} = 1,242$, $S_\infty = 1,250$
13. (B) $S_\infty = \frac{8}{5} = 1.6$ **15.** 0.999   **17.** About \$11,670,000   **19.** \$31,027; \$251,600

Exercise A-7

1. 720   **3.** 10   **5.** 1,320   **7.** 10   **9.** 6   **11.** 1,140   **13.** 10   **15.** 6   **17.** 1   **19.** 816
21. $C_{4,0}a^4 + C_{4,1}a^3b + C_{4,2}a^2b^2 + C_{4,3}ab^3 + C_{4,4}b^4 = a^4 + 4a^3b + 6a^2b^2 + 4ab^3 + b^4$
23. $x^6 - 6x^5 + 15x^4 - 20x^3 + 15x^2 - 6x + 1$ **25.** $32a^5 - 80a^4b + 80a^3b^2 - 40a^2b^3 + 10ab^4 - b^5$ **27.** $3,060x^{14}$

29. $5,005p^9q^6$ **31.** $264x^2y^{10}$ **33.** $C_{n,0} = \dfrac{n!}{0!n!} = 1$; $C_{n,n} = \dfrac{n!}{n!0!} = 1$ **35.** 1 5 10 10 5 1;   1 6 15 20 15 6 1

Index

Applications Index

■ Life Sciences

■ Social Sciences

Designer: Janet Bollow
Cover designer: John Williams
Cover photographer: John Jensen
Interior photographer: John Drooyan
Technical artists: Vantage Art, Art by AYXA
Production coordinators: Phyllis Niklas, Janet Bollow
Typesetter: Progressive Typographers
Printer and binder: R. R. Donnelley & Sons